In the Company of Others

In the Company of Others

AN INTRODUCTION TO COMMUNICATION

FOURTH EDITION

J. DAN ROTHWELL

CABRILLO COLLEGE, CALIFORNIA

NEW YORK | OXFORD
OXFORD UNIVERSITY PRESS

Oxford University Press, Inc., publishes works that further Oxford University's objective of excellence in research, scholarship, and education.

Oxford New York
Auckland Cape Town Dar es Salaam Hong Kong Karachi
Kuala Lumpur Madrid Melbourne Mexico City Nairobi
New Delhi Shanghai Taipei Toronto

With offices in
Argentina Austria Brazil Chile Czech Republic France Greece
Guatemala Hungary Italy Japan Poland Portugal Singapore
South Korea Switzerland Thailand Turkey Ukraine Vietnam

For titles covered by Section 112 of the U.S. Higher Education Opportunity Act, please visit www.oup.com/us/he for the latest information about pricing and alternate formats.

Published by Oxford University Press, Inc.
198 Madison Avenue, New York, New York 10016

http://www.oup.com

Library of Congress Cataloging-in-Publication Data
Rothwell, J. Dan.
In the company of others : an introduction to communication / J. Dan Rothwell.—4th ed.
p. cm.
Includes bibliographical references and index.
ISBN 978-0-19-986162-0
1. Communication. I. Title.
P90.R665 2012
302.2—dc23 2011026015

Printing number: 9 8 7 6 5 4 3 2 1

Printed in the United States of America
on acid-free paper.

To my family,
Marcy, Hilary, Geoff, Barrett, and Clare

BRIEF CONTENTS

CONTENTS

CHAPTER 2

Perception of Self and Others: Who Am I? Who Are They? 34

CHAPTER 3

Culture and Gender 62

CHAPTER 4

Language: Sharing Meaning with Words *94*

CHAPTER 5

Nonverbal Communication: Sharing Meaning Without Words *126*

PART 3 Group Communication

CHAPTER 10

The Anatomy of Small Groups 286

CHAPTER 11

Creating Effective Groups 310

CHAPTER 13

Presenting Speeches *376*

CHAPTER 14

Informative Speaking *410*

One student commented, anonymously, on an earlier edition of *In the Company of Others* that this is a textbook that "gets real." I consider that a supreme compliment. Too often mass-market books, and some textbooks, on human communication offer chirpy homilies encouraging readers to get along with others, be cooperative, improve self-esteem, listen intently, and the like. These are agreeable and worthwhile sentiments. Nevertheless, readers can be forgiven if they find themselves perplexed by how to accomplish getting along, being cooperative, enhancing self-esteem, listening well, and other admirable suggestions. When such books offer advice or a step-by-step plan, these are rarely given credibility by supporting research. My own preference, both as a teacher and as a textbook author, is to provide detailed practical ways, *supported by abundant research,* to address the myriad communication challenges each of us face in our complex lives. This "getting real" approach means that I embrace controversy, and I look for insights, explanations, and practical solutions revealed by voluminous research that addresses issues uppermost in students' minds. If little had changed in this regard since the third edition of this text was published, I would feel content to leave well enough alone. Much has changed in our increasingly technocentered world, and much has been learned in the interim to help us meet the new challenges. So I enthusiastically invite you to explore with me the ever-fascinating, ubiquitous, and preeminent human activity, communication, in its many modern manifestations.

Distinguishing Features

Almost all instructors agree that while covering all the standard topics in substantial detail, it is essential to remain faithful to the core material (verbal and nonverbal communication, perception, listening, conflict management, small-group processes, public speaking, etc.). Although remaining faithful to core material, *In the Company of Others* differs from other texts in significant ways. Here are the main distinguishing features.

Communication Competence Model: A Foundation for Students

The communication competence model is one of our discipline's unique contributions to understanding and improving human behavior. A premise of this book is that communication competence, whether in the arena of interpersonal relations, small-group work, public speaking, or communication technology, is critical to student success and achievement. The five components of the model—knowledge, skill, sensitivity, commitment, and ethics—for achieving communication effectiveness and appropriateness underscore the complexity of the communication process and provide direction and guidance for students. The model is integrated throughout the text, not merely discussed in the first chapter and then dropped entirely or mentioned only briefly in later chapters. Communication competence icons appear in margins throughout the text to highlight the pervasive influence of this model on material presented in every chapter. Most topics

and issues in the text, including perception of self and others, intercultural and gender communication, language use, listening, transacting power, managing conflict, and using communication technologies, are analyzed from the model's perspective. In addition, Developing Communication Competence boxes are included in each chapter to help students improve their communication.

Cooperation: A Recurring Theme

Cooperation is a recurring theme of this book. One of the great potential contributions of the communication discipline is that not only can we discuss cooperation theoretically, but we can also provide specific, concrete advice on how to structure human transactions so cooperation can become a reality. Many textbooks in several disciplines pay lip service to the need for human cooperation, but they are noticeably devoid of informed research-supported suggestions regarding how to make it happen. This does little more than frustrate students who are looking for practical guidance on working collaboratively. *In the Company of Others* thoroughly addresses the issue of cooperation in a variety of communication contexts. This book is based on the assumption that cooperation should be embraced, nurtured, and cultivated.

Integration of Gender and Culture

Gender and culture are important themes because we live in a world of increasing diversity. *In the Company of Others* treats gender and culture as integral parts of the overall discussion of communication. Gender receives special attention early in the text, and culture and gender are the main subjects of Chapter 3. This material is thoroughly integrated in subsequent chapters. Topics related to gender and culture include cultural differences in perception and nonverbal meanings, the role of gender and culture in powerful/powerless language, cross-cultural friendships and romantic relationships, gender and cultural bias in the workplace, the effects of communication technologies on cultural transactions, leadership and the glass ceiling in groups, and many others.

A Fresh Look at Communication Technologies

No one can doubt the enormous impact that communication technologies are having on our lives. How we cope with these technologies and the huge changes they bring are vital issues. Technological changes and advances are addressed in substantial detail throughout the text, but particular emphasis is given to the influence of technologies on social relationships (see especially Chapter 8). *In the Company of Others* provides the most extensive coverage of technology and its impact on our communication of any textbook on the market. Subjects include social online networks, cyberlove and cyberdating, e-dumping, text messaging and language, electronic technology and information overload, cyberaddiction, cyberconflicts, virtual groups, cell phone and online etiquette, *Wikipedia*, and Internet research and misinformation, among others.

Emphasis on Power

Power is inherent in every human transaction. It is perplexing that many textbooks give so little attention to the integral role power plays in all human relationships. The communication discipline has many valuable insights to offer on this important subject that require more than perfunctory, obligatory mention. Chapter 7 gives special focus and detailed analysis to the subject of power in relationships, and later chapters include additional discussions and applications. Such topics as the effects of power imbalances in relationships, sexual harassment in the workplace, sources of personal power, strategies for transacting power competently and cooperatively, and ways to empower ourselves and others are addressed.

Focus on Critical Thinking

Asking students to think critically and to determine which ideas and conclusions make sense may strike some students as promoting closed-mindedness. "Shouldn't all ideas be given an equal hearing?" Chapter 6 explores skepticism and the probability model like no other textbook, discussing the issue of open- and closed-mindedness in the process. Open-mindedness is explained as following where the evidence and reasoning lead, while closed-mindedness is accepting or rejecting an idea or conclusion despite what the evidence and reasoning suggest. Chapters 12, 13, 14, and 15 offer further coverage of critical thinking, with an emphasis on using sound reasoning and concrete evidence to build both informative and persuasive speeches. The Focus on Controversy boxes in every chapter also encourage critical thinking from student readers about current issues.

Focus on Controversy Boxes

Communication theory separated from the realities of a complex and not always pleasant world can seem sadly irrelevant to students faced with vexing problems. "Getting real" means to me that embracing a discussion of the tough realities of our challenging social relationships in a frenetic, hypercompetitive world has direct relevance to students' lives. Addressing important controversies directly can provide significant opportunities for student learning. The aim is to show students how to weigh evidence and draw conclusions supported by research. Examples of topics include the ethics of hypercompetitiveness, the issue of absolute honesty in relationships, excessive self-esteem, gender and relationship violence, verbal obscenity, texting as language, and plagiarism of public speeches. Every controversy receives a balanced treatment. Conclusions are drawn and thought-provoking questions are posed. Treatment of relevant controversies will certainly spark interesting discussion in the classroom and, more important, trigger critical thinking by students.

Extensive Treatment of Speech Anxiety and Attention Strategies

In the Company of Others provides the most extensive treatment of speech anxiety of any human-communication textbook. Speech anxiety is the most important concern on most students' minds when they are told that giving speeches will be a required activity in class. Also, no hybrid textbook on communication covers attention strategies as thoroughly as *In the Company of Others*. Let's face the facts: no one wants to listen to boring speeches, and no one wants to present a speech that puts the audience in a stupor. Attention strategies are a vital part of an effective speech.

Film School Feature Provides Opportunity to Apply Communication Theory

The very popular Film School segment at the end of every chapter identifies carefully selected movies on DVD that illustrate key concepts. Instead of doing the work for students by analyzing each film and applying it to chapter material, I have asked students to do this by answering critical thinking questions. More current films have been added to most chapter lists.

Carefully Composed Model Speeches

A major concern I had with general communication textbooks before I wrote *In the Company of Others* was the discrepancy between text descriptions and actual models of informative and persuasive speeches. Often the model speech even contradicted advice provided in the main text. Model informative and persuasive speeches have been carefully composed to illustrate the advice offered in the text.

Readability

Samuel Johnson's comment, "What is written without effort is in general read without pleasure," guided the writing of this textbook. Readability is a vital concern to me. Textbooks should not induce a coma, although it is understandable why some might cause eyelids to slam shut. Textbooks are not meant to read like the latest Stephen King novel, but they don't need to be a horror by reading like an instruction manual for installing and setting up your new flat-screen TV. Similarly, an overly dense, theoretical text written in technical language can impede clarity and understanding for students and create the kind of frustration many people experience when reading manuals for the latest computer software. Consequently, I searched in obvious and not-so-obvious places for the precise example, the amusing illustration, the poignant event, and the dramatic instance to engage readers, enhance enjoyment, and improve clarity. Colorful language and lively metaphors are sprinkled throughout the text to provide vividness. Humor is plentiful.

New to this Edition

The proven organization of the text remains firm, but much of the content has been updated to respond to current research and trends in our field.

Updates Throughout

- Almost 500 new references have been added. There are now more than 1,100 references dating from 2000 or sooner, more than half the total.
- Dozens of new studies, surveys, and statistics on technology and social media have been included throughout the text.
- More than a hundred new examples, stories, jokes, and anecdotes have been added so that the material is contemporary, resonates with readers, and sparks reader interest.
- Many new photos, cartoons, and graphics have been added or have replaced previous illustrations.
- Model informative and persuasive speeches have been thoroughly updated with more current research and statistics included, and the entire speeches have been edited for concision.

New Chapter Boxes

- "The Language of Texting" (Chapter 4)
- "The Uncritical Inference Test" (Chapter 4)
- "Reactions to Defensive and Supportive Communication" (Chapter 8)
- "What Is Your Leadership Style Preference?" (Chapter 10)
- "Are You a Difficult Group Member?" (Chapter 11)
- "Social Loafing: A Self-Assessment" (Chapter 11)

Chapter-by-Chapter Changes

Many chapter openings have been made more concise, and material previously included in openings has been developed into new segments in the chapters. Examples include the power of language (Chapter 4), the power of nonverbal communication (Chapter 5), and the significance of listening (Chapter 6).

- Chapter 1: There is added research and discussion of social networking and small talk and the effects of constant access from electronic technologies. There is also new material on breaking up relationships electronically (e-dumping), the inappropriateness of texting abbreviations in student-teacher communication, and the worst communication blunders made by those interviewing for jobs. The material on communication climate has been reorganized.
- Chapter 2: Research and examples of selective attention and texting with its dangers identified have been added. The dangers of social networking sites and self-disclosure also have been added. Research on how and why the negativity bias is built into our brains is discussed.
- Chapter 3: New, updated material has been added on gender differences in communication. A section on definitions of sex and gender and a section on self-disclosure have been added.
- Chapter 4: There is a new section on the language of abuse and exclusion, and a new section on language and identity has been included. Discussions of language and thinking, framing, and labeling have been moved to a new section on the power of language.
- Chapter 5: A new chapter opening has been constructed. New material on deception detection also appears. The section on tattooing has been extended with updates, statistics, and discussion. Rules of casual attire at work have been updated and discussed. Recent research on the importance of touch communication has been included and discussed. Recent research on gated communities has also been added.
- Chapter 6: The opening is entirely new. New research on the importance of listening has been added and discussed. Segments on information overload and the relationship between blogging sites and political true belief have been added.
- Chapter 7: Research on high-power individuals communicating like sociopaths is reviewed. New material on replications of the Milgram obedience studies has also been included.
- Chapter 8: Research on the fragility of relationships has been updated and discussed. A section on the primary reasons for forming relationships has been added. New material on "praise first, then describe" has also been added to the section on defensive versus supportive communication. More applications to friendships and workplace relationships have been added to the chapter. New material on "mate poaching" and relationship deterioration now appears in the chapter. The lengthy section on technology and social relationships has been extended and thoroughly updated with an added emphasis on workplace relationships and telecommuting challenges and relationships. The section on online romance has been revised.
- Chapter 9: New research on conflict between doctors and nurses and communication styles of conflict management has been added. Research on anger management in the workplace also appears in this chapter. A new section on workplace bullying has been included.
- Chapter 10: A new chapter opening has been written. A new section on the "rule of seven" is included in the discussion of group size. New research on binge drinking and conformity to norms has been included. The material on leadership in groups has been reorganized.
- Chapter 11: There is a new chapter opening. New research on "bad apples" in groups is included. Material on virtual groups has been revised. Material on group synergy and negative synergy has been moved from Chapter 10 to Chapter 11.
- Chapter 12: The opening has been revised. Recent research on generation gaps and audience analysis has been included. Using the Internet

for speech research has been revised. There is a reorganized section on developing arguments.

- Chapter 13: There is a new opening for the section on speech anxiety. Recent research on using unpleasant examples to gain attention also is discussed in this chapter.
- Chapter 14: An expanded discussion of narratives, telling stories, is included with a new section on narrative tips. There is greater emphasis on technology and the use of visual aids.
- Chapter 15: There is a new opening for the persuasive speaking strategies section. A new section on anger appeals as a persuasive strategy has been added. The ethics and emotional appeals section has been further developed. The section on persuasive strategies has been reorganized.
- Appendix B: A discussion of speeches for special occasions has been added as a second appendix.

Communication Theory Updates

- Channel richness theory appears in Chapter 1
- Attachment theory appears in Chapter 8
- Similarity attraction theory appears in Chapter 8
- Exchange theory also appears in Chapter 8
- Anger Activism Model appears in Chapter 15

Organization of the Text

In the Company of Others is divided into four parts. First, Chapters 1–6 lay the groundwork for the rest of the book. Subjects include the communication competence model, the role of perception in human transactions, intercultural and gender communication, the use and misuse of language, nonverbal communication, and the listening process. Each of these subjects crosses into every area of communication. Second, Chapters 7–9 on interpersonal communication discuss power in communication transactions, interpersonal dialectics, strategies for making relationships work, and conflict-management techniques. Third, Chapters 10 and 11 on group communication explain the anatomy of small groups, teambuilding, and teamwork in groups and organizations. Fourth, Chapters 12–15 on public speaking address preparing public speeches, presenting a speech to an audience, and constructing an effective informative or persuasive speech.

Supplements

An instructors manual with numerous activities, an extensive test bank for constructing exams, and a website with communication activities are available. Students can access the text website to take practice exams entitled "Quizzes without Consequences."

Acknowledgments

I owe a special debt to the reviewers for their very helpful critiques:

Karen Anderson, North Texas University

Marcanne Andersen, Johnson County Community College, KS

Charlotte Amaro, Lake Superior State University, MI

Kat Arnolfo, San Francisco State University

Tracie Babb, Bowie State University, MD

Andrew Barnes, James Madison University, VA

Peter Bicak, Rockhurst University, MO

Jeffrey Bineham, St. Cloud State University, MN

Jaime Bochantin, Western Illinois University/DePaul University

Martin Brodey, Montgomery College, MD

Lynda Brown, Texas A&M International University

Laura Carr, Eastfield College, TX

Michael Caudill, Western Carolina University, NC
Cathryn Chase, Indiana University–Purdue University Indianapolis
Scott Christen, Tennessee Tech University
Rosemary Collins, Pacific Union College, CA
Kim Cuny, University of North Carolina–Greensboro
Rebecca Curnalia, Youngstown State University, OH
Patti Cutspec, East Tennessee State University
Mike Davis, James Madison University, VA
George Denger, Lake Superior State University, MI
Alan DeSantis, University of Kentucky
William Ferreira, Houston Community College–Southwest, TX
Amber Finn, Texas Christian University
Crystal Fonseca, University of Rhode Island
James Gallagher, New Mexico State University
Gary Gillespie, Northwest College, WY
Stan Gwin, Southern Utah University
John Hart, Hawaii Pacific University
Kelly Herold, Winona State University, MN
Todd Holm, Concordia College, MN
David Hopcroft, Quinnebaug Valley Community College, CT
Debra Japp, St. Cloud State University, MN
Sarah Kercheval, William Penn University, IA
Jim Kimble, Seton Hall University, NJ
Stephen King, Delta State University, MS
Thomas Knutson, California State University–Sacramento
Branislov Kovacic, University of Hartford, CT
Gary Kuhn, Chemeketa Community College, OR
Sandra Lakey, Pennsylvania College of Technology
Kehbuma Langmia, Bowie State University, MD
Jaime Long, Kishwaukee College, IL
Louis Lucca, LaGuardia Community College, NY
Robin Mara, Hartnell College, CA
Bob Mild, Fairmont State University, WV
Donna Munde, Mercer County Community College, NJ
Jan Oehlschlaeger-Browne, South Seattle Community College, WA
John Phipps-Winfrey, Southeastern Community College, IA
Evelyn Plummer, Seton Hall University, NJ
Kelle Repinski, University of Toledo, OH
Adam Roth, University of Rhode Island
Kay Rutherford, Seattle Central Community College, WA
Marilyn Shaw, University of Northern Iowa
Margaret Smith, Bainbridge College, GA
Ronnie Stanley, Northwest Florida State College
Karen Staten, Wilkes Community College, NC
John Tapia, Missouri Western State University
Jason Teven, California State University–Fullerton
Ben Tyson, Central Connecticut State University
Beth Waggenspack, Virginia Polytechnic Institute and State University
Toni Whitfield, James Madison University, VA
Catherine Woells, Bellevue University, NE

I was often impressed by your insights and the eloquence with which you expressed your wisdom.

I would like to thank my Oxford editor Mark Haynes and development manager Thom Holmes. I offer a heartfelt thank you to senior production editor Keith Faivre for his careful oversight of the editing and production process, to art directors Paula Schlosser and Betty Lew for developing an outstanding design, and to assistant editor Caitlin Kaufman and editorial assistant Kate McClaskey for ably managing the photo selections and ancillary program for this text. I especially thank three people who worked closely with Oxford. Michael Davis of James Madison University prepared the Instructor's

Manual, Test Bank, and PowerPoint lecture notes for this edition. Joni Johnson Gray of West Virginia University and Robert E. Mild of Fairmont State University prepared the Student Success Manual.

Finally, to my wife, Marcy, a special thanks is due. She was unflagging in her support of me throughout this revision. Her support, love, and understanding during the hundreds of hours I spent isolated in my home office sustained me through many moments of frustration.

About the Author

J. Dan Rothwell is chair of the Communication Studies Department at Cabrillo College. He has a BA in American history from the University of Portland (Oregon), an MA in rhetoric and public address, and a PhD in communication theory and social influence. His MA and PhD are both from the University of Oregon. He has authored four other books: *In Mixed Company: Communication in Small Groups and Teams, Telling It Like It Isn't: Language Misuse and Malpractice,* (with James Costigan) *Interpersonal Communication: Influences and Alternatives*, and *Practically Speaking*, a public speaking text that is in the finishing stages of production with Oxford University Press. During his extensive teaching career, Dr. Rothwell has received numerous teaching awards, including most recently: the 2011 National Communication Association Community College Educator of the Year award; 2010 Ernest L. Boyer International Award for Excellence in Teaching, Learning, and Technology; and the 2010 Cabrillo College Innovative Teacher of the Year award.

Professor Rothwell appreciates feedback and correspondence from both students and instructors regarding *In the Company of Others.* Anyone so inclined may email him at darothwe@cabrillo.edu or send correspondence care of the Communication Studies Department, Cabrillo College, Aptos, CA 95003. Dr. Rothwell may also be reached by phone at 1-831-479-6511.

CHAPTER 1

Chapter Outline

Competent Communication

Effective and Appropriate

WHAT MAKES US LAUGH illustrates the richness and complexity of human communication. A study called LaughLab sought to determine the world's funniest joke (British Association for the Advancement of Science, 2002). More than 350,000 people from more than 70 countries logged on to an Internet site, contributed 40,000 jokes, and then, from a random selection, rated the jokes on a scale from 1 to 5. Here's the joke that received the highest overall rating:

> Two hunters from New Jersey are out in the woods when one of them falls to the ground. He doesn't seem to be breathing. The other whips out his mobile phone and calls the emergency services. He gasps out to the operator: "My friend is dead. What can I do?" The operator in a calm soothing voice says, "Just take it easy. First let's make sure he's dead." There is silence, then a shot is heard. The guy's voice comes back on the line. He says, "Okay, now what?"

By the end of this chapter, you should be able to:

1. Debunk common myths about communication.
2. Understand the transactional nature of human communication.
3. Diagnose communication problems using the communication competence model of effective and appropriate transactions—the theme of this text.
4. Understand the five global ways to achieve communication competence.
5. Recognize and create a cooperative, not a competitive, communication climate in a variety of contexts.

Humor is a matter of subjective perception. What is thigh-slappingly funny to one person may be offensive or lame to another. The LaughLab study found that men often favor jokes that put down women, involve sexual innuendo, or are aggressive (see also, Nicholson, 2010). For example,

> **Texan:** Where are you from?
> **Harvard graduate:** I come from a place where we do not end our sentences with prepositions.
> **Texan:** Okay, where are you from, Jackass?

Women often prefer jokes that are based on word play, such as: "A man walks into a bar with a piece of tarmac under his arm. He says to the bartender: 'A pint for me, and one for the road.'"

Culture also influences what is perceived to be funny. Americans preferred this joke:

> A man and a friend are playing golf one day at their local golf course. One of the guys is about to chip onto the green when he sees a long funeral procession on the road next to the course. He stops in mid-swing, takes off his golf cap, closes his eyes, and bows down in prayer. His friend says, "Wow, that is the most thoughtful and touching thing I have ever seen. You truly are a kind man." The man replies, "Yeah, well we were married 35 years."

The joke favored most by the British participants in the LaughLab study was this one:

> A woman gets on a bus with her baby. The bus driver says, "That's the ugliest baby that I've ever seen. Ugh!" The woman goes to the rear of the bus and sits down, fuming. She says to a man next to her, "The driver just insulted me!" The man says, "You go right up there and tell him off—go ahead. I'll hold your monkey for you."

The French liked this joke: "You're a high-priced lawyer! If I give you $500, will you answer two questions for me?" The lawyer responds, "Absolutely! What's the second question?"

Some humor, such as slapstick, crosses cultural boundaries easily, but sick jokes and dark humor do not (Lewis, 1996). Sarcasm, exaggeration, satire, and parody are usually unappreciated by Asians who value politeness and harmony, and jokes about religion, sex, and the underprivileged can cause deep offense (Lewis, 1996). Jokes that rely on ethnic stereotypes, especially if they elevate one group at the expense of another, are risky.

Humor is largely a social event that bonds us with others (Nicholson, 2010). Typically, we like to laugh, and we like people who make us laugh. This is one reason we might email jokes at work. Humor, however, can be a dicey proposition, especially if it contains sexual content. One person receiving an emailed joke about sex might be amused, but another might file sexual harassment charges against the sender. A salacious joke told during a speech could provoke a mass exodus by the audience.

We laugh harder and longer when a joke is told to us than when we merely read it (Provine, 2000). Often we laugh at a joke that doesn't seem funny because we don't want to embarrass the joke teller or because not laughing at a joke told by a more powerful person (your boss) can place you in an awkward position. How well you tell a joke also influences the response. This mostly involves nonverbal elements of facial expressions, eye movements, tone of voice, gestures, posture, and body movements.

Humor touches on virtually every main topic explored in this text—communication climate, perception, gender, culture, verbal and nonverbal communication, listening, power, conflict, relationships, groups, public speaking, and communication technologies. Knowing how to use humor well requires communication competence—the unifying theme of this text.

The purpose of this chapter is to explain the communication competence model. It serves as a map to guide your exploration of how to communicate well with others.

Benefits of Communication Competence

Communication is a central focus of your existence. It is mostly what we humans do. You spend most of your time in college communicating. As the National Communication Association states, "Communication is the foundation of all disciplines" (Rhodes, 2010, p. 13). You listen to and ask questions of your professors, give oral reports and speeches in classes, debate controversial issues, engage in class discussions, talk to, text, and tweet fellow classmates and roommates, and form friendships through conversation that may even blossom into true love. The entire academic enterprise is largely a communication event. Anything that occupies so much of your time is certainly worth serious attention. This section discusses two general reasons to study communication: (1) the social, personal, and workplace benefits of communicating competently, and (2) the need to improve our communication with others.

Humans are "the social animal"; we crave social connection through communication

Social Connection: Communicating with Others

We humans are "the social animal" (Aronson, 1999). This is an observation made by Aristotle almost 2,500 years ago and by others since. We have a powerful need to connect with others (Baumeister & Leary, 1995; Hawkley et al., 2005). Communication is the means by which we establish social connection and build relationships. Kids "talk friendships into existence" (Yingling, 1994), and technology has become an increasingly important tool for maintaining these friendships. Social networking sites have exploded in popularity, permitting unprecedented social connection. Facebook, for example, has a "limit" of 5,000 "friends" accessible per user. Text messaging, especially among teens, has become an increasingly pervasive means of remaining in almost constant contact with other people. A study by Nielsen Company found that American teenagers send and receive, on average, 3,339 text messages per month (Choney, 2010). Almost a fifth of adults 18 to 24 years old text message more than 200 messages per day or 6,000 per month ("Cell Phones and American Adults," 2010). There were an estimated 25 billion Twitter tweets sent worldwide in 2010 and 107 trillion emails from almost 1 billion email users ("Internet 2010 in Numbers," 2011).

The depth of our social connections in the digital age, however, has come into question. For example, a reporter for *The New York Times* observes that Facebook can too often be "a place of indiscriminate musings and minutiae, where people report their every thought, mood, hiccup, cappuccino, increased reps at the gym or switch to a new brand of toothpaste" (Ball, 2010). One study that conducted a content analysis of Twitter tweets found that 41% of the tweets were "pointless babble" of the "I am eating a sandwich now" variety (Kelly, 2009). I'm not suggesting that all conversations must be deep and meaningful. Sometimes we may need to "just talk" about meaningless "stuff" for many reasons. Another study, however, showed that "well-being is related to having less small talk and more substantive conversations" (Mehl et al., 2010, p. 539). Social networking sites provide a forum for social contact, but that social contact often may never rise beyond that of "friendsters," not genuine friends.

Now consider the reverse. Consider what your life would be like if you did not interact with another human being for a week, a month, or even a year. Ironically, we need to communicate with others to establish social connection and build relationships, but the lack of social connection retards our ability to communicate and to establish a human identity. Stories of feral or "wild" children growing up without any apparent human contact and horrific instances of children imprisoned in closets or basements demonstrate this (Newton, 2002). Despite intensive training, these unfortunate children do not learn to communicate normally unless their plight is discovered within the first six years of life. After age six, learning a language, any language, is very difficult, and shortly after puberty, the capacity to master a language virtually disappears if no language at all has been acquired (Clarke & Clarke, 2000; Kuhl et al., 2005).

Consider the sad case of Genie (see Rymer, 1993). From the time she was 20 months old, Genie's abusive father had imprisoned her in a bare room with the curtains drawn, strapped her naked to a potty chair, and sometimes bound her in a makeshift straitjacket. Genie's mother, almost blind and fearing her husband's brutality, left Genie isolated and deprived. When Genie was discovered, she could not walk, talk, stand erect, chew solid food, or control her bodily functions. Despite years of intensive training, Genie never lost her unnatural voice quality, and she never learned to master language. She constructed ungrammatical sentences, such as "I like elephant eat peanut" and "Genie have Momma have baby grow up." Her ability to communicate—a vital link to other human beings—had been profoundly impaired by her early isolation.

Personal Well-Being: Staying Alive

Competent communication is also linked to our personal well-being. Studies have shown that more than 60% of potentially lethal medication errors in hospitals and pharmacies are caused by mistakes in interpersonal communication (Maxfield et al., 2005). The recurrent "toxic talk" that usually accompanies bad relationships can literally talk us into heart disease, strokes, even cancer (Lynch, 2000). Our close relationships can also help us ward off the "torment of loneliness." Lynch (2000) calls chronic loneliness "one of the major diseases of our age," and based on his own research and a vast array of health statistics, he concludes, "We really do need human dialogue to stay alive" (p. 8). Social isolation can be as perilous to our health as high blood pressure and cholesterol, obesity, and smoking (Crowley, 1995; Lynch, 2000).

Another benefit of close relationships is that they can satisfy a need for intimacy with another human being (De Seve, 2003). They can meet our needs for affection, companionship, sex, and a purpose in life (Prager & Buhrmester, 1998). Communication is the "dynamic and essential force in the maintenance of relationships, and facilitates the development of the satisfied and healthy family" (Pearson & Sessler, 1991).

Workplace Benefits: Positions, Performance, and Promotion

Communication skills are critical to landing a job, performing effectively, and receiving promotions in the workplace. An annual study of more than 400 employers conducted by the National Association of Colleges and Employers in its 2011 survey ranked communication skills, for the thirteenth year in a row, as the *most important qualification* a candidate for employment can possess ("Top Skills for Job Candidates," 2011). A 2010 survey by Hart Research Associates for the Association of American Colleges and Universities showed that "the ability to communicate effectively" was chosen first by employers among a list of learning outcomes that should be given greater emphasis (Rhodes, 2010). A survey of 2,115 managers and executives conducted by the American Management Association found similar results ("AMA 2010 Critical Skills Survey," 2010). Moreover, once people are hired, skillful communication is the determining factor in how well they perform on the job and their likelihood of promotion (Morreale & Pearson, 2008). The CEO of Worthington Industries, John H. McConnell (1995), in his book *Are You Communicating? You Can't Manage Without It*, states emphatically, "Take all the speech and communication courses you can because the world turns on communication."

Communication Improvement: All Can Benefit

All of us can benefit from improving our communication with others, but not if we're convinced that no improvement is necessary. Most Americans believe they are better communicators than those of us on the receiving end might think. A national Roper poll of more than 1,000 Americans reported that 91% of the respondents see themselves as very or somewhat effective when communicating with other people ("How Americans Communicate," 1998). Numerous studies, however, question these self-assessments. Many national reports emphasize the need for college students to upgrade their oral communication skills. One such report notes, "Ironically, communication skills not only top employers' list of most-desired skills, but also their list of the skills most lacking in new college graduates" ("Job Outlook," 2007). One researcher concluded, based on a review of numerous studies, that students often graduate with "serious weaknesses" in communication knowledge and skills (Bollag, 2005).

A huge long-term study conducted in a wide variety of organizations found that the self-assessments of 600 team leaders were wildly more generous than those of the 6,000 team members who had to endure their inappropriate and ineffective communication (LaFasto & Larson, 2001). In fact, team members' assessments of leaders were a whopping *50% lower* than the team leaders' self-assessments. These same team members also noted the inadequacy of the entire team's communication. Finally, a survey of 61,000 individuals revealed that only 10% of the respondents rated their bosses good at communicating ("Key Survey Findings," 2007).

No one is a perfect communicator, so studying communication can benefit everyone. This is why more than a thousand faculty members surveyed from a wide variety of academic disciplines and colleges identified these *essential skills* for every college graduate: speaking, listening, problem solving, interpersonal skills, working in groups, and leading groups (R. Diamond, 1997). That previews the general content of this text.

Communication Myths

American humorist Will Rogers once remarked, "It isn't what we don't know that gives us trouble, it's what we know that ain't so" (Fitzhenry, 1993, p. 243). As used here, a **myth** is a belief that is contradicted by fact. Communication myths disrupt our ability to improve our communication knowledge and skills. If what we know about communication "ain't so," then what chance do we have to improve our communication competence? Because common misconceptions interfere with our understanding of what communication is, let's first discuss what communication is not.

Myth 1: Communication Is a Cure-All

Relationships can't always be fixed by better communication. Sometimes communicating clearly reveals just how far apart individuals in a relationship have grown. Skillful communication may ease the pain of breaking up, but it may not sufficiently heal the wounds of a bruising relationship. Similarly, despite its importance to your employment future, improving your interviewing skills may not be sufficient to land a job. If the most challenging aspect of any job you've held involved asking, "Would you like fries with that?" then your chances of landing a high-skills managerial or technical position are about the same as a snail's safe passage across a freeway.

Research also reveals that some problems that occur between individuals are not solvable (Gottman & Silver, 1999). Your partner may never learn to enjoy events attended by large crowds. Your coworker or boss may never develop a sunny disposition and a less cynical view of the world. Your roommate may never become a tidy person. Competent communication can help us cope with our recurring disagreements, but it may not change people.

Communication is a very important tool. When employed skillfully, communication can help solve numerous problems. Communication, however, is a means to an end, not an end in itself. It is not the basis of all human problems. Thus, not all problems can be solved even by textbook-perfect communication.

Myth 2: Communicating Is Just Common Sense

"Hindsight is 20–20" goes the adage. People often claim that they "knew" who would win an election once the victor became known, but when tested in advance of an election, most aren't very accurate (Powell, 1988). "Monday-morning quarterbacks" always seem to know what would have worked and why a coach's call failed because they have the benefit of hindsight.

This "I-knew-that-already" tendency is called the **hindsight bias** (Worthington et al., 2002). For example, everybody knows that opposites attract, correct? When psychologist David Myers (2002) told this to college students, most found the observation to be unremarkable. Yet, when another group of college students was told the *opposite* ("Birds of a feather flock together"), most also found this observation to be plain common sense. Sometimes what we know isn't so.

Because all of us have communicated all of our lives, it is seductively simple to get snared in the hindsight-bias trap by thinking as you read this text, "Oh, that's just common sense." The proof for such claims, of course, is whether you can provide the accurate information *before* you are told what the research says is true. I regularly quiz my students at the beginning of each term on their general knowledge of communication (see Box 1-1). I do not ask them technical definitions of concepts or query them about remote facts. I keep the questions within the realm of the average college student's communication experience. Thus, it is by far the easiest test I give. Consistently, students do very poorly. Such results are not unexpected and certainly not cause for ridicule. One of your primary purposes for taking a communication course should be to learn new information, to gain new insights, and to unlearn the misinformation popular culture often disseminates.

The "common-sense" notion of communication is contradicted by our all-too-common experience. If communication consists mostly of common sense, with no requirement for studying or training, then why do so many people exhibit inadequate communication knowledge and skills? Why is the divorce rate so persistently high, and why are breakups so often nasty, uncivilized battles? Why are most teams unsuccessful in achieving their desired goals (Ellis et al., 2005; Ju & Cushman, 1995)? Why does it seem that public speaking is almost a lost art, as far too many politicians anesthetize us with bland, ghostwritten speeches (Shachtman, 1995)? As you read this text, note that what passes in the popular media for knowledge and insight about communication, and what may seem like common sense, is often pure myth. How do we know? Because the research says so!

Myth 3: Communication Quantity Equals Quality

"One of our culture's most cherished ideas is that when it comes to communication in relationships, more is better" (Swann et al., 2003, p. 1104). Relentless criticism is more communication but hardly better communication. Persistently text messaging a boyfriend or girlfriend about a nasty argument may intensify the conflict, especially if the original argument centered on "smothering" with too much attention. If you have a disagreement with your professor about a grade, repeatedly approaching your teacher in the hope that persistence, or "nagging,"

BOX 1.1 Developing Communication Competence

HINDSIGHT BIAS TEST

INSTRUCTIONS Choose either TRUE or FALSE for each statement. Each correct answer is worth 2 points.

1. Research on communication between men and women shows that differences are so vast that women seem to be from Venus and men from Mars.

   TRUE FALSE

2. Personal relationships have a good chance of lasting and remaining strong as long as both partners balance negative, judgmental communication (criticism, blame) with an equal amount of positive, supportive communication (praise, recognition, affection).

   TRUE FALSE

3. Venting your anger (expelling it, not holding it in) so it doesn't build up steam until you explode is a productive and effective way to manage your anger.

   TRUE FALSE

4. Females, far more than males, have body image concerns.

   TRUE FALSE

5. Relationships cannot thrive if there is any deception between partners.

   TRUE FALSE

6. The greater the fear appeal (e.g., scaring people about health dangers of smoking), the likelier your audience will be persuaded by your message to change behavior (e.g., stop smoking).

   TRUE FALSE

7. Whenever we travel to another culture, we should attempt to be as direct, precise, and explicit in our communication as we can be to avoid misunderstandings.

   TRUE FALSE

8. Women rarely use violence against their male partners.

   TRUE FALSE

9. Most people can usually detect lying from others; college students, because of their general intelligence and education, are actually quite good at it.

   TRUE FALSE

10. Compromising is the most effective strategy for managing conflicts in relationships and groups because it is based on fairness.

    TRUE FALSE

11. Competition motivates the vast majority of individuals to give their very best performance.

    TRUE FALSE

12. Some stereotypes can be accurate depictions of groups in general.

    TRUE FALSE

13. Self-disclosure (communicating personal information about ourselves that others would not know unless we told them) should be plentiful on a first date to help determine whether a second date is desired.

    TRUE FALSE

14. Conflicts should not be avoided because this will only make things worse.

    TRUE FALSE

(continued)

BOX 1.1 *(Continued)*

15. Parents should take every opportunity possible to praise their children because an individual can never have too much self-esteem.
    TRUE FALSE
16. First impressions are usually inaccurate because they are based on very limited information.
    TRUE FALSE
17. You cannot think without language; just try thinking without words in your head.
    TRUE FALSE
18. You can stop sending messages of any sort to other people if you want to, even when they are observing you.
    TRUE FALSE
19. No one is ever completely powerless.
    TRUE FALSE
20. Converting a person from one strong belief to a contradictory belief is very achievable if you know how to use persuasive strategies effectively.
    TRUE FALSE

Determining your score: See answers at the end of the chapter. Explanations occur throughout this text.

might produce a favorable grade change will likely fail (Dunleavy et al. 2008). It may even harden your professor's resolve to stop listening to you. According to long-term studies of couples' communication, 69% of all marital conflicts never go away, and arguments about such conflicts recur year after year (Gottman & Gottman, 2006). Couples who argue sometimes keep resurrecting points of contention, and like someone picking a scab, they reopen old wounds again and again. Occasionally, agreeing to disagree and not discussing an issue at all may be the best choice. Finally, in a survey by LexisNexis of 1,700 white-collar professionals in five countries, almost 60% revealed that being constantly accessible via cell phone, email, and by other means was distracting and a serious interference with working effectively on tasks; more than half felt "demoralized" and close to a "breaking point" from information overload that resulted from easy access (Walsh & Vivona, 2010). *More communication isn't always better communication.*

Defining Communication

The *Oxford English Dictionary (OED)* takes about 1,200 words to define communication. Communication scholars and researchers have contributed more than 100 different definitions of their own. There is no ideal, or sacred, definition of communication. Authors, scholars, and students of human communication offer definitions suitable to their perspectives on the subject.

The definition that best fits the perspective presented in this textbook is as follows: **Communication** *is a transactional process of sharing meaning with others.* This seemingly simple 10-word definition requires explanation. Be thankful that you won't be asked to memorize or explain the *OED*'s definition.

Communication Is Transactional: The Evolving Perspective

Many communication models have been developed over the years, and each attempts to describe communication in concrete terms. In this section, I describe three communication models in the order of their development: linear, interactive, and transactional. Each of these models provides insights that explain how the communication process works.

Linear Model: The Straight Arrow View

The communication process has been described as a linear, one-way phenomenon. Communication, from this perspective, involves a **sender** (initiator and encoder) who sends a **message** (stimulus that produces meaning) through a **channel** (medium through which a message travels, such as oral or written) to a **receiver** (decoder of a message) in an atmosphere of **noise** (interference with effective transmission and reception of a message) (see Figure 1-1).

When the president of the United States addresses the nation on television, all the components of the linear model are present. The president is the sender who encodes the message (puts ideas into a spoken language). The message is composed of the ideas the president wishes to express (e.g., what this country should do about terrorism). The channel is the medium of television and is oral, aural (hearing), and visual. The receivers are members of the television audience who tune in to the address and decode the message (translate the president's spoken ideas). Noise might be the static in the television transmission or, perhaps, family members fighting over the remote control. *The linear model provides insight into the communication process, especially by highlighting the concepts of channel and noise.*

Channel Changing: The Medium Can Be the Message The choice of channel can make an enormous difference in the way a message is received. Do you ask your partner to marry you, for example, by sending a text message? By having a banner pulled across the sky by an airplane? Face to face on bended knee? By having your best friend do it because you're too chicken? By registered mail with a prenuptial agreement attached?

Conversely, channel choice can deeply affect the process of dumping your date or mate. In one study, 43% of women and 27% of men said they had been e-dumped by text messages ("Sex in the Digital Age," 2010). Emma Brady, a 35-year-old conference organizer in Great Britain discovered her marriage to Neil Brady was over when he posted the message, "Neil Brady has ended his marriage to Emma Brady" on his Facebook page (Farhanghi, 2009). She said she felt humiliated by the public nature of the breakup. How would you feel if you were dumped in such impersonal ways?

When it is especially important to remain civil in your communication with others, switching from electronic to face-to-face communication can prove to be a more productive channel choice. Face-to-face communication is **channel rich**; it incorporates multiple channels besides words, such as gestures, facial expressions, tone of voice, posture, and other nonverbal cues. Text-only

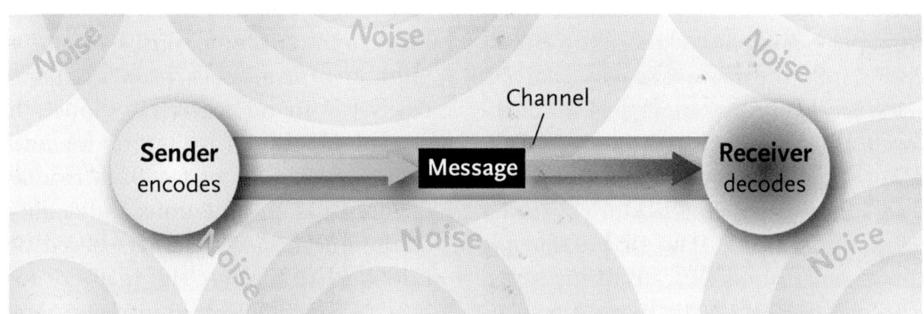

FIGURE 1-1 Linear Model of Communication

communication is **channel lean**; only a single channel devoid of the richness of nonverbal cues is available for understanding messages (Surinder & Cooper, 2003). We are more likely to be abusive, insulting, offensive, and intemperate in our communication with others when emailing, texting, or tweeting than we are in face-to-face conversation (Wallace, 1999; Zornoza et al., 2002). Text-only, channel-lean communication can be **disinhibiting**—less restrained and more spontaneous but also impersonal, abrupt, and often offensive. Statements you would never say to a person face to face can be said easily and sent abruptly in text messages because the immediate reactions and consequences are not apparent. We seem to know this even though we may not always practice what we know. Ilana Gershon (2010) found that all but 4 of the 472 respondents she surveyed felt breaking up face to face is the "ideal way to end a relationship." Choosing the wrong medium to communicate bad news "can signal to others the initiator's cowardice, lack of respect, callousness, or indifference" (p. 3). Even the act of "defriending" someone from your Facebook page poses questions. Do you want to break up but "remain friends"? Can you break up and still be friends? What message is conveyed by defriending someone on your social networking site?

Types of Noise: Beyond the Jackhammer The linear model is also important because it broadens the definition of noise to include interference that goes beyond mere loud or irritating sounds. Physical noise, or external, environmental distractions, such as startling sounds, poorly heated rooms, or the unfortunate periodic reappearance of bell-bottom pants and paisley ties, all divert our attention from the message sent by a source. Physiological noise, or biological influences, such as sweaty palms, pounding heart, and butterflies in the stomach induced by speech anxiety, or feeling sick or exhausted at work, can produce dramatic interference on both senders and receivers of messages. Psychological noise, in the form of preconceptions, biases, and assumptions, also interferes with effective message transmission and reception. For example, a 2010 Gallup poll found that 52% of Americans surveyed felt "a little" or a "great deal" of prejudice toward Muslims. This was more than twice the number who felt prejudice toward Christians (18%), Jews (15%), and Buddhists (14%) ("In U.S., Religious Prejudice," 2010). Such preconceived, dangerous biases make effective transmission and reception of messages between different ethnic and religious groups extremely difficult.

Semantic noise as reflected in word choice that is confusing or distracting also creates interference. Text messaging acronyms (DBEYR RBTL TTYL) are noise if you can't translate the text lingo. ("Don't believe everything you read. Read between the lines. Talk to you later" is the translation for the above message. See netlingo.com for up-to-date text term translations.) Racist, sexist, and homophobic labels and descriptions, even if unintended, easily derail productive conversation. Even a term for a particular ethnic group can cause difficulties. For example, is the preferred term "African American" or "black"? One study found more than a third of black Americans have a preference (24% for African American and 13% for black) (Newport, 2007). Should you use "Native American" or "Indian"? "Hispanic" or "Latino"? Different groups, even individuals within a group, prefer different terms. Choosing the "wrong" term can derail your message by drawing attention to terminology disputes while submerging the content of your intended message.

Despite its insights, application of the linear model is quite limited. Its most glaring weakness is the absence of **feedback**—the receiver's verbal and nonverbal responses to a message. The linear model assumes that communication consists of the transmission of a message from a sender to a receiver with no receiver response; listeners are merely passive targets for information. The absence of feedback is a serious flaw because all of us constantly adjust our communication with others based on the feedback we receive. The inability to read feedback accurately and to make appropriate adjustments is a serious communication competence issue.

Candorville

This cartoon illustrates the importance of (more than one answer could be correct)

1. psychological noise
2. channel
3. hindsight bias
4. physical noise

Answers at end of chapter

Interactive Model: The Ping-Pong View

The interactive model of communication includes feedback (Figure 1-2). The addition of feedback clearly indicates that communication is not a one-way but a two-way process. Receivers are actively involved in the process; they are not static targets. Receivers become senders, and senders become receivers of messages.

The importance of feedback to the communication process cannot be overestimated. Remember the study of managers and team members mentioned earlier (LaFasto & Larson, 2001)? Of the 35,000 assessments gathered from 6,000 team members, *two consistent problems emerged: giving feedback and receiving feedback*. As noted in the study, the ability to give and receive feedback effectively is key to any constructive self-correction that can occur in teams. The huge disparity previously identified between an individual's self-assessment of his or her communication skills and the assessments made by others exists primarily because too often we insulate ourselves from feedback. How else could managers deem themselves highly effective listeners when their employees view the managers' listening skills as woefully substandard?

A second component of the interactive model missing from the linear version is fields of experience. **Fields of experience** include our cultural background, ethnicity, geographic location, extent of travel, and general personal experiences accumulated over the course of a lifetime. Fields

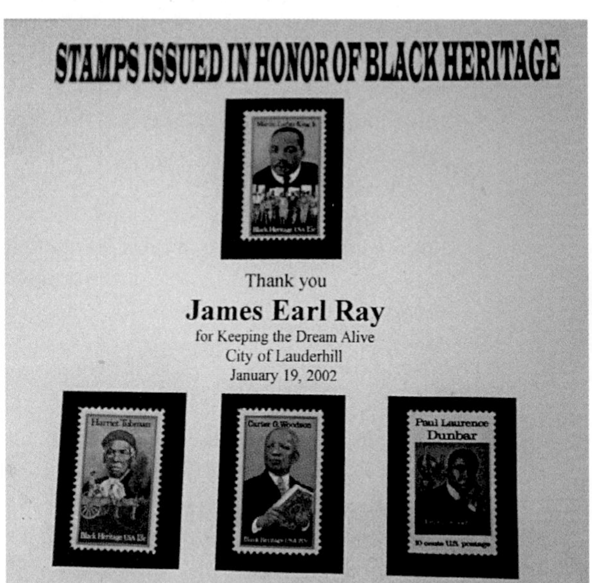

This plaque, to honor actor James Earl Jones at a celebration of civil rights legend Rev. Martin Luther King Jr., mistakenly honors James Earl Ray, the man who assassinated King. This is a startling example of

1. psychological noise
2. physical noise
3. channel choice
4. semantic noise

Answers at end of chapter

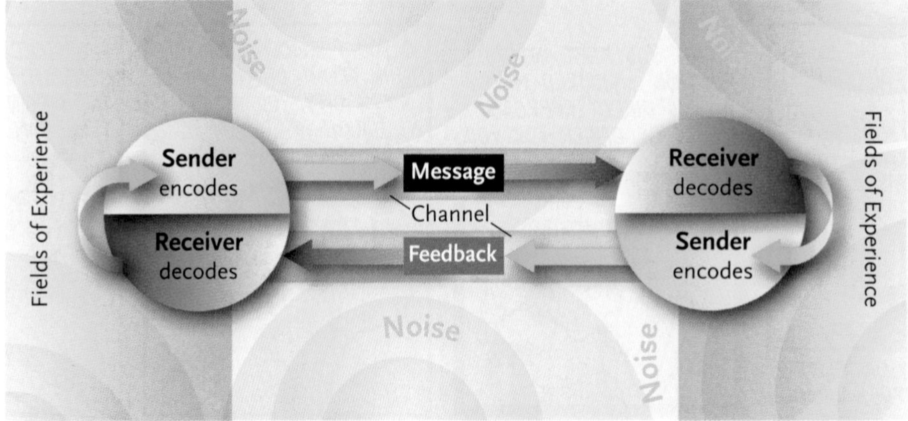

FIGURE 1-2 Interactive Model of Communication

of experience between individuals may be poorly matched and consequently produce misunderstanding. Parents, who know from their own experience how important education was to their attainment of important goals, want the same for their children. Their kids, however, don't have equivalent experience that might give them the same perspective. Languishing in a math or chemistry class may seem to teenagers more like torment than a pursuit of life goals. The more experiences we have in common, the more likely it is that misunderstandings can be avoided.

Despite these improvements offered by the interactive model, some complexities of human communication are not adequately depicted. Consequently, the transactional model was developed.

Transactional Model: The Sender-Receiver Impact View

The transactional model, by definition, assumes that people are connected through communication; they engage in a transaction. Viewing communication as transactional (see Figure 1-3) provides two insights. First, it recognizes that *each of us is a sender-receiver, not merely a sender or a receiver.* You may be the speaker in a conversation, but you are receiving feedback from your listeners simultaneously, mostly nonverbally. This feedback may encourage you to speak as you've been speaking or to make adjustments.

Second, the transactional perspective recognizes that *communication affects all parties involved.* We are defined in relation to each other as we send and receive messages, not as individuals separate from others. A teacher requires students. Parents require children. An interviewer must have an interviewee. A leader must have followers. The roles we play in life result from how we are defined in relation to others. Thus, transactional communication is not merely two-way interaction. Something more than movement of information back and forth occurs when humans communicate. We continuously influence each other and develop a relationship one to the other as we communicate (Anderson & Ross, 1994). We become interconnected. Your choice of words on your Facebook status updates, for example, can influence friends' emotions and subsequent postings. One study reported that use of positive words such as "happy" and "hug" provoked similarly positive word choices from Facebook friends and positive emotional states. Using negative words such as "sick," "vile," and "lame" provoked similarly negative word choices from Facebook friends and negative emotional states that lasted up to three days. As Adam Kramer, the study's author, notes, "If people are using more positive words, not only are their friends using more positive words, their friends also will use fewer negative words" (quoted in Swift, 2011).

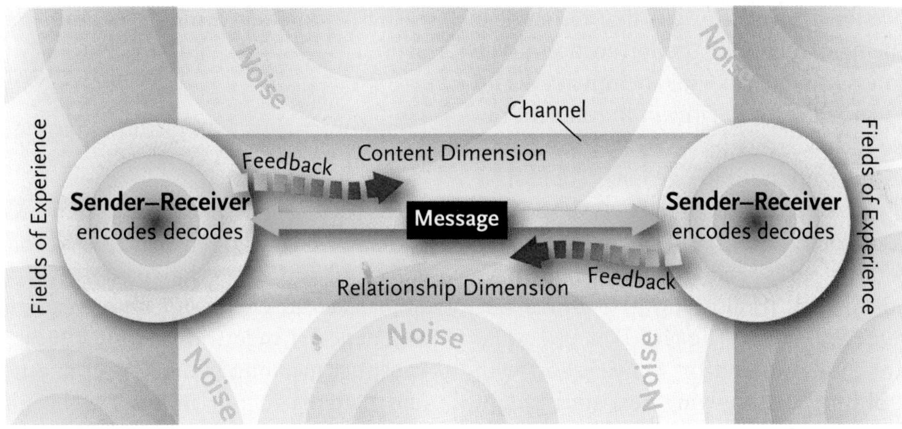

FIGURE 1-3 Transactional Model of Communication

We can see the influence we have on each other during communication more clearly by examining the two dimensions of every message: content and relationship (Watzlawick et al., 1967). The **content dimension** refers to what is actually said and done. The **relationship dimension** refers to how that message defines or redefines the association between individuals.

A college student might say, "Professor Tillson, I didn't like your test" or "Hey Tillson, your test sucks." Both messages have the same essential content (unhappiness with the test), but the relationship dimension is different. The first statement exhibits respect. The second statement, by contrast, is disrespectful, even abrasive. Of course, nonverbal cues can change the relationship. If a student jabbed an index finger in the professor's face while making the first statement in an aggressive tone of voice, then the relationship would clearly change. Likewise, if a student made the second statement with a big, knowing grin that signaled lighthearted playfulness, the nature of the relationship might be the opposite of what the words themselves indicate. This highlights the vast potential for misunderstanding that exists with email and text messages that restrict nonverbal cues.

Message content can also differ while the relationship dimension stays the same. "Will you please lend me 50 bucks?" and "Would you please help me study for my math final?" are messages that display different content but essentially the same relationship. Although the specific requests differ, respect is shown to the person receiving the request in both instances.

These illustrations show the content and relationship dimensions of messages, but they are not transactional. We don't see the reaction to the message and the impact it has on each party. Here is an example that shows transactional communication:

Student: "Hey Tillson, your test sucks."
Professor Tillson: "Did you actually study for the exam?"
Student: "No. I figured you'd give an easy test, so I didn't need to study. Besides, I had to party last night."
Professor Tillson: "Perhaps you should take this class *more* seriously?"
Student: "Perhaps you should take me *less* seriously. I'M KIDDING. I studied hard for your test, but I was confused on several questions. I want to go over the exam with you."
Professor Tillson: "Fine, but that'll cost you a five-point deduction on your exam score."
Student: "WHAT?"
Professor Tillson: "JUST KIDDING!"

The professor and the student are sparring with each other, defining their relationship as they converse. Will this be a formal relationship between teacher and student or will this be an informal relationship between relative equals? The nature of the conversation and their relationship shifts once the professor realizes that the student is being glib but has a serious concern. The professor then makes an attempt at the end to match the informality of the student but also to reassert status.

This conversation, of course, could have progressed in many different ways. The professor could have chastised the student for the "test sucks" remark. This would have defined their relationship as a formal one of unequal power. The professor also could have chosen to end the conversation with an abrupt "Try studying next time" retort while walking away. This would likely produce an unfriendly, distant relationship between teacher and student. In each case, both parties are affected not only by what is said (content) but also by how it is presented (relationship).

Communication Is a Process: The Continuous Flow

Communicating is a process of adapting to the inevitable changes that affect any relationship. The process view of communication recognizes "events and relationships as dynamic, ongoing, ever-changing, continuous" (Berlo, 1960, p. 24). In a relationship, "nothing never happens" (Johnson et al., 1974), or as the bumper sticker says, "Change is inevitable, except from a vending machine."

If you wanted to understand the ocean, you wouldn't just take a picture of a single wave or scoop up a cupful of water. The ocean can be understood only in terms of its entirety—the tides and currents, waves, plant and animal life, and so forth. Likewise, to understand communication, you need to focus not on single words, sentences, or gestures but on how currents of thoughts and feelings are expressed by both verbal and nonverbal means in the context of change.

Relationships can't be frozen in time, even though our memories of "the way we were" sometimes have this effect. Every conversation is a foothold on our next conversation, and we bring our accumulated experiences to each new conversation. Communication is an ongoing process, and each new experience influences future transactions.

Communication Is Sharing Meaning: Making Sense

The term *communication* is derived from the Latin word *communicare,* which denotes "to share." **Meaning** is "the conscious pattern humans create out of their interpretation of experience" (Anderson & Ross, 1994). We construct meaning by making connections and patterns in our minds which "make sense" of our world. When we seek help from friends or counselors about problems we are experiencing in our romantic relationships, we are trying to make sense of what may be too confusing for us to sort out by ourselves. We say something is "meaningless" when it makes no sense (someone speaking Chinese to us when we speak only English), but it is "meaningful" when it makes sense and has an impact on us in some way (Anderson & Ross, 1994).

Meaning doesn't occur in a vacuum. It is socially constructed. There is never a perfect "meeting of the minds" regarding meaning. The meaning I have for an experience, idea, relationship, concept, or symbol is an approximation of the meaning you have for the same thing. *Meaning is shared when there are overlapping interpretations between individuals.* For example, when you view a relationship as a friendship and the other person sees it likewise, there is an overlap and meaning is shared. The depth of that friendship or even what constitutes friendship, however, is not identical between two people. There are always subtle differences.

We attempt to share meaning both verbally and nonverbally. This is an imperfect process, however. Sometimes meaning doesn't get shared verbally even though words are transmitted from one person to another in a common language. For example, there is a story of a Catholic nun teaching religion to her third-graders and conducting standard catechism drills. She repeatedly asked her students, "Who is God?" Her students were to respond in unison, "God is a supreme being." Finally, she decided to test the fruits of her patient labor and called on one of the boys in the class. When asked, "Who is God?" he promptly and proudly replied, "God is a string bean." Words were transmitted, but meaning was not shared. *Supreme being* was meaningless to the third-grader. *String bean* at least could be grasped even if applying it to the divinity was a tad mysterious.

Sharing meaning between cultures poses its own unique problems. Electrolux, a Scandinavian manufacturer, discovered this when it tried selling its vacuum cleaners in the United States with the slogan, "Nothing sucks like an Electrolux." In preparation for the 2008 Beijing Olympic Games, David Tool, a retired army colonel living in the capital city, was hired to correct notoriously poor English on signs throughout the city. "Deformed Man Toilet" was thankfully replaced with "Disabled Person Toilet" and "Beijing Anus Hospital" was replaced with "Beijing Proctology Hospital" (Boudreau, 2007). As Ray Gordon, a sociologist and expert on Latin America, puts it, "If you know the language but not the culture in a country you visit, you will be able to make a fluent fool of yourself" (quoted in Brembeck & Howell, 1976, p. 205).

Sharing meaning nonverbally between cultures can be equally problematic (Axtell, 1998; Mancini, 2003). The "A-OK" gesture in the United States that forms a circle with the index finger and the thumb is obscene in Brazil, means "worthless" in France, and "money" in Japan. Raising the index finger to signify "one" means "two" in Italy; the thumb is one. In Japan, however, the upright thumb means "five"; counting begins with the index finger, and the thumb is the last digit. Nodding the head up and down means "yes" in the United States, and shaking it side to side means "no." In Bulgaria, Turkey, Iran, and Bengal, however, it is the reverse. In Greece, tipping the head back abruptly means "no," but the same gesture in India means "yes." (Nod your head if you understand all of this.)

Communication is a transactional process of sharing meaning with others. We are sender-receivers trying to make sense of our dynamic, ever-changing relationships with others. These relationships define who we are and what roles we play in life.

Common hand gestures can be offensive in many cultures. The "hook-em horns" gesture displayed by George W. Bush, a reference to the University of Texas Longhorns, is a salute to Satan in Norway. In Italy, it is an accusation of adultery.

Defining Communication Competence

Defining communication does not tell us how to communicate in a competent manner. For that, we need a map, or a theoretical model, to guide us. The communication competence model can serve a diagnostic function for you. When you begin to sense that all is not well in your transactions with others, this model can help you isolate the most likely sources of difficulty and recognize what competencies require your greater attention.

Communication competence *is engaging in communication with others that is perceived to be both effective and appropriate in a given context* (Spitzberg, 2000). This section explores the explanation and implications of this definition.

Effectiveness: Achieving Goals

Effectiveness is the degree to which we have progressed toward the achievement of our goals. Effectiveness is a litmus test of communication competence. If your cynical humor provokes hostility from your roommate, you may need to modify your humor if your goal is to remain roommates.

Degrees of Effectiveness: From Deficiency to Proficiency

Some people are proficient at establishing intimate relationships with a few individuals but feel awkward and ill at ease in large gatherings of strangers. Others would rather bite the head off of a rattlesnake than give a public speech. Our competence varies by degrees from highly proficient to severely deficient depending on our current set of circumstances. Thus, you may see yourself as highly proficient in social gatherings, moderately skillful in leadership positions in groups, and woefully inadequate in public speaking situations. We are more to less competent, not either competent or incompetent. Labeling someone a "competent communicator" makes a judgment of that individual's degree of proficiency *in a particular context,* but it does not identify an immutable characteristic of that person. Being a competent communicator is also not an idyllic state of perfection. Even the best communicators occasionally err.

We-Orientation: We-First, Not Me-First

Because communication is transactional, competence comes from focusing on "We" (what makes the *relationship* successful), not "Me" (what makes *me* successful). When you enter into an intimate relationship, for example, interdependence (a We-orientation) is primary, and independence (a Me-orientation) is secondary. A 20-year study of why marriages succeed and fail found that the more marriage partners, especially husbands, viewed their marriage as a joint undertaking, the more likely the marriage would succeed (Gottman & Silver, 1994). Problems for either partner are viewed as difficulties that affect both individuals together.

The "me-first" attitude also destroys teamwork in groups (LaFasto & Larson, 2001). In fact, a collection of individuals doesn't function as a group at all if the members are more interested in individual accomplishment than group achievement (Zander, 1982). In organizations, the Me-orientation "must be avoided at all costs. It [creates] winners and losers. When that happens, the organization is always shortchanged" (LaFasto & Larson, 2001, p. 172).

Not all individual goals clash with relationship or group goals, and some individual goals (intimacy) can only be accomplished in a context of interdependence. Nevertheless, trying to achieve individual goals at the expense of relationship, group, or organizational goals usually produces unsatisfactory outcomes for both you and others.

Effectiveness is not the sole determinant of communication competence, however, because goals are not always achievable. Your lack of effectiveness may be due to forces beyond your control (communication isn't a cure-all). A person can exhibit exemplary communication and still have relationships with family, friends, spouses, and coworkers fail (personality clashes perhaps). A public speech can be beautifully constructed and delivered, but listeners may still be unmoved because you don't share the same values and beliefs. Nevertheless, communication that often fails to achieve your goals is probably deficient in some way.

Appropriateness: Communicating by the Rules

Spitzberg (2000) defines **appropriateness** as behavior that "is viewed as legitimate for, or fitting to, the context" (p. 375). Appropriateness can be determined only within a specific context. **Context** is the environment in which communication occurs: *who* (sender-receiver) communicates *what* (message) to *whom* (receiver-sender), *why* a message is sent (purpose), *where* (setting) it is sent, and *when* (timing) and *how* (channel) it is transmitted. We determine the appropriateness of our communication by analyzing all of these elements.

Rules: Explicit and Implicit

Every communication context is guided by rules. A **rule** "is a followable prescription that indicates what behavior is obligated, preferred, or prohibited in certain contexts" (Shimanoff, 1980, p. 57). A family, for example, has many rules (Yerby & Buerkel-Rothfuss,

This cartoon illustrates
1. implicit rules of communication
2. explicit rules of communication
3. linear model of communication
4. all of the above
Answers given at end of chapter

1982). Rules stipulate who takes out the trash, who cooks the meals, who pays the bills, and so forth. There are also rules constraining and structuring communication transactions within the family unit, such as "We never go to bed angry," "Children will address a parent or stepparent in a respectful way at all times," and "Don't interrupt someone during dinner conversation."

Rules create expectations regarding appropriate behavior. Some rules are *explicitly* stated (directly expressed), such as "No shoes, no shirt, no service" and "No smoking." Social networking sites have explicit rules concerning text content and photos, even the number of characters allowed in text messages. Most rules, however, are merely *implied* (indirectly indicated) by patterns of behavior. You don't have to be told directly what to do or not do. For example, it is unlikely that you will find signs in a grocery store that read: "Don't eat cookies and put the half-empty bag back on the shelf," "Don't crash into other customers with your cart," and "Don't steal food from another person's cart." When you encounter a coworker or stranger who asks, "How ya doing?" you know better than to respond with a long-winded appraisal of your current state of affairs. Normally, you just say, "I'm fine, how are you?" Cultural greeting rules dictate that the question not be interpreted literally. Consequently, the greeting becomes ritualistic, even mindless, which is why I've caught myself on more than one occasion asking, "How are you?" and receiving the response from the other person, "I'm fine, how are you?" whereupon I give the slightly embarrassing response, "I'm fine, how are you?" (Oops, already asked that—trapped in a feedback loop.)

When you do encounter explicit rules that seem to underestimate your grasp of the implicit rules guiding social conventions, you're likely to take note. Wallace (1999), for example, tells of a tavern in rural Texas that conspicuously displays signs that read "No spitting" and "No fighting." There is even a sign in the men's restroom—meant to be amusing, I assume—that advises, "Do not eat the urinal cakes."

A violation of an implicit rule often leads to an explicit statement of the rule. College instructors take for granted that students won't interrupt the flow of a lecture or discussion by talking inappropriately with fellow students or texting during class. On occasion, however, this implicit rule must be made explicit to students whose enthusiasm for casual conversation outweighs their ardor for the classroom task.

Rule Violations: Consequential Effects

Communication becomes inappropriate if it violates rules when such violations could be averted without sacrificing a goal by choosing alternative communication behaviors (Getter & Nowinski, 1981). Consider two examples. First, students' communication with professors can be perceived as inappropriate. One study found that college faculty are concerned about students communicating with them in too casual, careless, or cocky a manner (Duran et al., 2005). Students could choose to do otherwise without jeopardizing, and probably enhancing, their goal attainment.

In a stunningly inappropriate act, Kanye West seized the microphone from Taylor Swift. She was about to give her acceptance speech for "best female video" award at the MTV Music Awards when West touted a music video by Beyonce, one of her competitors. What implicit rules were violated? The reaction to West's moment of hubris was swift (no pun intended) and vociferously negative from almost every circle.

Another study asked college professors to assess an email message from a student that read: "R U Able to Meat Me?" Professors especially disliked the "R U" acronym for "are you" and expressed strong dislike for using "meat" for "meet." There are implied rules about message formality, grammar, and spelling in student-teacher communication which, if violated, can produce very negative reactions. Messages such as the above made professors "like the student less, view them as less credible, have a lesser opinion of the message quality, and made them less willing to comply with students' simple email requests" (Stephens et al., 2009). A professor, of course, can signal to a student in an email that common rules of formality can be loosened somewhat by constructing a message with texting acronyms and occasional slang ("ain't"). The higher status person, however, has the greater flexibility to loosen the rules.

Second, in a survey of more than 2,400 "hiring managers" by Harris Interactive for Career Builder, a web-based employment organization, 71% of respondents said "answering a cell phone or texting during the interview" was the most common error made by job applicants. A close second (69%) was "dressing inappropriately." Rules create expectations (e.g., be polite, responsive, and attentive during job interviews). When job applicants demonstrate scant understanding or appreciation for common rules and corresponding expectations, they communicate disrespect, indifference, even insult toward interviewers. These are sure-fire ways to lose any chance of being offered the job.

Although rules for appropriate communication are determined by context, rules are not sacred. Some rules may need to be modified. When students share a dorm room or an apartment, rule modification is almost inevitable if communication is to remain competent. Difficulties living together will occur if one person expects a spotlessly clean, orderly environment and the other person is content with more casual surroundings. When rules clash, a modification of the rules will have to be negotiated unless one person is willing to accept the other's rules completely.

Achieving Communication Competence

Defining communication competence tells us what it is but not how to achieve it. There are five general ways the appropriateness and effectiveness of our communication can be improved. We can build *knowledge,* develop our communication *skills,* increase our *sensitivity,* enhance our *commitment,* and apply *ethics* to our communication choices (see Figure 1-4). Let's look at each of these in more detail.

Knowledge: Learning the Rules

Achieving communication competence begins with knowledge of the rules that create behavioral expectations and knowing what is likely to work effectively given the rules of the situation. Communication can be inappropriate and ineffective (deficient in every respect), appropriate but ineffective (a desire to please others at your own expense or uncontrollable circumstances preventing achievement), inappropriate but effective (lying, cheating, intimidating, or coercing others to achieve goals), or appropriate and effective (goal achievement while following the rules relevant to a context). Which of these four possibilities is most likely largely depends on your knowledge of the rules and the communication strategies that work in particular communication situations.

FIGURE 1-4 Communication Competence Model

Failure to know basic rules common in different cultures can produce embarrassment or even unpleasant international incidents. For example, in South Korea, men enter and exit through doors *before* women, and women assist men with their coats. In Zambia, you may go hungry at a dinner gathering unless you specifically ask for food. It is deemed impolite for the dinner host to offer food before it is requested. When American dignitaries and businesspeople travel to Japan, one source of awkward social interaction is the bowing ritual used as a social greeting. Axtell (1998) briefly describes the Japanese bowing ritual with its list of rules. When bowing to "business inferiors," always permit them to bow lower and longer. When bowing to those of equal status, match bows. When bowing to "the top man" (it usually is a man), "if he clearly outranks you, make sure you outbow him even if it takes your knuckles all the way to the floor. Also remember to keep your eyes respectfully lowered" (p. 44). Learning cultural rules helps you avoid serious misunderstandings and miscommunication.

Skills: Showing, Not Just Knowing

A **communication skill** is "the successful performance of a communication behavior . . . [and] the ability to repeat such a behavior" (Spitzberg & Hecht, 1984, p. 577). Clearly, fluently, concisely, eloquently, and confidently communicating messages are examples of skills. Knowledge about communication without communication skill will not produce competence. You can read stacks of books about public speaking, but there is no substitute for skill gained by practice and experience speaking in front of an audience. The ability to communicate a message concisely and precisely is an important skill. Speaking with long pauses and vocal fillers (ums and ahs), however, can nullify your effectiveness despite an otherwise concise and precise message.

Conversely, *skill without knowledge is equally unproductive.* Learning to "express your feelings honestly" can be an important communication skill in many situations. Expressing your honest feelings indiscriminately, however, no matter what the likely consequences, mimics the act of an innocent child, not a mature adult. Learning to be assertive—standing up for yourself by stating your thoughts and feelings to others with confidence and skill—is very useful generally. Encouraging a battered woman to be assertive with her abuser, however, might get her killed by challenging the abuser's desire for complete control (O'Leary et al., 1985). Confrontation—directly addressing a conflict with others—is an appropriate and effective strategy for dealing with interpersonal conflict generally (see Chapter 9). It is the worst strategy a stalking victim can choose because it feeds a stalker's desire for contact, any contact, with the victim (Wondrak & Hoffman, 2007). A one-size-fits-all skills package doesn't produce competent communication. *Being flexible and adaptive is essential to effective and appropriate (competent) communication* (Martin & Rubin, 1994).

One key to achieving communication competence is using a mixture of both knowledge and skills. Lack of knowledge constrains your understanding of what skills work in a given situation. Limited skills constrain your ability to respond appropriately even if you know what is required. Having a variety of skills gives you the flexibility to make choices appropriate to the specific context (Riggio, 2006).

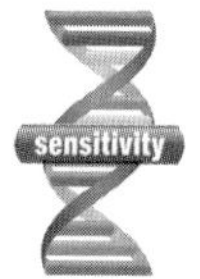

Sensitivity: Developing Receptive Accuracy

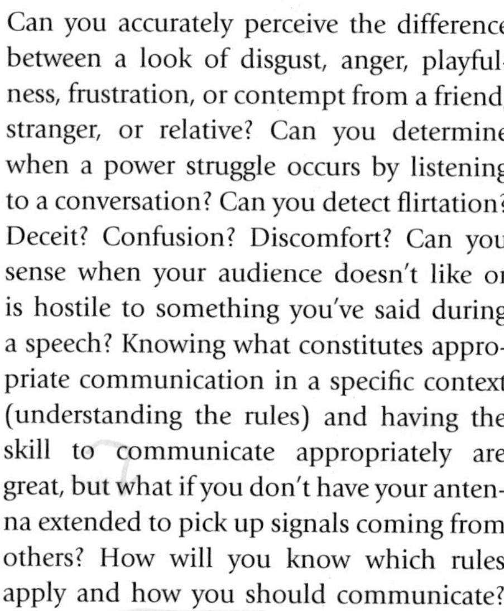

Can you accurately perceive the difference between a look of disgust, anger, playfulness, frustration, or contempt from a friend, stranger, or relative? Can you determine when a power struggle occurs by listening to a conversation? Can you detect flirtation? Deceit? Confusion? Discomfort? Can you sense when your audience doesn't like or is hostile to something you've said during a speech? Knowing what constitutes appropriate communication in a specific context (understanding the rules) and having the skill to communicate appropriately are great, but what if you don't have your antenna extended to pick up signals coming from others? How will you know which rules apply and how you should communicate?

Sensitivity is *receptive accuracy* whereby we can detect, decode, and comprehend signals in our social environment (Bernieri, 2001). Sensitivity can help us adapt our messages to a particular context in an appropriate and effective manner. Failure to recognize and to comprehend signals can severely limit our social effectiveness (Hall & Bernieri, 2001). If you are obviously angry but your partner doesn't have a clue that this is how you feel, you will easily perceive this cluelessness as insensitivity to your needs, and an argument will likely ensue. Competent communicators develop sensitivity to nuances and subtleties of communication transactions and respond to them.

Sensitivity can be learned (Hall & Bernieri, 2001). One of the functions of this text is to help you become more sensitive to your social environment by identifying patterns of communication that cause problems in relationships and by learning how to analyze an audience before giving a speech.

A major aspect of sensitivity is being mindful, not mindless, about your communication and that of others. We're **mindful** when "we think about our communication and continually work at changing what we do in order to become more effective" (Griffin, 1994, p. 406). For instance, we notice when friends or loved ones reach out to us for support and affection, and we respond in appropriate ways. We're **mindless** when we're not cognizant of our communication with others and we put little or no effort into improving it.

Gottman tells a story of a neurosurgeon he had as a client who exhibited mindlessness not from any desire to be mean but from emotional distance that served him well in his profession (Gottman & DeClaire, 2001). As a successful neurosurgeon, he practiced giving objective, clinical analyses of patients' afflictions. When he came home, he communicated with his wife in the same manner. His wife once asked him, "How do you think we're doing—as a couple?" He provided a long-winded, accurate analysis. His wife burst into tears and ran from the room, leaving him flummoxed. He hadn't been mindful of what her question was actually seeking from him. She desired reassurance, support, and affection. Had he thought about why his wife would ask in a serious manner about the state of their relationship, surely he would have realized that she was not seeking an emotionally detached analysis. If you don't attend to the signals that indicate other people's emotional needs because you aren't looking, then you can't connect with those who can make life a joyful experience. This doesn't mean that we are obliged to connect with everyone we encounter daily, but we surely must connect with those individuals who are important influences on our lives.

As email, text messaging, tweeting, and blogging are increasingly used to communicate with others, the channel-rich, nonverbal cues that we use to detect signals in our social environment are minimized. Consequently, our sensitivity is constrained. Think of the number of times that you've read an email or text message and mistaken the tone for irritation or hostility when the sender intended to communicate no such feeling. In one study of **virtual groups**, whose members communicate electronically and rarely if ever meet face to face, 94% of respondents found the "inability to read nonverbal cues" a significant problem (Solomon, 2010). Technological advances in communication pose new challenges to our sensitivity.

Commitment: Acquiring a Passion for Excellence

Knowledge, skills, and sensitivity are important ways to improve your communication competence. Communication effectiveness, however, also requires commitment. **Commitment** is a passion for excellence: accepting nothing less than the best that you can be and dedicating yourself to achieving that excellence. You strive for excellence by identifying your communication weaknesses, by learning constructive communication patterns, by dedicating considerable effort toward changing bad communication habits to good patterns, and by practicing your communication skills diligently.

To exhibit commitment, *attitude is as important as aptitude.* No one can force you to be a proficient communicator. You have to want to be proficient. In sports, athletes develop a high level of skills when they commit themselves to hard work, study, and practice. Academic success also does not come from lackluster effort. You must want to do well and be dedicated to making it happen. You make it a priority in your life. Sustaining love in an intimate relationship also requires commitment (Epstein, 2010). You have to want the relationship to remain successful, and you need to work hard to sustain that success. The same holds true for communication competence. You must want to improve, to change, and to grow more proficient in your communication with others.

Ethics: Determining the Right and Wrong of Communication

A few years ago, a national poll asked 5,500 Americans whether they would kill a stranger for $10 million; 7% said they would ("Amoral Majority," 1991). Applied to the total adult population of the United States, this response means that about 15 million people would be willing assassins for a big chunk of cash. How do we decide whether behavior is right or wrong?

In 1999, the National Communication Association (NCA) adopted a "Credo for Ethical Communication." The opening statement of this credo establishes the significance of and justification for including ethics in any communication competence model. The statement reads:

> Questions of right and wrong arise whenever people communicate. Ethical communication is fundamental to responsible thinking, decision making, and the development of relationships and communities within and across contexts, cultures, channels, and media. Moreover, ethical communication enhances human worth and dignity by fostering truthfulness, fairness, responsibility, personal integrity, and respect for self and others. We believe that unethical communication threatens the quality of all communication and consequently the well-being of individuals and the society in which we live.

Ethics is a system for judging moral correctness by using an agreed upon set of standards to determine what constitutes right and wrong behavior. In its entirety, the NCA credo identifies five ethical standards to guide our communication with others. They are:

1. *Respect.* "Some form of the Golden Rule is embraced by virtually all of the major religious and moral systems" (Jaksa & Pritchard, 1994, p. 101). Treating others as you would want to be treated is a central guiding ethical standard. Respect shows concern for others (We-orientation), not just concern for self (Me-orientation).

2. *Honesty.* Ethically responsible communicators try to avoid intentionally deceptive messages. Honesty is a cultural expectation. There is a "presumption against lying" (Bok, 1978, p. 32). All ethical systems condemn lying ("Lying Is Part," 1996). One poll found that honesty was the most prized attribute in a friend ("Lying in America," 1987).

3. *Fairness.* Prejudice has no place in the communication arena. Racism, sexism, homophobia, ageism, and all the other "isms" that plague the human spirit and divide nations and peoples would diminish if we applied the standard of fairness in our communication with diverse groups. Permitting some people to express their points of view but stifling others' expression of dissent is unfair. Fairness requires equal treatment.

4. *Choice.* Our communication should strive to allow people to make their own choices free of coercion (Jaksa & Pritchard, 1994). Persuasion allows free choice among available options. Coercion forces choice without permitting individuals to think or act for themselves. "Choice must be intentional and voluntary. . . . A communicator's intention is a prime consideration in ethical judgment" (Jensen, 1997, p. 4). When a person is forced to lie or mistreat others, the actions are unintentional. In such a circumstance, the person performing the unethical behavior is not culpable.

5. *Responsibility.* "People constantly struggle with the tension between rights and responsibilities, and conscientious people seek to balance the tensions in meaningful and fair ways. Individuals demand the right of free expression, but society demands that individual freedom not harm the larger community" (Jensen, 1997, p. 10). We have a responsibility to consider the consequences of our communication on others. Responsibility means that ethical communication requires a We-orientation. Competent communicators must concern themselves with more than merely what works to achieve personal or group goals. A person may be quite effective at accomplishing individual goals (Me-orientation), but if these goals produce bad outcomes for others, their appropriateness must be questioned.

In the abstract, these standards may seem straightforward and uncontroversial, but almost nothing in human communication is absolute and clear-cut. Human communication behavior is so complex that any list of standards for judging the ethics of communication, applied without exceptions, is bound to run into difficulty. In some cases, two or more ethical standards may collide. Free choice, for example, collides with parents' responsibility when parents insist that their children behave in certain ways and make certain choices that may ultimately depend on coercion (the threat of punishment). Also, what if honesty shows disrespect and a lack of concern for another person's feelings ("Yes, you are fat and unattractive")? Despite these difficulties, all five of these ethical standards are strong values in our culture, and they serve as important guidelines for our communication behavior.

In summary, you can achieve communication competence in five general ways: building your knowledge, developing your skills, increasing your sensitivity to verbal and nonverbal cues, enhancing your commitment to achieving communication excellence, and applying ethics to your communication choices. These global ways of achieving communication competence are explained in far greater detail and complexity throughout this text. Achieving communication competence, however, occurs within the context of a communication climate that either encourages or discourages communication proficiency.

Creating a Communication Climate

A **communication climate** is the emotional atmosphere, the pervading or enveloping tone that we create by the way we communicate with others. Communication climate is integrally linked to communication competence. Some communication climates promote proficiency, and others promote deficiency in goal attainment.

Types of Climates: Constructive and Destructive

A **constructive communication climate** is composed of two general elements: a pattern of **openness**, or a willingness to communicate, and a pattern of **supportiveness**, or a confirmation of the worth and value of others and a willingness to help others succeed (LaFasto & Larson, 2001). At their core, openness and supportiveness are We-oriented, whereby our individual agendas are secondary to the relationship, group, or organizational agenda.

A **destructive communication climate** is composed of two general elements: a pattern of **closedness**, or an unwillingness to communicate with others, and a pattern of **defensiveness**, or a protective reaction to a perceived attack on our self-esteem and self-concept. The protective reaction usually takes three forms (Ellison, 2009; LaFasto & Larson, 2001).

1. You *deny* the validity or accuracy of the perceived attack. "I did *not* study half-heartedly for the exam; I studied hard" is an example of denial.
2. You *counterattack* the person whose communication diminishes your self-perception. When Margaret Thatcher was prime minister of Great Britain, she was often called the "Iron Maiden" for her aggressive style and tactics stereotypically associated with men, not women. When she received the backhanded "compliment" from a male opposition Labour Party official, "May I congratulate you on being the only man on your team," she counterattacked, "That's one more than you've got on yours" (Barreca, 1991, p. 84).
3. You *withdraw.* This occurs when you psychologically and/or physically remove yourself from a threatening arena so no further attacks can be launched against you.

Individual instances of openness and supportiveness or closedness and defensiveness do not typically constitute constructive or destructive communication climates. This is analogous to weather climates. We say that a part of the country has a "temperate climate." We don't base this on a single 70-degree, sunny day. One critical comment, for example, is an *episode* that might provoke an immediate defensive response, but it doesn't create a destructive climate unless the episode is especially egregious (sexual abuse). A *pattern* of criticism (several episodes) can create a destructive climate. Although examples offered in this and later chapters (see especially Chapter 8) to illustrate communication climates are by necessity just episodes, keep in mind that repetitive episodes of the same kind of communication create climates.

Communication Patterns and Climates: Competition and Cooperation

Competitive and cooperative communication patterns typically produce different climates for human transactions. Before discussing their respective consequences to human relationships, however, some seemingly straightforward terms need to be defined for conceptual clarity.

Drawing Clear Distinctions: Conceptual Clarity

Competition is a process of mutually *exclusive* goal attainment (MEGA); for you to win, others must lose (Kohn, 1992). The single inescapable fact that defines competition is that the system of rewards inherently benefits the victorious. Thus, examples of competitive communication include engaging in public debates; waging battles to win arguments with friends, spouses, or partners; arguing over material possessions and child custody during a divorce; and criticizing and diminishing others to look superior to rivals at work. In all of these acts, communication is a *winner-take-all* vehicle to defeat others and to establish oneself as best at others' expense.

Cooperation is a process of mutually *inclusive* goal attainment (MIGA); for me to achieve my goal, you must also achieve your goal. We sink or swim together. Examples of cooperative communication include negotiating problems to the mutual satisfaction of all parties in a conflict; engaging in teamwork to solve problems and make decisions; teaching those with inadequate skills to improve and become more capable; and expressing support to those who are discouraged. The essence of cooperation is a *winners-all* effort to raise everyone to a high standard, not to drag anyone down to defeat for the sake of individual glory.

Competitive communication can be tumultuous, but cooperative communication also can be difficult, at times contentious, even frustrating. *Cooperative communication is a process, not an outcome* (King et al., 2009. Parties in a conflict, for example, may communicate cooperatively yet still not reach an agreement because they seek very different outcomes. *The cooperative communication process also doesn't mean yielding to others.* Management guru W. Edwards Deming relates a story to make the point. "I was stuck in an airplane waiting for several hours to disembark. When we finally were able to get off, the stewardess said, 'Thank you for your cooperation.' That's not cooperation. What choice do prisoners have?" (quoted in Aguayo, 1990, p. 230).

Individual achievement is the realization of personal goals without having to defeat an opponent. Giving a speech better the second time you perform it is an individual achievement. It becomes competitive when you try to outperform someone else, as in a speech contest or debate tournament. When 1,030 females from ages 11 to 49 were asked with whom they competed, 75% of the respondents chose "with myself; my own standards and goals" (Nelson, 1998). Saying that you compete with yourself makes little conceptual sense. What would you deduce from someone saying, "I ran faster than myself"? *Competition is not a solitary undertaking; it is interactive* (Kohn, 1992). What we often call competing with ourselves is more accurately termed individual achievement. Seeking to reach a higher goal without defeating someone else is a challenge, not a contest.

Hypercompetitiveness is the excessive emphasis on beating others to achieve one's goals. This *winning-is-everything* attitude is widespread in American culture. Americans "manifest a staggering cultural obsession with victory" (Aronson, 1999, p. 263). Kevin Daugherty, youth sports specialist for the American Sport Education Program, says, "Our culture bombards us with messages that winning is everything" (Krucoff, 1998, p. D3). One study of 198 elite athletes revealed that more than half would take a performance-enhancing drug if it would increase their chances of winning every competition for a five-year period. That probably doesn't surprise you, but here is the real stunner: these same elite athletes would take this drug even if they realized it would *kill them* at the end of the five years ("Superhuman Heroes," 1998). That's hypercompetitiveness.

Constructive competition occurs when competing against others produces a positive, enjoyable experience and promotes increased efforts to achieve victory without jeopardizing positive interpersonal relationships and personal well-being (Tjosvold et al., 2003, 2006). Friendly family rivalries, for example, can be a source of bonding. Verbal jousting with your intimate partner can be enjoyable and a cause for laughter. Some individuals, usually those who have the skills to win, thrive in competitive environments. Research supports three conditions that determine whether competition creates a constructive or destructive climate (D. W. Johnson, 2003; Tjosvold et al., 2006). They are

1. de-emphasis on winning,
2. competing against relative equals, and
3. competing fairly.

The more these three conditions for constructive competition are missing, the more we encourage closedness and defensiveness, the two components of a destructive communication climate.

Competitive and Cooperative Communication Climates: Consequences

Challenging the wisdom of competing can be difficult because the uncritical acceptance of the benefits of competition and the passion with which this view is often held are so widespread in the United States (Kohn, 1992). Nevertheless, a sober examination of the research will show that there are significant differences between competitive and cooperative communication climates, and we ignore this evidence at the expense of our relationships with others and our ability to achieve many of our goals in life.

Interpersonal Relationships: Stress and Strain No discussion of human communication can ignore competition—"the common denominator of American life" (Kohn, 1992, p. 1). Nathan Miller bitingly asserts that "conversation in the United States is a competitive exercise in which the

Hypercompetitiveness knows no bounds. Nathan's yearly hot dog eating contest encourages contestants to gorge themselves with stomach-churning quantities of hotdogs in buns.

This cartoon illustrates
1. individual achievement
2. cooperation
3. hypercompetitiveness
4. none of the above
Answers given at end of chapter

first person to draw a breath is declared the listener" (quoted in Bolton, 1979, p. 4). Competition saturates our society, and hypercompetitiveness profoundly influences our relationships with others. Competition is not structured to enhance interpersonal relationships. Trying to win an argument with your partner about who does the most cleaning or who is most responsible for making repairs has "victory" as the goal. "Losing" an argument doesn't usually foster friendliness toward your antagonist. Trying to win an argument with your romantic partner can be challenging and fun as long as this verbal jousting is playful or entertaining and doesn't wound. That is difficult to achieve, however, because what begins as playful can quickly deteriorate into a nasty hypercompetitive verbal battle if feelings are hurt.

As competitiveness increases, empathy decreases (Kohn, 1993). **Empathy** is "thinking and feeling what you perceive another to be thinking and feeling" (Howell, 1982, p. 108). Empathy is the We-orientation of communication competence. When you have empathy, you experience another person's perspective. Trying to win at someone else's expense clouds your ability to empathize. Your focus is on yourself, not on the other person or on what damage winning might produce. The more empathy you feel, the more difficult it becomes to view another person as a rival to be vanquished. Hypercompetitiveness can make empathy disappear.

Increasing levels of competitiveness can also incite increasingly hostile communication (Van Oostrum & Rabbie, 1995). In a survey of 60 high-school athletic associations, 76% of the respondents said increased verbal and nonverbal hostility are causing many officials of high-school sporting events to quit (Dahlberg, 2001). In Whitehall, North Carolina, one coach slashed the throat of a rival coach, spattering blood on one of the Little Leaguers. Parents have brawled at T-ball games in Florida, coaches across the nation have been threatened and physically harmed by parents and opposing coaches, and kids are regularly yelled at by parents during and after sporting events (Dahlberg, 2001; "Poor Sporting Behavior," 2007). Little League baseball, to some, seems like "institutionalized child abuse" because hypercompetitive parental behavior is so shameful (Kohn, 1992). Hostile communication drives people apart. Cooperation, in contrast, is structured to enhance interpersonal attraction, trust, and empathy (Kohn, 1992, 1993). Individuals become partners, working together to accomplish goals, not enemies to defeat.

The communication climate is critical to relationship effectiveness, team achievement, and organizational success. Even in the public speaking arena, the effectiveness of a speech is largely dependent on the

BOX 1.2 Focus on Controversy

ETHICS AND HYPERCOMPETITIVENESS

Competent communication involves ethical considerations, and hypercompetitiveness raises serious ethical concerns. Lying and deception clearly violate the ethical criterion of honesty, and hypercompetitiveness encourages dishonesty (Callahan, 2004). As Sissela Bok (1978), in her widely acclaimed book *Lying,* explains: "The very stress on individualism, on competition, on achieving material success which so marks our society also generates intense pressures to cut corners . . . Such motives impel many to participate in forms of duplicity they might otherwise resist" (p. 258).

Cheating, in addition to being dishonest, violates the ethical criterion of fairness because it gives an unfair advantage to the cheater. Cheating has become widespread in the United States, and hypercompetitiveness is the driving force behind it. For example, several studies show that more than three-quarters of college students cheat by copying off a fellow student's exam, plagiarizing term papers in whole or in part that are found or purchased on the Internet, or failing to attribute sources for facts and statistics presented in papers or speeches (McCabe et al., 2001; Yardley et al., 2009). This widespread cheating encourages other students, who might otherwise reject cheating as an option, to engage in such dishonesty to "level the playing field." They perceive a competitive advantage given to cheating students who do not get caught or who are rarely or only lightly punished for cheating when discovered. Intense competition for grades to gain entry to the best colleges or medical, business, and law schools, and to help land the most coveted jobs upon graduation, are primary reasons college students cheat (McCabe et al., 2001).

Another ethical standard, respect for others, is shown by communicating sportsmanship, empathy, and compassion. Hypercompetitiveness, which glorifies the victors with messages of praise and adulation and is indifferent to or even contemptuous of losers in a contest, teaches none of these elements of respect. As Alice Walker so eloquently notes, we live in a culture where "the only way I can bloom is if I step on your flower, the only way I can shine is if I put out your light" (quoted in Lanka, 1989, p. 24). Respect, not in the sense of being impressed by someone's talent as a potential rival but of valuing someone as a person, doesn't blossom in a hypercompetitive climate in which being called "a loser" is a common experience for many.

This is all well and good, you may be saying, but we live in a hypercompetitive society. Our children will have to face the disappointment of losing throughout their lives, and so will we. They'll lose jobs because others gave better interviews; they'll lose arguments with parents and teachers; they'll lose speech contests; they may even lose in divorce proceedings. Is it not the responsibility of parents to teach children how to lose?

Teaching children how to lose with grace and dignity is an important communication lesson, but just as important is teaching them how to communicate cooperatively with others. Our children will be afforded many opportunities to practice losing without any encouragement from us. Does it not make more sense to offer cooperative experiences for our children to counterbalance the competitive exposure they most surely will face without our assistance?

QUESTIONS FOR THOUGHT

1. Are the ethical questions raised here merely misplaced idealism that ignores the unavoidable realities of American society? Don't we have to deal with what is, not with what we might like our society to be?
2. Are the ethical questions raised here an indictment only of hypercompetitiveness, or can the same questions be raised about competition in general?

communication climate that exists between speaker and listeners. Repeatedly attacking your audience's beliefs or values, for example, will likely provoke a counterattack in the form of heckling or withdrawal as demonstrated by audience members leaving the speech in disgust.

Group Effects: Teamwork/Cohesiveness The degree of liking we have for members of a group, and the level of commitment to the group that this liking produces, is called **cohesiveness**. Cohesiveness nurtures teamwork, and it is best enhanced by a cooperative communication climate of openness and supportiveness (LaFasto & Larson, 2001).

A common notion is that intergroup (between groups) competition promotes intragroup (within a group) cohesiveness and teamwork. This is primarily true, however, for winning teams and not losing ones. Losing teams typically fall apart as members look for someone to blame (Stephan & Stephan, 1996; Van Oostrum & Rabbie, 1995). Communication within the group often becomes hostile when defeat becomes common.

Teamwork requires cooperation, not competition (Johnson & Johnson, 2003). The Me-orientation of competitiveness works against the We-orientation critical to teamwork. As former Los Angeles Dodgers manager Tommy Lasorda once said, "My responsibility is to get my 25 guys playing for the name on the front of the shirt and not the one on the back" (quoted in LaFasto & Larson, 2001, p. 100).

We've probably all experienced the thrill of victory and the agony of defeat. Here the U.S. women's soccer team celebrates its "miracle" victory against Brazil in the 2011 FIFA World Cup. Brazil suffers crushing disappointment, as the U.S. team would later against Japan in the finals.

Achievement and Performance: Not What You Might Think There is a widely accepted belief in the United States that competition enhances achievement and performance in schools, in the workplace, in virtually every walk of life. The evidence, however, does not support this assertion. A review of more than 750 studies in a variety of settings points to an inescapable conclusion: *achievement and performance are typically best enhanced by a cooperative climate, not a competitive one* (Johnson, 2003b; Johnson & Johnson, 2005). Why? Rivals typically hoard resources to gain a perceived advantage over adversaries, and they cheat and act dishonestly to vanquish opponents (Callahan, 2004; Kohn, 1992; Stanne et al., 1999). Such a communication climate is not conducive to achieving excellence and performing well (Van Oostrum & Rabbie, 1995). Also, the vast majority who realize they have no chance to win are unlikely to be motivated to perform optimally. They

TABLE 1-1 EFFECTS OF COOPERATION COMPARED TO HYPERCOMPETITIVENESS

COOPERATION	HYPERCOMPETITION
Builds interpersonal relations	Damages interpersonal relations
Creates empathy	Creates hostility/aggression
Develops connection	Disconnects
Encourages trust	Encourages distrust
Develops teamwork/cohesiveness	Teamwork occurs when winning
Improves achievement/performance	Impedes achievement/performance
Reduces incentive to cheat	Encourages cheating

are more likely to want to quit and often do. Of the 41 million youths ages 18 or younger who participate in organized sports in the United States, 70% quit by age 13 because the pressure to win is too great and most don't believe they have any chance of winning and reaping the rewards of victory (Emmons, 2005; Goodwin, 2010). In the workplace, individuals who feel incapable of competing effectively for promotions, bonuses, and merit pay typically want to quit their jobs (Tjosvold et al., 2003).

Openness and supportiveness, the two components of a constructive communication climate, are discouraged by hypercompetitiveness because they give an advantage to your opponent. Cooperation, unlike competition, requires the attainment of your goals by working with, not against, others. Thus, openness and supportiveness are encouraged because mutual goal attainment is more likely in such an atmosphere.

In some circumstances, however, a cooperative option doesn't exist. Interviewing for a job is unavoidably competitive whenever more than one applicant is vying for a single position. Encouraging individuals to hone their oral communication skills so that they might compete more effectively in such situations should be applauded. The knowledge and skills discussed in this text will give you distinct advantages over rivals when competition is unavoidable. *Encouraging greater cooperation in our communication with others merely calls for a better balance in a society awash in competition, not the impractical abolition of all competition and the substitution of some fairy-tale notion of total cooperation in a world of perfect harmony.*

Summary

COMMUNICATION is the transactional process of sharing meaning with others. The communication competence model acts as a map that can guide your transactions with others. Studying the human communication process increases your knowledge of how to behave appropriately and effectively in a specific context. Communication skill development allows you to use your knowledge of communication in useful ways. Knowledge and skills, however, don't automatically improve relationships. Being sensitive to your social environment by detecting, decoding, and comprehending signals increases effective communication. Sensitivity means monitoring your communication so you can improve. Being committed to improving your communication by investing time, energy, feelings, thoughts, and effort is also necessary. The communication competence model of knowledge, skills, sensitivity, commitment, and ethics will serve as the map directing your journey into a variety of communication environments that will be explored in later chapters. Developing a constructive communication climate is a first step in this journey.

Answers for *Critical Thinking* captions:

Candorville (p. 13): #2 and #4
James Earl Ray (p. 13): #4
Cathy (p. 28): #3

Answers for *Hindsight Bias Self-Test,* Box 1-1

T/F:

1. False	**11. False**
2. False	**12. True**
3. False	**13. False**
4. False	**14. False**
5. False	**15. False**
6. False	**16. False**
7. False	**17. False**
8. False	**18. False**
9. False	**19. True**
10. False	**20. False**

Calculating Your Scoring:
Each answer is worth *2 points.*

Your Score: _______

Maximum 40 points (20 × 2)

36–40 = A
32–34 = B
28–30 = C
24–26 = D
Below 24 = F

Quizzes Without Consequences

Test your knowledge before your exam!

Go to the companion website at www.oup.com/us/rothwell, click on the Student Resources for each chapter, and take the Quizzes Without Consequences.

Film School Case Studies

THIS activity section, found in every chapter, presents select films for you to analyze. A movie rating (PG-13, R, etc.) is included to assist you in deciding which films are appropriate. This is a critical thinking activity. A specific question or issue is raised that is relevant to each film listed. You are asked to explore this question or issue using chapter material for your analysis.

French Kiss (1995). Romantic Comedy; PG-13

This is a very amusing "relationship" movie with Kevin Kline and Meg Ryan turning in wonderful comic performances. Notice the influence of culture on communication transactions. Where do you see examples of all four types of noise (physical, physiological, psychological, and semantic)?

I Am Legend (2007). Drama; R

Will Smith is a man alone in New York City after a terrifying pandemic has occurred. Examine the influence of loneliness on one's well-being. Why is the death of his dog so traumatic?

Leatherheads (2008). Comedy; PG-13

Goofy comedy about the early days (1920s) of professional football starring George Clooney. Is the competition in all of its aspects depicted as constructive or destructive? Apply the three criteria for constructive competition.

Nell (1994). Drama; PG-13

This is the story of a socially isolated individual. Identify the powerful effects social isolation has on a person, especially in the main character's ability to communicate and establish connection with others.

Rachel Getting Married (2008). Drama; R

Anne Hathaway takes a departure from her usual roles. She plays a recovering addict temporarily away from rehab to attend her sister's wedding. Examine this movie for examples of the dictum that "quantity of communication does not always produce quality."

Return to Paradise (1998). Drama; R

Underrated film about a harrowing moral dilemma. You'll be contemplating what you would do in the same circumstances. Analyze the film for communication ethics. You'll find much material to chew over.

Up in the Air (2009). Drama; R

George Clooney travels across country delivering the bad news to employees that they have been "terminated." He also is a motivational speaker (nice combination). Apply the communication competence model, specifically concentrating on skills and commitment.

CHAPTER 2

Chapter Outline

Perception of Self and Others

Who Am I? Who Are They?

THERE IS NO "IMMACULATE PERCEPTION" that can objectively convince everyone of the single correct interpretation of your experience. This is particularly striking when comparing cultures. Consider widely varied food choices across cultures. The Scottish dish called haggis is a mixture of sheep innards blended with chunks of sheep fat, seasonings, and oatmeal, all cooked in the animal's stomach. It has little appeal to most Americans. Beetle grubs, which have the appearance of plump white worms, make most Americans gag at the thought of eating them, but they are a delicacy to the Asmat of New Guinea. The Inuit eat raw fish eyes like candy, and several East African tribes enjoy a tall drink of fresh cow's blood. To Americans, insects and raw animal blood don't qualify as food. Other cultures, however, find some of our food choices equally revolting (Archer, 2000). Many South Americans perceive our common peanut butter sandwich to be disgusting in taste, texture, and smell, and most people from India find our common practice of eating meat offensive. Imagine the revulsion many Indians must

By the end of this chapter, you should be able to:

1. Explain the three elements of perception: selecting, organizing, and interpreting.
2. Understand how self-concept is formed.
3. Recognize important issues associated with self-esteem.
4. Determine when self-disclosure is appropriate and when it is not.
5. Recognize and combat errors in your perceptions of others.
6. Use specific strategies to improve your communication effectiveness and appropriateness, given per-

experience walking down the aisles of our grocery stores seeing packaged meats displayed. Perhaps you can appreciate the perceptual difference better if you imagine seeing an entire grocery counter of packaged dog meat (beagle burger). Dog is a common food in some cultures.

Our culture teaches us what is food and what is inedible. This is largely a matter of learned expectation, not objective taste. If you are not told what you are eating, it may taste good until you are informed that it is lizard innards, at which point you may feel compelled to chuck your innards. Food preferences of all sorts can present communication challenges at mealtime when you don't want to cause offense by declining to eat the meal presented, but what is offered as food may be stomach churning.

The act of speaking also illustrates stark cultural differences in perception. Speaking is highly valued in the United States, and silence is not prized. Quiet individuals do not become leaders in groups (Bormann, 1990). Americans interpret silence mainly in negative ways, as indicating sorrow, criticism, obligation, regret, indifference, rejection, or embarrassment (Martin & Nakayama, 2008). The silence of some men is often a source of frustration for their female partners. Women sometimes prod men to talk more. There's an old story about President Calvin Coolidge, who was renowned for his taciturnity. Two women approached him and one said, "Mr. Coolidge, I just bet my friend that I could get you to say three words." Coolidge replied, "You lose." Famed wit Dorothy Parker, upon hearing that Coolidge had died, remarked, "How can they tell?"

Some cultures, however, value silence and devalue speaking (McDaniel, 2003). The Thai culture values quietness as a sign of humility (Knutson & Posirisuk, 2006). There is a Chinese proverb: "Those who know do not speak; those who speak do not know." Class participation is often encouraged, even required, as part of the grade in U.S. schools. Japanese students, however, initiate and maintain fewer conversations and are less apt to talk in class discussions (Ishii et al., 1984). Thai students rarely express their opinions in class, preferring to listen to the older, wiser teachers (Knutson et al., 2003). Students whose culture places little value on speaking are at a substantial disadvantage in U.S. classrooms, where open and frequent participation is often expected. When you've been taught to value silence, speaking up is difficult, especially in a public forum.

Disagreements and conflicts are bound to emerge over perceptual differences, not just between diverse cultures but also within one's own ethnic group, family, group of friends, and between intimate partners. A memorable scene from Woody Allen's Oscar-winning movie *Annie Hall* illustrates this point. When Annie's therapist asks her how often she and Alvie have sex, she replies, "Constantly. Three times a week." When Alvie's therapist asks him the same question, he responds, "Hardly ever. Three times a week." Imagine the difficulty two individuals like Annie and Alvie would have conversing about this issue. You can almost hear the argument: "You demand too much." "You want too little." "Too much." "Too little . . ."

Perception is not an unbiased process. Consequently, *the primary purpose of this chapter is to address how you communicate competently when your perceptions are inherently subjective and often markedly at odds with the perceptions of others.* We all behave as we do largely because of our perceptions of the world. Understanding the perceptual process is an important step toward improving our communication with others.

The Perceptual Process

The eye is not a camera, nor is the ear a tape recorder. Sight, sound, touch, taste, and smell are sensations, but *sensation and perception, although related, are not the same.* **Sensation** is the process by which our sense organs (eyes, ears, nose, skin, and tongue) that contain sense receptors change physical energy (light, sound waves, chemical substances) into neural impulses that are sent to our brains. Perception is the processing of these neural impulses so we go beyond merely sensing, and we begin to *make sense* of the impulses; we build meaningful patterns from them. "We sense the presence of a stimulus, but we perceive what it is" (Levine & Shefner, 1991, p. 1). Sound waves, for instance, are the raw materials of hearing, but they are not actual hearing. **Perception**, therefore, *is the process of selecting, organizing, and interpreting sensory data.*

In this section, I briefly explain the perceptual process. The three elements of perception—*selecting, organizing,* and *interpreting*—do not occur in isolation from each other. Perception is a process, so all three elements interact. Nevertheless, understanding the perceptual process requires that each element first be discussed separately.

Selecting: Forced Choices

The world is teeming with stimuli. We perceive what we can sense, but much of our world is hidden from us by the limitations of our senses. As discussed in this section, *perception is inherently subjective and selective.* Selecting which stimuli to notice begins the perceptual process. Selecting is determined by sensory limitations and selective attention.

Sensory Limitations: We're Mostly Blind and Deaf

What sensory data we select and how it will be organized and interpreted are influenced greatly by the capacity of our sensory receptors to be stimulated in the first place. As

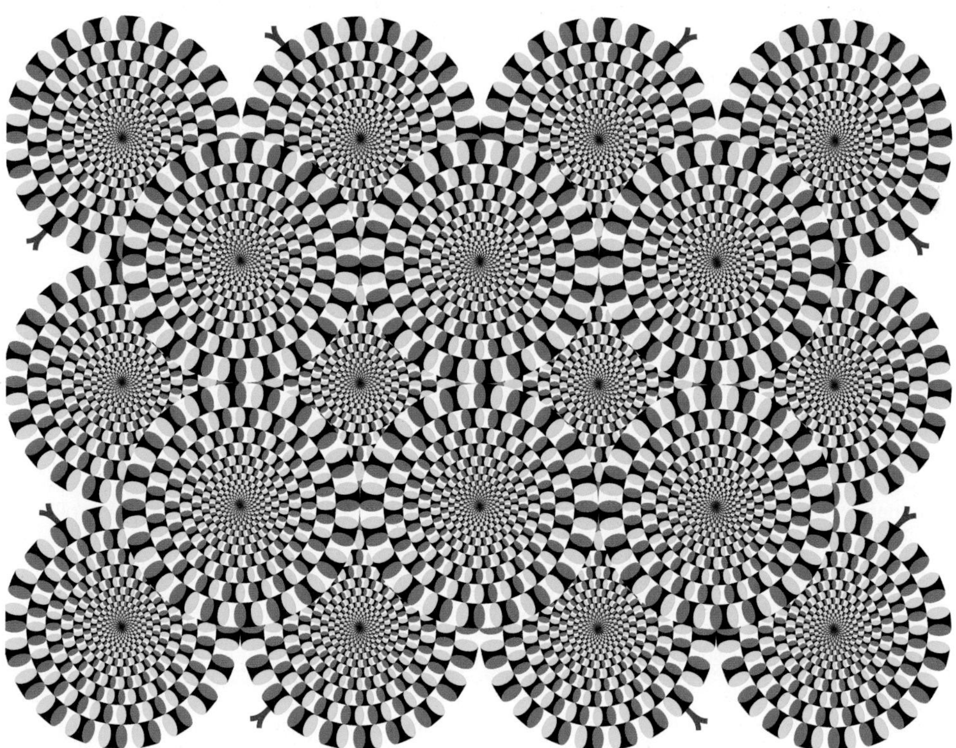

FIGURE 2-1 Rotating Snakes perceptual illusion. We may see movement where none exists because our sensory receptors can be tricked.

sensitive as these receptors are, they have a limited capacity to receive stimuli. Table 2-1 indicates the average **threshold**, or minimum amount of energy, that triggers a sensation for each human sensory system. Vision is our primary sense, but we do not see ultraviolet rays, X-rays, gamma rays, or cosmic rays, nor do we see radar or long radio waves. If we could see light energy of slightly longer wavelengths than we do, we would see warm-blooded animals glowing in the dark (Rathus, 1990). There are as many microscopic creatures on our bodies (e.g., fungi, bacteria, mites, etc.) as there are people on Earth, but fortunately, these are hidden from our view by the limitations of our eyesight.

Human hearing, likewise, is sensitive yet limited. The frequency of sound waves hitting your ear registers from about 20 cycles per second to a maximum of about 20,000 cycles per second. Frequency is perceived as **pitch**—how low or high the sound is (e.g., how low or high a human voice is during conversation). Human hearing may seem impressive, but it is not when compared to a dog that can hear up to 50,000 cycles per second (very high-pitch sounds), a mouse that can hear up to 90,000 cycles per second, or a bat that can hear up to 100,000 cycles per second (Roediger et al., 1991). This tells us that we cannot sense a huge amount of stimuli that envelops us each moment.

Sound also varies by **amplitude**, perceived as loudness. Normal conversation is 10,000 times louder than a human whisper, but have you ever been accused of mumbling? Cell phone conversations are typically a bit louder; they're sometimes referred to as the "cell yell." A passing subway train is 10 billion times louder than the minimum detectable sound to the human ear (Myers, 2004). Hearing loss occurs when you are exposed for a prolonged period to very loud sounds (rock concert), reducing your already limited hearing acuity. When parents or grandparents have substantially diminished hearing, conducting a conversation with them can be enormously frustrating and a test of your compassion as they repetitively ask, "What did you say?" Watching television with them can also be an ear-splitting experience when volume is pumped to the maximum.

Individual differences in **sensory acuity**, which is the level of sensitivity of our senses, add another element to the subjective perception of our world. About 25% of the population are supertasters; they have six times more taste buds than those with the fewest, also about 25% of the population ("Taste Intensity," 1998). About 35% of women but only 10% of men are supertasters (Hunt, 1997). If you are a supertaster, sugar seems twice as sweet as it does to average tasters, and bitter tastes can be overpowering (a reason brussels sprouts are not everyone's favorite food). Arguments about something being "too sweet" or "not sweet

TABLE 2-1 THE THRESHOLD OF HUMAN SENSES

SENSE	STIMULUS	RECEPTORS	THRESHOLD
Vision	Electromagnetic energy	Rods and cones in the retina	A candle flame viewed from a distance of about 30 miles on a clear night
Hearing	Sound pressure waves	Hair cells on the basilar membrane of the inner ear	The ticking of a watch from about 20 feet away in a quiet room
Touch	Mechanical displacement or pressure on the skin	Nerve endings located in the skin	The wing of a bee falling on a cheek from one-half inch
Smell	Chemical substances in the air	Receptor cells in the upper part of the nasal cavity	One perfume drop diffused throughout a small apartment
Taste	Chemical substances	Taste buds on the tongue	About one teaspoon of sugar dissolved in two gallons of water

Source: Adapted from Galanter (1962).

enough" are wasted effort. Sensory acuity is an individual subjective difference.

Your sense of smell is about 10,000 times more sensitive than your sense of taste (Reyneri, 1984). Recently, the issue of smell perception has become a source of interpersonal communication conflict. I have observed some rather nasty verbal exchanges between people in movie theaters, on elevators, and in other public places that were triggered by one person wearing "offensive" perfume. Signs have even begun appearing in public facilities asking people not to wear strong-smelling perfumes or colognes that might provoke allergic reactions from some individuals. Some people with a clearly diminished sense of smell do not realize that marinating themselves in potent perfume, aftershave, or cologne and leaving a vapor trail as they walk can be troublesome for others.

Selective Attention: Bombarded by Stimuli

We don't process what we don't see, hear, taste, touch, or smell. What is available to our senses, however, is too voluminous for our brains to process. Attention is unavoidably selective. By one calculation, our five basic senses are bombarded with 11 million bits of information *each second*, but at best, we attend to only about 40 bits (Wilson, 2002). Our senses have the potential to receive a wide range of data, but the channel capacity of our senses is limited. Consequently, we must selectively attend to stimuli.

Selectively attending to stimuli involves two processes: (1) focusing on specific stimuli and (2) screening out other data (van der Heijden, 1991). You do both when you're talking intently to your date at a restaurant. You focus on that person and what he or she says and does, and you screen out conversations occurring all around you (at least you do if you know what's good for you). The results of these two processes working at the same time can produce some interesting results. For example, in one study, a young man approaches a passerby on a college campus and asks for directions, then points to a campus map. The passerby looks at the map and begins directing the man, when two individuals carrying a wooden door step between the two conversing, blocking their view of each other momentarily. One of the men carrying the door changes places with the young man who asked directions. Once the door no longer obstructs the passerby's view, the "original" conversation continues except with a different person seeking directions. Half of the individuals who were stopped and asked directions did not notice that they were talking to a different young man who was dressed differently and was significantly taller (Simons & Levin, 1998). (See Chabris & Simons, 2010, for a thorough explanation of this "change blindness" phenomenon.) We can become so focused on selectively attending that even seemingly obvious changes go unnoticed (Simons & Ambinder, 2005).

Increasingly, people are becoming so focused on cell phone conversations and text messaging while walking that they run into street lamps, step off curbs into traffic, or trip and fall. Cathy Cruz Marrero was so intent on texting while walking in the Berkshire Mall in Reading, Pennsylvania, that she tumbled headfirst into a fountain. The security camera footage was subsequently posted on YouTube and viewed more than 2 million times ("Texting While Walking," 2011). The consequences of such focused attention can be more serious than embarrassment. A 39-year-old woman walked into an oncoming train and was killed when she became engrossed in a cell phone conversation. Another woman stepped off a curb in San Francisco while talking on a cell phone and was hit by a pickup truck and killed (Zimmerman, 2010). An Ohio State University study discovered that more than 1,000 pedestrians visit emergency rooms annually to tend to injuries incurred while engaging in sidewalk texting (Donald, 2010). Another study found that the vast majority of us (97.5%) are lousy multitaskers (driving and talking on a cell phone) despite the common belief that most of us can adeptly do two things at once (Watson & Strayer, 2010).

What we attend to at any given moment is influenced by the nature of the stimulus (Passer & Smith, 2004), a point that is explored in Chapter 13 when attention strategies for speeches are discussed. The *intensity* of the stimulus draws our attention without conscious effort on our part. For example, someone shrieking can snap our head around before we have a chance to think what it means. It may be a child excitedly playing with a sibling, or it might be a person in serious trouble. *Novelty* invites attention. Perhaps that is why some individuals channel surf, looking for anything different to watch on TV. *Movement* also draws attention. If a friend approaches you and feigns a punch to your stomach, you'll notice and reflexively protect yourself with your arms. *Repetition,* if it is irritating or annoying, triggers attention. If you're talking with someone at a party and they keep snorting when they laugh, you'll probably notice it if you find the noise bothersome. The constant repetition of sounds from other partygoers talking, however, likely fades into the background unnoticed. Finally, *contrast* invites attention. When conversation at that same party suddenly stops, you'll notice the contrast. You may even feel anxious or concerned.

What we attend to is also influenced by internal factors peculiar to each individual. Hunger can make you notice a friend eating a large pepperoni pizza. *Fatigue* can screen out important stimuli such as your partner's new hairdo or your teacher's announcement of an assignment due date. If your *interest* is riding horses, you will likely notice two people conversing about dressage. If you're fearful walking down a dark street at night because you've had an *experience* with a mugger, you'll likely notice strangers or anyone that might appear menacing.

Organizing: Creating Schemas

Perception does not operate apart from meaning, and we must organize selected stimuli to create meaning. Schemas organize perceptual stimuli. **Schemas** are mental frameworks that create meaningful patterns from stimuli. The three types of schemas discussed here are prototypes, stereotypes, and scripts (Wood, 2004).

Prototypes: Best Case

Humans categorize persons, places, events, objects, phenomena, ideas, and so forth. Categorizing helps us make sense of our world. One way we categorize is by forming prototypes in our minds. A **prototype** is the most representative or "best" example of something. You have prototypes of a "boss from hell," a "best friend," an "ideal relationship," a "great movie," and a "perfect date."

Poorly matched prototypes can be problematic. If one person's prototype of an "ideal date" is attending a ballgame and munching on hotdogs but the other person's prototype is dressing elegantly and eating at a five-star restaurant, then a second date may not be in the offing. A problem may also develop even if both parties share a similar prototype. The "made-in-Hollywood" prototype of a "perfect romance" may set a standard certain to be unreachable, and it may inevitably lead to

disappointment when your own relationship doesn't measure up to the prototype.

Stereotypes: Generalizing About Groups

A **stereotype** is a generalization about a group or category of people. Stereotypes organize individuals according to categories such as ethnic origin, socioeconomic status, age, gender, sexual orientation, religious affiliation, and even body type, and they attribute common traits to all individuals in that group. For example, research comparing the American stereotype of the elderly as warm but incompetent is shared in six other countries studied (Cuddy et al., 2005). Stereotypes of Asians are consistent with media representations that they are academically successful but nerdy (Zhang, 2010).

Some stereotypes are positive ("Artists are creative, interesting people"), and some are negative ("College professors are stuffy and arrogant"). *Stereotyping isn't always bad.* Positive stereotypes of others—such as, "Most Hispanics are good-hearted and hardworking people"—can lead to cooperative transactions. *Stereotypes are not necessarily completely incorrect, either* (Lee et al., 1995). Sometimes they are mostly true and accurate, such as, "College professors are intelligent and avid readers." Nevertheless, stereotypes can distort your perceptions and produce serious consequences, as discussed later in this chapter, because they allow for no individual differences within a group.

Scripts: Predictable Behavior

A **script** is a predictable sequence of events that indicates what we are expected to do in a given situation. When you are sitting at a table in a restaurant and the server hands you a menu, you don't ask, "What's this?" You already know that you're expected to choose a meal from the menu. You have a "restaurant script." The more predictable the sequence of events, the more scripted it is. A mental script operates the way a movie script works. The movie script tells you what to say and do. The script organizes our behavior into a sequence of activities. Your mental script does the same. We have scripts for greeting people, for expected behavior in classes, for asking someone for a date, and so on.

Scripts allow us to behave without having to think carefully. This can be positive and negative. When partners begin finishing each other's sentences, the script is well known to both individuals. Finishing your partner's sentences may be appreciated as "really knowing me." It may also be annoying because you are "too predictable." Partners may act out "conflict scripts" that repeat the same destructive behaviors. Without deviation from the script, the same ineffective arguing patterns get repeated seemingly without end.

Interpreting: Making Sense of Stimuli

Two men were arrested in Scottsbluff, Nebraska, when, on a "triple-dog-dare" from a friend, they bought women's thong underwear at a Wal-Mart, changed in the store's bathroom, then walked through the store wearing only the thongs and T-shirts. Why did these men, ages 35 and 36, act so strangely?

We select stimuli and organize them, but we also interpret what they mean. We try to make sense of the stimuli that we've organized. Principally, we make sense of our own behavior and our transactions with others by making **attributions**—assigning causes to behavior. We attribute two principal causes to behavior: the personal characteristics, or traits, of the individual (*dispositional causes*) and the environment (*situational causes*).

Deciding the causes of our own behavior is a highly subjective process. Did we fail the exam because we didn't care enough, or was the exam too difficult for a lower-division class? Some individuals assign personal reasons for their failure ("I'm not smart enough"), and other individuals attribute situational causes ("There wasn't enough time to do my best on the exam").

Accurately attributing causes to the behavior of others is particularly difficult because we usually do not have enough information to make valid conclusions. This doesn't stop us, however. *Social desirability* of a behavior can influence whether you choose dispositional or situational attributions for the behavior of others. Usually, when a behavior will be disapproved, observers make a dispositional attribution

(Jones & Davis, 1965). You may think the two men who wore thongs in Wal-Mart on a triple-dog-dare did it because they are just weird individuals (dispositional attribution), but the explanation they gave suggests strong influence from a friend's triple-dog-dare (situational attribution).

Consistency and *distinctiveness* of the information also influence attributions (Seibold & Spitzberg, 1982). For example, you're walking across campus, and a classmate, Felicia, passes you without acknowledging your existence. Why were you ignored? You notice during the week that she acknowledges other classmates when she passes them, but she does not acknowledge you on several occasions. Her behavior toward you is consistent and distinctive (she does it only to you). Perhaps you said something that offended her (situational cause). Felicia may be ignoring you because she is upset with what you said, not because she is unfriendly (dispositional cause). If, however, she ignores everyone she passes, perhaps she is shy (dispositional cause). Her behavior is consistent but not distinctive (she ignores everyone).

Person perception is not simply a linear, one-way process beginning with selecting, then organizing, and finally ending with interpreting stimuli. Our interpretations of self and others often double back and influence what data we continue to select and organize that influence our self-perceptions and our view of others.

Perception of Self

From the moment you are welcomed into the world, you begin the process of becoming who you are, a person separate from others but defined in relation to others. This section discusses the perception of self and the role it plays in human communication.

Self-Concept: Developing Perception of Self

Each one of you has a sense of who you are and what makes you a person distinct from other persons. This **self-concept** is the sum total of everything that encompasses the self-referential term "me." It is your *identity* or self-schemas: perceiving yourself as athletic, intelligent, compassionate, attractive, moody, awkward with others, and so forth. It is "a conviction of self-sameness—a bridge over the discontinuities which invariably creep or crash into our lives. It is the link between the child of seven and that same person at seventeen; between the seventeen-year-old and the seventy-year-old" (Kilpatrick, 1975, p. 31).

Self-concept is also a central point of reference for your communication with others. If you see yourself as a person of integrity, you likely feel compelled to speak up when promises are broken and injustices based on deceit emerge. If you see yourself as attractive, you are more likely to flirt with a stranger than if you see yourself as unattractive. If you see yourself as compassionate and caring, you likely find it difficult to reject a homeless person's request for "spare change" when you have a pocketful of money. We communicate from the perspective of how we see ourselves. Your self-concept intrudes on every communication event of your life.

Influence of Others: You Are Who We Say You Are

Your self-concept is not formed in isolation. *Self-concept is a social construction, a product of interpersonal communication.* "You find out who you are by meeting who you aren't" (Anderson & Ross, 1994, p. 116). Infants haven't formed a self-concept. Their self-concept gradually develops through communication with significant people over a long period of time. Parents, teachers, friends, relatives, coworkers, bosses, even strangers are instrumental in shaping your concept of self. You learn to think of yourself as humorous if others laugh at your jokes. You see yourself as a leader if you notice that others follow you. You see yourself as quiet if others tell you that you're taciturn in social circumstances.

Your self-concept is relatively stable, especially once you reach adulthood (Bergner & Holmes, 2000). Self-concepts don't change easily even in the face of contradictory evidence. You may see yourself as shy because when you were a child your parents, relatives, and teachers told you so. In later life, this may no longer be as true, yet you may still cling to an outdated view of self. I once attended a workshop composed of faculty, staff, and administrators from my college on negotiation approaches. The federal mediator who conducted the workshop began the first meeting with this instruction: "Each of you tell your group one thing about yourself that would surprise them. Identify a trait, not a behavior." When it came time for my revelation, I told my group of about a dozen individuals who had interacted with me many times on and off campus for years that I see myself as a shy person. The entire group burst into laughter. I was a little stunned by their reaction. As a child, I was painfully shy and was described as such by relatives and teachers. I still see myself as somewhat shy, even though this is definitely not my persona on campus.

Self-concepts can change, but change comes from characterizations by others that are numerous and consistent (all your teachers say you're smart), the characterizations must come from those whom you see as competent and important sources (parents, romantic partners), and they can't be radically dissimilar to how you perceive yourself (outgoing instead of shy) (Bergner & Holmes, 2000).

Perceptual Distortion: Body Image

"Our body image does not constitute the whole of the self, but it is a highly significant aspect of it" (Hamachek, 1992, p. 159). Body image is largely influenced by society's conception of an ideal body (prototype).

Women have been socialized to equate body size with self-worth (Grover et al., 2003). Social standards dictating what constitutes "overweight" and "thin" for women have changed drastically in the last few decades. Since 1979, the majority of Miss America contestants have been at least 15% below recommended body weight for their height, coming alarmingly close to a medical definition of anorexia (Rubinstein & Caballero, 2000). Despite these cultural images of the "ideal woman" as wafer thin, most men prefer a woman to be heavier and more curvaceous (Markey et al., 2004).

What is the result of this disparity between fantasy and reality? Between 70% and 90% of women report dieting at some time, even though a large portion of these women do not need to lose weight for health or aesthetic reasons (Markey, 2005). Nevertheless, in one study, a majority of women (57%) had participated in at least one unhealthy diet (Markey, 2005).

Body image distortion is also a problem for men. As one researcher concludes: "In our society, much is made of women's nagging anxieties about how they look. But if women ever really had a lock on such worries, those days are gone" (Pope, 2004, p. 1P). Cultural ideals for the male body communicated in the popular mass media have changed, alarming some researchers about distorted body images of boys and men (McCabe & Ricciardelli, 2004). In one study, 65% of men were dissatisfied with their bodies in some way compared to 77% of women (Markey, 2005). For men, however, the concern is often that they are too skinny (Cafri et al., 2006). Losing weight isn't the primary concern; becoming more muscular is (Grogan & Richards, 2002; Olivardia et al., 2004). When college men from the United States, Austria, and France were asked to take the Body Image Test and choose the body they thought women prefer in a man, on average they chose one with *30 pounds more muscle* than their own body possessed (Pope et al., 2000; see also Olivardia et al., 2004).

Do women have the same "ideal body" image for men that males expect them to have? When American and Austrian college women were given the same Body Image Test as male college students, they chose a male body image with *15 to 20 pounds less muscle* than what the men thought women preferred (Pope et al., 2000; see also Olivardia et al., 2004).

The male concern about insufficient muscularity can lead to a disorder called **muscle dysmorphia**—a preoccupation with one's body size and a perception that, though one is very muscular, one actually

Most people see a massively muscled young man. Muscle dysmorphs, however, perceive an embarrassingly scrawny man. Perception is inherently subjective.

looks puny (Thomas et al., 2011). Muscle dysmorphs perceive puniness when they look at themselves in a mirror even when other people perceive massiveness. One individual studied by researchers was 6 feet 3 inches tall, weighed 270 pounds, had a 52-inch chest, and had 20-inch biceps. Despite his huge, massively muscular physique, he confessed, "When I look in the mirror, I sometimes think that I look really small. . . . You'd be amazed at how hard it is, sometimes, for me to actually convince myself that I'm big" (quoted in Pope et al., 2000, p. 83). These researchers estimate that more than 1 million men have this disorder. Muscle dysmorphs give up jobs, careers, and social engagements so they can spend hours every day lifting weights to "bulk up." They may refuse to appear in public in a bathing suit, turn down dates, or refuse to go to social gatherings fearing that people will see their bodies as tiny and out of shape. Muscle dysmorphs report checking themselves in the mirror an average of 9.2 times a day. They also average *325 minutes*, more than 5 hours per day, worrying about their muscularity and body size.

Self-Esteem: Evaluating Your Personal Identity

Self-concept is the descriptive element of self-perception. **Self-esteem** is the evaluative element of self-perception (Hamachek, 1992; Myers, 2004). It is self-appraisal—the sum of all your self-schemas—your perception of self-worth, attractiveness, and social competence. "I am a quiet person" describes your perception of self without attaching an evaluation to the perception. "I'm *too* quiet," however, attaches an evaluation to the self-perception.

Influences on Self-Esteem: Appraisals, Comparisons, and Contingencies

There are three primary influences on our self-esteem: reflected appraisal, social comparison, and contingencies of self-worth. **Reflected appraisal**, a term coined by Harry Stack Sullivan (1953), refers to messages you receive from others that assess your self-concept. It is difficult for us to perceive ourselves as smart, for example, if every person important to us is saying that we are slow-witted or just average. Parents can have a particularly powerful effect on your self-esteem. They generally get the first crack at shaping your perception of self-worth. If parents persistently call you a failure, feeling good about yourself is challenging. You'll need to turn to other significant people in your life (friends, siblings, other relatives, teachers, professional acquaintances) to counteract parental negativity.

Your self-esteem is also a product of **social comparison**—evaluating yourself by comparing yourself to other people (Guest, 2007; Mussweiler et al., 2004). When we are in the presence of someone we perceive as impressive, even as superior, our self-esteem tends to diminish. When we are in the presence of someone we perceive as unimpressive, however, our self-esteem tends to inflate (Morse & Gergen, 1970). Research shows that young women who regularly compare themselves to strikingly thin professional models appearing in popular media develop negative images of their own bodies, which can lead to eating disorders (Han, 2003; Harrison & Cantor, 1997). Men also experience a similar dissatisfaction with their bodies when they view images of prototypically attractive muscular men (Blond, 2008).

Your self-esteem is also influenced by what is perceived as most important to you feeling good about yourself. This is called **contingencies of self-worth** (Crocker, 2002; Stefanone et al., 2011). Although people in general want to be perceived by others as attractive, smart, and capable, there are individual differences that add to the self-esteem equation. One study of Facebook postings of personal information found that women based their self-esteem on their appearance more than men (Stefanone et al., 2011). "One person may have self-esteem that is highly contingent on doing well in school and being physically attractive, whereas another may have self-esteem that is contingent on being loved by God and adhering to moral standards" (Crocker & Wolfe, 2001). Making the first person feel highly moral and the second person feel highly attractive won't necessarily raise self-esteem for either. The reverse, however, likely will. Students whose self-esteem is highly contingent on academic competence experience substantially greater increases in self-esteem when they are accepted into a graduate program and substantially greater decreases in self-esteem when they are rejected than students whose self-esteem is not so contingent on academic competence (Crocker et al., 2002). Our self-esteem is contingent on what we value most and whether we succeed or fail in the pursuit of valued goals (Crocker & Knight, 2005).

Self-Esteem Issues: Too Little or Too Much?

Despite the common notion that low self-esteem is a serious problem in the United States (see Box 2-1), research reveals otherwise. A global study of 17,000 respondents from 53 countries found that the United States ranked sixth among these nations on self-esteem, and all countries averaged higher than the midpoint on the self-esteem scale used as a measuring device. The United States scored especially high on self-competence, although not as strongly on self-liking (Schmitt & Allik, 2005).

Most of us feel quite accomplished, even more so than statistically makes sense. A survey of 829,000 high-school seniors by the College Entrance Examination Board reported that *all* of the respondents ranked themselves in the top half of the population on their "ability to get along with others"; 60% ranked themselves in the top 10% of the population, and 25% were convinced they qualified for the top 1%. The same study found that 70% of the participants ranked their leadership abilities in the top 25% of the population, and only 2% thought they had below-average leadership abilities (cited in Myers, 2004). Only 1% of online daters rate their appearance as "less than average" (Epstein, 2007). A robust 95% of respondents in close relationships think their romantic partner, a reflection on their own self-esteem, is above average in appearance, intelligence, warmth, and sense of humor (Gagne, 2004). Ninety-four percent of university professors believe they outperform their colleagues (cited in Reid et al., 2007). Individuals tend to think that anyone who outperforms them must be a genius (Lassiter & Munhall, 2001). One survey even found that 79% of respondents thought Mother Teresa was at least "somewhat likely" to go to heaven, but 87% of respondents believed they themselves would make it to heaven ("Oprah," 1997). Another national survey showed that when participants were asked, "How would you

BOX 2.1 Focus on Controversy

SELF-ESTEEM: MORE IS NOT ALWAYS BETTER

The *Final Report of the California Task Force to Promote Self-Esteem and Personal and Social Responsibility* (1990) asserted, "The lack of self-esteem is central to most personal and social ills plaguing our state and nation" (p. 4). It claimed, "People who esteem themselves are less likely to engage in destructive and self-destructive behavior, including child abuse, alcohol abuse, abuse of other drugs (legal and illegal), violence, crime, and so on" (p. 5). The conclusions of the task force report were based on what to most people may seem to be self-evident truths. California assemblyman John Vasconcellos, a member of the task force, had to admit, "We didn't claim to have proven it all. The science was not very far advanced" (Bauer, 1996, p. A20). Nevertheless, the report became the best-selling state document of all time. Most of California's 58 counties formed self-esteem task forces as a result of the report (Billingsley, 2010).

High self-esteem, so goes the reasoning of the task force, should provide a "social vaccine" that inoculates individuals against destructive communication that attacks self-concepts with criticism, insults, and demonstrations of disrespect. A review of more than 150 studies on self-esteem contradicts this reasoning (Baumeister et al., 1996; see also Baumeister et al., 2003). The most aggressively violent individuals, whether neo-Nazi skinheads, terrorists, Ku Klux Klan members, juvenile delinquents, gang members, psychopaths, or spouse abusers, do not suffer from low self-esteem. Rather, they exhibit superiority complexes, and their "self-appraisal is unrealistically positive" (p. 28). Nazis thought of themselves as members of the "master race," and they vilified Jews as "vermin." The image of a Mafia godfather suffering from low self-esteem as he orders the assassinations of rivals is difficult to visualize. Bullies and psychopaths seem contemptuous of the unfortunate victims they torment.

Perhaps bullies, godfathers, gang members, and the like camouflage their low self-esteem, as is often asserted, beneath the veneer of bluster and aggressiveness. Maybe favorable self-appraisals mask deep-seated insecurities. If this sounds reasonable to you, then try arguing the reverse proposition: that timid, reticent individuals don't suffer from low self-esteem. They simply mask their enormous self-confidence and deep-seated security. Both claims require us to ignore persuasive evidence to the contrary without providing supportive evidence for the validity of the assertions. One study of 540 college students showed that those with the biggest egos were the most aggressive, and when criticized, they delivered three times the intensity of painful noise (retaliatory punishment) to a victim (Bushman & Baumeister, 1998). As one researcher concludes, "A belief in undetected low self-esteem as a cause of undesirable behavior" is contradicted by "all the available evidence" (Dawes, 1994).

A major cause of aggression in human relations seems to be not low self-esteem, masked or otherwise, but "high self-esteem combined with an ego threat" (Baumeister et al., 1996, p. 8; see also Bushman & Baumeister, 1998; Rodkin et al., 2000). In other words, aggression, with its emphasis on competitive, adversarial communication, results from a discrepancy between two views of self: favorable self-appraisal but an unfavorable reflected appraisal from others. When others do not communicate "proper respect" worthy of a "superior person"—and instead criticize, insult, or show disrespect—an aggressive response is likely. "The higher . . . the self-esteem, the greater the vulnerability to ego threats. Viewed in this light, the societal pursuit of high self-esteem for everyone may literally end up doing considerable harm" (Baumeister et al., 1996, p. 30).

Is our society's emphasis on bolstering self-esteem completely misguided? If we are looking for a cure-all in raised self-esteem, the answer is "yes." In addition to having the potential for aggressiveness (Heatherton & Vohs, 2000; Menon et al., 2007), those with inflated self-esteem are more

BOX 2.1 *(Continued)*

likely than individuals with more moderate self-esteem to be obnoxious to others, interrupt more, and talk at others instead of listen carefully (Baumeister et al., 2003). When children's self-esteem is inflated by effusive praise for relatively trivial behavior ("Nice breathing"), the potential for later disillusionment and deflated egos increases. As psychologist Robert Brooks of Harvard explains, "There are well-meaning parents who have seen self-esteem as 'every little thing your kid does, praise them to the sky.' [But] if [teaching self-esteem] is done wrong, you can raise a generation of kids who cannot tolerate frustration" (quoted in Begley, 1998, p. 69).

Nevertheless, ignoring low self-esteem of our children and even adults is not desirable either. What good can possibly come from people feeling bad about themselves? Praising others for genuine performance, accomplishments, and effort, however, not for merely being themselves, is more likely to improve low self-esteem and to encourage socially beneficial behavior (Baumeister et al., 2003).

QUESTIONS FOR THOUGHT

1. In your estimation, how much should improving self-esteem be emphasized in our schools?
2. Is it ethical to praise children or adults indiscriminately for completion of commonplace tasks knowing that this might lead to egomaniacal self-centeredness in some individuals?

rate your own morals and values on a scale from 1 to 100 (100 being perfect)?" 50% rated themselves 90 or above; only 11% rated themselves 74 or below (Lovett, 1997).

Self-Serving Bias: Protecting Your Self-Esteem

Assigning causes (attribution) to our own behavior is not an objective process. We protect our self-concept and our self-esteem by exercising a self-serving bias. The **self-serving bias** is the tendency to attribute our successful behavior to ourselves (personal traits) but to assign external circumstances (situations) to our unsuccessful behavior (Major et al., 2003). Divorced individuals usually blame their partner for the marital split. Managers often blame poor worker performance on weak worker effort, but workers typically blame crushing workloads, ambiguous tasks, inadequate resources, or troublesome coworkers. Athletes tend to attribute their victories to personal prowess but blame their losses on bad officiating, weather conditions, or cheating by their opponents. Students who perform well on tests usually view exams as valid indicators of knowledge, whereas students who perform poorly on exams may see them as arbitrary, unfair measures of knowledge. Teachers may take credit for the success of their students but blame their students' lack of motivation, effort, or ability for their failures.

Our tendency to emphasize our accomplishments and downplay or deflect our shortcomings and failures is common. It is especially common in online virtual groups "where remote partners are unseen and ephemeral, [and] members are easy targets who can be blamed for the poor performances that an individual may have committed" (DeAndrea et al., 2011, p. 110). Unless we are mindful of this tendency to be self-serving, we are unlikely to learn new skills and gain new knowledge (Walther, 2008). Why seek to improve our communication skills if communication difficulties are usually perceived to be someone else's fault?

Optimal Self-Esteem: Pursuing Goals, Not Self-Esteem

When we see professional athletes strutting and posturing before their fans, insisting that they receive thunderous applause and accolades for relatively insignificant athletic accomplishments, modesty and humility are missing. *Optimal self-esteem comes from significant accomplishments without expecting a coronation* (Kohn, 1993). Optimal self-esteem is unlikely to occur if you place yourself at the mercy of other people's appraisals (Crocker, 2006; Crocker et al., 2006). Remaining in a relationship in which your partner persistently denigrates you can diminish self-esteem. Either your partner must be confronted and changes must occur, or your association with this negative influence should be curtailed or ended. Surrounding yourself with positive influences from warm and loving friends and partners is constructive.

Optimal self-esteem develops, paradoxically, when you don't strive to build self-esteem, but instead, you concentrate on goals that can be accomplished (Crocker, 2006). Setting goals to learn new things can build confidence. No one even has to know that you're learning a new language or studying economics, political science, or some other subject. Pursuing goals for self-improvement (internal reward), not for external rewards such as grades, money, or social approval, is more likely to produce optimal self-esteem (Kernis, 2003). Concentrating on developing your talents and personal relationships with others is also productive (Crocker & Park, 2004).

Self-Disclosure: Revealing Your Self to Others

Once you have formulated your self-concept and sense of self-esteem, you can communicate this perception of self to others by self-disclosing to them, and this self-disclosure, in turn, creates an impression others have of who you are. Revealing ourselves to others is how friendships are born and intimacy blossoms (see Chapter 8).

Self-disclosure is the process of purposely revealing to others personal information about yourself that is significant and that others would not know unless you told them. *Self-disclosure is purposeful, not accidental, communication.* You may unintentionally demonstrate that you're clumsy at sports, but this is not self-disclosure. If you tell a friend that you are afraid to give public speeches and it is news to your friend, however, that is self-disclosure.

There are gender and cultural differences in self-disclosure. Women disclose more than men (Dindia, 2000). Women typically disclose more about themselves on Facebook, sharing more photos and spending greater time managing their profiles on social networking sites than men (Stefanone et al., 2011). Female-to-female self-disclosure is the most frequent, and male-to-male self-disclosure is the least frequent (Dindia, 2002). Men typically disclose emotional revelations to women, especially a girlfriend or spouse, but not to other males, even male friends (Doyle, 1995). This may be more a cultural influence than a gender difference, however. Although U.S. culture suppresses intimate self-disclosure among men, cultures such as Jordan and Hong Kong encourage male-to-male self-disclosure (Reis & Wheeler, 1991).

Constructive Goals for Self-Disclosure

There are many possible goals for self-disclosing to others. Five primary constructive goals are addressed here.

Developing Relationships: Intimacy with Others Self-disclosure can be an important gateway to intimacy. The more you limit your self-disclosure to another person, the more you remain a stranger to that person. If you know little about someone, you have little that connects you to that person. *Self-disclosure is critical to the development of close personal relationships.*

Whether you and another person perceive each other as strangers, acquaintances, friends, or intimate partners depends largely on the breadth and depth of self-disclosure that takes place between the two of you (Altman & Taylor, 1973). **Breadth** refers to the range of subjects discussed. There may be several topics that you don't discuss with an acquaintance, but almost any topic is open for discussion with loved ones. **Depth** refers to how personal you become when discussing a particular subject. Intimate relationships usually have both breadth and depth, whereas impersonal, casual relationships usually have little of either. Breadth and depth of self-disclosure are critical factors in connecting with others.

Gaining Self-Knowledge: Self-Awareness Sharing information about yourself with others helps you gain perspective. If you disclose to another person that you lack self-confidence, that person may point out several instances where you appeared very self-confident in front of others. That may cause you to revise your perception of self in this regard.

Correcting Misperceptions: Countering Inaccuracies Others may have misperceptions about you. They may perceive you to be unfriendly, for example. Revealing to them that you are shy, and explaining that engaging in conversation has always been challenging and anxiety producing for you, can open them to a different perception of you: one that is more accurate.

Eliciting Reassurance: It's Okay When we have doubts about our body image, communication abilities, or other capabilities, disclosing these doubts often produces reassurance from others. Students frequently come to me with doubts about their public speaking abilities. I reassure them that they are fully capable of mastering the fundamentals of speaking in front of an audience. It is helpful to hear from others that we are capable.

Creating Impressions: The Image You Portray to Others We usually want others to like who we are. That's difficult to do if the other person knows little about you—your likes and dislikes, passions, goals, fears, and concerns. Self-disclosure is part of the process of creating favorable impressions. Be cautious, however, when self-disclosing online. Increasingly, employers are scouring social networking sites for information on job applicants. Posting potentially embarrassing photos that cast you in a bad light, and revealing personal information online about your private life could backfire.

Counterproductive Goals for Self-Disclosure: Inappropriate Me-Orientation

Two principal goals for self-disclosure are Me-oriented, not We-oriented. Both encourage incompetent communication.

Manipulation: You'll Disclose if I Disclose Research clearly shows that self-disclosure by one person induces self-disclosure by another (Dindia, 2000). Pretending to reveal important personal information about oneself merely to coax knowledge from another person that can be used against him or her is inappropriate and unethical communication. It may provide a competitive advantage—"So, Marissa doesn't like confrontation; how interesting"—but it is dishonest.

Using self-disclosure to deceive others is an ethical issue. Glenn Souther was a student at Virginia's Old Dominion University. He also was a Soviet spy. He successfully deceived students and professors alike. Virginia Cooper (1994), a communication professor at the university, knew Souther well, or so she thought. Souther was a student of hers, her research assistant, and a frequent guest in her home. Curious how Souther could have deceived her so totally, she examined four hours of audiotape she had of Souther working with a group on a project. She discovered that Souther "was skilled in relationship deception due, in part, to his strategic disclosures that projected a plausible false image." Souther manipulated people into believing that he was trustworthy by disclosing large amounts of personal information. He disclosed more personal information than any other group member. He seemed so "transparent" that no one suspected he was hiding an awful truth.

Catharsis: Getting Secrets Off Your Chest Spur-of-the-moment purging of personal information to "get it off your chest" or to relieve guilt is a poor reason to self-disclose.

This is especially true if it is likely to damage the relationship you have with another person. Getting it off your chest may put it on the other person's chest. It also may create real problems for couples going through a divorce. The American Academy of Matrimonial Lawyers notes that 81% of its members have used or faced evidence taken from social networking sites. "The desire to talk trash is great" when a marriage runs aground, but "just blabbing things all over Facebook" when a marriage breaks up is "the worst possible time to share your feelings online" (Italie, 2010). Online disclosures can be used in court in child custody cases, property settlements, and on other contentious issues. Social networking sites can make public what you may wish, upon reflection, to keep private.

Appropriate Self-Disclosure: When to Open Up; When to Shut Up

Several characteristics act as guidelines for appropriate self-disclosure. Here are five characteristics.

Trust: Can You Keep a Secret When you self-disclose to another person, you risk being hurt or damaged by that person. Some of the risks involved with self-disclosure are indifference, rejection, loss of control, and betrayal (Derlega, 1984). Disclosures we make to others may be used against us. Sometimes people betray our trust and reveal our secrets disclosed in confidence. Trusting another person to honor your feelings and to refrain from divulging the disclosure to anyone unless given permission says, "I value our relationship, and I trust that you will not hurt me."

Reciprocity: Two-Way Sharing Reciprocal, or mutual, self-disclosure demonstrates that trust and risk-taking are shared (Omarzu, 2000). If one person discloses but the other person does not, you should be wary of further disclosures until reasons for the one-way self-disclosure become apparent. Perhaps the other person is merely reticent and needs encouragement. One-way self-disclosure leaves you vulnerable and the other person protected. That asymmetry can spell trouble. Therapy, of course, is one exception. Counselors need to hear about you; they don't need to self-disclose in return. Individuals also reveal intimate details about their sex lives to doctors who monitor sexually transmitted diseases, but they don't expect their doctor to reciprocate.

Cultural Appropriateness: Openness Not Universally Valued Not all cultures value self-disclosure. Compared to North Americans, Japanese students disclose very little about their personal lives. During initial interactions, North American students will discuss gossip, politics, marriage, life goals, friends, and after-graduation plans, topics that Japanese students resist discussing (Nishida, 1991). Japanese students discuss universities, ages, and club activities more than North American students during initial conversations. Both North American and Japanese students discuss more neutral topics such as the weather, recent movies, music, and college life. Appropriate self-disclosure in one culture may not be appropriate in another culture.

Situational Appropriateness: Considering Context Public settings and private information are a poor fit. A public speech before a large audience is an awkward, uncomfortable setting for self-disclosure, as several political campaigns have demonstrated. The classroom also doesn't usually lend itself well to intimate self-disclosure.

A colleague of mine told of a surprising incident in her public speaking class that illustrates the importance of situational appropriateness. Students were assigned a four-minute speech in which they were to describe to the class some event that had altered their lives in an important way. My colleague expected to hear speeches about trips taken abroad, geographic relocations, the college experience, and so forth. She did hear this—and more. A female student in her 30s began her speech by informing the class that she had never achieved sexual fulfillment in her life until the previous weekend. She then proceeded to explain to her astonished classmates exactly what it was like. Such revelations might be appropriate in a professional counselor-client relationship whose purpose is to explore intimate issues in a comfortable setting. Such intimate self-disclosure might even be appropriate with certain close friends, but not in front of relative strangers in a classroom where the main purpose is to hone public speaking skills. She needed to consider her audience and the obvious embarrassment she caused her listeners.

Incremental Disclosure: Bit by Bit Overly zealous self-disclosure in which, for instance, you blurt out your whole life story in one sitting may overwhelm your listener and send him or her running to the nearest exit. This may provoke a reflected appraisal, "You're creepy." Test the waters. Gradually disclose personal information to another person and see whether it is reciprocated. There is no urgency required. A person usually needs to get to know someone before a proper perspective can be given to intimate revelations about self. "I've always hated guys like you" or "Women make me nervous" probably aren't very good openers. Once you get to know the person, these disclosures may seem funny. Initially, they might end the conversation and any potential for a relationship.

Most conversations concentrate on commonplace topics. Self-disclosure is important, especially during the initial stages of a relationship, but it isn't the principal focus of people's lives. There is only so much to disclose, then your partner has heard it all. Even couples in intimate relationships spend relatively little time divulging personal information to each other (Duck, 1991).

Perception of Others

Perceptions of self influence our communication, but so do our perceptions of others. In this section, I explain the impact our perceptions of others can have on our communication by discussing first impressions of others, attribution error, stereotyping, and self-fulfilling prophecies.

First Impressions: You Never Get a Second Chance

Speed dating is reducing the date-selection process to a quick first impression. In a few minutes, two strangers meet, conduct a quick conversation, then check a box on a short form indicating interest in that person. If both parties check the box, the couple is notified within 24 hours and email addresses are provided. Participants move from person to person conducting instant interviews, potentially widening their dating pool. Gladwell (2005) observed one such speed-dating event and heard a woman announce that she liked none of the dozen men she interviewed, remarking, "They lost me at hello" (p. 63).

Studies in which an image of an object or a face is flashed for an instant show that these images are evaluated as good or bad in as little as a *tenth of a second,* too quickly to think consciously about them (Olivola & Todorov, 2010; Willis & Todorov, 2006). This means *you cannot avoid virtually instantaneous impressions of others.* The human brain appears to be hardwired to make blink-of-the-eye judgments, probably because there is survival value in such quick determinations: "Which category do you fit, friend or foe?" (Krebs & Denton, 1997).

Accuracy of First Impressions: Thin Slicing

Some first impressions can closely match impressions formed over lengthy periods of time (Gaschler, 2005). For example, participants in one study were shown three 10-second slices of Harvard University graduate students teaching undergraduates. These brief snippets ("thin slices") were sufficient for participants to match very closely the ratings given by students who observed these teachers for an entire semester (Ambady & Rosenthal, 1992, 1993). Even thinner slices—three 2-second clips—still produced only slightly less comparable ratings.

First impressions, although vulnerable to biasing influences, can be remarkably accurate in certain circumstances. A few minutes of thoughtful observations (type of clothes, hairstyle, speaking ability) and face-to-face

BOX 2.2 Developing Communication Competence

WHERE DO YOU DRAW THE LINE??

Consider each of the following opportunities for self-disclosure. Indicate whether you view each option for self-disclosure as appropriate or inappropriate for you.

1. Tell a friend what your favorite movie is.
2. Inform your parents that you've run out of money.
3. Indicate how much you earn annually to a stranger on a bus.
4. Tell your college class that you didn't vote in the last election.
5. Reveal to a friend of the opposite sex that you viewed a pornographic website.
6. Text message a friend that you have a crush on a teacher.
7. Identify on your Facebook page what you really dislike about one of your parents.
8. Tell a person you are very attracted to that you wish he or she were dating you and not your roommate.
9. Tell a classmate whom you barely know that you had a dream about him or her.
10. Reveal to the class what your GPA is.

There are no "right" answers, but this self-disclosure test should pose some issues for you: Do you draw a line—do some revelations cross a line and become inappropriate? How do you decide what is appropriate to disclose and what is inappropriate? Identify the rules that you use to make such decisions. Does the means used to self-disclose (social network site, cell phone, face to face) matter? Explain. If you considered all the situations listed as appropriate, what would you not reveal and to whom? Why?

conversation can lead to relatively accurate perceptions of others. Quick glances and gut feelings, however, are not so accurate (Borkenau et al., 2004; Gaschler, 2005).

Even paying attention to "identity claims"—symbols that a person consciously creates to communicate an impression—can produce relatively accurate impressions (Gosling et al., 2002). A dorm room decorated with posters of Einstein, rock stars, or beer ads creates impressions of individuals' personality and intelligence. Rooms and offices decorated only with bookshelves stocked with classic novels or academic texts in neat rows say something about discipline, neatness, and academic interests. Accurate impressions of individuals' personality (especially degree of openness, extroversion, conscientiousness, and emotional stability) can even be garnered from inspecting personal websites (Vazire & Gosling, 2004). These are broad, general impressions, however, not complex, personal impressions of others.

Biased Impressions: Going Negative First

Thin slicing works fairly well on simple, broad impressions, but it is problematic on complex impressions. For example, the short, face-to-face job interview is a favorite method for hiring employees in institutions and organizations. Job interviews, however, usually require an assessment of more than one ability or attribute. Hiring for a college teaching position, for example, requires forming predictive impressions of ability beyond just teaching, such as candidates' capacity to perform appropriate research to stay current in their field, their ability to work cooperatively with colleagues, their rapport with students, and their decision-making ability. Most people are reasonably accurate when predicting from a thin slice of observed behavior whether a candidate will be *sociable* and *verbally skillful* (Levesque & Kenny, 1993). You're not likely to deduce from a first impression, however, whether an individual has integrity, conflict-management skills, and a strong work ethic.

A thin slice of observed behavior or even a half-hour face-to-face interview is a less precise predictor of *job performance* than tests of job knowledge, peer ratings of prior job performance, aptitude tests, and samples of a candidate's work in previous positions (Kaplowitz, 1986; Schmidt & Hunter, 1998).

Primacy Effect: The Power of Initial Information Although you cannot inhibit instant impressions of others because your brain makes them in a tenth of a second, you do not have to adhere steadfastly to the bias of the primacy effect. The **primacy effect** is the tendency to be more influenced by initial information about a person than by information gathered later. If an initial positive impression is formed during a job interview, that impression can act as a filter to excuse later revelations of potential concern ("Apparently, you learned from that disappointing failure") (Dougherty et al., 1994). College roommates who form positive first impressions of each other are likely to maintain positive relationships, manage their conflicts competently, and continue as roommates. Negative first impressions produce the opposite result (Marek et al., 2004).

Once aware of the primacy effect and the automatic nature of initial impressions, you can make a conscious effort to slowly, deliberately, and consciously consider more than the initial information about a person. The bias of the primacy effect can be overridden. This is especially true when people anticipate being held accountable for their impressions of others; they do not want to look foolish when they are asked to justify their judgments (Lerner & Tetlock, 1999).

First impressions are immediate, often negative, and sometimes startlingly wrong. When Susan Boyle, a plain-looking 47-year-old Scottish woman, first appeared on *Britain's Got Talent*, audience members laughed, some booed, and others hissed before she began to sing "I Dreamed a Dream" from *Les Miserables*. The audience gave her a standing ovation when she finished singing. Jackie Evanko appeared on *America's Got Talent* as a 10-year-old. Her beautifully mature operatic voice wowed the stunned audience. The bias of the primacy effect can be overcome.

Negativity Bias: Agile, Funny, Compassionate, and FAT Add to the primacy effect our strong tendency to be influenced more heavily by negative than positive information (Smith et al., 2006), which is called **negativity bias** (Kiken & Shook, 2011), and you can see how perceptions of others can become quite distorted. If I described a person to you as "outgoing, casual, fun-loving, articulate, and manipulative," would you want to be friends with that person? Would the single negative quality cause you to pause despite the four very positive qualities? Conversely, if I described a person as "abrasive, rude, domineering, closed-minded, and fun-loving," would the one positive quality even make a dent in the negative impression created by the first four qualities? Would you even want to meet such a person? This negativity bias is actually built into your brain. As comedian Stephen Colbert once observed, "Mother Nature is on your side, keeping fear alive." Your amygdala, "the alarm bell of your brain," uses about two-thirds of its neurons to search for bad news. Why? Because negative information is potentially threatening to human well-being, but positive information is merely pleasant with little likely risk to human survival (Hanson, 2010). Even though most negative information ("You are fat") isn't an immediate threat to a person's survival, your brain doesn't make that nuanced assessment. Hesitation when faced with a real threat could prove fatal. It's best to be on guard.

The negativity bias can be particularly strong during job interviews (Dougherty et al., 1994). In fact, negative information, especially if it is received early in the interview, is likely to lead to a candidate's rejection even when the total quantity of information about the candidate is overwhelmingly positive. In a hypercompetitive job market where differences in quality between candidates can be hard to discern, one poorly chosen phrase or inappropriate remark during an interview can negate a dozen very positive letters of recommendation.

Sometimes the negative information should outweigh the positive. Medical doctor Harold Shipman was England's worst serial killer. An official investigation determined that he murdered 215 of his patients by injecting them with a lethal dose of painkiller. Described by his patients as trustworthy, persuasive, and attentive, he conducted his killing spree over a 23-year period. He was finally caught in 1998 and sentenced to life in prison (Hoge, 2002). He hanged himself in his cell in January 2004. Not all qualities of a person are created equal. Some negative characteristics supersede even a host of positive traits.

When we formulate perceptions of others, initial information and negative information influence us more than later information and positive information. Sometimes this is appropriate. Often it is not. The negativity bias can be overridden in much the same way as the primacy effect. Presenting an abundance of positive information that contradicts the negative can overcome negativity bias (Smith et al., 2006). Also, being mindful of the negativity bias can reduce it and increase positive judgments (Kiken & Shook, 2011).

A first impression can encourage further transactions with others when it is positive, and it can prevent any further contact with a person when the impression is negative. You never get to make a second first impression, so you want to begin on a positive note.

Attribution Error: Underestimating Situational Causes

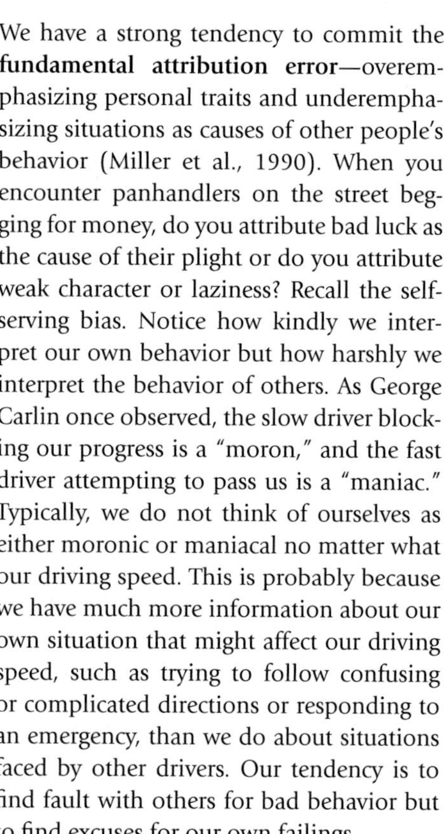

We have a strong tendency to commit the **fundamental attribution error**—overemphasizing personal traits and underemphasizing situations as causes of other people's behavior (Miller et al., 1990). When you encounter panhandlers on the street begging for money, do you attribute bad luck as the cause of their plight or do you attribute weak character or laziness? Recall the self-serving bias. Notice how kindly we interpret our own behavior but how harshly we interpret the behavior of others. As George Carlin once observed, the slow driver blocking our progress is a "moron," and the fast driver attempting to pass us is a "maniac." Typically, we do not think of ourselves as either moronic or maniacal no matter what our driving speed. This is probably because we have much more information about our own situation that might affect our driving speed, such as trying to follow confusing or complicated directions or responding to an emergency, than we do about situations faced by other drivers. Our tendency is to find fault with others for bad behavior but to find excuses for our own failings.

Marriage partners can experience difficulties because of attribution error. Partners are inclined to attribute relationship problems to personal traits rather than to situational forces (Bradbury & Fincham, 1990). A wife might complain that her husband does not help out sufficiently with the housework, leaves his clothes on the floor, and doesn't listen or pay attention to her. She then claims that her husband is lazy,

Zinedine Zidane head-butts Marco Materazzi in a championship soccer match between Italy and France. Zidane claimed that he did it because Materazzi insulted his mother and sister (situational cause). He denied that it was because he was a "bad sport" or had a "violent temper" (personal traits as causes).

sloppy, and uncaring, which are all personal traits. Her husband, however, is likely to assign situational causes such as stress at work, exhaustion, or other factors beyond his control. If his wife is unmoved by such interpretations, he is likely to attribute her anger and frustration to "moodiness" or "irritability," also personal characteristics.

Attribution patterns of communication can indicate whether couples have a happy or unhappy relationship (Fletcher & Fincham, 1991). Individuals in happy relationships, for instance, typically explain the nice behaviors of their partners as personal traits: "She did the grocery shopping after work because she is a caring, giving person." Negative behaviors are explained in situational terms: "He snapped at me because he's under a great deal of pressure."

Individuals in unhappy relationships typically exhibit the reverse attribution pattern. Positive behavior is explained in situational terms: "She picked up my clothes at the laundry because she had nothing better to do with her time." Negative behaviors are explained in dispositional terms: "He was irritable with me because he is a very impatient person."

Attribution patterns of communication do not automatically produce happy or unhappy relationships, but "the evidence supports the existence of a causal link between attributions . . . and relationship satisfaction" (Fletcher & Fincham, 1991, p. 14). Explaining your partner's positive behavior as situationally caused and his or her negative behavior as the result of character flaws creates a destructive communication climate from which there is little chance of escape. Attribution error can kill a relationship. Conversely, preferring to see your partner's negative behavior as caused by bad situations and his or her positive behavior as a reflection of strength of character can reinforce a sense of happiness in a relationship (Fincham et al., 2000).

It's not that traits are never the cause of bad behavior. Sometimes individuals just seem mean and disagreeable no matter what the circumstances (consistent and not distinctive). Attribution error, however, denies a person reasonable doubt. We begin by assuming character flaws explain antisocial communication patterns without adequately considering the influence of situational forces.

Stereotyped Distortions of Others: Inaccurate Impressions

Prejudice refers to *negative* feelings about members of a group. **Discrimination** is any behavior that manifests these negative feelings. Individuals act out their prejudice ("I hate them") through discrimination (barring club membership to Jews). This section discusses stereotyping and the role it can play in producing prejudice and discrimination.

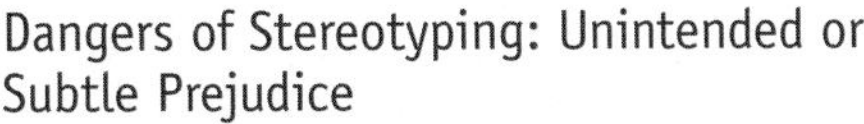

Dangers of Stereotyping: Unintended or Subtle Prejudice

Stereotyping is natural and unavoidable. It permits rapid judgments when instant decisions are required ("Is that a dangerous or safe person approaching?"), but it can lead to serious mistakes (Jonas & Sassenberg,

2006). One study that used a video game simulation had African American and white participants make quick decisions to fire at armed targets and to withhold fire when targets were unarmed. Stereotypes of African Americans as "violent" triggered significantly greater errors (firing at unarmed targets) when the targets were African American than when they were white. Both African American and white participants made about the same number of errors, so mere knowledge of the stereotype may be sufficient to trigger errors (Correll et al., 2002). Stereotyping can be so automatic that a person's conscious intent or disagreement with the stereotype can be irrelevant (Devine, 1989).

Stereotypes, although not necessarily prejudicial (they can produce *positive* feelings), can produce prejudice in some instances. For example, people acting as jurors saw a picture of a defendant and read some evidence about a crime. The defendant was an African American man. Some of the jurors read about a crime that was consistent with the negative stereotype for African American men (auto theft); other jurors read about a crime that was inconsistent (embezzlement). The defendant was more likely to be judged guilty of the stereotype-consistent crime than for the stereotype-inconsistent crime (Jones & Kaplan, 2003).

Benevolent Sexism

Benevolent sexism is a subtle form of discrimination that embraces the "positive" stereotype of women as "pure creatures" who deserve to be protected and shown affection, but only as long as they behave in the conventional manner. There are benefits to being protected, adored, and provided for, but people who have this view of women are likely to resist women's efforts to pursue education, careers, business opportunities, and full participation in the political life of the nation (Glick & Fiske, 2001). Challenging benevolent sexism would likely result in loss of benefits and could provoke **hostile sexism**—"antipathy toward women who are viewed as usurping men's power" (Glick & Fiske, 2001, p. 109). The seemingly positive stereotypes of women are not without their downside.

Men from diverse cultures tend to endorse benevolent sexism, and *women also tend to endorse it* (Glick & Fiske, 2001; Glick et al., 2004). Relinquishing the benefits is not always so easy, and it may appear that men are just being nice, not sexist. By rewarding women for maintaining a patriarchal, "chivalrous" status quo, however, benevolent sexism retards gender equality. Men can treat women well without making the benevolence a reward for women who "know their place."

Stereotype Distortions: Let Us Count the Ways

Stereotypes can distort our perceptions in several ways. First, stereotypes create cookie-cutter images of sameness that discount individual differences within a group (Rudman & Fairchild, 2004). Acclaimed African American poet Maya Angelou tells a story about a white friend of hers who mentioned a black woman they both had met some time ago. Maya Angelou couldn't remember who this woman was, so she asked, "What color is she?" Her white friend responded, "I already told you she is black." Ms. Angelou replied, "Yes, but what color of black?" (cited in Matlin, 1992). No shades of difference are perceived when we stereotype. All black people are perceived to be the same color.

Second, stereotypes distort our perceptions of others by creating a selective memory bias. **Selective memory bias** occurs when we tend to remember information that supports our stereotypes but forget information that contradicts them. In one study, men and women engaged in conflict remembered only behaviors of their partners that fit gender stereotypes ("Women are nags"; "Men are slobs") (Allen, 1998b). Our stereotypes produce a selective memory bias, and our memory bias, in turn, nurtures and hardens our stereotypes of others.

Third, negative stereotypes can influence our perceptions of self and produce poor performance. Several studies on **stereotype vulnerability**—a perceived threat from apprehension that a person will be evaluated based on a negative stereotype—demonstrate this point (Cadinu et al., 2005;

Shih et al., 1999; Steele et al., 2002). Asian American women posted high scores on a standardized math test when reminded of their ethnicity before taking the test, but they scored much lower when reminded of their gender identity. When told that Asian students typically do better than whites on a test, white students bombed the test. Female students scored as well as male students on a rigorous math exam when told beforehand that the exam didn't measure gender differences. They scored far lower, however, if made to think gender differences would be measured.

Fourth, and closely related to stereotype vulnerability, is the problem of **self-fulfilling prophecy**—acting on an erroneous expectation that produces the expected behavior and confirms the original impression. Hundreds of studies in a wide variety of circumstances and settings demonstrate the power of self-fulfilling prophecies (McNatt, 2000). Expect individuals to be unfriendly, act according to that expectation by not smiling, backing away, and making little effort to engage in conversation, and watch them fulfill the prophecy by becoming unfriendly even though that may not have been their inclination. Those individuals who expect to be rejected by others behave in ways that fulfill the prophecy; they ultimately get rejected (Downey et al., 1998).

Self-fulfilling prophecies make inaccurate stereotypes appear valid (Snyder, 2001). If you expect an Asian student to be very quiet in group discussions, you may ignore him or her whenever an attempt is made to contribute. When the Asian student gives up trying to be heard by the group, the expectation is confirmed, though this particular student may not typically be quiet in groups. Those individuals who most expect to be negatively stereotyped tend to avoid opportunities that could counter prejudicial stereotypes (Pinel, 1999). Women who expect stigmatizing stereotypes behave more critically toward men who they expect to be sexist. Not surprisingly, such reactions to expected stereotypes trigger negative responses from men, making them appear sexist (Pinel, 2002).

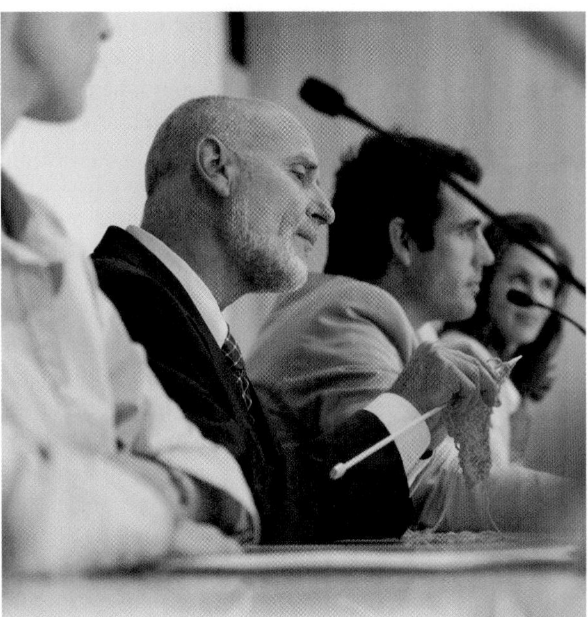

A man knitting during a public meeting. "Only 4% of knitters are men" (Penn & Zalesne, 2007). This photo illustrates which of the following?

1. Some stereotypes are mostly true
2. Stereotypes are negative generalizations about a group
3. Stereotypes don't allow for individual differences among members of a group
4. Stereotypes are always inaccurate depictions of members of groups

Answers at end of chapter

Combating Stereotypes: Reducing Prejudice Through Competent Communication

There are several communication strategies that change stereotypes and reduce prejudice. First, confront the stereotypes head-on. Three studies show that both a hostile confrontation that accuses another person of being racist and a calm appeal for fairness ("They don't get equal treatment in our society") significantly reduce negative stereotyping and prejudiced attitudes (Czopp et al., 2006). Hostile confrontations, however, produce greater anger and irritation toward the confronter by those confronted than the less threatening appeal to fairness.

Second, contradict the stereotype by using multiple examples. For instance, presenting only a single example contradicting stereotypes of African Americans (success of Condoleezza Rice) can easily be discounted as an exception. Presenting *several* examples (Barack Obama, Colin Powell, Oprah Winfrey, etc.), however, especially when they are presented as typical, can erode the stereotypes (Wilder et al., 1996).

Finally, **contact theory** predicts that interacting and becoming more familiar with members of stereotyped groups can diminish prejudice resulting from stereotyping (Hodson, 2011). An analysis of 515 studies supports the general wisdom of this theory (Pettigrew & Tropp, 2006). Interacting works best under certain conditions: (1) contacts are more than just superficial, (2) status differences among group members are de-emphasized, (3) contact occurs between relative equals (e.g., skill and education levels), and (4) groups pursue a common, valued goal, preferably a **superordinate goal**—one that requires mutual effort by both groups to achieve a desired end (Brewer & Brown, 1997; Pettigrew & Tropp, 2006).

Communication Competence and Perceptual Challenges

This final section explains competent communication strategies that overlap more than one perceptual problem or issue. These strategies will help you connect the discussion of perception of both self and others to an interrelated whole.

Monitor Perceptual Biases

Self-serving bias and attribution errors need to be carefully monitored. If you see yourself rationalizing your mistakes and taking credit for successes that may be more luck and good fortune than personal achievement, recognize your self-serving bias.

Resist attributing personal characteristics to the negative behaviors of others and situational causes to the positive behaviors of others. Practice the reverse. Try explaining the communication behaviors of your partner, coworker, friend, or relative that irritate or anger you with a situational attribution. Try explaining communication behaviors that please you with a personal characteristic attribution. In other words, be experimental. Test new ways of communicating with others and see what happens.

Recognize Cultural Differences

There is a cultural component to our self-appraisals. A common question during most job interviews in the United States is "Why should we hire you?" You are asked to promote yourself for the position. You are, after all, competing against other candidates, and the hiring committee is presumably looking for the best person. In contrast, Asian cultures encourage the denial of self-importance. Reticence, not self-assertion, is valued. Promoting yourself is considered boastful. Your possible contribution to the group is important, as well as your likely conformity to the norms of the group or organization (Brislin, 1993). Consequently, the self-serving bias is found far more in the American culture than in Asian cultures (Anderson, 1999).

Attribution error also occurs more often in U.S. culture than in some other cultures. In one study, participants from India made primarily situational attributions for behavior, and Americans made primarily personal trait attributions (Miller, 1984; see also Na & Kitayama, 2011). There were similar findings when comparing American and British students with Korean and Nigerian students. American and British students attributed criminal behavior to personal traits of offenders more than Korean and Nigerian students did (Na & Loftus, 1998; Pfeiffer et al., 1998).

Manage Impressions

It is not enough to know that perceptual biases occur frequently in the human communication arena. Try taking an active approach, not a reactive one. Attempt to prevent perceptual biases before they occur. Create the impression you wish others to perceive. Of the many aspects of self, consider which you want to emphasize in a given situation. In a job interview, would you display your articulateness, friendliness, sense of humor, and dynamism, or would you display your irritability, cynicism, sarcasm, and interpersonal remoteness? These all may be aspects of your self-concept, but you can choose to display some aspects in a given situation and keep private other aspects of your self. This is especially important given the power of the negativity bias.

This is not meant to encourage phoniness or dishonesty, only communication flexibility. When you are interviewed for a job, you make choices regarding which aspects of your self-image you wish to display. You put forward your best self to create a positive impression. This is not dishonest. It is adapting to the expectations of your audience. Communication is situational. We don't show the same self to strangers as we do to intimate partners—at least we don't if we know what's good for us.

Practice Empathy

You can counter attribution errors by practicing empathy. Empathy has three dimensions (Stiff et al., 1988). The first is *perspective taking*. Here you try to see as others see, perceive as they perceive. You try on the viewpoint of another to gain understanding of his or her perspective. You don't have to accept the viewpoint of another to be empathic, just understand it. A second dimension is *emotional understanding*. You participate in the feelings of others, experiencing their joy, anxiety, frustration, irritation, and so forth. The last dimension of empathy is *concern for others*. You care what happens to them.

One study (Regan & Totten, 1975) found that attribution errors were countered by empathy. College students were instructed to list their impressions of individuals either shown in a video or described in a short story. Those who were instructed to empathize with the person as deeply as possible and attempt to picture how that person was feeling were prone to attribute situational causes to behavior. Participants given no instructions to be empathic were inclined to choose personal traits as causes of behavior. Not all behavior is situationally caused, of course, but the fundamental attribution error predisposes us to assign personal characteristics as causes of the behavior almost to the complete exclusion of situational causes. Empathy can provide attribution balance.

Check Perceptions

Perhaps the most obvious yet most often ignored method for dealing with perceptual biases and distortions is perception checking. That is, we should not assume our perceptions of others are accurate without checking to see whether they are. The perceptual process of selecting, organizing, and interpreting is inherently subjective and prone to biases.

Assuming another person is angry, for example, can lead to misunderstanding. Statements such as "You're so irritable" and "I know you're bored, but try to look interested" may assume facts not in evidence.

An effective perception check usually has three steps:

1. A behavior description
2. An interpretation of the behavior
3. A request for verification of the interpretation

Consider this example: "I noticed that you left the room before I was finished speaking (behavior description). You seemed offended by what I said (interpretation). Were you offended (request for verification)?" All three steps are present in this perception check. Sometimes an effective perception check is more abbreviated: "You looked very angry. Were you?" Here the behavior description is implied along with the interpretation, and the verification request follows.

Perception checking is a cooperative communication strategy. The goal is mutual understanding, a We-orientation. If you assume your perceptions are accurate without checking with the other person, you may elicit a defensive, competitive response.

Summary

PERCEPTION is the process of selecting, organizing, and interpreting data from our senses. This is an inherently subjective process with much potential for error both in the perception of self and perception of others. Our self-concept and self-esteem are protected by the self-serving bias. Our perception of others is biased by the primacy effect, negativity bias, attribution error, and stereotyping. Our perception of self and others is a fundamental starting point of human communication. We reveal who we are to others by self-disclosing. To be a competent communicator, monitor your perceptual biases, recognize cultural differences, manage the impressions you make with others, practice empathy, and check your perceptions with others.

Answers for *Critical Thinking* caption:

Man knitting (p. 57): #1 and #3

Quizzes Without Consequences

Test your knowledge before your exam!

Go to the companion website at www.oup.com/us/rothwell, click on the Student Resources for each chapter, and take the Quizzes Without Consequences.

Film School Case Studies

Before Sunset (2004). Romantic Drama; R

This is the wonderful sequel to *Before Sunrise*, a tale of a young man and woman who meet by chance on a train traveling through Austria and share an intimate but brief romance. This sequel has the two meeting for a few hours in Paris nine years later. Explore the process of self-disclosure. Why do they hesitate to reveal feelings and experiences? What are the risks of opening up and the potential drawbacks of resisting self-disclosure?

Bridget Jones's Diary (2001). Romantic Comedy; R

This is the somewhat underrated story of Bridget Jones (Renée Zellweger) and her battle with self-esteem issues. Analyze what influences her self-esteem most by applying concepts of reflected appraisal, contingencies of self-worth, and social comparison.

Brokeback Mountain (2005). Drama; R

Heath Ledger and Jake Gyllenhaal tend sheep on Montana's Brokeback Mountain. They become friends and eventually lovers kept secret from their wives and children. Examine how self-concept and self-disclosure interconnect. How do the two characters engage in impression management?

Catch Me If You Can (2002). Drama; PG-13

Leonardo DiCaprio plays a character who assumes several false identities and cons his way through life earning riches, respect, and admiration from others. In the process, he loses his own sense of identity. Analyze the cost of failure to self-disclose to others, to reveal one's true identity. Who pays the price?

City Island (2009). Comedy/Drama; PG-13

Andy Garcia is a prison guard who secretly wants to be an actor. In fact, just about everyone in the Rizzo family is keeping secrets. Examine this movie from the perspective of self-disclosure—when to open up and when to shut up.

Crash (2005). Drama; R

This intercultural clash of ethnicities provides gripping entertainment and poignant moments. Analyze the movie from the perspective of stereotypes.

I, Robot (2004). Drama; PG-13

Will Smith plays a suspicious cop of the future who does not trust the robot society being created to serve humankind. Analyze the many questions raised regarding what constitutes self-concept and personal identity.

Precious (2009). Drama; R

Gabourey Sidibe plays Claireece "Precious" Jones who is surrounded by abusive people. Analyze what part reflected appraisal, social comparison, and contingencies of self-worth play in the formation and tenacity of her self-concept and self-esteem.

CHAPTER 3

Chapter Outline

Culture and Gender

NEW YORK TIMES reporter Nicholas Kristof (1995) describes the falsetto voice used by Japanese women in formal settings, on the phone, or during conversations with strangers or business customers this way: "The Voice is as fawning as her demeanor, as sweet as syrup, and as high as a dog whistle. Any higher, and it would shatter the crystal on the seventh floor" (p. A27). Historically, Japanese women have used this unnaturally high-pitched voice to communicate politeness and femininity (Hiramoto & Anderson, 2006), much as a person in the United States might raise his or her voice at the end of a sentence to sound tentative or questioning. Julie Saito, a reporter at *Asahi Shimbun*, explains, "A lower voice sounds too bullying, too aggressive, too manly. . . . A high voice sounds more cute, more like a girlish image of women" (Kristof, 1995, p. A27).

By the end of this chapter, you should be able to:

1. Recognize the deep structural value differences among cultures that strongly affect communication.
2. Identify communication challenges and problems resulting from ethnocentrism, misunderstanding, and miscommunication.
3. Understand ways to address these cultural challenges.
4. Evaluate to what degree gender differences in communication exist.
5. Recognize the value of several perspectives that explain gender differences, large and small, in communication.
6. Choose effective and appropriate communication strategies to address gender differences in commu-

Speaking in a falsetto voice reflects a gender stereotype of women in Japan (Yamashita, 2009). Even if it were possible for men to match the falsetto voice (usually men's voices are an octave lower than women's), it would sound "too feminine." A man doesn't want to "sound like a woman" for good reason. In one study, males with the deepest voices were perceived by women as more attractive, older, and more likely to have well-developed muscles and a hairy chest (Collins, 2001). The voice of David Prowse, the six-foot-seven-inch actor who played Darth Vader in *Star Wars*, was replaced with the deep, rumbling voice of James Earl Jones. Reportedly, Prowse's voice was too high pitched to communicate "masculine" power and stature (Adam, 2001).

As these examples illustrate, *gender is integrally connected to culture*. What is considered masculine or feminine is culturally determined (Hofstede & Hofstede, 2005). "Every known human society has rules and customs concerning gender. Members of every society have expectations and beliefs—sometimes explicit, sometimes unspoken—concerning what boys and girls, or men and women, are supposed to do, or not do" (Maccoby, 1998, p. 2). These gender-role expectations vary across cultures from highly constraining to barely noticeable. Gender influence operates within the context of culture. For example, traditional Arab women are expected to follow a few steps behind their husbands, an expectation that is wholly incompatible with expectations of both men and women in U.S. culture. In some instances, however, there is sad uniformity across cultures in gender treatment. For example, despite enormous strides made recently, especially in the United States, women the world over continue to experience gender inequality (Hausmann et al., 2010).

The principal purpose of this chapter is to explain how you can competently address the challenges of intercultural and gender differences in communication. Culture is discussed before gender because culture provides the broader context for gender differences in communication.

Culture and Communication

You don't have to travel far to experience the challenges of cross-cultural transactions. Intercultural opportunities within the United States are wide and varied.

Intercultural Opportunities: It's a New World

Recent, vast demographic changes mean that the ever-mobile U.S. population is constantly exposed to diverse cultures and ethnicities. Minorities comprised 35% of the population in the United States and 46% of children under 15 years old in 2010. By 2050, Latinos and Mexican Americans, African Americans, and Asian Americans will collectively constitute the majority of the population in the United States (Garrido, 2010). International student enrollment in U.S. colleges and universities rose to almost 700,000 in 2010 ("International Student Enrollments," 2010). More than 260,000 students from the United States study in other countries each year ("Study Abroad by U.S. Students," 2010). Almost 60% of students in one survey said that they had dated someone from a different cultural group (Farrell, 2005). A survey of more than 14,000 college students on 136 campuses in the United States revealed that more than half were committed to "improving my understanding of other countries and cultures"

(Marklein, 2007). Despite some residual resistance to interracial dating and marriage in the United States, about 8% of marriages are mixed race (Yen, 2010). This doesn't include couples that are cohabiting.

The development of electronic technologies has expanded opportunities for intercultural communication beyond anything our world has ever experienced. Where once a person had to hop onto a plane and travel for hours or was severely constrained by the prohibitive cost of international phone calls, the Internet and satellite transmission have made transactions with members of diverse cultures highly accessible. Online virtual groups allow members from diverse cultures to transcend time and space. Group members may represent many cultures and live in widely separate time zones. Electronic technologies have also expanded the opportunities for intercultural misunderstandings because, as you'll see, cultural values impact our communication with others (Hofstede & Hofstede, 2005).

Inescapable intercultural communication tells us why we need to know how to communicate competently with others from diverse cultural backgrounds. It doesn't explain why intercultural miscommunication occurs, however. Before discussing this, a few critical terms need defining. **Culture** is a learned set of enduring values, beliefs, and practices that are shared by an identifiable, large group of people with a common history. **Values** are the most deeply felt, generally shared view of what is deemed good, right, or worthwhile thinking or behavior. Values constitute a shared conception, not of what is, but of what ought to be. **Beliefs** are what a person thinks is true or probable. Two individuals may *value* human life, but one may *believe* that capital punishment preserves life by deterring homicides, while the other may believe the contrary. Finally, a **co-culture** is a group of people who live in a dominant culture yet remain connected to another cultural heritage that typically exhibits significant differences in values, beliefs, and practices from the dominant culture. African Americans, Asian Americans, Native Americans, and Mexican Americans are some examples of co-cultures within the United States.

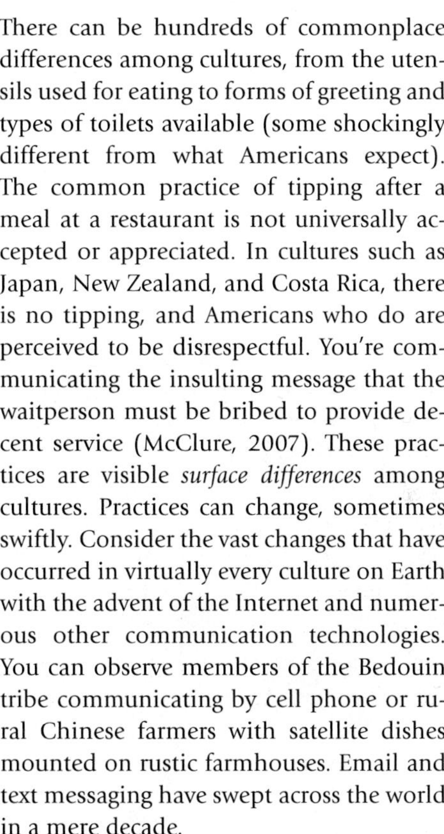

Cultural Values: Deep, Not Surface, Differences

There can be hundreds of commonplace differences among cultures, from the utensils used for eating to forms of greeting and types of toilets available (some shockingly different from what Americans expect). The common practice of tipping after a meal at a restaurant is not universally accepted or appreciated. In cultures such as Japan, New Zealand, and Costa Rica, there is no tipping, and Americans who do are perceived to be disrespectful. You're communicating the insulting message that the waitperson must be bribed to provide decent service (McClure, 2007). These practices are visible *surface differences* among cultures. Practices can change, sometimes swiftly. Consider the vast changes that have occurred in virtually every culture on Earth with the advent of the Internet and numerous other communication technologies. You can observe members of the Bedouin tribe communicating by cell phone or rural Chinese farmers with satellite dishes mounted on rustic farmhouses. Email and text messaging have swept across the world in a mere decade.

Bedrock core values of a culture, however, are highly stable and resistant to change (Hofstede, 2012; Hofstede & Hofstede, 2005). What we "ought to do" becomes the hardened cement of our culture. It can be changed, but about as easily as jackhammering concrete. Perhaps this is because "cultural values and experiences shape neurocognitive processes," or put another way, "culture wires the brain" (Park & Huang, 2010). We see the world differently partly because culture has shaped the neural networks in our brains to perceive the world differently. **Value dimensions**—varying degrees of importance placed on those deeply felt views of what is right, good, and worthwhile—are the *deep structural reasons* many cultural differences that provoke serious miscommunication and intense conflict exist.

Geert Hofstede (1980) conducted the largest cross-cultural survey ever attempted to identify significant value dimensions that distinguish cultures from each other. Initially involving more than 100,000 workers at IBM subsidiaries in 40 countries, his research eventually encompassed 50 countries and 3 geographic areas (Hofstede & Hofstede, 2005). Several value dimensions emerged from this abundance of data. Two have received considerable attention and substantial additional supporting research (see Hofstede, 2012; Hofstede & Hofstede, 2005, for a summary). *These two value dimensions are individualism-collectivism and power-distance.*

Children from collectivist cultures such as most Asian cultures are typically taught that "the nail that sticks up gets hammered down" and are encouraged to blend into the group. Children from individualist cultures such as the Unites States are typically taught that "the squeaky wheel gets the grease" and are encouraged to stand out from the group by being overtly expressive.

Individualism-Collectivism: Prime Value Difference

The individualism-collectivism dimension is thought to be the most important of all value dimensions that distinguish cultures (Hui & Triandis, 1986). It clearly has received the most voluminous research and interest.

General Description: The Me-We Dimension An **individualist culture** has a "me" consciousness. Individuals see themselves as loosely linked to each other and largely independent of group identification (Hofstede & Hofstede, 2005; Triandis, 1995). They are chiefly motivated by their own preferences, needs, and goals. Personal achievement and initiative are stressed. Emphasis is placed on the self: self-help, self-sufficiency, self-actualization, and personal growth. People communicate as individuals and pay little heed to a person's group memberships. Decision making is based on what is best for the individual, sometimes even if this sacrifices the group welfare. Words such as "independence," "self," "privacy," and "rights" permeate cultural conversations. "I gotta be me; I gotta be free" is the anthem of the individualist. Finally, individualist cultures are characterized by an emphasis on a rational assessment of the benefits and drawbacks of relationships. Those that are perceived to be, on balance, disadvantageous are typically severed.

A **collectivist culture** has a "we" consciousness. Individuals see themselves as closely linked to one or more groups. Commitment to valued groups (family, organization) is paramount (Hofstede & Hofstede, 2005; Triandis, 1995). People take notice of a person's place in the hierarchy of a group. Individuals often downplay personal goals in favor of advancing the goals of a valued group. The Chinese proverb "No need to know the person, only the family" and the African adage "It takes a village to raise a child" express the collectivist perception. Words such as "loyalty," "responsibility," and "community" permeate collectivist cultural conversations. The decision regarding whom to marry must involve the wishes and preferences of family members and other interested parties. As Francis Hsu (1981) explains, when in love, "an American asks, 'How does my heart feel?' A Chinese asks, 'What will other people say?'"

All cultures vary in their emphasis on individualism and collectivism, and no culture is entirely one way or the other. Hofstede, however, was able to rank cultures on the basis of the relative importance placed on individualist or collectivist values (see Figure 3-1). In general, North American, Western European, and European-influenced cultures such as Australia, New Zealand, and South Africa are individualist, with the United States ranking number one among them. East Asian, North African, and most Latin American cultures are collectivist. Approximately 70% of the world's population lives in collectivist cultures (Triandis, 1990; see also Hofstede & Hofstede, 2005). The individualism-collectivism dimension also applies to co-cultures. The Mexican American co-culture, for example, expresses its collectivism in proverbs: "Better to be a fool with the crowd than wise by oneself" and "He who divides and shares is left with the best share" (Zormeier & Samovar, 2000).

Differences between individualist and collectivist cultures can be seen in a variety of ways. First, in a poll, 131 businesspeople, scholars, government officials, and professionals in eight East Asian countries and the United States were asked, "Which of the following are critically important to your

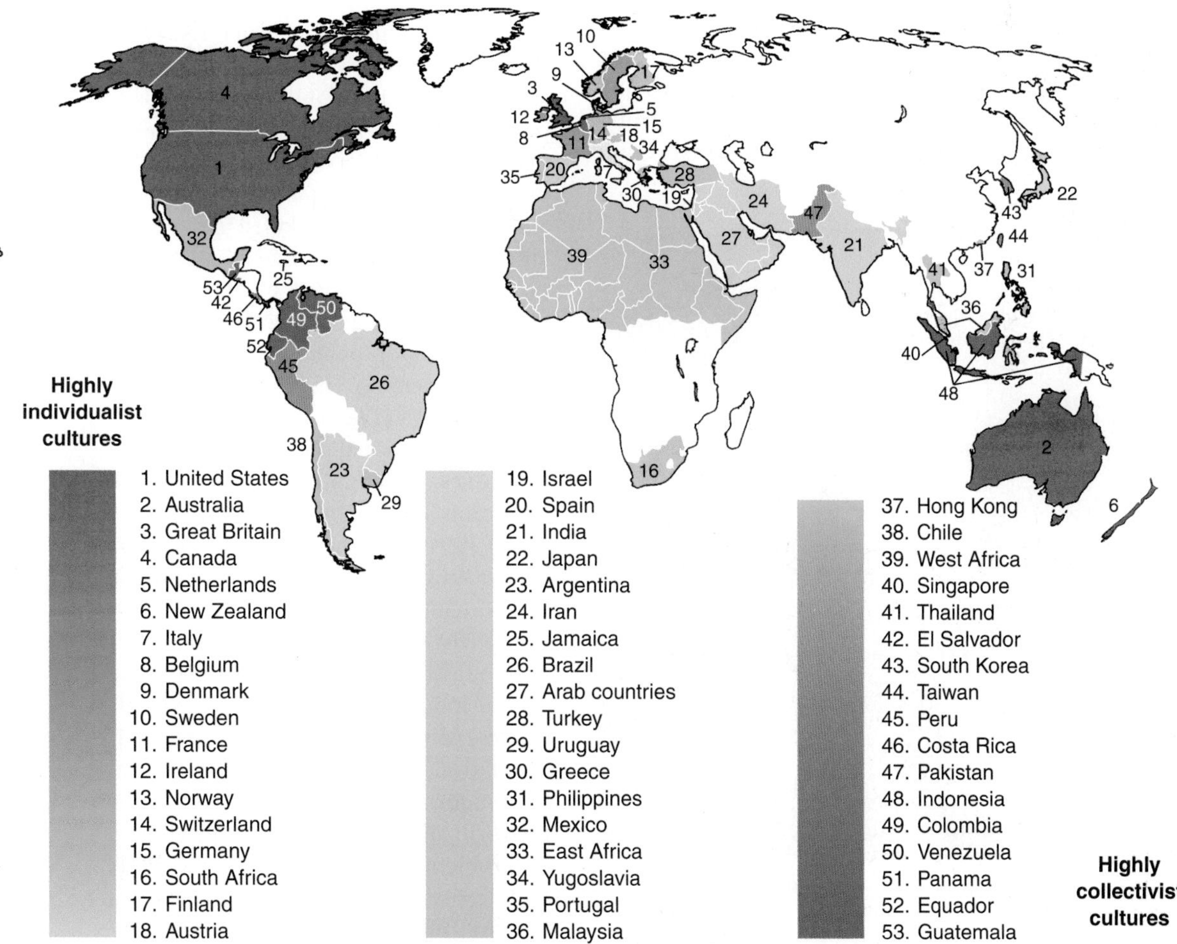

FIGURE 3-1 Individualism-Collectivism Rankings for 50 Countries and 3 Regions. (Source: Hofstede, 1991)

people?" (Simons & Zielenziger, 1996, p. A22). The results were as follows:

	Asians	Americans
1. An orderly society	70%	11%
2. Personal freedom	32%	82%
3. Individual rights	29%	73%

The 2011 Supreme Court decision *Snyder v. Phelps* starkly illustrates structural (law) support given to individual rights, personal freedom, and less concern for an orderly society in the individualistic United States. A group of protesters from the Westboro Baptist Church demonstrated at hundreds of funerals for dead American soldiers killed in Iraq and Afghanistan. The demonstrators believed that God killed American soldiers as punishment for homosexuality and the nation's sinful policies. Picket signs were offensive slurs against gays and celebrations of dead soldiers. The demonstrations were peaceful but emotionally disruptive for mourners burying their dead sons and daughters. The group was sued for disrupting the funerals. Nevertheless, the Court ruled 8-1 that the Westboro protesters engaged in protected speech guaranteed by the First Amendment to the U.S. Constitution (Savage, 2011). A collectivist culture would likely arrest the demonstrators for disrupting the peace.

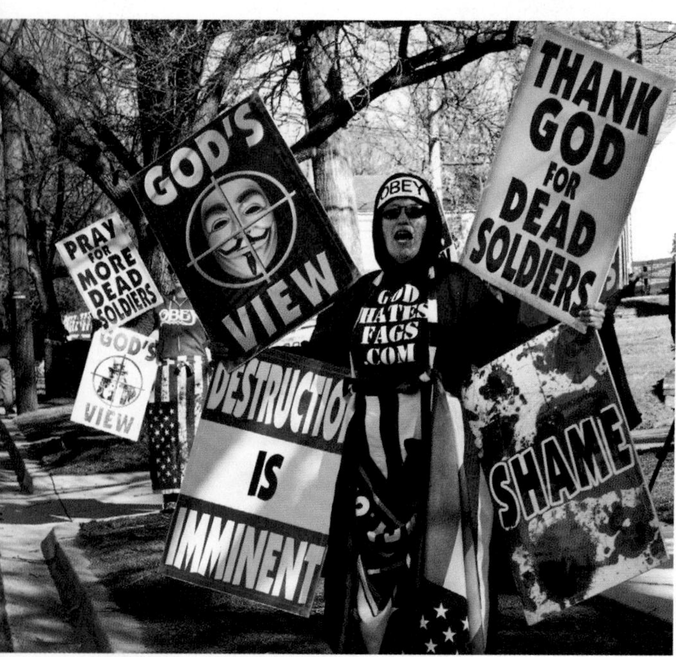

Shirley Phelps-Roper of the Westboro Baptist Church protests freely in Hyattsville, Maryland. Individualist cultures such as the United States tolerate, even protect, such offensive speech. Collectivist cultures view offensive speech as disharmonious and typically outlaw such protests.

Second, students from collectivist cultures such as China are far less likely than students from the United States to complete the statement "I am . . ." with personal traits ("I am generous"; "I am honest"). More likely, they are inclined to finish the statement with a social identity ("I am the second daughter in my family"; "I am a university student") (Dhawan et al., 1995; Triandis, 1989).

Third, attributions (causes) for behavior (dispositions/traits and situations; see Chapter 2) can be vastly different. A tragic incident in November 1991 shows differences in attributions. Gang Lu, who had recently received his doctorate in physics from the University of Iowa, methodically walked through two campus buildings shooting six people: the winner of a prestigious award that Lu felt he deserved, three physics professors, the associate chair of student affairs, and her receptionist. He killed five and then killed himself. *The New York Times* focused on dispositional causes of Lu's behavior ("very bad temper"; "deeply disturbed"; "psychological problems"). In stark contrast, reporters for the Chinese-language newspaper *World Journal* attributed Lu's behavior to situational causes ("isolated from the Chinese community" and "the availability of guns" in the United States) (Morris & Peng, 1994). North Americans are more likely to give greater weight to dispositional causes than Asians are (Choi et al., 1999). Collectivist cultural values with their focus on groups place greater emphasis on situational influences (Lu's isolation from the Chinese community), whereas individualist cultural values with their focus on individual uniqueness place greater emphasis on personal characteristics (Lu's psychological problems) (Markus & Kitayama, 1991). Clearly, people from individualist and collectivist cultures and co-cultures perceive the world in markedly different ways (Na & Kitayama, 2011).

People learn individualist or collectivist values from **socialization**—the communication of shared cultural practices, beliefs, and values from generation to generation (Maccoby, 1998). Socialization imbeds individualist or collectivist value systems into the marrow of a culture. This socialization process begins early. In the United States, those parents who can afford to place their infants in a separate "baby's room." Sleeping apart from a child is the beginning of training for independence in an individualist culture. Parents from many collectivist cultures, however, exhibiting a greater emphasis on interdependence, find this "abandonment" of a child in a lonely, dark room to be cruel (Morelli et al., 1992).

Despite socialization, *no culture's population is uniformly of one mind* (see Box 3-1). For example, the falsetto voice used by Japanese women to communicate politeness and femininity in public situations is not universally practiced. Mari Shimakura, a teenager in Tokyo, expresses the viewpoint of many: "When girls speak in really high voices, I just want to kick them in the head. It's totally fake and really annoying. It gives me a headache. Mom tells me I speak in too low a voice, and that I should raise it. But I can't change it" (quoted in Kristof, 1995, p. A27). Within the United States, individualist tendencies are strongest in the Mountain West and Great Plains states, but collectivist tendencies are quite strong in the Deep South (Vandello & Cohen, 1999). An analysis of 35 studies involving thousands of respondents revealed that African Americans place significantly higher emphasis on

BOX 3.1 Developing Communication Competence

BE YE INDIVIDUALIST OR COLLECTIVIST?

How closely do you personally reflect individualist or collectivist values of your culture or co-culture? Consider the following statements and, using a scale from 1 (strongly disagree) to 9 (strongly agree), indicate your degree of disagreement or agreement with each statement.*

1. I prefer to be direct and forthright when I talk with people.
2. I would do what would please my family, even if I detested that activity.
3. enjoy being unique and different from others in many ways.
4. I usually sacrifice my self-interest for the benefit of my group.
5. I like my privacy.
6. Children should be taught to place duty before pleasure.
7. like to demonstrate my abilities to others.
8. I hate to disagree with others in my group.
9. When I succeed, it is usually because of my abilities.
10. Before taking a major trip, I consult with most members of my family and many friends.

Total your score for all odd-numbered statements (1, 3, etc.), then total your score for even-numbered statements (2, 4, etc.). All *odd-numbered statements* reflect *individualism* and all *even-numbered statements* reflect *collectivism*. Which are you? Do you agree overall more with individualist statements (higher score on odd-numbered statements) than with collectivist statements (lower score on even-numbered statements)? If so, you reflect the prevailing individualist values of American culture. If not, can you explain why your values do not mirror those of mainstream U.S. culture? Are you influenced more by co-cultural influences? What communication challenges has this difference presented to you?

*For the entire 63-statement measuring instrument, see Triandis (1995).

individualism than European Americans (white participants), but both are substantially more individualist than are collectivist Asian Americans (Oyserman et al., 2002).

Communication Differences: Self-Promotion Versus Group Support Differences in emphasis on individualism and collectivism create differences in communication. Useful communication skills in an individualist culture include getting to know people quickly, engaging easily in conversation on a wide variety of subjects, being interesting enough to make an impression on others, and employing public speaking skills in meetings (Samovar et al., 2010). Individualist cultures expect a person to initiate a job search and engage in personal promotion. You're largely on your own in social interactions, and dating, flirting, and small talk play an important part in self-promotion. In fact, receiving help from friends or family can make you appear somewhat desperate and ineffectual, such as getting set up with a blind date. Selection of a mate is considered a personal choice. Parental approval is desirable but not necessary, and marriage will occur even in the face of parental disapproval. During conflict, individuals tend to be direct, competitive, and more concerned with protecting their own self-esteem than worrying about the self-esteem of others (Ting-Toomey et al., 1991).

Collectivist cultures do not require the same communication skills as individualist cultures. Self-promotion is discouraged because it is competitive. Cooperative communication within valued groups is emphasized for its promotion of harmony and diminishment of conflict with others (see Box 3-2). Competitive self-promotion can incite envy, jealousy, and friction within groups, and self-promotion is thought to divert energies away from the welfare of the group. In exchange for loyalty to the group and contributions to the group's effectiveness, members of collectivist cultures receive help from influential members of the group or organization in finding jobs and making social contacts. Parents often arrange mate selection because family approval is important (Hofstede & Hofstede, 2005).

Hall (1981) was the first to identify a specific difference in communication styles between individualist and collectivist cultures. *Individualist cultures typically use a low-context style, and collectivist cultures typically use a high-context style* (Ambady et al., 1996; Holtgraves, 1997). The chief difference between the two styles is in verbal expression. A **low-context communication style** is verbally precise, direct, and explicit. There is little assumption that others will be able to discern what you mean without precise verbal explanation. Self-expression and speaking ability are highly valued. Points of view are openly expressed, and persuasion is an accepted goal of speech (Chen & Starosta, 1998b). Using a computer provides a technological example of low-context communication. Nothing can be left out of an email or Internet address. Every space, period, number, and letter must be exact or the computer will exhibit how truly dumb it can be. Instructions given to computers must be precise and explicit; close doesn't count. Low-context human communication is similarly precise and explicit. "Say what you mean," "Tell me what you want," and "What's your point?" are statements that reflect a low-context communication style in individualist cultures.

In collectivist cultures, context is paramount, not the explicit message. A **high-context communication style** uses indirect verbal expression. You are expected to "read between the lines." Significant information must be derived from contextual cues, such as the relationship, situation, setting, and time. The contrast between the high- and low-context communication styles is aptly explained by a Japanese manager working in the United States, "When we say one word, we understand 10, but here you have to say 10 to understand one" (quoted in Kameda, 2003). For example, here is a seemingly confusing English message written by a Japanese manager: "Our office has moved to Kawasaki. I'm going to buy a Honda." To Americans, this likely seems to be two unrelated sentences. To a Japanese, the meaning is unmistakable: "Our office has moved to Kawasaki. It's too far from the station to walk, so I'll have to buy a car. I'm thinking of getting a Honda" (Kameda, 2003). "If you hear 'one' part of a message you are supposed to understand all the other unsaid 'nine' so that with 'one' part you must understand the whole 'ten' parts" (Kameda, 2007).

Harmony is highly regarded in collectivist cultures, and verbal messages tend to be vague to avoid causing offense. When a Japanese person says "maybe," it is a polite way of saying "no." "We will take that into consideration" also means, "Sorry, but we have no interest" (Kameda, 2003). Imagine how American directness and in-your-face communication are perceived by cultures that value harmony between people. A Chinese proverb states, "The first man to raise his voice loses the argument." Chinese culture promotes "a conflict-free and group-oriented system of human relationships" (Chen, 1993, p. 6). Filipinos see bluntness and frankness as uncivilized. In a meeting, they will often agree outwardly, even if they have objections, to preserve smooth interpersonal relations and show respect for the feelings of others (Samovar et al., 2010). This can be very frustrating to Americans who expect—with some exceptions, such as not "airing dirty laundry" in public—that everyone will speak openly and straightforwardly, and we tend to view public agreement but private disagreement as deceptive or manipulative.

When cultural populations are quite similar, there is less need to be verbally explicit because there is historical understanding of the rules, roles, norms, and customary practices of the culture. Thus, *a high-context, implicit communication style is appropriate in collectivist cultures because they tend to have more homogeneous (similar) populations* (Samovar et al., 2010). Individualist cultures tend to have more heterogeneous (dissimilar) populations. With a culturally diverse population comes uncertainty. The rules, roles, norms, and customary practices are not immediately known by individuals from co-cultural backgrounds. There is a compelling need to be verbally explicit in individualist cultures to prevent misunderstanding and miscommunication. Thus, *a low-context, explicit communication style is appropriate in individualist cultures.*

Power-Distance: Does Bill Gates Deserve Special Treatment?

Cultures vary widely in their attitudes concerning the appropriateness of power imbalances. These variations in the *acceptability of unequal distribution of power* in relationships, institutions, and organizations are called the **power-distance dimension** (Hofstede & Hofstede, 2005). The extent to which members of a culture, both relatively powerful and powerless, endorse the society's overall level of inequality determines its place on the power-distance dimension (hereafter referred to as PD) (Hofstede, 2012).

General Description: Horizontal and Vertical Cultures All cultures are **stratified**—divided into various levels of power that put distance between the haves and the have-nots. *The difference on the power-distance dimension lies in whether the culture tends to accept or reject stratification even though it is a fact of life.* A **low-PD culture**, or what Triandis (1995) calls a *horizontal culture*, values relatively equal power sharing and discourages attention to status differences and ranking in society. Challenging authority, flattening organizational hierarchies to reduce status differences between management and employees, and using power legitimately are encouraged in a low-PD culture. Low-PD cultures do not expect power disparities to be eliminated. Nevertheless, in low-PD cultures such as the United States, Great Britain, Sweden, Denmark, Austria, Israel, and New Zealand (see Figure 3-2), norms that minimize power distinctions act as guides for appropriate behavior.

High-PD cultures, or what Triandis (1995) refers to as *vertical cultures*, have a relatively strong emphasis on maintaining power differences. The norms of cultures in Malaysia, Guatemala, the Philippines, Mexico, India, Singapore, and Hong Kong encourage power distinctions (see Figure 3-2). Authorities are rarely challenged, the most powerful are thought to have a legitimate right to exercise their power, and

BOX 3.2 Focus on Controversy

COMPETITION: CULTURAL INFLUENCE

In a highly competitive society such as the United States, it is easy to assume that intense competition is a natural part of being human. Seeing individuals from other cultures responding to competition in a way dramatically different from our own can help us understand the powerful influence of cultural values on exhibitions of competitive or cooperative behavior (Ehrlich, 2000). A story makes this point apparent.

> A newly trained teacher named Mary went to teach at a Navajo Indian reservation. Every day, she would ask five of the young Navajo students to go to the chalkboard and complete a simple math problem from their homework. They would stand there, silently, unwilling to complete the task. Mary couldn't figure it out. . . .
>
> Finally, she asked the students what was wrong. . . . It seemed that the students . . . knew that not all of them were capable of doing the problems. . . . They believed no one would win if any students were shown up or embarrassed at the chalkboard. So they refused to compete with each other in public.
>
> Once she understood, Mary changed the system so that she could check each child's math problem individually, but not at any child's expense in front of classmates. They all wanted to learn—but not at someone else's expense. (Canfield et al., 1997, pp. 175–176)

In many cultures, the emphasis on being "the star" at someone else's expense is discouraged. As Henry (1963) explains, "To a Zuni, Hopi, or Dakota Indian, [besting another student] would seem cruel beyond belief, for competition, the wringing of success from somebody else's failure, is a form of torture" (p. 35).

Competitiveness is not an innate part of being human; it is socially constructed (de Waal, 2010). There is abundant evidence that American competitiveness is primarily a product of an individualist value system that is learned, not an evolutionary imperative common to all species (Chatman & Barsade, 1995; Cox et al., 1991; Wright, 2000). Two studies compared people from cultures that vary widely on the individualism-collectivism dimension: Americans (extremely individualist) and Vietnamese (extremely collectivist). The first study showed that the Vietnamese "cooperated at an extraordinarily high rate." The Americans were inclined to be competitive. In the second study, Vietnamese subjects exhibited high rates of cooperation even when faced with competitive strategies from other participants. Americans showed far less cooperative and more competitive communication. The authors of these studies conclude: "The difference between the extremely individualistic and extremely collectivistic cultures was very large and consistent with cultural norms" (Parks & Vu, 1994, p. 712). When members of collectivist cultures perceive a threat from an outside group, however, they can be hypercompetitive in "protecting" their valued group (Ting-Toomey & Chung, 2005; Triandis, 1994).

QUESTIONS FOR THOUGHT

1. Can you imagine a culture entirely free from competition? Would that be a desirable society? Could you avoid mass conformity in such a culture?
2. How might competitive and cooperative cultural environments affect the educational process? How might students address students and students address teachers?
3. How might you assess a group's comfort level with competitive transactions when you enter a new group? How would this assessment affect your communication behavior?

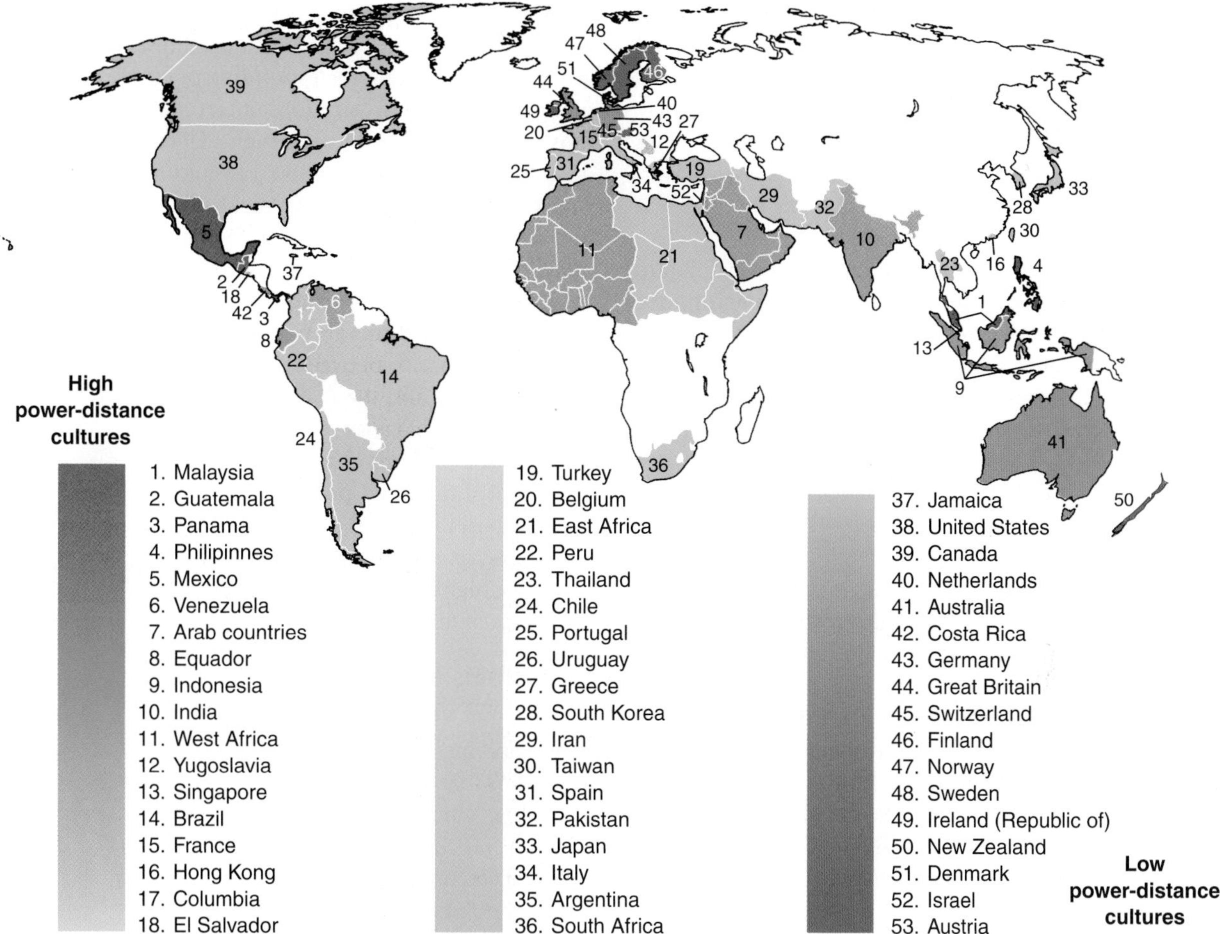

FIGURE 3-2 Masculinity-Femininity Ratings for 50 Countries and 3 Regions (Source: Hofstede, 1991)

organizational and social hierarchies are nurtured (Lustig & Koester, 2003). In Japan, for example, seeking a second opinion on a health issue is taboo; it is an affront to the primary care physician's expertise and power position (Ricks, 2000). In India, a massive 7.7-magnitude earthquake struck parts of the country on January 26, 2001, killing almost 20,000 people, injuring more than 60,000, and leaving about a million individuals homeless (Coleman, 2001). The biggest impediment to the distribution of desperately needed aid to those afflicted was India's traditional caste system—a social hierarchy, outlawed long ago but still strong in practice, with Brahmans at the top and the "untouchables" at the bottom. As Catholic Relief Services worker Mayuri Mistry explained, "Whatever the distribution of aid, it first goes to the upper castes" (Coleman, 2001, p. 7A). Although the wealthy and privileged in America may, on occasion, receive preferential treatment, it is difficult to imagine a similar dispersal of emergency aid occurring in the United States during a natural disaster. Can you imagine the outcry that would ensue if such preferential treatment were to occur?

Communication Differences: With Whom May You Communicate? Communication in low-PD cultures reflects the minimization of power disparities. Workers may disagree with their supervisors; in fact, some bosses may encourage disagreement. Socializing outside the work environment and communication on a first-name basis between workers and bosses are not unusual. Students can question and disagree with their teachers. Some professors also encourage students to address them by their first names (Hofstede & Hofstede, 2005).

When I taught at Western Washington University in Bellingham, Washington, one of the hottest issues was a proposal to establish a pub on campus. Three-quarters of the students favored the proposal. The most common argument used to support the proposal was that students and professors would have an informal place to meet, relax, sip a brew, and discuss philosophy, politics, or the state of the world. The pub would diminish power disparities between professors and students. Not surprisingly, the administration was not enthusiastic about the proposed pub—but primarily for legal and liability reasons, not out of any desire to maintain power disparities. The pub was never established. In a high-PD culture, the issue would never be raised.

Communication in high-PD cultures reflects the desire to maintain power disparities. Children raised in high-PD cultures are expected to obey their parents without question. Workers typically do not disagree with their bosses. Friendship between a worker and his or her boss would appear inappropriate. Students do not question or disagree with their teachers. Reticence to speak during class discussions unless asked to do so personally by the teacher underlines the acceptance of power disparities (Hofstede & Hofstede, 2005). The teacher is the expert. Students are in class to receive the wisdom of the instructor, not to challenge the more knowledgeable teacher or to show off their own knowledge (Samovar et al., 2010). Even a student admitting to a teacher that they "don't understand" something covered in a lecture is perceived as insulting the teacher. It implies that the teacher provided an inadequate explanation of the material.

Cultural differences on the power-distance dimension do not mean that high-PD cultures never experience conflict and aggression arising from power imbalances. Members of low-PD cultures, however, are more likely to respond to power imbalances with frustration, anger, and hostility than members of high-PD cultures. This occurs because low-PD cultures subscribe to power balance even though the reality of everyday life in such cultures may reflect significant power disparities. African Americans, Mexican Americans, and Native Americans in particular recognize this disparity between the "ideal" of power balance and the reality of socioeconomic disadvantage in the United States. In a low-PD culture, the battle to achieve the ideal of balanced power is more compelling, and the denial of power is likely to be viewed as more unjust and intolerable than in a high-PD culture where power balance is seen differently ("Occupy" protest).

Relationship of Two Dimensions: Connecting the Dots

Remembering all the details of value dimensions that distinguish cultures can seem daunting. When trying to condense all this material on cultural value differences, concentrate less on the details and more on two primary points. First, recognize that individualism-collectivism is probably "the crucial dimension of cultural variability" (Griffin, 2003, p. 421). Be particularly familiar with this dimension because it has the greatest support in cross-cultural research.

Second, there is a strong relationship between the individualism-collectivism and the power-distance dimensions (Hofstede & Hofstede, 2005). *High-PD cultures tend to be collectivist, and low-PD cultures tend to be individualist.* Thus, the United States, for example, being a highly individualist culture, is also a low-PD culture. Duane Alwin, a sociologist at the University of Michigan, illustrates this combination in a study he conducted of parental values in the United States. His study found that parents placed the highest value on "thinking for oneself" as the quality that will best prepare children for life. Questioning authority (low-PD) also emerged as an important parental value (see Frerking, 1995). This exhibits an individualist, low-PD value system.

Intercultural Miscommunication

With differences in core values come numerous opportunities for miscommunication between members of differing cultures, making appropriate and effective intercultural communication a significant challenge. This section discusses *basic intercultural miscommunication in the framework just presented of differences in core value dimensions (individualism-collectivism; power-distance)*.

Ethnocentrism: Intercultural Prejudice

Imagine two different ways to approach eating dinner. In the first version, the family believes dinner is a ritual that allows family members to put aside diversions and distractions of the day. The focus should be on the family and what each person did that day—exciting things, happy experiences, problems, troubling issues, and the like. The family begins by saying grace before eating, thanking God for the bounty. Each person seated at the table formally requests that food be passed to him or her. They also say "Thank you" after the food is passed. No one reaches across the table and grabs anything. That is considered rude. Conversation is encouraged. Silence is noticed and discouraged. No one leaves the table without first asking to be excused. When dinner is over, everyone busses their dishes and pitches in on cleanup.

In the second version, the family rarely eats at the dinner table. Food is usually consumed in front of the TV. When dinner is eaten together at the table, everyone grabs for the food as though this were the final meal on Earth. No one asks for anything. Dinner is more a feeding frenzy like sharks smelling blood in the water than a relaxed, social affair. No one thanks anyone for passing food. Grace is not said. When dinner is over, the women take care of the dishes, and the men go about their business of relaxation or television watching.

Here we have two distinctly different ways of carrying out commonplace dinner activities. Do you deem superior the version that is closest to the way you were raised to conduct dinner and the other version to be inferior? If so, you have captured the fundamental essence of ethnocentrism: the way we do things is good, and the different way others do things is not so good.

The term *ethnocentrism* is derived from two Greek words: *ethnos*, meaning "nation," and *kentron*, meaning "center" (Klopf, 1998). Literally, it means, "Our nation is the center of all things." **Ethnocentrism** "is the notion that one's own culture is superior to any other. It is the idea that other cultures should be measured by the degree to which they live up to our cultural standards" (Nanda & Warms, 1998, p. 9). The degree of difference between your own and other cultures determines ratings on a superiority-inferiority scale. The bigger the difference found in a culture distinct from your own, the greater is the perceived inferiority of that culture.

Ethnocentrism: Cultural Superiority Complex

All cultures to some degree are ethnocentric (Hofstede & Hofstede, 2005). Ethnocentrism usually involves "comparisons that ennoble one's culture while degrading those of others" (Stewart & Bennett, 1991, p. 161). This ethnocentric bias is often shocking, even brutal, in its judgment of other cultures. Names of various tribes and groups sometimes reflect this bias. Kiowa means "real or principal people." Laplander means "human being." Jews are the "chosen people"; gentiles are everyone else. Historically, among Christians "gentile" meant heathen or pagan. Greeks and Romans referred to outsiders as "barbarians" (Klopf, 1998). Immigrants to the United States are referred to as "aliens," legal or otherwise. Common definitions of alien include "strange," "unnatural," "repugnant," "outsider," and of course, "visitor from another galaxy."

Ethnocentrism is a learned belief. Experiencing another culture's customs, practices, and beliefs that are different from what we are accustomed to may seem weird and wrong. For example, if you were spat on by your date at the end of an evening, you undoubtedly would not feel complimented. Members of the Masai tribe of East Africa, however, regard being spat on as highly complimentary, especially if a member of the opposite sex does the spitting (Wierzbicka, 1986). The dating scene would certainly take on a different flavor if this were common practice in America. I have visited Great Britain a half-dozen times over the years. Early visits revealed a frustrating lack of showers in my accommodations. I am not a bath person unless left with no alternative. I find sitting in a tub of water ("Dan soup," as my son refers to it), with a dirty oil slick formed on the surface of the tub water after washing, not particularly appealing.

A high power-distance country such as India values the right of parents to arrange their children's marriages. A low power-distance country such as the United States accords no such right to parents. What is your view of arranged marriages and cultures that promote them?

My first reaction to the shower scarcity was ethnocentric ("What a goofy culture"). I have since learned to relax my expectations and flow more with the difference-is-not-deficiency perspective (and lately, finding showers in Great Britain is not uncommon).

Consider differences in teaching and learning in schools (Samovar et al., 2010). In Russia, China, Japan, Korea, Vietnam, and Cambodia, learning is passive. Teachers read to their students. Students are mostly silent unless called on to answer questions or recite. Rote memorization is common. In Mexico, students are more active. They talk and learn through group work. In Germany, southern Italy, and the West Indies, students rise in unison when the teacher enters the classroom. In an Israeli kibbutz, students wander around the classroom, talk to each other, sharpen pencils, or get a drink without formal permission. They talk during lessons, even hum to themselves while working on an assignment. American classrooms are a mix of many of these practices, and they are less formal and more active places of learning than in most other cultures.

So which cultural communication practices are correct? Every culture believes the way it operates is preferable; otherwise, the practices would change (unless enforced by an authoritarian regime). Ethnocentrism is prejudice on a global scale.

Core Values and Ethnocentrism: Bedrock Cultural Bias

The core value differences of individualism-collectivism and power-distance previously discussed highlight how markedly diverse cultures can be. Although even surface differences can provoke ethnocentrism, core value differences can easily serve as a bedrock foundation for ethnocentrism. Consider arranged marriages. A high-PD culture such as India values the right of parents to arrange their children's marriages. About 95% of marriages in India are arranged (Epstein, 2010). Usually, the bride and groom don't meet until the wedding. A low-PD culture such as the United States accords no such right to parents. So do you view a culture that promotes arranged marriages as just a little "strange" and not as "progressive" as the United States? It's difficult to resist judging cultures based on the core values of our own culture. Yet, high-PD cultures are different but not necessarily deficient. India with its arranged marriages has one of the lowest divorce rates in the world, and "the love experienced by Indian couples in arranged marriages appears to be even more robust than the love people experience in 'love marriages'" (Epstein, 2010, p. 31).

Consider also the Thai preference for what some researchers have called "unwillingness to communicate" (Knutson et al., 2002). Thais are slow to engage in conversation with strangers. To Americans, this may seem unfriendly. Research reveals, however, that Thais delay conversing with strangers to reflect carefully and choose communication that furthers social harmony and avoids giving offense (Knutson & Posirisuk, 2006). This exhibits a strong regard for sensitivity (receptive accuracy) in the communication competence model explained in Chapter 1. Thailand, the "Land of Smile," is a collectivist culture with unspoken rules that encourage modesty, humility, and harmony. Instead of seeing the Thai "unwillingness to communicate" as deficient from an American perspective, perhaps we could learn the potential value of listening more and talking less (see Chapter 6).

Cultural Relativism: Differences, Not Deficiencies

In an effort to combat ethnocentrism, anthropologists offered the cultural relativism viewpoint (Harrison & Huntington, 2000). **Cultural relativism** views cultures as merely different, not deficient. From this viewpoint, "all phenomena can be assessed only from the perspective of the culture in which they exist" (Moghaddam, 1998, p. 506). We must respect all cultures and their inherent right to engage in practices, rituals, and communication behaviors that may appear strange, even repugnant. The "West is best" ethnocentrism should not be imposed on cultures that depart from the West's values. Men and women communicate openly with each other in Western cultures; they are far more restricted in most Arab cultures. Americans usually expect to speak without interruption and are often irritated when not accorded this privilege. Arabs have no such expectation and will exuberantly join a conversation that will appear to most Americans to be a chaotic shouting match (Lewis, 1996). Cultural relativism dictates that we respect these different cultural practices despite personal misgivings.

In the abstract, cultural relativism appears egalitarian and unprejudiced. The ethical and moral correctness of an act can only be judged within the value system of the culture in which it takes place. Confusion, however, can arise from the use of the term "relativism." It seems to imply that there are no universal standards for judging cultural practices. There are practices in cultures around the world, however, that are condoned within the culture but contradict universal human rights. Female genital mutilation (female circumcision), denial of education and political participation to women, wife beating, "honor killings" (murdering women because they have "dishonored" the family by extramarital affairs, divorce, etc.), the selling of children, slavery, and myriad other practices are behaviors that some cultures and co-cultures condone.

The United Nations Universal Declaration of Human Rights declares that every human being has certain basic rights that include the right to life, liberty, security, freedom of speech and belief, equal protection under the law, participation in the political process, a decent standard of living, necessary social services, and education (Harrison, 2000). Customs, practices, and communication behaviors that do not deny these human rights should not be rejected as inferior simply because they are different from our own cultural ways of operating. Sexism, racism, homophobia, and all the "isms" that breed "ethnic cleansings" and genocidal wars, however, deserve no defense. Cultural relativists typically condemn these inhumane practices, which makes the term *cultural relativism* more confusing than clarifying.

Multiculturalism: Recognition of Human Rights

An alternative to cultural relativism is multiculturalism. Flowers and Richardson (1996) define **multiculturalism** as a "social-intellectual movement that promotes the value of diversity as a core principle and insists that all cultural groups be treated with respect and as equals" (p. 609). Multiculturalism assumes universal human rights. As Moghaddam (1998) explains,

> In order for multiculturalism to work, there must be certain universal rules to allow communication and understanding to take place. For example, without mutual respect and orderly turn taking, there can be no meaningful dialogue. Furthermore, in a situation in which universal rules of justice are not accepted, the weak will necessarily suffer because they cannot use the law to protect their interests. (p. 506)

Multiculturalism incorporates the five ethical standards discussed in Chapter 1: honesty, respect, fairness, choice, and responsibility. To be a competent intercultural communicator, you must accept cultural diversity and eschew ethnocentrism, but always you are guided by these ethical standards. Inhumane behavior that degrades and diminishes others cannot be accepted with the justification, "That's just the way they do things in their culture." Diversity is part of the colorful tapestry of humankind, but inhumanity is a blight on any culture's fabric.

Misunderstanding: Mismatched Communication

What is appropriate and expected communication in your own culture may be perceived as rude, arrogant, or uncivilized by individuals from other cultures. We often do not sufficiently understand the rules, norms, customs, and common practices of other cultures, so misunderstandings are common. *Understanding is a core element of communication competence.* Individuals are too late for appointments or too early, too talkative or too quiet, express their anger too openly or hide their anger too much, stand too close or too far apart when conversing, look too directly at the other person or look down or away too often. Looking down when conversing with another person could be interpreted as a sign of a weak, easily intimidated person in American culture. The same behavior, however, when viewed by a member of an Asian culture, might be interpreted as an indication of a respectful, polite person. You don't have to be ethnocentric to be confused by the communication differences among cultures.

The warm, friendly, say-whatever-you-feel communication style familiar to Americans that typifies an individualist, low power-distance culture can produce awkward confusion when it clashes with communication styles more typical of collectivist cultures. Brislin (1993) cites an apt example of poorly matched communication styles:

> If a young man from an Asian culture interacts with an American woman who employs the warm and exuberant style . . . the man may attribute the style to a romantic interest in him, personally. For example, assume that an American woman helps an Asian male on a class assignment. The Asian (following norms in his culture) offers a small gift to show his appreciation. The American

> woman responds, "I just love it! It's great! How thoughtful of you!" The Asian may conclude that the comment about "loving it" extends to him, personally. (p. 225)

Confusion over romantic intentions can be embarrassing and potentially nasty. Toning down her response would, of course, be the simple solution to this clash of communication styles. The woman would have to know there was a stylistic clash in the first place, however, as would the man if he were to draw a different interpretation of her response. This again underlines the importance of knowledge in the communication competence model. Individuals using low-context styles typically try to clarify issues and misunderstandings by being increasingly direct and explicit. Individuals using high-context styles, however, continue to be vague and indirect, as is their habit. This further frustrates both parties, as the clash of poorly matched communication styles continues and misunderstandings abound.

Interpersonal Miscommunication: Not Knowing the Rules

Lustig and Koester (2003) provide a prime example of interpersonal miscommunication stemming from not knowing the rules of appropriate communication within a specific culture:

> Brian Holtz is a U.S. businessperson assigned by his company to manage its office in Thailand. Mr. Thani, a valued assistant manager in the Bangkok office, has recently been arriving late for work. Holtz has to decide what to do about this problem. After carefully thinking about his options, he decides there are four possible strategies:
>
> 1. Go privately to Mr. Thani, ask him why he has been arriving late, and tell him that he needs to come to work on time.
> 2. Ignore the problem.
> 3. Publicly reprimand Mr. Thani the next time he is late.
> 4. In a private discussion, suggest that he is seeking Mr. Thani's assistance in dealing with employees in the company who regularly arrive late for work, and solicit his suggestions about what should be done. (p. 65)

If you were Holtz, what choice would you make? Which one is likely to be both appropriate and effective? The first choice is a typical American solution. It is direct and a typical response in an individualist culture with a low-context communication style. It would probably be effective in curbing Mr. Thani's tardiness. As already noted, in Thai culture, however, an individual does not directly criticize another person. This causes a loss of face and threatens harmony (collectivist value). The first choice would be very inappropriate, even embarrassing.

The second choice, ignoring the problem, would be appropriate but ineffective since Mr. Thani would likely continue arriving late to work. Mr. Holtz would view this as intolerable. Ignoring a problem is not direct and assertive.

The third choice, public reprimand, would be neither appropriate nor effective. Mr. Thani, a valuable employee, would likely resign in shame. Public rebuke invites loss of face. It is aggressive and domineering.

Thus, the first three options, if chosen, would be examples of miscommunication. Such communication would likely aggravate the problem. The fourth choice, a problem-solving approach, is preferred because it is likely to be both appropriate and effective (Lustig & Koester, 2003). Mr. Thani can receive the message indirectly that he must arrive at work on time without losing face. Mr. Holtz can comment to Mr. Thani that he needs his help solving a problem. "Tardiness has recently increased in the office." No specific person is identified. "I would be very pleased if you would help solve this problem." Mr. Thani can recognize that his tardiness is a problem without any public acknowledgment or humiliation. He can "solve" the problem by changing his own behavior in the context of assisting his boss.

Interpersonal miscommunication can occur even in intercultural circumstances in which you might attempt to be helpful or caring. Frequent interaction between supervisors and subordinates in work situations may be highly appreciated by members of some cultures but resented by others. In Japan, it is typically perceived as caring, but in the United States, it is often perceived as micromanaging or "spying" on workers to evaluate their performance. Close supervision of teenagers by parents is usually perceived by teens as showing love in collectivist cultures but as interference in individualist cultures (Triandis, 1995). Being an interculturally competent communicator is highly challenging.

Intercultural Communication Competence

Later chapters will delve into specific ways intercultural communication competence can be enhanced. In this section, I discuss general ways to develop appropriate and effective communication between cultures

Become Mindful: Monitor Your Communication

Cultural values are so deep seated, and communication that flows from these values is so automatic, we often take no notice. We see differences in the content of messages and the outcomes, but we often fail to see the communication process that separates members of diverse cultures.

One general way to take notice is to be mindful. As discussed in Chapter 1, mindfulness is thinking about our communication with others and persistently working to improve it. It is the process of exhibiting sensitivity in your communication with members of diverse cultures. When we are mindful, we recognize our ethnocentrism, and we resolve to recognize our biases and correct our misperceptions.

We exhibit mindfulness in three ways (Langer, 1989). First, we make more careful distinctions. We aren't as prone to stereotype. We look for information that contradicts stereotypes. Second, we are open to new information, especially that which focuses on the process, not the content, of communication. It is easy to identify disagreements over the content of messages—"You've asked for more office space, but we have none to spare." The disagreement on content of messages is usually so apparent that we often fail to examine the communication process that is essential to resolving differences. When individuals from diverse cultures communicate, a content-only focus can trigger ethnocentrism and misunderstanding. Third, we exhibit mindfulness when we recognize different perspectives. This is the essence of empathy, and it is critical to competent intercultural communication. Members of differing cultures perceive the world from their own cultural perspectives, and each person believes his or her perspective is reasonable and comfortable.

When we lock into our own cultural perspective, we respond to cultural differences in an unthinking, "mindless" way. Mindless communication is a universe away from competent communication. Remember, sensitivity is recognizing signals that can alert us to potential difficulties or possible solutions to problems. You have to extend your antenna. Mindfulness raises your antenna. Mindlessness keeps your antenna lowered.

Become Acculturated: Strangers in a Strange Space

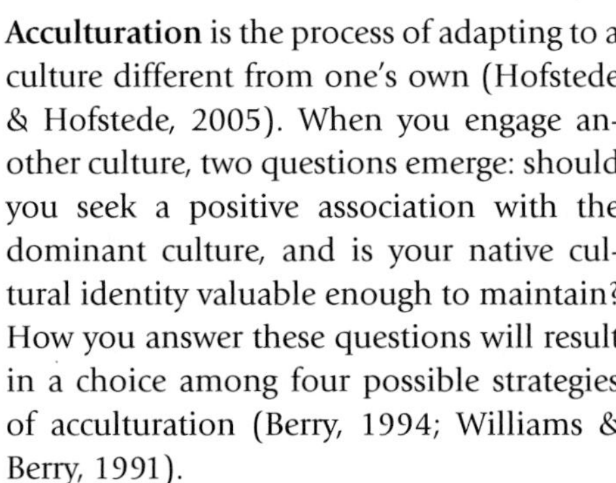

Acculturation is the process of adapting to a culture different from one's own (Hofstede & Hofstede, 2005). When you engage another culture, two questions emerge: should you seek a positive association with the dominant culture, and is your native cultural identity valuable enough to maintain? How you answer these questions will result in a choice among four possible strategies of acculturation (Berry, 1994; Williams & Berry, 1991).

The first strategy is *assimilation*—the abandonment of the customs, practices, language, identity, and ways of living of one's heritage for those of the host culture. The original idea of the United States as a "melting pot" encouraged immigrants to assimilate and become Americans: to blend, not to stand apart. Recently, the idea of assimilation has been criticized as a way of eradicating cultures and destroying the unique heritages of diverse peoples. The second strategy of acculturation is *separation*—maintaining one's ethnic identity and avoiding contact with the dominant culture. Individuals who separate may refuse to learn the language of the dominant culture, reside in homogeneous neighborhoods populated by others from the same ethnic heritage, and socialize predominantly with members of their own ethnic group.

A third strategy of acculturation is *integration*—maintaining one's ethnic identity while also becoming an active part of the dominant culture. For example, many Irish Americans, Asian Americans, Mexican Americans, and other groups celebrate their heritage with St. Patrick's Day parades, Chinese New Year street celebrations, and Cinco de Mayo activities, among other manifestations of ethnicity. At the same time, they express pride in their new culture by becoming American citizens, joining the military, and working in the outside community. A fourth strategy of acculturation is *marginalization*—maintaining no ties to either one's native or new culture. These individuals experience feelings that they don't belong anywhere.

Which of these four strategies of acculturation is most effective? Berry (1997) concludes that "integration is usually the most successful; marginalization is the least; and assimilation and separation strategies are intermediate. This pattern has been found in virtually every study, and is present for all types of acculturation" (p. 24). Acculturation, however, in any form is more likely the longer the exposure to the dominant culture, and it is easier for those who are relatively young (Cheung et al., 2011).

Reduce Uncertainty: Egads, Nothing's the Same!

Uncertainty Reduction Theory (URT) posits that when strangers first meet, their principal goal is to reduce uncertainty and to increase predictability (Berger & Calabrese, 1975; Witt & Behnke, 2006). We are so motivated because uncertainty often produces anxiety. This is particularly true of intercultural communication (Neuliep & Ryan, 1998). Managing uncertainty and its attendant anxiety (called anxiety uncertainty management, or AUM) is an important part of competent intercultural communication (Gudykunst, 2005). It directly affects your communication effectiveness. You can see this most apparently when you reside in a culture distinctly different from your own. Initially, you will likely experience **culture shock**, or what more recently has been termed **acculturative stress**—the anxiety that comes from the unfamiliarity of new cultural surroundings, rules, norms, and practices and the attempt to adapt to these new circumstances (Williams & Berry, 1991). You may feel helpless, isolated, even depressed because so much is different from what you are used to seeing and experiencing.

Uncertainty reduction can improve the effectiveness of your communication in unfamiliar cultural contexts. Engaging others in conversation and contact is an important aspect of uncertainty reduction. If your acculturative stress prods you into withdrawing from communication transactions with members of the unfamiliar culture, uncertainty will not be reduced. Merely spending time in another culture, however, is not sufficient to counter acculturative stress and reduce uncertainty, but making friends with indigenous members of a culture is effective (Torbiorn, 1982). Proceed cautiously, gently, and respectfully when interacting with individuals from other cultures.

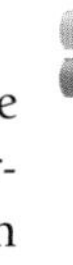

Promote Convergence: Bringing Us Together

DeVito (1990) offers an apt example of the difficulties we face when trying to determine what is appropriate communication in an intercultural context:

> An American college student, while having a dinner party with a group of foreigners, learns that her favorite cousin has just died. She bites her lip, pulls herself up, and politely excuses herself from the group. The interpretation given to this behavior will vary with the culture of the observer. The Italian student thinks, "How insincere; she doesn't even cry." The Russian student thinks, "How unfriendly; she didn't care enough to share

her grief with her friends." The fellow American student thinks, "How brave; she wanted to bear her burden by herself." (p. 218)

Here we see divergent interpretations of a single event. **Divergence** refers to differences that separate people. The American college student is insincere, unfriendly, or brave depending on your cultural perspective. Ethnocentrism nourishes divergence. It makes difference a reason to dislike, hate, avoid, or feel contempt for individuals from other cultures.

Divergence widens the gap between cultures; convergence closes the gap. **Convergence** refers to similarities that connect us to others. Convergence doesn't erase, or attempt to change, core differences between cultures.

There are two primary ways to create convergence in intercultural transactions. First, *adjust your style of speaking*. Minor adjustments can promote convergence. For example, more closely align your speaking rate, pitch, vocal intensity, frequency of pauses, and silences with those of the other person. The issue of speaking style can be controversial. Historically, relatively powerless groups (African Americans, Latinos) have been expected by the mainstream U.S. culture to shift their style of speaking to the mainstream speech style (Hecht et al., 1993). Weber (1994) cites an example. While she was lecturing to her class, a vocal black student began a "call and response" with encouraging "all right," "make it plain," and "teach" responses to her lecture. Soon a few more black students joined. Startled white students, quizzed afterward, found the vocal responses disruptive, annoying, and rude. Social norms in mainstream American culture do not endorse "call and response" in college classrooms. Nevertheless, convergence requires effort from all parties, not just members of the mainstream culture or individuals from co-cultures.

Second, *find common ground*. Ask what interests members of other cultures. Let them introduce topics of possible mutual interest and explore those topics with them. You are not trying to change people's interests; rather, you are attempting to share interests. Interest in sports, religion, politics, history, and so forth may offer opportunities to find commonalities.

Gender and Communication

Statements such as, "The first duty of a woman with young children is to home and family" and "When a man and a woman live together, she should do the housework and he should do the heavier chores" receive greater agreement from respondents in Cuba, Nigeria, Pakistan, and South Africa than from respondents in Australia, Great Britain, the Netherlands, and the United States (Glick et al., 2000; Williams & Best, 1990). Thus, there is an intersection of culture and gender.

Before exploring this intersection, let's first clarify the difference between sex and gender. **Sex** is *biology* (female-male); it is genes, gonads, and hormones. One sex difference is that a male can impregnate a female, and a female can become pregnant. It doesn't work in the reverse. **Gender** is social role *behavior* (feminine-masculine) learned from communicating with others (Hofstede & Hofstede, 2005). Each culture's gender role expectations, what is perceived as appropriate behavior to be considered masculine or feminine, powerfully influence our communication with others (Lindsey & Zakahi, 2006). "It is through pervasive cultural value patterns—as filtered through family and media systems—that persons define meanings and values of identities, such as gender . . ." (Ting-Toomey & Chung, 2005, p. 86).

Masculine-Feminine Value Dimension: Rigidity Versus Flexibility

The intersection of gender and culture serves as the basis for a third deep structural value identified by Hofstede (2001) called the **masculine-feminine dimension**. A **masculine culture** exhibits stereotypic masculine traits such as male dominance, ambitiousness, assertiveness, competitiveness, and drive for achievement (Hofstede & Hofstede, 2005). *Gender roles are rigid and distinct*

in masculine cultures. In Japan, for instance, women comprise a scant 0.1% of the board members of Japan's top companies, and those who do work in the corporate world are confined mainly to clerical or ceremonial jobs (French, 2001). A survey of 3,500 Japanese (males and females) revealed that a scant 4% thought a husband should clean the house, a mere 3.5% thought he should wash dishes, and only 1.2% thought he should cook ("More Japanese Think," 2005). Cultures ranking high on masculinity include Japan, Austria, Venezuela, Italy, Switzerland, and Mexico. The United States ranks relatively high on masculinity (see Figure 3-3).

A **feminine culture** exhibits stereotypic feminine traits such as affection, nurturance, sensitivity, compassion, and emotional expressiveness (Hofstede & Hofstede, 2005). *In feminine cultures, however, gender roles are less rigid and more overlapping*, equality between the sexes is more typical, and individual achievement and competitiveness are de-emphasized for both men and women (Hofstede & Hofstede, 2005). In Sweden, for example, equality between the sexes is highly valued. Sweden has a well-entrenched social support system of pregnancy leave, lengthy paid vacations, and time off to tend to sick children because a very high proportion of the workforce is composed of women. Cultures ranking high on femininity include Sweden, Norway, the Netherlands, Denmark, Costa Rica, Finland, and Chile.

In **masculine cultures**, men typically communicate in ways that will enhance their esteem (e.g., speak often, control the

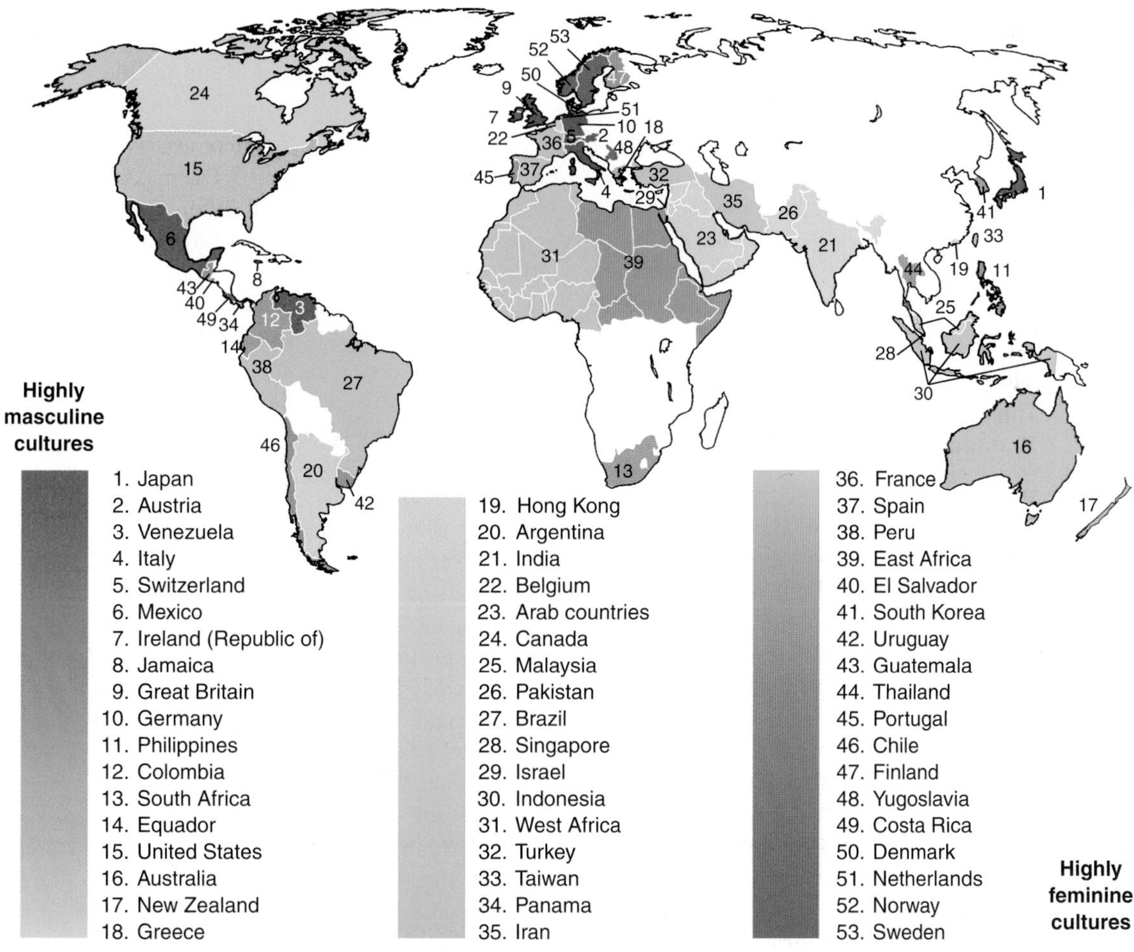

FIGURE 3-3 Masculinity-Femininity Ratings for 50 Countries and 3 Regions (Source: Hofstede, 1991)

floor, interrupt). Women in masculine cultures typically communicate in ways that will enhance relationships (e.g., express support, encourage, listen well). In feminine cultures, both men and women communicate in ways that emphasize relationships over power. In Sweden, for example, management in organizations is democratic. Managers don't give orders to employees; they make suggestions or offer guidelines (Lewis, 1996). Nurturance and the creation of a caring society are paramount concerns.

It is important to note here that the rankings of cultures on the masculinity-femininity dimension are relative, not absolute. A high ranking on femininity doesn't mean that a culture treats women as well as men. It simply means that feminine cultures have less rigid gender roles than masculine cultures, with their distinctly different behaviors for males and females.

Given the masculine-feminine dimension of cultures, you might think gender differences in communication would be quite large. This is probably true when comparing a strongly masculine culture to a strongly feminine culture, but the size of gender differences in communication and the reasons for such differences, be they large or small, within the culture of the United States are both hotly debated issues, as you will see in this section.

The Gender Differences Hypothesis: Mars and Venus—Really?

When it comes to communicating, are women and men mostly similar or different? John Gray (1992) asserts that "men are from Mars and women are from Venus." He's built a multimillion-dollar empire based on this metaphorical premise that men and women are dramatically different from each other. He's peddled this premise in books, seminars, audiotapes, DVDs, and even franchised counseling centers (Marano, 1997). He's proven that "not only does sex sell, but sex differences sell" (Dindia, 2006, p. 13). Are men and women so different that they seem to exist in separate alien worlds?

If you listen to stand-up comedians or consult numerous Internet sites, you would certainly think that John Gray is correct (see Cameron, 2007, for a comprehensive critique of Gray's work). Consider a few examples from the Internet. "Why does it take 1 million sperm to fertilize one egg? The sperm won't stop to ask for directions." "When do women stop advocating equality? When they have to kill large, hairy spiders." "Give a man an inch and he thinks he's a ruler." "How do you impress a woman? Compliment her, cuddle her, caress her, love her, listen to her, support her, and spend money on her. How do you impress a man? Show up naked. Bring beer." Television series repeatedly characterize men and women as hugely different beings. There are some large gender communication differences that support the **gender differences hypothesis**—the assertion that men and women communicate in vastly divergent ways. Let's examine a few significant examples.

Sexual Interest: One-Night Stand or One Right Man

"You know that look women get when they want sex? Me neither." Drew Carey is underlining the perceived difference between men and women regarding interest in sex. The stereotype is that men are sex hounds. Women, so goes this notion, have to resist the incessant overtures from men. They simply aren't as interested. Is there any truth to this popular gender stereotype? One review of studies on this question concluded that men do have more frequent and intense sexual desire than women (Baumeister et al., 2001). Men initiate sex about twice as often as women do (Byers & Heinlein, 1989; O'Sullivan & Byers, 1992), although this may be the communication expectation of both sexes. This gender difference has been validated across many cultures (Segall et al., 1990) and is true for straight and gay men alike (Bailey et al., 1994). It is also true for those over the age of 45 (Crary, 2010). In addition, research shows that women are about twice as likely as men to engage in **compliant sex**—having sexual intercourse when you don't want to, but your partner does, in circumstances that do not involve duress or coercion (Impett & Peplau, 2003). Compliant sex is not necessarily negative. It can communicate affection for your partner.

The relationship between desire for sex and communication can be seen in the marked difference between women and men on the willingness to accept an offer of casual sex. One study had attractive confederates of the experimenters approach individuals of the other sex and say, "I have been noticing you around campus and I find you to be very attractive. Would you go to bed with me tonight?" *None* of the women would have casual sex with the stranger, but *75%* of the men were willing (Clark & Hatfield, 1989). The study was repeated two more times with similar results even when the stranger was recommended by a close personal friend (Clark, 1990).

Men want and do have more sex partners, a surprise only to someone new to the planet (Buss & Schmitt, 1993). Interest in casual, "no strings" sex is much higher for men than for women. A review of 177 studies on casual sex shows that this gender difference is among the largest ever discovered (Oliver & Hyde, 1993). For the majority of women (85%), emotional involvement is a prerequisite for sex (Carroll et al., 1985). Conversely, for many men, sex may be viewed as just a pleasant recreation but not a very significant event. As Billy Crystal once quipped, "Women need a reason to have sex. Men just need a place." There is an element of truth to this stereotype. Only a minority of men (40%) feel emotional involvement is a precondition for sex (Hatfield et al., 1989). More recent research, however, suggests that emotional involvement is important to women but that there are multiple reasons women have sex (Meston & Buss, 2009).

There are many potential communication problems associated with gender differences in sexual interest. First, there is greater pressure on women to engage in compliant sex out of fear that their partner will terminate their relationship or lose interest in them if they resist sexual overtures (Impett & Peplau, 2000). Second, conflict in relationships can be triggered by differential interest in sex. Individuals with the greater sexual interest may become angry when their partners are not compliant. Consenting to sex to prevent a partner's anger is associated with feelings of shame, fear, and anger (Impett & Peplau, 2003). Concerns that a partner might end the relationship or withhold love and affection if sexually rebuffed is associated with riskier sexual practices and unplanned pregnancies (Cooper et al., 1998). Third, there may even be some association with sexual violence against women if a woman is less interested in sex and must "disappoint" her male partner (Impett & Peplau, 2003).

Social Support and Social Skills: Caring About and for Others

We typically think of women as more supportive in times of stress and bereavement than men. This is among the largest gender differences in communication ever supported by research. A review of 30 studies reveals that men tend to "go it alone" in times of stress and emotional difficulty far more than women, whereas women draw on social-emotional support from family members, friends, and neighbors (Luckow et al., 1998). Women also provide help and comfort in such circumstances far more than men. This same pattern can be found cross-culturally (Belle, 1987, 1989; Taylor, 2002).

Men are also significantly more **emotionally restrictive**—"having difficulty and fears about expressing one's feelings and difficulty finding words to express basic emotions" (O'Neill et al., 1995, p. 176)—than women (see also Wong et al., 2006). When it comes to the social skill of expressing how one feels, men generally are far more challenged than women (Burleson et al., 2005). This typically has a negative effect on the health of a romantic relationship (Rochlen & Mahalik, 2004). One important exception, however, involves display rules associated with emotional expressions. Men tend to express what are sometimes perceived to be negative emotions, such as anger or hatred, more easily than positive emotions, such as affection and joy. Women, conversely, have some difficulty expressing anger but little difficulty expressing the positive emotions (Simpson & Stroh, 2004). When women do express anger, it tends to be expressed by crying; men tend to express anger in outbursts, even rage (Domagalski, 1998; Girion, 2000; Hoover-Dempsey et al., 1986). Women generally cry about *five times more often* than men (Walter, 2006), unless you're Republican Speaker of the House John Boehner, teasingly dubbed "Weeper of the House" by some for his well-known penchant for crying with seemingly little provocation.

Negotiating for Salaries: Do You Want a Million Dollars?

Women are vastly more hesitant than men to ask for higher starting salaries. In a study of students graduating with master's degrees from Carnegie Mellon University, only 7% of the female students but 57% of the male students asked for higher starting salaries. Those students that asked for more money received, on average, $4,053 in additional starting compensation—the difference in average starting salaries between men and women generally (Babcock, 2002; see also Babcock & Laschever, 2003). Two professors of management, Robin Pinkley and Gregory Northcraft (2000), estimate that women who consistently negotiate salary increases will earn more than *$1 million additional compensation* by retirement than will those who accept only what is offered.

Why don't women typically ask for more money? A primary reason is that women are more inclined to believe that their individual circumstances are controlled by outside forces—"life happens." Men are more likely to believe that circumstances can be changed by individual action—"we make life happen" (Wade, 1996). In one study of salary negotiations, the male applicants were almost *six times more likely* than the female applicants to see their worth determined by themselves, not the company (Barron, 2003). This gender difference was found to be true not just in the United States but in 14 other diverse cultures (Smith et al., 1997). Another reason women usually don't ask for more money is that they are more than twice as likely as men to admit "a great deal of apprehension" about negotiating (Babcock et al., 2002). Women tend to see negotiation as an unpleasant conflict or contest that may disrupt interpersonal relations (Babcock & Laschever, 2003). Men focus on accomplishments and less on relationships with others when negotiations occur, whereas women focus more on relationships (Cross & Madson, 1997). Barron (2003) found that men were two-and-a-half times more prone than women to view a job negotiation as a means to advance their interests, but women were two-and-a-half times as likely to see a job negotiation as a method for furthering their acceptance by others.

There are other significant gender differences in communication besides sexual interest, social support, and salary negotiation.

Some of these additional significant differences will be highlighted throughout the rest of this text.

Gender Similarities Hypothesis: United States and Canada

Some researchers don't think gender differences in communication are significant (Cameron, 2007). Janet Shibley Hyde (2005) calls this perspective the **gender similarities hypothesis**. According to this perspective, although there are a few large gender differences, most are small. Instead of men and women being from different planets, it seems they are more Earth bound, like neighbors from similar adjacent nations, such as the United States and Canada.

Consider a few common examples. Although men are more likely than women to check their email over the weekend (69% to 62%) and to check their email in the middle of the night (44% to 36%), the gender differences are small according to a national survey (Conlon, 2007). Consider further some common communication activities while driving. A national survey of 502 U.S. drivers (251 males; 251 females) revealed that 24% of both males and females admitted to texting at least once a week while driving. Additionally, 43% of men and 41% of women used their car horn to express displeasure to another driver, and 50% of men and 43% of women admitted to using a rude gesture when expressing this displeasure (Burfeind & Witkemper, 2010). The gender differences are small to nonexistent.

One review of a large number of studies on gender differences in communication found, in aggregate, that men and women are 99% similar in their communication and only 1% different (Canary & Hause, 1993). Others, however, disagree with this perspective and argue that important research was omitted in the review (Andersen, 2006; Wood, 1998).

Assuming for the moment that gender differences in communication are small, please note that *even small differences can produce large effects* (Eagly, 1995). Chimpanzees and humans, for example, are almost 99% similar in chromosomes; yet consider the enormous differences in performance and behavior (not even counting looks). A computer simulation study of organizational hiring practices found that when gender accounted for a mere 1% difference in performance ratings that favored men over women, 65% of the highest-level positions in the organization were filled by men (Martell et al., 1996).

One review of research found 16 language features (e.g., use of personal pronouns, length of sentences, etc.) that distinguish male-female communication patterns. Each difference is small. Nevertheless, these "subtle language differences have substantial consequences in how communicators are evaluated. The inescapable conclusion is this: The language differences really do make a difference" (Mulac, 2006, p. 238).

Although gender differences in communication are mostly small, and men and women are far more similar than different in their communication patterns, that message hasn't been well publicized. **Gender role stereotypes** *magnify even small gender differences* (Lindsey & Zakahi, 2006). These stereotypes are important because they suggest not merely how men and women might differ, but they specify how they *should* differ. For instance, historically, men's gender roles in most cultures have been to be the providers, protectors, and decision makers. Women's roles have been to be the nurturers, caregivers, and emotional supporters. Men have been dominant; women have been submissive. Stereotypic descriptions of men's positive characteristics relate to respect and power; stereotypic descriptions of women's positive characteristics relate to liking (Wajciszke et al., 1998). These stereotypes may have reflected real significant differences at one time, but they are far less credible as society changes. Thus, these gender differences have become smaller, but the stereotypes linger and nurture the misperception that men and women still behave in markedly divergent ways.

In addition to stereotypes, context should be considered. Studies of interruptions during conversations have consistently shown that men far more than women interrupt intrusively to seize the floor or

The gender similarities hypothesis is partially supported by the strong similarities in male and female use of communication technologies—for good or ill.

dominate a conversation in a variety of settings (Anderson & Leaper, 1998). Despite the stereotype that women talk more than men, a review of 63 studies shows that men speak far more than women in committee meetings, classroom discussions, problem-solving groups, other formal settings, and even in less formal contexts as well (Crawford & Kaufman, 2006). Nevertheless, *context can virtually eliminate some apparent gender differences in communication*. For example, despite the general finding that men are more talkative than women, with close friends and family there is little difference (Leaper & Ayres, 2007).

Explaining Gender Differences: No Consensus

Clearly, there is no consensus among researchers and theorists regarding how numerous and how large the gender differences in communication are (see especially Dindia & Canary, 2006). It is also clear, however, that men and women do not communicate in identical ways. The large gender differences that are well supported by research, even if relatively few, concern some of the most important aspects of our lives (sex, social support and social skills, negotiating for financial security) with powerful communication implications, and even small gender differences can produce large effects. Why do these gender differences in communication exist? This section briefly discusses several perspectives.

Styles Perspective: Status Versus Connection

Deborah Tannen (1990) popularized the different-styles perspective with her international bestselling book *You Just Don't Understand: Women and Men in Conversation*. She claims, as do others (Bruess & Pearson, 1996; Noller, 1993; Wood, 2000), that males and females learn *different communication styles* as the outgrowth of cultural expectations and socialization processes (see also Maccoby, 1998). Every conversation has two dimensions: status and connection (Tannen, 2010). *Status* is hierarchical, and conversation perceived from this dimension is a "negotiation in which people try to achieve and maintain the upper hand if they can" (Tannen, 1990, p. 24). When status is the focus, an individual asks, "Am I one-up or one-down?" *Connection* is nonhierarchical, and conversations perceived from this standpoint view talk between self and others as a "negotiation for closeness" (p. 25). When connection is the focus, an individual asks, "Are we closer or farther apart?" Men and women are concerned with both status and connection, but *men typically give more focus and weight to status, and women typically give more focus and weight to connection* (Tannen, 2010; see also Wood, 2007). Note the supporting research, previously discussed on male and female patterns of negotiating salaries, in which men were far more prone than women to view a job negotiation as a means to advance their interests (status enhancing), whereas women were far more likely to see a job negotiation as a method for furthering their acceptance by others (connecting). Also, with strangers, men focus more on influencing the listener while women focus more on affirming a connection with the listener (Leaper & Ayres, 2007). Women make phone calls and use instant messaging more for maintaining relationships, and they share more personal photos and maintain social networking sites more than men do (Lacohee & Anderson, 2001; Ramirez & Broneck, 2009; Rosen et al., 2010). Finally, men perform humor (status enhancing) far more than women, but women appreciate and laugh at humor offered by others (connecting) far more than men do (Nicholson, 2010).

According to Tannen, men usually see conversation as a contest, a competitive opportunity to increase status (see also Coates, 1993; Wood, 2007). Thus, men typically display their knowledge and expertise on a subject for all to appreciate (sometimes they play "expert" when they know little about the subject). They offer solutions to problems, even when not solicited, because this spotlights their expertise (status enhancing). This explains the male propensity for cruising the globe rather than stopping to ask for directions when lost. Asking for directions diminishes status—someone else solves the problem. Conversely, women typically make references to personal experiences, share their feelings, and listen intently to establish cooperative rapport with others. This explains the female propensity to talk on the phone for long periods of time. Conversation, regardless of topic, connects the parties conversing.

Perceptual misunderstandings between genders often result from style differences in communication (Wood, 2007). Women interpret men's refusal to ask for directions as pigheaded, exasperating stubbornness, and men interpret women's long phone conversations as gossipy and pointless. Both interpretations can be misperceptions that emerge from differing communication styles.

If men and women often approach simple conversation from conflicting perspectives, then conversation is often a negotiation between individuals with two different perceptions. This negotiation can be a competitive, adversarial contest of wills that can threaten the very future of a relationship, or it can be a cooperative effort to find areas of agreement and to work out areas of disagreement.

Dominance Perspective: Unequal Power

Tannen's style-differences explanation for gender communication has been criticized for seriously underemphasizing the *dominance of men* (see Cameron, 2007; Freed, 1992; Talbot, 1998). "The fact that women are the outsiders, not that they have some universal conversational style, is what creates differences between the sexes" (Tavris, 1992, p. 300). Women communicate in ways typical of most people who are in a relatively powerless position, and men communicate in ways typical of those with more power. These power disparities that disadvantage women result from cultural gender role expectations and the rigidity of these roles typical of a masculine culture.

There is evidence to support this dominance perspective. Because women have historically been in subordinate positions to men, they have been forced to use a communication style that is relatively noncompetitive, friendly, accommodating, and unassertive. When you have little status and authority, adopting the "male style" which emphasizes status would be self-defeating. Bosses can order employees to perform certain tasks. Employees would be foolish to try the same with their bosses. When women have been in positions of relatively equal power to men, however, they are likely to communicate in ways strikingly similar to men (Rosenthal & Hautaluoma, 1988; Sagrestano, 1992).

Tannen (1990) does not ignore the obvious power differences between men and women. She simply offers the different-styles perspective as an additional view. She explains, "Male dominance is not the whole story. It is not sufficient to account for everything that happens to women and men in conversations—especially in conversations in which both are genuinely trying to relate to each other with attention and respect" (p. 18). As women increasingly gain power, communication differences are unlikely to disappear. The "men-are-dominant" perspective is also complicated by research on conflict. When one partner in a male-female relationship is dominant during a conflict (raises disagreements, insists on certain actions), women are about twice as likely to be the dominant partner, not to gain a personal advantage but to resolve relationship troubles (Gottman, 1994). Research on leadership in groups and organizations also diminishes the men-are-dominant perspective on gender differences. "Rather than being less powerful, women may in fact be equally or more powerful than their male counterparts" because the typical leadership style of women that is more interpersonally friendly (connecting) is better suited to today's business and institutional environment than the typical male style (status enhancing) (Kalbfleisch & Herold, 2006; see also Eagly, 2007; Eagly & Carli, 2007). Finally, research on nonverbal communication shows inconsistent support for the dominance perspective (Hall, 2006b).

Deficiencies Perspective: Communication Inadequacies

Some communication experts argue that, contrary to the different-styles or dominance-of-men perspectives, some gender differences can be better explained by *deficiencies in communication skills* (Kunkel & Burleson, 2006). They argue that if men and women have distinctly different communication styles, then men should prefer the "masculine style" and women should prefer the "feminine style." One's own gender style should be more familiar, more comfortable, and make better sense. Both men and women, however, prefer the female communication modes of providing comfort and emotional support. Thus, women are more often sought for comfort and emotional support by *both* men and women because women have been socialized as part of cultural gender role expectations to develop these skills; men have not. In contexts where persuasive skills are highly valued, however, such as in organizational meetings and legal proceedings, the female style might prove to be deficient. "Members of each sex tend to specialize in some skills while incurring deficits in other skills" (Kunkel & Burleson, 2006, p. 151). Thus, gender differences in communication reflect communication deficiencies encouraged by our culture's gender role expectations. The appropriate advice, then, would not be to accommodate gender style differences uncritically but to encourage skills development in areas where deficiencies exist.

Communication Competence and Gender

The issue of gender differences in communication is not settled. The magnitude of gender differences and their importance to communication competence are still hotly debated. *The research, however, does not support a conclusion that no important differences exist.* A couple of observations regarding how to approach gender differences in your communication with others can be offered.

Don't Magnify Gender Differences

John Gray's success with his Venus-Mars metaphor that argues a biological determinism, asserting that men and women are inherently and hugely different creatures, "does more than reflect gender stereotypes; he reproduces them (amplifies them to the level of intergalaxy differences). . . . His prescriptions are sexist. . . . He provides an excuse for bad behavior" (Dindia, 2006, p. 13). Gray is a pop psychologist with dubious credentials (Salerno, 2005). His claims are not based on credible research. For example, one stereotype he nurtures is that men need alone time to deal with stress at work, and women need to talk. He advises women to permit men to "go to their cave," to work out their feelings in private (Gray, 1992). Dindia (2006) notes, "I have asked thousands of women who work outside the home whether they would like to come home from work and 'go to their cave,' and they overwhelmingly say yes. This has nothing to do with whether you are a man or a woman" (p. 18). She continues, "When you have been interacting all day long with others, you want to come home and be left alone; when you have been home alone (or home with the kids) all day, you want to engage in some (adult) interaction" (p. 18). Don't magnify gender differences in communication by nurturing gender role stereotypes.

Embrace the Value of Many Perspectives

There are some large, important gender differences in communication, and there are many small differences, some with potentially large effects. There are three primary explanations offered: different communication styles, dominance of men, and deficiency in communication skills. Picking any one of the three as the correct explanation ignores the insights the others provide. When power disparities exist between men and women, communication differences will likely emerge. Diminishing the power imbalances, a subject discussed in Chapter 7, will diminish communication differences. It will not eradicate them, however. Many such differences can be accurately explained as legitimate variation in styles. If, however, a clear skills deficiency exists (men are worse listeners; women are less assertive), then this may be the reason for communication differences. Skills training to diminish the gender differences would then be appropriate. So look to create power balance, correct skill deficiencies, and accommodate style differences that still account for some gender differences in communication.

Summary

INTERCULTURAL communication is a fact of life. The United States is thoroughly multicultural. With cultural diversity come new challenges. We tend to misunderstand individuals from other cultures and co-cultures because deep-seated cultural values differ. The main value dimensions are individualism-collectivism and power-distance. Cultures vary widely on these dimensions. These value differences and the communication patterns and styles that emerge from them can result in ethnocentrism, or the attitude that your own culture is the measure of all things and cultures that differ from your own culture are deficient. This ethnocentric attitude can produce misunderstandings and miscommunication. Finding ways to become acculturated to different cultures, to reduce uncertainty and create convergence while de-emphasizing divergence, can help produce competent intercultural communication.

Recognizing the interconnectedness of gender to culture is also important. Cultures can be ranked on a masculine-feminine dimension that reflects rigidity or flexibility of gender role expectations. Gender role expectations create stereotypes. These stereotypes occur within cultures. Although gender differences in communication clearly do exist, the magnitude and importance of these differences are still debated. Nevertheless, even small differences can produce large effects.

Quizzes Without Consequences

Test your knowledge before your exam!

Go to the companion website at www.oup.com/us/rothwell, click on the Student Resources for each chapter, and take the Quizzes Without Consequences.

Film School Case Studies

For Love of the Game (1999). Drama; PG-13

This charming film ostensibly about baseball and a pitcher's swan song is much more complex and multitextured than most sports movies. Identify gender differences in behavior, especially between the Kevin Costner and Kelly Preston characters. Applying the difference, dominance, and deficiency models of gender communication, what could these characters have done to make their relationship progress more smoothly?

Pride and Prejudice (2005). Romantic Drama; PG

This is a magnificent rendering of the Jane Austen novel. Keira Knightley is splendid as the main character in this period piece. Analyze the gender role stereotypes and the verbal combat between the main characters of Elizabeth and Mr. Darcy resulting from these stereotypes.

Spanglish (2004). Comedy/Drama; PG-13

This surprisingly touching film about a Mexican mother and her child who struggle to subsist in Los Angeles is an entertaining delight. Analyze the issue of assimilation versus multiculturalism in the context of ethnocentrism. Does this movie mostly support or challenge the desirability of assimilation? Provide arguments and evidence from the movie to defend your answer.

The Joy Luck Club (1993). Drama; R

This film version of Amy Tan's critically acclaimed novel is a wonderful depiction of intercultural dynamics. See if you can identify all the instances of difficulties caused by the individualism-collectivism and power-distance dimensions of culture. Analyze this film for low-context and high-context communication patterns and their consequences. Does ethnocentrism play a part in the communication difficulties exhibited?

The Namesake (2006). Drama; PG-13

Gogol Ganguli (Kal Penn), raised as an American by immigrant Bengali parents, is torn between Indian culture and modern Boston. Analyze assimilation and multiculturalism depicted in this film.

The Wedding Banquet (1993). Comedy; R

What happens when a New York real estate agent agrees to marry one of his tenants so she can get a green card and he can stop his parents' attempt to find him the "perfect Chinese wife," all with the knowledge of the agent's male lover? Check out this very amusing film and identify examples of convergence and divergence depicted in the movie.

CHAPTER 4

Chapter Outline

- The Nature of Language
- The Abstracting Process
- The Power of Language
- Competent Language Use

Language

Sharing Meaning with Words

IMAGINE LIFE WITHOUT LANGUAGE. Individuals with Alzheimer's disease don't have to imagine because it is their reality. During the early phase of Alzheimer's disease, victims exhibit great difficulty retrieving appropriate words (Price et al., 1993). For example, a 77-year-old man afflicted with this disease—he was a college graduate and former businessman—when asked to name a pen, replied, "a unit . . ." He substituted *pop* for watch, *sheet* for shoe, and *twice* for second floor (Clark et al., 2003). In the middle phase of Alzheimer's, a "verbal casserole" is common in which spoken thoughts become disconnected and words are invented (Coste, 2003). This same man, when trying to say his first name, Paul, instead said "Parma" and later "Pisei." In the final phase, language ability all but disappears. Again, this same man at 79 years old could utter only a single meaningful sentence, "I'm going to die"—a few months before he did. Those afflicted with Alzheimer's usually become extremely agitated by their inability to communicate coherent thoughts, eventually seeking sad refuge in silence.

By the end of this chapter, you should be able to:

1. Explain the basic elements of language.
2. Describe the language abstraction process.
3. Understand and appreciate the power of language.
4. Recognize common sources of inappropriate and ineffective language use.
5. Understand ways to improve your use of language.

Oliver Sacks (1990) calls deficiency in language "one of the most desperate of calamities, for it is only through language that we enter fully into our human estate and culture, communicate freely with our fellows, acquire and share information" (p. 8). Prior to the creation of sign language, the prelingually deaf were labeled as "dumb" and "mute," treated outrageously by society as little more than "imbeciles" incapable of learning beyond menial tasks (Sacks, 1990). Sign language freed the deaf community from its communication imprisonment.

Language facilitates human survival (Krauss, 2001). With language, you are not limited to direct experience, so you can learn from and avoid the fatal mistakes of others. You can also make requests, share your feelings, and get your needs met. Infants are limited mostly to crying and flailing their arms and legs to draw attention to their needs. Once language is learned in early childhood, you progress beyond flailing and wailing, although you may know some adults who occasionally regress to such infantile communication. Without the ability to read, write, and speak a language, there would be little or no science, literature, history, or philosophy. Many concepts would be extraordinarily difficult to teach and learn without language (Jackendoff, 1996). Try teaching the concept "being" or "nothingness" nonverbally.

Without language, human communication is enormously restricted. Even with language, humans often use it ineffectively and inappropriately. *The primary purpose of this chapter is to explain how you can use language competently.*

The Nature of Language

Language is a structured system of symbols for communicating meaning. There are about 6,800 spoken languages in the world (Grimes, 2004). On the surface, they seem distinctly different from each other. If you are a native speaker of English, it would be difficult for you to mimic the sounds of Chinese, Arabic, or Bengali without practice, much less understand what is said. Nevertheless, all languages share four essential elements: structure, productivity, displacement, and self-reflexiveness.

Structure: Saying by the Rules

Structure is the most essential element of any language and easily the most complicated. Without structure, you have no language. Every language has a grammar that provides this structure. **Grammar** is the set of rules that specify how the units of language can be meaningfully combined. Grammar is divided into phonology, morphology, syntax, and semantics (Krauss & Chiu, 1998).

Phonology: Patterns of Sound

The individual units of sound that compose a specific spoken language are called **phonemes**. These sounds correspond to consonants (such as *b, c, d*), vowels (*a, e, i, o, u*), and consonant combinations (such as *ch, th*). The human vocal apparatus is capable of producing many sounds, but no single language encompasses more than a fraction of the clicks, croaks, hisses, squeaks, snorts, and other noises—many of them considered rude, crude, or lewd—that people can produce. In fact, linguists have identified 869 phonemes in the almost 500 languages studied (Maddieson, 1984). The English language, however, has only about 44 of this total, the Hawaiian language has 13, and some African languages have more than 100 (the southern African language !Xu has 141) (Crystal, 2005).

The number of English phonemes is approximate, not precise, because of variations in pronunciations. For example, do you say *hair* with a hard "*h*" sound or do you drop the "*h*" sound and say *air?* The *h*-pronouncing speakers have one more phoneme than the *h*-droppers. Most Americans pronounce the *h*, but many speakers in England drop it (Trask, 1999).

Phonology is a part of grammar that describes the patterns of sound in a language. Put another way, "Phonology is the study of how we find order within the apparent chaos of speech sounds" (Crystal, 2005). Phonemes cannot be strung together helter-skelter. They follow phonological rules. *Shirt* is a recognizable English word. *Shtri* is not, yet the exact same letters appear in both examples. No English word begins with the *shtr* phoneme combination. English words can begin with up to three consonants, but no more, before a vowel (e.g., *strap*) (Crystal, 2005). (In the word *crystal*, the *y* is considered a vowel—see "Is the Letter Y a Consonant or a Vowel?" 2011.) Every language has phonological rules indicating which sounds to use, how to pronounce these sounds, and how to combine these sounds in meaningful ways (Crystal, 2005).

Morphology: Transforming Phonemes into Meaningful Units

Your ability to combine the 44 phonemes in highly complex ways permits your verbal communication to rise above the level of a primitive human being. You combine phonemes to create morphemes. A **morpheme** is the smallest unit of meaning in language. **Morphology** is the part of grammar that describes how morphemes are constructed meaningfully from phonemes. Morphemes are more than just words. A morpheme may be a stand-alone word (*friend*) called a **free morpheme** or a unit of meaning called a **bound morpheme** that has no meaning until it is attached to a stand-alone word (e.g., prefixes such as *un* in *unfriend* or suffixes such as *ing* in *Facebooking*). *Bat* is a free morpheme composed of three phonemes (the *b, a,* and *t* sounds). Add an *s*, making *bats*, and there are two morphemes (one free and one bound) because the *s* means "more than one" when attached to the stand-alone word. Adding *ly* to the word *loud* changes an adjective (the *loud* cry) into an adverb (he cried *loudly*). The suffix *ly* by itself is meaningless.

Once morphemes are constructed from phonemes, you are faced with a challenging problem: multiple meanings. This is made apparent by a famous Groucho Marx quip: "Time *flies* like an arrow; fruit *flies* like a banana." There also is a big difference between a movie *buff* and seeing a movie in the *buff*. A *booty call* can be a treasure hunt or a pursuit of a different sort. The word *set* has almost 200 meanings, more than any other word in the *Oxford English Dictionary* (Bryson, 1990). Some words are especially challenging because they can have contradictory meanings. *Sanction*, for example, can mean either "permit" or "forbid." *Fast* might denote "move quickly" or "stick firmly." A *blunt* instrument is dull but a *blunt* remark is sharp and pointed. Multiple meanings for a word can cause confusion because of ambiguity, as actual newspaper headlines reported in several issues of the *Columbia Journalism Review* illustrate: "Kids Make Nutritious Snacks"; "Panda Mating Fails—Veterinarian Takes Over"; and "Prostitutes Appeal to Pope." Typically, we try to resolve the ambiguity in each case by interpreting from the context the correct meaning of the words. This is no small feat. Joshua Hartshorne (2011) notes in an article entitled "Where Are the Talking Robots?" that "language has proved harder to understand than anyone had imagined. Our ability to perform such tasks as choosing the correct meaning of ambiguous words is in fact the fruit of millions of years of evolution. And we accomplish these feats without knowing how we do so, much less how to teach the skill to an artificial being" (p. 46).

Syntax: Word-Order Rules

Using single, isolated words is very limited—insufficient for complex communication to occur. That's why humans combine words into phrases ("the woman in the blue dress") and sentences ("She is the woman in the blue dress"). "Workers hoisted the iron girders" is a meaningful sentence, but "Hoisted girders workers iron the" is not. Why? There are rules, called **syntax**, that govern combining words into phrases and phrases into sentences. The article (the) and adjective (iron) come before the noun (girders), and the verb (hoisted) comes after the subject (workers). Subject-verb-object (SVO) is, syntactically, the typical English word order. That is why the speech of Yoda,

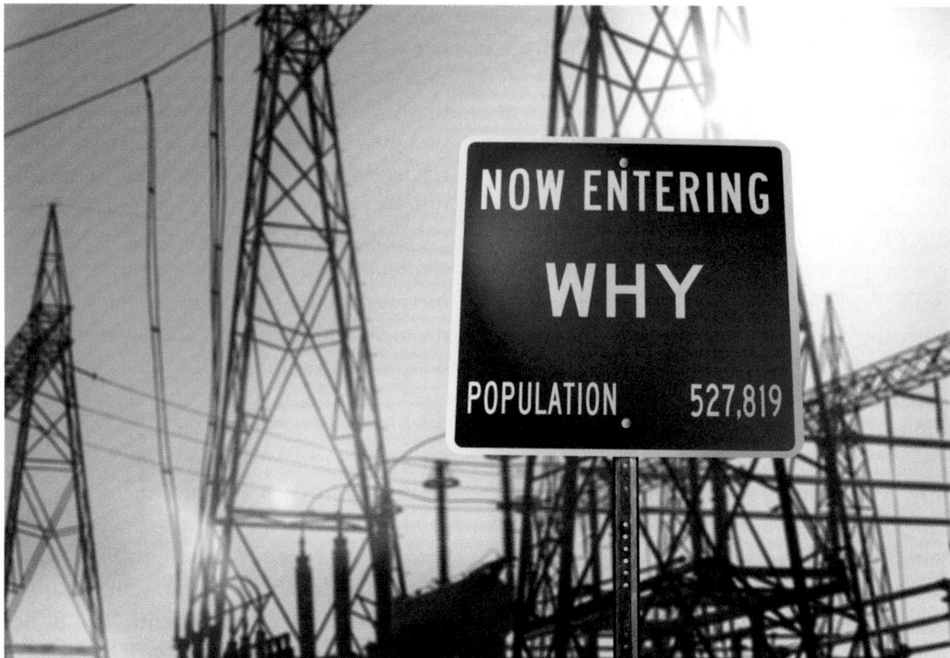

This photo illustrates which of the following?

1. The multiple meanings for words that can produce confusion or misunderstandings
2. Grammatical rules of language are arbitrary conventions
3. The phonology of words
4. The structure of language

Answers at end of chapter

the Jedi Master in the *Star Wars* films, seems so strange. "Sick have I become" and "Your father he is" have an object-subject-verb (OSV) order that is very unusual for English. Yodaspeak, in fact, is an unusual construction in all but a few rare languages (Crystal, 1997).

The English language is highly dependent on word-order rules for communicating meaning. For example, the sentence "Skateboarding is not a crime" has a far different meaning than "Not skateboarding is a crime." Word-order rules are a part of the grammar of language, but not all languages have the same word-order rules.

Semantics: Rules of Meaning

"Swift flowers smell noisy bells" is a syntactically correct sentence. It has a standard subject-verb-object order with the modifiers placed immediately before the nouns. Nevertheless, the sentence is semantically incorrect. **Semantics** is the set of rules that governs the meaning of words and sentences. *Flowers* cannot be swift, and although they can emit a fragrance, they cannot actively smell anything. The meaning of the words, even though those appear in appropriate order, makes the sentence nonsensical. George W. Bush once urged listeners to put themselves in the role of a single mother "working hard to put food on your family" (see www.snopes.com). This is a semantic problem. Normally, we put food *on the table*, not on family members. They seem to prefer it that way. Bush also coughed up this linguistic hairball: "Families is where wings take dream" (see www.snopes.com). Here we see both a syntactic and semantic problem. "Families is" violates subject-verb agreement because a plural subject requires a plural, not a singular, verb. The sentence is also semantically nonsensical because wings can't "take dream."

Each person constructs meaning from symbols that appear in the form of sounds, words, phrases, and sentences by interpreting those symbols in a context. **Symbols** are arbitrary representations of objects, events, ideas, or relationships. **Referents** are the objects, events, ideas, or relationships referred to by the words. For example, the referent for "table" is the physical object upon which we place the evening meal. Korzybski (1958) notes that *a word (symbol) is to a referent as a map is to a territory*. A map of New York City is obviously not the city of New York, only a representation of it. You would be viewed as more than just a little odd if you spread a map of New York City in front of your car, then drove your car onto the map and happily announced your arrival in "the Big Apple." Similarly, the word *sandwich* won't take the edge off of anyone's hunger. Words are not their referents anymore than maps are their territories.

Thus, a basic semantic rule is that *word origin is arbitrary but word usage is conventional*. What we initially choose to call something, as long as it doesn't violate phonological rules, is arbitrary. A *house* could be called a *fadoydlehoffer* (but not a *zxchltz*). Sniglets—words that are simply made up—also illustrate the arbitrariness of word origin (see Unwords.com and urbandictionary.com). Here are a few examples: *arachnidiot* (a person who, having wandered into an "invisible" spiderweb, begins gyrating and flailing about wildly); *fornicorium* (a single man's apartment); *snowbooking* (constantly updating your status or post on Facebook during a snowstorm); *masogyny* (hatred of giving back rubs to women); *PHOBAR* (Photo Shopped Beyond All Recognition); and *downloafing* (surfing the net when you should be working). None of these "made-up words," however, will have meaning and become part of the English **lexicon**—total vocabulary—without conventionality, common agreement to use these words with these specific meanings. Shakespeare invented more than 1,700 words (Bryson, 1990). *Barefoot, critical, leapfrog, monumental, excellent, summit, obscene,* and *submerged* are just a few of his creations. Other made-up words of his, however, did not achieve common usage and fell into obscurity. Some examples are *barky, brisky, vastidity,* and *tortive*.

In brief review, there are rules for which sounds may be included in a particular language (phonology), how these sounds may be linked into words (morphology), in what ways words and phrases may be ordered (syntax), and how words and sentences gain meaning (semantics). The next essential language element is productivity.

Productivity: Inventing Words and Expressing Thoughts

"There are hundreds of millions of trillions of thinkable thoughts" (Pinker, 1997, p. 118). There are only a few dozen phonemes in English to communicate these thoughts, but these phonemes can be transformed into about 100,000 morphemes that can be combined into a lexicon of more than 600,000 words, the total vocabulary listed in the *Oxford English Dictionary (OED)*, the largest lexicon of any language. This lexicon is forever expanding. New words in English added to the *OED* in 2011 included *muffin top* (a protuberance of flesh above the waistband of a tight pair of trousers) and *couchsurfing* (moving from one friend's house to the next and sleeping wherever available). New words sprout up like mushrooms in loamy soil to accommodate new products, scientific discoveries, abstract concepts, and technologies. For example, the emergence of Twitter produced a growing lexicon: *twitterspeak, twitizens* (citizens in the *Twitterverse*—the universe of Twitter), *twitterpated* (a borrowed term from the Disney movie *Bambi* that meant infatuated but now also means getting addled by too many *tweets*), and *twaffic* (traffic on Twitter) (Keats, 2011). You could even be a *twit* for tweeting too much. About 10,000 words are added to an English dictionary every decade (Gorlick, 2005).

This capacity of language to transform a small number of phonemes into whatever words, phrases, and sentences that you require to communicate your abundance of thoughts and feelings is called **productivity**. This essential element of language allows you to express a virtually infinite number of thoughts and feelings in an amazing variety of ways. There are approximately 1 million grammatically correct 6-word sentences possible in the English language and an astounding 100 million trillion 20-word sentences possible (Pinker, 1999). It is very likely that most sentences of about average length (10-15 words) that you might produce, aside from clichés and quotations, have never been spoken or written before, and they will never be randomly reproduced exactly by anyone in the future. That is why it is frustrating for a communication instructor, listening to thousands of student speeches, to hear repeatedly terms such as *like, you know, know what I mean*, and *absolutely* (and new variants sure to be added). When Shakespeare is the measure of human language potential, why settle for the commonplace?

Displacement: Beyond the Here and Now

Your ability to use language to talk about objects, ideas, events, and relations that don't just exist in the physical here and now is called **displacement**. You can talk about things that don't exist, such as unicorns, fairies, hobbits, and corporate responsibility. You can discuss past vacations or future adventures. You can ask questions about impossible things—"If I were 10 feet tall and weighed 450 pounds, would you consider me fat?"—and receive answers. You can ponder abstract ideas, such as this bumper sticker "logic": "I'm nobody, nobody is perfect, therefore I'm perfect." The displacement capacity of language helps us all learn from past mistakes and consider potential solutions for anticipated problems.

We can ponder abstract ideas, such as comedian Stephen Wright's questions: "If you are in a spaceship that is traveling at the speed of light, and you turn on the headlights, does anything happen?" or "So what's the speed of dark?" We can contemplate: "Would I rather have a free bottle in front of me or a prefrontal lobotomy?" Language gives each of us the freedom to communicate about the past, present, or future; about things that may exist, don't exist, or can't exist; about the imaginary and ethereal as well as the concrete and physical.

Self-Reflexiveness: The Language of Language

Language has the capacity to be **self-reflexive**—the ability to use language to talk about language (DeVito, 1970). All languages are self-reflexive. This chapter is a detailed example of self-reflexiveness. We are using

This cartoon makes which of the following points about language?

1. Grammar is not a fixed set of rules
2. Language structure varies from language to language
3. Word origin is arbitrary but word usage is conventional
4. Language has the capacity to be self-reflexive

Answers at end of chapter

English to analyze and discuss English and languages in general. A vocabulary has been created to identify and discuss the nature of languages (phonemes, morphemes, syntax, etc.). We use our language to reflect on how we might improve our use of it, which has the benefit of assisting us in solving life's problems by communicating clearly and effectively. The meaning we can communicate with language includes an analysis of language itself.

Considering all four elements—structure, productivity, displacement, and self-reflexiveness—must a language have the

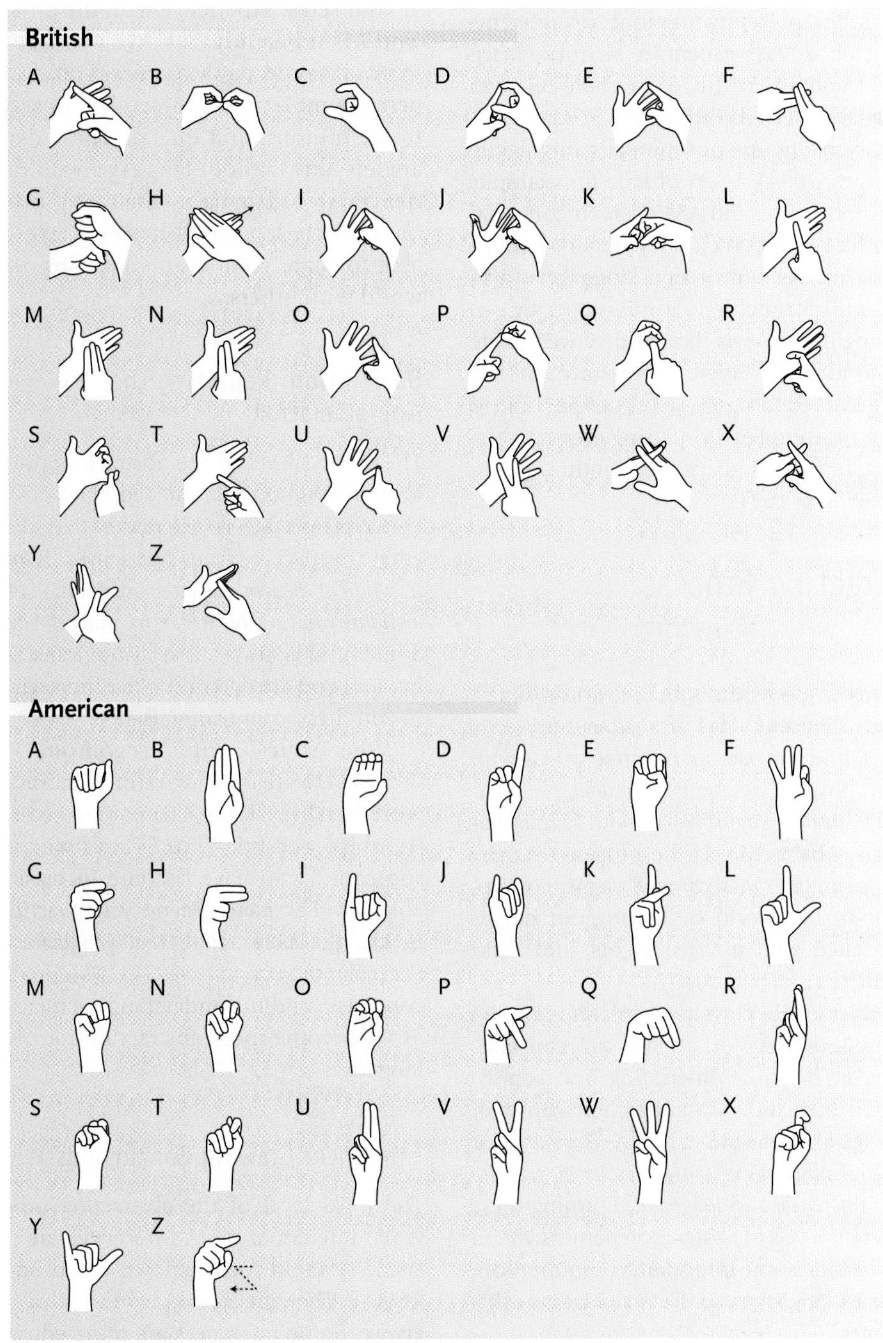

FIGURE 4-1 Comparison of Signs in British and American Sign Languages

capacity to be spoken or written to qualify as a true language? For example, do sign languages qualify? Yes, they do (Crystal, 2005). They have a structured system of symbols that can be expanded to accommodate any thought or feeling, concrete or abstract, immediate or far away, real or imaginary, and sign languages can use signs to discuss signs. Most signs, like words in spoken languages, are arbitrary representations of referents (Crystal, 2005). American Sign Language (ASL) and any of the more than 100 sign languages, such as British (BSL) or Japanese (JSL) versions, are not mutually intelligible (Grimes, 2004). Users of BSL, for example, will not understand ASL users in conversation (see Figure 4-1). They require a translator. Any version of sign language is also not understandable to a non-signer by observing the signs as though they were mere pantomime. "Everyone can gesture; but few have learned to sign. . . . It is not possible to tell a complicated story using everyday gestures. In sign language, it is routine" (Crystal, 2005, p. 163).

The Abstracting Process

All words are symbols, but all words do not reflect the same level of abstraction. *Comb, jacket,* and *hammer* are concrete words with clear physical referents. *Freedom, anarchy,* and *justice* are vague words with fuzzier referents. **Abstracting** is the process whereby we formulate increasingly vague conceptions of our world by leaving out details associated with objects, events, and ideas (Littlejohn & Foss, 2008).

Abstracting permits displacement and self-reflexiveness. It allows our conversations to be more interesting and sophisticated than the communication efforts of average one-year-old children. *There are four levels of abstraction: sense experience, description, inference,* and *judgment.* Learning these different levels of abstraction permits you to understand some important common problems of language use discussed later in this chapter.

Sense Experience: Approximating Our Physical World

Abstracting begins with your sense experience of the physical world. Figure 4-2 illustrates the abstracting process. The parabola represents the world we live in, the territory (a reference to Korzybski's map-territory analogy). As discussed in Chapter 2, your sense experience with the physical world is inherently selective and limited. In your day-to-day existence, you do not perceive molecules, atoms, electrons, neutrons, protons, and quarks. These details are left out. Without language, your experiences would remain essentially private ones. With language, however, you are able to share your approximations of the world with others.

Description: Reporting the Approximation

The second level of the abstracting process is a description of our sense experience. **Descriptions** are *verbal reports* that sketch what we perceive from our senses. *Your description of the world is an approximation of the world as you perceive it, not an exact duplicate.* Something is always lost in the translation because you are describing to others what is in your head, not reality itself.

When your descriptions go from "I am in a committed, long-term relationship with Fran" to "I am in a committed relationship" and finally to "I am living with someone," you have become increasingly abstract. *The more general your description is, and the more details that you leave out, the more abstract you are.* The potential for confusion and misunderstanding increases as we become more abstract in our use of language.

Inference: Drawing Conclusions

The third level of the abstracting process is the inferential stage. **Inferences** are conclusions about the unknown based on the known. They are *guesses,* educated or otherwise. Some inferences are more educated

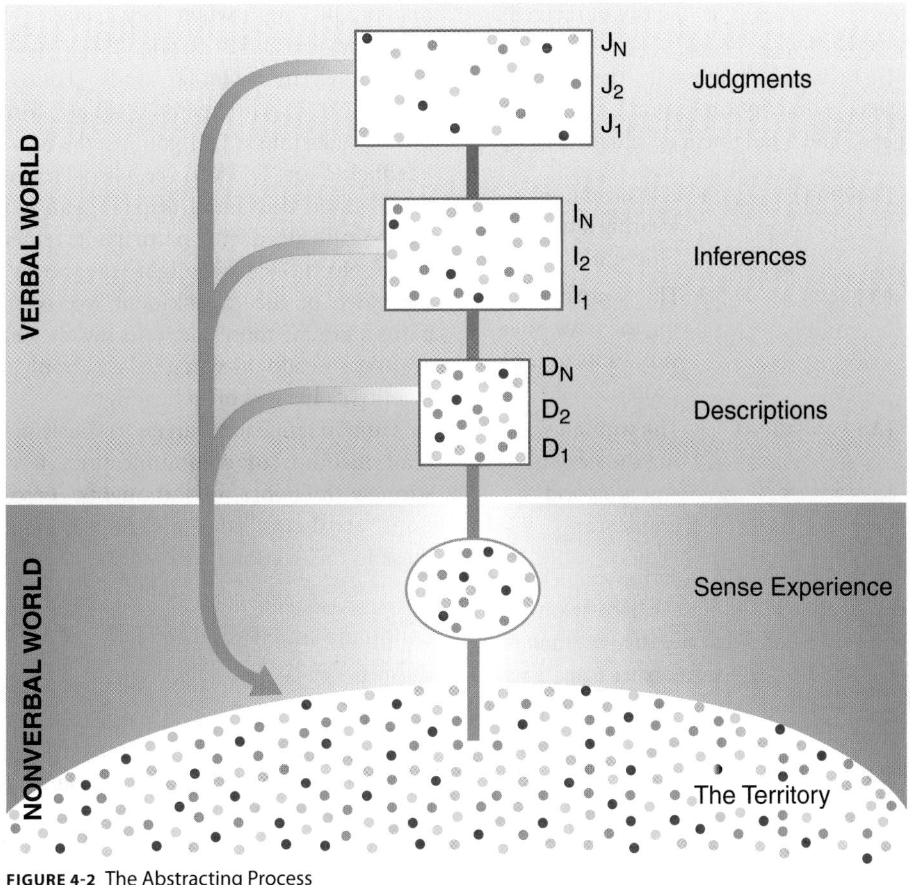

FIGURE 4-2 The Abstracting Process

than others because their probability of accuracy is higher. You can infer that a neighbor is not home (the unknown) because newspapers have accumulated on the front porch, the mailbox is crammed, and repeated phone calls connect with a message machine (the known). This is a relatively safe inference, probably true, but it is an inference and not a fact. Your neighbor may be sick in bed, unable to attend to the newspapers, mail, and phone calls.

Inferring that your neighbor is away on vacation is more abstract than the first inference because a greater range of possibilities exists, but the details upon which the inference is based (newspapers, mail, and unanswered phone calls) remain the same. Your neighbor may be away on business, visiting relatives, attending a funeral, searching for a new house, or hiding from the law.

Judgment: Conclusions That Assign Value

The fourth level of abstraction is making judgments. **Judgments** are subjective *evaluations* of objects, events, or ideas. We attach a subjective positive or negative value such as right or wrong, good or bad, and ugly or beautiful. "My partner is a generous person" is a judgment. It appears to be a description, but it is a subjective evaluation, not a factual report. Generosity is in the mind of the beholder. The statement is also more than just an inference because it does more than draw an indifferent or neutral conclusion from what is known. Generosity is usually perceived as praiseworthy.

In review, let's illustrate the difference between a description (report), an inference (guess), and a judgment (evaluation).

(A report)	1. The woman is wearing a navy blue suit.
(A guess)	2. The woman wearing the navy blue suit wants to look professional.
(An evaluation)	3. The woman wearing the navy blue suit is a good employee.

The first statement is descriptive because it merely reports a simple observation. The second is inferential because it makes a guess based on the woman wearing a navy blue suit without assigning a value (some might see it as stuffy, others might see it as setting a good example, but neither is stated or implied). The third statement is judgmental because it expresses a positive opinion. It is more than just a guess (inference), and it's not a mere report (description). It's an evaluation.

The Power of Language

So far, I've discussed what constitutes language, its nature, and abstracting process. Now let's discuss the power of language more specifically than the few brief comments introducing this chapter. Imagine, for example, that you view a videotape of an automobile accident. You are then asked to estimate how fast the cars were traveling when they *hit*. Do you think your estimate would be different if instead of *hit*, an experimenter used *smashed*, or *collided*, or *bumped*, or *contacted*? Loftus and Palmer (1974) found that changing the descriptive word influenced participants' estimates. When the cars *smashed* into each other, the average estimated speed by participants was 40.4 mph. It was 39.3 mph when the cars *collided*, 38.1 mph when they *bumped*, 34.0 when they *hit*, and 31.8 when they *contacted* each other. In a similar study (Loftus & Zanni, 1975), participants were asked one of two questions: "Did you see *the* broken headlight?" or "Did you see *a* broken headlight?" Even this small difference in word choice influenced what participants remembered. No broken headlight was shown in the video of the car accident, yet participants were far more likely to say they saw a broken headlight when asked about "*the* headlight" instead of "*a* headlight."

Human language is an enormously powerful medium of communication. It can strongly influence our thoughts, perceptions, and behaviors. I discuss all three of these in this section.

Language and Thinking: Related but Different

Edward Sapir, an anthropologist, asserted in 1929 that human beings "are very much at the mercy of the particular language which has become the medium of expression for their society" (quoted in Mandelbaum, 1949, p. 162). He later argued that meanings are "not so much discovered in experience as imposed upon it, because of the tyrannical hold that linguistic form has upon our orientation in the world" (Sapir, 1931, p. 572). Sapir ignited a debate that has lasted for decades concerning the power of language to affect thought and perception.

Sapir-Whorf Hypothesis: Linguistic Imprisonment

It was left to Sapir's student Benjamin Whorf to be the principal advocate for what became known as the **Sapir-Whorf hypothesis**. There are two versions of this perspective: one that claims we are the prisoners of our native language, unable to think certain thoughts or perceive in certain ways because of the grammatical structure and lexicon of our language (**linguistic determinism**); the other version claims that the grammar and lexicon of our native language powerfully influence but do not imprison our thinking and perception (**linguistic relativity**).

Whorf noticed certain grammatical differences among languages. Some languages have few, if any, *tenses*—changes in the verb form to indicate time differences—such as *like* to *liked*. Other languages have many tenses. Do these tense differences determine our capacity to think in terms of time? No! "Whether a language has eleven tenses, three tenses, two tenses, or no tenses at all, its speakers have not the slightest difficulty in talking about any desired point in time, past, present, or future" (Trask, 1999, p. 62).

Whorf also claimed that the size of the vocabulary for various objects and concepts could determine how precisely a person can think about those objects and concepts. The Inuit language has seven words for *snow* (not the dozens or even hundreds asserted on many Internet sites), the Masai of Africa have 17 words for *cattle*, and Italian has more than 500 words related to types of *pasta*, some of which have unappetizing literal translations (e.g., *vermicelli* means "little worms" and *strozzapreti* means "strangled priests") (Bryson, 1990).

Is Whorf correct about the size of vocabulary and perception? It hardly seems so. The Dani tribe in New Guinea, for example, has only two color terms, *mili* (black) and *mola* (white), yet they can perceive distinctions among a variety of colors (Rosch, 1973; see Davidoff et al., 1999, however, for another view). Egyptian businessman Tarek Haggy in a September 2002 article in the Egyptian newspaper *Al-Ahram* asserted that there is no Arabic word for *compromise*, giving the impression that if you have no word for compromise, how could you think the thought? The absence of a single word for compromise, however, doesn't mean Arabs can't, and don't, talk of "reaching a middle ground" (Nunberg, 2003). English has no handy single word that denotes the pleasure one takes in the misfortune of others, as the Germans have with the word *Schadenfreude*. Does this mean that developers of Facebook could not think joyful thoughts about the decreased popularity of Myspace as a social networking site during Facebook's popularity explosion? A limited vocabulary may make it more difficult to perceive subtle differences, but it doesn't make it impossible.

A principal problem with linguistic determinism is that it assumes thought is dependent on language, yet *we can think without language*. All of us have had the experience of not being able to express a thought in words, yet the thought exists. If thinking were dependent on language, did humans not begin thinking until language was created, and how did that creation occur without thought? Does a child's thinking remain in a dormant stage until a first word is uttered, then BAM, the child's brain suddenly kicks into gear and thinking is activated? The simple answer is no (Damasio & Damasio, 1999). Thus, linguistic determinism is generally unsupported.

Although linguistic determinism, the so-called strong version of the Sapir-Whorf hypothesis, has no merit, research does provide support for linguistic relativity, the weaker version of the hypothesis (Boroditsky, 2001; Gentner & Goldin-Meadow, 2003). Looking at just one avenue of research, studies on the influence of **masculine-generic** gender references in English, reveals an easily understood instance of support for the linguistic relativity perspective.

Consider the use of masculine nouns and pronouns to refer to both women and men (*man, mankind, he, him,* and *his*). Sentences such as "*Man* is the master of *his* own destiny" and "A doctor should treat *his* patients compassionately" use masculine generic language. Research shows that these sentences trigger mental images of men more often than women, creating gender bias (Cronin & Jreisat, 1995). Masculine-generic terms are far more likely than gender-neutral terms (*humankind, they*) to produce mental images of men to the exclusion of women (Foertsch & Gernsbacher, 1997; Gastil, 1990; Hardin & Banaji, 1993). Similarly, terms ending with the *-man* suffix (*chairman, businessman, fireman*) promote gender-biased stereotyping, but gender-neutral terms (*chair, businessperson, firefighter*) do not (McConnell & Fazio, 1996).

Gender-biased language makes women virtually invisible, and it tacitly brands them as less powerful and less important than men. Statements that use gender-biased language leave women guessing (having to

Look closely at this picture. Can you discern what it is? If you can't identify the image (it is unmistakable once you see it), ask a classmate or your instructor. Now can you see it? Language labels help us see what may remain hidden without the label, validating the linguistic relativity view of language.

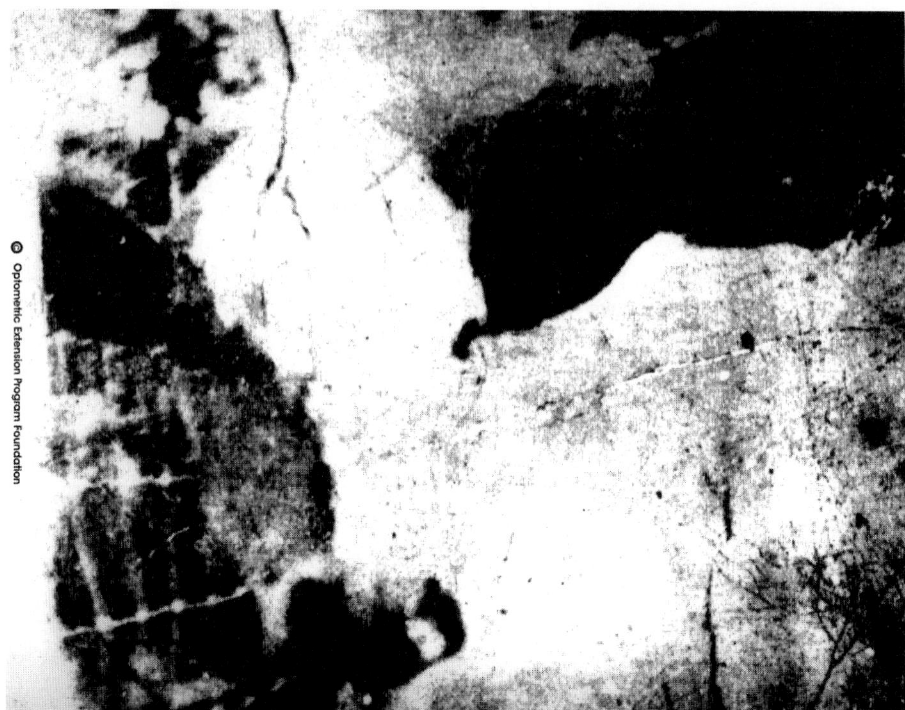

make inferences) whether they are ever really included. There has been a concerted effort in recent years to address the problem by making small but important changes in language (*worker's* for *workman's* compensation; *husband* and wife for *man* and wife). Research clearly shows that, although we are able to form images of women when gender-biased language is used (invalidating linguistic determinism), it is far more difficult (supporting linguistic relativity). Language may not create a mental prison from which there is no escape, but it certainly can narrow our thinking, making more expansive views of the world difficult to contemplate.

Although much discussion and research on the power of language have centered on grammatical and lexical differences between specific languages, the power of all languages to influence perception and behavior may provide a more compelling case for studying and improving language use (Ng, 2001).

Labeling: The Name Game

Advertisers and producers of myriad products know the importance of labels. *Chinese gooseberries* didn't sell well until renamed *kiwi*. The California Prune Board approved a move to call prunes *dried plums* to escape negative connotations attached to this wrinkled fruit.

A **label** is a name or a descriptive word or phrase. Labels can powerfully influence perceptions. In one study, participants were asked to sniff a test odor (either isovaleric acid with cheddar cheese flavor or clean air) while it was described as "cheddar cheese" or "body odor." For both test odors, participants rated the smell as significantly more unpleasant when labeled "body odor" than when labeled "cheddar cheese" (de Araujo et al., 2005). Labels can influence a subjective perception of smell.

Besides perceptions, labeling can also strongly influence behavior. Research showed that labeling a game either "community game" or "Wall Street game" significantly influenced whether participants would be competitive or cooperative when playing the game (Ross & Samuels, 1993). Labeling can produce prosocial (positive and helpful) behavior. In one study, children were told that they were *kind* and *helpful*. These prosocial labels encouraged children to give prizes they received in the experiment to other children (Grusec et al., 1978). Even three weeks later, children labeled kind and helpful were more willing to aid others than children not so labeled (Grusec & Redler, 1980). Prosocial labels influence adults as well. New Haven, Connecticut, residents were more likely to give a donation to the Multiple Sclerosis Society when they were described as *generous* and *charitable* one to two weeks prior to the donation request (Kraut, 1973).

Framing: Influencing Choices

Two Catholic priests, Father O'Leary and Father Kelly, strongly disagreed with each other on the question of whether smoking and prayer are compatible behaviors. They each decided to write the pope, plead their own case, and ask for his wisdom. When they received the pope's reply, both priests were triumphant. Puzzled that the pope could agree with both of them when only two contradictory choices seemed available, Father O'Leary asked Father Kelly, "What question did you ask the pope?" Father Kelly responded, "I asked the pope if it was permissible to pray while smoking. The pope said that praying should always be encouraged no matter what you are doing." Father O'Leary chuckled to himself. "Well, I asked the pope whether it is permissible to smoke while praying, and the pope said that I should take praying very seriously and not trivialize it by smoking." The way each question was framed by the priests dictated the answer they received from the pope.

Framing is a close associate of labeling. **Framing** is the influence wording has on our perception of choices. Framing, more specifically than just labels, narrows our perceptions. It "captures a viewpoint" (Fairhurst & Sarr, 1996). Much like a photographer frames a picture to communicate a point of view, language frames choices. When a photographer changes the frame so that a person is no longer the center of interest but is rather a mere bystander, our thoughts and perception of the picture change. The focus shifts. Likewise, changing language that describes or identifies our choices can change our focus and perception. As Fairhurst and Sarr (1996) explain, our "frames determine whether people notice problems, how they understand and remember problems, and how they evaluate and act upon them" (p. 4).

Malamuth (as cited in Rottenberg, 2000) offers a disquieting example of the power of framing to shape perceptions. "When men are asked if there is any likelihood they would force a woman to have sex against her will if they could get away with it, about *half* say they would. But if you ask them if they would rape a woman if they knew they could get away with it, only about 15% say they would" (p. 244). Studies abound showing the power of wording to shape our perception of choices. When subjects were presented with the option of treating lung cancer with surgery, 84% chose surgery when it was framed in terms of the odds of *living*, but 56% chose surgery when this option was worded in terms of the chances of *dying* (McNeil et al., 1982). Most subjects thought condoms were an effective method of preventing AIDS when they were told that condoms have a "95% success rate," but a majority did not view condoms as effective prevention when told that they had a "5% failure rate" (Linville et al., 1992). When business students and managers were told that a specific corporate strategy had a 70% chance of *success*, most favored the strategy. When it was framed as having a 30% chance of *failure*, however, the majority opposed it (Wolkomir & Wolkomir, 1990). In all instances, the two choices compared have identical outcomes, but they are perceived differently because of how the wording frames them.

Clearly, language significantly influences our perception and behavior. It is important to remain aware of the power of framing and its capacity to alter perception and change behavior (Clark, 1996).

Identity: Languages R Us

The principal language that one uses to communicate can also mark an individual's or group's educational level, socioeconomic class, and ethnic and cultural identity. When India won its independence from Great Britain in 1947, an attempt was made to unify the Indian population by imposing the Hindi language on the entire country, in which 200 languages were spoken. Riots ensued and many thousands were killed in years of conflict. A more benign language war has been waged in Canada. Quebec has passed numerous laws making French the principal language of this province, restricting the use of English. "Language police" enforce the laws.

America has not escaped the language wars. Following World War I, a wave of prejudice against immigrants produced laws in 35 states mandating English-only instruction in public schools (Crawford, 1996). Efforts continue even now to recognize English as the official language of the United States (Welch, 2008). For some, the English-only movement is a genuine attempt to unify an increasingly multicultural nation, but for others, it provides acceptable cover for ethnic prejudice.

The dominance of English on the Internet, especially in business, commerce, and academia, also raises concerns about ethnic and cultural identity. "Only a small share of Internet content is in some of the world's most commonly spoken languages, like Arabic or Hindi" (Swift, 2011, p. A23). As linguist John McWhorter observes, "English is dominant in a way that no language has ever been before" (quoted in Mydans, 2007) primarily because of the Internet. This dominance of English is an oft-stated concern worldwide.

The increasing globalization of business makes the choice of language to communicate within and among multicultural groups and organizations a significant issue. "Those who share a mother-tongue have a linguistic bond that differs from those who speak the same language as a second language" (Victor, 2007, p. 3). The choice of language to conduct business can directly affect teamwork and long-term business relationships for good or ill (Chen et al., 2006; Swift & Huang, 2004). Major advances in automatic machine translations to neutralize the dominance of English and permit even broader intercultural communication on the Internet have been made, but "it is extraordinarily complex to translate informal speech and text—laden with jargon, localized expressions, inconsistent grammar, and the 'ums' and 'aahs' that pepper everyday conversation—from one language to another" (Swift, 2011, p. A23).

Clearly, language is more than a mere neutral vehicle of information transmission (see Box 4-1). Language can help us improve the human condition by promoting tolerance and cooperation, or it can fan the embers of prejudice, ignite aggression, or fuel the flames of violence.

Competent Language Use: Problems and Solutions

The power of language makes it a vehicle for both positive and negative communication. In this section, I discuss several principal problems that occur when we use language ineffectively and inappropriately. I also explore competent language usage for each problem identified.

Signal Reactions: Responding, Not Thinking

A **signal reaction** is an automatic, emotional response to a symbol (Rothwell, 1982). In several experiments, participants reacted to "hot button" terms such as "affirmative action" and "death penalty" and names such as "Gore" and "Bush" in about a quarter of a second (Lodge & Taber, 2005). This is too swift to process information relevant to these terms. Strong emotional reactions to verbal obscenity, vulgar language, ethnic slurs, pledges, oaths, slogans, ritualized greetings, chants, and buzzwords in advertising and politics are other instances of signal reactions to words.

Source of Signal Reactions: Connotative Meaning

The source of most signal reactions is connotative meaning. **Connotation** is personal

BOX 4.1 Focus on Controversy

THE LANGUAGE OF TEXTING: G9

Texting has become a hugely popular form of communication worldwide. An estimated 7 trillion text messages are sent annually, and the quantity continues to increase ("More Than Seven Trillion Messages," 2010). Texting has produced a substantial controversy. Claims such as texting is destroying language, destroying students' literacy, and "fogs your brain like cannabis" are common. David Crystal (2008), an internationally recognized linguist, in his book *Txtng: The gr8 db8*, comments that "It is the extraordinary antipathy to texting which has surprised me. I don't think I have ever come across a topic which has attracted more adult antagonism" (p. xiii). He goes on to note, "All the popular beliefs about texting are wrong, or at least debatable" (p. 9).

Texting is not a new language or slang. "Texting is just another variety of language, which has arisen as a result of a particular technology" (p. 164). Texting language follows grammatical rules for Standard English. Claims that teens accustomed to frequent texting slip into using texting abbreviations when writing essays for composition classes are highly suspect (Crystal, 2008). Linguist Naomi Baron (2008) discovered from her research on college students that "abbreviations were rare, contractions were less common than expected, and that when it came to emoticons, students seemed to have a stunted vocabulary." She continued by noting that students usually realize the difference between writing essays and texting and typically respond appropriately except for an occasion slip-up. The assertion that teens are becoming illiterate as a result of texting addiction is also highly dubious. A series of studies actually showed the opposite. There proved to be a strong positive relationship between use of text language and success in usage of Standard English (Plester et al., 2008). Students "could not be good at texting if they had not already developed considerable literacy awareness" (Crystal, 2008, p. 162). As Crystal concludes, "Texting is one of the most innovative linguistic phenomena of modern times, and perhaps that is why it has generated such strong emotions . . . Yet all the evidence suggests that belief in an impending linguistic disaster is a consequence of a mythology largely created by the media" (p. 173). In a word, it's g9 (genius).

QUESTIONS FOR THOUGHT

1. Is texting ever an appropriate communication medium in a college classroom?
2. Although texting itself is not merely slang, can there be slang in texting?
3. Are there any ideas or concepts that cannot be communicated in texting abbreviations?

meaning. It is the volatile, individual, subjective meaning of a word. Connotations have three dimensions (Osgood, 1969): *evaluation* (e.g., good/bad), *potency* (e.g., strong/weak), and *activity* (e.g., active/passive). Connotation changes from individual to individual, sometimes in barely perceptible shades of difference and sometimes in spectacular ways (see Box 4-2). Connotative meaning is different from denotative meaning. **Denotation** is shared meaning. It is the objective meaning of words commonly agreed to by members of a speech community and usually found in a dictionary (although some words are left out of dictionaries, all have denotative meaning). The denotation of Rottweiler, for example, is "a large breed of dog characterized by a short tail and short, black hair with tan markings." Connotations for Rottweiler, depending on your experience with such a dog, might vary from "cute" to "vicious" (evaluative), "powerful" to "indifferent" (potency), and "perpetual motion" to "sleepy" (activity).

Signal reactions to connotative meaning can launch individuals from their recliners and spring them into action with little thought about the consequences. Signal reactions can provoke offense, aggression, and violence. The U.S. Supreme Court recognized this decades ago in its precedent-setting decision *Chaplinsky v. New Hampshire*, which ruled that "fighting words" are not protected speech. More recently, "speech codes" banning "hate speech"—derogatory references to "race, sex, sexual orientation, or disability"—have emerged on college campuses, leading to court challenges and national debate over free speech. The hate speech issue reached prominence especially in April 2007 when shock jock Don Imus lost his talk radio show after referring to the Rutgers University women's basketball team as "nappy-headed hos." (He was back on the radio, however, in 2008.)

Competence and Signal Reactions: Developing Semantic Reactions

Here are two suggestions for avoiding problems of signal reactions and making your language usage appropriate and effective:

1. *Learn to follow signal reactions with semantic reactions.* A **semantic reaction** is a delayed, thoughtful response that seeks to decipher the user's intended meaning of a word, thus short-circuiting a behavioral response to the hair-trigger emotional

BOX 4.2 Developing Communication Competence

MEASURING CONNOTATIVE MEANING

Osgood (1969) originated the semantic differential to measure the varying connotative meaning between individuals. Individuals can be compared by asking each to respond to a word by assigning a number from 1 to 7 on a series of bipolar scales. For example,

RAPPER:

Good	1	2	3	4	5	6	7	Bad
Hot	1	2	3	4	5	6	7	Cold
Active	1	2	3	4	5	6	7	Passive
Strong	1	2	3	4	5	6	7	Weak
Pleasant	1	2	3	4	5	6	7	Unpleasant

Try it yourself. Complete the semantic differentials for the word *rapper*. Have a friend and a parent do likewise without them seeing your responses in advance. Now compare the results. Do you see any differences? You can do the same for any word (try *textbook* or *tweeting*).

reaction. A helpful way to delay your behavioral response until meaning has been confirmed is to ask the question "What do you mean?" or "Why are you saying that?" If someone calls you a "racist," you can instantly react with verbal abuse or physical violence, or you can delay such behavioral responses by asking, "What do you mean by racist?" or "Why do you think I'm racist?" This encourages a thoughtful response to your questions. The initial response would occur too swiftly (a quarter of a second) to short-circuit the *emotional* response, but that does not prevent training yourself to delay your *behavioral* response (acting on your emotional response) until meaning has been clarified.

2. *Refrain from using words that will likely trigger signal reactions.* Verbal obscenity or fighting words may cause no signal reaction within certain groups, but they will likely trigger signal reactions in many contexts (see Box 4-3). Consequently, it is advisable to adapt your language use to the context, avoiding words that will likely provoke aggression and violence with certain individuals and groups.

Provoking a signal reaction isn't always undesirable. Shouting "Look out!" when someone is about to step on a slippery patch of oil on the street, for example, should elicit an immediate response; otherwise, that person is liable to take a bite out of the asphalt. Nevertheless, there are relatively few instances when careful thought is not superior to immediate behavioral reactions. Speakers should be mindful not to provoke unnecessary signal reactions, and listeners should resist being baited into acting on signal reactions.

Language of Abuse and Exclusion

John Gottman's research with more than 2,000 couples persuasively shows that the language of contempt, criticism, and defensiveness has a corrosive effect on personal relationships (Gottman & Silver, 1994). Extensive research by James Lynch (2000)

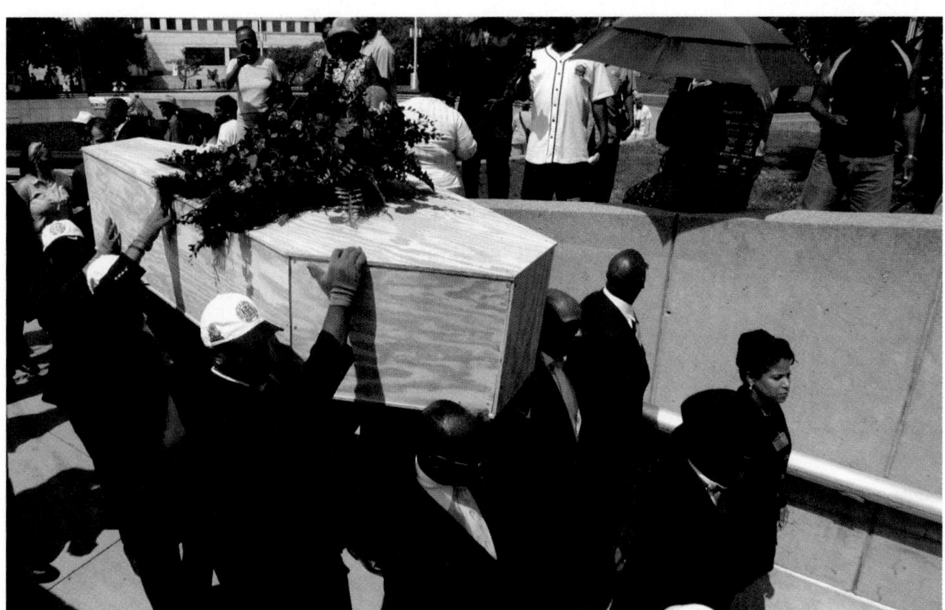

The NAACP burying "the N word." This photo illustrates which of the following?

1. Some words are inherently, naturally offensive
2. The source of signal reactions to "the N word" is its denotative meaning
3. Language can powerfully influence perceptions and behavior
4. "The N word" can never be used inoffensively no matter the context

Answers at end of chapter

BOX 4.3 Focus on Controversy

VERBAL TABOOS: A QUESTION OF APPROPRIATENESS

One of my friends, whose daughter was four years old at the time, told this story. His daughter's name was Janie, and while playing with a boy in the neighborhood about her same age, she became very angry by something the boy did to her. Janie turned to the little boy and yelled, "I'm going to shit on your head." Janie's mom heard this outburst and sternly admonished her daughter, "Janie, we don't talk like that." Janie paused, then turned to the boy and said, "I'm going to shit on your arm."

Janie's mom clearly had a signal reaction to Janie's use of an offensive word. Denotative meaning doesn't appear to be the real problem, however. The objectionable word was used for centuries in England without causing offense before becoming taboo in the early part of the 19th century (Bryson, 1990). Do you think Janie's mother would have been so alarmed and stern if Janie had said, "I'm going to toidee on your head" instead? If denotative meaning is producing the signal reaction, why can a doctor ask you for a *feces* or *stool* sample without inviting reproach (even though mild embarrassment might accompany the request)? The denotation of all three terms for excrement is identical, yet the connotative meaning is not. It is the word itself that offends quite apart from its denotative meaning. A signal reaction to "obscene words" is a learned behavior. Janie didn't seem to realize that she had uttered a "bad word." She apparently thought that the location of the threatened act was the problem (the head would indeed be a more objectionable target than the arm).

When we consider English words from Great Britain that incite similar signal reactions, it is even more apparent that denotation is not the source of the response. In England, *bloody* is a swear word as objectionable as Janie's offending term (Pinker, 2007). *Bloody* has no potency for Americans; it sparks no strong negative evaluation. We don't have the cultural associations that condition us to react negatively.

We denounce the use of "obscene and profane words" even though their denunciation may make little logical sense (Pinker, 2007). *Virgin, slut, tart, sex, virtuous*, and *bum* were all banned from U.S. newspapers and motion pictures until the second half of the 20th century. The prohibition on taboo words has relaxed in recent years, but despite the widespread and frequent use of taboo words among adults and especially college students (Jay, 1992), some strictures still remain. George W. Bush caused a stir when caught on an open microphone at the 2006 Group of 8 Summit in Russia using little Janie's expletive while conversing with Britain's Prime Minister Tony Blair. At the 2003 Golden Globe Awards, U2's lead singer Bono joyfully blurted an obscenity when receiving his award, and *Simple Life* star Nicole Richie used two obscenities later in the same program. Viewers were outraged and complained to the Federal Communications Commission. Ironically, a bill banning the broadcasting of any obscenities and increasing fines for violations to a hefty $325,000 was signed into law by President Bush in June 2006. Woody Allen once noted his response to someone who angered him, "I told him to be fruitful and multiply, but not in those words." Apparently, the FCC, Congress, and the president want those appearing on the mass media to avoid using "those words." More recently, when Barack Obama was told he had to relinquish his Blackberry for security reasons, his response was "WTF!" United States Senator Carl Levin publicly used Janie's expletive repeatedly when referring to a deal with Goldman Sachs that he disliked (D'Souza, 2010).

Despite the questionable logic of banning a small list of words whose denotative meaning is identical to nonobjectionable words, we know that taboo words can provoke negative respons-

(continued)

BOX 4.3 *(Continued)*

es. An August 1999 Gallup poll found that 24% of respondents thought frequent use of profane and obscene language in movies was extremely offensive, and another 52% thought it was somewhat offensive ("Movie Content," 1999). A Gallup survey of teens found that 75% agreed that "foul language" should be restricted in written assignments for a class (Ray, 2005). Taboo words can also incite aggression and violence, as many historical examples attest (Rothwell, 1982). The "police riot" that occurred at the Democratic National Convention in Chicago in 1968 was attributed largely to the provocation by demonstrators who shouted obscenities at the police.

Individuals, however, respond to taboo words in various ways. Some people find even relatively mild epithets completely objectionable—fighting words. Others are not bothered in the least even by the most outrageous obscenities. A poll conducted by the Shorenstein Center at Harvard's Kennedy School of Government found that only 18% of those who were aware of George W. Bush's use of the vulgar expletive "asshole" during the 2004 presidential campaign reported that it had affected their opinion of the candidate, and 7% said that it had *improved* their estimation of him. A 2011 Associated Press-MTV poll of 1,355 respondents ages 14-24 reported that half feel free to use racial epithets and offensive slang terms when texting on their cell phones or posting to sites such as Facebook. Most respondents perceived the slurs to be funny not hurtful (Cass & Agiesta, 2011). Again, this underlines the connotative, personal meaning of taboo words. More recently, a study showed that swearing in formal settings (e.g., in courtrooms and formal meetings at work) is typically unexpected and therefore highly objectionable. Those who violate the expectation of appropriate language use in formal situations are considered incompetent communicators. Even less formal social gatherings at work in which the expectation is that offensive language usage is inappropriate invites the conclusion that the speaker is incompetent when using taboo language (Johnson & Lewis, 2010). If the expectation is that coarse and vulgar language is permissible, even encouraged, in some situations (taverns, auto repair shops), the reaction to it obviously would be quite different. The appropriateness or inappropriateness of verbal obscenity is dependent on context (Jay, 2009).

QUESTIONS FOR THOUGHT

1. Is it ever appropriate to use obscene language? Should children be forbidden to use obscene and profane language? Why?
2. Are there ethical reasons to ban certain words? Which words would you ban, if any? Why?
3. Does the who, what, where, when, why, and how of communication contexts (see Chapter 1) influence our perception of verbal obscenity? Explain.

reveals that repeated exposure to "poisoned language" leads "inexorably to an increased sense of loneliness and social alienation, and ultimately to disease and premature death" (p. 6).

Abusive language has severe consequences for targets of hurtful words. One study found that verbal abuse is comparable to "witnessing domestic violence or nonfamilial sexual abuse" (Teicher et al., 2006). Verbal abuse from peers is also equivalent to parental verbal abuse in producing anxiety, depression, hostility, and drug use (Teicher et al., 2010). Peer abuse has the added dimension of often appearing on the Internet, so "these very public insults and virtual assaults can 'go viral,' taking on lives of their own and persisting long after they would have otherwise lost their immediacy" (Putnam, 2010).

Verbal abuse of nurses by doctors has become a serious national problem only recently recognized. The 2009 survey of 2,100 doctors and nurses by the American College of Physician Executives found that 85% of respondents experienced degrading comments and insults, 73% yelling, and 50% cursing (Johnson, 2009). In one instance, a doctor said to a nurse, "You don't look dumber than my dog. Why can't you at least fetch what I need?" In another case, a surgeon shouted that "monkeys could be trained to do what scrub nurses do" (Johnson, 2009). Verbal abuse by doctors has consequences. The more that abuse is showered on nurses, the more likely they are to quit their jobs (Grenny, 2009). Aside from the negative effects on nurses, patient care is also at risk. A study called "Silence Kills," conducted by VitalSmarts and the American Association of Critical-Care Nurses, showed that more than 20% of health-care professionals have witnessed harm to patients because of disrespectful and abusive communication mostly by doctors toward nurses (Maxfield et al., 2005). Hospitals across the country, as a result of these survey findings, are instituting zero tolerance policies to end such verbal abuse.

Language can also lead to feelings of social exclusion. "We all feel the pain of ostracism about equally, no matter how tough or sensitive we are" (Williams, 2011, p. 32). Sometimes we feel ostracized at work when coworkers speak Spanish when we speak only English, or vice versa. This social exclusion elicits a variety of negative outcomes, including hurt feelings, lowered self-esteem, and aggressive communication (Hitlan et al., 2006). This is life for many Latino baseball players who have joined major league teams (Almond & Gervas, 2003). Initially, most struggle with English, and many admit that it is the biggest obstacle in their career advancement. They often feel others perceive them as dumb when their initial attempts to speak English go awry. Willie Montanez spoke little English when he came from Puerto Rico to play for the San Francisco Giants. He was advised to answer "yes" to any question so he wouldn't appear perplexed. On the first morning of training camp, a Giants' coach asked him if he had eaten. "Yes," he answered. The coach had breakfast at a coffee shop without him. The next morning, determined to be included for breakfast, he changed his strategy. When the coach asked him, "Do you want any breakfast?" Montanez replied, "No." He missed breakfast a second time.

Learning the language of connection and inclusion can be an effective antidote to poisonous language and ostracism, as I discuss extensively in Chapter 8. The short version is to avoid abusive language. Treat people with respect as you would want them to treat you (remember ethical communication discussed in Chapter 1). Be sensitive to the feelings of exclusion that others may experience (pick up the signals) when the standard language spoken in groups and in the workplace is not a person's native language.

False Dichotomies: The Inaccuracy of Either-Or Framing

Advice columnist Ann Landers once raised a fuss when she coyly asked her female readers to answer the question: "Would you be content to be held close and treated tenderly and forget about 'the act'?" Landers was swamped with more than 90,000 responses. A stunning 72% of these respondents said they would prefer hugs to sexual intercourse. The talk show circuit went crazy. Experts, self-appointed and otherwise, all wanted to comment on the results. Typically, Landers' survey results were interpreted as proof that men are jerks. Women are starved for affection from their insensitive lovers, so went the "analysis," and they are willing to forego sexual consummation for tender caresses from their partners.

If you recognized that Landers asked a question that presented two choices as mutually exclusive alternatives (sex or hugs), when a third choice exists, congratulations;

you recognized a false dichotomy. A **false dichotomy** is using either-or language to frame a choice as though only two opposing possibilities exist, when at least a third option is clearly available. Do you think the "men are jerks" debate would have been stimulated by an Ann Landers survey that offered a third choice? How many women do you think would have answered "hugs only" if offered "both hugs and sexual intercourse" as a third choice?

If a thousand people were randomly chosen and plotted on a graph according to height, weight, or age, most of these individuals would bunch in the middle (average height, weight, etc.), and only a few would fit the extremes (very tall or extremely short). This result is called a bell-shaped curve, or normal distribution. A dichotomy (*either* this *or* that) becomes false when our thinking and perception are focused on the extremes of the distribution while we ignore the vast middle.

Most people can't be accurately described as short or tall, fat or thin, smart or dumb, young or old, strong or weak. We fall somewhere in between. Consider, for example, Tiger Woods. He has been dubbed the greatest *black* golfer in history and thus an African American. Did you know that his heritage is a combination of Caucasian (white), African American (black), American Indian, and Asian in almost equal proportions (White, 1997)? As a young boy, Woods concocted the term *Cablinasian* to describe his mixed heritage. It would seem that the answer to the question "Is Tiger Woods black or white?" should be "Both and neither." Similarly, Barack Obama is half black and half white—both and neither. Even the issue of sexual orientation typically gets framed as "gay or straight," but psychologist Robert Epstein (2006) notes that it "lies on a continuum" from "exclusive same-sex attraction" to "mainly same-sex attraction" to "mainly opposite-sex attraction" to "exclusive opposite-sex attraction. . . . It is not an all-or-nothing state" (p. 56).

False dichotomies can have a significant impact on how we think and act. Earlier, I cited several studies that showed the power of framing on the choices people make. Huspek (2000) studied the 1980 riot at the Penitentiary of New Mexico that resulted in 407 serious injuries and 33 deaths. He concludes that *oppositional codes* "provided their respective users with diametrically opposed views of the world and ways of acting upon it" (p. 144). A "model prisoner" to the penitentiary's administration was a "punk" to inmates; a "trouble maker" to prison officials was a "bad ass" to prisoners; a "cooperative informant" to officials was a "snitch" to inmates; a "psychopathic personality" to officials was a "gladiator" to prisoners. Given the intractable oppositional codes (false dichotomies) prevalent in the prison, the riot was probably "inevitable." As the riot erupted, these oppositional codes provided agents representing the two sides "with increasingly few meanings that might have been used effectively to derail the ever-escalating locomotion of violence" (p. 157).

"Next question: I believe that life is a constant striving for balance, requiring frequent tradeoffs between morality and necessity, within a cyclic pattern of joy and sadness, forging a trail of bittersweet memories until one slips, inevitably, into the jaws of death. Agree or disagree?"

In some instances, a dichotomy is not false because there are only two opposing choices possible. Being "sort of pregnant," "almost a virgin," or "slightly dead" isn't a realistic third option. Most dichotomous framing, however, inappropriately implies that the only possibilities are the two extreme choices, when clearly this is not accurate.

There are two steps you can take to avoid false dichotomies:

1. *Think pluralistically*. When presented with a dichotomous choice, search for additional options. Ask the questions, "Are these our only two choices? Can't we think of other options?" These questions reframe our thinking from dichotomous (considering only two contradictory choices) to pluralistic (expanding the choices).

2. *Recognize degrees of difference when using language*. Although it is true that some individuals are fat (obese) or skinny (anorexic), it is inaccurate to describe most people with such extreme language. To be appropriate and effective, your language should attempt to approximate reality, but false dichotomies allow for only gross approximations. Strive to use language more precisely. This means using terms such as *slightly, moderately, occasionally, rarely, sometimes, often*, and *usually*. This is not the language of the wishy-washy fence straddler but the language of precision.

Mislabeling: Inaccurate Descriptions

The power of labels can also produce significant problems. Langer and Abelson (1974) showed therapists a videotape of an ordinary-looking man being interviewed. Half of the therapists were told in advance that the man was a "job applicant" and half were told he was a "psychiatric patient." Those therapists who thought they were watching a job interview described the man using terms such as *ingenious, open, straightforward, ordinary, candid*, and *upstanding*. Those therapists who thought they were observing a psychiatric patient described the man as *rigid, dependent, passive aggressive, impulsive*, and "frightened of his own aggressive impulses." Both groups of therapists saw exactly the same videotaped interview, but each group perceived a different reality. Labels can have a powerful biasing effect.

Bias and Stigma: Distorting Perceptions

Labels can stigmatize and diminish people. Label a child *smart* and you may boost the child's self-esteem, but label a child *slow* and the child's self-esteem may suffer. Teachers sometimes treat students differently when either a desirable or undesirable label has been attached (Oakes, 1985; Rosenthal & Jacobson, 1968). Research shows that people with highly unusual first names, such as Oder and Lethal, are more likely to be labeled psychotic than individuals with more common first names (Branan, 2007). The Reuters news agency reported that Germans with unflattering surnames such as Dumm (stupid), Schwein (pig), Kotz (vomit), and Dreckman (filth man) admitted having problems as children because of their easily ridiculed names. Imagine a Dumm, Schwein, Kotz, and Dreckman law firm ("Go see stupid, pig, vomit, and filth man for legal advice"). Would you be inclined to retain their legal services? Picture introducing Mr. Pig (Schwein) to Ms. Vomit (Kotz). Now there's an awkward social moment.

The power of labels is particularly evident when mislabeling occurs. For example, eight individuals, none with any real psychiatric problems, gained admission to 12 psychiatric hospitals (some did it twice). This was the initial stage of a controversial study conducted by David Rosenhan (1973). These eight "pseudopatients" gained admittance under slightly false pretenses. They were instructed to complain to the admissions staff at each hospital that they heard voices that said "empty," "hollow," and "thud." Once admitted, none of the pseudopatients was to complain of these symptoms again. Eleven of the pseudopatients were diagnosed (mislabeled) as *schizophrenic*, and one was said to have *manic-depressive psychosis* (bipolar disorder). The pseudopatients had to remain in the hospital until the staff recognized the mistaken diagnosis or until they were simply freed. The stays in the hospital ranged from

7 to 52 days, and the average was 19 days. Ironically, 35 of the 118 actual patients in the hospital recognized the ruse of the pseudopatients and said so openly, but none of the staff ever questioned the initial diagnosis. Even when the pseudopatients were released, hospital records showed that their "psychiatric disorder" was merely "in remission," not cured or a mistaken diagnosis. Rosenhan replicated these disturbing findings in later studies (see Greenberg, 1981).

Psychiatric labels can stigmatize. They are particularly troublesome when misapplied. The stigma attached to these labels can linger even after full recovery from a real mental disorder. Individuals so labeled often become social lepers. Mislabeling mentally healthy individuals has the potential to ruin their lives. No one wants to be mislabeled, especially if the labels can stigmatize. Imagine how traumatic it would be if you were mislabeled as a child abuser, spouse abuser, rapist, or murderer.

The problem of mislabeling can be profoundly abusive. Renowned speech pathologist Wendell Johnson, in one study, purposely mislabeled children as "stutterers" who previously exhibited no such speech problem. This mislabeling actually induced lifelong stuttering with ruinous consequences. The study was kept secret for 60 years and only discovered by an enterprising investigative reporter for the *San Jose Mercury News* (Dyer, 2001). Even though Johnson's purpose was laudable—to determine the cause of stuttering—the study was subsequently labeled the "Monster Study" and correctly blasted as unethical.

Competence and Mislabeling: Operational Definitions

So how do you prevent the problem of mislabeling? Consider two steps:

1. *Operationally define significant labels.* An **operational definition** grounds a label by specifying which measurable behaviors or experiences are subsumed under the label and which are ruled out. When you ask someone to "be specific" or to "provide an example," you are asking them to operationalize their language. Operational definitions say, "For our purposes, an *'A' student* is anyone who scores 90% or above in the class." The Harvard School of Public Health operationally defines "binge drinking," a problem that afflicts almost half of the college students in the United States, as "consuming five or more drinks at one sitting for men, and four or more drinks for women" (Kalb & McCormick, 1998). Operational definitions clarify the meaning of labels to avoid misunderstanding and misapplication.

Operational definitions may produce some surprises. A study of Virginia mental health and legal professionals revealed that the "child abuse" label could be loosely applied. Twenty percent of those sampled believed frequent hugging of a 10-year-old constitutes child abuse and justifies intervention by state authorities. More than half defined "sexual abuse" as including a parent giving a child a brief good-night kiss on the lips (Okami, 1992). Remember, word usage is conventional. Thus, *the accuracy of any label depends on common agreement.* We should not be labeling someone a child abuser if we have no common agreement on which behaviors constitute child abuse.

2. *Apply the labels accurately once they have been operationalized.* Don't apply a label more broadly than the operational definition allows. Labeling older people *senile* simply because they have minor memory problems is inaccurate and inappropriate.

Dead-Level Abstracting: Ineffective Sense Making

Wendell Johnson (1946) coined the term **dead-level abstracting**, which refers to the practice of remaining stuck at one level of abstraction. As explained earlier, words operate at different levels of abstraction, from very vague to concrete or precise. Note the progression from high-level (vague) to low-level (concrete/precise) abstraction in the following statements:

George likes *sports*.
George likes *team sports*.
George likes *contact team sports*.
George likes *ice hockey and football*.

The first statement is fairly vague. The term *sports* includes many different kinds of sports. The second statement is more precise because it specifies "team" sports, but there are still many team sports from which to choose. The third statement is even more precise because "contact" team sports is specified. Nevertheless, there are still many contact team sports. Finally, the last statement is the most precise and concrete because the particular team sports are indicated.

Dead-Leveling: Rigid Use of Vague or Concrete Words

Dead-level abstraction occurs when we stick rigidly either to vague or to concrete words, thus making little sense. When politicians give speeches using vague, undefined terms such as *family values* or *patriotism*, voters can be forgiven for not knowing precisely what is meant. When they propose "comprehensive medical care for all," it's fair to ask, "What does that mean?" If they respond, "Really great coverage for everyone," you have dead-level abstracting. The response is as vague as the original statement. Research by Paivio (1969) found that the degree of concreteness or vagueness of words could be the most important determinant of how easy or difficult it is to form mental images. Forming a clear image of a *horse, clown,* or *baseball* is easy. Forming a clear image of *truth, justice,* and the *American way* is difficult (although it may produce signal reactions). Concrete words produce concrete images; vague words can remain imprecise in our minds.

The solution to the problem of dead-level abstracting, however, does not lie in always speaking in concrete terminology. *Never rising above the level of the concrete and precise is also dead-level abstracting.* A neighbor who insists on telling you every insignificant detail of his or her recent trip abroad easily produces tedium and a desire to flee. The conversation is so concrete that you may want to bang your head on concrete. Where's the significance of all this detail? A professor who tells many jokes and stories may keep interest for a while, but eventually, students will ask the question,

This photo illustrates which of the following?
1. Mislabeling
2. Words can be too concrete to be useful
3. Operational definitions
4. Dead-level abstracting
Answers at end of chapter

"What does this have to do with the class?" The details need to be tied to a higher-level abstraction. All the jokes and stories need to be connected to concepts, principles, and generalizations. Otherwise, the professor is teaching trivia—unconnected factoids. Connecting the jokes and stories to the concepts and generalizations can produce learning.

Communication Competence and Dead-Level Abstracting: Three Ways

To make your language use more effective, consider three suggestions for avoiding dead-level abstraction.

1. *Avoid by-passing.* When you assume that everyone assigns the same meaning to a word, without checking to see if it is true, it is called **by-passing**. Vague, undefined words easily produce by-passing and consequent misunderstanding. For example, a December 22, 2004, Harris poll of 1,833 U.S. adults asked, "How important were moral values to you in deciding which candidate (Bush or Kerry) to vote for?" Almost half (45%) answered "very important," and an additional 35% responded "somewhat important." Yet when asked, "What do you mean by moral values?" 25% of Bush voters included "marriage protection/marriage defined as between a man and a woman," but only 1% of Kerry voters did likewise. In addition, 22% of Bush voters included "pro-life/against abortion," but only 3% of Kerry voters agreed. Conversely, 12% of Kerry voters included "caring/respect/compassion for others," but only 3% of Bush voters did. Finally, 15% of Kerry voters included "peace in Middle East," but only 1% of Bush voters agreed. We generally agree that moral values are important, but we don't agree on a definition. If you by-pass such a definition, letting individuals remain in the fuzzy clouds of abstraction, there will be a lot of head-nodding affirmations among these individuals who are not aware that they sharply disagree.

2. *Operationally define abstract terms.* When a couple seeks help from a therapist, the therapist will likely request operational definitions frequently. If the husband says, "My wife and I are having a problem," the therapist undoubtedly will ask, "What specific problem are you experiencing?" If the husband then responds, "We argue all the time," the therapist will pursue this abstraction by requesting, "What do you argue about?" "We argue about money," might be the response, whereupon the therapist might continue to ground the husband's language by further requesting, "Can you give me an example of a recent argument you had about money?" Each time, the therapist attempts to move the language from vague and abstract to precise and concrete. Thus, the husband moves from *problem* to *argument* to *argument about money* to a *specific behavioral example* of an argument about money.

3. *Use language flexibly.* Do not get stuck using either concrete or vague terms alone. Use both fluidly. When others get stuck at one level of abstraction, help them get traction and become unstuck by asking for examples or clearly identifiable behaviors that might clarify vague terms. If others remain frozen at the level of excessive concrete detail, ask them to clarify the significance or relevance of the detail.

Inferential Errors: Ineffective Guessing

There's a story of two women from the United States (a grandmother and her granddaughter), a Romanian officer, and a Nazi officer seated together in a train compartment. As the train passes through a dark tunnel, the sounds of a loud kiss and a slap are audible. When the train emerges from the tunnel, no words are spoken but a noticeable welt forming on the face of the Nazi officer is observed by all. The grandmother muses to herself, "What a fine granddaughter I have raised. I have no need to worry. She can handle herself admirably." The granddaughter thinks to herself, "Grandmother packs a powerful wallop for a woman of her years. She sure is spunky." The Nazi officer, none too pleased by the course of events, ruminates to himself, "How clever is this Romanian. He steals a kiss and gets me slapped in the process." The Romanian chuckles to himself, "I am indeed clever. I kissed my hand and slapped a Nazi."

This story illustrates **inferential error**—a mistaken conclusion that results from the assumption that inferences are factual descriptions of reality instead of interpretations of varying accuracy made by individuals (see Box 4-4). The facts reported are that the four characters in the story heard what sounded like a kiss followed by a slap. The Nazi officer had a welt on his face. Any conclusions drawn from these facts is an inference (a conclusion about the unknown based on the known). It was completely dark in the tunnel, and inferences were made that the sounds heard were that of a kiss and a slap. These are reliable inferences because we've all heard the sounds of a kiss and a slap many times. The visible welt on the face of the Nazi officer is further evidence of the reliability of the slap inference. Each person made an inferential error, however, because each leaped to a conclusion regarding who kissed and slapped whom based on superficial information. Only the Romanian knows the truth.

The Bush administration, based on faulty intelligence, inferred that Saddam Hussein possessed weapons of mass destruction. The inference turned out to be incorrect, but the United States went to war with Iraq using WMD as a prime justification (Daniel, 2008). The unfortunate practice of some law enforcement agencies in the United States of disproportionately stopping African American male drivers for drug possession or drug dealing based solely on race and a few additional details such as type of dress, automobile, and so forth (called "racial profiling") produces many more inferential errors than valid inferences (Lamberth, 1998). This is because the information upon which the inference is based is extremely limited and often of poor quality. Elmo Randolph, a New Jersey dentist, was stopped more than 100 times during a four-year period while driving his BMW from his home to his office. Dr. Randolph, guilty only of "driving while black," finally sold his automobile.

There are two ways to avoid inferential errors:

1. *Base inferences on a substantial quantity of information.* Limited information can lead to inaccurate inferences in the form of such practices as gossip and rumors.

2. *Base inferences on high-quality information.* Weak evidence produces weak inferences. You don't have to check every inference you make, but you should check important ones, especially if the quantity and quality of information on which the inference is based are limited or questionable.

Jargon, Euphemisms, and Slang: Promoting Misunderstanding

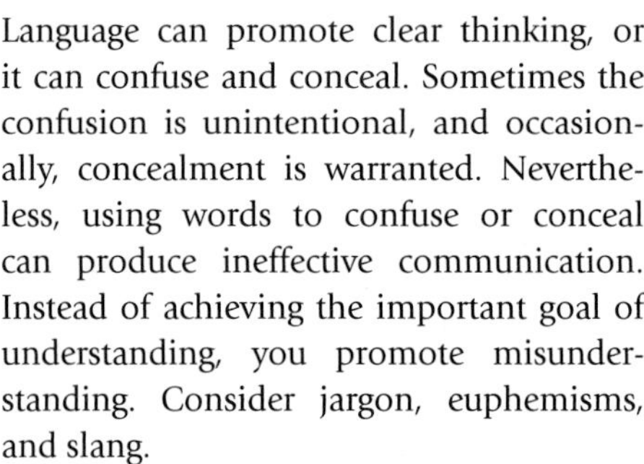

Language can promote clear thinking, or it can confuse and conceal. Sometimes the confusion is unintentional, and occasionally, concealment is warranted. Nevertheless, using words to confuse or conceal can produce ineffective communication. Instead of achieving the important goal of understanding, you promote misunderstanding. Consider jargon, euphemisms, and slang.

Jargon: Verbal Shorthand

Every profession, trade, or group has its specialized language called **jargon**. *Jargon is not inherently a poor use of language.* One study (Bross et al., 1972) found that medical jargon allowed surgeons to communicate important factual information briefly and clearly. Jargon is a kind of verbal shorthand. When lawyers use terms such as *prima facie case* and *habeas corpus*, they communicate to other attorneys and officers of the court very specific information without tedious, verbose explanation. "To the initiated, jargon is efficient, economical, and even crucial in that it can capture distinctions not made in the ordinary language" (Allan & Burridge, 1991, p. 201). *Signal reactions, false dichotomies, dead-level abstracting,* and *inferential error* are apt examples from this chapter.

Jargon, however, can pose problems for those who do not understand the verbal shorthand. When doctors use terms such as *bilateral periorbital hematoma* (black eye), *tinnitus* (ear ringing), *agrypnia* (sleeplessness), *cephalalgia* (headache), and *hyperemesis* (excessive vomiting), they communicate very specific conditions to medical staff, but they more than likely mystify patients and

BOX 4.4 Developing Communication Competence

THE UNCRITICAL INFERENCE TEST

Read the following story. For each statement about the story, choose **T** if it can be determined from the information provided in the story that the statement is true, **F** if the statement directly contradicts information provided in the story, or **?** if you cannot determine from the information provided whether the statement is either true or false. *Read the story only once* and *don't check the story while answering the statements that follow.*

THE STORY: Pat Doyle was sitting behind the receptionist's desk typing rapidly on a computer. The executive director of the Atlantic Sports Equipment Company walked briskly by the receptionist and hurried into the office, grunting a hasty "Good Morning" to Pat. A man with a briefcase, which had "Wilson's Sporting Goods" engraved on it, was leafing through a copy of *Wired* magazine while waiting in a chair. A few moments later, the director came out, made a beckoning motion, and said, "Hi, Jim! How's the sales racket?"

1. Pat, the executive director's receptionist, was typing rapidly on a computer.
   T F ?
2. Pat was sitting behind a desk while she typed rapidly.
   T F ?
3. Pat's boss walked briskly by the receptionist's desk.
   T F ?
4. Pat was sitting behind the desk when the executive director walked by and said, "Good Morning."
   T F ?
5. The executive director hurried into his office.
   T F ?
6. A man with a briefcase was sitting in a chair.
   T F ?
7. A man was reading a copy of *Wired* magazine.
   T F ?
8. The man worked for Wilson's Sporting Goods.
   T F ?
9. The man was waiting to see the executive director.
   T F ?
10. The story involves only three people: a receptionist, the executive director of the company, and a salesman.
    T F ?

Haney (1967) originally devised the "Uncritical Inference Test." This is a different version. The correct answer for ALL of these statements is **?**. Without exception, every statement is based on guesses (inferences) regarding what is likely but not verifiably true from the information provided. The reasons are as follows:

1. It can't be determined that Pat is the executive director's receptionist. Pat is merely sitting behind the receptionist's desk.
2. Is Pat a *she*? It can't be determined.

(continued)

BOX 4.4 *(Continued)*

3. We don't know whether the executive director is Pat's boss.
4. Pat may not have been sitting behind the desk *when* the executive director walked by. Pat may have stood up (sign of respect?).
5. Is the executive director male ("his" office)? It can't be determined.
6. The man was "waiting" in a chair. May not have been sitting (ever see kids in a doctor's office?).
7. The man was "leafing through" *Wired* magazine. That may include some reading or not.
8. An engraved briefcase doesn't automatically mean that the man worked for Wilson's Sporting Goods any more than a "Harvard University" sweatshirt means that you actually attend that institution.
9. We don't know whom the man was waiting to see.
10. There is Pat, "a receptionist" who may or may not be Pat, an executive director, a man waiting in a chair, and someone named "Jim" who may or may not be the man in the chair. We don't know how many people there are.

NOTE: All statements are inferences, but some are better inferences than others. The man was very likely sitting in the chair because that is what most adults would do. That's a reliable inference. The executive director referred to as male, however, decades ago might have been a fairly reliable inference because most executive directors were male, but today, that is assuredly not the case. It's an unreliable inference.

turn common conditions into dangerous diseases in the minds of the linguistically uninitiated (Wagner, 2011). The message is concealed when it should be revealed to those who most need to know.

Edspeak, the sometimes bewildering jargon of educators (Ravitch, 2007), can intimidate parents who may hesitate revealing their unfamiliarity with the jargon. Parents can be forgiven if they are flummoxed by jargon used to "explain" their child's strengths and shortcomings: *phonemic sequencing errors, phonological process delays, normed modality processing, morphosyntactic skills, word-attack skills, psychometrics, deficit model,* and *additive model,* to name just a few. To most parents, this bushel basket of buzzwords probably sounds closer to Klingon than any language they speak. Parents become the "outsiders," disconnected from teachers and administrators who "speak the language." There are two guidelines for the competent use of jargon:

1. Cut the use of jargon when conversing with someone unfamiliar with the jargon.

2. If jargon is necessary, operationalize terms unfamiliar to the receiver. Some school districts offer free jargon handbooks to parents.

Euphemisms: Linguistic Novocain

Businesses and corporations don't lay off workers anymore; they engage in "force management programs" and "duplication reduction," or they give employees a "career-change opportunity." These are euphemisms. *Euphemism* is derived from the Greek *euphemismos*, meaning "to speak well of." It substitutes "kinder, gentler" terms for words that hurt, cause offense, or create problems for us. **Euphemism** is a form of linguistic Novocain whereby word choices numb us to or camouflage unpleasant or offensive realities.

Not all euphemisms are inappropriate. Using *passed away* instead of *dead* is unlikely to cause harm to anyone, and it may cushion an ugly reality for grieving relatives and friends. Nevertheless, euphemisms can create mischief. When the nuclear power industry refers to out-of-control nuclear reactors simply going on "power excursions" or experiencing "rapid oxidation" (a major fire), the public is left in a fog. When "unplanned hypercriticality" (approaching a meltdown of the reactor core) can result in "spontaneous energetic disassembly" (a catastrophic explosion), the potential danger is hidden from us. When our government calls killing enemy soldiers "servicing the target," which results in "decommissioned aggressor quantum" (dead bodies), who can guess what's really occurring? When doctors refer to "therapeutic misadventures" (operations that kill patients), we have a clear case of inappropriate language use.

Official-sounding terminology used by hospitals and HMOs across the country has contributed to the U.S. Government Accounting Office's estimate of $10 billion a year in overpayments by patients (Palmer, 2000). With increasing out-of-pocket payments, patients are baffled by charges of $57.50 for "cough-support devices" (a teddy bear for pressing against one's chest to ease the pain of coughing after surgery), $10 for "mucus-recovery systems" (a box of tissues), and $18 for a "gauze collection bag" (an ordinary trash bag). Pat Palmer, author of *The Medical Bill Survival Guide*, provides this suggestion for frustrated patients who suspect medical fleecing camouflaged by euphemisms: "Pop open a mucus-recovery system, give your cough-support device a big hug, then get on the phone and give the billing office a piece of your cerebral control center" (Palmer, 2000, p. 82).

Here are two suggestions for dealing competently with euphemisms:

1. *Use euphemisms cautiously and wisely*. This is a judgment call. Substituting euphemisms for profanities and obscenities should cause few, if any, problems. Using euphemisms to confuse, however, can be more problematic. Normally, your communication goal should be clarity, not confusion. Confusing with language isn't always evil, but you wouldn't want to make it standard practice.

2. *Expunge dangerous euphemisms*. Euphemisms that simply lie to us to hide ugly, dangerous truths should be eliminated from our communication in all but the rarest instances.

Slang: Casual Language

Unless you are confident that your listeners will comprehend and identify with such casual speech, be very cautious using **slang**—the highly informal words not in standard usage that are employed by a group with a common interest. Slang acts as a means to identify individuals who belong to a group and those who are outsiders. If you don't speak the slang, you don't belong. Using terms such as *warez* (pirated software, music, or movies copied from a friend or downloaded from the Internet), *off the hinges* (outstanding or great), or *dot gone* (failed Internet company) may leave your listeners in a fog of confusion (check www.urbandictionary.com or SlangSite.com for translations and updates of constantly changing slang). Slang usually emerges and becomes popular among teens, college students, musicians, or marginalized groups in society (gays and lesbians; gangs).

It is typically inappropriate to use slang in formal speeches and presentations or at formal gatherings. Research shows, however, that creating a mildly informal classroom climate by using some positive slang ("awesome," "props," etc.) is well received by students and more effective than lectures entirely free of slang (Mazer & Hunt, 2008a, 2008b). Using slang that is an awkward fit for you personally (an older person trying to sound young and *cool*), however, can be embarrassing. Slang also can become dated quickly, making you sound hopelessly "uncool."

Summary

Language is a structured system of symbols for communicating meaning. It is our unique communication system. All languages have phonological, morphological, syntactic, and semantic sets of rules that allow us to share meaning with others. Every language has structure, productivity, displacement, and self-reflexiveness capabilities. Language influences thought, perception, and behavior in a wide variety of ways.

Language is a window to our minds and a catalyst of behavior. It is our chief means of communicating with other human beings. As Pinker (1999) so nicely puts it, to notice the "deep parallels in the languages of the French and the Germans, the Arabs and the Israelis, the East and the West, people living in the Age of the Internet and people living in the Stone Age, is to catch a glimpse of the psychic unity of humankind" (p. 239). Language is our connection to the world, and we pay dearly for misusing it. We need to replace gender-biased language with gender-neutral references, signal reactions with semantic reactions, abusive language with nonabusive terminology, false dichotomies with pluralistic thinking, dead-level abstracting with flexible language use, mislabeling with accurate operational definitions, inferential errors with more reliable conclusions based on high quantity and quality information, and we need to use jargon, euphemisms, and slang clearly and carefully.

Answers for *Critical Thinking* captions:

"Why" sign (p. 98): #1
Calvin & Hobbes (p. 100): #3 and #4
Blurry photo (p. 106): a cow
NAACP (p. 111): #3
Signs (p. 118): #4

Quizzes Without Consequences

Did you understand all the material in this chapter? Test your knowledge before your exam!

Go to the companion website at www.oup.com/us/rothwell, click on the Student Resources for each chapter, and take the Quizzes Without Consequences.

Film School Case Studies

Doubt (2008). Drama; PG-13

Meryl Streep plays a Catholic nun who begins to suspect a highly popular priest (Philip Seymour Hoffman) of child molestation. Identify examples of uncritical inferences and euphemistic and evasive language.

Mean Girls (2004). Comedy/Drama; PG-13

This is the story of Cady Heron (Lindsay Lohan), raised by her zoologist parents in the African bush country and thrown into the unfamiliar environment of public high school in the United States. Examine Cady's experience with slang terminology to infiltrate the Plastics (high-status girl clique). How does language affect Cady's thoughts, perceptions, and behavior?

My Fair Lady (1964). Musical; PG

If you like musicals, you'll love this movie that's all about language (okay, there is a love story, too). Analyze the movie for the power of language to stigmatize and identify individuals and groups, and explore the argument presented that some languages are inferior to others.

Nell (1994). Drama; PG-13

This is a story about a socially isolated individual. Identify the powerful negative influence social isolation has on Nell's ability to master language. What are the specific consequences of

Nell's isolation on her ability to communicate with other people? Does the movie accurately depict the "critical period" for language acquisition? Explain.

The N Word (2007). Documentary; R

This documentary explores the many uses and abuses of perhaps the most inflammatory word in the English language. Do you have signal reactions while watching? Are all uses of the word offensive to you? Do we give this word too much power by calling it "the N word"? Explain.

CHAPTER 5

Chapter Outline

PART 1

Nonverbal Communication

Sharing Meaning Without Words

ON NOVEMBER 14, 2009, PRESIDENT BARACK OBAMA bowed to Japanese Emperor Akihito as a gesture of greeting. A controversy ensued. Former Vice-President Dick Cheney asserted: "There is no reason for an American president to bow to anyone. Our friends and allies don't expect it, and our enemies see it as a sign of weakness." Fox News anchor Steve Doocy asserted: "For 233 years of precedent dating back to the very founding of this Republic, American leaders do not bow to leaders of other countries." Actually, Richard Nixon bowed to Chairman Mao of China, and Dwight Eisenhower bowed to French President Charles De Gaulle. George W. Bush even held hands and kissed Saudi Crown Prince Abdullah (Harris, 2009).

By the end of this chapter, you should be able to:

1. Understand the power of nonverbal communication.
2. Compare and contrast nonverbal and verbal communication.
3. Recognize and understand the many channels of nonverbal communication.

In June 2009, an official White House photograph showed President Obama talking on the phone to Israeli Prime Minister Benjamin Netanyahu. Why was this notable? Obama was shown with his feet propped on his Oval Office desk and the soles of his shoes prominently displayed. An article in *Haaretz*, a liberal-leaning Israeli daily, interpreted the photo this way: "As an enthusiast of Muslim culture, Obama surely knows there is no greater insult in the Middle East than pointing the soles of one's shoes at another person. Indeed, photos of other presidential phone calls depict Obama leaning on his desk, with his feet on the floor." The article also offered further interpretation: "The president is seen with his legs up on the table, his face stern and his fist clenched, as though he were dictating to Netanyahu: 'Listen up and write Palestinian state a hundred times'" ("Obama Shoe Photo," 2009).

First Lady Michelle Obama stirred a controversy in the same year when she briefly touched the back of Queen Elizabeth II as the two chatted amiably during a reception. The British media sputtered at this breach of protocol. This wasn't the first such breach, however. A former Australian prime minister similarly touched the queen and was branded "the Lizard of Oz." George W. Bush even once winked at the queen (Chua-Eoan, 2009).

National controversy about nonverbal communication had occurred many times prior to these instances. During the 2008 presidential campaign, Hillary Clinton became the target of late-night talk shows and political pundits when she wore an outfit on the Senate floor that revealed a slight amount of cleavage. Her pantsuits and makeup were also dissected, but probably no other aspect of her persona was as ridiculed and debated as her laugh. It was variously called a cackle, a caterwaul, and a bray, and conservative talk show host Sean Hannity questioned whether it was presidential (Dickerson, 2007). Presidential candidate John Edwards was similarly criticized vociferously for his primping in front of a mirror before a televised debate, and his $400 haircut became an issue that wouldn't die. And finally, Sarah Palin's $150,000 wardrobe and the $22,000 reportedly spent on a makeup artist to capitalize on her physical attractiveness became a public obsession.

Our gestures of greeting, soles of our shoes, touches, dress, appearance, laugh, and a host of other nonverbal cues become headline stories, even international incidents. Those of us who are less celebrated and powerful also experience the impact of nonverbal communication on our daily lives, but we often don't recognize its role in our communication with others until problems emerge. Then we experience difficulties knowing how to be nonverbally effective and appropriate nonverbally. *The principal purpose of this chapter is to show how you might improve your nonverbal communication with others.*

The Power of Nonverbal Communication

The city council of Palo Alto, California, once proposed a code of conduct that would ban elected officials from nonverbal expressions of disagreement, such as rolling their eyes, shaking their heads, or frowning during discussions and debates. The proposal was meant to encourage civility at a time of great bickering during council meetings. The proposed code garnered national media coverage, worldwide attention, and no small amount of ridicule. Opponents defended their "right to frown" and wondered if the "demeanor police" might extend the code to include those who are caught "grinning too much." The proposal was subsequently dropped, but it underlined awareness of the power that nonverbal communication can have.

Nonverbal communication is central to emotional expression, impression management, and much of what facilitates healthy relationships (Giles & Le Poire, 2006). Research shows that you can determine the nationality (e.g., American vs. Australian) of individuals just by seeing them walk, wave in greeting, or exhibit emotional facial expressions (Marsh et al., 2007). You can also determine the socioeconomic status of individuals by observing people's level of disengagement when you speak to them. If they are fidgeting, yawning, doodling, or otherwise showing disinterest, they may not be just rude, but they may also be from the wealthy class. Greater engagement typically indicates that one is likely not from the privileged class (Kraus & Keltner, 2009). Those born into privilege may feel less need to foster a good first impression, and so they become disengaged. Mundane conversation may be viewed as "beneath them." Those of less fortunate means may feel more compelled to make a strong first impression and so remain engaged even if bored with the conversation.

Surprisingly, artifacts such as a flag can significantly influence our perceptions and behavior. Even brief exposure to the American flag, for example, can markedly influence voters' choices in political elections without their conscious awareness of such an impact. Two studies showed that a single exposure to the flag "resulted in a significant increase in participants' Republican voting intentions, voting behavior, political beliefs, and implicit and explicit attitudes, with some effects lasting 8 months . . ." (Carter et al., 2011).

How important nonverbal communication is to the communication process in general, however, has been badly overstated in some instances. Some communication texts and numerous Internet sites misinterpret research by Mehrabian and assert that 93% of all meaning of messages is communicated nonverbally (see Lapakko, 1997, for a critique). Mehrabian (1971) never drew such a broad conclusion from his research. In fact, he repudiated it directly: "Clearly it is absurd to imply or suggest that the verbal portion of all communication constitutes only 7% of the message" (Mehrabian, 1995). He repudiated it for good reason because it makes no sense. Turn off the sound when watching a movie scene of two characters quarreling and see if you can ascertain 93% of the meaning of their argument. Yes, you can know they are quarreling

and even ascertain emotion (anger), but can you discern specific meaning? Travel to Paris without understanding French and observe Parisians in animated conversation. Can you understand more than a hint of the meaning in this transaction?

Another somewhat less extreme claim is that communication is 65% nonverbal based on limited research by Birdwhistell (1970). The exact percentage is unimportant and certainly dubious for the same reasons stated earlier. Nonverbal communication, however, often does play a predominant part in communication with others (Giles & Le Poire, 2006). This is a remarkable conclusion considering the power of language to shape thought, perception, and behavior. The strength of your handshake can communicate degree of confidence. The intensity of your anger is exhibited mostly nonverbally (tone of voice, facial expressions, gestures, posture). Anxiety is communicated nonverbally unless you openly self-disclose this to others. As noted in Chapter 1, 94% of virtual group members found the "inability to read nonverbal cues" a significant problem (Solomon, 2010). If nonverbal communication were merely incidental to verbal messages, few would find constraints on nonverbal communication when conveying messages electronically to be a problem. The power of nonverbal communication, regardless of the dubious percentages of import assigned to it, is rendered obvious as this chapter unfolds.

Distinctions Between Verbal and Nonverbal Communication

Communication is a lot more than just words. "Actions speak louder than words" is a cultural cliché. **Nonverbal communication** is sharing meaning with others nonlinguistically. This definition means that there are important differences between verbal and nonverbal communication. Before I explain these distinctions, however, take the self-assessment test in Box 5-1 to get a glimpse of what you know about nonverbal communication.

Number of Channels: Single- Versus Multichanneled

Verbal communication is single-channeled, but nonverbal communication is multichanneled. You can express anger verbally by saying, "I hate you" or "I hope you grow hair on your palms and your breath smells permanently like vomit." The statements change, but the channel (using words) is the same.

The same anger can be expressed nonverbally through multiple channels (channel-rich): shaking a fist, extending a middle finger, jumping up and down, glaring, screaming, kicking a wall, to name just a few possibilities. The multichanneled nature of nonverbal communication can add impact and believability to a message. For instance, it's easy to lie with words as long as you can remember to keep your story consistent, but it is more challenging to lie convincingly in multiple nonverbal channels (Vrij, 2006). If the nonverbal channels reveal inconsistent messages, credibility is questioned. When you say "I'm telling the truth," but your nonverbal communication says "No, I am not," we tend to believe the nonverbal message. Because nonverbal communication is more spontaneous, is physiologically based, and has to be consistent in more than one channel, it seems more believable and genuine, even though it may not be.

The adult pattern of relying on nonverbal messages when verbal and nonverbal messages conflict is not typical of children. Infants begin life depending solely on nonverbal communication. Once language develops, however, children rely primarily on verbal communication (Morton & Trehub, 2001). Verbal comments are taken literally by young children. Sarcasm, which is indicated by tone of voice and facial expressions, belies the verbal message. One study found that children only gradually learn to understand sarcastic messages (Andersen et al., 1985).

BOX 5.1 Developing Communication Competence

NONVERBAL COMMUNICATION TEST

Answer the following questions either TRUE or FALSE.

1. Young people are significantly worse than older adults at both signaling emotions nonverbally and correctly interpreting them.
2. Averting one's eyes (looking away) is a strong indicator of lying.
3. Eye contact should be direct whenever conversing with someone, especially with a person of higher status than you.
4. Putting your hands behind your back is a gesture that clearly signifies power and status.
5. Folding your arms across your chest should be interpreted as a defensive gesture meaning "stay away" or "I'm not comfortable with you."
6. A smile is a sure sign of happiness.
7. There are no universal standards of beauty because beauty is in the eye of the beholder and therefore subjective.
8. All cultures have pretty much the same touch taboos.
9. There are no universal facial expressions of emotions; different cultures interpret facial expressions of emotion differently.
10. In a singles bar, when a woman smiles at a man she has never met, this is likely to be a sexual invitation.

ANSWERS: End of chapter. How did you do? If you did well, did you make lucky guesses? If you did poorly, don't fret. Much of what we "know" about nonverbal communication isn't so. The mass media are notoriously gullible purveyors of misinformation about nonverbal communication.

Degree of Ambiguity: No "Reading a Person Like a Book"

Nonverbal communication is at least as ambiguous as language, probably more so. This point was made abundantly clear by rock legend Frank Zappa when he appeared on a television talk show hosted by an obnoxious individual named Joe Pine. This incident occurred in the 1960s, when a person's physical appearance, especially hair length for men, communicated nonconformity, rebelliousness, and antiwar sentiments. The most distinctive aspect of the show was Pine's shabby treatment of his guests, whom he tried to make look foolish. Pine had an amputated leg, but this was unremarkable until Zappa appeared on the show. When Zappa, sporting shoulder-length hair, was introduced to the audience, the following exchange took place:

> **Pine:** I guess your long hair makes you a girl.
> **Zappa:** I guess your wooden leg makes you a table. (quoted in Cialdini, 1993, p. 224)

Zappa's laser-quick ad lib exposed the absurdity of treating a nonverbal cue (e.g., hair length) as though only a single meaning could be attached. Meaning isn't embedded in the nonverbal *cue*—whatever triggers meaning. Hair length has no meaning apart from those who observe it anymore than a wooden leg has an inherent meaning. We have to interpret nonverbal cues. With interpretation comes ambiguity.

Can you "read a person like a book," as is so often asserted in the popular media? Consider deception detection. Can you spot a liar? A review of 217 studies over a 60-year period involving tens of thousands of subjects showed participants correctly distinguish liars from truth tellers an average of only 55% of the time (see Lock, 2004). That's slightly better than chance (flipping a coin—"heads" you're lying, "tails" you're telling the truth). Psychologist Maureen O'Sullivan (2005) has tested more than 13,000 individuals, and only 31 achieved 80% accuracy on detecting lying. She dubs them "truth wizards." The television series *Lie to Me* depicts truth wizards, but Paul Ekman, who is the prototype for the Dr. Lightman character, warns on his website, "Dr. Lightman is not as tentative about interpreting behavior as I am. Lies are uncovered more quickly and with more certainty [on this television program] than it happens in reality." Some researchers question the existence of actual truth wizards (Bond & Uysal, 2007).

Even "experts" in deception detection do poorly when trying to determine truth tellers from liars. In one study, 509 such experts—individuals who administer lie-detector tests, psychiatrists, court judges, police detectives, and Secret Service agents—were asked to detect deception. All of these people worked in professions where lying is a common occurrence and an important issue. Nevertheless, only the Secret Service agents did better than chance detecting lies from nonverbal cues, and they were wrong more than a third of the time (Ekman & O'Sullivan, 1991). College students as nonexperts were also included in the study. They did the worst (48% accuracy). In another study, highly educated, well-trained child abuse experts, confident that their intuition and experience would enable them to discern true from false allegations of abuse, actually performed *worse* than chance. They concluded that the children who gave the greatest amount of misinformation were most credible (Horner et al., 1993).

Why are we such poor deception detectors? It is primarily because "there is no sign of deceit itself—no gesture, facial expression, or muscle twitch that in and of itself means that a person is lying" (Ekman, 1992, p. 80; see also Vrij, 2006). We think there is, however, and there lies the misperception. Two global studies of thousands of people from 75 countries found that the number one answer to the question "How can you tell when people are lying?" was "Liars avert their eyes" (Bond & DePaulo, 2006; see also Porter & ten Brinke, 2010). Ekman (2001) found one group that excels at making direct eye contact and not averting gaze—pathological liars. Liars don't avert their gaze, shift their weight, touch their noses, clear their throats, or exhibit any other single nonverbal cue more often than truth tellers.

Also, most people have a **truth bias**; they believe most messages are truthful (we normally tell many more truths than lies in daily transactions) (Burgoon et al., 2008). We tend to be moderately good at spotting truthful statements but lousy at spotting lies. One review of 37 studies showed that subjects were 67% accurate in detecting truthful statements but only 44% accurate in detecting lies (Vrij, 2000). The truth bias is particularly strong in intimate relationships. Individuals are usually confident that they can spot deception in their romantic partners because they "know them well," so a partner wouldn't even try to lie for fear of being caught, but research does not support the confidence (Vrij, 2000, 2006). Prison inmates, however, exhibit a **lie bias**; they expect most messages to be deceptive (lying can be a way of life in prison). They are moderately good at spotting lies but lousy at spotting truthful statements (Bond et al., 2005).

Detecting lying is only marginally improved by training individuals to look for "micro-expressions" that suggest lying (Levine et al., 2005). Individual differences in personality make detecting lies from micro-expressions tricky. Introverted, socially awkward individuals provoke greater suspicion of lying even when they aren't deceiving (Vrij, 2006). Some people are just good liars because they are good actors, or they experience no guilt or fear when lying, or their attractiveness is mistaken for virtue and honesty (Vrij et al., 2010). Your best shot at detecting lying is by collecting a variety of nonverbal evidence over a period of days, weeks, or even months and by seeking information from third parties ("Did you see him with another woman?") (Park et al., 2002). There is also some evidence that liars provide fewer details than truth tellers when giving narratives (Vrij et al., 2010). The more details a liar provides while telling a story, the more opportunity to be exposed.

Culture can interject an additional source of ambiguity into the accurate perception of lying and truth telling. Detecting lies when interacting with members of cultures different from your own is even more difficult than spotting lies within your own cultural group (Bond & Rao, 2004). Some cultures, for example, consider maintaining direct eye contact during conversation as rude and eye aversion as polite, having nothing to do with lying (Vrij, 2000).

Despite a tendency toward overconfidence, *most of us don't read nonverbal cues very well.* One supermarket chain told its employees to make eye contact and smile when interacting with customers to communicate a customer-friendly message. Several employees filed grievances as a result because customers misperceived the friendly nonverbal cues as sexual invitations. Despite our general shortcomings when trying to read nonverbal cues accurately, women tend to be more accurate decoders of nonverbal messages than men, and middle-aged people tend to be better at reading nonverbal communication than younger people (Andersen, 2006; Hall, 2006b; Rosenthal, 1979). Can we "read a person like a book"? It is unlikely, but we certainly can become more sensitive to nonverbal cues and improve our accuracy.

The women in both of these photos appear distraught and profoundly sad if you concentrate on the nonverbal communication. In fact, Halle Berry is profoundly thrilled by the honor of receiving an Oscar—the first ever given to an African American female for best actress. The woman below has suffered from the tragedy of a major tsunami. Nonverbal cues alone can be ambiguous.

Discrete Versus Continuous: Stop and Go

Verbal communication has discrete beginnings and endings. We begin it when we start talking, and we end it when we stop talking. Nonverbal communication, however, has no discrete beginning and end. We continuously send messages for others to perceive, even when we may wish not to do

Victoria Beckam is rarely photographed smiling. This absence of smiling illustrates which of the following?

1. Not smiling doesn't mean "not communicating"
2. Nonverbal communication is discrete
3. Nonverbal communication is continuous
4. Nonverbal communication is single-channeled

Answers at end of chapter

so. Robert Noel was convicted of involuntary manslaughter as the owner of a Presa Canario (a breed of dog) that viciously mauled and killed Diane Whipple. Noel seemed oblivious to the continuous nature of nonverbal communication. After the trial, jurors in the case offered their impressions of Noel. They saw him as a man who seemed unremorseful and generally unpleasant in his demeanor. Staring stoically into space for most of the trial, Noel gave this assessment of the jurors' characterization of him: "I made up my mind not to react one way or another. I'm sitting there just watching what was going on, making notes for the attorneys. . . . And it's just amazing that I could just sit there doing nothing and that gets twisted into, 'Oh, he's a cold-hearted son of a bitch'" (May, 2002, p. 18A).

Noel apparently believed that by sitting expressionless and "doing nothing," he would communicate nothing to a jury. Unfortunately for him, it communicated volumes. We can't communicate "nothing" as long as others are observing us. Consider facial expressions, for example. Try not to display any facial expressions at all while another person looks at you. It can't be done. Even a blank stare is a facial expression that communicates a message. Others may perceive your blank stare to mean that you're introspective and are thinking deeply, or that you don't want to be bothered by anyone, or that you're inattentive, sullen, or disdainful.

Gestures and eye contact may seem to be discrete, not continuous, because a specific gesture begins and ends, and eye contact also begins and ends. Not gesturing, however, can indicate boredom, relaxation, or awkwardness. Lack of eye contact can indicate disinterest, intimidation, distraction, or a host of other messages.

Nonverbal communication is sometimes unintentional. We blush, blink our eyes rapidly, and shuffle our feet without necessarily intending to do so. We are sharing meaning with others without necessarily wanting to share. Individuals standing before an audience giving speeches may want desperately to hide their nervousness. Nevertheless, their hands may shake, their voices may quaver, and perspiration may form on their brows. The nonverbal message that is likely received by their audience is that they are experiencing speech anxiety. Audience members, in turn, may want to hide their recognition of the anxiety to ease the tension, but averting eye contact with speakers or moving restlessly in their seats may, on the contrary, indicate such recognition.

Interconnectedness of Verbal and Nonverbal Communication

Verbal and nonverbal communication are interconnected. We don't speak without embellishing the words with gestures, facial expressions, tone of voice, eye contact, and so forth. This section discusses several ways verbal and nonverbal codes interconnect.

Repetition: Same Message, Different Channels

We say "yes" and then nod our head. We give verbal directions, then point in the appropriate direction. We profess our love for individuals and then hug them. All of these nonverbal cues repeat the verbal message. This repetition diminishes ambiguity and enhances accuracy of message perception. *Consistency of verbal and nonverbal communication increases the clarity and credibility of the message.*

Accentuation: Intensifying Verbal Messages

When we use vocal emphasis such as "*Please* don't touch anything in the store," this accents the message. It adds emphasis where it is desired. "Don't you *ever* say that word" accents the unqualified nature of the verbal message. Pounding your fist on a table as you express your anger nonverbally repeats the message but also accents the depth of your emotion. Accentuating enhances the power and seriousness of verbal messages.

Substitution: No Words Necessary

Sometimes nonverbal cues substitute for verbal messages. A yawn can substitute for the verbal "I'm bored" or "I'm tired." A wave can substitute for a "good-bye." Shaking your head "no" doesn't require a verbalized "no." We signal interest in courting another person without actually having to express

We accentuate verbal messages (in this case, most likely spewing obscenities at the computer) by screaming the message (vocal characterizer) and shaking the computer or putting your fist through the screen.

this message in words. Eye contact, smiling, forward leans, room-encompassing glances, close distance, frequent nodding, and hair smoothing are just some of the nonverbal flirting cues (Brown et al., 2009; Muehlenhard et al., 1986). A later stage of courtship, sexual initiation, is usually accepted nonverbally but rejected verbally (Metts et al., 1992).

Regulation: Conversational Traffic Cop

Conversation is regulated by nonverbal cues. Turn taking is signaled by long pauses at the end of sentences and eye contact in the direction of the person expected to speak next, especially if the conversation occurs in a group. Interruptions may be prevented by speeding up the rate of speech, raising one's voice over the attempted interruption, or holding up one's hand to signal unwillingness to relinquish the floor. A teacher can recognize a student's desire to speak by pointing to the person. This means "your turn."

Contradiction: Mixed Messages [S]

"Sure, I love you," when said with eyes cast downward and flat vocal tone, doesn't exactly inspire belief. Sometimes we contradict verbal messages with nonverbal cues. These are **mixed messages**—inconsistencies between verbal and nonverbal messages. The words say one thing, but gestures, facial expressions, eye contact, posture, tone of voice, and physical proximity leak contradictory information. Leathers (1979) found that mixed messages had a highly disruptive impact on problem-solving groups. Mixed messages produced tension and anxiety, and group members found it difficult to respond to mixed messages in socially appropriate ways (Leathers, 1986). Young children are especially confused by mixed messages (Morton & Trehub, 2001).

Types of Nonverbal Communication

Let's now explore the main types of nonverbal communication used during transactions with others. I begin with the vast potential of our bodies and their accoutrements to communicate: physical appearance, face, gestures, touch, and voice. At the end, I discuss space and environment. In each instance, note the power of nonverbal communication and the potential for misunderstandings and miscommunication.

Physical Appearance: Looks Matter

How we physically look to others often is the first nonverbal message communicated. Our physical appearance is strongly related to perceptions of physical attractiveness. In this section, I explore beauty bias, body shape and size, body adornments, clothing, and hair.

Physical Attractiveness: The Beauty Bias

There is a popular belief that men place greater emphasis and value on physical attractiveness when choosing a mate than women do. Several reviews involving hundreds of studies show that physical attractiveness is equally significant for men and women (Eagly et al., 1991; Feingold, 1992; Langlois et al., 2000). Physically attractive people get more dates, and this is of interest to both women and men.

This **beauty bias**—a perceived advantage accorded those who are viewed as attractive—goes beyond simple interpersonal attraction and the advantage attractive people have in garnering dates, fostering romance, and choosing mates. Beautiful people are thought to be more sociable, poised, independent, happy, sensitive, sexy, and successful than unattractive individuals (Dion & Dion, 1987; Eagly et al., 1991; Lorenzo et al., 2010). There is some evidence that suggests parents give preferential treatment to their better-looking children (Harrell, 2005). The beauty bias also seems to produce a "beauty premium"—namely, higher wages. Two economists calculated from survey data that above-average-looking individuals tend to earn 5% more per hour than average-looking individuals. "Plain-looking" individuals apparently suffer an actual penalty of 9% less per hour in wages (Hamermesh & Biddle, 1994). In these beauty premium studies, the advantage seems to be significantly greater for men than for women.

Two other economists determined that a self-fulfilling prophecy may be partially responsible for this beauty premium/penalty. Physically attractive employees tend to be more self-confident and consequently are wrongly perceived by employers to be more able workers (Mobius & Rosenblat, 2006). Knowing that others find you attractive and being treated favorably because of your good looks can bolster self-confidence, and this in turn can be exhibited in positive ways in the workplace.

Supermodel Linda Evangelista once remarked, "It was God who made me so beautiful. If I weren't, then I would be a teacher." (If you're not attractive, become a teacher. Really?) Actually, her beauty would likely help her be a successful teacher in the eyes of students. A study of 94 faculty members in 463 courses at the University of Texas, Austin, found that professors rated as very attractive (on a 10-point scale) by students received teaching evaluations (on a 5-point scale) that averaged 4.5, but those rated at the bottom on attractiveness received an average of 3.5 (Hamermesh & Parker, 2005). Teachers are not immune to the beauty bias. Teachers perceive attractive students as more intelligent, popular, and friendly than less attractive students (Ritts et al., 1992).

This attractiveness bias, however, is likely to occur during initial attraction to a person, but it may not be enduring "with the weight of additional information about the person" (Berscheid & Walster, 1974, p. 205). The attraction may be fleeting indeed if good-looking individuals' egos swell like pufferfish the moment they open their mouths. Being hypercritical of people or generally acting "like a jerk" significantly reduces a person's perceived physical attractiveness. Also, romantic love and commitment to your partner decrease attention to opposite sex, physically attractive individuals (Maner et al., 2009; Plant et al., 2010). The allure is lessened in happy relationships. As psychologist John Lyman of McGill University explains, "The more committed you are the less attractive you find other people who threaten your relationship" (quoted in Parker-Pope, 2010).

Plastic surgery and vigorous physical exercise can improve a person's looks, but attractiveness can be enhanced in ways other than engaging in an "extreme makeover." Kindness is perceived as a mate preference for both men and women (Li et al., 2002). Women rated men as more physically and sexually attractive if they were considerate of others and showed sensitivity (Jensen-Campbell et al., 1995). Chalk up another advantage for the competent communicator. Offering compliments, expressing affection, and purchasing gifts for your partner can make you appear more physically attractive (the "bling-beauty bonus"?" (Albada et al., 2002). Less attractive individuals, if given a chance, may exhibit a very attractive personality and consequently increase their perceived physical attractiveness (Newman, 2000). As we get to know others over time and grow to like them, they become more physically attractive in our eyes (Bazil, 1999). This reverses the "beauty is good" stereotype to "good is beautiful" (Gross & Crofton, 1977). It thus behooves us all to follow Hatfield and Sprecher's (1986) advice to put more focus on attempting to be nice to others and communicating competently.

Body Shape and Size: Universal Standards of Attractiveness

You've heard the adage "Beauty is in the eye of the beholder." Is beauty entirely a matter of individual, subjective preferences? Some women find the male bodybuilder physique extremely attractive, but other women think it is repellent (Pope et al., 2000). Individual preferences do play a part in our judgment of physical attractiveness.

Cultural differences also exist, making beauty appear highly subjective. Ubangi women insert wooden disks into their mouths to stretch their lips up to 10 inches in diameter to enhance their attractiveness. Unlike the United States, some cultures prefer plump over skinny. One study of 54 cultures discovered that heavy women are preferred to slender women in cultures where food is often limited (Anderson et al., 1992). In Niger and other countries in West Africa, fat is the female beauty ideal (Onishi, 2001). At one festival in Niger called *Hangandi*, women compete for a prize given to the heaviest contestant. Women train for this beauty contest by gorging themselves and drinking lots of water on the day of the contest. Women also take steroids to bulk up, and some even ingest animal feed advertised as a means to increase body weight. In Nigeria, the Warirke people have "fattening rooms" established to help young women pile on the pounds. For four weeks, young women gorge themselves to improve their marriage prospects (McGirk, 1998).

Despite cultural and individual differences that are learned, there are universal standards of physical attractiveness. First, **bilateral symmetry**—the right and left sides match each other—seems to be a universal attractiveness characteristic (Floyd, 2006; Rhodes et al., 2001). Lopsided features of the face (one eye slightly lower than the other, a crooked mouth or nose, uneven ears) are perceived to be less attractive than more symmetrical features.

Second, the size of the female body seems to be less important than the body shape. The lower the **waist-to-hip ratio**—the smaller the waist is compared to the hips (an hourglass shape)—the greater the perception of attractiveness. This ratio in women was found to be a more important characteristic than facial features, height, body weight, and other physical attributes (Singh, 1993). This was true whether those judging the female shape were 8 or 80 years old and regardless of culture or background (Furnham et al., 2003; Springen, 1997). The "ideal" shape was a 0.70 waist-to-hip ratio (the waist is 70% the size of the hips). This same preference was reported for lesbians and bisexual women, although a heavier body with the 0.70 ratio was considered the "ideal" (Cohen & Tannenbaum, 2001). Even men blind from birth, when touching a mannequin, preferred a preference for low waist-to-hip ratio, although sighted men had a stronger preference (Karremans et al., 2010). *Playboy* centerfolds and Miss America winners from 1923 to 1990 stayed within the narrow waist-to-hip ratio of 0.68 to 0.72 even though height and total weight varied significantly (Singh, 1993). Despite the "ideal" shape, perceived attractiveness in general varies rather broadly from a 0.60 to a 0.80 ratio (Springen, 1997).

Although research on the male body shape is limited, an attractive physique for men appears to be relatively broad shoulders and narrow waist and hips, or a **wedge shape** (Hughes & Gallup, 2003; Singh, 1995). Thus far, however, no ratio similar to the waist-to-hip ratio in women has been well supported for male attractiveness across cultures.

Body Adornments: Tattoos and Taboos

He got his first tattoo—a rosary with a cross, etched on the back of his right hand—when he was 11 years old. At 13, he had Chinese characters that translate to "trust no man" tattooed on his left shoulder. At 16, an ornate cross that memorialized his dead older brother was added to his right hand. All of these tattoos were rites of passage into gang life in Watsonville, California, for Mando. After his brother's death, however, he began questioning his way of life and looking for alternatives. When he searched for a job, he found that potential employers would eye his gang tattoos and say that no jobs were available.

Tattoo removal has become a popular business. A Harris poll showed that 17% of tattoo wearers regret having them (Sever, 2003). The most often cited reason is "because of the person's name in the tattoo." Sometimes removal is desired because what was thought to be a cool tattoo turned out to be a joke played on the wearer. For example, one customer thought he was getting a trendy Chinese-language tattoo but later discovered that the Chinese language figures translated to "gullible white boy" ("Some Tattoos," 2006). More women than men seek tattoo removal (Armstrong et al., 2008). "Society supports men, because tattoos are related to a macho image, so we don't question it. But for women, having a tattoo seems to be a transgression of gender boundaries" ("More Women Seeking Tattoo Removal," 2008).

Despite the stereotyping, tattoos and body piercings are more popular than ever. The Food and Drug Administration estimates that 45 million Americans sport at least one tattoo (May, 2010). A survey by the American Academy of Dermatology shows

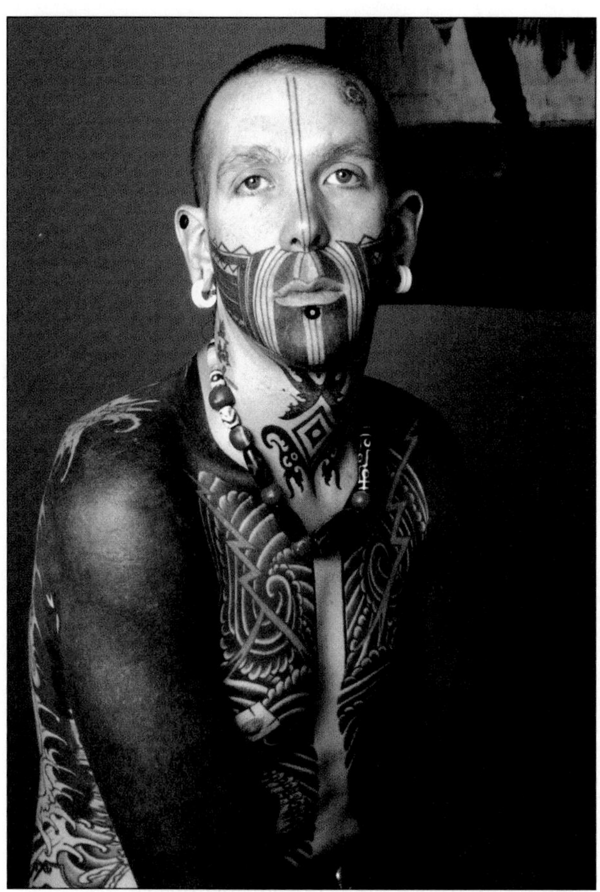

What's your first impression of this man with tattoos?

that among those in their 20s, 36% have at least one tattoo and 22% have body piercings in places other than earlobes ("Body Art," 2006). Reasons for getting tattoos vary: 34% feel sexier for having them, 29% say tattoos make them feel rebellious, and 26% feel attractive wearing them (Sever, 2003).

Tattoos can be taboo with a large portion of the population. According to the Harris poll, 42% of Americans who do not have tattoos perceive those who do to be less attractive, 35% see tattoo wearers as less sexy, and 31% view them as less intelligent (Sever, 2003). According to a survey conducted by career information website Vault.com, 85% of respondents believe that tattoos and body piercings hinder job seekers' chances of finding employment (Ridley, 2007). A Vault survey also found that 60% of employers admitted that they were less likely to hire an applicant with tattoos and piercings (Icon, 2011).

Such body adornments have led to stricter dress codes at workplaces. According to Kelli Thompson, an employment lawyer, "For the vast majority of the hospitality industry, the public generally does not want to be greeted by a customer service person or server with a nose ring, a pin in their ear or a tattoo that covers their arm." She continues, "There is a strong legal basis for limiting tattoos and piercings in the workplace, especially if employers have reason to believe that tattooed or pierced employees will hurt their image with customers" (quoted in Holtzman, 2010).

The type of job, however, dictates how strict or loose dress codes are in the workplace. Wal-mart, for example, does not permit facial piercings but does allow inoffensive tattoos. Ford Motor Company permits everyone, including senior executives, to wear tattoos and piercings unless they interfere with safety (metal getting caught in machinery) (Icon, 2011). Again, context and communication interconnect.

Clothing: Not Just for Warmth

Physical appearance can be enhanced or diminished in a variety of ways. Clothing expresses a person's identity. "It is impossible to wear clothes without transmitting social signals. Every costume tells a story, often a very subtle one, about its wearer" (Morris, 1977, p. 213). One study of dress in an international airport reported Tongans wearing ceremonial gowns, Sikhs in white turbans, Africans in white dashikis, and Hasidic Jews in blue yarmulkes next to Californians in running shorts and tank tops (McDaniel & Andersen, 1995). The variety of clothing choices is astonishing.

Clothing matters. In Afghanistan, the traditional burqas worn by women became a symbol of subjugation in the eyes of most Americans during our war with the Taliban. The burqas covered women from head to toe, making them unrecognizable. In France and Great Britain, laws and court rulings have permitted banning Muslim students from wearing full-face veils in class. The bans have provoked tumultuous protests and controversies in both countries. On April 11, 2011, a French law went even further and banned women from wearing full-face veils in any public place. Dress communicates social position, economic status, level of sophistication, social background, educational level, personal identity, even moral character and religious affiliation.

Just observe the reactions to dress codes. School uniforms have become increasingly popular in elementary and high schools around the nation—unpopular with students but popular with administrators and parents. Parents and school boards opt for uniforms to combat gang violence at schools provoked by gang colors and attire and to instill a stronger focus on schoolwork, not wardrobe. Strict dress codes often substitute for uniforms in schools. Again, students object to the restriction on their "freedom of expression" and the conformity that rigid dress codes require.

Workplace dress codes are also a subject of debate. The trend toward dress codes that permit more casual dress at work seems to be waning. According to a report by the Society of Human Resources Management, the number of companies permitting casual dress in the workplace has been declining steadily from an all-time high of 97% in 1998. In Great Britain, the number of companies still permitting casual attire has fallen to 36% (Dumont, 2010). Typically, casual dress at work does not include tight-fitting clothes (too provocative), cutoffs and bare midriffs (too sloppy and unkempt), tank tops (too recreational), sleeveless muscle shirts (too self-absorbed), or running shorts, sweatpants, and sweatbands (gym attire). Clothes that are neat, clean, unwrinkled, loose fitting, and undamaged (no rips or holes) are usually more appropriate for most workplaces. Clothing choices communicate messages. Casual attire for too many workers often became sloppy and inappropriate attire as dress codes were relaxed. Such attire communicated an image of sloppy, careless work. Employers increasingly decided to tighten their dress codes in response.

Appropriate dress is an issue for teachers. One study (Morris & Gorham, 1996) found that formal professional attire receives the highest instructor competence ratings from students, with casual professional dress a close second. Casual dress, however, produced the highest sociability ratings (e.g., sociable, cheerful, good-natured) from students. Interesting presentation of material was also associated with casual instructor dress. Casual professional dress seems to make instructors more approachable for discussions and more interesting from the student vantage point. Again, there are rules for every communication context. What is appropriate in one workplace context may be inappropriate in another workplace environment.

Hair: Styling

Another significant element of physical appearance is hair. In the late 1800s, American Indians were forced to attend federal boarding schools. Upon their arrival, their long hair, a tie to their spiritual heritage, was shorn to "civilize" them. It was a traumatic introduction to white society (Arrillaga, 2001).

Hairstyle expresses self-concept. The Taliban brutally enforced a law in Afghanistan mandating that all men wear the traditional beard. When the Taliban were driven from power by the U.S. military, many Afghan men shaved off their beards as a symbolic act of freedom from oppressive rule (Filkins, 2001).

Hair has enormous communicative potential. That is why hair is big business. In the United States, there are approximately 70,000 hair-care salons and barbershops generating about $19 billion of business annually ("Hair Salons," 2011). Hairstyles create an image and follow normative trends (long hair in the 1960s was popular with men; short hair is more popular now). Baldness is a continuing issue for millions of men and some women. Annually, about $3.5 billion are spent in the United States on stopping hair loss or regenerating lost hair ("Cure for Baldness," 2011).

More recently, a trend among men is called *manscaping*—removing body hair by having it waxed or lasered off (James, 2009). This hair removal involves more than just back and shoulder hair. Men are manscaping chest, arms, hands, even pubic areas. The message communicated is that body hair is "gross" and should be removed for a person to be more attractive, a subjective view not universally shared.

Facial Communication: Your Personal Billboard

"Faces express emotions, thoughts, and character. Brows knit, mouths gape, lips grin, cheeks blush, jaws clench, eyes weep, and pupils dilate with libidinal enthusiasm" (Garland-Thomson, 2009). Your eyes and face are the most immediate cues people use to form first impressions. Speed dating preferences are heavily influenced by facial appearance (Olivola & Todorov, 2010). Happy looking faces are perceived to be trustworthy, and angry looking faces create the opposite impression (Said et al., 2009). This section explores how your eyes and face influence communication with others. A discussion of gestures follows. The study of both facial communication and gestures is referred to as **kinesics** by social scientists.

Eyes: Your Personal Windows

"Eyes wink, gleam, glitter, twinkle, glaze over, cut, make contact, pierce, penetrate, and assist the mouth in fashioning a frown or smile" (Garland-Thomson, 2009). They also blink. Boston College neuropsychology professor Joe Tecce claims stress can be measured by how often someone blinks, and perceptions of self-confidence and being in control can be subtly affected by blinking rates. He goes further by concluding that presidential candidates with the lower blink rate win elections (Tecce, 2004). The normal blink rate of someone speaking on television, according to Tecce, is between 30 and 50 blinks per minute. Tecce's hypothesis that blinking rates are strongly correlated with presidential victory has been correct in six presidential elections examined. The 2000 election between Bush and Gore, however, deviated from the norm. Gore averaged 36 blinks per minute to Bush's 48, and we all know how that election turned out. Of course, Gore did win the popular vote. The 2004 election, however, reverted to form. Bush averaged 40 blinks and Kerry averaged 50 blinks per minute. The 2008 Obama-McCain presidential debates saw Obama with far fewer blinks per minute than McCain in all three debates (Hebel, 2008). Polls showed that Obama was viewed as the winner of all three debates by a majority of respondents, and Obama won the presidency.

The Tecce blink-rate-equals-stress-level hypothesis is interesting and may have validity. Generalizing from a single-channel nonverbal cue requires caution, however, especially when predicting presidential elections—a dubious undertaking. The blink rate of Jack Kemp in the 1996 vice-presidential debate was exceedingly low at a sleepy 31 blinks, yet anyone observing Kemp during the debate would have noticed the sheen of perspiration on his face and his stiff posture as well as several verbal miscues ("Eyes Wide Open," 2000). Perspiration, rigid posture, and verbal mistakes suggest stress and nervousness. Gore also manifested greater stress than his eye blinks appeared to indicate. His stiff posture, downward glances, and head movements were that of a person feeling ill at ease. Nonverbal communication is multichanneled. Thus, one nonverbal cue may suggest relaxed demeanor while other nonverbal cues may contradict this observation. Eye-blink rates may also be affected by factors other than anxiety, such as the glare of TV lights on sensitive eyes, mild allergy reactions, wearing contact lenses, lack of sleep, and so forth. None of this was taken into account by Tecce.

Besides blinking, eye contact is also important, and its study is called **oculesics**. Eye contact regulates conversational turn taking, communicates involvement and interest, manifests warmth, and establishes connection with others. It can also command attention, be flirtatious, or look cold and intimidating (Andersen, 1999).

Interpersonal communication is quite dependent on eye contact, especially in the United States. Eye contact invites conversation. Lack of eye contact is usually perceived to be rude or inattentive. Too much eye contact in the form of staring can be viewed as rude and intrusive (Garland-Thomson, 2009). One study found that individuals interviewing for a job were less successful when they averted eye contact than those who maintained eye contact with the interviewer (Burgoon et al., 1985). As discussed in later chapters, eye contact is a critical element of effective public speaking.

Cultures differ regarding the appropriateness of direct eye contact (Samovar et al., 2010). Indonesians, Chinese, Japanese, and many Latin Americans will show deference to others by lowering their eyes. This is a sign of respect. It is also easy for "look-you-in-the-eye" Americans to misread this nonverbal cue and assume that Asians and Latin Americans lack self-confidence and can be easily manipulated. In Egypt, men and women who are strangers to each other avoid eye contact to communicate modesty and to act in accordance with religious rules widely practiced in the culture (Meleis & Meleis, 1998). In India, individuals from differing socioeconomic classes avoid eye contact with each other (Luckmann, 1999).

Co-cultures within the United States also show different preferences regarding eye contact. Hopi dislike direct eye contact. Navajos have a creation story about a "terrible monster called He-Who-Kills-with-His-Eyes." This story teaches Navajo children that "a stare is literally an evil eye and implies a sexual and aggressive assault" ("Understanding Culture," 1974).

Our eyes are highly communicative even when we might prefer they weren't. Pupil dilation (pupil opening) offers a subtle but significant cue that suggests arousal or attraction. Experienced gem buyers wear sunglasses to hide pupil dilation that might reveal how much they want to buy a particular gem. Poker players often do the same to hide any indication of a good or bad hand. In an amazing study (Hess & Goodwin, 1974), students were shown two photos of a mother holding her baby. The photos were identical in all respects, except one photo was retouched to show constricted pupils and the other retouched to show dilated pupils. The students were asked, "Which mother loves her baby more?" Every student chose the mother with the dilated pupils. Most student participants gave reasons other than the dilated pupils, even though pupil dilation was the only difference between the two photos. "She's holding her baby closer," "She has a warmer smile," or "Her face is more pleasant" were some of the explanations offered.

Not surprisingly, heterosexual men display increased pupil dilation when viewing photos of attractive women, and gay men display greater pupil dilation when viewing photos of attractive men (Hess et al., 1965). Pupil dilation is subconsciously perceived during interpersonal interactions and actually may increase the observer's attraction for the person with dilated pupils (Andersen et al., 1980). Candlelight dinners, moonlight walks, and conversations by firelight produce wider pupils due to the soft light. This is probably part of the reason such experiences increase romantic attraction (Andersen, 1999). Again, be careful not to read too much into the single nonverbal cue of pupil dilation. A dimly lit restaurant can dilate your pupils even as you're thinking of graceful ways to end the evening with your date.

Facial Expressions: The Look of Emotions

Seven-year-old Chelsey Thomas underwent facial surgery on December 16, 1995, to correct her perpetually grumpy facial expression. Chelsey suffered from an unusual condition called Moebius syndrome. She couldn't smile because the nerves that trigger the facial muscles that control smiling were missing. Chelsey's mother described how the inability to smile affected her daughter: "It's been hard for her because people think she's unfriendly or ignoring them or bored. . . . Kids stare at her. Adults are pretty understanding, but she has a worse time with kids" ("Girl Undergoes," 1995).

Surgery grafted leg muscles and nerves from her leg to her facial muscles used for chewing, and Chelsey now has a smile. Imagine what it would be like to be unable to smile when we feel joy or perceive humor. Imagine how others would respond to you if you always seemed to be frowning and you had no way of changing the sour expression on your face. Think of what that would do to your self-esteem and to your ability to communicate with others. Smiling is a primary cue that exhibits friendliness and warmth. A smile makes a person approachable. "We know that genuine smiles may indeed reflect a 'sweet soul.' The intensity of a true grin can predict marital happiness, personal well-being, and even longevity" (Jaffe, 2010). A person who doesn't smile at us can seem distant, even mean. Teachers who rarely if ever smile during class lectures and activities make it difficult for students to ask questions, disagree, or participate in discussions.

Chelsey's inability to smile may even have affected her emotional experience of happiness. Emotions clearly influence facial expressions, but according to the **facial feedback hypothesis** (Adelmann & Zajonc, 1989), the reverse is also true; facial expressions can influence emotions. In one study (Strack et al., 1988), those individuals who held a pen between their teeth parallel to their mouth rated cartoons as funnier than individuals who held a pen with their lips when it was pointed perpendicular to the mouth. Why? Because holding a pen between your teeth parallel to your mouth forces you to smile, but holding a pen perpendicular to your mouth with your lips forces you to constrict your mouth. Try it. Which way seems happier?

There has been extensive research on facial expressions. Research on facial expressions in 20 Western cultures and 11 nonliterate and isolated cultures showed that members of all these cultures recognized the same basic emotions from photographs of specific facial expressions. *These universal emotions identified by all cultures from specific facial expressions are fear, anger, surprise, contempt, disgust, happiness, and sadness* (Ekman, 1994, 2003; Schubert, 2006). (See photos on page 144)

Members of diverse cultures recognize the same emotions from specific facial expressions, but they don't necessarily perceive the same intensity of emotion (e.g., from annoyance to rage). One study asked members in 10 different cultures to rate the intensity of the perceived emotions exhibited by facial expressions. Significant differences were found. Non-Asian cultures rated the emotions as more intense than did Asian cultures (Ekman & Friesen, 1987). Not surprisingly, accurately interpreting emotions from facial expressions is improved when a person views another member from an in-group (same ethnicity, nationality, regional location) (Elfenbein & Ambady, 2002).

There are also differences in display rules for facial expressions. **Display rules** are culture-specific prescriptions that dictate the appropriateness of behaviors (Ekman, 1993). The Japanese would be more likely than Americans to suppress negative emotions (anger, contempt) if the emotion occurred during a private conversation and the target of the emotion were an in-group member (Jaffe, 2010). If, however, the target of the negative emotion were a rival group or individual, Japanese would be more likely than Americans to display the emotion. Showing contempt or anger toward one of your own group members creates disharmony and may hurt the group. Showing anger or contempt to a competitive rival, however, may create in-group cohesion (Matsumoto, 1990).

Gestural Communication: Bodies in Motion

Gestures are everywhere. When we communicate with others, gestures accompany our verbal messages even when we aren't aware that we're using them. People who talk on the telephone usually gesture while they are talking even though the person on the other end cannot see the gestures. When we communicate with others, we often are a wiggling, fidgeting, finger-tapping, hand-waving, toe-tapping, arm-flailing body in motion.

There are three main categories of gestures: manipulators, illustrators, and emblems (Ekman, 1992). **Manipulators** are gestures made by one part of the body, usually the hands, that rub, pick, squeeze, clean, or groom another part of the body. They have no specific meaning, although people observing such manipulators may perceive nervousness, discomfort, or deceit. Manipulators, however, also occur when a person is relaxed and feeling energized and when no deceit is occurring. Nevertheless, studies show that people will mistakenly judge deceitfulness when a person exhibits many manipulators (Ekman, 1992). The

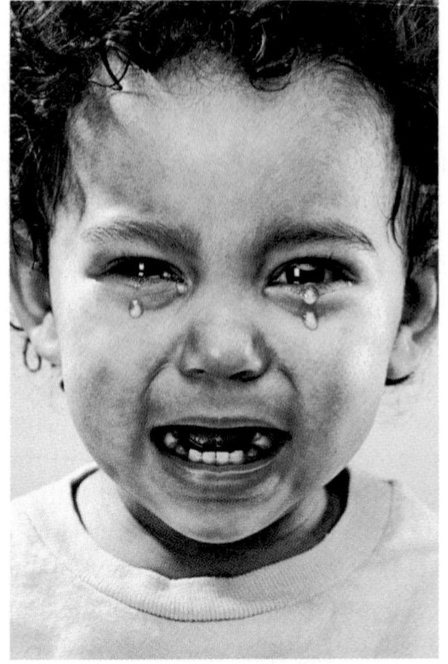

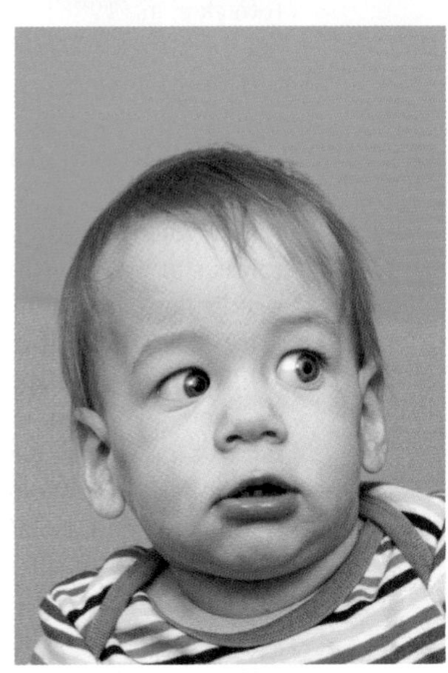

Universal facial expressions of emotions are exhibited naturally by infants. They don't have to be taught expressions for (from top left and clockwise) happiness, sadness, disgust, fear, anger, and surprise. Recently, contempt has been added to the list of universally expressed and recognized expressions of emotions.

important point is not to jump to conclusions concerning what manipulators mean.

Illustrators are gestures that help explain what a person says to another person. They usually occur simultaneously with the verbal message, but sometimes they begin while the speaker is still formulating the words. Activating the brain's motor function is simpler than constructing grammatically appropriate sentences. If the words don't come fast enough, the gesture will stop in midstream (Wachsmuth, 2006). Telling a person to go to the left, then pointing in the appropriate direction, is an example of an illustrator. Describing how to "zigzag" while drawing the movement in the air is another example. Many of the unconscious gestures we make that emphasize what we are saying are illustrators. Public speakers, for example, punctuate their points with hand and arm movements (a stabbing motion with the index finger and hand to illustrate intensity of commitment; arms spread widely to illustrate desire to include everyone in the audience). These are rarely planned, and when they are, they often come across as stilted and artificial.

Emblems are gestures that have precise meanings separate from verbal communication. The hand wave communicates "goodbye" in the United States. There are fewer than 60 emblems used in the United States. Israel, however, uses more than 250 (Ekman, 1992). No emblems are unique to the United States. The French, however, have a unique gesture for "He's drunk." The gesture is a fist placed around the nose and twisted. Germans have a unique "good luck" emblem that consists of two fists with the thumbs inside pounding an imaginary table (Ekman et al., 1984).

Many common emblems, especially obscene or vulgar ones, have spread to other cultures around the world (Tibit, 2011). The extended middle finger is recognized almost everywhere as an obscene gesture and is used widely beyond the borders of the United States. Some Latin American cultures add to the gesture by extending the middle finger while raising the arm abruptly and grabbing the arm with the other hand.

The competent communicator needs to be mindful of the vast potential for misunderstanding inherent in the gestural code. Consider one example. A young photographer was flown to a remote area of Alaska one summer. When the weather turned bad, the photographer's father became concerned and sent a plane to look for his son. The pilot spotted the young man's camp and soon saw him waving a red jacket liner, which to a pilot is a signal to leave. The young photographer then showed a thumbs-up gesture as the plane flew over. The pilot kept on flying, concluding that the thumbs-up gesture meant everything was fine. Weeks later, the frozen body of the young man was found. He left a diary. In it he wrote that he was ecstatic to see the plane and waved the red jacket liner to flag down the pilot. He showed the thumbs-up gesture to communicate his happiness at being rescued. He was dumbfounded to see the plane fly away. When he finally ran out of firewood, he used the last bullet in his gun to end his misery (Burgoon et al., 1996).

Very few gestures are emblems with precise meanings in all contexts. Most gestures are far more ambiguous and require sophisticated interpretation tied specifically to the transactions and contexts in which they occur. Folding your arms across your chest, for example, may mean that you are closing yourself off to others in a defensive gesture, or it may simply be a comfortable way for you to rest your arms. In Fiji, it is a sign of respect when talking to others (Mancini, 2003). Be cautious when interpreting the meaning of gestures. When you do interpret the meaning of gestures, match them with other nonverbal cues and look for consistency of meaning.

As cultures increasingly mix and countries become multicultural, misunderstanding can occur when a specific emblem has different meanings in two cultures. The thumb inserted between the index and middle fingers is an old American gesture commonly used playfully with children that typically means, "I've got your nose!" This same gesture is a nonverbal invitation to have sex in Germany, Holland, and Denmark, but in Portugal and Brazil, it wishes a person good luck or protection. The extended middle finger is obscene in most cultures, but in Uruguay, it means "I don't believe you." Pointing to objects with the index finger in parts of Central Africa is deemed vulgar and crude. A large study of 40 different cultures isolated 20 common hand gestures, all of which had different meanings in each culture (Morris et al., 1979).

Touch Communication: Hands-On Experience

Social scientists call the study of touch **haptics**. There are approximately 5 million touch receptors in our skin, about 3,000 in a single fingertip, all sending messages to our brain. Skin is the largest organ in the human body, covering about 19 square feet on the average-sized human (Colt, 1997). Touching skin is an enormously powerful and important communication code. Anger, fear, disgust, love, gratitude, sympathy, happiness, and sadness all can be decoded fairly accurately by those receiving touch even while blindfolded (Hertenstein et al., 2009). Social psychologist Dacher Keltner notes that touch is "our richest means of emotional expression" (quoted in Carey, 2010).

Significance of Touch: Life Changing

American playwright Tennessee Williams testified to the power of touch when he wrote, "Devils can be driven out of the heart by the touch of a hand on a hand, or a mouth on a mouth" (quoted in Colt, 1997). Premature babies studied at Miami's Touch Research Institute show the remarkable benefits of touch to human well-being. With just three 10-minute gentle massages each day, premature babies are more alert, responsive, and active than infants of the same size and condition who are not massaged. Premature infants who are massaged tolerate noise, sleep more soundly, gain weight 47% faster, and leave the hospital an average of six days sooner than premature babies who are not massaged (Colt, 1997). With almost half a million premature babies born in the United States each year, the six-day earlier departure from the hospital would translate into billions of dollars in annual savings if gentle baby massage were practiced in all hospitals.

Voluminous research on infant and child development reveals that touch is not only beneficial but even critical for life itself (Hertenstein, 2002; Loots & Devise, 2003). Infants in orphanages who do not receive much, if any, touch from other humans are usually maladjusted and quiet; they show difficulty learning and maturing normally (Andersen, 1999). During Romania's strife in the early 1990s, thousands of infants were warehoused in orphanages, virtually alone in their cribs for two years. They were found to be severely impaired by the lack of physical contact, and some even died.

Touch has an impact on emotional health and well-being. Massage is a stress reducer. Approximately 20 million Americans visit massage therapists each year according to the National Institutes of Health, and the number increases each year (Barnes et al., 2008). Volunteer therapists gave massages to exhausted rescue workers, traumatized survivors, and medical pathologists to help them cope with the bombing of a federal building in Oklahoma City in 1996 and to rescue workers at the 9/11 collapse of the Twin Towers in New York City.

Touch is essential to the expression of love, warmth, intimacy, and concern for others (Andersen et al., 2006; Prager, 2000). It can promote trust and cooperation (Kraus et al., 2010). Misuse of touch can repel, frighten, or anger others. Touch communicates power. Sexual harassment is often an issue of inappropriate, unwanted touch communication (see Chapter 7). Touch can also be quite influential. When teachers touched students on the arm in the beginning and at the end of a conference, there was a 25% increase in positive evaluations of the teacher-student conference compared to the no-touch condition (Steward & Lupfer, 1987). Waitresses receive bigger tips, on average, when they touch patrons subtly (Crusco & Wetzel, 1984). Psychologists gain greater compliance from their clients when they touch them appropriately (Patterson et al., 1986). Even shoppers purchase more merchandise when they are unobtrusively touched (Smith et al., 1982).

Despite the clear benefits of touch communication, Americans are "touchy about touch." Psychologist Tiffany Field, director of the Touch Research Institute, worries that Americans are becoming touch-phobic (Colt, 1997). The growing concern about sexual harassment and child abuse has created a "touching is taboo" atmosphere. The National Education Association, the voice of 2 million teachers in the United States, advocates the slogan: "Teach, but don't touch" (Simpson, 2006).

Compared with other cultures, Americans are a "nontactile society." Field found that French parents and children touch each other three times as often as American parents and children, a pattern that doesn't vary with age. Field compared French and American teenagers in Paris and Miami McDonald's restaurants. French adolescents engaged in significantly more casual touch (leaning on a friend, putting an arm around another person's shoulder) than American teens. Field also concludes that "French parents and teachers alike are more physically affectionate and the kids are less aggressive" (cited in Colt, 1997, p. 62). The French, however, are not the "touchiest" culture. One study found that Italian and Greek dyads (pairs) touched more than French, English, and Dutch dyads (Remland et al., 1995).

Types of Touch: Function, Usage, and Intensity

There are several types of touching. Knowing which type of touch is appropriate for which context is a vital concern to the competent communicator. Heslin (1974) identified five types of touching based on their function, usage, and intensity.

The **functional-professional touch** is the least intense form of touching. The touch is instrumental communication that takes place between doctors and patients, coaches and athletes, and the like. Lately, teacher-student touch communication is limited to this type, if engaged in at all. Functional-professional touching is businesslike and limited to the requirements of the situation. A nurse helping a patient sit up in bed or a football coach demonstrating the "bump-and-run" are examples.

The **social-polite touch** occurs during initial introductions, business relationships, and formal occasions. The handshake is the standard form of social-polite touch in American culture. Many European cultures greet strangers with a hug and a perfunctory kiss on each cheek.

The **friendship-warmth touch** is the most ambiguous type of touch and leads to the most misunderstandings between people. The amount of touch has to be negotiated when showing friendship and warmth toward others. Too little touch may communicate unfriendliness, indifference, and coldness. Too much touch that seems too intimate communicates sexual interest when such interest may not be wanted. Friendly touches, especially those taking place in private, can mistakenly be perceived as sexual, especially by males (Andersen, 1999).

The **love and intimacy touch** is reserved only for a very few special individuals—close friends, family members, spouses, and lovers. This is not sexual touch, although it may blend with sexual touch. Tenderly holding a friend's hand, softly touching the cheek of a spouse, or hugging are examples of this type of touch. Couples that touch frequently have more satisfying relationships (Oveis, 2010).

The **sexual touch** is the most personal, intimate touch and the most restricted. Mutual consent is the most important consideration to the competent communicator. Engaging in this type of touch when it is unwanted will produce serious repercussions.

Appropriateness of touch largely depends on understanding which type of touch is acceptable and desirable in which situation. *Types of touch help define relationships between people.* If one person initiates a friendship touch but the other person recoils because no real friendship has been established, clearly this type of touch is inappropriate. Both parties must define their relationship similarly or problems will occur. Ignoring the social-polite touch during introductions can provoke a negative response from the party shown such indifference and disrespect. Choosing to engage in too much or too little touch communication in a particular situation can send a powerful message.

Touch Taboos: Keeping Your Hands to Yourself

At the Group of 8 Summit in St. Petersburg, Russia, in July 2006, George W. Bush approached German Chancellor Angela Merkel, the only female leader present, and proceeded to give her an unexpected, and apparently unwelcome, neck and shoulder massage. Her reaction became international news. She responded to the Bush touch as though he had stun gunned her. Her shoulders hunched, then she threw up her arms wildly, and her face showed a look of utter dismay. One German tabloid paper headlined the event, "Bush: Love Attack on Merkel." Political scientist and oft-quoted political pundit Larry Sabato of the University of Virginia noted that "almost any male alive today knows that you don't offer uninvited massages to any female, much less the chancellor of Germany" (Vennochi, 2006).

There are many touch taboos both within our own culture and in other cultures. According to research conducted in the United States (Jones, 1994), about 15% of all touches on a daily basis are unwanted and rejected. A manual published by the University of California at San Francisco instructs nurses not to touch Cambodians on the head. That is where they believe their soul resides. Greeting a Muslim by shaking his or her left hand is an insult because the left hand is reserved for toilet functions. Although not always enforced, couples break the law in Dubai if they hold hands, hug, or kiss in public (Surk, 2008). In Korea, young people are forbidden to touch the shoulders of their elders. Kim (1992) notes: "Southeast Asians do not ordinarily touch during a conversation, especially one between opposite sexes, because many Asian cultures adhere to norms that forbid displays of affection and intimacy" (p. 321).

Touch is taboo in many situations, such as Richard Gere's overly familiar embrace and kiss of Bollywood movie star Shilpa Shetty, which produced a huge uproar in India.

There are several forms of taboo touching in the United States. The competent communicator manifests sensitivity by recognizing these forbidden forms of touch and adopting more appropriate communication behavior (Jones, 1994). These touch taboos are:

1. *Strangers are the "untouchables."* Nonfunctional touch is usually perceived as too intimate and personal. Inevitable jostling and bumping take place in crowded elevators, buses, stores, and the like. The American norm is to apologize when we bump or otherwise touch a stranger. Sexual touch by a stranger is highly inappropriate, even cause for arrest. Although President Bush wasn't entirely a stranger to Chancellor Merkel, they didn't know each other well at the time of the massaging incident. This alone should have cued him to the inappropriateness of the massage.
2. *Harmful touches should be avoided.* Children have to learn early that hurting a person by hitting, biting, scratching, or otherwise damaging someone is forbidden. Even if the person who inflicts the hurt is a spouse or partner and the hurt is accidental, the recipient of the painful touch will cry out in protest. The initial handshake of a job applicant predicts who is likely to be offered the job after a pool of applicants has been interviewed (Ambady et al., 2000). A crushing handshake that inflicts pain on the interviewer is not likely to create a favorable impression (nor is the limp handshake that seems perfunctory). A handshake that matches the firmness applied by the interviewer tends to be received more favorably.
3. *Avoid startling touches.* Sneaking up on a person and tapping them on the shoulder when they think they are alone will likely startle them and produce a strong negative response. There is no equivalent immediate countermove a person can use. You can't startle the person who tapped you on the shoulder. Even though the startling touch is sometimes done playfully, most people resent

being startled. President Bush may have intended to be playful or considerate when he massaged the German chancellor's shoulders and neck, but he clearly startled her.

4. *Avoid the interruption touch.* Touches should not interfere with principal activities. Throwing your arms around your partner and hugging him or her tightly while your partner desperately tries to mix ingredients for dinner interrupts the primary activity. It will likely produce rejection of the touch. Trying to kiss your partner on the lips when he or she is watching an engrossing movie will also likely produce rejection. The Bush massage of Chancellor Merkel interrupted a conversation among the G-8 leaders.

5. *Don't move others.* This is especially important advice when dealing with strangers. Ushering people from one place to another without warning or permission is usually seen as an aggressive act. Warning people that they need to move and offering a quick explanation, however, can nullify the negative reaction to being moved by someone. "Excuse me, I need to get through" or "Watch out, this coffee is very hot," followed by a touch gently moving a person out of the way, usually will not produce the response that touch alone will produce.

6. *Avoid "rub-it-in" touches.* Don't intensify a negative remark with a touch. A husband pinching the thigh of his wife and remarking, "That's pretty fattening," as she orders dessert, inappropriately rubs in the nasty dig. A woman who tells her male partner to "walk your mother to her car" while slapping his arm intensifies the rebuke.

Dealing with those who violate touch taboos is fairly straightforward (Jones, 1994). Determining how accidental or purposeful the violation is will guide you in your response. Unintentional lapses of touch protocol are easily forgiven. Intentional violations usually require a stronger response.

Competence and Touch: Some Suggestions

Here are some suggestions for dealing competently with touch violations:

1. *Begin by assuming the violation is accidental.* Your nonverbal rejection—pulling away, frowning, and so forth—may be all that's required to convey the message that the touch is unwanted and inappropriate.

2. *Use descriptive statements* to identify your reaction and the behavior that ignited it. "I don't like to be moved out of the way like that. It seems aggressive, so please don't do it" is an example.

3. *Use intense nonverbal cues when faced with a purposeful violator.* Hard-core touch violators are fond of putting the person who is upset on the defensive with statements such as, "Don't be so touchy" or "Lighten up, I didn't mean anything by it." There's no need to engage in a tit-for-tat verbal competition. A prolonged glower, a disgusted look held for a bit longer than usual, or a penetrating stare without comment can make the violator very uncomfortable and communicate the appropriate message.

4. *Repeat offenders require strong nonverbal signs of rejection plus a direct, firm command.* "Don't ever touch me that way again" or "Don't ever grab my shoulder" are examples.

5. *A brief apology should follow your own touch violation.* If you inadvertently violate a touch taboo, simply apologize. "Oh, I'm sorry. I didn't mean to bump you."

Voice Communication: How You Sound

Our voice is second only to our face in communicating our emotions (Simon-Thomas et al., 2009), perhaps even as important (Johnstone & Scherer, 2000). As is true of universal facial expressions of emotion already discussed, there is preliminary evidence that suggests universal recognition of emotions from languagefree voice samples (Scherer, 2003).

Our voice communicates information about our age, sex, socioeconomic status, ethnicity, and regional background. Vocal cues, or **paralanguage**, are usually divided into three classifications (Samovar & Porter, 2004): *vocal characterizers* (laughing, yelling, moaning, crying, whining, belching, yawning), *vocal qualifiers* (volume, tone, pitch, resonance, rhythm, rate), and *vocal segregates* ("uh-hum," "uh," "mm-hmm," "oooh," "shh"). A whispering soft voice may indicate speech anxiety when it is heard in front of a large audience. A flat, monotone voice can induce sleep in listeners. Speaking at hyperspeed may communicate nervousness and excitement. Typically, listeners prefer a speaking rate that approximates their own speech pattern (Buller & Aune, 1992).

There are cultural differences regarding vocal communication. Arabs speak very loudly because it connotes strength and sincerity. Israelis view high volume as a sign of strong beliefs on an issue. Germans assume a "commanding tone that projects authority and self-confidence" (Ruch, 1989, p. 191). People from Thailand, Japan, and the Philippines tend to speak very softly, almost in a whisper. This communicates good manners and education. In Japan, laughing signals joy, but it also often camouflages displeasure, anger, embarrassment, and sorrow (McDaniel, 2000).

Space Communication: Distance and Territoriality

Space communicates in very powerful and significant ways. Much of human history has been a narration about wars fought over who controls what space. This section is about the influence that distance and territoriality—called **proxemics** by social scientists—have on our communication.

Distance: Defining Relationships

Anthropologist Edward Hall (1969) has identified four types of spatial relationships based on distances between individuals communicating. *These four types are intimate, personal, social, and public distances*. The distance zones identified by Hall are averages. The actual distances in each category vary according to culture, and individual preferences vary within a culture. The distances, their usages, and overlapping nonverbal cues for the mainstream culture of the United States appear in Table 5-1.

Typically, strangers stepping into an intimate zone will produce great discomfort, even hostility. This is usually perceived as an aggressive act. An intimate partner, however, who avoids the intimate zone signals a distancing in the relationship. Counselors look for such cues to signal trouble or disagreement between relationship partners even when couples verbally insist that a problem doesn't exist. One study found that distressed romantic partners stay 25% farther apart from each other than happy romantic partners (Crane, 1987). We signal that we are "far apart" in negotiations by literally moving away from our adversaries in the bargaining process.

Sometimes we are forced into intimate zones with strangers. A crowded elevator is an example. Being forced to rub elbows with individuals we've never met before is uncomfortable. Usually, when the intimacy zone is violated through nobody's fault, we try to establish a psychic distance from others. That is why occupants of crowded elevators often stare at the numbers indicating what floor is coming up next. This act distances us mentally from strangers and allows us to cope with an uncomfortable situation.

The personal space of short people is more often violated than that of tall people. In one observational study (Caplan & Goldman, 1981), short males (five feet five inches) had their personal space invaded more than twice as often (69% to 31%) as tall males (six feet two inches). Males

TABLE 5-1 FOUR TYPES OF SPATIAL RELATIONSHIPS AND THEIR CHARACTERISTICS IN MAINSTREAM U.S. CULTURE

TYPE	DISTANCE	USAGE OF NONVERBAL CUES	OVERLAPPING NONVERBAL CUES
Intimate	0–18 in.	Loving; showing tenderness	Limited eye contact; touch; smell
Personal	18 in.–4 ft.	Conversing with intimates, friends	Eye contact; some touching; gestures
Social	4 ft.–12 ft.	Business talk; social conversing	Formal vocal tone; gestures; eye contact
Public	12 ft. or more	Lectures; speeches	Eye contact; gestures; vocal tones

also claim a larger personal spatial bubble around themselves than do women (Mercer & Benjamin, 1980). Observe males sitting on a couch, for example, and notice how much space they often take by spreading out their arms and legs. In a multicultural country such as the United States, opportunities for misunderstanding associated with spatial zones are plentiful (Martin & Nakayama, 2007). Comfortable social distance for an Arab may violate personal or even intimate zones of Americans. Arabs typically move very close when conversing. Part of the reason is that Arabs perceive a person's smell to be an extension of the person and, thus, important (Hall, 1969). Not recognizing the cultural differences associated with distance can make an individual seem pushy and aggressive or distant and standoffish.

Territoriality: Defending Your Space

"To have a territory is one of the essential components of life; to lack one is one of the most precarious of all conditions" (Hall, 1969, p. 45). **Territoriality** is a predisposition to defend a fixed geographic area, or territory, as one's exclusive domain (Burgoon et al., 1996).

We stake out our territory in a variety of ways (Burgoon et al., 1996). We use *markers* such as hedges, small fences, and signs saying "Keep Out." A coat left on the back of a chair marks temporary possession of that specific seat. Resting a lunch tray on a table in a cafeteria signals "That's my eating area." We also claim a territory by erecting *barriers to entry*, such as walls, locked doors, security guards, and snarling dogs (see Box 5-2). When office space is limited, we erect partitions that make our environment look like a rabbit warren. A third way that we stake out our territory is by *occupancy*. Students who sit in the same chair every class period quickly assume the chair is their recognized place. Homeless people often establish their spot on the street by consistently occupying that small territory.

Invasions of territories (homes, offices) by others are usually met with physical and verbal aggression. One notable form of such territorial invasion is loud, obnoxious noise from neighbors. Walls prevent outsiders from physically intruding into one's home. Loud noise from megadecibel stereos, however, penetrates the walls. You can't move your home like you can your automobile to escape the intrusion.

Commuter train cars everywhere from Seattle to Washington, D.C., are being refitted with only rows of paired seats, no three-seat rows, because passengers often refuse to sit in the middle seat even if it means standing for an hour when riding the train. Richard Wener, an environmental psychologist at Polytechnic University in Brooklyn, suggests that a less drastic alternative may work equally well—armrests between seats, as in airplanes (Marantz, 2005).

Environment: Creating Atmosphere

Winston Churchill once said, "We shape our buildings, then our buildings shape us." The design of our environment shapes communication. Airports and fast-food restaurants design brightly lit buildings with uncomfortable plastic furniture to hurry people along and limit communication transactions. Such spaces are not meant for loitering, intimate communication, or relaxation. The environment communicates "Do your business and leave." Living in dilapidated public housing can produce aggressiveness, violence, and mental fatigue (Kuo & Sullivan, 2001). Students perceive professors as more credible when their offices are attractively decorated and organized than when their offices look like mine does (Teven & Comadena, 1996). Simply removing the desk in a physician's office makes patients feel five times more at ease during office visits than having the desk act as a barrier separating doctor and patient (Sommer, 1969).

Some jails and prisons have been designed with communication in mind, primarily because of the dismal failure of traditional prisons to control violence and reduce recidivism (repeat offenders) (Gilligan & Lee, 2004). The traditional prison environment provides little privacy and personal space, separates prisoners from guards, and restricts inmates' mingling. The Federal Bureau of Prisons began building prisons with a different design to encourage direct supervision of inmates (Wener,

BOX 5.2 Focus on Controversy

GATED COMMUNITIES: FORTRESS AMERICA?

Millions of households in the United States live in gated communities. Gated communities have become a worldwide phenomenon. They are popular in China, Argentina, Australia, Brazil, Mexico, Great Britain, and many other countries. Gated communities come in many varieties. Some are housing projects that require using a keypad code to open a metal gate blocking access to the community. Others have erected much more elaborate barriers to entrance. Gates may be accompanied by fences surrounding the community, armed guards, security patrols, and tire-piercing devices that are triggered by improper entrance. The Hidden Valley community in Santa Clarita, California (a gated neighborhood of 400 homes), discourages intruders with a military-style antiterrorist device that launches a three-foot metal cylinder from ground level into the bottom of any car trying to sneak past the gate. This device disables and seriously damages the intruder's car.

Protection of personal property and security against crimes of violence are the primary motivators for gating a community (Nonnemaker, 2009). Proponents claim they feel safer and that gated neighborhoods promote a sense of community where everybody knows everybody else. Opponents see it differently. Edward Blakely, dean of the School of Urban Planning and Development at the University of Southern California, warns, "Gated communities will accelerate the economic and social fragmentation of the nation" (Diamond, 1997a, p. 4). Robert Lang, director of the Metropolitan Institute at Virginia Tech, states, "You create enclaves of stability in seas of decay. That's worrisome" (quoted in El Nasser, 2002).

The desire to be safe in person and property cannot be taken lightly. Do gated communities afford real security or merely the illusion of safety? Ed Cross, member of the San Antonio planning commission and a real estate broker, claims, "People are living with a false sense of security. It's a marketing gimmick; it's a fad" (Diamond, 1997a, p. 5). Blakely and Mary Gail Snyder (1997), authors of *Fortress America*, note that crime rates typically drop in the first year or two after a neighborhood becomes gated, but thereafter, crime rates rise to levels equivalent to outside areas. Research at the University of Wisconsin showed no difference in crime rates between gated and ungated communities (Wilson-Doenges, 2000; see also Benfield, 2010). The 4,800 residents of Sudden Valley, a gated community in Bellingham, Washington, voted to tear down their five gates. Most residents felt that the gates enticed burglars instead of deterring them. When the gates were removed, crime rates went down (Diamond, 1997a). In Atlanta, burglars targeted gated communities in a crime spree that netted the robbers a million dollars in jewelry, cash, and silver from more than 90 homes (El Nasser, 2002). The gated community acted like a flashing neon sign: "Great Stuff; Come Steal."

Regardless of who's right in this debate, gated communities manifest an adversarial, competitive territoriality (Blakely & Snyder, 1997). They communicate to the outside world "Keep Out!" Gated communities segregate in-groups from out-groups (Vesselinov, 2008). Dividing America into thousands of enclaves homogenizes neighborhoods and very likely promotes divisiveness and conflict between groups. We see ourselves as adversaries competing for space. Out-group members resent the restraint on their freedom of travel. One study showed that gated communities create a false sense of security and a significantly lower sense of community (Wilson-Doenges, 2000). Another study in England showed "a dynamic pattern of separation that goes beyond the place of residence" (Atkinson & Flint, 2004). Social groups insulate themselves from unwanted encounters with outsiders.

(continued)

BOX 5.2 *(Continued)*

Typically, gated communities are affordable only to the well off or the rich. A poor family's gated community consists of a locked apartment building. When we wall ourselves in against those who look and act differently from us, it is probably more difficult to find common ground between ethnic groups and socioeconomic classes, develop opportunities for cooperation, and work together as teams to make decisions and solve personal and societal problems. As Blakely puts it, "The nation's dream was equality and mutual assistance and the melting pot. . . . Take that away and we're just people who live on a piece of territory" (Diamond, 1997a, p. 5).

Perhaps the downsides of gated communities have diminished their attraction. A study by GfK Roper Consulting found that many Americans are leaving gated communities, and fewer than one-fifth of Americans want to live in them. Only 15% consider gated communities "ideal" (Jefferson, 2007). The luster of gated communities has diminished primarily because of the perceived loss of community.

QUESTIONS FOR THOUGHT

1. Do you like the idea of gated communities? Would you like to live in a gated community? Is it ethical to create these enclaves that keep out mostly minorities and the poor?
2. Can you think of alternatives to gated communities that might produce the benefits proponents claim without closing off communication with groups who can't afford to live in such neighborhoods?
3. Are there external signs that would keep a community safer without advertising wealth and attracting thieves?

2006). Prisons were built with open areas for inmate interactions. Guards mingle directly with prisoners, developing ongoing relationships with the inmates and spotting trouble before it explodes. There are no enclosed booths for officers. Inmates have small rooms, not cells with bars. They control the lights in their rooms. There are more televisions available to reduce conflicts over which programs to watch. Furniture is "soft" (cushy and comfortable), not institutional "hard" (plastic and resistant), and floors are carpeted. These new prisons, despite their innovativeness, actually cost less to build than traditional jails (Wener, 2006; Wener et al., 1987).

Violent incidents are reduced 30% to 90% in the new prisons compared to traditional prisons. Inmate rape is virtually nonexistent, and vandalism and graffiti drop precipitously. Guards, hesitant at first, feel safer, and tension between inmates is reduced (Wener, 2006; Wener et al., 1987). The inmates still perceive direct-supervision jails to be prisons, but the communication outcomes are dramatically different from traditional jails.

Communicating Competently with Nonverbal Codes

Knowledge of the myriad ways nonverbal codes influence our communication with others is the first step toward competent nonverbal communication. As indicated repeatedly throughout this chapter, appropriateness and effectiveness of nonverbal communication are key parts of the competence equation. Suggestions have been offered already on how you might improve your understanding and skill in nonverbal communication. This section will tie together common threads linking various nonverbal codes to communication competence.

Monitor Nonverbal Communication

Knowledge is not useful if it isn't applied. Use your knowledge of nonverbal codes to monitor your own communication and the communication of others. Observe nonverbal communication in action. Become sensitive to the subtleties of these codes. Try experimenting. Maintain eye contact during interviews or in conversations with others. Observe how this affects the outcome of the communication. Try appropriate touching to see if it produces greater closeness and more positive responses from others. If you tend toward a monotone voice, enliven it on purpose. If your facial expressions tend to be constrained, try to communicate your emotions with more dramatic facial expressions.

Resist Jumping to Conclusions

By now, you should be aware that nonverbal communication can be highly ambiguous. Don't make the mistake that others have made. Don't assume that you can "read a person like a book," especially if you don't know that person well. Knowing the person well reduces the ambiguity of nonverbal cues. Nonverbal cues suggest certain messages, but you must consider them in their appropriate context. The easiest way to determine if you have interpreted nonverbal cues correctly is to ask. Check your perceptions with others. "I noticed you tapping your fingers and tugging at your ear. Are you nervous or upset about something?" is a quick way to determine if your nonverbal read is accurate.

Observe Multiple Nonverbal Cues

Relying on a single nonverbal cue will often produce a false perception. Slow blinking rate may suggest relaxed demeanor, but observe other nonverbal cues as well (e.g., posture, gestures). Silence may indicate disagreement, but do other nonverbal cues contradict this assessment? Be careful not to make a broad generalization based on a single nonverbal cue. Look for nonverbal clusters to determine more accurately what is being communicated.

Recognize Cultural Differences

The vast differences in cultural use of nonverbal codes have been stressed repeatedly. When you communicate with individuals from another culture or co-culture in the United States, recognize the nonverbal communication differences. If you come across a nonverbal cue that puzzles you, don't assume anything. Observe members of other cultures to determine what is appropriate behavior. If you still feel doubtful about your interpretation, check your perception by asking someone who would know.

Strive for Consistency

Try to match verbal and nonverbal communication. Mixed messages confuse those who communicate with us. Exhibiting nonverbal behavior that contradicts what we are saying will produce a negative reaction from others.

Summary

NONVERBAL communication affects our communication with others in powerful ways, yet it is often ambiguous and difficult to read. Much of the advice offered in the popular media on nonverbal communication is incorrect or overstated because a single nonverbal cue is given too much emphasis. Specific advice on communicating competently has been offered for each of the numerous types of nonverbal communication (physical appearance, facial communication, gestures, touch, voice, space, and environment), but general, overlapping advice also has been offered: monitor your nonverbal communication, resist jumping to conclusions based on a single nonverbal cue, observe multiple nonverbal cues before drawing conclusions about others, recognize vast cultural differences in nonverbal communication, and strive for consistency in your verbal and nonverbal communication to avoid mixed messages.

Answers for Self-Assessment Test, Box 5-1

1. True—older adults have more experience.
2. False—there is no single nonverbal cue indicating lying.
3. False—in many cultures, direct eye contact would be perceived as rude or disrespectful.
4. False—can just as easily be perceived as suspicious or untrustworthy.
5. False—too many other interpretations are possible; may just be comfortable.
6. False—smiles can show contempt, sarcasm, fear, misery; different types of smiles.
7. False—at least two research studies supported universal standards of beauty.
8. False—cultures can vary widely on touch taboos. Unmarried couples holding hands in public is strictly forbidden in some cultures but certainly not in the U.S.
9. False—there are at least seven universal facial expressions of specific emotions.
10. False—female friendly smiles are often misinterpreted by males as a sexual invitation.

Answers for *Critical Thinking* caption: Victoria Beckham (p. 135): #1 and #3

Quizzes Without Consequences

Did you understand all the material in this chapter? Test your knowledge before your exam!

Go to the companion website at www.oup.com/us/rothwell, click on the Student Resources for each chapter, and take the Quizzes Without Consequences.

Film School Case Studies

The Birdcage (1996). Comedy; R

A very amusing remake of *La Cage aux Folles* about a gay couple "acting straight" to fool a conservative U.S. senator. Analyze the main characters' nonverbal behavior, especially when Robin Williams attempts to teach Nathan Lane to act like a straight male. Are these merely stereotypic male behaviors or is there truth in the depiction?

Enchanted (2007). Fantasy/Romance; PG

Fantasy about Princess Giselle's (Amy Adams) idyllic life in the kingdom of Andalasia until she is exiled by evil Queen Narissa (Susan Sarandon) to New York City, where she meets her Prince Charming (Patrick Dempsey). Examine the many nonverbal cues that produce misunderstandings and comic results.

Hitch (2005). Romantic Comedy; PG-13

Will Smith plays a date doctor, teaching New York guys how to romance a woman. Smith teaches his latest pupil, played by Kevin James, the intricacies of nonverbal communication. Analyze whether Smith's depiction of nonverbal "masculine" behaviors is accurate, and why does his romancing of his dream woman go badly at first?

Mrs. Doubtfire (1993). Comedy; PG-13

Robin Williams assumes the role of an Irish nanny to be near his children when he and his wife (Sally Field) split up. Does Williams get the "feminine" behaviors correct? Analyze the different types of nonverbal behavior exhibited by Mrs. Doubtfire. Are these merely stereotypic feminine behaviors?

Quest for Fire (1982). Drama; R

An original film about humankind's initial attempts to make fire. Concentrate on the importance of nonverbal communication, especially since the "language" depicted in the movie is very limited. What are the limitations on nonverbal cues to communicate?

Tootsie (1982). Comedy; PG

This is the classic "cross-dressing" film. Dustin Hoffman's portrayal of Dorothy Michaels, who is actually the out-of-work actor Michael Dorsey, was Oscar worthy. Why does Hoffman's portrayal seem genuine? Did he make any mistakes in his nonverbal portrayal of a middle-aged woman?

CHAPTER 6

Chapter Outline

Listening to Others

CABRILLO COLLEGE FACULTY AND STAFF were understandably shaken after one of our instructors, a good friend of mine, was seriously injured when attacked with an ax handle by a mentally ill student of his. As a result, the college hired a consultant to address safety in the workplace. The speaker opened with a personal story. When driving from the cemetery after visiting the grave of her five-year-old son who had died the week before her visit, through tears from unimaginable sadness, she inadvertently ran a stop sign, pulling in front of another driver who had to brake hard to avoid a collision. The driver who screeched to a halt was a highway patrolman. The grieving mother pulled over to the curb. The officer got out of his patrol car and walked up to the passenger side of her vehicle. He tapped, indicating for her to roll down her window. He leaned over and asked, "May I get in?" She nodded her head, continuing to sob. The officer sat in the passenger seat for about five minutes without saying a word, then he asked, pointing to the cemetery, "Do you have someone in there?" Her eyes welled with tears, but she found comfort in telling him about her little boy. When she finished, the officer asked her how far away she lived and then offered to follow her home to be sure she got there safely. He never mentioned the traffic violation.

By the end of this chapter, you should be able to:

1. Understand the significance of listening to the human communication process.
2. Define and explain the listening process.
3. Describe and avert several listening problems that you may experience.
4. Distinguish different kinds of listening and prevent problems unique to each kind.
5. Identify specific ways that you can become a competent listener.

The speaker made several points from this poignant story, but an unstated point that struck me the most was the officer's compassionate willingness to listen silently to a grieving mother. He didn't interject any comments. He didn't offer advice. He didn't warn her about her driving or admonish her for the traffic violation. He just listened quietly to her story, then made certain that she got home safely. Listening is just such a fundamental, essential part of human communication, of connecting with others, but it is often too little appreciated.

The principal purpose of this chapter is for you to learn how to listen competently.

Significance of Listening

We have speech contests but no listening contests. We give awards to great speakers but not to great listeners. A list of the 100 greatest speakers of all time doesn't seem ludicrous, but a list of the 100 greatest listeners of all time seems odd at best. Speaking, not listening, earns us power and status. Until recently, listening has been an underappreciated part of communication in our hypercompetitive society. The necessity to train people to be effective listeners is a relatively recent revelation. Thirty years ago, finding a college course on listening would have been a challenge. Today, many colleges offer such a course, but those that don't usually offer a listening unit within a communication course.

There is abundant research that indicates the importance of listening. College students, on average, spend 11% of their total time communicating by writing, 16% speaking, 17% reading, but a whopping 55% listening (Emanuel et al., 2008). Poor listening in college produces poor academic performance. If you sleep or daydream your way through classes, you had better get used to saying, "Do you want to supersize that drink?"

Business leaders spend more time listening than any other type of communication. General managers ranked listening as the most important communication behavior from a list of eight possibilities (Brown, 2009; Flynn et al., 2008). "Listening is central to competence" and is a "key management skill" (Dodd, 2012, p 69). Numerous studies identify listening as the most important on-the-job communication skill (Darling & Dannels, 2003; Gabric & McFadden, 2001; Landrum & Harrold, 2003).

Interpersonally, listening is extremely important (Gottman & Gottman, 2006). Research shows "Good listening skills can help you to feel easy in all sorts of social situations, and to build the kind of rapport that leads to solid emotional bonds" (Gottman & DeClaire, 2001, p. 198). When college students listened to taped conversations, the persons who talked substantially more than they listened were the least liked (Wolvin & Coakley, 1996).

Competent listening has the power to create substantial bonds and build strong relationships with others, to avoid misunderstanding when clarity is essential to achieving important goals, to enhance your learning process both in school and outside as well, to make you a critical consumer of ideas so you can make intelligent, well-informed decisions, and to make you a more knowledgeable, skillful, and valued worker in your chosen career (Donoghue & Siegel, 2005).

Despite the impressive rewards available from competent listening, however, most people don't listen very well. Most individuals receive scant instruction regarding how to improve their listening despite the fact that instruction and training can produce significant improvement (Lane et al., 2000; McGee & Cegals, 1998). We all have extensive experience listening to others, but experience alone may simply reinforce bad habits. Some individuals have had "non-listening habits for so long that they are

DOONESBURY **BY GARRY TRUDEAU**

almost incapable of listening—if they had a listening gland, it would be atrophied from disuse" (Elgin, 1989, p. 90).

Poor listening may have contributed to the *Columbia* space shuttle disaster in 2003. According to the Columbia Accident Investigation Board (2003), "Managers' claims that they didn't hear the engineers' concerns were due in part to their not asking or listening." College students exhibit difficulties listening effectively. Professor Paul Cameron confirmed a principal concern of college instructors delivering a lecture to a room full of students (cited in Adler & Proctor, 2007). At random intervals during a nine-week course, he had students record their thoughts when he signaled them to do so. Only 20% were mildly attentive to the lecture, and a mere 12% were actively listening. Others were pursuing erotic thoughts (20%), reminiscing (20%), or worrying, daydreaming, or thinking about lunch or religion (8%). This study was conducted before the widespread availability of text messaging and social networking that have become common distractions in college classrooms. A more current study of 269 college students showed that 90% of respondents admitted to text messaging during class lectures. It is now the number one classroom distraction. Text messaging distracts fellow students, not just those doing the texting. This study also found that cell phones ringing during class was a considerable distraction (Mayk, 2010).

Doctor-patient communication is a particularly important context for effective listening, but competent listening often doesn't occur. One study found that more than half of the patients seeking medical care do not understand their diagnosis and instructions for taking proper medications and treatments, and doctors often fail to understand the complaints and concerns of patients because they aren't listening carefully (Christensen, 2004; Scholz, 2005). In another study, doctors interrupted, on average, approximately 20 seconds into a conversation with a patient. Physicians expected patients to be long-winded (to talk nonstop for an estimated three-and-a-half minutes, on average) when explaining their health concerns. When physicians were instructed not to interrupt, their patients actually talked for an average of only 92 seconds. When doctors were forced to just listen, they felt that the patients were providing significant information (Langewitz et al., 2002). Improving physicians' listening skills can reduce physicians' errors (Kertesz, 2010; Weiner et al., 2010). It can also result in fewer malpractice lawsuits from patients (Lenckus, 2005).

The Listening Process

The International Listening Association adopted an official definition of listening. With slight modification, the ILA defines **listening** as "the process of receiving, constructing [and reconstructing] meaning from, and responding to spoken and/or nonverbal messages" (Brownell, 2002, p. 48). This definition implicitly highlights listening as a dynamic, active process, not a passive activity. In the next several sections, I explore the listening process by looking at its three primary elements: comprehending, retaining, and responding.

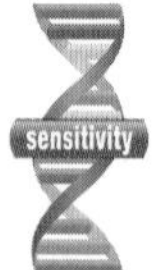

Comprehending: Discriminating for Understanding

An airline pilot, beginning the takeoff down the runway, glances at his copilot, who looks glum. The pilot encourages the copilot to "cheer up." The copilot, set to hear "gear up," promptly raises the plane's wheels—before they've left the runway (Reason & Mycielska, 1982). The copilot didn't comprehend the message from the pilot, and the plane skidded down the runway. **Comprehension** is shared meaning between or among parties in a transaction. The listening process begins with comprehension.

Discriminating Speech Sounds: Comprehending Phonemes

The first challenge facing the listener operates at the most basic level of comprehension—namely, accurately discriminating speech sounds (phonemes) and understanding these sounds as words (morphemes; see the Chapter 4 discussion of phonemes and morphemes). Making sense out of phonemes and morphemes is a complex mental process. When speaking, the average adult produces about 15 phonemes *per second* (Kuhl, 1994). This means that a listener must process 900 sounds each minute and make sense of this seeming cacophony. More rapid speakers, such as those annoying hucksters speeding through disclaimers and exclusions at the tail end of ads for bank loans or credit cards, can double these numbers and still communicate intelligibly.

Adults have difficulty distinguishing phoneme differences that do not appear in their native language. Japanese, for example, exhibit difficulty distinguishing between an *r* and *l* sound because no such distinction is meaningful in the Japanese language (Gopnik et al., 2001; Logan et al., 1991). Thus, "flied lice" and "fried rice" sound identical, provoking dubious mimicry from some smug English speakers. When the word *rake* is repeated and then followed by the repetition of the word *lake*, Japanese speakers do not hear the shift despite straining to recognize the change (Gopnik et al., 2001). Native English speakers, however, struggle to distinguish the *b* and *p* phonemes in Spanish. *Besar* meaning "to kiss" and *pesar* meaning "to weigh" get confused, which could translate the sentence "I want to kiss you" to "I want to weigh you." That could cause trouble in romance land!

Infants universally have no difficulty recognizing phoneme distinctions in any of the world's languages. Infants begin as linguistic "citizens of the world" (Kuhl, 2004). They start to have difficulty with phoneme distinctions that are not found in their native language, however, around six months old (Kuhl, 1993; Kuhl et al., 2005). Babies master the phonemes of their native language first, and this phoneme mastery facilitates learning words (Gopnik et al., 2001). Phoneme mastery is easier if infants begin to ignore phonemes that do not exist in their native language, much as they must learn to ignore nonlinguistic sounds. Gradually, the child loses the ability to hear phoneme distinctions not common to the native language. Japanese and American seven-month-old infants easily distinguish the *r* from the *l* phoneme, but at ten months, Japanese infants are no longer able while American infants become even better at making the distinction (Gopnik et al., 2001).

Speech Segmentation: Comprehending Morphemes

Listeners must be able to discern breaks between recognizable words, a process called **speech segmentation**, when speakers often make no apparent pauses to signal distinct words. The childhood chant "I scream, you scream, we all scream for ice cream" makes no apparent distinction between "I scream" and "ice cream" based on sound alone. You have to determine the meaning of the entire sentence before the correct segmentation emerges. When you hear an unfamiliar language, the morphemes seem to blend into one continuous auditory cluster. For instance, say aloud the following sentence:

Kamaunawezakusomamanenohayawewenimtuwamaanasana.

Can you segment the sentence? Not likely. If you speak Swahili, however, the sentence divides easily into this:

Kama unaweza kusoma maneno haya, wewe ni mtu wa maana sana. It means, "If you can read these words, you are a remarkable person" (Wade & Tavris, 2008, p. 81).

Comprehending meaning from phonemes combined into morphemes is more challenging than you might expect even if you are familiar with the language. In numerous classes, I have played an audiotape that was created by Dr. John Lilly. The tape repeats a single English word hundreds of times with no variation. In every class, within a 10-minute period, students report hearing 50 to 75 different words or phrases, often in several languages. Most insist that there is more than one word on the tape. Most cannot give the correct word, but many will insist that an incorrect word is actually the one on the tape. Lilly played the tape at a meeting of the American Association of Linguists, attended by almost 300 linguists who spoke 22 different languages. He tortured the linguists by playing the tape for 25 minutes (students grow restless after a few minutes). The linguists "heard" 2,730 different words in 22 languages.

Ordinary conversational speech is typically full of sloppy pronunciations, hesitations, and mumbled words, making recognition of individual words in a sentence difficult. One study isolated individual words taken from a recording of ordinary conversation. When the words were played back to participants one at a time, only 47% were correctly identified. When these same words were replayed in the context of the original conversation, however, almost 100% of the words were correctly identified (Pollack & Pickett, 1964). Determining the context (noun or verb placement in the sentence; companion words that clarify the meaning) is essential to comprehending a sentence such as "At the *present* time it is important to *present* the *present* to you."

Comprehending a single word may seem ludicrously simple, but such comprehension is more challenging than you might suppose because *hearing and listening are different processes*. **Hearing** is the physiological process of registering sound waves as they hit the eardrum. The particular sounds have no meaning until we construct meaning for them. Listening is the active effort to construct meaning from verbal and nonverbal messages. Constructing meaning from the messages of others is, in reality, more a process of reconstruction. The speaker constructs the original message. A listener reconstructs that message to match the original intended message as closely as possible. This involves a significant amount of interpretation, and with interpretation comes potential misunderstanding. One study showed a lot of misunderstanding by listeners, but speakers were convinced that listeners understood their utterances even when their statements were clearly ambiguous. "The daughter of the man and the woman arrived." "When you learn gradually you worry more." Can you discern the two different meanings for each sentence (Keysar & Henly, 2002)?

Comprehension is an important first element of listening, but if ignored, listening becomes little more than hearing background noise. One study found only 5 of 200 college students exhibited any interest in comprehending the messages of others. They were mostly interested in persuading others of the correctness of their own viewpoints (Trosser, 1998).

Retaining: Memories

Memory is essential to the listening process. This may seem obvious once you ponder what you do when you listen to a lecture in a college course. If you listen to the lecture and retain none of the information, of what value was it to you? All of those multiple-choice exams would truly become multiple-guess tests. You can't construct meaning from nothing. The information we retain when engaged in the listening process is the raw material from which meaning is constructed.

Fallibility of Memory: You Can't Retain Everything

Naturally, our minds do not retain every morsel of information as we listen to someone. One study found that married couples remembered only 35% of what they discussed in the past hour (Sillars et al., 1990). Another study found that individuals recall only about 9% of what was discussed days earlier (Stafford & Daly, 1984). Hunt (1982) notes that by the time college students receive their diplomas, they have forgotten, on average, almost 80% of what they learned. Part of the reason this occurs may be a result of cramming information into short-term memory, only to have it forgotten before it moves into long-term memory. Wurman (1989) calls this cramming process **information bulimia**. You're undoubtedly familiar with it. You binge on information to pass an exam, then purge it from your mind once the exam is over.

The **forgetting curve**—the rate at which we no longer retain information in our memory—drops rapidly at first but levels out and remains almost constant for many years thereafter (Bahrick, 1984). For example, students who took Spanish in high school or college but didn't continue using it, when tested three years later, had forgotten much of the vocabulary they had learned. After three years, however, forgetting leveled off, and retention of vocabulary showed only slight diminishment after *fifty years* (see Figure 6-1). Those students who took the most Spanish in school and learned it well remembered best. Even

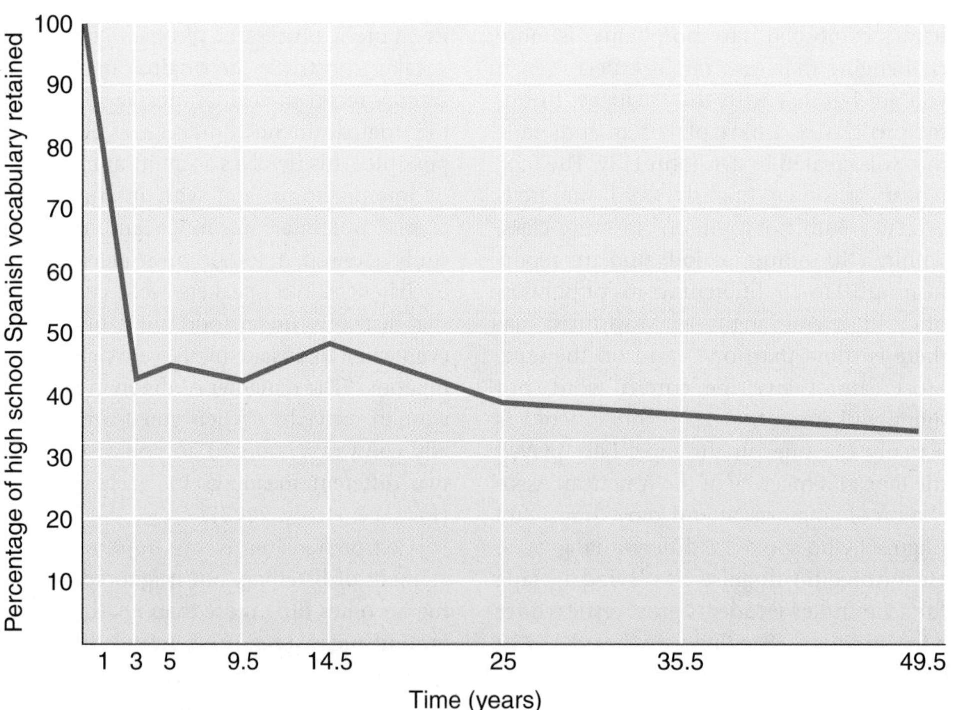

FIGURE 6-1 Long-Term Forgetting Curve (Source: Bahrick, 1984)

students who hadn't used Spanish for years still retained a significant vocabulary if they learned it well initially.

Using information immediately enhances retention. "Use it or lose it," as they say in the memory business. If you immediately apply what you have learned in college to your life's profession or to your relationships, your retention will improve markedly and last longer. The forgetting curve will be far less pronounced.

Benefits of Forgetting: Curse of the Infallible Memory

Retention is important, but remembering everything you hear would be a curse. Imagine what it would be like forgetting nothing. Every telephone number, email address, advertising jingle, slogan, song lyric, irritating noise, angry moment, embarrassing episode, and painful event would be available to clutter up your ability to think clearly and analytically. Imagine how this would affect your relationships with others. Wouldn't reliving every painful memory and embarrassing moment make it difficult for you to be optimistic and constructive in your relationships? Forgetting sometimes has a very constructive effect.

James McGaugh, a renowned memory researcher at the University of California at Irvine, and his colleagues have studied Jill Price, a woman who seems to remember virtually every detail of her life experiences (see Parker et al., 2006). Price wrote a book, *The Woman Who Can't Forget*, to publicize her amazing memory of autobiographical facts. McGaugh and his colleagues extensively tested Price's memory. If given a specific date, she can remember instantly what she was doing and what day of the week it was. The recalled personal facts of her life were checked against more than 50,000 pages of journal entries Price wrote over a period of several decades. Is her memory a blessing or a curse? She writes in her book that she became a "prisoner" of her own memory. She explains:

> The emotional intensity of my memories, combined with the random nature in which they're always flashing through my mind, has, on and off through the course of my life, nearly driven me mad. As I grew older and more and more memories accumulated in my mind, my memory became not only a horrible distraction in trying to live my life today, but also the cause of my terrible struggle to come to terms with my feelings about my past. . . . So many painful memories kept asserting themselves. (Price & Davis, 2008)

The inability to forget any detail of a past argument or the feelings you experienced when engaged in past conflicts, for example, presents challenges that we don't normally face when entering into relationships with others. Sometimes it is better to forget past slights and painful events so we can move on to better moments.

Why You Forget: Inattention, Meaninglessness, and De-motivation

You forget information for a variety of reasons. Sometimes you just don't pay attention. You are introduced to strangers, and you are concerned with what kind of impression you are making on them. Their names glance off the edges of your memory and promptly skip irretrievably into space. You are forced to say, "I'm sorry, but I've forgotten your name." You may also forget because you don't properly organize the information you hear. You don't attach the information to any meaningful concept, idea, event, or phenomenon. The numbers 1865, 1945, and 1953 don't mean much unless you realize that they are the ending dates of three significant American wars. You can remember the dates more easily knowing that. Forgetting also results from lack of motivation to listen carefully and remember. Imagine if your professor stated at the start of a lecture, "You don't need to know this for the test." Would you pack up your notebook or close your laptop and hunker down in your seat with no concern about your attention drifting or your eyelids slamming shut? Would you listen to the lecture? Finally, an amnesia dubbed the "Google effect" has been supported by four separate studies. Researchers found that the ready accessibility of the Internet and Google searches primes our memory for where to find information but lowers our ability to recall the information itself (Sparrow et al., 2011). The information is stored on the Internet so why commit it to memory?

We forget a great deal for many reasons. A perfect memory would be a curse, but what we do remember is vital to our ability to comprehend what another person communicates to us. As linguist Herbert Clark observes: "We bring to bear an enormous amount of knowledge to even the simplest utterances, in order to comprehend them" (quoted in Hunt, 1982, p. 119).

Whenever you listen, you depend on your memories to fill in the blanks. Speakers presume knowledge of their audiences. If you had no common experiences with others and no common language to communicate those experiences, you couldn't communicate even rudimentary messages effectively. Retention of information is an integral part of the listening process. Retention is diminished when our listening is *mindless*—little effort is made to attend to a speaker's message. Retention is enhanced when listening is *mindful*—careful attention is given to a speaker's message. *Mindful listening is active listening;* you're engaged in the communication transaction with others. You're not merely a passive observer. Mindful listening is not always appropriate, however. It's impossible to listen mindfully to every message you receive daily. Your brain circuits would figuratively fry, and you would be mentally exhausted if you tried this unrealistic task. Every conversation is not deep and meaningful; some are pointless or peripheral. Mindful listening can occur because we focus on meaningful conversations, speeches, and learning opportunities while ignoring the trivial.

Responding: Providing Feedback

Responding is a third essential element of listening (Barker & Watson, 2000; Pasupathi, et al.,1999; Purdy & Borisoff, 1997). Listening is a transactional process between speaker and audience. Effective listening depends on both participants in the transaction. Speakers look for responses from listeners to determine whether a message is being processed or ignored. Without a response from the listener, you have no way of knowing whether listening actually occurs. You determine the quality and type of listening from the responses of listeners. These responses can be both verbal and nonverbal. As listeners, we indicate confusion by frowning or by asking a question for clarification. If listeners are staring out a window, doing a face plant onto the desktop, doodling, talking to the person next to them, or reading the sports page when you are talking, then listening to you probably isn't a top priority.

One study revealed that responsiveness is a key determinant of effective listening (Lewis & Reinsch, 1988). Analyzing 195 incidents in medical and banking environments, researchers determined that listeners' attentiveness to the speaker was critical. Verbally, listeners exhibited attentiveness by answering questions and sharing ideas. Nonverbally, listeners exhibited attentiveness by maintaining eye contact and using facial expressions that showed interest (smiles, raised eyebrows).

In the next three sections of this chapter, I discuss informational, critical, and empathic listening. Each type, in its own way, incorporates the basic elements of listening: comprehending, retaining, and responding.

Competent Informational Listening

Informational listening attempts to comprehend the message of a speaker. Your goal is to understand what the speaker has said. When listening to others, it is usually better to be sure that you comprehend the speaker's message before you critically evaluate it. Too often we are prone to judge another person's ideas without fully understanding what the person actually said and believes. Consider several problems that thwart competent informational listening and steps a competent communicator should take to correct these problems.

Information Overload: Too Much of a Good Thing

A study by LexisNexis on international workplace productivity asked workers to respond to the statement: "It is difficult to maintain my focus on the task at hand when I get distracted by the constant flow of emails and other information." Workers in five countries—United States, Great Britain, China, South Africa, and Australia—responded. Agreement with this statement varied from a low of 57% in China to a high of 85% in Australia. Respondents from the United States registered 60% agreement (Walsh & Vivona, 2010). Workers also responded to the statement: "Being constantly accessible through mobile phone, email and other means, makes it harder for me to get my job done." Affirmative responses to this statement were: 58% (United States), 45% (Great Britain), 63% (China), 50% (South Africa), and 71% (Australia).

We live in a world of information overload aided and abetted by communication technologies barely conceived of two decades ago. When do we have time to listen to others? We so easily become swamped in the tsunami of information that listening to others speak becomes noise—interference. Elsewhere, I provide a detailed list of solutions for addressing information overload (Rothwell, 2010). Briefly, begin by occasionally shutting off the technological marvels that inundate us with information both useful and useless. Find times to listen and converse with others without the intrusive interruptions of cell phones ringing, vibrating, or otherwise demanding your attention. During meetings at work, shutting off cell phones, PDAs, and the like is important. It permits focused attention on the meeting's agenda without outside distractions. Screen information whenever possible. Spam filters on your email can reduce the trivia and provide more time for you to engage others in conversation instead of sorting information.

Shift Response: Conversational Narcissism

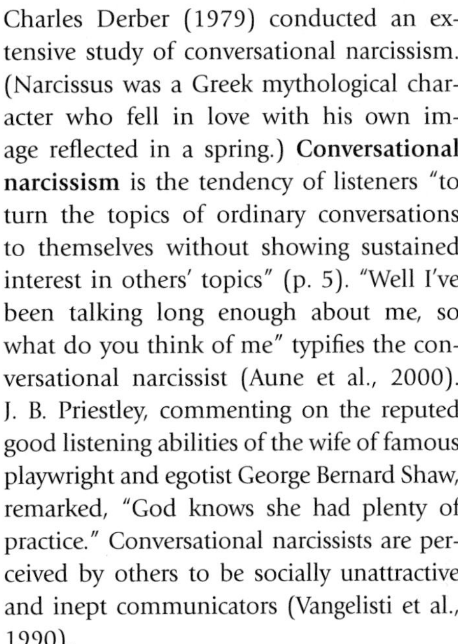

Charles Derber (1979) conducted an extensive study of conversational narcissism. (Narcissus was a Greek mythological character who fell in love with his own image reflected in a spring.) **Conversational narcissism** is the tendency of listeners "to turn the topics of ordinary conversations to themselves without showing sustained interest in others' topics" (p. 5). "Well I've been talking long enough about me, so what do you think of me" typifies the conversational narcissist (Aune et al., 2000). J. B. Priestley, commenting on the reputed good listening abilities of the wife of famous playwright and egotist George Bernard Shaw, remarked, "God knows she had plenty of practice." Conversational narcissists are perceived by others to be socially unattractive and inept communicators (Vangelisti et al., 1990).

Derber recorded and transcribed 100 dinner conversations among 320 friends and acquaintances conducted in restaurants, dining halls, and homes. The predominant pattern found in these conversations was the strong inclination to employ the attention-*getting* initiative, called the shift response, as opposed to the attention-*giving* initiative, called the support response (see also Vangelisti et al., 1990). The **shift response** is a competitive vying for attention and focus on self by shifting topics. It is Me-oriented. The **support response** is a cooperative effort to focus attention on the other person. It is We-oriented. You can see the difference between the two responses in these two conversations:

Boris: I'm feeling pretty depressed.
Natasha: Oh, I felt really depressed last week when I flunked a math exam. (*Shift response; provides information about self that shifts focus*)
Boris: I'm feeling really depressed.
Natasha: Why are you feeling depressed? (*Support response; seeks information for understanding*)

As you can see from these examples, the shift response sets the stage for a competitive battle for attention; the support response does not. Conversational narcissism can be exhibited by a single person, or it can be a pattern of interaction by both parties in a conversation, neither of whom may be prone to shift responses. One person's shift response, however, will likely be countered with the other person's shift response, and a narcissistic transaction may ensue, as in this example:

Boris: I love listening to jazz.

Natasha: I hate jazz, but I love country. Don't you think country is more truly native to the U.S.? (*Shift response*)

Boris: I think country is weird. All those silly lyrics like "My baby left me high and dry and now I have altitude sickness and skin like a lizard" are for Gomers. Have you ever listened to jazz, I mean really listened to it? (*Shift response*)

Natasha: No, and I don't plan to. It's just a bunch of noise. Sounds like kids first learning to play instruments. Let me play some country tunes for you. You'll like them if you put aside your prejudice. (*Shift response*)

In this conversation, the two individuals construct a narcissistic pattern of communicating. Each attempts to make his or her topic the focus of the conversation by quickly making a shift response. Neither party seems interested in understanding the other person's point of view.

Support responses encourage elaboration of the topic initially introduced. Three types of support responses encourage the speaker to explore the topic initiated. They are the *background acknowledgment* (e.g., "Uh huh," "really," "yeah"), the *supportive assertion* (e.g., "That's great," "I didn't think of that," "You must have considered this carefully"), and the *supportive question* (e.g., "How is jazz different from blues?" "Why do you hate math?").

Conversational narcissism is a pattern of overusing the shift response and underusing the support response. The shift response may be necessary in some conversations when individuals drift from the main task. The shift response becomes an informational listening problem, however, when it becomes a patterned response. *The competent communicator primarily uses the support response, not the shift response.*

Competitive Interrupting: Dominating Conversations

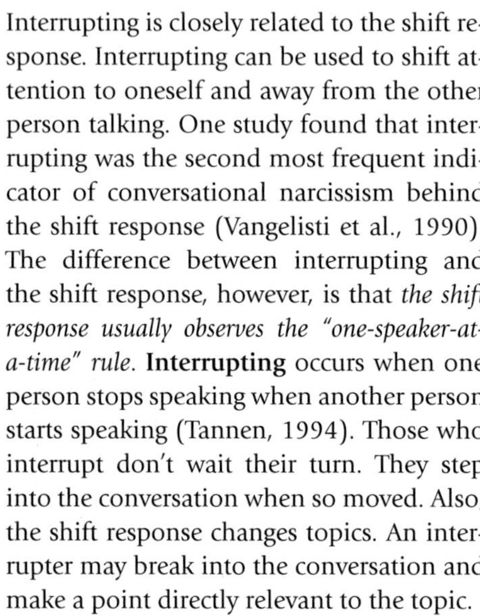

Interrupting is closely related to the shift response. Interrupting can be used to shift attention to oneself and away from the other person talking. One study found that interrupting was the second most frequent indicator of conversational narcissism behind the shift response (Vangelisti et al., 1990). The difference between interrupting and the shift response, however, is that *the shift response usually observes the "one-speaker-at-a-time" rule.* **Interrupting** occurs when one person stops speaking when another person starts speaking (Tannen, 1994). Those who interrupt don't wait their turn. They step into the conversation when so moved. Also, the shift response changes topics. An interrupter may break into the conversation and make a point directly relevant to the topic.

Interrupting can be competitive, just like the shift response. **Competitive interrupting** occurs when we dominate the conversation by seizing the floor from others who are speaking. Competitive interrupting can create reciprocal interrupting where both parties battle each other for conversational control.

Interrupting also can be used for a variety of reasons that are noncompetitive. Expressing support ("She's right"), showing enthusiasm for the speaker's point ("Great idea"), stopping the speaker to ask for clarification of a point ("Hold on! I'm lost. Could you give me an example to clarify that point?"), warning of danger ("Stop! You're going to tip over the computer"), or giving a group a break from a talkaholic's nonstop monologue all are noncompetitive forms of interrupting. Most interruptions are noncompetitive (see James & Clarke, 1993, for a review of 56 studies).

Informational listening problems occur with competitive interrupting but only rarely with noncompetitive interrupting. In competitive interrupting, the focus is Me-oriented narcissism. Interrupters are not

Interpersonal arguments often produce competitive interrupting.

concerned with listening to the speaker for understanding or to learn something. The agenda of interrupters is to break into the conversation and make their own point—to "inform" others. Competitive interrupting creates winners and losers in ordinary conversation. Fighting for the floor, trying to dominate the conversation, and hogging the stage by cutting off other speakers in midsentence create rivalry, hostility, and in some instances, reticence to continue with the conversation. *Typically, competent communicators refrain from competitive interrupting.* When others attempt to interrupt competitively, you need to ask them calmly and politely to allow you or others to continue without interruption ("Please let me finish.").

Glazing Over: The Wandering Mind

A prominent informational listening problem is what researchers call glazing over (Vangelisti et al., 1990). **Glazing over** occurs when listeners' attention wanders and daydreaming occurs. Listening is an active process. You have to be committed to listening carefully. The average listener can think at a rate of about 500 words per minute, but a normal conversational speaking pace ranges between 140-180 wpm (McCoy et al., 2005). This leaves plenty of opportunity for daydreaming and glazing over. Listeners may benefit from a faster speaking rate. Listeners' comprehension of speech doesn't decline markedly until the speaker's rate exceeds 250 wpm (Foulke, 2006). A lethargic speaking rate may put listeners to sleep. Linguist Deborah Tannen (2003) also notes that a very slow speaking rate (fewer than 100 wpm) is stereotyped as slow-witted and unintelligent in every culture studied. If the pace is slow, *the competent communicator should try to put the differential between the rate of speaking and thinking to good use.* Think about the speaker's message. Apply the message to your life experience.

Pseudolistening: Faking It

When Franklin Roosevelt was president, he once decided to test whether people that he greeted in a receiving line actually listened to him. As he received each person, Roosevelt remarked, "I murdered my grandmother this morning." Listeners typically responded, "Thank you," "How kind of you," and the like. Many people passed in the receiving line pretending to listen before someone actually listened to the president and retorted, "I'm sure she had it coming to her" (Fadiman, 1985). This pretend listening is called **pseudolistening**. It is slightly different from glazing over. When listeners glaze over, they are not even pretending to listen. Staring blankly while another person is speaking shows no effort to disguise inattention to the message. Pseudolisteners attempt to disguise inattention to the message. Responding with "Mmm-hmm," "really," and "uh-huh" as someone speaks fakes attention if one's mind is not focused on the speaker's message. Pseudolistening typically is easier to enact over the phone, where visual cues are unavailable.

People pretend to listen for many reasons. Often we engage in pseudolistening to keep from making a romantic partner upset with us. We don't really want to put any energy into listening because we're not really intending to understand our partner's point or issue, but we don't want to be accused of not listening because that could start a quarrel. So we nod our heads to indicate listening, when all the time our minds are out in the Andromeda galaxy floating far away from the topic of conversation.

WE THE JURY, WHOSE SELECTION WAS BASED ON OUR LACK OF KNOWLEDGE, FIND THE EVIDENCE MAKES US SLEEPY, SO WE FLIPPED A COIN AND WANT TO GET HOME BEFORE OUR FAVORITE SOAPS COME ON
MURIEL'S CIVICS LESSON...
WILEY
NON-SEQUITUR.COM

Students can be skillful pseudolisteners. Pretending to listen to a boring lecture, nodding your head when the professor asks the class, "Does everyone understand what I just explained?" and focusing eye contact on the professor can fake listening. *The listening process is effortful, not effortless.* This is why listening to a cell phone call while driving can be dangerously distracting. Neuroscientist Marcel Just of Carnegie Mellon University studied subjects who used a driving simulator while conducting a cell phone conversation. Listening to someone speak led to significant deterioration of driving proficiency. In some cases, drivers hit simulated guardrails and veered out of their lanes (Just et al., 2008). A study by the American Journal of Public Health showed that fatalities from cell phone and texting while driving has hit about 6,000 individuals per year (Richards, 2010).

Competent listening necessitates focused attention. We do not remember what has not received our focused attention (see Box 6-1 and take the test to see that what does not receive your focused attention, for all practical purposes, does not exist for you). Texting during class prevents your attention from being focused on the teacher.

For informational listening to be proficient, *speakers should make their points meaningful to listeners.* That which is meaningless, mere trivia, rarely is remembered. As a speaker, answer the question for listeners, "Why should they care?" *Listeners should focus their attention on what is being said by speakers.* This means coming prepared to listen by bringing a notepad or laptop computer to take notes or by mentally reviewing key points made by the speaker.

Ambushing: Focused Attention with Prejudice

We don't necessarily listen openly and without bias. Sometimes we ambush a speaker. **Ambushing** occurs when we listen for weaknesses and ignore strengths of a speaker's message. An ambusher's bias is to attack

BOX 6.1 Developing Communication Competence

FOCUSED ATTENTION

Listening requires focused attention. The airline industry recognizes this. In an effort to get passengers to listen carefully to safety instructions at the beginning of flights (critical information if an emergency were to occur), flight attendants have tried singing the safety message accompanied by a ukulele, impersonating famous people while reciting the instructions, and performing a rap version of the safety message (Riechmann, 2001). Cebu Pacific Airlines had flight attendants give a safety demonstration to the tune of Lady Gaga's "Just Dance" and Katy Perry's "California Gurls" (Cebu Airlines, 2010). Even humor has been tried, especially by Southwest Airlines: "In the event of a sudden loss of cabin pressure, oxygen masks will descend from the ceiling. Stop screaming, grab the mask, and pull it over your face" or "Your seat cushion can be used for flotation, and in the event of an emergency water landing, please take them with our compliments." To make the point that we do not retain information unless we listen with focused attention, answer the following questions:

1. On which side of the Apple icon for Macintosh computers is the bite located, left or right?
2. How many sides on a stop sign?
3. In which hand does the Statue of Liberty hold her torch?
4. On which side of their uniforms do police officers wear their badges (to them, not to you)?
5. When you look at a dime, which way does Franklin Roosevelt face, left or right?
6. How many geometric shapes are in the CBS "eye" logo?
7. Is the top stripe on an American flag red or white?
8. What is in the center of the backside of a $1 bill?
9. Every number key on the main portion of a standard computer keyboard has a symbol on it as well. What symbol is on the #5 key?
10. Which of the following can be found on all current U.S. coins?
    a. "United States of America"
    b. "E Pluribus Unum"
    c. "In God We Trust"
    d. "Liberty"

The correct answers (don't sneak a peek until you've finished) for these 10 questions are: **1.** *right side*, **2.** *eight sides*, **3.** *right hand*, **4.** *left*, **5.** *faces left*, **6.** *two geometric shapes: a circle twice and a football shape*, **7.** *red*, **8.** *ONE*, **9.** *%*, **10.** *all of them*.

How did you do? It is not unusual to answer many of these questions incorrectly. What you don't pay attention to because it isn't meaningful to you isn't remembered. A coin collector would answer correctly the Franklin Roosevelt question because coin collectors spend a great deal of time examining coins for minute details. Such an examination is part of their business. Most of us, however, pay little attention to the details on coins aside from recognizing what coin it is. Even this can be attended to rather casually, as many people discovered when they used Susan B. Anthony silver dollars as quarters, necessitating the withdrawal of these silver dollars from circulation (recently replaced with a larger "gold" dollar coin).

If you don't focus your attention during conversations, those conversations will be little more than a blur. If your conversational partner asks, "What did I just say?" you'll look very foolish having to admit you heard next to nothing said. Such indifference to others can threaten the quality, even the continuation, of relationships.

what the speaker says. This is focused attention with prejudice. Ambushers may distort what a speaker says to gain an advantage. Ambushing is competitive and Me-oriented.

Some of the most obvious examples of ambushing occur in the political arena. Candidates for political office are coached to ambush their opponents. It's called "going negative." The listener is looking to tear down his or her opponent. Journalists also can be ambushers. They're drawn to the mistakes made by public officials and celebrities (Tannen, 1998). They're listening to frame a story as a scandal, a blooper, or an egregious error. If you're always ready to pounce on a speaker who may send messages that oppose your viewpoint, then you may miss important qualifying statements, put words in the speaker's mouth, and reject what was not said or meant in the first place. Don't ambush. It's poor informational listening.

Competent Critical Listening

Listening involves more than accurately understanding the messages of others. Once we understand the message, we need to evaluate it. All opinions are not created equal. People used to think that the earth was flat, that pus healed wounds, that bloodletting cured diseases, and that drilling a large hole in an afflicted person's skull cured mental illness by letting evil spirits escape (called trephining). A book published in 1902 entitled *The Cottage Physician*, written by a group of "the best physicians and surgeons of modern practice," claims that cataracts can be cured by generous doses of laxatives, tetanus can be treated effectively by "pouring cold water on the head from a considerable height," and difficulty urinating can be relieved by marshmallow enemas (cited in Weingarten, 1994).

We hear a dizzying variety of claims every day. As critical listeners, you need to know the difference between prime rib and baloney, between fact and fantasy. Consider one example that illustrates this point. Despite voluminous data from thousands of scientific studies and conclusions drawn from these studies by the Centers for Disease Control, the National Institutes of Health, the Pasteur Institute, and others (see Nattrass, 2007; "The Evidence," 2005), Christine Maggiore, a former executive in the garment industry with no scientific training or even a college degree, waged a vigorous campaign to discredit the link between HIV and AIDS (France, 2000; Nattrass, 2007). Having tested positive for AIDS, she nevertheless wrote a book on the subject challenging the scientific evidence, posted numerous emails, gave frequent speeches, and appeared at medical conventions on AIDS to publicize her protest. Surprisingly, people were convinced by her campaign (France, 2000; Nattrass, 2007).

She gave birth to two children. She refused to take any antiretroviral drugs, such as AZT, that could have prevented passing the AIDS virus on to her children during pregnancy, and she breastfed her children, thereby increasing the odds of them contracting the virus. She adamantly maintained that a healthy lifestyle provides sufficient protection, she discouraged the use of condoms that prevent transmission of the disease, and she claimed that the use of antiretroviral drugs is a primary cause of AIDS deaths, not HIV. Tragically, her three-year-old daughter, Eliza Jane, died in 2005 from what the Los Angeles coroner's report deemed pneumonia caused by AIDS. Dr. James Ribe, the senior deputy medical examiner, called the autopsy report's conclusion "unequivocal" ("Did HIV-Positive Mom's Beliefs," 2005; see also "Autopsy Report," 2005). Maggiore disputed the findings and continued her campaign to discredit the HIV and AIDS connection after the death of her child. Maggiore died in December 2008 from pneumonia. No autopsy was performed, but it seems likely her pneumonia, like her daughter's, was AIDS related.

You separate the likely facts from the almost certain fantasies and nonsense by listening critically. **Critical listening** is the process of evaluating the merits of claims as they are heard. A **claim** is a generalization that remains to be proven.

Skepticism, True Belief, and Cynicism: Differences

Skepticism is the essence of critical listening. **Skepticism** is a process of listening to claims, evaluating evidence and reasoning supporting those claims, and drawing conclusions based on probabilities. Skeptics may seem to be annoying nags, always asking for evidence and challenging people's beliefs. The term *skeptic,* however, is derived from the Greek *skeptikos,* which means thoughtful or inquiring, not doubtful and dismissive.

Conversely, **true belief** is a willingness to accept claims without solid reasoning or valid evidence and to hold these beliefs tenaciously even if a googol of contradictory evidence disputes them. As Winston Churchill put it, a true believer is "one who can't change his mind and won't change the subject." Often belief rests on little more than the power of a charismatic or revered person who can press our "awe buttons" (Sagan, 1996). Columnist Leonard Pitts (2011) puts it aptly when commenting on the state of journalism, political discourse, and the rise of blogging sites on the Internet: "If we are all journalists, we all ought to be governed by journalism's most sacred directive. Meaning accuracy. Get the facts straight." He continues, "One encounters little fealty to that directive in surveying the landscape of new media, overrun as it is by *true believers* for whom accuracy is subordinate to ideology and facts useful only to the degree they can be bent, shaped or outright disregarded in service to ideology." This true belief results in "increasing incoherence and intellectual incontinence, an empty shouting match better suited to a fifth-grade schoolyard than to adults analyzing the great issues of the day" (p. A13). Nowhere is critical listening a part of true belief.

Cynicism is nay-saying, fault finding, and ridiculing. H. L. Mencken once described a **cynic** as someone who "smells flowers and looks around for a coffin." Cynics have "a feeling that things will pan out for the worse" (Mole, 2002, p. 45). They are quick to pounce on human frailties and imperfections. I mention cynicism because skepticism is often confused with cynicism (Mole, 2002). In some instances, skeptics have exhibited condescension and arrogance when commenting on questionable beliefs, justly deserving the criticism leveled at them. *True skeptics, however, are hard on the claim but soft on the people making the claim* (Sagan, 1996). Skepticism requires humility because no one's ideas and beliefs are immune to challenge. Nobody can honestly claim to be entirely free of foolishness. Skeptics operate in between the extremes of true belief and cynicism.

True belief, as used here, does not simply mean "strong belief." Skepticism also does not mean "no belief." Ruggeiro (1988) notes, "It is not the embracing of an idea that causes problems—it is the refusal to relax that embrace when good sense dictates doing so." *The key distinction between a true believer and a skeptic is not the strength of the belief but the process used to arrive at and maintain a belief.*

So how should a skeptic critically listen to a true believer and respond without belittling or showing contempt? Consider this dialogue:

True Believer: You should join my group. We show our true commitment to the group by freeing ourselves of individual material ties.

Skeptic: Does this involve selling all of my possessions and giving the proceeds to the group?

True Believer: Yes, we believe that living frugally in service to the leader is a path of enlightenment and a better life.

Skeptic: Doesn't it bother you that the leader of your group uses those proceeds to buy expensive cars and live a lavish lifestyle, while group members are required to wear inexpensive robes and live frugally?

True Believer: We believe our leader is the exalted one and should have, as you put it, "a lavish lifestyle." We are merely his servants.

Skeptic: It seems contradictory to me to teach commitment and to attack materialism but expect only you to make sacrifices while your leader lives very comfortably without visible sacrifice.

True Believer: That simply shows how little you understand us and our leader.

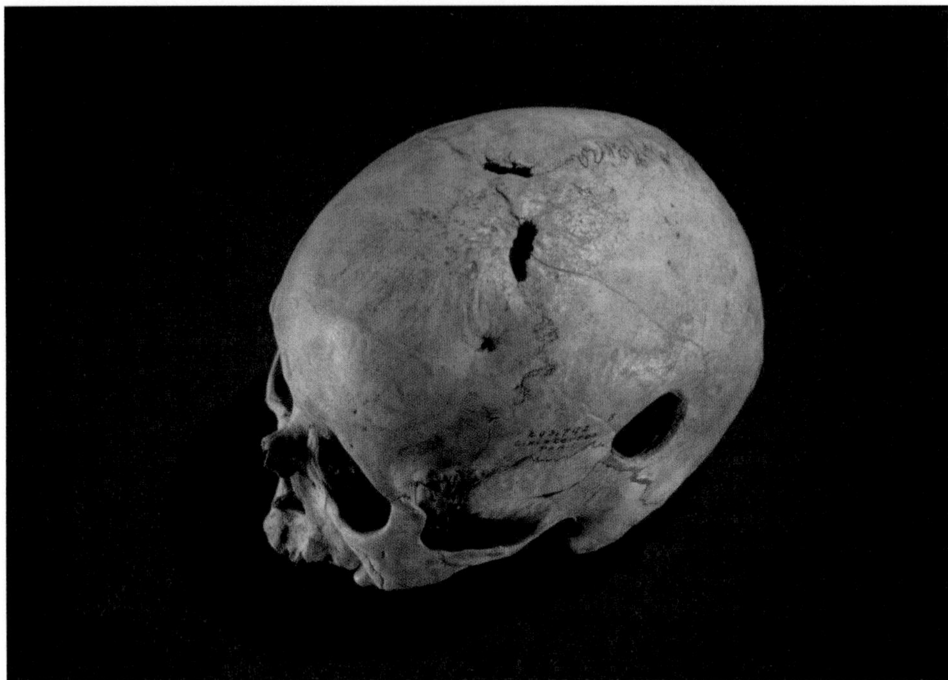

Trephining was a primitive procedure that involved cutting a hole in a person's skull to release evil spirits or "mad thoughts." Clearly, some ideas are better than others, and it is the critical listener's responsibility to make such determinations. Our knowledge can build only if we act as skeptics who critically evaluate claims and reject those that aren't supported by quality evidence.

Skeptic: Perhaps, but I'm trying to understand. Are you ever allowed to doubt the teachings of your leader?

True Believer: No! Doubt leads to confusion and weak commitment.

Skeptic: Well, this is where we really disagree, because I have serious reservations about a group that requires me to accept without question what a group leader teaches.

Throughout this dialogue, respect is shown to the true believer even though differences in belief are obvious and strong. You can disagree, even strongly, with a true believer without being disagreeable. There can be reasonable disagreement even among skeptics. Show others respect when discussing beliefs because few people take their beliefs lightly. Listen carefully and respectfully but also listen critically.

The Process of True Believing: Uncritical Listening

True beliefs vary widely, and in some instances, they can be contradictory. Nevertheless, despite the differences in the details, true believers all operate in essentially the same way, as I discuss in this section.

Confirmation Bias: Searching for Support

The TV show *Nightline* once discussed frivolous lawsuits. Host Ted Koppel first questioned a representative of the insurance industry. This representative told a story of a man who was paralyzed by an automobile that went out of control and crashed into a phone booth where he was making a call. The victim sued the phone company, or what is commonly referred to as the "deep pocket," or the party with the cash, and won millions of dollars. The insurance representative asserted vehemently that this was a classic case of a frivolous lawsuit. Why sue the phone company? Sue the driver of the car! Koppel, however, turned to the lawyer who represented the injured man and requested a response. The lawyer noted that the phone company on several occasions had been notified that the phone booth in which the victim was injured had a defective door that stuck, trapping individuals inside. The phone company did nothing to correct the problem. When the victim saw the car careening out of control and heading for him, he tried desperately to vacate the phone booth, but the jammed door trapped him inside. It was determined that the man would have had a reasonable expectation of escaping unharmed if the door had not jammed. The phone company was deemed negligent.

Many viewers (myself included) likely jumped to the conclusion that the wrong party was sued before listening to the counterargument from the victim, thus engaging in a very common behavior called confirmation bias. **Confirmation bias** is the tendency to seek information that supports one's beliefs and to ignore information that contradicts those beliefs (Evans, 1989). If your prevailing belief is that Americans sue frivolously, the presentation by the insurance representative seems persuasive. Once your belief has been confirmed, you are not inclined to seek or listen to disconfirming evidence.

One of the hallmarks of true belief is confirmation bias. *True believers are belief driven, not evidence driven.* Their beliefs are formed first, and then they look for confirming evidence. Research shows that confirmation bias is pervasive (Jonas et al., 2001; Nickerson, 1998). Psychologist Drew Westen presented to the 2006 Conference of the Society for Personality and Social Psychology results of a study he conducted of partisan Democrats and Republicans demonstrating uncritical listening. Prior to the 2004 presidential election between George W. Bush and John Kerry, self-described "strong" Democrats and Republicans were presented video-recorded statements in which each candidate clearly contradicted himself. Democrats consistently ignored contradictions by Kerry and Republicans consistently did the same for Bush, but both partisan groups were keenly aware and strongly critical of the contradictions from the opposing candidate ("Political Bias," 2006).

People generally do not give themselves a chance to spot faulty claims while listening because they listen only for supportive assertions and information for their beliefs and ignore contrary information (Schittekatte & Van Hiel, 1996; Snyder & Swann, 1978). *Competent critical listeners must be prepared to say to themselves consistently, "So why would some people disagree with this speaker?" You're listening with an ear for both sides on an issue, not just one side.*

Rationalization of Disconfirmation: Clinging to Falsehoods

There is a story of a client with an odd problem who came to see a therapist. The client believed that he was dead. The therapist made several attempts to convince the client that he was not dead. Nothing worked. Finally, the therapist asked her client, "Do dead men bleed?" The man said no. The therapist then took a pin out of the drawer in her desk, grabbed the man's hand, and stabbed it. Blood spurted. The man looked at his bleeding hand and responded, "Well I'll be damned; dead men do bleed."

Even when true believers are confronted with strong, disconfirming evidence, they usually hold tenaciously to their beliefs. True believers use **rationalization of disconfirmation**—inventing superficial, even lame, alternative explanations for contradictory evidence. Thirty-nine members of the Heaven's Gate group who died by suicide in 1997 exhibited rationalization of disconfirmation. They bought a high-powered telescope to see a spaceship they steadfastly believed was traveling in the wake of the Hale-Bopp comet—a spacecraft that was to transport Heaven's Gaters to a new cosmic life. The telescope was returned, however, and the owner of the store was politely asked for a refund because they saw the comet but not the spacecraft (Aronson, 1999). To Heaven's Gaters, the telescope must have been defective, but the original belief of a spaceship trailing the comet remained.

Christian preacher Harold Camping adamantly predicted that the Rapture—Judgment Day—would occur on May 21, 2011 (he originally predicted that 1994 would see the Rapture). He posted 1,200 billboards around the country to advertise his prediction. For reasons beyond strange, the popular media gave Camping's prediction wide coverage. As you know, his prediction did not come true. Did he admit his prediction was a fantasy based on no credible evidence? Nope! He "revised" the date to October 21, 2011, claiming that May 21 was the "spiritual" Rapture and October 21 would be the "physical" Rapture (Maher, 2011). You already know that he was wrong again. Like the man who believed he was dead, true believers' view of reality is invulnerable to challenge because some rationalization can always be concocted.

Shifting the Burden of Proof: Whose Obligation Is It?

The **burden of proof** is the obligation of the person making the claim to present compelling evidence and reasoning to support it (Fisher, 2003). As a speaker, whenever you make a claim to an audience (e.g., "texting can become addictive"), you assume the burden to prove that claim. As a critical listener, you should be looking to see whether a speaker meets his or her burden of proof when making claims. When those making a claim challenge a skeptic to "prove us wrong" before they have offered compelling evidence to support their claim, they are **shifting the burden of proof**—inappropriately assuming the validity of a claim unless it is proven false by another person who never made the original claim (Gilovich, 1991). No one should have to prove that another person's claim is false when that person has failed to present credible reasoning and evidence to show that the original claim might be true. If it were otherwise, skeptics would have to disprove all manner of absurd, unsupported claims: humans can suddenly burst into flames for no apparent reason (spontaneous human combustion); humans can train themselves to live without food but on air alone (claim of breatharians). Remember, *whoever makes the claim has the burden of proof.*

Your burden of proof increases the more extraordinary your claim. *Extraordinary claims require extraordinary proof* (Gracely, 2003). If you claim that the 9/11 attacks on the Twin Towers were not the work of terrorists but of our own government (as asserted in the "documentary" *Loose Change*), your burden of proof requires extraordinary evidence to support such an extraordinary and wholly implausible claim. If your claim requires rewriting the laws of physics, no ordinary evidence will do. Participants in many self-help and empowerment workshops are told by charismatic speakers conducting the workshops that they can walk barefoot on red-hot coals without suffering injury using a mind-over-matter mantra (Radford, 2001). If participants can walk over burning coals, so goes the argument, surely they can accomplish anything by willing it with their minds. The mind-over-matter explanation is hard to swallow, however, because "the very idea that brain activity could alter the physical properties of burning carbon compounds or the reactivity of skin cells to extreme heat contradicts volumes of well-established scientific data" (McDonald, 1998, p. 46). Fire-walking looks impressive, but it is a matter of physics, not mind over matter. As physicist David Willey explains, wood coals, despite their intense heat, are poor thermal conductors (Noelle, 1999). Fire-walkers do not walk across heated metal rods. If they did, the moment their feet hit the metal they would hear the same sound a steak makes when it first hits the barbecue grill—SIZZLE. Metal is an excellent heat conductor. Heat an oven to 400 degrees. If you touch the metal grill inside the oven, you will instantly sear your fingertips. Touch a cake cooked in the same 400-degree oven. Your finger will not burn for a second or two of continuous contact. That is because the cake is a poor thermal conductor. Wood coals are like the cake; they transfer the heat relatively slowly.

Fire-walking is not called fire-*standing*. Individuals do not remain immobile in the middle of the hot coals for even a few seconds reciting mantras and making speeches that exhort others to join them in demonstrating mind over matter. Think about it, though. If minds truly can control matter, why do participants have to move at all?

Extraordinary claims require extraordinary proof, not sensational-looking demonstrations that exhibit a poor grasp of simple physics. As competent critical listeners, you cannot ignore mountains of evidence and substitute a molehill of wishful thinking that nurtures ignorance.

The Skepticism Process: Exercising Competent Critical Listening

This section explains the process of becoming a skeptical, critical listener. This same process is also relevant to being a competent speaker (see later chapters on public speaking, especially the discussion of fallacies). Claims people make assert varying degrees of likelihood (Adler, 1998). Note the differences in the following claims:

> *Possibility:* You could receive an "A" in your communication class even though you flunked all the tests, skipped all the assignments, and rarely came to class.
>
> *Plausibility:* There is at least one other galaxy besides our own with intelligent life.
>
> *Probability:* Leaping out of an airplane from 2,500 feet without a parachute will result in death.
>
> *Certainty:* Everybody dies.

In this section, I discuss differences in claims of possibility, plausibility, probability, and certainty to clarify the critical listening process that separates skeptics from true believers.

Possibility: Could Happen, but Don't Bet on It

That a student could receive an "A" in a communication class without passing any tests, completing any assignments, or attending class is possible but highly unlikely. A student could receive an "A" because of clerical error by the instructor or a computer glitch. True belief often rests on the "anything is possible" rationale. This allows for no distinctions to be drawn between sense and nonsense, fact and fiction.

Suppose, for example, a stranger asks you to walk blindfolded across a busy highway. Would you do it? What if you saw someone else do it without getting hit by a car? Now would you do it? One successful crossing proves that it is possible to cross a busy highway blindfolded and not get catapulted into the next county by a speeding automobile. It is possible but not likely. "Anything is possible" is insufficient justification for gambling with your life or accepting an unsupported claim.

Plausibility: Making a Logical Case

The next step up from possibility is plausibility. The claim that at least one other galaxy has incubated intelligent life forms can be supported by a rational argument that rests on related knowledge. Astronomers report that there are approximately 100 billion galaxies, each composed of about 100 billion stars. With numbers that large, it does not defy logic to think that life exists elsewhere besides this flyspeck in the universe called Earth (Tarter, 2006). Conditions necessary to sustain life could have developed elsewhere. Scientists at SETI (Search for Extraterrestrial Intelligence) scan the inky darkness of space for signals from any intelligent species that might be out there. SETI bases this search on plausibility alone. There is no proof extraterrestrial life exists, and members of SETI only claim that there is reason to believe that it *might* exist. They are searching. Initially, the search for knowledge may have no better rationale than plausibility.

The assertion that Earth has already been visited by extraterrestrial life, however, is implausible. Consider three reasons. First, other galaxies are thousands of light years away. Thus, only travel far faster than the speed of light, which is contrary to known laws of physics, would make the arrival of alien tourists feasible (Paulos, 1988). Second, most people's accounts of alien abduction consistently describe extraterrestrials as having humanoid form (heads, eyes, mouths, arms, and legs). Since these beings would have had a separate evolutionary history, it is implausible that they should look so similar to us (Sagan, 1996). Third, two surveys conducted in the 1990s, one by Roper and the other by Gallup, found that approximately 3 million Americans believed they had been abducted by aliens. Assuming aliens do not discriminate by picking only on Americans, this suggests that more than 60 million people worldwide have been abducted. "It's surprising more of the neighbors haven't noticed" (Sagan, 1996, p. 64).

A claim must be at least plausible to be worthy of serious consideration and further exploration. Alien visitation does not even pass this minimal test. *Plausibility is a basis for inquiry, but it is an insufficient basis for acceptance of a claim. Skepticism requires probability.*

Probability: Likelihood of Events

The claim that falling from an airplane from 2,500 feet without a parachute will result in death is not only plausible; it's probable. People usually injure themselves falling from an 8-foot ladder. A 2,500-foot free fall does not bode well for the person hurtling toward the earth. Death is highly likely but not certain. On September 25, 1999, Joan Murray, a 47-year-old bank executive and skydiving enthusiast, struggled to open her parachute during a jump, but without success. Finally, a reserve parachute opened at 700 feet from the ground but became tangled and deflated. Murray slammed into the ground at an estimated 80 miles per hour. She suffered multiple serious injuries, but she survived. Two years later, she resumed skydiving ("Beating the Odds," 2002).

Probability is a concept not well understood by most people (Paulos, 1988). There's a difference in probabilities between making a general claim and a specific claim. The **Law of Very Large Numbers** notes that with large enough numbers almost anything is likely to happen to *somebody*. On August 14, 1992, a small meteorite hit a boy in Uganda (Krieger, 1999). The odds of this particular little boy being hit by a meteorite are astronomical (specific claim). Given the 7 billion people on our planet and the great regularity of meteorites hitting Earth, however, it is highly probable that someone, somewhere, sometime will be hit (general claim). If some event happens to only one person in a million each day, with 300 million people in the United States, you can expect 300 such events daily.

Certainty: Without Exception

Claims of true believers are frequently stated as absolute certainties. A true believer by definition exhibits no doubt. *Skepticism, however, can aspire to no stronger claim than very high probability.* Skepticism does not allow the assertion that any phenomenon is "impossible," although some skeptics have intemperately made such a claim. Consider doubts about homeopathy, an "alternative" medical treatment widely used in the United States (Kutschera, 2008; Park, 2000). Homeopathy is based on the so-called law of infinitesimals. This means "less is better." Homeopathic solutions are composed of extracts of herbs, minerals, or animal organs diluted in water many times. At the standard dilution of 30 times, patients would have to drink 7,874 gallons of the solution to consume a *single molecule* of the medicine (Park, 2000). Carrying the less-is-better belief to even greater extremes, some homeopathic remedies, such as the standard flu remedy Oscillococcinum, are diluted 200 times or more. It is virtually certain that homeopathic remedies, the "no-medicine medicine," could not have any beneficial effects on patients (Ernst, 2010; Kutschera, 2008; Park, 1997). Nevertheless, skepticism allows for no greater claim than that it is "virtually" certain homeopathic remedies are bogus. Although nothing is deemed impossible, however, this does not open the door to the everything-is-possible "open-mindedness" justification for true belief (see Box 6-2).

Self-Correction: Progressing by Mistake

In 1983, Barry Marshall, an internal-medicine resident from Perth, Australia, startled the medical world. He argued that most stomach ulcers are not caused by a stressful lifestyle. Instead, he claimed that they are caused by a simple bacterium. Martin Blaser of the Vanderbilt School of Medicine reflected the initial response of the medical community to Marshall's claim when he called it "the most preposterous thing I'd ever heard" (Monmaney, 1993). Marshall's claim seemed outlandish because it contradicted what the medical community thought it knew about ulcers. Marshall, however, was soon proven correct when the bacterium, now called *Helicobacter pylori*, was discovered and shown to be the cause of most stomach ulcers. This meant that

BOX 6.2 Focus on Controversy

SKEPTICISM AND OPEN-MINDEDNESS: INQUIRING MINDS, NOT EMPTY MINDS

Although skeptics avoid claims of certainty, this does not open the door to the everything-is-possible "open-mindedness" justification for true belief. Years ago, I explored a variety of alternative medical treatments and New Age therapies partly from curiosity and partly from a need to help a sick friend. I investigated herbal remedies, homeopathy, psychic healing, polarity therapy, crystal healing, iridology, pyramid power, radiasthesia, dowsing, marathon fasts, megavitamin therapy, therapeutic touch, and faith healing. Whenever I expressed doubt concerning the validity of these alternative approaches to health and disease, I was denounced as "closed-minded." It seemed that open-mindedness was equated with never discounting any claim no matter how poorly supported or implausible.

Open-mindedness does not require us to listen to obviously false claims or to give them a forum for expression (Hare, 2009). Do you really want to listen to a speaker argue that the world is flat or that gravity does not exist? As the bumper sticker says: "Gravity: Not just a good idea; it's the law!" An open mind should not equate with an empty mind. "What truly marks an open-minded person is the willingness to follow where evidence leads" (Adler, 1998, p. 44).

We don't always follow where the evidence leads, however. A Zogby survey of 1,200 Americans reported on the NBC *Today* show revealed that 7% of respondents don't believe that the *Apollo* astronauts ever landed and walked on the Moon, and an additional 4% were not sure. Since there are about 230 million adult Americans (Liptak, 2008), these results suggest that about 16 million adult Americans think the Moon landing, one of the most thoroughly documented events in human history, was a hoax, and an additional 9 million think it might have been faked. Attempting to capitalize on this apparent doubt, the Fox TV network aired *Conspiracy Theory: Did We Land on the Moon?* Striving for the sensational and achieving the nonsensical, the program clearly intimated that the U.S. government faked the Moon landing. The Internet is replete with sites alleging the Moon landing was a hoax.

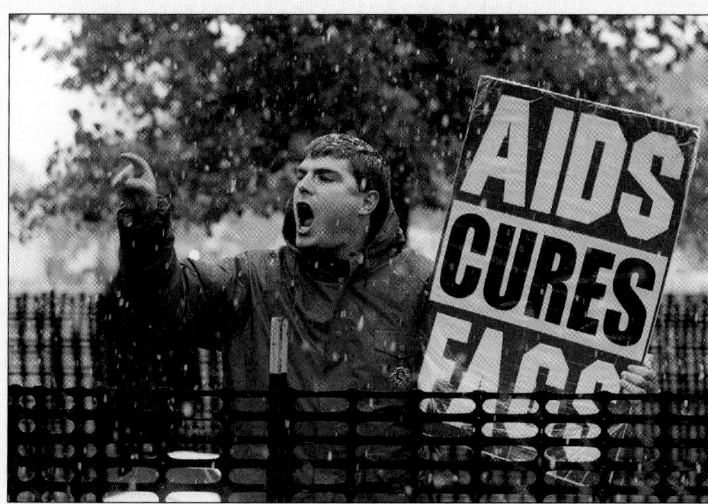

This anti-gay protester expresses his point of view. Open-mindedness doesn't mean that we have to listen to hateful bigotry.

The Moon landing was documented by scientists from around the world. There is no legitimate "other side" or reasonable debate on this topic. A Moon hoax conspiracy is completely implausible because it would have to involve thousands of NASA collaborators. The principle of parsimony rules out such an implausible scheme because you have to assume a grand conspiracy of thousands of collaborators who all have remained silent for more

(continued)

BOX 6.2 *(Continued)*

than four decades. If any credible evidence of fakery were discovered by Soviet scientists who were monitoring the *Apollo* Moon flights, they surely would have announced it to the world because the Soviet Union was our Cold War nemesis and was racing us to the Moon. If you engage in a debate with those who deny the Moon landings, or other equally discredited claims such as Holocaust denial, that is your choice, and you may just be exercising your intellectual muscles for fun. Remember, though, that all claims are not created equal, and being open-minded doesn't mean having to listen to speakers espousing false claims that have already been demolished by careful reasoning and abundant evidence. Be open-minded by following where the evidence leads you.

QUESTIONS FOR THOUGHT

1. Can you have too much skepticism and become closed-minded? Explain.
2. Should we listen "open-mindedly" to claims that women are the inferior sex and men make poor parents?
3. Is it ethical to steadfastly maintain a belief that you know is wrong but makes you feel comfortable nevertheless? Explain.

antibiotics, not psychotherapy or antacids and a bland diet, were the effective cure. Despite initial doubt, the medical community now accepts the bacterial cause of most ulcers (Atwood, 2004).

Skepticism goes where the evidence leads, and if the evidence compels change, then change must occur. *Skepticism and self-correction are inseparable*. All academic disciplines build on knowledge acquired through various methods of research, discarding what proves to be incorrect. All the fields of true science have shown an exponential accumulation of knowledge and a corresponding heavy dose of self-correction. Self-correction should be embraced, not resisted. If, while listening to a speech, strong evidence is presented that clearly contradicts one of your cherished beliefs, defending that erroneous belief is ethically questionable. Honesty demands self-correction. Skepticism mandates tough choices and the courage to correct errors.

Parsimony: Making Fewer Assumptions

It was the end of a term, and students were selling their textbooks to a buyer working for the university bookstore. Repeatedly, I received reports from my students that the textbook buyer would quickly fan a stack of \$1, \$5, or \$10 bills and hand the correct amount of money to the students. Each time, there was serious doubt that he had given the correct amount of money, but in every case, seemingly without counting the bills, he unerringly gave the correct amount. How could he so quickly peel off the exact number of bills without counting? My students began to speculate. Maybe he had been a professional card player in Las Vegas who, after years of practice, could manipulate stacks of currency like a deck of cards. Perhaps he had some paranormal power to read the bills and "see" the correct amount instantaneously. Possibly he merely estimated the thickness of the stack of bills that would provide the correct amount of money, and he was just incredibly lucky each time to guess correctly.

Curious, I walked to the bookstore to see for myself. Sure enough, the book buyer unfailingly fanned the stacks of bills and provided the correct amount of money to each student. I approached the book buyer, mentioned the stir he was creating among my students, and asked him to explain his feat. Amused, the book buyer revealed that before each visit to a college to buy textbooks, he went to his bank and requested several thousand dollars divided into three denominations. He also requested that each stack of bills have sequential serial numbers. Thus, he merely looked at the last three digits in the serial numbers, did some quick arithmetic, fanned the stack quickly for the correct serial number, and handed the seemingly uncounted stack of bills to the amazed student.

There was more than one possible explanation for the book buyer's behavior before his method was revealed, and each was far more complicated than his unspectacular explanation. Faced with multiple explanations for an event or phenomenon, skeptics follow the **principle of parsimony**—when competing explanations or theories fit the facts, the simplest is preferred. A theory that uses fewer concepts or makes fewer assumptions is less likely to be wrong (see Box 6-2).

Parsimony (pronounced *par* se mo ne) can help with the common response to psychics who manage an occasional "hit." When the psychic offers a very specific piece of information, such as the exact name of a dead relative or the cause of death of a loved one, the typical response from an often amazed listener is, "There's no way he (or she) could have known that." Having had no previous contact with the psychic, individuals are understandably amazed. When they cannot immediately explain how a stranger could know personal information about their lives, some people are inclined to choose the paranormal instead of a more commonplace explanation. The paranormal explanation requires acceptance of a vast number of assumptions about the nature of our physical world that are contradicted by observable evidence.

A more parsimonious explanation for a psychic's success is that he or she has learned the specific information before ever performing the psychic reading. How simple it would be for an associate or friend of the psychic to stand in line before a performance and listen for information from individuals conversing while they wait to enter the auditorium. The information could then be given to the psychic before the performance so a "hit" can be manufactured. Instances of spying on conversations before a show to obtain specific information on audience members have been revealed on many occasions (Polidoro, 1999; Wiseman, 1997).

Competent Empathic Listening

Informational listening and critical listening achieve important goals for the competent communicator. Informational listening expands our knowledge and understanding of our world. Critical listening helps us sort through bad ideas to discover good ideas that will solve problems and help us make quality decisions that improve our lives. There are times, however, when the point of conversation is to establish a relationship with another person or to help him or her through an emotional event. The police officer in the opening story to this chapter illustrated empathic listening. **Empathic listening** requires us to take the perspective of the other person, to listen for what that person needs and wants. Research shows that more personal and impersonal information alike is disclosed when listeners exhibit perspective-taking behaviors (paraphrasing, perception checking, etc.). Perspective taking also improves comprehension and retention of another person's viewpoint in conflict situations (Johnson, 1971; Johnson & Johnson, 2000). Failure to perceive another person's perspective is a frequent communication problem for couples (Vangelisti, 1994).

Response Styles: Initial Response Patterns

Listener **response styles** are the types of initial verbal reactions we make when another person comes to us with a problem, reveals a frustrating event, or is experiencing an emotional crisis. This next section covers seven styles, some that are nonempathic and others that are empathic (Rogers & Roethlisberger, 1952).

Evaluative Response: Making Judgments

A friend comes to you, obviously upset, and says, "I hate my job. I've got to find something different to do." You respond, "You haven't given the job much of a try. Perhaps you'd like it better if you put more effort into it." This is an **evaluative response**; it makes a judgment about the person's conduct. It assumes a standard of evaluation has or has not been met. As you read the evaluative response, perhaps you said to yourself, "I wouldn't respond that way." Perhaps not, but the most frequent response people make in situations like the one just presented is to evaluate (Rogers & Roethlisberger, 1952).

A hypercompetitive, individualistic culture such as ours promotes the evaluative response. Competition focuses us on discerning weaknesses in our adversaries. Even when we are conversing with a friend, there is a tendency to focus on weaknesses. Competitors don't try to bolster their opponents. Adversaries try to diminish each other to win. Evaluating a friend who comes to you with a problem is nonempathic.

Evaluation is the least effective response when we need to be empathic. Harold Kushner (1981), author of *When Bad Things Happen to Good People*, makes this point:

> It is hard to know what to say to a person who has been struck by tragedy, but it is easier to know what not to say. Anything critical of the mourner ("don't take it so hard," "try to hold back your tears, you're upsetting people") is wrong. Anything which tries to minimize the mourner's pain ("it's probably for the best," "it could be a lot worse," "she's better off now") is likely to be misguided and unappreciated. (p. 89)

When you're suffering, the last things you need are criticism and judgment. You want an empathic response (see the section "Supporting Response: Bolstering Others").

Advising Response: Telling Others How to Act

"My roommate drives me crazy. She has so many odd quirks." How would you respond to this? If you would respond in this fashion, "Why don't you change roommates?" you are offering advice. The **advising response** tells people how they should act. It is a common initial reaction to those who make a complaint or reveal a problem. Despite its frequency, advice is as likely to be unhelpful as helpful to others in distress (Goldsmith & Fitch, 1997; Goldsmith & MacGeorge, 2000). The distressed person may resent being offered unrequested advice, and the advice may be disastrously incorrect (telling a violently abused partner to "stand up and fight back").

Men more than women tend to offer advice when others come to them with a problem or complaint (Tannen, 1990). Giving advice under these circumstances does two things (Wood, 1994). First, it fails to acknowledge the other person's feelings. Second, it communicates superiority by the person giving the advice. Giving advice presumes that the person with the problem hasn't figured out the solution, so the listener offers advice. Take the perspective of the other person before giving advice. Does the person seem interested in receiving advice from you? Is that what he or she is seeking? Have you considered your advice carefully, or is it merely a glib response made without thoughtful examination? Do you have expertise that can provide helpful advice?

Interpreting Response: Explaining Meaning

When we give an **interpreting response**, we express what we think is the underlying meaning of a situation presented to us. A friend says to you, "I don't understand why he says such embarrassing things to me in front of my family." You respond, "Perhaps he is just uncomfortable around your parents and doesn't really know quite what to say, so he says silly things that embarrass you because he's socially clumsy." This is an interpreting response. You are explaining the meaning of the situation for the other person. Interpreting responses are what we pay counselors, psychiatrists, and therapists to do for us when we can't make sense of our relationships, feelings,

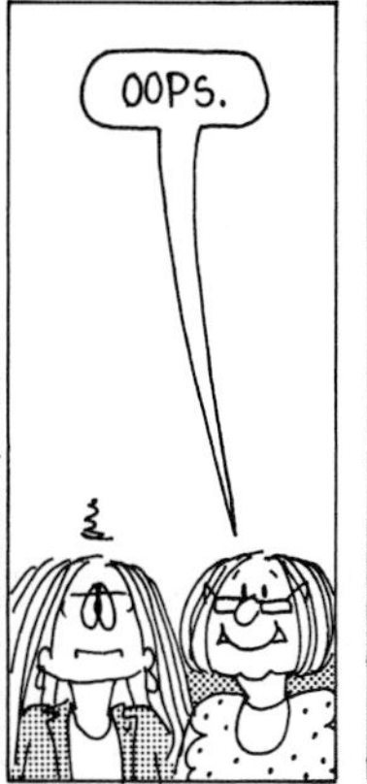

conflicts, and traumas. The interpreting response is useful in some situations, but like advising, it tends to place the listener in a superior position. One can "play guru" too often if the interpreting response becomes frequent.

Content-Only Response: Ignoring Feelings

A **content-only response** comprehends the literal meaning of messages from others but doesn't recognize the feelings that ride piggyback. Consider this example:

> **Bettina:** I can't believe we're so far in debt. Those student loans are killing us.
> **Jeremy:** I've been in worse trouble.
> **Bettina:** Look at these Visa bills, and the MasterCard is maxed out, too.
> **Jeremy:** Actually, we haven't hit the limit on the MasterCard yet. We have another $800 to go.
> **Bettina:** That's small comfort. What if we lose our house because we can't pay the mortgage?
> **Jeremy:** We could use the MasterCard to buy food and pay some bills up to the $800 that's still short of the limit. Then we could use our paychecks to cover the mortgage next month.

Nowhere does Jeremy, the content-only responder, ever acknowledge Bettina's fears and concerns by perspective taking. ("I understand your fear. I'm feeling very anxious, too, about our pile of debt.") Every response only increases her fears that they are in debt up to their eyebrows and that they may lose their home.

Content-only responding ignores feelings and is nonempathic. Natural disaster communication expert Peter Sandman notes that public officials need to acknowledge people's fears immediately in a crisis situation before presenting clear, concise information regarding what steps to take to deal with a disaster (see Tallmadge, 2007). Failure to exhibit empathy will likely diminish fearful individuals' ability to listen to critical emergency information.

Probing Response: Asking Questions

The **probing response** seeks more information from others by asking questions. As a listener, you're showing interest in the other person's distress by inquiring further about the problem. Several types of questions qualify as a probing response (Purdy & Borisoff, 1997).

> *Clarifying Question:* "Can you give me an example of what you mean when you say that she is insensitive?"

> *Exploratory Question:* "Can you think of some ways to defuse her anger?" "Can you think of any alternative besides resigning from your position?" Exploratory questions urge the speaker to examine possibilities posed by a problem or situation.

> *Encouraging Question:* "You didn't have any other choice, did you? Who could blame you for sticking to your principles?" Encouraging questions inquire about choices made and imply agreement at the same time.

Probing responses show interest in the speaker by seeking more information from and being attentive to the plight of the other person. Probing questions do not make a person feel like someone being grilled on a witness stand by a prosecutor. "Why did you ever agree to go out with him in the first place?" or "Didn't you realize she couldn't be trusted with money?" smacks of evaluation, not sincere inquiry. These questions seem intended to make a point, not help you grasp the nature of the other person's distress.

Supporting Response: Bolstering Others

A **supporting response** includes "expressions of care, concern, affection, and interest, especially during times of stress or upset" (Burleson, 2003, p. 552). There are several types of supporting responses.

Reassurance: "First day on the job can be a little nerve-racking, but you have the skills to do the job really well."

Agreement: "You're right! Your boss is completely out of line."

Praise: "You did a fantastic job even if she doesn't recognize it."

Assistance: "I can help you move out if you need me."

Validating Feelings: "You should be angry; I know I would be!" (Burleson, 2003)

When a person is suffering the loss of a loved one, he or she needs empathy. In our struggle to help someone shoulder a burden, we may choose the wrong response. One survey found that bereaved individuals considered 80% of the responses made to them during mourning unhelpful (Davidowitz & Myricm, 1984). Almost half of the responses were advice ("You need to get out more"; "You have to accept his death and move on with your life"), but they were hardly ever perceived as helpful to the bereaved. Acknowledging and validating the feelings of the bereaved were the most helpful responses. ("I can see how much you miss her. She was a warm and sensitive person.")

Don't provide "cold comfort" responses (Hample, 2006). These include *denying the right to feel a particular way* ("Stop worrying about it" or "Don't take it so hard; he wasn't worth your tears"), *minimizing the significance of the situation* ("It was only your first real job; there will be others" or "It was just a silly party; so what if you didn't get invited"), or *focusing on the future* ("You'll feel better tomorrow" or "You'll find another girlfriend soon"). When a person is distressed, such responses are unlikely to seem helpful. Have you ever stopped worrying just because someone told you to?

Women generally are more likely to provide emotional support to others in need, they are more skillful in providing comfort, and they are more prone to seek supporting responses from others than are men (Burleson et al., 2005). This is why, as noted in Chapter 3, both men and women usually seek and prefer support and comfort from women.

Understanding Response: Paraphrasing and Perception Checking

The **understanding response** requires a listener to check his or her perceptions for comprehension of the speaker's message or to paraphrase the message to check accuracy. **Perception checking** was discussed in Chapter 2. Briefly, you begin with a behavior description, follow with an interpretation of the behavior, and finish with a request for verification of your interpretation. **Paraphrasing** "is a concise response to the speaker which states the essence of the other's content in the listener's words" (Bolton, 1979, p. 51). Paraphrasing is not a parroting of a person's message ("I'm Arturo"—"I hear you saying that your name is Arturo"). Paraphrasing is concise and to the point. For example,

Francine: My roommate hums to himself while he studies. He hums stupid, irritating little tunes that stick in my head like annoying ads on TV. I'm trying to study, and I can't concentrate with his humming. I have a major exam in chemistry class tomorrow, and old hum-till-we're-all-dumb never grows tired of the sound of his own noise. I've got a lot riding on this exam.

Teresa: Sounds to me like you're really worried that your roommate's annoying humming will make you flunk your chemistry exam.

Francine: Yeah, and I've never flunked an exam! Got any suggestions what I should do about him, or to him?

Paraphrasing helps a listener understand the essence of a speaker's message. However, it should be used only occasionally during a conversation. Look for the significant points in a conversation and then paraphrase. Details and elaborations of important points usually don't require paraphrasing.

Now that you have read about these response styles, test yourself by identifying the listening response in Box 6-3.

Response Styles and Empathic Listening: Making Choices

Different responses produce different results. Some of these response styles are empathic and some are nonempathic.

Empathic Response Styles: Probing, Supporting, and Understanding

Empathic listening is composed of probing, supporting, and understanding responses. All three put the focus on the speaker and are therefore **confirming responses**—they enhance the person's self-esteem and confidence. Hamachek (1982) explains:

> An understanding response is a way of letting a person know that you're listening to both the content of what's being said and the feeling accompanying it; a probing response lets a person know that you want to know more and, on a deeper level, that he or she is worth knowing more about; a supportive response is a way of saying that you care and that you hope things will get better. (p. 214)

When building a relationship and connecting with a person are the principal goals of your communication, then probing, supporting, and understanding responses establish trust, deepen the connections between you and another person, and keep communication open.

Nonempathic Responses: Evaluating, Advising, Interpreting, and Content-Only

Responses that tend to be **disconfirming** —they diminish the person and reduce

BOX 6.3 Developing Communication Competence

DISTINGUISHING LISTENING RESPONSES

Read the following situation, then identify which type of response it is. Mark **A** for advising, **E** for evaluation, **I** for interpreting, **P** for probing, **S** for supporting, **U** for understanding, and **C** for content-only.

My boss is a total jerk. She's always giving me these huge projects to do, then yelling at me for not getting my other work done. She never has anything nice to say to anyone, and she actually times us when we take breaks to make sure we don't take longer than we're allowed. I feel like quitting.

_____ Aren't you being a little unfair? She can't be that bad.
_____ What have you tried so far to deal with your boss?
_____ Your situation is a classic power struggle.
_____ I think you should quit and find a job more to your liking.
_____ You feel overworked and underappreciated.
_____ I know you'll make the right decision because you usually know what is right to do.
_____ Your boss could be worse.

Which response do you think would be the best? Second best? Explain.

Answers: E, P, I, A, U, S, C.

confidence—are nonempathic. These include evaluating, advising, interpreting, and content-only responses (Hamachek, 1982). Should you therefore avoid such responses? *Empathy is not always the type of listening that is competent in a given situation*, so the answer is "no." Therapists interpret meaning for clients. Interpreting is an important listening response when someone is confused and wants clarity. Advising others can be constructive and helpful, especially if a person seeks our advice. Evaluating a person's self-destructive behavior may save that person's life.

Choosing Competent Response Styles: Frequency, Timing, and Solicitation

Three variables influence the appropriateness and effectiveness of evaluating, advising, interpreting, and content-only responses. The first variable is frequency. *Frequency* refers to how often you use disconfirming responses. Occasional evaluation, interpretation, advice, or content-only responses, especially in a strong relationship, will rarely cause more than a ripple of disturbance. The frequent use of such disconfirming responses, however, can swamp even resilient relationships.

Timing is a second variable. *Timing* refers to when you use nonempathic responses. "This is politics, pure and simple. You've handled them wrong. Stand up to these thugs." This statement begins with interpreting, follows with evaluating, and closes with advising—the triple crown of disconfirmation. Such a statement early in a relationship, when the two parties hardly know each other, would likely be received negatively. The same statement much later in a relationship, when the two parties are familiar with each other's style and trust each other, might be received in a more neutral, even positive, way. Additionally, evaluating, interpreting, advising, or content-only responses used when a person is feeling fragile and in need of support will likely disconnect speaker and listener. Such responses can make a person feel inferior and diminished.

Finally, evaluating, advising, interpreting, and content-only responses are more appropriate and likely to be more effective when the speaker solicits them (Goldsmith, 2000). *Solicitation* refers to whether you are asked to evaluate, interpret, advise, or concentrate on the content, not the feelings, of the speaker. A person may simply want to be heard by you, not told what to do. He or she may reject unsolicited advice, even resent it. "I already thought of that, and it won't work" is a typical rejoinder to unsolicited advice. If individuals request such advice, however, they will more likely perceive it to be helpful. People who seek help from a therapist implicitly request an interpreting response. People rarely request evaluation, but if they do, it is more likely to be accepted than if a critique is unsolicited.

Summary

LISTENING is the most frequent type of communication any of us do on a daily basis. Listening is first and foremost an active process. You cannot comprehend information, retain it, or respond appropriately to what you hear from others without focused attention. Listening is effortful, not effortless. The competent communicator recognizes when informational, critical, and empathic types of listening are appropriate and effective. Be an informational listener when the principal focus of the communication is learning or retaining information. Be a critical listener when you need to find solutions to problems or make decisions that have consequences for yourself and others. Be an empathic listener when you are trying to build or maintain

PART 2

Power

The Inescapable Interpersonal Dynamic

POWER IS INESCAPABLE in human transactions. "There is power in a word or a gesture. There is power when women and men live together, work together, talk together, or are simply in each other's company. There is power in a smile, a caress, and there is power in sex." There is also "power in how we choose to resolve our conflicts, and how we negotiate the most intimate aspects of our lives" (Kalbfleisch & Cody, 1995, p. xiii). Relationships between parents and children, doctors and nurses, teachers and students, judges and lawyers, supervisors and employees, or coaches and athletes are hierarchical and fundamentally power oriented. Parents, doctors, teachers, judges, supervisors, and coaches have the power to tell others what to do. There is power when a person speaks as an expert to a large group. Organizations and institutions are typically structured as hierarchies with the powerful at the top and the less powerful below. "To be human is to be immersed in power dynamics" (Keltner, 2007).

By the end of this chapter, you should be able to:

1. Define power and explain the differences between types of power.
2. Describe the principal indicators and five main sources of power.
3. Recognize power imbalances and their consequences to you and others.
4. Contrast competitive with cooperative use of power.
5. Develop competent communication strategies to balance power in your transactions with others.

Power, however, is often thought of as a negative dynamic. Power may connote negative communication transactions ("power plays," "power struggles," "power politics"). "Power tends to corrupt, and absolute power corrupts absolutely," Lord Acton reputedly observed. This is a popular perspective. In a low power-distance culture such as the United States, exercising power can seem questionable (Carl et al., 2004). We are inclined to think of power as illegitimate or even evil, unless, of course, we are the individual with the power. Then, as former Secretary of the Navy John Lehman once quipped, "Power corrupts. Absolute power is kind of neat."

Research on the behavior of high-power individuals doesn't help diminish the generally negative view of power. There is a "wealth of evidence that having power makes people more likely to act like sociopaths. High-power individuals are more likely to interrupt others, to speak out of turn, and to fail to look at others who are speaking." More unsettling, "They are also more likely to tease friends and colleagues in hostile, humiliating fashion. Surveys of organizations find that most rude behaviors—shouting, profanities, bald critiques—emanate from the offices and cubicles of individuals in positions of power" (Keltner, 2007; see also Gonzaga et al., 2008).

Exercising power, however, can be corrupting or altruistic. Some may use power to bulldoze, bully, and intimidate others for personal gain. Others may use power to build schools and feed starving children in Africa. *You achieve your individual goals, resolve conflicts, and sustain relationships by exercising power competently*. Education, for example, empowers you to improve your life because it gives you choices unavailable to those who lack a college degree. Without a college degree, you can't even apply for most well-paying jobs because you don't qualify. Your choices are narrowed; your options are few.

There is no virtue in exercising little power. Feeling powerless creates apathy, shrivels our desire to perform at work, and strains personal relationships (Wilmot & Hocker, 2011). It creates interpersonal disconnection and erodes self-esteem (Lee, 1997). Feeling powerless inhibits the direct expression of ideas and produces withdrawal from interactions with others. Feeling powerless can strangle your spirit and stifle your motivation to improve your life and the lives of those you love. It can lead to self-destructive behavior or aggression toward others (Keltner et al., 2003).

Your choice is not between using and not using power. "We only have options about whether to use power destructively or productively for ourselves and relationships" (Wilmot & Hocker, 2011, p. 115). *The primary purpose of this chapter is for you to learn ways to exercise power effectively and appropriately.*

Definition of Power

Power is the ability to influence the attainment of goals sought by you or others. This is a general definition. More specifically, this section explores the nature and forms of power. Above all, power is transactional. As noted in Chapter 1, every message has two basic dimensions: content and relationship. The content of a message communicates information regarding events and objects. The relationship dimension identifies, among other things, how power is being distributed between individuals. This means that power is constantly being negotiated during conversations with others. Consider this dialogue and the comments interjected in parentheses that indicate the power dynamics in the conversation:

> Jennifer is washing the dishes. Geoff seems not to notice.
>
> "I'm tired of dealing with my mother's demands on me," begins Jennifer (***control is an issue***).

> Geoff responds, "Don't let her make you feel guilty for not spending every holiday with her and your father" (***advising as a parent to a child***).
>
> Jennifer says, "I'm not letting her make me feel guilty (***asserting control***). I just get emotionally exhausted having to explain over and over again why we aren't coming to her house on Christmas."
>
> Geoff picks up a towel and begins to dry some dishes. "Tell her just once why we won't be coming for the holidays; then refuse to talk about it any further. Stand up to her" (***encouraging assertion of power***).
>
> Jennifer scrubs a plate a bit more vigorously than necessary (***exhibiting tension when implicitly accused of being weak***). "It isn't a question of standing up to my mother (***rejecting Geoff's characterization of weakness***). You make it sound like I'm putty in her hands."
>
> "Well, maybe not putty; more like sculpting clay," Geoff says with a chuckle (***reasserting weakness by Jennifer***).
>
> "You're one to talk," says Jennifer. "You haven't stood up to your father in years. Why don't you practice what you preach?" (***takes the offensive in battle to win the argument; asserts weakness by Geoff***).
>
> Geoff moves next to Jennifer, looking down at her with an unpleasant expression on his face (***dominance posture***). He responds in a stern voice (***power in tone of voice***), "That's hitting below the belt."
>
> "Now you know how it feels to receive such flip advice," Jennifer retorts (***continues with powerful offensive***).

Power, who has it and how it is being exercised, is central to this conversation. "Whenever you communicate with another, what you say and do exercises some communicative control—you either go along with someone else's definition of the conflict, struggle over the definition, or supply it yourself" (Wilmot & Hocker, 2011, p. 114). Jennifer and Geoff are struggling to define the main issue of contentiousness in an interpersonal tug-of-war for dominance. Both are quick to reject characterizations by the other of weakness. Offering advice becomes a source of dispute because to accept advice is perceived as an acknowledgment of subordination to the person advising. There is friction regarding who should be able to tell whom to do what. Power is the main topic of conversation as well as the subtext, the meaning beyond the words.

The Nature of Power: No Powerless People

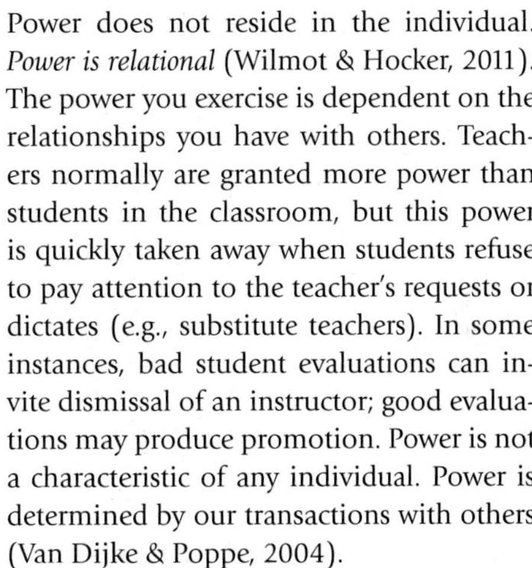

Power does not reside in the individual. *Power is relational* (Wilmot & Hocker, 2011). The power you exercise is dependent on the relationships you have with others. Teachers normally are granted more power than students in the classroom, but this power is quickly taken away when students refuse to pay attention to the teacher's requests or dictates (e.g., substitute teachers). In some instances, bad student evaluations can invite dismissal of an instructor; good evaluations may produce promotion. Power is not a characteristic of any individual. Power is determined by our transactions with others (Van Dijke & Poppe, 2004).

Power is not dichotomous. We often identify individuals as powerful or powerless. No one, however, is all powerful or completely powerless, not even an infant, as many weary parents can attest when they have tried to attend to their crying baby's needs in the middle of the night. If each person has some degree of power in a relationship, the appropriate question is not the false dichotomy, "Is Person A powerful or powerless?" The apt question is, "How much power does Person A have compared to Person B?"

Forms of Power: Dominance, Prevention, and Empowerment

There are three forms of power: dominance, prevention, and empowerment (Hollander & Offerman, 1990). **Dominance** is the exercise of power over others. Dominance is a competitive, win-lose transaction. This form of power results from dichotomous, either-or thinking. You're perceived to be either a winner or a loser in a power struggle.

Prevention is power used to thwart the influence of others. Prevention is the flip side of dominance. When someone tries to dominate you, you may try to prevent the dominance. The willingness to say "no" can be formidable, even in the face of dominating attempts. Prevention power is competitive. Dominators and preventers engage in power struggles to become winners and to avoid becoming losers.

It is another false dichotomy to assume that power can be exercised only as dominance or prevention. There is a third alternative—empowerment. **Empowerment** is power derived from enhancing the capabilities, choices, and influence of individuals and groups (Rothwell, 2010). It is power used positively and constructively. It is a cooperative form of power. You do not have to defeat anyone to achieve personal or group goals. Empowered individuals feel capable, effective, and useful because they performed well, not because they beat someone. You become empowered by successfully accomplishing an important task. That accomplishment has an impact on you and on others (Frymier & Shulman, 1996; Thomas & Velthouse, 1990).

Power Struggles and Power Sharing: A Comparison

The three forms of power—dominance, prevention, and empowerment—are considerably different from each other. Those who try to dominate see power as an active effort to advance personal goals at the expense of others. Power is a zero-sum contest. This means that for every increment of power I gain, you lose an equivalent amount of power. From this perspective, the power pie can't be enlarged, so the battle is for the biggest possible slice.

Those who seek to prevent domination by others see power as reactive. Prevention power is competitive. Individuals who attempt to prevent domination react to the power initiatives of others by fighting back. Preventive power is self-protective. You're trying to keep the slice of the power pie that you have, even enlarge your portion if possible by decreasing the portion of those trying to dominate (see Figure 7-1).

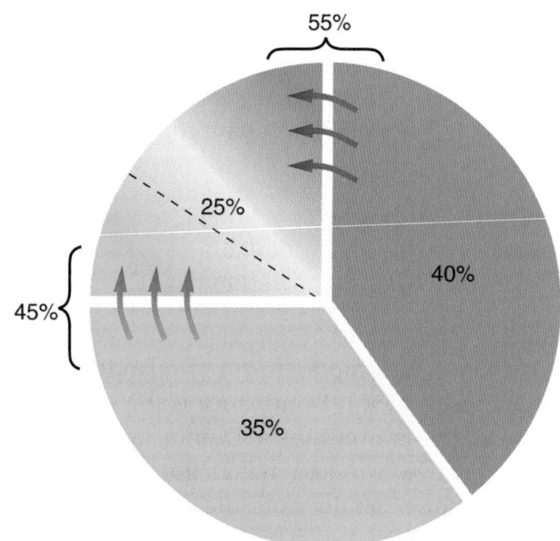

FIGURE 7-1 Power Struggle Dynamic

The dominance-prevention power struggle can be seen in commonplace transactions. Access to bathrooms on the job rarely poses a problem for white-collar workers, but for workers in factories, telephone-calling centers, food-processing plants, and construction sites, using the restroom when nature calls can be a serious power struggle, especially for women (Linder & Nygaard, 1998). Lawyers, business executives, and college professors don't need to ask for permission to relieve themselves, nor do they have their bathroom activities monitored. Employees on the lower rungs of the employment ladder, however, may not be so lucky. Workers who perform the heavy lifting and "grunt" work can be refused permission when they request a bathroom break; they can be timed with stopwatches while they are in the restroom; they can be disciplined for frequent restroom visits; they can even be hunted like quarry by supervisors if they remain in the stalls too long. The courts have ruled that these common practices by supervisors are not necessarily illegal (McAllister, 2008; Souto, 2007). Workers have in some instances taken to wearing adult diapers while working on assembly lines because bathroom breaks are not permitted often enough. Increasingly, workers have fought back by complaining to supervisors, filing formal grievances, taking court action, and protesting their treatment.

Train operators on the Norfolk Southern Railway protested the lack of flush toilets by taking the waste-filled plastic bags they were forced to use and flinging them off their moving trains. Norfolk Southern responded by printing employee numbers on the bags and monitoring which employees brought back the full bags (Walsh, 2000). A dominance-prevention power struggle can quickly deteriorate into outlandish power tactics.

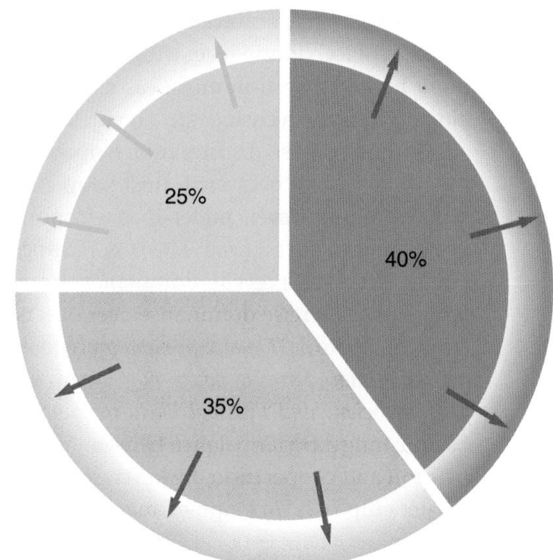

FIGURE 7-2 Empowerment—Expanding Resources

Those who seek to empower themselves and others see the power pie as expandable (see Figure 7-2). When the power pie is expanded, there is more for everyone. Thus, no zero-sum competitive game needs to take place. "Empowerment takes an abundance mentality—an attitude that there is plenty for everybody and some to spare, and the more you share the more you receive. People who are threatened by the successes of others see everyone as competitors. They have a scarcity mentality. Emotionally they find it very hard to share power, profit, and recognition" (Covey, 1991, p. 257).

Empowerment is proactive. Individuals take positive actions to assist themselves and others in attaining goals cooperatively (Table 7-1). For example, a football team may have a great quarterback, but it takes a team to be successful and win games. If the offensive line performs poorly, the quarterback will be running for his life, not throwing touchdown passes. The empowerment perspective encourages improvement by working together, not against each other. By helping each other to improve blocking techniques, players on the offensive line improve the entire team's performance. Protecting the vulnerable quarterback so he can have time to spot open receivers, score points, and stay healthy benefits everyone. I should also note here that empowerment can occur even in the larger competitive arena, in this instance, professional football. You can have intragroup (within the group) empowerment for the purpose of intergroup (between groups) competitive success. Intergroup rivalry is not necessary for intragroup empowerment, but different forms of power sometimes operate at the same time.

If you have a negative view of power, you are more than likely responding to the dominance form of power and its companion, prevention.

TABLE 7-1 THE THREE FORMS OF POWER

TYPE	DEFINITION	DESCRIPTION
Dominance	Competitive	Active: zero-sum
	Power struggle	(I win; you lose)
Prevention	Competitive	Reactive: zero-sum
	Power struggle	(You win; I lose)
Empowerment	Cooperative	Proactive: multi-sum
	Power sharing	(We all win)

It would be naive, however, to argue that we could replace dominance with empowerment in all, or even in most, cases. If individuals in a relationship are satisfied with an unequal power distribution, empowerment may not be necessary. Most people in our culture, however, prefer to have more power than others (Van Dijke & Poppe, 2004) either to prevent dominance from others or to exercise dominance over others (to be in control). *Dominance and prevention are the primary forms of power in a hypercompetitive society, and this will likely remain so.* Establishing a better balance between competition and cooperation, however, requires greater emphasis on empowerment.

Communication Indicators of Power

To understand the role of power in all of your transactions with others, you have to recognize its inherent presence. You can become adept at recognizing power dynamics by understanding three types of power indicators: general, verbal, and nonverbal.

General Indicators: Defining, Following, Opposing, and Inhibiting

There are several general indicators of power. First, *those who can define others are typically recognized as having power in relationships and groups*. Teachers define students (e.g., smart, slow learner), physicians define patients (e.g., healthy, hypochondriac, addict), psychiatrists define clients (e.g., paranoid, schizophrenic, psychotic), parents define children (e.g., incorrigible, obedient), and bosses define employees (e.g., hard worker, sluggard).

Definitional prerogative as an indicator of power can be seen from our attitudes about rape and sexual abuse in prisons. A study by the U.S. Department of Justice in August 2010 estimated that 88,500 adults in prisons and jail in this country are raped or sexually abused annually. "Overall, the survey paints a grim picture of a system of mass incarceration where all too many prisoners, stripped of their autonomy or ability to defend themselves, spend their sentences terrorized by sexual predators" (Froomkin, 2010; see also Beck, 2010). Rape and sexual abuse in prisons are largely ignored, and male inmates' victimization is even the subject of television sitcom humor. Prisoners, male or female, have no power to define rape inside the prison as either a crime or at least a serious problem to be solved. Prisoners are dependent on judges, prosecutors, and lawmakers to define prisoner rape as a criminal act worthy of sanction. We recognize those who can define the actions of others as more powerful than those who might try to define the actions of others but are not accorded legitimacy.

A second general indicator of power is *who cares less about maintaining a relationship*. The **principle of least interest** indicates that the person who cares less about continuing a relationship is typically recognized as having more power (Attridge et al., 1995; Waller & Hill, 1951). The person with the greater interest and investment in maintaining the relationship can be held hostage by his or her partner's lack of interest, forced to try resurrecting an intimacy that only one partner cares much to rejuvenate. The partner with less interest is in the dominant position because of the implied or stated threat to terminate the relationship. The only person controlled by a threat to end a relationship is a partner who cares about maintaining it.

A third general indicator of power is *whose decisions are followed*. Employees follow the directives of supervisors, not vice versa. Children obey parents. Wouldn't it be odd to see parents obeying children? ("Dad! Be home by 10 o'clock, and gas up the BMW before you return.") We recognize those whose decisions are followed as having power.

Finally, *behavioral inhibition* is a general indicator of power (Keltner et al., 2003). The more powerful are usually more vocal in groups, more expressive of opinions and ideas, and more assertive or aggressive in pushing those ideas and opinions. The less powerful are more inhibited. They are more passive and withdrawn in groups. They are more likely to be quiet and not express ideas, especially if those ideas might be unpopular or challenge more powerful individuals.

Verbal Indicators: Language Choices

Power is indicated by the way we speak and by how listeners evaluate these speech patterns. The speech of a less powerful person is often flooded with self-doubt, approval seeking, overqualification, hesitancy, and personal diminishment.

Powerful and Powerless Language: Communicating Status

Examples of speech patterns commonly viewed as relatively powerless in U.S. culture include the following (Mulac & Bradac, 1995):

Hedges: "*Perhaps* the best way to decide is . . ." "I'm a *little* worried that this *might* not work."

Hesitations: "Well, *um,* the central point is . . ." "Gosh, *uh,* shouldn't we, *um,* act now?"

Tag question: "Dinner will be served at 6 o'clock, *okay?*" "This section of the report seems irrelevant, *doesn't it?*"

Disclaimers: "You may *disagree* with me, but . . ." "This idea is probably very *silly,* but . . ."

Excessive politeness: "I'm *extremely sorry* to interrupt your conversation, but . . ."

Powerless speech suggests lack of confidence, uncertainty, indecisiveness, vacillation, and deference to authority. It advertises a person's subordinate status. Powerful speech, by contrast, is generally direct, fluent, declarative, commanding, and prone to interrupt or overlap the speech of others. It advertises superior status, dynamism, and credibility (Haleta, 1996; Hosman, 2002).

Powerful forms of speech are not always appropriate. Abusive and obscene language sounds powerful because it is shocking, but it will likely offend others. Sometimes deferential language is a sign of respect and not merely powerless speech. Even tag questions can sometimes be used powerfully. If your boss says, "You'll see that this is done, won't you?" this may be more a directive than a request. If so, the tag question is authoritative, not weak. Competent communicators understand that in some contexts it is important to use language that acknowledges another person's power.

Gender and Cultural Influences: Powerful Language Differences

Verbal indicators of power in U.S. culture show several clear gender differences. Men are typically more verbose, more inclined to give long-winded verbal presentations, and more talkative in mixed-sex groups than women (Crawford & Kaufman, 2006; Leaper & Ayres, 2007). Talkativeness is associated with leadership. Men in general are more verbally aggressive, direct, opinionated, and judgmental than women (Brownlow, 2003; Mehl & Pennebaker, 2002). They are also more inclined to attack the self-concepts of others (dominance), and they are more argumentative than women, meaning that men are more likely to advocate controversial positions or to challenge the positions on issues taken by others (Stewart et al., 1996). Women are inclined to view verbal aggressiveness and argumentativeness as strategies of dominance and control, a hostile, competitive act (Nicotera & Rancer, 1994). Women also tend to use tag questions, hedges, and disclaimers more than men (Brownlow, 2003).

Women's tentative use of language and men's more direct use are generally apparent, but the topic of discussion can have a marked influence on these patterns. If the topic is more typically masculine (sports and cars), men use more powerful language, but if the discussion topic is more typically feminine (shopping, fashion), men become more tentative and women become more direct (Palomares, 2009). Tannen (2010) also notes how seemingly powerless or powerful speech can be misinterpreted between the genders: "If men often mishear women's ritual indirectness as lacking confidence (or even competence), women often misinterpret *less* indirect rituals as overbearing—and also lacking in confidence. Her thinking goes: he must really lack self-esteem if he has to throw his weight around like that" (p. 57).

The issue of powerless versus powerful speech takes on even more complexity when culture is added to the mix (Den Hartog, 2004). What is viewed as powerful speech is culture specific. Japanese, for example, and most Asian cultures would view our version of powerful speech as immature because it indicates insensitivity to others and is likely to make agreement more difficult (Wetzel, 1988). Collectivist Asian cultures desire harmony; the group is more important than the individual. In Western societies, verbal obscenity and swearing are perceived as powerful language. Individualistic Western cultures place a high value on personal uniqueness. Verbal obscenity marks you as an individual willing to flout cultural values that discourage verbal obscenity. Neither Japanese men nor women use such language except in rare instances (De Klerk, 1991), but it is increasingly common among Americans.

When cultures clash over significant issues, these different views of powerful and powerless speech can pose serious problems. When negotiating teams from Japan and the United States meet, misunderstandings easily arise (Hellweg et al., 1994). The language of Japanese negotiators is rife with indirect phrases typical of a high-context communication style (see Chapter 3). Japanese negotiators use expressions such as "I think," "perhaps," "probably," and "maybe" with great frequency because they strive to preserve harmony and cause no offense that would result in loss of face for anyone (Kameda, 2003, 2007). This indirect language is viewed as powerless by American negotiators more accustomed to the direct, explicit, "powerful" language of a low-context communication style.

Nonverbal Indicators: Silent Exercise of Power

Anyone who has experienced the "silent treatment" from his or her intimate partner recognizes the power dimension of nonverbal communication. You become a nonperson; your connection to your partner is separated. This experience can be enormously frustrating, even depressing (Burgoon & Dunbar, 2006).

There are numerous nonverbal indicators of power in relationships (see Burgoon & Dunbar, 2006; Hall et al., 2005). *Clothing* is recognized as a strong indicator of power. We typically associate uniforms with power and authority. The "power suit" indicates to most people a stature and status associated with financial success and position in an organization. Tattered clothing scrounged from the trash communicates powerlessness associated with poverty.

Touch is another important nonverbal power indicator. The more powerful per son can usually touch the less powerful person more frequently and with fewer restrictions than vice versa (Henley, 1995). Sexual harassment laws recognize this difference and try to protect subordinates from tactile abuse.

Eye contact indicates a power difference. Staring is done more freely by the more powerful person (Garland-Thomson, 2009). Less powerful individuals must monitor their eye contact more energetically. A boss can show lack of attentiveness or interest by looking away from a subordinate, but a subordinate doing the same to his or her boss may invite a reprimand. Submissiveness is typically manifested in both the animal and people worlds by lowering one's eyes and looking down.

Space is a clear nonverbal indicator of power. The more powerful usually have more of it. Those who dream of winning the lottery imagine buying a large house, not a cramped studio apartment. The master bedroom in a house is reserved for the more powerful parents, and the children often share smaller bedrooms, often sleeping stacked vertically in bunk beds. The higher up in the corporate hierarchy you travel, the bigger is your office space. Reserved parking spaces, part of the "parking wars" on college campuses across the United States, clearly designate power differences. Reserved faculty parking spaces often are closer to classroom and office buildings. Student parking spaces often are located somewhere in the next time zone.

Much more could be added here, but the point seems clear. You can ascertain the relative distribution of power between individuals by observing general communication patterns and specific verbal and nonverbal communication.

Power Resources

A **power resource** is anything that enables individuals to achieve their goals, assists others to achieve their goals, or interferes with the goal attainment of others (Folger et al., 1993). The range of power resources is broad. This section lays out the primary resources from which power is most extensively derived.

Information: Scarce and Restricted

We live in the Age of Information, where information is power. Not all information, however, becomes a power resource. *Information has power potential when it is not easily or readily available* (Sell et al., 2004). Lawyers can charge eye-popping fees because they have information about the law that clients must have but do not. Information that is *restricted* and *scarce* can be a powerful resource.

J. Z. Knight, who portrays herself as a celestial "channeler" in contact with a 35,000-year-old Cro-Magnon prophet named Ramtha from the lost city of Atlantis, runs a School of Enlightenment in rural Washington (Lydgate, 2007). The main attraction for Ramtha devotees is to hear the "wisdom" of this prophet as he speaks to small gatherings of fascinated followers (although recently Knight has taken to the Internet to spread the word). Ramtha "speaks" through Knight in a guttural voice with a fake-sounding English accent.

It's not every day that you get an opportunity to hear from a 35,000-year-old guru from another spirit dimension. The scarcity of such elder prophets makes what Ramtha has to say more inviting. What Ramtha says, among other things, is that every orgasm brings you nearer to death (the same could be said, of course, for every breath you take). When you die, do not seek the light because "light beings" are waiting and they will suck experience from your spirit and leave you to reincarnate with no memory of your last life. Instead, Ramtha entreats, seek the darkness, the void. Ramtha claims mirrors are portals to a parallel universe, mind-reading is possible, aging can be reversed, you can travel through time, and that Twinkies contain a life-extending ingredient (Lydgate, 2007).

If a 35-year-old guy named Fred provided the same information as Ramtha, do you think anyone would pay much attention? More likely, we'd suspect that Fred's off his meds. Many do pay attention to Ramtha, however, because his "wisdom" is viewed as scarce, restricted information from a supposed prophet who communicates only through Knight. So Knight has the power of information because she is the only conduit for Ramtha's "enlightenment." Her fame and fortune are built on the exclusive access she has to information from Ramtha.

Information can be a positive power resource. Teachers are accorded stature because they have information that is valuable for students to learn. Sharing this information can empower students. Ministers, priests, and religious leaders have information that brings them respect and prestige, and the information, when shared, is spiritually empowering for laypersons. The information teachers and ministers share is a power resource because it is restricted to students and laypersons by their limited background and experience. Teachers and ministers can translate the information so it is understandable.

Expertise: Information Plus Know-How

There is an old story told about an expert who was called in to fix a brand-new diesel locomotive that wouldn't start. The railroad that owned the diesel engine requested an itemized billing once the expert had successfully finished his labor. His bill was for $1,500. He broke the bill into two items: $15 for swinging a hammer and $1,485 for knowing the right spot to hit and how to hit it. We pay big money to experts for knowing what to do and how to do it.

Information and expertise are closely related, but a person can have critical information without being an expert. You might possess a valuable technical report without being able to decipher any of the information. You may also know the law but not be capable of practicing it skillfully in the courtroom. Expertise is more than just having information. *An expert knows how to use the information wisely and skillfully.*

No individual or group could ever hope to function effectively without at some time requiring the services of experts. Families require financial advisers, roofers, carpenters, exterminators, counselors, physicians, hairstylists, mechanics, and those who repair our appliances, phones, computers, broken pipes, and broken hearts. Expertise can be a very positive power resource.

Expertise functions as a power resource under two conditions. First, the person is perceived to *have the requisite skills, abilities, knowledge, and background* to function as a real expert. Normally, real expertise includes appropriate education and training, intelligence, experience, and demonstrated mastery of relevant information.

A second condition for individuals to be perceived as experts is that they *be considered trustworthy*. People everywhere are more influenced by experts who stand to gain nothing personally than they are by those who would gain personally by lying or distorting information (McGuinnies & Ward, 1980).

Legitimate Authority: You Will Obey

Participants were told to deliver increasingly painful electric shocks to an innocent victim for every wrong answer on a word-association test. No one, neither the experimenters, groups of psychiatrists, college students, nor middle-class adults, thought any of the participants would deliver the maximum shock of 450 volts. Nevertheless, two-thirds of the participants in some of the studies obeyed the experimenter and delivered the maximum shock to the victim, who in some cases screamed in agony. No shocks were actually delivered, but the experiments were made to seem real, and none of the participants suspected trickery.

In all, 19 variations of these obedience-to-authority studies were conducted (Milgram, 1974), and others have replicated the results (Blass, 2000). More recently, a number of television shows have offered various versions of the Milgram studies. Psychologist Jerry Burger at Santa Clara University in 2007 for *ABC Primetime* showed results that paralleled previous obedience studies (Burger, 2007). British illusionist Derren Brown copied Milgram's main study for his UK TV program called *The Heist*. More than half of the participants obeyed to the end ("Milgram Experiment—Derren Brown," YouTube). A French documentary film crew in March 2010 reframed the obedience study as a game show called *The Game of Death*. They added the "entertaining" twist of live audience participation with shouts for "punishment" from the highly vocal crowd and an eager host who encouraged delivery of greater shocks. A whopping 80% of the participants went to the extreme (Crumley, 2010). None of these television versions of the Milgram studies, with the possible exception of the Burger replication, are completely credible because there is no way of determining how much editing or fakery occurred to make the programs entertaining to a television audience. Nevertheless, they suggest that nothing much has changed since Milgram conducted his original experiments five decades ago.

Participants in the Milgram studies followed orders not because they were evil or sadistic but because they couldn't resist legitimate authority (Milgram, 1974). The experimenter was the legitimate authority. He insisted that participants continue to deliver increasing levels of electric shock to the victims. A **legitimate authority** is someone who is perceived to have a right to direct others' behavior because of his or her position, title, role, experience, or knowledge.

The strength of legitimate authority can be seen outside the experimental laboratory. David Cline, a driver education instructor at Northern High School in Durham, North Carolina, ordered a teenage student driver to chase a car that cut them off. When they caught up to the offender, Cline jumped out of the car and punched Jon David Macklin in the nose. Macklin took off. Cline ordered the student driver to chase after him again, which the student did. A police officer pulled them over for speeding. The student broke traffic laws and endangered several people on the orders of a legitimate authority—her driver education instructor. They ultimately obeyed a higher authority, the police officer. Cline resigned from his teaching post.

No individual possesses legitimate authority. It is conferred by others. Babysitters sometimes face a predicament. Parents put them in charge of their children, but the children's perception that the sitter is not a "real parent" can undermine this power resource. Parents exercise legitimate authority over their children by virtue of their caregiver role. They typically use their legitimate authority to guide, protect, and teach their children. Once children become adults, however, a parent's authority is minimized. In some instances, it is perceived as illegitimate. ("I'm not your little boy anymore. You can't tell me what to do.")

The competent communicator must adopt the skeptical view and distinguish between appropriate and inappropriate use of authority. Blindly refusing to obey police officers, teachers, parents, judges, and bosses is as dangerous as blindly obeying authority. Ethical criteria—respect, honesty, fairness, choice, and responsibility—provide the means for determining when we should defy and when we should comply with dictates from authority.

Rewards and Punishments: Pleasure and Pain

Distributing rewards and punishments can be an important source of power. Salaries, bonuses, work schedules, perks, hirings, and firings are typical job-related rewards and punishments. Money, freedom, privacy, and car keys are a few of the rewards and punishments found in family situations.

The power potential of punishment depends on the degree of certainty that the punishment will be administered. Idle threats have little influence on behavior. Parents who threaten spankings or denial of privileges—but never follow through—soon realize that their children have learned to ignore such impotent bluster. Punishment is a source of power if it can be, and likely will be, exercised.

Punishing as a power source, however, is delicate business. Punishing can be used positively to change behavior from antisocial to prosocial. Punishing, however, is coercive and reinforces dominance. Consequently, it easily triggers backlash (Kohn, 1993). Individuals on the receiving end of punishment typically rebel. Those who punish create interpersonal distance between themselves and those punished. We don't normally like our tormenters.

Reward as a power resource tends to induce rewarding behavior. If you disseminate rewards, you become more attractive in the

Personal qualities can be a power resource. Which personal qualities account for Lady Gaga's power?

eyes of those rewarded. This, of course, depends on whether rewards are used to promote competition or cooperation. Rewards, especially when used to bribe a person to behave in a certain way, can be used as a strategy of dominance. "Do what I say and I'll buy you a computer" seeks compliance from the person rewarded.

Personal Qualities: A Powerful Persona

We all know individuals who exert some influence over us without using any of the power resources already discussed. They exhibit personal qualities that we find attractive. Mother Teresa, the pope, several U.S. presidents, some sports figures, political leaders, teachers, and parents exhibit these personal qualities that draw people to them and make them positive role models. This constellation of personal attributes that people find attractive is often referred to as **charisma**.

Good looks, an attractive personality, dynamism, persuasive skills, warmth, and charm are some of the personal qualities that make an individual charismatic. There is no precise formula for determining charisma. What is attractive to you may be unattractive to others. Your friends may be flabbergasted by your choice for a date. Who can adequately explain the grief exhibited by Elvis worshipers on the anniversary of his death? Many of the grief stricken weren't born until after Elvis died. The cult of celebrity and personality can be a very powerful resource.

Before leaving this section on power resources, one final point should be emphasized. *A person does not possess power but is granted power by others*. Your relationship partner, a group, or an organization must endorse the power resource for it to be influential. Charisma means little in a job interview if a hiring committee prefers diligence, expertise, and efficiency. Charisma might look like flash without follow-through. Arnold Schwarzenegger (flash) ousted Governor Gray Davis (appropriately named Gray—dull) in a recall election in California in 2003 largely on the strength of his charisma as an international celebrity. As one columnist for *The Atlantic* notes, "A year after being sworn-in as California's governor in 2003, Arnold Schwarzenegger's popularity was so great there was talk of a constitutional amendment so the GOP's Austrian-born action hero could run for president. The movement failed, which might have been just as well. Schwarzenegger leaves office today with an approval rating of 22 percent and a state budget deficit of $28 billion" (Gustini, 2011). Power is transactional. No one has it unless others grant it to you, as every dictator toppled in the Middle East in 2010–2011 learned. A reward that nobody wants will influence no one. Information that is irrelevant to the needs of individuals or groups has no power potential.

Problems of Power Imbalance

In this section, I discuss five effects of power imbalances: relationship failure, physical violence, verbal and nonverbal abuse, sexual harassment, and commonplace difficulties in ordinary transactions. The first four effects are part of what some researchers have called the "dark side" of communicating with others (Cupach & Spitzberg, 2011). The desire to present communication transactions in a sunny, "positive" framework is understandable. Ignoring the dark side because it is unpleasant, however, would make this text seem sadly unrelated to the all-too-frequent experience of readers. As two communication experts observe, "To fully understand how people effectively function requires us to consider how individuals cope with social interaction that is difficult, problematic, challenging, distressing, and disruptive" (Cupach & Spitzberg, 1994, p. vii). As another puts it, the "dark side is integral to the experience of relationships, not separate from it" (Duck, 1994, p. 6). Few problems in life, especially significant difficulties, are solved by ignoring them. If relationship failures, verbal and physical violence, abuse, and harassment were infrequent, insignificant occurrences, ignoring them here would be appropriate and welcome. These problems, however, occur frequently in our communication transactions, and they are significant. We ignore them at our own peril.

Ultimately, this examination of the more unpleasant side of communicating with others has a very positive goal: to help you recognize the often subtle encroachment of the dark side into your communication transactions. Such recognition is the first step toward preventing the dark side from intruding into your life.

Relationship Failure: Why Share Power?

Sharing power with your intimate partner is critical to relationship satisfaction and success for most couples. *When men refused to share power with their wives, there was an 81% chance that the marriage would fail* (Gottman & Silver, 1999). When power is unequally distributed and dominance becomes the focus, power struggles often ensue (Wilmot & Hocker, 2011). This is not only significant for heterosexual couples, but several studies of gay and lesbian couples reveal that sharing relatively equal power leads to higher satisfaction and greater commitment (Eldridge & Gilbert, 1990; Kurdek, 1989, 1998).

Power is shared when partners accept each other's influence (Gottman & Gottman, 2006; Gottman & Silver, 1999). When partners disagree, they search for common ground. They solve problems; they discuss issues without insisting that one viewpoint is accepted outright. Everything is open to negotiation—careers, cooking and housework responsibilities, paying bills, and child rearing. Decisions are not made on the basis of gender role stereotypes (the man is the breadwinner; the woman is the child rearer). Responsibilities are viewed as shared, not the sole obligation of one partner or the other. Raising children is a coparenting process, not the principal responsibility of the mother. Partners do not try to dominate each other in a grab for power. Attempting to drown out a partner's expressed viewpoint, exhibiting contempt for a partner's feelings, heaping criticism on one's partner, or trying to bully a partner into capitulating during an argument is the opposite of power sharing.

Equal-partner relationships have the greatest potential for success in most instances, and according to a Pew Research study, they are becoming more common (George, 2008). Sociologist Andrew Cherlin, commenting on the study, notes, "I think the big story over time is the rise in shared decision making. It's not the same as the '50s and '60s, where 'father knew best'" (quoted in George, 2008). Equal-partner relationships are not the only avenue to success (Gottman & Gottman, 2006), but such relationships greatly increase the odds of success.

Relationship Aggression: Battle for Dominance

Comedian Elayne Boosler once remarked, "When women are depressed, they either eat or go shopping. Men invade another country." The stereotype is that men are far more aggressive than women. There is truth to the stereotype. Although cultures vary widely in their frequency of homicides, *men commit more than 80% of all homicides in every culture* (Daly & Wilson, 1998), and close to 90% of all homicides in the United States are committed by men (Lilienfeld & Arkowitz, 2010). Males commit a wide range of aggressive acts more frequently than women (Harris, 1996). Men are arrested for more than 80% of violent crimes committed each year (Archer, 2000). Research also reveals that male-initiated violence against women is a serious problem worldwide (Haj-Yahia, 1999). Many of these acts of aggression qualify as catastrophic events that ignite significant stress for the victims (being held up at gunpoint can be a shattering experience).

Aggression Types: Direct and Indirect

The substantial gender difference in the tendency to commit aggressive acts, however, is not as clear-cut as quoting crime statistics suggests. First, a review of 64 studies revealed that men are far more likely to engage in unprovoked aggression (sticking up a liquor store for money) than are women, but the gender difference in aggression is small when there is provocation—for example, communication that frustrates or insults (Bettancourt & Miller, 1996).

Second, **aggression** is any physical or verbal communication that is intended to inflict harm, so there are two kinds. **Direct aggression** is hostile communication that targets the victim openly, such as pushing, shoving, physically assaulting, or shouting insults. **Indirect aggression** is hostile communication that intends to harm a targeted person while avoiding identification as an aggressor, such as gossiping, spreading malicious rumors, or sabotaging behind the victim's back (Bjorkqvist et al., 1994; Willer & Cupach, 2011). Men far more than women engage in direct aggression, accounting for their disproportionate representation in crime statistics. Women far more than men engage in indirect aggression (Card et al., 2008; Willer & Cupach, 2011). These gender differences in direct versus indirect aggression have been found in Australia, Finland, Italy, Poland, and Sweden in addition to the United States (Owens et al., 2000).

Third, although men far more often than women initiate direct aggression outside intimate relationships, there is substantial direct aggression initiated by women against their male partners within intimate relationships. Archer (2000) conducted a review of 124 studies and concluded that women resort to physical violence in relationships as often as men. A more recent extensive review of voluminous research on this issue led Spitzberg (2011) to conclude: "Compared to males, females use approximately equal, or greater, amounts of violence in their intimate relationships" (p. 335). Straus (2008) conducted an international study of university students in 32 nations and concluded that almost one-third of *both male and female students* "physically assaulted a dating partner" in a 12-month period. Straus concludes that there is "overwhelming evidence that women assault their partners at about the same rate as men." Are the assaults minor or major aggressive acts? Most are minor, but many are severe. Straus operationally defined a *severe assault* as using a knife or gun, punching, choking, slamming a partner against a wall, beating, burning or scalding on purpose, or kicking a partner. Women engaged in severe assaults *more frequently* than men (Straus, 2001, 2008). These conclusions, though strongly supported by voluminous research, have not gone unchallenged (see Box 7-1; *read it now*).

Solutions: The Communication Link

Ultimately, solutions to problems of relationship aggression require concerted and systematic efforts by individuals and entire cultures. This is particularly true regarding intimate

BOX 7.1 Focus on Controversy

GENDER AND RELATIONSHIP AGGRESSION: A WHITE-HOT DEBATE

Research showing about equal amounts of gender violence in intimate relationships startles many, and it has provoked passionate debate among partisan groups. Women's groups often point to crime reports to support the claim that men are more directly aggressive than women. Males, however, are reluctant to label a physical attack by a female partner as a criminal assault, so it is underreported (Archer, 2000). On the other hand, survey data probably vastly underreport male battering of women because batterers are reluctant to fill out surveys that require them to admit their criminal acts (Johnson, 2006a).

Michael Johnson (1995, 2006a, 2006b) reviewed a vast number of studies and concluded that the gender violence debate is muddied by mixing differing and conflicting sets of data. He identifies four types of relationship violence, two that are predominant. First, **intimate terrorism** is the most extreme form that involves "a violent attempt to take complete control of, or at least to generally dominate, a relationship." According to Johnson, 97% *of intimate terrorism is committed by men against women*. It is most likely to increase in frequency and escalate to severe acts of aggression, including murder. Women rarely counter intimate terrorism with violence (2006a).

Second, **situational couple violence** "is a product of particular conflicts or tensions within relationships" (Johnson, 2006b). Individuals quarrel with their partners, anger and frustration erupt, and an assault occurs. Here *both partners commit roughly equal amounts of direct aggression* (Johnson, 2006a; Klein & Johnson, 1997). Situational couple violence afflicts a much broader range of couples than the less-common intimate terrorism (Straus, 2008), *occurring among about half the heterosexual couples in the United States* at some point in their relationship (Johnson, 1995; Klein & Johnson, 1997). Dating couples experience more violence than married couples (Straus, 2001), and newlyweds experience greater violence than more seasoned married couples (Frye & Karney, 2006). Gay and lesbian couples experience about the same frequency and level of violence as heterosexual couples (Spitzberg, 2011; Waldner-Haugrud et al., 1997). Situational violence is typically less severe, less frequent, and less likely to escalate than what occurs during intimate terrorism (Johnson, 2006a).

Female violence is not primarily used in self-defense during situational couple violence. Self-defense is pegged at a mere 7% of female violent acts by Straus (2008). Pearson (1997) found that 90% of the women she studied reported that they assaulted their male partners because they were furious, frustrated, or jealous, not because they needed to defend themselves. Numerous studies

This is the image most people have when partner abuse is an issue. Hundreds of studies, however, reveal substantial violence is also initiated by women against their partners.

(continued)

BOX 7.1 *(Continued)*

report from both males and females that women initiate violence against their male partners as often or *more often* than vice versa (Straus, 2001, 2008). Women are more likely to initiate physical aggression against men if they believe that their male partners are unlikely to retaliate or that their male partners may simply try to physically restrain the attack (Archer, 2000).

Given that women are physically smaller and weaker than most men, should we take female violence as seriously as male violence no matter who initiates the aggression? Certainly, a woman slapping a man across the face is less severe than a man hitting a woman with his fists, even though both acts might qualify as "severe violence." By far, the most frequent acts of severe violence by women—kick, slap, bite, punch, hit with an object (Archer, 2002)—may rarely produce severe injuries. Men's far more likely choices—strangle, choke, beat up their partners—are severe violence of a different magnitude. Even seemingly identical acts of aggression ("hit with fist") also can produce markedly different physical injuries (Christopher & Lloyd, 2000). Female severe violence, however, is not inconsequential. A kick to the male groin may not require a trip to the emergency room or even show bruising, but as every male knows, it can reduce a man to a whimpering, writhing blob on the ground. The humiliation that men may feel, however, from being kicked or slapped in the face by their female partner, even though no obvious severe physical injury has been suffered, should not be trivialized. Initiating physical aggression, even if it doesn't result in the loss of blood or broken bones, leaves its mark emotionally on the victims, be they male or female (Spitzberg, 2011).

Thus, the evidence supports several conclusions. First, men are almost exclusively responsible for intimate terrorism, making women feel more menaced because they typically are physically weaker and almost always the victims. Second, the more frequent form of direct aggression in intimate relationships is situational couple violence, initiated about equally by men and women (Johnson, 2006a). Third, the significant level of female aggression deserves greater attention than it usually receives. Some have argued that this may become a strategy to obscure men's violence (Berns, 2001). This certainly is not my intention. The fact that women violently attack men, usually not in self-defense, should make us no less concerned about males battering women. We should, however, be more concerned about female-initiated violence than perhaps we are currently because it is far more frequent and severe than often supposed. Relationship violence should not be framed as a competition to determine who is the bigger victim, women or men. Our aim should be to stop the aggression. We can't do that well if we look at only male abusers and female victims.

QUESTIONS FOR THOUGHT

1. Are you surprised by the research results showing substantial female-initiated violence in intimate relationships? What should be done to help male victims of female-initiated violence?
2. Do you think men fear violence from their female partners as much as women fear violence from male partners?
3. How can college students address violence in dating relationships? Would this differ from approaches used by married couples with children?

terrorism (see Box 7-1), for which there is no easy or quick-fix communication solution. Treatment programs for batterers, unfortunately, have not proved to be very effective in reducing this serious problem (Johnson, 2001). Focusing on women's safety and the male perpetrator's criminality is the most appropriate approach, at this point, to minimize the effects of intimate terrorism.

Addressing situational couple violence, however, is more promising. Our society is not noted for its adept conflict-management skills (see Chapter 9). When conflict arises, small arguments can easily explode into major episodes of aggression if competent communication is absent. Verbal aggression (insults, ridicule, yelling, contempt) often precedes physical aggression (McKibbin et al., 2007), making verbal aggression a likely signal that a couple is in jeopardy of becoming violent (Schumacher & Leonard, 2005). In addition, communication deficiencies such as poor argumentative skills (inarticulate presentation of claims and weak ability to support claims made during a conflict) contribute to relationship violence (Infante et al., 1989, 1990). Situationally violent couples exhibit more verbal aggression and deficiencies in argumentation than nonviolent couples (Infante & Rancer, 1996; Sabourin, 1996). Violence, in a perverse way, compensates for the communication deficiencies, especially if the deficient individual has a verbally skillful partner. The incompetent communicator "levels the playing field" by acts or threats of violence. Learning communication competence, especially when dealing with conflict in relationships, strengthens the likelihood that violence can be avoided and constructive problem solving engaged.

Finally, an imbalance of power, whether actual, perceived, or desired, is a central element in relationship violence (Leonard & Senchak, 1996; Sabourin, 1995). Dominance is perceived through communication (who must ask for permission to party with friends or skip cooking a meal; who participates in decision making; who makes final choices on significant issues—one or both partners—etc.). *Violence is far more prevalent in relationships where power is unequally distributed than in relationships where the power distribution is relatively equal* (Cahn & Lloyd, 1996; Straus, 2008). Either male or female dominance in relationships is more likely to provoke severe violence than minor aggression (Straus, 2008). As Straus (2008) concludes, "Whenever there is dominance of one partner, there is an increased risk of violence by the dominant partner to maintain the dominant position or by the subordinate partner to achieve something blocked by the dominant partner, or to change the power structure." Working to establish a more equitable distribution of power is an important step toward nonviolent intimate relationships.

Verbal and Nonverbal Abuse: Expressing Contempt

Power struggles in relationships that take on a dominance-prevention quality do not always end in violence. In fact, more likely than not, no fists will fly, nor will any pots and pans. Partners will simply abuse each other verbally and nonverbally by tearing apart each other's self-esteem and self-worth (Spitzberg, 2011). Communicating contempt for one's partner has a corrosive effect on a relationship (Gottman, 1994a; Gottman & Gottman, 2006).

Contempt is intended to insult and emotionally abuse a person. Robert G. Ingersol once described three-time presidential candidate William Jennings Bryan's mind as "an insane asylum without a keeper." A 36-year-old female trucking company executive describes men in power positions as "a bunch of shallow, bald, middle-aged men with character disorders. They don't have the emotional capacity it takes to qualify as human beings. One good thing about these white, male, almost extinct mammals is that they are growing old. We get to watch them die" (Gates, 1993, p. 49). Now that's contempt! When couples argue as adversaries trying to win a verbal exchange, contempt can easily become a verbal weapon both for the dominant partner trying to exert control and for the weaker partner trying to equalize the power distribution.

There are four ways to communicate contempt (Gottman, 1994a, 1994b). First, contempt can be communicated by verbal insults and name-calling. *Bastard, bitch, moron, jerk, imbecile, fathead,* and even cruder, more vicious insults are targeted at tearing apart the self-esteem of one's partner.

Second, hostile humor communicates contempt. Camouflaged as "only a joke," hostile humor, if you're the target, aims to make others laugh at your expense. "Marsha's so sweet I fear getting diabetes just being around her" and "Harry's a very passionate lover—of himself" ridicule the person shown contempt. Respect, a key ingredient of competent communication, is nowhere to be seen.

Third, mockery communicates contempt. You mock others by imitating them derisively. A man says to his partner, "I really do love you," and his partner responds with a contorted facial expression and fake, exaggerated voice, "You really do love me." Mockery is meant to make fun of a person. It assaults that person's sincerity.

Fourth, certain body movements communicate contempt. Sneering, rolling your eyes, curling your upper lip, and using obscene gestures are all signs of contempt for your partner. When a person leaves the room while a partner or coworker is speaking, this nonverbally communicates contempt.

Sexual Harassment: When "Flirting" Is Hurting

Sexual harassment is generally defined as verbal or nonverbal communication of a sexual nature that is unwelcome by the recipient and is likely to interfere with the victim's work (Maass et al., 2003, p. 854). The law defines two principal types of sexual harassment: quid pro quo (you give something to get something) and hostile environment (Wiener & Gutek, 1999; Witteman, 1993). **Quid pro quo harassment** occurs when the more powerful person requires sexual favors from the less powerful person in exchange for keeping a job, getting a high grade in a class, landing an employment promotion, and the like. **Hostile environment harassment** is not so easily defined. The Supreme Court in 1986 endorsed the hostile work environment interpretation of sexual harassment. According to the Court's decision, employees have a right to work in situations free from discriminatory insult, ridicule, or intimidation (Paetzold & O'Leary-Kelly, 1993).

Quid pro quo sexual harassment is blatant, unethical communication behavior. It is disrespectful to victims, often covered by lies, and unfair because preferential treatment is given for sex. Choice is removed when threats of job loss are involved. It is irresponsible Me-oriented behavior.

The hostile environment form of sexual harassment, however, can also be crude and unethical communication in the extreme. A District of Columbia court awarded Elizabeth Reese $250,000 for damages incurred while she worked for the architectural design firm Swanke, Hayden, and Connell. Reese's male supervisor repeatedly made lewd comments to her, incessantly asked about her sex life, encouraged her to prostitute herself for the firm, then told fellow workers that she had.

Sexual harassment is an explosive issue partly because of serious disagreements regarding what it means. Researchers in one study asked female faculty and graduate students whether they had experienced any of 31 acts legally defined as sexual harassment. Almost 90% of the study participants had. Yet only 5.6% of the faculty and 2.8% of the graduate students surveyed answered "yes" to the question that directly asked them if they had been sexually harassed (Brooks & Perot, 1991; see also Mecca & Rubin, 1999; Shepela & Levesque, 1998). A similar result was found for male college students, with only 1 of 40 labeling inappropriate behavior by their professor as sexual harassment (Kalof et al., 2001). Although only a minor gender difference exists regarding agreement with what the courts define as quid pro quo sexual harassment (sexual coercion), larger differences emerge between men's and women's views of hostile environment sexual harassment—for example, sex-stereotyped jokes or repeated requests for dates after refusal (Rotundo et al., 2001).

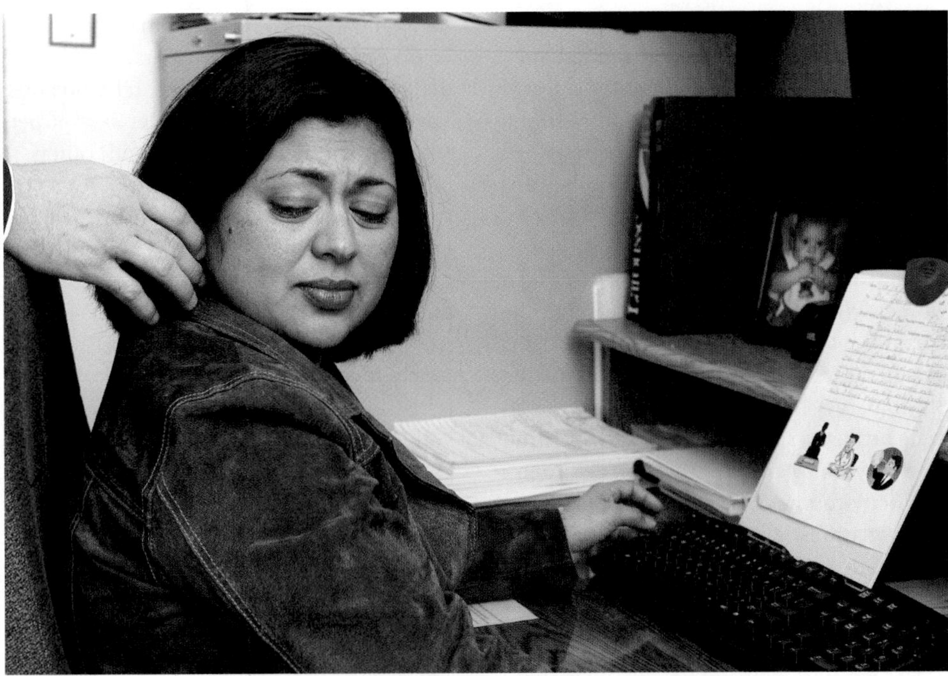

Sexual harassment is often more nonverbal than verbal, and it usually involves a power imbalance.

What is flirtation to men may be harassment to women.

Most instances of sexual harassment victimize women. On average, 58% of women have experienced sexual harassment on the job (Berdahl & Moore, 2006; Ilies, 2003). *Sexual harassment against males, however, is not an insignificant problem.* The U.S. Equal Employment Opportunity Commission (2006) reports that men file almost 20% of all complaints of sexual harassment. In some states, such as California and Michigan, about a quarter of complaints come from men (Mittioli, 2010). The consequences to the victims of sexual harassment, both male and female, have been well documented: psychological distress, depression, shame and embarrassment, and diminished job performance (Jorgenson & Wahl, 2000; Kelly, 2005; Magley, 2002).

Sexual harassment is fundamentally an abuse that stems from power imbalances (Dziech & Hawkins, 1998). Quid pro quo harassment is a clear instance of dominance by perpetrators against less powerful victims. Dealing with this kind of sexual harassment is extremely difficult because the harasser has legitimate authority and can punish the victim for openly complaining. Laws forbidding such behavior, policies that explicitly punish such harassment, and the enforcement of laws and policies are all helpful in combating quid pro quo harassment. Firm, unequivocal rejection of such harassment by the target of an unwanted sexual advance is also an important communication approach. ("Do not ever make sexual remarks to me.")

Hostile environment sexual harassment is also promoted by power imbalances. It is particularly prevalent where women try to compete in traditionally male occupations (Parker & Griffin, 2002). Smith Barney, a Wall Street brokerage firm with 400 offices nationwide, established a pattern of hostile environment sexual harassment that led to a class action lawsuit by 25 female stockbrokers. Male employees gawked at the women's breasts and made lewd and suggestive remarks. Senior male managers in the Garden City, New York, office maintained a basement room dubbed the "Boom-Boom Room," where female employees were confronted with unwanted sexual advances, groping, and kissing on the lips. Women at work were sent condoms and food shaped in the form of penises. Plaintiffs claimed that their complaints to superiors were ignored. In some cases, women were punished with menial tasks and public humiliations for complaining. Pamela Martens, one of the plaintiffs, noted, "It's like they have a manual in their heads as to how to crush women" (Jackson, 1997). Even though the harassment often came from fellow brokers of equal position and power, most of the Smith Barney brokers were men. This put female brokers in a decidedly weaker position when trying to combat the hostile "men's club" environment. Individual women were fighting against a group of men. Smith Barney finally settled the case in October 2010 ("Today in Labor History," 2010).

Sometimes the hostile environment is the product of misperceptions and misreading signals, not ugly intentions (Bingham, 1991). For example, men often misread women's communication as flirting signals (Abbey, 1987; Saal et al., 1989). Men more than women interpret eye contact, a brush against an arm, an innocent smile, a friendly remark, a gift, or a compliment as a sexual come-on (Kowalski, 1993). Men traditionally are expected to be the initiators of romantic transactions, so they are more likely to make mistakes than women, who typically wait to be approached.

Combating hostile environment sexual harassment is difficult. A firm, clearly defined policy staunchly supported by those in power positions goes a long way toward diminishing sexual harassment. With such a policy, those who are harassed can more safely and confidently reject poor treatment. Communication strategies of assertiveness, threat of formal complaint, or deflection of sexual remarks by diverting discussion to neutral topics can be successful when hostile environment harassment is clearly not tolerated in the workplace or educational environment (Bingham, 1991).

Commonplace Difficulties: Lighter Side

Power imbalances don't always lead to violence, verbal or physical abuse, and harassment. Many, perhaps most, instances of power imbalance never graduate to the dark side of interpersonal relationships. They remain part of the lighter side of personal difficulties experienced with others.

Consider the remote control wars. Invented for Zenith Corporation by Dr. Robert Adler, the remote control made its debut on June 8, 1956. According to a study conducted by sociologist Alexis Walker, men were the predominant channel surfers, much to the displeasure of most women (cited in McCall, 1996; see also Bellamy & Walker, 1996). Walker herself recalls, "My parents bought a second TV set because my mother said to me, 'I will not watch TV with your father any more because of the way he uses that remote control'" (p. D1). Women told Walker that they recorded their preferred shows to view at a later time so they could still be with their male partners while they watched sports.

More recent evidence shows that the remote control wars are subsiding, or at least becoming less male dominated. A study by Pew Research Center showed that 27% of respondents said that women control the remote, 26% said men do, and another 25% said it was a joint decision (George, 2008).

Power imbalances are apparent in a wide variety of daily occurrences. At work, the shift from work to personal talk is usually initiated by the most powerful person (Tannen, 1994). If the office manager takes a break and begins telling stories and chatting, everyone else in the office sees fit to follow suit. Taking breaks and chatting, however, can be perceived as goofing off unless sanctioned by a more powerful person. Such power imbalance can make employees wary, even resentful, of the "double standard."

Doctor-patient relationships are rarely equal. Patients wait for doctors, sometimes for unreasonably long periods of time, not vice versa. My doctor developed a reputation for mistreating his patients by making them wait for up to two hours. On one occasion, after a tedious delay, I felt compelled to leave before seeing him, whereupon he raced out into the parking lot, chased me down, and cajoled me into returning for immediate treatment. The less powerful do have options.

Doctors usually wear white coats as symbols of their authority. Patients wear casual clothes, humiliating hospital gowns with a breezy backside, and sometimes no clothes at all. Patients refer to the physician as "Dr. Schmidt" or "Dr. Martinez," not "Harry" or "Maria." The physician, however, often addresses patients by their first names. This pattern is not always displayed, however, when the doctor is female. Some male patients may inappropriately try to upset the power imbalance by referring to female physicians informally (e.g., "Hi Kate") or even by making lewd or suggestive remarks (Tannen, 1994). Such references are insulting, and they make the doctor's task of caring for the patient exceedingly difficult.

Apologies for mishaps or misdeeds are expected from the less powerful, reminding them of their subservient position. Children are expected to apologize to parents for cracking up the car, but parents do not normally apologize to their kids for a similar mishap, even though the children may be seriously inconvenienced by the car being out of commission. Nevertheless, apologizing can cement relationships between unequal individuals.

Competent Communication and Balancing Power

The quick answer to relationship problems caused by power imbalances is to balance the power. This is easier said than done, especially when some individuals would rather maintain their dominance in relationships and groups. There are many ways to balance unequally distributed power; some involve competent communication, and others are clearly incompetent communication. I discuss both in the next two sections.

Dominance-Prevention: Competitive Power Balancing

Dominance-prevention power struggles produce several methods of balancing power. These methods are coalition formation, defiance, and resistance. Although none of these methods inherently produce incompetent communication, as you will see, each is prone to produce negative outcomes.

Coalition Formation: Pooling Power

Individuals form temporary alliances, called **coalitions**, to increase their power relative to others (Simpson & Macy, 2001). Coalitions occur in group situations when there are disputes and group members jointly use their combined power to control a decision and to take action. One study found that arguments and disagreements in families lead to coalitions about 30% of the time (Grusky et al., 1995). Coalitions can balance the power in a group when the relatively powerless form a coalition and increase their strength, but they can create power imbalances when the more powerful group members move to consolidate their strength by banding together against the weaker members.

In most families, the father is considered the most powerful person, followed by the mother, then the oldest child, followed by the younger siblings (Grusky et al., 1995). Parental coalitions predominate in a four-person family, and they are virtually unopposable. Such coalitions maintain the family structure and support the status differences between parents and children. The next most frequent coalition is a parent and an older child. Children-only coalitions are the least frequent and least successful (Grusky et al., 1995).

Coalitions may be useful in the political arena, but they can be destructive in family situations (Rosenthal, 1997). Coalitions create a "them-versus-us" competitive mentality. Parental coalitions are sometimes necessary to present a united front when a dispute with children arises. Parent-child coalitions, however, can disrupt the family structure. Parental stability is the most vital part of family stability. Asking children to choose sides in a dispute between parents can rip a family apart, especially if the issue is significant and the dispute is recurrent. It is usually more constructive and effective when parents work out their differences without seeking allies among their children.

Defiance: Digging in Your Heels

Low-power persons sometimes overtly defy higher-power persons. **Defiance** is unambiguous, purposeful noncompliance. It is a refusal to give in to those with greater power. Defiance is the prevention form of power where one stands against those who attempt to dominate.

Defiance can be contagious. A defiant child can embolden siblings to defy parents, unless the parents take effective action. A single worker who defiantly walks off the job may encourage a wildcat strike. Those in authority are anxious to halt defiance before it spreads.

Defiant individuals hoping to counter dominance from others occasionally convert an entire group to their point of view. If a person cannot be expelled from the relationship or group (e.g., family member), remaining unalterably and confidently defiant provides the best chance of successfully countering pressure to comply (Gebhardt & Meyers, 1995). When a group has the power to expel a person, however, remaining unalterably defiant will likely prove to be an impotent choice. Remaining uncompromisingly defiant until the group is about fed up, then switching to a more compromising position, is an option likely to produce better results (Wolf, 1979).

Remaining uncompromisingly defiant risks straining friendships and jeopardizing relationships with partners, relatives, and coworkers. Any time individuals are defiant, they run the risk of alienating those who disagree with them and sometimes even those who agree. Defiance is a highly competitive communication behavior. It will make a person a loser far more often than a winner because the very nature of defiance is disagreeable to those who want compliance, and they usually are the majority. In most cases, consider defiance an option of last resort.

Resistance: Dragging Your Feet

Although defiance is chosen in some instances, resistance is more often the choice of the less powerful to prevent dominance from others (Wilmot & Hocker, 2011). Defiance is overt, unambiguous noncompliance.

Defiance is an overt act of noncompliance. This lone unarmed man stands against tanks in the 1989 Tiananmen Square uprising in China. Most defiance is the product of a power imbalance, vividly evident here.

Resistance is covert, ambiguous noncompliance. It is often duplicitous and manipulative. Resisters are subtle saboteurs. The sabotage is ambiguous because truly successful resistance leaves people wondering if resistance even occurred.

Resistance has an advantage over defiance. It is often safer to use indirect means of noncompliance than direct confrontation when faced with a more powerful person or group. Those who are defiant dig in their heels and openly cause trouble, but those who resist merely drag their feet.

There are several resistance strategies (Rothwell, 2010). Resistance strategies are sometimes referred to as *passive aggression* (Wilmot & Hocker, 2011).

Strategic Stupidity: Smart People Acting Dumb This is the "playing stupid" strategy. When children don't want to do what their parents tell them, they sometimes act stupid when they know better. "But Mom, I don't know how to fold the laundry" may simply be an effort to frustrate the parent, who may give up in disgust and fold the laundry rather than show the child for the "bazillionth" time what should be plainly obvious.

Strategic stupidity works exceedingly well when the low-power person claims stupidity, is forced to attempt the task anyway, and then performs it ineptly. In one study of 555 married adults, 14% of the men admitted purposely botching house chores to get out of doing them again ("Home Chores," 1993). The poor performance becomes "proof" that the stupidity was real. The passive aggressor can assert, "I told you I didn't know how to do laundry."

Loss of Motor Function: Conscious Carelessness This resistance strategy is an effective companion to strategic stupidity. The resister doesn't act stupid, just incredibly clumsy, often resulting in costly damage. There is a mixed message here of resistance on one hand but apparent effort on the other. "I tried really hard not to let dishes slip out of my hands; I'm sorry I broke two plates" may be an honest apology from your housemate for accidental behavior. If it becomes repetitive, however, it may be an effort to avoid doing dishes.

The Misunderstanding Mirage: Confusion Illusion This is the "I thought you meant" or the "I could have sworn you said" strategy. The resistance is expressed "behind a cloak of great sincerity" (Bach & Goldberg, 1972, p. 110). Students sometimes excuse late assignments by using this strategy. "You said it was due Wednesday, not today, didn't you?" they'll say hopefully. The implied message is that since this is a simple misunderstanding, penalizing the student for a late paper would be unfair.

Selective Amnesia: Fake Forgetfulness Have you ever noticed that some people are particularly forgetful about those things that they clearly do not want to do? This temporary amnesia is highly selective when used as a resistance strategy. Selective amnesiacs rarely forget what is most important to them. No outward signs of resistance are manifested. Resisters agree to perform the task—but conveniently let it slip their minds.

In a sophisticated version of this strategy, the individual remembers all but one or two important items. A person shops for groceries and purchases all but two key items. Hey, no one's perfect. He or she remembered almost everything. The dinner menu, however, will have to be altered because the main course wasn't purchased.

Tactical Tardiness: Late by Design When you really don't want to attend a meeting, a class, a lecture, or a party, you can show contempt by arriving late. Tactical tardiness irritates and frustrates those who value the event. It can hold an entire group hostage while everyone waits for the arrival of the person who is late. Consistently arriving late for class is disruptive, especially if the resister requests an update on material missed.

Tactical tardiness may be used on occasion by high-power persons to reinforce their dominance and self-importance. Celebrities often arrive late to functions. They may hope to underscore their prestige by making fans wait for them.

Purposeful Procrastination: Deliberate Delays Most people put off doing what they dislike. There is nothing purposeful about this. Purposeful procrastinators, however, pretend that they will pursue a task "soon." While promising imminent results, they deliberately refuse to commit to a specific time or date for task completion. They delay completion of tasks on purpose. Trying to pin down a purposeful procrastinator is like trying to nail Jell-O to a wall—it won't stick. If those waiting for the task to be completed express exasperation, they appear to be nagging or fussing. Parents who try to get their kids to clean their rooms are often faced with this maddening strategy. When parents grow weary of monitoring their children's room-cleaning progress, they may give up in disgust and perform the task themselves or leave the room chaotic. This makes the resistance successful.

All six of these resistance strategies result from power imbalances. It is difficult to know for sure when such strategies are being used. A single occurrence of forgetfulness or tardiness doesn't indicate resistance necessarily, although resistance may be occurring. If the behavior becomes repetitive, it is safe to conclude that resistance strategies are being used.

Resistance strategies are dishonest. In extreme cases, however, they may be the only feasible option available to prevent evil. In most instances, there are better ways to prevent dominance, as you will see later in this text. There are two principal ways for competent communicators to discourage resistance strategies.

1. *Confront the strategy directly*. Use first-person singular language to describe the resistance strategy (see Chapter 8). Discuss why the strategy has been used, and work cooperatively with the resister to find an equitable solution so resistance strategies are not employed.

2. *Produce consequences for resistance*. We become enablers when we allow ourselves to become ensnared in the resister's net of duplicity. When we continue to wait for the tactically tardy, we encourage the behavior. If we perform the tasks for those who use loss of motor function or strategic stupidity, we reward their resistance and guarantee that such strategies will persist.

You thwart the enabling process by making sure consequences result from resistance. If staff members "forget" important items when shopping for office supplies, send them back for the items. Encourage

▶ This cartoon illustrates which of the following?

1. Defiance
2. Resistance
3. Purposeful procrastination
4. Selective amnesia

Answers at end of chapter

them to make a list and check off items as they shop. If people are persistently late for meetings, continue without them and do not interrupt the meeting to fill them in on missed information. Encourage them to be punctual. Continued tardiness may necessitate punishment or expulsion from the group. Refrain from rescuing those who use strategic stupidity or loss of motor function. Compensation for damage caused by such resistance strategies should be the responsibility of the resister.

Despite the negative aspects of resistance strategies, the primary focus should not be on how to combat resistance. Instead, focus on how to reduce power imbalances and dominance-submissiveness transactions that foster a desire to resist.

Empowerment: Exercising Positive Power

Empowerment is a constructive form of power. Individuals become empowered by learning to communicate competently. Acquiring communication knowledge and developing a broad range of communication skills can give us the confidence to adapt our communication appropriately whatever the context. We are empowered by this knowledge and these skills because more options are available to us. In this section, I explain several ways to empower people.

Developing Assertiveness: Neither Doormat nor Boot Wiper

The terms *assertive* and *aggressive* are often confused. **Assertiveness** is "the ability to communicate the full range of your thoughts and emotions with confidence and skill" (Adler, 1977, p. 6). Those who confuse assertiveness with aggressiveness tend to ignore the last part of this definition. Assertiveness isn't merely imposing your thoughts and emotions on others. It requires confident and especially skillful expression of thoughts and emotions. Assertiveness falls between the extremes of aggressiveness and passivity and is distinctly different from both. Aggressiveness puts one's own needs first; you wipe your shoes on other people. Passivity underemphasizes one's needs; you're a doormat in a world of muddy shoes. *Assertiveness considers both your needs and the needs of others.*

Although assertiveness can be used to defy others, it is primarily an empowering skill. We are most often assertive to assure that our needs, rights, and responsibilities are not ignored or to make a relationship or group more effective. Assertive individuals try to enhance their significance in the eyes of others, not alienate anyone. When passive, reticent individuals learn assertiveness, they become more productive contributors in groups. When aggressive individuals learn to be assertive, they are more likely to receive a fair hearing than if they try to bulldoze through a disagreement that stands in their way.

Assertiveness is conspicuous by its absence in our culture (see Box 7-2). Despite the renowned American individualism, we tend to talk the talk but not walk the walk. In one study, small groups of four members congregated to decide which 12 individuals from a list of 30 were best suited to survive on a deserted island. During discussions, a male group member (a confederate of the experimenter) made three sexist remarks: "We definitely need to keep the women in shape"; "One of the women can cook"; "I think we need more women on the island to keep men satisfied." What would you do in this situation? Would you assert yourself by protesting such sexist remarks? Would you sit silently and endure the offensive remarks? When college students were asked what they would do, only 5% said they would passively remain quiet. When female participants were put to the test, however, 55% remained silent and only 16% objected to the sexist remarks. The rest mostly joked nervously or asked questions (Swim & Hyers, 1999). These results parallel more recent evidence that generally women are not as assertive as men (Leaper & Ayres, 2007). Assertiveness takes confidence and skill. Remember the studies discussed in Chapter 3 that showed women rarely negotiate for higher starting salaries, resulting in the loss of a million dollars over the course of a lifetime career. Passively accepting whatever starting salary is offered can be a serious disadvantage.

The practice of being assertive involves four key communication steps (Bower & Bower, 1976).

1. *Describe* your needs, rights, and desires or the basis of your conflict with others. Use first-person singular language.
2. *Express* how you think and feel. "It upsets me when my ideas are ignored" is an example.
3. *Specify* the behavior or objective you are seeking. "I want to be included in future decision making" specifies the objective.
4. *Identify* consequences. The emphasis should be on the positive, not the negative, consequences. "I like working here, and I will continue for as long as I'm treated fairly" is better than "If you continue to treat me unfairly, I'll be forced to quit."

It is important to note that assertiveness doesn't mean being impolite to others. Competent communicators show respect to others. You can remain firm and direct and still be unwaveringly polite and respectful. Assertiveness is ethical communication.

Assertiveness isn't always appropriate. Asian cultures typically do not value the low-context directness that characterizes assertive communication (Den Hartog, 2004). Standing up for yourself and speaking your mind are seen as disruptive and provocative acts likely to create disharmony. Even in an individualist culture like the United States, where a low-context communication style is encouraged, overly persistent assertiveness can result in less favorable evaluations from supervisors, lower salaries, greater job tension, and greater personal stress than less vigorous assertion of one's needs and desires (Schmidt & Kipnis, 1987). The competent communicator analyzes the context to determine the appropriate use of assertiveness.

Increasing Personal Power Resources: Expanding Choices

Individuals can empower themselves in numerous ways by developing their power resources. Women who have been homemakers may significantly empower themselves by returning to college, earning a degree, and finding employment. The additional income benefits the entire family. Self-esteem may be bolstered by her sense of independence resulting from a college education and employment in her field of study.

Husbands who assume a greater portion of the domestic chores and child rearing may increase their value in the family. They do not have to depend on the expertise of their partners to perform domestic activities competently. The stereotype of the bungling husband and father burning the dinner and falling prey to the antics of his children when his wife is away doesn't have to be the reality. Men can empower themselves to handle domestic responsibilities and tasks with dexterity. They don't have to become the passive victims of their own self-imposed ineptitude.

Developing expertise can be empowering. Learning computer skills can make you a valuable asset in a group or organization. Developing public speaking and interpersonal skills is empowering. Such skills open up new horizons, new capabilities, and options. Becoming informed on topics, especially if the information is specialized, can make you a valuable group member. The more we develop our personal power resources, the more empowered and significant we can become.

Employing Cooperative Argumentation: Deliberations, Not Combat

When someone tells us that they just had an argument with another person, it is usually perceived to be a negative event. Arguments usually involve strong disagreements between "opponents" engaged in disagreeable verbal combat where the goal is to "win the argument" even if this means using unethical personal attacks, deception, and manipulation. It is little wonder that most people shrink from such unpleasant engagements. The willingness and ability to engage in argument, however, are signs of one's degree of power. Those who feel highly capable in the arena of advocacy feel powerful. Those who feel ill equipped to so engage feel relatively powerless in such situations.

Makau and Marty (2001), however, offer an empowering alternative to the

BOX 7.2 Developing Communication Competence

ASSERTIVENESS SELF-ASSESSMENT QUESTIONNAIRE

Fill out the following Assertiveness Self-Assessment Questionnaire. Be as honest as you can. This is not an assessment of your "ideal self." This should be your "real self." For each situation, indicate how likely you would be to take the action indicated by using the following scale:

5 = Very likely 4 = Likely 3 = Maybe 2 = Unlikely 1 = Very unlikely

_______ 1. You have been invited to a party but you don't know anyone except the friend who invited you, who is not present when you enter the room. You see dozens of strangers. You walk up to a group of people, introduce yourself, and begin a conversation.

_______ 2. There is a definite undercurrent of tension and conflict in your group. You are feeling that tension as your group begins discussing their project for class. You stop the discussion, indicate that there is unresolved conflict in the group, and request that the group address this issue.

_______ 3. You strongly disagree with your group's choice for a symposium project. Nevertheless, you say nothing and go along with the majority decision.

_______ 4. During class, your instructor makes a point that angers you greatly. You raise your hand, are recognized by the instructor, and you vehemently challenge your instructor's position, raising your voice to almost a shout.

_______ 5. You're sitting in the back of the class. Two students sitting beside you engage in an audible conversation that is distracting. You can't concentrate on the instructor's lecture. You lean over and calmly ask them to stop talking so you can listen to your instructor.

_______ 6. At a family holiday dinner gathering, your uncle makes a blatantly racist remark, then tells a sexist joke. You sit silently.

_______ 7. While on vacation, you sign up to receive a group lesson in a new sport (jet skiing, rock climbing, snow skiing). After the instructor has explained the basics, everyone in the group appears to understand perfectly. You, however, are unclear about a couple of instructions. You raise your hand and ask the instructor to repeat the instructions and explain them more fully.

_______ 8. Three individuals representing a religious group knock on your door. When you answer, they begin to proselytize, trying to sell you on their religious point of view. You stand there waiting patiently for them to finish, wishing they would go away.

_______ 9. A small group of teenagers talk loudly during a movie you attend at a local theater. You become increasingly annoyed but say nothing to them.

_______ 10. You live in a dorm room with two roommates. Next door, loud music is playing, making it impossible for you to study. Your roommates seem not to care, but you are becoming increasingly annoyed by the noise. You walk next door, pound on the door, and when the door is opened, you demand that the music be turned way down immediately.

_______ 11. A member of your group couldn't afford to buy the textbook for the class. He asks you if he can borrow your book for "a couple of days." You agree. He has had the book for more than a week and shows no sign of returning it to you. You wait for him to return the book or to explain why he hasn't mentioned it.

_______ 12. At work, you are a member of a project team. Every member of the team makes considerably more money than you do, yet your jobs are equivalent. You believe that you deserve a hefty raise. You make an appointment with your boss to ask for a substantial raise.

(continued)

BOX 7.2 *(Continued)*

_____ 13. You receive an email from a team member that has a condescending tone. It angers you that this team member, whom you view as a bit of a screw-up, lectures you on the "right way" to approach your part of the group task. You write back a sarcastic, biting reply.

_____ 14. The coach of your sports team berates players at a team meeting for "lackluster play" and "lackadaisical attitudes." The coach is shouting and abusive. You believe the criticism is mostly unfair and doesn't apply to most of the players. You remain silent, wishing the coach would wind down.

_____ 15. A group member pulls you aside and begins accusing you of "unethical behavior." She is shouting at you, her face is flush red, and she is wildly gesturing. People are noticing. You shout back at her.

_____ 16. The family that lives next door has a dog that barks all hours of the night. It is disturbing to you and your family members. You meet one of the dog owners during a walk through the neighborhood. You stop, begin to talk, and you calmly bring up the barking-dog problem.

_____ 17. You are taking an exam. You notice several students cheating on the exam. You're upset because this gives these students an undeserved advantage and may lower your own grade because the instructor grades on a curve. The instructor doesn't notice the cheating. You report the cheating to the instructor after class.

_____ 18. During a group discussion, your point of view clashes with that of another group member. You want very much to convince the group that your viewpoint should be accepted. You interrupt when the member who disagrees with you tries to voice her opinion, you keep talking when she tries to disagree with a point you make, and you insist that she is wrong and you are right.

_____ 19. At work, a member of your project team "steals" your idea and takes credit for work you have done. You angrily denounce him in front of the entire team and insist that he own up to his deception.

_____ 20. One of your team members has extremely bad breath. This is a common problem when you meet. His bad breath bothers you a great deal. Nevertheless, you say nothing and try sitting as far away from him as possible during meetings.

_____ 21. You are waiting in line to be served at a local store. Just as you are about to be waited on, a group of three individuals steps in front of you. You demand that they step aside, insisting that you were in line ahead of them.

SCORING DIRECTIONS: Total your scores for numbers 4, 10, 13, 15, 18, 19, and 21 (aggressiveness). Now total your scores for numbers 1, 2, 5, 7, 12, 16, and 17 (assertiveness). Finally, total your scores for numbers 3, 6, 8, 9, 11, 14, and 20 (passivity). Enter these raw totals in the appropriate blank below.

____ Aggressiveness ( ) ____ Assertiveness ( ) ____ Passivity ( )

Now average each raw score by dividing by 7 (e.g., 21 on aggressiveness divided by 7 equals 3.0 average). Put averages in parentheses above.

NOTE: Generally speaking, you want to average between 4.0 and 5.0 on assertiveness and average 2.0 or less on aggressiveness and passivity. This reflects the general desirability of assertiveness and the

(continued)

BOX 7.2 *(Continued)*

general undesirability of aggressiveness and passivity. A low score on a specific assertiveness scenario or a high score on a specific aggressiveness or passivity scenario may also mean a need for improvement in these particular situations. Please note, however, that the appropriateness of assertiveness, aggressiveness, and passivity is situational. Assertiveness, although generally a desirable skill, is not always appropriate, especially if harm may come to you by being assertive. Conversely, aggressiveness, although generally an undesirable communication pattern, is not always inappropriate. Likewise, occasionally, the appropriate choice is passivity.

typical hypercompetitive argument—namely, cooperative argumentation. **Cooperative argumentation** is engaging in a process of deliberation with understanding and problem solving as ultimate goals. Cooperative argumentation focuses on the problem or issue, not on the people deciding. Participants disagree without being disagreeable. Civility is the overarching principle that guides discussions. Critical listening is emphasized, not fighting for the floor to dominate the conversation. In typical arguments, there is a dominance-prevention power struggle with winners and losers. Cooperative argumentation balances the power by providing a supportive atmosphere where all participants can feel free to join the discussion. Those who are hesitant to disagree are encouraged to participate. Having an opportunity to be heard can be profoundly empowering, especially to those unaccustomed to being taken seriously.

Cooperative argumentation is conducted in a supportive climate, whereas competitive argumentation produces defensiveness and a desire to counterattack or withdraw entirely from the clash of ideas. Thus, participants in cooperative argumentation describe objections they have to particular ideas instead of criticizing "rivals" to achieve a personal advantage. Participants solve problems instead of attempting to force other participants to agree. They assert their points of view instead of aggressively attacking those who disagree. They treat everyone as equals by eschewing arrogance. They are careful to avoid absolute statements that shut off discussion, and they let the force of their arguments change minds instead of employing manipulative strategies of influence, such as ridiculing a rival's idea or being deceptive about the weakness of a proposal.

Seeking Mentors and Networking: Looking for Assistance

Mentors are knowledgeable individuals who have achieved some success in their profession or job and who assist people trying to get started in a line of work. Mentors can provide information to the novice that can prevent mistakes by trial and error (Lavin & Young, 2006). Mentoring seems to be especially empowering for women (Liang et al., 2002). Mentoring is necessary for women to rise to upper echelons of organizations (Noe, 1988). One study showed that women who have mentors move up the organization ladder much faster than women without mentors. Women also receive more promotions faster when they are assisted by mentors (cited in Kleiman, 1991).

Networking is another form of empowerment. People with similar backgrounds, skills, and goals come together on a fairly regular basis and share information. Networks also provide emotional support for members, especially women's networks.

Encouraging Leadership That Empowers: Delegating, Not Ordering

Leaders can take actions that empower individuals and groups. Encouraging meaningful participation in decision making, providing opportunities to perform complex and challenging tasks, giving greater responsibility, and providing opportunities to expand knowledge and expertise all empower individuals in groups and organizations (Burpitt & Bigoness, 1997; Eagly & Carli, 2007). Teams evaluated as the most innovative actively sought out, learned, and applied new knowledge and skills. Becoming a competent communicator is empowering.

Summary

POWER is the ability to influence the attainment of goals sought by you or by others. It is inherent in all human relationships. There are three forms of power: dominance, prevention, and empowerment. Power imbalances produce several consequences: relationship failure, physical violence, verbal and nonverbal abuse, sexual harassment, and commonplace difficulties. Power imbalances also produce anger, frustration, wariness, and resentment in common everyday situations. Information, expertise, legitimate authority, rewards and punishments, and personal qualities are the primary power resources. Coalition formation, defiance, and resistance strategies are the chief power-balancing approaches employed in dominance-prevention power struggles. Although dominance and prevention forms of power can produce the "dark side" of interpersonal relationships, empowerment is a very positive form of power. Becoming empowered is an important step in becoming a competent communicator. Empowerment is a win-win cooperative approach to power balancing.

Answers for *Critical Thinking* caption:

Cartoon (p. 210): #2 and #3

Quizzes Without Consequences

Did you understand all the material in this chapter? Test your knowledge before your exam!

Go to the companion website at www.oup.com/us/rothwell, click on the Student Resources for each chapter, and take the Quizzes Without Consequences.

Film School Case Studies

Cool Hand Luke (1967). Drama; Not rated

Paul Newman wowed audiences with his portrayal of Luke, an irrepressible, spirited man imprisoned and forced to endure a repressive Southern chain gang. Analyze the instances of passive aggression and defiance that exemplify the point that no one is completely powerless.

Disclosure (1994). Drama; R

An intriguing plot twist propels this film. Michael Douglas plays a business executive who files sexual harassment charges against his female superior. Analyze the issue of power imbalance and sexual harassment. Does it seem like a stretch to portray a man as the victim of sexual harassment?

Lincoln Lawyer (2011). Drama; R

Matthew McConaughey plays a sketchy defense lawyer who operates from the backseat of his Lincoln town car. While representing a high-profile client (Ryan Phillippe), he becomes immersed in some nasty, tricky business. Examine power resources employed by the various characters, concentrating on McConaughey's character. Apply the three types of power and the results of power imbalances.

Michael Clayton (2007). Drama; R

This dramatic thriller stars George Clooney in an Oscar-nominated role of a burned-out corporate lawyer whose main task is to clean up his clients' messes. Analyze the power resources depicted in this film.

One Flew Over the Cuckoo's Nest (1975). Drama; R

The role of Randle P. McMurphy made Jack Nicholson an international star and earned him his first Oscar. This film depicts a power struggle in a mental institution. Analyze the dominance-prevention dynamic that propels the story. Are there any resistance strategies used by the Jack Nicholson character? Does empowerment emerge?

Reign Over Me (2007). Drama; PG-13

Don Cheadle is a dentist in New York City who one day stumbles upon his college roommate, played by Adam Sandler. The Sandler character is suffering mental illness following the loss of his entire family (wife and two daughters) in the 9/11 terrorist attacks. Examine the power dynamics, especially the verbal and nonverbal indicators of power, imbalances in power, and the consequences these produce, and instances of resistance and defiance. Does empowerment emerge anyplace in the movie?

CHAPTER 8

Chapter Outline

Making Relationships Work

JESSICA TANDY AND HUME CRONYN were married for 52 years, and the marriage ended only when Tandy died. Their relationship was the more remarkable for its longevity because they stayed happily married even though they were both successful, acclaimed actors. Hollywood is legendary for chewing up marriages. Yet Tandy and Cronyn remained steadfast partners for five decades despite great notoriety and professional success, each of them winning numerous stage and screen awards. They starred, sometimes separately and sometimes together, in a variety of successful movies. Given a choice among models of romance that included several famous relationships, respondents to one survey picked Tandy and Cronyn's relationship as the ideal (Kanner, 1995). Contrary to the enduring success of their relationship, both had been married previously. Why does one marriage last until death and another survive for what seems like the blink of an eye? What makes relationships succeed or fail? *The purpose of this chapter is to discuss why interpersonal relationships at home, at work, at school, and at play succeed, struggle, or sink, and what you can do to make them more durable and rewarding.*

By the end of this chapter, you should be able to:

1. Explain the main reasons that we form relationships.
2. Identify the 10 phases of intimate relationships.
3. Recognize communication strategies that work or fail during each stage.
4. Use competent communication strategies to sustain relationships that are important to you.
5. Recognize and adjust for the significant influence technology has on interpersonal relationships.
6. Address the many challenges posed by intimate intercultural relationships.

Main Reasons for Forming Relationships

Our relationships with others can seem so fragile. Marriage rates in the United States have dropped to their lowest level (52% of adults) ever recorded by the U.S. Census Bureau (Mather & Lavery, 2010). According to Pew Research Center, only 43% of married couples in the United States are "very happy" ("Is Marriage Bliss?" 2011). Stephanie Coontz, director of public education for the Council on Contemporary Families, notes that American adults now spend half their lives unmarried (cited in Roberts, 2007).

The flavorful wine of a new marriage may gradually turn into the bitter vinegar of divorce. Rates of divorce dropped slightly during the 1990s but remain high today. About 50% of first marriages, 60% of second marriages, and 75% of third marriages end in divorce (Epstein, 2010). Cohabitations (intimate couples living together but unmarried) are even less stable. A mere 10% of couples who cohabit remain together for more than five years (Crooks & Baur, 2011). High-school sweethearts rarely stay together for life. Gay and lesbian relationships are at least as fragile as heterosexual relationships (Kurdek, 2005).

Despite their apparent fragility, most people crave stable, long-term relationships. The U.S. Census Bureau has consistently shown that in the last three decades more than 95% of the American public want to be married now or in the future. The probability that an adult living in the United States will get married at some time during his or her life is almost 90% (Mather & Lavery, 2010). That figure would be higher if gays and lesbians were granted legal civil marriages.

Sustaining relationships has never been more challenging, and making friendships work is no exception. One study found that American adults, on average, had only two close friends, down from three in 1985 (Hampton et al., 2009; see also "Social Networking Sites," 2011). They may have 5,000 "friends" on Facebook, but truly close friends are few for most people. Fewer close friends mean a weakening social support network in stressful times. In addition, 80% of respondents to a face-to-face survey of 1,467 individuals reported that they discuss important matters in their lives only with family members, up significantly from 57% in 1985 (McPherson et al., 2006). About 10% confide only to a spouse and no other person, almost double compared to 1985. Sustaining friendships during your college experience can be especially challenging given the typical high stress associated with a college education, close proximity of dorm living, and competitive atmosphere that often pervades college life. One key problem is that friendships are often taken for granted (Guerrero & Chavez, 2005). Less effort to sustain friendships is made than occurs with romantic partners and family members (Canary et al., 1993).

Why do we seek close relationships if they often end poorly and they are so challenging to sustain? Generally, most of us don't enter relationships expecting them to fail. Most newlyweds think there is *zero chance* that they would ever get divorced (Baker & Emery, 1993). On average, both singles and married couples put their own probability of divorce at about 10% (Fowers et al., 2001). There are several other more specific reasons, however, that, despite frequent setbacks, we continue to seek meaningful relationships with others. In this section, I briefly discuss the main reasons.

Need to Belong: Like Food and Water

Humans have a deep-seated need to belong, to make social connections with other humans. We are "the social animal" (Aronson, 1999; Brooks, 2011). In Chapter 1, I related the story of Genie who was raised in almost total isolation from other human beings with but brief and abusive interactions with her parents. The results were disastrous. Our need for human connection is an imperative, as necessary to our well-being and development as food and water (Baumeister & Leary, 1995). "We humans are social animals down to our very cells. Nature did not make us noble loners" (Parks, 2007, p. 1), although loners at least get to decide how the toilet paper roll gets placed on the dispenser (over or under).

Nature has provided each of us with an "affiliative neuropeptide" called *oxytocin*. "The levels of this chemical rise when couples watch romantic movies, hug, or hold hands. . . . Oxytocin is also related to the feelings of closeness and being 'in love' when you have regular sex . . ." (Amen, 2007). This "love hormone" also seems to increase feelings of trust. "Oxytocin is nature's way of weaving people together" (Brooks, 2011, p. 64).

These human attachments we make, especially in the early formative stages of our development, are particularly meaningful (Sroufe et al., 2005). **Attachment theory** argues, "Children born into a web of attuned relationships know how to join in conversations with new people and read social signals. They see the world as a welcoming place. Children born into a web of threatening relationships can be fearful, withdrawn, or overaggressive" (Brooks, 2011, p. 62). Communication forms attachments with others, and the quality of these attachments influences the competence of our communication.

Interpersonal Attraction: What Draws Us Together

There are several basic factors that attract us to other people and make the idea of developing a relationship with them desirable. These include physical attractiveness, similarities, and reciprocal liking.

Physical Attractiveness: Looking Good

In Chapter 2, I discussed the beauty bias. Physically attractive individuals have advantages that those with more average looks often do not. Speed dating necessitates quick decisions based on blink-of-an-eye first impressions. Looks tend to dominate as a criterion for these rush-to-judgment decisions whether to seek further contact. Hundreds of studies show that physical attractiveness is equally significant for men and women (Eagly et al., 1991; Langlois et al., 2000). One study of online dating preferences found that both men and women had a strong preference for "very good looks" from their online prospects (Hitsch et al., 2010). Evolutionary psychologists argue that physically attractive people are more likely to be physically healthy and have good genes. This makes them a good prospect for a mate to produce healthy children (Buss, 2003). This is a debatable point of view, but physical attractiveness is unquestionably a predominant characteristic of interpersonal attraction, at least initially.

Similarity: Birds of a Feather

There's a well-known adage: "Birds of a feather flock together." Is it true that we are drawn to those who are similar to us, or do "opposites attract"? Research resoundingly supports **similarity attraction theory** (Byrne, 1997). We are drawn to individuals who seem to share our interests, values, attitudes, and personality (McCrae et al., 2008). Our level of communication skill also plays a part in attraction, friendship, and relationship satisfaction. Highly skilled communicators are drawn to other highly skilled communicators, and less skilled communicators are drawn to each other (Burleson & Samter, 1996). In addition, a study of online dating found that both men and women prefer a partner with about the same educational level, same ethnicity, and same or similar religion. Divorced online daters also prefer divorced partners (true mostly for women), and those with children prefer dating someone who also has children (Hitsch et al., 2010).

Why are we attracted to those who are similar to us? First, similarity of values, attitudes, personality, background, and communication skills makes relationships less stressful and easier to manage. There is less likelihood of frustration, bickering, and strife (Duck & Pittman, 1994). Second, individuals who share our attitudes and values validate the correctness of our perceptions (Bryne & Clore, 1970). Their worldviews match.

This *matching effect* based on similarities seems tied to relationship success or failure. Physically mismatched couples (one is attractive and the other is not) usually don't stay together long term. The Boston Couples Study showed that dissimilarity in physical attractiveness between partners was a significant factor in the eventual split-up of the relationship (Hill et al., 1976). The more attractive partner may see opportunities available with more physically attractive prospects—the wandering eye.

The matching effect also applies to language styles. College students engaged in four-minute speed dates were three times as likely to want future contact with their partner when their language style (use of prepositions, pronouns, etc.) matched. A second study of casual online chats between dating partners showed that couples whose language style matched were far more likely to be together three months later than those who didn't match (Ireland et al., 2010). This matching effect seems to apply to nonverbal communication as well. When the hand gestures, eye gazes, and postures of two people match when they first meet, they are more inclined to like each other (Shockley et al., 2009). Finally, a sense of humor is a highly desirable quality in a date or mate, and those who exhibit similar senses of humor will likely discover interpersonal attraction, but attraction is less likely to occur if senses of humor are mismatched—you're telling gross jokes and your date finds that kind of humor repulsive (Cooper, 2008).

The matching effect also appears to apply to same-sex friendships and even roommates (Carli et al., 1991; Cash & Derlega, 1978). Less attractive friends and roommates are seen as holding back the social lives of more attractive friends and roommates. It can be a cold world out there!

Reciprocal Liking: I Like You If You Like Me

We tend to like those who we perceive like us. The perception that others like us can even compensate for the lack of similarities. In one study, for instance, male participants revealed that they liked a female very much when she communicated interest by maintaining eye contact, listening carefully, and leaning toward them. Even though the male participants knew that the female disagreed

The matching effect is apparent when very attractive individuals are paired; unmatched couples (one person is notably more attractive than the other) typically have a greater failure rate.

with them on significant issues (dissimilarities in attitudes and values), they still liked her because she appeared to like them (Gold et al., 1984).

If we assume that others do not like us, we may create a self-fulfilling prophecy by responding negatively to them. This negative response could easily invite a reciprocal negative response from a person who may have been primed to like us but begins to dislike us because of our unlikable behavior toward them (Curtis & Miller, 1986).

Rewards: Exchange Theory

Sometimes we seek relationships based on **exchange theory**—a cost-benefits analysis that weighs the benefits of a particular relationship against any costs incurred (Jeffries 2002). We seek *rewards*, anything that we consider desirable, and these rewards may compensate for any perceived imperfections in our partners and friends. We may not be a perfect fit (some dissimilarities), but certain rewards may compensate. A substantial income may compensate for short stature in men (Hitsch et al., 2010). We tolerate some irritating quirks or even difficult moodiness from our partners because they offer us rewards that are equal to or greater than the costs. Our partner or friend talks too much at parties, laughs too loudly, or tells inappropriate jokes to our boss. Yet close friends and romantic partners can provide social support for us when we are stressed, so we overlook the inappropriate behavior (Rusbult & Van Lange, 2003).

A partner or friend can also offer kindness, sensitivity, and thoughtfulness as compensation for only average looks or a small income (Epstein, 2010). Kindness, in fact, is the most important quality desired in an intimate partner by both men and women across many cultures (Buss, 2003). Although social exchange theory can seem coldly calculating, we do tend to make a cost-benefits analysis of our relationships. When the costs of a relationship (conflict, stress, unhappiness, personal safety) outweigh any benefits (companionship, friendship, sex), we usually look for the door to escape.

Forming Close Relationships

Despite the challenges and disappointments, we are driven to find those lasting, happy relationships that prove to be so rewarding and life affirming. In this section, I discuss intimacy and love and the developmental stages of relationships.

Intimacy and Love: Friends, Family, and Romantic Partners

The previous chapter included a discussion of the "dark side" of personal relationships. Our personal relationships also have a very "bright side." We have many relationships in our lives. Some are casual, some professional, and others are intimate and loving. Intimacy and love are two of the most fulfilling, satisfying experiences humans can enjoy.

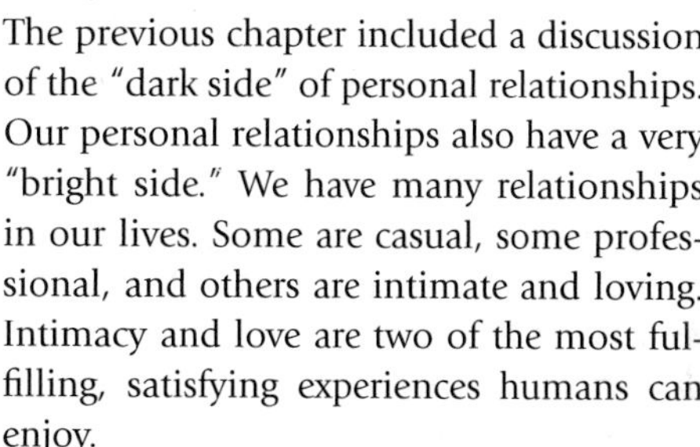

Intimacy: Close Connection

An **interpersonal relationship** is a connection two people have to each other because of kinship (brother-sister), an attraction (lovers and friends), or a power distribution (boss-employee). An **intimate relationship** is a type of interpersonal relationship that is characterized by strong emotional bonding, closeness, and interdependence, in which individuals meaningfully influence each other.

Although intimacy is sometimes associated with sex ("We were intimate last night"), intimacy occurs in different types of relationships, some nonsexual and nonromantic. One study (Berscheid et al., 1989) of several hundred college students found that respondents' "most intimate relationship" was with a romantic partner (47%), a friend (36%), or a family member (14%). In another study, three-quarters of college students reported that intimacy could occur without sex and romance (Floyd, 1996).

Men and women, however, do not always express and nurture intimacy in the same ways (Wood, 2007). Women typically draw close to one another through talking about personal matters and discussing experiences. When you equate intimacy with only self-disclosure (sharing personal information), it would appear that women are better at establishing intimacy than men. Wood (2007) calls this mistaken notion the *male deficit model*, and she criticizes it as too narrow in perspective. She notes that men typically talk less about personal matters and share feelings less with other men, but men achieve closeness by sharing meaningful activities and helping each other (Radmacher & Azmitia, 2006; Wood & Inman, 1993). Engaging in building or repair work, watching or playing sports, and getting stuck in mud while off-roading and having to dig out together are all ways to achieve intimacy (Coontz, 2009).

If styles of communicating intimacy differ between men and women, then it is important that the partners recognize this early in the relationship. Otherwise, misunderstandings will emerge. For example, a man fixes an annoying squeak in a door hinge that has bothered his female partner for some time. He assumes that she will recognize this as an act of affection because he perceives it as such. His partner, however, may see this as simple maintenance and not recognize it as an expression of intimacy. Thus, she experiences no act of closeness, and he's probably upset that his act of affection went unrecognized. Men also may think that physical proximity (being in the same room; watching television while sitting on the same couch together) is intimate. Women may see this as the "slouch on the couch." These style differences in communicating intimacy should be discussed.

Love: An Ocean of Emotion

Richard Barnfield described it as "a fire, a heaven, a hell, where pleasure, pain, and sad repentance dwell." Germaine Greer called it "a drug." Then there's the story of a four-year-old whose next-door neighbor had recently lost his wife. The man was crying in his backyard. The little boy came over and sat on the grieving man's lap. Asked later by his mother what he'd said to the man, the little boy replied, "Nothing. I just helped him cry." Love almost defies definition, principally because there is not just one kind of love.

Although we tend to think of love in terms of passion, not all types of love are fever pitched. Robert Sternberg (1986, 1988, 1997) has offered his **triangular theory of love** to explain the different types (see Figure 8-1). The three elements of love according to this theory are intimacy, passion, and commitment. *Intimacy* has already been defined as feeling emotionally close to and strongly influenced by another person. *Passion* refers to both the physiological drives that produce intense physical attraction and sexual responses and psychological desires and needs expressed as the idealization of a loved one and constant thinking about that person (Yela, 2006). *Commitment* refers to a decision to continue a relationship long term. There are seven types of love related to these three key elements.

1. *Liking*—intimacy without passion or commitment, such as in some friendships.
2. *Infatuated love*—passion without intimacy or commitment, such as "puppy love."
3. *Empty love*—commitment without passion and intimacy, such as in a stagnating, unsatisfying marriage.
4. *Romantic love*—passion and intimacy without commitment, such as a romantic affair.
5. *Companionate love*—intimacy and commitment without passion, such as a long-term marriage where partners are more friends than lovers.
6. *Fatuous love*—passion and commitment without intimacy, such as a "love at first sight" relationship.
7. *Consummate love*—combines intimacy, passion, and commitment and is the most satisfying adult relationship.

It is not unusual to mistake passion for consummate love. Passion without intimacy or commitment, however, is more a "one-night stand" than a consummate love. In the absence of intimacy and commitment, passion can flame out quickly, leaving emptiness and disappointment. *Personal*

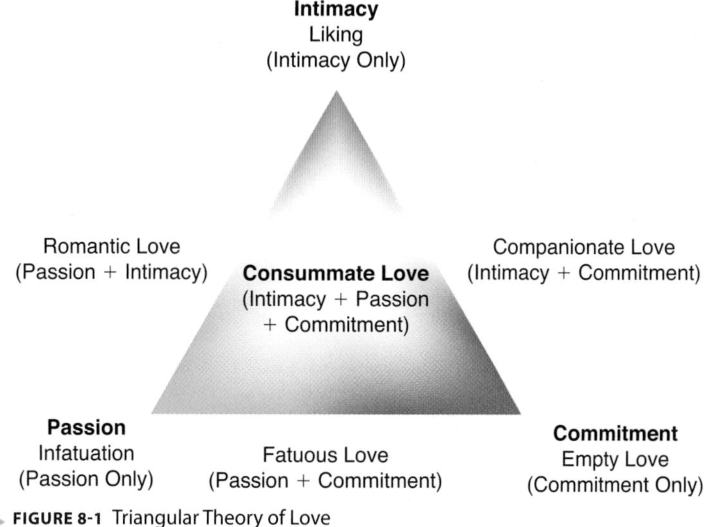

FIGURE 8-1 Triangular Theory of Love

relationships that have the greatest longevity and satisfaction are those in which partners are constantly working on sustaining intimacy and reinforcing commitment to each other. This is the companionate love of friendships that plays an integral part in making our lives rewarding.

Passion does not inevitably disappear as a romantic relationship grows long term, but the giddy levels of passion characteristic of the early stages of romance cannot be realistically sustained (Gonzaga et al., 2006; Tucker & Aron, 1993). In fact, such desperate longing often equated with obsessive passion ("I can't live without you") is detrimental because it controls you, ultimately making the relationship less satisfying than a passionless relationship (Pileggi, 2010, p. 38).

Not to depress anyone, but the average rate of sexual intercourse for married couples declines by half after only a single year of marriage (Hatfield & Rapson, 1996). As romantic relationships mature, passion will be more episodic, appearing sometimes but seeming to disappear at others. When the fires of passion seem to flicker or diminish overall, the warmth of intimacy and the comfort of commitment sustain a long-term relationship (Sprecher & Regan, 1998). Engaging in enjoyable activities can cultivate a healthy passion over the long term when passion becomes more episodic. These activities, however, should not be competitive "because the point of the outing should not be winning but enjoying time together" (Pileggi, 2010, p. 39). Expecting romantic relationships to remain as they were when passion first ignited sets expectations that doom relationships. We form powerful emotional attachments in committed relationships, but these attachments mature and change over time (Hazan & Shaver, 1994a & b).

Relationship Development: Coming-Together Phases

Knapp and Vangelisti (1992, 2005) examined a large body of research on phases of relationships and communication patterns (see especially Honeycutt et al., 1989; Honeycutt et al., 1992). They synthesized this research into their **stages of relationships model** that has five "coming-together" and five "coming-apart" phases (see Figure 8-2). The model applies equally well to mixed-sex and same-sex intimate relationships (Haas & Stafford, 1998; Peplau & Spalding, 2000).

Particular patterns of communication occur in each phase; some advance the development of your relationships, and others lead to deterioration. Recognizing the difference can make or break interpersonal relationships. Movement through the phases may be rapid, especially the early phases, or it may be slow when one partner wants

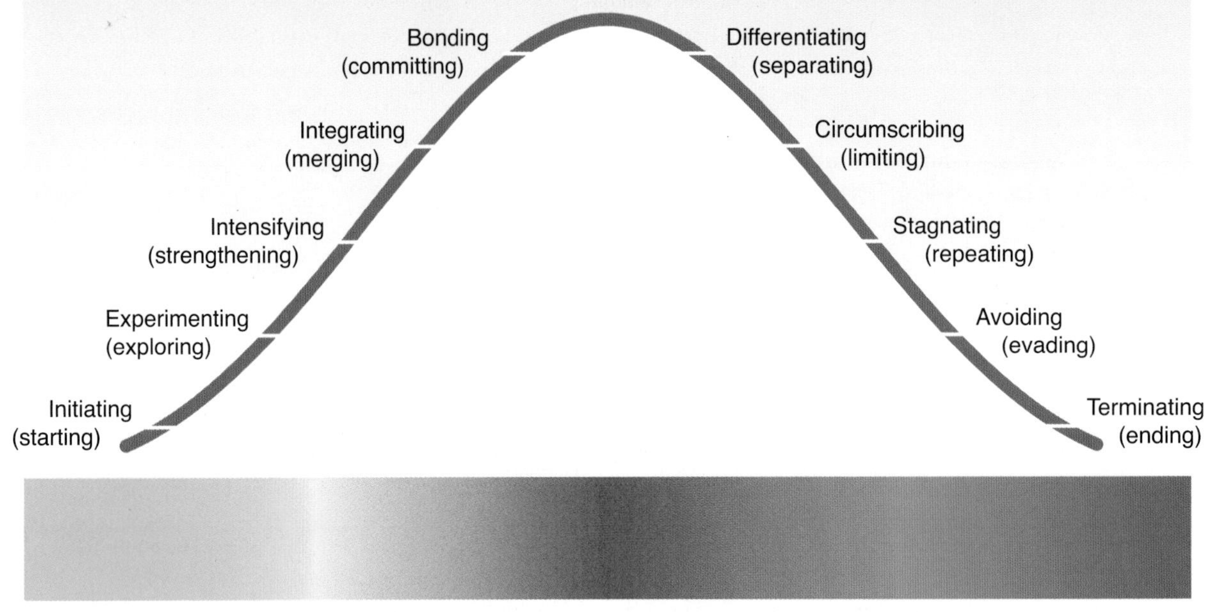

FIGURE 8-2 Stages of Relationship Development

to move forward or backward but the other partner resists. There may be substantial overlap between phases as you move in either direction. Movement may not even be sequential because sometimes phases are skipped. Let's look at each of these phases, recognizing that we're describing intimate relationships. Other relationships, such as those with coworkers, follow different patterns.

Initiating: Taking the Plunge

During the initiating phase, we are surveying the interpersonal terrain. We try to put our best foot forward by appearing friendly, open, and approachable. Communication approaches that seem to work effectively during this phase were revealed in one study (Douglas, 1987). *Networking* (learning about a person from someone who knows him or her), *offering* (making yourself available for conversation by sitting in an adjacent seat or being in a place the person usually frequents), *approaching* (signally an interest verbally or nonverbally with a smile or a self-introduction), and *sustaining* (keeping the conversation going by asking questions) all work well.

Communication approaches that don't work effectively during this phase of personal relationship development include *expressing deep feelings* ("I'm afraid to love again"), *keeping silent* to create an air of mystery (there's no mystery in looking doltish), *asking for big favors* ("Will you help me move?"), and *diminishing oneself* (Woody Allen: "My one regret in life is that I am not someone else"). Using a cell phone, talking about an "ex," and not making eye contact are additional "don'ts" during the initiating phase noted in a survey by the dating service It's Just Lunch ("Navigating Today's Complex Dating Scene," 2011).

So what about clever opening lines? A man approaches a woman in a bar and says, "How much does a penguin weigh?" The woman replies, "How much?" The man responds, "Enough to break the ice." Does this work for you? What about this opener: Man says, "Did it hurt?" Woman replies, "What?" Man responds, "When you fell from heaven?" Then there's the man asking a woman, "Was your dad a thief when he stole the stars for your eyes?" (Goldston, 2007). A basic problem with all of these opening lines is that they are not customized for the individual who is of interest to you. Research shows that attempting to find the perfect opening line is wasted effort ("What Social Science Can Tell You about Flirting," 2007). Most openers are awkward, silly, or embarrassingly lame. Some are clever, but the best openers are simple introductions ("Hi, I'm Glen. What's your name?") or conversation starters ("What do you think about this crazy weather we've been having?"). Just K.I.S.S.: Keep It Simple and Straightforward.

This shouldn't discourage you from using humor, however. In the initial stages of relationship formation, humor can have a very large, positive impact on the future prospect of a relationship if the humor is viewed as appropriate (Cooper, 2008). You want a dating prospect to laugh with you, not at you.

Experimenting: Auditioning for the Part

The experimenting phase is when we "audition" for the part of boyfriend or girlfriend. We experiment by engaging in small talk to discover areas of commonality: "What's your major?" or "Do you like ice skating?" We're casually probing, searching for ways to connect with others. All of us have superficial contacts with hundreds of people that never develop to any extent. Most of our transactions do not progress beyond the experimenting phase of development.

Intensifying: Warming to the Relationship

The intensifying phase is when relationships deepen. Individuals use a variety of communication approaches to intensify relationships (Taraban et al., 1998). The top 10 approaches identified in one study are these (Tolhuizen, 1989).

1. *Increased contact* (39.2%)—seeing or phoning partner more often.
2. *Relationship negotiation* (29.1%)—openly discussing feelings about the relationship.
3. *Social support and assistance* (26.1%)—requesting advice from a parent or friend.
4. *Increased rewards* (17.6%)—doing favors such as doing partner's laundry or fixing partner's car.
5. *Direct definitional bid* (16.6%)—asking for a commitment from partner.
6. *Tokens of affection* (16.1%)—giving gifts, sending flowers, giving cards.
7. *Personalized communication* (15.1%)—listening to partner or friend.
8. *Verbal expressions of affection* (14.1%)—saying "You're really sweet"
9. *Suggestive actions* (13.1%)—flirting.
10. *Nonverbal expressions of affection* (12.1%)—gazing, touching.

Women use relationship negotiation far more often than men; men use direct definitional bid and verbal expressions of affection more often than women (see also Owen, 1987). Which of these approaches do you use most frequently?

The success of any of these approaches depends on the unique dynamics of a particular relationship. What is effective in one relationship may fail disastrously in another. Be careful not to move too quickly and exuberantly to intensify a relationship. Your partner may knock over furniture in a determined effort to flee the scene.

Trying to intensify a relationship is one thing; determining if the effort is working is quite another. Individuals conduct "secret tests" during the intensifying phase to check out the success of their intensification efforts. *Endurance* requires a partner to tolerate unpleasant behavior such as criticism and inconvenient requests (taking care of a slobbering, ill-trained dog big enough to saddle and ride). If your partner endures the test, commitment is assumed. *Public presentation* tests the intensity of the relationship by introducing your partner as "my boyfriend/girlfriend" to see if the partner is comfortable with the label. *Separation* tests the relationship by keeping the partners away from each other for a period of time to see if the relationship will remain viable. This, of course, is a risky test because, although "absence makes the heart grow fonder," "out of sight out of mind" may occur instead. *Third-party questioning* occurs when one partner asks a friend to check out the other person's depth of feeling about the relationship and then reports the results to the interested party. *Triangle tests* involve asking a friend to make the partner jealous by seeming to express interest in the partner concocting the test (Baxter & Wilmot, 1984).

Women are more likely to employ these "secret tests" of a relationship because they monitor relationships more than men (Baxter & Wilmot, 1984). In particular, separation and triangle tests are the most frequent choices. *Endurance, separation, and the triangle tests are also the least constructive.* The triangle test in particular is the most dangerous. Feeling the need to induce jealousy in a partner is a sign that the relationship is of low quality, and the triangle test is unlikely to be constructive. Secret tests generally are "more common in deteriorating [versus stable] relationships" (Goodboy et al., 2010, p. 74). Nevertheless, public presentation and third-party questioning are relatively harmless ways to test the depth of a relationship.

Integrating: Moving Beyond "Just Friends"

The integrating phase fuses a relationship. Individuals seem to merge into a distinct couple. Social circles of friends mix. Nonverbal markers of intimacy are displayed, such as pictures, pins, or clothing belonging to the other person. Self-disclosure is more revealing and potentially risky. Life goals and aspirations are shared. A sexual relationship often occurs at this stage (sex on a first date or "one-night stands" are not included as examples of this stage). Partners may begin living together, indicating that they have moved beyond the "just friends" phase.

Bonding: Strings, Rings, and Other Things

The public-ritual phase that institutionalizes the relationship is called *bonding*. We are communicating to the world that we have a committed relationship, not just a "no-strings" attachment. An engagement ring may be worn. There may be a public contract, of which marriage is the most obvious example. Gay couples do not have this option in most states. Nevertheless, any public announcement, ceremony, gesture, or proclamation that the relationship is considered exclusive and binding moves the couple into the bonding phase.

This phase usually signals a turning point. A **turning point** is "any event or occurrence that is associated with change in a relationship" (Baxter & Bullis, 1986, p. 470). Disclosing a personal secret for the first time or lending your classic car that is in mint condition might be turning points in a relationship. Having sex for the first time, moving in together, or saying "I love you" are typical turning points (Mongeau et al., 2006). Although "I love you" can be a powerful turning point in a relationship, one survey found that the words women most want to hear are "You've lost weight" (see Cameron, 2002).

Interestingly, almost half the time, partners in heterosexual relationships do not identify the same turning points in their relationship (Baxter & Bullis, 1986). For example, having sex may be a momentous turning point for a woman that may suggest a long-term intimate relationship, even marriage, but it may be merely a pleasant but not very significant event for a man (Mongeau et al., 2006). Realizing for the first time that his female partner enjoys watching sports or backpacking in the wilderness, however, may be turning points for a man.

As we all know, reaching the bonding phase does not guarantee that partners will remain bonded. Also, *bonding is not an idyllic state*. You may not wish to remain bonded with your partner. Nevertheless, this chapter will offer several key ways to improve your chances of remaining bonded with your romantic partner if that is your desire.

Relationship Deterioration: Coming-Apart Phases

Rita Rudner once joked, "My boyfriend and I broke up. He wanted to get married and I didn't want him to." Romantic relationships often don't move in just one direction—from friendly to intimate to happy to blissful. Relationships can move forward (coming together) or backward (coming apart), and the outcome is not inevitable. Couples who were once happy but become dissatisfied don't necessarily end their relationship. The direction of a relationship can turn around in an instant. A sexual affair can provoke a partner to leapfrog from bonding to termination, skipping four phases in between that are typical of a relationship that is coming apart. A friendship that is just beginning to intensify may fall apart suddenly because of an act of violence or a perceived betrayal of trust. Nevertheless, some relationships do dissolve, not in an instant but painfully over what may seem a lifetime. *If you want to prevent the demise of a relationship, recognizing the early phases of relationship deterioration can help.* Once you get too far down the path of deterioration, it may be too late to turn around the relationship. Let's look briefly at the five coming-apart phases (see Figure 8-2).

Differentiating: Disintegrating Begins

The first phase of disengagement is differentiating. What were thought to be similarities are discovered to be differences. The pretense of being alike in most ways begins to erode. Assertions of individuality become more frequent. Conflict occurs, although differentiating can occur without conflict. Differentiating is an expected phase in romantic relationships. In the beginning of an intimate relationship, partners may be inseparable. Later in the relationship, giving each other "some space" may be a welcome way to respond. Excessive differentiating, however, can mean trouble ahead.

Circumscribing: Don't Ask, Don't Tell

When we establish limits and restrictions on communication with our partner, we are circumscribing. Both the breadth and the depth of our communication become constrained. Fewer topics are perceived to be safe to discuss for fear of igniting a conflict, and topics that are addressed are discussed superficially. "Let's not talk about that again" becomes a familiar refrain. Communication interactions become less frequent. You've entered the danger zone in your deteriorating relationship.

Stagnating: Treading Water

Stagnating relationships aren't growing or progressing. The feeling is "nothing changes." Communication becomes even more restricted, narrow, hesitant, and awkward than in the circumscribing stage. Even stabs at discussing relationship problems are likely to provoke yet another conflict with an unhappy outcome. Communication begins resembling interactions with strangers. The relationship is barely above water and in danger of sinking.

Avoiding: The End Is Near

In the avoiding phase, partners keep a distance from each other, hoping not to interact. Separation, not connection, is desired. Partners stay away from home by working late, or they spend more time with friends. If physical separation is not possible because children need to be parented, partners' communication may be impersonal and infrequent.

Terminating: Stick a Fork in It

This is the final pulling-apart phase. The relationship is finished—cooked, ceased, done, dead, kaput! Who initiates the termination of a romantic relationship is about equal between men and women (Akert, 1998). Women, however, typically anticipate the demise of a relationship sooner than men, but men take the termination harder. Men are more depressed, lonelier, and unhappier than women following the end of a personal, romantic relationship (Unger & Crawford, 1996). Whether men initiate the breakup or are dumped, they usually prefer not to remain friends with their ex-partner. Women more often wish to remain friends regardless of who initiated the dumping. When the initiation of the breakup is mutual, men and women are about equally desirous of remaining friends (Akert, 1998).

Relationship termination can be traumatic for one or both parties. One study found that individuals who had been rejected by the person they loved spent more than 85% of their waking hours thinking about the person who jilted them. They became love zombies, lurching through life with only one thing on their minds. In addition, they exhibited lack of emotional control repeatedly for weeks or months.

Examples of such lack of emotional control included inappropriate contact by phoning, emailing, texting, pleading for reconciliation, and by dramatic entrances and exits from the rejecter's home, workplace, or social space. Uncontrollable weeping for hours and drinking excessively are other examples. This is passion gone awry that looks remarkably like withdrawal from addiction (Fisher et al., 2010).

Although there is a tendency to view the coming-together stages of relationships as good and the coming-apart stages as bad, especially given the often dramatic responses to rejection, this is not necessarily true. Some romantic relationships that appear promising initially prove to be less satisfying as we get to know the other person better. Some relationships may even be destructive to one or both parties and should not progress. Terminating abusive relationships is positive, not negative. Sometimes relationship participants have to step back before they can step forward. *Stages of relationships merely describe what is, not necessarily what should be.*

Sustaining Relationships: Friends, Relatives, Lovers, and Coworkers

Sustaining relationships of all kinds can be an enormous challenge. Competent communication is central to meeting this challenge. Chapter 1 discussed the importance of creating a constructive communication climate of cooperation. In this section, I expand this discussion.

Connecting Bids: Keeping Us Together

You enter your living room after a long day at work. Your partner asks you, "How was your day?" Do you utter a dismissive "Same stuff, different day"? You're having lunch with your father at a local café. You attempt several times to engage him in conversation, but invariably, his cell phone rings and he conducts business while you both eat.

These exchanges involve what Gottman terms bids for connection. A **connecting bid** is any attempt to engage another person in a positive transaction, sometimes at a deep and enduring level and other times at a superficial and fleeting level. It says, "I want to feel connected to you" if only for a brief moment (Gottman & DeClaire, 2001). A bid could be verbal, in the form of a question, statement, or comment whose content includes thoughts, feelings, observations, opinions, or invitations. A bid could also be nonverbal, in the form of a gesture, look, touch, facial expression, or vocalization (grunt, sigh).

Making Bids: Reaching Out to Others

Connecting bids vary in importance. There are the hugely significant bids such as, "Let's move in together" or "Do you want to start a business with me?" Some are seemingly insignificant requests characteristic of day-to-day communication: "Honey, will you get me a beer?" or "Mommy, will you help me tie my shoe?" or "Did you read the email I sent to you?" Some bids are subtle attempts to connect: "You look very nice today," "Good morning," or "How was your vacation?" Others can be very direct: "Do you still love me?" or "Do you think of me as a good friend?" or "May I have your phone number?" A vague bid may protect our vulnerable self-esteem, whereas a direct bid may be too risky. For example, instead of asking directly, "Do you want to see a movie with me on Saturday?" you might ask, "What's your favorite movie?" followed by "Maybe sometime we could check out one of those classic movies you love." The vague bid doesn't risk outright rejection as a more direct bid might.

Everybody makes connecting bids every day because we want to feel as though we are a part of the human experience, not alone and separate. We also want to draw close to those most important in our lives. *Not all transactions with others, of course, require us to connect.* When a telemarketer calls you in the middle of dinner, you probably want to be disconnected. Obnoxious individuals who harass you for a date are only encouraged by a positive response to their

connecting bids. Nevertheless, making bids is a central communication process for establishing and sustaining close relationships (Gottman & DeClaire, 2001). *How you respond to those bids markedly influences the communication climate for relationships to blossom or wilt.*

Responses: Turning This Way and That

Every bid provokes one of three responses: turning toward, turning away, or turning against the bid (Gottman & DeClaire, 2001). The **turning-toward response** is a positive reaction to the bid. Your partner tells a joke and you laugh. A parent calls to ask for help moving furniture and you agree without complaint. A friend wants to talk and you engage in conversation. A coworker invites you to lunch and you accept.

Sometimes a response may appear to be negative unless you recognize an understanding that exists between two people. For example, a good male friend and I regularly engage in verbal jousting for fun. We ridicule each other, sometimes with seemingly brutal put-downs. To outsiders, it may appear that we do not like each other until they observe us laughing and amused by our verbal sparring. We perceive this feigned fighting as friendly banter, and it connects us in friendship. Even though on the surface our put-downs appear to be turning against the other person, we understand that this is merely a friendly verbal game, and our participation is actually a turning-toward response to connecting bids. Such verbal jousting may seem odd, even repellant to some people, especially to women, who do not engage in such banter nearly as much as men do (Tannen, 2010). Nevertheless, it is a reminder that communication is not always what it seems on the surface.

The **turning-away response** occurs when we ignore a bid or act preoccupied when a bid is offered. You ask your partner if she wants her wash put in the dryer, and she waves dismissively as she focuses intently on her computer screen. You ask a friend at work for advice on a project, and without looking up from reading a report, he mutters, "Can't help you now." These turning-away responses are rarely malicious. The turning-away response, however, communicates, "You're not very important to me right now," at least not as important as my primary focus of attention (which is something other than you).

The **turning-against response** is an overtly negative rejection of a connecting bid. You ask your partner, "Do you want to watch some TV?" and your partner responds, "All you ever want to do is watch that lobotomy box. Get a life!" You offer to help your roommate clean up the clutter in your dorm room. Your roommate remarks, "Don't get your tights in a twist. I know how psycho you can get about a little mess." You approach a coworker and ask for assistance figuring out how to use a new software program. The coworker responds, "Can't help now. Try reading the manual for a change." Unlike the turning-away response, a turning-against response seems harsh, even malicious. In essence, the turning-against

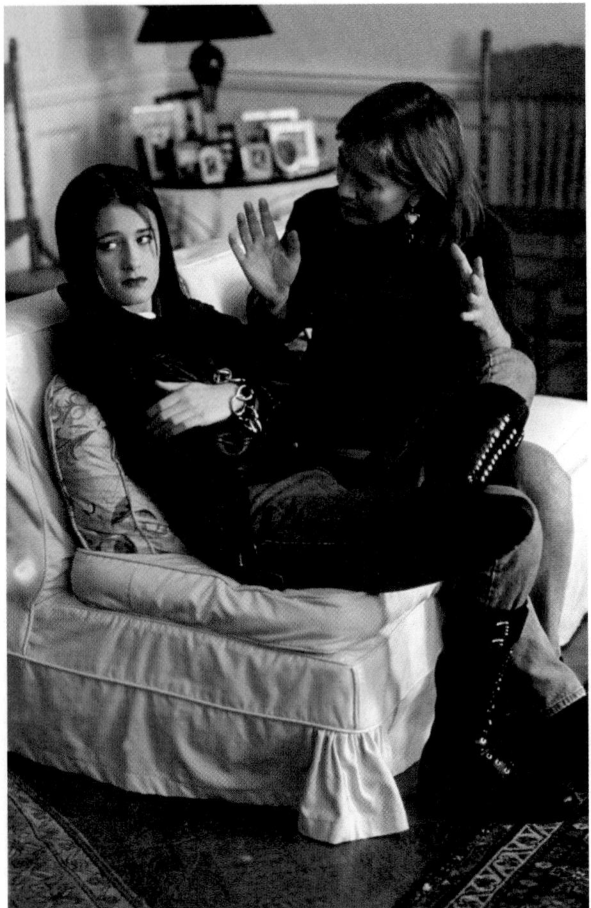

A turning-away response can be as destructive to a relationship as a turning-against response. Which is this?

response says "Get lost" or "I'm angry or irritated with you."

Consequences: The Glad, the Bad, the Sad

According to research, husbands heading for divorce turn away from their wives' bids 82% of the time. Wives in similar unhappy circumstances turn away from their husbands' bids 50% of the time. Husbands and wives in strong relationships, however, rarely turn away from their spouse's bids (Gottman & DeClaire, 2001). When we turn away from the connecting bids of others, we dampen further attempts to connect. The bidder easily loses heart when a bid is ignored. In fact, attempts to **rebid**, to try again after an initial bid has been ignored or rejected, are *near zero*. This is a classic withdrawal reaction typical of a destructive communication climate (see Chapter 1). *No one can turn toward every connecting bid, but a pattern of turning away can destroy relationships* (Gottman & Levenson, 1999).

Not surprisingly, turning against the bids of others also destroys relationships. Negative responses to connecting bids typically produce hostility or withdrawal. Although turning-against responses may seem to be the worst possible reaction one can make to a bid for connection, the research shows that *turning-away and turning-against responses are about equally destructive to relationships* (Gottman & DeClaire, 2001).

Emphasize Supportive Communication: How to Talk to Others

"The principle of openness implies that it is better to talk things over. The principle of supportiveness implies that it makes a great deal of difference *how* you talk things over" (LaFasto & Larson, 2001, p. 17). This section explains "how to talk things over" so we can prevent a defensive, competitive communication climate and establish a supportive, cooperative communication climate, a subject introduced only generally in Chapter 1 (see also Gibb, 1961) (see Box 8-1).

Evaluation Versus Description

A friend of mine was in his townhouse when the 6.9-magnitude Loma Prieta earthquake hit central California. Objects flew across the rooms, kitchen cabinets emptied onto the counters and floor, and glass shattered throughout his home. When those 15 seconds of tumultuous shaking subsided, the timid voice of my friend's four-year-old daughter came from the back room: "Daddy, it wasn't my fault." We are quick to defend ourselves if we even think an evaluation might be offered.

Evaluations are value judgments made about individuals and about their actions. Statements of praise, recognition, admiration, or flattery are positive evaluations. One study found that lack of praise for accomplishments was the number one reason employees left their companies ("Praise Thy Employees," 1994). Praise for significant accomplishments plays an important part

BOX 8.1 Developing Communication Competence

REACTIONS TO DEFENSIVE AND SUPPORTIVE COMMUNICATION

Project yourself into each situation below and imagine how you would react. Choose a number for each situation that reflects how much you would like or dislike the statements presented.

1. You live with your roommate in a studio apartment. You forgot to clean your dishes three times this week. Your roommate says to you, "Do your dishes. I'm tired of cleaning up your mess."

   STRONGLY DISLIKE 5 4 3 2 1 STRONGLY LIKE

2. You're working with your partner on a class project. Your project partner says to you, "I'm feeling very concerned that we will not finish our project on time. We're barely halfway, and we only have three days before our presentation. What do you think?"

   STRONGLY DISLIKE 5 4 3 2 1 STRONGLY LIKE

3. You are a member of a softball team. Your coach takes you aside and says, "You blew the game last week. Are you prepared to do better this game?"

   STRONGLY DISLIKE 5 4 3 2 1 STRONGLY LIKE

4. At work, you tripped and badly bruised your shoulder. Your boss says to you, "I heard that you injured yourself yesterday. That must really hurt. Do you need time off? Can I do anything to make you more comfortable while you work in your office?"

   STRONGLY DISLIKE 5 4 3 2 1 STRONGLY LIKE

5. You want to discuss a nagging issue with your friend. When you approach her to address the issue, she responds, "I haven't got time to hear from you now. I have more important things on my mind."

   STRONGLY DISLIKE 5 4 3 2 1 STRONGLY LIKE

6. You're trying to resolve a dispute that you have with your romantic partner. Your partner says to you, "I have a suggestion that might solve our problem. Perhaps this will move us forward."

   STRONGLY DISLIKE 5 4 3 2 1 STRONGLY LIKE

7. You ask for a meeting with your boss at work. You discuss a problem that you're having with inappropriate behavior from a coworker. Your boss finally says after some dialogue, "We obviously don't agree on this issue, but since I'm the boss, I'll make the final decision."

   STRONGLY DISLIKE 5 4 3 2 1 STRONGLY LIKE

8. During a family meeting, one family member says, "I know we all have strong feelings on this issue, but let's put our heads together and see if we can find a solution everyone can support. Does anyone have ideas they wish to share?"

   STRONGLY DISLIKE 5 4 3 2 1 STRONGLY LIKE

9. During a heated discussion with a fellow classmate, your classmate says, "I know I'm right and there's no way you will convince me that I'm wrong."

   STRONGLY DISLIKE 5 4 3 2 1 STRONGLY LIKE

10. You approach your teacher and propose an idea for a paper that your teacher initially dislikes. She says, "I can see that you really like this idea, but it doesn't satisfy the requirements of the project. I suggest that you keep brainstorming."

    STRONGLY DISLIKE 5 4 3 2 1 STRONGLY LIKE

(continued)

BOX 8.1 *(Continued)*

11. You're a member of a hiring panel. During a break from an interviewing session, one member of the panel takes you aside and says, "Look, we've been friends a long time. I want you to support my candidate. This is important to me. Whaddaya say? Can I count on you to back me up?"

    STRONGLY DISLIKE 5 4 3 2 1 STRONGLY LIKE

12. You've been asked to work on a committee to solve the parking problem on campus. The chair addresses the committee: "It is my hope that this committee can come to a consensus on solutions to this parking problem. I'll conduct our meetings, but I have only one vote, the same as everyone else."

    STRONGLY DISLIKE 5 4 3 2 1 STRONGLY LIKE

Answers 1, 3, 5, 7, 9, and 11 = **defensive communication** (control, evaluation, indifference, superiority, certainty, and manipulation—in that order); 2, 4, 6, 8, 10, and 12 = **supportive communication** (description, empathy, provisionalism, problem orientation, assertiveness, and equality—in that order). Find your average score for each set (divide by 6 both the sum of the odd-numbered items and the sum of the even-numbered items). Which do you like best (*lower average score*)—defensive or supportive communication?

in constructing supportive communication climates.

Negative evaluation is the culprit in provoking defensiveness. Interpersonal relationships are strained by even moderate amounts of criticism, contempt, and blame (Gottman & Silver, 1994; Stone et al., 1999). We typically don't respond constructively when we're treated like IRS agents at the ceremony for a state lottery winner. Criticism produces more conflict in the workplace than mistrust, personality clashes, power struggles, or pay (Baron, 1990).

Blame, a close cousin of criticism, is no better (Stone et al., 1999). Blame seeks to pin responsibility for a perceived failure on an individual. Focusing on blame makes what *has* occurred more important than what *should* occur to solve problems. It usually leads to **self-justification**—the creation of excuses that absolve us of blame. "How can I be expected to remember to pick up a wedding gift when I have so much on my mind? You might try helping out more" is an example of self-justification followed by a counterattack. Self-justification "is the prime suspect in the murder of a marriage" (Tavris & Aronson, 2007, p. 172). We're focused on protecting our ego, even at the expense of our relationships.

Relationships, even casual associations with coworkers, supervisors, or distant relatives, are strained by negative evaluations. Gottman's research found that *it takes at least five positive communication acts to counterbalance every negative one* (Gottman & Gottman, 2006; Gottman & Silver, 1999). Failure to maintain this five-to-one **magic ratio** leads to relationship failure in almost all cases. Couples headed for divorce communicated fewer than one positive behavior directed toward their partners for every negative one (Gottman & Gottman, 2006). Further research reveals that even *twenty acts* of kindness toward your partner does not usually anesthetize the pain of a single, extremely negative "zinger" ("I hope you didn't pay for that haircut"; "You're not nearly as good as my previous boyfriend") (Notarius & Markman, 1993). How would you react if someone described you as caring, generous, sensitive, friendly, funny, and DUMB? Would even five glowing descriptors counteract the single zinger? (Remember the negativity bias discussed in Chapter 2.)

The antidote to poisonous negative evaluations is not to ignore the troublesome behavior of others and glide through life uttering the cheery nostrum to "think positive." Enacting the magic ratio of positive to negative communication helps prevent negative evaluations from emerging, but when they do emerge (notice the ratio is 5 to 1 not 5 to none), being positive doesn't address the problem. The antidote is to be descriptive. A **description** is a first-person report of how we feel, what we perceive to be true in specific situations, and what behaviors we desire from others. As Aronson (1999) observes, "Feedback expressed in terms of feelings is a lot easier for the recipient to listen to and deal with than feedback expressed in the form of judgments and evaluations" (p. 423). Four primary steps can help you become more descriptive.

1. ***Praise first, then describe***. Begin with praise before describing behavior that is problematic ("This is a well-written paper. I do have a few suggestions, however, for improvement"). This inclines recipients to accept suggestions for change, and the motives of those giving the suggestions are also more likely to be viewed as constructive (Hornsey et al., 2008). There is the risk, of course, that a "praise first" strategy might be perceived as patronizing and manipulative. "By design, humans are exquisite insincerity detectors" (Fredrickson, 2009a). Sincere praise for real accomplishment, however, minimizes defensiveness (Hornsey et al., 2008). If there is nothing worth praising or if any praise offered would appear lame and superficial, however, then skip this step.

2. ***Use I-statements, not You-statements*** (Narcisco & Burkett, 1975; Notarius & Markman, 1993). I-statements begin with an identification of the speaker's feeling followed by a description of behavior connected to the feeling. "I feel ignored when my contributions receive no response" is an example. If no significant feelings emerge, simply suggest recommendations for improvement ("I have a few changes I'd like you to consider"). Any suggestion that you change something carries with it the implication that you haven't "measured up" in some way (criticism), but framing your message as an I-statement can appear less like a disapproving edict ("You need to make these changes").

A You-statement of negative evaluation, on the other hand, makes you a target for blame. "You have ignored me and you make me feel like I don't matter to you" is a statement that blames and criticizes. Expect denial from anyone so accused ("I've never ignored you") or a counterattack ("What do you expect when you act like you're starring in a Jackass movie?"). Eschewing You-statements is not always warranted to minimize defensiveness (e.g., "You might find these suggestions useful"), but try getting into the habit of using I-statements instead.

3. ***Make your descriptions specific, not vague***. "I feel sort of weird when you act inappropriately around my boss" is an inexact description. "Sort of weird" and "inappropriately" require more specific description. "I feel awkward and embarrassed when you tell jokes to my boss that ridicule gays and women" makes the description much more concrete.

4. ***Eliminate editorial comments***. "I get annoyed when you waste my time by talking about silly side issues" uses the first-person singular form but adds editorial language. "Waste my time" and "silly" are editorial asides that spark defensiveness and may lead to a pointless argument. Instead, say, "I get annoyed when you introduce side issues." Then provide specific examples of side issues. If the tone of voice used is sarcastic or condescending, facial expressions are contemptuous, or gestures are abusive, of course, the editorial remains.

Control Versus Problem Orientation

"He who agrees against his will, is of the same opinion still," observed English poet Samuel Butler. Most people dislike being controlled by others. Control is communication that seeks to regulate or direct a person's behavior, such as "Get off the phone" or "Bring me food."

Controlling communication can easily lead to a contest of wills brought about by psychological reactance (Brehm, 1972). **Psychological reactance** means that the

"And just who the hell are you to tell me I'm entitled to my opinion?"

more someone tries to control our behavior and restrict our choices, the more we are inclined to resist such efforts, especially if we feel entitled to choose. For example, if upon returning to your parked car you realize that another car follows you then waits for your space, are you inclined to leave faster or slower? What if your parking stalker honked you to encourage a faster exit? One study found that most people slow their exit, especially if honked (Ruback & Jweng, 1997).

If the pressure to restrict becomes intense, we may be strongly attracted to that which is prohibited. As advice columnist Ann Landers (1995) observed: "There are three ways to make sure something gets done: Do it yourself, hire someone to do it, or forbid your kids to do it" (p. D5). When parents oppose romantic relationships, such as a teenage daughter dating an older boy, it often intensifies feelings of romantic love (Driscoll et al., 1972). The more strongly parents admonish their children not to take drugs, smoke, or get their tongue pierced, the more likely the kids are to do those very behaviors to restore their sense of personal freedom (Dowd et al., 1988; Graybar et al., 1989). Parents step into the psychological reactance quicksand when they insist that their children obey them. Nevertheless, parents want to protect children from foolish or dangerous behavior. All controlling communication can't be eliminated, but it can be kept to a minimum and used only when other choices are not practical.

We can prevent defensiveness from occurring when we collaborate on a problem and seek solutions cooperatively instead of demanding obedience. Parents and children can work together, brainstorming possible solutions to troublesome conflicts instead of engaging in power struggles.

Consider some examples differentiating controlling and problem-solving communication:

Controlling	**Problem Orientation**
Clean up your room—now!	I've asked you repeatedly to clean your room. You haven't done it. I have a problem with the chores I expect you to perform not getting done. How do you see our situation?
Stop talking on the phone.	I need to make an important call. Please let me know when you're finished.
If you don't start pulling your weight, I'll fire you.	We need to talk about how to improve your performance.

Manipulation Versus Assertiveness

Imagine that you have just met an interesting person at a party. This person seems very open, honest, and attentive. You are complimented by the attention this person pays you. Then imagine that you hear later from a friend that this same person was using you to gain favor with your older sibling. You were a pawn in a chess game. How would it feel to be manipulated in such a callous and deceptive way? **Manipulative communication** is an attempt by one person to maneuver another toward the manipulator's goal. Most people resent manipulation, especially if it is based on deception. One study of 6,000 team members in organizations found that playing politics, a particularly cutthroat form of manipulative communication, destroys interpersonal relationships and team effectiveness (LaFasto & Larson, 2001).

One summer, I sold encyclopedias for a brief time door to door, when such things were done. Working out of Denver, Colorado,

I dutifully knocked on doors. The first person to invite me in was a young, friendly woman who had no idea I planned to pitch the benefits of owning encyclopedias. I was trained to camouflage what my actual purpose was for knocking on doors. Upon entering the woman's home, I was met by her inebriated husband and his unfriendly German shepherd. "If you're selling something," the unpleasant husband grumbled at me, "I'm sicking my dog on you." I manufactured an excuse and quickly left. I found refuge in the house of an elderly couple from the former Czechoslovakia who served me tea and cake and engaged in friendly conversation about "the old country" for almost three hours. I gave up trying to sell encyclopedias for the evening, having recognized how intensely people resented being disturbed by a stranger attempting to hawk his wares. I've since pondered whether that sweet couple remembered the young man who came to visit them for no apparent reason. I quickly retired from the encyclopedia business.

Assertiveness, a skill discussed at length in Chapter 7, is the antidote to manipulation. Assertiveness requires thought, skill, and concern for others. Assertive communication says, "No games are being played. This is how I feel, and this is what I need from you." It is honest and direct, unlike manipulative communication.

Indifference Versus Empathy

The Fatherhood Project at the Families and Work Institute in New York concluded, "It is presence, not absence, that often lies at the heart of troubled families. It is common for family members to be in the same room and be oblivious to each other's thoughts and feelings" (Coontz, 1997, p. 160). This indifference toward others is a sign of a disintegrating family. It also encourages further family deterioration and conflict.

The lowest self-esteem among teenagers occurs in two-parent families in which the father shows little interest in his children (Clark & Barber, 1994). Children often grow resentful of an indifferent or absent parent. This resentment can turn into outright hostility, making future reconciliation between parent and child difficult.

You counter indifference with empathy. **Empathy**, as defined in Chapter 1, is "thinking and feeling what you perceive another to be thinking and feeling" (Howell, 1982, p. 108). During "difficult conversations," each party tends to see the disagreement from his or her own perspective (Stone et al., 1999). Consequently, each person thinks that the other person is the problem. You don't defuse defensiveness by attacking or by assuming that all rationality and truth resides with you. Strive for understanding, not retaliation. How might a child feel when a father refuses to pay child support? What message does that send to the child? Can you feel the child's pain and understand why he or she might experience it in such a circumstance? That's empathy.

Part of empathy is promoting the positive in your relationships. You can't be indifferent to your partner while also appreciating your partner for small acts of kindness or special favors. *Sustaining relationships requires you to give your partner regular, copious amounts of positive, genuine feedback verbally* ("You look great," or "I love you") *and nonverbally* (don't forget flowers or small acts of kindness) (Pileggi, 2010). Promoting the positive in your relationships strengthens attachments, and expressing gratitude is a particularly meaningful way of emphasizing the positive. *Expressing gratitude* for acts of kindness or generosity enacted by your partner ("Thanks for doing those dishes when I know you're really tired") is the antithesis of indifference. Expressing gratitude is one of the most powerful communication behaviors for sustaining relationships (Fredrickson, 2009b).

Superiority Versus Equality

The line "No matter what this guy does, he thinks that no one can hold a candle to him, although a lot of people would like to" (Perret, 1994, p. 92) expresses the typical feeling most people have to expressed superiority. The superiority attitude, which alleges others don't measure up, invites defensiveness. Who likes to be viewed as inferior in anyone's eyes? Research on boastfulness, when we brag about our superiority, reveals that braggarts are generally disliked (Holtgraves

& Dulin, 1994). Research in the classroom reveals that teachers who communicate an air of superiority are also generally disliked (Rosenfeld, 1983). Leaders in groups who act superior undermine their credibility and influence with group members (Reicher et al., 2007).

Whatever the differences in our abilities, talents, and intellect, treating people with respect and civility, as equals on a human level, is supportive and encourages harmony and cooperation. Treating people like gum on the bottom of your shoe will invite defensiveness, even retaliation.

Note the difference between these examples of expressed superiority and equality:

Superiority	Equality
That's wrong!	Can you think of why that might be incorrect?
When you get to be a parent then you'll know I'm right!	Can you see why I might not agree with you on this?
I'm the boss and I know what's best.	Let's discuss this and see if we can find agreement.

Certainty Versus Provisionalism

Few things in this world are certain. Death, taxes, your dryer will eat your socks, and your computer will crash at the most inopportune moment are a few that come to mind. Because most things are not certain, however, there is room for discussion and disagreement. When people make absolute, unqualified statements of certainty, they close off discussion and disagreement. Those who communicate certainty easily slip into using terms such as *always, never, impossible, must, can't,* and *won't*, as in, "You always ignore me and you never listen." The result is often that the other party withdraws from the conversation or counterattacks with an attempt to prove the know-it-all wrong (Leathers, 1970).

Provisionalism is an effective substitute for the certainty attitude. **Provisionalism** means qualifying your statements by avoiding absolutes (remember the probability model discussed in Chapter 6). It is communicated by using terms such as *possibly, probably, perhaps, sometimes, occasionally, maybe, might, seems,* and *could be*. Problems and issues are approached as questions to be investigated and discussed.

Defuse Defensiveness: When a Cooperative Climate Isn't Enough

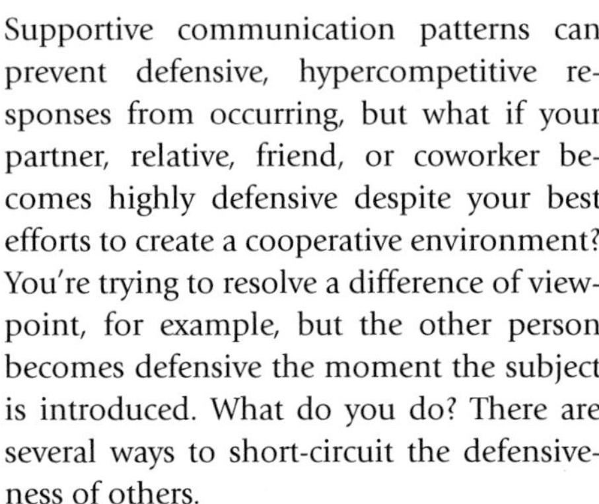

Supportive communication patterns can prevent defensive, hypercompetitive responses from occurring, but what if your partner, relative, friend, or coworker becomes highly defensive despite your best efforts to create a cooperative environment? You're trying to resolve a difference of viewpoint, for example, but the other person becomes defensive the moment the subject is introduced. What do you do? There are several ways to short-circuit the defensiveness of others.

Avoid Defensive Spirals: I Didn't Do It, and Besides, They Deserved It

Lady Astor, the first female member of the British Parliament, was exasperated by Winston Churchill's opposition to several of the causes she espoused. Frustrated, she acerbically commented, "If I were your wife I would put poison in your coffee." Churchill shot back, "And if I were your husband, I would drink it" (Sherrin, 1996, p. 160). An attack produces a counterattack that can easily spiral out of control. Refuse to be drawn into a defensive spiral in which you begin sounding like two kids arguing: "You did so. You did not. Did so. Did not. . . ." This means that you speak and listen nondefensively, even if your partner, friend, relative, or coworker exhibits defensive communication patterns. This takes discipline and patience. You have control over your communication. Try using that control to create a constructive dialogue, not a malignant spiral of defensiveness.

Focus on the Problem, Not the Person: Keep Your Eye on the Prize

Unless the problem is the other person, stick to the agenda for discussion. Do not make turning-against responses even if the connecting bid is provocative. For example, this kind of diverting response is not advisable:

Shasha: We need to go out more. We don't do anything exciting.
Mike: Do you have to tap your fingers on the table all the time? It drives me nuts. Maybe we'd go out more if you didn't irritate me so much.

When serious issues get detoured by irrelevant remarks about the person, not the problem, and turning-against responses are made to connecting bids, defensiveness is encouraged (Fisher & Brown, 1988). Mike's response diverts attention from the issue raised and centers the discussion on irritating mannerisms. That shifts the agenda and will likely induce a counterattack. Shasha could respond to the criticism of her finger tapping this way: "We can talk about my finger tapping another time. Let's discuss going out more often, and let's do it without insulting each other." Staying focused on the problem and being constructive can defuse defensiveness.

Address Relationship Deterioration: Beyond Sustaining

As relationships fall apart, the desire to turn the direction around and rebuild the connection is typically stymied by the negative atmosphere that pervades the deteriorating relationship. It is difficult to short-circuit a failing relationship and recapture the "magic" that once existed between people. It is especially difficult if infidelity is an issue. Depending on the survey, about 25% of married men and women will cheat on their spouses sometime during their lifetime (Tafoya & Spitzberg, 2007). *Mate poaching*—"trying to woo an individual away from a committed relationship to begin a relationship with them instead" (Tsapelas et al., 2011)—is even more prevalent, running at 60% for men and 53% for women (Schmitt & Buss, 2001).

Sometimes we don't recognize threats to our relationships soon enough or see that our relationships are deteriorating. We're too busy to notice, or there's too much going on in our lives to respond effectively and quickly to the erosion of love and intimacy and the infidelity that often ensues. It is critical that you respond quickly to the first signs of deterioration in your relationships. Waiting until you're standing at cliff's edge may be too late to save what once was an important part of your life. All the suggestions for sustaining relationships supported by extensive research must be applied with extra vigor if you want to salvage a relationship in crisis.

1. *Resist the temptation to reciprocate negative communication.* Fighting fire with fire will make toast of your relationship. Remain unconditionally constructive. Negativity bias is especially problematic in a relationship in crisis, so avoid the negative comments.
2. *Seek opportunities to praise, compliment, and bolster your partner.* Supportive communication is critical when a relationship begins to hit the skids. "You sure have been working hard," "You look nice," and "That place couldn't run without you" are examples of the type of communication that can begin to turn around a negative communication climate.
3. *Avoid at all costs turning-away and turning-against responses to connecting bids.* You don't repair relationships by choosing communication responses that tear apart bids that connect two people. Find every opportunity to make turning-toward responses to bids of your partner. Make this your raison d'être, your vital concern.

Cross-Sex Friendships: Sustaining with Complications

Cross-sex friendships are becoming more common and significant (Monsour, 2002). They also can be especially fragile and challenging to sustain (Werking, 1997). Part of the reason is that we typically make a stronger effort to sustain same-sex friendships than cross-sex friendships (Afifi et al., 1994; Rose, 1985). Cross-sex friendships are complicated by ambiguity regarding romantic and sexual potential (Guerrero & Chavez, 2005). This uncertainty can inhibit maintenance efforts (Dainton, 2003).

There are four types of cross-sex friendships, each requiring different maintenance behaviors to sustain the relationship (Guerrero & Chavez, 2005). They are *mutual romance* (you believe that both of you want the friendship to become romantic), *strictly platonic* (you believe that you and your friend both want the relationship to remain nonsexual and nonromantic), *desires romance* (you want the relationship to become romantic but you believe your friend does not want this), and *rejects romance* (you do not want the relationship to become romantic but you believe your friend does).

Behaviors aimed at sustaining cross-sex friendships are many and varied. They include being pleasant and complimentary, self-disclosing private information, sharing activities, being supportive, sharing tasks, incorporating circles of friends, flirting, engaging in humor, talking about the relationship, and acting jealous or trying to change the friend in some way (Guerrero & Chavez, 2005). The more uncertainty in the cross-sex relationship, the less routine contact and activities, relational talk, self-disclosure, and humor are used. The avoidance of such activities and conversations attempts to maintain the relationship as it is, not as one partner may wish it to be. If one person wants romance but the other does not, the person rejecting the romance may avoid frequent contact and joint activities to discourage any misunderstandings. The person hoping for romance with a partner who seems uninterested may avoid such contact and activities as well for fear of rejection or to safeguard the friendship (Messman et al., 2000). Disclosing romantic feelings (expressing a desire to move from platonic to romantic) inevitably complicates a friendship if one party doesn't want romance to flower.

Research on sustaining cross-sex friendships is in its infancy. Clearly, most people sense that cross-sex friendships can be complicated by uncertainty and asymmetry (contradictory desires for the friendship such as one person wanting romance and the other not wanting it). If you are in the situation of wanting romance to develop but are uncertain whether your friend shares this, approach carefully. If you offer subtle hints of romantic interest and they are avoided or discouraged by your friend, recognize that continuing along the path of pursuing romance may result in the demise of your friendship. You have to decide whether you can keep the relationship platonic when you desire more.

Technology and Competent Interpersonal Relationships

Communication technologies markedly influence our relationships with others and our lives in general. Whether this influence is positive or negative is a subject of lively debate. Let's examine the interpersonal effects of communication technologies.

Social Contact: The Influence of Technology

In 2010, 240 million Americans were using the Internet, second only to China with 420 million users. That's more than three-quarters of the American population ("Internet World Statistics" 2010). Cell phone use among adults in the United States hit 82% by 2011 ("Cell Phones and American Adults," 2011), making those who don't use a cell phone a rarity (some would say dinosaurs). These two technologies in particular have markedly changed our social lives and our communication with others.

Benefits: Expanding Social Networks

The technological advances provided by the Internet and cell phones offer a number of social benefits (Bargh & McKenna, 2004). Internet sites such as Facebook, which had 600 million users worldwide by 2011, and Twitter, which had 175 million users worldwide by the same year ("Internet," 2011), have provided an opportunity for individuals to expand their social networks beyond anything possible in previous historical periods. An early study of Internet and social media use provoked some concern about social isolation spawned by overuse of social

Electronic communication technologies can bring us together or separate us. They can also produce a generational divide regarding appropriate uses of these technologies.

networking and Internet sites. More time spent online may lead to less time spent with family and friends engaged in face-to-face social activities (see Kraut et al., 1998). Concern was also raised about online addiction (see Box 8-2). Despite these initial concerns, *the great bulk of more recent research shows no such negative effects when the Internet is used in moderation* (DiSalvo, 2010; Rainie et al., 2011). An Associated Press-Viacom poll reported that 9 out of 10 high school and college students surveyed saw social networking as a tool to keep in close touch with family and friends ("Social Media," 2011). A Pew Research study concludes: "Although some commentators have expressed fears that technology pulls families apart, this survey finds that couples use their phones to connect and coordinate their lives, especially if they have children at home. American spouses often go their separate ways during the day, but remain connected by cell phones and to some extent by internet communications" (Kennedy et al., 2008). Another Pew Research study found that Facebook users, on average, have more close relationships, receive more social support from others, and are more politically engaged than non-users ("Social Networking Sites," 2011). Cell phones and the Internet have largely been responsible for less television watching, not less connection with others.

Romantic relationships are also affected by the new technologies. One study found that the more the use of voice calls by individuals in romantic relationships "the stronger the love and commitment with their partners" (Jin & Pena, 2010). Mobile voice calls seem to allow couples to experience the feeling of continuous connection. Texting, however, does not appear to have a positive effect on romantic couples. Different channels produce different results (see Chapter 1), and texting may be too restrictive or devoid of emotional complexity to function effectively in romantic contexts.

A three-year study in Sweden, Portugal, Great Britain, and Ireland shows that older people get a psychological boost from online communication (cited in Marcus, 1999). Family therapist Howard Adelman encourages his older patients to use email to counteract loneliness and depression. "Seniors are often depressed, and with depression comes withdrawal. Email brings them back to the world" (Marcus, 1999, p. 62). Although older Americans are the least likely to use the Internet and social networking sites, their numbers are mushrooming rapidly. By 2011, 42% of adults 65 or older were using the Internet, up from 10% a decade earlier (Wolverton, 2011). The age group 50–64 has gone from 11% who used social networking sites in 2008 to

BOX 8.2 Focus on Controversy

ADDICTION TO TECHNOLOGY

In Chapter 1, I mentioned a study by Nielsen Company that reported American teenagers send and receive, on average, 3,339 text messages per month (Choney, 2010). Also, close to a fifth of adults 18 to 24 years old send more than 200 messages per day or 6,000 per month ("Cell Phones and American Adults," 2010). A survey by Samsung Telecommunications America found that 33% of men and 31% of women would prefer keeping their cell phones to engaging in sex if forced to make a choice (Kruger, 2009). Another study found that lonely individuals with poor social skills are prime candidates for compulsive use of the Internet (Kim et al., 2009).

Whether addiction to electronic communication technologies is a real psychological disorder is open to question. As already noted, the use of electronic communication technologies has pros and cons. So how much use is too much? There is no firm answer to this question. It's debatable and controversial. If a person is sick and alone, is it Internet addiction to spend more than five hours per day communicating with online friends? Is tweeting 200 times a day addiction but talking to friends in person for two to three hours a day perfectly normal? If a person were to spend hours each day reading books, would we call that an addiction? If Facebook use is primarily focused on playing games for hours each day with family members and friends who live in distant locations, is that also an addiction or is it socially constructive activity?

There is no precise formula for determining if or when overuse has been reached. There are some guidelines, however. When our most important relationships suffer from too much use of electronic communication technologies, it is time to cut back. When we fail to meet our responsibilities at home, at work, or at school, it is time to reduce the use. When we find ourselves losing sleep because we can't resist checking our Facebook site or our tweets or our emails, it's probably time to either exercise discipline and refuse to be leashed to our electronic devices or seek help from a counselor or therapist if such discipline is lacking.

QUESTIONS FOR THOUGHT

1. Do you think Internet addiction is a serious problem? Have you ever spent excessive amounts of time on the Internet at the expense of your interpersonal relationships? Can you be addicted to cell phone use?
2. Is it likely that some Internet addicts spend large amounts of time developing interpersonal relationships online without ignoring important relationships?
3. In India and in other cultures as well, close friends spend a great deal of time together, most days of every week. That is how a close friendship is defined. Would you classify this as a friendship addiction?
4. Does what kind of communication and with whom you communicate matter in labeling the use of electronic communication technologies as an addiction?

47% who did by mid-2010. Those aged 65 and older went from 5% in 2008 to 26% by mid-2010 (Swift, 2010).

Online support groups can also connect people who face troublesome physical or emotional problems (Barnes, 2001). "These groups are focused on a mutually recognized need for emotional support and feedback. Members offer each other encouragement in dealing with a medical or mental affliction that they share in common with other members of the group" (King, 1995). People with physical limitations that make face-to-face support group participation difficult and individuals who could never get together in person because of geographic distances can meet in virtual support groups. Although online support groups are still not widely used, one study found that those with serious and chronic health conditions used support groups far more than those in better health (Owen et al., 2010).

Business can be more easily conducted with cell phones and the Internet. A study by Plantronics of more than 1,800 business professionals from six countries revealed that 83% consider email "critical" to their work success and productivity, and 81% said the same about cell phones (only 38% said the same about instant messaging and 19% about social networking) ("Plantronics Study," 2010). **Telecommuting**, what the U.S. Department of Labor defines as "pay for work at an alternate site," has become widespread. In 2011, 34 million adults in the United States telecommuted at least part time. That number is expected to increase to 63 million by 2016 (Winters, 2011). According to the Telework Research Network, however, only a fraction of this number (about 3 million) work exclusively at home ("Statistics," 2011). Telecommuting provides more flexible hours for employees to work (not strictly a 9 to 5 workday), results in significantly less work-life conflict and stress than office-based employees experience (Fonner & Roloff, 2010), and typically saves resources (less driving) and can put less wear and tear on one's health (less stress from sitting in traffic jams or traveling long distance to and from a worksite).

Drawbacks: Negative Transactions

Telecommuting definitely has its advantages. Unfortunately, the ease and flexibility often obtained from telecommuting can be offset by workaholism (Amour, 2007). With Smartphones, computer laptops, and notebooks, escape from work responsibilities has become increasingly difficult—at the expense of relationships. As Ken Siegel, president of The Impact Group, a collection of psychologists who consult with management of leading global companies, explains, "Extreme work is real. The technological age has exacerbated this problem beyond belief. You can take work into the shower or bath. There's no escape" (quoted in Amour, 2007).

Sticking with drawbacks in work environments, Nucleus Research in Boston determined that almost half of workforce employees access Facebook during work hours. The average time spent on the site was 15 minutes a day. Avid users averaged two hours per day on the site. Most employees (87%) were not using Facebook for work-related tasks. Most usage was for social networking on the job. This "social notworking" costs companies 1.5% in total lost productivity. This is a small percentage, but it runs into the billions of dollars ("Facebook," 2009).

There are some potential drawbacks on the psychological front as well. Lonely people who access the Internet and social networking sites do not assuage their feeling of social isolation. Psychologist Laura Freberg notes that "chronic loneliness makes people act in ways that push others away. Social networking isn't equipped to handle that and can actually make it worse" (quoted in DiSalvo, 2010, p. 52). Obsessive-compulsive individuals also may use social networking sites in obsessive ways. "A consistent factor across many of the studies in this realm is that social networking is simply a new forum for bad habits" (DiSalvo, 2010, p. 55).

Cell phones can also be a source of some concern. In an elegant San Antonio, Texas, nightclub, a jazz singer was entertaining the crowd when a cell phone rang. The patron answered the phone, then shushed the singer so the patron could hear the call. In Palo Alto, California, a food fight nearly broke out when one customer complained loudly about eight cell phone calls disrupting his meal. One survey by Harris Interactive for Intel found that 63% of respondents were irked by loud talking on cell phones in a restaurant or other public places (Johnson, 2009). Cell phone users can be seen conducting conversations while walking down the street, bouncing off passersby like balls in a pinball machine, seemingly oblivious to their surroundings. Restaurants, theaters, and museums from coast to coast have begun creating "cell phone-free zones" or banning cell phone conversations entirely by posting "No Cell Phones" signs at entrances. Cell phone use while driving has become a legislative issue in most states. Movie theaters routinely flash requests to turn off cell phones during the showing of films. Such requests are often ignored by cell phone junkies who feel compelled to text message every five minutes during the movie, distracting others with their brightly lit phone screens. Teachers at all education levels regularly instruct students to turn off cell phones before classes begin, but it is rare that at least one cell phone doesn't interrupt a class session.

Personal conversations formerly relegated to one's home, private office, or possibly an enclosed phone booth now regularly take place in crowded restaurants, buses, airport waiting areas, even in public bathrooms. "By engaging in a call, mobile phone users are capable of transforming public space into their own private space, often at the expense of others around them" (Campbell, 2008, p. 70). The Harris survey found that 55% of respondents reported that they were bothered by private cell phone discussions in public places. One study found that overhearing someone engaged in conversation on a cell phone is more irksome than overhearing two physically present individuals engaged in conversation because in the latter they hear a dialogue but in the former they hear only a "halfalogue." A **halfalogue**—hearing only half the conversation—is more distracting because your brain tries to figure out the unheard part of the conversation (Emberson et al., 2010). It's more difficult to tune out the cell phone conversation.

Cell phone conversations in public places such as theaters and classrooms are considered particularly intrusive and inappropriate among individualistic Americans ("You're disturbing *me*"). In collectivist countries, public cell phone use is more tolerated because keeping in contact with

members of an in-group (family, work, etc.) is considered more important than preventing strangers who are not in a preferred group from becoming irritated (Campbell, 2008). Etiquette, our set of rules for appropriate public communication, has not kept up with technological change (see Box 8-3).

Online Romance: Cyberlove

Online dating services have become increasingly popular and enormously lucrative. Dating sites such as Match.com and eHarmony were raking in about $4 billion annually by 2011 (Whysall, 2011). The depth of online relationships, however, certainly can be questioned, and since there is no physical proximity, you can hardly separate the truth from fiction (Epstein, 2007). Pictures on profiles can be 20 years old, or may even be photos of other, presumably better-looking people. A study of more than 5,000 online daters reported that there is a fair amount of lying and exaggeration on these sites. Women are inclined to lie about their weight, and men are inclined to lie about their age, income, personality, and interests (Hall et al., 2010). One study asked almost 5,000 online daters to respond to the statement: "People who I have met online have said they were dating only me when they were also involved with someone else." Thirty-nine percent responded that this happened to them "constantly," and another 19% said it occurred "frequently" or "occasionally" (Albright, 2007).

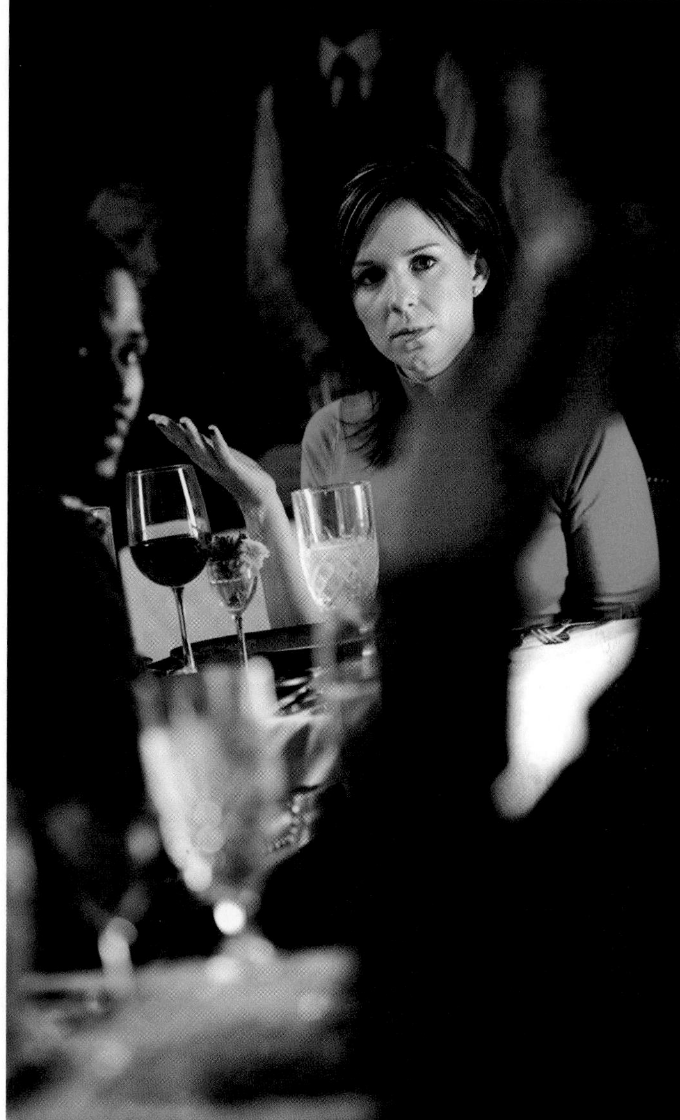

Cell phone use in restaurants and other public places is particularly annoying for those listening only to the halfalogue—only one side of the conversation.

Despite effusively positive advertising from eHarmony, Match.com, and other dating services extolling the virtues of online dating ("find your soul mate"), independent studies show that satisfaction among the users is low (Thompson et al., 2005). A survey of more than 2,000 online subscribers by Jupiter research reported that barely a quarter were satisfied with online dating services (cited in Epstein, 2007). A Pew Internet and American Life Project survey found that 66% of Internet users consider online dating dangerous ("Pew Internet," 2006). A team of psychologists, in a white paper about online dating services, concluded: "When eHarmony recommends someone as a compatible match, there is a 1 in 500 chance that you'll marry this person. . . . Given that eHarmony delivers about 1.5 matches a month, if you went on a date with all of them, it would take 346 dates and 19 years to reach [a] 50% chance of getting married." The paper goes on to conclude that "there is no evidence that . . . scientific psychology is able to pair individuals who will enjoy happy, lasting marriages" (Thompson et al., 2005; see also Epstein, 2007).

Perhaps enduring, joyful marriages are unlikely to develop from online dating, but what

BOX 8.3 Developing Communication Competence

CELL PHONE ETIQUETTE FOR THE COMPETENT COMMUNICATOR

Cell phone use is pervasive and potentially intrusive, making cell phone etiquette essential. A 2009 survey by LetsTalk revealed less tolerance for cell phone use in several contexts. Only 19% felt it is appropriate to use a cell phone in the bathroom, down from 38% in 2003 in another survey by Harris Interactive (Davis, 2006). Only 1% found it acceptable to use a cell phone at the movies or in a theater. Acceptability of cell phone use in restaurants fell from 29% in 2003 in the Harris survey to 5% in the 2009 LetsTalk survey ("Survey Says," 2009). Based on these and other survey results, LetsTalk, an online wireless retailer that commissions annual surveys on the use of communication technologies, offers guidelines on appropriate cell phone etiquette. Based on this and a consideration of the communication competence model, here are some etiquette guidelines:

1. Do not answer a cell phone on a date, during a business meeting, or while conducting a face-to-face conversation unless you know that an emergency has arisen. Most people perceive such behavior as rude and insensitive. It appears that your cell phone conversation takes precedence over your face-to-face conversation. Use the phone's caller ID function to screen calls and let voice mail handle all calls that aren't clearly urgent.
2. Don't text message while conversing with another person face to face. Such "multitasking" is cloddish behavior. This is obvious pseudolistening (see Chapter 6).
3. Never use a cell phone (for calls or text messaging) in a restaurant, theater, or during any public performance when such use could disrupt others' enjoyment. If you absolutely must receive a call or must text message a response in such venues, excuse yourself, and take the call or text message in a more private location.
4. When using a cell phone in public, *do not raise your voice*. Speak in a normal manner, not a "CELL YELL." Most people do not care to listen to your personal conversations.
5. Don't conduct nonessential business or personal conversations on public transportation, in checkout lines, or in any public place where strangers are a captive audience. Recognize the difference between public and private communication.
6. Avoid using annoying rings. Switch to the vibrating feature when possible.
7. Do not use a cell phone while driving. It's likely to divert your attention from the safe operation of your vehicle. Pull off the road and take a call that seems urgent.
8. Use the camera feature with discretion. Most strangers do not welcome being photographed without permission.

Which of these eight guidelines do you adhere to and which do you violate?

about merely pursuing a good time by dating online? Even this limited pursuit doesn't seem to pan out for most people. Respondents to one study found that participants spent an average of 5.2 hours each week looking through profiles and 6.7 hours responding to emails. On a question asking about enjoyment of online dating, respondents averaged 5.5 on a 10-point scale (10 = very much and 1 = not at all) (Frost et al., 2008). Only 3% of committed relationships typically result from online dating services ("More Think It Is Important," 2006). The effort required to search multitudinous profiles and the high expectations created by inflated profiles often lead to disappointment when in-person dates materialize (Sprecher, 2011).

Conflict: Hurling Electronic Flames

Messages communicated by email, texting, or tweeting can be easily misinterpreted.

Sarcasm, for instance, or teasing without the requisite tone of voice, facial expressions, and physical cues that signal how the message should be interpreted can be mistaken for serious personal attacks. **Emoticons**, graphic notations that indicate emotional information, can help in this regard. Emoticons for a smile (:)), or a frown (:() can indicate a proper tone for a message. Men, however, especially when conducting business by email, may resist using emoticons because they are more closely associated with female communication patterns, and they may seem unprofessional. Emoticons also don't produce understanding if receivers are unfamiliar with them.

Email also reduces the natural constraints on incivility and hostility that come from facing a person directly (Thompson & Nadler, 2002; Van Kleef et al., 2004). Conflict can turn destructive more easily when mediated by technology than when conducted face to face (Holahan et al. 2008; Zornoza et al., 2002). **Flaming** is a cyberterm for an abusive, attacking written message between Internet users (emailed; text messaged; blog comment, Playstation interplay). Typical attributes of an electronic flame include profanity, the use of all capital letters, and excessive exclamation points or question marks (Turnage, 2007). The absence of normal constraints on incivility and hostility that come with in-person transactions (e.g., implicit rules against ugly public displays of anger) often couple with the ease and swiftness of email to the detriment of relationships (Wallace, 1999). As Brin (1998) explains,

> Electronic conversations seem especially prone to misinterpretation, suddenly and rapidly escalating hostility between participants, or else triggering episodes of sulking silence. When flame wars erupt, normally docile people can behave like mental patients. . . . Typing furiously, they send impulsive text messages blurting out the first vituperation that comes to mind, abandoning the editing process of common courtesy that civilization took millennia to acquire.
> (p. 166)

Flaming is competitive, defensive communication. Those given to flaming often experience *sender's regret*—they wish they hadn't sent the angry, emotionally damaging message in the heat of the moment. Once it is sent, however, the damage is done.

So, what can you do if using communication technologies increases hostile conflict? Here are four suggestions.

1. *Use communication technologies selectively*. The cell phone can be an *electronic lasso* that binds us to others, or what Shenk (1997) calls "electronic leashes," if we can never escape their intrusiveness. Plan for times during each day when you will have no access to any of these technologies. Shut off the computer, switch off the cell phone, and turn off the television set. Decompress your stress that can trigger flames. Try simple conversation or social activities with no technological distractions.
2. *Delay sending any email message that has strong emotional content*. If you want to avoid sender's regret, delay sending any email or text message written in the heat of the moment. Flaming email messages should always be put aside overnight. Never send an angry response to someone else's flame until you have had time to cool down. If an immediate response is required, simply ask for time to reflect on what was said and the way it was said.
3. *Do not use email to fire or to reprimand an employee, to offer negative work appraisals, or to tender resignations*. These highly personal matters should be conducted face to face (Zornoza et al., 2002).
4. *Exercise etiquette on the Net*. See Box 8-4 for details.

Intercultural Relationships and Communication Competence

Different cultures have different perspectives on love and intimacy. When individuals from cultures with different perspectives develop friendships or romantic relationships, difficulties inevitably arise.

BOX 8.4 Developing Communication Competence

NETIQUETTE

The competent communicator wishes to function within the social norms of a specific community. In this regard, there are certain communication norms that specify appropriate behavior on the Internet. Barnes (2001) offers several guidelines for **netiquette**—etiquette on the Internet:

1. *Be brief.* Lengthy messages make email management difficult and can be irksome. Get to the point.
2. *Flame off.* Common courtesy is expected of all netizens. Blogs are notorious for offensive rants. Curb the incivility.
3. *Observe good form.* Grammar, spelling, rules of capitalization, and accepted spacing between words and paragraphs should be observed. Take the same care in composing emails that you would writing a standard letter. It demonstrates respect for the reader. Proofread before sending to avoid embarrassing yourself.
4. *Avoid spamming.* **Spamming** is sending unsolicited email, especially advertisements for products or activities. Spamming clutters people's email inboxes.
5. *Assume publicity.* When composing emails, assume that anything written could be published on the front page of the local newspaper. If you'd be embarrassed to see what you've written published for all to read, consider carefully whether you should write it at all. Deletion of messages does not wipe out all traces of emails.

Although exceptions can be found to each of these guidelines, most communication should follow them carefully. Which have you followed and which have you violated?

Intercultural Friendships: Additional Challenges

The very definition of friendship varies among cultures (Martin & Nakayama, 2008). Americans have many types of friendships. Other cultures do not have casual friends and close friends. The "special emotional relationship" that exists in only some close friendships in America is a requirement for *any* designation of friendship in Germany and India, for example. If you are accorded friendship status, there has to be that special emotional bond.

The initial stages of a developing friendship between individuals from different cultures present three problems (Martin & Nakayama, 2007). First, the differences in values, perceptions, and communication style can be troublesome. These are deep-seated, not superficial, differences (see Chapter 3). Second, anxiety is a common experience in the initial stages of any friendship, but intercultural friendships are likely to induce greater anxiety. We experience greater fear of making mistakes and causing offense when we are unfamiliar with the norms and rules of another culture. Third, overcoming stereotypes about a different culture and resisting the impulse to be ethnocentric can be difficult (see Chapter 3).

A study of American and Japanese students who were friends revealed some interesting ways to nurture intercultural friendships (Sudweeks et al., 1990). First, some similarities that transcend the cultural differences must be discovered, whether they are sports, hobbies, lifestyle, or political attitudes. Bridges must be constructed from common experience. Second, making time for the relationship is critical. It takes more time to develop a friendship with a member of another culture because we are typically drawn to others who are like us, not to those who are unlike us. Third, sharing the same group of friends can be very important. A shared group of friends can lend support to an intercultural relationship. Finally, capitalizing on key turning points (requesting a favor; revealing a personal secret) is especially vital in developing cross-cultural friendships. Reluctance to respond positively to a turning point may be perceived as an insult and might end the relationship.

Ultimately, cross-cultural friendships require more "care and feeding" (Pogrebin, 1987) than do friendships between similar individuals. More explaining and understanding must take place. "Mutual respect, acceptance, tolerance for the faux pas and the occasional closed door, open discussion and patient mutual education, all this gives crossing friendships—when they work at all—a special kind of depth" (Pogrebin quoted in Gudykunst & Kim, 1992, p. 318).

Intercultural Romance: Tougher Than Friendships

Romantic relationships can be even stickier than friendships. Once the difficulties of developing a friendship have been overcome, additional problems can develop when romance flowers. Families may raise a stink about cross-cultural friendships, and romance may intensify this opposition (Kouri & Lasswell, 1993). Opposition from one's family isn't necessarily based on prejudice, although surely bigotry sometimes plays a part. Concerns about child-rearing styles, religious differences, politics, gender roles, power issues, place of residence, and

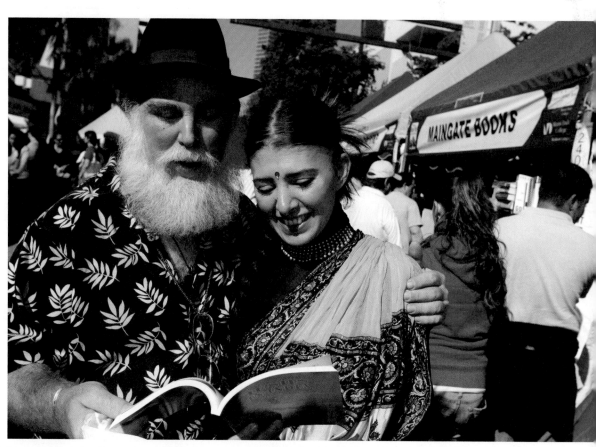

Intercultural relationships present extra challenges for couples. Consensus, learning about and adopting aspects of each other's culture, is an effective strategy for meeting intercultural relationship challenges.

rituals and ceremonies may also increase opposition.

Romano (1988) identifies four strategies that are used in intercultural marriages. Submission is the most common strategy. One partner abandons his or her culture and submits to the partner's culture, adopting the religion, value system, politics, and so forth. This is rarely effective because individuals find it enormously difficult to erase their core cultural values and background. A second strategy, compromise, means giving up only part of one's cultural beliefs, values, and habits. This is also very difficult in most situations. Asking one partner to forego Christmas decorations and celebration while the other partner is asked not to observe the Muslim holy month Ramadan isn't likely to be a smooth compromise. A third strategy, obliteration, is sometimes used. Obliteration occurs when both partners attempt to erase their respective cultures from the relationship. This is difficult to accomplish, and it means avoiding basic support groups such as family and friends. Finally, there is consensus, which seems to work best. Consensus is based on negotiation and cooperation. Learning the partner's language, studying the religion, and learning about the cuisine erect bridges between partners. Consensus is built by emphasizing similarities and commonalities in relationships and by de-emphasizing differences. Consensus is difficult even among culturally similar individuals. It is doubly difficult between culturally dissimilar individuals who plan to marry.

Summary

DEVELOPING relationships with others is a human imperative. Nature inclines us toward such connections. We form relationships because we have a need to belong, because we are attracted interpersonally to those who are physically attractive, similar to us, and reciprocate our liking them, and because relationships with others can provide benefits that outweigh costs. Relationships are more challenging than ever. Every relationship travels through specific stages. Recognizing what communication behaviors work best at each stage is important to the development of intimate romantic relationships and close friendships. Keeping a relationship from moving into the coming-apart stages is a principal concern. We sustain relationships in a variety of ways; the most important are by understanding the value of connecting bids and our responses to those bids, avoiding defensive communication patterns, and encouraging supportive communication. Advances in technology influence our relationships with others in powerful ways. Technology can help sustain relationships, or it can become an electronic leash that adds stress to our lives and threatens the health of our relationships. Intercultural relationships are probably the most challenging of all. Individuals from collectivist cultures have a We-emphasis, but persons from individualist cultures have a Me-emphasis. This fundamental distinction in cultural values can put a strain on an intercultural relationship.

Quizzes Without Consequences

Did you understand all the material in this chapter? Test your knowledge before your exam!

Go to the companion website at www.oup.com/us/rothwell, click on the Student Resources for each chapter, and take the Quizzes Without Consequences.

Film School Case Studies

The Break-up (2006). Romantic Comedy (sort of); PG-13

Vince Vaughn and Jennifer Aniston play a couple struggling to make their relationship work. Well, actually the Aniston character struggles, and the Vaughn character mostly acts clueless and belligerent. Examine the coming-apart stages of this relationship. Look for connecting bids and responses to those bids. Examine defensive and supportive communication patterns.

Fifty First Dates (2004). Romantic Comedy; PG-13

Adam Sandler woos Drew Barrymore, who suffers from short-term memory loss. Analyze this repetitive courtship from a stages-of-relationship-development perspective.

(500) Days of Summer (2009). Romantic Comedy; PG-13

Offbeat romantic comedy about a young woman (Zooey Deschanel), who doesn't believe in true love, and a young man (Joseph Gordon-Levitt), who falls hard for her. Examine the coming-together and coming-apart stages of their relationship.

Knocked Up (2007). Romantic Comedy; R

Highly popular, unrealistic pairing of Seth Rogen and Katherine Heigl, who play characters that meet at a bar, get drunk, and have sex (really?) that gets the Heigl character pregnant. Apply the similarity attraction theory to this film.

Martian Child (2007). Drama; PG

John Cusack plays a widower who decides to adopt a troubled little boy who thinks he's a Martian. This is a very tender, sweet story. Examine defensive and supportive communication patterns in Cusack's relationship with his new son.

My First Mister (2002). Comedy/Drama; R

An unusual relationship develops between the Albert Brooks and Leelee Sobieski characters. Analyze their relationship using the triangular theory of love model.

Notting Hill (1999). Romantic Comedy; PG-13

The charming and extraordinarily entertaining story of a London bookstore owner whose chance encounter with an internationally acclaimed American actress begins an on-again off-again romance. Analyze the complex, fitful development of their relationship in terms of the stages of relationships. Do the several reversals of direction in the relationship between the Hugh Grant and Julia Roberts characters coincide with the stages-of-relationships material presented in this chapter? Are there any turning points? Explain.

Second Skin (2008). Documentary; R

This documentary follows three sets of online gamers, exploring ways that social media influence interpersonal connections. What are the pros and cons depicted in this film of mediated relationships and life in cyberspace?

CHAPTER 9

Chapter Outline

Interpersonal Conflict Management

CONFLICT IS AN UNAVOIDABLE FACT OF LIFE. A survey of 31,000 first-year college students revealed that 29% reported having conflicts with their roommates (Warters, 2005). Because most incoming first-year students have never shared a room before they land on campus, the potential for conflict to occur as new roommates adjust to each other is high. In addition, student-faculty disputes regarding grades, assignments, attendance policies, and the like are relatively common on college campuses. One study found that students are usually unsatisfied with instructors' responses when conflict arises (Tantleff-Dunn et al., 2002).

By the end of this chapter, you should be able to:

1. Define conflict in both its constructive and destructive forms.
2. Explain the inevitable contradictions in relationships that provoke conflict.
3. Understand the five principal communication styles available for managing conflict.
4. Manage conflict competently through appropriate choices of communication styles of conflict management, anger management, forgiveness, and intercultural understanding.

Research on marital conflict indicates that the more couples engage in conflict, the more they become verbally aggressive, and verbal aggression can provoke physical violence (Schumacher & Leonard, 2005). Contributing to the frequency of couple conflict is the tension created by trying to juggle both work and family responsibilities. Too much time spent at work robs time spent with your partner, and if kids are involved, they get ignored as well. Friction with your intimate partner is a likely result. Conversely, too much time spent on your personal relationships can cause friction at work because job responsibilities are not met. With more than 70 million individuals in the United States in dual-earner relationships (both work), the opportunities for conflict increase (Lapierre & Allen, 2006; Matthews et al., 2006).

Marital conflict also has significant effects on children (Cummings & Keller, 2007; Cummings et al., 2006). When couples fight in front of their kids, or even ignore each other in response to disputes, this can be very distressful for the children and can also lead children to view conflict itself in a negative light (Davies et al., 2006). Frequent marital conflict is associated with a wide range of problems for children, including depression, weak academic performance, poor social skills, and discipline difficulties (Hetherington et al., 1998). These results are likely to be more serious as the frequency of conflict increases. Children of intact (nondivorced) families with frequent conflict, for example, have greater problems with psychological adjustment and self-esteem than do children living in both low-conflict divorced and nondivorced families (Amato & Loomis, 1995).

The main purpose of this chapter is to discuss ways to manage inevitable relationship conflict in a competent manner.

Definition of Conflict

In this section, I define conflict in its general form. Then I identify and explain the differences between destructive and constructive conflict.

General Definition: Essential Elements

Janice Lightner is a student in Professor Winthrop's Human Communication intensive six-week summer course that meets four times per week. Professor Winthrop has a strict policy on attendance. Four absences result in an automatic "F" for the course. Janice has earned an "A" on all tests and assignments through the fourth week of the class, and she has perfect attendance. The sudden death of her grandfather, however, requires Janice to fly from Eugene, Oregon, to Toronto, Canada, to attend his funeral. She must be absent from class for an entire week. She asks Professor Winthrop for an exemption from the attendance policy, revealing the news of her grandfather's sudden death. She promises to make up the work and miss no other classes. Professor Winthrop expresses regret but tells Janice that she will not pass the course if she misses a week of class. Janice becomes upset and tells Professor Winthrop that her attendance policy is unreasonable and unfair. "What do you expect me to do, miss his funeral?" Professor Winthrop defends the policy as essential for her students to learn difficult class material. She and Janice part feeling angry.

Conflict is the expressed struggle of interconnected parties who perceive incompatible goals and interference from one or more parties in attaining those goals (Wilmot & Hocker, 20011). The Professor Winthrop–Janice Lightner situation illustrates each element of this definition.

First, conflict is an *expressed struggle* between two or more parties. If Janice had accepted Professor Winthrop's attendance policy without confronting her about it, no conflict would have existed. Even if Janice had been angry about the policy, for a conflict to exist Janice had to indicate her unhappiness to Professor Winthrop in some fashion. The expression of the struggle could be obvious, such as Janice talking directly to Professor Winthrop. The expression could also be very subtle, even exclusively nonverbal, such as cold stares or slouching posture by Janice during class.

Second, conflict involves *interconnected parties*. The behavior of one party must have consequences for the other party. Professor Winthrop and Janice are interconnected. Janice faces a dilemma because of Professor Winthrop's attendance policy. Professor Winthrop affects the choice Janice must make. Does she miss her grandfather's funeral so she can pass her class, or does she attend her grandfather's funeral and flunk the class? Janice affects Professor Winthrop because Janice is a disgruntled student challenging her attendance policy. Professor Winthrop may wonder whether her policy is too harsh or unfair.

Third, *perceived incompatible goals* must be present for conflict to occur. The goals of Professor Winthrop and Janice seem incompatible. Professor Winthrop's goal is to have students attend class regularly so they can learn difficult material. Janice's goal is to attend the funeral without failing the class. Professor Winthrop's attendance policy and Janice's desire to attend her grandfather's funeral clash directly.

Finally, *perceived interference from parties* who pursue incompatible goals is necessary for conflict to occur. For two people to have a conflict, either one or both must interfere with the other's goal attainment. Professor Winthrop clearly interfered with Janice's goal to attend her grandfather's funeral without affecting her class grade. If Janice attends the funeral, she thwarts Professor Winthrop's goal. Janice will fall seriously behind in the class.

Perception plays an important role in conflict. Goals may not be incompatible, and goal attainment may not be interfered with by anyone. Nevertheless, if you act as though your goals are incompatible with your partner's goals and as though your partner is trying to interfere with your goal achievement, conflict will occur until perceptions are clarified and accepted.

Types of Conflict: It's Not All Bad

To most people, conflict always seems destructive. Conflict can make us angry, fearful, and frustrated, and it can trigger verbal, even physical, aggression. Nevertheless, there are two general types of conflict: destructive and constructive (Holahan et al., 2008). *Our communication determines to what degree conflict will be destructive or constructive.*

Destructive Conflict: Taking No Prisoners

Destructive conflict is characterized by escalation, retaliation, domination, competition, defensiveness, and inflexibility (Lulofs, 1994; Wilmot & Hocker, 2011). Typical communication tactics employed during destructive conflict include threats, intimidation, condescension, dishonesty, and personal assaults (verbal or physical). A conflict between two coworkers at the Fresh Vegetable Package Company in Denver, Colorado, is such an instance. The victim accused her assailant of throwing fruit at her because she "laughed at her." The conflict escalated to vegetables, at which point the assailant "for no reason" hurled a four-inch-diameter carrot at the victim. The victim, who was five months pregnant, complained about stomach pains and was rushed to Denver General Hospital. A detective investigating the altercation reported, "All she [the victim] wants is that the suspect leave her alone. I'm going to call up and talk to the supervisor and have the assailant moved from the dangerous weapon section—back from vegetables to fruit." No charges were filed against the assailant, presumably because it would have been difficult to prosecute the attacker for "assault with a deadly vegetable" (Isenhart & Spangle, 2000).

Donohue and Kolt (1992) argue that the key to recognition of destructive conflict is the ability to say to oneself in the middle of a conflict, "*Gee, I'm getting stupid*" (p. 24).

When you begin to lose sight of why you're battling with someone and you become petty, even infantile, in your tactics to win a conflict (throwing vegetables), you're getting stupid. When hurting your adversary becomes your principal goal, not problem solving, you're getting stupid. When you can no longer think clearly because conflict triggers emotional reactions that clog the brain's ability to reason, then you are moving into destructive conflict territory. Gottman calls this flooding. He operationally defines **flooding** this way: "The body of someone who feels flooded is a confused jumble of signals. It may be hard to breathe. People who are flooded inadvertently hold their breath. Muscles tense up and stay tensed. The heart beats faster and it may seem to beat harder" (Gottman & Silver, 1994, p. 112). *Men are far more likely than women to experience flooding.* According to Gottman, "the male cardiovascular system remains more reactive than the female and slower to recover from stress" (Gottman & Silver, 1999, p. 37).

Constructive Conflict: Working It Out

Despite its negative potential, conflict can be constructive (Dovidio et al., 2009). Conflict can signal that change needs to occur for a relationship to remain vital. Women, but usually not men, may use conflict to provoke attention to a relationship problem and trigger discussion of a possible solution (Haefner et al., 1991). Conflict can also encourage creative problem solving in the workplace by raising tension, which may encourage an energetic search for innovative answers.

Constructive conflict is characterized by communication that is cooperative, supportive, and flexible (Lulofs, 1994; Wilmot & Hocker, 2011). The focus is on achieving a solution that is mutually satisfactory to all parties in the conflict. Participants work together flexibly to deal effectively with their conflicts by de-escalating them. Partners in happy marriages, for example, approach each other in gentle, positive ways when conflict arises. They listen respectfully, and they work to find solutions that benefit both partners (Gottman & Gottman, 2006). Reducing the severity of conflict episodes by learning conflict-management techniques is a key to constructive conflict (Canary et al., 1995).

Constructive conflict doesn't mean you have to feel all warm and fuzzy as you work

Remaining unconditionally constructive during a conflict can be a huge challenge, but returning abuse with abuse merely angers both parties and produces destructive conflict. Flooding fogs the brain during shouting matches.

out your differences with others. *Constructive conflict can be contentious, frustrating, and difficult.* It is constructive, however, because supportive communication patterns are employed; participants are assertive, not aggressive or passive; and there is an overriding commitment to cooperating, not competing. Thus, certain communication styles of conflict management are emphasized, a subject discussed later in this chapter.

Destructive Versus Constructive Conflict: It's All About Communication

The distinctions between destructive and constructive conflict (see Figure 9-1) are apparent from studies of parents engaged in conflict in front of their children (Cummings et al., 2006; Sturge-Apple et al., 2006a, 2006b). Interparental conflict handled destructively involves verbal hostility (yelling), personal insults, threats of violence, nonverbal hostility manifested by angry fist shaking or threatening body posture, the silent treatment, and crying and trembling. These are especially distressing to children. Interparental conflicts handled constructively produce the opposite effects; they actually increase children's emotional security and help them feel more positively about themselves and their families (Cummings et al., 2003). These interparental constructive conflicts are characterized by calm discussions of disagreements, careful listening to try to understand each other, and outward indications of affection such as holding hands while addressing issues of disagreement.

Distinctions between destructive and constructive conflict are also apparent during and after divorce, especially when children make contact between estranged parents unavoidable. Cooperative, mutually supportive coparenting reduces the frequency and severity of conflicts (Hetherington et al., 1998). Children adapt more effectively to their parents' divorce and accept remarriages more readily. Unfortunately, only about one-quarter of divorced parents manage such conflicts constructively (Maccoby & Mnookin, 1992). Conflicts in stepfamilies (sometimes called "blended families") are destructive 95% of the time (Baxter et al., 1999).

When divorced parents express contempt for each other in front of children, insist that children choose sides in a conflict, use children as leverage in a power struggle, or ridicule their ex-spouse's new partner, they are engaged in destructive conflict. Actor Alec Baldwin, locked in a bitter seven-year battle with his ex-wife, Kim Basinger, left a voice mail for his 11-year-old daughter calling her "a thoughtless little pig." Baldwin admitted later, "I took it out on the wrong person."

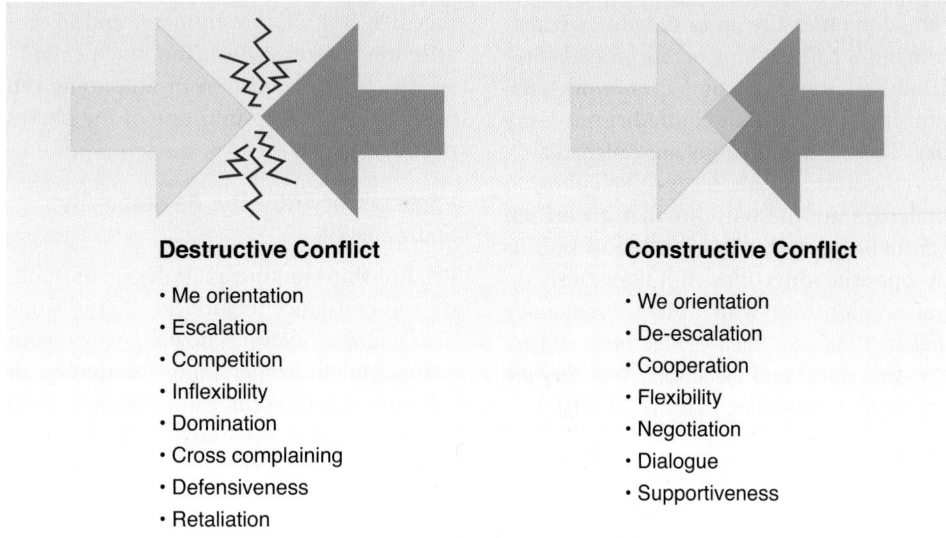

Destructive Conflict
• Me orientation
• Escalation
• Competition
• Inflexibility
• Domination
• Cross complaining
• Defensiveness
• Retaliation
Constructive Conflict
• We orientation
• De-escalation
• Cooperation
• Flexibility
• Negotiation
• Dialogue
• Supportiveness

FIGURE 9-1 Destructive Versus Constructive Conflict

When Bill Sears was 8 years old, his divorced parents literally engaged in a tug-of-war in a Wal-Mart parking lot, each parent pulling on one of his arms while shouting, "He's coming with me!" That's "getting stupid." Sears lived with his dad in their "testosterhome" and reflected, "You know your parents are better than this. They just hate each other right now" (Smolowe, 2007, p. 132). When divorced couples encourage children to have contact with both parents, focus on supportive communication patterns, and maintain respect for former spouses and their new partners even while they themselves disagree on important issues, they are engaged in constructive conflict.

Relationship Dialectics

Relationships are often messy. As we move through the phases of relationships (see Chapter 8) and become increasingly intimate, relationships will rarely follow the profile for textbook-perfect communication. Many romantic partners talk to each other, on average, for a mere hour a day, rarely self-disclose, often fight, even become violent verbally and sometimes physically, are less polite to each other than they are to strangers, and are more concerned with task accomplishment than with sharing intimacies (Baxter & Montgomery, 1996). We typically don't measure up to the ideal because romantic partnerships, close friendships, family relationships, and even work relationships face difficult contradictions every day. These contradictions are called dialectics, the focus of this section. Relationship **dialectics** are the tensions that arise from contradictory needs that push and pull us in opposite directions simultaneously in our relationships with others. *Relationship dialectics can be a fundamental source of relationship conflict and meltdown when they are not managed competently* (Erbert, 2000).

Dialectics Within Relationships: Pushing Us/Pulling Us

Dialectics are an intrinsic part of romantic partner-partner, friend-friend, parent-child, and boss-employee relationships. Individuals have many motives, goals, and needs, and in relationships, these often unavoidably clash. *Dialectics never disappear from these relationships* (Baxter & Montgomery, 1996; West & Turner, 2007). They are managed, not eradicated. Three common dialectics (there are others) that occur within these interpersonal relationships are connection-autonomy, predictability-novelty, and openness-closedness (Baxter & Erbert, 1999; Baxter & Montgomery, 1996; Petronio, 2002).

Connection-Autonomy: Hug Me/Leave Me Alone

The desire to come together with another person (connection) yet remain independent and in control of one's own life (autonomy) is called the **connection-autonomy dialectic**. We want to be an "us" without losing the "me." Adult children, for example, want to be connected to their parents in a loving relationship, but they usually rebel when parents interfere in their lives too much or make them feel as though they are still children to be supervised.

Excessive emphasis on connection usually leads to feeling smothered by partners, parents, or personal friends, to feeling entrapped and controlled by others, and to having no independent life. Excessive emphasis on autonomy, however, leads to complaints of insufficient time spent together, lack of commitment, and loss of affection (Baxter, 1994). Too much emphasis on either connection or autonomy can push a relationship into one of the phases of coming apart.

Predictability-Novelty: Be Stable/Be Spontaneous

Relationships require a fair degree of stability and constancy to survive—that is, some predictability. Never knowing when your partner might come home for dinner, or even if that will occur, can produce tension and conflict. Predictability can be comforting because you know what to expect.

Predictability, however, can induce boredom, possibly leading to the stagnating phase of a relationship. As relationships become increasingly predictable, a desire for novelty, for excitement and unpredictability, easily surfaces (Tsapelas et al., 2009). Thus, you are faced with the **predictability-novelty dialectic**—a desire for both stability and change in interpersonal relationships.

The early phases of relationships—initiating, experimenting, intensifying—are inherently novel. Everything seems new and different, and that can be exciting. Interacting with a new college roommate can be an interesting and challenging enterprise. Dating someone for the first time can be exciting because both individuals are exploring and discovering. At some point, however, dating partners may wish to settle into a long-lasting partnership to provide some predictability because of the comfort and stability it produces.

The predictability-novelty dialectic is particularly challenging for long-distance relationships (Sahlstein, 2006). According to the Center for the Study of Long Distance Relationships, there are almost 4 million married people living apart for reasons other than marital discord (de la Vina, 2008) and more individuals trying long-distance relationships who are unmarried. There is built-in unpredictability in relationships in which infrequent face-to-face interactions can occur ("When can I see you again?"). Even making plans that appear to provide predictability may be disrupted more often in long-distance relationships than in more proximate relationships. The complexity involved in planning when two people are not physically present, and distance acts as a barrier to smooth organization, can be daunting.

Openness-Closedness: Tell Me More/Tell Me Less

U.S. culture encourages openness and discourages closedness (Klapp, 1978). We view an open mind and an open society with admiration. We usually view a closed mind and a closed society with disdain. Open expression of feelings and self-disclosure are necessary for bonding and intimacy to occur in a relationship. Some privacy, however, is also necessary if a relationship is to survive. Sharing every thought that enters your head, aside from being annoying, can provoke embarrassment, hurt, or conflict. This tension between accessibility and privacy is called the **openness-closedness dialectic**.

The openness-closedness dialectic is an important dilemma that every relationship faces, especially romantic partnerships (Baxter & Erbert, 1999). How much self-disclosure and openness is enough, and how much is too much (see Box 9-1)? Indiscriminate self-disclosure strains most relationships and is incompetent communication (see Chapter 2). Openness is a matter of appropriateness of context. Excessive closedness, however, makes you a silent partner. Friendship and intimacy

Life in the same old routine can make a relationships overly predictable and boring, creating friction and a need for greater novelty to prevent potential relationship conflict ("We never do anything fun!"). Relationships need some excitement!

don't flourish when you share little with another person about who you are.

The three relational dialectics discussed—connection-autonomy, predictability-novelty, and openness-closedness—typically emerge as more intense and challenging at different phases of a personal relationship (Baxter, 1990). During the initial phases of a developing relationship, openness-closedness is of paramount concern. How much should you self-disclose to your friend or romantic partner? Is your self-disclosure reciprocated? As a relationship becomes more established, however, connection-autonomy often predominates. Are you losing your identity and independence? Are you becoming distant from each other, burdened by the daily concerns of work and earning a living? Are you both still strongly committed to the relationship? Finally, as a relationship settles in for the long term, predictability-novelty often becomes a primary concern. Has the relationship become tediously predictable and boring? One study showed that significant boredom in year 7 of a marriage predicts significant dissatisfaction with the relationship in year 16 (Tsapelas et al., 2009).

Dialectics with Outsiders: Us and Them

Dialectics occur not only within relationships but also with outsiders. Anyone who is not directly involved in a specific relationship is considered an outsider. In a parent-child relationship, for instance, everyone who is neither the parent nor the child is an outsider. In a marriage, anyone outside the marriage is an outsider, even a parent of either one of the spouses. Three common dialectics with outsiders are inclusion-seclusion, conventionality-uniqueness, and revelation-concealment (Baxter & Montgomery, 1996).

Inclusion-Seclusion: Be Together/Be Alone

In a relationship with another person, you may be pulled in two directions when outsiders enter the picture. You may want your partner to spend time with outsiders (inclusion), yet you may also want time alone together to nurture your relationship (seclusion). This is called the **inclusion-seclusion dialectic**. Including

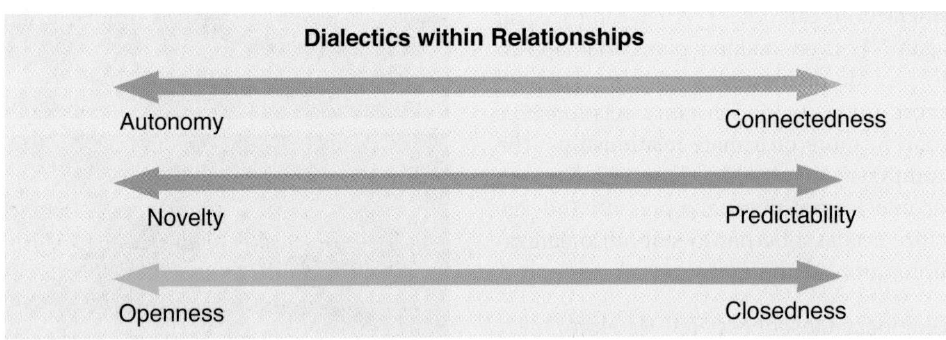

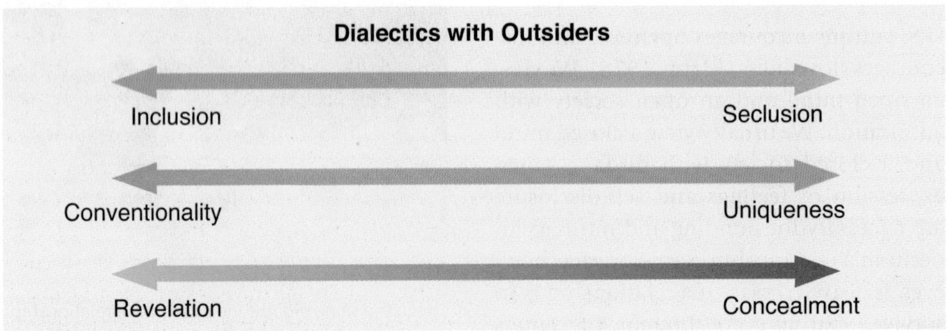

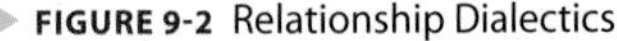
FIGURE 9-2 Relationship Dialectics

a larger network of friends and family can provide emotional support and encouragement that bolster the relationship. Too much involvement of outsiders, however, can provide few moments for relationship partners to connect. Thus, you may be torn between larger "family responsibilities," such as spending holidays together, and a desire to be alone with your partner without stress from outsiders.

Conventionality-Uniqueness: Conform/ Don't Conform

When we have relationships with others, we usually want to "fit in" and conform to certain family and societal expectations. Such conventionality just makes life less difficult generally. We're not bumping against how others believe we should act. Yet, by conforming to familial and societal expectations, our relationships may begin to look like everyone else's. Considering the high divorce and breakup rates for most relationships, this can be unsettling. If your relationship is "unique," perhaps you have a better chance of sustaining it over the long haul. When we are torn between wanting our relationships to be the same yet different, we are experiencing the **conventionality-uniqueness dialectic**.

Consider marriage, for example. The conventional institution of marriage has not lost its appeal. Very few adults will live out their entire lives never having been married. About three-quarters of divorced parents remarry (Gottman, 1994). Cohabiting couples are still relatively unconventional. A significant portion of cohabiting couples will eventually get married. Among gays, 85% view legal marriage as "very" or "somewhat important" (Leland & Miller, 1998). At the same time, couples typically want outsiders to view their relationship as unique. Talk of a "soul mate" expresses a desire to have a special relationship with an "irreplaceable" person.

Revelation-Concealment: Go Public/Be Private

Both romantic relationships and friendships face this dilemma: how much do we reveal to outsiders about the relationship and how much do we keep private? This is the **revelation-concealment dialectic**. Revealing too much breaks the confidentiality that intimacy requires, but revealing too little denies the couple an important source of support and legitimation.

The revelation-concealment dialectic is a key dilemma present in office romances. A survey by Vault.com, a career information website, found that 59% of respondents admitted being involved in an office romance at some time ("2011 Office Romance," 2011). Almost a quarter of office romances end in marriage (Fisher, 2007). Despite their frequency, and contrary to most couples' desire to announce their romance to friends and coworkers, office romances are often concealed. Couples fear coworkers' strong disapproval, or they fear being fired (Eng, 1999).

Battered women are faced with the revelation-concealment dialectic. Most abused women wrestle with the impulse to conceal their abuse because they fear triggering further violence from a partner angry that others know what occurs. They also want to avoid public embarrassment and perceived shame from the revelation that abuse occurs. Public revelation, however, can be a first step in escaping an abusive relationship (Dieckmann, 2000).

Addressing Dialectics: Not a Balancing Act

It may be tempting to assume that the most effective means of addressing dialectics in relationships is to achieve a balance between the contradictory needs that produce tension. *There is no balancing of these contradictory impulses, however, because they are always in flux* (Littlejohn & Foss, 2008). As one theorist puts it, dialectics are always the "unfinished business" of relationships (Duck, 1990). This is so because change is the inevitable constant in all relationships. What was important to us yesterday may be relatively unimportant today. Our moods and circumstances change, so we must constantly adapt to the seesaw of dialectical tensions. There is no ultimate resolution of these dialectics, no single balancing point

BOX 9.1 Focus on Controversy

ETHICAL CONUNDRUM: IS HONESTY ALWAYS THE BEST POLICY?

You are gay. You are celebrating Christmas with your parents and siblings, and you want to bring your partner to the festivities. Your father is intensely homophobic. Do you pretend that your partner is just a friend, or do you reveal the true nature of your relationship (revelation-concealment)?

Your spouse asks you whether you've ever had an affair. You have, but it ended two years ago. There is little chance that the affair would ever be discovered unless you confess. Your spouse would be devastated to know that you had cheated, even though you have no intention of ever being unfaithful again. It was a "horrible mistake," a moment of "temporary insanity" fueled by mass quantities of alcohol. Would you be honest with your spouse (openness-closedness)?

Your close friend at work has a body-image concern. Your friend asks whether you think she or he is fat and unattractive. Your friend is very overweight and poorly groomed. Would you tell the truth (openness-closedness), or would you make an excuse, then run like a cheetah?

You feel smothered by your partner. You have little time alone. When you plan outings with friends, your partner wants to come along. Do you tell your partner that you need time alone or with friends, knowing that your partner will feel excluded (connection-autonomy)?

Dialectical forces pose a challenge to the oft-stated claim that honesty is always the best policy in relationships. The issue of lying brings into focus a principal dilemma we all face in relationships. Honesty is an important ethical guideline and the cornerstone of trust, but relationship dialectics complicate the glib, chirpy advice to "just be honest."

Lying is widespread in the United States. One study found that undergraduates lied in one of every three interactions they had with others (DePaulo et al., 1996). Nonstudent participants lied in one of every five interactions. Another study found that 60% of college students lied at least once during a 10-minute conversation (Feldman et al., 2002). On average, three lies were told during this short conversation. Lying is common in job interviews. Applicants want to look good, and they are prone to lie to create a favorable impression, especially the more unqualified they are for the job (Weiss & Feldman, 2006). Deceit is also common in Internet chat room conversations and in online dating (Epstein, 2007; Wood & Smith, 2001).

Lying is pervasive, but even outright lies rarely are told to cause psychological damage to another ("so he'd look like a fool"). Fewer than 1% of lies told by college students and slightly more than 2% of lies told by nonstudent adults are of this damaging variety (DePaulo & Kasby, 1998). Most of our fabrications are minor fibs, or "white lies," not whoppers. About a third of our lies are told to spare the feelings of another person (DePaulo et al., 1996).

Complete honesty can sound very good in the abstract, but total honesty has the potential to destroy relationships. Most people recognize that lying in some circumstances is justified (Gamer, 2009; Knapp, 2006). As psychologist Bella DePaulo explains, "It would be a disaster if everyone tried to tell the truth all the time. If you tell the whole truth, you start alienating people. You'd have to go back and apologize because you've made a mess of your interpersonal relationships" (quoted in "Lying Is Part," 1996).

We teach children to look pleased by a birthday gift, even when the gift is a dud, so the gift giver's feelings aren't hurt. We lie about Santa Claus and the Easter Bunny to give pleasure to our children. Lying is pervasive but not because honesty is no longer valued. In fact, when asked to choose among telling a hurtful truth, telling a face-saving lie, or equivocating, only 6% chose ly-

(continued)

BOX 9.1 *(Continued)*

ing, about 4% chose the truth, and more than 90% opted for equivocation (Robinson et al., 1998). **Equivocation** occurs when our language permits more than one plausible meaning. For example, when asked, "Do you like the dinner?" you might respond, "It is most unusual." The questioner can interpret the answer as either approval or disapproval. Equivocation spares the feelings of the questioner and avoids the brutal truth that dinner is headed for the dog dish at the first opportunity. Equivocation can also allow others to draw their own conclusions without you having to be pinned down. For example, an ambiguous job reference for an incompetent worker might be: "You will be lucky to get this person to work for you." One for an applicant with no talent could be: "I recommend this candidate with no qualifications" (cited in Adler &Proctor, 2007, p. 321).

So, when is it appropriate to tell the truth, and when is lying acceptable?

1. *Honesty should be the norm, and lying should be the exception.* Communication with others would be chaotic if we could never trust what others say to us. Relationships must have a foundation of honesty even if an occasional lie for selfless reasons seems warranted.
2. *Try to determine what the questioner is seeking.* This requires sensitivity—picking up signals from the person. If it is clear that the person is seeking support and encouragement, not absolute honesty, then a small lie may be appropriate.
3. *Weigh the likely consequences of an honest response versus a lie.* Lying to a friend or spouse about his or her weight may encourage the person to continue an unhealthy lifestyle. An honest response may sting initially, but it may also motivate change.

Bok (1978) summarizes the issue this way: "To say that white lies should be kept at a minimum is not to endorse the telling of truths to all comers. Silence and discretion, respect for the privacy and for the feelings of others must naturally govern what is spoken" (p. 76). *Honesty isn't always the best policy, but it usually is.*

QUESTIONS FOR THOUGHT

1. How would you have answered the questions posed in the situations described at the beginning of this box? Explain your answers.
2. Do you agree that honesty is usually the best policy? Why or why not?
3. What would occur in your own relationships if dishonesty were the norm?

to maintain, because when that imagined "ideal balance" allegedly occurs, it soon changes and we must adjust. "Dialectical thinking is not directed toward a search for the 'happy mediums' of compromise and balance, but instead focuses on the messier, less logical, and more inconsistent unfolding practices of the moment" (Baxter & Montgomery, 1996, p. 46). This means strategies for effectively addressing dialectics must be dynamic, not static.

Some dialectics also seem to play a more important role in relationships than others. One study found that for young married couples, connection-autonomy was the biggest source of tension, predictability-novelty was second, and inclusion-seclusion was third (Pawlowski, 1998). For romantic couples generally, connection-autonomy and openness-closedness appear to be the most significant to address (Baxter & Erbert, 1999; Erbert, 2000).

Amalgamating Dialectics: Addressing Both Needs

Relationships need openness *and* closedness, connection *and* autonomy, predictability *and* novelty. Addressing both impulses is usually preferable to addressing one need at the expense of the other (Baxter & Montgomery, 1996). This **amalgamating** of dialectics, in which both contradictory forces are addressed without compromising on either impulse, can be a highly effective approach to dialectics (Miller, 2005). Relationships can provide an abundance of novelty (exciting new events) and plenty of predictability as well. Both needs can be satiated without compromising or diluting either contradictory need by leaving room to satisfy both. Taking frequent vacations to locations never visited before or carefully planning a variety of exciting, new events amalgamates the novelty of new experiences and the predictability of careful planning. Novelty can thwart relationship boredom (Tsapelas et al., 2009), but as most people recognize, it is also enjoyable to return to the fond predictability of home and hearth, relaxing with your partner.

Selecting: Choosing One Need Only

Giving attention to one contradictory impulse while ignoring the other is called **selecting** (Wood, 2004). It is a weak method for managing relational dialectics because attention to only one of the two contradictory forces inevitably creates a stronger impulse from the other direction (Baxter, 1990). Spending "quality time" together on a rare pleasurable vacation, for example, may not satisfy the partners' need to connect on a more regular basis. The residual "glow" from a wonderful vacation may not sustain a relationship for 11 months until the next booster shot of connection is administered.

Segmenting: Categorizing

When partners divide certain parts of their relationship into domains, or categories, they are **segmenting** (West & Turner, 2007). In dealing with the openness-closedness dialectic, for instance, partners may designate certain subjects as "off limits" for sharing with each other to reduce the possibility of hurting each other's feelings or provoking jealousy. They also may express closeness at home but more distance at work or in public. Previous boyfriends or girlfriends may be segmented as a taboo topic. How each partner spends money from a personal bank account may also be categorized as off limits. Couples might set aside certain holidays to visit parents and relatives (inclusion) but keep certain special occasions, such as birthdays or New Year's, just for themselves (seclusion). Couples might also agree that career and work-related matters fall under the category of autonomy (each person decides independently) but relationship issues and social situations fall under the connected category. Segmenting is usually an effective means of managing relational dialectics (Baxter & Montgomery, 1996).

Communication Styles of Conflict Management

Despite conventional wisdom, research indicates that marital happiness has less to do with whom you marry and more to do with how you both manage conflict (Notarius & Markman, 1993). There is a cognitive element, a thought process, in conflict management. Attributions (see Chapter 2) for negative events that occur in relationships can promote either constructive or destructive conflict. If a negative event occurs, such as one partner showing up late for dinner, a conflict-promoting attribution would be "He is so self-absorbed that he can't even call me to tell me he'll be late." A conflict-diminishing attribution for the same negative event would be "He's been working so hard that he probably just forgot that I'd scheduled dinner earlier than usual." The first attribution assigns a dispositional (character) cause to the behavior, and the second attribution assigns a situational cause. Conflict-promoting attributions produce less effective conflict management and less satisfying relationships overall than do conflict-diminishing attributions (Bradbury & Fincham, 1992; Fletcher & Fincham, 1991).

The role attributions play in impeding effective conflict management is important. Conflict management, however, is essentially a communication process. We can't be mind readers. Our attributions will not promote conflict if they remain thoughts that aren't communicated to our partners either verbally or nonverbally. It is therefore critical that we explore research on communication styles of conflict management.

A **communication style of conflict management** is a typical way a person addresses conflict (DeChurch et al., 2007). There are five communication styles: collaborating, accommodating, compromising, avoiding, and competing (Blake & Mouton, 1964; Kilmann & Thomas, 1977). Styles are contextual (Wilmot & Hocker, 2011). At work, your style may be competing, but with your spouse or romantic partner, your style may change to avoiding conflict.

Collaborating: Looking for Win-Win Solutions

The collaborating style means working together to maximize the attainment of goals for all parties in a conflict. This is a cooperative style of conflict management. The collaborating style has three key components: confrontation, integration, and smoothing.

Confrontation: Addressing the Problem

Confrontation is the overt recognition of conflict and the direct effort to manage disagreements effectively. Confrontation brings the conflict out into the open for careful examination and discussion. Although mass media often use the term *confrontation* in a negative sense (e.g., "There was a violent confrontation between police and protesters"), this is not the meaning that applies here. Confrontation should utilize all the elements of supportive communication already discussed in Chapter 8 (describe, problem solve, empathize, be assertive, treat others as equals, and qualify your statements). In fact, the initial effort to address a conflict is usually crucial to the subsequent pattern of the entire conversation. *Gottman (1994) found that in only 4% of the instances he examined did couples reverse a negative beginning to a conflict conversation (attack, demand, criticism, contempt)*. Furthermore, research by Gottman revealed that he could predict the outcome of a 15-minute conversation within the first 3 minutes with 96% accuracy (Gottman & Gottman, 2006). It's probably all downhill after an opening such as, "What could you possibly have been thinking?" or "Is it laziness or just plain stupidity that makes you so insensitive?"

Someone once quipped that, for men, the most terrifying statement in the English language is, "Let's talk about our relationship." *In more than 80% of the instances of confrontation, women raise the issue, not men* (Gottman & Silver, 1999). This gender difference undoubtedly arises from men's greater difficulty handling conflict and women's greater difficulty tolerating emotional distance in a relationship (Notarius & Markman, 1993). This gender difference in itself is not necessarily a sign of a troubled relationship because how men respond to the confrontation, not who initiates it, is a more important concern.

Integration: Finding Mutually Satisfactory Solutions

Integration is a collaborative strategy that meets the goals of all parties in the conflict. Two integrative tactics are expanding the pie and bridging (Pruitt & Rubin, 1986).

Expanding the pie refers to finding creative ways to increase resources, typically, money. Scarce resources often cause conflict (power struggles). As Michael Sion (2011), author of *Money and Marriage*, notes, money isn't what couples fight about most, but intense conflict over finances is a leading source of turning "'Til death do us part" into "'Til debt do us part" (p. A11). School districts across the nation have found creative ways to increase their usually inadequate budgets, saving teachers' jobs and minimizing the inevitable conflict that results from layoffs, while helping to maintain educational quality. Some districts have established private foundations that solicit funds from private donors. One district foundation in California purchased a vacant school site, developed it, and sold it for a $4 million profit.

Bridging considers the goals of all parties in the conflict and offers a new option that satisfies the interests of everyone involved. For example, consider partners who want to take a vacation together, but one wants the full resort experience (goal: comfort) and the other wants to camp and commune with nature (goal: get away from stressful urban life and a demanding job). Initially, this may appear to be mutually exclusive. Taking their vacation at a resort with nearby camping facilities, however, may bridge the supposed gap in partners' vacation goals. The couple could then share certain mutually interesting activities such as hiking, fishing, swimming in the pool, taking a sauna, and eating at the resort restaurant, but each also has the opportunity to either camp or be pampered in a comfortable room. This may not satisfy every couple with a similar problem, but it can't hurt to explore this potential solution.

Smoothing: Calming the Storm

Smoothing is the act of calming the agitated feelings of others during a conflict episode. When tempers flair and anger turns to screaming or shedding tears, no collaborating is possible. You want to postpone problem solving until you've addressed inflamed emotions (Gottman & Gottman, 2006).

Smoothing addresses the emotional side of conflict. It can make integrative solutions possible by defusing emotionally volatile situations. Gottman calls smoothing *repair attempts* (Gottman & Gottman, 2006). You might call it self-preservation. The ultimate repair attempt is probably saying "I'm sorry" and meaning it when an apology is deserved. These are also useful: "Can I take that back?" "How can I make things better?" "I see your point." "Let's start over." "I understand." "I didn't say that out loud did I?" Using humor, especially self-deprecation, is also an effective smoothing technique (Gottman et al., 1998).

Accommodating: Yielding to Others

When we yield to the needs and desires of others during a conflict, we are using the **accommodating style**. Less powerful individuals such as employees are expected to accommodate more often and to a greater degree than more powerful individuals such as bosses (Lulofs, 1994).

Regardless of relative power, when you are clearly wrong about an issue or point of contention, it makes sense to yield on it. This yielding demonstrates reasonableness and enhances your relationship with the other person. It shows commitment to the relationship (Wieselquist et al., 1999). Yielding also makes sense if the issue is more important to the other person. This flexibility is an aspect of constructive conflict management. The roles may be reversed in the future, and it may be appropriate for the other party to yield. Accommodating by others is more likely when there is a history of mutual flexibility.

Accommodating can be an appropriate style of conflict management in some contexts (DeChurch et al., 2007). A less powerful person may need to adjust to a more powerful person to keep a job, maintain a relationship, or avoid nasty consequences. Yielding can sometimes maintain harmony in a relationship. Demonstrating a willingness to sacrifice personal benefit to cement a relationship, but not to avoid disagreements, can strengthen the bonds between partners (Impett et al., 2005). This is an especially important consideration in collectivist cultures that typically emphasize harmonious relationships (Ting-Toomey et al., 2000). Nevertheless, being too accommodating, making too many sacrifices, particularly when the sacrifices become lopsided toward your partner, can make you someone's lackey.

Compromising: Halving the Loaf

When we give up something to get something, we are **compromising**. The compromising style of conflict management occurs most often between parties of relatively equal power. More powerful individuals do not usually consider compromising necessary. They can dominate, and they do.

Compromising emphasizes workable, but not optimal, decisions and solutions.

Some have referred to compromising as a lose-lose style of conflict management because trade-offs and exchanges are required to reach agreement. Despite the limitations and disadvantages of compromising, it may be the only feasible goal in some situations. Half a loaf is better than starvation, so goes the thinking. Compromising can be a useful strategy when an integrative decision is not feasible, when issues are not critical, when essential values are not undermined, and when such a settlement is to last only until a better solution can be found and negotiated.

Avoiding: Ignoring Conflict

When we sidestep or turn our back on conflict, we are **avoiding**. The avoiding style is exhibited in many ways (Wilmot & Hocker, 2011). We avoid conflict when we ignore it or deny it exists, even though it does. When we shift topics so we don't have to address a conflict, we avoid. We may crack jokes to deflect a focus on disagreeable issues. We may quibble about the meaning of a word used by another who is probing uncomfortably about a subject of some dispute, or we may simply not respond to a question (turning-away response). One study revealed the interesting finding that students have become so accustomed to communicating online and in text messages that they often avoid direct face-to-face communication to address conflicts. They'll complain to others but not directly to roommates who are causing them distress and provoking their anger. Research reveals that some students text message their roommate about a conflict even though the roommate is sitting a few feet away (Warters, 2005). They confront, but they avoid turning and talking to their roommate face to face.

Stonewalling is an especially troublesome form of avoiding. **Stonewalling** occurs when one partner refuses to discuss problems or physically leaves when the other partner is complaining, disagreeing, or attacking. It is "like talking to a stone wall" (Gottman & Gottman, 2006, p. 5). Stonewallers often justify their withdrawal from conflict by claiming that they are merely trying to remain under control and not make the contentiousness worse by responding. Stonewalling can be extremely frustrating to those faced with the withdrawal. It can also communicate disapproval, conceit, self-righteousness, and cold indifference—a defensive communication pattern.

Earlier it was noted that women far more than men confront issues in relationships that trigger conflict. Men, conversely, are far more prone than women to avoid such issues and to withdraw (Canary et al., 1995). *About 85% of the stonewalling in relationship conflicts comes from men* (Gottman & Silver, 1999). Men are more likely to stonewall because they experience flooding more easily than women, and they may hope to prevent it by clamming up or retreating (Gottman & Carrere, 1994). Avoiding is more apt to be dissatisfying for women than men, and the more partners are dissatisfied with their relationship, the more likely they are to avoid conflicts (Afifi et al., 2009).

Avoiding is not always an inappropriate and ineffective style of conflict management. We can avoid trivial issues without damaging our relationships. Avoiding "hot button" issues that trigger intense disagreements and may not be resolvable can be appropriate. Reminding a partner of an affair confronted long ago, for instance, dredges up anger and hurt feelings with no constructive outcome likely. Older couples tend to avoid escalating conflicts much more than younger couples, who tend to approach conflicts more aggressively. Consequently, "Older adults typically report better marriages, more supportive friendships, less conflict with children and siblings, and closer ties with social-network members than do younger adults" (Fingerman & Charles, 2010, p. 172).

Competing: Power-Forcing

When we approach conflict as a win-lose contest, we are competing. The **competing style** is exhibited in a variety of ways that are likely to produce defensiveness: threats, criticism, contempt, hostile remarks and jokes, sarcasm, ridicule, intimidation, fault

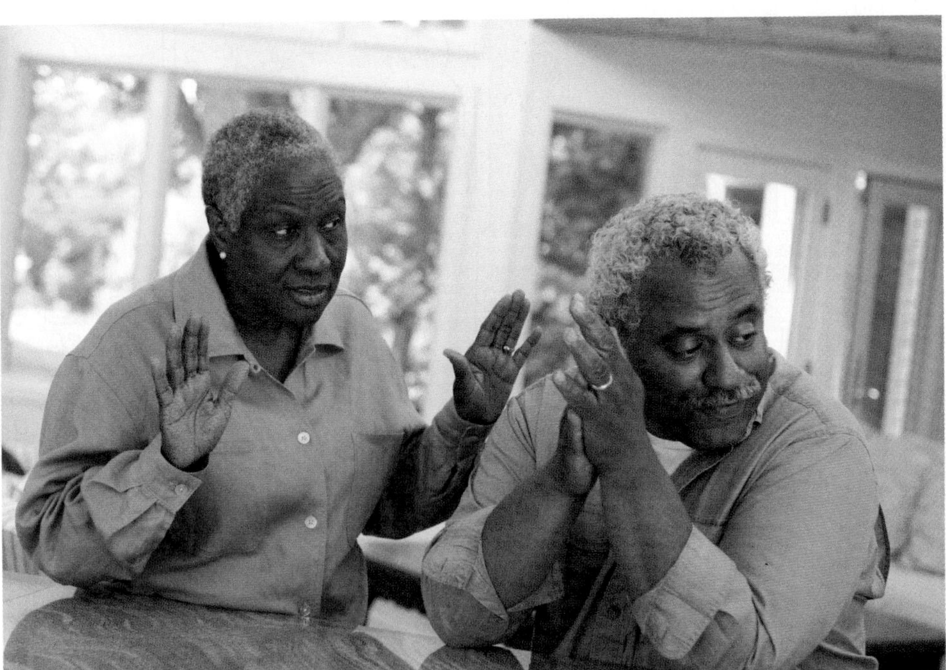

Men stonewall far more than women. Notice the differences in nonverbal communication between the man and the woman.

Power-forcing is sometimes an unavoidable conflict-management style, but it should be a last resort, used only when other styles have proved ineffective or can't be used because of an emergency.

finding and blaming, and denials of responsibility (Wilmot & Hocker, 2011). The competing style is aggressive, not assertive. It is not confrontation as previously defined; it is an attack. The chief flaw of the competing style is that the focus is on victory for oneself, not on a mutually satisfactory solution for all parties involved. This is particularly evident in celebrity divorce disputes.

Managing Conflict Competently

This section addresses how to transact conflict competently. Topics include appropriate and effective use of communication styles of conflict management, anger management, communicating forgiveness, workplace bullying, and the communication challenges presented when cultures clash.

Styles in Action: Smooth Sailing to White-Water Rafting

In my small-group communication classes, at least one group every semester approaches me about problems with a group member. Typically, the group member is unreliable, fails to show for group meetings, and hasn't shared the group workload on class projects. Consistently, their first question to me is, "Can we kick Josh [or Jamie, Janine, or whomever] out of the group?" When I ask if they have confronted this person and expressed the group's concerns and feelings, virtually every time they admit that they have yet to confront their slacker. They avoid the problem because it makes them uncomfortable to confront, but when the problem keeps getting worse, they choose power-forcing. This is not surprising in a hypercompetitive society.

The five communication styles of conflict management have been explained, as well as the types of situations in which each is likely to be appropriate and in what contexts the reverse is likely. In general, however, how do these five styles rank in terms of overall probability of effectiveness in conflict situations? Research shows clearly that the collaborating style has the greatest likelihood of managing conflicts effectively (DeChurch et al., 2007; Holman & Jarvis, 2003; Johnson & Johnson, 2000; Kuhn & Poole, 2000). For example, field research on a program called Peacemakers involving students from kindergarten to ninth grade supports the efficacy of the collaborative method of conflict management. An analysis of 17 studies on the Peacemaker program found that students trained in the collaborative method that specialized in finding integrative solutions to conflicts almost always used the method in actual conflict incidents. As a result, student conflicts referred to teachers for resolution decreased by 80%, and referrals to the principal dropped to *zero*. Student conflicts became less severe and destructive. Students untrained in the collaborative method *never* used integrative negotiations, and the results were negative (Johnson & Johnson, 2000).

Satisfaction in romantic relationships is positively associated with the use of integration to manage conflict episodes (Canary & Cupach, 1988; Canary & Spitzberg, 1989). The same is true in the workplace. The number of disputes at Toyota's U.S. subsidiary, for instance, fell from 178 in 1985 to 3 in 1992 when the company instituted a problem-solving (collaborative) method for dispute resolution (Carver & Vondra, 1994). "Integrative solutions are almost always the most desirable. They tend to last longer and to contribute more to the relationship between parties and the welfare of the broader community than do compromises and agreements about how to choose the winner" (Fry & Fry, 1997, p. 12).

Yielding is a mixed style of conflict management (Impett et al., 2005). When you sacrifice your own needs out of genuine concern for your partner's well-being, this can be constructive. When you sacrifice your needs to prevent further conflict, however, the results are typically unhappiness, increasing resentment, and a weakened relationship (Neff & Harter, 2002).

The compromising style has already been dubbed a lose-lose style because you begin with an expectation of achieving only part of what you hope to achieve. A principal drawback of compromising occurs when you start with an expectation that no better than partial success can be accomplished, instead of first seeking a collaborative approach that may produce an integrative solution to a conflict. You may end up compromising because an integrative solution is not always possible, but why start with compromising as the end goal?

The avoiding style increases the frequency of marital disagreements because unresolved issues keep re-emerging (Cramer, 2002; Gottman & Gottman, 2006; McGonagle et al., 1993). Managers who avoid critiquing employees' poor work performance typically become increasingly annoyed by the continued bad performance. When the annoyance rises to extremely high levels, they give feedback that is usually biting, sarcastic, harsh, threatening, and personal (Baron, 1988). This merely intensifies the anger of both parties. Similar patterns are likely to result when roommate disputes are avoided. The avoiding style is only slightly better than the competing style (Canary & Spitzberg, 1987; Holman & Jarvis, 2003).

The competing style is the least effective because of the disadvantages of competition and the drawbacks of the dominance form of power previously discussed in Chapters 1 and 7 (DeChurch et al., 2007; Kuhn & Poole, 2000; Van de Vliert et al., 1995). "Competitive strategies fail to address the long-term, underlying needs of relationships, organizations, or communities" (Isenhart & Spangle, 2000, p. 23). One study by Markman (cited in Edwards, 1995) of 135 married couples, 21 of whom later divorced, showed that escalating conflicts into ugly verbal battles (competing) and refusing to face conflicts directly (avoiding) *predicted divorce in almost every instance.*

Collaborating depends on dialogue. Dialogue is central to the management of conflict provoked by dialectics in relationships (Baxter & Montgomery, 1996). Competing and avoiding both stifle dialogue. Competing sets up a power relationship that discourages dialogue. If you can force your point of view on others, you don't have to engage in dialogue. You can demand compliance. Those with less power also have little motivation to engage in dialogue. Expressing dissenting viewpoints might invite retaliation from the more powerful individual. Avoiding dialogue and controversial viewpoints becomes an act of self-protection in a competitive, power-imbalanced situation.

Despite the clear advantages of the collaborating over the competing style, research shows that *typically we use the least effective and most inappropriate style when trying to manage conflict* (Johnson & Johnson, 2000). The "I'm going to kick your butt" power-forcing style of conflict management is modeled everywhere—in movies, television dramas, sitcoms, video games, even advertisements for consumer products. Can you find any examples in "reality" television programs when conflict is handled in a productive way? Mostly, we see profanely abusive individuals "acting stupid" by viciously attacking each other.

One study showed that only 5% of supervisors, middle managers, top managers, and administrators used the collaborating style in specific conflict situations. Instead, 41% of this same group selected competing, and 26% chose avoiding. This was true of both male and female supervisors and managers (Gayle, 1991). Another study found that managers often avoid giving negative feedback to employees because they are reluctant to stir up a conflict (Larson, 1989). A third study reported that students use avoiding in more than half of their conflicts (Sillars et al., 1982; see also Warters, 2005). Additional studies report that avoidance is a chief style used by nurses when faced with abuse from doctors (Johnson, 2009; Maxfield et al., 2005). One of these studies showed that fewer than 7% of nurses confronted abusive doctors (Maxfield et al., 2005). The consequences not only to nurses but to patients under their care are serious. "The Silence Kills study found countless examples of caregivers who delayed action, withheld feedback or went along with erroneous diagnoses rather than face potential abuse from a colleague" (Grenny, 2009).

A key to appropriate and effective use of conflict-management styles is more than which style was chosen. For example, despite the clear advantages of collaborating, some conflicts are too trivial to warrant confrontation. Incessant confrontation can also become annoying and counterproductive. "Can't you just let some things slide?" will be the likely response to excessive use of confrontation.

Timing is also important. Sometimes the timing is wrong. Individuals may wake up irritable or arrive home from work exhausted. Confrontation is best attempted at a time when people are able to work constructively on problems. When couples aren't stressed by time pressure, they can exercise more effortful processing and make more appropriate and effective responses (Yovetich & Rusbult, 1994). Substance abuse also escalates conflicts into hypercompetitive episodes with potentially destructive consequences. Wait to address difficult conflict issues until no drugs and alcohol are involved (MacDonald et al., 2000).

Timing is also relevant concerning when to employ any of the five conflict-management styles. If you begin by using a competing style, the likely result will be anger, hostility, and retaliation. Realizing that the competing style isn't working well, you may decide to try the collaborating style. Good luck! Once you have competed, it is much more difficult to cooperate. Suspicion and mistrust will permeate your transactions. It is far better to begin with the collaborating style. If collaborating does not work, you may want to use other styles to manage the conflict. If the issue is not very important, accommodating or avoiding might work.

You could use compromising as an interim style until you find a more integrative solution. Ultimately, you may have to use the competing style.

The students in my small-group communication course must first confront group members who are not producing and try to resolve the conflict cooperatively. If these efforts are unsuccessful, I do allow the students to inform their slacker that he or she will be booted out of the group unless these behaviors change. *Competing is the style of last resort, but you may have to use it when all other styles fail or are inappropriate.* Employees who are frequently tardy or absent, do not complete required work on time, and manifest a negative attitude may have to be fired if no other style changes their behavior. Divorce is often a power-forcing style, especially when one partner wants out of the relationship and the other does not. Divorce may be the last-resort solution to years of bitter conflict. It isn't pretty, but it may be necessary in some circumstances.

"Just another of our many disagreements. He wants a no-fault divorce, whereas I would prefer to have the bastard crucified."

This cartoon illustrates which of the following communication styles of conflict management?

1. Avoiding
2. Compromise
3. Collaborating
4. Competing

Answers at end of chapter

Transforming Competing into Collaborating: Cooperation Revisited

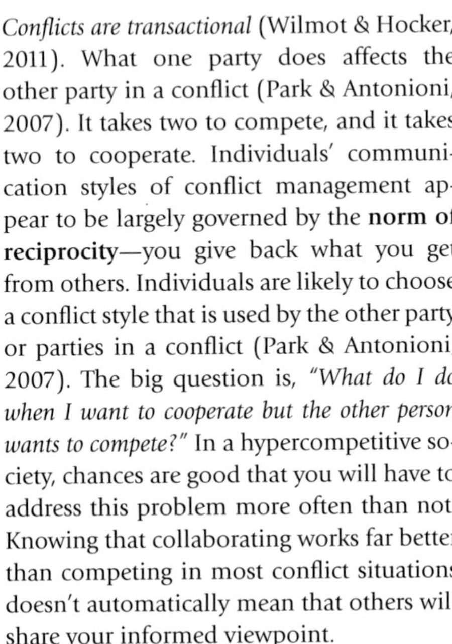

Conflicts are transactional (Wilmot & Hocker, 2011). What one party does affects the other party in a conflict (Park & Antonioni, 2007). It takes two to compete, and it takes two to cooperate. Individuals' communication styles of conflict management appear to be largely governed by the **norm of reciprocity**—you give back what you get from others. Individuals are likely to choose a conflict style that is used by the other party or parties in a conflict (Park & Antonioni, 2007). The big question is, *"What do I do when I want to cooperate but the other person wants to compete?"* In a hypercompetitive society, chances are good that you will have to address this problem more often than not. Knowing that collaborating works far better than competing in most conflict situations doesn't automatically mean that others will share your informed viewpoint.

Here are some suggestions for how you might transform a competitor into a collaborator.

1. *Always be "unconditionally constructive"* (Fisher & Brown, 1988). Refuse to be abused, but also refuse to be abusive. Break the norm of reciprocity when it encourages hypercompetitiveness. Don't return contempt with contempt, intimidation with intimidation. If others become abusive, remain civil. If they confuse issues to hide their weak position, clarify. If they try to intimidate you, don't bully back. Attempt to persuade them of the merits of your viewpoint. If they lie, neither trust nor deceive them. Remain vigilantly trustworthy at all times. If they don't actively listen to you, encourage them to listen carefully. Always listen actively and empathically to them. Meet defensive communication with supportive communication. This is not a guide to sainthood, although you probably deserve some small award for remaining composed when dealing with certain individuals. Remaining unconditionally constructive serves

your own interests. As Fisher and Brown (1988) explain, "If you are acting in ways that injure your own competence, there is no reason for me to do the same. Two heads are better than one, but one is better than none" (p. 202).

2. *Ask problem-solving questions* (Ury, 1993). Your goal is to move the other party from a power-forcing, controlling communication pattern to a problem-solving, collaborative pattern. One way to do this is to engage the other person in joint problem solving (encouraging a cooperative norm of reciprocity). Encourage joint effort to find an integrative solution. Ask "Why?" "Why not?" and "What if?" questions. "Why is it a problem for you that I don't talk much when I come home from work?" "Why not do it as I suggested? Can you see some problems?" "What if you let me do extra credit? What would happen?" You should not ask these questions, of course, as if you are cross-examining a terrorist on the witness stand.

3. *Confront the process* (Ury, 1993). Confronting the process can encourage collaborating. Don't attack; be assertive. Simply make an observation about the process. "Have you noticed that every time I try to explain my point of view, I am interrupted before I can finish my thought? Perhaps we can both agree to listen to each other without comment for one minute. What do you think?" If the other party gets nasty and belligerent, don't return fire. Address the process. "Do we really want to get nasty with each other? I don't see any good coming of it, do you?" This forces the other party to justify the nastiness, which is not an easy thing to do. Notice that the phrasing uses "we" to express inclusiveness. This removes the appearance of accusation. Sitting next to each other to discuss a family budget or credit card debt instead of across from each other also nonverbally shows inclusiveness, not exclusiveness.

4. *Ask for advice* (Ury, 1993). "What would you do if you were in my position?" This requires some empathy—taking the perspective of the other person. "What do you suggest we do to satisfy both of our needs?" Again, the focus is on mutually solving problems and moving away from power-forcing strategies. To paraphrase Ury (1993), you're trying to bring others to their senses, not bring them to their knees.

Remaining unconditionally constructive is the most crucial of these four suggestions. Don't try to learn all four steps at once. Concentrate on remaining unconditionally constructive first until it becomes second nature to you. Then gradually use and refine the other three suggestions, one at a time.

Styles and Partner Abuse: Addressing Aggression

Physical abuse is directly relevant to students because Straus (2001) studied university students in 31 countries (including the United States) and determined that, on average, 29% of the students admitted physically assaulting a dating partner in the previous 12-month period. The lowest rate for any university was 17%, and the highest was 45%.

The problem of partner abuse has been addressed at length in Chapter 7. The relationship between partner and date abuse and communication styles of conflict management, however, has not been discussed. *A person's style of handling conflict can be an important indicator of potential abuse early in a relationship.* The competing (power-forcing) style is the most common style used in abusive relationships (Sabourin, 1995). If a partner's chief style of resolving conflict is competing, you should take this as a warning sign of possible future abuse. In particular, controlling behaviors such as wanting to know whom you were with when you weren't with your partner, trying to specify which friends you should associate with, and attempting to dictate with whom you can socialize are troublesome power-forcing behaviors. Even if your partner presents these controlling behaviors as requests rather than demands at first, be concerned. Yielding to such requests or demands won't end disagreement, and it may feed the abuser's desire to control you.

Psychologically abusive communication such as contemptuous remarks, ridicule, and humiliating comments are dominance strategies aimed at keeping a partner "in line." Verbal threats of physical violence when resistance is offered, of course, are even more serious power-forcing behaviors. Verbal aggression often leads to physical aggression (Infante et al., 1992). Verbal aggression in relationships either precedes or accompanies physical violence in 99% of abuse cases (Straus & Sweet, 1992). Psychological abuse as an intimidating power-forcing conflict strategy is dangerous and cause for alarm.

Accommodating is normally an ineffective conflict style to use when signals of possible abuse first appear. Yielding to power-forcing demands may be necessary in the immediate situation if one's partner is showing signs of losing self-control. Nevertheless, accommodating the demands of a partner out of fear for one's safety places the potential abuser in charge of his or her partner's life.

Compromising usually doesn't satisfy a potential abuser. Abusers, especially outright batterers, want total control and obedience (Jacobson & Gottman, 1998). There should be no compromise on the goal of eradicating verbal and physical aggression. Do not try to defend or rationalize "a little bit of abuse."

Avoiding is the most common style used by women to deal with physical abuse from their partners, especially in cases of intimate terrorism, as previously discussed (Gelles & Straus, 1988). It reduces the frequency of physical violence in relationships by avoiding "hot buttons" that trigger violence in a partner. This style, however, is difficult to recommend except in the most dire situations, where avoiding might be a temporary expedient necessary for self-protection. As a long-term style, it is woefully deficient. It reinforces power imbalances and perpetuates intimate terrorism.

Confrontation is most effective for dealing with potential or actual abuse in relationships. As Gelles and Straus (1988) explain, "Delaying until the violence escalates is too late. A firm, emphatic, and rational approach appears to be the most effective personal strategy a woman can use to prevent future violence" (p. 159). They suggest *confronting the very first incident of even minor violence* and stating without equivocation that such behavior will not be tolerated and must never occur again.

In a study of college students, almost a third of college women admitted slapping their partners, and almost a fifth admitted slapping a partner in the face (Vitanza & Marshall, 1993). During my first year in college, I dated a woman who, when angry at me, would slap me in the face. The first time it happened, I avoided discussing it, mostly because I was embarrassed. When it happened a second time, months later, I still did not confront her. Finally, when it happened a third time, I confronted her. I described how it made me feel when she slapped me. I explained to her that when she slapped me my first reaction was to slap her back, but that might injure her physically. I further explained that I hated the feeling of wanting to strike her in retaliation. Finally, I said to her, "I cannot and will not hit you when you slap me, but you put me in an embarrassing and unfair position. You can hit me, but I can't hit back. What am I supposed to do?" She responded by saying that she had never considered her actions from my perspective. She promised never to slap me again, and during a long relationship, she never did. It is vital that even relatively minor acts of aggression be confronted before they escalate into tragic abuse. I should have confronted my partner sooner than I did.

If physical or psychological abuse continues after you confront it, you should seriously consider ending the relationship. Abuse that is excused, rationalized, or ignored almost always recurs and grows worse (Jacobson & Gottman, 1998). *The best way to handle abuse is assertively, directly, and unequivocally at the outset.* Partners can stop their abuse, but it is infinitely more difficult and more dangerous once it has become standard practice. If there is a threat of imminent serious injury from your partner, avoid, don't confront, and put distance between yourself and your abuser.

Overall, the evidence is clear. Cooperation has distinct advantages over competition. Collaborating instead of power-forcing has greater potential for the constructive management of conflict. Start with collaborating and be committed to making it work. With few exceptions (a parent demanding that a child stop hurting a younger sibling), only when all else has failed should competing, or power-forcing, be seriously considered.

Anger Management: Controlling the Beast Within

The issues that create conflict are virtually infinite in number. Conflict over serious issues or silly ones is a natural part of marriages and all close relationships. Anger is a frequent companion of such conflicts. Workplace anger often increases during trying economic times and spills into verbal and physical aggression (Szivos, 2010). The most common communication behaviors associated with workplace anger include yelling, swearing, flinging insults, criticizing, using sarcasm, crying, giving dirty looks, making angry gestures, throwing things, and physical assault (Glomb, 2002; Johnson, 2009).

Learning to manage anger is an important step in managing conflicts competently. Ahrons (1994) notes that the chief difference between divorced parents who were effective coparents to their children and those who were ineffective "was that the more cooperative group managed their anger better" (p. 145). Also, anger decreases integrative offers proposed by parties in conflict and heightens the likelihood of competitive, not cooperative, behavior (Liu, 2009).

Constructive and Destructive Anger: Intensity and Duration

Twenty-nine-year-old Rene Andrews pulled onto I-71 near Cincinnati, Ohio. Apparently upset by the way Andrews pulled into her lane, 24-year-old Tracie Alfieri attempted to pass Andrews on the right shoulder of the freeway, then passed on the left, cut in front of Andrews, and slammed on the brakes. Andrews swerved and crashed into a stopped tractor-trailer rig. Andrews died in this accident. Alfieri suffered multiple injuries, and her 6-month-old fetus died. Alfieri was convicted of aggravated vehicular homicide and was sentenced to 18 months in prison. Clearly, road rage is an example of destructive anger. Unfortunately, it is quite common. One survey found that 90% of drivers "in the past year" were either victims of road rage or had witnessed such an event (Arkowitz & Lilienfeld, 2009).

Two conditions determine how destructive or constructive anger is (Adler & Proctor, 2007). The first condition is the

Road rage produced four wrecked cars and three dead people in this horrific Washington, D.C., crash.

intensity, or relative strength, of the anger. Anger can vary in intensity from mild irritation to rage. Mild, even moderate, anger can be constructive. It can signal the existence of a problem, and it can motivate necessary change. Rage, however, is destructive (Glomb, 2002). Temper tantrums and screaming fits are never endearing. In relationships, rage frightens partners and children. In the workplace, rage is never appropriate because it "shows you've lost control—not to mention that it's tough to be articulate if you're having a conniption" (Black, 1990a, 1990b). Ranting and raving make you look like a lunatic. When used to get your way on an issue, rage is a power-forcing style of conflict management that will likely produce an equivalent response. *Rage times rage equals rage squared.*

Duration, or how long something lasts, is the second condition that determines to what degree anger is constructive or destructive. The length of an anger episode can vary from short-lived to prolonged. Quick flashes of temper may hardly be noticed by others. Even fairly intense expressions of anger, if short-lived, can make the point powerfully that you are upset. If your anger goes on for too long, however, you and anyone listening will lose sight of the issue that caused the anger. Protracted anger episodes can make conflict management extremely difficult. When expressions of anger are highly intense and long lasting, the combination can be extremely combustible.

There is a popular notion that venting one's anger is constructive and that suppressing anger is unhealthy. This popular notion is wrong. *Venting anger, or "blowing off steam," usually increases one's anger* (Bushman, 2002; Lohr et al. 2007). Replaying our anger about past events, especially if the anger is unresolved, simply rehearses it. When we tell friends of past "injustices," blood pressure rises, heartbeat increases, and the face flushes. We are experiencing the anger all over again. This doesn't put the anger to rest. It awakens it, pops it out of bed, and starts it doing jumping jacks.

Anger and Attribution: Is It Intentional?

Anger and the desire to lash out at others are choices. Imagine, for instance, that you are stopped at an intersection in your car and another car "steals" your right of way by moving into the intersection before you do. Will you get angry? Do you make an obscene gesture? Do you shout at the driver? Now imagine what your reaction would be if you saw that it was your best friend or your mother driving the car. Would your reaction be the same? Probably not. We can be righteously indignant or we can choose to be calm, even amused, by the same stimulus.

Anger can be a thoughtful choice unless our anger reaches the level of rage (Zillmann, 1993). Rage floods our thought process: we can't think straight, and we "get stupid." Attributing meanings, causes, or outcomes to conflict events shapes the way we think about and respond to disagreements and perceived poor treatment. Attribution can influence enormously whether we get stupid or we get smart on potentially volatile issues (Baron, 1990).

Intent and blame are two common forms of attribution that ignite anger (McKay et al., 1989). Trying to ascertain the intention of another person is mind reading, or "intention invention" (Stone et al., 1999). Unless a person tells us, we must guess about motivation, and unfortunately, we often assume the worst. Negative behaviors from others that we perceive to be intentional, not accidental, easily trigger our anger. Deliberately shoving someone is perceived to be more worthy of anger and hostility than accidentally tripping and shoving a person while trying to regain your own balance.

Blaming someone for negative behavior is the companion of intent. If the behavior of others is intentional and negative, it "deserves" reproach. We can justifiably blame them for unfortunate outcomes. If their behavior is not intentional, we can still blame them for the outcome, but it doesn't seem as justified to be angry with them. How we frame potential conflict-producing events influences our emotional response.

Consider an example. A patient named Margaret had her hip replaced by a prominent surgeon, a man she perceived to be gruff and difficult to confront. When Margaret appeared for her first office visit following the surgery, she was informed that the doctor had unexpectedly extended his vacation. Margaret was furious. She imagined her doctor soaking up sun on some Caribbean island, probably with his wife or girlfriend. When Margaret returned for her postponed appointment, she asked her doctor curtly how his vacation had turned out. He replied that the vacation had been wonderful. "I'll bet," Margaret responded in a sarcastic tone. Her doctor, however, continued before Margaret had a chance to express her anger about being so cavalierly inconvenienced. "It was a working vacation. I was helping set up a hospital in Bosnia. The conditions there are just horrendous" (Stone et al. 1999, p. 47). Understandably, Margaret's anger subsided with this news.

Managing Your Own Anger: Seizing Control

There are several ways to defuse and de-escalate anger, both your own and others' (Gottman & Gottman, 2006). Try these suggestions for managing your own anger:

1. *Reframe self-talk*. Thoughts trigger anger. Reframing the way we think about events can deflate our anger before it has a chance to escalate (Baron, 1990; Gottman & Gottman, 2006). Very often we have no way to know whether the act of another person was intentional or not. Instead of assuming it was intentional, assume it was unintentional. "He probably didn't see me." "She looked stressed out." "Her day isn't going too well." This kind of self-talk reframes events as unintentional, even haphazard, not intentional.

2. *Speak and listen nondefensively*. Criticism, contempt, and cross-complaining ignite angry passions (Baron, 1990). Refuse to become defensive. Insulting your partner or hurting his or her feelings dooms the possibility of constructive conversation (Gottman & Gottman, 2006). Reframe criticism as a problem or challenge. Use supportive communication.

3. *Deliberately calm yourself*. Exercise some discipline and refuse to vent your anger. You will feel your heartbeat increasing when your anger starts to rise. This is a signal that your anger is escalating. Check your pulse if you are uncertain whether you are feeling overwhelmed. A pulse rate that climbs 10% higher than your normal resting pulse rate is cause for concern. If your normal resting pulse is 80 beats per minute, be concerned if it increases to 88. If your pulse reaches 100, you are in the throes of flooding (Gottman & Gottman, 2006).

Be prepared to take steps to calm yourself (Fisher & Shapiro, 2005). When you feel the adrenaline surge, deliberately take slow, deep breaths and concentrate on reducing your heartbeat. Count to 10 before responding. A cooling-off period may be necessary in serious cases. A cooling-off period works well to calm a person's anger (Gottman & Gottman, 2006). Typically, it takes 20 minutes to recover from an adrenaline surge. Take the 20 minutes and stay away from the person or situation that triggers your anger. Go for a walk, shoot a basketball, or do whatever diverts your attention and moves you out of the situation. Return to discuss your anger with others only when you are certain that flooding has subsided. Then express your anger to others in a calm, descriptive manner (first-person singular language).

4. *Change your focus*. Don't rehearse your anger. Revisiting past injustices won't change your history. You can't get beyond old issues if you keep replaying them in your mind (Gottman & Gottman, 2006). Change your focus when old hurts resurface. Read the newspaper, watch television, or make plans for a family outing. Just get your mind off your anger for a little while (Rusting & Nolen-Hoeksema, 1998).

Don't attempt to learn all four of these suggestions at once. Pick one and work on learning it until it becomes virtually automatic. Then you can attempt a second suggestion and so forth.

Managing the Anger of Others: Communication Jujitsu

You can defuse and de-escalate the anger of others so you can confront issues constructively. It is usually best to address the person's anger first, then deal with the substance of the dispute that triggers the anger (Donohue & Kolt, 1992). Dialogue cannot take place when tempers are white hot. Try these suggestions to defuse another person's anger and restore a climate conducive to dialogue.

1. *Be asymmetrical.* When a person is exhibiting anger, particularly if it turns to rage, it is critical that you do not strike back in kind. Resist reacting signally to words of criticism. Be asymmetrical; that is, you do the opposite. Counteract rage with absolute calm. Stay composed (Black, 1990a, 1990b). Hostage negotiators are trained to defuse highly volatile individuals by remaining absolutely calm throughout the negotiations and employing the smoothing technique to quiet the enraged person. Matching a person's rage with rage can produce ugly, violent outcomes.

2. *Validate the other person.* Validation is a form of the smoothing technique of collaborating. Let the person know that his or her point of view and anger have some validity, even though you may not agree. Validation is particularly vital for men to use because men tend to respond to a woman's emotional upset by becoming hyperrational (Gottman, 1994). Offering advice or trying to solve a problem while a person is extremely upset invalidates that person's feelings by ignoring them.

You can validate another person in several ways. You can take responsibility for the other person's anger. "I upset you, didn't I?" acknowledges your role in provoking anger. You can apologize. "I'm sorry. You're right to be angry" can be a very powerful validation of the other person. Don't apologize, of course, unless you really bear some responsibility. Sometimes a compliment can defuse another person's anger: "I actually think you handled my abrasiveness rather well." Finally, actively listening to the other person and acknowledging what the person has said can be very validating. "I know it upsets you when I play my music too loudly while you're trying to study" makes the other person feel that he or she has been heard, even if conflict still exists.

3. *Probe.* Seek more information from the other person so you can understand his or her anger (Gottman & Gottman, 2006). When you ask a question of the angry person, it forces the person to shift from emotional outburst to rational response. Simply asking, "Can we sit down and discuss this calmly so I can understand your point of view?" can momentarily defuse another person's anger. If your partner angrily criticizes you, listen and then probe. "Wow! Any chance you might give me some examples so I can understand why you think I'm such a jerk?" probes for specific information necessary to resolve the conflict.

4. *Distract.* When a person is really out of control, distracting that person by introducing a topic that shifts the focus can sometimes divert attention away from the source of the rage (Rusting & Nolen-Hoeksema, 1998). A humorous quip, an odd question, pointing to some event unrelated to the anger, and requesting help on a thorny problem not associated with triggering the rage are ways to distract and short-circuit the tirade.

5. *Assume a problem orientation.* This is a supportive communication pattern. This step should occur once you have calmed the angry person by the previous steps. Approach the emotional display as a problem to be solved, not a reason to retaliate. The question "What would you like to see occur?" invites problem solving.

6. *Refuse to be abused.* Even if you are wrong, feel guilty, or deserve another person's anger, do not permit yourself to be verbally battered (McKay et al., 1989). Abusive assaults are unproductive no matter who is at fault in a conflict. "I cannot discuss this with you if you insist on being abusive. I can see that you're upset, but name-calling won't lead to a solution" sets a ground rule on how anger can be expressed.

7. *Disengage.* This is the final step when all else fails to calm a person's anger. This step is particularly important if the person continues to be abusive and enraged. Simply and firmly state, "This meeting is over. I'm leaving. We'll discuss this another time."

Keeping track of all seven of these steps, especially when faced with an enraged person, is too much to expect. Concentrate on one or two steps until you have learned them so well that they become a habit. Being asymmetrical is the crucial step, with validation a close second. The remaining steps can be learned gradually. Being asymmetrical provides the greatest chance that the other person's anger will be defused and that you will remain safe in the process.

Anger is a central element in conflict. The constructive management of conflict can occur only when you keep anger under control. This does not mean squelching anger. A person can feel angry for excellent reasons. Anger acts as a signal that changes need to occur. Anger should not, however, be used as a weapon to abuse others. We need to learn ways to cope with and express anger constructively, not be devoured by it.

Typically, it is best to express your anger directly to the person with whom you are upset, not to innocent bystanders (Tavris, 1989). Coming home and chewing out your roommate because your boss at work angered you are inappropriate. Express your anger when you have calmed yourself and can confront the person in a descriptive manner. Expressing anger is most satisfying when the behavior that caused the anger changes. Gaining behavioral change from others happens more often when both parties engage in constructive dialogue, taking the problem-solving approach to communication.

Workplace Bullying: Conflict and Anger Meet

Workplace bullying is an especially challenging problem because conflict, anger, and power are melded. **Workplace bullying** is "persistent verbal and nonverbal aggression at work" that "includes public humiliation, constant criticism, ridicule, gossip, insults, and social ostracism—communication that makes work tasks difficult or impossible, and socially isolates, stigmatizes, and discredits those targeted" (Lutgen-Sandvik, 2006, pp. 406, 408). Workplace bullying is unethical behavior. It is egregiously disrespectful and irresponsible action against others. "Adult bullying at work is shockingly common and enormously destructive" (Lutgen-Sandvik et al., 2009, p. 41). In a survey by the Workplace Bullying Institute and Zogby International, 35% of U.S. employees report being victims of workplace bullying ("Results," 2010). In the same survey, 62% of bullies are identified as men and 58% of their targets are women. The majority (68%) of bullying, however, is same-gender harassment.

Descriptions reported in one study of victims of bullying indicate the intensity of bullying events. As one victim described such an event: "[She was] intimidating—right in your face—less than an inch away from your face, where her spit would hit you in the face. She would scream at us, her face getting all red and her eyes watering. It was almost like she wanted to reach out and choke you." Another victim described it this way: "He'd scream and yell every day. Veins would pop out of his head; he'd spit, he'd point, he'd threaten daily, all day long to anyone in his way, every day that I was there. *Every single day*. . . . He'd swear profusely" (quoted in Lutgen-Sandvik, 2006, p. 411). Rage and flying spit appear to be common manifestations of workplace bullying.

Workplace bullying is fundamentally a dominance-prevention power struggle. Between 60% and 80% of bullies at work are supervisors and upper management (Einarsen et al., 2003; Lutgen-Sandvik et al., 2007). Bullying is allowed to persist primarily because transgressors are in more powerful positions than victims (legitimate authority); even higher-ups who could address the problem constructively often implicitly or explicitly approve of the aggressive behavior, or the problem is simply ignored. In many cases, those who complain are reprimanded for making complaints, or they are fired from their jobs. Most bullies suffer no negative consequences; some are even promoted (Lutgen-Sandvik & Sypher, 2009).

How victims should address bullies is a complicated challenge. What works well in other conflict situations may not work well with more powerful bullies. Confrontation may get you fired, or more abuse is heaped on you until you quit. Some victims use resistance strategies. They choose to drag their feet, a frequent choice of the relatively powerless, not openly defy the more powerful bully. For example, they might use the *work-to-rule* resistance strategy where they perform the absolute minimum amount of work necessary to keep their job according to work rules in place. This is emotionally satisfying because it likely results in lowered

Workplace bullying has become a serious problem. A boss screaming at employees is "acting stupid."

productivity for the organization. It doesn't really end the abuse, however. Some victims try avoidance by keeping as much distance between themselves and the bully at work, but you can't become invisible, so this is only a temporary fix at best. Other workers withdraw completely and quit their jobs. In tough economic times, however, this may not be a feasible option. Finally, victims of workplace bullying individually, or collectively in the form of coalitions with other abused workers, may adopt the power-forcing conflict style by filing formal grievances with external authorities (unions, courts, governmental agencies) (Lutgen-Sandvik, 2006; Lutgen-Sandvik & Sypher, 2009). This usually takes years and doesn't guarantee a satisfactory outcome for abused workers.

Ultimately, prevention is far more effective than any of the preceding strategies. A zero tolerance policy in organizations for any acts of bullying is the place to start. This would, of course, need to be backed up with confrontation and integration strategies such as addressing directly the first signs of bullying behavior and providing training for bullies to change their ways. This would be followed eventually by power-forcing, firing the offender, if bullying persisted. Developing a constructive communication climate is also essential. A supportive communication climate at work can significantly diminish workplace bullying if the constructive climate is modeled by those in positions of legitimate authority.

Forgiveness: Healing Conflict's Wounds

Forgiveness plays an important role in resolving conflict and dealing with anger (Exline & Baumeister, 2000). Studies show that forgiveness seems to promote marital adjustment and satisfaction (Fenell, 1993;

Woodman, 1991) and to reduce hostile anger (Williams & Williams, 1993). "Forgiveness is the final stage of conflict and is the one thing that is most likely to prevent repetitive, destructive cycles of conflict" (Lulofs, 1994, p. 288).

Forgiveness Defined: Healing, Not Hurting

In Neil Simon's play *California Suite*, a woman catches her husband committing adultery and says to him, "I forgive you. And now I'm going to go out and spend all your money." Good line, but this isn't forgiveness. **Forgiveness** is "letting go of feelings of revenge and desires to retaliate" (Lulofs, 1994, p. 276). The focus of forgiveness is on healing wounds, not inflicting them on others.

Forgiveness is not simply forgetting what happened. When we forgive, we remove the desire to mimic the behavior we hate. Forgiveness is also not tolerating reprehensible behavior ("Oh, that's okay."). Forgiveness "still allows for holding the offender responsible for the transgression, and does not involve denying, ignoring, minimizing, tolerating, condoning, excusing or forgetting the offense" (Witvliet et al, 2001, p. 118). The best indicator that you have forgiven someone is honestly wishing that person well when you think of him or her (Smedes, 1984). Forgiveness, therefore, is the opposite of the bumper sticker "Don't get mad—get even."

Forgiveness is particularly difficult when the offense is severe, intentional, repeated, and the transgressor is unrepentant (Bachman & Guerrero, 2006; Exline & Baumeister, 2000). When a friend ridicules your style of dress or taste in music in front of others, it can hurt and make you angry, but you usually can forgive the insult easily. In fact, as Smedes (1984) explains, "It is wise not to turn all hurts into crises of forgiving. . . . We put everyone we love on guard when we turn personal misdemeanors into major felonies" (p. 15). Stealing your boyfriend or girlfriend from you on purpose (mate poaching) with no apparent guilt, however, makes forgiving a bit more difficult.

Revenge may be our first impulse in response to transgressions, but seeking revenge doesn't resolve conflict. It stimulates anger and perpetuates and escalates conflict. Revenge fantasies and blaming can lead to psychopathology, criminality, poor recovery from bereavement, and health problems (Exline & Baumeister, 2000).

The Process of Forgiveness: Four Stages

Forgiveness is a process that occurs in stages. Smedes (1984) offers a *four-stage model*: we hurt, we hate, we heal, and we come together. Hurting and hating are natural results of the painful actions of others. Dwelling on the hating stage, however, paralyzes us. Hate is like a parasite drawing our life's energy from us, making us too weak to move forward. The only way to break free from the grip of hatred is to forgive. Forgiveness starts the healing process.

Perhaps you're thinking, "Easy for you to say, but there are just some things that can't be forgiven." Remember that forgiveness doesn't mean acceptance or tolerance of bad behavior by others. It doesn't mean you shouldn't get angry when you are mistreated. It also doesn't mean you necessarily return to a relationship (Morse & Metts, 2011; Wade & Worthington, 2005). Think, though, what the alternative is to forgiving. Holding on to hatred and seeking revenge do nothing constructive to enhance your life. Hatred and desire for revenge are physically and psychologically damaging (Lulofs, 1994).

Mary Nell Verrett is the sister of James Byrd Jr., a 49-year-old African American who was beaten and dragged to death behind a pickup truck in Jasper, Texas, on June 7, 1998. Despite her terrible loss, Verrett eloquently testifies to the futility and danger of hating: "Our family has no use for destructive hate . . . it tears away at you. You become sick. You become a victim all over again. It can keep you from sleeping, eating, and thinking straight. It can keep you from going forward" (quoted in "Message of Hope," 1998, pp. 9-10). If Mary Nell Verrett can forgive what racist white men did to her beloved brother, surely we can forgive those who hurt us.

Forgiveness is a transactional process. Although some people can readily forgive others, it is extremely difficult for others to forgive. In such cases, what the transgressor does to encourage forgiveness can help. Individuals who have inflicted pain on us can take two steps to initiate the forgiveness process. First, they can openly and sincerely accept responsibility for what they have done. "What I did to you was wrong and totally unprovoked" accepts responsibility. Second, transgressors can apologize: "I'm very sorry for hurting you." An apology is a particularly important step that encourages forgiveness (McCullough et al., 1997). *Elaborate, sincere apologies work best when the transgression is serious* (Morse & Metts, 2011; Weiner et al., 1991). As one study showed, "the perception that one received a sincere apology was a fairly good predictor of forgiveness" (Bachman & Guerrero, 2006, p. 54).

Others can start the forgiveness process, but ultimately, we have to forgive in our hearts. *As victims, we can forgive by reframing the event.* We recast the behavior that hurt us into an uncharacteristic departure from the norm. The hurtful act doesn't have to become a defining moment in our relationship with the other person. A friend can hurt us and still remain a friend. We can also reframe the event by attributing situational causes for the act. "He stole my money because he lives in desperate circumstances, not because he is evil" reframes the event for forgiveness.

The final stage of the forgiveness process is the coming-together part. There are three forms of communicating our forgiveness of others (Merolla, 2008). First, *direct forgiveness* is explicit and unambiguous ("I forgive you"). Second, *indirect forgiveness* is "just understood." There is no direct acknowledgment of the forgiveness. Third, *conditional forgiveness* attaches stipulations that make it clear any further transgression will not be tolerated ("Stay off the booze or I'm leaving you"). *Coming together occurs most completely with direct forgiveness when the victim openly communicates forgiveness to the transgressor.* A hug or some expression of affection, if possible, is helpful in bringing parties together. In cases of serious transgressions, indirect forgiveness or conditional forgiveness is likely, and this tends to delay actual coming together until trust is rekindled (Merolla, 2008). The transgressor may have to demonstrate his or her commitment to make amends (Tavris, 1989). If the transgressor, for instance, stays off alcohol for three months as promised, this might serve as an outward sign that regaining trust is important. It indicates that commitment to the relationship is firm.

Personal injury inflicted on us by others becomes a part of who we are, but it need not be the whole of who we are (Lulofs, 1994). Expressing forgiveness and acting in ways that show forgiveness can heal.

Culture and Conflict: Different Styles

"Recent research on conflict management strategies indicates that there are no universal resolutions to conflict. In fact, attempts to remedy conflict may be culturally inappropriate, yield unfavorable results, and even increase the propensity toward future conflict" (Gibson & McDaniel, 2010, p. 456). The value differences between cultures discussed extensively in Chapter 3 highlight the potential for intercultural conflict. Misinterpretation of a person's intentions and behavior is common when value differences are pronounced. The ways individuals from different cultures manage conflict can pose significant problems as we become a more multicultural society.

Individualist and collectivist values markedly influence the communication styles of conflict management that are preferred when conflict erupts (Ting-Toomey & Chung, 2005). For example, avoidance of confrontation is "a core element of Thai culture. Expressions of emotion and excitement are seen as impolite, improper, and threatening" (Knutson & Posirisuk, 2006, p. 211). From the Thai viewpoint, a competent communicator is one who avoids conflict, exhibits respect, tactfulness, modesty, and politeness, and controls emotions (Knutson et al., 2002; Sriussadaporn-Charoenngam & Jablin, 1999). For collectivist cultures, expressing anger during conflict-management efforts is likely to evoke negative reactions (Brescoll & Uhlmann, 2008).

Consider also differences between Chinese and Americans. Chinese culture, far more collectivist than American culture, emphasizes harmony as a goal. "The Chinese consider harmony as the universal path which we all should pursue. Only when harmony is reached and prevails throughout heaven and earth can all things be nourished and flourish" (Chen & Starosta, 1998a, p. 6). A conflict-free interpersonal relationship, therefore, is the ultimate goal (Chen & Starosta, 1998a).

The Chinese philosophy of harmonious relationships translates into a strong desire to avoid a conflict with a friend or member of an in-group (e.g., family). When conflicts are unavoidable, there is a preference for accommodating—not confronting—the dispute, so harmony is maintained (Chen & Starosta, 1998a). Handling a dispute ineptly can bring shame, a loss of face, not just on the individual but also on the individual's entire family. Thus, one must avoid stirring up trouble for fear of bringing shame on the family (Yu, 1997).

Conflicts with individuals from an out-group, however, are often handled quite differently among Chinese than are conflicts within the group. Although not the initial choice, competing is a common way to approach conflict with outsiders, especially if the interests of the opposing parties are highly incompatible. Vicious quarrels, even physical fights, are not uncommon in such circumstances (Chen & Starosta, 1998a; Yu, 1997).

Imagine the difficulty that would occur when an American and a Chinese try to resolve a conflict. Americans favor direct, competing, or compromising styles of conflict management. These styles clash with the avoiding and accommodating styles initially favored by Chinese. Consider a slightly different intercultural conflict with similar difficulties. Tannen (1998) cites an example of a Japanese woman married to a Frenchman. The French love to argue; in fact, they may change topics at the dinner table until they find one that ignites a disagreement. For the first two years of marriage, this Japanese woman spent a great deal of time in tears. She tried accommodating her husband and avoided arguing with him. This seemed to frustrate him. He would try to find something to start an argument. Finally, she couldn't take it anymore, and she began yelling at him. Her husband was thrilled. To him, starting an argument with his wife showed that he valued her intelligence and that he was interested in her. Enthusiastic debate between partners was considered a sign of a solid relationship.

The key to effective intercultural conflict management is flexibility (Knutson et al., 2003). If you find yourself in a situation or relationship that calls for intercultural conflict management, try broadening your approach to conflict. Learn to use all communication styles well, not just those you are most comfortable with or are accustomed to using. Change to a different style when one style seems to clash with another person's cultural values. If you know that someone comes from a collectivist culture, don't abandon collaborating because one study found this cooperative approach to conflict worked well for Chinese employers in a variety of industries when the strategy was employed (Chen et al., 2005). Be prepared, however, to seek accommodation wherever possible. In any case, *recognize that competing is as ineffective and troublesome to use interculturally as it is to use intraculturally*. When you make mistakes, and you will, be prepared to apologize. Seek forgiveness for embarrassing or shaming the other person. Elaborate apologies work best when the insult or embarrassment seems to be great. Above all, try to empathize with people whose cultural values and standards are different from your own. Consider their perspective and respect their right to disagree. Find ways to build bridges between culturally diverse individuals, not tear them down.

Summary

Most people view conflict with some dread. Conflict, however, can be constructive as well as destructive. Our communication determines the difference. Destructive conflict is typified by escalating spirals of conflict that can easily turn ugly. Constructive conflict is characterized by controlling or de-escalating conflict by using a We-orientation, cooperation, and flexibility in applying communication styles of conflict management. There are five communication styles of conflict management. They are collaborating, accommodating, compromising, avoiding, and competing. Collaborating has the greatest potential for appropriately and effectively managing conflict; competing has the least potential. Learning to control our anger and to manage the anger of others is an important part of dealing with conflict effectively. The final stage of conflict management is forgiveness. Forgiveness is letting go of the desire for revenge and retaliation. Intercultural conflicts can be extremely difficult to manage because members of individualist and collectivist cultures differ dramatically in how they view conflict and how best to manage it.

Answer for *Critical Thinking* caption:

***New Yorker* cartoon (p. 272): #4**

Quizzes Without Consequences

Did you understand all the material in this chapter? Test your knowledge before your exam!

Go to the companion website at www.oup.com/us/rothwell, click on the Student Resources for each chapter, and take the Quizzes Without Consequences.

Film School Case Studies

An Unfinished Life (2005). Drama; PG-13

Morgan Freeman, Robert Redford, and Jennifer Lopez star in this story about grief and forgiveness. Examine this film for conflict-management styles and elements of forgiveness.

Changing Lanes (2002). Drama; R

Gavin Banek (Ben Affleck) and Doyle Gipson (Samuel L. Jackson) are strangers who collide as a result of a traffic accident. Examine the elements of destructive conflict depicted in this film.

The Holiday (2006). Romantic Comedy; PG-13

A fairly predictable, but somewhat charming, entertaining piece of fluff. Analyze the many dialectics portrayed in the relationships. Is it possible that the Kate Winslet character could really be attracted to the Jack Black character? (That's just a personal aside.)

Horrible Bosses (2011). Comedy; R

Three friends plot to murder their horrible bosses. Identify all the communication patterns that make these bosses horrible. Besides assassination, an obviously silly and morally reprehensible option but cathartically funny in a perverse way, what if anything could the three friends have done to deal with their horrible bosses?

Juno (2007). Romantic Comedy; PG-13

Juno, a pregnant teenager played by Ellen Page, must deal with finding the perfect couple to raise her child in this offbeat, coming-of-age comedy. Examine the dialectics depicted throughout the film.

Knocked Up (2007). Romantic Comedy; R

Continuing the pregnancy theme, Alison (Katherine Heigl) has a one-night stand with slacker-loser Ben (Seth Rogen) and a pregnancy results. The comedy is raunchy and often sophomoric, but the opportunity to analyze conflict is apparent. Focus your analysis on dialectics, conflict-management styles, and anger management.

The Invention of Lying (2009).
Comedy; PG-13

Ricky Gervais plays an average guy in an alternate reality in which lying does not exist; there isn't even a word for it. He realizes that lying can be beneficial to him and to others, but there is a downside. Analyze the conditions in which lying may or may not be appropriate. Apply the five criteria for ethical communication.

The Upside of Anger (2005). Drama; R

This movie has an interesting perspective on anger. Does it depict anger in ways that coincide with this chapter's material? Does it deviate from what has been presented from a research standpoint?

The War of the Roses (1989). Black Comedy; R

This is destructive conflict in graphic detail. Kathleen Turner and Michael Douglas go toe to toe in an increasingly mindless escalation of verbal and physical aggression. Identify instances that fit the definition of destructive conflict. What might the characters have done in each instance to de-escalate the conflict?

What's Cooking? (2000). Comedy/Drama; PG-13

Diversity is not lacking in this portrayal of four interrelated families trying to celebrate Thanksgiving. Look for the many dialectical sources of conflict. Is honesty always the best policy? Identify the communication styles of conflict management depicted in the film.

CHAPTER 10

Chapter Outline

PART 3

The Anatomy of Small Groups

WE LIVE IN A WORLD of groups, and we reap significant rewards from our group experiences, some quite profound (Rains & Young, 2009). The rewards include feelings of belonging and affection from *primary groups* (family and friends) and *social networks* (Facebook, Twitter, LinkedIn); social support from *self-help* and *support groups* (Parents Without Partners; Alcoholics Anonymous, Cancer Survivors Network); satisfaction from solving challenging problems in *project groups* (ad hoc groups, self-managing work teams); achieving social justice from *advocacy* and *judicial groups* (civil rights groups, Supreme Court); increased knowledge from *learning groups* (study groups, mock trial teams); thrills and entertainment from *activities groups* (athletic teams, bridge clubs); a sense of community from *neighborhood groups* (homeowners associations, PTA); an identity and pleasure from helping others through *social* and *service groups* (fraternities, sororities, Rotary, Lions, and Kiwanis clubs); and a creative outlet in *music* and *artistic groups* (bands, choirs, quilting circles). These are the many rewards

By the end of this chapter, you should be able to:

1. Define groups and recognize their strengths and pitfalls.
2. Understand the structure of small groups and how groups function.
3. Recognize evolving theories of leadership.
4. Understand how competent leadership occurs in small groups.

derived from participation in groups, and these provide the main reasons we join groups: desire to belong, attraction to group activities, desire to achieve group goals, excitement, personal growth, and a boost in self-esteem and development of self-identity.

Group experiences, however, don't always prove to be rewarding. Winston Churchill once described a committee as "the organized result of a group of the incompetent who have been appointed by the uninformed to accomplish the unnecessary." On my own campus, committees metastasize like cancer, devouring the time and energy of faculty, staff, and administrators alike, threatening to suck the lifeblood from the institution. A serious proposal was once offered to establish a committee on committees in the misguided hope to rein in the proliferation of campus work groups. The proposal was sent to a committee where it died.

Often groups seem to be an impediment to decision making and problem solving, not an aid. Groups can be time consuming, sometimes indecisive, conflict provoking, and slow to react to urgent needs. Group members may not all exhibit the same level of motivation and attention to task accomplishment. Frequent group meetings at work can make employees feel fatigued, and this can put everyone in a surly frame of mind (Luong & Rogelberg, 2005). Sorensen (1981) coined the term **grouphate** to describe how troublesome the group experience is for many people. Surveys of students reflect prevalent grouphate (Karau & Elsaid, 2009; Myers & Goodboy, 2005).

Why are some group experiences pleasurable and rewarding whereas others are like downing cough syrup? Finding answers to this question is important because there is no escaping the group experience. The American Association for the Advancement of Science, the National Council of Teachers of English, the National Council of Teachers of Mathematics, and the National Communication Association all promote frequent group activity in college courses. By the start of the 21st century, most large companies worldwide were using work teams regularly in their organizations (Wright & Drewery, 2006). Virtual teams have also become a worldwide phenomenon (Godar & Ferris, 2004; Kozlowski & Ilgen, 2006). A major study of multinational corporations concluded that "virtual teams are an ever-growing component of global business" (Solomon, 2010). The "virtual classroom" is an increasingly popular distance learning choice at colleges and universities globally. In the United States in 2010, almost 5 million students enrolled in online degree programs and courses ("More Than One in Four College Students," 2010). Most of these courses require online group discussions and team activities and projects.

Sorenson (1981) noted a direct relationship between communication competence and diminishment of grouphate. Two studies, for example, show that negative attitudes about group meetings disappear when meetings are conducted competently (Rogelberg et al., 2006). Groups are much more likely to be successful when group members are competent communicators. Thus, *the primary purpose of this chapter is to learn how to improve your communication in groups by first understanding the nature of small groups.*

The Structure of Small Groups

Every group has a discernible **structure**, a form or shape characterized by an interrelationship among its parts. In this section, I begin with defining key terms; then I explore group structure, which is composed of group size, task and social dimensions, norms, and roles.

Definitions: Setting the Scope

A **group** is composed of three or more individuals, interacting for the achievement of some common purpose(s), who influence and are influenced by one another. Two people qualify as a couple, or **dyad**, not a group (Moreland, 2010). They engage in *interpersonal* communication. One study revealed that two individuals working together to solve complex problems performed no better than two individuals working alone. Three individuals working together, however, proved to be the "tipping point" for significant improvement in problem solving compared to individuals working alone (Laughlin et al., 2006). A group dynamic appears to begin with no fewer than three individuals. Also, a group is not merely any aggregation of people, such as 10 strangers waiting in line to buy tickets to a rock concert. These strangers are not standing in line to achieve a common purpose, such as helping each other buy tickets. The same is true for a crowd in a shopping mall or a collection of people waiting to board a plane. In both cases, the presence of other individuals is irrelevant to the achievement of a common purpose, which is buying tickets or clothes or traveling from point A to point B. *To qualify as a group, three or more people must succeed or fail as a unit in a quest to achieve a common purpose.* The essence of a group, therefore, is a We- not Me-orientation. Any of these examples, of course, could qualify as a group if circumstances required united action to achieve a mutual goal (e.g., flash mob in a shopping mall).

Group Size: Influencing Structure

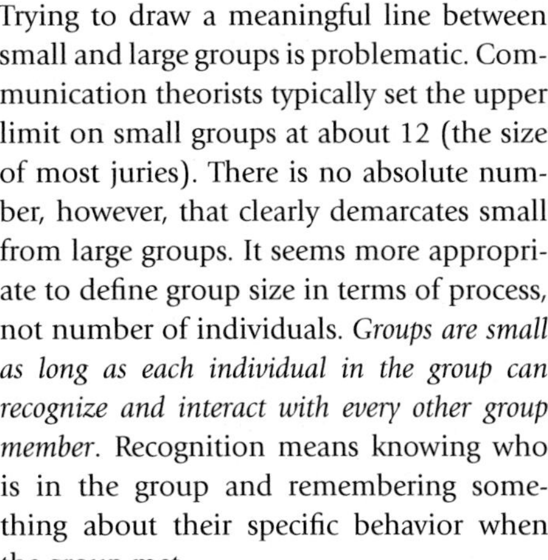

Trying to draw a meaningful line between small and large groups is problematic. Communication theorists typically set the upper limit on small groups at about 12 (the size of most juries). There is no absolute number, however, that clearly demarcates small from large groups. It seems more appropriate to define group size in terms of process, not number of individuals. *Groups are small as long as each individual in the group can recognize and interact with every other group member.* Recognition means knowing who is in the group and remembering something about their specific behavior when the group met.

Group size largely determines group structure. All small groups are not created equal. A group composed of 3 members doesn't function the way a group of 8 does. As the size of the group increases, complexity of group transactions and decision making increases enormously, affecting its structure. The possible number of interpersonal relationships between group members grows exponentially as group size increases. Bostrom (1970) provides these calculations:

Group Size	# of Possible Relationships
3	9
4	28
5	75
6	186
7	441
8	1,056

A triad, or three-member group, has 9 possible interpersonal relationships, a four-person group has 28, and so forth, as shown in Figure 10-1.

The relationship member A has with member B may not be the same as the relationship member B has with A. Member A may see the relationship with member B as close; B may see it as just a work relationship and nothing more. Different perceptions of relationships increase the complexity of transactions between group members. Individual members also can have very different

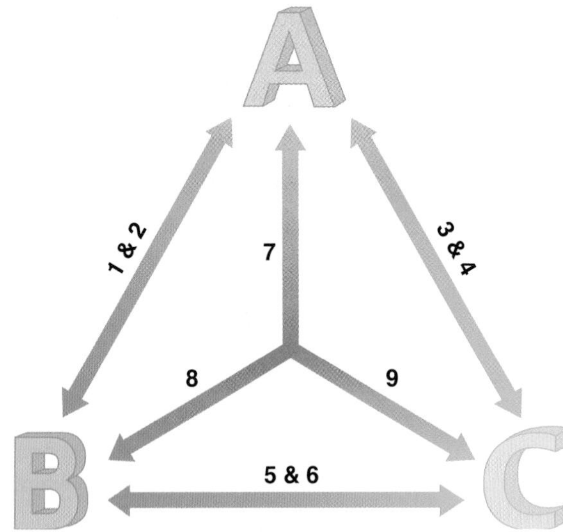

FIGURE 10-1 Nine Possible Relationships in a Group of Three

relationships with two or more other members (see 7, 8, and 9 in Figure 10-1). Adding even one member to a group is not an inconsequential event. As newscaster Jane Pauley once observed, "Somehow three children are many more than two."

Increasing Group Size: Several Challenges

Several challenges emerge as groups increase in size and complexity (Lowry et al., 2006). First, the number of nonparticipants in group discussions increases when groups grow much beyond seven members. Reticent members may be intimidated by the prospect of speaking to a group, especially a large one. Second, larger groups easily become *factionalized*—members of like mind may splinter into smaller, competing subgroups—to withstand the pressure from other members to conform to the majority opinion on an issue. Third, larger groups may take much more time to make decisions than smaller groups. With more members, there are potentially more voices to be heard on the issues discussed. Fourth, even scheduling a meeting at a time when all members are available can be a daunting task when groups grow large. Schedule conflicts are almost inevitable with groups of more than eight. Finally, group productivity typically decreases as groups grow larger. Research shows that each member added to a decision-making group that starts with seven members reduces decision effectiveness by 10%. If you take this *rule of seven* to its logical conclusion, a group of 17 members or more "rarely makes any decisions" (Blenko et al., 2010, p. 88). Too many group members can create decision paralysis. Another study of 2,623 members in 329 work groups shows that groups composed of three to eight members are significantly more productive than groups composed of nine or more members. Groups of three to six members proved to be the most productive (Wheelan, 2009).

So, given the many challenges that emerge as groups increase in size, what is the ideal group size? Amazon.com CEO Jeff Bezos uses the "two-pizza rule." A group is too large if it can't be fed by two pizzas (Yang, 2006). That's obviously not a very precise rule (size of pizzas and size of group members' appetites aren't considered). There is no single ideal-sized group for all situations. Each group experience is unique. For example, complex, politically charged issues may require much larger groups (10 or more) just to give a voice to all interested factions. Groups may be faced with a trade-off between *speed* and *quality* of decision making. Smaller groups of three or four members are faster, but somewhat larger groups often produce higher-quality decisions because their knowledge base is larger. Groups of about five members are a nice compromise when speed and quality are equally important (Pavitt & Curtis, 1994). Offering a precise number, however, is arbitrary and debatable. Instead, *the smallest size capable of fulfilling the purposes of the group should be considered optimum* (Sawyer, 2007). The key point is to keep groups relatively small to reap the greatest advantages. As groups grow in size, complexity increases, and formal structure becomes necessary. Some small groups even evolve into large organizations.

Groups Versus Organizations: Structural Differences

What began as a very small business in 1937 with a half-dozen employees grew into 30,000 establishments worldwide employing about 1 million workers, exceeding any other American organization, public or private. One of every eight workers in America has at some time been employed by this organization (Schlosser, 2002). Can you guess what it is? If you guessed McDonald's, you are correct.

Small groups sometimes grow into large organizations. The transition produces changes in structure and attendant communication processes. Small groups typically operate with an informal structure. Communication is usually conducted informally as conversation rather than formally as public presentations. Procedures for managing conflict also remain informal. There is little need for formal grievance procedures. Differences among three group members can usually be handled through discussion and a meeting. Power also can be easily shared. A meeting of a three-person group certainly doesn't require formal communication rules of parliamentary procedure, such as Robert's Rules of Order, although larger groups may require such procedures. Smaller groups would appear silly using such formal rules. "Point of order," "call the question," "I move to table the motion," and "I rise to a point of privilege" are assertions of such rules, but they sound goofy when communicating in a group of three or four friends or colleagues. "Dude, relax! You're among friends."

As groups increase in size, complexity increases. Thus, when small groups become large groups and eventually organizations, structure typically becomes more formal to cope with increased complexity. Individuals receive formal titles with written job descriptions. Power is distributed unevenly. Those with the most prestigious title typically are accorded the most status and decision-making power. The larger the organization, the more likely the structure will become **hierarchical**, meaning that members of the organization will be rank ordered. This pyramid of power has those at the top—the CEOs, presidents, and vice-presidents—wielding the most power, with middle managers coming next, then the "worker bees" or low-level employees with the least influence and autonomy.

Changes in communication follow changes in structure (Adler & Elmhorst, 2008). Formal communication networks emerge in large organizations. In most organizations, low-level employees' communication with those at the top of the power pyramid is restricted. If everyone in the McDonald's organization, all 1 million workers, felt free to email or text message those at the top, information overload would overwhelm decision makers. Formal lines of communication, or networks, are established to control information flow. These chains of command can make **upward communication** (also called vertical communication)—messages that flow from subordinates to superordinates in an organization—very difficult. Typically, there are risks for low-level employees who communicate with bosses, especially if the information is negative. Criticism and complaints can get you fired, ostracized, or perceived as a troublemaker.

Downward communication—messages that flow from superordinates to subordinates in an organization—also can be problematic. Communicating policy changes, giving rationales for assignments, explaining proper procedures and practices for the smooth running of the organization, motivating workers, and offering sufficient

This cartoon illustrates which of the following?

1. Hierarchical structure of organizations
2. Upward communication is difficult in organizations
3. As groups increase in size complexity increases
4. Communicating negative information to higher-ups within organizations is risky.

Answers at end of chapter

feedback to subordinates so they know when they have performed well and when improvement is needed are vital messages. What you don't want in an organization is what former United Airlines president Ed Carlson called NETMA—Nobody Ever Tells Me Anything.

Horizontal communication—messages between individuals with equal power, such as office workers in the same department—is another common communication pattern in organizations. Horizontal communication coordinates tasks, aids problem solving, shares information, enhances conflict management, and builds rapport (Adler & Elmhorst, 2008). It is predominately informal, even casual.

Task and Social Dimensions: Productivity and Cohesiveness

Every group has two primary interconnected dimensions: task and social. The **task dimension** is the work performed by the group and its impact on the group. The **social dimension** consists of relationships between group members and the impact these relationships have on the group.

Walter V. Clarke Associates, a consulting firm, conducted a study of more than 700 professional athletes, NFL draft choices, and college players. They found that skill at performing tasks is not enough to be successful (cited in Goleman, 1998). Gifted athletes who haven't mastered how to work cooperatively with team members can create havoc. Athletes who listened poorly, wouldn't take directions, and came late to meetings were rated by their coaches as less motivated, harder to coach, less talented, and less likely to be leaders. Although technical, task-oriented skills are important, a study by the U.S. Department of Labor Employment and Training Administration showed that the critical skills are all socially oriented—oral communication, interpersonal communication, and teamwork abilities (Carnevale, 1996; see also "Top Skills," 2011).

Productivity is the goal of the task dimension. The extent of a group's productivity is determined by the degree to which it accomplishes its work efficiently and effectively. Five workers performing the same amount of work with the same proficiency as ten workers doubles the group productivity.

Cohesiveness is the goal of the social dimension. The extent of a group's cohesiveness depends on the degree to which members identify with the group and wish to remain in the group. Cohesiveness is developed primarily by encouraging compatible membership when possible, developing shared goals that members find challenging and exciting to achieve, accomplishing important tasks that meet these shared goals, developing a positive group history of cooperation, and promoting acceptance of all group members by making each feel valued and welcome in the group (see Rothwell, 2010, for more details).

Cohesiveness and productivity (performance) are interconnected; one affects the other (Cohen & Bailey, 1997). High cohesiveness alone doesn't guarantee group success, but it seems to be a necessary condition for successful task accomplishment. When groups lack cohesiveness, their productivity typically suffers (Beal et al., 2003; Gammage et al., 2001). Small groups of exceedingly talented individuals will not accomplish tasks well if interpersonal relations among members are immersed in disharmony, anger, resentments, hostilities, and rivalries. Low cohesiveness almost always dooms a group to poor performance and low productivity. Members who do not like each other and wish they weren't a part of the group typically exhibit feeble effort and poor performance. Competitiveness among group members, especially when combined with time pressure to accomplish tasks, diminishes cohesiveness (Klein, 1996).

Group members can be so cohesive, however, that they become too concerned with maintaining harmony. When disagreement is avoided because members fear disrupting group cohesiveness, error correction may be sacrificed. This is one aspect of groupthink, a problem discussed in Chapter 11.

Finding the proper relationship between productivity and cohesiveness is a persistent dialectical struggle in all groups. Too much focus on productivity can strain interpersonal relationships within a group. Too much focus on cohesiveness can lead to anemic effort on the task (Hardy et al., 2005). Strong cohesiveness combined with a strong group work ethic is an effective combination (Langfred, 1998). Both task and social dimensions should be addressed, not one at the expense of the other.

Norms: Rules Governing Group Behavior

Every group, large or small, has norms that guide behavior. **Norms** are rules that indicate what group members have to do (obligation), should do (preference), or may not do (prohibition) if they want to accomplish specific goals. This section discusses small-group norms. We explore types of norms, their purpose and source, and conformity to norms.

Types of Norms: Explicit and Implicit

There are two types of norms: explicit and implicit. **Explicit norms** specifically and overtly identify acceptable and unacceptable behavior. Explicit norms are typical of a low-context communication style. You want group members to know unambiguously what behavior is expected, preferred, and prohibited, so you tell members explicitly. "No Smoking" signs posted around

Imagine if the people on the top were at a rock concert and those on the bottom were attending the opera. It doesn't work, does it? Every social situation has norms for appropriate attire and conduct.

campus and in public buildings indicate an explicit norm. Laws of society and bylaws of a group are explicit norms. When your instructor tells the class not to interrupt a student during discussions or to attend regularly and be on time, he or she is providing explicit norms.

In small groups, however, most norms are implicit. **Implicit norms** are observable patterns of behavior exhibited by group members that identify acceptable and unacceptable conduct. Examples might include the following: all group members sit in the same seats for every meeting, no one eats or drinks during meetings, all members dress neatly, everyone is polite, humor is never sarcastic or offensive, and no one says anything derogatory about any other member. These patterns indicate implicit norms. There is no book of rules on how to behave during such meetings, yet members all act as though there were.

Implicit norms may become explicit on occasion, especially when there is a norm violation. Instructors rarely feel compelled to tell students at the beginning of a school term that loud talking during lectures is unacceptable. This is an implicit norm that is taken for granted. It is unlikely that you would find such a rule in the college catalogue, on the schedule of classes, or on a syllabus. If students have ignored this implicit rule, however, instructors may make the implicit norm explicit by pointedly telling the class that talking while a lecture is in progress should cease. It should also be apparent that listening to an iPod, checking or sending text messages, answering cell phones, perusing websites from a laptop, or blogging during class violates implicit norms of appropriate student behavior, but probably every instructor has had to note the norm violation to some students.

Purpose of Norms: Achieving Group Goals

The primary purpose of norms is to achieve group goals. Shimanoff (1992) provides the example of Overeaters Anonymous to illustrate the goal-oriented nature of norms. Losing weight is the principal goal of Overeaters Anonymous groups. Norms help achieve this goal. Members are permitted to talk about food only in general terms (carbohydrates, proteins, etc.) but not in terms of specific foods (e.g., candy bars, burgers, or ice cream). The norm is based on the assumption that references to specific foods will induce a craving for those foods and make losing weight more difficult. References to foods in general terms, presumably, will produce no such cravings.

Apparently, you won't hear the refrigerator calling your name when merely talking about carbohydrates, but mention Ben and Jerry's ice cream and there better be an unobstructed path to the Frigidaire or somebody's going to get trampled.

Conforming to Norms: Being Liked and Being Right

Group members tend to conform to group norms. **Conformity** is the inclination of group members to think and behave in ways that are consistent with group norms. Conformity creates a sense of belonging, helps groups accomplish important goals, and can be a positive force. Groups couldn't exist without some conformity. Group discussion would be tumultuous if there were no rules governing such interactions (e. g., take turns speaking).

Conformity can also be negative. **Binge drinking**—consuming five or more drinks for men and four or more for women in a two-hour period—among college students illustrates the power of social norms to promote conformity and the sometimes negative consequences of such conformity. The Harvard School of Public Health found that 44% of college students binge drink, and almost 25% binge drink often (Wechsler & Wuethrich, 2003). Subsequent studies found that rates of binge drinking among college students have remained steady for years (Nelson et al., 2009). More than 80% of students living in fraternities and sororities binge drink.

Drinking to excess is encouraged by group norms (Wechsler & Nelson, 2008). The social norm at many college sporting events, fraternities and sororities, and college parties is to drink to excess. A Zogby International survey reported that 56% of the 1,005 college students polled felt group pressure to binge drink ("Poll: College Students," 2000). College students primarily binge drink to "fit in" with a valued group (Kirn, 1997).

Members conform to group norms for two principal reasons: to be right and to be liked (Cialdini & Trost, 1998). We typically do not want to suffer the embarrassment of being wrong in front of our group, so we look to the group for information on correct behavior. Conformity can keep lines of communication open. Sources of information are likely to be shared when we conform to group norms. Failure to conform, however, can lead to the severing of informational sources that may be critical to meeting

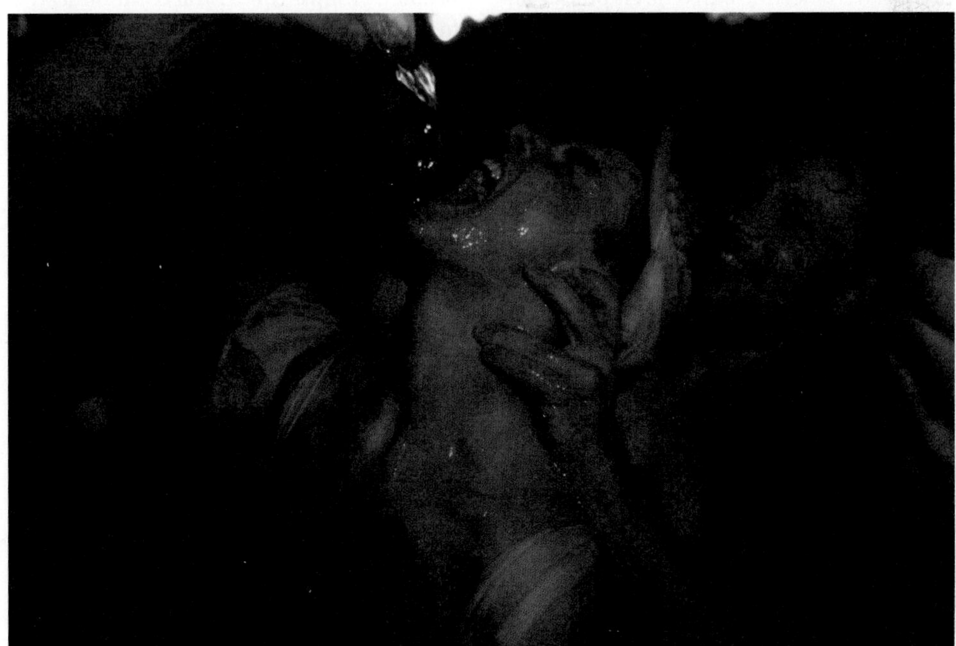

Binge drinking is encouraged by group norms. Almost half of all college students binge drink with often calamitous consequences.

personal goals within the group. We also are inclined to strive for acceptance from our group. We "go along to get along." Social acceptance, support, and friendship are often the rewards for conformity. Nonconformity typically triggers a negative response from the group such as social ostracism, personal attack, or expulsion from the group.

Group conformity is strongest when cohesiveness is high, when members expect to be in the group for a long time, and when members perceive that they have somewhat lower status in the group. Groups have little leverage against members who are not committed to the group, don't plan on remaining in the group for long, or have high status that gives them "the right" to occasional nonconformity.

Given the discussion of cultural values in Chapter 3, you should not be surprised that *conformity to group norms is greater in collectivist cultures* (Smith & Bond, 1994). Content analysis of advertisements comparing Korea and the United States reveals that personal-uniqueness themes appear almost twice as often in American advertisements (89% to 49%), and conformity themes appear a third more often in Korean advertisements (95% to 65%) (Kim & Markus, 1999). Parental enforcement of norms when children misbehave reflects a different emphasis on conformity. American parents frequently chastise nonconforming children by taking away highly valued rights and privileges ("You're grounded until the next Ice Age"; "Don't even think about watching TV or playing video games"). Chinese parents, however, are more likely to suggest that social ties to the group are jeopardized by misbehavior ("We don't like children who disobey"; "People will ridicule you if you act badly") (Miller et al., 1996).

Roles: Expected Patterns of Behavior

Roles and norms are interconnected. Small-group **roles** are "patterns of expected behavior associated with parts that you play in groups" (Rothwell, 2010, p. 135). Norms are broad rules that stipulate expected behavior for *every* group member, whereas roles stipulate specific behaviors expected of *individual* group members, not the entire group.

There are two general types of roles: formal and informal. **Formal roles** assign a position. They are a standard part of the structure of organizations. Titles such as "president," "chair," or "secretary" usually accompany formal roles. Formal roles do not emerge naturally from group transactions; they are assigned. Normally, an explicit description of expected behaviors corresponds to each formal role.

In small groups, roles are mostly informal. **Informal roles** identify functions, not positions. They usually emerge naturally from group transactions. The informal roles a group member plays are identified by observing patterns of communication. If a member often initiates group discussions, the member is playing the role of initiator-contributor. The group does not explicitly tell a member how to play an informal role. Groups do, however, indicate degrees of approval or disapproval when a member assumes an informal role.

Informal roles are generally divided into three types: task, maintenance, and disruptive roles. **Task roles** advance the attainment of group goals. The central communicative function of task roles is to extract the optimum productivity from the group. **Maintenance roles** address the social dimension of small groups. The central communicative function of maintenance roles is to gain and maintain group cohesiveness. **Disruptive roles** are Me-oriented. They serve individual needs at the expense of group needs and goals. Group members who play these roles often deserve the label "difficult group member." The central communicative function of disruptive roles is to focus attention on the individual.

Because competent communicators recognize the interconnectedness of task and social dimensions of groups, they look for the optimum balance between task and maintenance roles to achieve group success. They also avoid disruptive roles. Table 10-1 identifies some common task, maintenance, and disruptive roles found in small groups (Benne & Sheats, 1948; Mudrack & Farrell, 1995). This list is not exhaustive.

Assuming appropriate task and maintenance roles during group discussion is a matter of timing. A devil's advocate is

TABLE 10-1 SAMPLE OF INFORMAL ROLES IN SMALL GROUPS

Task Roles

1. *Information giver*—provides facts and opinions; offers relevant and significant information based on research, expertise, or personal experience.
2. *Information seeker*—asks for facts, opinions, suggestions, and ideas from group members.
3. *Initiator-contributor*—provides ideas; suggests actions and solutions to problems; offers direction for the group.
4. *Clarifier*—explains ideas; defines the group position on issues; summarizes proceedings of group meetings; raises questions about the direction of group discussion.
5. *Elaborator*—expands the ideas of other group members; helps the group visualize how an idea or solution would work if the group implemented it.
6. *Coordinator-director*—pulls together the ideas of others; promotes teamwork and cooperation; guides group discussion; breaks the group into subgroups to work effectively on tasks; regulates group activity.
7. *Energizer*—tries to motivate the group to be productive; acts as a task cheerleader.
8. *Procedural technician*—performs routine tasks such as taking notes, photocopying, passing out relevant materials for discussion, finding a room to meet, and signaling when allotted time for discussion of an agenda item has expired.
9. *Devil's advocate*—gently challenges prevailing viewpoints in the group to test and evaluate the strength of ideas, solutions, and decisions.

Maintenance Roles

1. *Supporter-encourager*—offers praise; bolsters the spirits and goodwill of the group; provides warmth and acceptance of others.
2. *Harmonizer-tension reliever*—maintains the peace; reduces tension with gentle humor; reconciles differences between group members.
3. *Gatekeeper*—controls the channels of communication, keeping the flow of information open or closed depending on the social climate of the group; encourages participation from all group members and open discussion.

Disruptive Roles

1. *Stagehog*—recognition seeker; monopolizes discussion and prevents others from expressing their points of view; wants the spotlight.
2. *Isolate*—withdraws from group; acts indifferent, aloof, and uninvolved; resists inclusion in group discussion.
3. *Fighter-controller*—tries to dominate group; competes mindlessly with group members; abuses those who disagree; picks quarrels, interrupts, and generally attempts to control group proceedings.
4. *Blocker*—expresses negative attitude; looks to tear down other members' ideas without substituting constructive alternatives; incessantly reintroduces dead issues.
5. *Zealot*—attempts to convert group members to a pet cause or viewpoint; delivers sermons on the state of the world; exhibits fanaticism; won't drop an idea that has been rejected or ignored by the group.
6. *Clown*—interjects inappropriate humor during discussions and meetings; engages in horseplay; diverts attention from the group task with comic routines.

not needed during initial discussion. You do not want to kill potentially creative ideas by immediately challenging them. A harmonizer-tension reliever is needed when conflict emerges and threatens to derail the group discussion. It is irrelevant if there is no tension and disharmony. Disruptive roles embody incompetent communication. Deal with those who act out disruptive roles the way you would approach difficult group members (discussed in Chapter 11).

Role playing is a fluid process. During a single meeting, a group member may play several informal roles. Groups usually function better when members exhibit flexibility by playing several roles depending on what is required to make the group effective. **Role fixation**, when a member plays a role rigidly with little or no inclination to try other roles, will decrease group effectiveness. The chosen role will be appropriate only some of the time but irrelevant or inappropriate most of the time. Every group needs an energizer, but no group needs an energizer bunny all of the time. Constant cheerleading grows tiresome. If that is the only role a member chooses to play, the member will be mostly an annoyance for the group.

Leadership

The leader is often thought to be the most important group role, and learning how to be an effective leader is a fascination for many people. Scholars, philosophers, social scientists, even novelists have written and spoken

BOX 10.1 Developing Communication Competence

PLAYING BY THE ROLES: A SELF-ASSESSMENT

Fill out the self-assessment on roles for any important group that you choose: family, study group, project group, and so on. (Optional) Have members of your chosen group fill out this same form about you. Compare the results.

1. What was your degree of participation in group activities?

   Low 1 2 3 4 5 High

2. How task oriented (showed interest in meeting group goals) were you?

   Low 1 2 3 4 5 High

3. How socially oriented (concerned about the relationships among group members) were you?

   Low 1 2 3 4 5 High

4. How much influence did you have on the group's decisions?

   Low 1 2 3 4 5 High

Using the scale above, indicate the degree to which you played the following roles by writing the appropriate number:

TASK

____ **Information giver**	____ **Information seeker**
____ **Initiator-contributor**	____ **Clarifier**
____ **Elaborator**	____ **Coordinator-director**
____ **Energizer**	____ **Procedural technician**
____ **Devil's advocate**	

MAINTENANCE

____ **Supporter-encourager**	____ **Harmonizer–tension reliever**
____ **Gatekeeper**	

DISRUPTIVE

____ **Stagehog**	____ **Isolate**
____ **Fighter-controller**	____ **Blocker**
____ **Zealot**	____ **Clown**

extensively about effective leadership. "Authors have offered up over nine thousand different systems, languages, principles, and paradigms to help explain the mysteries of management and leadership" (Buckingham & Coffman, 1999, p. 53). If you type "leadership" in the Google search window, you'll get millions of hits. Business executives and management consultants regularly author books on leadership, mainly offering an abundance of anecdotes that purport to provide allegedly sage advice gained from years of corporate experience or management training. Matthew Stewart (2009), a former management consultant turned disapproving critic, offers this assessment: "Upon putting the gurus' books down, however, I find that I get the same feeling I get after reaching the bottom of a supersized bag of tortilla chips. They taste great while they last, but in the end, what am I left with?" (p. 8). He later answers, "platitudes," "bundles of nonfalsifiable truisms," and "transparently unsubstantiated pseudotheories."

Echoing Stewart's criticism, what I see most of these "business experts" frequently offering is ego gratification for the authors who tout their self-proclaimed mastery of leadership based on experience only as CEOs, and sometimes not even that. Untroubled by the paucity of social scientific research to support their advice, they share it anyway with those who aren't CEOs of major corporations but must adapt to markedly different situations and circumstances than a corporate CEO might face (Vroom & Jago, 2007). Stewart argues that they "write with complete indifference to or even against the academics" (p. 249). I offer this assessment because abundant, insightful academic research on leadership effectiveness too frequently is ignored while these flashy, quick-fix books are lionized by the press, the public, and the popular culture. With few exceptions, they have minimal merit.

Fortunately, you don't have to depend on the self-promotional, peppy platitudes of these personal testimonials on leadership. One communication scholar estimated more than a decade ago that nearly 8,000 research studies had been published on group leadership (Pavitt, 1999), and hundreds more have been produced since (Vroom & Jago, 2007). One highly acclaimed, bulky reference book on leadership fills more than 1,500 pages to review the vast research and theory on leadership (Bass & Bass, 2008).

This reservoir of research serves as the basis for my discussion of leadership effectiveness in small groups. In far fewer than 1,500 pages, much to your relief I'm sure, I define leadership, discuss how to gain and retain leadership, and I explore several perspectives on what constitutes effective small-group leadership.

Defining Leadership: A Process of Influence

There are as many definitions of leadership as there are individuals attempting to define it. Despite myriad definitions, most agree that leadership is primarily a social influence process (Northouse, 2007; Vroom & Jago, 2007). Leaders influence followers, but followers also influence leaders by making demands on them to meet expectations and by evaluating their performance in light of those expectations (Avolio, 2007). A person may have an authoritative title, a position that comes with an expectation of leadership, but if no one follows the designated leader, then this person is the drum major in a phantom marching band. Longtime leadership researcher Warren Bennis (2007) observes that "the only person who practices leadership alone in a room is the psychotic" (p. 3). He further notes that leadership requires the willingness of followers to be led, so leadership is grounded in the relationship leaders and followers establish.

The term *follower* evokes negative connotations, such as passive, sheeplike, even unintelligent. This vision of followers has been relegated to the trash heap of archaic thinking. Modern researchers and theorists see leadership as a partnership. Leaders and followers act like ballroom dancers. One leads and the other follows, but they influence each other, and they must operate in tandem to be effective. "Leadership, in short, is very much a 'we thing'" (Haslam et al., 2011, p. xxi).

Thus, *"Leadership is a process and not a person"* (Hollander, 1985, p. 487; see also Vroom & Jago, 2007). When you look at leadership from this perspective, focusing only on leaders without analyzing the complex communication transactions that occur between leaders and followers is largely irrelevant. For example, one study addressed whether angry leaders (e.g., chef Gordon Ramsay on *Hell's Kitchen*) motivate followers better than leaders who are generally positive (e.g., Barack Obama). The answer depends on the degree of agreeableness among followers. *Agreeableness* is an inclination to be pleasant and accommodating with others. Groups composed of members with higher average levels of agreeableness performed more effectively when their leader was supportive and generally positive, whereas groups composed of members with low levels of agreeableness performed more effectively when their leader expressed anger, even though they may have disliked the emotional outbursts (Van Kleef et al., 2010). There is no one-size-fits-all leader-follower relationship. Some followers can tolerate a leader's anger and be motivated to improve personal performance, although disrespectful expressions of anger, such as screaming "You idiot," are ethically questionable. Other followers may be completely demoralized by a leader's anger.

Some communication theorists refer to *transactional leadership* as a type different from *transformational leadership* based on distinctions originally offered by Burns (1978). Transformational leadership inherently involves change. Transactional leadership does not. Transactional leadership, however, should be equated with being a manager, not a leader, because change is not the focus and all leadership involves social influence (change). Being a manager and being a leader are different processes (Kotter, 1990; Northouse, 2007). "There are many institutions that are very well managed and very poorly led. They may excel in the ability to handle all the routine inputs every day, yet they may never ask whether the routine should be preserved at all" (Bennis, 1976, p. 154).

There are two primary differences between managers and leaders (Hackman & Johnson, 2004; Rost, 1991). First, managers ("transactional leaders") operate from positional authority—they have a title. Equating a title with leadership is squarely at odds with prevailing theory and research that posits leadership as a process, not a person (Vroom & Jago, 2007). Persons in authority may have the power to instill fear in followers because they can fire employees, but this makes for an odd concept of leadership. Second, managers maintain the status quo; they implement policy, but they don't try to change it. They engage in "management by exception" (Northouse, 2007; Powell & Graves, 2006). They monitor follower performance and intervene to correct "exceptions" when follower performance strays from policy rules and regulations of a group or organization. In other words, they enforce the rules, but they don't change them. *The primary goal of managing is efficiency (getting the job done); the primary goal of transformational leadership is change* (Kotter, 1990; Rost, 1991). If someone functioning in a management position is an agent of change, then that person is operating not as a manager but as a transformational leader. Managers can exercise leadership, and leaders can exhibit good management practices (balance budgets, implement policies efficiently, etc.). Some argue that this is the ideal (Kotter, 1990). Again, it's the process (working to produce change), not the person (someone in a position with the title "leader"), that typifies leadership.

Thus, *all leadership is transformational* because all leadership involves change or innovation, either promoting it or adapting to its inevitability (Rost, 1991). A follower is not influenced by a leader if no change in attitude or behavior occurs. A leader is not influenced by followers if he or she persists in repeating the same behaviors toward followers regardless of outcomes. (One definition of stupidity is stubbornly repeating the same failed action but expecting different results to occur.) "People expect leaders to bring change about, to get things done, to make things happen, to inspire, to motivate" (Husband, 1992, p. 494).

Leaders perceived to be *extremely* transformational, capable of producing great change, are sometimes called *charismatic leaders* (Judge & Piccolo, 2004). Hackman and Johnson (2004) refer to these leaders as the "superstars of leadership" (e.g., Gandhi, Mother Teresa, Martin Luther King, or Pope John Paul II). Charismatic leaders are visionary thinkers, highly inspirational, decisive, and self-sacrificing (House & Javidan, 2004). They exhibit "high standards for moral and ethical conduct" (Bono & Judge, 2004, p. 901).

With this brief theoretical foundation, **leadership** is defined as a leader-follower influence process with the goal of producing positive change that reflects mutual purposes of group members and is largely accomplished through competent communication (Hackman & Johnson, 2004; Rost, 1991). Defining leadership, however, neither informs us regarding how leaders emerge nor, more important, indicates what constitutes *effective* leadership.

Leader Emergence: A Process of Elimination

In formal groups and organizations, the role of leader is often assigned. In certain cases, it is a formally elected position. In some small groups, the leader role is designated (chair of a committee), but in most small groups, a leader emerges from group transactions. The emergence of a leader is an important event in the life of a small group. Geier (1967) studied sixteen small groups for four months. In five of these groups, a leader did not emerge, and none of these groups was successful in completing tasks and tending to social relationships. All of the groups in which leaders did emerge were successful.

Leader emergence is a process of elimination (Bormann, 1990). Small groups typically know what they don't want in a leader but are less certain about what they do want. The first to be eliminated from consideration for the leader role are quiet, uninformed, seemingly unintelligent, and unskilled members (Riggio et al., 2003). Group members who express strong, unqualified assertions and those perceived to be poor listeners are also quickly eliminated as candidates for the role of leader (Bechler & Johnson, 1995). A second phase of this process of elimination rejects bossy, dictatorial members and individuals with irritating or disturbing communication styles.

If a leader hasn't emerged after these two phases, the group typically looks for a member who provides a solution to a serious problem or helps the group manage a crisis. Members who are perceived to be effective listeners also frequently emerge as leaders during this stage (Johnson & Bechler, 1998). A member may acquire a *lieutenant*, an advocate who promotes him or her for the leader role. This member will become the leader unless another member acquires a lieutenant. If there are competing lieutenants, a stalemate may ensue, and no clear leader will emerge.

Groups expect more from leaders who emerge naturally from group transactions than they do from assigned leaders (Hackman & Johnson, 2004). Emergent leaders are held to a higher standard, and failure is tolerated less because the group has more invested in its chosen leader. How the leader performs reflects well or badly on the group. When an outsider (i.e., supervisor, executive) assigns a leader to a group, gaining credibility with group members may be the biggest hurdle for the leader. Gaining credibility to become leaders and to function effectively as leaders in groups is especially difficult for women and ethnic minorities (see Box 10-2).

Competent Leadership: Evolving Perspectives

Emerging as the leader of a group and exercising effective leadership may be distinctly different processes. Emergent leaders aren't always effective leaders. In this section, I discuss several perspectives on leadership effectiveness.

Traits Perspective: Born Leaders

Do you have the "right stuff" to be an effective leader in small groups? That is the core question of the traits approach to leadership. This is the "leaders are born, not made" perspective, sometimes referred to as the "heroic model" of leadership (Vroom & Jago, 2007). Thus, we search for the heroic, exceptionally talented individuals to idolize as model specimens of leadership. This journey has taken us to odd places. You can buy books on the leadership secrets of Jesus, Colin Powell, Meg Whitman, Donald Trump, Attila the Hun, and Osama bin Laden. Clearly, mixing such vastly different individuals into the leadership recipe suggests a perspective with significant limitations.

The first systematic scientific investigations of leadership looked for a list of traits that distinguish leaders from followers. **Traits** are relatively enduring characteristics of a person that highlight differences between people and that are displayed in most situations. There are physical traits, such as height, weight, physical shape, physique, and beauty or attractiveness. There are personality traits, such as being outgoing or sociable. There are traits associated with inherent capabilities, such as intelligence and quick-wittedness. There are traits associated with consistent behaviors, such as integrity, trustworthiness, and confidence.

Hundreds of studies have generated separate lists of traits that identify leaders. The traits often differ, are even contradictory in some cases, when lists are compared (see

BOX 10.2 Focus on Controversy

GENDER AND ETHNICITY: GLASS CEILING OR TRICKY LABYRINTH?

Group bias against women and ethnic minorities is still an issue in leader emergence and leader effectiveness. How much bias still exists remains a controversy. Groups tend to favor white men when selecting and evaluating leaders (Eagly, 2007; Forsyth et al., 1997; Shackelford et al., 1996). This bias in choosing group leaders occurs despite impressive evidence that women exhibit leadership effectiveness equivalent to or greater than that of men (Eagly, 2007; Eagly et al., 2003). One study of 58,000 individuals showed that women outranked men on 20 of 23 leadership skills. Another study of 2,482 executives showed women again outranked men on 17 of 20 leadership skills (Sharpe, 2000). Regarding ethnicity and leadership, one study showed that African Americans (male and female) were perceived to have more leadership ability than whites (Craig & Rand, 1998).

Nevertheless, the **glass ceiling**, an invisible barrier of subtle discrimination that excludes women and ethnic minorities from top leadership positions in corporate and professional America, appears resilient. In 2010, only 13 women were CEOs for the 500 largest companies in the United States. Only two women headed a company in the top 50. Another 14 women were CEOs of the next 500 largest U.S. corporations ("Women CEOs," 2010). Thus, there were 27 women and 973 men running the 1,000 largest U.S. companies in 2010. Women sat on a scant 15.7% of Fortune 500 corporate boards of directors' seats in the same year, and only 14.4% of executive officers in the same companies were women ("Women in U.S. management," 2010).

In politics, the situation is only marginally better. Women held only 17 of the 100 U.S. Senate seats in 2011, 76 (17.4%) of 435 House seats, 1,811 (24.5%) of state legislative seats, 71 (22.5%) of statewide elective offices, and 202 (17.5%) of all mayors of U.S. cities with more than 30,000 people. The United States ranked a miserable 73rd in the world in 2010 on women's representation in national legislatures or parliaments out of 186 direct election countries ("Member FAQs," 2011; "Women in Government," 2010; "Women in the Senate," 2011).

That's the bad news. The good news is that significant gains have been made in women's rise to positions of leader in the workplace. In 2010, women held more than half (51.4%) of all managerial and professional positions in the United States ("Women in U.S. Management," 2010). Women dominate in 13 of 15 categories projected to grow the most in the coming decade (Rosin, 2010). All of these positions, of course, are in organizations, not small groups. Nevertheless, they provide a snapshot of societal leadership opportunities for women, and all of these top positions offer plentiful chances for leading small groups within organizations (budget committees, planning councils, cabinet groups, etc.) and promoting change (transformational leadership), not merely enforcing current policies (managing).

Gaining access to the halls of power, of course, does not automatically ensure leadership effectiveness. Women often have less power and authority than men who occupy comparable leader positions. Eagly and Carli (2007) argue that this is less a problem of the glass ceiling and more the challenge of a complex labyrinth to negotiate. Women must work far more than a 40-hour week to rise to the highest levels of an organization, but greater family responsibilities than men typically embrace limit women's ability to put in such long hours, resulting in slower promotion to higher levels of power and authority. Many quit before opportunities emerge to become CEOs and presidents. When women exercise leadership by being assertive, reactions from followers are often negative, but if they act in stereotypic ways by showing a kind, gentle approach, they are often viewed as ineffectual and a poor leader (Eagly, 2007; Eagly & Carli, 2007).

The situation for ethnic minorities gaining important leadership positions is not very encouraging. In 2010, only one African American woman

(continued)

BOX 10.2 *(Continued)*

and only four African American men were CEOs of a Fortune 500 company (Buchanan, 2010; Woertz, 2010). A scant 1% of senior corporate officers were African American women, and only 3% were African American men in 2009 (Washington, 2009). A mere 2% of directors of Fortune 500 companies were Hispanic, and less than 2% were Asians in 2010 (Choo, 2010; Kuznia, 2010).

Women and ethnic minorities can improve their chances of emerging as group leaders in several ways.

1. *Increase the proportion of women and ethnic minorities in groups* (Carli, 2001; Shimanoff & Jenkins, 1996). Consider the **Twenty Percent Rule** (Pettigrew & Martin, 1987). Discrimination decreases when at least 20% of group membership is composed of women or minorities. Flying solo is the most difficult position for women and minorities (Taps & Martin, 1990; Yoder, 2002). Being the only woman or minority in a group can brand a person as a "token," thus diminishing his or her chance of emerging as leader.
2. *Encourage mingling and interaction among members before choosing a leader.* Getting to know group members while working on a project puts the emphasis on individual performance instead of gender and ethnicity (Haslett, 1992).
3. *Emphasize task-relevant communication during group discussions.* Play task roles. This can be empowering. Task-oriented female group members are as likely to become small-group leaders as are task-oriented male group members (Hawkins, 1995). This suggestion applies primarily to work groups. Support groups may prefer a more social-oriented leader, which can favor women (Eagly & Carli, 2007).
4. *Women and minorities should be among the first to speak in the group, and they should speak often* (Shimanoff & Jenkins, 1996). One study of all-male groups found that token white males (one white male, three Chinese males) were judged to be leaders in every instance, whereas token Chinese males (one Chinese male, three white males) were never seen as leaders (Kelsey, 1998). The key factor was not ethnicity, however, but degree of participation. Token white males spoke much more often and longer than did the majority Chinese males in every instance. Speaking first and often marks a person as leadership material in U.S. culture.
5. *Hone communication skills and become a competent communicator* (Hackman & Johnson, 2004). Communication is the core of leadership, and communication skills are empowering. The best communicators have the best chance of emerging as group leaders. Those who combine high quantity and high quality of contributions during group discussions have the best chance of being perceived by group members as effective leaders (Jones & Kelly, 2007).

QUESTIONS FOR THOUGHT

1. Have you experienced discrimination in small groups that prevented you from emerging as leader? Discuss the ethics of this discrimination.
2. Will men easily accept greater representation of women and ethnic minorities in groups? What about historically male-dominated occupations and professions (firefighters, coal miners, airline pilots)?

Northouse, 2007). The limitations of the trait approach can be seen by considering the case of Amy Henry, the front-running candidate on Donald Trump's "reality" television series *The Apprentice*. Henry appeared to be a surefire winner right up to the show's final episodes. A panel of experts consisting of CEOs, management experts, and entrepreneurs chosen by *USA Today* was asked to identify the leadership traits Henry possessed that made her such an obvious choice for the show's ultimate prize. Panel member Jay Sidha noted Henry's clear vision and human skills. Stephen Covey asserted that character and moral authority were her most important leadership traits. Joe Moglia identified spiritual soundness, dedication, love, and courage. Deborrah Himsel said that strength, humility, and being a team player were her admirable qualities. Jeffrey Sonnenfeld offered intelligence, confidence, and an upbeat personality. Alfred Edmond noted her sense of humor and cool demeanor under pressure. Necole Merritt said she had "an engaging personal style" and "a really neat haircut" (Jones, 2004, p. 4B). Amy Henry may have possessed all of these qualities or only some of them; that's debatable. The list of traits was very broad and unfocused. The traits experts claimed she had weren't enough, however, to win the ultimate prize. Trump, after noting she was beautiful, fired her.

Despite some disillusionment with the trait approach after decades of research and contradictory results, there do seem to be some universal traits associated with effective leadership, such as persistence, tolerance for ambiguity, honesty, drive, achievement motivation, and self-confidence, to name a few (Avolio, 2007). The trait approach to leadership, however, is no more than a starting point, not an end in itself, for determining competent leadership because, in addition to inconsistent lists of leadership traits, other problems exist.

First, certain negative traits can predict who will not become leader (arrogance, dishonesty, laziness), but positive traits don't permit accurate predictions regarding who is likely to emerge as leader and exhibit effective leadership because negative traits may cancel positive traits. Physical attractiveness and sociability may be outweighed by lack of integrity. Intolerance may cancel verbal skills. Arrogance may cancel intelligence or self-confidence. "Acting superior or failing to treat followers respectfully or listen to them will undermine a leader's credibility and influence" (Reicher et al., 2007, p. 27). How does one predict which traits, the positive or the negative, will be most important with which group?

Second, *certain sets of traits may be necessary but not sufficient to become an effective leader*. Fiedler and House (1988) claim that "effective leaders tend to have a high need to influence others, achieve, and they tend to be bright, competent, and socially adept, rather than stupid, incompetent, and social disasters" (p. 87). Intelligence, social and verbal skills, integrity, sense of humor, confidence, or other traits may influence a group. Such traits, however, are not sufficient to be an effective leader. Why? *The trait approach assumes that leadership is a person, not a process.* Such a view is too narrow to be very useful (Hollander, 1985; Vroom & Jago, 2007). Meg Whitman, former CEO of eBay, spent $178.5 million in 2010 trying to become governor of California ("Meg Whitman Spent Fortune," 2011). She tried to translate her leadership in business to the political arena. She lost to Jerry Brown, who had been governor 30 years prior, by an embarrassing margin of 13%. Traits that prove to be effective in one context (business) may prove to be ineffective in others (politics). What is considered intelligent in one culture may not translate as such in another culture (Sternberg, 2004). Appearing to be too clever may alienate followers in some groups. One study by John C. Turner and Alexander Haslam found that when students were presented with a rival group that had an intelligent leader who also exhibited inconsiderateness, they wanted their own leader to be *un*intelligent. When the rival leader was unintelligent, however, they preferred an intelligent leader for their own group (cited in Reicher et al., 2007). They wanted a leader who was different from the disliked out-group. The trait approach provides an incomplete explanation of competent leadership.

Styles Perspective: The Autocrat and the Democrat

There are two general leadership styles (see Box 10-3). The **directive style**, originally called *autocratic*, puts heavy emphasis on the task dimension with slight attention to the social dimension of groups. Member participation is not encouraged. Directive leaders assume that they have greater power than other group members. Such leaders tell members what to do, and they expect obedience. The **participative style**, originally called *democratic*, places emphasis on both

The trait perspective on leadership explains very little. What do Barack Obama, Mark Zuckerberg, Bono, German Chancellor Angela Merkel, Michele Bachmann, and George Stephanopoulos have in common that would explain their leadership? Certainly not looks, personality, gender, ethnicity, intelligence, physical size, vocal quality, or a host of other traits.

the task and social dimensions of groups. Task accomplishment is important, but social relationships must also be maintained. Unlike the directive style, which uses the dominance form of power, the participative style is empowering. Group members are encouraged to participate meaningfully in discussions and decision making. Participative leaders work to improve the skills and abilities of all group members.

Another style, the laissez-faire, was originally offered by Lewin (see Lewin et al., 1939). The **laissez-faire style** is a sit-on-your-derriere approach to leadership, which is to say no leadership at all is exercised (Kozlowski & Ilgen, 2006). There is theoretical consensus that leadership is a social influence process. The laissez-faire style by definition makes no attempt to influence anyone. Thus, it provides no insight into effective leadership in groups. As Zaccaro (2007) concludes, "Successful and effective leadership means, fundamentally, influencing others by establishing a direction for collective effort and managing, shaping, and developing the collective activities in accordance with this direction" (p. 9). So-called laissez-faire leaders perform none of these functions for a group.

BOX 10.3 Developing Communication Competence

WHAT IS YOUR LEADERSHIP STYLE PREFERENCE?

Fill out the self-assessment on leadership styles. ***Note***: The rating scale ALTERNATES.

1. I like it when my supervisor at work admits openly that he/she made a mistake.

   STRONGLY AGREE 1 2 3 4 5 STRONGLY DISAGREE

2. I want to be told what to do on the job, not have to figure it out for myself

   STRONGLY AGREE 5 4 3 2 1 STRONGLY DISAGREE

3. If my team were hiring a new applicant, I prefer that the entire team interview the candidate and make the final decision, not the team leader only.

   STRONGLY AGREE 1 2 3 4 5 STRONGLY DISAGREE

4. I don't want my boss to be my friend; I prefer that my boss remain aloof from the group so he/she can be objective when decisions need to be made.

   STRONGLY AGREE 5 4 3 2 1 STRONGLY DISAGREE

5. I do not think that my boss should reverse the decision of his/her team except in extraordinary circumstances (dangerous mistake).

   STRONGLY AGREE 1 2 3 4 5 STRONGLY DISAGREE

6. I prefer to be told what decisions have been made then informed what I should do to implement these decisions, not engage in time-consuming debate.

   STRONGLY AGREE 5 4 3 2 1 STRONGLY DISAGREE

7. I prefer having many opportunities to provide input before my team leader makes a final decision.

   STRONGLY AGREE 1 2 3 4 5 STRONGLY DISAGREE

8. I want my boss to make the important decisions, not get me and others on our team involved; that's why he/she gets paid the big bucks.

   STRONGLY AGREE 5 4 3 2 1 STRONGLY DISAGREE

9. I want my boss to encourage robust debate and differences of opinion before any decisions are made.

   STRONGLY AGREE 1 2 3 4 5 STRONGLY DISAGREE

10. I want my boss to be decisive, to make decisions confidently, and model a person who is totally in charge.

    STRONGLY AGREE 5 4 3 2 1 STRONGLY DISAGREE

Tally your total score and divide by 10. The *lower* your average score, the more you prefer *participative* leadership from supervisors/bosses/team leaders. The *higher* the average score, the more you prefer the *directive* leadership style. Taken from Rothwell, J. D. (2013).

Initially, researchers thought the participative style would prove to be superior. Research results, however, have been mixed (Gastil, 1994). Both directive and participative leadership styles can be productive. Although the participative style fosters more member satisfaction than does the directive style (Van Oostrum & Rabbie, 1995), the difference is neither large nor uniform (Gastil, 1994). Some groups don't want their leaders to be participative. The military wouldn't function effectively if every soldier got to vote on the wisdom of a military action: "All those in favor of attacking the heavily armed enemy on the ridge signal by saying aye; those opposed, nay. Okay, the nays have it. We'll stay put and live another day."

Again, as you might expect from the discussion in Chapter 3, high power-distance cultures tend to expect and prefer the directive leadership style (Brislin, 1993). In such cultures, the participative style may not work as well as the directive style. The directive style also tends to be more effective when groups face stressful circumstances or time constraints (a cardiac surgical team performing a heart transplant), whereas the participative style is usually more effective in unstressful situations (that same cardiac surgical team, when not performing surgery, discussing ways to improve surgical procedures and improve patient survival) (Rosenbaum & Rosenbaum, 1985). These research results indicate that the effectiveness of leadership style depends on the situation.

Situational Perspective: Leadership Development

Leader traits and styles must operate within a context. The context is the situation a leader confronts. No set of traits will provide effective leadership in every group, and no single style of leadership will be suitable for all situations. In fact, it is probably more accurate to speak of directive (autocratic) *situations* and participative (democratic) *situations* faced by a leader than separate styles isolated from context (Vroom & Jago, 2007).

The Hersey and Blanchard situational leadership model is one of the most widely recognized approaches to leadership effectiveness (Hersey et al., 2007). It recognizes the process nature of leadership and the importance of adapting to changing contexts. The model subdivides the directive and participative leadership styles into four types: telling/directing, selling/coaching, participating/supporting, and delegating. The telling style emphasizes task, not relationships; the selling style emphasizes both task and relationships; the participating style emphasizes relationships, not task; and the delegating style has little focus on either task or social dimensions of groups. The key situational variable that every leader must consider to determine which style is appropriate is the development level of followers (see Figure 10-2). **Development** (sometimes called *readiness*) is composed of the ability of group members, their motivation, and their experience with relevant tasks. Lots of experience and strong motivation to accomplish a task aren't enough if a member's ability is poor. Likewise, substantial ability and experience don't compensate for weak motivation.

When the development level of followers is low, the telling and selling styles are most appropriate. As development levels increase, effective leaders choose the participative and delegating styles. When someone is hired for a job, for example, effective leaders begin diagnosing the development level of the employee. Development levels vary from D1 (low task competence, high motivation to tackle the task) to D4 (high competence, high commitment). Normally, a person at the D1 level would not be hired. Who would want someone of this caliber? Thus, the telling style would mostly be used with an employee whose development level falters because of stress, personal trauma, or technological advances beyond the employee's abilities. Using the telling style with an able worker would seem like micromanaging. The selling style requires interaction between leader and follower. This style would normally be used with a new employee as the supervisor and the employee begin to establish a relationship. With greater development comes a further shift in leadership style. The participating style is appropriate

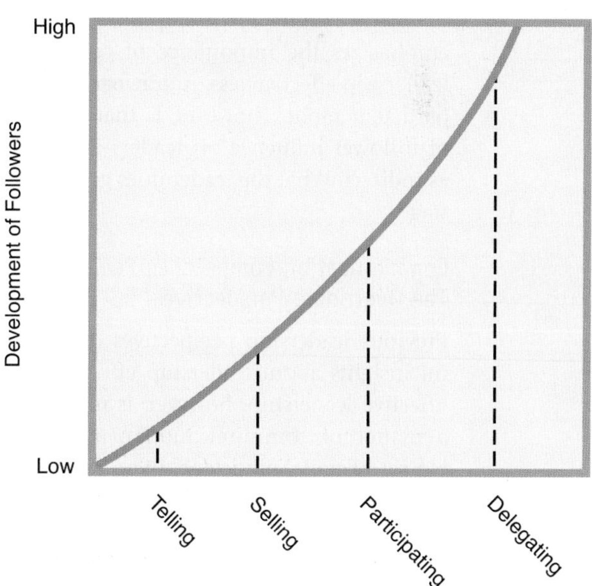

FIGURE 10-2 Situational Leadership Model: The Telling (S1), Selling (S2), Participating (S3), and Delegating (S4) Leadership Styles Related (Source: Situational Leadership is a registered trademark of the Center for Leadership Studies, Inc. Reprinted with permission. All rights reserved)

for the worker who now knows the ropes and has sufficient readiness to offer suggestions and engage in decision making. Finally, when the development level is high, an effective leader steps out of the way and delegates responsibility and decision making to the worker.

The situational leadership perspective makes intuitive sense, although the research to support this perspective is somewhat skimpy, even contradictory (Northouse, 2007; Vecchio et al., 2006; Yukl, 2006). One leadership style does not fit all situations. An effective leader matches the style with the development level of followers and the group as a whole. Newly formed groups require greater supervision and direction than experienced groups. Experienced, capable groups work best when leaders are "guides on the side." They offer relational support and encouragement but allow the group to perform its task without much interference. Leaders can become more directive (telling or selling) if groups or individual members slip in their development levels because of stressful events or personal difficulties. This means that leaders should be sensitive to signals from group members that development levels have diminished and a different style of leadership is required.

The situational leadership model rightly emphasizes the importance of context to leadership effectiveness. A drawback of this particular model, however, is that the role of follower influence on leaders is viewed as indirect. What the leader does gets center stage.

Communication Competence Perspective: The Overriding Perspective

Previous leadership perspectives offer useful insights about leadership effectiveness. Effective leadership, however, is ultimately a matter of communication competence. No set of traits, particular styles, or matching of styles with situational development will be effective without competent communicators. The most effective leaders are the most proficient communicators. As Hackman and Johnson (2004) conclude, "Extraordinary leadership is a product of extraordinary communication" (p. 98).

The We-orientation of the communication competence model is crucial for leadership effectiveness. Larson and LaFasto (1989) studied 75 highly diverse teams (e.g., mountain climbing, cardiac surgery, and professional football teams). Their conclusion was unequivocal: "The most effective leaders . . . were those who subjugated their ego needs in favor of the team's goal" (p. 128). Bennis and Nanus (1985) interviewed 90 successful leaders from a broad range of environments and concluded that "there was no trace of self-worship or cockiness" among these leaders (p. 57). Effective leaders try to empower group members, not stand out as dominant and deserving of adoration or blind obedience. Garfield (1986) interviewed more than 500 top leaders and concluded that they use three primary skills: delegating, stretching the abilities of group members, and encouraging thoughtful risk-taking. All three skills empower group members. As Larson and LaFasto (1989) concluded, "leaders create leaders" (p. 128).

Competent communication is critical to effective leadership because a leader sets the emotional tone of the group. Top executives who fail as leaders exhibit insensitivity to others, are brutally critical, and are too demanding (Goleman, 1998). When a leader expresses rage, shows disrespect for members, berates those who make mistakes, humiliates members in front of the group, and exhibits arrogance and pettiness, the entire group is tarnished by this incompetent communication. Such "emotional incontinence," as Birgitta Wistrand calls it, ripples throughout the group (Goleman, 1998). When leaders fail to control themselves emotionally, members become hesitant, anxious, fearful, angry, and depressed.

Effective leaders create a supportive climate, encourage open communication, stimulate cooperation and a collaborative spirit, show empathy, and express optimism and a positive attitude (Goleman, 1998). Effective leaders adapt to changing circumstances and a variety of styles and personalities.

Summary

MANY benefits can be derived from working effectively in groups. Communication competence is central to our attitude about groups. Those who have little communication training typically find the group experience daunting and frustrating. Those who learn to communicate competently typically find the group experience far more beneficial.

The structure of small groups is largely shaped by group size, and it is composed primarily of norms and roles. Norms are rules that govern the behavior of group members. Roles are patterns of behavior that group members are expected to exhibit. The leader role is central to group structure. Playing the role of leader, however, does not equate with effective leadership. Effective leadership is not a person; it is a transformational process. Effective leadership requires competent communication. Leaders should be sensitive to the changing needs and situations within the group, assume the appropriate style for a given situation, and resist displays of competitive, defensive communication when dealing with group members.

Answers for *Critical Thinking* caption:

Dilbert (p. 292): #1, #2, #3, and #4

Quizzes Without Consequences

Did you understand all the material in this chapter? Test your knowledge before your exam!

Go to the companion website at www.oup.com/us/rothwell, click on the Student Resources for each chapter, and take the Quizzes Without Consequences.

Film School Case Studies

A League of Their Own (1992). Comedy/Drama; PG

This is director Penny Marshall's amusing and entertaining treatment of the first women's professional baseball league. Analyze leadership styles, especially those used by the Tom Hanks character. Does Hanks change leadership styles as the movie progresses?

Crimson Tide (1995). Drama; R

Taut drama about a nuclear submarine given an order (or so it seems) to launch a preemptive strike against a dissident rebel group in Russia. Examine the leadership style of the two main characters, played by Gene Hackman and Denzel Washington. Further analyze the leader-follower relationship and the ethics of leadership.

Hairspray (2007). Musical; PG

You'll need to like musicals as a film genre to enjoy this story of Baltimore teen life in 1962. Nevertheless, there is much to analyze from the viewpoint of norms and conformity. Examine explicit and implicit norms. What are some responses to norm violations, and how do these responses parallel research on the typical group responses to nonconformity?

Miracle (2004). Drama; PG-13

This is a faithful re-creation of the 1980 U.S. Olympic hockey team in Lake Placid when it defeated a far more talented Soviet team and proceeded to win the gold medal. Explain group synergy and the process that produced the synergistic "miracle on ice."

Pleasantville (1998). Comedy/Drama; PG

The two main characters (Tobey Maguire and Reese Witherspoon) are zapped into the black-and-white world of the 1950s. This is a trippy little movie with a nice message. Analyze the impact of norms on behavior and the reactions to nonconformity.

The Jane Austen Book Club (2008). Romance; PG-13

Several women and one man form a book club to read and discuss all six books by Jane Austen. Examine the roles that develop in the group. Identify who plays task, maintenance, and disruptive roles. Analyze leadership emergence and leadership effectiveness.

Twelve Angry Men (1957 or 1997). Drama; PG-13

Either version of this film is terrific. This is the classic jury movie, copied many times but never equaled. Examine the roles played by jury members during intense deliberations. Analyze leadership dynamics.

CHAPTER 11

Chapter Outline

- Challenges of Group Composition
- Competent Group Decision Making and Problem Solving
- Teambuilding and Teamwork
- Virtual Groups and Teams

PART 3

Creating Effective Groups

THE UNITED STATES fielded an imposing lineup for the 2006 World Baseball Classic, which included superstars Derek Jeter and Ken Griffey Jr. This was the first year that teams from around the world, comprised of professional players, competed for the world title in baseball; some viewed it as the real World Series. The U.S. team was embarrassed when it lost to Mexico, Canada, and South Korea and failed to make even the semifinal round. In the second baseball classic in 2009, the team from the United States did better, but they lost to Japan 9–4 in the semifinals even though they fielded a team whose aggregate professional salaries amounted to $160 million.

By the end of this chapter, you should be able to:

1. Recognize and combat the significant challenges you may face when working in small groups.
2. Promote competent group decision making and problem solving.

In stark contrast, the 1980 U.S. Olympic ice hockey team was a group of college players who had never participated on the same team until six months before the Olympic Games. At the time, the Soviet Union had the most powerful hockey team in the world (maybe ever) with a 44–0 win-loss record in international competition. The Soviet team was capable of defeating a professional group of NHL all-stars, which it did before the Olympics (score was 6–0). The Soviet team was a quasi-professional team claiming technical amateur status (no professional players were allowed in the Olympics at the time). In one of the most stunning upsets in modern sports history, the U.S. team defeated the Soviet team 4–3 in the "miracle on ice." The Americans went on to win the gold medal.

Why do some groups and teams succeed and others fail? Why doesn't assembling a group of the most highly skilled individuals assure success? Shouldn't the best produce the best? *The primary purpose of this chapter is to examine why groups succeed and fail.*

Challenges of Group Composition

Group membership presents many complex challenges. There may be vast differences among members in levels of motivation to work and accomplish group goals (task dimension). Members may dislike each other (social dimension). In this section, I discuss the challenges you face from difficult group members, social loafers, and diverse membership.

Difficult Group Members: Addressing Disruption

In one of my small-group classes, a group of six women was formed to work on a class project. Their communication was warm, friendly, and harmonious. They appeared enthusiastic about working together. They brainstormed a long list of ideas for their project and settled on one option within a short period of time. The following class period, a male student needed to join a group because he had missed the previous class. He joined the all-women group because other groups in the class were already somewhat larger. This new group member single-handedly transformed a harmonious, task-effective group into a frustrating group experience for everyone. This particular individual enjoyed telling sexist jokes, making derogatory remarks to the other members, and fighting any suggestions that were not his own. He proudly (and loudly) proclaimed to the entire class that he was the "leader of a chicks group." He also told his astonished group members that he "hoped PMS wouldn't be a problem" when they worked on their project.

The women were stunned. After class, they all approached me and requested that this disruptive individual be assigned to another group. I turned down their request, not wanting to pass the problem to another group. When I asked what steps they had taken to deal with their difficult group member, they confessed that none had yet been taken. This is not unusual. When faced with a difficult group member, ridding the group of the troublemaker is a common first response. As previously discussed, however, the power-forcing conflict style should be used as a last resort, not as a first option.

Difficult group members exhibit a wide variety of troublesome behaviors (see Box 11-1). *The disruptive roles identified in Chapter 10 provide a common list of such behaviors.* The male student who disrupted the previously all-female group adopted the fighter-controller and clown roles. One troublesome member's inappropriate behavior can cause disharmony and prevent a group from operating as a cohesive, fully functioning team (Wellen & Neale, 2006).

Research on **bad apples**—disruptive members who poison the group ("One bad apple spoils the barrel")—demonstrates just how disturbing such a group member can be (Felps et al., 2006; "Ruining It for the Rest of Us," 2008). A skilled student actor portrayed three versions of "bad apple" behavior in several groups. He played a *jerk* who made insulting comments to other group members, such as "Do you know anything?" and "That's a stupid idea." He played a *slacker* who refused to contribute during a 45-minute difficult group task, but text messaged a friend and responded with "whatever" or "I really don't care" to other group member's ideas. Finally, he played a *depressive pessimist* who called the task boring, predicted group failure, and placed his head on the table.

The results were stunning. Regardless of team talent and capabilities, those groups that had a single bad apple scored 30%-40% lower on a challenging task than teams with no bad apple. The bad apple's disruptive behavior was also contagious. When playing the jerk, the bad apple's insults triggered counterinsults from group members. When playing the slacker, his lethargic behavior encouraged slacker behavior from group members who said things such as "Let's just get this over with. Put down anything." When playing the depressive pessimist, other group members became cynical and disengaged.

Another study showed that a disruptive member of a work team who exhibited rude behavior toward coworkers had prompted half of those who were interviewed to contemplate leaving their jobs, and 12% actually quit (Pearson et al., 2000). The best employees are the most likely to leave a job to escape a disruptive coworker because they have a better chance of finding a new job (Mitchell & Lee, 2001). This leaves less capable coworkers and leads to a further deterioration in group performance (Felps et al., 2006).

You can take several steps to deal with difficult group members.

1. *Make certain a cooperative climate has been created by the group.* Are communication patterns supportive or defensive (see Chapter 8)? Is meaningful participation encouraged? Are all group members treated with respect? Developing a cooperative group climate is an essential first step in minimizing opportunities for disruptive behavior to emerge.

2. *Don't encourage disruptive behavior.* Laughing nervously at a disrupter's offensive "jokes" encourages the antisocial behavior. All six women laughed nervously at the

BOX 11.1 Developing Communication Competence

ARE YOU A DIFFICULT GROUP MEMBER?

Rate honestly your likely behavior in each of the scenarios that follow. This should reveal whether you are a difficult group member. Optional Alternative: After answering this questionnaire, ask fellow class or team members to complete this same assessment about you but only if you feel comfortable making such a request. If team members are hesitant, encourage them to complete the assessment without identifying themselves in the questionnaire (ideally, all team members should complete the assessment to preserve anonymity). Compare the results by following the scoring system at the end of this assessment.

1. When a topic of great interest to me is discussed in my group, I tend to talk much longer and more forcefully than I know I should.

   FREQUENTLY 5 4 3 2 1 RARELY
2. During group discussions, I typically remain silent, exhibiting lack of interest in the proceedings.

   FREQUENTLY 5 4 3 2 1 RARELY
3. When my group attempts to work on a task, especially one of little interest to me, I prefer to joke around and be comical instead of focusing on the task.

   FREQUENTLY 5 4 3 2 1 RARELY
4. When I oppose what my group decides, I am inclined to reintroduce the issue already decided even though I know there is little chance the group will change its decision.

   FREQUENTLY 5 4 3 2 1 RARELY
5. I often quarrel openly with group members by raising my voice, interrupting other members to forcefully interject my own opinion and criticizing those who disagree with me.

   FREQUENTLY 5 4 3 2 1 RARELY
6. I have strong opinions that often color my participation during group discussions, and I attempt to convert group members to my way of thinking even if they are unresponsive.

   FREQUENTLY 5 4 3 2 1 RARELY
7. I'm inclined to predict failure of the group, especially if a risk is involved, and I tend to focus on what will go wrong, not on what will go right with my group's decisions.

   FREQUENTLY 5 4 3 2 1 RARELY

Total your responses for all seven of your answers (maximum score = 35; minimum score = 7). Determine your average score (divide total score by 7). If your average score is 3.0 or higher, you tend toward being a difficult group member. Any single answer that is 3, 4, or 5 indicates trouble for your group on that particular behavior. These seven scenarios correspond to the disruptive informal roles discussed in Chapter 10.

disrupter's sexist jokes and remarks. He had no antenna, no sensitivity, to pick up fairly obvious signals from his group members that they were offended and embarrassed by his behavior. When a feedback form was filled out weeks later by all group members, his self-assessment showed that he believed the female group members thought he was funny and liked his humor. He was flabbergasted when all six women wrote on their feedback form that his humor was offensive and disruptive. Don't allow the disrupter to dominate conversations, interrupt other members, or in any way intimidate the group. Giving the troublemaker a soapbox only encourages the bad behavior. Simply ask the disrupter to wait his or her turn, respect other members, and listen.

3. *Confront the difficult person directly* (see Chapter 9). If the entire group is upset with the disrupter, the group should confront the troublemaker. Follow the guidelines for supportive communication when confronting a difficult member (see Chapter 8).

4. *If all else fails, remove the disrupter from the group* (LaFasto & Larson, 2001). In one study of 75 diverse teams, a very clear message emerged: "There is no longer any room on teams for people who cannot work collaboratively" (Larson & LaFasto, 1989, p. 71). If the troublesome group member cannot be removed for some reason, keep interactions with this person to a minimum.

5. *Always be unconditionally constructive.* Model constructive communication. Imitating the disrupter's troublesome behavior produces a conflict spiral. Only one group in the "bad apple" study resisted the disrupter's negative influence. This group had a strong member who didn't return insults with insults, didn't get angry, but instead listened intently to everyone and asked lots of questions. He set a constructive tone and refused to be sidetracked. His father was a diplomat, so perhaps he learned to be diplomatic from him.

So how did the six women in my class manage their disruptive member? None of them would confront him directly despite my prompting. All of them, however, remained unconditionally constructive. They eventually stopped laughing nervously at his jokes, and they refused to let him bully them. Since there were six of them and only one of him, they managed to silence him on several occasions by ignoring his disruption and focusing on the task, thereby giving him no soapbox and no appreciative audience. They all performed wonderfully during their group presentation to the class. He, on the other hand, embarrassed himself by performing ineptly. Sometimes the most you can hope for is containment, not transformation, of the disrupter.

Social Loafers: Dealing with Lackluster Effort

Call them goof-offs, freeloaders, energy sappers, participatory parasites; academics call them social loafers. Social loafing is one of the most common complaints about working in groups. Members do not share the same level of commitment to the group and the task (see Box 11-2). Those who are fully committed, even inspired, to work in the group become demoralized and frustrated by the apathy and disinterest shown by one or more group members. **Social loafing** is the tendency of individuals to reduce their work effort when they join groups (Karau & Hart, 1998). Social loafers "goof off" when tasks need to be accomplished. They miss some meetings and show up late to others. They fail to complete tasks important to overall group performance. Social loafers exhibit scant effort because of weak motivation, disinterest in the group, or poor attitude. *Social loafing is not the same as shyness.* Shy individuals may be strongly committed to the group but are reluctant to participate in discussions because of communication anxiety or fear of disapproval (McCroskey & Richmond, 1992). Shy members may attend all meetings and never be tardy.

Why Social Loafing Occurs: Sizing Up the Problem

Social loafing increases with group size (Chidambaram & Tung, 2005). It is easier to reduce effort expended in a larger group than in a smaller group and not be noticed. One study asked participants to clap and cheer "as loud as you can." These efforts were measured as individuals, dyads (two partners), and four- or six-person groups. Dyads performed at 71% of each person's individual capacity, four-person groups at 51%, and six-person groups at only 40% (Latane et al., 1979).

Social loafing occurs because individual group members often do not see the connection between their personal effort and the outcomes desired by the group (Karau & Williams, 1993). It occurs in a broad range of groups working on a variety of tasks. Males and females of all ages and from many different cultures may be social loafers. *Social loafing is more common in an individualist culture* such as that of the United States than it is in collectivist cultures such as those of Singapore, China, Thailand, Pakistan, and Indonesia (Early, 1989; Gabreyna, 1985). People in individualist cultures are not as heavily influenced

BOX 11.2 Developing Communication Competence

SOCIAL LOAFING: A SELF-ASSESSMENT

Make honest assessments of your participation in small-group decision making and problem solving.

1. I am on time for small-group meetings.
   Rarely 1 2 3 4 5 Almost Always
2. I leave small-group meetings early.
   Rarely 1 2 3 4 5 Almost Always
3. I am quiet during small-group discussions.
   Rarely 1 2 3 4 5 Almost Always
4. My attention during small-group discussions is focused on the task.
   Rarely 1 2 3 4 5 Almost Always
5. I am strongly motivated to perform well in small groups.
   Rarely 1 2 3 4 5 Almost Always
6. When other group members show little interest in accomplishing a task successfully, I lose interest in achieving success.
   Rarely 1 2 3 4 5 Almost Always
7. When other group members seem uninvolved in participating on the group task, I also reduce my participation.
   Rarely 1 2 3 4 5 Almost Always

Determine your average score on statements 1, 4, and 5 (add the scores and divide by 3), then determine your average score on items 2, 3, 6, and 7 (add the scores and divide by 4). Your average score on statements 1, 4, and 5 should be high (4–5), and your average score on statements 2, 3, 6, and 7 ideally should be quite low (1–2)—little social loafing.

as those in collectivist cultures by what the group might think of a person's effort. Individual group members may establish their "uniqueness" by showing how uninvolved they can be, even in the face of group pressure to perform. In collectivist cultures, however, pleasing the group, maintaining group harmony, and submerging individual accomplishment for the sake of the group encourage strong group commitment and discourage loafing. The collectivist attitude is "don't let the group down." Lackluster performance by loafers could bring loss of face.

Addressing Social Loafing: The Three C's of Motivation

How can you diminish or eliminate the disadvantage of social loafing associated with group work? Motivation is the root of this problem. Before discussing what might motivate loafers, let's be very clear regarding what doesn't motivate them. Exhortations from motivated group members usually have no lasting effect on loafers. This is analogous to hiring a "motivational speaker" to lecture employees in the workplace. Kohn (1993) sums up the failure of this approach: "At best, the result is a temporary sense of being re-energized, much like the effect of eating a doughnut. When the sugar high wears off, very little of value is left in the system" (p. 187). Cheerleading doesn't address a loafer's lack of interest in the group and its tasks. It assumes that every member can be inspired, even if the group task is tedious and uninspiring.

Performance evaluation tied to some kind of reward system also is unlikely to jump-start a loafer (Aguayo, 1990; Kohn, 1993). In the workplace, performance evaluations are often tied to wages and other forms of compensation. Exceptional work earns a bonus. Poor appraisal of a worker typically results in no pay increase or even a pay reduction. Consultant Peter Scholtes (1990) says, "Using performance appraisal of any kind as a basis for reward is a flat out catastrophic mistake" (p. 46). The likely result of such schemes is de-motivation of workers given mediocre or poor appraisals for lackluster performance. *Any step that creates a competitive, defensive environment is unlikely to motivate social loafers* (Kohn, 1993).

Kohn (1993) offers "the three C's of motivation" that encourage cooperation, not competition. The three C's are collaboration, content, and choice. *Collaboration* is the cooperative style of conflict management (see Chapter 9). It is also synonymous with teamwork (LaFasto & Larson, 2001; Sawyer, 2007). Developing teamwork through cooperation and cohesiveness (see discussion later in this chapter) can motivate loafers because they no longer see themselves as individuals separate from the group (Hoigaard et al., 2006). They identify with the group. Groups that achieve success and receive rewards for such success typically have little problem with loafers. This is especially so when each group member perceives that his or her individual effort is necessary for the group to succeed on a valued task (Hart et al., 2001; Karau & Williams, 1993). If a group member's individual performance can be identified separately from the group's, social loafing also decreases (Karau & Williams, 1993). When a group member has been given a specific task to perform and he or she does not complete the task because of weak effort, the entire group notices. Not wanting to let the team down can be a powerful motivator for some members.

Content refers to the group task. What work are group members asked to perform? "Idleness, indifference and irresponsibility are healthy responses to absurd work," claims Frederick Herzberg (quoted in Kohn, 1993, p. 189). Few group members will be motivated to work on tasks that hold no interest for them. Granted, not all tasks can be motivating. Some tasks must be performed even though they are dreary, mind-numbing jobs. Nevertheless, busy work should be kept to a minimum so the totality of a group's work is viewed as involving and interesting. Group members need to see the value of performing a task before they are likely to take responsibility for meeting their individual obligations to the group effort. Social loafing decreases when group members see work as meaningful (Karau & Williams, 1993).

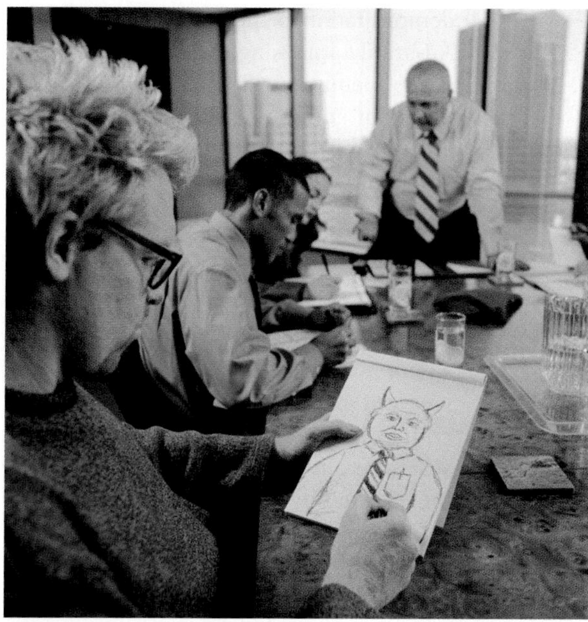

Social loafing

1. Is the same as shyness exhibited by a group member
2. Decreases as the size of the group increases
3. Occurs because individual group members often do not see the connection between personal effort and group outcomes
4. Is, at root, a lack of group member motivation

Answers at end of chapter

Choice is a nice complement to content. One way of making group projects and tasks challenging and interesting to group members is to allow as much choice as possible. Try letting group members choose which part of a project they would most like to tackle. Some members may enjoy doing Internet research, others may enjoy interviewing experts on a topic, and still others may enjoy constructing a PowerPoint demonstration or developing a web page. Arbitrarily imposing task assignments on group members will quickly produce loafing, even grumbling. Group tasks become meaningful when members have a say in what is done and how it is accomplished.

Group Member Diversity: The Challenge of Difference

Chapter 3 documented the increasing diversity of our population. The likelihood that you will participate in groups composed entirely of individuals very much like yourself is becoming ever more remote. This is an opportunity and a challenge. Research shows that gender diversity in small groups enhances team performance (Curseu & Schruijer, 2010). Another study showed that groups composed of Asian, African, Latino, and Anglo American members outperformed groups that contained only Anglos (whites) (McLeod et al., 1996). Also, groups that include a mix of genders and ethnicities combat biases more effectively than more homogeneous groups (Marcus-Newhall et al., 1993).

Member diversity, however, poses significant challenges to groups and individuals alike (Chao & Moon, 2005; Mannix & Neale, 2005). Older students in a group of mostly teenagers may have a challenge identifying with younger members, and vice versa. Individuals fresh out of college and thrown into the corporate world of much older and more experienced individuals may find it intimidating working with more mature, experienced members. With diversity may come greater difficulty finding agreement in the group. Cohesiveness and group satisfaction may also be more difficult to develop and maintain (Barker et al., 2000). There may be a perceived competition for power and resources between majority and minority members that can result in hostile communication and discrimination (Mannix & Neale, 2005). Competent communication provides a promising approach to meeting these challenges that group member diversity poses. Using communication to develop perceptions of commonality among diverse group members to create a sense of strong group identity that transcends stereotypes and issues of gender, race, socioeconomic status, and power differences is particularly essential if small groups are to succeed.

Competent Group Decision Making and Problem Solving

James Surowiecki (2005), author of *The Wisdom of Crowds*, claims that groups can often outsmart individuals working alone (see also Laughlin et al., 2006). Surowiecki cites the example, among many others, of the television game show *Who Wants to Be a Millionaire?* When contestants are stumped by a question, they may consult a trusted friend or family member (allies) or the studio audience. The trusted allies produce correct answers 65% of the time, but the studio audience chooses the right answer 91% of the time. Psychologist Keith Sawyer (2007) refers to this collective wisdom as "group genius."

Synergy: Creating Group Genius

Groups often outperform individuals, and sometimes they outperform individuals spectacularly. This group genius effect is called synergy. **Synergy** (syn = together; ergon = work) occurs when the work of group members yields a greater total effect than the sum of the individual members' efforts could have produced. When this joint action of group members produces performance that exceeds expectations based on the perceived abilities and skills of individual members, synergy has occurred (Salazar, 1995). Thus, the whole is not equal to the mere sum of its parts but is greater than the sum of its parts. Synergy is like combining cancer-fighting drugs to produce far greater effects than taking the drugs separately could produce. This is the basis of chemotherapy.

The 1980 U.S. hockey team is a stunning example of group synergy. Comparing the individual abilities of players on the U.S. and Soviet teams, it should have been no contest. The Soviet team, on paper, was the far superior team. In fact, a couple of weeks before the Olympics, the U.S. team played a practice match against the Soviet team and lost badly 10–3. Sometimes, however, less capable individuals working smoothly as a team pull off a synergistic miracle.

A June 23, 1998, *NBC News at Sunrise* report provides another apt example of synergy. A Little League team in Tucson, Arizona, called the Diamondbacks, was composed of players no other teams wanted because they were considered misfits who were not good enough to play. These misfits compiled a perfect record of 18–0 to win the league championship. The group effort far exceeded expectations of success based on the individual abilities of the players.

How does synergy happen? Synergy is typically the product of cooperation within a group (Sawyer, 2007). It occurs primarily by individuals working together, unselfishly, in a coordinated effort to achieve a common goal. Rafael Aguayo (1990) draws from his own experience as a Little League soccer coach to explain how synergy occurs. Aguayo emphasized having fun, improving skill levels, and teamwork. He de-emphasized winning. Before each game, he told his players that scoring goals and winning weren't important. Playing hard, improving skills, and acting like a team were important. After a game, he would ask his players, "Who scored that first goal?" At first, the player who scored the first goal would raise a hand. "No!" Aguayo would cry. "We all scored that goal. Every person on a team is responsible for scoring a goal." Then he repeated his question, "Now, who scored that goal?" All the players on the team raised their hands. Aguayo never singled out any player as better than any other. Instead, he gave every team member a "best player" trophy at the end of the season. Each player got to be captain at least once. What were the results of this experiment in cooperation, teamwork, and a We- not Me-orientation? Synergy was the result. In the four years Aguayo coached Little League soccer, his team lost only a single game.

In addition to cooperation, groups composed of members with **deep diversity**—substantial variation among members in task-relevant skills, knowledge, abilities, beliefs, values, perspectives, and problem-solving strategies—have greater potential to produce synergy than groups with little diversity (Harrison et al., 2002). "Group genius can happen only if the brains in the team don't contain all the same stuff" (Sawyer, 2007, p. 72). In one simulation study comparing groups with deep diversity and those without, the deeply diverse groups produced a synergistic effect, the groups outperformed even their best individual member, and cooperative interaction among members during problem solving benefited the performance of these groups. Groups without deep diversity didn't perform nearly as well (Larson, 2007).

Negative Synergy: Collective Failure

Groups don't always produce the group genius of synergy, however. If you're sharing ignorance about a subject, no good is likely to come of it. The National Geographic-Roper Public Affairs Geographic Literacy Study (2006) shows some gaping holes in geographic knowledge among young Americans ages 18–24. Only 54% of the questions were answered correctly by the 510 respondents chosen randomly. More than six in ten (63%) were unable to locate Iraq on a map, 75% couldn't locate Iran or Israel, and 88% could not locate Afghanistan despite heavy media coverage of major U.S. involvement in these countries. More than half (51%) couldn't find Japan on a map, and 65% couldn't locate our "Mother Country" Great Britain. Half also couldn't locate New York on a map of the United States; 6% couldn't even locate the United States on a world map. (When asked the trivia question on a roll sheet I circulate in each class, "What is the tallest mountain in the world?" one student wrote "Mountain Dew." I laughed, but having just read the results of this geography study, I wasn't completely confident it was meant to be a joke.) These results prompted authors of the report to conclude: "Americans are far from alone in the world, but from the perspective of many young Americans, we might as well be" (p. 6). Some reassurance comes from the result that those with at least some college education and those who use the Internet for world news updates did somewhat better on this geography quiz (64% accuracy). Nevertheless, groups aren't likely to perform magic in the absence of knowledge. That is why you don't want a group of geography-challenged individuals making decisions about U.S. Middle Eastern policy when these group members can't locate countries in the Middle East on a map. Ignorance of geography indicates a staggering lack of essential knowledge about the very cultures for which such policies are aimed. No good can come of such shared ignorance.

When groups produce results that are beyond bad, it is called negative synergy. **Negative synergy** is the product of joint action of group members that produces a result worse than that expected based on perceived individual abilities and skills of members (Salazar, 1995). Negative synergy is like mixing alcohol and tranquilizers, which can cause accidental death. The mixture is far worse than the sum of the effects produced when taking each separately.

I give cooperative exams in my classes. Group members work on the exam together and turn in a single answer sheet. An individual accountability test, which sets a minimum standard of performance to earn the group grade, follows the group exam. Most groups score much higher than the average of individual test scores (synergy) and usually higher than any member of the group scores on the individual test. Occasionally, however, negative synergy occurs. On one exam, all the groups but one scored in the 80s or 90s. One group of six, however, scored 50. Their group score was actually lower than the average of their individual scores. The group performed worse than any group member. I had listened to their discussion during the test, and I heard members talk the group into choosing incorrect answers. The group was capable of scoring much higher on the test, but lack of motivation, poor communication in the group, lackluster preparation, and conflict diminished the result.

Synergy won't occur simply because individuals form a group. A single expert on a technical topic can provide better advice than a group of uninformed members. If you have a legal question, go see a good lawyer. Seeking legal advice from a group of friends who know next to nothing about the law is inviting prison (criminal charges) or poverty (civil suit). Nevertheless, groups can often produce exceptional results because they can share the labor required to research even technical or complex subjects, they can pool knowledge and share information, and they can correct errors more readily because there are more heads devoted to spotting mistakes and misjudgments (for a more comprehensive treatment of this, see Rothwell, 2010). As the Japanese proverb says, "None of us is as smart as all of us."

Manage the Meeting Monster: Stop Wasting Time

The major difference between meetings and funerals is that "most funerals have a definite purpose. Also, nothing is ever really buried in a meeting." So claims humorist Dave Barry (1991, p. 311). Columnist George Will adds this: "Football combines two of the worst things about American life. It is violence punctuated by committee meetings" (quoted in Fitzhenry, 1993, p. 426). The so-called Mitchell's Law states: "Any simple problem can be made insoluble if enough meetings are held to discuss it." Meetings are an indispensable means of making group decisions and solving problems (Blenko et al., 2010; Luong & Rogelberg, 2005), but they can be a horror if handled poorly. Having to attend meetings is perceived by many to be a serious disadvantage of group work. The more meetings attended, the greater is the fatigue felt by participants, and the greater is the perception of excessive workloads (Luong & Rogelberg, 2005). Grouphate is nourished by the prevalent belief that group meetings are mostly a waste of time. Studies have found that about a third of the time spent in meetings is wasted, costing billions of dollars to organizations and businesses and more than a few headaches (Green & Lazarus, 1990; Lazar, 1991).

Admittedly, meetings can eat up a large chunk of one's day. One study reported that individuals attended meetings, on average, for more than two-and-a-half hours each working day (Luong & Rogelberg, 2005). Nevertheless, group meetings can actually increase the productivity of groups. Cecilia Sharpe, head of an auditing team of six accountants, decided to calculate the effects of eliminating the team's weekly meeting while encouraging team members to maintain direct communication with each other to coordinate task accomplishment. When a single proposal to revise work schedules for her auditing team arose, she found that eliminating the team's weekly meeting to discuss this proposal resulted in a net loss of 18 person-hours in productivity, 102 disruptions of team members because of phone calls to discuss proposals (compared to 7 disruptions of any kind during regular team meetings), a decision that was two days late, and significant team-member dissatisfaction with the final decision (see Shaffner, 1999).

Group meetings don't have to be time wasters, but they often are. Business consultant Mitchell Nash (see Dressler, 1995) identifies six common complaints made about group meetings: (1) the meeting has an unclear purpose, (2) participants are unprepared, (3) key individuals are absent or tardy, (4) discussion drifts into irrelevant conversation, (5) some group members dominate discussion, and (6) decisions made at meetings often are not implemented.

Whoever chairs a meeting can take steps that will make the meeting productive and efficient. Here are some suggestions.

1. *Don't call a meeting unless no other good alternative exists.* Hold a meeting if immediate action is required, group participation is essential, group members are prepared to discuss relevant issues, and main players can be present. If objectives can be met without a meeting, don't meet. One of life's small pleasures is the unexpected notification, "Meeting has been canceled."

2. *Identify the specific purpose of the meeting.* Notify each group member of where the meeting will be held, when, and how long it will likely last. Let participants know if they should bring certain materials or resources to the meeting. Encourage each member to be prepared to discuss important issues. Typically, only about a quarter of group members are prepared for most meetings (Green & Lazarus, 1990).

3. *Prepare a clear agenda.* An **agenda** is a list of topics to be discussed in a group meeting presented in the order in which they will be addressed. An agenda typically includes a time allotment for discussion of each issue (see Box 11-3). Provide any necessary information, along with the agenda, that may help members understand topics to be discussed.

4. *Above all, keep the discussion on track.* Don't allow drifting. Aimless discussion sucks the life out of meetings and causes eyelids to droop. As Ronald Reagan once quipped, "I have left orders to be awakened at any time in case of national emergency, even if I'm in a cabinet meeting." Also, squelch stagehogs. No one should be permitted to dominate the discussion. A simple "Let's hear from some other individuals" is usually sufficient to short-circuit the stagehog. Encourage participation from all members.

5. *Start the meeting on time and be guided by the "what's done is done" rule* (Tropman, 1996). Do not interrupt the flow of the meeting by bringing latecomers up to speed, except to indicate which item on the agenda is under discussion. Latecomers can be filled in briefly after the meeting or during a break, if necessary. Instructors don't restart classes each time a student comes in late. Nothing would get accomplished. Concerts aren't stopped in midstream to accommodate those who amble in late. Movies aren't begun again when latecomers appear. Punctuality discourages late arrival, especially when the meeting moves forward and isn't derailed by tardiness.

6. *Do not discuss an issue longer than the time allotted unless the group decides to extend the time.* This prevents talkaholics from pointlessly extending the meeting well beyond expectations. Three of four meetings don't end on time (Green & Lazarus, 1990). Meetings that end ahead of time are cause

BOX 11.3 Developing Communication Competence

A SAMPLE AGENDA FOR GROUP MEETINGS

Meeting of the Student Senate
November 15
Boardroom
2:00–4:00 P.M.

Purpose: Biweekly meeting

I. Call meeting to order
II. Approval of the minutes of last meeting (5 minutes)
III. Additions to the agenda (2 minutes)
IV. Committee reports
 A. Student clubs committee (5 minutes)
 B. Student transportation committee (5 minutes)
 C. Student activities committee (5 minutes)
V. Officers' reports
 A. Treasurer's report (3 minutes)
 B. President's report (10 minutes)
VI. Old business (previously discussed but unresolved)
 A. Campus security problems (15 minutes)
 B. Cost of textbooks (10 minutes)
 C. Parking garage proposal (10 minutes)
 D. Student credit card proposal (5 minutes)
VII. New business
 A. Hate speech on campus (15 minutes)
 B. Expanding the bookstore (10 minutes)
 C. Open access computer use (10 minutes)
 D. Student elections (5 minutes)
VIII. Agenda building for next meeting (5 minutes)
IX. Adjournment

for celebration; those that end late are cause for exasperation.

7. *Take a few minutes at the end of the meeting to determine if all objectives were accomplished.* Two-thirds of meetings fail to accomplish stated objectives (Green & Lazarus, 1990). Schedule time in the next meeting to consider any unresolved issues.

8. *Distribute minutes of the meeting to all participants as soon as possible.* The minutes should indicate what was discussed, who said what, what action was taken, and what remains to be discussed and decided.

The meeting monster can be slain and grouphate quelled if these simple steps are followed to keep meetings efficient and productive. Meetings do not have to be a form of torture.

Structure Decision Making: Using the Standard Agenda

Conducting efficient meetings in which problems can be explored is a good beginning, but much more is required for competent group decision making and problem solving. Without a structure for decision making, groups often leap to consideration of solutions before adequately discussing and exploring the causes of problems. Free-floating discussions usually result in poor time management, aimless conversation, high-status members' domination of discussions, squelching of minority viewpoints, and escalation of conflict spirals (Sunwolf & Frey, 2005). This leads to ineffective decision making. Thus, successful groups typically have a systematic, structured method of decision making and problem solving; unsuccessful teams typically do not (LaFasto & Larson, 2001).

The **Standard Agenda** provides one such highly effective structured method of decision making and problem solving. It is based on the **reflective thinking model** of John Dewey (1910)—a sequence of logical steps that incorporates the scientific method of defining, analyzing, and solving problems. These are the six steps in the Standard Agenda.

1. *Identify the goal(s)*. Establish a clear, specific goal or set of goals. Let's say that your group has a project assigned in your group-discussion class. Your instructor has told the class that each group must choose a project from a list of five options. The group's overall specific goal might be to choose an option that will earn the team an "A" grade. A secondary goal might be to work on a project that interests all group members.

2. *Analyze the problem*. When we analyze a problem, we break it down into its constituent parts. We examine the nature of the problem. The group project assigned in class might produce an analysis of the pros and cons for the five options available. Group members might consider how much research will be required and what information is readily available for each option, how much time the group has to do the necessary research, how much background knowledge is necessary to do the project well, and how interested members are in each option.

3. *Establish criteria*. Criteria are standards for judgment, guidelines for determining effective decision making and problem solving. When I visited the National Gallery of Modern Art in Washington, D.C., I was immediately drawn to a huge painting. The entire canvas, which covered most of an interior wall, was painted off-white except for a solitary red dot about the size of a basketball in the lower-right quadrant. Why was this painting chosen as special enough to hang in the National Gallery? Why would the National Gallery pay tens of thousands of dollars for such a painting? Could it be the reputation of the painter? Perhaps its attention-getting quality made it a worthy choice. I couldn't help thinking that I could duplicate this work. "If I can do it, it can't be great art" has always been my starting criterion for assessing the relative merit of art works. Knowing what criteria art experts who chose this painting used to make their decision would have helped me understand why their choice made sense. I never found out what criteria were applied to this painting, and my appreciation of its merits remains minimal.

Without establishing criteria in advance of final decisions, it is very difficult to gauge whether group choices will likely prove to be effective. In the case of a class project, the instructor will normally provide the specific criteria for the groups. In other circumstances, the group should discuss criteria and choose three to five before proceeding with the next step. Criteria should answer the question, "What standards should be met for the decision/solution to be a good one?" Some possible criteria for a group project in a class might be the following:

a. Stay within the prescribed time limits for the class presentations.
b. Exhibit clear organization.
c. Use at least one clear attention strategy and cite at least three credible sources of information during each group member's presentation.
d. Employ one visual aid per member's speech.

The extent to which the group meets these criteria will determine whether members all earn an "A" on their project.

4. *Generate solutions*. When weighing the merits and demerits of each project option,

don't assume that the objections to each option can't be solved. Let's suppose that the group is torn between two options: exploring a campus problem such as parking or researching an international problem such as global warming. Initially, the parking problem might seem a less satisfactory choice. Finding credible sources and sufficient quality information in the limited time available for preparation might seem to be insurmountable impediments. If the group has a greater interest in the parking problem than in global warming, however, group members might brainstorm possible solutions to these impediments. Perhaps the group could conduct a campus survey to generate credible information where a lack of such information might be a problem. School officials and campus security could be interviewed.

5. *Evaluate solutions and make the final decision.* Before deciding on the project, the group should consider each option in terms of the criteria. Which option will best allow the group to achieve its goals? Will exploring a campus problem such as parking or an international problem such as climate change best permit the group to reach its goal of an "A" grade? Which option is most interesting to group members? The likelihood of satisfying the criteria will allow group members to make a reasonable decision.

It is particularly important during this step that group members consider both the positive and the negative aspects of each choice. Groups often become enamored with a solution without considering **Murphy's Law**, which is, anything that can go wrong likely will go wrong. When the Boeing Company builds an airplane, designers account for Murphy's Law in the plans. An airplane with four engines is designed to fly temporarily with but a single engine. Boeing doesn't expect three engines to malfunction during the same flight, but just in case, it is better to err on the side of safety. Expect the unexpected and build it into your group decision.

6. *Implement the decision.* Group decisions don't amount to much if they aren't implemented, and implementation takes planning, which is something groups often fail to do. To implement the group's decision, divide labor among the members in a coordinated fashion. Each member must be given a clear role to perform that contributes to the eventual implementation of the group decision. One or two members might do interviews, another might write a survey, other members might research the parking problem. All of these tasks are interdependent; leave any out and successful implementation may be jeopardized. Merely talking about doing the project doesn't get it done. Deadlines for completion of each stage of the project should be set so all members know what is expected of them and when the product of their labor is due. Members should then discuss the results, condense the material into usable form, and organize the presentation of results to outsiders.

Some groups don't stick rigidly to the Standard Agenda. They may jump around from step to step. Two points are critical, however. First, the problem should be explored thoroughly before any solutions or options are considered. Second, establish criteria before making any important decisions.

Employ Decision-Making Rules Competently: Making Choices

Choices must be made at every step of the Standard Agenda. How those decisions will be made depends on rules of decision making. There are three chief decision-making rules for small groups: unanimity or consensus, majority rule, and minority rule. Each has its benefits and drawbacks. Groups may choose to use more than one decision-making rule depending on developing circumstances.

Consensus: It's Unanimous

Some groups operate under the unanimity rule. This is usually referred to as consensus decision making. **Consensus** is "a state of mutual agreement among members of a group where all legitimate concerns of individuals have been addressed to the satisfaction of the group" (Saint & Lawson, 1997, p. 21). Juries are one example of consensus groups. Criminal trials in most instances require all jurors to agree. All legitimate concerns of jurors must be addressed to achieve a consensus. If jurors ignore a legitimate concern, even a single dissenter can hang the jury and force a retrial or dismissal of charges.

Consensus requires unanimity, but it doesn't mean that every group member's preferred choice will be selected. Consensus is reached when all group members can support and live with the decision that is made. This means that group members interact cooperatively (see Box 11-4). Members exhibit give-and-take during discussions. Some group members may have to modify a preferred choice before every group member can climb aboard and sail with the decision. Conversely, giving in too easily will negate the value of the unanimity rule. Airing differences of opinion is constructive.

There are several advantages to using the unanimity rule to structure decision making. First, consensus requires full discussion of issues, which improves the chances that quality decisions will be made. Every group member must be convinced before a decision becomes final. Minority opinions will need to be heard. Those who disagree can't be ignored because they can stymie the group (e.g., most jury decisions). All points of view must be considered. Second, team members are likely to be committed to the final decision and will defend the decision when challenged by outsiders. Dissenters may undermine a group decision that is less than unanimous. Third, consensus usually produces group satisfaction. Members typically are satisfied with the decision-making process and the outcome (Abramson, 1994; Miller, 1989).

The unanimity rule has two chief drawbacks. First, consensus is very difficult to achieve; the process is time consuming and sometimes contentious. Members can become frustrated by the length of deliberations and perturbed with holdouts who resist siding with the majority. Second, consensus

BOX 11.4 Developing Communication Competence

HOW TO ACHIEVE A CONSENSUS

Achieving a consensus is a major challenge for any group. Here are several suggestions that can guide a team toward achieving consensus (Hall & Watson, 1970; Saint & Lawson, 1997).

1. Follow the Standard Agenda, and use suggestions for running productive meetings. Consensus requires structured deliberations, not aimless, brain-killing conversation.
2. Encourage supportive patterns of communication throughout discussions. Discourage defensive patterns that creep into discussions. A cooperative group climate is essential.
3. Identify the pros and cons of a decision under consideration. Write these for all to see.
4. Discuss all concerns and try to resolve those concerns to everyone's satisfaction. Look for alternatives if concerns remain.
5. Avoid arguing stubbornly for a position. Be prepared to give in when possible. Look for ways to break an impasse.
6. Ask for a *stand-aside.* Standing aside means a group member still has a reservation about the decision but does not feel that it warrants continued opposition to the final decision.
7. Avoid conflict-suppressing methods such as coin flipping and swapping ("I'll vote for your proposal this time if you vote for mine next"). A straw vote to ascertain the general level of acceptance for a decision or proposal is useful, but the goal should be unanimity.
8. If consensus cannot be reached, seek a *supermajority* (minimum two-thirds agreement). This at least captures the thrust of consensus decision making by requiring substantial, if not total, agreement.

becomes increasingly unlikely as groups grow larger. Teams of 15 or 20 will find it difficult to achieve consensus on anything (even a time to meet). Some large groups can't even achieve consensus on whether to meet again.

Consensus is not the only way groups make decisions, but consensus decision making is useful when policy, priorities, and goals are being considered (Romig, 1996). Consensus is most relevant for important group decisions.

Many choices made by group members, however, do not require consensus. The group does not need to reach a consensus on where research should be conducted to gather information. Presumably, the group member who plays the information-seeker role will be knowledgeable about where to look. Members can provide suggestions, but insisting on a consensus in such situations micromanages group members and will likely build resentment. If you've ever tried to reach a family consensus when choosing a restaurant for dinner or a movie preference, then you know consensus cannot always be reached. If consensus cannot be reached, other decision-making rules can be used to break a deadlock.

Majority Rule: Effective but Not Always Appropriate

The most popular method of decision making in the United States is majority rule. The U.S. political system depends on it. It has determined winners on *American Idol, Dancing with the Stars, Survivor*, and other media-created contests. Majority rule has important benefits. It is efficient and can provide rapid closure on relatively unimportant issues. In large groups, majority rule may be the only reasonable way to make a decision. Unlike consensus, majority rule can usually break a deadlock. Once a majority emerges, a decision can be made.

Majority rule also has significant disadvantages. First, majorities sometimes support preposterous, unethical positions. Majorities have supported racism, sexism, and homophobia at various times in the history of the United States. The majority in the South accepted slavery as a "peculiar institution" worth defending, and crowds (including women and children) assembled to watch lynchings of African Americans. Prior to 1920, the majority in the United States thought women should not be allowed to vote, own property, serve on juries, or be members of Congress. Sometimes the "tyranny of the majority" can produce awful decisions.

Second, groups using majority rule may encourage a dominance power dynamic within the group. Those with the most power (the majority) can impose their will on the less powerful minority. This could easily lead to a competitive power struggle within the group.

Third, majorities may be tempted to decide too quickly, before proper discussion and debate have taken place, squelching the chance of creating synergy. Groups can make reckless, ill-conceived decisions. Minority opinion can be ignored.

Typically, *effective groups use majority rule when consensus is impossible or when quick decisions about commonplace issues must be made*. A consensus decision regarding where the group should meet, when, and for how long is useful, but bogging down from lengthy discussions about such "housekeeping" tasks will quickly grow old. A simple majority vote may prove satisfactory to move the group along.

Minority Rule: Decision by Expert or Authority

Majorities don't always make decisions in small groups. Occasionally, a group will designate an expert to make the decision for the group. Sometimes a group merely advises a person in authority but doesn't actually make decisions. The authority can choose to listen to the advice or ignore it because he or she has the power of the position granted by the larger organization. On rare occasions, a forceful faction, a small but powerful subgroup, can intimidate a group and assert its will on the majority.

Minority rule has serious disadvantages. First, a designated expert can ignore group input or simply not request it. Second, members may engage in power plays to seek favor with the authority figure who makes

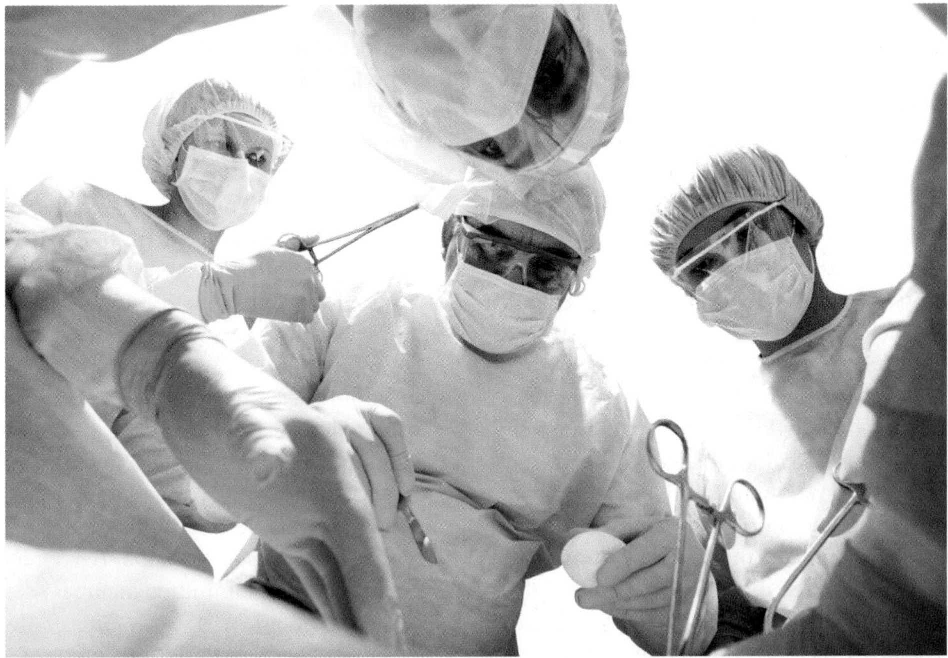

Consensus and majority vote both would be inappropriate for a surgical team performing an operation. "All those in favor of cutting here raise your hand"—it doesn't work! Split-second decisions must be made, so minority rule (chief surgeon) makes the decisions.

the decision. Third, group members will likely have weak commitment to the final decision because they had little participation in the outcome.

Despite significant drawbacks, minority decision making may be warranted in some limited circumstances. For example, *consensus with qualification* is a two-step decision-making process. First, the group tries to reach a consensus on an important issue. If consensus is reached, the decision is made. If consensus cannot be reached, a supervisor, manager, or expert makes the final decision using input from all group members. Thus, consensus with qualification begins with the unanimity rule and ends with minority rule.

Avoid Groupthink: Preventing Decisions Beyond Bad

How could the United States have been caught sleeping when the Japanese executed a sneak attack on Pearl Harbor, resulting in the worst naval disaster in U.S. history? Why did John Kennedy and his cabinet advisers ever launch the Bay of Pigs invasion? After all, 1,400 Cuban exiles were facing a 200,000-strong Cuban army in a fruitless attempt to overthrow Fidel Castro. Kennedy lamented afterward, "How could I have been so stupid to let them go ahead?" (quoted in Janis, 1982, p. 16). Add to these disasters the escalation of the Vietnam War under Lyndon Johnson, the Nixon Watergate scandal, Jimmy Carter's failed mission to rescue hostages in Iran, the Iran-Contra scandal during the Ronald Reagan presidency, the space shuttle *Challenger* disaster, and the U.S. entry into the Iraq War. Each of these events is an instance of "groupthink" (Janis, 1982; Mansfield, 1990; Senate Select Committee on Intelligence, 2004).

Groupthink is a process of group members stressing cohesiveness and agreement instead of skepticism and optimum decision making. Too much emphasis is placed on members being "team players," and too little emphasis is placed on the group making quality decisions. Consensus seeking, cooperation, and cohesiveness are all part of competent group decision making, but these normally vital and constructive elements can produce terrible consequences when taken to an extreme (Esser, 1998). The more cohesive a group is, the greater is the danger of groupthink (Rovio et al., 2009). This is especially true as group size increases (Mullen et al., 1994).

Groupthink has several specific characteristics (Janis, 1982; Mohamed & Wiebe, 1996; Street, 1997). First, disagreement is discouraged during group discussions because it is viewed as disruptive to group cohesiveness. Second, there is strong pressure to conform, so there is at least the appearance of group unity. The team usually has a self-appointed "mindguard" whose task is to discourage ideas and viewpoints that might threaten group unity. Dissenters are pressured to be "team players." Third, the group lacks a structured decision-making process that encourages consideration of divergent options and opinions. Confirmation bias (see Chapter 6) is prevalent. Lack of structured decision making combined with a high concern for maintaining group cohesiveness produces poor group decisions (Mullen et al., 1994). Fourth, there is an in-group–out-group competitive group mentality. Everyone who is not a group member is considered part of the out-group. This in-group–out-group mentality gives rise to feelings that the in-group is morally superior to out-groups; outsiders are often negatively stereotyped or branded as evil. An offshoot of this in-group–out-group view of the world is a strong group identity that gives members a feeling of pride and prestige from belonging to the group (Street, 1997).

Janis (1989) offers four suggestions to prevent groupthink. First, the group could consult an impartial outsider with expertise on the problem discussed. This would reduce the danger from excessive cohesiveness leading to poor group decisions. This is sometimes why consultants are hired from outside an organization or group to give advice and counsel. Second, to reduce pressure on group members to conform, the group leader could withhold his or her point of view during early discussions. In this way, the appearance of dominance in power relationships between a more powerful group leader and less powerful members can be avoided, and members will be more inclined to express honest opinions.

John Kennedy, anxious to avoid committing another blunder after the Bay of Pigs fiasco, instituted leaderless discussions with his advisory group. On occasion, especially during the early stages of discussion when alternatives were brainstormed, Kennedy would leave the group. This proved to be especially effective during the 1962 Cuban missile crisis, when the United States and the USSR took the world to the brink of nuclear war over the USSR's secret installation of nuclear missiles in Cuba. Ted Sorenson, an Executive Committee member who worked on the crisis, noted, "One of the remarkable aspects of those meetings was a sense of complete equality . . . I participated much more freely than I ever had . . . and the absence of the president encouraged everyone to speak his mind" (cited in Janis, 1982, p. 144).

Third, the group could assign the devil's advocate role (see Chapter 10) to a specific member (Valacich & Schwenk, 1995). This role, in which an individual "for the sake of argument" challenges a prevailing group viewpoint, combats the excessive concurrence seeking typical of groups that slide into groupthink. The devil's advocate tests the strength and validity of group ideas to prevent poor decision making.

Fourth, the team can set up a "second chance" meeting where members can reconsider a preliminary decision. This allows teams to reflect on any proposal and avoid making impulsive decisions. *Ultimately, what is required to combat groupthink is a group climate that encourages robust discussion of opposing viewpoints.*

Although Janis originally saw groupthink as a process that *leads to* inept decision making, more recent research shows that the same process can occur *after* the group makes a terrible decision (Henningsen et al., 2006). Even when faced with strong evidence that the group decision is terribly flawed, group members attempt to hold the consensus together, thus producing groupthink characteristics.

Enhance Creative Problem Solving: Becoming Unstuck

Four deer hunters hire the same floatplane every hunting season, fly into northern Maine, and "bag" a deer apiece. This season is no different. The pilot of the plane looks at the four deer carcasses and informs the hunters that he can't fly all the men and deer in one trip. The hunters complain, the pilot resists; the hunters complain more strenuously, the pilot wavers; they finally load the plane. The pilot taxies the plane across the lake, guns the engine, picks up speed, and lifts off. A few minutes into the flight the plane crashes. The men crawl from the wreckage, and one hunter asks, "Where are we?" The pilot looks around and answers, "Looks like we're about 100 yards from where we crashed last year."

Groups can get into ruts. Creative problem solving requires breaking free from thinking that is repetitive, ritualistic, and rigid. The rigid thinking that characterizes the hunters' problem solving is an impediment. They continue to repeat the same mistake because their thinking is stuck.

This section explains ways to unstick a group's thinking so creative, original, and effective solutions to problems can be devised. Creative problem solving is a vital aspect of competent small groups (Miura & Hida, 2004). As Carnevale and Probst (1998) note, "Successful conflict resolution often requires that disputants develop novel alternatives, new perspectives, and a fresh outlook on the issues. Creative problem solving is often required in negotiation" (p. 1308). Solving problems is a primary purpose of small groups working on a task, and doing it effectively requires creativity.

Promoting Group Creativity: Necessary Conditions

Several conditions can promote creative problem solving in groups. First, *a cooperative expectation is most conducive to creativity*. Competitive expectations can freeze thinking (Carnevale & Probst, 1998). When group members anticipate an adversarial exchange, thinking often becomes rigid, and counterproductive power struggles can distract the team. "An individual who anticipates competition may use precious cognitive resources in the effort to beat the other negotiator rather than develop creative optimal solutions. Cognitive resources may be used to plan, strategize, and coerce rather than to problem solve and collaborate" (p. 1308). A cooperative expectation can unfreeze thinking. Group members have little reason to be combative, and the focus is on solving a problem together to everyone's satisfaction.

Second, *creativity is promoted by challenges*. As the adage says, "Necessity is the mother of invention." Trying to discover a solution to a previously insoluble problem can stir the creative juices. Attempting to do what others have not been able to accomplish can be a powerful motivator.

Third, *creativity flourishes when there is a moratorium on judging ideas*. Create an atmosphere where any idea, no matter how zany, can be offered without fear of ridicule. Ideas must be evaluated for their practicality and effectiveness, but instant assessments are creativity killers (Goleman, 1998). Group members should withhold critiques of ideas until there has been an opportunity to explore the solution and to tinker with it.

Fourth, *relaxing deadlines as much as possible can free team members' thinking*. Creativity can flourish under pressure, but relentless and unreasonable deadlines can panic a group. Panic doesn't usually spur creativity, but it can lead to a mental meltdown.

Fifth, *a fun, friendly atmosphere usually promotes creativity best* (Goleman, 1998). Fun relaxes group members and reduces concerns about power, status, and esteem. Having fun is the great equalizer among diverse individuals. Having fun means modifying some nonessential rules. Casual dress instead of more formal work attire may help signal a looser, friendlier, less power-conscious atmosphere.

Brainstorming: Generating Ideas

"Encourage Wild Ideas" reads the sign on the wall of each brainstorming room at

IDEO Product Development in Silicon Valley, California. Brainstorming rooms are sanctuaries for creativity where product design teams composed of engineers, industrial designers, and behavioral psychologists hurl ideas back and forth in a frenzy of mental activity (O'Brien, 1995). IDEO brainstormed designs for Levolor blinds, virtual reality headgear, AT&T's telephones and answering machines, medical devices, and a host of other diverse products. IDEO has even brainstormed functional spatial designs for entire hospitals and worked with some of the largest corporations in the world (Hyatt, 2010). One of its most notable and early accomplishments was the design for the Apple computer's original point-and-click mouse. Steve Jobs, Apple's cofounder, went to Xerox first for the design. Xerox had a crude idea for a mouse, but it would have cost the consumer $1,200. This wasn't very practical for a computer that would cost only $1,000. Next, Jobs consulted Hewlett-Packard engineers, who claimed it would take three years to design a practical mouse, and it would cost the consumer $150. Jobs finally consulted David Kelley, owner and president of IDEO. Kelley assembled a team and in three weeks designed a workable mouse. "We made the outside from a Walgreen's butter dish. It cost $17 to make," explains Kelley (O'Brien, 1995, p. 14).

Team creativity is enhanced by structured methods of problem solving (Romig, 1996). Edward DeBono (1992), author of several books on creativity, argues that unstructured creativity "is a dead end. It appears to be attractive at first, but you really can't go far" (p. 37).

The first and most popular structured approach is brainstorming. **Brainstorming** is a creative problem-solving method characterized by encouragement of even zany ideas, freedom from initial evaluation of potential solutions, and energetic participation from all group members. The brainstorming method was originally introduced in 1939 by Alex Osborn, an advertising executive. Team members produce the best results when several rules (a structure) are followed (Kelley & Littman, 2001; Nussbaum, 2004).

1. *All members should come prepared with initial ideas.* Most research that shows disappointing results from group brainstorming excludes this vital first step (see Rothwell, 2010, for detailed discussion). Team members must be prepared adequately to brainstorm in the group. Provide necessary background information to all team members. Make certain the problem is clearly defined. Each member generates ideas prior to team interaction.

2. *Don't criticize any idea during the brainstorming process.* Idea slayers, such as "You can't be serious," "What a silly idea," "That'll never work," or "We don't do it that way" will quickly defeat the purpose of brainstorming. This is especially true if the more powerful members make these criticisms of ideas offered by less powerful, hesitant members. An air of equality is important for productive brainstorming. If less powerful members concentrate on what more powerful members will think of them, they will be overly cautious about contributing ideas. Prohibiting instant evaluations of ideas can reduce initial reluctance to participate fully in brainstorming sessions because all ideas are treated as equal during the brainstorming.

3. *Encourage freewheeling idea generation.* Even zany ideas may provoke a truly terrific solution to a problem by causing team members to think "outside the box." You want team members to expand their thinking and to think in new ways. This is where the fun atmosphere is important. A loose, relaxed, enjoyable brainstorming session encourages freewheeling idea generation, and it can minimize power distinctions between members. When team leaders are as zany and relaxed as other members, it momentarily equalizes power in the group. Team members see the leader as "one of them." This can be empowering for the more hesitant, cautious members.

4. *Don't clarify or discuss ideas during the idea-generation phase.* That will slow down the process (Dugosh et al., 2000). Clarification can come later.

5. *Do not engage in task-irrelevant discussion.* Idea generation is significantly diminished when conversation is permitted during brainstorming sessions (Dugosh et

al., 2000). With conversation often comes irrelevant chatter. A brainstorming facilitator should invoke this rule whenever talking interrupts idea generation.

6. *Stay focused on the topic.* You want all suggestions to be related to the topic. Wild ideas that are not on topic are not helpful.

7. *Piggyback on the ideas of others.* Build on suggestions made by team members by modifying or slightly altering an idea.

8. *Record all ideas for future reference.* Don't edit any ideas during the initial phase of the brainstorming.

9. *Encourage participation from all team members.* Keep the brainstorming fun and fast paced so all members will want to offer suggestions.

10. *Wait to evaluate ideas generated until the brainstorming session is completed,* but do evaluate ideas afterward to garner the best suggestions (Sawyer, 2007). The group must decide what ideas generated are best to implement.

The proper brainstorming technique is exhibited by IDEO. Brainstorming is a key element in the designs they concoct. Presented with the challenge to design a commuter coffee cup that allows pedaling a bicycle without spilling the drink, the brainstormers rapidly fire questions at the customer who requests the product. "Do you want to sip or suck the coffee as you ride?" "Sip" is the response. The brainstormers quickly draw designs of 15 contraptions; among them are a "camelback" that puts a container with a plastic hose in a backpack, a coffee cup (with temperature gauge) attached to a helmet, and a "Sip-o-matic" with a suction valve. The brainstorming atmosphere is kept lighthearted and fun. No idea is too goofy during the idea-generation phase of the brainstorming session, and all ideas are written on "writable walls." Brainstormers repeatedly piggyback on the ideas of other team members, and all team members are totally engrossed, enjoying the challenge. The final prototype is determined by an assessment process (voting with Post-It notes or asking the customer for a preference). The Sip-o-matic is a hit with the customer.

Nominal Group Technique: Averaging Individual Brainstorming

Nominal group technique is a second structured method of creative problem solving. **Nominal group technique** involves these steps.

1. Team members work alone to generate ideas.
2. The team is convened, and ideas are shared in round-robin fashion. All ideas are written on a chalkboard, tablet, or easel. Clarification of ideas is permitted, but evaluation is prohibited.
3. Each team member selects five favorite ideas from the list generated and ranks them from most to least favorite.
4. Team members' rankings are averaged, and the ideas with the highest averages are selected.

Initial research comparing nominal group technique and brainstorming found a surprising result: nominal group technique produced ideas in greater quantity and quality than brainstorming despite the popularity of brainstorming (Diehl & Stroebe, 1987). Other researchers, however, criticized this and subsequent studies that concurred with these initial findings (Sutton & Hargadon, 1996). The artificiality of untrained laboratory groups with no history of working together and brainstorming ideas for which members had no apparent interest in the outcome constituted the main criticisms (Offner et al., 1996). More recent research shows brainstorming is as effective or slightly more effective than nominal group technique in generating a high number of ideas and high-quality ideas when a trained facilitator guides group brainstorming and when a videotape of effective versus ineffective brainstorming is shown to group members prior to idea generation (Baruah & Paulus, 2008; Kramer et al., 2001).

The nominal group technique is more impersonal than brainstorming, tends to be less fun and involving, and does not capitalize on the benefits of working in groups. Nominal groups also show no advantage to brainstorming groups in the final evaluation of ideas once brainstorming has concluded (Rietzschel et al., 2006).

Nominal group technique may be a relevant option, however, when teams experience substantial unresolved interpersonal friction and tension but need to make creative choices "now." Brainstorming, because of its emphasis on high participation, may prove to be ineffective in such an atmosphere.

Reframing: Breaking Rigid Thinking

Another method of creative problem solving is reframing. **Reframing** is the creative process of breaking rigid thinking by placing a problem in a different frame of reference. A service station proprietor put an "Out of Order" sign on a soda machine. Customers paid no attention to the sign, lost their money, then complained to the station owner. Frustrated and annoyed, the owner changed the sign. It now read "$5" for a soda. No one made the mistake of putting money in the soda pop dispenser. The problem was reframed. Instead of wondering how to get customers to recognize that the machine was out of order, the owner changed the frame of reference to what would make customers not want to put money in the dispenser. Reframing opens up possible solutions hidden from our awareness by rigid thinking. Reframing a team dispute from a competitive, adversarial contest of wills to a cooperative problem to be solved by mutual effort and goodwill can prevent conflict from becoming destructive. Winning a contest and solving a problem are distinctly different frames of reference.

When teams become stumped by narrow or rigid frames of reference, asking certain open-ended questions can help reframe the problem so new solutions might emerge. "What if . . . ?" is a very useful question. "What if we don't accept the inevitability of worker layoffs and downsizing?" "What if we tried working together instead of against each other?" "What if management is telling the truth about the budget?" All these questions encourage a different frame of reference and a different line of thinking. Additional reframing questions include these:

Why must we accept what we've been told?

Why are these the only choices?

Could there be a different solution than the one we've discussed?

Can the problem be described in any other way?

Is there any way to make this disadvantage an advantage?

Brainstorming, nominal group technique, and reframing are three useful methods of creative problem solving. In some instances, methods can be combined, such as brainstorming ways to reframe a problem before brainstorming ideas to solve the problem.

Teambuilding and Teamwork

A 1999 Institute of Medicine report estimated that hospital errors produce 98,000 deaths and a million injuries each year. More recent research shows that this disturbing result has not improved (Grady, 2010). To address this shocking reality in medical care, a pilot program called the Unit Based Clinical Leadership Program (UBCL) was begun in 2007 at Pennsylvania Hospital in Philadelphia. The UBCL trained participants to improve communication, collaborate, and share responsibility and ownership for patient care so physicians and nurses could function as a team. "The UBCL pilot not only resulted in breakthrough improvements in quality and patient safety, but also forged better physician-nurse collaboration and job satisfaction as well" (Buckley et al., 2009).

Developing effective teams is an important concern for all of us, not just to those who need medical care in hospitals. Discussing teamwork and teambuilding marks the culmination of research on competent small-group communication. Teams are not merely another type of small group. They have the potential to be super small groups capable of extraordinary accomplishment far beyond everyday small groups. Effective teams have launched humankind successfully into space, produced the personal computer, invented and developed the

Internet, solved many of the world's most vexing problems, and provided many enthusiastic sports fans with endless hours of exciting entertainment and pride in team accomplishment.

Most of us have our first exposure to teams from our early participation in sports. More than 260 million Americans play at least one sport (Penn & Zalesne, 2007). Basketball, baseball, softball, football, ice hockey, field hockey, and soccer provide common experiences with teams for millions of girls and boys, women and men, every year. In addition, theater productions in high school and college require team effort, as do fund-raising activities to support college clubs and service groups. Also, group projects in college classes are most successful when approached from a team perspective.

Perhaps our most important and long-term exposure to teams, however, occurs in the workplace. The annual survey of employers from across the nation conducted by the National Association of Colleges and Employers ranks "teamwork skills" among its most important qualities in job applicants ("Top Skills," 2011). The Center for Creative Leadership conducted a study of top U.S. and European executives whose careers went sour. They found that the inability to build and lead teams was the common reason for executive failure (Spencer & Spencer, 1993).

Defining a Team: Not Just a Small Group

Every team is a group, but not every group is a team (Hackman & Johnson, 2004). There are three primary distinctions between small groups and teams. First, teams commonly exhibit a higher level of cooperation and cohesiveness than standard groups. Teams are inherently We-oriented. Each member develops skills "for the good of the team." A forward may have to switch to playing center to help his or her basketball team, even though this may mean scoring fewer individual points. Teams may function within a competitive, intergroup environment, but to be successful, they depend on intragroup cooperation. Second, teams normally consist of individuals with more diverse skills. Not everyone can be a goalie in soccer or a pitcher in baseball. A team requires complementary, not identical, skills. Third, teams usually have a stronger group identity. Teams see themselves as an identifiable unit with a common mission. Thus, a **team** is "a small number of people with complementary skills who are equally committed to a common purpose, goals, and working approach for which they hold themselves mutually accountable" (Katzenbach & Smith, 1993b, p. 45).

Boards of directors, standing committees, student and faculty senates, and similar groups are not usually teams. These groups often lack cohesiveness and cooperation, and group members may have similar rather than diverse skills. Members are asked to attend periodic meetings where discussion occurs and an occasional vote is taken, but members do not have to work together. Members may factionalize and even work against each other. Contact with fellow members may never take place except indirectly and formally during meetings.

Although some groups are not and never will become teams, *most groups can profit from acting more teamlike*. The more teamlike small groups become, the more likely they will function effectively. *Teams embody a central theme of this text*—that cooperation in human communication arenas has distinct advantages. These benefits of cooperation should be exploited far more than occurs at present.

Establishing Team Goals: An Important First Step

Teambuilding begins with goal setting (LaFasto & Larson, 2001). A team needs a purpose, and goals provide that focus. In addition, team goals improve task performance (Crown, 2007). Goals should be clear, challenging, and cooperative, and team members must be committed to achieving them.

Clear Goals: Knowing Where You're Headed

An ancient Chinese proverb states, "If you don't know where you are going, then any road will take you there." Groups that have no particular focus drift aimlessly. They achieve little because little is planned. Without exception, every effectively functioning team studied by Larson and LaFasto (1989) had clear, identifiable goals, and members had a clear understanding of those goals. In their study of 600 teams and 6,000 team members, they conclude, "Goal clarity is critical for team members to have confidence in their direction and to be committed to making it happen" (LaFasto & Larson, 2001, p. 101). Vague goals such as "do your best" or "make improvements" provide no clear direction. "Complete the study of traffic congestion on campus by the end of the term" or "raise $100,000 in donations for a campus child-care center within one year" are clear, specific goals. For a group to become a team, clearly focused goals are essential.

Romig (1996) found one department in an organization had developed 60 goals to achieve in a single year. This department accomplished none of its goals but threatened the future of the entire organization by losing huge sums of money flailing in all directions. Too many goals can diffuse effort and scatter group members. A few clear goals are preferable. Each member should be able to recite from memory the primary goals of the team. This allows all team members to have a shared mission and a common vision. *Goals for a team work best when they are clearly stated and limited in number.*

Challenging Goals: Putting a Dent in the Universe

Accomplishing the trivial motivates no one. Groups need challenging goals to spur interest among members. Challenging goals can stretch the limits of group members' physical or mental abilities. Problems never faced or solved present a challenge. Finding solutions to problems when time is short and the need is urgent can also challenge a group. Groups are elevated to teams when they see their mission as important, meaningful, and beyond the ordinary.

The team that developed the original Macintosh computer had this elevated sense of purpose. Randy Wigginton, a team member, puts it this way: "We believed we were on a mission from God" (quoted in Bennis & Biederman, 1997, p. 83). Steve Jobs, the team leader, promised team members that they were going to build a computer that would "put a dent in the universe" (p. 80). They may not have put a dent in the universe, but subsequent creations from Apple teams, such as the iPod, iPhone, and iPad, certainly became cultural icons and shaped an entire consumer market.

Cooperative Goals: Requiring Team Effort and Interdependence

In individualist cultures such as the United States, the cooperative aspects of team-building are a bit more challenging than in collectivist cultures such as those of Singapore, China, and Malaysia. Competitive goal structures abound in the United States. Developing cooperative goal structures can seem perplexing initially.

There are two primary elements that compose cooperative goals. First, cooperative goals require interdependent effort from group members. This is achieved by all members working together in a coordinated fashion. *Collaborative interdependence is essential to teamwork* (Johnson & Johnson, 2003b).

Second, cooperative goals necessitate a We-orientation. A study at Cambridge University of 120 teams found that assembling highly intelligent team members didn't produce stellar results (Belbin, 1996). High-IQ members were intensely competitive. Instead of working together, they exercised their intellectual abilities by striving to impress each other with their brilliance. Each member's individual status became more important than any group goal. Teams composed of members with more ordinary intellectual abilities outperformed the high-IQ teams. They exhibited a We-orientation by putting personal agendas aside for the sake of team goals. The result was synergy.

Commitment to Goals: Stimulating the Passion Within Members

Teams need unified commitment from all members to be effective (Aube & Rousseau, 2005). "The essence of a team is common

The Blue Angels illustrate which of the following?

1. Clear goals
2. Challenging goals
3. Cooperative goals
4. Commitment to goal achievement

Answers at end of chapter

commitment. Without it, groups perform as individuals; with it they become a powerful unit of collective performance" (Katzenbach & Smith, 1993a). Those members who do not demonstrate sufficient commitment and effort necessitate the use of suggestions for dealing with social loafers and difficult group members.

Goals established by team members, not imposed by outsiders or a team leader, usually gain greater commitment (Romig, 1996). Cooperative goals are the product of member participation. It is very difficult for members to get excited about goals foisted on them.

The U.S. women's Olympic basketball team in 1996 illustrates the importance and value of team goals. This team soundly defeated its longtime nemesis, Brazil, for the gold medal. Brazil, a powerful team that had humbled previous U.S. teams in the 1991 Pan American Games, the 1992 Olympics, and the 1994 world championships, was no match for the smooth teamwork of the U.S. women. The final score was 111–87. The U.S. total was the most points ever scored by a women's basketball team in the Olympics.

The U.S. women's success was achieved primarily by establishing cooperative goals from the outset. Interdependence and a We-orientation were critical to the team's success. Sportswriter Ann Killion (1996) summed it up when she attributed the U.S. women's success to "setting [their] sights on a goal and working for it, [and] sacrificing one's self for the team" (p. D1). Tara VanDerveer, the U.S. women's basketball coach, explained her team's success this way: "There's a stereotype that women can't work together. What makes this special is that people had a team agenda. They weren't individuals. This team put the gold medal as their mission" (Killion, 1996, p. D3).

All players on the team were passionately committed to achieving their clear, challenging goal—to win the gold medal. The team traveled 100,000 miles during the year prior to the Olympic Games to play international powerhouse teams such as China and Russia. Players endured intensive physical training. They participated in teambuilding exercises in Colorado Springs. As a result of a carefully constructed teambuilding effort, the women's team won all 52 preparation games, then scored wins in all 8 Olympic contests for a perfect 60–0 record.

Contrast this example of flawless teamwork with the 2004 U.S. men's Olympic basketball team. Composed of top NBA players such as Allen Iverson and Tim Duncan, this new version of the "dream team" was embarrassed in a preliminary round by Puerto Rico 92–73. The U.S. team went on to lose three games, equal to the total losses in all previous Olympic Games. Collaborative interdependence was missing. Players operated as individuals, not as teammates. Initially, most players seemed to view the entire Olympic event as not very challenging. After all, what contest could there be in playing teams from tiny countries that, at best, had only one or two NBA players? Coach Larry Brown remarked, after the embarrassing loss to Puerto Rico, "We have to become a team in a short period of time. Throw your egos out the window" (quoted in Killion, 2004, p. 3D). The U.S. team improved but still lost to Lithuania and earned the bronze medal. There's much more to building a team and establishing teamwork than choosing the best players.

The 2008 U.S. Olympic men's basketball team learned from its previous disappointing showings by concentrating on developing teamwork and foregoing individual stardom. In its eight games, all victories, the U.S. team had more assists than its opponents in every game, exhibiting the players' willingness to pass and engage in team play. In the final game against Spain, all five starters scored in double figures, showing a willingness to spread the scoring around, not seek personal glory ("Olympic Basketball," 2008). This "redeem team" won the gold medal with teamwork.

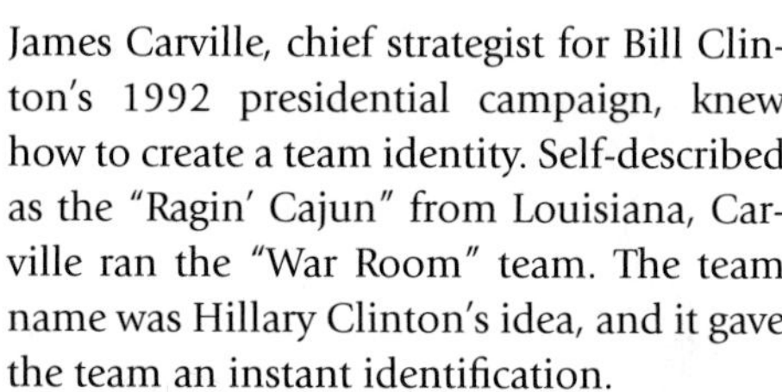

Developing a Team Identity: Who Are You?

James Carville, chief strategist for Bill Clinton's 1992 presidential campaign, knew how to create a team identity. Self-described as the "Ragin' Cajun" from Louisiana, Carville ran the "War Room" team. The team name was Hillary Clinton's idea, and it gave the team an instant identification.

The War Room was the political nerve center of the Clinton campaign. Located in Little Rock, Arkansas, the team responded to every perceived threat, every attack from the Bush campaign, and every stumble or miscue by Clinton with lightning speed. As Carville put it, "You create a campaign culture, and ours was based on speed" (quoted in Bennis & Biederman, 1997, p. 93).

The War Room team's identity combined speed with informality. The T-shirt was part of the War Roomers' uniform. Carville liked wearing one that read, "Speed kills . . . Bush." He also wore ragged jeans with holes. There was a constant air of immediacy and high drama. Team members ran to copy machines; they didn't walk. Carville promoted a 24-hour-a-day sense of urgency. Like him or hate him—and he does have vociferous detractors—Carville unquestionably built a remarkably effective team. Hillary Clinton's run for the presidency in 2007–2008 tried to mirror the original War Room approach. Barack Obama, who eventually bested Hillary Clinton and ultimately John McCain for the presidency, chose a less intense team identity: "No Drama Obama." Stay cool under fire!

Every team is a group, but not every group is a team. What stands out immediately as a means of showing team identity?

Group identity is an important part of building a team. There isn't a single way to do this. Often team identity is fostered by a uniform or style of dress common to team members. A team name is not essential, but it helps. An identifiable style of behaving, such as the War Room's focus on speed, also creates an identity, especially if the style is different from other groups. Offering awards and prizes for team accomplishments, creating rituals and ceremonies unique to the group, establishing a clearly identifiable space that belongs to the team, and sometimes creating an air of secrecy all contribute to team identity. Every team will create its own identity in its own way. Part of being an effective team, however, is building that identity early in the group's life.

Designating Clear Team Roles: Avoid Duplication

Roles emerge informally in most small groups, but teams require greater structure than groups in general. Group members won't function as a team if they are uncertain of the roles they are supposed to play or if too many team members want to play the same role and other roles are left unfilled. You don't want 10 quarterbacks and a dozen wide receivers but no punter or cornerback on a football team. A team of lawyers will divide the responsibilities among members. One lawyer may be the chief researcher (information giver). Another may write the legal briefs (clarifier-elaborator). A third may challenge the briefs to find flaws in the arguments (devil's advocate), and a fourth lawyer may direct the entire team (leader). In each case, team members are given specific responsibilities befitting their talents, experience, and expertise. The team leader often makes this assignment of roles, but in some cases, team members volunteer to play specific roles.

Poor role clarity can produce confusion, duplication of effort, and overall weak team performance. Team members need to demonstrate coordinated activity to be successful. Clear designation of roles can produce high performance. Dr. Don Wukasch, a respected open-heart surgeon, describes what happened when a hurricane hit the Texas Heart Institute while his surgical team was performing a heart operation.

> A hurricane again—the power went out, and the patient was on the heart-lung machine. When the power goes off, the heart-lung machine goes off. You have about a minute or two before the patient starts to die. I didn't know we had them, but there are hand cranks under each heart-lung machine. The team started cranking, and within 15 seconds we were going at normal. Here again, no panic, just a smooth operation. That's real professionalism. That's a high-performance team. (quoted in Larson & LaFasto, 1989, p. 54)

Each member of the surgical team played his or her part in the performance of a successful operation. No one tried to play all the roles. Every team member had a specific set of tasks to perform well, and all roles were coordinated. Clearly defining each team member's role is critical to team effectiveness.

The leader role is usually designated in advance (coach, project director, task force chair, etc.). Although there are exceptions, the general pattern of leadership for most teams should be participative. Team leaders encourage participation from team members. "The guide on the side, not the sage on the stage" is the typical model of team leadership (see Rothwell, 2013, for further discussion). Leaders should emphasize development and maintenance of constructive communication climates (see Chapter 8). Conflict management should focus on collaboration and avoid power-forcing (see Chapter 9).

Virtual Groups and Teams

Have you ever taken an online "distance education" course and been required to work with class members you have never met and will never communicate with face to face? Welcome to the world of virtual groups. Members of a virtual group rarely if ever communicate face to face but instead communicate by means of electronic technology. Virtual groups have three characteristics that distinguish them from conventional face-to-face groups (Fisher, 2000). First, virtual-group members are spread across multiple locations, even across multiple time zones (Rutkowski et al., 2007). Second, members often come from more diverse backgrounds and cultures in which multiple languages are spoken and organizational allegiances may be varied. Third, membership tends to be less stable, with members dropping out more frequently. In short, virtual group members are "working together apart" (Fisher, 2000).

Although distinctions between virtual groups and virtual teams are rarely offered by researchers and theorists, there are differences. They have electronic technologies and remote communication in common, but they differ in the same ways that conventional face-to-face groups and standard teams differ: degree of cooperation, diversity of skills, level of group identity, and commitment of members. For example, online class discussion groups are virtual groups but not virtual teams. Class members join online discussions to fulfill class requirements and share opinions. Little cooperation is required, class members are not chosen because of skill diversity, no real group identity is necessary, and commitment to the online discussion may be lackluster and sporadic.

The worldwide opportunities for collaboration are enormous with the development of the Internet and complementary technologies (Sunstein, 2006; Tapscott & Williams, 2006). Virtual groups are a natural result of this global electronic network that has emerged. Virtual teams are becoming the norm for businesses and government globally. With the emergence of virtual teams come new and varied communication challenges (Poole & Zhang, 2005). First, language choice may be an issue if group membership spans diverse cultures with widely varying languages. Switching from one language to another may result in serious misunderstandings and give rise to ethnocentrism ("Why wouldn't we use English?"). Second, virtual-group members may have difficulty determining the meaning of long silences. When a group member fails to answer emails, for example, the tendency is to assume that the member lacks commitment and is a social loafer instead of assuming another possibility—namely, that there has been a technical difficulty preventing a timely response (Cramton, 2001).

Third, virtual-group members are more likely than members of conventional groups to make negative dispositional attributions (lazy, unskilled) for behavior that perturbs the group (failure to meet deadlines, long silences, etc.) than situational attributions (family or work difficulties intruding on virtual-group time). Such attributional bias can lead to greater conflict than what occurs in conventional groups (Cramton, 2002). Managing conflict in virtual groups is especially tricky because of the lack of face-to-face contact to resolve issues (Solomon, 2010). Fourth, lack of nonverbal cues, in the absence of video- or audioconferencing, limits the ability of members to accurately discern emotional states of those emailing or blogging (Solomon, 2010).

Fifth, social loafing is a potentially greater problem in virtual groups than in conventional groups (Driskell et al., 2003). A survey of 600 employees of multinational corporations who participate actively in virtual groups found that 75% saw social loafing as a serious challenge (Solomon, 2010). Confronting a loafer is problematic in text-only formats. If the loafer refuses to read the messages, deletes them, or does not respond to the confrontation, group members have few options. Members can try working around the loafer by ignoring lackluster participation, but this merely increases the workload of more motivated members. Sixth, developing cohesiveness may be a bigger challenge because virtual-group members may never meet each other face to face (Solomon, 2010). Seventh, if virtual-group members are spread across several time zones, the timing of virtual meetings can be a stumbling block. Nine P.M. on the West Coast is five A.M. in London.

These challenges can be addressed. First, there are "degrees of virtuality" (Poole & Zhang, 2005). Occasional face-to-face meetings of virtual-group members can help build social relationships and enhance cohesiveness (Kirkman et al., 2002; Maznevski & Chudoba, 2000). If some face-to-face contact is impossible, videoconferencing may suffice as an alternative (Lipnack & Stamps, 1997). Videoconferencing has developed to the point that the quality of the video production can allow members to forget that they are in completely different locations, even thousands of miles away. Members have been known to offer each other refreshments during videoconferences, forgetting that they are communicating in a virtual world. Videoconferencing has its own set of potential problems (technical glitches; cost of equipment, production, and maintenance; member unfamiliarity with the technology), but in most instances, these can be overcome with experience. The ready availability of Skye videoconferencing on standard laptops and computers makes accessibility less of an issue for most people.

Second, it is helpful to set agendas, draft timelines and deadlines for projects, and schedule regular communication among group members (Connaughton & Daly, 2005; Yoo & Alavi, 2004). Also, agreeing to specific times for meetings so all can attend is important (Poole & Zhang, 2005). Third, decide on which language will be used for all meetings and communication. Switching back and forth between different languages leads to difficulties and less effective virtual groups (Knoll & Jarvenpaa, 1998). Fourth, members of virtual groups should agree to explicit norms regarding responsiveness and punctuality, etiquette (no flaming), and so forth. Finally, confronting any conflicts immediately so they don't fester and grow is essential.

Virtual groups present new challenges for group members. These challenges, however, are likely to diminish with time as we become more accustomed to working in virtual groups (van der Kleij et al., 2009).

Summary

THE advantages of working in groups are many. Groups can pool knowledge and information, correct errors often missed by an individual working alone, accomplish broad-range tasks by sharing the load among members, and above all, produce synergy. The main disadvantages of groups—factionalism, disruptive group members, scheduling conflicts, negative synergy, social loafing, groupthink, and wasting time in meetings—are correctable. The group experience can be unpleasant if we allow it to be, but it need not be that way.

Teams are cooperative groups. Teambuilding provides the structure for teams: clear, challenging, and cooperative goals and commitment to these goals; clear roles; use of the Standard Agenda; and consensus decision making whenever possible. Teamwork often requires creative problem solving. There are three structured methods of creative problem solving: brainstorming, nominal group technique, and reframing. Finally, virtual groups present additional challenges, but with experience, these challenges will probably diminish significantly.

Answers for *Critical Thinking* captions:

Social loafing (p. 317): #3 and #4
Blue Angels (p. 335): #1, #2, #3, #4

Quizzes Without Consequences

Did you understand all the material in this chapter? Test your knowledge before your exam!

Go to the companion website at www.oup.com/us/rothwell, click on the Student Resources for each chapter, and take the Quizzes Without Consequences.

Film School Case Studies

Flight of the Phoenix (1966 and 2004). Drama; PG-13

The original 1966 version of this taut drama about a plane crash and efforts of survivors to rebuild their damaged plane into a smaller flying machine to escape their plight in the desert is probably better than the remake. In either case, examine the creative group problem solving required. What methods were used to fashion the final product? What decision-making rules (unanimity, majority, or minority rule) were used?

Glory Road (2006). Drama; PG

Dramatic depiction of coach Don Haskins's effort to mold a winning team at Texas Western University in the early 1960s, eventually making it to the finals of the NCAA basketball tournament and fielding an all-black starting five against an all-white Kentucky team when racial tensions were heightened nationally. Examine the major elements of teambuilding and teamwork.

O Brother, Where Art Thou? (2000). Drama; PG-13

Three convicts escape from a Depression-era chain gang and stumble through the countryside. Their problem-solving knowledge and skills are sorely deficient. Contrast the problem-solving mistakes of this small group of convicts with suggestions in this chapter on effective problem solving.

Remember the Titans (2000). Drama; PG

In this film based on a true story, Denzel Washington plays a high-school football coach who must integrate his team in the face of racism and ignorance. Analyze how Washington accomplishes the feat of molding a championship team from warring factions. Focus especially on types of team goals and team identity.

The Cove (2009). Documentary; PG-13

A team of environmental activists exposes the mass slaughter of dolphins in this Oscar-winning documentary. It's a tough film to watch but an important one. Examine how the team handles decision-making and problem-solving challenges.

The War Room (1993). Documentary; PG

This documentary on the 1992 Clinton presidential campaign earned an Oscar nomination. Whatever your political leanings, this is a fascinating inside look at politics in action. Analyze how Clinton's campaign team capitalized on the elements of teambuilding and teamwork to forge a winning combination.

CHAPTER 12

Chapter Outline

PART 4

Preparing Speeches

FREEDOM OF SPEECH is the bedrock of a democratic society. There is an inherent recognition in the First Amendment to the U.S. Constitution that articulate speech can give voice to the voiceless and power to the powerless. Eloquence can influence the course of our history. Virtually every major and minor protest that occurs in our sometimes tumultuous society relies on public speaking to move the populace. The powerful oratory of Martin Luther King and others was the engine of the civil rights movement. The Tea Party that emerged in 2009 and the Occupy Wall Street movement that sprang to life in 2011 both relied heavily on public speeches at large rallies to marshal support. The entire history of student protest in this country exhibits the power of public speaking. From the Free Speech Movement at Berkeley in 1964, through the Vietnam War era and the protracted wars in Iraq and Afghanistan, and continuing with the battles on college campuses over tuition increases, the high cost of textbooks, abortion, climate change, terrorism, and prejudice of all kinds, students have depended on public speaking to incite change. Ideas

By the end of this chapter, you should be able to:

1. Analyze audiences.
2. Choose and narrow your speech topic appropriately.
3. Research your topic effectively.
4. Develop competent supporting materials for your speech.
5. Outline and organize your speech effectively.

have to be framed, issues have to be crystallized, and arguments must be presented for change to occur. Public speaking is an essential part of this process.

There are many other important reasons to learn effective public speaking besides producing change in society (Morreale & Pearson, 2008). College courses in diverse disciplines increasingly assign oral presentations. One survey of 260,000 students at 523 four-year colleges revealed that 84% of first-year college students and 95% of seniors gave formal class presentations. Among first-year students, 31% gave oral class presentations "often" or "very often," and 61% of seniors did likewise ("National Survey," 2006). The more you progress in college, the more you need public speaking knowledge and skills. Those of you who do acquire such knowledge and skills early in your college studies enjoy an enormous advantage when giving class presentations. Whether viewing oral presentations with reluctance or relish, you will undoubtedly be required to give them in your classes, so learn to do them well.

Public speaking is also essential to career building. It is difficult to identify a profession that does not rely on or benefit from competent public speaking. Teaching, law, religion, politics, public relations, marketing, and business require substantial knowledge and skill in public speaking. A survey of employers shows public speaking as a highly desirable job skill ("Top Skills," 2011). Employers also don't believe most job applicants possess public speaking proficiency ("Job Outlook," 2009).

Public speaking knowledge and skills are also quite useful in other circumstances. Average citizens are frequently called upon to give speeches of support or dissent at public meetings on utility rate increases, school board issues, and city or county disputes. Toasts at weddings or banquets, tributes at awards ceremonies, eulogies at funerals for loved ones, and presentations at sales group meetings are additional common public speaking situations.

Competent public speakers know how to present complex ideas clearly and fluently, keep an audience's attention, critically analyze important issues, conduct effective research, make reasonable arguments, and support claims with valid proof. They entertain and also move people to listen, to contemplate, and to change their minds. This is an impressive array of practical knowledge and skills for anyone to possess, and its application is virtually boundless.

The communication competence model serves as a guide throughout this discussion of public speaking. Public speakers must make choices regarding the appropriateness and likely effectiveness of topics, attention strategies, style and delivery, evidence, and persuasive strategies. When you are giving a speech, you must be sensitive to the signals sent from an audience that indicate lack of interest, disagreement, confusion, enjoyment, support, and a host of additional reactions. This allows you to make adjustments during the speech if necessary. Finally, the effectiveness of a speech must be tempered by ethical concerns. What works may not always be honest, respectful, responsible, noncoercive, or fair.

Thus, *the principal purpose of this chapter is to explain how to prepare a competent speech*. Ensuing chapters discuss the competent presentation of informative and persuasive speeches.

Audience Analysis

A well-known and high-priced speaker was invited to address the Cabrillo College faculty. She was articulate, poised, and dynamic. For 45 minutes, she told stories and anecdotes that brought frequent laughter from her audience. It appeared that she had succeeded admirably. Faculty broke into groups following the speech to discuss the subjects the speaker had raised. In contrast to the apparent positive response the speaker received during her speech, an avalanche of criticism followed. The chief complaint was that the speaker had entertained everyone, but she hadn't presented substantial material that warranted a generous speaker fee. The speech was so dissatisfying for most that the college was hesitant for several years afterward to invite any outside speaker to address the faculty. This speech failed because it was poorly suited to the audience. A competent speech is far more than good style and delivery. Your thoughts have to resonate with listeners. *Audience analysis is the core of any public speech.* Both speech preparation and presentation are audience-centered processes.

Edmund Muskie, a former U.S. senator, once remarked: "In Maine we have a saying that there's no point in speaking unless you can improve on silence." Improving on silence requires careful audience analysis. Almost 2,500 years ago, Aristotle wrote: "Of the three elements in speechmaking—speaker, subject, and person addressed—it is the last one, the hearer, that determines the speech's end and object" (cited in Cooper, 1960, p. 136). Meeting audience expectations is a key element in competent public speaking.

Think of audience analysis as the process of discovering ways to build bridges between yourself and listeners, to identify with their needs, hopes, dreams, interests, and concerns. In general, *you construct your speech with the audience always in mind.* In this section, I discuss types of audiences and audience composition as the basis of audience analysis.

Types of Audiences: The Five Cs

Begin analyzing your audience by considering what type of audience will hear your speech. There are five general types of audiences: captive, committed, contrary, concerned, and casual.

Captive Audience: Disengaged Listeners

A captive audience assembles to hear you speak because it is compelled to, not because listeners expect entertainment or intellectual stimulation. A required speech class is an example of a captive audience. Formal ceremonies, luncheon gatherings of clubs and organizations, and most meetings conducted in places of business are other examples. Power, especially in its dominance form, can be an issue with captive audiences. Listeners may attend a speech only because those with greater power (supervisors, teachers) insist.

Gaining and maintaining the interest of a captive audience are primary considerations. When listeners prefer to be elsewhere, snaring their attention and keeping them listening to you are no small accomplishments. (Chapter 13 discusses many attention strategies necessary to meet these challenges.)

Committed Audience: Agreeable Listeners

A committed audience voluntarily assembles because members want to invest time and energy listening to and being inspired by a speaker. A committed audience usually agrees with the speaker's position already and is presumably interested because it consists of people who voluntarily appeared to hear the speech. Listeners who gather for Sunday sermons, political rallies, and social protest demonstrations are all examples of committed audiences. Gaining and maintaining the interest and attention of a committed audience are not nearly as difficult as doing the same with a captive audience. Inspiring action, persuading, and empowering listeners to act decisively are primary considerations for a speaker addressing a committed audience. Committed listeners want to be inspired to act, and as the speaker, you want to "rally the troops," provide listeners with a "can do" attitude, and motivate change.

Contrary Audience: Hostile Listeners

You don't usually get to choose your audience, so sometimes the audience that forms is initially hostile to your position on issues. School board meetings, public meetings of the county board of supervisors, meetings on public utility rates, and political gatherings often attract hostile listeners ready to do battle. Listeners of this sort are more likely to engage in ambushing (see Chapter 6), looking for weaknesses in your arguments and preparing to pounce on perceived mistakes in your facts. It is vitally important in such circumstances that you have researched your topic and are well prepared. Your demeanor when addressing a hostile audience must remain unconditionally constructive. Dealing with a hostile audience is adversarial and hypercompetitive. You want to defuse audience anger, not ignite it against you. Be prepared for personal attacks but resist personal counterattacks. Ask audience members who get rowdy to disagree without becoming disagreeable.

Concerned Audience: Eager Listeners

A concerned audience is one that gathers voluntarily to hear a speaker because listeners care about issues and ideas. A concerned audience is a motivated audience. Unlike a committed audience, however, listeners haven't attended the speech to show commitment to a particular cause or idea. Concerned listeners want to gather information and learn. Listeners who gather for book and poetry readings or lecture series are examples of concerned audiences. Your main consideration is to be informative by presenting new ideas and new information in a stimulating and attention-getting fashion. Concerned listeners may eventually become committed listeners.

Casual Audience: Unexpected Listeners

A casual audience is composed of individuals who become listeners because they hear a speaker, stop out of curiosity or casual interest, and remain until bored or sated. When I was in Bath, England, I happened upon a street performer, or busker as they are called in England. He gathered an audience mostly with clever banter, corny jokes, audience interaction, and whimsical tricks. Curious about the gathering crowd, I joined the audience. Within minutes, I was picked out of the crowd to "assist" the busker in performing one of his "daring" tricks. My job was to tie the busker's hands tightly behind his back with a chain, put a bag over his head, and count to 30 while the performer "escaped" from his confinement while on his knees with his head submerged in a one-gallon bucket of water. Not surprisingly, he performed this "underwater escape" successfully and garnered great laughter and applause from his casual audience.

Your primary consideration when addressing a casual audience is to connect with listeners immediately and create curiosity and interest. The busker did this well. Unlike a captive audience, members of a casual audience are free to leave at a moment's whim.

Each type of audience—captive, committed, contrary, concerned, or casual—presents its own challenge to a speaker. Each audience has its own expectations that a speaker must address to be successful.

Audience Composition: Making Inferences

Your speech should be prepared with your audience always in mind, so knowing something about your audience is critical. The appropriateness of your remarks and their effectiveness with a specific audience depend in large part on connecting with your listeners.

Connection comes from framing your speech to resonate with listeners' attitudes, beliefs, and values. An **attitude** is "a learned predisposition to respond favorably or unfavorably toward some attitude object" (Gass & Seiter, 2007, p. 42). In Chapter 3, I defined a **belief** as what a person thinks is true or probable, and a **value** as the most deeply felt, *generally* shared view of what is deemed good, right, or worthwhile thinking

This is an example of a casual audience that assembled for a street performance.

or behavior. Women in the United States are "disproportionally sensitive to and critical of the human costs of armed conflict" compared to men (Eichenberg, 2003). This is a value difference. A gender difference on how effective the Iraq War was conducted is a difference in beliefs. In the 2006 national election, women and men differed significantly on the importance of the Iraq War, health care, and the economy (Carmany, 2006). These are attitude differences. This moves from the abstract value (generally what is deemed right or wrong) to the more specific belief (what is true from your perspective) to a particular attitude (what is important in this instance).

The strength of an audience's attitudes, beliefs, and values determines interest level. You may have an opportunity to survey listeners and determine their basic values, beliefs, or attitudes. Students sometimes poll classmates about issues and problems before composing their speeches. Often, however, you must make educated guesses (inferences; see Chapter 4) about an audience based on **demographics**—characteristics such as age, gender, culture and ethnicity, and group affiliations. Even then, audiences often are composed of diverse members, so there are competing attitudes, beliefs, and values among listeners, making audience adaptation especially challenging. Recognize that few audiences are entirely of one mind.

Age: Generation Gap

The average age of an audience can provide valuable information for a speaker. College instructors, for instance, must speak to the experience of college students, and most of you weren't even born before 1985. This means that most of you have no direct experience of the Vietnam War, Watergate, the Beatles, eight-track tapes, rotary dial telephones or "car" phones the size of a small piece of luggage, ditto machines, or manual typewriters. You haven't experienced a time when space travel was not possible, color television didn't exist, computers wouldn't fit on a desktop or in your hand, the Internet or cell phones were unavailable, and remote controls didn't operate all your electronic entertainment systems.

Generalizations based on age define what we consider to be a **generation gap** in cultural beliefs and practices. Assumptions about age-based cultural divides should be embraced cautiously, but a study by the Pew Research Center (2009) reports the largest generation gap in the United States in 40 years. For example, 66% of respondents 65 and older said religion is a very important part of their lives, but only 44% of 18 to 29 year olds felt the same. Only 5% of those 65 and older used a cell phone almost exclusively instead of a land line and only 11% text messaged, but 72% of adults under 30 used cell phones almost exclusively instead of land lines and 87% text messaged. The under 30 crowd believes old age begins at 60; those over 65 believe it begins at 74. Another Pew Research Center (2007) study also found large differences between older and younger Americans on gay parenting, couples living together before marriage, and the morality of unwed women having children.

As a speaker, develop the content of your speech so it relates to the experience of your listeners. References to insider trading, mutual funds, problems of leadership in corporations, and retirement accounts don't speak directly to the experience of a young audience. Older audiences, however, may relate to detailed explanations of such topics. Conversely, don't assume older audiences are necessarily technologically proficient or that they embrace technology, its advantages, and its necessity as readily as younger generations.

Gender: Avoiding Stereotyping

Gender differences in perception and behavior do exist, as discussed in Chapter 3. Competent audience analysis, however, means going beyond simplistic stereotypes. Present your material in a way that interests all audience members but is sensitive to the shades of difference between genders.

Develop your speech from different perspectives to include all listeners. A speech on sexual harassment, for instance, could be linked to both men and women by discussing effects on victims who are typically women but increasingly men (see Chapter 7). Offering ways to avoid charges of sexual harassment should concern particularly men but also women in positions of power. In addition, men can relate to the indignity and powerless feelings associated with sexual harassment indirectly by seeing what wives, girlfriends, or daughters experience when victimized. Men don't want to see the women they love or care about subjected to indignity and injustice.

Ethnicity and Culture: Sensitivity to Diversity

Students who fail to analyze the multicultural makeup of college audiences can create embarrassing speaking situations. Despite my efforts to encourage sensitivity to individuals from diverse cultures, I have witnessed several student speeches that ignited awkward, even hostile, moments in class. One Jewish student gave a speech on peace agreements in the Middle East. She referred to Palestinians as "terrorists and warmongers." This did not sit well with several Arab students in the class. Policies and issues can be questioned and debated without resorting to insults and sweeping generalizations. Avoid ethnocentrism (see Chapter 3).

Group Affiliations: Points of View

The groups we belong to tell others a great deal about our values, beliefs, and attitudes. Membership in Save Our Shores indicates a strong belief in protecting our ocean environment. Working with Habitat for Humanity indicates an interest in charitable work and a concern for poor people with inadequate housing. Membership in clubs, sororities, fraternities, national honorary societies, or educational groups provides information about your listeners that can be helpful in shaping your speeches, especially informative and persuasive presentations (see later chapters).

Be cautious, however, not to assume too much. Group affiliations suggest possible aspects to consider about your audience, but religious affiliations, for example, can be tricky. A huge majority of Catholics consistently defy the Vatican ban on contraception (Catholics for Choice, 2008). A quarter of white evangelicals, traditionally conservative and Republican, voted for Barack Obama in the 2008 election (Goodstein, 2008).

There are additional audience composition factors besides those just covered that can affect your audience analysis, such as sexual orientation, income, and education level. With some exceptions, however, these may not be so apparent. Some people purposely hide their sexual orientation or consider it nobody else's business, and others consider it rude to ask or discuss income level. Nevertheless, be sensitive to these elements of audience composition.

Topic Choice and Analysis

A frequent concern of students is what topic to choose for a speech. In some instances, you may be asked to give a speech on a particular subject because of your expertise (e.g., a nurse asked to give a speech on flu shots; a student volunteer for Food Not Bombs asked to speak about homelessness). In a speech class, however, the choice, within broad limits, will likely be up to you. This section covers how to choose a topic that is appropriate for you, your audience, and the occasion. I also explain how to narrow your topic to a specific purpose statement.

Potential Topics: Important Choice

If you choose a bad topic, you are stuck with a bad speech. If you choose a good topic, the potential for a great speech looms large. There are three primary ways to explore potential speech topics systematically: do a personal inventory, brainstorm ideas, and scan popular books, periodicals, newspapers, and blogging sites.

Personal Inventory: You as Topic Source

Begin your exploration of appropriate topics by looking at your own personal experiences and interests. Make a list. What are your hobbies? What sports do you play? List any unusual events that have occurred in your life (e.g., caught in a tornado, observed a bank robbery). Have you done any volunteer work? What forms of entertainment interest you? Do you have any special skills? Have you traveled to any interesting places (e.g., Ayers Rock, Machu Picchu)? Have you met any exciting people? What's the worst thing that's ever happened to you? What's the best? How do you spend your free time? This list contains many possible choices for a speech topic.

Brainstorm: New Possibilities

Take your list of interests and choose five topics that seem most promising. Write down each topic on a separate list and, with each topic, brainstorm new possibilities. For example, brainstorm "trip to London" by letting your mind free-associate with any related topics, such as double-decker buses, driving on the left, the Thames River, British accent, Parliament, Buckingham Palace, William and Kate's royal wedding, the relevance of royalty, Hyde Park, Soho, British money, and British rock groups. Each of these topics is rather general. Consider each one and try to brainstorm a more specific topic. British money, for example, might lead to a comparison of British money to American currency. Driving on the left could lead to an interesting presentation on why the British drive on the left, yet we drive on the right. Parliament could trigger a comparison between the U.S. Congress and the British Parliament. If this approach does not generate excitement, try a third method—scanning.

Scanning for Topics: Quick Ideas

Scanning books can help generate ideas for speech topics. Check the nonfiction shelves of your local bookstore for books on current controversies and topics of general interest. Log on to Amazon.com and scan the latest nonfiction best sellers. This process can produce some real surprises. My

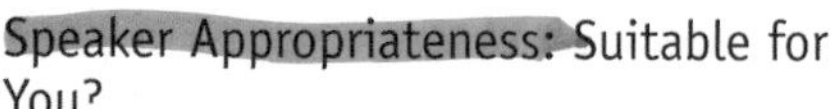

own casual search for interesting books to read led me to a book by Dennis Diclaudio (2006) entitled *The Hypochondriac's Pocket Guide to Horrible Diseases You Probably Already Have*. In it, the author identifies 45 terrible diseases, among them alien hand syndrome, "in which your own hand may attempt to choke you to death," and candiru infestation, "in which you don't even want to know what happens." This book could prove to be a useful resource for developing an interesting informative speech on hypochondria, on serious diseases and prevention, or on a history of human disease epidemics.

Scan magazines, such as *Newsweek, Time, Consumer Reports, Ebony, Jet, Sports Illustrated, People, Psychology Today, Entertainment, Ms., Men's Health*, or *Scientific American Mind*. Look at the table of contents and leaf through the articles. Don't spend time reading them. You're scanning quickly to get ideas. If you see a promising topic, write it down and note the magazine, the article, and the date. Do the same with newspapers. Your library will have local, national, and international newspapers that are filled with hundreds of potential topics for speeches.

Finally, scan blogging sites such as *Huffington Post*, which has a potpourri of articles and opinion columns on politics, sports, news items, gossip, comedy, business, entertainment, and fashion. If you can't find a topic of appropriate interest after scanning this site, you aren't looking hard enough.

Appropriateness of Topic: Blending Topic and Audience

Appropriateness and effectiveness are the two variables that define communication competence. Choosing a topic that is inappropriate for a particular audience virtually guarantees that your speech will be ineffective. Appropriateness is contextual. A speech topic that works in one instance may be an abysmal failure in another. There are three central elements to consider when analyzing the appropriateness of your topic choice: speaker, audience, and occasion.

Speaker Appropriateness: Suitable for You?

If a topic is chosen merely to fulfill an assignment but you find it uninteresting, then it is not appropriate for you, the speaker. Choose a topic that interests or excites you. An appropriate topic can motivate your desire to research the topic and build a quality speech. An inappropriate topic will make researching and constructing your speech drudgery. If you're interested and excited about your topic, you can communicate that to your audience. It is a rare individual who can take a topic that he or she finds as dull as watching slugs race and successfully fake interest to an audience. If you think the subject is dull, what must your audience think?

You and the topic may be a poor fit. A white person speaking about "black experience in America" is an awkward fit. Similarly, young people talking about "what it's like being old" sounds goofy. Men speaking about female menopause or women discussing the care and feeding of a prostate gland are also awkward. No matter how gifted you are as a speaker, some topics will sink your chances of presenting an effective speech. Choose a topic that suits your interests and fits who you are.

Audience Appropriateness: Suitable for Listeners?

Over the years, my colleagues have shared many horror stories about student speeches that were startlingly inappropriate, such as "how to assassinate someone you hate," "proper methods of inducing vomiting after a big meal" (accompanied by demonstrations), "spitting for distance," "effective nail-biting techniques," "harassing the homeless," "opening a beer bottle with your teeth," "constructing a bong," and "shoplifting techniques that work." These topics are inappropriate because they are offensive, trivial, demeaning, or they encourage illegal, unethical behavior. Most of them are pointless, adolescent silliness.

There are other reasons a topic might be inappropriate for an audience. An audience may find a topic difficult to relate to or appreciate. Giving a speech on how to surf to people living in Kansas is a bit weird. A topic can also be too technical or complex. Students occasionally try to refute evolutionary theory when explaining the origins and development of the universe by referring to the Second Law of Thermodynamics. Their explanation is almost always wildly incorrect and confusing because it requires an understanding of physics.

The increasingly multicultural makeup of audiences provides an additional risk for inappropriate topic choice. Even without intending to, a speaker's topic choice can insult individuals from other cultures or co-cultures. Giving a speech on religion or politics should be approached cautiously lest insult be given to those with different cultural perspectives.

Occasion Appropriateness: Suitable for the Event?

When you're speaking at a particular event, topic choice must be appropriate to the occasion. A graduation ceremony invites topics such as "employment possibilities for the future," "skills for success," and "thinking in the future tense." A sermon at a Sunday religious service warrants a topic related to ethical or moral behavior. Don't choose a topic unrelated to the occasion. It won't fulfill audience expectations. Soliciting support for a political cause at a graduation ceremony or an awards banquet will get you booed off the stage.

Eleven days before the 2002 national election, Paul Wellstone, democratic U.S. senator from Minnesota, died in a plane crash. With the expectation that former U.S. Senator Walter Mondale would replace Wellstone on the ballot, the memorial service for Wellstone, attended by 20,000 people, became a pep rally for the Mondale campaign. In a "eulogy" for Wellstone, Rick Kahn made this plea: "Can you not hear your friend calling you, one last time, one step forward on his behalf, to keep his legacy alive and help us win this election for Paul Wellstone" (Wilgoren, 2002). Most of the crowd sprang to its feet and began chanting, "Mondale! Mondale!" With many Republicans and independents in attendance, this burst of partisanship ignited a firestorm of controversy.

Narrowing the Topic: Recognizing Constraints

Sometimes you are given a very broad topic on which to speak. Other times you find an interesting topic, but it is too broad and general for the time available to speak. Narrowing your topic to fit the audience and the occasion is a significant task for the competent speaker.

Time Constraints: Staying in Bounds

President Woodrow Wilson, a former college professor and the only U.S. president to earn a PhD, took his public speaking very seriously. A reporter interviewed him once regarding his speech preparation. "How long do you spend preparing a 10-minute speech?" Wilson was asked. He replied, "About two weeks." "How long do you spend preparing an hour-long speech?" the reporter queried. "About a week," answered Wilson. Surprised, the reporter then asked Wilson how long he prepared for a two-hour speech. Wilson replied, "I could do that now." Giving a long-winded speech takes less effort than narrowing the speech to fit neatly into a shorter time allotment.

Once you have settled on a general topic that is appropriate for you the speaker, the audience, and the occasion, begin narrowing the topic to fit your time limit. A 5-minute speech obviously requires much more narrowing than a 15-minute speech. Don't choose a topic that is so broad and complex that you couldn't possibly do it justice in the time allotted. Heed Mark Twain's observation, "Few sinners are saved after the first 20 minutes of a sermon." *Staying within your time limit is critical.* If you are asked to address a luncheon meeting of a civic organization and you are scheduled for a 15-minute presentation, you'll be addressing a roomful of empty chairs if you go much beyond the time limit. People attending luncheon meetings often have only an hour, of which your speech is but a small part.

Abraham Lincoln's Gettysburg Address, considered one of the great American speeches, lasted about *two minutes*. Famed orator Edward Everett, who preceded Lincoln, gave a two-hour-plus speech. He later wrote Lincoln, "I shall be glad if I could flatter myself that I came as near to the central idea of the occasion in two hours as you did in two minutes" (cited in Noonan, 1998, p. 65). Stay within your time limits. That requires preparation.

Purpose Statements: Intent

Once you have narrowed a general topic into more specific subtopics, identify a general purpose and compose a specific purpose statement. A **general purpose** identifies the overall goal of your speech; it tells the audience why you're giving the speech (to inform, describe, explain, demonstrate, persuade, celebrate, memorialize, entertain, eulogize).

The general purpose will be given to you if your speech is a classroom assignment (e.g., give a demonstration speech). If you have no direction from others, you must decide what general purpose is appropriate for the audience and occasion. Once you have determined the general purpose, decide what will be your central idea (sometimes referred to as your *theme*). The **central idea** identifies the main concept, point, issue, or conclusion that you want the audience to understand, believe, or feel. The central idea becomes the one concise thought, separate from all the details provided in the speech, that audience members are likely to remember.

We compose a specific purpose statement when we have a clear central idea in mind. A **specific purpose statement** is a concise, precise infinitive phrase composed of simple, clear language that encompasses both the general purpose and the central idea and indicates what the speaker hopes to accomplish with the speech. For example,

TOPIC: Cost of a college education.

NARROWED TOPIC: The high cost of textbooks.

GENERAL PURPOSE: To inform.

CENTRAL IDEA: Complaining about the high cost of textbooks is not as helpful as knowing why textbooks are so expensive.

SPECIFIC PURPOSE STATEMENT: To explain the three primary reasons textbooks are expensive.

Once you have constructed your specific purpose statement, test its appropriateness and likely effectiveness. Ask the following questions:

1. *Is your purpose statement concise and precise?* You should be able to phrase an effective purpose statement in 15 words or fewer. If your purpose statement is much beyond 15 words, rephrase it until it is more concise and precise.
2. *Is your purpose statement phrased as a declarative statement?* Phrasing a purpose statement as a question asks your listeners to provide the answers (e.g., "Why are textbooks so expensive?"). Make your purpose statement declarative (i.e., declare the direction of your speech) and begin with an infinitive phrase (i.e., to inform, to persuade, to celebrate, to teach, to demonstrate, to eulogize).
3. *Is your purpose statement free of figurative language?* Keep your purpose statement plain and direct. Figurative language is fine for the body of your speech, but it can be confusing in a purpose statement. For example, "To tell you why textbooks are the golden fleece of education" will likely leave your listeners mystified. Those who speak English as a second language may really be puzzled.
4. *Is your purpose statement more than simply a topic?* "To inform my audience about the cost of textbooks" is a topic statement, not a specific purpose statement. What about the cost of textbooks? Listeners are provided with no direction for your speech. Tell them specifically what you seek to accomplish. "To discuss the feasibility of a private college bookstore to lower textbook prices" provides direction.
5. *Is your purpose statement practical?* Can your listeners accomplish what you ask them to do? "I want to teach you to be a top-notch computer programmer" will not happen in a single speech, even a lengthy one. "My purpose is to inform you about the many changes in the new tax code" is too technical and complex for a single speech

to an audience of mostly uninformed taxpayers. Make your specific purpose statement practical: "I want to convince you that taking a computer programming course is worthwhile."

Now you know how to choose a topic, determine its appropriateness for the speaker (you), the audience, and the occasion, and how to construct a specific purpose statement that appropriately narrows your topic for the time allotted. The next step is to research your topic so you have something useful to say.

Researching the Topic

Researching your topic should be a focused undertaking. Wandering aimlessly through a library or searching randomly on the Internet will waste time and accomplish little. This section explains how to research a speech topic systematically.

The Internet: First Stop

The Internet has quickly become a primary source for research. A survey of 272,000 first-year college students revealed that 76% frequently used the Internet for research (Marklein, 2008). Using the Internet efficiently and effectively for researching your speech requires some basic knowledge.

Search Tools: Finding What You Need

Often your research effort will begin with an Internet search engine. A **search engine** is an Internet tool that computer generates indexes of web pages that match, or link with, keywords typed in a search window. There are far too many search engines to provide an exhaustive list here. A comprehensive list of search engines can be found at the Library of Congress website (http://www.lcweb.loc.gov/global/search.html). These are some of the more popular ones.

Google (http://www.google.com)
MSN Search (search.msn.com)
Bing (www.bing.com)

A **directory** is an Internet tool in which humans edit indexes of web pages that match, or link with, keywords typed in a search window. The important difference between a search engine and a directory is that a directory has a person trained in library or information sciences choosing prospective sites based on the quality of the site. *Search engines are more likely than directories to provide overly broad, often irrelevant sites.* These are three popular directories.

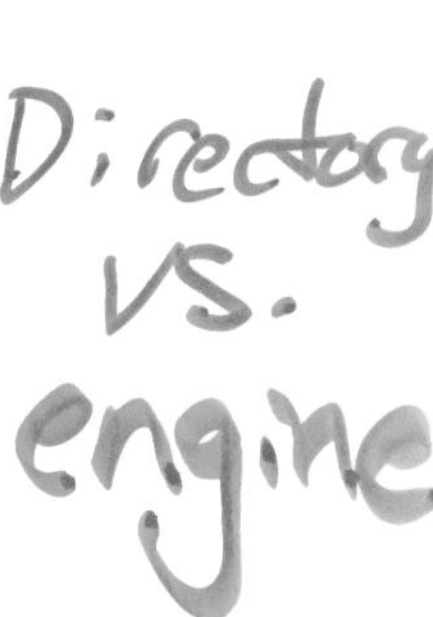

TradeWaveGalaxy (www.einet.net)
Yahoo (http://www.yahoo.com)
About (www.about.com)

A **metasearch engine** will send your keyword request to several search engines at once. *They work best when your request is a relatively obscure one,* not a general-interest topic. When you want to narrow your search to about a dozen sites, try using a metasearch engine. These are some popular metasearch engines.

Dogpile (http://www.dogpile.com)
Ask Jeeves (www.ask.com)
MetaCrawler (www.metacrawler.com)

Because there is much on the web that is irrelevant, misinformed, or plain nutty, virtual libraries have been created to provide more selective, higher-quality information on the Internet. A **virtual library** is a search tool that combines Internet technology and standard library techniques for cataloguing and appraising information. Virtual libraries are usually associated with colleges, universities, or organizations with strong reputations in information dissemination. These are some of the more popular virtual libraries.

Internet Public Library (http://www.ipl.org)
Social Science Information Gateway (http://www.ariadne.ac.uk/issue2/sosig/)
WWW Virtual Library (http://vlib.org)

Internet Search Tips: Navigating the Web

Information overload is a significant problem when you conduct only a general search on the Internet. Type "technology" into a search window and you'll access millions of sites. Obviously, so much information is unhelpful.

Use the Internet search tools on a website homepage to help access relevant information. Click on the Help, Frequently Asked Questions, Tutorial, or Search Tips button on the homepage. Instructions will appear on screen for using the search engine, directory, or virtual library effectively.

Another tip is to *do a subject search*. Many web homepages have lists of subjects. Clicking on one of the subjects produces smaller categories. Clicking on one of these subcategories produces even smaller subtopics and so on until you find the websites that work for you.

Evaluating Websites: Using Basic Criteria

The survey of 272,000 first-year college students found that only 35% of those who use the Internet for research evaluate the quality or reliability of the information (Marklein, 2008). Websites that show up first on Google, for example, are not necessarily those with the most reliable information. This is a problem because the Internet can be a prime source of misinformation. For example, I received the following attachment in an email from a friend:

> These are actual comments made on students' report cards by teachers in the New York City public school system. All teachers were reprimanded but boy, are these funny!!
>
> 1. Since my last report, your child has reached rock bottom and has started to dig.
> 2. I would not allow this student to breed.
> 3. Your child has delusions of adequacy.
> 4. Your son is depriving a village somewhere of an idiot.
> 5. Your son sets low personal standards and then consistently fails to achieve them.
> 6. The student has a "full six-pack" but lacks the plastic thing to hold it all together.
> 7. This child has been working with too much glue.
> 8. When your daughter's IQ reaches 50, she should sell.
> 9. The gates are down, the lights are flashing, but the train isn't coming.
> 10. If this student were any more stupid, he'd have to be watered twice a week.
> 11. It's impossible to believe that the sperm that created this child beat out 1,000,000 others.
> 12. The wheel is turning but the hamster is definitely dead.

Confident that these "actual comments" would not have been made by public school teachers, especially on a report card, I chose one of the comments and typed it verbatim in the Google search window. I located websites that printed the same list of comments but claimed that the list was garnered from British military officer fitness reports, employee performance evaluations, military performance appraisals, and appraisals of federal employees. There were 672 websites dating as far back as 1997 that printed this exact list of comments attributed to various sources. The list is almost certainly fabricated. What teacher would risk legal action or loss of their job by making such comments on a report card sent home to parents? Who has access to student report cards to compile such a list?

The Internet is a rich source of rumor, gossip, and hoaxes (check the validity of Internet rumor at http://www.snopes.com/). So how do you separate the high-quality information on the Internet from the hokum? Follow these three easy steps.

First, *consider the source*. Are you looking at medical information from the Mayo Clinic or from a Fred Smith with no accompanying credentials? You may be able to find the credentials of an author by consulting *Biography Index* or by logging on to Virtual Reference Desk (www.refdesk.com) or ProfNet's Expert Database (www.profnet.com). In some instances, no source is identified for an article. In that case, be doubly cautious. Check to see if sources are cited in the article and make a quick check of some of them to see if they exist and are from credible sources.

Second, *try to determine if the source is biased*. No matter what the source, if the website uses a hard sell to peddle products, therapies, or ideas, be wary. Look for sites that have no vested interest, no products to peddle, and no ax to grind. Look at the website address. If it is a "dot-gov" or a "dot-edu," this means that the website is sponsored and maintained by a governmental or educational institution with a reputation to protect. If the address is a "dot-com" site, it is commercial and therefore more likely to be biased. Websites with "dot-org" in their address are sponsored by organizations with varying credibility.

Third, *determine whether the document is current.* Websites sometimes indicate when the site was last updated. Many documents indicate the date at the beginning or at the end. You can also make a rough estimate of the currency of the document from the recency of the information in the article. Be as current as possible.

Libraries: Bricks-and-Mortar Research

The Internet is a wonderful virtual resource, but the bricks-and-mortar library buildings still house books, documents, and reference works that can't be found on the Internet. College libraries also are computerized, and most allow students to access the Internet on library computers. Thus, college libraries provide "one-stop shopping" for information on speech topics.

Every college library offers one or more tours of its facility. Take the tour. Even if you are already knowledgeable about using a library, the tour will familiarize you with where materials are located in a specific library.

Librarian: Expert Navigator

If you do not know quite where to begin, ask the librarian; there is no better single source of information on researching a speech topic. They are the experts on information location. Use them. Do not expect the librarian to do your research for you, but he or she will guide you on your journey through the maze of information if you get stuck.

Library Catalogues: Computer Versions

For decades, the card catalogue was a standard starting point for most research. Now the old card catalogues have been

The Library of Congress is the world's largest library, housing more than 138 million items, including 32 million books, 2.9 million recordings, 13.7 million photographs and films, 5 million maps, and 61 million manuscripts. Conveniently, many of the Library's resources are available online at www.loc.gov. "I couldn't find anything on my topic" used to be a problem for students. Not anymore.

BOX 12.1 Focus on Controversy

WIKIPEDIA: CREDIBLE SCHOLARSHIP OR MOB RULE?

Wikipedia is often cited as a credible reference. This online collaborative encyclopedia is the most widely used general reference source on the Internet. In late 2010, *Wikipedia* was the fifth most visited website. There are 17 million articles, and counting, in multiple languages. As Association for Psychological Science President Mahzarin Banaji (2011) notes, "It is the largest collaboratively produced knowledge repository that has ever existed."

One serious problem with *Wikipedia* is that it takes contributions from almost anyone willing to make entries. Information can be unreliable, even wrong. An assessment by the Project on Psychology of 935 articles on *Wikipedia* found only 2% were above "B level" in quality, and many were woefully inadequate, even inaccurate (Banaji, 2011). Sources of articles contributed are omitted. Even though *Wikipedia* articles often include links to valid and credible sources, and some articles are first-rate scholarly works, nevertheless you may be quoting merely an interested party with no expertise and a decidedly biased view. This "anyone can contribute and edit" approach runs the risk of providing misinformation (Banaji, 2011). Comedian Stephen Colbert urged his fans to change the *Wikipedia* entry for African elephants to reflect his satirical campaign for "truthiness" by claiming that the elephant population had not declined but tripled in the previous six months. His fans made the change (Morrison, 2007). During the 2008 presidential campaign, partisans engaged in an editing war concerning whether Senator John McCain's *Wikipedia* entry should refer to him as a conservative, moderate, or liberal. When McCain announced Sarah Palin as his running mate, within hours more than 1,200 edits had been made to her *Wikipedia* entry in a battle of partisans (O'Brien, 2008).

Longtime and respected journalist John Seigenthaler was victimized by an anonymous entry in *Wikipedia*. The purported biography claimed that Seigenthaler was "thought to have been directly involved in the Kennedy assassinations of both John, and his brother, Bobby. Nothing was ever proven." Seigenthaler (2005) was outraged

(continued)

computerized in almost all libraries in the United States. The computer catalogue, like its predecessor, lists books according to author, title, and subject. An important distinguishing characteristic of the computer catalogue is that you can do a keyword search. Type in "mountain climbing" and a list of titles will appear related to this subject. You can also keyword search by author names. Computer catalogues also indicate if the book is available or checked out, saving you time.

Periodicals: Popular Information Sources

The Reader's Guide to Periodical Literature provides current listings for articles in hundreds of popular magazines in the United States. Articles are listed by both author and subject. There is also a computer version entitled *Reader's Guide Abstracts and Full Text*. This computer version is faster to use, and it includes a brief abstract, or summary, of the listed magazine articles and full-text articles from more than 100 periodicals. There are many other periodical indexes. Check with your librarian to discover which are available at your college library.

Newspapers: An Old Standby

Newspapers are one of the richest available sources of information on current topics. Your college library undoubtedly subscribes to the local newspaper. *The New York Times Index* is a valuable resource. Database

BOX 12.1 *(Continued)*

by this slander, but because the entry was anonymous, he was unable to seek legal recourse. The "Internet character assassination" stayed on *Wikipedia* for 132 days before it was removed. By that time, the "malicious biography" had circulated to other websites such as Reference.com and Answers.com. Beginning in 2010, *Wikipedia* began "flagged revisions" which are designed to check the accuracy of new material on famous people. Nevertheless, Jim Redmond, a *Wikipedia* administrator and editor, counsels: "Students shouldn't even be tempted to use *Wikipedia* as an original source" (quoted in Daniels & Johnson, 2007).

The criticisms are harsh, but are they entirely fair? Duke University interdisciplinary studies and English professor Cathy Davidson (2007) thinks not. She views *Wikipedia* as "the single most impressive collaborative intellectual tool produced at least since the *Oxford English Dictionary*" (p. B20). She further claims that criticisms are overblown. She notes that studies have shown *Wikipedia* is no more error-prone than some standard encyclopedias, and *Wikipedia* has the added advantage that errors can be corrected sometimes within hours of discovery. *Wikipedia* "is not just an encyclopedia. It is a knowledge community, uniting anonymous readers all over the world who edit and correct grammar, style, interpretations, and facts" (p. B20). As a starting point for research, *Wikipedia* can be "a quick and easy reference before heading into more-scholarly depths" (p. B20). Davidson's points have merit. Nevertheless, be cautious using *Wikipedia*. It is probably best to use it as Davidson suggests—as one possible starting point for your research, but not as a primary, reliable reference.

QUESTIONS FOR THOUGHT

1. Do you see any ethical concerns using *Wikipedia* as a primary source?
2. Can you think of ways to improve the accuracy and integrity of *Wikipedia*?

indexes for newspapers include *Newsbank Index*, the *InfoTrac National Newspaper Index*, and *UMI's Newspaper Abstracts*.

Reference Works: Beyond *Wikipedia*

Encyclopedias are standard references used for researching a wide variety of topics. The most widely known encyclopedias are the *Encyclopaedia Britannica, Collier's Encyclopedia, World Book Encyclopedia*, and *Encyclopedia Americana*. Many encyclopedias can be accessed by computer. *Wikipedia* is probably the most controversial (see Box 12-1).

Other useful general reference works besides encyclopedias are *Statistical Abstracts of the United States, World Almanac, Monthly Labor Review, FBI Uniform Crime Report, Vital Statistics of the United States, Facts on File*, the *Guinness Book of World Records*, and *Who's Who in America*. References for government-related information include the *Monthly Catalogue of United States Government Publications, Congressional Quarterly Weekly Report, Congressional Record, Congressional Digest*, and *Congressional Index*.

Interviewing: Questioning Experts

Research interviews are sometimes a very productive resource for your speeches. Interviewing local artists about standards for determining the difference in quality between a Picasso painting and a three-year-old's crayon drawing could be quite useful.

Interviewing an expert on hybrid car technology might be a great place to begin your research on this topic. Experts can often guide your search by telling you where to search and what to avoid.

Student speakers often assume that no expert would want to be interviewed by just a student. That is usually untrue, especially when you consider how many experts are college professors on your campus. If your topic is a campus issue, such as parking problems or theft of car stereos, interviews with the campus chief of security could provide valuable information for your speech.

Interview Plan: Be Prepared

No research interview should be conducted without a specific plan of action. Your plan should include what you hope to find, who you will interview and why, a specific meeting time and place arranged with the interviewee, and prepared questions that will likely elicit helpful information. Avoid questions that ask the obvious or tell you what you already know. Avoid leading questions such as, "You couldn't possibly believe that this campus has no parking problem, could you?" Also avoid hostile or belligerent questions such as, "When you screwed up the arrest of that student accused of stealing car stereos on campus, did you make the arrest because you are biased against Middle Eastern people?" Ask difficult questions if you need to, but be respectful to the interviewee. Open-ended questions are usually a good way to begin a research interview. Consider a few examples:

Do you believe we have a parking problem on campus?

What actions have been taken to address the parking problem on campus?

What more should be done about campus parking?

Interview Conduct: Act Professionally

The manner in which you conduct yourself during the interview will usually determine whether the interview will be a success and provide useful information. Dress appropriately. Sloppy or bizarre dress will likely insult the interviewee. Always be on time for your meeting. If you are late, the interview may be canceled. Never record your interview without the expressed permission of the interviewee. Stay focused and don't meander into unfruitful side discussions. Take careful notes. Stay within the allotted time for the interview. Thank the interviewee for answering your questions. Review your notes after the interview and write down any additional clarifying notations that will help you remember what transpired during the interview.

Plagiarism and Ethics: Cutting Corners on Research

In 1987, when Joe Biden was a U.S. senator from Delaware, he ran for president of the United States. Biden, a gifted orator, was given a decent chance of securing the Democratic nomination. His candidacy went into the dumpster, however, when news accounts revealed that Biden had plagiarized his conclusion to a speech he gave at the Iowa State Fair. He lifted his conclusion almost verbatim from a speech by British Labor Party leader Neil Kinnock. Biden had even cribbed Kinnock's personal history. For example, Kinnock asked rhetorically, "Why am I the first Kinnock in a thousand generations to be able to get to university? Why is Glenys [his wife] the first woman in her family in a thousand generations to be able to get to university?" (cited in Jamieson, 1988, p. 221). Biden's conclusion asked rhetorically, "Why is it that Joe Biden is the first in his family ever to go to a university? Why is it that my wife, who is sitting out there in the audience, is the first in her family to ever go to college?" (p. 222). Biden was not the first in his family to receive a college education (Jamieson, 1988).

Confronted with the charge of plagiarism, Biden claimed that the similarity between his speech and Kinnock's was merely coincidental. The news media, however, sensed a bigger story and discovered that Biden had also lifted passages from speeches by Hubert Humphrey and Robert Kennedy. Biden was further damaged by his admission that he had plagiarized when he was a law student at Syracuse University. Biden's presidential campaign came to a screeching halt, and he didn't attempt another presidential bid until the 2008 campaign, ultimately winning the consolation prize—vice-president.

Some might pass off Biden's plagiarism as a lot of huffing and puffing about very little. Plagiarism, however, is unethical behavior. Speaking someone else's words without giving attribution is dishonest and disrespectful and, therefore, incompetent communication. How do we know who the real Joe Biden is if he speaks the unattributed words of another and even assumes someone else's personal history to sound eloquent?

The issue of plagiarism emerged again in the political realm when journalist Geoffrey Dunn (2009) accused Sarah Palin of lifting whole passages of a November 1, 2005, article written by Newt Gingrich and Craig Shirley. In a speech she gave in June 2009 at the Alaska Center for the Performing Arts, Palin very closely paraphrased the article ten times, making this vague attempt to reference her paraphrases: "Recently, Newt Gingrich, he had written a good article about Reagan." She made one further oblique reference to the Gingrich article later in the speech. Is this plagiarism? Jonathon Bailey (2009), who founded the website Plagiarism Today, thinks not. Technically, I agree. Palin would have been guilty of plagiarism if she had never attributed anything she said in her speech to Gingrich. Nevertheless, her attempt at attribution is extremely vague, and it makes it impossible for her audience to know what are her words and what specifically are those of Gingrich unless they check the original Gingrich article, an unlikely prospect. She also never references the second author of the article, Craig Shirley. That is not acceptable. It isn't strictly plagiarism, but it certainly is extremely sloppy and unprofessional. Merging your words and those of others without clearly identifying the difference is inappropriate.

With the explosive growth of the Internet and the easy availability of whole speeches by others, student plagiarism has become an increasing problem (Noguchi, 2008). Documented cases of students stealing lines, even entire passages, from the graduation speeches of other students for use in their own graduation speeches have produced lively debate on YouTube, a frequent resource used by students for such plagiarism.

These student speakers and Joe Biden were guilty of selective plagiarism, or stealing portions of someone else's speech or writings. That is bad enough, but plagiarism becomes even more serious when entire speeches are stolen and presented as one's own. Some students attempt such blatant theft of another's words usually because the development of a speech has been left until there is too little time to conduct adequate research. Stealing someone's words is pilfering a part of that person's identity. That is never an inconsequential act.

Developing Supporting Materials

Supporting materials are the examples, statistics, and testimony used to bolster a speaker's viewpoint. Supporting materials answer the three primary questions listeners are likely to ask: "What do you mean?" "How do you know?" "Why should we care?" (Johnson, 1946). This section covers the purposes for supporting materials, types, argument development, and criteria for evaluating supporting materials.

Purposes: Why Important

Supporting materials accomplish four specific goals: to clarify points, to amplify ideas, to support claims, and to gain interest. *This is an audience-centered process.* For example, some audiences require greater clarification of points than others; a group of lawyers won't require examples to clarify legal procedures nearly as often as a lay audience assuredly would.

Clarify Points: What Do You Mean?

When we don't understand a point someone has made, we commonly ask, "Can you give me an example?" Examples can clarify your point. Consider this:

> Races exist in name only! Classifying "races" according to skin color is like arbitrarily categorizing books in a library by the color

> of their covers. Nothing of substance is revealed by such categorization. Skin color is a superficial human trait that reveals nothing significant about the content of the group. We might as well have a freckle-faced race, a short or tall race, maybe a bow-legged, a bald-headed, or a belly button race ("inny" or "outy"). No one seriously suggests that these superficial inherited physical traits should be the basis of racial designations, yet who can be heard laughing at the suggestion that a black, white, or yellow race exists?

Merely asserting that races exist in name only leaves listeners guessing as to the basis of such a claim. Providing clear examples lessens opportunities for misunderstanding by listeners.

Support Claims: How Do You Know?

A claim without evidence is like a haystack in a hurricane—it is easily blown apart from lack of support. Using supporting materials is essential to establishing the probability of your claims (remember the probability model discussed in Chapter 6). Without evidence, the validity of your claims is possible, but not necessarily plausible, and hardly highly probable. As you will see in Chapters 14 and 15, claims supported by quality evidence strengthen a speech by answering the question, "How do you know?"

Gain Interest: Why Should You Care?

Clarifying, creating impact, and supporting the points made in your speech are important goals that can be satisfied by using supporting materials. Perhaps less central, but still helpful, is the use of supporting materials to gain the interest of listeners. As you put together your speech, you should choose material with an eye cast specifically toward riveting your audience's attention. This takes planning and thought. In some instances, further research may be required to find more attention-grabbing supporting materials to jazz up the interest level of your speech.

Create Impact: Why Should You Care Deeply?

Scott Branton (2006), as a student at Florida Community College and participant in the 2006 Interstate Oratorical Association contest, makes a powerful case for eco-friendly "green funerals."

> According to . . . the Glendale Memorial Preserve website, last updated February 14, 2005, each year in the U.S., we bury roughly 827,000 gallons of embalming fluid which is enough to fill nearly four Olympic-size swimming pools. John Konofes, director of the Iowa Waste Reduction Center at the University of Northern Iowa, has found that embalming fluids have contaminated groundwater. . . . On top of that, caskets and vaults produce roughly 104,272 tons of steel, 2,700 tons of copper and bronze, 1,636,000 tons of reinforced concrete, and 30 million board feet of hardwoods. Now, you don't have to be a "granola tree-hugging hippie" to see that these practices are having significant impacts on our environment. Ask yourself, why are we trying so hard to preserve the inevitable decompositions of our bodies from nature? Or more importantly, what will happen when we run out of space to bury everyone in a mausoleum or metal vault? Try visualizing this—if you laid out everyone buried last year from head to toe, it would form a line from Los Angeles to New York City. (p. 5)

Most of us probably haven't thought much about this issue that Scott raises, but his plentiful use of supporting materials establishes well the significance of his point of view.

Types of Supporting Materials

There are several types of supporting materials. The principal types are examples, statistics, and the testimony of authorities.

Examples: Various Types

What would the Bible be without examples? Imagine the story of Jesus without inclusion of his parables. A well-chosen example is often memorable for audiences and may have a great impact on listeners. There are four types of examples: hypothetical, real, brief, and extended.

Hypothetical Examples: It Could Happen A **hypothetical example** describes an

imaginary situation, one that is concocted to make a point, illustrate an idea, or identify a general principle. Hypothetical examples help listeners envision what a situation might be like, or they call up similar experiences listeners have had without having to cite a historically factual illustration that may not be readily available. *As long as the hypothetical example is consistent with known facts, it will be believable.*

A hypothetical example can help an audience visualize what might occur. Imagine what it would be like to experience a hurricane, tornado, or tsunami. In what ways would your life be changed if you suddenly lost your job, were laid up in a hospital for three months, or became permanently disabled? These hypothetical examples help listeners picture what might happen and motivate them to take action that might prevent or prepare them for such occurrences.

Real Examples: It Did Happen During the tumultuous protests in Iran following the disputed presidential election in June 2009, 26-year-old Neda Agha-Soltan stepped from her car to get fresh air while caught for an hour in traffic clogged by mass protests. Within seconds, she was shot in the chest from a suspected government sniper ("Who Was Neda?" 2009). Caught on a video cell phone by a bystander, her agonizing death almost instantly became a rallying cry for the antigovernment protesters in the streets. The video was posted on YouTube and seen by millions around the world. Protesters brandished copies of a picture showing her last moment of life. Mehdi Karroubi, an opposition leader and presidential candidate, called Neda a martyr. "A young girl, who did not have a weapon in her soft hands, or a grenade in her pocket, became a victim of thugs who are supported by a horrifying intelligence apparatus," he wrote (quoted in Fathi, 2009). Neda Agha-Soltan became a symbol of the Iranian uprising.

Actual occurrences are **real examples**. Because real examples are factual, they are more difficult to discount than hypothetical examples. A real example can personalize a problem. Hypothetical examples can be discounted as simply "made up." Unlike hypothetical examples, real examples can sometimes profoundly move an audience.

Brief and Extended Examples: Timing and Impact Often a brief example or two make a point well. The examples are clear, and no explanation or elaboration is required. An **extended example** is a detailed story or illustration. I have provided several such examples throughout this text. The Joseph Biden plagiarism narrative told a few pages back is a real and an extended example. A story's length must fit the confines of the time permitted for your speech, but for full impact, a story sometimes must have at least minimal elaboration.

Statistics: Figures for Facts

Statistics are measures of what is true or factual expressed in numbers. They can provide magnitude and allow comparisons. For example, the first Internet website was info.cern.ch, created by Tim Berners-Lee in December 1990 ("How We Got," 2008). The number of websites (not web pages) worldwide jumped to 24 million by 2000, and by March 2010, it exploded to more than 200 million sites ("March 2010 Web Server Survey," 2010). The magnitude of the Internet today and its astronomical growth in just two decades (comparison) are exhibited by these statistics. A well-chosen statistic can support claims, show trends, correct false assumptions, validate hypotheses, and contradict myths, perhaps not as dramatically and memorably as a vivid example, but often more validly and effectively (Lindsey & Yun, 2003).

Statistics, however, can be manipulated to distort truth. Later in this chapter, I present several fallacious uses of statistics. Nevertheless, when statistics are used validly, they can add real substance to your speech.

Testimony of Authorities: Quoting Experts

We live in an often baffling world of mind-boggling complexity. None of us can be expected to know enough to make rational, informed decisions without the help of experts. A discussion of expert testimony appears in the next section when I present

Neda Agha-Soltan was killed, sparking a huge outcry and massive demonstrations in Iran. Real examples can be far more powerful than hypothetical examples. Picture the difference between saying, "Someone could get killed" and "My mother was actually killed."

criteria for evaluating supporting materials. For now, simply recognize that the testimony of authorities is very useful supporting material.

Developing an Argument: Staking Your Claim

When a speaker wanders into controversial territory (e.g., "Gay marriage should be legalized"; "Guns should be allowed on college campuses"), arguments are required to make a case for such claims. An **argument** "implicitly or explicitly presents a claim and provides support for that claim with reasoning and evidence" (Verlinden, 2005, p. 5). **Reasoning** is the thought process of drawing conclusions from supporting materials. **Evidence** consists of supporting materials just discussed whose purpose is to bolster claims that are controversial.

Toulmin Model: Informal Logic

As discussed in Chapter 6, human decision making and problem solving navigate in a sea of relative uncertainty. Probability, not certainty, is the best we can hope to achieve. Thus, informal logic described by British philosopher Stephen Toulmin aptly depicts how people usually conduct argumentation and decision making (Rieke et al., 2005; Verlinden, 2005).

Toulmin (1958) identified and explained the six elements of an argument (see also Figure 12-1). They are

1. *Claim*—that which is asserted and requires support.
2. *Grounds* (Reasons/Evidence)—reasons to accept a claim and the evidence used to support those reasons. Reasons justify the claim, and evidence provides firm ground for these reasons.

3. *Warrant*—the reasoning that links the grounds to the claim. It is usually implied, not stated explicitly.
4. *Backing*—the reasons and relevant evidence that support the warrant.
5. *Reservations*—exceptions or rebuttals that diminish the force of the claim.
6. *Qualifier*—degree of truth to the claim (possible, plausible, probable, highly probable).

Everyday reasoning follows this pattern known as the **Toulmin structure of argument**. For example, suppose you are a guy who wants to date a supermodel. Your train of reasoning might proceed as follows:

Claim: I can date supermodel Jasmine.

Grounds: I am a brainy, average-looking, very nice, sensitive guy with an average income.

Warrant: She dates brainy, average-looking, very nice, sensitive guys with average incomes.

Backing: The last three guys she dated were brainy. Two of them had college degrees, and one had a PhD. All three were average looking according to five girls I asked at random. All three had very average incomes and drove three- or four-year-old sedans. I read interviews with Jasmine in which she said that all of these guys were very nice, sensitive, caring human beings, and that was attractive to her.

Reservations: She's a supermodel who could date almost any guy she wanted. I'm a stranger to her. I don't know anyone who is friends with her who could introduce me. She has a bodyguard who could inflict grievous harm on my person if I tried to approach her. I can't just call her. She might think I'm a stalker.

Qualifier: Possibly she would accept a date with me—when pigs can fly and taxes are abolished.

Evaluating Arguments: Criteria

There are three primary criteria, or standards, to evaluate reasoning and evidence used to support controversial claims: credibility, relevance, and sufficiency. In this section, I explain these criteria and discuss errors in evidence and reasoning called **fallacies** that violate these criteria.

Credibility: Is It Reliable and Valid?

A key criterion for evaluating evidence, as you listen to speakers make claims and

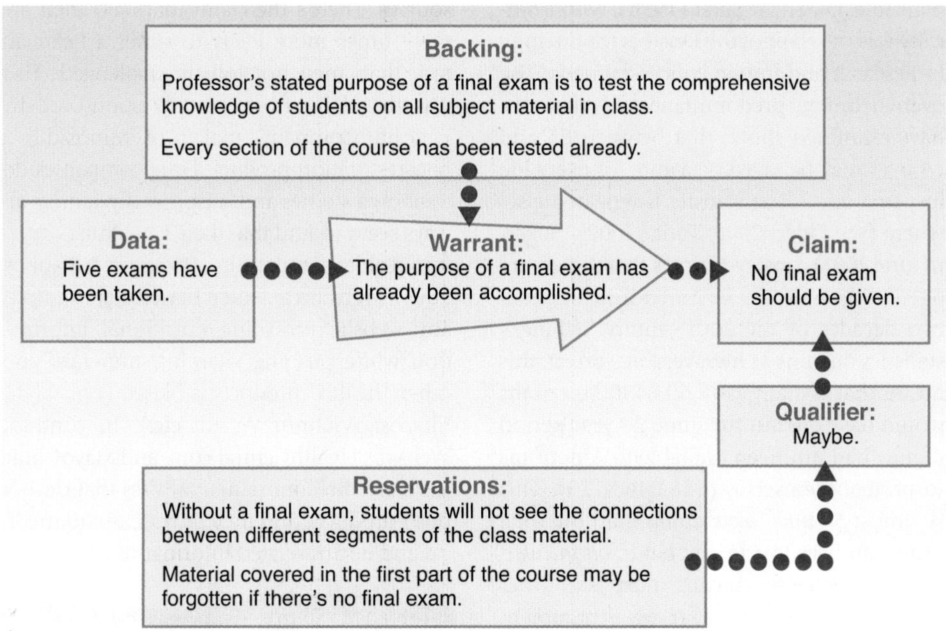

FIGURE 12-1 The Toulmin Structure of Argument

you plan your own arguments for a public speech, is credibility. **The credibility** of evidence used to support claims is determined by its reliability and validity. **Reliability** means consistency, and **validity** means accuracy. A source of information should not be quoted as support for claims if that source has been inconsistent in citing facts and interpreting data or guilty of bending or breaking the truth even occasionally. If cited "facts" prove to be inaccurate, the credibility of any source of those inaccuracies should suffer. Quoting the Centers for Disease Control on the likelihood of a serious outbreak of the West Nile virus or the swine flu is credible because the CDC is consistently objective, relying on scientific studies to support claims about diseases. It has a track record of providing accurate information based on the best currently available data. The CDC is an internationally recognized authority often called upon to investigate outbreaks of disease all over the world.

Evidence used to support claims is often not credible, however. Several fallacies significantly diminish the credibility of evidence presented and therefore do not warrant the claim based on the evidence.

Questionable Statistic: Does It Make Sense Some statistics must be questioned as implausible. Dr. Edgar Suter (1994), who ironically was the chair of the Doctors for Integrity in Research and Public Policy, claimed: "The overwhelming predominance of data we have examined shows that between 25 and 75 lives may be saved by a gun, for every life lost to a gun." The statistic is repeated elsewhere (see Elder, 2000; Faria, 2002). Sugarmann (2001), however, notes that there were 648,046 gun deaths in America in the final two decades of the 20th century. If Suter's statistics on guns as lifesavers are correct, this means that as many as 48,603,450 Americans would have died in the same 20-year period if guns had not been available to Americans to protect themselves (648,046 × 75). This is almost *50 times more deaths* than the total American lives lost in combat in *all the wars in U.S. history*. The skeptic must ask, "Does this statistic make sense?" A cogent argument can be made for opposing gun control (see Kates et al., 1994; Kleck, 2005), but Suter's statistics are not credible.

Question every statistic you plan to use in your speeches by asking yourself whether the statistic seems sensible and accurate. In January 2011, the headline "Shocking numbers behind cell phone usage" was trumpeted on hundreds of websites (type the headline into the Google search window and check it out). The most shocking number was that *"200 trillion* text messages are received in America *every single day."* I checked dozens of these websites and not one questioned the plausibility of the statistic. Simple arithmetic shows that for this to be true, every person (including infants) in the United States (310 million) would receive, on average, *645,161* text messages *each day*. The statistic is wildly implausible.

Biased Source: Grinding an Ax Special-interest groups or individuals who stand to gain money, prestige, power, or influence if they advocate a certain position on an issue are biased sources of information. You should consider their claims as dubious. Look for a source that has no personal stake in the outcome of a dispute or disagreement—a source that seeks the truth, not personal glory or benefit.

Consider several examples of biased sources. There's the claim that bald men are three times more likely to suffer a heart attack than men not follicly challenged. This was the claim from a study sponsored by Upjohn Company, maker of Minoxidil, a hair-restoration product. Drug companies do their own studies and, suspiciously, almost always seem to find that their new drug outperforms older competitors (Rampton & Stauber, 2001). Websites are often biased. For example, any website providing nutritional information while pushing vitamins, minerals, and other "health" products is biased (e.g., GNC, Vitacost, Vitamin World, etc.). In contrast, WebMD, HealthCentral.com, and MayoClinic.com are three more neutral sites that do not push products, and they provide useful medical and health-related information.

Incomplete Source Citation: Something to Hide? A complete citation of the source of your information adds credibility to your argument if your source is qualified. A complete citation includes, as a minimum, (1) the name of the source, (2) the specific title or expertise of the source if not obvious, and (3) the specific publication in which the evidence can be found with the relevant date of the publication.

It is easy and common to cite sources incompletely, leaving out one or more of the minimum requirements, but the skeptic holds speakers to a higher standard. Citations with references only to a vague title, such as Dr. Smith or Professor Jones, are incomplete. What type of doctor or professor is being cited? What are his or her specific credentials to speak as an expert on a particular topic? Even references to qualified experts leave us wondering how current they are if they are missing citation of the publication source and date. When you cite your sources completely, you signal to your audience that you have nothing to hide. Your transparency likely increases your credibility.

Expert Quoted Out of Field: No Generic Experts Iben Browning, the chief scientist for Summa Medical Corporation, has a doctorate in physiology and a bachelor's degree in physics and math. He predicted a major earthquake for December 3 and 4, 1990, along the New Madrid Fault in the Midwest. Schools in several states dismissed students for these two days as a result of Browning's prediction. Browning had some scientific expertise, but not in the area of earthquake prediction. In fact, earthquake experts around the country denounced Browning's predictions. No earthquake, large or small, occurred on the dates Browning predicted. There wasn't even a sizable earthquake on the Madrid fault until April 17, 2008, and it was considered "moderate" by quake experts, causing little damage. Quoting experts outside their field of expertise runs the substantial risk of promoting inaccurate claims supported by invalid and unreliable evidence.

Relevance: Does It Follow?

Evidence used to support claims must have **relevance**; it must relate directly to those claims, or the claims are unwarranted. Consider two fallacies that fail the relevance test: ad hominem and ad populum fallacies.

Ad Hominem Fallacy: Diversionary Tactic In December 2006, Rosie O'Donnell, apparently irked that business tycoon and beauty pageant sponsor Donald Trump gave Miss USA Tara Conner "a second chance" to redeem herself and not lose her beauty crown after revelations of underage drinking and drug use, attacked Trump. "Left his first wife, had an affair, left the second wife, had an affair. Had kids both times, but he's the moral compass for 20-year-olds in America" ("Donald and Rosie," 2007; "Donald Trump Tells FNC," 2007). Later she called Trump a "snake-oil salesman," "a hot bag of wind with bad hair," a "pimp," and she made fun of his "comb-over" hairdo. Trump fired back by calling O'Donnell "a loser," "despicable," "a degenerate," "a fat slob," "ugly," a "mental midget," and "a stumbling buffoon" ("Trump Versus Rosie," 2006). These are ad hominem (Latin meaning "to the person") attacks, personal character assaults, but are they ad hominem fallacies?

The **ad hominem fallacy** is a personal attack on the messenger *to avoid the message*. It is a diversionary tactic. In the Rosie-versus-Donald verbal food fight, O'Donnell challenges Trump's "moral authority" to speak to young people about "second chances." Trump's response is pure vitriol. He never responds directly to the challenge to his moral authority but instead assaults O'Donnell's character and physical attractiveness. This is diversionary character assassination, not a reasonable or relevant response to her initial claim. In effect, Trump is making the irrelevant argument, "Your allegation is weak because you're a fat, ugly slob." O'Donnell, on the other hand, minimized the force of her main claim that Trump has no credibility as a "moral compass" by mixing in irrelevant and distracting personal attacks on Trump's physical attractiveness. Both, then, are guilty of the ad hominem fallacy.

Not all personal attacks are ad hominem fallacies. If a claim raises the issue of a person's credibility, character, or trustworthiness, the attack is not irrelevant to the claim made. Criticisms that led to Richard Nixon's resignation and Bill Clinton's impeachment involved legitimate questions about their character and credibility. O'Donnell's charge that Trump has no moral authority is a character attack but not in itself an ad hominem fallacy. It's an issue that could be reasonably debated.

Ad Populum Fallacy: Arguing from Public Opinion A 2005 national survey conducted by a research team at UCLA found 63% of more than 260,000 first-year college students agreed that "only volunteers should serve in the armed forces" (Engle, 2006). Advocating that the U.S. Army remain all volunteer because a majority of first-year students, the age group most vulnerable to a draft, take this position is an example of the **ad populum fallacy**—basing a claim on popular opinion. Whether the military remains voluntary or becomes mandatory should not be decided just on the basis of popular opinion at some moment, even the opinion of the most affected group. Popular opinion can be fickle and unsound.

Typically, in annual surveys, about two-thirds of the American people favor capital punishment (Newport, 2010). That doesn't mean that it is right or a good policy. Claims should be weighed on the basis of valid reasoning and substantial high-quality evidence, not on the whim of the majority, which could change in a flash.

Sufficiency: Got Enough?

The person who makes a claim has the burden to prove that claim (see Chapter 6). This means that sufficient evidence and reasoning must be used to support a claim you make. Sufficiency is a judgment. There is no precise formula for determining it. Generally, strong, plentiful evidence and solid reasoning meet the sufficiency criterion. Several fallacies, however, clearly exhibit insufficiency.

Self-Selected Sample: Partisan Power Any poll or survey that depends on respondents selecting themselves to participate provides results that are insufficient to generalize beyond the sample. A **random sample** is a portion of the population chosen in such a manner that every member of the entire population has an equal chance of being selected. A **self-selected sample** attracts the most committed, aroused, or motivated individuals to fill out surveys on their own and answer polling questions. Printing a survey in a magazine and collecting those that have been returned is an example of a self-selected sample. Calling an 800-number to answer questions about politics or social issues is another example.

On July 26, 2007, I accessed a continuing MSNBC online "live poll" that asked whether President Bush should be impeached. The results from 487,217 respondents showed 88% for impeachment and the rest opposed or unsure ("Politics," 2007). All surveys taken during July 2007 using a random sample showed a deeply divided country on the impeachment question, but *none* showed majority support (e.g., *USA Today*/Gallup showed 36% favored impeachment).

Online surveys attract partisan respondents. Surveys using self-selected samples are unrepresentative and thus produce bogus results. Note that the problem is not an insufficient sample. Self-selected samples often involve huge numbers of respondents. For example, social analysis company Crimson Hexagon examined more than 190,000 Twitter tweets nationally on a court ruling striking down a ban on gay marriage. Only 17% were opposed to the court ruling despite polls with random samples that show a country deeply divided on the subject ("Prop 8 Twitter Reaction," 2010). Only those with strong feelings on the subject likely tweeted. Increasing the number of respondents does not improve the results (unless you survey everyone in the population) because the sample is unrepresentative.

Inadequate Sample: Large Margin of Error The mass media tend to sensationalize each new scientific study that gets published. *A single study, however, proves very little and is insufficient to draw any general conclusion.* In science, studies are replicated before results are given credence because mistakes can be made that may distort the results. The greater the number of carefully controlled studies that show similar or identical results, the more it meets the sufficiency standard.

Praising a product that you have used is called a **testimonial**. Testimonials are not sufficient proof for a claim because a single endorsement of a product is an inadequate sample. One person can make a mistake. Even a dozen testimonials, although potentially persuasive, don't make the claim any stronger because a dozen people can also be wrong. Testimonials are also confirmation bias in action. Advertisers don't seek testimonials from consumers who hate the product. Only the believers are sought for their testimonial.

So, what is an adequate sample size? In general, the **margin of error**—a measure of the degree of sampling error accounted for by imperfections in sample selection—goes up as the number of people surveyed goes down. *Margin of error applies only to random samples,* not self-selected samples. An adequate sample size will have a margin of error no greater than 3%–4% plus or minus. A poll of 1,000 people randomly selected typically has a margin of error of about plus or minus 3%. This means that if the poll reports 65% of respondents approve of the job the president is doing, the actual result, if every adult American were surveyed, would be between 62% and 68%. No poll is without some margin of error because it is usually impractically expensive and time consuming to survey every person in a population, but increasing the sample size improves the chances that the poll is accurate if the sample is random, not self-selected.

My favorite questionable survey is a study of 103 California companies testing job applicants for drug use ("Pre-employment," 1990). The study revealed that 17.8% of applicants tested positive. The margin of error was an astounding 7.8%. Thus, the findings of this study are highly questionable because drug use among applicants could have been 25.6% (17.8% plus 7.8% margin of error) or 10% (17.8% minus 7.8%). Is there a really big drug use problem at these companies or a relatively minor problem? Who knows!

When you draw a conclusion based on too few or unrepresentative samples, this is called a **hasty generalization**. Seek more credible information, ask questions, and research the issue before making a conclusion.

Correlation as Causation: How Related We humans are intensely interested in discovering causes of events that remain unexplained. For example, why do some people live to be 100 years old, and others die at a much younger age? Scientists, journalists, and health seekers have visited Vilcabamba, Ecuador, for a half-century to discover the causes of their unusual longevity. Manuel Picoita, 102 years old, thinks getting along with his neighbors is the cause of his reaching centenarian status (Kraul, 2006, p. 16A). Josefa Ocampa, 104, believes the secret to her long life is that each morning she drinks a glass of goat's milk with a bit of her own urine added. Aurora Maza, a mere 96, attributes her longevity to working in the fields all her life. Legendary comedian George

Burns was fond of arguing that he made it to 100 years old because he smoked a cigar and drank martinis every day. We all are prone to draw causation (x causes y) from mere correlation (x occurs and y also occurs, either sequentially or simultaneously). "The invalid assumption that correlation implies cause is probably among the two or three most serious and common errors of human reasoning" (Gould, 1981, p. 242).

A **correlation** is a consistent relationship between two variables. A **variable** is anything that can change. Finding a strong correlation between two variables doesn't necessarily have significance. A large research team explored variables that might determine causes of contraceptive use in Taiwan (Li, 1975). The number of electric appliances (ovens, irons, toasters) found in the home correlated most strongly with birth control use. As the number of appliances increased, the use of contraceptives also increased. So, based on this study, do you think distributing free blenders and microwave ovens would likely reduce teen pregnancies? More probably, this correlation merely reflects socioeconomic status that is also strongly correlated with contraceptive use and is a better candidate for causation.

Correlations suggest possible causation, but correlations alone are an insufficient reason to claim probable causation. Gould (1981) notes that "the vast majority of correlations in our world are, without doubt, noncausal" (p. 242). Kids with big feet are better readers than those with small feet. Why? Do big feet cause reading proficiency? Not likely. Children with big feet are usually older, and older children have had more experience reading.

False Analogy: Mixing Apples and Oranges A claim based on an analogy alleges that two things that resemble each other in certain ways also resemble each other in further ways. Thus, both things should be treated in similar ways. Apples and oranges have much in common (skin, seeds, juice, grow on trees). If you like the taste of apples, you'll like the taste of oranges also, so goes the analogical reasoning. The analogy is often made between the Vietnam and Iraq Wars. Both seem to follow similar paths of escalation with frustratingly minimal progress leading to quagmire and popular dissatisfaction.

Analogies are false when significant points of difference exist despite some superficial similarities between the two things being compared. Consider this analogy: "In Turkey, farmers grow poppies as a cash crop. In the United States, farmers grow corn and soybeans for cash crops. Why outlaw poppies in the United States when we don't outlaw corn and soybeans?" Sound reasonable to you? Poppies, corn, and soybeans are all cash crops, but that doesn't warrant similar treatment. This is a superficial similarity. Poppies are outlawed in the United States because they are a source of heroin, a dangerous drug. Corn and soybeans are grown in the United States to feed the world, not to produce narcotics. Poppies are not an indispensable crop. Corn and soybeans are indispensable crops.

This ends my identification of specific fallacies. I have focused on only a handful of fallacies, the most common ones, among the more than 100 that could be identified, but this should serve you well in constructing speeches and discussing and debating controversial issues.

Competent Outlining and Organizing

The quality of speech organization directly influences how well your listeners understand your key points (Thompson, 1960; Titsworth, 2004). A very disorganized speech arouses negative perceptions from your listeners. Speakers who are well organized impress listeners as more credible than speakers who are disorganized. A speaker who doesn't seem able to connect two thoughts doesn't inspire confidence (Chesebro, 2003).

Effective Outlining: Connecting Your Points

The organizational process begins with an understanding of the rudiments of outlining your thoughts. There is a standard form

of outlining that has stood the test of time. Standard outlining follows a few basic criteria for appropriate formatting.

Symbols: Standard Formatting

Standard outlining form uses a specific set of symbols, shown in brief here.

I. Roman numerals for main points
  A. Capital letters for primary subpoints
    1. Standard numbers for secondary subpoints
      a. Lowercase letters for tertiary subpoints

Each successive set of subpoints is indented to separate the main points visually from the primary, secondary, and tertiary subpoints. Thus, you would not format an outline as follows:

I. Main point
A. Primary subpoint
1. Secondary subpoint
a. Tertiary subpoint

You can readily see that lack of indentation merges all of your points and can easily lead to confusion for the speaker.

Coherence: Logical Consistency and Clarity

Logical consistency and clarity are qualities of an effective outline. Begin with your topic, narrow the topic to your specific purpose statement, and from that statement, develop main points that break down further into subpoints. Work from the most general to the most specific. For example,

[TOPIC] The aging U.S. population.

[CENTRAL IDEA] Longer life spans pose new challenges.

[PURPOSE STATEMENT] To explain in what ways longer life spans stress fragile support systems for elderly Americans.

I. [MAIN POINT] Americans are living longer than ever before.
II. [MAIN POINT] Longer life spans stress fragile support systems for the elderly in three significant ways.

Coherence requires that main points flow directly from the purpose statement. Subpoints, however, should also flow from main points. For example, look at the development of Main Point I:

I. [MAIN POINT] Americans are living longer than ever before.
  A. [PRIMARY SUBPOINT] Average life span of an American is at its highest level in history.
  B. [PRIMARY SUBPOINT] Americans are living increasingly to 100 years old and beyond.

Each primary subpoint flows from the main point on "living longer."

Each primary subpoint can be further divided into secondary subpoints. For example,

  A. [PRIMARY SUBPOINT] The average life span of an American is at its highest level in history.
    1. [SECONDARY SUBPOINT] Average life span of an American is a record 77 years old.
    2. [SECONDARY SUBPOINT] Average life span of an American has increased from 69 years old just two decades ago.
  B. [PRIMARY SUBPOINT] Americans are living increasingly to 100 years old and beyond.
    1. [SECONDARY SUBPOINT] A record 30,000 Americans are 100 years old or older.
    2. [SECONDARY SUBPOINT] There will be an estimated 800,000 Americans at least 100 years old by the year 2050.

Following this pattern of working from the most general to the increasingly specific will assure coherence.

If primary subpoints relate directly to a main point, secondary subpoints relate to primary subpoints, and tertiary subpoints relate directly to secondary subpoints, every point will then flow logically from the purpose statement.

Completeness: Using Full Sentences

Your first attempt to outline your speech will prove to be more successful if you use complete sentences. Complete sentences communicate complete thoughts. A word or phrase may suggest a thought without communicating it completely or clearly. For example,

PURPOSE STATEMENT: To explain hazing (initiation rituals).

I. Hazing
   A. Campus hazing
   B. Military hazing
   C. Corporate hazing
II. Solutions
   A. Laws
   B. Policies
   C. Penalties
   D. Education

This word-and-phrase outline creates informational gaps and questions that can't be answered merely by referring to the outline. The purpose statement provides no direction. What will be explained? Will you explain how to do hazing? Why it is a problem? How it can be controlled? Why shouldn't it be controlled?

The main points and subpoints are no clearer. Main Point I is about hazing, and subpoints indicate three types: campus, military, and corporate. Still, no direction or complete thought is communicated. Are these three types of hazing serious problems? Should they be prevented? Should we find them amusing? Should we encourage hazing on campus, in the military, and in the corporate world? Main Point II suffers from the same problem. Solutions are suggested, but solutions imply a problem has been described when no problem is indicated in the previous main point or in the purpose statement. If a problem exists, what type of legal, policy, and educational solutions are offered? This remains unclear.

Consider how much more complete a full-sentence outline is when compared to the incomplete and confusing word-and-phrase outline.

PURPOSE STATEMENT: To explain specific ways to prevent the problem of hazing.

I. Hazing is a growing problem in the United States.
   A. More than 50 deaths and numerous injuries have occurred from hazing in just the last decade.
   B. The number of hazing incidents requiring intervention by authorities has doubled in the last decade.
II. There are several ways to prevent hazing.
   A. Hazing could be outlawed in all states.
   B. College, corporate, and military policies could specifically ban hazing rituals.
   C. Penalties for violations of laws and policies could be increased.
   D. Students, employees, and soldiers could receive instruction on the dangers of hazing and the consequences of violating laws and policies banning the practice.

Balance: No Lopsided Time Allotment

Each main point deserves substantial development. This does not mean that you have to allot an equal amount of time during your speech to each main point. Nevertheless, you want a relatively balanced presentation. If you have three main points in the body of your speech, don't devote four minutes to the first main point and only a minute or less to your two remaining main points. Such a lopsided time allotment means either that your second and third main points aren't really main points at all or that you haven't developed your last two main points sufficiently. Increase the development of main points given insufficient treatment, combine points insufficiently developed into a single point and give the point some beef, or drop the two underdeveloped points and replace them with more substantial points.

Division: Dividing the Pie

Main points divide into subpoints. Note the plural on subpoints. Logically, you don't divide something into one. You divide a pie into two or more pieces. Likewise, *you divide main points into two or more subpoints.* If you can't divide a point into at least two subpoints, this should signal to you that your point probably doesn't need division

or that the point isn't substantial enough. It's time to rethink the development of your speech (see Box 12-2).

Even when you have only a single example to illustrate a point, the principle of division still applies. For example,

I. Professional baseball players' salaries are astronomical.
   A. Average player salaries are more than $3 million per year.
   B. Example: Alex Rodriguez makes $25 million per year.

You can't generalize from a single example, so don't let it dangle as a subpoint all its own.

Competent outlining requires the proper use of symbols, coherence, completeness, balance, and appropriate division of points. An outline maps the flow of a speaker's ideas.

Effective Organization: Creating Patterns

There are several patterns for organizing a speech. The most common ones used in U.S. culture are topical, chronological, spatial, causal, problem-solution, and problem-cause-solution.

Topical Pattern: By the Subjects

A topical pattern shapes information according to types, classifications, or parts of a whole. For example,

PURPOSE STATEMENT: To explain the three types of prisons in the United States.

I. The first type is minimum security.
II. The second type is medium security.
III. The third type is maximum security.

A topical pattern doesn't suggest a particular order of presentation for each main point. You could begin with maximum and work to minimum security prisons as easily as the reverse.

Chronological Pattern: According to Time

Some speeches follow a time pattern. A chronological pattern suggests a specific sequence of events. When speeches provide a biographical sketch, explain a step-by-step process, or recount a historical event, chronological order is an appropriate pattern of organization. For example,

PURPOSE STATEMENT: To explain the renovation plan for our local downtown city center.

I. The old Cooper House and Del Rio Theatre will be demolished.
II. Main Street will be widened.
III. A Cinemax theater complex will replace the Del Rio Theatre.
IV. A new, twice-as-large Cooper House will replace the old Cooper House.

Each main point follows a logical sequence. You don't replace buildings on the same sites until the old buildings are demolished. There is a sequence that must be followed.

Spatial Pattern: According to Space

Some speeches provide information based on a spatial pattern. This spatial pattern may be front to back, left to right, north to south, top to bottom, bottom to top, and so forth. Explaining directions to a particular place requires a spatial order—a visualization of where things are spatially. Explaining how the Brooklyn Bridge was built would necessitate starting the explanation at the base of the bridge and working up spatially. Or consider this example of a backpack.

PURPOSE STATEMENT: To explain how to load up a backpack for camping.

I. Certain items must go on the bottom of the pack.
II. Some items are best packed in the middle.
III. There are several items that pack well on top.
IV. A few items fit well lashed to the outside of the pack.

The outline focuses on segments of space. Actually loading a backpack while you explain your four points is an essential visual aid.

Causal Pattern: Who or What Is Responsible

A standard organizational pattern is causes-effects or effects-causes. The causes-effects

BOX 12.2 Developing Communication Competence

A STUDENT OUTLINE: ROUGH DRAFT AND REVISION

Constructing a competent outline can be a struggle, especially if appropriate outlining form and criteria are not well understood. Initial attempts to outline a speech may prove challenging, and first attempts may produce seriously flawed results. Don't despair. Outlining is a process that trains our minds to think in an orderly fashion. It takes time to learn such a sophisticated skill.

Compare this rough draft of a student outline to the revised outline constructed by the same student (my comments appear in *italics*).

Rough Draft Outline

PURPOSE STATEMENT: To eliminate the drug problem by making drug testing mandatory. (*Where's your central idea? You overstate the potential outcomes of mandatory drug testing. Try "significantly reduce drug use," not "eliminate the drug problem." General purpose is only implied—will you try to convince us?*)

I. The drugs among society. (*No clear direction is provided. What do you want to say about "the drugs among society"? This is also not a complete sentence.*)
   A. The effects of drugs. (*Are you concerned with only negative effects? Unclear! This is not a complete sentence.*)
      1. The immediate effects of drugs.
      2. The permanent effects of drugs. (*1 and 2 are not complete sentences.*)
   B. The effects of using drugs. (*This seems to repeat "A" above. Do you have a different idea in mind? Unclear! This is not a complete sentence.*)
      1. Memory loss.
      2. Addicted babies.
      3. Brain damage.
      4. Physical harm. (*1–4 are not complete sentences.*)
II. Ways to solve drug abuse. (*Your purpose statement indicates only one solution—mandatory drug testing. Stay focused on your purpose statement.*)
   A. The first step is to be aware of the problem. (*"Awareness" doesn't seem related to mandatory drug testing. Let your purpose statement guide your entire outline.*)
      1. Establish drug testing in all companies.
      2. Establish stricter laws against drug users.
      3. Start more drug clinics. (*Good use of complete sentences. Subpoints 1–3 do not relate directly to "A"—they are not kinds of awareness. Subpoints 2 and 3 also seem unrelated to mandatory drug testing. These are coherence problems.*)

(*You have an "A" point without a "B" point—problem of division. Also, Main Point II is less developed than Main Point I—problem of balance.*)

Revised Version

CENTRAL IDEA: Drug use in the workplace is a serious problem requiring a new approach to solving this problem.

(continued)

BOX 12.2 *(Continued)*

PURPOSE STATEMENT: To convince my audience that every place of employment should start a mandatory drug-testing program. (*This is a much-improved purpose statement. "Every place of employment," however, seems a bit drastic. Try narrowing the application of your proposal to workers who might jeopardize the health and safety of others if drugs were used—airline pilots, bus drivers, etc.*)

I. Drug use in the workplace is a serious problem. (*Good clear main point.*)
   A. Drug use in the workplace is widespread.
      1. Many employees in large companies use drugs.
      2. Many employees in factories use drugs.
   B. Drug use in the workplace is dangerous.
      1. Workers injure and even kill themselves.
      2. Customers have been injured and killed. (*Doesn't the risk go far beyond customers? If a plane crashes on a neighborhood because the pilot was loaded on drugs, dead and injured include far more than customers.*)

(*This entire main point with its subpoints is much improved. One question—are you focusing only on drugs used on the job or do you include drug use that occurs hours before starting work?*)

II. Mandatory drug testing in the workplace will reduce drug abuse. (*This is a solid second main point that flows nicely from your purpose statement.*)
   A. Drug testing will catch drug users.
      1. Testing is very accurate.
      2. Drug testing will provide absolute proof of drug use by workers. (*"Absolute proof" seems overstated. Try "solid proof."*)
   B. Drug testing will prevent drug use in the workplace.
      1. Workers will worry about getting caught using drugs.
      2. Drug testing can prevent drug users from being hired. (*Second main point is coherent, balanced, divided appropriately, and complete sentences were used throughout. One final question: What do you propose should happen to employees who use drugs? Rehabilitation? Immediate job termination?*)

pattern looks for why things happen and then discusses the consequences. For example,

> PURPOSE STATEMENT: To explain the causes and effects of yearly flu viruses.
>
> I. There are several causes of yearly flu viruses.
> II. Flu viruses result in serious illness and death for millions of people worldwide.

Your speech can also begin with the effects of an event and then move to what caused the event. For example,

> PURPOSE STATEMENT: To show that grading systems create learning deficiencies at the elementary-school level.
>
> I. There are serious deficiencies in student learning from grades 1 to 6.
> II. Grading systems promote these learning deficiencies.

Problem-Solution Pattern: Meeting Needs

The problem-solution organizational pattern explores the nature of a problem and proposes a solution or possible solutions.

PURPOSE STATEMENT: To argue for a flat income tax to replace the current graduated income tax.

I. The present income tax system has several serious problems.
II. A flat income tax will solve these problems.

Problem-Cause-Solution Pattern: Knowing Why and How

The problem-cause-solution organizational pattern expands on the problem-solution pattern by exploring causes of the problem and addressing these causes in the solution.

PURPOSE STATEMENT: To argue for a government-sponsored program to prevent hearing loss among teenagers and young adults.

I. Teenagers and young adults are suffering serious hearing loss.
II. There are several causes of this hearing loss.
III. A government-sponsored program to prevent hearing loss is critical.

Monroe's Motivated Sequence: Five-Step Pattern

The Monroe Motivated Sequence was first designed for sales presentations. It is an organizational pattern with five steps (Gronbeck et al., 1998).

I. *Attention:* Create interest; use attention strategies.
II. *Need:* Present a problem to be solved and relate it to your audience.
III. *Satisfaction:* Provide a solution to the problem that will satisfy your audience.
IV. *Visualization:* Provide an image for your audience of what the world will look like if your solution is implemented.
V. *Action:* Make a call to action; get the audience involved and committed.

A lengthy example of this organizational pattern is presented in Chapter 15 in a sample speech.

For years, Monroe's Motivated Sequence has been touted as a "persuasive" organizational pattern. *There is no credible evidence to support this claim.* One of the few studies conducted on this organizational pattern found no unique persuasive effect across four different groups, but there was a significant improvement in comprehensibility of ideas using this pattern (Micciche et al., 2000).

All of the organizational patterns discussed here are commonly used in the predominant U.S. culture. Other cultures and co-cultures may use additional patterns (Jaffe, 1998). Space does not permit an explanation of less standard, though valid, forms of speech organization. Learning the standard forms of organizing, however, is an excellent beginning for the novice public speaker.

Summary

ALL speeches begin with audience analysis. Determining which of the five types of audiences—captive, committed, contrary, concerned, or casual—you're speaking to is the first step. Demographic features also help you make inferences about the attitudes, beliefs, and values of that audience. Choosing a topic is a matter of appropriateness and effectiveness. Tailor your choice to your audience. Researching your speech is a lengthy process. There are many valuable sources of information available. Developing your supporting materials requires a careful look at the reasoning and evidence used. Developing arguments on controversial issues requires the use of competent reasoning and evidence. Finally, organizing and outlining your ideas in a logical, understandable pattern are essential.

Quizzes Without Consequences

Did you understand all the material in this chapter? Test your knowledge before your exam!

Go to the companion website at www.oup.com/us/rothwell, click on the Student Resources for each chapter, and take the Quizzes Without Consequences.

Film School Case Studies

All the President's Men (1976). Drama; PG

In the days when the Internet was only a futurist's dream, Bob Woodward (Robert Redford) and Carl Bernstein (Dustin Hoffman) do research the hard way. Identify how these reporters who exposed the Watergate scandal during the Nixon presidency managed to extricate important information from key individuals during interviews.

40 Inspirational Speeches in 2 Minutes (2010); available on the Internet

Mostly for laughs, but this compendium of super-brief excerpts from movie speeches permits a glimpse of how audiences are the core element of effective and appropriate speeches. Pin each speech segment to a specific audience and analyze whether it works or not and why.

Speechless (1994). Romantic Comedy; PG-13

Imperfect comedy about two competing speechwriters who fall in love. Analyze the speechwriters' attention to audience analysis and careful construction of political speeches.

CHAPTER 13

Chapter Outline

Presenting Speeches

SUCCESSFUL ACTING IS largely a matter of presentation. Shakespeare's great literature, spoken by an inept actor, can sound like gibberish. A joke told badly produces a collective groan from an audience. Some people can butcher a terrific line, and others can make an ordinary line thigh-slappingly funny. Poetry read poorly can leave listeners preferring fingernails on a chalkboard; poetry presented skillfully can be a sublime experience. The greatest script, the wittiest joke, and the cleverest poetry are diminished or enhanced by how they are presented. Likewise, the effectiveness of a speech can depend largely on its presentation. Even ordinary ideas can seem extraordinary when said well. As James Russell Lowell notes poetically,

> Though old the thought and oft exprest,
> 'tis his at last who says it best.

The previous chapter discussed ways to develop the substance of your speech. *The purpose of this chapter is to explain how to present the substance of your speech competently.*

By the end of this chapter, you should be able to:

1. Address speech anxiety effectively.
2. Gain and maintain audience attention.
3. Present effective introductions and conclusions.
4. Present supporting materials competently.
5. Use methods of effective speech style.
6. Identify and implement the basic elements of a competent delivery.

Addressing Speech Anxiety

Ricky Henderson, longtime baseball star for the Oakland Athletics, fretted before giving a speech at the ceremony inducting him into baseball's Hall of Fame at Cooperstown on July 26, 2009. As he described it, giving a speech, especially of this magnitude, is like "putting a tie too tight around your neck . . . I've sweated to death about it and then wondered why" (quoted in Steward, 2009a, pp. C1, C5). Henderson wisely sought help from speech instructor Earl Robinson at Laney College. He also received critiques from Robinson's students who were taking a summer public speaking class and heard Henderson's speech. He practiced his speech for two weeks. One journalist who listened to Henderson's 14-minute presentation at the Hall of Fame ceremony offered this assessment: "He seized the stage in Cooperstown, N.Y., and commanded it as he did as a player. . . . He wasn't perfect, but he was pretty close. Moreover, he was gracious, highly effective and suitably entertaining" (Poole, 2009, pp. 1A, 6A). Another journalist remarked that his speech "was stunning for its clarity, poignancy, humor and humility" (Steward, 2009b, p. 1A). Ricky Henderson's experience says two things. First, speech anxiety is a significant problem for many people about to present a speech. Second, with proper knowledge and training, speech anxiety can be addressed successfully.

Speech anxiety is fear of public speaking and the nervousness that accompanies that fear. In this section, I discuss the pervasiveness and symptoms of speech anxiety, its typical causes, and several strategies for managing it.

Pervasiveness: You're Not Alone

Mark Twain once remarked, "There are two types of speakers: those who are nervous and those who are liars." Overstated perhaps, but about 85% of the population fears public speaking (Motley, 1995), and of these, almost 75% experience moderately high to very high speech anxiety (Richmond & McCroskey, 1995). In fact, the instant a speech assignment is announced, many students manifest high levels of anxiety (Behnke & Sawyer, 1999a). Some surveys show that many people fear public speaking more than they fear death (Bruskin & Goldring, 1993; Thomson, 2008), prompting Jerry Seinfeld to quip that if you attend a funeral, you would prefer being in the casket to delivering the eulogy. These dubious "death before public speaking" preferences are a reflection of some individuals' intense speech anxiety. Public speaking is a challenge, but not a fate worse than death, and it should not be avoided at all costs.

Speech anxiety isn't a challenge only novice speakers must address. A substantial majority of experienced speakers also have anxiety before presentations (Hahner et al., 1997). Even college instructors must manage it (Gardner & Leak, 1994). Biographies of famous speakers such as Demosthenes, Cicero, Abraham Lincoln, Henry Clay, Daniel Webster, and Winston Churchill reveal that these giants of history overcame their fear of public speaking by taking every opportunity to mount the speaker's platform. Actor Harrison Ford feared public speaking his entire career. Even when the character he was playing in a movie was required to make a speech as part of the script (e.g., *Air Force One*), he admitted feeling speech anxiety (Bailey, 2008). Jennifer Aniston, Fonzworth Bentley, Beyonce Knowles, Cheryl Cole, Courtney Cox, Matt Damon, Charlize Theron, Natalie Portman, Adam Sandler, and Liv Tyler are just a few of the celebrities who have confessed to fear of public speaking.

Symptoms: Fight-or-Flight Response

Howard Goshorn observed, "The human brain is a wonderful thing. It operates from the moment you are born until you stand up to make a speech." "Going blank" is one of the commonest concerns of novice speakers. Why does the human brain seem to stop working when giving a speech? Learning to manage your speech anxiety begins with identifying its common symptoms and explaining why these symptoms occur. Remaining uninformed about managing your speech anxiety reduces your chances of exhibiting competent public speaking skills.

Basic Symptoms: Responding to Threat

Walter Cannon (1932) labeled the physiological defense-alarm process triggered by stress the **fight-or-flight response**. The myriad physiological changes that are activated by a perceived threat prepare both animals and humans either to fight the foe or flee the fear-inducing threat.

The fight-or-flight response produces a complex constellation of physiological symptoms. Some of the more pronounced symptoms are accelerated heartbeat and increased blood pressure (increases oxygen supply); blood vessel constriction in skin, skeletal muscles, brain, and viscera (cuts off blood supply to less necessary functions); increased perspiration (enhances cooling); increased respiration (supplies oxygen); inhibited digestion (stalls unnecessary energy drain); stimulated glucose release from the liver (increases energy supply); increased blood flow away from extremities and to large muscles (supplies oxygen and glucose to major muscles used to fight); stimulated adrenal gland activity (improves alertness, motion, and strength); spleen release of red blood corpuscles (aids in clotting a wound); and bone marrow stimulation to produce white corpuscles (fights possible infection) (Zimbardo, 1992).

Some of the more prominent corresponding verbal and nonverbal symptoms are quivering, tense voice and weak projection (constricted throat muscles); frequent dysfluencies such as "ums" and "uhs"; and of course, going blank (restricted blood flow to the brain causing confusion of thought); rigid, motionless posture (constricted muscles of legs and torso); dry mouth that makes speaking difficult (digestive system shutdown); even long pauses and silence (scared speechless) (Lewin et al., 1996).

Appropriateness of Symptoms: Relevance

The physiological symptoms of the fight-or-flight response make sense if you are about to grapple with a crazed grizzly or to run with the bulls at Pamplona. Increased perspiration (cooling), respiration (oxygen), glucose (energy), and blood flow to major muscles (strength) would certainly help with the grappling and running. There are few times, however, in which fighting or fleeing would be an appropriate response to speech anxiety. There is little likelihood that you will be grappling with anyone during your speech (the fond wish of every speech instructor that no grappling occur), and it is doubtful that you would sprint from the classroom when called to begin a speech. Granted, if the speech is lengthy, the room hot and stuffy, and the occasion momentous, increased glucose, respiration, perspiration, and adrenaline will help sustain you throughout your presentation. Adrenaline can also assist you in performing at a peak level, very similar to athletes "psyching up" for an important contest. Clothes saturated with perspiration, increased red and white corpuscles, nausea, a pounding heart, a quivering voice, dry mouth, and rigid posture, however, are unnecessary and often distracting when making a speech—unless your life is in jeopardy (an unlikely classroom occurrence). Nevertheless, your sympathetic nervous system, which controls the fight-or-flight response, doesn't pick and choose relevant symptoms (Wilson, 2003). When the response is triggered, you get the whole package. Thus, *the useful approach to speech anxiety is to moderate the fight-or-flight response, not hope to activate only selective symptoms.*

Causes: Dysfunctional Anxiety

Dysfunctional speech anxiety occurs when the intensity of the fight-or-flight response prevents an individual from giving a speech effectively. **Functional speech anxiety** occurs when the fight-or-flight response is managed and stimulates an optimum presentation. *The degree of anxiety and your ability to manage it, not anxiety itself, determine the difference.* Individuals who experience low to moderate anxiety that is under control typically give better speeches than individuals who experience little or no anxiety (Motley, 1995). Low to moderate anxiety means you care about the quality of the speech. Anxiety can energize you and enhance your performance. You deliver a more dynamic, forceful presentation when energized than when you feel so comfortable that you become almost listless and unchallenged.

Causes of dysfunctional speech anxiety fall primarily into two categories: self defeating thoughts and situational factors. I briefly explain each because understanding the causes of dysfunctional anxiety is the first step in learning to maintain your anxiety at a level that is functional.

Self-Defeating Thoughts: Sabotage

Some individuals see giving a speech as a challenging and exciting opportunity, whereas others see it as an experience equivalent to being swallowed by a python. How you think about speaking to an audience will largely determine your level of speech anxiety. Self-defeating thoughts that can sabotage your speech are grounded in the excessive concern that your audience will judge and reject you (Cunningham et al., 2006).

Catastrophic Thinking: Fear of Failure Wildly exaggerating the magnitude of potential failure is a common source of stress and anxiety (Ellis, 1995, 1996). Those with irrational fears predict not just momentary memory lapses of no real consequence but a complete mental meltdown. They fear that audiences will laugh and hoot them off the stage and view them as irredeemable fools. Minor problems of organization during a speech are magnified in the speaker's mind into graphic episodes of total incoherence and nonstop babbling.

Predictions of public speaking catastrophes are unrealistic because they are highly unlikely to occur (Peterson, 2000; Seligman, 1991). I personally have listened to more than 20,000 student speeches. I have witnessed some unimpressive presentations, but not more than a handful of these qualified as outright unforgettable disasters, and the obvious cause of the disaster in each case was a complete lack of preparation.

Catastrophic thinking sees only failure, not an opportunity for exhilarating success produced by embracing challenges. Thomas Edison made more than 2,000 attempts to invent the electric light bulb. When asked how it felt to fail so many times, Edison responded, "I never failed. It just happened to be a 2,000 step process." Don't paralyze yourself with catastrophic, unrealistic thinking.

Perfectionist Thinking: No Mistakes Permitted Perfectionists anguish over every perceived flaw, and they overgeneralize the significance of even minor defects. For example,

"I tanked—I forgot to preview my main points."

"My knees were shaking. The audience must have thought I contracted rabies."

"I feel so stupid. I kept mispronouncing the name of one of the experts I quoted."

Flawless public speaking is a desirable goal, but why beat up on yourself when it doesn't happen? Even the most talented and experienced public speakers make occasional errors in otherwise riveting and eloquent speeches. Acclaimed public speaker Martin Luther King Jr. stumbled twice during his famous "I Have a Dream" speech. Who noticed? These were only fleeting blips in an otherwise smoothly delivered masterpiece. Ironically, the imperfections so glaring to perfectionists usually go unnoticed by their audiences.

Desire for Complete Approval: Trying Not to Offend It is highly unlikely that you will please everyone who listens to your speech, particularly if you take a stand on a controversial issue. Making complete approval from your audience a vital concern is an unrealistic goal and merely sets you up for inevitable failure. When you set standards for success at unreachable heights, you are bound to take a tumble.

Anxiety-Provoking Situations: Context

Several anxiety-provoking situations are relevant to public speaking. There are three principal ones: novelty, conspicuousness, and types of speeches.

Novelty of the Speaking Situation: Uncertainty We often fear what is unpredictable or unfamiliar (Witt & Behnke, 2006). For inexperienced speakers, the mere novelty of the speaking situation may trigger speech anxiety (Kelly & Keaten, 2000). What if your listeners seem bored? Is your speech too long or too short? Is the audience likely to be supportive or hostile? What if someone heckles? Based on uncertainty reduction theory, as you gain experience speaking in front of groups, the novelty wears off and anxiety diminishes because you gain a reservoir of knowledge from giving speeches that helps you handle almost any situation that might occur (Roby, 2009).

Conspicuousness: In the Spotlight I have polled more than 1,000 students in public speaking classes. When asked what causes their speech anxiety, most identify being "on stage" or "in the spotlight." Being conspicuous, or the center of attention, can increase your anxiety. You feel as if you are under a microscope being meticulously examined. As the size of an audience grows, conspicuousness increases in most individuals' minds. Gaining confidence from experience speaking often to a variety of audiences large and small is a strong antidote for alleviating speech anxiety provoked by conspicuousness.

Types of Speeches: Varying Responses Types of speeches combined with situational challenges affect whether you experience anxiety. Telling a story in front of a class of fellow students may give you no pause, but giving a lecture as a teaching demonstration while interviewing for an important job may be an anxiety-producing situation (Young et al., 2004). Suddenly being asked to "say a few words" with no warning typically stirs greater anxiety than giving a more prepared speech (Witt & Behnke, 2006). Giving a speech to an audience hostile to your expressed point of view may also engender high levels of anxiety (Pertaub et al., 2002).

All of these causes of speech anxiety, both self-defeating thoughts and anxiety-provoking situations, can produce a spiraling effect that feeds on itself. If you begin by viewing a speech as a performance, you've already created unrealistic expectations for yourself. This, in turn, stimulates a physiological fight-or-flight arousal. If you then interpret the physical symptoms as fear, this can trigger catastrophic thinking which stimulates more intense physical symptoms, greater fear, and so forth (Motley, 1995). *A key to managing your speech anxiety is to prevent the spiral of fear from ever occurring.*

Strategies: Managing Anxiety

One surefire way to experience absolutely no anxiety prior to and during a speech is to not care about the quality of your speech. You will be very relaxed, but you will also give a poor speech. Your goal should not be to eliminate speech anxiety but instead to manage the anxiety that you do experience and use it to energize and stimulate peak accomplishment.

Many individuals, from famous actors to celebrities of various kinds, have suggested strategies for managing speech anxiety. These include swearing at your audience backstage, sticking a pin in your backside (pain as diversion), and imagining members of your audience clothed only in their underwear or in diapers. Although these are dubious solutions, if these suggestions work for you, then that's fine, but there is no good evidence that they have widespread application. They are unquestionably limited because they are diversionary tactics rather than strategies that directly address the primary causes of speech anxiety. In this section, I offer several ways to manage your speech anxiety that are supported by research.

Prepare and Practice: Novelty to Familiarity

As in most social situations, whether it is making small talk with strangers at parties or playing a musical instrument in front of a crowd, you tend to be less anxious when you are confident of your skills. You fear making a fool of yourself when you don't know what you're doing. First and foremost, this means don't delay preparing and practicing your speech until the night before you give it. *Procrastination increases anxiety* (Behnke & Sawyer, 1999b).

When you are adequately prepared, you will remove most of the novelty and uncertainty from the speaking situation. This will reduce your anxiety (Menzel & Carrell, 1994). So prepare your speech meticulously. Begin the necessary research well in advance, organize and outline your speech carefully, and practice your presentation. Practice your speech while taking a shower. Give it in your car on your way to class. Give it to your dog; they're eager listeners (cats not so much). *Practice, practice, practice*! When you have practiced your speech "enough," practice it again. Do a dress rehearsal for friends or family members, or video record your performance and play it back so you can study parts to improve (Svoboda, 2009).

Experience giving speeches to a variety of audiences will gradually build your confidence and reduce your anxiety (Finn et al., 2009). Speaking experience, of course, won't reduce anxiety if you stumble from one traumatic disaster to the next. If you make speech after speech, ill prepared and untrained, do not expect your anxiety to diminish. Your dread of public speaking will likely become dysfunctional. "Practice makes perfect" if it is practice based on knowledge of effective public speaking for appropriate skill building. Without the requisite knowledge, practice will make perfectly awful any speech that you give because you will be rehearsing incompetent public speaking.

Poor physiological preparation also will sabotage the most carefully prepared and practiced speech. You require appropriate nutrition to manage the stress of public speaking. Do not deliver a speech on an empty stomach. Complex carbohydrates (whole grains, pastas, legumes) work well to stoke your energy, but eat lightly. You want blood traveling to your brain, not to your stomach. Avoid the empty calorie foods (doughnuts, Twinkies). High intake of caffeine, simple sugars, and nicotine can stoke the physiological symptoms of fight or flight (increased heart rate, sweating). I once had a student with significant speech anxiety who drank a 32-ounce "Big Gulp" cola and chain smoked before each speech. He was a wreck each time he presented his speech, and so were those of us who had to endure his agitated, overwrought, staccato presentation. Despite my best efforts, he continued to ignore the proper physiological preparation necessary for competent public speaking.

Alcohol and tranquilizers are also counterproductive solutions. Alcohol restricts oxygen to your brain and dulls mental acuity. Tranquilizers can send you on a valium vacation in which you feel pleasantly numb but mentally dumb. You never want to take even a mild amphetamine. Speed kills a speech. It will increase your heart rate beyond what anxiety already induces.

There is no substitute for preparation and practice. If you do both, most of your anxiety will melt away, and your confidence will soar (Ayres & Hopf, 1995).

Gain Perspective: Rational Thinking

Understanding the progression of your speech anxiety can give you a realistic perspective on what is a reasonable amount to expect. It will improve naturally (see Figure 13-1). There are four phases to speech anxiety symptoms (Witt et al., 2006). There is the *anticipation phase*, when your symptoms elevate just prior to giving your speech. The *confrontation phase* occurs when you face the audience and begin to speak. There is a tremendous surge of adrenalin, heart rate soars—sometimes to 180 beats per minute—perspiration and other symptoms increase. Next the *adaptation phase* kicks in about 60 seconds into the speech. Adaptation takes place even more swiftly for low-anxiety speakers, usually 15 to 30 seconds into the speech. During this phase, symptoms steadily diminish, reaching a more comfortable level within a couple of minutes. Finally, there is the *release stage*—the 60 seconds immediately following the speech.

Recognizing that your anxiety will diminish dramatically and quickly as you speak should provide some comfort. By learning to monitor your adaptation, you can accelerate the process. As you begin to notice your heart rate diminishing, say to yourself, "It's getting better already . . . and better . . . and better." *Anxiety levels, even for*

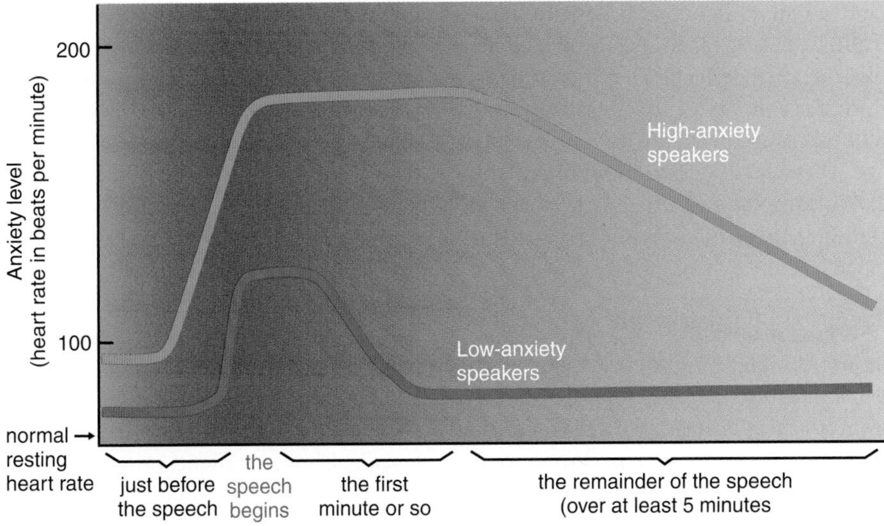

FIGURE 13-1 Heart-Rate Patterns of Typical High- and Low-Anxiety Speakers (Motley, 1995)

the inexperienced, high-anxiety speaker, will diminish rapidly during the course of a speech.

Another aspect of gaining a realistic perspective is learning to recognize the difference between rational and irrational speech anxiety. A colleague of mine, Darrell Beck, concocted a simple formula for determining the difference: *the* ***severity*** *of the feared occurrence times the* ***probability*** *of the feared occurrence.* This formula gives a rough approximation of how much anxiety is rational and when you have stepped over the line into irrational territory.

Severity is approximated by imagining what would happen if catastrophic failure did occur. Typically, when I ask my students for their worst imagined case of speech anxiety, they offer examples such as stuttering, flop sweating, knees and hands shaking violently, forgetting everything, even fainting or vomiting in front of the class. Imagine all of this occurring, not just one or two of these manifestations of catastrophic failure, but the entire mess. Would you renew your passport and make plans to leave the country? Would you hide from friends and family, afraid to show your face? Would you drop out of college? None of these choices seems likely. You might drop the class, but even this choice is unlikely. Students are an understanding lot (this is not high school), and you will have other opportunities in class to redeem yourself. Even a disastrous speech does not warrant significant life changes. A few moments of disappointment, mild embarrassment, or discouragement because you received a mediocre grade is about as severe as the consequences get.

Then consider the probability of this nightmare scenario happening. It is highly improbable that all of these feared occurrences would transpire. No one has ever fainted or vomited in my classes despite the thousands of speeches I have witnessed. If you stutter and it is not an actual speech pathology, you can gain control by deliberately slowing your rate of speech and carefully enunciating your words. Other occurrences are mitigated with conscientious preparation and practice. When you consider the probability of the "worst-case scenario," you should realize that there is not much to concern you. *Concentrate on the probable (low-severity occurrences), not the improbable (high-severity occurrences).*

Even individuals for whom English is a second language will benefit from gaining a realistic perspective on their speech anxiety. Giving a speech in a second language can increase anxiety (McCroskey et al., 1985). There is an unrealistic expectation that English should be spoken perfectly. I have witnessed hundreds of speeches by non-native speakers of English. Never have

I observed an audience of college students be rude to that speaker because his or her English was not perfect. Normally, students admire a speaker who tries hard to give a good speech in a relatively unfamiliar language. They usually listen more intently as well. Working yourself into a lather over an impending speech simply lacks a realistic perspective.

Communication Orientation: Reframing

Desiring complete approval, engaging in perfectionist thinking, and fretting over your conspicuousness onstage all occur when you view public speaking as a **performance**—an attempt to satisfy an audience of critics whose members are focused on evaluating your presentation (Motley, 1997). Giving a speech is not an Olympic event; you're usually not competing to score more points than someone else or to earn a gold medal and get your face on a cereal box. Your audience won't hold up cards indicating your score immediately after you sit down. Granted, your speech instructor will likely give you a grade on your speech, but even here the performance orientation is counterproductive. No speech instructor expects silver-tongued oratory from novice speakers. You're expected to make mistakes, especially during your first few speeches. Speech classes are learning laboratories, not speech tournaments.

Reframe the performance orientation with a communication orientation. The **communication orientation** focuses on making your message clear and interesting to your listeners. Motley (1995) makes the case for reframing to the communication orientation: "I have never encountered an anxious speaker who did not have a performance orientation, or one whose anxiety was not substantially reduced when the communication orientation replaced it" (p. 49).

The irony is that you will perform more effectively as a speaker if you move away from the competitive performance orientation (Motley, 1995). Your speaking style and delivery will seem more natural, less forced, and not as stiff. When conversing with a friend or stranger, you rarely notice your delivery, gestures, and posture. You are intent on being clear and interesting, even having some fun. Approach your speech in a similar way. Choking under pressure occurs most often when you overthink your performance while it is occurring (e.g., "vary your voice," "use gestures," "don't pace," "look at your audience," etc.). Scrutinizing your performance while speaking is counterproductive (Svoboda, 2009). Simply concentrate on communicating your message clearly to your audience, and the rest will follow if you have practiced well.

One way to develop the communication orientation is to practice your speech conversationally. Choose a friend or loved one with whom you feel comfortable. Find a private location and sit in chairs or on a couch. Using a conversational style, just begin describing the speech that you have prepared. Do not give the speech. Merely talk about it—what the speech covers and how you plan to develop it. Use notes if you need to but refer to them infrequently. In subsequent practice sessions with your listener, gradually begin to introduce elements of the actual speech such as an introduction. Eventually, deliver the entire speech while sitting down. Finally, present the entire speech standing, using only an outline of the speech for reference.

Does the communication orientation work? *When compared to other methods of anxiety reduction and control, the communication orientation is the most successful* (Motley, 1995). Simply concentrating on communicating with an audience, not impressing them, reduced anxiety levels of speakers from high to moderately low.

These methods for reducing and controlling your speech anxiety work so well that little else needs to be said. Nevertheless, I briefly cover the remaining methods because they are your insurance policy.

Coping Statements: Rational Reappraisal

Negative self-talk leads to catastrophic thinking. You stumble at the outset of your speech and say to yourself, "I knew I couldn't do this well" or "I've already ruined the introduction." You're immediately scrutinizing your performance. Negative, disaster thinking triggers high anxiety. A rational reappraisal can help you cope effectively with your anxiety (Ellis, 1995, 1996). Try making coping statements when problems arise. "I'm past the tough part," "I'll do better once I get rolling," and "The best part is still ahead" are examples of positive coping statements. Coping statements shift the thought process from negative and irrational to positive and rational self-talk (O'Donohue & Fisher, 2008). Make self-talk constructive, not destructive.

Positive Imaging: Visualizing Success

Mental images can influence your anxiety either positively or negatively (Holmes & Mathews, 2005). Prepare for a speech presentation by countering negative thoughts of catastrophe with positive images of success, sometimes called **visualization**. This can be a very effective strategy for addressing your speech anxiety (Ayres, 2005; Ayres et al., 2001; Martin et al., 1999). Novice speakers typically imagine what will go wrong during a speech. To avoid this pitfall, create images in your head that picture you giving a fluent, clear, and interesting speech. Picture your audience responding in positive ways as you give your speech. Exercise mental discipline and refuse to allow negative thoughts to creep into your consciousness. Keep imagining speaking success, not failure.

Relaxation Techniques: Reducing Fight or Flight

There are a number of simple relaxation techniques that can reduce physiological symptoms of the fight-or-flight response (O'Donohue & Fisher, 2008). First, deep, slow, controlled breathing is very helpful. Five to seven such breaths per minute are optimal (Horowitz, 2002). Do not allow yourself to breath in rapid, shallow bursts. This will likely increase your anxiety.

Relaxing your muscles through a series of tense-and-relax exercises also can be beneficial, especially right before giving a speech (if you can be unobtrusive about it—perhaps backstage or outside). Lifting your shoulders slowly up and down, then rotating them slowly is relaxing. Wiggling your facial muscles by moving your cheeks, jaw, mouth, nose, and eyebrows and by smiling broadly may seem silly, but it loosens tight muscles. Even big, exaggerated yawns can help. Another muscle relaxation exercise is tensing and then relaxing sets of muscles (diaphragm, stomach, legs, arms, etc.).

Finally, sitting in a hot bath can be very soothing and infinitely relaxing. This, of course, is a rather impractical technique right before giving a speech. You are not likely to launch into your speech immediately after exiting the bathtub, but the relaxing effects can last for an hour or two, so you might be able to squeeze it in just before class. If not, a restful night's sleep induced by a hot bath will keep you mentally alert before giving your speech the next day.

Systematic Desensitization: Step by Step

Systematic desensitization is a technique used to control anxiety, even phobias, triggered by a wide variety of stimuli (O'Donohue & Fisher, 2008). The technique operates on the principle that relaxation and anxiety are incompatible and do not occur simultaneously (Wolpe, 1990). Systematic desensitization involves incremental exposure to increasingly threatening stimuli coupled with relaxation techniques. This method of managing anxiety is very effective (Spiegler & Guevremont, 1998). It is time consuming, however, so you must be committed to this technique of anxiety reduction.

Applied to giving speeches, systematic desensitization involves making a list of perhaps 10 progressive steps in the speaking process, each likely to arouse increased anxiety. Find yourself a comfortable, quiet place to sit. Read the first item on your list (e.g., your speech topic). When you experience anxiety, put the list aside and begin a relaxation exercise. Tense the muscles in your face and neck. Hold the tensed position for 10 seconds, then release. Now do the same with your hands and so on until you've tensed and relaxed all the muscle groups in your body. Now breathe slowly and deeply as you say the word "relax" to yourself. Repeat this for one minute. Pick up the list and read the first item again. If your anxiety remains pronounced, repeat the process. If your anxiety is minimal, move on to the second item (e.g., gathering your speech material) and repeat the tense-and-relax procedure. Work through your entire list of 10 items, stopping when you are able to read the final item (e.g., beginning the introduction of your speech) without appreciable anxiety. Use systematic desensitization several days in a row before your speech presentation. Your anxiety level should fall to lower levels. The final step is exposure to the actual anxiety-provoking stimulus—giving the speech.

Gaining and Maintaining Attention

An enormously popular British ad that featured a sexy model progressively removing her clothing as she climbed inside a sleek automobile drew attention to the wrong stimulus. One survey showed that the gorgeous model commanded attention while the automobile being advertised was virtually invisible to almost everyone watching (Clay, 2002). As noted in Chapter 2, attention is unavoidably selective. Gaining and maintaining attention are processes of directing listeners' awareness toward the stimulus you provide and steering them away from competing stimuli. Herein lies the challenge for any speaker. How do you induce an audience to attend to your message and ignore all others? Minds easily wander (Kane et al., 2007; McVay & Kane, 2009).

One national survey of individuals from a wide variety of professions revealed that the top-ranked skill for preparing and delivering a speech was keeping an audience's attention (Engleberg, 2002). Corporate media consultant Steve Crescenzo (2005) observes, "In today's short-attention-span, sound-byte society, the one thing people cannot afford to be is boring" (p. 12). Why prepare and present a speech that induces a nap? You want your listeners excited, engaged, touched, and anxious to hear what comes next. You don't want them yearning for those signal words "In conclusion." It's a lesson every teacher learns when lecturing to students for an entire class period and every religious leader comprehends when delivering a sermon or homily to a congregation. Most speeches are not meant to be purely entertainment, but if listeners are bored when you speak to them about significant issues, then your substantial ideas fall on deaf ears.

The next chapter addresses very specific ways to gain attention during the introduction to your speech that extend from this chapter's discussion. It is important to note here, however, that *grabbing an audience's attention initially is far easier than maintaining attention for an entire speech*. Whether for five minutes or fifty, keeping your listeners' rapt attention is a supremely difficult task, making it a topic worthy of considerable discussion and illustration. The rewards of presenting a truly galvanizing speech are considerable.

Attention Strategies: Involuntary Triggers

Gaining and maintaining the attention of your listeners require a fairly sophisticated understanding of key stimulus triggers that can be exploited to ignite listeners' attention involuntarily throughout your entire speech. Specific types of stimuli trigger attention involuntarily (see Chapter 2). These include appeals to that which is novel, startling, vital, humorous, or intense (Passer & Smith, 2004). When a direct effort is made to exploit such triggers, they become strategies for galvanizing audience attention.

Novelty: The Allure of the New

Novelty attracts attention (Escera et al., 1998). Audiences are naturally drawn to the new and different. The commonplace can produce a comalike stupor. Recognizing this means never beginning your speech with a snoozer, such as "My topic is . . ." or "Today I'd like to talk to you about . . ." Stimulate interest in your subject before giving your purpose statement. There are several ways to make novel appeals.

Unusual Topics: Choosing Creatively In this age of high-tech weapons systems and so-

Novelty is an exceptional attention strategy.

phisticated counterterrorism tactics, sometimes it's the low-tech solutions that save lives. American troops in the Iraq War were constantly faced with potential booby-trapped dwellings. A solution? Shoot Silly String across a room before entering to locate possible tripwires attached to bombs. This is an unusual topic for a great speech: low-tech creative solutions to significant problems. For instructors who may have heard a gazillion speeches on legalization of marijuana or the abortion controversy, unusual topics presented by students can be refreshing.

Unusual Examples: The Antisedative Sprinkle your speech with unusual examples that illustrate important points. For instance, consider using real examples such as these pulled from a newspaper story.

> "The check is in the mail" used to be the standard ploy to ward off bill collectors. Not so anymore. Delinquent customers have adopted more original stalling tactics. One woman claimed that she had run over her husband with a car, breaking both of his arms, thereby making it impossible for him to write checks or pay by computer. A flower-shop owner insisted that she couldn't pay her bills until someone died and had a funeral. "Business should pick up soon," she said hopefully. These are silly excuses for failing to pay one's bills, but mounting personal debt is no laughing matter.

Compare this opening to the more commonplace "I want to talk to you about how to handle personal debt." The more novel opening with unusual examples invites attention. The commonplace opener encourages a nap.

Unusual Stories: Nothing Like a Good Tale We all love a good story, especially one we haven't heard. Newspapers are filled with novel stories. For example,

> In November 2009, Matt Blea, a 16-year-old high school football player at San Jose High Academy in California took a legal blindside tackle that slammed him to the turf during a Thanksgiving day game against Lincoln High. His head bounced off the ground producing severe head trauma. He suffered a skull fracture, underwent emergency brain surgery, and was placed in a drug-induced coma. Fortunately, he survived and "woke up" from his coma almost two weeks after his surgery.
>
> Doctors estimated that Hall of Fame Pittsburgh Steelers' center Mike Webster suffered the equivalent of 25,000 car crashes

> without a seatbelt in the 25 years he played football from high school through the NFL. After retiring, he experienced amnesia, dementia, and depression from his football-induced head trauma. The experiences of both Blea and Webster reflect a serious problem that until recently has received relatively little attention. Football at all levels, from high school to the NFL, is hazardous to your brain. Stronger regulation of football injuries must be implemented.

Stories such as these invite attention because they are not trivial, commonplace episodes we've heard many times. They make us sit up and take notice.

Unusual Phrasing: It's in the Wording Colorful phrasing or unusual wording can transform an ordinary statement into a novel, memorable one.

> **Ordinary:** Most books are carried less than 60 days by bookstores unless they become best sellers.
>
> **Novel:** The shelf life of the average book is somewhere between milk and yogurt. (Calvin Trillin)
>
> **Ordinary:** Choosing the right word is important.
>
> **Novel:** The difference between the right word and the almost right word is the difference between lightning and the lightning bug. (Mark Twain)
>
> **Ordinary:** She really said nothing of importance.
>
> **Novel:** She plunged into a sea of platitudes, and with the powerful breast stroke of a channel swimmer made her confident way towards the white cliffs of the obvious. (W. Somerset Maugham)
>
> **Ordinary:** Our office was way too small.
>
> **Novel:** He and I had an office so tiny that an inch smaller and it would have been adultery (Dorothy Parker)

Startling Appeal: Shake Up the Audience

Daniel Hale, a pediatric diabetes specialist, commenting on a study documenting pervasive childhood obesity, notes: "These kids will have strokes and heart attacks in their 20s and 30s. The diseases we thought of as being problems in their grandparents are on their way to being diseases in their grandchildren" ("The Week," 2006, p. 2P). Hale's startling appeal tries to shake his audience out of its complacency.

Startling Statements, Facts, or Statistics A startling statement, fact, or statistic can rouse audience attention. Kathy Levine (2001), a student at Oregon State University, offers this startling revelation in her speech on dental hygiene.

> As the previously cited *20/20* investigation uncovered, the water used in approximately 90% of dental offices is dirtier than the water found in public toilets. This means 9 out of 10 dental offices are using dirty water on their patients. Moreover, the independent research of Dr. George Merijohn, a periodontist who specialized in dental waterlines, found that out of 60 randomly selected offices from around the nation, two-thirds of all samples taken contained oral bacteria from the saliva of previous patients. (p. 77)

Startling statements, facts, and statistics can be unsettling (wondering if I'm rinsing my mouth with someone else's saliva when I go to the dentist certainly disturbs me). They are meant to alarm, shock, and astonish an audience into listening intently to what you have to say. Researchers David Brenner and Eric Hall of Columbia University attempted to raise an alarm about excessive use of diagnostic CT scans which superimpose multiple X-ray images to form a three-dimensional picture of a patient. They noted a study in the *New England Journal of Medicine* that reported the amount of radiation patients receive during each scan varies between 1,000 and 10,000 millirems. That statistic isn't likely to mean much to the average person. They liken the radiation amount per scan, however, to doses received by Japanese survivors of Hiroshima and Nagasaki who were a mile or two from the ground zero blast of atomic bombs during World War II (see Sternberg, 2007). The average radiation dose for survivors was 3,000 millirems. That is a startling fact likely to cause real concern, especially since detection of minuscule radiation levels in the United States from the 2011 Japanese nuclear catastrophe following a tsunami spiked near panic among many Americans. There was a run on potassium iodide pills to counteract the effects of radiation, even though it is not a cure-all for radiation poisoning if such an event were to occur in the United States (Goldwert, 2011).

Inappropriate Use: Beware Bizarre Behavior Every speech instructor remembers notable examples of student miscalculations when using a startling appeal to gain an audience's attention. My colleagues have shared some with me. For instance, one student punched himself so hard in the face that he was momentarily staggered and he produced a large bruise under his eye (the speech was on violence in America). Another student shrieked obscenities to his stunned audience (the speech was on FCC legislation banning verbal obscenity and profanity on the media airwaves).

The competent public speaker exercises solid judgment when choosing to startle his or her listeners. *The speaker's goal should not be to gain attention by being outrageous, irresponsible, or by exercising poor judgment.* The competent public speaker considers the implied or stated rules of a speech context when choosing appropriate attention strategies. An audience can turn on a speaker and become an adversary, not an ally, when angered or offended. Startle an audience, but make certain your attention strategy is appropriate.

The Vital Appeal: Meaningfulness

We attend to stimuli that are meaningful to us, and we ignore stimuli that are relatively meaningless (Ruiter et al., 2006). Problems and issues that vitally affect our lives are meaningful. In this sense, audiences tend to be Me-oriented. Listeners heed warnings when a societal problem affects them personally. The AIDS epidemic was slow to seize the attention of the average American when it was erroneously thought to be a "gay disease." When the disease became rampant in the general population of heterosexual males and females, however, more people started to pay attention.

Nicolle Carpenter (2004), an Orange Coast College student when she gave a speech at the Interstate Oratorical Association contest, shows how to make your message vital and thus meaningful to your audience. After a brief opening story about a man named Jack Spratt who died of a food-borne illness caused by eating contaminated green onions at a restaurant, she proceeded with this effective vital appeal.

> What happened to Spratt and some 175,000 other people who are hospitalized each year due to contaminated produce is frightening; even more disturbing is the fact that it could happen to anyone. . . . In a November 23, 2003, *Seattle Times* news article Dr. Glen Morris, chairman of the department of epidemiology and preventive medicine at the University of Maryland, said, "Produce is emerging as an important cause of food-borne illness in this country" and we must understand how real the risk is. (p. 5)

Nicolle leaves no one in her audience unaffected by her speech.

When attempting to grab the attention of your listeners, don't just make a general appeal, citing the seriousness of the problem for nameless, faceless citizens. Personalize the appeal to all of your listeners. Jake Gruber (2001), a Northern Illinois University student, did exactly this when he stated in his speech on heart disease in women: "Whereas one in 28 women will die of breast cancer, one in five will die of heart disease. And guys, before you take the next nine minutes to decide what you'll eat for lunch, ask yourself one question: what would my life be like if the women who make it meaningful are not there? Clearly, this is an issue that concerns us all" (p. 16). Vital concerns that affect us personally focus our attention.

Humorous Appeal: Keep 'Em Laughing

"We've childproofed our house, but they keep finding a way in." This ironic, anonymous quip has been circulating on the Internet for years. Its humor gives it staying power. Humor is a superior attention strategy if used adroitly. Using humor effectively, however, can be very tricky. Issues

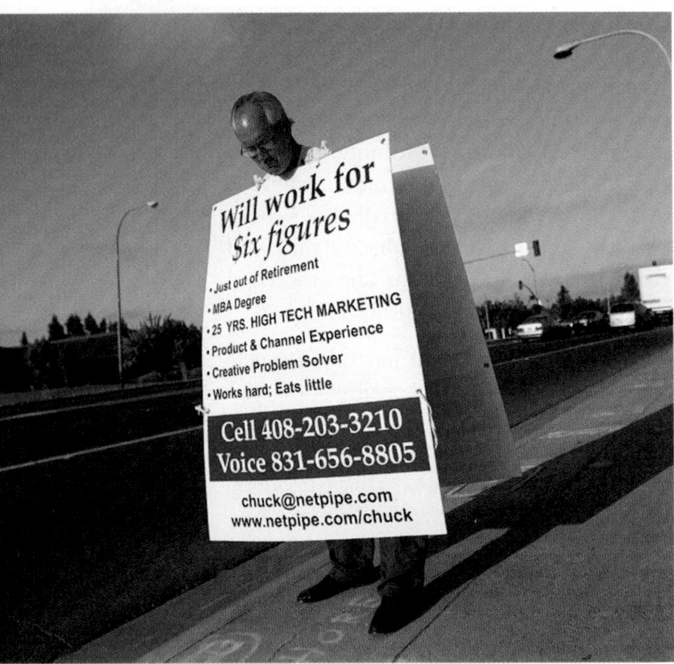

Use of humor is a wonderful attention strategy.

of appropriateness and effectiveness are always present. There are several guidelines for using humor competently as an attention strategy.

Don't Force Humor: We're Not All Funny If you've never told a joke without flubbing the punch line, avoid humiliating yourself. Listening to a speaker stubbornly try to be funny without success can be an excruciatingly uncomfortable experience for all involved. Nevertheless, you can still use humor. Use humorous quotations; tell funny stories or amusing occurrences to amplify or clarify points. Don't telegraph stories as intentionally humorous, however, by using a risky lead-in such as, "Let me tell you a really funny joke." Such a lead-in invites embarrassment if your listeners do not laugh.

Use Only Relevant Humor: Stay Focused Humor should amuse listeners while making a point. Tie the humor directly to a main point or principal theme. For example, "Someone once said, 'I want to die peacefully in my sleep like my grandfather, not screaming in terror like his passengers.' You've all experienced it—the nerve-racking anxiety every time you see an old person driving a car. I want to convince you that greater restrictions on elderly drivers should be instituted." The humor is simple and it leads to the specific purpose of the speech.

Be Sensitive to Context: Humor Can Backfire Glib one-liners and slapstick do not mesh well with funeral services. Sexist, racist, and homophobic "jokes" exhibit poor taste and a lack of ethics. Coarse vulgarities, obscenities, and sick jokes invite comparisons to the *Jackass* movies—not everyone's idea of amusement. Humor that rests on stereotypes and putdowns may alienate vast sections of an audience (unless it is an official "roast"). I heard a speaker crack this "joke" to his mixed-sex audience: "What's the difference between a terrorist and a woman with PMS? You can negotiate with the terrorist." Watching the audience's reaction was instructive. Some laughed. Some started to laugh, then thought better of it. Others not only didn't laugh; they booed the speaker. The speaker seemed surprised by the mixed response and searched for a graceful recovery. He never found one.

Use Self-Deprecating Humor: "I'm Not Worthy" Humor that makes gentle fun of one's own failings and limitations, called **self-deprecation**, can be quite appealing. Abraham Lincoln was a master of self-deprecation. During the famous Lincoln-Douglas debates, U.S. Senator Stephen Douglas called Lincoln "two-faced," whereupon Lincoln calmly replied, "I leave it to my audience. If I had another face, do you think I would wear this one?" Bob Uecker, a major league baseball player of no consequence, was inducted into the Hall of Fame as a broadcaster after announcing Milwaukee Brewers' games for 33 years. On July 27, 2003, in his acceptance speech at Cooperstown, New York, Uecker displayed his well-known propensity for self-deprecating humor. "I remember Gene Mauch telling me, 'Grab a bat and stop this rally'" (Bodley, 2003, p. 5C). Uecker also made this comment at a Brewers' winter banquet: "Look, people have differing opinions on many

issues. Take my career. Half the people thought I was the worst player they've ever seen, and the other half thought I was a disgrace to the uniform" (quoted in "Chatter Box," 2007, p. 2C).

Self-deprecating humor can disarm a hostile audience. On May 21, 2001, George W. Bush was the commencement speaker at the Yale University graduation. An alumnus who had partied hard and earned mediocre grades, Bush faced his most hostile audience. More than 170 faculty members boycotted the graduation ceremony, and scores of graduates greeted Bush with protest signs. Many thought he had "stolen" the 2000 election from Gore. Bush encouraged mediocre students, "You, too, can be president of the United States." Referring to his party animal reputation while at Yale, Bush remarked, "If you're like me, you won't remember everything you did here. That can be a good thing." Making fun of his penchant for using tortured syntax, Bush remarked, "As I recall, one of my academic advisers . . . said I should focus on English. I still hear that quite often" ("President George W. Bush," 2001). Bush likely did not change many minds, but he defused the overt hostility, and his audience listened to his speech because it is tough to be angry when the person you dislike is making you laugh.

Intensity: Concentrated Stimuli

We attend to the intense (Pashler, 1998). **Intensity** is concentrated stimuli. It is an extreme degree of emotion, thought, or activity. Relating a tragic event, a moving human-interest story, or a specific instance of courage and determination plays on the intense feelings of your audience. For example, a youth minister, Melvin Nurse, at the Livingway Christian Fellowship Church International in Jacksonville, Florida, wanted to make his point emphatically that sin is like Russian roulette. His congregation of 250 parents and youngsters saw him place a .357-caliber pistol to his temple and pull the trigger. Nurse apparently expected that the blank cartridge in the pistol's chamber would cause him no harm. Unfortunately, in front of his wife and four daughters, the blank cartridge flew apart on impact and shattered Nurse's skull. He died instantly. His attempt to capture attention was successful but with a horrifying result.

This is an intense example because it provokes a sense of profound tragedy. Who could be callous or indifferent to such painful human drama? The example, however, is also unpleasant, and this raises an issue: should speakers use unpleasant examples to capture attention? Might your listeners be repelled by such stark, negative examples? *There is often a potential risk when you employ intensity as an attention strategy.* Any time deep human emotion is aroused, your listeners may respond in a variety of ways, both positive and negative. Nevertheless, research shows that highly unpleasant stimuli can be highly interesting and attention grabbing, whereas highly pleasant stimuli can be so uninteresting that attention is easily diverted (Turner & Silvia, 2006). Whether to use an unpleasant yet intense example such as the Melvin Nurse story is a judgment. Unpleasant examples are likely to work most effectively when they are used occasionally. A steady diet of unpleasantness can be mind numbing and counterproductive. The extremely difficult challenge you face as a speaker to gain and maintain the attention of your audience, however, may require moving beyond just happy stories and uplifting examples, as pleasant and comforting as these can be. Human interest runs the gamut from pleasant to unpleasant, so don't restrict yourself to only one or the other.

Intensity can be created in ways other than by powerful stories and examples. Direct, penetrating eye contact can be riveting. If you doubt this, try staring at someone for a prolonged period of time. The intensity can be quite powerful. When you don't look directly at your audience, listeners' minds can easily wander.

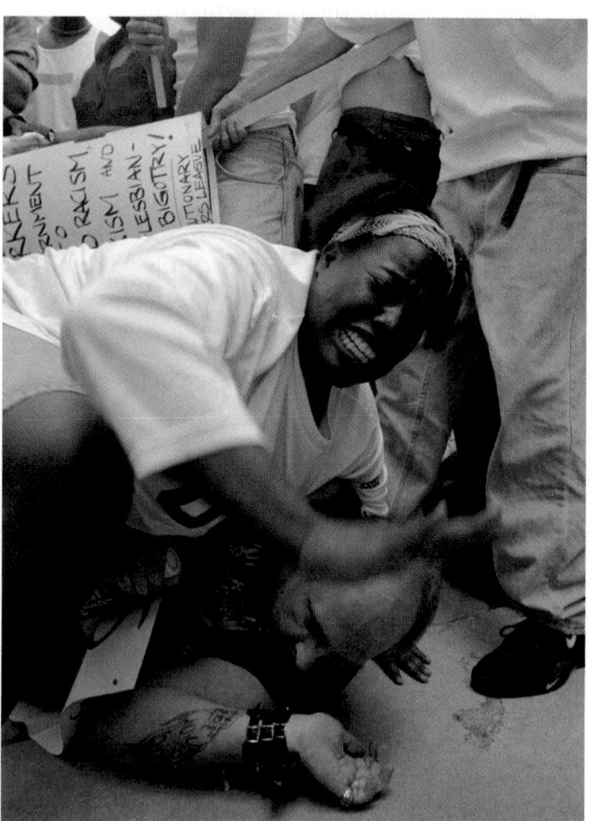

This picture epitomizes intensity. It is also startling and novel. An African American woman protects a White Ku Klux Klan member from an angry mob.

Competent Presentation of Introductions and Conclusions

The beginning and ending can be as important as the body of your speech. Getting off to a good start presenting your speech alerts your audience to expect a quality presentation. Ending with a bang leaves a lasting impression on your listeners. Kerry Konda (2006), as a student from Northern State University, began a speech delivered at the Interstate Oratorical Association contest this way.

> On the roof of an old airport hangar outside of Fallujah, the Marine credo, "No One Left Behind," is spelled with crudely arranged sandbags. Inside this hangar was where Marine Sgt. Daniel Cotnoir, father of two, tried to put that credo into practice. His job on the mortuary unit was to crawl along, sifting through the blood-soaked debris of blast areas, finding pieces of his fallen comrades, and then, put them back together. For his outstanding service in Iraq, the *Marine Corps Times* honored him as "Marine of the Year." However, this glory quickly faded. According to the *Boston Herald* on August 15, 2005, Cotnoir pointed a 12-gauge shotgun out his second-floor window and fired a single shot into a crowd of noisy revelers who were leaving a nightclub and nearby restaurant in retaliation for a bottle that was thrown through his window. After police arrived, Cotnoir broke down crying saying he had to protect his family. Cotnoir is just one of the many soldiers returning from Iraq, who in military terms, has "temporary adjustment disorder," but in reality is suffering from something far greater. That something is PTSD, post-traumatic stress disorder. (p. 74)

This is a very powerful beginning to a speech. The story is novel, startling, and intense. Kerry's conclusion is equally impressive.

> Claiming post-traumatic stress disorder is just a temporary adjustment soldiers must go through is unacceptable. Our soldiers, like Daniel Cotnoir . . . made it through the hell that is war, but we cannot lose them to the battles that still rage in their minds. As Americans we cannot sit idly by and deny

> them the right to lead a normal life when they sacrificed so much. Instead, we must do what is humanly possible and answer the call in their time of need; we must follow the example of Sgt. Daniel Cotnoir and leave no one behind. (p. 76)

Tying the introduction and conclusion together with the Marine slogan "No One Left Behind" neatly packages the speech. The speech ends as poignantly as it began.

Competent Introductions: Four Requirements

There are four principal requirements for a competent introduction to a speech: gain attention, make a clear purpose statement, establish the significance of your topic, and preview your main points. Before explaining each requirement, it should be noted that these requirements in some cases might overlap. Your attention strategy may establish the significance of your topic and purpose statement, making additional focus on significance redundant. Some gatherings for speeches make a direct reference to significance during the introduction unnecessary because the audience has assembled in recognition of the importance of the topic (e.g., ceremonies commemorating the victims of the September 11 terrorist attack). Nevertheless, make certain that all four requirements are addressed directly if no such exceptions exist.

Gain Attention: Focusing Your Audience

The previous section covered general attention strategies you can use throughout your entire speech. For the introduction to your speech, however, more specific suggestions apply. Getting your speech off to a good start sets the stage for the rest of your presentation.

Begin with a Clever Quotation: Let Others Grab Attention Opening with a clever quotation can capitalize on the wit and wisdom of others. For example,

> President John F. Kennedy, in a speech at a White House dinner honoring several Nobel Prize winners, said: "I think this is the most extraordinary collection of talent, of human knowledge, that has ever been gathered together at the White House with the possible exception of when Thomas Jefferson dined alone." President Kennedy deftly complimented his esteemed honorees without becoming effusive in his praise. He demonstrated skill in giving compliments. Complimenting others is an important but often overlooked way to cement interpersonal relationships, build teamwork, and promote goodwill among coworkers and friends. Giving compliments unskillfully, however, can provoke embarrassment and awkwardness between people. Today I will discuss three effective techniques for giving compliments.

Note that the quotation not only grabs attention with ironic humor, but it relates specifically to the purpose statement.

Use Questions: Engage Your Audience Asking questions of your audience can be an effective technique for gaining listeners' attention immediately. A question asked by a speaker not intended to be answered out loud is a **rhetorical question**. Consider this example:

> When you walk downtown and are approached by street people begging for change, do you oblige them? When members of the Salvation Army stand in front of stores during Christmas shopping season ringing their bells and asking for donations, do you drop change into their pots? Have you ever wondered what happens to the money donated to the poor? Well, I plan to inform you where that money goes and on what it is spent.

Rhetorical questions can involve the audience and invite interest in the subject. A powerful rhetorical question asked more than once by those opposed to U.S. involvement in the Iraq War, and originally asked by John Kerry about the Vietnam War, was "Who will be last to die for a mistake?" The question turns the wheels of thought to what purpose the great sacrifices of our men and women in combat serve if the war was a tragic error in policy and practice. On the other side, the rhetorical question "How can we ask our young men and women to make the ultimate sacrifice in combat when we are unwilling to make even a token sacrifice to pay for the war?" raises the issue of hypocrisy when there is resistance to tax increases to pay for a war many supported.

Make sure, however, that your rhetorical questions are meaningful and not merely a commonplace device to open a speech. "Have you ever wondered why our college doesn't have a chess team?" is likely to produce a "not really" mental or even verbal response from the audience. The question doesn't spark interest if interest is already lacking.

You may want to ask questions that seek overt responses. "Raise your hands, please—how many of you have attended a rock concert?" or "Let's see a quick show of hands—have you tried an exercise program in the last year?" are examples. Polling an audience can be engaging and even amusing. "How many in this audience have used a dangerous, illegal drug in the past six months? Whoa, two of you actually raised your hands; that's a first. You might want to check the Fifth Amendment protections against self-incrimination. Americans revere the Bill of Rights, but how many of you can even identify the first 10 amendments to the U.S. Constitution?" This example uses both actual and rhetorical questions to engage the audience.

Expecting listeners to respond overtly to a question can be tricky business. Asking an audience to cop to illegal behavior is questionable in its own right even if it offers an opportunity for humor and playfulness with the audience. It could also easily produce an awkward silence with no hands raised. Conversely, you may expect (and hope) no hands are raised. A student began his speech this way: "How many of you have ever played Frisbee golf?" Almost every student raised a hand. "Wow, I didn't expect that response," blurted the speaker. Some listeners may even see your question as an opportunity to heckle or ridicule you. "How many of you have difficulty losing weight?" might trigger "Not as much trouble as you seem to have." Only certain audiences would likely be so boorish (high school comes to mind), but skip polling your audience unless you feel comfortable ad libbing responses.

Begin with a Simple Visual Aid: Show and Tell Carrie Clarke (1995), a student at Southern Utah University, began her speech with a simple visual aid apparent from her introductory sentence: "When I flip this coin, I have a 50-50 chance of getting heads. You have the same odds of getting a qualified physician in an emergency room" (p. 103). Another example might be holding a Smartphone for your audience to see while noting:

> This tiny, wafer-thin device has more computing power than the super computers of only 40 years ago that filled a large portion of a room. So why hasn't there been an equivalent downsizing of solar cells and enhancement of solar power in the same time period? Shouldn't we be able to replace huge, bulky solar panels with Smartphone-size solar cells with the capacity to power an entire house?

Beginning with a simple visual aid can draw in your audience and also make a point.

Tell a Relevant Story: Use Narrative Power Juan Roberto Melendez-Colon languished on Florida's death row for "17 years, 8 months, and 1 day." He became the 99th death-row inmate in the United States to be exonerated and freed since 1973. He told his story at the 2007 Los Angeles Religious Education Congress. The room was packed to hear his tragic story of dehumanization, of wrongful imprisonment that nearly led him to commit suicide. I was there and I was deeply moved to hear his story and witness his spirit of forgiveness.

A short, entertaining story is usually called an **anecdote**. Research shows that introductions that begin with an anecdote motivate your audience to listen and promote understanding and retention of your message (Andeweg et al., 1998). Anecdotes that have a personal relevance can be particularly captivating. Buey Ruet (2006), as a student at the University of Nebraska at Omaha, gave this introduction at the Interstate Oratorical Association competition. It is not only novel but intense.

> On October 15, 1994, a woman by the name of Workinsh Admasu opened a letter, which required her 8- and 13-year-old boys to immediately report to military training camp. Three weeks after basic training, the boys, along with another 300,000 8- to 14-year-olds, strapped on AK-47s that were half their body weight and headed off to fight in Sudan's civil war. . . . If you are wondering why I care about this topic so much, that 8-year-old boy was me. My 13-year-old brother and I were forced to experience things that no other child should ever have to experience. (p. 49)

The Sudan War can seem extremely remote for most Americans until a victim is standing in front of them telling his personal story of tragedy and outrage.

Refer to Remarks of Introduction: Acknowledge Your Audience In some cases, your planned introduction may need to be altered slightly following remarks made about you by the person introducing you to the audience. A simple, clean reference to those remarks is sufficient before launching into your prepared speech. Walter Mondale, former U.S. senator from Minnesota, had a standard response when he was extravagantly introduced to an audience: "I don't deserve those kind words. But then I have arthritis and I don't deserve that either." Former President Lyndon Johnson also had a standard line prepared if his introduction to an audience was effusive in its praise: "That was the kind of very generous introduction that my father would have appreciated, and my mother would have believed." Following an underwhelming, bland introduction to his audience, Mondale would begin: "Of all the introductions I've received, that was the most recent" (cited in Noonan, 1998, p. 148).

Make a Clear Purpose Statement: Providing Intent

Purpose statements were discussed in some detail in Chapter 12. The purpose statement provides the intent for your entire speech. Consider this example.

> Matthew Shepard, a gay 21-year-old University of Wyoming student, was lured away from a bar in October 1998 by two young males pretending to be gay. Shepard was then robbed, beaten senseless, and tied to a fence outside of Laramie, Wyoming, and left for dead. He was found in a coma, and five days after his horrific assault, Shepard died. This tragic instance of gay bashing aroused the entire nation. At his funeral, more than a thousand mourners showed up to pay their respects to "this gentle soul," as he was described by those who knew him. During the funeral, however, a dozen protesters stood across the street from the church holding signs that read, "No Tears for Queers" and "Get Back in Your Damn Closet." It was a tasteless and insensitive protest. Soon after his death, a prominent conservative Christian church created a web photo of Matthew Shepard burning, with a link allowing visitors to hear him "scream in hell."
>
> More than a decade after Matthew Shepard's tragic murder, hate speech continues unabated. The vileness of hate speech may incline us to support laws that ban it. I hope to convince you, however, that outlawing hate speech would be disadvantageous.

The opening example invites attention because it is novel and intense, and it leads directly to a clear purpose statement.

Establish Topic Significance: Making Your Audience Care

Audiences tend to be Me-oriented, not We-oriented. When told about a local, national, or international problem, listeners typically want to know "How does this affect me?" As a speaker, you must answer that question. During your introduction, establish the basis for why audience members should care to listen. If you are an avid golfer, surfer, card player, quilter, or woodworker, your audience will see your enthusiasm for your topic. Why should listeners be enthusiastic, though, if they haven't ever tried such activities or if they proved to be inept when they did try? Relate your purpose statement to your audience. For example, suppose your listeners never considered playing golf because it seemed uninteresting. You could make the topic relevant and significant to your listeners this way.

> Mark Twain once said that golf was a good walk spoiled. For many of you, that may seem true. Most members of my family tell me that watching golf on television is as exciting as watching mold form on rotting food. I beg to differ with these assessments. Golf can be a wonderful activity to watch and play. Golf is a good walk, but it is only spoiled if you lack knowledge of the strategy behind the game and your skill level is deficient. Understanding the strategy, and learning to play golf well, can make for an extremely enjoyable few hours of recreation in the bright sun and fresh air. Also, millions of dollars' worth of business are negotiated on the golf links every day. Even if you don't foresee a business deal on the horizon, it's never too early to begin learning the game in case your big chance comes unexpectedly. To put it succinctly, golf can be entertaining and it can enhance your life physically, psychologically, economically, and occupationally.
>
> I can't teach you to play golf well in a five-minute speech. You'll want to find a qualified golf instructor to help you do that. I can, however, briefly explain four qualities to consider when choosing a golf instructor.

Some topics are more challenging to make relevant to an audience's interests than others. Nevertheless, every topic needs to be made relevant to an audience, or listeners will quickly tune out and let their minds wander freely.

Preview the Main Points: The Coming Attractions

A preview presents the coming attractions of your speech. A speech will normally have two to four main points that flow directly from the purpose statement. For example, "I want to explain how you can save money when purchasing a new car. There are three ways: comparison shopping, lowering your interest payments, and purchasing at the end of the year."

Although the purpose statement and the significance can be reversed in order, attention is always the first requirement. The preview is the final requirement of an introduction. Some speech experts suggest that there is a fifth requirement for a good introduction: ***establishing the credibility of the speaker***. If you have expertise relevant to your purpose statement that is unknown to your audience, don't hesitate to mention it. That you have surfed for ten years, worked as an auto mechanic for three years, or have a degree or certificate in computer science would likely induce your listeners to grant you credibility on those subjects. If you are asked to make a presentation because you are viewed as a credible expert or authority on a subject, however, no effort to establish credibility is necessary, especially if your credentials are listed when you're introduced to the audience. Student speakers and laypersons often cannot establish their credibility in this way during the introduction to their speech. They may have no particular experience or expertise on a subject that would produce initial credibility with an audience. Even informing an audience that you have conducted extensive research on the subject can sound self-serving. Why not let your evidence and command of the facts make that point obvious and leave it at that?

Credibility is created primarily by developing your purpose with logic and supporting materials throughout the body of your speech. If you sound as though you know what you are talking about, listeners will be inclined to perceive you as credible. Establishing credibility in this way, however, takes an entire speech, not merely a few statements during the introduction. Credibility will be discussed in greater detail in Chapter 15. At this point, *establishing credibility may be one element of an introduction, but it is not always a requirement.*

Requirements for Competent Conclusions: Finishing Well

Conclusions should do what introductions do, except in reverse. Your conclusion should create a sense of unity like completing a circle. You want your introduction to begin strongly, and you want your conclusion to end strongly.

Summarize the Main Points: Connecting the Parts

In your introduction, you preview your main points as a final step. In your conclusion, you summarize those main points, usually as a first step. For example, "In brief review, we learned a little history of the martial arts, I explained how to choose a qualified martial arts school, and I demonstrated some common martial arts defense techniques." Summarizing your main points during your conclusion reminds the audience of the most important points in your speech.

Refer to the Introduction: Bookending the Speech

If you used a dramatic story or example to begin your speech, referring to that story or example in your conclusion provides closure. This is how Moorpark College student Tara Kubicka (1995) concluded her speech on tainted organ transplants.

> Clearly, by examining the problems associated with the unregulated organ industry and the factors leading to this tragedy, we can see that such steps are necessary. Only then can we insure that when the Ruth Glors and Brian Clarks of the world receive their long awaited saving transplant that it is indeed life saving and not a death sentence. (p. 11)

She finishes by making reference to opening examples used to grab the attention.

Make a Memorable Finish: Sizzle Don't Fizzle

Surely one of the most powerful speech conclusions came in Martin Luther King's "I Have a Dream" speech in 1963. He concluded: "When we allow freedom to ring, when we let it ring from every village and every hamlet, from every state and every city, we will be able to speed up that day when all of God's children, black men and white men, Jews and Gentiles, Protestants and Catholics, will be able to join hands and sing in the words of that old Negro spiritual, 'Free at last! Free at last! Thank God Almighty, we are free at last!"

You begin your speech with an attention strategy, and you should end your speech in similar fashion. A strong quotation, a moving rhetorical question, an intense statement, a moving example or story, or a humorous statement makes an effective attention grabber for introductions. They serve the same purpose for effective conclusions. Student Chris Griesinger (2006) finished his speech on inadequate pain management for terminally ill patients by telling the story of 15-year-old terminally ill leukemia patient John Wandishin. He concluded with this statement: "Leukemia robbed him of a future, but pain robbed him of his present. Every last one of us came into this world kicking and screaming, but there is no reason why anyone should be forced to leave this world doing the same" (p. 38). Student Tina Lynn Wheeler (2004) finished her speech on the dangers of dietary supplements with this quotation: "As Dr. Sidney Wolfe, director of Public Citizen's Health Research Group stated in the previously cited *Business Week* article, 'Studies should be done first, rather than counting the bodies after'" (p. 52).

One final note about conclusions: *do not end abruptly, apologize for running short on time, or ramble until you fizzle like a balloon deflating.* Be concise and to the point when finishing your speech. Your conclusion should be no more than about 5% to 10% of your total speech. Don't diminish the effect of a great speech with a bloated, aimless conclusion.

Competent Presentation of Supporting Materials

In Chapter 12, I discussed in detail criteria for selecting valid and reliable supporting materials. These valid and reliable supporting materials, however, do not automatically make a speech interesting or inspiring for listeners. There are specific ways to present supporting materials effectively.

Examples: Appropriateness and Effectiveness

Knowledge and skill are keys to presenting examples competently. In this section, I discuss examples in terms of relevance, vividness, representativeness, and stacking.

Use Relevant Examples: Stick to the Point

Use examples that are relevant to the point you make. A young Abraham Lincoln, acting as a defense attorney in a courtroom trial, explained what "self-defense" meant by using a relevant story to clarify his point. He told the jury a story about a man who, while walking down a country road with pitchfork in hand, was attacked by a vicious dog. The man was forced to kill the dog with his pitchfork. A local farmer who owned the dog asked the man why he had to kill his dog. The man replied, "What made him try to bite me?" The farmer persisted, "But why didn't you go at him with the other end of the pitchfork?" The man responded, "Why didn't he come at me with the other end of the dog?" (cited in Larson, 1992, p. 181). Lincoln made his point that the degree of allowable force depends on the degree of force used by the attacker.

Choose Vivid Examples: Create Strong Images

Examples should be vivid. A vivid example triggers feelings and provokes strong images (Pratkanis & Aronson, 2001). Kittie Grace (2000), a student at Hastings College, in a speech at the 2000 Interstate Oratorical Association contest, uses a vivid example to evoke a strong image on her main theme that hotels in America are unsanitary.

> According to the August 8, 1999, *Hotel and Motel Management Journal* or *HMMJ*, in Atlantic City, New Jersey, two unsuspecting German tourists shared a motel room which had been cleaned that morning, but a foul smell permeated through the room. After the third complaint, housekeeping cleaned under the bed finding the body of a dead man decomposing, all because housekeeping failed to clean under the bed in the first place. (p. 86)

This example is so vivid that it quite likely will stick in many of your memories the next time you stay at a motel or hotel.

Stack Examples: When One Is Not Enough

Sometimes a single example does not suffice to make a point clear, memorable, interesting, or adequately supported. Note the value of using plentiful examples stacked one on top of another in the following:

> Male residents of Boonville, California, who obviously had lots of time on their hands, created a lingo of their own in the late 1800s, mostly to talk around women without them understanding what was being said. The rules for Boontling are those of English. The lexicon (total vocabulary) of more than 1,300 words, however, is mostly unintelligible to speakers of standard English. Those individuals who *harp Boont* (speak Boontling) concocted some colorful words. Examples include *burlapping* (having sexual intercourse), *fence-jumpy* (given to adultery), *grey-matter kimmie* (college professor), *mink* (a female of easy morals), *wheeler* (lie), *shoveltooth* (medical doctor), and *high-split* (very tall, slender man). Knowing just these few Boont words gives you the ability to translate this sentence: "The high-split, fence-jumpy, grey-matter kimmie told a wheeler to cover up his burlapping with a mink, daughter of the local shoveltooth." There are still a few speakers of Boontling, but most have *piked to the dusties* (died).

In this instance, using only one or two examples of Boontling wouldn't clarify the main point well, create much impact, support claims well, or spark much interest.

Statistics: Quantifying Your Points

Statistics can be powerful supporting material. There are three ways to use statistics effectively and not degenerate into a boring recitation of figures and numbers.

Use Accurate Statistics Accurately: Be Careful with Statistics

A statistic should be accurate, but the speaker should also use an accurate statistic accurately. News media and even health-care professionals commonly claim that a woman's chance of developing breast cancer is 1 in 9. This is not a fallacious statistic, but it is somewhat misleading. The 1 in 9 chance is the cumulative probability of getting breast cancer if a woman lives to an age of 85 years or older. The chances of developing breast cancer by age 50, however, are about 1 in 52, or less than 2% (Paulos,

1994). The risk gradually increases beyond the age of 50. Scaring young women into getting mammograms every year when their chances of getting breast cancer are slim results in unnecessary expense and creates unreasonable fear.

Make Statistics Concrete: Clarify Meaning

Large statistics don't always communicate meaning to listeners. For example, the difficulty in sending a spaceship to even the closest star to Earth is hard to grasp. Alpha Centauri, the nearest star, is 4.4 light years from the Sun; that's equivalent to about 26 trillion miles (Angier, 2002). These statistics are so large that they have little meaning beyond "really big." Dr. Geoffrey Landis of the NASA John Glenn Research Center in Cleveland, however, provides a concrete referent for us. Referring to the *Voyager* interplanetary probes, the fastest objects humans have ever launched into space, he explains: "If a caveman had launched one of those during the last ice age, 11,000 years ago, it would now be only a fifth of the way toward the nearest star" (Angier, 2002). Landis doesn't merely present the statistics. He presents them effectively by providing a clear, concrete example that gives perspective.

Make Statistical Comparisons: Gain Perspective

An effective way to make a technical statistic meaningful is to compare it with a more familiar statistic closer to a layperson's experience. For example, a speech by Sarah Werner (2005), a student at the University of Maryland and a contestant at the 2005 Interstate Oratorical Association contest on federal mandatory minimum prison sentences, notes that Weldon Angelos, convicted of selling marijuana on a first-time offense, was sentenced to *63 years* in prison "despite the fact that a jury of his peers—the jury that convicted him—favored a sentence of 15–18 years." She further notes that "the federal maximum sentencing for hijacking an airplane is 24½ years, for detonating a bomb in a public place, 19½ years" (p. 60). The comparison greatly enhances the impact of her central claim that mandatory minimum sentences are unjust.

Stack Statistics: Create Impact

Jon Celoria (1997), as a student at William Carey College, effectively stacked statistics for maximum impact in a speech on counterfeit airline parts.

> *Aviation Week & Space Technology* of July 29, 1996, reports that since 1978, U.S. air traffic has grown ten times faster than the inspector force employed by the FAA. As a result, the FAA's nearly 3,000 inspectors currently have the unthinkable task of overseeing 7,300 jets, 200,000 other planes, 4,700 repair stations, 650 pilot training schools, 190 maintenance schools, and nearly 700,000 active pilots. (p. 80)

This is an impressive stack of statistics supporting the point that thwarting the flood of bogus airline parts is an impossible task for inspection teams. Stacked statistics, however, should be used sparingly and only to create an impact on the central points in a speech. Audience members will tune out if they become weary hearing you stack a mountain of statistics.

Competent Style of Presentation: A Signature Event

British author Oscar Wilde once said, "One's style is one's signature always." Your speaking style reveals an identity. It is part of who you are. A speech is a combination of substance and style. Your **style** is composed of the words you choose to express your thoughts and the ways you use language to bring your thoughts to life for an audience. A verbose style may tag you as boring or confused, a clear and precise style as interesting or instructive, and a vivid style as exciting, even inspiring. Take your style seriously because it is the picture that you project to your audience. Your style may leave a more lasting image with your audience than any specific points made in your speech. In this section, I examine the differences between written and oral style as well as the primary elements of an effective and appropriate style.

Oral Versus Written Style: An Essay Is Not a Speech

There are distinct differences between oral and written style. First, *when we speak, we usually use simpler sentences than when we write.* An audience must catch the speaker's meaning immediately. When you read a sentence, however, you can reread it several times if necessary to discern the correct meaning, even consult a dictionary if you don't know the meaning of unfamiliar words. In a speech, very complex sentence structure can confuse listeners, who cannot normally rewind the speech.

Second, *oral style is highly interactive; written style is not.* When speaking, you can look directly into the faces of your listeners. If you sense that they do not understand your point, you can adjust by rephrasing your point, adding an example, even asking if they are confused. Feedback is immediate from listeners, but feedback from readers is delayed even in text messaging, and it is often nonexistent. The speaker and the audience influence each other directly. If you crack a joke and no one laughs, you may decide to dump other attempts at humor.

Third, *oral style is usually less formal than written style.* Spelling errors only occur in written language. Even highly educated individuals diminish their credibility when they send emails or letters with obvious spelling mistakes. My auto insurance company sent me a letter with this sentence in the opening paragraph: "You may not know that the reputation of our Auto Insurnance is equally outstanding." Grammar errors may go unnoticed when words are spoken but may jump off the page when words are written. More slang and casual forms of address creep into spoken language than appear in written form. We tend to be more conversational when we speak than when we write.

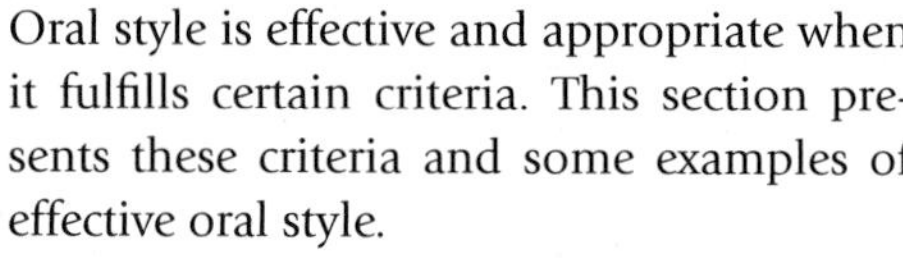

Standards of Competent Oral Style: The Language of a Speech

Oral style is effective and appropriate when it fulfills certain criteria. This section presents these criteria and some examples of effective oral style.

Clarity: Say What You Mean

Oral style works more effectively when language is clear and understandable. This often means avoiding jargon, euphemisms, and slang (see Chapter 4). *Clarity comes from a simple, concise style.* John F. Kennedy asked his speechwriter, Ted Sorensen, to discover the secret of Lincoln's Gettysburg Address. Sorensen noted this: "Lincoln never used a two- or three-syllable word where a one-syllable word would do, and never used two or three words where one word would do" (National Archives, 1987, p. 1). There are 701 words in Lincoln's second inaugural address, of which 505 are one syllable and 122 are merely two syllables (Zinsser, 1985). Inexperienced speakers may think that big ideas require big words. When listeners start noticing the big words, however, the big ideas shrink into the dark shadows of obscurity. Don't try to impress

an audience with a vocabulary that sounds as though you consulted a thesaurus on a regular basis. Remember, oral style requires greater simplicity than written style.

A clear style is simple but not simplistic. Lincoln's second inaugural address included this memorable line: "With malice toward none, with charity for all, with firmness in the right as God gives us to see the right." The words are simple, yet the meaning is profound, even moving. Including an occasional complex sentence or more challenging vocabulary, however, can also work well. Although Lincoln used a simple, clear style, his sentence structure and phrasing were not always simple. In his Gettysburg Address, he included several lengthy, complex sentences. He also included this sentence: "We cannot dedicate, we cannot consecrate, we cannot hallow this ground." He could have said, "We cannot set aside for the special purpose of honoring, we cannot make holy this ground." Sometimes more challenging vocabulary provides an economical use of language. By occasionally using more sophisticated vocabulary, Lincoln spoke more concisely, clearly, and eloquently. If in doubt, however, default to simple sentence structure and vocabulary.

Precision: Pick the Apt Words

Baseball great Yogi Berra once observed this about the game that made him a household name: "Ninety percent of this game is half-mental." Yogi also said, "When you get to a fork in the road, take it," and "Our similarities are different." Yogi was not renowned for his precise use of the English language (or his mastery of arithmetic). Deborah Koons Garcia, wife of the Grateful Dead's Jerry Garcia, was equally imprecise when she remarked, "Jerry died broke. We only have a few hundred thousand dollars in the bank" (cited in White, 1998). Wouldn't you love to be that broke? Everyone has misused a word or gotten tangled on syntax occasionally. Nevertheless, you should strive to be as precise in your use of language as possible. Using words imprecisely or inaccurately diminishes your credibility and can make you appear foolish.

Sometimes our attempt to be precise leads to redundant phrases such as "twelve noon," "true fact," "circle around," "close proximity," "end result," "revert back," and "the future to come." Eliminate repetitive phrases. Also be careful, when using acronyms, that you don't add redundant words such as "ATM machine" (**A**utomatic **T**eller **M**achine machine), "HIV virus" (**H**uman **I**mmunodeficiency **V**irus virus), and "AIDS syndrome" (**A**cquired **I**mmune **D**eficiency **S**yndrome syndrome).

Vividness: Paint a Picture

Simple, concise, precise use of language doesn't mean using words in a boring fashion. Referring to parents who hover over their children on academic concerns as "helicopter parents" is colorful and memorable (Mathews, 2007). A vivid style paints a picture in the minds of listeners and makes a speaker's ideas memorable. William Gibbs McAdoo, twice an unsuccessful candidate for the Democratic nomination for president, vividly described the speeches of President Warren G. Harding this way: "His speeches left the impression of an army of pompous phrases moving over the landscape in search of an idea." The words are simple and the point is clearly drawn. The style, however, is quite vivid. Oscar-winning actor George Clooney, speaking about the importance of directing, his real passion, once remarked, "Directing is the key to filmmaking. Everything else is just paint" ("As 'Sexiest Man Alive,'" 2006, p. 2A). Student Meaghan Hagensick (2008) delivered a speech at the Interstate Oratorical Association national competition in which she referred to those who claim that sitting in the backseat of a car makes wearing a seatbelt unnecessary as "backseat bullets." Sarah Hoppes (2008), a student giving a speech at the same contest, noted that a proposal to sell ad space on the Golden Gate Bridge to cover an $80 million deficit would turn a national landmark into "The Google Gate Bridge." Each of these examples leaves a visual impression in the listener's mind.

Consider the difference vivid style makes by comparing the phrasing of several famous statements with a plainer version of the same statements.

> Vivid: "Friends, Romans, countrymen, lend me your ears."
>
> (Shakespeare's version of a speech by Mark Antony)
>
> Plain: "Friends, Romans, countrymen, may I please have your attention?"
>
> Vivid: "Don't fire until you see the whites of their eyes."
>
> (Colonel William Prescott at the Battle of Bunker Hill)
>
> Plain: "Don't shoot until they get really close."
>
> Vivid: "I have a dream."
>
> (Martin Luther King)
>
> Plain: "I have an idea."
>
> Vivid: "I have nothing to offer but blood, toil, tears and sweat."
>
> (Winston Churchill, The Battle of Britain speech)
>
> Plain: "I have nothing to offer but a struggle."

Here are a few suggestions for making your style move from commonplace to vivid.

Metaphor and Simile: Figures of Speech Two main figures of speech that can add vividness to your speeches are metaphors and similes. A **metaphor** is an implied comparison of two seemingly dissimilar things. In a speech delivered on January 6, 1941, Franklin Roosevelt said that selfish men "would clip the wings of the American eagle in order to feather their own nests." Hillary Clinton, addressing the 2008 Democratic National Convention as the runner-up candidate for president, used metaphor when she described the "Supreme Court in a right-wing headlock and our government in partisan gridlock" ("Transcript," 2009). Patrick Buchanan, a Republican candidate for president, in a speech at the Republican National Convention in 1992, characterized the Democratic National Convention held weeks before as a "giant masquerade ball [where] 20,000 radicals and liberals came dressed up as moderates and centrists in the greatest single exhibition of cross-dressing in American political history." You can differ with the points of view expressed, but these speakers created vivid images that enlivened their ideas. Metaphors may also influence listeners' attitudes (Sopory & Dillard, 2002).

Be careful not to mix your metaphors; otherwise, your vivid imagery may sound laughable. A **mixed metaphor** is the use of two or more vastly different metaphors in a single expression. Famous movie producer Samuel Goldwyn once remarked, "That's the way with these directors. They're always biting the hand that lays the golden egg." Then there's Alabama Senator Jeff Sessions who, in his opening statement at the Judiciary Committee confirmation hearings for Sonya Sotomayor as Supreme Court justice in July 2009, argued for a "blindfolded justice calling the balls and strikes fairly and objectively" (quoted in Goodman, 2009, p. A13). A blindfolded justice metaphorically symbolizes lack of bias, but a baseball umpire, making inherently subjective perceptual judgment calls, surely doesn't. Even more to the point, would you ever want an umpire of any sort to be blindfolded when they "call the balls and strikes"? Mixing metaphors can sound goofy.

A **simile** is an explicit comparison of two seemingly dissimilar things using the word *like* or *as*. Curt Simmons described what it was like pitching to Hank Aaron: "Trying to get a fastball past Hank Aaron is like trying to get the sun past a rooster." Bill Clinton, in a speech at Galesburg, Illinois, on January 23, 1995, used simile in an amusing way: "Being president is like running a cemetery; you've got a lot of people under you and nobody's listening."

Similes and metaphors can enhance a speech but not if they become clichés. A **cliché** is a once-vivid expression that has been overused to the point of seeming commonplace. "Dull as dishwater," "dumb as a post," and "smooth as a baby's butt" are a few overused similes. "It's not rocket science," "It's an emotional roller coaster," and "I'm between a rock and a hard place" are metaphors that have become shopworn. A survey of 5,000 individuals in 70 countries, conducted by the British-based Plain

English Campaign, showed that "at the end of the day" is the most annoying cliché in the English language across all cultures. Other clichés vying for most annoying are "touching base," "pushing the envelope," and "singing from the same hymn sheet" ("Touching Base," 2004).

Alliteration: Several of the Same Sounds The repetition of the same sound, usually a consonant sound, starting each word is called **alliteration**. It can create a very vivid cadence. Classic examples of alliteration were spoken by the Wizard in the movie "Wizard of Oz." He called the Tin Man a " clinking, clanking, clattering collection of caliginous junk." He referred to the Scarecrow as a "billowing bale of bovine fodder." Student Kittie Grace (2000) noted in her speech on poorly cleaned hotel rooms that the rooms had become "a biological banquet for bugs and bacteria that cause us physical harm" (p. 87). When Spiro Agnew was vice-president of the United States during the Nixon presidency, he became famous for phrases such as "nattering nabobs of negativism" and "pusillanimous pussyfooters." The problem with Agnew's use of alliteration, however, was that most listeners couldn't decipher what he had said because he loved to use silver dollar words when nickel and dime words would have been more effective.

Parallelism: Vivid Rhythm A parallel construction has a similar arrangement of words, phrases, or sentences which create a rhythm. Here are two examples.

> From now on, it will be unremarkable for a woman to win primary-state victories, unremarkable to have a woman in a close race to be our nominee, unremarkable to think that a woman can be the president of the United States. And that is truly remarkable. (Hillary Clinton, 2008)

> When we have faced down impossible odds, when we've been told we're not ready or that we shouldn't try or that we can't, generations of Americans have responded with a simple creed that sums up the spirit of a people: Yes, we can. Yes, we can. Yes, we can. . . . Yes, we can, to opportunity and prosperity. Yes, we can heal this nation. Yes, we can repair this world. Yes, we can. (Barack Obama, 2008)

As is true of any stylistic device, a little goes a long way. *Be careful not to overuse parallel constructions.*

Antithesis: Using Opposites Charles Dickens began his famous novel *A Tale of Two Cities* with one of the most memorable lines in literature: "It was the best of times; it was the worst of times." This is an example of the stylistic device called **antithesis**, the use of opposites to create impact. Former First Lady Barbara Bush offered this example of antithesis: "Your success as a family, our success as a society, depends not on what happens at the White House, but on what happens inside your house." Perhaps the most famous example of antithesis in public speaking is from John F. Kennedy's inaugural address in 1961: "Ask not what your country can do for you, ask what you can do for your country." The effectiveness of antithesis is in the rhythmic phrasing. Four months before his inaugural address, Kennedy made this statement: "The new frontier is not what I promise I am going to do for you. The new frontier is what I ask you to do for your country." This also used antithesis, but it wasn't memorable. It seems more verbose. Be concise when using antithesis.

Ultimately, your style must be your own. Work on clarity, precision, and vividness by listening to successful speakers, but explore what fits you well. Metaphors and similes may come easily to you, but antithesis may seem artificial and awkward. Develop your own style by experimenting. Try including metaphors in your conversations with others. Play with language informally before incorporating stylistic devices in your formal speeches. Remember, style is your signature.

Competent Delivery of Speeches

Cornell University psychology professor Stephen Ceci had been receiving average student evaluations of his teaching. He decided to change his delivery of class lectures. He spoke more loudly than usual, varied the pitch of his voice more dramatically, and gestured more emphatically than normal. The student ratings for his class and his instruction went up noticeably from an average of between 2 and 3 on a 5-point scale to a 4-plus (Murray, 1997). Ceci was perceived by students to be more effective, knowledgeable, and organized because of the change in delivery. Surprisingly, students found the textbook more interesting to read and Ceci's grading policy (unchanged) fairer than in previous terms when he had used a more commonplace delivery. Students also believed they had learned more material even though their test scores were identical to those of previous classes. Does delivery make a difference? Unquestionably, it does.

The next section begins with a brief discussion of common delivery problems. Then I will look at various methods of delivery a speaker can use.

Common Delivery Problems: Distractions

Inexperienced public speakers often fail to notice problems of delivery that interfere with the effectiveness of their message. Most are commonplace problems that are easily corrected.

Weak Eye Contact: Avoiding Your Audience

Earlier, I noted the importance of eye contact to gaining and maintaining the attention of your audience. Weak eye contact is a common delivery problem. This is often the case when speakers make PowerPoint presentations. They look at the slides, not the audience. There are simple ways to improve your eye contact when delivering a speech. First, be very familiar with your speech so you won't get pinned to your notes or read from a manuscript. Second, practice looking at your entire audience, beginning with the middle of your audience, then looking left, then right, then to the middle again, and so forth. With practice (an imaginary audience will do fine), your eye contact will become automatic.

Monotone Voice: Flat and Uninteresting

The tone of your voice can influence the mood of your audience. One study showed that people listening to a speaker deliver a message in either a happy tone or a sad tone experienced **emotional contagion**—they felt happy or sad depending on the speaker's tone of voice (Neumann & Strack, 2000). Some individuals have very little range in their voices when giving a speech (a monotone). Their voices sound flat and uninteresting. Strive for vocal variety. You can avoid attention-killing monotony by raising and lowering the pitch of your voice. The singing voice has a range of pitch from soprano to bass. Similarly, you can vary your speaking voice by moving up and down the vocal range from high sounds to lower sounds and back.

Monotony can also be avoided by varying the loudness or softness of your voice. A raised voice signals intense, passionate feelings. It will punctuate portions of your presentation much as an exclamation point punctuates a written sentence. Using vocal volume to gain attention, however, can be overdone. As Mark Twain noted, "Noise proves nothing. Often a hen who has merely laid an egg cackles as if she laid an asteroid." Incessant, unrelenting, bombastic delivery of a message can irritate and alienate your audience. Speak loudly only when you have an especially important point to make. All points in your speech do not deserve equal attention.

Speaking softly can also induce interest. When you lower the pitch and loudness of your voice, the audience must strain to hear. This can be a nice dramatic twist in a speech if used infrequently. Vocal variety signals shifts in mood and does not permit an audience to drift into the hypnotic, trancelike state produced by the white noise of the monotone voice. Practice vocal variety on your friends during casual conversations. Experiment with different voice inflections, volume, and pitch.

Vocal Fillers: Um, Know What I Mean?

A common delivery problem is the tendency to include **vocal fillers**—the insertion of *um, ah, like, you know, know what I mean,* *whatever*, and other variants that substitute for pauses and often draw attention to themselves. A Geneva, Nebraska, high-school senior, Jessica Reinsch, won a $1,000 prize in the Nebraskaland Foundation's "you know" contest for recording a 15-minute radio interview during which that phrase was used unintentionally 61 times ("Best English Lesson," 1999). A website called Interview Stream.com, founded by Miles Muntz, produced a top-ten list of "all-star" vocal-filler users among celebrities, politicians, and athletes. Britney Spears made the list for uttering 73 "likes" and "ya knows" in a five-minute YouTube interview. A companion website, UmmLike.com, included Eminem, who also "like, ya know" likes to use "like" and "ya know." Golfer Michelle Wie also made the list for using "ya know" 15 times in a one-minute interview (Kitchen, 2007).

The fluency of your delivery suffers mightily when vocal fillers are used more than occasionally. Almost all speakers use vocal fillers once in a while, and an audience will not notice infrequent use. When they become frequent, however, it may be the only part of your speech that is memorable. Don't be concerned about filling in a few pauses in your delivery. Recent brain research shows that a one- to two-second pause powerfully combats wandering attention. Brief silence can awaken the brain (Swaminathan, 2007).

Practice not using vocal fillers during casual conversation with friends and family. Focus on noticing how often other people use vocal fillers during conversation. Practice your speech in front of a friend or videotape it. Have your friend tap a pencil on a table every time you use a vocal filler during your speech. When you review the videotaped practice speech, count the number of vocal fillers. With time, you will eliminate the habit.

Rapid Pace: Speed Speaking

Steve Woodmore of Orpington, England, spoke 637.4 words per minute on a British TV program called *Motor Mouth*. Sean Shannon, a Canadian residing in Oxford, England, recited the famous soliloquy "To be or not to be . . ." from Shakespeare's *Hamlet* at a 650-words-per-minute clip. Normal conversation ranges between 140 and 180 wpm (McCoy et al., 2005). This pace can allow an audience to scrutinize complex messages (Miller et al., 1976). The slower end of this range (around 140 wpm) also may be appropriate when discussing sensitive subjects such as medical problems, safe sex, or a personal trauma. A swift speaking rate may communicate insensitivity or coldness to listeners as though you're in a rush to blow town (Giles & Street, 1994; Ray et al., 1991). Moderately fast and fast speaking rates (180 to 210 wpm), however, increase the audience's perception of you as intelligent, confident, and effective compared to slower paced speakers (Smith & Shaffer, 1995). Speaking fast shows that you are quick on your feet and can handle ideas swiftly. Most speakers, however, are unintelligible when speaking faster than 300 wpm, and most audiences become twitchy when a speaker motors along at much above 200 wpm. A very slow speaking pace (about 100 wpm), however, can induce a stupor in an audience.

Speaking pace should be lively enough to keep attention but not so fast that you appear to have consumed too many café espressos. A speaking pace of 175 to 200 wpm is usually appropriate. Without actually measuring your speaking pace, *you can get a rough idea of the appropriate pace by enunciating your words carefully and pausing to take breaths without gasping for air.*

Awkward Body Movements: Physical Distracters

Too little movement when speaking can anesthetize an audience. A speaker stands before an audience, grabs the podium in a viselike grip (white knuckles clearly visible to everyone), assumes an expressionless face reminiscent of a marble statue in a museum, and appears to have feet welded to the floor. This is an example of too little body movement. Excessive body movement, however, can be a distraction. Aimlessly pacing like a caged panther, wildly gesticulating with arms flailing in all directions, or awkwardly wrapping legs and arms around the podium diverts attention away from the speech's message. *Strive for a balance between excessive and insufficient body movement.* An animated, lively delivery can excite an audience, but you don't want to appear to have insects in your underwear. Posture should be erect without looking like a soldier standing at attention. Slumping your shoulders, crossing and uncrossing your legs, and lurching to one side with one leg higher than the other call attention to awkward movements. Practice speaking in front of a mirror or record your practice speech to determine whether you have any of these awkward movements.

Proper gesturing can be a concern for the inexperienced public speaker. Don't let it overly concern you. Unless you have adopted some really odd or distracting gestures while speaking, your gestures will rarely, if ever, torpedo your speech. Let gestures emerge naturally. You don't need to plan gestures. As Motley (1995) explains, gestures "are supposed to be non-conscious. That is to say, in natural conversation we use gestures every day without thinking about them. And when we do consciously think about gestures, they become uncomfortable and inhibited" (p. 99). Focus on your messages and your audience, and gestures will follow.

Distracting Behaviors: Stop Clicking the Pen

She crawled on her hands and knees across the courtroom floor while the jury watched transfixed. She kicked the jury box, cried, flailed her arms, and screamed. One journalist said she "behaved like she needed a rabies shot during the trial" (Hutchinson, 2002, p. 9A). Defense attorney Nedra Ruiz's delivery during the emotion-charged trial of Marjorie Knoller and Robert Noel, in the highly publicized 2002 dog mauling murder case in Los Angeles, became a subject of considerable comment. Laurie Levenson, a law professor at Loyola University in Los Angeles, remarked, "Most people I talk to just shook their heads. . . . It's borderline bizarre" (Curtis, 2002, p. A4). As Levenson explained, "There's a pretty decent defense here, but it's getting lost in her [Ruiz's] mannerisms and her theatrics. She's not smooth. She's not polished. She crosses the line from what I think is effective advocacy to cheap theatrics" (Curtis, 2002, p. A4).

At one point in the trial, Ruiz asked prosecution witness Janet Coumbs to stand and show how tall one of the dogs that savagely attacked and killed Diane Whipple was when he licked Coumbs's face (presumably to show how friendly the dog normally acted). Ruiz acted as the dog (again) and placed her "paws" on Coumbs's shoulders. A startled Judge Warren, apparently concerned about Ruiz's extreme delivery, instructed, "I think we'll leave it to the jury's imagination about the licking" (Mikulan, 2002).

This is a case of delivery subverting substance. One of the jurors, Don Newton, remarked after the trial that Ruiz's flamboyant performance was "in some ways counterproductive. She was so scattered at times and it threw you off" (May, 2002, p. 8A).

There are dozens of possible quirky behaviors that speakers can exhibit, often without realizing that they are distracting an audience's attention from the message. Playing with change in your pocket while speaking is one example. Playing with a pen or pencil is another. Sometimes a speaker will unconsciously click a ballpoint pen or tap the podium while speaking. Distracting behaviors can easily be eliminated. Don't hold a pen in your hand and you won't play with it while speaking. Take change out of your pocket before speaking if you have a tendency to jiggle coins when you put your hand in your pocket. Distracting behaviors won't destroy a quality speech unless the behavior is beyond weird (Ruiz's). Nevertheless, eliminating them helps create the impression of a polished performance.

Methods of Delivery: The Big Four

There are four primary methods of delivery, each with its own pros and cons. They are manuscript, memorized, impromptu, and extemporaneous speaking.

Manuscript Speaking: It's All There in Black and White

Speakers often refer to "writing their speeches." In my lifetime, I have delivered thousands of speeches. No more than a handful were written word for word. Remember that oral and written styles have distinct differences. It is very difficult to write

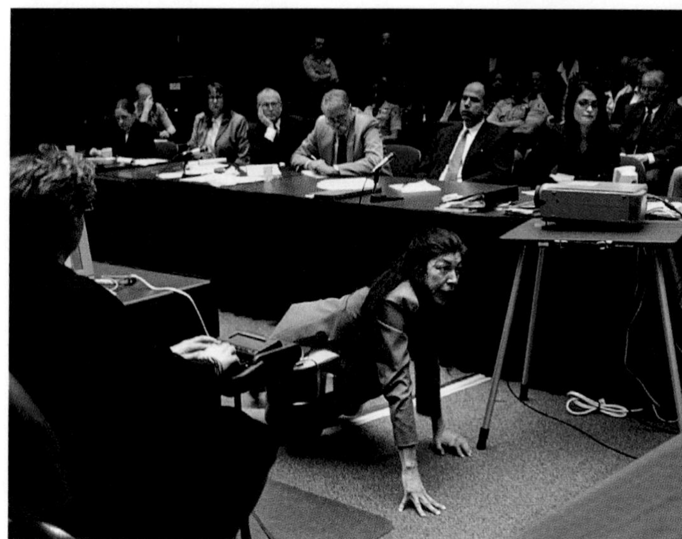

Lawyer Nedra Ruiz's presentation was vivid and memorable during her animated defense in a California dog mauling trial. Nevertheless, it was so extreme, including crawling like a dog, that she was more distracting than effective.

a speech for oral presentation that won't sound like an essay read to an audience. I often tell my students that I do not have to look at a speaker to know immediately that the speaker is reading his or her speech. A read manuscript has a distinct sound and rhythm. Effective speeches are not merely spoken essays. An essay read to an audience can sound stilted and overly formal.

A manuscript speech may be an appropriate method of delivery in certain situations. If you must be scrupulously precise in your phrasing for fear of being legally encumbered or causing offense, then a manuscript may be necessary. Political candidates spend millions of dollars for television and radio ads. They cannot tolerate mistakes in phrasing or wordy speeches. Their speeches are precisely written and delivered from a teleprompter—an electronic device that scrolls a manuscript speech, line by line, for the speaker to read while looking right at the audience or the television camera. A television audience does not see the manuscript scrolling in front of the speaker. Most speakers, however, neither need a teleprompter nor have access to one.

It takes extensive practice to present a manuscript speech effectively. A chief drawback of manuscript speaking is that the speaker will appear too scripted, and ownership of his or her ideas becomes suspect. On February 19, 2010, Tiger Woods presented a carefully scripted apology to his fans, colleagues, sponsors, employees, and family members for cheating on his wife with multiple sex partners. One columnist called it "an infomercial" and a "weirdly scripted and strangely robotic appearance" that "had all the soul of one of his prepared releases" and "looked like a bad Saturday Night Live skit" (Dahlberg, 2010, p. C3). Another said that Woods "stayed too on script" and that "it was as awkward to watch as it must have been painfully uncomfortable for him to deliver" (Inman, 2010, p. 1D).

Another drawback is that the speaker usually gets buried in the manuscript and fails to establish eye contact with an audience. Reading to an audience can disconnect the speaker from listeners. John McCain won the New Hampshire presidential primary on January 8, 2008. His victory speech, however, was tarnished badly by a lackluster performance that was ridiculed by political pundits. Katrina vanden Heuvel on MSNBC criticized McCain for reading his speech. Joe Scarborough remarked, "If this is your introduction to America in 2008, do not have your head looking straight down into a speech." Another drawback of a manuscript speech is that digressions from the prepared manuscript are difficult to make smoothly, yet such changes may be critical if the audience does not respond well to a portion of the speech. Generally, manuscript speaking should be left to professional speakers who have substantial experience using this delivery method.

Memorized Speaking: Memory, Don't Fail Me Now

Some speakers attempt to memorize their speeches. A short toast at a wedding, a brief acceptance speech at an awards ceremony, or a few key lines in a lengthy speech may benefit from memorization, especially if what you memorize is emotionally touching or humorous (no one wants the punch line of a joke to be read). Memorizing a speech of five minutes or more, however, is a bit like stapling oatmeal to a ceiling—it takes lots of energy, it's usually pointless, and it probably won't stick anyway.

It's too likely that you'll forget portions of your speech; your script won't stick in your mind. Have you ever grown frustrated or felt uncomfortable when someone tries to remember a joke or funny story and keeps forgetting important details, and then, following an agonizing oral search for the correct version ("Oh wait, that's not the way it goes . . . "), he or she finally flubs the punch line? Forgetting can be painful for listeners and speaker alike. Awkward silences while you desperately attempt to remember the next sentence in your speech can be embarrassing. Also, making a memorized speech sound natural, not artificial and robotic, requires considerable experience (those who have acted on stage know this well).

Impromptu Speaking: Off-the-Cuff Presentations

An **impromptu speech** is one delivered without preparation, or so it seems. You are asked to respond to a previous speaker without warning or to say a few words on a subject without advance notice. Although impromptu speeches can be challenging, a few simple guidelines can help.

First, *anticipate impromptu speaking.* If you have any inkling that you might be called on to give a short speech on a subject, begin preparing your remarks. Don't wait until you are put on the spot.

Second, *draw on your life experience and knowledge for the substance of your remarks.* F. E. Smith once remarked, "Winston Churchill has devoted the best years of his life to preparing his impromptu speeches." Churchill had clarified his ideas and points of view in his mind. When called on to speak in an impromptu fashion, he was already prepared. Life experience is preparation for impromptu speaking. Draw from that experience.

Third, *formulate a simple outline for an impromptu speech.* Begin with a short opening attention strategy—a relevant story, a humorous quip you've used successfully on other occasions, or a clever quotation you've memorized. State your point of view or the theme for your remarks. Then quickly identify two or three short points that you will address. Finally, summarize briefly what you said. You are not expected to provide substantial supporting material for your points during an impromptu speech, but if you have some facts and figures memorized, you will impress your audience with your ready knowledge. Impromptu speaking is usually less formal than a standard speech, so be conversational in tone and presentation.

Extemporaneous Speaking: The Virtues of an Outline

Most public speaking classes stress extemporaneous speaking, usually called "extemp" speaking for short. An **extemp speech** is delivered from a prepared outline or notes. There are several advantages to extemp speaking. First, even though fully prepared in advance, *an extemp speech sounds spontaneous* because the speaker does not read from a manuscript but instead glances at an outline or notes, then puts his or her thoughts into words on the spot. In this sense, extemp speaking falls between impromptu and manuscript speaking. It sounds impromptu and has the detail and substance of a manuscript speech without being either.

Second, *extemp speaking permits greater eye contact with the audience.* The speaker isn't buried in a manuscript, head down. Of course, an outline can take on the form of a manuscript if it is too detailed. It is possible to write an entire speech, word for word, on a three-by-five index card. In such cases, the manuscript is merely tiny. Typically, a speaker prepares an extemp speech by constructing an outline composed of full sentences. The speaker delivers the speech, however, from an abbreviated outline composed of simple words or phrases that trigger complete thoughts.

Third, *extemp speaking allows the speaker to respond to audience feedback as it occurs.* You can adjust to the moment-by-moment changes in audience reactions much more so than with manuscript or memorized speeches.

The one drawback of extemp speaking is that learning to speak from notes or an outline takes practice. There is no substitute for practicing extemp speaking. Once you learn how to do it, you may never want to use any other method of delivery.

Here is one final note: *delivery should match the context for your speech.* A eulogy calls for a dignified, formal delivery. The speaker usually limits body movements and keeps his or her voice toned down as a sign of respect. A motivational speech, however, requires a lively, enthusiastic delivery. Your voice may be loud, body movements dramatic, eye contact intense, and facial movements expressive. During a motivational speech, the podium is usually moved aside or ignored, and the speaker moves back and forth across a stage or even moves into the audience. An after-dinner speech or "roast" calls for a lively, comic delivery. Facial expressions consist mostly of smiles, gestures may be gross or exaggerated, and a speaker's voice may be loud, even abrasive, for effect. Match your delivery to the speech context.

Summary

THE substance of your speech, no matter how well prepared, will make little difference to an audience if presented poorly. Speech anxiety can significantly interfere with competent presentation. Addressing this potential problem is critical. Gaining and maintaining the attention of your audience throughout your speech increase the likelihood that your carefully prepared speech will resonate with listeners. An effective introduction gets your speech off to a good start, and an effective conclusion ends it with a bang. Style should be clear, precise, and vivid. Delivery should incorporate strong eye contact, vocal variety, moderate body movements, and be free of distracting mannerisms. Extemporaneous speaking is the type of delivery to master for most occasions.

Quizzes Without Consequences

Did you understand all the material in this chapter? Test your knowledge before your exam!

Go to the companion website at www.oup.com/us/rothwell, click on the Student Resources for each chapter, and take the Quizzes Without Consequences.

Film School Case Studies

And Justice for All (1979). Dark Comedy/Drama; R

Al Pacino delivers a very famous speech ("You're out of order") in a courtroom. Analyze his style and delivery for appropriateness and effectiveness.

Malcolm X (1992). Historical Drama; PG-13

Denzel Washington plays Malcolm X in this Oscar-worthy performance. Analyze the numerous public speeches delivered by Washington for both style and delivery. Do they match well with his varied audiences?

The King's Speech (2010). Drama; PG-13

This is the story of King George VI of Great Britain, played by Oscar-winning actor Colin Furth, who suffered terribly from a pronounced stutter. Forced to give numerous speeches, especially upon his ascension to the throne, he was helped by a speech therapist, played by Geoffrey Rush. Examine the depiction of the king's speech anxiety for symptoms of fight-or-flight and analyze the methods of treatment offered by the therapist.

To Kill a Mockingbird (1962). Drama; Not rated

Gregory Peck's character is a lawyer in a small southern town who defends a black man accused of raping a white girl. Peck earned an Oscar for his touching performance. Analyze the lengthy speech delivered to the jury for its style and delivery. Contrast the style and delivery with the Al Pacino character in *And Justice for All.*

CHAPTER 14

Chapter Outline

PART 4

Informative Speaking

TWO THEORISTS SPEAK METAPHORICALLY of surfing, swimming, and drowning in information to underline the need to manage it effectively (Crawford & Gorman, 1996). Although discussing information in the context of electronic technology, their metaphors seem applicable to informative speaking. An informative speech that presents too little information is unsatisfying to an audience. This is analogous to surfing, merely skimming the top of a subject without delving deeply. Presenting too much information is analogous to drowning, swamping an audience in a tidal wave of information too voluminous to appreciate or comprehend. An informative speech works best when the speaker swims in the information, finding the right balance between too little and too much information for the audience.

By the end of this chapter, you should be able to:

1. Distinguish between informative and persuasive speaking.
2. Explain the five different types of informative speeches.
3. Use guidelines and strategies to deliver a competent informative speech.
4. Use visual aids to enhance your informative speeches and other types of speeches as well.

Everywhere you look, informative speaking occurs. Infomercials are pervasive on the mass media. YouTube and other Internet sites provide access to all manner of informative speeches from education and industry, some great (see especially www.Ted.com) and some not so great. Teachers spend the bulk of their time in the classroom speaking informatively. Managers present information at meetings. Military officers give briefings. Religious leaders speak informatively when interpreting religious doctrines and organizing fund drives, charitable activities, and special events. Students give informative presentations in a wide variety of courses and disciplines. Competent informative speaking is a valuable skill.

The principal purpose of this chapter is to explain how you construct and present a competent informative speech.

Distinguishing Informative from Persuasive Speaking

The overriding difference between an informative and persuasive speech is your general purpose. *The general purpose of an informative speech is to teach your audience something new, interesting, and useful.* You want your listeners to learn. *The general purpose of a persuasive speech is to convince your listeners to change their viewpoint and behavior.* You want your listeners to think and act differently.

Don't think of informative and persuasive speeches as dichotomous. They differ more by degree than in kind. A teacher, for example, is primarily interested in informing students, but controversial issues arise and advocacy of a particular theory or perspective may occur. So teaching isn't purely informative. Persuasive speeches also inform. You often have to teach your audience about the magnitude of a problem that listeners may not have been aware of before advocating solutions. Nevertheless, two specific distinctions between informative and persuasive speeches can help you understand where a speech falls on the informative-persuasive continuum.

Noncontroversial Information: Staying Neutral

Informative speeches do not usually stir disagreement and dissension. It's hard to imagine any audience getting worked into a froth if you offered study tips to improve students' test scores or ways to avoid the common cold as long as the information is accurate. Some information, however, has the potential to ignite disagreement without prompting. For example, the *New England Journal of Medicine* has reported that more money each year is spent out of pocket (not covered by insurance) on alternative medical therapies than on traditional medical treatments. This mere fact can upset those who view alternative therapies as massively inferior to traditional medicine.

Nevertheless, presenting all relevant sides on an issue in a neutral fashion, as most journalists report the news, focuses on teaching something new, interesting, or useful, not on advocating a specific point of view. "I've explained three ways that you can build your finances for the future. Whichever one you choose, know that there is a strong financial future awaiting you" doesn't advocate; it informs. You aren't being told which choice to make. If, however, conclusions are drawn regarding which side is correct after weighing the evidence and a specific choice is advocated, then you are trying to persuade.

Precursor to Persuasion: No Call to Action

An informative speech may arouse your listeners' concern on a subject. This concern may trigger a desire to correct a problem. Your informative speech may act as a precursor, or steppingstone, to a subsequent persuasive speech advocating strong action. If you hear a speech informing you of the pros and cons of hybrid cars, you might be encouraged without any prompting from the speaker to investigate such cars further or even to buy one. If a speaker relates a personal story about the rewards he or she experiences teaching young children, you might begin to consider teaching as a profession, even though the speaker never makes such an appeal.

In some cases, you may be presenting interesting information to your audience without connecting it to any particular issue, but someone in the audience might. For example, do you know who Otis Blackwell was? He died May 6, 2002, at the age of 70. Otis Blackwell was credited with writing more than 1,000 songs that were recorded by such international stars as Elvis Presley, Ray Charles, Billy Joel, The Who, Otis Redding, James Taylor, Peggy Lee, and Jerry Lee Lewis (Edwards, 2002). His songs sold more than 185 million copies. Providing further details about the life of this remarkable African American talent would be an interesting informative speech. Someone listening to such a speech, however, might wonder why mainstream America is mostly oblivious that Blackwell ever lived. A persuasive speech that advocates teaching more African American history to American college students might be triggered by an informative speech on Otis Blackwell.

If you are given an assignment by your teacher to present an informative speech to the class, are told by your boss to make a report to a committee or group, or are asked to explain a new software package to novice computer users, remember that your focus will be on teaching, not convincing your listeners. The more neutral and even-handed your presentation, the more essentially informative it is. When you take a firm stand, present only one side without critique, or advocate a change in behavior from your listeners, you have moved into persuasive territory.

The competent public speaker recognizes when persuasion is appropriate and when the specific context calls for a presentation more informative in nature. When teachers use the classroom as a platform for personal advocacy, they may step over the not always clear line between informative and persuasive speaking. Advocacy on issues directly relevant to the teaching role—such as advocating the scientific method as a means of critical thinking—is appropriate. Advocacy of "correct" political points of view, however, can run dangerously close to proselytizing, or converting the "unbelievers," not teaching. Again, *it can be a blurry line that separates informative from persuasive speeches.*

Types of Informative Speeches

The issue of what constitutes an informative speech becomes clearer by looking at different types. There is some overlap between the types, but each one has its own unique qualities.

Reports: Facts in Brief

A report is usually a brief informative presentation that fulfills a class assignment, updates a committee about work performed by a subcommittee, reveals the results of a study, provides recent findings, or identifies the latest developments in a current situation of interest. Students give reports in classes and during meetings of student government. Scientists give reports on research results. Press secretaries give reports, or briefings, to members of the mass media. Military officers give briefings to fellow officers and to the press.

Reports need to be clearly presented. Make sure you have your facts straight and that all information presented is accurate. Complex, detailed information should be summarized succinctly. Present the main points and the most significant specifics. Don't get lost in minutia.

Explanations: Deeper Understanding

Unlike a simple report which merely states the facts to an audience that often is already familiar with the topic (press corps at a presidential press conference), speeches that seek to explain are concerned with advancing deep understanding of complex concepts, processes, events, objects, and issues for listeners who are typically unfamiliar with the material presented. For example, Gary Lauder gave a six-minute lecture on the advantages of replacing Stop or Yield signs at intersections with a "Take Turns" sign and replacing standard intersections with traffic circles (http://www.ted.com/talks/gary_lauder_s_new_traffic_sign_take_turns.html). Richard St. John gave a three-minute, amusing lecture on "The 8 Secrets of Success," which included transforming yourself from a workaholic to a "workafrolic" (having fun) (see this at: http://www.ted.com/talks/richard_st_john_s_8_secrets_of_success.html).

The lecture is a common example of informative speeches that explain. Students are most familiar with this type of informative speech, having heard hundreds of lectures from numerous instructors. Unlike reports that typically run about 15 minutes or fewer, lectures often last an hour or more. Also unlike most reports, lectures work best when they are highly entertaining. Attention strategies discussed extensively in Chapter 13 are extremely important to the success of a lecture. Maintaining the attention of a sometimes captive audience for long periods of time is a huge challenge. Celebrities, famous authors, politicians, consultants, and experts of all types use the lecture platform to share ideas.

Demonstrations: Acting Out

A demonstration is an informative speech that shows the audience how to use an object or perform a specific activity. Dance teachers demonstrate dance steps while explaining how best to perform the steps. Cooking and home improvement television programs are essentially demonstration speeches. Demonstration speeches require the speaker to show the physical object or

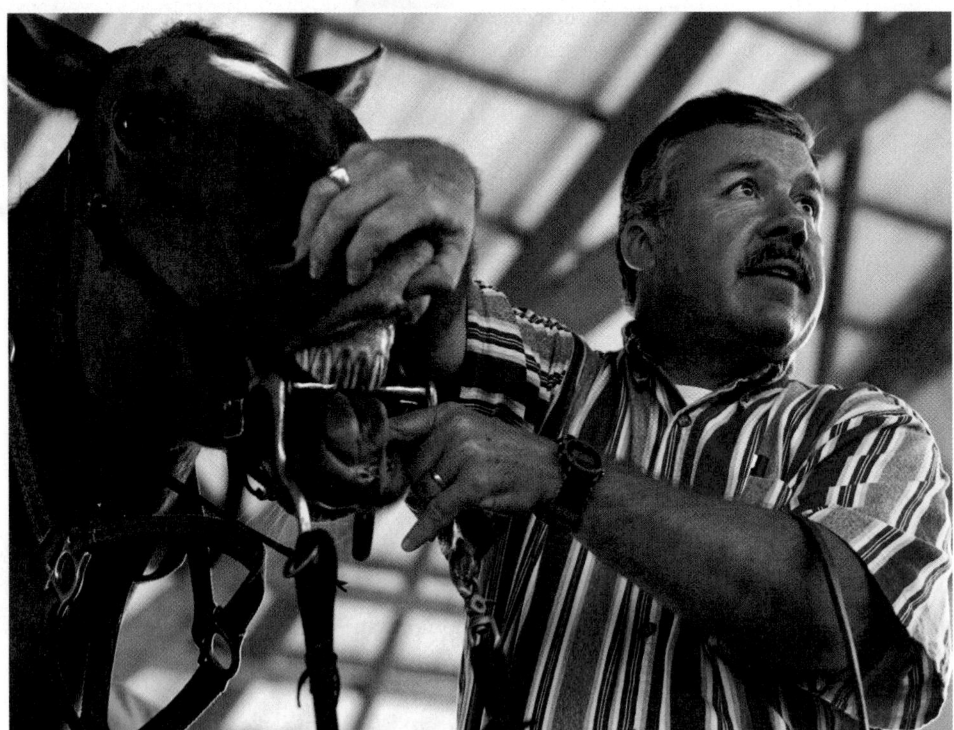

A live animal may be an effective visual aid for a demonstration speech, but animals can be very difficult to control and are mostly impractical for classroom demonstrations.

to display the activity for the audience. A demonstration is not a mere description of objects or activities. If you are going to give a speech on martial arts, show the audience specific movements and techniques; don't just ask your audience to imagine them. A speech on how card tricks and magic are performed must demonstrate the trick slowly and clearly so the audience can understand.

Neuroanatomist Dr. Jill Bolte Taylor suffered a severe stroke and told her story at a TED lecture entitled *My Stroke of Insight* (also the title of her book).

Narratives: Storytelling

One morning, a blood vessel burst in neuroanatomist Jill Bolte Taylor's brain. She was 37 years old. As a brain scientist, she realized she had a rare opportunity to witness her own stroke and understand what was happening while it occurred: movement, speech, memory, self-awareness all became impaired. As she observed, "How many brain scientists have been able to study the brain from the inside out? I've gotten as much out of this experience of losing my left mind as I have in my entire academic career" (quoted in "Jill Bolte Taylor," 2008). She spent eight years recovering her ability to walk, talk, and think. She tells her amazing story of what it was like experiencing a stroke and what it took to recover from it in a best-selling book entitled *My Stroke of Insight: A Brain Scientist's Personal Journey*. She also gave an 18-minute narrative presentation at the TED (Technology, Entertainment, Design) conference in Monterey, California, on February 27, 2008, explaining what her stroke was like and what insights she learned. Her story is intensely moving. By the conclusion, she is in tears and so are many in the audience. It became one of the top 10 presentations for the TED organization (see "Jill Bolte Taylor's Stroke of Insight" at www.TED.com).

A story well told such as Dr. Taylor's fascinating journey can be thoroughly engaging. Taylor's speech is highly engaging. She shows a real human brain with spinal cord attached (a captivating visual aid), and she provides insights about your own brain. Narratives may be about you or about other people. Instructors may give a short presentation at the beginning of a course informing students about their number of years spent teaching, where teaching occurred, the joys and challenges of teaching, and prospects for teaching in the future. Some also relate really dumb things tried in the classroom that went embarrassingly wrong, which can make a professor seem more human and approachable. Narratives may be historical ("The Struggles of Thurgood Marshall"), personal ("My Life as a Surgeon"), self-disclosing ("I Once Lived a Life of Drug Addiction"), or merely amusing ("What It's Like Being a Technophobe"). Narratives are most effective when they entertain an audience.

Comparisons: Pros and Cons

Some informative speeches explain serious problems that exist and then compare a variety of potential solutions without taking a stand on any of the remedies offered. For example, the increasing prices of college textbooks is a recognized national problem. There are several possible solutions: increasing the availability of used books, using multiple-source public domain materials, establishing textbook rental programs, urging professors to adopt only textbooks that have minimal ancillaries (websites, CDs, etc.), discouraging publishers from producing new editions sooner than every three or four years, encouraging customized versions of textbooks, and offering more "stripped down" versions of standard textbooks that can be priced more cheaply than more elaborate versions. Each of these solutions has pros and cons. For instance, expanding the availability of used books means more students can purchase textbooks at three-quarters the cost of a new textbook ($75 used compared to $100 new), but as the availability of used books increases, textbook publishers are pressured to increase the cost of new versions of textbooks to counter losses engendered by used books. Presenting the positives and negatives of various solutions without taking a stand on any of them is structured as an informative speech. You leave it to the audience to make choices based on a balanced presentation of possible remedies for a problem.

These five types of informative speeches can overlap. A report may occasionally veer into a demonstration when listeners don't appear to understand what is reported. A teacher typically lectures for a majority of a class period, but the teacher may do demonstrations to add variety and make a point more memorable and meaningful. I have used a fairly lengthy demonstration of a polygraph, or lie detector machine, with student volunteers, to drive home several points related to nonverbal communication and connotative meaning related to words. It never fails to engender interest, even fascination, from the class. Years later, students tell me they still remember that particular demonstration and what it showed.

Guidelines for Competent Informative Speaking

In general, informative speeches work best when the information presented is clear, accurate, and interesting instead of opaque, wrong, and boring. Thus, review Chapters 12 and 13 for tips on outlining and organizing, reasoning and the use of evidence, and attention. In this section, I provide additional tips for presenting effective informative speeches.

Inform: Tell Us What We Don't Know

An informative speech, first and foremost, must tell your audience something it doesn't already know. Your first guideline, and seemingly the most obvious, is to provide new information to your listeners. I say seemingly obvious because I've sat through far too many "informative" presentations that never told me a thing I didn't know previously, and in some cases, the speaker should have known that the points made were trivial and lacked any insight. You don't want your listeners saying after your presentation, "I didn't learn a thing." This doesn't mean that everything you present must be new information, but the emphasis should be on providing that which is not widely known.

Adapt: Audience Analysis

How do you know whether your informative speech goes beyond what your listeners already know? That requires an analysis of your audience (see Chapter 12). If the topic choice is at your discretion, then choose what will likely interest your listeners and is well suited to their knowledge, concerns, and expectations. If the subject of your speech is too high level, complex, and abstract for the educational level of your audience, then you've chosen poorly. Presenting

Info. structure

information on systems theory or thermodynamics won't resonate with very young audiences because the information is well over their heads. Set theory in mathematics will probably baffle a lot of adult audiences. If the choice is not up to you and the topic is very high level, complex, and abstract (a professor teaching quantum physics to students), your challenge is to explain clearly each facet of your subject using multiple examples, personal stories, visual aids, metaphors, analogies, and demonstrations to clarify difficult material. Albert Einstein, when faced with explaining his immensely complex theory of relativity to laypeople, offered this as a starting point: "When you sit with a nice girl for two hours you think it's only a minute. But when you sit on a hot stove for a minute you think it's two hours. That's relativity" (quoted in "Famous Quotes," 2009). Remember that oral style requires simpler language than written style. Strive for language simplicity as discussed in Chapter 13, and avoid highly complex language that may confuse even a well-educated audience.

If your subject is fairly simple and you're addressing an educated audience, be careful not to condescend to your listeners. Acting as though they are third graders is patronizing and will insult them. If your audience is already knowledgeable about your subject, more difficult material can be included earlier and with less need to elaborate extensively.

Organize Carefully: Clarity Is Critical

Because the primary purpose of an informative speech is to teach, organization of the speech is vitally important. Any of the standard organizational patterns discussed in Chapter 12 can work well depending on your topic and purpose statement. Several additional organizational tips are also useful.

Basic Structure: The Cultural Challenge

The basic structure of most speeches, but especially informative ones, divides the speech into an introduction, body, and conclusion. The introduction grabs attention, explains the significance of the topic to the audience, provides a clear purpose statement, and previews the main points of the speech. The body of the speech, which takes the most time to present, develops the main points previewed in the introduction. The conclusion provides a quick summary of the main points, often makes reference to the introduction, and offers a memorable finish.

This basic structure may seem unusual to individuals from cultures or co-cultures accustomed to high-context communication patterns. In high-context cultures (see Chapter 3), speakers typically do not provide such explicit organization when communicating messages to audiences. A purpose statement and main points won't normally be precisely stated. Listeners are expected to understand the principal message of a speech from the context. Previous knowledge about the speaker and the message helps listeners interpret meaning.

The United States, however, is a low-context culture (see Chapter 3). There is a general expectation that messages will be communicated explicitly and that ambiguity will be kept to a minimum. Because of this prevailing expectation, individuals from high-context cultures will be more effective public speakers in the United States if they organize their speeches explicitly, fulfilling standard requirements for a competent introduction, body, and conclusion. Explicit organization by a speaker can also help listeners from cultures whose native language is not English to understand the speaker's message.

Clarify Key Terms: Definitions

Key terms, especially unfamiliar or technical ones, should be defined clearly and precisely. For example, do you know what hemochromatosis is? How about endocrine disruptors? Jennifer Bazil (1997), a student at West Chester University, gave a speech on hemochromatosis. She defined the term, unfamiliar to most listeners, in this way: "Hemochromatosis is a genetic blood disorder resulting in iron overload. It begins to take effect when an error in the metabolic system causes people to absorb too much iron from their diet" (p. 119).

Adam Childers (1997), a student at the University of Oklahoma, does an equally effective job when he defines *endocrine disruptors* as "human-made chemicals that have an uncanny ability to mimic some of the human body's most powerful hormones" (p. 103). Even though most people have a passing familiarity with the term *hormone*, many may have a difficult time giving a precise definition. Childers anticipates this and defines hormones as "little more than messengers of the endocrine system. They are released by the pituitary gland, and then they circulate throughout the body, telling different cells what to do. For example, the hormone adrenaline tells our heart when to beat faster" (p. 104). This is a nice definition of hormones. You can picture what hormones do in the body.

Make Connections: Signposts and Transitions

Signposts and transitions both have the same purpose. They guide the listener during a speech. Although not unique to informative speeches, signposts and transitions are extremely important when the principal aim is to help listeners understand. They may be especially helpful to listeners whose native language is other than English. **Signposts** are organizational markers that indicate the structure of a speech and notify listeners that a particular point is about to be addressed. **Transitions** connect what was said with what will be said. They are bridges between points. Box 14-1 offers examples of typical signposts and transitions.

Clarifying as You Go: Internal Summaries

When you say "summary," most people think of a final wrap-up to a speech or essay. There is another type, however, called an internal summary, which is useful for both informative and persuasive speeches. An **internal summary** restates a key point in a speech. It occurs in the body of the speech, not in the conclusion. Internal summaries help listeners follow the sequence of ideas, connecting the dots so the picture drawn by the speaker comes into focus. "As you can now see, protecting homes from wildfires begins with clearing a defensible space

BOX 14.1 Developing Communication Competence

EXAMPLES OF SIGNPOSTS AND TRANSITIONS

Signposts

My first point is	The key points are
My second point is	There are two ways
There are three points to explore	My final point is

Transitions

So what does this mean?	However
For example	Why should we care?
Nevertheless	Along the same lines
In summary	Therefore
Consequently	Granted
Conversely	But

Check papers you have written for classes and see if you can identify signposts and transitions. It will help you recognize each. Would your papers have been better organized with more transitions and signposts?

around each home" is an example of an internal summary. It signals that a main point has concluded and suggests a new point is about to be addressed. "Closely related to this, a second way to protect homes from wildfires . . ." is a transitional statement with a signpost that both follow the internal summary.

Supporting Materials Revisited: Follow the Rules

Much has been said already in Chapter 12 about using supporting materials competently. This section covers how to use supporting materials specifically in an informative speech. This is a reminder to review the material in Chapter 12 on fallacies. No matter how interesting your informative speech might be, presenting misinformation to your audience is not competent public speaking. Your information should be credible, relevant, and sufficient.

Choose Interesting Supporting Materials: Counteracting Boredom

Learning doesn't usually occur when listeners are uninterested in the subject matter. This doesn't mean substituting a colorful but weak supporting material for a strong but bland one. Your first consideration when choosing supporting materials should be their credibility and strength. Nevertheless, a strong, credible, but interesting supporting material is the best of all choices. Startling statistics, dramatic examples, and clever quotations by experts add interest to a speech that could become tiresome if supporting materials are dull and lifeless. Use the strategies explained in Chapter 13 for effective use of supporting materials to enliven an informative speech (see complete example in Box 14-2).

Abbreviate Source Citations: Brief Reference Reminders

The initial citation of a source should be complete, but subsequent references to the same source can be abbreviated to avoid tedious repetition, unless the abbreviation might cause confusion (e.g., two articles from the same magazine). Abby Norman (2006), a student at Ball State University, abbreviates this way: "On the governmental level, the previously cited *Humanist* article advocates . . ." (p. 18). Buey Ruet (2006) of the University of Nebraska at Lincoln offers this form of abbreviating a source: "The *Economist* further explains that . . ." (p. 50).

Avoid Information Overload: Don't Drown in Data

The ready availability of huge quantities of information because of computer technologies can tempt a speaker to provide way too much detail and complexity in a speech. Don't make your speech a tedious "data dump." Know when to quit. Preparation and practice are essential. Prepare a well-organized informative speech, then practice the speech and *time it precisely* before giving it. Timing your speech will immediately indicate whether you have provided too much information for the time allotted. Be careful not to offer needless details. Ask yourself, "Does my audience really need to know this?"

Tell Your Story Well: Narrative Tips

Stories can be short vignettes or lengthy detailed narratives. Randy Pausch, a 47-year-old Carnegie Mellon University computer science professor who contracted pancreatic cancer in 2007, gave a lecture at his university on September 18, 2007, to a crowd of 500 students, faculty, and friends. In a 75-minute presentation, Pausch told many stories about his life, each relating to his central idea about achieving his childhood dreams. His stories were humorous, poignant, and very entertaining. Although he knew he was dying, he conducted himself as though he were perfectly healthy, at one moment dropping to the floor and doing pushups both one- and two-handed. When he finished his final lecture, his audience gave him a prolonged, standing ovation. The video of his lecture was seen by millions on YouTube, and it became a book entitled *The Last Lecture*.

How do you tell an effective story when giving a public speech (see Collins

BOX 14.2 Developing Communication Competence

OUTLINE AND TEXT OF AN INFORMATIVE SPEECH

Here is an outline and the text of an informative speech. Each incorporates the suggestions offered for constructing a competent informative speech.

Introduction

I. *Attention strategy:* Use startling examples.
   A. Describe the Spanish flu pandemic of 1918–1919.
   B. Refer to the 1957 Asian flu pandemic and 70,000 deaths.
   C. Mention the 1968 Hong Kong flu pandemic.
   D. Note the 1976 scare, the 2003 avian flu concern.
   E. Mention the 2009 swine flu pandemic.

II. *Significance:* We should all be concerned about yearly flu viruses for two reasons.
   A. A serious flu epidemic could strike again.
   B. Everyone is susceptible to deadly flu viruses each year.

III. *Central idea:* Flu is a serious problem, but there are effective ways to prevent contracting this yearly disease.

IV. *Purpose statement:* To inform my audience about ways to prevent contracting the flu.

V. *Preview:* Three main points will be discussed.
   A. Flu viruses pose serious health hazards to all of us.
   B. Flu viruses are difficult to combat.
   C. There are several ways to prevent contracting the flu.

Body

I. Flu viruses pose serious health hazards to everyone.
   A. Flu viruses are killers.
      1. Seasonal flu deaths vary from 3,000 to 49,000 annually.
      2. The avian flu potentially could kill 81 million people worldwide.
   B. Flu viruses can make you very sick.
      1. Flu produces symptoms such as high fever, sore throat, aches, cough, and severe fatigue.
      2. "Stomach flu," however, is a misnomer.
   C. Flu viruses are highly contagious.
      1. Children easily catch the flu.
      2. Children infect adults.
      3. Adults spread flu to coworkers.

II. Flu viruses are difficult to combat.
   A. "Influenza" was thought to be the "influence" of the stars, making it exceedingly difficult to combat.
   B. There are many strains of flu, even in a single flu season.
      1. There are two types of flu: Types A and B.
      2. There were three strains of flu during the 2010–2011 flu season.
   C. Occasionally, a flu virus will mutate, causing a pandemic.

III. There are three primary ways to prevent contracting the flu.
   A. Stay generally healthy.
      1. Get exercise.

(continued)

BOX 14.2 *(Continued)*

2. Eat a healthy diet.
3. Avoid crowds during flu season.
4. Practice good hygiene.

B. Get a flu shot.

1. Flu shots are 70%–90% effective.
2. Flu shots could prevent 80% of deaths and serious complications if everyone got immunized.
3. Flu shots cannot cause the flu.

C. Take an antiviral prescription drug.

1. Antiviral drugs are almost as effective as vaccines.
2. An antiviral drug is an effective option for those who fear shots or have allergic reactions to eggs.

Conclusion

I. Provide summary of main points.

A. Flu viruses can be hazardous to humans.
B. Combating flu viruses can be difficult.
C. Flu viruses can be prevented.

II. Make reference to the introductory example of Spanish flu.

III. Give a memorable finish by making a reference to this annual plague.

Bibliography

Advisory Committee on Immunization Practices. (2002, May 5). Recommendations of the Advisory Committee on Immunization Practices (ACIP). [Online]. Available at: http://www.cdc.gov/mmwr/preview/mmwrhtml/rr5103a1.html

Centers for Disease Control. (2006, January 11). Flu vaccine effectiveness: Questions and answers for health professionals. [Online]. Available at: www.cdc.gov/flu/professionals/vaccination/effectivenessqa.htm

Centers for Disease Control. (2007, August 7). Community measures prevent deaths during pandemic, new study finds. [Online]. Available at: http://www.cdc.gov/od/oc/media/pressrel/2007/r070807.htm

Centers for Disease Control. (2010, August 27). Estimates of deaths associated with seasonal influenza—United States, 1976-2007. [Online]. Available at: http://www.cdc.gov/mmwr/preview/mmwrhtml/mm5933a1.htm?s_cid=mm5933a1_e%0d%0a

Centers for Disease Control. (2011, February 8). Reconstruction of the 1918 influenza pandemic virus. [Online]. Available at: http://www.cdc.gov/flu/about/qa/1918flupandemic.htm

Centers for Disease Control. (2011, February 8). The nasal-spray flu vaccine (live attenuated influenza vaccine [LAIV]. [Online]. Available at: http://www.cdc.gov/flu/about/qa/nasalspray.htm

Centers for Disease Control. (2011, February 9). What you should know about flu antiviral drugs. [Online]. Available at: www.cdc.gov/flu/antivirals/whatyoushould.htm

Flu pandemic could kill up to 81 million people. (December 21, 2006). *MSNBC*. [Online]. Available at: www.msnbc.com/id/16313464/print/1/displaymode/1098/

Garrett, L. (1994). *The coming plague: Newly emerging diseases in a world out of balance*. New York: Penguin Books.

Haney, D. (1998, November 8). Researchers breaking new ground on flu front. *San Jose Mercury News*, p. 10A.

Kolata, G. (1999). *Flu: The story of the Great Influenza Pandemic of 1918 and the search for the virus that caused it*. New York: Farrar, Straus & Giroux.

(continued)

BOX 14.2 *(Continued)*

National Institutes of Health. (May 8, 2007). Commentary discusses why predicting the next influenza pandemic is difficult and how scientists can best prepare. [Online]. Available at: www3.niaid.nih.gov/news/newsrelease/2007/predictflu.htm

U.S. Department of Health & Human Services. (June 5, 2007). *General information*. [Online]. Available at: www.pandemicflu.gov/general/index.html

U.S. lab-verified swine flu infections. (2011, April 27). [Online]. Available at: http://www.flucount.org/

THE ANNUAL PLAGUE

(Prepared summer 2011—application of text material in brackets)

It killed 50 million people worldwide and sickened 1 billion more, half the world's population at the time, according to a February 8, 2011, report from the Centers for Disease Control. [CREDIBLE SOURCE] The CDC further notes that half a million Americans died of the disease in a single year, a greater loss of life than Americans suffered in all of the wars in the 20th century combined. [USE OF STARTLING STATISTICS GAINS ATTENTION; COMPARISON MAKES STATISTIC CONCRETE] According to Laurie Garrett, health and science writer for *Newsday* and the award-winning author of the 1994 book *The Coming Plague*, the virus was so severe that some died from it within one day, a few within hours. Women who boarded the New York subway at Coney Island, feeling only mild fatigue, were found dead when the subway pulled into Columbus Circle 45 minutes later. [VIVID, REAL EXAMPLE MAKES STATISTICS MORE CONCRETE AND PROVOKES STRONG, MEMORABLE IMAGE] This lethal disease began in Europe and spread to every corner of the globe. Almost 20% of the population of western Samoa died from the illness, and entire Inuit villages in isolated parts of Alaska were wiped out.

What was this killer disease? [TRANSITION] The Black Death of the 14th century revisiting the human species? Some biological warfare agent? Cholera, smallpox, or diphtheria? [RHETORICAL QUESTIONS INVOLVE AUDIENCE, CREATE CURIOSITY] None of these were the cause of this massive loss of life. The global killer was the flu! [STARTLING STATEMENT FOR MOST LISTENERS] That's right, the so-called Spanish flu of 1918-1919 caused this pandemic, or worldwide epidemic. According to Gina Kolata, science reporter for *The New York Times* and author of the 1999 book *Flu*, victims of this disease suffered agonizing deaths from high fever and fluid that filled their lungs, causing them to drown in their own juices. [VIVID DESCRIPTION KEEPS ATTENTION]

In 1957, a flu pandemic struck again. The U.S. Department of Health and Human Services website at pandemicflu.gov noted that 70,000 Americans died from the Asian flu, and 2 million fatalities occurred worldwide. The same source noted that in 1968, yet another flu pandemic, the Hong Kong flu, felled the human population. The Hong Kong flu hit the United States with sledgehammer force, sickening a huge portion of the country, killing 34,000 Americans and 1 million worldwide. [USE OF COLORFUL LANGUAGE; EXAMPLES MAKE A NOVEL OPENING TO GRAB ATTENTION] In 1976, the swine flu initially was feared to be a return of the Spanish flu, but it never developed into a serious illness. In 2003, the highly deadly H5N1 avian flu virus emerged, resulting in the deaths of more than 250 million birds in 55 countries by 2007 and, according to the World Health Organization website on August 31, 2007, the deaths of 199 people who came in close contact with infected birds. Finally, in 2009, the World Health Organization issued a global public health emergency warning of the H1N1 swine flu pandemic. According to an April 27, 2011, report from the flucount.org website, there were almost 11,000 confirmed deaths in the United States from the 2009 swine flu.

Why should we care about flu epidemics of the past? [RHETORICAL QUESTION INVOLVES AUDIENCE, MAKES TRANSITION] There are two good reasons to be interested in such notable events: (1) a flu pandemic could strike

(continued)

BOX 14.2 *(Continued)*

again, and (2) everyone in this room is a potential victim of a deadly flu virus. [SIGNIFICANCE OF TOPIC TO THE AUDIENCE IS ESTABLISHED] Since every person here probably has suffered from the flu at least once, you'll want to listen carefully as I inform you about ways to prevent contracting the flu. [CLEAR PURPOSE STATEMENT] I have three main points: I will show that flu viruses are a serious health hazard, that flu viruses are difficult to combat, and that there are several ways to prevent the flu. [CLEAR, CONCISE PREVIEW OF MAIN POINTS; PROBLEM-CAUSE-SOLUTION ORGANIZATIONAL PATTERN USED]

Let's begin by discussing the serious health hazards produced by a normal flu season. [SIGNPOSTING FIRST MAIN POINT] Even ordinary flu viruses that hit the United States every year between the months of October and April are killers. An August 27, 2010, report by the CDC notes that the number of deaths from seasonal flu can vary from a low of 3,000 to a high of 49,000. [STARTLING STATISTIC MAINTAINS ATTENTION AND INTEREST; USE OF CREDIBLE SOURCE FOR ALL STATISTICS] Annual flu, directly or indirectly, kills more people than AIDS. [COMPARISON MAKES STATISTIC CONCRETE] The threat of a not-so-normal flu season is real. The H5N1 avian flu might mutate and become more contagious to humans and emerge as a new pandemic. Medical researcher Chris Murray of Harvard University, in a December 20, 2006, issue of *Lancet* estimates that the avian flu could kill as many as 81 million people globally if this were to occur. No one knows if or when this could happen.

Most of you won't die from a common flu virus, but you may wish you were dead. [TRANSITION] Typical flu symptoms include high fever, sore throat, intense muscle aches, congestion, cough, and severe fatigue. My friend Terry once described how he feels when he gets the flu: "It's like being suddenly hit by a speeding car, catapulted into a concrete wall, roasted in an oven, then forced to participate in the Ironman marathon. Death, by comparison, seems pleasant." [VIVID USE OF SIMILES; INTENSITY USED TO MAINTAIN ATTENTION] Symptoms of flu can last from a few days to several weeks. The flu can often lead to severe complications, such as bronchitis and pneumonia, which may require hospitalization.

Although nausea sometimes occurs with the flu, the "stomach flu" is a misnomer. According to the Centers for Disease Control website, severe vomiting is rarely a prominent symptom of flu. [CREDIBLE SOURCE] The so-called stomach flu is actually a gastrointestinal illness caused by microorganisms that cause food poisoning. So if you're "tossing your cookies" or "clutching the porcelain throne," it is unlikely that you have contracted the flu. [VIVID SLANG TO KEEP ATTENTION]

In addition to the severity of its symptoms, [TRANSITION] flu is hazardous to humans because it is highly contagious. According to Daniel Haney, science reporter for the Associated Press, in a November 8, 1998, article in the *San Jose Mercury News*, young children are "flu incubators." [CREDIBLE SOURCE; DATE IS INCONSEQUENTIAL, SINCE PHENOMENON DOESN'T CHANGE] Haney continues, "In epidemiological terms, children are in the same category as ticks, rats, and mosquitoes: they are vectors of disease." [COLORFUL QUOTE] Day-care centers and classrooms are flu breeding grounds where sick children spew the virus everywhere by coughing, sneezing, and wiping their runny noses. [VIVID DESCRIPTION CREATES ATTENTION] Children also bring the flu home and infect adult parents, who pass it along to coworkers, and so it spreads throughout the population.

Naturally, [TRANSITION] we're all interested in why flu is an annual event about as welcome as flies, frogs, and the other plagues God visited upon the ancient Egyptians in the biblical story of the Exodus. This brings me to my second main point, [SIGNPOSTING MAIN POINT] which is that flu viruses are difficult to combat.

(continued)

BOX 14.2 *(Continued)*

Previous centuries produced many theories as to the cause of flu. Influenza, flu being the shortened version of this term, reflects the 15th-century astrological belief that the disease was caused by the "influence" of the stars. According to Laurie Garrett, previously cited, [*CREDIBLE SOURCE*] prominent American physicians of the time thought the 1918 Spanish flu might have been caused by nakedness, fish contaminated by Germans, dirt, dust, Chinese people, unclean pajamas, open windows, closed windows, old books, or "some cosmic influence." [*HISTORICAL EXAMPLES ARE NOVEL ATTENTION GETTER*]

Unlike our predecessors, [*TRANSITION*] we know that a virus causes flu, but a flu virus is difficult to combat. There are many strains, not just a single type. For instance, according to the CDC website (cdc.gov), there were three strains of flu in 2010–2011: A/California, A/Perth, and B/Brisbane. Flu strains are divided into A and B types and designated by the primary locale where the flu is first reported. There are many strains of flu because flu viruses continually change over time. Sometimes they change their genetic structure only slightly. This genetic "drift" means that your immune system's antibodies, produced to fight a previous flu, will not combat the disease as well when exposed to a slightly altered virus. Occasionally, a flu strain will mutate, altering the genetic structure of the virus so greatly that human antibodies from previous exposures to flu will be useless. Type A flu viruses are usually more serious than type B, partly because, according to the CDC, [*CREDIBLE SOURCE PREVIOUSLY CITED*] type A viruses genetically drift more rapidly than type B flu viruses. According to Laurie Garrett, [*CREDIBLE SOURCE*] the pandemics of 1918, 1957, and 1968 were mutated flu strains, and the CDC notes that the 2009 swine flu also was a mutated strain. [*REFERENCE TO EARLIER EXAMPLES PROVIDES CONTINUITY TO THE SPEECH; CREDIBLE SOURCE*] The changing structure of flu viruses and their many strains make finding a cure very challenging. [*INTERNAL SUMMARY OF MAIN POINT*]

So what can be done about the yearly flu and potential flu pandemics until a lasting cure is discovered? [*USE OF RHETORICAL QUESTION TO INVOLVE AUDIENCE; TRANSITION*] This brings me to my final main point [*SIGNPOSTING MAIN POINT*] that there are several ways to prevent catching the flu. First, [*SIGNPOSTING SUBPOINT*] stay generally healthy. Those in a weakened or vulnerable physical state, such as the very young, the elderly, those with chronic health conditions, and pregnant women, are most likely to catch the flu. All reputable health-care professionals encourage a series of preventive steps, including exercise, healthy diet, sufficient rest, frequent hand washing, and avoiding touching your eyes, nose, and mouth. Not everyone contracts the flu, even in the worst pandemics. Robust health and a few precautionary actions are strong preventives. Also, avoid large crowds and confined spaces as much as possible, where flu sufferers can spread the disease. Airplanes, classrooms, and offices are flu factories. [*ALLITERATION FOR VIVIDNESS*] Scientists at the CDC and the University of Michigan Medical School's Center for the History of Medicine conducted an extensive study of the effects of school closures, voluntary isolation and quarantines of infected individuals, and staying clear of sick individuals during the 1918–1919 pandemic. In their report entitled "Community Measures to Prevent Deaths During Pandemic," released August 7, 2007, they concluded that such measures were effective in limiting the spread of the Spanish flu. Such measures were considered to combat the 2009 swine flu but became unnecessary when the severity of the pandemic proved to be less than anticipated.

Second, [*SIGNPOSTING SUBPOINT*] a yearly flu shot is the best preventive. The mass worldwide immunization campaign to combat the 2009 swine flu is credited by the CDC with significantly diminishing the severity of the pandemic. The CDC website cdc.gov notes that flu shots are 70%–90% effective in preventing flu among healthy adults, and close to 80% of deaths from flu and its complications could

(continued)

BOX 14.2 *(Continued)*

be prevented with mass immunization each year. [*CREDIBLE SOURCE; CREDIBLE STATISTICS*] Because flu viruses change, last year's vaccination won't protect you against this year's flu strains. Despite common belief, a flu shot cannot give you the flu because, as the CDC website explains, flu shots contain no live virus. [*CREDIBLE SOURCE*] The most frequent side effect is brief soreness at the site of the shot.

For those who get weak in the knees at the simple sight of a syringe, there is FluMist, a vaccine in the form of nasal spray. [*COLORFUL LANGUAGE; USE OF ALLITERATION; TRANSITION*] The CDC website, February 8, 2011, reported that FluMist is 92% effective in preventing the annual flu. The CDC recommends FluMist for healthy children and adolescents ages 5–17 and healthy adults ages 18–49. FluMist does contain live virus, so there is a small chance of experiencing flulike symptoms from the spray. Its side effects are minimal, however, especially when compared to some things people shoot up their noses. Pain phobics take note—it doesn't hurt! Researchers are also working on a pain-free skin patch to inoculate against flu.

A third way to prevent catching the flu is to take an antiviral drug. There are two principal antiviral drugs—Tamiflu and Relenza. The CDC website on February 9, 2011, [*CREDIBLE SOURCE*] reported that these prescription drugs are almost as effective as vaccines in preventing the flu. These antiviral drugs were stockpiled by the U.S. government to target infected swine flu victims. Developing effective vaccines against a new flu strain takes time. The antiviral drugs can be used immediately. They also have the added benefits, according to the CDC, of shortening the duration of the flu and reducing the severity of the symptoms, if taken immediately after the onset of the flu. So for those who faint at the thought of receiving a shot or who cannot be vaccinated because of allergic reactions to eggs (a component of the vaccine), antiviral drugs are a good option.

In review, [*SIGNPOST*] I have shown that flu viruses can be hazardous to humans, that combating flu can be difficult, but that catching the flu can be prevented. [*SUMMARY OF MAIN POINTS*] I began with a reference to the 1918 Spanish flu. Nobody knows where the Spanish flu virus went or whether it will surface again. [*REFERENCE TO THE SPANISH FLU EXAMPLE IN THE INTRODUCTION GIVES CLOSURE TO THE SPEECH*] Until we find a lasting cure for the flu, we'll have to be vigilant in our effort to prevent this annual plague. [*REFERENCE TO SPEECH TITLE, "ANNUAL PLAGUE," MAKES A MEMORABLE FINISH*]

& Cooper, 1997; Hendricks et al., 1996)? First, *choose a story that fits your audience*. A story about a Jewish rabbi and a Catholic priest told to an audience filled with Muslims probably won't resonate. Second, *make sure the story fits your purpose and illustrates a key point*. Don't tell stories just to entertain if they have no relevance. Third, *keep the stories concise*. Don't get bogged down in details that can become confusing or tedious for your listeners or lose sight of the key theme. If a detail doesn't advance the story but sidetracks it, cut it. Fourth, *practice telling your story*. Tell it to friends, to family members, or to anyone who will listen. Fifth, *do not read your story to your listeners*. You want to sound natural, not artificial. Sixth, *be animated, even visual, when telling a story*. If you're not interested in telling the story, why should your listeners care? Pausch was very engaging because he was unafraid to do pushups, wear a crazy looking Jabberwocky hat, and walk around with fake arrows in his back while lecturing.

Terry Hersey is a Protestant minister who for more than two decades has presented enormously popular lectures at the annual Religious Education Congress in Anaheim, California. He tells this story often at this conference (I've seen him tell it many times)

Dr. Randy Pausch delivers his "The Last Lecture" before a packed arena at Carnegie Mellon University. Knowing he was dying from pancreatic cancer, Pausch nevertheless displayed great storytelling ability and injected humor throughout his presentation. He joked that he had experienced a near-deathbed conversion—he bought a Macintosh computer.

to make the point that we learn very early in life to fear making mistakes.

> There's a terrific story about a first-grade Sunday school class. The children were restless and fussy. The teacher, in an attempt to get their attention, said, "Okay kids, let's play a game. I'll describe something to you. And you tell me what it is."
>
> The kids quieted down. "Listen. It's a furry little animal with a big bushy tail, that climbs up trees and stores nuts in the winter. Who can tell me what it is?" No one said anything. The teacher went on. "You are a good Sunday school class. You know the right answer to this question. It's a furry little animal with a big bushy tail, that climbs up trees and stores nuts in the winter." One little girl raised her hand. "Emily?" "Well, teacher," Emily declared, "it sounds like a squirrel to me, but I'll say Jesus." (see Hersey, 2000, pp. 100–101)

Unfailingly, when Hersey tells this story, the audience roars with laughter. The story is brief, humorous, fits the audience perfectly because it has religious overtones and a moral, is delivered in an animated style (you had to be there), and is told fluently as though Hersey has told this story many times.

Terry Hersey is a great storyteller because he has clearly practiced the art of telling a narrative. He also has written many inspirational books, each of which have numerous stories he's collected over the years. Each of you have stories to tell, whether they be personal experiences, stories told to you by parents, relatives, or friends, or perhaps they are stories you've seen and heard presented on television, on the Internet, or at Sunday sermons. When you're researching your topic, don't fail to notice clever, amusing, poignant, and powerful stories told by others. You can retell many of these to make a point. "Let me tell you a story" immediately perks up an audience (see Box 14-2 for a comprehensive informative speech).

Visual Aids

I once had a student who realized five minutes before his speech that a visual aid was required for the speaking assignment. I actually saw him take his lunch bag, pour out the contents, take a black marker pen, and quickly sketch a drawing for his visual aid. When he gave his speech and showed his lunch bag drawing, audience members had to stifle their laughter. When discussing visual aids, it's important that you recognize both words in that term. The visual part is necessary, but so is the aid part. You don't choose just anything visual to show during your speech. You choose something that aids your presentation and doesn't invite ridicule or serve as a distraction.

Visual aids should only be used if they serve a clear purpose.

First, they *clarify difficult points* or descriptions of complex objects. Showing an object to an audience helps listeners understand. Many topics are truly difficult to describe without a visual aid. Consider the difficulty of using words alone to explain the operation of a computer motherboard or an internal combustion engine.

Second, effective visual aids *gain and maintain audience attention*. A riveting image can capture attention during the opening of a speech, reinforcing your words by engaging the visual perception of the audience.

Third, visual aids *enhance speaker credibility.* Presenting impressive statistics in a graph, chart, or table drives home an important point in your speech and improves your credibility.

Fourth, visual aids can *improve your delivery.* Novice speakers find it difficult to stray from notes or a manuscript. A good first step toward an extemporaneous delivery (see Chapter 13) is to make reference to a visual aid. When you are showing a visual aid, you move away from reading your speech, and you assume a more natural delivery when you explain your visual aid to your listeners. Finally, effective visual aids can be *memorable.* Demonstration speeches rely heavily on visual aids. We can remember a magic trick, a martial arts move, the proper way to arrange flowers, or how to decorate wedding cakes when we have seen them demonstrated.

The purpose of this section is to explain how to use visual aids competently. I discuss the types of visual aids available and presentational media for the competent use of visual aids.

Types: Benefits and Drawbacks

There are several types of visual aids, each with its advantages and disadvantages. I discuss both strengths and limitations of each type in this section.

Objects

Sometimes there is no substitute for the actual object of your speech. For example, giving a speech on playing different types of recorders really requires demonstrating with the musical instruments. "Bass and tenor recorders have very different sounds" just doesn't work if you merely show a photograph of the instruments. You must actually play the recorders.

There are limitations, however, to the use of objects as visual aids. Some objects are too large to haul into a classroom. One student in my class wanted to show how the size of surfboards has changed over the years, so he brought in four different-sized boards. His immediate problem was that his long board hit the ceiling when it was placed on its end, punching a hole in the ceiling tiles. Some objects are also impractical to bring to most speaking venues. A speech on building a bullet train in the United States may benefit from a visual aid, but you surely can't drive a real train into a classroom or auditorium.

Some objects are illegal, dangerous, or potentially objectionable to at least some audience members. One of my students long ago thought it was a good idea to bring in a live marijuana plant he had been cultivating as a "show-and-tell" object. Another student wanted to show students "how to roll a doobie." He began his speech by pulling out a plastic bag of marijuana and papers to roll a joint. In both cases, the speech had to be halted because the objects were illegal. Firearms, poisons, combustible liquids, or sharp objects are dangerous. One student wanted to give a speech on "the dangers of pornography." She asked me in advance, thank goodness, if she could bring in explicit pornographic photographs as a visual aid. I nixed her idea. Offending an audience with a visual aid, as abortion protesters often do with graphic pictures of aborted fetuses, can easily backfire and call into question a speaker's credibility and good taste. Simply exercise responsible judgment. Check for rules or laws that could invite trouble before using any visual aid that seems questionable.

Inanimate objects are usually preferable to living, squirming objects. Puppies are unfailingly cute and great attention grabbers, but they are also very difficult to control. A student of mine brought a puppy to class for her speech. The puppy whined, barked, and howled throughout her presentation. At first, it was cute. But after five minutes, the audience was thoroughly annoyed. My student ended her speech as the puppy urinated on the classroom carpet.

Some living objects can frighten audience members. A live snake, especially one not in a cage, will make some audience members extremely uneasy, even agitated. One student brought a live tarantula to class for her speech. She let the spider walk

Consider enlarging visual aids to show detail and inform your audience. Large visual aids, such as this gigantic lottery check, garner attention as well.

across a table as she presented her informative speech. Audience members were transfixed—not by what she was saying but by the hairy creature moving slowly in front of them.

Models

When objects relevant to your speech are too large, too small, expensive, fragile, rare, or unavailable, models can often act as effective substitutes. A speech on dental hygiene is an apt example. Speakers usually bring in a larger-than-normal plastic model of a human mouth full of teeth. It isn't practical or effective to ask for a volunteer from the audience to open wide so the speaker can show the volunteer's teeth. The teeth will be too small to see well, especially for audience members in the back row. Such a demonstration will also be extremely awkward. The speaker may have to point out tooth decay, gum disease, and fillings in the volunteer's mouth—not something most people want others to notice, much less have spotlighted.

Demonstration speeches on cardiopulmonary resuscitation (CPR) require a model of a person. You can't ask for an audience member to serve as a victim for the demonstration. Pushing forcefully on a person's chest could be dangerous and potentially embarrassing.

Graphs

A graph is a visual representation of statistics in an easily understood format. There are several kinds. Figure 14-1 is a bar graph. A bar graph compares and contrasts two or more items or shows variation over a period

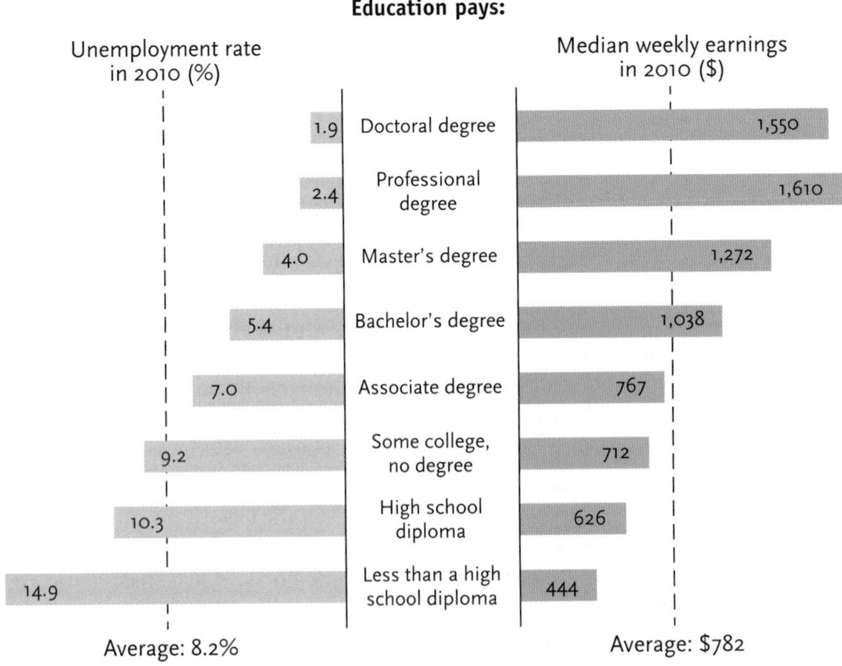

FIGURE 14-1 A Bar Graph Illustrating the Monetary Advantage of Education (Source: Bureau of Labor Statistics)

of time. Bar graphs can make a dramatic visual impact. Figures 14-2 and 14-3 are line graphs. A line graph is useful for showing a trend or change over a period of time. A pie graph, as shown in Figure 14-4, depicts a proportion or percentage for each part of a whole.

Graphs are effective if they are uncluttered. Too much information in a graph makes it difficult for an audience to understand. A graph must be immediately understandable to an audience. More detailed graphs published in print media can be effective because readers can examine the graphs carefully. During a speech, this is neither possible nor desirable.

Maps

A map helps audience members see geographic areas to make important points. Commercial maps are normally too detailed to be useful as a visual aid for a speech. The most effective maps are large, simple, and directly relevant to the speaker's purpose. Figure 14-5 is an example of an effective map. Some speakers attempt to

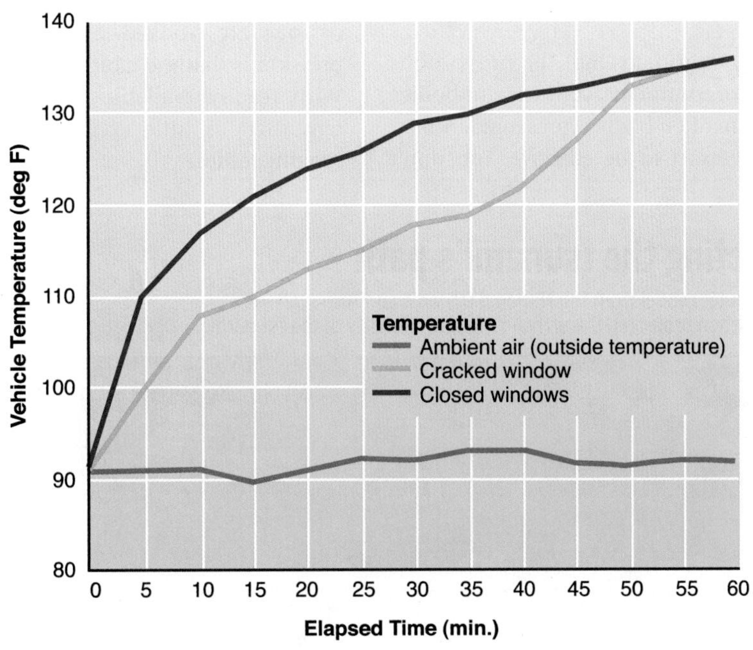

FIGURE 14-2 A Line Graph Comparing Interior Temperature over time in Cars with Closed or "Cracked" Windows (Source: McLaren et al., 2005)

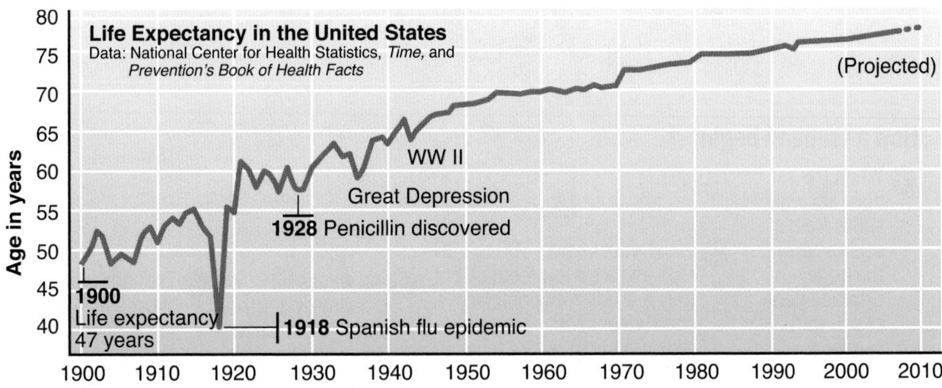

FIGURE 14-3 A Line Graph Illustrating Life Expectancy in the United States (Source: *San Jose Mercury News*)

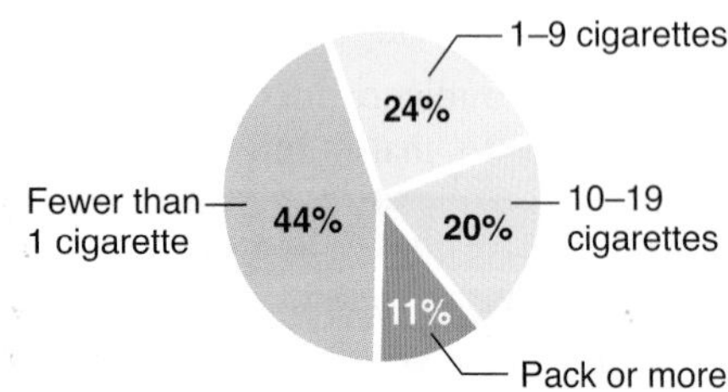

FIGURE 14-4 A Pie Graph Showing Smoking Rates Among College Students (Source: Knight Ridder/Tribune Information Services)

draw their own maps, but the proportions and scale of continents, countries, or bodies of water are often badly represented. A map should be exact to be effective. You don't want the United States to look three times bigger than Asia.

Tables

A table is an orderly depiction of statistics, words, or symbols in columns and rows. Tables 14-1 and 14-2 are examples. A table can provide easy-to-understand comparisons of facts and statistics. Tables, however, are not as visually interesting as graphics. Tables can also become easily cluttered with too much information.

Tables will be a visual distraction if the headings are too small to read, the columns or rows are crooked, and the overall impression is that the table was hastily drawn. With readily available computer technology, there is little excuse for amateurish looking tables.

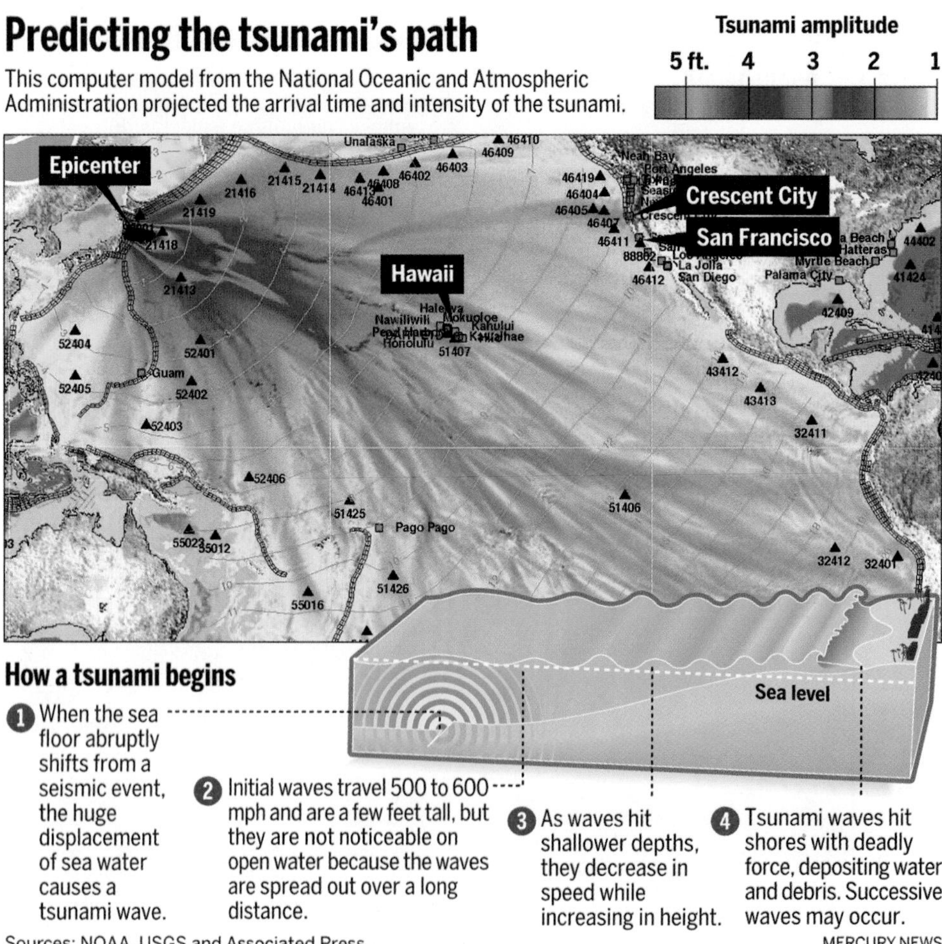

Predicting the tsunami's path
This computer model from the National Oceanic and Atmospheric Administration projected the arrival time and intensity of the tsunami.
Tsunami amplitude
5 ft. 4 3 2 1
Epicenter
Hawaii
Crescent City
San Francisco
Unalaska
Neah Bay
Port Angeles
La Jolla
San Diego
Myrtle Beach
Palama City
Hatteras
Haleiwa
Nawiliwili
Honolulu
Kahului
Kawaihae
Guam
Pago Pago
How a tsunami begins
1 When the sea floor abruptly shifts from a seismic event, the huge displacement of sea water causes a tsunami wave.
2 Initial waves travel 500 to 600 mph and are a few feet tall, but they are not noticeable on open water because the waves are spread out over a long distance.
3 As waves hit shallower depths, they decrease in speed while increasing in height.
4 Tsunami waves hit shores with deadly force, depositing water and debris. Successive waves may occur.
Sea level
Sources: NOAA, USGS and Associated Press
MERCURY NEWS

FIGURE 14-5 A Map of 2011 Tsunami Whose Epicenter Was off the Northeast Coast of Japan.

TABLE 14-1 AVERAGE ANNUAL MAJOR LEAGUE BASEBALL SALARIES 2002–2011

YEAR	AVERAGE ANNUAL SALARY
2002	2.38 million
2003	2.58 million
2004	2.49 million
2005	2.63 million
2006	2.83 million
2007	2.92 million
2008	3.15 million
2009	3.26 million
2010	3.27 million
2011	3.32 million

SOURCE: *USA TODAY*

Photographs

The many photographs included in this textbook underline the effectiveness of this visual aid to make a point, clarify a concept, and draw attention. When objects are too big or unwieldy, unavailable, or too fragile to use as visual aids, photographs may serve as effective substitutes. Instead of bringing the wiggling, fussing, barking, urinating puppy to class, perhaps several photographs of the cute pet will suffice. Instead of violating the law by displaying a real marijuana plant in class, show a photograph of the plant.

Photographs have some drawbacks. They may need to be enlarged. Recent technological advances with digital photography and Photoshop have made this relatively easy to do if you have access to the technology and know how to use it. Postage-stamp-size photographs are worthless as visual aids. When a speaker says to his or her audience, "So as you can see in this photograph," and no one can because the photograph is minuscule, the photo becomes not an aid but an embarrassment. The photograph should be large enough for everyone in the audience to see easily.

Drawings

When photographs are unavailable, a careful drawing might be an effective substitute (see Figure 14-6). Drawings of figures performing ballet moves or pole-vaulting techniques could be instructive for an audience. If the drawings are sloppy, distorted, small, and appear to have been drawn by a five-year-old with no artistic talent, find a different visual aid.

TABLE 14-2 WORLD'S DEADLIEST EARTHQUAKES LAST 100 YEARS

LOCATION	MAGNITUDE	DEATHS
1. Tangshan, China (1976)	7.5	255,000
2. Sumatra, Indonesia (2004)	9.1	228,000
3. Haiti Region (2010)	7.0	223,000
4. Haiyuan, China (1920)	7.8	200,000
5. Kanto, Japan (1923)	7.9	143,000
6. Turkmenistan (1948)	7.3	110,000
7. Eastern Sichuan, China (2008)	7.9	88,000
8. Northern Pakistan (2005)	7.6	86,000
9. Chimbote, Peru (1970)	7.9	70,000
10. Western Iran (1990)	7.4	40,000

SOURCE: U.S. Geological Survey

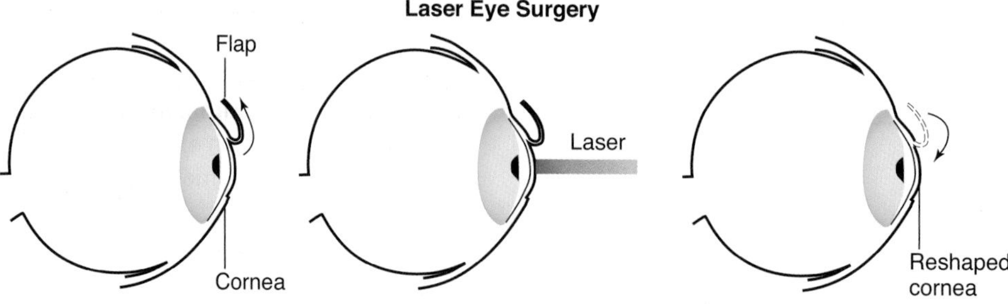
Laser Eye Surgery
Flap
Laser
Cornea
Reshaped cornea
How vision is corrected
• Myopia, nearsightedness: Cornea is flattened
• Hyperopia, farsightedness: Curve of cornea is made sharper
• Astigmatism: Curve of cornea is evened out

FIGURE 14-6 Drawings That Illustrate Laser Eye Surgery (Source: Eye Surgery Education Council)

knowledge
skills

Media: Simple to Complex Technology

There are many media, or means of communicating, with visual aids. Tables or graphs, for example, can appear on chalkboards, posters, PowerPoint slides, or other media. I discuss the most frequently used media next.

Chalkboard and Whiteboard: All Dinosaurs Aren't Extinct

Every student is familiar with the chalkboard or whiteboard. Despite its "dinosaur" reputation of late, the chalkboard or whiteboard is a useful visual aid medium when time and resources don't permit the use of more sophisticated media. Chalkboards and whiteboards are widely available and allow great flexibility. Tables, drawings, and graphs all can be drawn on them. Lecture material can be outlined. Mistakes can be immediately, and easily, erased.

Chalkboards and whiteboards, however, do have several serious drawbacks. The quality of the table, drawing, or graph is usually inferior. Students are sometimes tempted to draw on a chalkboard or whiteboard during their speech, consuming huge portions of their allotted speaking time creating their visual aid. If a student uses the chalkboard or whiteboard prior to his or her speech, the class waits impatiently while the speaker creates the visual aid. It is too time consuming. Turning to write or draw on the board also breaks eye contact with your audience. Most instructors discourage the use of both as a visual aid medium for student speakers, but if you become a teacher, the chalkboard and whiteboard, unlike the dinosaurs, likely will have avoided extinction because they are cheap and easy to use.

Poster Board: Simplicity Itself

A poster board is a very simple medium for visual aids. Available in most college bookstores or stationery outlets, you can draw, stencil, and make graphs or tables using poster board. Making the poster appear professional, however, is a primary challenge. Several guidelines can help. First, all lettering and numbering should be large enough for anyone in the back of the room to see easily. Second, your poster should be neat and symmetrical. Headings, lettering, and numbering should be even, not sloping downward, upward, or any combination that looks like a roller coaster. Use a ruler to keep lines straight. Letters and numbers should be of the same size or font. Third, strive for simplicity. Don't clutter the poster with a collage of pictures that meld into a blob of images unless the assignment requires a collage. Generally avoid using newspaper clippings whose print is too small and too detailed to read quickly. Resist ornate, flowery borders. Glitter, feathers, and other "accessories" are distracting and rarely beneficial.

Posters are usually attached to an easel for display. Simply standing them on a chalk tray, however, will usually result in the poster curling at the top and flopping onto the ground unless the poster is made of very stiff, sturdy material. Watching a speaker repeatedly fuss with a poster trying desperately to keep it upright is awkward for everyone. Tape it to a wall if necessary.

Handouts: An Old Standby

Distributing a handout is a popular form of visual aid. Tables, maps, drawings, PowerPoint slides, or even photographs can be copied onto a handout. One significant advantage of a handout is that the listeners can keep it long after the speech has been presented. It can serve as a useful reminder of the information presented.

Handouts have several potential disadvantages, however. Passing out a handout in the middle of your speech wastes time, breaks the flow of the speech, and can be a huge distraction when you try to regain audience attention. If your listeners are busy reading your handout while you're speaking, they will not be attending to your message. You may be speaking on a different point while audience members are still reading your handout on a previous point.

Distribute a handout just prior to giving your speech if the handout will be an integral part of your presentation. If the handout is necessary for explanation of important points throughout your speech, the handout will not distract but will assist audience members to maintain focus and increase their understanding of your message. A handout can be distributed during a speech if you are lecturing for a long time (an hour or two) and the handout is vital to a later portion of your presentation. During short speeches (five to ten minutes), however, don't distribute a handout in the middle of your presentation. It's too disruptive to the flow of your short speech. Sometimes a handout can be passed out after the speech has ended. A handout with names, email addresses, and phone numbers of organizations or agencies that provide additional information on your subject can be distributed after your speech.

Video Excerpts: DVDs, YouTube, and Visual Power

An excerpt from a movie, YouTube, or a video segment you shot yourself can be a valuable visual aid. Videos can be dramatic, informative, and moving. They often are great attention grabbers. Videos used during a speech, however, have several limitations. First, the sound on a video will compete with the speaker for attention. Shut off the sound when you are trying to explain a point while the video is playing unless the video excerpt is very short (30 seconds or less) and sound is essential. (Longer video excerpts with sound may be effective in lengthy presentations.) Second, a video with its dramatic action can make your speech seem tame, even dull, by comparison. It is tough to compete with a Hollywood production. Third, *a video isn't a speech*. There is a real temptation to show a video as a major portion of a speech without any narration or direct reference to it while it is playing.

If you use a video excerpt during your speech, cue it properly ahead of time so you won't have to interrupt the flow of your presentation by looking for the right place to start the excerpt. Downloading several short excerpts onto a blank DVD is preferable to loading several separate DVDs. Also, downloading any YouTube excerpts onto a blank DVD is less cumbersome and time consuming to set up and use than accessing the YouTube site. YouTube video excerpts should also be embedded into any PowerPoint presentation to avoid interrupting the flow of your presentation by accessing YouTube sites (see youtube.com and search for "Embed YouTube video"). Typically, use only very short video excerpts (30 seconds) when your speech is relatively short (10 minutes).

Tim Berners-Lee, credited with inventing the World Wide Web, delivered a TED (Technology, Education, Design) lecture in February 2010 entitled "The Year Open Data Went Worldwide." During his 20-minute lecture, he used slides and brief video excerpts effectively. Since the video excerpts required no sound, he narrated the excerpts, always talking directly to his audience and not to the large video screen behind him. (You can access this lecture at: http://www.ted.com/talks/tim_berners_lee_the_year_open_data_went_worldwide.html). Harsha Bhogle explained how the rise of the game of cricket paralleled the rise of modern India, effectively using very short video excerpts during a 20-minute TED lecture (http://www.ted.com/talks/harsha_bhogle_the_rise_of_cricket_the_rise_of_india.html). Since the video excerpts included necessary sound, Bhogle kept the excerpts very short so his presentation didn't deteriorate into merely viewing a video without a speech.

Projection Equipment: Blowing It Up

There are several options for projecting images onto a large screen. Slide projectors were very common, but they have neared extinction as a visual aid medium, mostly replaced by PowerPoint slide presentations. Kodak stopped manufacturing slide projectors in 2004.

Overhead projectors are another type of projector that, despite being an aging technology, continues to be used in some circumstances. Overhead projectors can be used to display enlarged images. They are still around because they are easy to use, relatively problem free, and a flexible piece of equipment. Transparencies are placed on the overhead projector, enlarging a table, map, picture, graph, or drawing. Transparencies are very simple to prepare. Whatever can be photocopied can be made into a transparency. The relative ease with which this equipment can be used tempts speakers to overdo the number of transparencies shown during a speech. Be careful not to substitute transparencies for an actual speech.

Computer projectors are a more recent development. Pictures taken directly from computer software presentations can be shown on a large screen. The time required to prepare the computer presentation and technical breakdowns in the middle of the presentation are potential drawbacks.

PowerPoint: Computer-Assisted Presentations

By now, you should be familiar with the many options available for computer-assisted presentations. PowerPoint is probably the most widely available and utilized example of this visual aid medium. Space does not allow a "how-to" explanation for using this technology. There are several excellent sites on the Internet that provide step-by-step instructions (see http://office.microsoft.com/en-us/powerpoint-help/create-your-first-presentation-RZ001129842.aspx). For relatively short presentations (five- to ten-minute speeches), this technology may be overkill. If you have critically important slides to show (e.g., pictures of a Southeast Asia trip to illustrate cultural differences), then PowerPoint slides are appropriate. For longer speeches (an hour-long lecture), computer-assisted presentations can be wonderful. The biggest drawbacks are the time it takes to prepare the slides, the potential for glitches to occur during the actual speech, and the tendency to become so enamored with the software capability that it detracts from the speech (see Box 14-3).

Consultant Cliff Atkinson (2008), author of *Beyond Bullet Points*, offers several research-based suggestions for improving PowerPoint presentations. Unlike some conventional suggestions, such as the "rule of seven" (no more than seven bulleted lines on a slide or seven words per line), Atkinson translates theory and research on communication into solid advice for improving PowerPoint presentations. First, *don't overwhelm listeners with complicated slides*. Text-heavy slides with numerous bullet points (what Atkinson calls the "grocery list approach") that require listeners to read for 10 to 15 seconds or more distract from your speech and are not visually interesting. Second, *do not read the slides to your audience*, and do not wait for your listeners to read lengthy slides. This interrupts the flow of your presentation. Research also shows that reading a list of bulleted points diminishes learning the information (Mayer, 2005). Attention fades. Third, *narrate your PowerPoint slides*. You tell the story that focuses listeners on your main points as you advance your slides.

Fourth, *most slides should have a full-sentence headline at the top with a descriptive graphic (picture) underneath*. Exceptions would be some photographs or cartoons that need no explanation or slides that convey easy-to-grasp points. Use a full-sentence headline for the same reasons full-sentence outlines work better than word or phrase outlines (see Chapter 12); full-sentence

BOX 14.3 Focus on Controversy

POWERPOINT: LOTS OF POWER, LITTLE POINT?

The year 2007 marked the 20th anniversary of PowerPoint, "one of the most elegant, most influential and most groaned-about pieces of software in the history of computers" ("PowerPoint Turns 20," 2007, p. B1). Edward Tufte (2003), Yale political scientist and specialist in graphic display of information, wrote an editorial in *Wired* magazine in 2003 entitled "PowerPoint Is Evil: Power Corrupts, PowerPoint Corrupts Absolutely." Tufte claimed that PowerPoint "elevates format over content, betraying an attitude of commercialism that turns everything into a sales pitch." Tufte even suggested that PowerPoint might have played a role in the *Columbia* shuttle disaster because vital technical information was swamped in the glitzy PowerPoint slides and endless bullet points. The report by The Columbia Accident Investigation Board (2003) seemed to agree: "It is easy to understand how a senior manager might read this PowerPoint slide and not realize that it addresses a life-threatening situation." The report then went on to criticize "the endemic use of PowerPoint briefing slides" as a substitute for quality technical analysis. Inventors of the software, Robert Gaskin and Dennis Austin, agree with Tufte's criticisms. "All the things Tufte says are absolutely true. People often make very bad use of PowerPoint" (quoted in "PowerPoint Turns 20," 2007, p. B1).

The heavy reliance on PowerPoint during speeches, what consultant Nancy Stern (2004) calls "slideswiping" and others call "death by PowerPoint" or "hypnotizing chickens," should be discouraged. As Brig. Gen. H. R. McMaster, who banned PowerPoint presentations when he led forces in Iraq, notes, "Some problems in the world are not bullet-izable" (quoted in Bumiller, 2010). Imagine a bullet point presentation of Martin Luther King's inspiring "I Have a Dream" speech.

"I Have a Dream" (several dreams, actually)—M. L. King

- Dream #1: Nation live true meaning of "all men created equal"
- Dream #2: Sit down at table of brotherhood
- Dream #3: Mississippi: transformed into oasis of freedom/justice
- Dream #4: My 4 children—judged by content of character not color of skin
- Dream #5: Alabama: black and white boys/girls become sisters/brothers

PowerPoint drains the vitality from a powerful, beautifully composed speech (Witt & Fetherling, 2009). No one is likely to feel moved to march for freedom from reading this lifeless laundry list of longed for "dreams."

Organizations such as the Pentagon have instructed employees to curtail the use of PowerPoint presentations because they turn meetings into marathon sessions (McGinn, 2000). As chief executive of Sun Microsystems, Scott McNealy ordered a ban on all PowerPoint demonstrations. The ban was never enforced, but more and more business conferences are prohibiting PowerPoint presentations because it places too much focus on the bells and whistles—the surface "gee whiz" computer capabilities—and too little on the content (Zuckerman, 1999). As Atkinson (2008) notes, "When you finish the presentation, you want the audience to talk about your special ideas, not your special effects" (p. 323).

Consider carefully whether multimedia presentations are appropriate and whether they really enhance the content of your presentation. PowerPoint can be very powerful and useful but only if used effectively (Atkinson, 2008). Too often, speakers obsess about font size and choices for animation that frequently distract an audience's attention instead of concentrating on developing a quality speech.

(continued)

BOX 14.3 *(Continued)*

If you do choose to use PowerPoint, avoid listing every point in your outline. This is tedious and uninteresting. Remember that the power of PowerPoint is in its ability to make presentations far more interesting than your standard chalkboard or whiteboard listing of main points. When PowerPoint becomes little more than a high-tech version of a chalkboard or overhead transparencies, little is gained by using this computer technology. PowerPoint slides should meet the same criteria as visual aids in general (see next section).

QUESTIONS FOR THOUGHT

1. Should PowerPoint be banned so it can't be misused?
2. Is there any technology that can't be misused by someone unskilled?
3. What do you think is the best use of PowerPoint—what can't be presented in a speech nearly as well without using PowerPoint?

headlines explain the main point, but word or phrase headers only suggest what the point might be. Research shows that full-sentence headlines improve listeners' knowledge and comprehension when compared to sentence fragments or phrase headings (Alley, 2005). A simple but interesting graphic for each slide recognizes that PowerPoint is a *visual* aid, so it should be visually interesting (seven bulleted points are a snooze). Fifth, *don't get graphic crazy.* Heavy use of animation and clever graphics can make the razzle-dazzle memorable but the main points of your speech opaque and unmemorable. Animation to create humor may be appealing if used infrequently. Finally, *use a remote to advance slides.* Having to press a key on the keyboard chains you to the computer. Either you must stay next to the computer keyboard throughout your presentation, which makes your presentation stilted, or you must keep running back to the keyboard to advance the slides, which can look comical and unprofessional.

There are always exceptions to every rule (a list of bulleted points may be necessary in some circumstances and a single word or phrase header may work well in some situations), but Atkinson's suggestions are excellent guidelines for using PowerPoint effectively. PowerPoint can be a wonderful *visual* aid.

Guidelines: Aids, Not Distractions

Poorly designed and clumsily presented visual aids will detract, not aid, your speech. Here are some guidelines for the competent use of visual aids.

Keep Aids Simple

Complex tables, maps, and graphics can work well in print media such as magazines and newspapers. Readers can closely examine a visual aid. Listeners do not have the same option. Complex visual aids do not work well for speeches, especially short ones, where the information needs to be communicated clearly and quickly. Your audience will be intent on figuring out a complex visual aid, not listening to you speak. Keep visual aids simple.

Make Aids Visible

The general rule for visual aids is that people in the back of the room or auditorium should be able to see your visual aid easily. If they can't, it is not large enough to be effective. Audience members should not have to strain to see words or numbers. Your

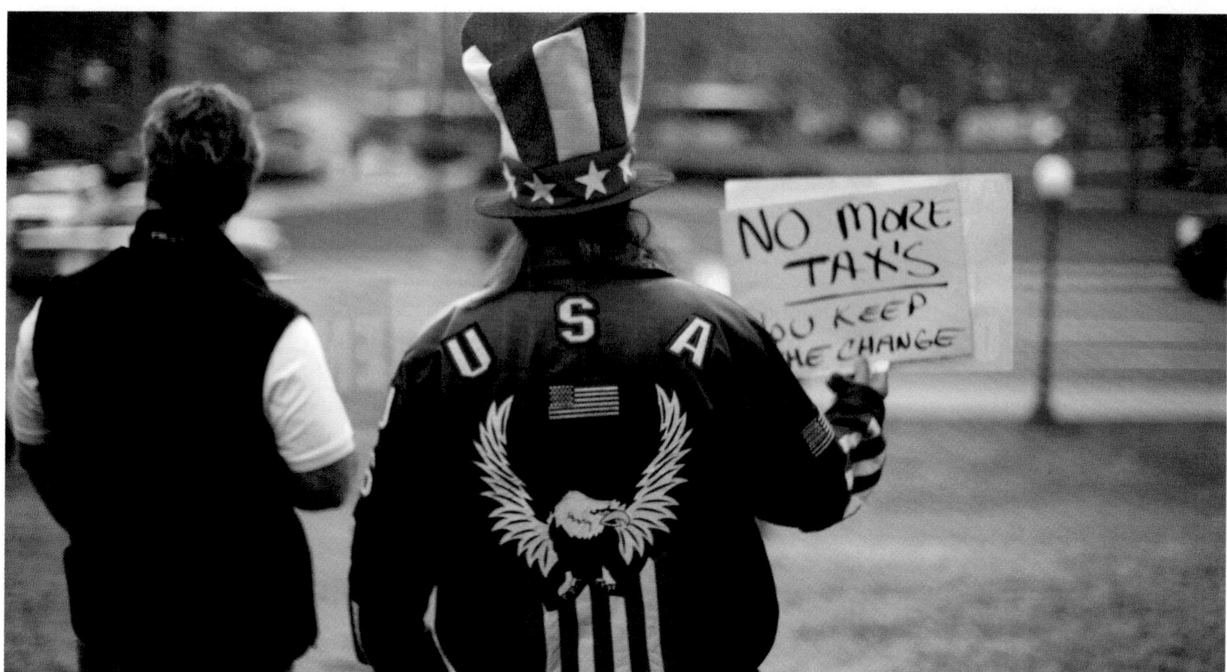

Grammatical and spelling mistakes on a visual aid diminish credibility.

audience will quickly grow uninterested in your visual aid if it is not large enough to be easily seen. Effective font size depends on the size of the screen and the room. A huge screen in a large auditorium requires a larger font size for PowerPoint presentations—typically 44 points for headlines, 32 points for main points, and 24 points for subpoints—than a regular-sized classroom (Earnest, 2007). Transparencies usually work well in standard classrooms when the font size is 16 to 20 points.

Make Aids Neat, Attractive, and Accurate

Don't embarrass yourself by showing a visual aid of poor quality. When you use a visual aid, you want it to look neat and attractive. This means you have to take time to prepare the visual aid. Sloppy drawings, posters, tables, and the like won't suffice. Take time to proofread your aids before showing them. Misspelled words or grammatical mistakes on PowerPoint slides, posters, charts, or tables scream "*carelessness!*" Tea Party protesters at 2010 rallies carried signs reading "No Pubic Option," "Politians Are Like Dipers: They Need to Be Changed Often," "Get a Brain Morans," and "Crisis of Competnce." The impression created by even a few such misspelled signs is that Tea Party protesters are uneducated (note the vividness effect produced by stark examples). Yet a *New York Times*/CBS survey of April 14, 2010, shows Tea Party supporters are better educated than the general public (Zernike & Thee-Brenan, 2010). Carelessness kills credibility.

Don't Block the Audience's View

A very common mistake made even by professional speakers is that they block the audience's view of the visual aid. Standing in front of your poster, graph, drawing, table, or PowerPoint slide while you talk to the visual aid, not to your audience, is awkward and self-defeating. You want your audience members to see the visual aid. Audience members should not have to stand and move across the room to see a visual aid, crane their necks, or give up in frustration because a speaker's big pumpkin head is blocking their view. Simply stand beside your poster, drawing, graph, or video excerpt while you explain it to the audience. Point the toes of your shoes toward the audience and imagine that your feet are nailed to the ground. If you don't move your feet, you will continue to stand beside, not in front of, your visual aid. *Talk to your audience, not to your visual aid.*

Keep Aids Close to You

Don't place a visual aid across the room from where you speak. This is particularly problematic when using PowerPoint (Atkinson, 2008). You don't want to split the listeners' attention and create the look of a crowd at a tennis match shifting eye contact back and forth from projection screen to you speaking across the room.

Put the Aid Out of Sight When Not in Use

Cover your poster or drawing, graph, or photo when not referring to it. Simply leaving it open to view when you no longer make reference to it or showing it before you actually use it distracts an audience. Atkinson (2008) suggests including blank slides between images on PowerPoint slides when you are not referring to them for a while (a minute or more). Shut off the overhead projector or video player when you are finished using the visual aid.

Practice with Aids

Using visual aids competently requires practice. At first, using a visual aid may seem awkward, even unnatural. Once you have practiced your speech using a visual aid, however, it will seem more natural and less awkward. Practice will also help you work out any problems that might occur before giving your speech for real.

Don't Circulate Your Aids

Don't pass around photos, cartoons, drawings, objects, or anything that can distract your audience from paying attention to you while you're speaking. If audience members want to see your visual aid again, let them approach you after the speech for a second viewing.

Don't Talk in the Dark

I have had to advise student speakers not to turn off the classroom lights when they are showing video clips during their presentations. When the lights are off, the room becomes so dark that they become disembodied voices. The audience can't see nonverbal elements of their presentation, and it all comes off as just weird. I've seen professional speakers do the same thing. With a huge screen and PowerPoint slides flashing one after the other, had the speakers merely provided a voice-over for the slides, their actual presence would have been unnecessary. They become "little more than well-educated projectionists whose major role is to control the PowerPoint and video displays projected on the screen" (Nevid, 2011, p. 54). If possible, dim the lights so slides or video excerpts show more effectively without putting everyone in darkness. If there is no dimmer switch to partially lower the lights, try bringing in a lamp with a low-wattage bulb and lighten the room that way with the main lights switched off. If the room is very large and there is no way to merely dim the lights, try focusing a light on you at a podium so the audience can at least see you as you speak.

Anticipate Problems

The more complicated your technology the greater the likelihood that problems will occur before or during your presentation. Projection bulbs burn out unexpectedly, computers crash, programs won't load. Have a backup plan. If the audience is small (30 or fewer), a hard copy of PowerPoint slides, for example, can be prepared just in case your computer fails. Overhead transparencies of slides also can be prepared if the audience is large. Show up early and do a quick test to see if all systems are GO! If your easel falls over during your presentation, be prepared with a casual remark to lighten the moment ("Just checking to see if everyone is alert; obviously, I wasn't"). Think about what might go wrong and anticipate ways to respond appropriately.

Summary

A KEY difference between informative and persuasive speaking is that informative speeches attempt to teach listeners something new, and persuasive speeches, although oftentimes informative, move beyond and attempt to change behavior. There are five types of informative speeches that sometimes overlap during the same presentation: those that report, explain, demonstrate, tell a story, or compare pros and cons of a proposal without taking a position. Competent informative speaking is achieved by considering your audience when choosing a topic, organizing carefully, avoiding information overload, keeping your audience interested, using supporting materials competently, and telling stories well.

Visual aids must be both visually interesting and an actual aid to your speech. Sloppy, poorly prepared, and poorly selected visual aids can bring you ridicule and embarrassment. Always choose and prepare your visual aids carefully. Visual aids can clarify complicated points, gain and maintain audience attention, enhance your credibility, improve your delivery, and make your information memorable. You have many types of visual aids to choose from, but make sure that you don't become enamored with the technologically sophisticated and glitzy aids when you aren't well versed in their use. If you do, your speech could be diminished by too much flash and not enough substance. Follow the guidelines for using visual aids.

Quizzes Without Consequences

Did you understand all the material in this chapter? Test your knowledge before your exam!

Go to the companion website at www.oup.com/us/rothwell, click on the Student Resources for each chapter, and take the Quizzes Without Consequences.

Film School Case Studies

Dangerous Minds (1995). Drama; PG

Michelle Pfeiffer, probably miscast, plays a teacher in an inner-city school. Contrast her informative speaking with that of the Robin Williams character in *Dead Poets Society*. Consider especially differences in audience analysis that are required when comparing the two.

Dead Poets Society (1989). Drama; PG

Robin Williams delivers an effective performance as an English teacher in a private New England prep school. Evaluate his use of the lecture format for informative speaking. Does the Williams character remain informative or does he move into persuasive territory? Is he proselytizing inappropriately? Is his communication always ethical?

Mona Lisa Smile (2003). Drama; PG

This is a vehicle for Julia Roberts, who plays a free-spirited professor at staid Wellesley College in the 1950s. Examine the Roberts character and the quality of her audience analysis. Does her informative speaking mesh well with the Wellesley crowd? Compare the Roberts character to the Robin Williams character in *Dead Poets Society* regarding whether she sticks to informative speaking or crosses the blurry line into proselytizing and persuasion.

CHAPTER 15

Chapter Outline

Persuasive Speaking

IT WAS THE 60TH ANNUAL CONVENTION of the California Federation of Teachers. Keynote speaker Charles Kernaghan, director of the National Labor Committee, was addressing an audience of California teachers. His central idea (theme) was that extreme poverty of much of the world's workforce accrues from economic globalization and the exploitation of workers. His speech was a rousing antisweatshop call to arms. Kernaghan held up garments produced overseas, and he told stories of the exploitation of workers who made these garments, most of whom are between the ages of 6 and 16. Referring to a Nike document from the Dominican Republic, he noted: "There are 22 steps to the production of a t-shirt, which in total take 6.6 minutes, or 11% of an hour's labor. The worker gets 8 cents for that time—0.3% of the retail price. Advertising that same shirt costs them $2.32. They spend 32 times more on branding (brand identification) than they do on the worker" (quoted in "Anti-sweatshop activist," 2002, p. 4). He argued that young people "have a right to ask, how do the people live who produce the clothes they wear?" (p. 4). Kernaghan discussed the Students Against Sweatshops

By the end of this chapter, you should be able to:

1. Understand the relationship between attitudes and behavior.
2. Identify the principal goals of persuasion.
3. Distinguish between peripheral and central processing of persuasive messages.
4. Use competent persuasive speaking strategies.

movement in the United States and its hundreds of chapters on college campuses. The audience cheered when he thundered, "These kids are on fire!" Kernaghan brought his listeners to their feet when he concluded, "There can never be peace without social justice, or in a world with child labor" (p. 4).

Kernaghan's speech was masterful and an enormous success. "Of all the speakers at the 60th annual convention, none stirred delegates as deeply as Charles Kernaghan" (p. 4). His speech was successful for several reasons. First, the CFT convention had social justice as one of its prime themes. Kernaghan's keynote address was well suited to this theme. As members of a powerful teachers union, listeners were receptive to his message that nonunion workers can be and are exploited as "cheap labor." He knew his audience and tailored his message to audience members' expectations. Note, however, that this same speech would likely trigger a much less favorable reaction from an audience composed of Chamber of Commerce members or small-business owners who depend on selling inexpensive clothing to stay competitive in a tough business climate. Second, he evidently researched his topic very carefully. He had the facts to support his claims. Third, he used very effective attention strategies. His speech was not a dry recitation of facts and figures; it was a passionate presentation that was at times intense, startling, and vital in its depiction of the plight of garment workers in countries around the world. It aroused anger at injustice. He told stories about young women he interviewed who worked in deplorable sweatshop conditions. They struggle to stay alive on a day's wage of $4.80 when it costs them $1.14 for bus fare to and from work, 91 cents for breakfast, and $1.37 for lunch, leaving them $1.38 after expenses. Fourth, his conclusion didn't just fade out. He ended with a rousing appeal to stamp out exploitation of workers worldwide. Clearly, Kernaghan developed his persuasive speech carefully so it would be a smashing success with CFT members.

Possessing the persuasive knowledge and skills demonstrated by Kernaghan has practical significance. One study found that when economists totaled the number of people whose jobs depend predominantly on persuading people—lawyers, counselors, managers, administrators, salespersons, and public relations specialists—persuasion accounts for 26% of the gross domestic product of the United States (Bennett, 1995). Individuals often are required to speak persuasively in our culture. News networks interview individuals every day who engage in persuasive speaking before the cameras. Most talk shows display persuasive speaking from panelists and audience members, although many persuasive attempts are dismal efforts by unskilled and untrained speakers. *Court TV* and several "people's court" programs show average citizens defending themselves in court cases.

Almost 2,500 years ago, Aristotle systematically discussed persuasion in his influential *The Rhetoric*. The scientific study of persuasion, however, began less than a century ago in the United States. Much has been learned from this research on persuasion, and it will provide you with many useful insights. Capitalizing on this research and insight, *the primary purpose of this chapter is to explain how you can construct and present a competent persuasive speech.*

Foundations of Persuasion

Persuasion is a communication process of converting, modifying, or maintaining the attitudes and/or behavior of others. In Chapter 12, an **attitude** was defined as "a learned predisposition to respond favorably or unfavorably toward some attitude object" (Gass & Seiter, 2007, p. 42). "The iPhone is better than the Droid phone" is an attitude and so is "Consistency requires you to be as ignorant today as you were a year ago" (Bernard Berenson). An attitude sets our mind to draw certain judgments.

In this section, I discuss foundational elements of persuasion upon which persuasion strategies for public speeches are based. I explain the relationship between persuasion and coercion, attitude change and behavior change, the goals of persuasion, the elaboration likelihood model that explains how persuasion works generally, and the influence of culture on persuasion.

Coercion Versus Persuasion: Choice

Although much effort to persuade audiences is aimed at attitude change, the behavior of others can change without attitude change. Threats of violence may produce behavioral change without changing attitudes. Forced compliance from threats of physical harm, damage to one's reputation, financial ruin, and the like, however, are usually seen as coercion, not persuasion.

So what is the difference? *The essential difference between coercion and persuasion is the perception of free choice* (Perloff, 2010; Strong & Cook, 1990). Those who coerce seek to eliminate choice by force, threats of force, or intimidation. As noted in Chapter 1, coercion raises serious ethical concerns because free choice is taken away. In 2009, town hall meetings around the nation organized to inform concerned citizens about health-care proposals being considered in Congress often deteriorated into shouting matches as polarized participants attempted to silence each other (Urbina, 2009). A similar situation occurred in 2011 at town hall meetings convened for members of Congress to discuss a Republican bill that would fundamentally change the Medicare system in the United States. Hecklers opposed to this plan shouted down proponents of the bill, and audience members on both sides of the issue engaged in shouting matches ("House Republicans," 2011).

Does this mean heckling a speaker is always unethical? No! Heckling may be the only option an audience member has to voice opposition to a speaker commanding the stage. Heckling, however, steps across the ethical line when it becomes so boisterous and abusive that a speaker is given no opportunity to respond completely to the heckling. If the goal is to shut down speech, then it is coercive and unethical.

Conversely, those who persuade seek to limit choice to the most acceptable options by using logical and emotional appeals, not by threats, force, and intimidation. Logical and emotional appeals can influence your listeners, but your listeners are still free to choose what to believe and how to behave. *Ethical persuasive speaking is a communication process of convincing through open and honest means.* When your listeners can choose for themselves which attitude to accept or which behavior to perform, they are in charge of their decision making. If your listeners refuse to pay attention to your speech, ignore your persuasion effort, or do not heed your advice or plea, your persuasive speaking simply fails.

Attitude-Behavior Consistency: Variables

Although attitudes often predict behavior, there isn't always a consistent relationship between the two (Wallace et al., 2005). For example, most Americans think the Ten Commandments should guide our lives (we embrace them as strong attitudes—killing is wrong, coveting is bad, stealing is immoral, etc.). Yet everyone violates at least some of the commandments as though they were merely the Ten Suggestions. Thus, our behavior doesn't always match our attitudes. Energy conservation is socially desirable. Few people would argue that consumers should waste energy. One study found that 85% of those surveyed considered the energy crisis serious (Costanzo et al., 1986). This same study, however, found little relationship between stated attitudes on the energy crisis and actual conservation of energy.

Very often changing attitudes is not sufficient. It is behavior that needs to change. Consider the abstinence-only programs to prevent premarital sex among teenagers. Despite a vigorous campaign to convince teenagers to take a public pledge to abstain from premarital sex, a careful analysis of data reveals that those who took the "virginity pledge" were just as likely as nonpledgers within a five-year period to have premarital sex, but they were less likely to use birth control (Rosenbaum, 2009). If a principal purpose of abstinence-only programs is to prevent teen pregnancy and all the problems associated with it, then this study's results are quite disheartening. The pledge (stated attitude) doesn't produce the desired behavior. There are other ways to strengthen abstinence-only persuasive efforts (see Jemmott, 2010), but inducing teens to make public pledges of abstinence is, by itself, unlikely to produce abstinence.

Why aren't our attitudes and behaviors always consistent? Several variables affect how consistent our attitudes and behaviors are likely to be.

Direct Experience: No Secondhand Attitudes

Attitudes that are formed from direct experience usually conform more closely to actual behavior than those formed more indirectly (Fazio, 1986). When you have encountered a problem in your life, thought about it, felt its implications, and considered appropriate responses, your relevant attitude has been formed through direct experience. Have you ever been unemployed, experienced poverty, or had to solicit money from strangers? Have you ever been a small-business owner who has worried about high taxes jeopardizing your ability to thrive or even survive? That's direct experience. Your attitudes about food stamps for the poor, unemployment benefits, and business taxation are likely influenced strongly by these directly related experiences. Your behavior toward those similarly disadvantaged is more apt to coincide with these attitudes than if you have only indirect experience of such things (Perloff, 2010).

Those attitudes that are shaped more indirectly by media images, what friends and others have told you, or by your participation in discussions on blogging sites tend to be inconsistently related to behavior. These "second-hand attitudes" (Gass & Seiter, 2007) derived from indirect experience usually serve as weak predictors of behavior because, when faced with actual situations, the attitudes are more borrowed than personal. For example, it's far easier to ignore panhandlers begging for money when you've never had the desperate, frightening experience of joblessness and homelessness. Directly formed attitudes derived from personal experience are also likely to be more strongly held than secondhand attitudes.

These strong attitudes are more likely to predict behavior than weakly held, borrowed attitudes (Wallace et al., 2005). For instance, you may steadfastly avoid drinking alcohol because you have experienced firsthand what alcoholism can do to a family. Perhaps a parent was an alcoholic, became abusive, and provoked constant discord in your family that eventually led to parental divorce. Your attitude about alcohol has been formed directly through personal experience, and your attitude about the dangers of alcoholism is strongly held. If your attitude about alcohol is mostly formed indirectly from watching public service announcements on the dangers of alcohol and is only weakly held, however, when prodded to drink by friends and peers, you may cave in to the pressure more easily. The more directly you can make your audience feel that they are affected by the problem you describe (e.g., general state budget cuts threaten your access to higher education), the greater is the chance that their behavior will move in the direction you desire (support tax increases).

Social Pressure: Heat from Others

Social pressure has been shown to be a very strong influence on human behavior, and it is a significant reason that your attitudes and behavior may be inconsistent at times (Wallace at al., 2005). You may want to speak up when someone makes a racist or sexist remark, but you may remain quiet if you fear social disapproval from others for being a "troublemaker." You may not particularly enjoy drinking alcohol, but maybe you drink to excess at parties because it is the social expectation of your peer group. Previously, I cited a Zogby International survey that showed 56% of the 1,005 college students polled felt group pressure to binge drink ("Poll: College Students," 2000). Social pressure and fear of disapproval make standing before an audience and giving a speech that you know will incite a negative reaction very challenging.

Effort Required: Make It Easy

Despite the best intentions, attitudes and behavior will often be inconsistent because consistency may require too great an effort to perform the behavior (Wallace et al., 2005). You likely see recycling your cans, bottles, and newspapers as too labor intensive if you have to separate each item into separate bins, load them into the trunks of your cars, then drive to the nearest recycling center to unload the waste. Increasingly, however, communities around the country are recognizing the benefits of curbside recycling. Participation in recycling programs grows explosively when it is no more difficult than hauling a trash bin to the curb in front of your home. The effort required is minimal, so recycling is almost universal. Half the U.S. population had access to curbside recycling by 2010 ("Curbside Recycling," 2010).

When trying to persuade an audience to act on a problem, find the easiest ways for listeners to express their support. Signing a petition or donating a dollar on the spot is an easy way to show support. Asking people to canvass neighborhoods, to call strangers on the phone to solicit support for a cause or a candidate, or to raise money for a program is hampered by the effort required to perform the behavior. Far less participation in such activities should be expected as a result.

Consider how Sean McLaughlin (1996), a student at Ohio University, offers simple, yet effective, solutions for the problem of food poisoning.

> First, wash hands well and wash them often. . . . If you prefer to use sponges and dishcloths, be sure to throw them in the dishwasher two or three times a week. Also, try color coding your sponges—the red one for washing dishes and a blue one for wiping up countertops. . . . Experts also suggest using both sides of a cutting board—one side for meats and the other side for vegetables. And those who wash dishes by hand, be careful. Scrub dishes vigorously with an antibacterial soap and rinse with hot water. Air drying is preferred to drying with a towel. . . . Finally, and perhaps the best advice—don't become lax when it comes to food safety in your home. Don't write your congressperson, write your mom. As we have seen today, re-educating yourself and spreading the word on kitchen safety can significantly reduce chances of food poisoning. (p. 75)

The speaker provides several easy steps that will protect you from food poisoning. One step, air drying dishes, actually reduces labor. Towel drying requires effort; air drying requires merely waiting.

Solutions to serious problems cannot always be simple and easy to implement. Nevertheless, try to offer ways that even complex solutions can be implemented in relatively simple, straightforward steps.

Goals of Persuasion: Not Always Change

Persuasive speaking can have several goals. Choosing the appropriate goal for the situation will largely determine your degree of success or failure.

Conversion: Radical Persuasion

Psychologist Muzafer Sherif and his associates (1965) developed the **social judgment theory** of persuasion to explain attitude change (see also Littlejohn & Foss, 2008). Their theory states that when listeners hear a persuasive message, they compare it with attitudes they already hold. The preexisting attitude on an issue serves as an **anchor**, or reference point. Surrounding this anchor is a range of possible attitudes an individual may hold. Positions a person finds tolerable form his or her **latitude of acceptance**. Positions that provoke only a neutral or ambivalent response form the **latitude of noncommitment**. Those positions the person would find objectionable because they are too far from the anchor attitude form the **latitude of rejection**. Figure 15-1 depicts this range of possible opinions on an issue.

Research found that persuasive messages that fall within a person's latitude of rejection almost never produce a change in attitude (Sherif et al., 1965). The further away a position is from the anchor attitude, the less likely persuasion will be successful (Littlejohn & Foss, 2008; Sherif et al., 1973). This is especially true when the listener has high ego involvement with the issue. **Ego involvement** refers to the degree to which an issue is relevant or important to a person (Littlejohn & Foss, 2008). Students who work hard for a political candidate, for example, are highly unlikely to vote for the opponent.

Social judgment theory strongly suggests that setting conversion as your goal for persuasion is unrealistic. Conversion asks your listeners to move from their anchor position to a completely contradictory position. This is especially unlikely when conversion is sought during a brief persuasive speech. Students often make the attempt to convert the "unbelievers" in speeches on abortion, religion, and other emotionally charged topics. Such efforts are doomed from the start. If your message seeks conversion from your audience, it will likely meet with quick resistance, especially if your listeners have strongly formed attitudes on the subject.

Unless a *significant emotional event* occurs, conversion almost never happens from a single persuasive attempt. If you have been a strong gun control advocate but experience a home invasion in which your life and those of your loved ones were threatened, you may think seriously about purchasing a hand gun for future protection. Absent such an emotional event, however, conversion from strong gun control advocate to a defender of relatively unrestricted gun ownership is unlikely. Hearing a 10-minute persuasive speech, no matter how eloquent, rarely converts anyone holding strong views. Conversion, then, is an unrealistic goal for most persuasive speeches.

Modification: Don't Ask for the Moon

Research suggests that moderate, not extreme, positions relative to a particular audience are most persuasive (Edwards & Smith, 1996). Positions that lie at the outer fringes of a listener's latitude of acceptance may become the new anchor position as a result of a persuasive speech. For example, very restrictive gun control legislation may be a person's anchor. A strong persuasive speech, however, may realistically modify this person's position to an outright ban on *handguns*. Once this position is embraced, it may become the new anchor. Subsequent persuasive efforts may move the anchor incrementally until the person eventually accepts a complete ban on ownership of *all guns*. The change in attitude occurs bit by bit. It is rarely a one-shot effort. Modification of

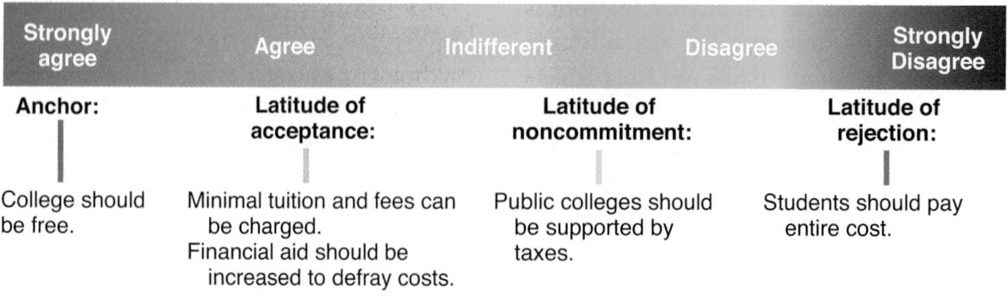

FIGURE 15-1 Social Judgment Theory

attitudes and behavior is an appropriate, realistic goal for a persuasive speech.

Maintenance: Keep 'Em Coming Back

When most people think of persuasion, changing attitudes and behavior immediately comes to mind. Much persuasion, however, does not aim to produce change. Charles Kernaghan's speech to the CFT was mostly "preaching to the choir." Few in that audience of active labor organizers and members would have disagreed with much of what Kernaghan said in his rousing oration. Most advertising of well-established products, such as Coke or the Toyota Camry, aims to maintain the buying habits of the public. The goal is to keep consumers purchasing your products over and over and preventing purchases of competing products. In political campaigns, initial persuasion is usually aimed at "securing the base." This means motivating Democrats to keep voting for Democratic candidates and to keep Republicans voting for Republican candidates. The message is "do what you've been doing." Sunday sermons usually change few minds because most people who attend a church service require no such change. They already believe the religious dogmas articulated by the minister, priest, or rabbi. Preaching to the choir, however, can inspire the faithful, energize believers, and reinforce preexisting attitudes.

Part of maintaining current attitudes and behavior of your audience is inducing resistance to **counterpersuasion**, or attacks from an opposing side. Inducing resistance to counterpersuasion helps maintain current attitudes. There are two principal ways you can induce resistance to counterpersuasion. First, *forewarn* your audience members that an attempt to change their attitudes, beliefs, or behavior will occur (Benoit, 1998; Quinn & Wood, 2004). Prosecution and defense attorneys often use forewarning in their opening statements to juries ("The defense will try to appeal to your emotions by presenting her client as a desperate father trying to save his dying child. Don't be fooled. The defendant is a cold, calculating murderer."). Forewarning gives your listeners time to generate counterarguments that thwart attempted persuasion and to rehearse their responses (Gass & Seiter, 2007).

A second way to induce resistance to persuasion is to *inoculate* your audience (McGuire, 1964). When you are inoculated against disease, you are exposed to a weakened version of the virus to trigger an immune response. Likewise, inoculating your audience to counterpersuasion exposes your listeners to a weakened version of counterarguments. Studies aimed at preventing teenagers from starting to smoke cigarettes found that merely mentioning arguments for smoking (e.g., smoking is cool; peers will like you) and then refuting these weakly presented arguments did induce resistance to peer persuasion to start smoking (Pfau & Van Bockern, 1994). There is substantial evidence that inoculation can be an effective way to induce resistance to persuasion (Pfau et al., 2005; Szabo & Pfau, 2002; Wood, 2007).

Elaboration Likelihood Model: Mindful or Mindless Persuasion

The **elaboration likelihood model** (ELM) of persuasion is an overarching explanation for how listeners cope with the bombardment of persuasive messages by sorting them into those that are important, or central, and those that are less relevant, or peripheral (Petty & Cacioppo, 1986a, 1986b). The *central route* requires mindfulness; the content of the message is scrutinized for careful reasoning and substantial, credible evidence. Counterarguments are considered and weighed. Questions come to mind, and a desire for more information (elaboration) emerges. The *peripheral route* is relatively mindless; little attention is given to processing a persuasive message. The listener looks for mental shortcuts to make quick decisions about seemingly peripheral issues. Credibility, likability, and attractiveness of a persuader, how other people react to the message, and the consequences that might result from agreeing or disagreeing with the persuader are some of the shortcuts used in the peripheral route (Shadel et al., 2001).

To illustrate the two routes to persuasion, consider an example offered by Gass and Seiter (2007). Let's say that Michael and Maria are on a date and about to order dinner at a nice restaurant. The waiter suggests several specials, all of them meat or fish. He even volunteers which one is his favorite. Maria orders first. She is very careful to choose only vegetarian dishes from the menu. She asks the waiter whether an entrée is cooked in animal fat, is there any butter on the pasta, and does the sauce contain any dairy products? After ordering, Maria turns to Michael and says with an animated delivery that he should eat vegetarian because it is healthier and reduces animal deaths. Michael has no strong opinion on the subject, but he is very attracted to Maria. He tells the waiter, "I'll have what she ordered." Maria used the central route to decide her order. She was very mindful of her decision. She considered her decision very carefully because it was important to her. Michael, on the other hand, used the peripheral route. The decision was relatively unimportant to him, so he based his order on a cue unrelated to the menu, the waiter's preference, or the arguments offered by Maria. He ordered vegetarian because he hoped to gain favor with Maria.

Your listeners use both central and peripheral routes, called **parallel processing**, when presented with persuasive messages (Petty et al., 1987). They tend to use one route more than the other, however. The degree to which a receiver emphasizes the central or peripheral route depends primarily on his or her *motivation* and *ability* to think about and carefully assess the quality of a persuasive message (Petty et al., 2004). We are more motivated to use the central route when the issues affect us personally. We are more likely to use the peripheral route when issues seem tangential to our interests, are largely inconsequential to our lives, and our knowledge of a subject is limited and we are distracted or preoccupied. If you were Michael in the situation described, you are motivated to please your date, not to learn about vegetarianism. Your knowledge of issues related to vegetarianism is superficial at best, and you are distracted by your attraction to your date. It is a wonder you can think at all.

Also, some persuasive messages are too complex and require technical knowledge to evaluate. In such cases, our ability to use central processing is limited. Typically, peripheral cues, such as how other audience members respond to the messages, will be used.

Attitude change produced by the central route tends to be more persistent, resistant to change, and predictive of behavior than attitude change produced by the peripheral route (Petty et al., 2004). If Michael never again went on another outing with Maria, he probably would eat dead cow flesh with relish because his flirtation with vegetarianism was arrived at by peripheral influences.

Clearly, *central processing of persuasive messages should be encouraged*. Central processing is what skeptics do primarily when presented with a persuasive message (see Chapter 6). You can increase central processing by making issues relevant to listeners' lives. Complex, technical issues can be simplified for lay audiences. If listeners understand the basic concepts, they can analyze the arguments and evidence presented. Even highly involved listeners, however, will use parallel processing. Because of time constraints and information overload, we sometimes have no choice but to use peripheral processing. Persuasive strategies that typically trigger parallel processing will be discussed later.

Culture and Persuasion: A Question of Values

The scientific investigation of persuasive speaking is a peculiarly Western interest. In Asian countries, for instance, spirited debates to influence decision making have been viewed as relatively pointless. Debates create friction and disharmony, and they usually end inconclusively (Jaffe, 1998). Japan, for example, began implementing a jury-style system in its criminal courts in 2009 (Kawatsu, 2009). This is a momentous change from the long-standing practice of judges making decisions in criminal cases. To acclimate a hesitant populace to the new system, 500 mock trials were held. Nevertheless, 80% of Japanese surveyed about the new jury system expressed dread at the prospect of participating. Japanese reluctance emerges from a deeply rooted cultural revulsion to expressing personal opinions, arguing with others in public, and questioning authority (Onishi, 2007).

Persuasion works best when it is adapted to the cultural context. Persuasive strategies that may successfully change attitudes and behavior in an individualistic country such as the United States may not be so successful in collectivist countries (Murray-Johnson et al., 2001). A survey cited in Chapter 3 showed clearly that respondents from the United States highly valued individual rights but not an orderly society. Respondents from Asian, collectivist countries expressed opposite preferences. Thus, appeals to order should be more persuasive in collectivist cultures, and appeals to individual rights should be more persuasive in individualist cultures.

One study examined slogans used in magazines for their cultural persuasiveness (Han & Shavitt, 1994). Slogans such as these were considered (see also Gass & Seiter, 2007).

1. The art of being unique.
2. We have a way of bringing people closer together.
3. She's got a style all her own.
4. The dream of prosperity for all of us.
5. A leader among leaders.
6. Sharing is beautiful.

Which of these slogans do you think would work best in individualist cultures, and which would work best in collectivist cultures? When comparing the United States and Korea, it was found that slogans like the first, third, and fifth were used more in the United States and were more persuasive than the other slogans. These three appeal to individual success, personal benefits, and independence. Slogans like the second, fourth, and sixth were used more in Korea and were more persuasive than the others. They appeal to group harmony, cooperation, and collective benefit. An American ad shows a young man at the wheel of a Cadillac CTS and presents a choice between "The nail that sits up gets hammered down" or "You can be the hammer." The first is an aphorism well known in Japan that expresses a collectivist viewpoint. The second is clearly an individualist viewpoint. Cadillac is obviously appealing to individualist values of American culture to sell cars when the ad implies being the hammer is the preferred position. Such an ad would likely backfire in Japan.

Another study found that when attempting to convince roommates to quiet down, individuals from the United States preferred direct statements such as "Please be quiet," "You are making too much noise," or "If you don't quiet down, I'll be as noisy as possible when you are trying to study." These statements pay little attention to face saving or harmony. They address individual needs. Persons from China, however, used more indirect strategies of persuasion, such as hinting that less noise would be preferred or making statements invoking group awareness ("Your noisiness shows a lack of consideration for others") (Wiseman et al., 1995). Clearly, your choice of persuasive strategies should be influenced by the diversity of your audience. It is only one element of the complex persuasion equation, but it is an important one.

Persuasive Speaking Strategies

A driver can be easily distracted by signs, many of which have no bearing on getting from one place to another. Signs are everywhere, competing for our attention. "Drop Your Pants Here and You Will Receive Prompt Attention" says the sign outside a dry cleaners. "Kids with Gas Eat Here Free" says another. "Parking for Drive-Thru Service Only" and "Hidden Entrance" read two other signs. They can be funny, but signs are a critical element of our everyday transit from place to place. Signs warn us of impending dangers ("Soft Shoulder, Blind Curves, Steep Grade, Big Trucks, Good Luck!"), notify us of our driving responsibilities ("Slow

Down or Die") and help us find where we are heading ("Emergency Phone 174 Km Ahead"). Poor signage can be infuriating and even dangerous. Have you ever looked for a sign telling you how to find a freeway or turnpike in an unfamiliar city, only to be left pounding your steering wheel in frustration (some of us don't have a GPS)? An April 2008 study by psychologists Oliver Clark and Simon Davies from the University of Hull presented at the British Psychological Society conference even found that too many signs bunched together can cause accidents. Poor signage shouldn't be life threatening. Therefore, Congress should mandate that all public signs receive advanced governmental approval for clarity, simplicity, and accuracy.

In this opening paragraph, I use humor, anger, fear, and evidence as potential persuasive strategies. These are but four ways that a speaker can attempt to persuade an audience. Their effectiveness is not sure fire because they must be used under the right conditions. Consideration of all possible persuasive speaking strategies would require a lengthy book. In this section, I discuss how to use significant persuasion strategies and under what conditions they are most likely to be effective.

Establish Identification: Connecting with Your Audience

Identification is the affiliation and connection between speaker and audience. Finding commonalities that resonate with audience members can move you beyond perceived initial differences in attitudes, beliefs, and values.

Likability: I Can Relate to You

A key element of identification is likability of the speaker. Even when your audience is composed of highly diverse members, if your listeners grow to like you, they are more inclined to listen. Compliance and assent on controversial positions are more probable than if you are not liked (Cialdini, 1993). One national tracking poll conducted October 6–8, 2000, several days following the first presidential debate between Al Gore and George W. Bush, found that respondents generally rated Gore smarter, but they liked Bush more (Benedetto, 2000). Gore exhibited heavy sighing, pained facial expressions, and head shaking to communicate contempt for his debate opponent. Catholic University of America political scientist Mark Rozell explained that Gore's "smart alecky" debate performance was poorly received. "Voters found his demeanor snide, rude and offensive, characteristics they don't like in a president." Also, "Gore just came across as not very likeable, while Bush, verbal stumbles and all, just seemed more human" (Benedetto, 2000, p. 1A).

How do you enhance likability? Praising and complimenting your audience ("This class did better on the exam than any previous class"), saying you like your audience ("What a great group"), and expressing genuine concern and showing empathy for problems and pain faced by audience members are just some quick ways (Cialdini, 1993). Telling stories well is also a very effective means of creating likability. Substantial research shows that storytelling promotes **social cohesion**—it binds us together in mutual liking (Hogan, 2003). Our brains even seem to be wired to relish good stories. "Storytelling is one of the few human traits that are truly universal across culture and through all of known history" (Hsu, 2008, p. 46). An audience can be highly diverse, but who doesn't love a great story and like the person who tells it well?

Stylistic Similarity: Looking and Acting the Part

We tend to identify more closely with individuals who appear similar to us. One way to appear similar is to look and act the part. This is called **stylistic similarity**. For example, when you go for a job interview, you should dress, look, and speak as an interviewer would expect from someone worthy of the job. Showing up in baggy pants and a T-shirt emblazoned with an imprint of your favorite local rock band when applying for a teaching job won't likely work in your favor. Throwing in an occasional verbal obscenity during a teaching demonstration also won't likely endear you to an interview panel.

When the situation is formal, such as a valedictory speech at a graduation ceremony, dress and speak formally. Slang and offensive language should be avoided. When the situation is less formal, such as some classroom speeches, country fair presentations, many protest marches, and public gatherings, however, you need to shift styles and speak, dress, and act more casually so your audience can relate to you.

Finding the appropriate level of formality can be tricky when the situation doesn't call for a clear-cut choice. For example, as a student, how do you respond to your instructor dressing formally, insisting you address him or her as "Professor" or "Doctor" so and so, and being required to always raise your hand to be recognized before speaking? Would you relate better if your instructor were more casual, or do you appreciate the formality? A formal style communicates seriousness of intent and significance of the event. An informal style communicates less seriousness, perhaps even playfulness, and sets a more casual atmosphere that encourages student participation. Your style needs to match your expectations and goals. Teachers make choices about formality or informality based on their goals for the class.

Substantive Similarity: Establishing Common Ground

Highlighting similarities in positions, values, and attitudes also encourages identification. This **substantive similarity** creates identification by establishing common ground between speaker and audience. If listeners can say, "I like what I'm hearing," they can identify with the speaker. If you're speaking to a contrary audience, it is helpful to build bridges by pointing out common experiences, perceptions, values, and attitudes before launching into more delicate areas of disagreement. Listeners will be more inclined to consider your more controversial viewpoints if they initially identify with you. For example, a November 30, 2010, poll by CNBC-AP reported that 85% of respondents were concerned about the mounting federal deficit (Dauble, 2010). These same respondents were split on how to solve the problem, however. Before addressing solutions to the federal deficit, you as a speaker would want to make a clear statement that expresses strong agreement with the prevailing majority on the seriousness of the problem before offering more controversial solutions. You establish common ground before launching into areas of potential disagreement.

Build Credibility: Can We Believe You?

O'Keefe (1990) defines **credibility** as "judgments made by a perceiver (e.g., a message recipient) concerning the believability of a communicator" (pp. 130–131). In *The Rhetoric*, Aristotle identified the ingredients of credibility, or **ethos** in his terminology, as "good sense, good moral character, and good will." Recent research affirms Aristotle's observation and expands the list of dimensions somewhat. The primary dimensions of credibility are competence,

What elements of credibility do you think Jon Stewart exhibits, pictured here at his "Restore Sanity" rally? Does it depend on which audience is listening to him: conservatives, moderates, or liberals?

trustworthiness, dynamism, and composure (Gass & Seiter, 2007; Pornpitakpan, 2004). All four are developed throughout your speech.

Competence refers to the audience's perception of the speaker's knowledge and experience on a topic. It addresses the question "Does this speaker know what he or she is talking about?" You can enhance your credibility when you identify your background, experience, and training relevant to a subject. Citing sources of evidence used, speaking fluently, and avoiding vocal fillers ("uhm," "ah," "like," "you know") also enhance credibility (subjects discussed in earlier chapters) (O'Keefe, 1990).

Trustworthiness refers to how truthful or honest we perceive the speaker to be. It addresses the question "Can I believe what the speaker says?" We don't feel comfortable hiring a dishonest plumber, electrician, or carpenter. We hesitate to buy anything from a salesperson we perceive to be dishonest.

One way to increase your trustworthiness is to argue against your self-interest (Pratkanis & Aronson, 2001). If you take a position on an issue that will cost you money, a job, a promotion, or some reward or benefit, most listeners will see you as presenting an honest opinion. Conversely, few people trust the explanations for rapid increases in gas prices provided by spokespeople for the oil companies because the oil companies make huge profits when gas prices are inflated. Oil giant ExxonMobil Corporation raked in an almost $11 billion profit in the first quarter of 2011 as gas prices at the pump simultaneously soared well above $4 a gallon (Rooney, 2011). If ExxonMobil lobbied hard in Congress for substantial increases in gas mileage standards for automobiles (against its self-interest), however, it might improve its credibility with the public.

Dynamism is a third dimension of credibility. It refers to the enthusiasm, energy, and forcefulness exhibited by a speaker. Sleepy, lackluster presentations lower your credibility. Over-the-top enthusiasm, however, can be equally problematic. Those who pitch products on infomercials are invariably enthusiastic, sometimes bordering on frenzied. Howard Dean killed his presidential campaign in 2004 when, after a disappointing showing in the Iowa caucuses, he gave what political pundits labeled his "I Have a Scream" speech when trying to whip up enthusiasm from his disappointed supporters. As his vocal volume escalated, he seemed almost maniacal. Too little dynamism can diminish your speech, but too much can backfire.

A final dimension of speaker credibility is **composure**. Audiences tend to be influenced by speakers who are emotionally stable, appear confident and in control of themselves, and remain calm even when problems arise during a speech. Bill O'Reilly and Geraldo Rivera engaged in a shouting match over the topic of illegal immigration on an April 5, 2007, episode of Fox network's *The O'Reilly Factor*. It became a "most watched" video on YouTube. Both appeared emotionally overwrought. To some, these episodes are entertaining, but it is doubtful that any listeners are impressed by witnessing two verbal combatants savage each other to the point where unleashing fire hoses on them to dampen their tempers almost seems appropriate.

Women have to be more careful expressing anger than men in professional settings. One study showed that women were accorded less status and were perceived as less competent when they became overtly angry (Brescoll & Uhlmann, 2008). Men, on the other hand, were not so diminished when they expressed anger but lost status when they expressed sadness. Stereotypes remain troublesome still for both men and women.

Displaying emotion overtly, however, does not always destroy a speaker's credibility. Too much composure may be perceived as hard-heartedness or insensitivity. Shedding tears at a funeral or expressing outrage at an atrocity may enhance your credibility with some listeners. *The appropriateness of displaying composure depends on the context.*

Humor has been discussed as a superior attention strategy, but does it play a role in persuasive identification and credibility? It does in some circumstances. *Humor can enhance listeners' perceptions of your communication competence* (Wanzer et al., 1996). It can also increase your likability and help establish rapport with your audience (Weinberger & Gulas, 1992). In June 2009, comedian Stephen Colbert took his *Colbert Report* to Iraq and performed four shows for the troops. He dubbed the series of shows *Operation Iraqi Stephen: Going Commando*. To great applause and laughter from the troops assembled, Colbert marched on stage dressed in a camouflage business suit and tie. Later he had his head shaved by Gen. Ray Odierno to exhibit solidarity with our soldiers. The crowd roared its approval. One soldier, Ryan MacLeod, remarked afterward, "Definitely the highlight was seeing him sacrifice his hair" (quoted in Baram, 2009). Later Colbert declared, "By the power vested in me by basic cable, I officially declare we have won the Iraq war" (quoted in Baram, 2009).

Inappropriate humor, however, can diminish perceptions of your credibility (Derks et al., 1995). Self-deprecating humor can also make you seem incompetent if used excessively (see Chapter 13 for a discussion).

Build Arguments: Persuasive Logic and Evidence

Much has already been said about the importance of logic and evidence in Chapters 12 and 13. In this section, however, I address building arguments based on logic and evidence, what Aristotle called **logos**, with a specific focus on persuasion.

Propositions: Fact, Value, and Policy Claims

The Toulmin structure of an argument begins with a claim (see Chapter 12). The primary, overriding claim for a persuasive speech is called a **proposition**. The proposition becomes the essence of your persuasive purpose statement. Propositions define and focus the argument, limit issues to what is relevant, and set standards for what should be addressed (Inch & Warnick, 1998).

There are three types of propositions: fact, policy, and value. A **proposition of fact** alleges a truth ("Open carry gun laws would provide significant protection against criminals"). A **proposition of value** calls for a judgment that assesses the worth or merit of an idea, object, or practice ("Abortion is immoral"). A **proposition of policy** calls for a significant change from how problems are currently handled ("Smoking should be banned in all public places"). Main reasons (the grounds) offered to support the proposition (principal claim) that calls for a ban on smoking in public places include:

1. Secondhand smoke is dangerous to nonsmokers.
2. Secondhand smoke is annoying to nonsmokers.
3. Smokers violate nonsmokers rights to breathe unpolluted air.
4. Employees in bars and restaurants cannot escape the smoke.

Skeptics, those who make a strong effort to analyze and evaluate arguments presented by speakers attempting to persuade, are more likely to be moved by strong, carefully developed arguments (the central route) than by peripheral issues and concerns. Strong arguments, of course, do not persuade everyone.

Persuasive Arguments: Quality and Quantity

The quality and number of arguments advanced for a proposition can be factors in

NASA astronaut Joan Higginbotham has credibility working for her the moment she addresses an audience on her area of expertise—the space program. Higginbotham was the third African American woman in space, and she actively participated in 53 space shuttle launches.

persuasive speaking. One study tested to what degree students could be persuaded that completing comprehensive examinations as a condition for graduating from college is a good proposal. Student groups were told either that the exams would begin in one year (meaning they would have to take the exams) or in ten years (meaning they would not have to take the exams). Presumably, those directly affected by the proposal (must take the exams) would scrutinize the persuasive message, whereas those unaffected by the proposal would see the message as peripheral and see the number of arguments, even if weak, as decisive (Petty & Cacioppo, 1984).

The quantity and quality of arguments made a big difference. Mindful students directly affected by the proposal were not persuaded by nine weak arguments. In fact, the more weak arguments they heard, the more they disliked the proposal. They were persuaded only when strong arguments were used, especially many strong arguments. For students unaffected by the proposal, however, the quality of the arguments was relatively unimportant. They were more persuaded that the proposal was a good idea when nine arguments were presented than when only three were offered, no matter how strong or weak the arguments.

When constructing your persuasive speech, don't be satisfied when you find one or two strong arguments to support your proposition. If several strong arguments emerge when you research your proposition and if time permits, present them all. Several strong arguments can be persuasive to listeners who process your message either peripherally (quantity of arguments) or centrally (quality of arguments).

Persuasive Evidence: Statistics Versus Narratives

"The use of evidence produces more attitude change than the use of no evidence" (Reynolds & Reynolds, 2002, p. 428). To be persuasive, however, your evidence must be attributed to a highly credible source, should be seen by audience members as legitimate (free of fallacies), must gain the attention of your audience and not put your listeners to sleep, and should not overwhelm your audience with an excessive abundance (Perloff, 2010).

What about types of evidence? Vivid narratives and examples can be more persuasive than statistics (Glassner, 2000), partly because they typically are more interesting and memorable (Green & Brock, 2000; Kopfman et al., 1998). A strong narrative can be "a potent persuasive tool" (Hsu, 2008, p. 51). Finding vivid stories more interesting and memorable, however, doesn't automatically make them more persuasive than statistics. Research is mixed on which is more persuasive (Allen & Preiss, 1997; Feeley et al., 2006). So, what should you conclude? Use both narratives and statistics as your optimum strategy, thereby capitalizing on the strengths of both forms of evidence (Allen et al., 2000).

Use Emotional Appeals: Beyond Logic

We are not like Spock or Data on *Star Trek*. Although logic and evidence can be enormously persuasive, especially for highly involved listeners, emotional appeals—what Aristotle termed **pathos**—are also powerful motivators. As social psychologist Drew Westen (2007) observes, "We do not pay attention to arguments unless they engender our interest, enthusiasm, fear, anger, or contempt. . . . 'Reasonable' actions almost always require the integration of thought and emotion . . ." (p. 16).

General Emotional Appeals: Motivating Change

Appeals to sadness, pride, honor, hope, joy, guilt, envy, and shame all have their place as persuasion strategies that ignite emotional reactions and change behavior (Gass & Seiter, 2007). Research, however, on the persuasiveness of these particular emotional appeals is sparse. Nevertheless, there is some evidence that these emotional appeals have persuasive potential (Dillard & Nabi, 2006; Nabi, 2002). Hope, for example, is sometimes a cornerstone of an entire political campaign. Barack Obama's successful run for the presidency revolved around a strong appeal to hope. He made this appeal in a victory speech the night of the 2008 Iowa presidential caucus.

> We are choosing hope over fear. . . . Hope is what led me here today—with a father from Kenya, a mother from Kansas, and a story that could only happen in the United States of America. Hope is the bedrock of this nation, the belief that our destiny will not be written for us, but by us, by all those men and women who are not content to settle for the world as it is; who have the courage to remake the world as it should be. ("Remarks," 2008)

Appeals to hope and other emotions can be persuasive. Unquestionably, however, fear is the number one emotional appeal used to change the attitudes and behavior of audiences.

Fear Appeals: Are You Scared Yet?

"Don't put that in your mouth. It's full of germs." "You'll poke your eye out if you run with those scissors." "Don't ever talk to strangers. They may hurt you." "Never cross the street before looking both ways. You could be killed." From childhood, we are all familiar with fear appeals. Our parents give us a heavy dose to keep us safe and out of trouble. Fear appeals are used on adults as well. In 2001, Canada began using the most shocking, fear-inducing warnings on cigarette packages ever used anywhere in the world (Bor, 2001). Photos of blackened, bleeding gums, a diseased heart, a lung tumor, or a gangrenous foot appeared on a rotating basis on all cigarette packs along with information on the hazards of smoking. The Food and Drug Administration followed the Canadian example by requiring tobacco marketers to cover the top half of cigarette packs and 20% of tobacco advertisements with nine extremely graphic anti-smoking images, effective as of October 2012.

Do fear appeals work? More research has been conducted on the efficacy of fear appeals than on all other emotions combined. In general, the more fear is aroused in listeners, the more vulnerable they feel and the more likely they will be convinced (Dillard, 1994; Witte & Allen, 1996). In Montana, a state plagued by methamphetamine use, young people were targeted during 2005-2007 for a barrage of extremely graphic, terrifying video ads of teens hooked on the drug ("Montana Meth Project," 2008). The fear appeals appeared to work (Siebel & Mange, 2009). A dramatic shift occurred in attitudes about meth use according to two reports from Mike McGrath (2007, 2008), Montana's attorney general. Teens' perceptions of great risk from trying meth even one time increased substantially to 93% of respondents, and 87% of young adults believed their friends would give them a hard time for using meth. Behavioral changes also followed attitudinal changes. Montana went from 5th in the nation in meth abuse to 39th, teen meth use declined 45%, meth-positive employee drug testing declined 70%, and meth-related crime decreased 53% (McGrath, 2007; "Montana Meth Project," 2008). Other states have subsequently followed the Montana meth persuasive model.

Fear appeals, however, don't always work with audiences. *Five conditions determine whether high fear appeals will likely produce constructive action* (Gass & Seiter, 2007).

First, *your audience must feel vulnerable.* We don't all fear the same things (Witte et al., 2001). Some people fear heights, whereas others relish jumping out of planes and skydiving. Some individuals fear pit bulls, whereas others see them as wonderful pets. Teens feel more threatened by social rejection than physical harm caused by drug use (Schoenbachler & Whittler, 1996). Recognizing this, the antimeth campaign in Montana tried to create strong social disapproval for meth use in addition to fear appeals about physical harm ("Montana Meth Project," 2008). There are also cultural differences in what we fear most. A cross-cultural study showed that audiences from individualist cultures were more persuaded by fear appeals that described personal harm, but collectivist cultures were more persuaded by fear appeals that described harm to the family (Witte et al., 2000).

Second, *a clear specific recommendation for avoiding or lessening the fear is important* (Devos-Comby & Salovey, 2002). A vague recommendation (e.g., get financial aid) is

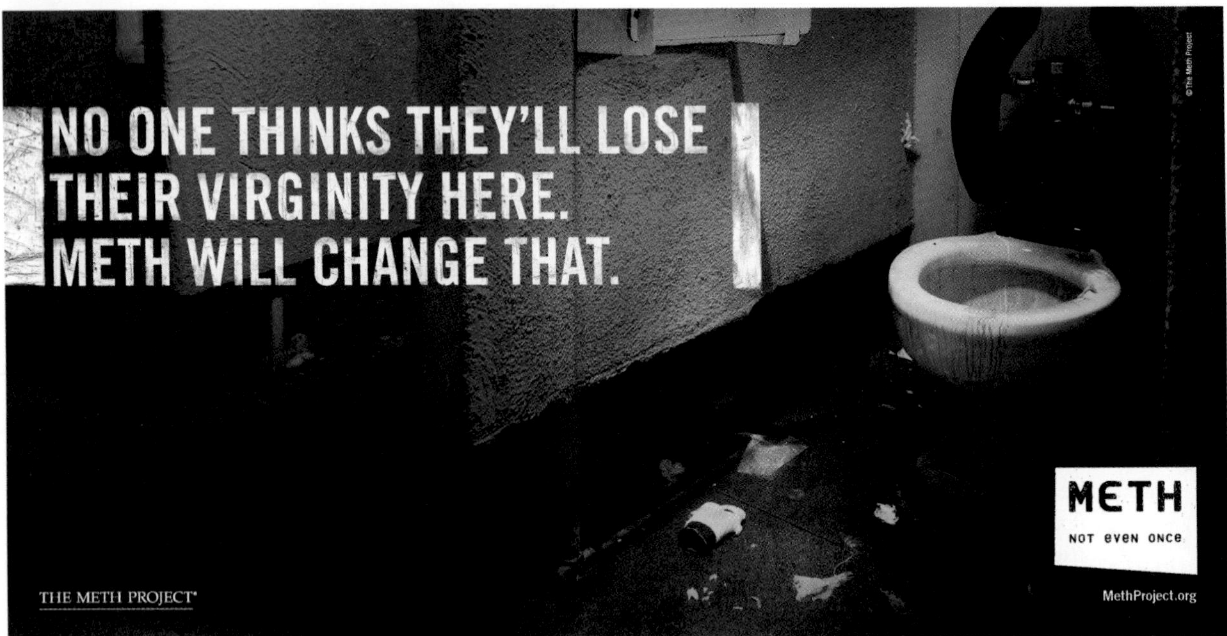

Carefully handled fear appeals can be very effective. Montana's gruesome anti-Meth ad campaign has been credited with a 30 percent decline in teen use of the drug.

not as effective as a specific recommendation (e.g., fill out this application for a Pell grant) to assuage the fear of having to drop out of school and be left with an uncertain future.

Third, *the recommendation must be perceived as effective* (Cho & Witte, 2004; Keller, 1999). Getting a vaccination against the flu is an effective recommended behavior. Wearing a mask to avoid infection is not nearly as effective and is often impractical. Imagine your professors lecturing through a mask, or you and fellow classmates working on group activities in class while all wearing masks.

Fourth, *listeners must perceive that they can perform the actions recommended.* Again, the effort required to perform the behavior is a key variable. Giving up sugary sodas entirely for the rest of your life to avoid dental and health problems may not be possible for most people. The effort is too great. Cutting soda consumption in half, however, may be realistic.

Finally, studies have shown that *fear appeals are more persuasive when combined with high-quality arguments* (Gleicher & Petty, 1992; Rodriguez, 1995). The fear appeal becomes more believable when it is bolstered by credible arguments.

In conclusion, fear appeals can be highly effective motivators of behavior but only under certain conditions (Witte, 1998). When a threat is perceived by listeners to be low, no action is likely. Thus, the speaker's fear appeal must be strong, and the threat must be shown to have a personal impact on individuals to arouse concern. When the personal threat is perceived to be high but the solution is viewed as ineffective by listeners or too difficult to implement, denial ("We can't do anything anyway, so why worry?") or rationalization ("You've got to die of something") typically neutralizes fear-arousing messages. Finally, when the personal threat is perceived by listeners to be high and a solution is viewed as effective and relatively easy to implement, fear-arousing messages will likely be successful in producing constructive action.

Anger Appeals: Make 'Em Mad

Arousing anger is often used to persuade listeners. Note how Hope Stallings (2009), a student at Berry College competing in the Interstate Oratorical Association contest, intended to trigger anger: "Now that we understand the catastrophic impact of DPAs [deferred prosecution agreements] on our economy and personal economic well-being, we should be sufficiently angry to do something about it" (p. 15). Attempting to ignite anger in an audience is a common persuasive appeal because anger can provide a strong motivation to act.

Anger doesn't always provoke constructive behavior. People sometimes become verbally and/or physically violent when angry (Guerrero, 1992; Tavris, 1989). The intensity of the anger is key. Intense anger can short-circuit an individual's ability to think clearly and act responsibly (Fein, 1993). Intensely angry individuals may lash out at any perceived source of their anger, real or imagined (Lazarus, 1991; Pfau et al., 2001). Hecklers at town hall meetings across the nation who convened to discuss the health care law sometimes became so enraged with the speaker or other audience members that security had to drag them screaming from the room. This creates a volatile, even dangerous, situation. As a speaker, you want to keep calm, be unconditionally constructive in your comments even when others are losing their heads, and you should not taunt a heckler in your audience, especially if your audience is predominantly hostile. You could provoke a physical confrontation or even a riot. Arousing anger in your audience can be persuasive, but it can also backfire.

The target and context of anger arousal largely determine its persuasive implications (Nabi, 2002). The **Anger Activism Model** helps explain the relationship between anger and persuasion (Turner et al., 2007; see also Turner, 2006). This model posits that anger provokes desired behavior change when (1) the target audience initially agrees with your persuasion message, (2) the anger produced by your message is intense, and (3) your audience members perceive that they can act effectively to address their anger. Two studies show that if all three of these conditions are met, intense anger has the potential to motivate action even if the action required to quell or satiate the anger is very difficult to perform (Turner et al., 2007). Remember that the more difficult it is to perform a behavior, the less likely our attitudes and behavior will be consistent. Intense anger, however, can rouse people even if action requires great effort. Intense anger appeared to be the prime motivator for tens of thousands of people to protest "big government" and "taxation" at Tea Party rallies across the country on April 15, 2010. Some traveled long distances to participate. Anger fomented the "Occupy" movement. Living in tents is tough.

How can you use anger in a speech to persuade? Consider this:

> Abdullah al-Kidd, a United States citizen and former University of Idaho student and running back for the football team, was detained for more than two weeks as a witness in a federal terrorism case in 2003. He was handcuffed, strip-searched, and repeatedly interrogated. There was no evidence of wrongdoing by al-Kidd. He was jailed and then investigated, not the other way around as required by the U.S. system of justice. A three-judge panel from the 9th Circuit Court ruled in September 2009 that his incarceration was "repugnant to the Constitution and a painful reminder of some of the most ignominious chapters of our national history" (quoted in Boone, 2009, p. A5). As a result of the illegal detention, al-Kidd lost a scholarship to graduate school, lost security clearance and subsequently lost a job with a government contractor, lost his passport, and was ordered to live with in-laws in Las Vegas. We should all be furious that our government so blatantly abused one of our citizens.

This story is one way anger can be used as a persuasive appeal.

Ethics and Emotional Appeals: Is It Wrong to Be Peripheral?

Emotional appeals can be very persuasive, but are they ethical? It depends. Shouldn't we be angry about racism, sexism, homophobia, and all manner of injustice? Shouldn't we fear terrorism, drunk drivers, food poisoning, and flu pandemics? Shouldn't we feel guilt about the treatment of Japanese Americans during World War II? Emotional appeals are not inherently unethical just because they aren't a logical appeal. An emotional appeal is considered a peripheral route to persuasion, and the central route should be encouraged. Nevertheless, emotion in the service of logic and truth can equal constructive action to do what is good. Emotional appeals motivate action. They also create attention so we might listen more intently to a clearly reasoned and supported argument.

Emotional appeals are ethical as long as they compliment the central route to persuasion (skepticism). Emotional appeals in the service of fabrications, distortions, and rumors are unethical. During the "debate" on health-care reform in the summer of 2009, Sarah Palin asserted that a proposal in a congressional bill would require "my parents or my baby with Down Syndrome . . . to stand in front of Obama's death panel so his bureaucrats can decide, based on a subjective judgment of their level of productivity in society, whether they are worthy of health care" (quoted in "Report," 2009). The allegation was explosive but utterly false and was denounced by more than 40 media outlets. *PolitiFact.com,* the nonpartisan fact-checking website of the *St. Petersburg Times* and winner of the 2009 Pulitzer Prize, called it a "pants on fire" lie and voted it "Lie of the Year" (Holan, 2009; "Report," 2009). The nonpartisan Factcheck.org. dubbed it "whopper of 2009" (Weiner, 2009). A skeptic must ask why any politician would even suggest euthanizing the elderly (e.g., Palin's parents), the most active voting bloc in America? It is completely implausible. The "death panels" allegation, however, scared a lot of older people who showed up at town hall meetings understandably outraged by the misinformation. The death panels accusation was a combined fear and anger appeal in the service of dishonesty. That's unethical persuasion.

Similarly, liberal MSNBC television talk show host Keith Olbermann, on his *Countdown* show, made this wildly unsupported characterization of Scott Brown, a soon to be elected conservative Republican U.S. senator from Massachusetts: "Scott Brown [is] an irresponsible, homophobic, racist, reactionary, ex-nude model, teabagging supporter of violence against women and against politicians with whom he disagrees" (quoted in Sheppard, 2010). Jon Stewart, on *The Daily Show,* ripped Olbermann for wallowing "in the fetid swamp of baseless name-calling." Stewart noted that Olbermann had in past "commentaries" called Chris Wallace "a monkey posing as a newscaster," Rush Limbaugh a "big bag of mashed up jack-ass," and Fox News contributor Michelle Malkin "a mindless, morally bankrupt, knee-jerk, fascistic . . . mashed-up bag of meat with lipstick on it" (quoted in Sheppard, 2010). Olbermann soon after apologized on his show for his "over-the-top" comments.

Name-calling is unethical if there are no solid facts to support the labels. If a person has clearly lied, then you can call him or her a liar, although this may not be effective persuasion because it can alienate listeners who dislike such abrasive labeling. If a person hasn't lied, then it is wrong to fling the label. Emotional appeals should not be a substitute for logic and evidence. If an emotional appeal contradicts sound logic and solid evidence, then it becomes the tool of the true believer (see Chapter 6).

Induce Cognitive Dissonance: Creating Tension

When we want to persuade others to change their attitudes or behavior, one of the most common strategies is to point out inconsistencies between two attitudes or between attitudes and behavior. A student asks her professor for more time on an assignment. The professor says "no." The student retorts, "But you gave extra time to Jamie. Why won't you give me the same extension?" The professor sees herself as a very fair-minded person. Faced with this apparent inconsistency in the treatment of two students, the professor feels tense and uncomfortable. Festinger (1957) called this unpleasant feeling produced by apparent inconsistency **cognitive dissonance**.

Whenever a person holds two inconsistent ideas, beliefs, or opinions at the same time, or when an attitude and a behavior are inconsistent, dissonance likely occurs (McKimmie et al., 2003; Tavris & Aronson,

2007). Parents often confront this persuasive strategy from their children. "Why can't I stay up past midnight on weekends? You let Tommy when he was my age." "Why do I have a curfew? You never gave a curfew to Jose or Magdalena."

We want to be perceived as consistent, not hypocritical or nonsensical, so dissonance emerges when inconsistencies are pointed out to us (McKimmie et al., 2003; Tavris & Aronson, 2007). If we view ourselves as unbiased but laugh at a sexist joke, some dissonance will likely surface. If we consider ourselves honest but use a copy machine at work for personal projects, we will likely experience some dissonance, especially if the inconsistency is pointed out to us. This arousal of cognitive dissonance seems to be a universal phenomenon, appearing in a variety of cultures studied (Hoshino-Browne et al., 2005).

"Cognitive dissonance is a motivating state of affairs. Just as hunger impels a person to eat, so does dissonance impel a person to change his [her] opinions or his [her] behavior" (Festinger, 1977, p. 111). According to this theory, you have to awaken dissonance in listeners for persuasion to occur. Without dissonance, there is little motivation to change attitudes or behavior. Therefore, *the strategy for the persuader is to induce dissonance in the audience, then remove the dissonance by persuading listeners to change their attitudes or behavior in the direction desired.*

> The [persuader] intentionally arouses feelings of dissonance by threatening self-esteem—for example, by making the person feel guilty about something, by arousing feelings of shame or inadequacy, or by making the person look like a hypocrite or someone who does not honor his or her word. Next, the [persuader] offers one solution, one way of reducing this dissonance—by complying with whatever request the [persuader] has in mind. The way to reduce that guilt, eliminate that shame, honor that commitment, and restore your feelings of adequacy is to give to that charity, buy that car, hate that enemy, or vote for that leader. (Pratkanis & Aronson, 2001, p. 44)

Does inducing dissonance change behavior? It certainly can (Aronson et al., 1991; Stone et al., 1997). Important decisions arouse more dissonance than less important ones (Gass & Seiter, 2007). Pointing out to a teacher that he or she was not consistent when grading a test could elicit varying degrees of dissonance. If the inconsistency involves a single point on a 100-point exam, the teacher can easily downplay the inconsistency as minor and inherent to any subjective grading system. If the inconsistency involves an entire grade difference and seems based on gender bias, however, the dissonance could be quite large.

Notice how Gary Allen (1996), a student at Northeastern State University, uses cognitive dissonance on the topic of drug testing in the military.

> The final problem is caused by a double standard, because a program is only as good as the goal it achieves. While alcohol is universally recognized as the most commonly abused drug, the military does not test for alcohol as regularly as for other drugs. . . . Soldiers caught drunk on the job are given 45 days extra duty, that is work that must be performed after the regular duty day, they have a letter put into their permanent file, and they are returned to light duty. Yet the soldier who receives a positive [drug] test result is, currently, kicked out of the military with a dishonorable discharge. Let me say that again. Every day soldiers are required to undergo a test of their innocence without suspicion of guilt. The soldier who is found guilty is kicked out and marked for life with a dishonorable discharge, while soldiers drunk on the job, endangering everyone's life, are returned to duty with a slap on the hand. (p. 82)

The speaker points out a glaring inconsistency to induce dissonance in the audience. Supporting such a "double standard" is hypocritical and unjust, so the speaker implies. One could argue that there is a big difference between alcohol and other drugs—namely, legality. Nevertheless, concerning possible dangerous effects of use, an inconsistency does seem apparent. Cognitive dissonance can be an effective persuasive strategy (Tavris & Aronson, 2007).

Use the Contrast Effect: Minimize the Magnitude

You're a salesperson, and a woman comes into the dress store where you work. Most of your pay is based on commission, so you want to sell as much merchandise as you can at the highest prices possible. Do you show the woman the inexpensive dresses first, then gradually show her more expensive dresses, or do you begin with very expensive dresses probably outside of her price range, then show her less expensive dresses? Which will net you the biggest commission? According to research on the contrast effect, you'd make a better choice if you began expensive and moved to less expensive (Cialdini, 1993). The **contrast effect** says listeners are more likely to accept a bigger second request or offer when contrasted with a much bigger initial request or offer. If shown a really nice dress that costs $250, most shoppers will balk at purchasing it because it is "so expensive." If shown a $475 dress first, however, and then shown the $250 dress, the second dress just seems less expensive by contrast with the first. Once the $250 dress is purchased, "accessorizing" it with $30 worth of jewelry, scarves, or whatever will seem like very little by contrast.

The contrast effect, sometimes referred to as the **door-in-the face strategy**, is used in all types of sales. I once purchased a recliner for $250. It was not "on sale." About two months later, I was browsing through a furniture store and spotted the identical recliner advertised as part of a "giant blowout sale." The price tag showed $800 marked out, then $600 marked out, then $475 marked out, and finally the "sale price" of $400. A casual customer who hadn't shopped around might see this recliner as a super bargain. The price had been cut in half. Yet this store was asking $150 more than what I paid for the same recliner at the regular price from another store.

Cialdini (1993) provides a stellar, amusing example of the contrast effect in action in parent-child persuasion. Although this example is a letter, you can easily see how this strategy could apply in a persuasive speech.

Dear Mother and Dad:

Since I left for college I have been remiss in writing and I am sorry for my thoughtlessness in not having written before. I will bring you up to date now, but before you read on, please sit down. You are not to read any further unless you are sitting down, okay?

Well, then, I am getting along pretty well now. The skull fracture and the concussion I got when I jumped out the window of my dormitory when it caught on fire shortly after my arrival here is pretty well healed now. I only spent two weeks in the hospital and now I can see almost normally and only get those sick headaches once a day. Fortunately, the fire in the dormitory, and my jump, was witnessed by an attendant at the gas station near the dorm, and he was the one who called the Fire Department and the ambulance. He also visited me in the hospital and since I had nowhere to live because of the burnt-out dormitory, he was kind enough to invite me to share his apartment with him. It's really a basement room, but it's kind of cute. He is a very fine boy, and we have fallen deeply in love and are planning to get married. We haven't set the date yet, but it will be before my pregnancy begins to show.

Yes, Mother and Dad, I am pregnant. I know how much you are looking forward to being grandparents and I know you will welcome the baby and give it the same love and devotion and tender care you gave me when I was a child. The reason for the delay in our marriage is that my boyfriend has a minor infection which prevents us from passing our premarital blood tests and I carelessly caught it from him. I know that you will welcome him into our family with open arms. He is kind and, although not well educated, he is ambitious.

Now that I have brought you up to date, I want to tell you that there was no dormitory fire, I did not have a concussion or skull fracture, I was not in the hospital. I am not pregnant, I am not engaged, I am not infected, and there is no boyfriend. However, I am getting a "D" in American History and an "F" in Chemistry, and I want you to see those marks in their proper perspective.

Your loving daughter,

SHARON

As a strategy to use in a persuasive speech, *the contrast effect works well when presenting your solution to a problem.* For example, say you have argued that taxpayer dollars don't begin to cover the costs of educating college students. You could begin the solution portion of your speech this way.

> Clearly, we cannot expect taxpayers to continue shouldering almost the entire burden of higher education expenses. I think it would be entirely justified if our state legislature immediately doubled tuition for every student in the state. This would provide some tax relief for already over-burdened taxpayers while still covering less than half the cost of educating each student.
>
> Although doubling student tuition is justified, fair, and beneficial, I can see that such a proposal probably isn't entirely practical for a number of reasons, not the least of which is the suddenness of such a large tuition increase. Having weighed the potential merits and demerits of such a proposal, let me propose instead that the state phase in a much smaller tuition increase over the next decade to ease the burden on students and still provide taxpayer relief in the long run.

Peruse the sample speech in Box 15-1 for another example of the contrast effect.

Use a Two-Sided Strategy: Refutation

Is it better to present arguments in favor of your proposition and ignore opposing arguments (one-sided message), or should you make your case and then refute opposing arguments (two-sided message)? *Two-sided persuasive messages are more effective than one-sided messages in convincing listeners to change attitudes* (Allen, 1991, 1993, 1998a).

A two-sided organizational pattern begins with a presentation of main arguments supporting your proposition. After you have laid out your case, you then answer common objections, or opposing arguments, against your case. This, of course, means that you need to anticipate what an audience might question about your position. Answering opposing arguments is called **refutation**. (The sample speech in Box 15-1 provides a detailed example of two-sided organization with refutation.)

There are four steps to refutation. First, *state the opposing argument.* "A common objection to colleges shifting from a semester to a quarter system is that not as much subject matter will be covered each term" is a statement of an opposing argument. Second, *state your reaction to the opposing argument.* "This isn't true. Courses that meet three hours per week could meet five hours per week under the quarter system" is a statement of response to an opposing argument. Third, *support your response with reasoning and evidence.* Failure to present strong arguments backed by solid evidence may backfire and promote more entrenched attitudes instead of changing attitudes (Rucker & Petty, 2004). Weak refutation can be worse than no refutation at all because listeners may deduce that poorly supported counterarguments mean currently held attitudes are meritorious. Fourth, *indicate what effect, if any, opposing arguments have had on the strength of your case.* If some disadvantage will occur from your proposal, admit it, but weigh the damage against the claimed advantages of your proposal. "No quarter system is perfect. Yes, students will be pressured in some instances to work more intensely in a condensed period of time. Overall, however, the advantages of a quarter system—greater number and variety of courses, more diversity of instructors, better vacation schedules, and greater retention and success rates—far outweigh the minor objections to my proposal."

BOX 15.1 Developing Communication Competence

A SAMPLE OUTLINE AND PERSUASIVE SPEECH

Here I present a sample outline and the text of a persuasive speech. This is approximately a 15-minute persuasive speech. That is a longer speech than most in-class presentations but shorter than many public presentations. This somewhat lengthier speech is presented to provide a more comprehensive illustration of several persuasive strategies than could be included in a shorter version.

This speech uses the Monroe Motivated Sequence organizational format discussed in Chapter 12. Steps in this sequence are identified in square brackets.

Introduction

I. [*ATTENTION STEP*] Begin with notable examples of big money in college sports.
   A. CBS paid NCAA $6.2 billion for TV rights for "March Madness" basketball championship.
   B. Athletic department budgets have ballooned to an average of $34.5 million among 117 Division I-A schools.
   C. Corporate sponsorship of college athletics has never been bigger.
      1. Coors pays $5 million to University of Colorado.
      2. Most colleges seek corporate deals.

II. Proposition: To convince you that colleges and universities should significantly reduce the scale of their athletic programs.

III. Establish significance to the audience.
   A. All college students partially pay for athletic programs with tuition, fees, and taxes.
   B. Student scholars must compete with student athletes for scholarships.

IV. Preview the main points.
   A. Big-time athletic programs contradict the educational mission of colleges.
   B. A specific plan will be offered to solve this problem.
   C. Common objections to such a plan will be addressed.

Body

I. [*NEED STEP*] Big-time intercollegiate athletic programs contradict the educational mission of colleges and universities.
   A. Athletic prowess, not academic ability, is often given priority.
      1. Athletes are given $1.2 billion in college scholarships to play ball.
      2. SAT scores for athletes are, on average, 108 points lower than for nonathletes.
   B. Student nonathletes and athletes alike are academically harmed by the emphasis on athletic ability.
      1. Student scholars may be bumped from academic admittance to make space for the student athlete with lower academic qualifications.
      2. Admitting marginal students because of their athletic ability is also harmful to the athlete and the college.
         a. Athletes struggle to survive academically.
         b. Colleges spend $150 million on tutors for athletes.
   C. Colleges' primary mission is often diminished by athletic department deficits and out-of-control spending.
      1. Most colleges suffer big athletic department deficits.
      2. By 2020, budgets will exceed $250 million at top schools.

(continued)

BOX 15.1 *(Continued)*

3. Huge deficits and out-of-control spending threaten academic programs.
   a. Deficits and wild spending siphon precious resources from academic programs.
   b. University of Oregon is a notable example.

II. [*SATISFACTION STEP*] Take the money out of college sports.
   A. Drop all college sports entirely (contrast effect).
   B. The real plan is as follows:
      1. Provide no scholarships based on athletic ability.
      2. Student athletes must maintain minimum 2.5 GPA.
      3. Team practice sessions will be limited to 20 hours per week.
      4. No corporate sponsorships, logos, names on arenas, and so forth allowed.
      5. No money from TV rights will go to college athletics, only to academic programs.
      6. College coaches will be paid equivalent professors' salaries.
      7. Football and basketball must be self-supporting; no general college funds may be used.
      8. Plan will be enforced by the NCAA where legally possible and by all member colleges individually or in concert within each league where antitrust laws prohibit NCAA action; enforcement sanctions include probation, suspension, and/or banishment from league play.

III. Three common objections to this proposal will be addressed.
   A. Objection 1 is that disadvantaged student athletes will lose scholarships and be denied an education.
      1. This is true.
      2. Total number of student scholarships, however, will not decrease.
      3. Student athletes will realize importance of academics.
   B. Objection 2 is that career training for pros will be lost.
      1. This is also true, but colleges shouldn't be farm teams for sports corporations.
      2. A minuscule percentage of college athletes go on to be professionals.
   C. Objection 3 is that sports fans lose an entertainment source.
      1. There will still be college sports programs.
      2. There will still be gifted athletes entertaining us.
      3. There just won't be big money distorting academics.

IV. [*VISUALIZATION STEP*] Imagine what it will be like when money is removed from college sports.
   A. Colleges won't need to reduce or eliminate academic programs because of athletic department deficits.
   B. More scholarship money will be available for academic merit.
   C. Colleges will no longer contradict their mission.
   D. Student tuition and fees will not be raised to pay for athletics.
   E. Failure to implement this plan means increased deficits and reductions in academic programs.

Conclusion

I. [*ACTION STEP*] Take action now.
   A. Summary of main arguments.
      1. Big money has corrupted college sports, thwarting colleges' academic mission.
      2. The proposed plan takes the money out of college sports.
      3. Common objections were found to be meritless.

(continued)

BOX 15.1 *(Continued)*

B. Take action.
   1. Contact your student representatives.
   2. Discuss this proposal with college administration.

C. Memorable finish.

Bibliography

Brand, M. (2006, October 30). National Press Club speech. [Online]. Available at: http://www.neuro.uoregon.edu/~tublitz/COIA/News%200f%20interest/

Eitzen, D. S. (1997, December 1). Big-time college sports. *Vital Speeches*, pp. 122–126.

Gillum, J. (2010, April 1). Schools raising fees to keep up with costs of college sports. *USA Today*. [Online]. Available at: http://www.usatoday.com/sports/college/2010-04-01-college-sports-subsidies_N.htm

Gilmore, R. (2007, January 17). College football players deserve pay for play. *ESPN*. [Online]. Available at: http://sports.espn.go.com/ncf/columns/story?columnist5gilmore_rod&id52733624

Knight Foundation Commission on Intercollegiate Athletics. (2001). A call to action. [Online]. Available at: www.Knightcommission.org/about/a_call_to_action_foreward/

Massey, D. S., & Mooney, M. (2007, February). The effects of America's three affirmative action programs on academic performance. *Social Problems*, 54, 99–117.

Restoring the balance. (2010). *Knight Commission on Intercollegiate Athletics*. [Online]. Available at: http://www.knightcommission.org/images/restoringbalance/KCIA_Report_F.pdf

Sperber, M. (1998). *Onward to victory: The crisis that shaped college sports*. New York: Holt.

Tublitz, N., & Earl, J. (2007, January 14). Ducking education. *Eugene Register-Guard*. [Online]. Available at: http://www.registerguard.com/news/2007/01/14/ed.col.tublitz.0114.pl.p

U.S. Secretary of Education backs Knight Commission's call for changing NCAA basketball tournament eligibility standards and financial rewards. (2011, March 17) *Knight Commission*. [Online]. Available at: http://www.knightcommission.org/

Wolverton, B. (2007, January 19). Athletics participation prevents many players from choosing majors they want. *Chronicle of Higher Education*. [Online]. Available at: http://chronicle.com/cgi-bin/printable.cgi?article5http://chronicle.com/Weekly/v53/i20/20a03601.htm

GET BIG MONEY OUT OF COLLEGE SPORTS

(Prepared summer 2011—application of text material in brackets)

[*ATTENTION STEP—MONROE'S MOTIVATED SEQUENCE*] Intercollegiate athletic programs are being corrupted by massive mountains of money. Intercollegiate sports programs have become a multi-billion-dollar enterprise. CBS contracted with the National Collegiate Athletic Association to pay $6.2 billion from 2003 to 2013 to broadcast the men's college "March Madness" basketball tournament. The NCAA's research director, Todd Petr, reported to the Knight Foundation Commission on Intercollegiate Athletics in May 2007 that the average total expenditure on each athletic program at the 117 colleges in Division 1-A is $34.5 million annually, and spending has skyrocketed since that report. That's more than the total operating budget of many small colleges and universities in the United States.

Corporate sponsorship of college athletics has never been greater. Coors Brewing Company paid $5 million to the University of Colorado for naming its new field house "Coors Events Center." University of Oregon has had a longtime, lucrative relationship with Nike. Is this increasing commercialization of college sports compatible with the educational mission of institutions of higher learning? Sociology Professor Emeritus Stanley Eitzen, in a December 1, 1997, speech printed in *Vital Speeches*, observed: "Big-

(continued)

BOX 15.1 *(Continued)*

time college sport confronts us with a fundamental dilemma. Positively, college football and basketball offer entertainment, spectacle, excitement, festival, and excellence. Negatively, the commercial entertainment function of big-time college sport has severely compromised academia. Educational goals have been superseded by the quest for big money. And, since winning programs receive huge revenues from television, gate receipts, bowl and tournament appearances, boosters, and even legislatures, many sports programs are guided by a win-at-any-cost philosophy." Professor Eitzen said this more than a decade ago when the corrupting influence of big money on intercollegiate sports programs was relatively tame by today's standards.

Let's be honest: college athletics, especially Division I-A big-time football and basketball programs, are a commercial entertainment venture far removed from the educational mission of colleges and universities. College sport has become so gigantic that it distorts the priorities of colleges and universities and compromises their educational mission. Because this is a serious problem, I will try to convince you that colleges and universities should significantly reduce the scale of their athletic programs. [*PROPOSITION OF POLICY*]

Every college student listening to me speak today is affected by this commercialization of college sports. [*PERSONAL IMPACT*] As I intend to prove, it is you who partially pay for big-time athletic programs with increased student fees, tuition, and taxes. Student scholars are forced to compete against student athletes for scholarships and resources. Academic programs central to your educational goals and dreams may be jeopardized by huge deficits incurred by athletic programs, especially those with losing records.

I can guess what some of you are thinking. "He wants to reduce college athletic programs because he hates jocks and was a geek who always lost at sports." Not true! Baseball and basketball were my two favorite sports, and I earned my share of trophies and accolades playing both. I am an avid University of Oregon Ducks and San Francisco Forty-Niners football fan. You can question my choice of teams to support, but I do not propose reducing the scale of college athletics because I hate sports. [*IDENTIFICATION*] A college education, however, can open the doors of success for each and every one of you. It is your ticket to a better future. College sports should never serve as a substitute for academic success or impede any student's chance to acquire the best education possible, but the commercialization of college athletics threatens to do just that. [*PERSONAL IMPACT*]

Let me make several arguments to support my proposal to significantly reduce the scale of college athletic programs. Please listen to these arguments before making a judgment. I will show how big-time athletic programs contradict the educational mission of colleges. I will offer a specific plan to rectify this serious problem. Finally, I will respond to primary objections you may have to my proposal.

[*NEED STEP*] Returning to my first argument, that big-time athletic programs contradict the educational mission of colleges, let me begin with what I think we all know is true. The principal mission of a college or university is to provide a quality education for all students. As the 2010 Knight Commission Report on Intercollegiate Athletics notes, "Spending on educational activities should not be compromised to boost sports funding." Excessive emphasis on sports programs, however, contradicts this mission in three ways. [*COGNITIVE DISSONANCE*] First, athletic prowess, not academic ability, is often given priority by colleges. Athletes receive $1.2 billion in scholarships to attend colleges and universities, according to NCAA President Myles Brand in an October 30, 2006, speech at the National Press Club. They receive scholarships, not to become great scholars or even to receive a quality education, but to play ball and entertain fans. The Knight Commission reported on its website on March 17, 2011, that men's basketball teams that failed to

(continued)

BOX 15.1 *(Continued)*

meet even minimum academic standards raked in $179 million from success in the past five NCAA basketball playoff tournaments. As U.S. Secretary of Education Arne Duncan, quoted on the same website, argues: "It's time to end rewarding teams millions of dollars for winning basketball games when they are failing to graduate their players." A study by two Princeton University researchers, Douglas Massey and Margarita Mooney, reported in a February 2007 issue of *Social Problems* that 70% of college athletes had SAT scores that averaged 108 points "below their institution's average." Clearly, athletic prowess, not academic potential, is what counts.

Second, excessive emphasis on athletic programs contradicts the educational mission of colleges because student athletes and nonathletes alike are harmed by the emphasis placed on athletic ability. [*CONTINUATION OF COGNITIVE DISSONANCE*] Admitting less-qualified students because of their athletic abilities prevents other more academically qualified students from gaining entrance to some of the best colleges and universities. Some of you may have been denied entrance to the college of your choice and had to settle for a second, third, or even fourth choice because athletes with far weaker academic records were granted preferential admittance. [*MILD ANGER APPEAL*] Does this seem fair to you? It didn't to students a decade ago. Professor Murray Sperber, former chair of the National Alliance for College Athletic Reform, conducted a study on college sports that he reported in his book *Onward to Victory*. A huge majority, 83% of undergraduate respondents to the survey, agreed with the statement "Athletic scholarship winners should meet the same college entrance requirements as regular students." Surely, you feel the same way today!

In addition, admitting marginal students with superior athletic ability does no favors for the student athletes. A study conducted by James Shulman and William Bowen, researchers at the Andrew Mellon Foundation, reported in their 2001 book *The Game of Life* that athletes entering college with weaker academic records "consistently underperform academically." Marginal students struggle to keep up in classes, often requiring tutors at college expense. NCAA President Myles Brand, in an October 30, 2006, National Press Club speech, notes that Division I colleges spend more than $150 million annually on tutoring and "educational support" to help athletes pass classes. The 2010 Knight report shows that median spending on student athletes at NCAA colleges and universities is 4 to 11 times more than median spending on education-related activities per student.

Third, the primary mission of colleges and universities, to educate students, is often diminished by athletic department deficits. [*CONTINUATION OF COGNITIVE DISSONANCE*] The same Knight Commission report notes that "only a tiny number of college athletics programs actually reap the financial rewards that come from selling high-priced tickets and winning championships." The report continues to note that in the five years previous to the issuance of its report in 2010, only 7 athletic programs each year generated enough revenue to finish in the black out of 117 programs nationally. "Almost all programs must rely on allocations from general university funds, fees imposed on the entire student body, and state appropriations to meet funding gaps." The report added: "reliance on institutional resources to underwrite athletics programs is reaching the point at which some institutions must choose between funding sections of freshman English and funding the football team." [*USE OF PERSUASIVE EVIDENCE; STARTLING AND UNUSUAL STATISTICS*]

Despite significant deficits, college athletic departments are engaging in out-of-control-spending. The 2010 Knight report warns that by 2020, budgets for top athletic programs will exceed $250 million annually for each college. "Even for the largest and best-positioned universities, a $250 million athletics budget serving an average of 600 student-athletes is untenable." These massive budget increases, like

(continued)

BOX 15.1 *(Continued)*

the deficits, threaten academic programs. [MILD FEAR APPEAL] The Knight Commission report also notes that athletic spending since 2005 is increasing twice as fast as spending on academic programs. The situation became so outrageous at the University of Oregon that 92 faculty members signed a January 14, 2007, open letter printed in the *Eugene Register-Guard* newspaper complaining of skewed priorities. The letter noted that the athletic department budget had increased 224% since 1994. During this time of crazy spending on athletics at the university, faculty salaries dropped to the lowest among the American Association of Universities. Meanwhile, the athletic department furnishes its offices with plush furniture, pays multi-million-dollar salaries to coaches, and charters private jets to travel during recruiting season.

So, what should be done about this problem? Clearly, since football and basketball programs are typically the source of all these problems, we should eliminate them from all colleges and universities. [CONTRAST EFFECT] If we were to eliminate football and basketball, less visible and far less costly sports such as baseball, golf, gymnastics, and field hockey could provide some athletic opportunities for students. Intramural football and basketball programs could be established for students who prefer those sports at virtually no cost to the college. Let's face facts—getting the money out of college sport is essential if we are going to solve the problems I've outlined.

Total elimination of football and basketball except for intramural programs solves the problems I've underscored. Perhaps, however, we don't need such a radical solution. As a sports fan and former athlete, I would be disappointed if colleges dumped their football and basketball programs entirely. [IDENTIFICATION] I do strongly believe, however, that the big money must be taken out of college sports.

[SATISFACTION STEP] My plan to do this is simple.

1. There will be no scholarships for students based on athletic ability. Scholarships and grants must be based on academic potential and financial need. This is a strong recommendation of the National Alliance for College Athletic Reform. It is also the current practice of Division III NCAA schools.
2. Student athletes must be admitted according to the same standards as all other students. They must maintain a minimum 2.5 GPA to participate in athletic programs.
3. Team practice sessions will be limited to no more than 20 hours per week as per a current NCAA rule.
4. Absolutely no corporate money goes to athletic programs. No corporate logos or names should appear on any sports facilities, equipment, or apparel of any kind.
5. No money from television rights or bowl games will go to college athletic programs. Any revenue earned from television or other media programming must be used exclusively for academic programs.
6. College coaches must be paid salaries equivalent to any professor. This is the current practice of Ivy League colleges. The 2010 Knight Commission report called escalating salaries of college athletics coaches "the single largest contributing factor to the unsustainable growth of athletics expenditures." In 2010, coaches' salaries averaged $1.3 million according to a *USA Today* study reported on April 2, 2010. College professors responsible for your education are fortunate if they make one-tenth of the average college coach's annual salary. An article in *USA Today* by columnist Jack Gillum reported on April 1, 2010, stated that coaches' compensation accounted for more than $1 billion, not counting severance payments and other "hidden" benefits.

(continued)

BOX 15.1 *(Continued)*

7. Football and basketball must be self-supporting. Ticket sales and sports merchandise will be primary sources of funds.
8. My plan will be enforced by the NCAA where legally possible and by all member colleges individually or in concert within each league where antitrust laws prohibit NCAA action; enforcement sanctions include probation, suspension, and/or banishment from league play.

This plan will substantially reduce college athletic programs without eliminating them. I have merely taken the big money out of college sports. Leagues, championships, and bowl games can continue, but without the huge financial incentives to distort the academic mission of colleges. Academic programs will no longer be threatened by huge athletic department debts. Without the big money, colleges can return to their primary mission—to provide a quality education for all students.

[*SATISFACTION STEP CONTINUED*] In case you're not completely convinced that my plan is a good idea, let me address common objections to my proposal. [*TWO-SIDED PERSUASION*] The first objection might be that disadvantaged student athletes will lose scholarships and be denied a college education. That's true, but the NCAA has cracked down some recently by reducing the number of scholarships a school can offer to athletes if academic performance and graduation rates of athletes sink too low. The NCAA, however, has not gone nearly far enough. Eliminating all athletic scholarships could save money for general scholarships and grants at each college. The net effect on students as a group would be zero. The faces would change, but the same number of students could receive financial help. In addition, if student athletes realize that they cannot play college sports unless they qualify academically, this will provide an incentive for them to take their studies seriously or risk ineligibility.

A second objection [*TWO-SIDED PERSUASION CONTINUED*] might be that, without scholarships, many academically unprepared student athletes will lose a training ground for a career in professional sports. This may be true, but is it relevant? Should a college be a farm team for professional sports corporations? Why should a college create false hope for athletes, most of whom will never make it into professional sports? According to NCAA statistics reported in the January 15, 2007, *Birmingham News*, only 2% of senior college football players ever get drafted by the NFL, and a mere 1.3% of male senior college basketball players are selected by the NBA. Although this is not reported, female senior basketball players have a similar dismal chance of graduating to the WNBA. These students are attending college to play ball as a way of auditioning for professional teams. Educational success often gets lost in the hoopla and hubbub over athletic accomplishment. Colleges should not be a party to exploitation of college athletes. [*COGNITIVE DISSONANCE*] Colleges should be working hard to prepare students for important professions because that is their primary mission. They should stop serving as a farm team for professional sports corporations interested only in profit.

Finally, won't sports fans lose a key source of entertainment if my plan is implemented? [*TWO-SIDED PERSUASION CONTINUED*] This is not true. Notre Dame and USC will still remain archrivals on the football field. Bowl games will still exist. Championships will still be contested, simply in scaled-down versions as they once were in the 1950s and 1960s before big money began exerting its corrupting influence. The difference will be that academic programs will not be diminished because of huge deficits from athletic programs, and the academic mission of colleges will not be distorted to pay for a bloated athletic program. The scale of college athletics will be substantially reduced, but the excitement and spectacle can remain.

[*VISUALIZATION STEP*] Imagine what my plan will accomplish. No longer will colleges be tempted or forced to reduce or eliminate an academic program, perhaps a program in your major, to pay for deficits

(continued)

BOX 15.1 *(Continued)*

incurred by bloated athletic programs. Millions of dollars in scholarships and grants will be available for academically qualified and needy students. Colleges will no longer serve as mere farm teams for profit-motivated corporations. Colleges will no longer appear hypocritical, espousing an educational mission on one hand while undermining it on the other. Your student fees and tuition will not have to be raised to support a faltering, expensive sports program.

Imagine what will happen if this problem is ignored. Athletic budgets will continue to swell and deficits will rise. Your tuition and fees will increase, academic programs will be cut, and some programs and majors will be eliminated to cover the athletic department deficits. The quality of your education and your opportunities for academic success will be threatened. [*MILD FEAR APPEAL*] As the 2001 Knight Foundation Commission report concluded, "If it proves impossible to create a system of intercollegiate athletics that can live honorably within the American college and university, then responsible citizens must join with academic and public leaders to insist that the nation's colleges and universities get out of the business of big-time sports." I submit to you that we have now reached that point.

[*ACTION STEP*] College sports have become too closely connected to corporate interests. Big money has corrupted college athletics and the primary mission of colleges and universities. I have proposed a solution that will work by taking money out of college sports. I have responded to common objections raised against my plan, and these objections have been found meritless. I ask that you support my proposal to significantly reduce college athletic programs. Stop the erosion of academic values and quality. Speak to your Student Senate officers and representatives. [*EFFORT REQUIRED IS MINIMAL*] Discuss the issues I have raised with the college administration. This college can be a beacon of light signaling the way for other colleges to follow. Change begins with us. Get big money out of college sports!

Summary

WHEN you attempt to persuade an audience, you try to convert, modify, or maintain your listeners' attitudes and/or behavior. Conversion is the least likely achievable goal. Attitudes do not always predict specific behavior. Reasons for possible inconsistency include whether the attitudes are derived from direct or indirect experience, the degree of effort required to perform the behavior, and the amount of social pressure applied to behave differently from your attitudes. The elaboration likelihood model explains persuasion in general by noting that there are two paths to persuasion. These are the peripheral route that includes likability, attractiveness, and emotional appeals of the speaker, and the central route that embraces skepticism and its emphasis on reasoning and evidence. Persuasion that works well in American culture may be ineffective in other cultures, especially those that are collectivist.

There are many persuasive strategies a speaker can use. Among these are establishing identification, building credibility, building strong arguments, inducing cognitive dissonance, making emotional appeals, using the contrast effect, and using a two-sided organizational pattern. Competent public speakers will find success if they utilize some or all of these strategies to persuade others. There are conditions that determine the likelihood of success using each strategy, so make sure that you are cognizant of these conditions and that you adapt your persuasive strategy to meet those conditions.

Quizzes Without Consequences

Did you understand all the material in this chapter? Test your knowledge before your exam!

Go to the companion website at www.oup.com/us/rothwell, click on the Student Resources for each chapter, and take the Quizzes Without Consequences.

Test yourself as many times as you like. It's a great way to confirm what you have learned before it counts in your classroom grade.

Film School Case Studies

American History X (1998). Drama; R

Powerful depiction by Edward Norton of a young man lured into a white supremacy movement in Venice, California. Examine this film for differences between coercion and persuasion. Apply the social judgment theory and elaboration likelihood model to Norton's conversion and attempt to steer his brother from a life of racist violence

Boiler Room (2000). Drama; R

Young sales reps (Giovanni Ribisi, Vin Diesel, and Ben Affleck) for a brokerage house pushing junk stocks adopt questionable persuasive strategies. Analyze the ethics of their persuasion, applying the five key elements of ethical communication explained in Chapter 1.

My Cousin Vinny (1991). Comedy; R

This is a "must see" comedy if you haven't already had the pleasure of viewing this hilarious account of a bumbling New York lawyer (Joe Pesci) attempting to free his cousin (Ralph Macchio) from a murder charge in a small town in Alabama. Analyze this film for the persuasive, and often not so persuasive, use of identification in the courtroom.

The Great Debaters (2007). Drama; PG-13

This is a surprisingly entertaining drama about college debaters, with Denzel Washington playing the debate coach (he also directed the film). Analyze the different persuasion strategies depicted in the movie.

Interviewing

Interviewing is a common communication event. **Interviewing** is defined as "a purposeful, planned conversation, characterized by extensive verbal interaction" (Peterson, 1997, p. 288). In every instance, communication competence is a central element of effective job interviewing.

The principal purpose of this appendix is to offer ways to improve your interviewing skills. By the end of this appendix, you should be able to:

1. Identify and avoid common mistakes made during job interviews.
2. Improve your own interviewing skills.

The informational interview conducted for research purposes is discussed in Chapter 12.

Preinterview Mistakes

We live in the Age of Technology. Thus, you must be cognizant that prospective employers may use technology to investigate your background and gain an impression of you from sources other than your résumé or in-person interview. An increasingly common research tool used by employers is to access your social networking sites. Much can be learned from viewing photos, comments, humor, and so forth included on your site. A survey by CareerBuilder.com reported that 45% of employers research candidates by accessing their social networking sites. Of the employers surveyed, 35% responded that they had found content on social networking sites that caused them not to hire a candidate. The most frequently cited examples of objectionable content that caused rejection included provocative or inappropriate photos or information (53%), content that revealed drinking and using drugs (44%), candidate bad-mouthed a previous employer (35%), candidate showed poor communication skills (29%), candidate made discriminatory comments (26%), and candidate obviously lied about qualifications (24%) (Grasz, 2009).

Conversely, 18% of employers who responded to the same CareerBuilder survey noted that they hired a candidate based primarily on information also found on a candidate's social networking site. The most frequently cited examples included network profile provided a positive feel for the candidate's personality (50%), profile supported professional qualifications (39%), site showed candidate was creative (38%), site showed candidate had strong communication skills (35%), site showed candidate was a well-rounded person (19%), and site showed candidate received awards and accolades (15%). The moral of this story is clean up your social networking site before submitting any job applications.

Job Interview Mistakes

Few events are as anxiety producing and as significant to our lives as a job interview. So much can be riding on such a brief encounter. Communicating competently during a job interview can be crucial to securing a job.

This section addresses common mistakes and effective communication strategies.

There is probably no such thing as a perfect interview. Communication strategies that work in one interview may not work as well in another. Nevertheless, there are some behaviors that seem destined to torpedo any chance of success in an interview for a job. A CareerBuilder.com survey (Grasz, 2011) cited in Chapter 1 listed the following candidate blunders reported by employers:

- Provided detailed list of what made candidate mad about a previous employer
- Hugged the prospective employer when the interview concluded
- Ate all the candy in the candy bowl while answering questions
- Constantly bad-mouthed spouse
- Talked about an affair that cost the candidate a job
- Had a friend interrupt the interview to ask "How much longer?"

These examples are clearly cases of clueless communication behavior on the part of interviewees. The same survey also listed more common problems displayed by candidates. They include:

- Answering a cell phone during the interview
- Dressing inappropriately
- Seeming disinterested or arrogant
- Chewing gum
- Providing evasive and indirect answers to questions
- Asking poor questions about the job and the place of employment

Peterson (1997) also identified typical interviewing mistakes. They include weak eye contact, irrelevant response to a topic, disorganized response to questions, poor listening skills, unclear response to questions, problems with response fluency, weak voice projection, inadequate volume control, and lack of preparation for the interview.

In addition to making these mistakes, interviewees commonly err in general ways during the interview. First, they approach the interview as though it were a sales pitch and they were the product. Most people are mildly, sometimes profoundly, repelled by a hard sell no matter what the product. Using a hard sell to land a job will likely produce a similar response from an interviewer or hiring panel. Second, interviewees sometimes attempt to relate their entire life story when answering a question. Too much detail can make interviewers weary and cause their attention to fade. Third, interviewees sometimes try to fake their knowledge and experience by inflating the importance of relatively minor background and accomplishments. If an interviewing committee senses that you are unreasonably padding your résumé, they may doubt your credibility across the board. Fourth, interviewees who are obviously unprepared to answer tough questions have little hope of being chosen for the job.

Competent Interviewing Skills

Anderson and Killenberg (1999) identify three qualities that are necessary for an interview to be a success: empathy, honesty, and respect. Empathy puts us in the position of seeing from the other person's perspective. This is a vital quality for an interviewee. Empathy allows you to anticipate questions that will be asked and to frame answers that will speak to the concerns of those interviewing you. Honesty is vital because no one is likely to hire a person he or she does not perceive to be candid and straightforward. If a person lies on his or her résumé and the lie is discovered, it can be grounds for immediate dismissal from the position. Embellishing minor accomplishments walks close to the precipice of dishonesty. Respect, the final quality, shows sensitivity and concern. Respect, of course, is a two-way street. Interviewers should show the applicant respect by addressing him or her in a manner that is not demeaning. Similarly, interviewees should show respect for interviewers. Some of the previous examples of clueless behavior during interviews show disrespect for the interviewer. Taking cell phone calls during the interview and chewing gum are too casual and display indifference.

There are several ways to improve your interviewing skills. First, *be prepared*. Do research on the job you seek. Most job announcements specify what experience, skills, and knowledge are essential to the performance of the job. Be prepared to adapt your background to the specific requirements of the job. If the job calls for knowledge of specific software or computer technology, be prepared to list your experience with such software and technology. If the job announcement expressly identifies "effective interpersonal skills" as desirable in an applicant, have a list ready that speaks to this qualification directly. For example, if you have taken a college course in interpersonal communication, if communication is your college major or minor, if you have taken any workshops in conflict management or couples communication, or if you have conducted workshops or classes in interpersonal communication, list these on your résumé. Have these examples ready in case you are asked questions on such background during the interview.

Second, *rehearse for your interview*. Have a friend ask typical interview questions.

What are your strengths and weaknesses?
Why did you apply for this particular job?
Why did you leave your previous job?
Have you ever had difficulty working for a boss or supervisor?
What problems did you encounter at your last position?
Where would you like to be professionally in five years?
What's the worst job you've ever had?
Would you have difficulty contradicting your boss if you thought he or she was about to make a bad decision?
Do you work well on a team?
Have you had good or bad experiences working in groups?

Frame your answers as positive reflections of your work ethic and determination to excel. For example, the question "Have you ever had difficulty working for a boss?" could be answered this way: "Yes, and it taught me a lot about how to deal with difficult people . . ." "Where would you like to be professionally in five years?" could be answered this way: "I'd like to have my work recognized and receive a promotion because of it." You certainly don't want to answer such a question by indicating that the job you are seeking is merely a steppingstone to a better position elsewhere. Honesty doesn't require an answer that wasn't sought.

Third, *look and act the part of a credible candidate for the job*. Professional jobs require professional attire. Show that you care about the position by arriving on time, appearing well groomed and neat, and dressing in professional clothing. During the interview, speak so everyone can easily hear you. Listen carefully to all questions, and if in doubt, ask for clarification or elaboration. Answer questions directly and eliminate nervous mannerisms (tapping fingers on the table, cracking knuckles, twirling hair, tapping a pen or pencil, or biting nails). Humor is often welcome, but avoid sarcasm or ethnic humor. Self-deprecating humor often works well as long as it doesn't diminish your qualifications for the position. Establish direct eye contact with the interviewer. If a panel conducts the interview, establish initial eye contact with the panel member who asks you the questions and then gradually direct your eyes to all panel members as you develop your answer. Do not express anger or hostility for previous bosses that have "done you wrong." Interviewers are looking for composure as an indicator of credibility. Speak fluently. Avoid long vocal pauses and dysfluencies (um, uh, you know, like). Don't be reticent, fail to smile, look unfriendly, or demonstrate a lack of enthusiasm for the position.

Fourth, *provide sufficient elaboration when answering questions*. Very brief answers ("Yes, I did that") with no detail leave interviewers guessing about your qualifications for the position. Successful applicants for jobs use focused elaboration when asked questions (Anderson & Killenberg, 1999). This means they provide considerable detail when answering questions, and the detail is always directly relevant to the questions asked. Unsuccessful applicants usually provide no elaboration, or their answers drift to irrelevant experiences, stories, or knowledge. When providing detail, look for signals from interviewers that you've answered the question sufficiently. When interviewers glaze over, fidget, glance around the room, stare at a pencil, look at the clock, or shift in their chairs, it is usually time to wrap up your answer.

Fifth, *organize your answers*. If you have prepared sufficiently for the interview, you should be able to answer most questions clearly and in an organized fashion. "What experience do you have working with people from diverse cultural backgrounds?" might be one question asked. A possible answer is "I've worked with three very diverse groups. At Datacom West, a third of the workers were Asian. When I worked at Silicon Software, several of the workers I supervised were from India and Pakistan. When I ran my own printing business, most of my workers were either African American or Jewish. As you can see, I've worked with a rich mixture of ethnic groups, and I feel such diversity has produced synergy."

Sixth, *provide sufficient evidence of your qualifications for the job.* **Behavioral interviewing** has become increasingly popular, especially in the business world. It involves asking interviewees for specific examples of behavior that illustrates an answer (Eng, 1997). Here are some typical behavioral interviewing questions.

Describe a time when you tried to persuade a person or group to do something they opposed.

Give an example of a time when you faced many obstacles to achieving a goal and explain how you handled the situation.

Identify a stressful experience and discuss how you dealt with it.

Describe a conflict you've had with a fellow worker.

Tell us about when you had to meet strict deadlines.

Provide an example of a situation when you were forced to make an important decision without adequate information.

All of these questions seek evidence of your skills on the job. Answers to these behavioral questions reveal an applicant's knowledge of real-life situations. Be prepared to provide specific evidence of your talents and abilities. Brainstorm examples that illustrate your strengths. Use the STAR interviewing method for answering such behavioral questions. *ST* stands for *situation/task*, *A* is *action*, and *R* stands for *result*. Thus, you identify the situation or task, explain what action you took, and describe what resulted from that action.

Seventh, *be prepared to ask relevant questions of interviewers*. An interview is a conversation, not an interrogation. Unlike a witness in a court trial, you have a right to ask questions of your interviewers. Your interviewers want to know if you are right for the job, but they also want to know if the job is right for you. Use the behavioral interviewing technique when asking questions of your interviewers. Don't ask, "Do people get promoted in this company?" Instead, ask, "Can you give me an example of the last person to receive a promotion and how that person earned it?"

Answering Illegal Questions

Employers may ask you an illegal question, such as requesting your marital status, national origin, religion, sexual orientation, cause of a disability, or your age. Such questions can all be sources of potential discrimination against a candidate. Illegal questions usually result, not from malicious intent, but from carelessness, misplaced curiosity, or ignorance of legal restrictions.

Despite legal restrictions on what interviewers may ask of a candidate, you may be asked questions that are out of bounds. How should you respond? You have several options. First, you can view the question as relatively harmless and answer it directly.

"What is your marital status?"—"I've been married for 10 years! You aren't going to hold that against me are you?" Second, ask for clarification: "How old are you? "—"Perhaps you could clarify why that is relevant for this job? Are you seeking further detail about my experience?" Third, you could simply refuse to answer the question: "Are you a religious person?"—"I consider my religious views and status a personal matter unrelated to the description of this job." Fourth, you could simply terminate the interview: "These questions are inappropriate, and I can see that I would not feel comfortable working here. I thank you for your time." There is no correct option. You have to decide how uncomfortable the illegal questions make you, what these questions say about the place of employment, how much you want the job, and the degree of objection you have to specific questions.

Summary

Interviews are important events in our lives. An interview is a purposeful, planned conversation characterized by extensive verbal interaction. Empathy, respect, and honesty should imbue every interview. Preparation is a major element of an interview from the standpoint of both the interviewee and the interviewer. The interview should be focused. Questions and answers should be direct, relevant, and purposeful. Anticipate how you will respond if illegal questions are asked.

Speeches for Special Occasions

Speeches for special occasions should be special. They are different from informative and persuasive speeches. Although a special occasion speech may impart knowledge and information or briefly persuade, that is not its main purpose. Audience expectations are critical to the effectiveness of a special occasion speech. The occasion sets the expectation for the audience, and your primary goal is to meet your audience's expectations. An inspirational occasion requires an inspirational speech. Listeners want to be moved, not merely informed. Listeners at a roast expect to laugh heartily and often. Little effort should be made to offer deep insights or persuade anyone to action.

The primary purpose of this appendix is to explore ways to give effective and appropriate special occasion speeches.

By the end of this appendix, you should be able to:

1. Recognize a variety of special occasion speeches, including eulogies, tributes, commencement addresses, after-dinner speeches, introductions, and award ceremony presentations.
2. Identify guidelines for delivering effective special occasion speeches.

Eulogies

Comedian George Carlin once remarked, "I'm always relieved when someone is delivering a eulogy and I realize I'm listening to it." Eulogies pay tribute to someone who has died. Given the sadness that typically surrounds a funeral, your challenge is to show respect for those grieving and provide a sense of closure for those feeling the profound loss of a loved one. The word *eulogy* originates from the Greek word that means "to praise." A **eulogy** is a speech delivered in praise of a deceased friend or family member. You want to capture the essence of the person eulogized. For years, I required my speech students to deliver their own eulogy, to play the role of someone paying tribute to them after their death. It offered a way of getting in touch with how my students saw themselves, who they wanted to become, and what they would want others to say about them after they died. The assignment was always instructive and often quite moving and insightful.

Eulogies do not have to be somber speeches, or as newscaster Tom Brokaw said at the funeral of his colleague Tim Russert, there would be "some tears, some laughs and the occasional truth" (quoted in Wilson, 2008, p. 2D). Capturing the essence of the person may mean paying tribute to their infectious sense of humor and their uniqueness as a human being. My father was just such a person. In my eulogy, I wanted to capture who my father was in life without excessively diminishing his faults or magnifying his admirable qualities. He could be irascible and enormously impatient, yet he could exhibit random acts of stunning kindness. I described not just my father's many acts of kindness, but I also tried to transform his legendary impatience into moments of gentle humor that all could appreciate. For example,

> Dad hated to get behind slow drivers (which was anyone obeying the speed limit). When Dad was in his 70s, he barely slowed down. I remember Mom and Dad picking me up at the airport one time. Dad was driving his Thunderbird. The freeways were jammed so Dad took a back route home. At one point he was flying down the boulevard. From the back seat I gently inquired: "Dad, when exactly will our flight be leaving the ground?" He reduced his speed only slightly.

Using humor in a eulogy can be tricky. You want to show the utmost respect for the deceased, and you certainly don't want to cause offense for the grieving. Listeners typically welcome gentle humor that humanizes and explores the principal personal characteristics of the deceased.

In constructing an effective and appropriate eulogy, follow these guidelines.

1. *Your opening should capture attention and set the theme.* A few possibilities are a relevant quotation, a short story that reflects the core characteristics of the deceased, or a novel example from the life of the lost loved one. I began my eulogy at my father's funeral this way: "There's a Jewish saying, 'The only truly dead are those who have been forgotten.' My dad won't be forgotten. One reason is that he was such an unforgettable character."

2. *Your organizational pattern is typically narrative.* You're briefly telling a story of the person's life, capturing the important plot lines about this individual. This is not a mere biography of the person. Don't simply list the person's résumé of awards, degrees, professional publications, and the like. Tell a story about what this person was like. Personal attributes are more important and heartfelt than personal accomplishments unless the accomplishments illustrate important and personal laudatory attributes.

3. *Strive for emotional control.* Your audience doesn't need to feel grief more than comes naturally from the loss of a loved one. A eulogy is a tribute. It should offer uplifting praise. You want the audience to feel a little better after your speech, not worse.

4. *Be balanced and realistic in your praise.* Senator Ted Kennedy, in his eulogy of his brother Robert who was assassinated during his California campaign for president in 1968, chose the perfect line to make this point: "My brother need not be idealized, or enlarged in death beyond what he was in life; to be remembered simply as a good and decent man, who saw wrong and tried to right it, saw suffering and tried to heal it, saw war and tried to stop it" (quoted in "Ted Kennedy's Eulogy," 1968).

5. *Relate what you will most remember and miss about the person.* Here are a few things I related about my father: "I will miss his puns—most of them real groaners. I will miss him teaching me golf, or trying to. I will miss Dad and Mom dancing to the big bands played on their stereo. I will remember Dad getting up in restaurants, grabbing the coffee pot and serving himself and other customers because the service was too slow. I will remember Dad hip deep in the Oxford Canal, saying 'Dammit Dorothy Mae,' as if Mom had something to do with his falling into the British muck. Most of all, I will remember Dad's unconditional love, unfailing support, and boundless generosity."

6. *Finish strong.* After telling several stories about my father that illustrated his uniqueness, the final line of my eulogy said this: "Heaven will be a more interesting place now that Dad has entered the Kingdom." This closing statement reflects again on the theme of my father as a unique and unforgettable character and offers mild comfort to those grieving. Ted Kennedy finished his eulogy for his brother Robert this way: "As he [Robert] said many times, in many parts of this nation, to those he touched and who sought to touch him: 'Some men see things as they are and say why. I dream things that never were and say why not'" (quoted in "Ted Kennedy's Eulogy," 1968). When the space shuttle *Challenger* exploded in 1986 with the loss of the entire crew, Ronald Reagan delivered a nationally televised eulogy commemorating our fallen heroes who risked their lives to explore space.

Delivering one of the most powerful, touching eulogies ever presented by a president of the United States, a speech ranked eighth on the Top 100 American Speeches of the 20th century (Lucas & Medhurst, 2008), Reagan captured the essence of the moment with these final few sentences.

> The crew of the space shuttle *Challenger* honored us by the manner in which they lived their lives. We will never forget them, nor the last time we saw them, this morning, as they prepared for their journey and waved goodbye and "slipped the surly bonds of earth" to "touch the face of God."

Using the words from a sonnet entitled "High Flight," a poem many pilots know well and some keep on their person, Reagan gave nobility to the deaths of our astronauts in the moving, eloquent finish to his eulogy.

Tribute Addresses

Although eulogies are tribute addresses, they are specifically related to the death of someone. There are other types of tribute speeches, however. **Tribute speeches** praise or celebrate a living person. They honor the person. You hear tribute speeches at retirement parties, birthdays, anniversaries, going-away parties, and award ceremonies. Brief tribute speeches can be roasts and toasts. A **roast** is a purposely humorous tribute to a person. Although the humor can be sarcastic, ribald, even wildly exaggerated, everyone in attendance knows and expects that the entire affair is meant to praise the honoree. You poke fun at the honoree as a way of expressing your admiration and affection for the person. Here are some guidelines.

1. *Humor is the key ingredient of any roast.* This is not meant to be a serious event. It is supposed to be lighthearted and amusing. Follow the guidelines in Chapter 13 on using humor appropriately and effectively.
2. *Keep the tone positive.* A roast is meant to be a good-natured kidding of the honoree, not an opportunity to embarrass the person in front of friends and relatives.
3. *Be brief.* This is not an opportunity for you to audition for stand-up comedian of the year. Usually, each speaker at a roast addresses the audience for about three to five minutes. Stick to the time limit.
4. *Finish on a heartfelt, serious note.* Playfully making fun of the honoree should be amusing, but don't forget that a roast is meant to express admiration and affection for the person roasted. "All kidding aside, you know how much I respect and admire my dear friend. He is a beacon of light in a sometimes dark world, and I will miss his smiling face at work every day" is one way to close your roast on a serious note.

Another type of tribute is the toast. A **toast** is a brief tribute to a person or couple. Weddings usually have several toasts offered by the best man and maid of honor and sometimes by bridesmaids and friends and family members of the bride and groom. Keep them brief. A well-known, oft-quoted Irish toast goes:

> May the road rise to meet you.
> May the wind be always at your back.
> May the sun shine warm upon your face.
> And rains fall soft upon your fields.
> And God hold you in the hollow of His hand.

If so inclined, you could play off this well-known toast and give it your own unique twist, such as:

> May the road rise to meet you, and may you avoid the potholes of life.
> May the wind be always at your back, unless a cool breeze in the face offers refreshment.
> May the sun shine warm on your face, but never burn you.
> And may rain fall softly, washing away any sadness you may feel.

Because a toast is often accompanied by a drink of wine or other alcoholic beverage, be cautious about the effect alcohol can have on your ability to offer a coherent and effective toast. Your toast may follow many others. I have heard some head-shaking, profoundly embarrassing toasts offered by those already toasted by excessive alcohol consumption. You don't want to make a fool of yourself and make others uncomfortable. Always be appropriate. Remember, weddings almost always have young children present. Your humor should be playful but PG rated—"To keep your marriage brimming, with love in the wedding cup, whenever you're wrong, admit it; whenever you're right, shut up" (Ogden Nash) or "If I'm the best man, why is she marrying him?" (Jerry Seinfeld) or "Love is an electric blanket with someone else in control of the switch" (Cathy Arlyle). Your toast should also be addressed to the couple. You stand and deliver the toast while everyone else remains seated. At the finish, you raise your glass and salute the couple.

A tribute to someone leaving due to retirement or moving to another place of employment has its own expectations and requirements. Such a tribute is very similar to a eulogy except the person is still living and is present for the tribute. The departure may not be welcome by the audience because a good colleague and friend is leaving, but it should be a cause for a happy send-off. This type of tribute speech should be lighthearted and should emphasize the contributions made by the person who is leaving and any notable qualities that everyone will miss.

Recently, I was asked to give a tribute speech for a friend and long-time colleague. I began:

> I'd like to begin this tribute to Jack with a short poem I've written for this occasion. I apologize in advance.
> There is a professor named Jack.
> Who deserved a most elegant plaque.
> With flattering comments and a turn of a phrase.
> Abundant awards and plentiful praise.
> But instead he must settle for this sorry rhyme.
> Knowing full well that he'll be teaching part-time.
> Because try as he might; no matter what he may say
> Old teachers never die, they just grade away.

The point of this opening was to create a lighthearted tone and to be a bit playful. The last line is a glancing reference to the famous line from Gen. Douglas MacArthur in his April 19, 1951 address to the U.S. Congress, "Old soldiers never die, they just fade away." I continued by reflecting on some of my friend's accomplishments during his long career as a teacher and administrator. I finished as I began, with a "bit of doggerel" or bad poetry (a lighthearted finish).

> The power of one is so often unclear.
> But let voices be raised and perhaps a dark beer.
> To proclaim across campus for all to hear.
> There's one special man whose impact is felt.
> And although his physique is no longer so svelte.
> Our dear friend and colleague will surely be missed.
> But let's all make a vow to steadfastly resist.
> Dwelling long on Jack's parting, no need for redundance.
> And instead wish he and Diane joy in abundance.

No one in the audience expected great poetry from me, and they certainly didn't hear any, but listeners were amused and attentive to hear something a bit different than the previous tribute speeches. Don't be afraid to take a small risk and produce a speech that tries something different. My attempt was greatly appreciated by my friend who recognized immediately that I had put some effort into constructing the tribute. It's the apparent effort that you put into a tribute speech that sends the message, "I care about you and you will be missed."

Commencement Addresses

A **commencement address** is an inspirational speech that occurs at graduation ceremonies. You want to move your listeners to think in news ways, to participate in a cause, or to help your community to solve problems. The primary focus is on engaging your listeners and imparting wisdom. This is no small task. Celebrities, comedians, actors, CEOs of major corporations, politicians, members of the news media, and individuals who have overcome great obstacles in life are invited every year to give commencement addresses at colleges and universities all across the United States. Even presidents of the United States give commencement addresses. As a student, you may be asked to give one type of commencement address, the valedictory speech.

Commencement addresses usually have a serious message to impart to graduates, but the best such addresses blend abundant humor with a serious theme. Barack Obama gave a commencement address at the University of Michigan on May 1, 2010, before 92,000 people. He began: "It is great to be here in the Big House, and may I say 'Go Blue!' I thought I'd go for the cheap applause line to start things off." Obama continued by quoting letters he received from a kindergarten class in Virginia. These youngsters asked him a number of questions, such as, "Do you work a lot?" "How do you do your job?" and "Do you live next to a volcano?" The last question he read, however, was more serious and became the theme of his address, "Are people being nice?" The rest of his speech developed the theme of the proper role of government in a democracy and the inability to succeed as a democracy when incivility reigns supreme in our political discourse ("Obama Michigan," 2010).

Harry Potter author, J. K. Rowling, in her 2008 Harvard commencement address, began this way: "The first thing I would like to say is 'thank you.' Not only has Harvard given me an extraordinary honour, but the weeks of fear and nausea I have endured at the thought of giving this commencement address have made me lose weight" ("The Fringe Benefits," 2008). Her amusing opening tapped beautifully into her theme—fear of failure and the fringe benefits of experiencing failure.

Rock star Bono began his commencement address to graduates at the University of Pennsylvania on May 17, 2004, this way: "My name is Bono and I am a rock star. Don't get me too excited because I use four letter words when I get excited. I'd just like to say to the parents, your children are safe, your country is safe . . . Doctor of Laws, wow! I know it's an honor, and it really is an honor, but are you sure? I never went to college, I've slept in some strange places, but the library wasn't one of them." Bono identified the central theme of his speech this way: "So what's the problem that we want to apply all this energy and intellect to? Every era has its defining struggle and the fate of Africa is one of ours" ("Because We Can," 2004).

Stephen Colbert delivered a commencement address to graduates at Knox College on June 3, 2006. Not surprisingly, there was abundant humor throughout his presentation. At one point, he said, somewhat mocking a cliché heard at so many commencements, "It has been said that children are our future. But does that not also mean that we are their past? You are here to replace us. I don't understand why we're here helping and honoring them. You do not see union workers holding benefits for robots." On a more serious note, Colbert remarked, "Cynicism masquerades as wisdom, but it is the farthest thing from it. Because cynics don't learn anything. Because cynicism is a self-imposed blindness, a rejection of the world because we are afraid it will hurt us or disappoint us. Cynics always say no. But saying 'yes' begins things." He finished on a humorous note, offering advice to graduates (sort of) that is traditional in commencement addresses, "And lastly, the best career advice I can give you is to get your own TV show. It pays well, the hours are good, and you are famous. And eventually some very nice people will give you a doctorate in fine arts for doing jack squat" ("Stephen Colbert's Address," 2006).

Inspirational commencement addresses should appeal to our better nature. You want to touch deep feelings of your audience, encouraging pure motives and greater effort to achieve a common good. This is a commencement, a new beginning.

After-Dinner Speeches

An **after-dinner speech** is a presentation that typically occurs at a formal gathering of some group. After-dinner speeches are not always presented after dinner. Developed in England in the 19th century as a formal type of presentation, such speeches were literally delivered right after a dinner, usually to a large gathering for some occasion. More recently, these presentations may occur after a luncheon or even a breakfast gathering of business or civic groups. They probably should be renamed *after-meal speeches* or *postprandial public speeches* (eh, maybe not), but after-dinner speech remains the common term still used.

An after-dinner speech is meant to entertain. Although your topic can be a serious one, you need to take an amusing approach to it. For example, a speech on vegetarianism could be informative if you describe the pros and cons of eschewing meat, it could be persuasive if you argue forcefully that we should convert to vegetarianism, and it could be an after-dinner speech if you made light of the vegetarian substitutes for meat (e.g., lentil loaf, soy burgers). The tone should be whimsical, not serious. This makes some topics more appropriate than others. AIDS doesn't lend itself easily to whimsy, nor does child abuse, terminal illness, or torture. "The Most Ridiculous Things People Do with Cell Phones" or "My Top 10 List of Irritating Behaviors in Restaurants" or "The World's Most Pointless Signs" all suggest humorous potential. Again, review the dos and don'ts for using humor effectively and appropriately discussed in Chapter 13.

Despite the whimsical nature of after-dinner speeches, this is not stand-up comedy. Don't deliver a series of one-liners unrelated to any theme or thoughtful point. Your after-dinner speech should have a central theme and a serious point relevant to that theme even though you accomplish this with humor. Often the topic and theme are your choice, or the group that invites you to speak considers you an authority on certain topics and wants you to speak on one of them. The occasion and makeup of your audience may also dictate certain topic choices. If you're speaking before an environmental group, there should be an environmental flavor to your theme (e.g., common mistakes the public makes about the environmental movement in America). Skip the canned jokes. Telling lawyer jokes to a group of attorneys will likely backfire. They probably have heard every lawyer joke ever made. Be original and creative.

Speeches of Introduction

A **speech of introduction** prepares an audience for a speech that is about to be presented. Sometimes an audience is very familiar with the speaker, requiring a very brief introduction. You want to create enthusiasm for the speaker, but remember that you are not the main focus. Identify who you are if the audience is unfamiliar with you, but place the focus on the speaker being introduced.

If I were introducing American humorist Dave Barry, a well-know personality in most circles, I would keep the introduction very brief because the audience isn't excited to hear me speak. They have gathered to hear the featured speaker. I would mostly quote his own self-description taken from his website because it is so amusing, places the focus squarely on him, and sets the mood for his speech. For example,

> Thank you for attending this anxiously anticipated event. It is my great honor to introduce to you a man who describes himself in these words: Dave Barry is a humor columnist. In 1988 he won the Pulitzer Prize for Commentary. Many people are still trying to figure out how this happened. Dave has also written a total of 30 books, although virtually none of them contain useful information. In his spare time, Dave is a candidate for president of the United States. If elected, his highest priority will be to seek the death penalty for whoever is responsible for making Americans install low-flow toilets. Anything else I might add about Dave Barry would pale in comparison to his

own self-description, so without further ado, please welcome Dave Barry.

Notice that the last statement asks the audience to welcome the speaker. This cues the audience to applaud the speaker as a welcoming gesture.

Less familiar speakers require a bit more information for an audience. You may need to build the speaker's credibility by briefly listing awards, titles, accomplishments, and the like: "Jerald Grayson has advanced degrees in geotechnical engineering and has investigated some of the worst natural disasters in our recent history, including our own all too familiar and tragic collapse of the counties earthen dam. He is a recognized geological expert internationally, and he has won numerous awards for his service to our country." Remember, the audience doesn't assemble to hear you speak, so keep the credential building short. Also, make sure that you pronounce the speaker's name correctly. If you are unsure, ask the speaker before introducing him or her. Finally, never provide any potentially embarrassing details about the speaker. Making a speaker and the audience uncomfortable at the outset sets an awful tone for the ensuing speech.

As a featured speaker, responding well to an introduction, especially an effusively positive one, can ingratiate you to your audience. Henry Shelton, when general chairman of the Joint Chiefs of Staff, responded to just such an effusive introduction this way: "Thank you, Mr. Secretary, for that incredible introduction. If I had known you were going to eulogize me, I would have done the only decent thing and died" ("Victory, Honor," 2000). For more standard introductions, simply offer a gracious thanks, express enthusiasm for appearing before this audience, then begin your speech.

Speeches of Presentation

Awards ceremonies have become commonplace. It's hard to find a week on television in which there is a total absence of some award program. As journalist and editor Joanne Lipman noted, "Hollywood has its Oscars. Television has its Emmys. Broadway has its Tonys. And advertising has its Clios. And its Andys, Addys, Effies, and Obies. And 117 other assorted awards. And those are just the big ones" (quoted in Foley, 2010). This list doesn't even include the awards in the music entertainment industry, which seem to metastasize uncontrollably.

As a student, you may not have many opportunities to present an award, but you may find occasions on campus and off when you are responsible for giving a presentation speech. A **speech of presentation** must communicate to the audience assembled the meaning and importance of the award. "The Floyd Younger award for excellence in teaching is offered each year to the one instructor on our campus, chosen by committee from nominations made by his or her colleagues, who has exhibited outstanding effectiveness as a teacher" is an example. Also, a presentation speech should identify why the recipient has earned the award. For example, "Karen Follett has taught creative writing on this campus for 15 years. Her students adore her. One student remarked, 'I've never had a teacher who was so enthusiastic, so encouraging, so down right fun in class.' Another student said this, 'Professor Follett rocks! She's simply the best instructor in the universe.' It is my great pleasure to give the Floyd Younger award for excellence in teacher to Karen Follett." Present the award to the recipient with your left hand so you are free to shake the recipient's right hand.

Speeches of Acceptance

How many times have you watched the Academy Awards presentations and heard a winner begin an acceptance speech, "I didn't think I would win so I didn't prepare a speech"? Every time I hear that, I cringe. It's false humility and it's lame. Actors especially should have a prepared script. It is the essence of their business. Some of the worst, most cringe-inducing acceptance speeches have occurred at the Oscars. If you have any inkling that you might win an award, large or small, prepare a brief acceptance speech. Don't embarrass yourself.

Your acceptance speech should be appreciative, genuine, and humble. No one wants to hear the winner gloat. "I knew I would win this" or "Boy I deserve this" doesn't endear you to the audience. Express your pleasure at receiving the award—"This is such an honor. I am so happy to receive it." Show your appreciation with a simple statement—"Thank you so much for this great honor." Thank the most important people who helped you and those who gave you the award. Thanking your parents for conceiving you is not usually appropriate or effective. Keep the list of those you wish to thank short. When Kim Basinger won the best actress Oscar in 1998, she said, "I just want to thank everybody I've ever met in my entire life." Thankfully, she didn't proceed to list each person by name. Host Billy Crystal, after a series of Oscar winners gave acceptance speeches for "Lord of the Rings," remarked, "It's now official. There is no one left to thank in New Zealand." An audience easily grows restless when a laundry list of people, most of whom may be unknown to audience members, is presented by the award recipient.

Summary

Special occasion speeches are different from informative and persuasive speeches. Each type has its special guidelines to be effective and appropriate. In most cases, such speeches work best when they are relatively brief, heartfelt, entertaining, and well suited to audience expectations. Make your special occasion speeches truly special.

Abstracting The process of selective perception whereby we formulate increasingly vague conceptions of our world by leaving out details associated with objects, events, and ideas.

Accommodating style Yielding to the needs and desires of others during a conflict.

Acculturation The process of adapting to a culture different from one's own.

Acculturative stress The anxiety that comes from the unfamiliarity of new cultural surroundings, rules, norms, and practices and the attempt to adapt to these new circumstances.

Ad hominem fallacy A personal attack on the messenger to avoid the message.

Ad populum fallacy Basing a claim on popular opinion.

Advising response Listeners telling individuals how they should act.

After-dinner speech An entertaining presentation that typically occurs at a formal gathering of some group.

Agenda A list of topics to be discussed in a group meeting presented in the order in which they will be addressed.

Aggression Any physical or verbal communication that is intended to inflict harm.

Alliteration The repetition of the same sound, usually a consonant sound, starting several words in a sentence.

Amalgamating Both contradictory forces (dialectics) are addressed without compromising on either impulse.

Ambushing When we listen for weaknesses and ignore strengths of a speaker's message.

Amplitude Variation of sound that is perceived as loudness.

Anchor attitude A preexisting attitude on an issue that serves as a reference point for how close or distant other attitudes and positions are.

Anecdote A short, entertaining story.

Anger Activism Model Helps explain the relationship between anger and persuasion; posits that anger provokes desired behavioral changes.

Antithesis A stylistic device that uses opposites to create impact.

Appropriateness Behavior that is viewed as legitimate for, or fitting to, the context.

Argument An implicit or explicit presentation of a claim and support for that claim with reasoning and evidence.

Assertiveness The ability to communicate the full range of thoughts and emotions with confidence and skill.

Attachment theory Children raised in families whose communication is supportive learn to join in conversations with new people and read social signals accurately while those raised in families whose communication is threatening and fear arousing produces adults who are withdrawn or overaggressive.

Attention Focused awareness on a stimulus at a given moment.

Attitude A learned predisposition to respond favorably or unfavorably toward some attitude object.

Attribution Assigning a cause, either situations or personal characteristics, to people's behavior.

Avoiding Sidestepping or ignoring conflict.

Bad apples Disruptive group members who poison the group.

Beauty bias A perceived advantage accorded those who are viewed as attractive.

Behavioral interviewing Interviewers ask for specific examples of behavior by an applicant that illustrate an answer given to a question.

Belief What we think is true or probable.

Benevolent sexism A subtle form of discrimination that embraces the "positive" stereotype of women as "pure creatures" who deserve to be protected and shown affection, but only as long as they behave in a conventional manner.

Bilateral symmetry The right and left sides of the human body match: eyes are straight across from each other, not one higher than the other, and so forth.

Binge drinking Consuming five or more drinks for men and four or more for women in a two-hour period.

Bound morpheme Unit of meaning that has no meaning until it is attached to a stand-alone word.

Brainstorming The creative problem-solving process characterized by encouragement of even zany ideas, freedom from initial evaluation of potential solutions, and energetic participation by all group members.

Breadth (of self-disclosure) The range of subjects discussed.

Burden of proof The obligation of the claimant to support a claim with evidence and reasoning; whoever makes the claim has the burden to prove it.

By-passing When you assume that everyone assigns the same meaning to a word without checking to see if it is true.

Central idea (of a speech) Identifies the main concept, point, issue, or conclusion that a speaker wants an audience to understand, believe, or feel.

Channel Medium through which a message travels, such as oral or written.

Channel lean A single channel devoid of the richness of nonverbal cues

Channel rich Incorporates multiple channels besides words, such as gestures, facial expressions, tone of voice, posture, and other nonverbal cues.

Charisma Constellation of personal attributes that people find attractive and that causes them to accord influence to a person perceived to have such attributes.

Claim A generalization that remains to be proven.

Cliché A once-vivid expression that has been overused to the point of seeming commonplace.

Closedness An unwillingness to communicate with others.

Coalitions Temporary alliances formed by individuals to enhance their power relative to others.

Co-culture A group of people who live in a dominant culture yet remain connected to another cultural heritage that typically exhibits significant differences in communication patterns, perceptions, values, beliefs, and rituals from the dominant culture.

Cognitive dissonance The unpleasant feeling produced by seemingly inconsistent thoughts.

Cohesiveness The degree to which members identify with the group and wish to remain in the group.

Collaborating Style of conflict management in which parties work together to maximize the attainment of goals for all involved in the conflict.

Collectivist culture A culture that has a "we" consciousness; individuals see themselves as being closely linked to one or more groups and are primarily motivated by the norms and duties imposed by these groups.

Commencement address An inspirational speech that occurs at graduation ceremonies.

Commitment A passion for excellence, accepting nothing less than the best that you can be and dedicating yourself to achieving that excellence.

Communication A transactional process of sharing meaning with others.

Communication climate The emotional atmosphere, the pervading or enveloping tone that we create by the way we communicate with others.

Communication competence Engaging in communication that is perceived to be both effective and appropriate in a given context.

Communication orientation Public speakers focusing on making their message clear and interesting to listeners to assuage anxiety.

Communication skill The successful performance of a communication behavior and the ability to repeat such a behavior.

Communication style of conflict management A typical way an individual addresses a conflict.

Competence (of speaker) An audience's perception of a speaker's knowledge and experience on a topic.

Competing style (of conflict management) Exhibited by threats, criticism, contempt, hostile remarks and jokes, sarcasm, ridicule, intimidation, fault finding and blaming, and denials of responsibility. This style tries to "win" the argument.

Competition A process of mutually exclusive goal attainment (MEGA); for you to win, others must lose.

Competitive interrupting When we dominate the conversation by seizing the floor from others who are speaking.

Compliant sex Having sexual intercourse when you don't want to, but your partner does, in circumstances in which no duress or coercion is involved.

Composure A speaker's emotional stability, confidence, and degree of control over himself or herself when under stress.

Comprehension Shared meaning between and among parties in a transaction.

Compromising Attempting to resolve a conflict by giving up something to get something in return.

Confirmation bias The tendency to seek information that supports our beliefs and values and to ignore information that contradicts our beliefs and values.

Confirming response Enhances the person's self-esteem and confidence.

Conflict The expressed struggle of interconnected parties who perceive incompatible goals and interference from one or more parties in attaining those goals.

Conformity The inclination of group members to think and behave in ways that are consistent with group norms.

Confrontation A strategy of the collaborating style of conflict management in which there is an overt recognition of a conflict and a direct effort to find creative ways to satisfy all parties in the conflict.

Connecting bid An attempt to engage another person in a positive transaction, sometimes at a deep and enduring level and other times at a superficial and fleeting level.

Connection-autonomy dialectic The desire to come together with another person (connection) yet remain apart, independent, and in control of one's own life (autonomy).

Connotation The volatile, personal, subjective meaning of words, composed of three dimensions: evaluation, potency, and activity.

Consensus A state of mutual agreement among members of a group in which all legitimate concerns of individuals have been addressed to the satisfaction of the group.

Constructive communication climate Composed of two general elements: a pattern of openness, or a willingness to communicate, and a pattern of supportiveness, or a confirmation of the worth and value of others and a willingness to help others be successful.

Constructive competition Occurs when competing against others and produces a positive, enjoyable experience and promotes increased efforts to achieve victory without jeopardizing positive interpersonal relationships and personal well-being.

Constructive conflict Conflict that is characterized by communication that is cooperative, supportive, and flexible.

Contact theory Predicts that interacting and becoming more familiar with members of stereotyped groups can diminish prejudice resulting from stereotyping.

Content dimension (of messages) What is actually said and done.

Content-only response Focuses on the content of a message, but ignores the emotional side of the communication.

Context The environment in which communication occurs; the who, what, where, when, why, and how of communication.

Contingencies of self-worth Your self-esteem is influenced by what is perceived as most important to you feeling good about yourself.

Contrast effect A persuasive strategy that begins with a large request that makes a smaller request seem more palatable.

Control Communication that seeks to regulate or direct a person's behavior.

Conventionality-uniqueness dialectic Wanting your relationship to be perceived as the same yet different from other relationships.

Convergence Similarities that connect us to others.

Conversational narcissism The tendency of listeners to turn the topics of ordinary conversation to themselves without showing sustained interest in others' topics.

Cooperation A process of mutually inclusive goal attainment (MIGA); for you to achieve your goals others must also achieve their goals.

Cooperative argumentation Engaging in a process of deliberation with understanding and problem solving as ultimate goals.

Correlation A consistent relationship between two variables.

Counterpersuasion Attacks from an opposing side on an issue of controversy.

Credibility (of evidence) Believability of supporting material determined by its reliability and validity.

Credibility (of speaker) Judgments made by listeners concerning the believability of a communicator.

Critical listening The process of evaluating the merits of claims as they are heard.

Cultural relativism The view that cultures are merely different, not deficient, and each culture's norms and practices should be assessed only from the perspective of the culture itself, not by standards embraced by another culture.

Culture A learned set of enduring values, beliefs, and practices that are shared by an identifiable, large group of people with a common history.

Culture shock The anxiety that comes from the unfamiliarity of new cultural surroundings, rules, norms, and practices.

Cynicism Nay-saying, fault finding, and ridiculing the beliefs and values of others.

Cynics Those who unthinkingly mock, ridicule, and tear down other people and their ideas.

Dead-level abstracting The practice of freezing on one level of abstraction (getting stuck using mostly very vague or very concrete words).

Deep diversity Substantial variation among members in task-relevant skills, knowledge, abilities, beliefs, values, perspectives, and problem-solving strategies.

Defensiveness A protective reaction to a perceived attack on our self-esteem and self-concept.

Defiance Unambiguous, overt, purposeful noncompliance with the dictates of others who exercise greater power.

Demographics Characteristics of an audience such as age, gender, culture, ethnicity, and group affiliations.

Denotation The socially agreed-upon meaning of words; it is the meaning shared by members of a speech community.

Depth (of self-disclosure) How personal you become when discussing a particular subject that reveals something about yourself.

Description A first-person report of how we feel, what we perceive to be true in specific situations, and what behaviors we desire from others.

Destructive communication climate Composed of two general elements: a pattern of closedness and a pattern of defensiveness.

Destructive conflict Conflict that is characterized by escalation, retaliation, domination, competition, cross-complaining, defensiveness, and inflexibility.

Development Composed of the ability of group members, their motivation, and their experience with relevant tasks.

Dialectics Impulses that push and pull us in opposite directions simultaneously within our relationships with others.

Direct aggression Hostile communication that targets the victim openly, such as pushing, shoving, physically assaulting, or shouting insults.

Directive style (of leadership) Leaders tell group members what to do and they expect compliance.

Directory An Internet tool in which humans edit indexes of web pages that match, or link with, keywords typed in a search window.

Disconfirming response Diminishes the person and reduces his or her confidence.

Discrimination Any behavior that manifests negative feelings about members of a group.

Disinhibiting Impersonal, abrupt, even offensive communication from lean channels of communication.

Displacement The human ability to use language to talk about objects, ideas, events, and relations that don't just exist in the here and now and may not exist at all except in our minds.

Display rules Culture-specific prescriptions that dictate appropriateness of behaviors.

Disruptive roles Group roles that serve individual needs at the expense of group needs and goals.

Divergence Differences that separate people.

Dominance The exercise of power over others.

Door-in-the-face strategy The contrast effect used as a persuasive strategy.

Downward communication Messages that flow from superordinates to subordinates in a hierarchical organization.

Dyad A couple or two-person, interpersonal relationship.

Dynamism The enthusiasm and energy exhibited by a speaker.

Dysfunctional speech anxiety When the intensity of the fight-or-flight response prevents a person from performing a speech appropriately and effectively.

Effectiveness How well an individual progresses toward the achievement of his or her goal.

Ego involvement The degree to which an issue is relevant or important to a person.

Elaboration likelihood model (of persuasion) Theory of how persuasion works positing two routes to persuasion—the central route that requires mindfulness and the peripheral route that is relatively mindless.

Emblem A gesture that has a precise meaning separate from verbal communication and is usually recognized across an entire culture or co-culture, sometimes even across cultures.

Emoticons Graphic notations that indicate emotional information.

Emotional contagion Feeling emotion communicated by speaker's tone of voice.

Emotionally restrictive Having difficulty and fears about expressing one's feelings and difficulty finding words to express basic emotions.

Empathic listening Requires listeners to take the perspective of the other person and to listen for what that person needs.

Empathy Thinking and feeling what you perceive another to be thinking and feeling.

Empowerment Power derived from enhancing the capabilities, choices, and influence of individuals and groups.

Equivocation Using language that permits more than one plausible meaning, often as a substitute for outright lying.

Ethics (in communication) A system for judging moral correctness by using an agreed-upon set of standards to determine what constitutes right and wrong behavior.

Ethnocentrism The notion that one's own culture is superior to any other. It is the idea that other cultures should be measured by the degree to which they live up to one's own cultural standards.

Ethos Aristotle's version of credibility characterized by "good sense, good moral character, and good will" of the speaker.

Eulogy A speech delivered in praise of a deceased friend or family member.

Euphemism Form of linguistic novocaine whereby word choices numb us to or camouflage unpleasant or offensive realities.

Evaluations Value judgments made about individuals and about their performance, exhibited as praise, recognition, admiration, criticism, contempt, or blame.

Evaluative response A judgment by a listener about a person's conduct.

Evidence Statistics, testimony of experts and credible sources, and verifiable facts.

Exchange theory A cost-benefits analysis that weighs the benefits of a particular relationship against any costs incurred.

Explicit norms Norms that specifically and overtly identify acceptable and unacceptable behavior in groups.

Extemp speech A speech delivered from a prepared outline or notes.

Extended example A detailed story or illustration.

Facial feedback hypothesis Facial expressions can influence emotions.

Fallacies Errors in evidence and reasoning.

False dichotomy Using either-or language to frame a choice as though only two opposing possibilities exist, when at least a third option is clearly available.

Feedback The receiver's verbal and nonverbal responses to a message.

Feminine culture A culture that exhibits stereotypic feminine traits such as affection, nurturance, sensitivity, compassion, and emotional expressiveness.

Fields of experience Cultural background, ethnicity, geographic location, extent of travel, and general personal experiences accumulated over the course of a lifetime that influence messages.

Fight-or-flight response Myriad physiological changes that are activated by a threat prepare both animals and humans either to fight the foe or flee the threat.

Flaming A cyberterm for an abusive, attacking message sent electronically to others.

Flooding When you can no longer think clearly because conflict triggers intense emotional reactions.

Forgetting curve The rate at which we no longer retain information in our memory.

Forgiveness Letting go of feelings of revenge and desires to retaliate.

Formal roles Assigned positions usually in an organizational structure.

Framing The influence wording has on our perception of choices.

Free morpheme A stand-alone word

Friendship-warmth touch Touch communication that can be ambiguous but is intended to express friendship.

Functional-professional touch Instrumental touch communication that is limited to the requirements of the situation.

Functional speech anxiety When the fight-or-flight response is managed and stimulates an optimum speech presentation.

Fundamental attribution error Overemphasizing personal characteristics and underemphasizing situational causes of other people's behavior.

Gender Social role behavior that is learned from communicating with others.

Gender biased language Language variants that make women virtually invisible and tacitly brands them as less powerful and less important than men.

Gender differences hypothesis View that men and women communicate in vastly divergent ways.

Gender role stereotypes The set of expectations defined by each culture that specifies what is appropriate behavior for men and women (what is considered "masculine" or "feminine").

Gender similarities hypothesis View that men and women communicate in mostly similar ways.

General purpose (of speech) Identifies the overall goal of a speech (to inform, describe, explain, demonstrate, persuade, celebrate, memorialize, entertain, or eulogize).

Glass ceiling An invisible barrier of subtle discrimination that excludes women and ethnic minorities from top leadership positions in corporate and professional America.

Glazing over When listeners' attention wanders and daydreaming occurs.

Grammar The set of rules that specify how the units of language can be meaningfully combined.

Group Three or more individuals, interacting for the achievement of some common purpose(s), who influence one another.

Grouphate The significant dissatisfaction, even dread, many people experience when working in groups.

Groupthink An ineffective process of group decision making in which members stress cohesiveness and agreement instead of skepticism and optimum decision making.

Halfalogue Hearing only half the conversation typical of cell phone calls by others that often produces irritation from outside listeners.

Haptics The study of touch.

Hasty generalization A broad claim based on too few or unrepresentative examples.

Hearing The physiological process of registering sound waves as they hit the eardrums.

Hierarchy Members of an organization are rank ordered.

High-context communication style Indirect verbal expression; significant information is derived from contextual cues, such as relationships, situations, setting, and time; typically found in collectivist cultures.

High power-distance cultures Cultures with a relatively strong emphasis on maintaining power differences.

Hindsight bias The tendency to look back after a fact or outcome has been revealed and say to yourself, "I knew that all along."

Horizontal communication Messages that flow between individuals with equal power in organizations.

Hostile environment sexual harassment Insult, ridicule, humor, or intimidation of a sexual nature that makes the work environment an unpleasant, even threatening, place to remain.

Hostile sexism Antipathy toward women who are viewed as usurping men's power.

Hypercompetitiveness The excessive emphasis on beating others to achieve one's goals.

Hypothetical examples Instances that describe an imaginary situation, one that is concocted to make a point, illustrate an idea, or identify a general principle.

Identification (in persuasion) The affiliation and connection between speaker and listeners.

Illustrators Gestures that help explain what one person says to another person.

Implicit norms Observable patterns of behavior, exhibited by group members, that identify acceptable and unacceptable conduct.

Impromptu speech A speech delivered off-the-cuff, without notes.

Inclusion-seclusion dialectic The desire to spend time alone with one's partner and also spend time together with others outside the relationship.

Indirect aggression Hostile communication that intends to harm a targeted person while avoiding identification as an aggressor, such as gossiping, spreading malicious rumors, or sabotaging behind the victim's back.

Individual achievement The realization of personal goals without having to defeat an opponent.

Individualist culture A culture with an "I" consciousness; individuals see themselves as loosely linked to each other and largely independent of group identification.

Inferences Conclusions about the unknown based on the known.

Inferential error A mistaken conclusion that results from the assumption that inferences are factual descriptions of reality instead of interpretations of varying accuracy made by individuals.

Informal roles Roles that identify functions, not positions; they usually emerge naturally from group transactions.

Information bulimia Cramming information into short-term memory.

Informational listening Attempting to comprehend the message of a speaker.

Integration A collaborating strategy that finds alternatives that meet the goals of all parties in a conflict.

Internal summary Restates a key point or points of a speech in the body of the speech.

Interpersonal relationship A connection two people have to each other because of kinship (brother-sister), an attraction (lovers and friends), or a power distribution (boss-employee).

Interpreting response A listener expressing what he or she thinks is the underlying meaning of a situation presented by another person.

Interrupting When one person stops speaking when another person starts speaking.

Interviewing A purposeful, planned conversation, characterized by extensive verbal interaction.

Intimate relationship A type of interpersonal relationship that is characterized by strong emotional bonding, closeness, and interdependence, in which individuals meaningfully influence each other.

Intimate terrorism Involves "a violent attempt to take complete control of, or at least to generally dominate, a relationship."

Jargon The specialized language of a profession, trade, or group.

Judgments Subjective evaluations of objects, events, or ideas.

Kinesics The study of both facial communication and gestures.

Label A name or a descriptive word or phrase.

Laissez-faire style (of leadership) A sit-on-your-derriere approach to leadership, which is to say no leadership at all is exercised.

Language A structured system of symbols for communicating meaning.

Latitude of acceptance Positions a person finds acceptable or at least tolerable.

Latitude of noncommitment Positions that provoke only a neutral or ambivalent response from people.

Latitude of rejection Positions people find objectionable because they are too far from their anchor attitude.

Law of Very Large Numbers With large enough numbers almost anything is likely to happen to *somebody*.

Leadership A leader-follower influence process with the goal of producing positive change that reflects mutual purposes of group members and is largely accomplished through competent communication.

Legitimate authority Someone who is perceived to have a right to direct others' behavior because of his or her position, title, role, experience, or knowledge.

Lexicon The total vocabulary of a language.

Lie bias When we expect most messages to be deceptive.

Linguistic determinism The claim that we are prisoners of our native language, unable to think certain thoughts or perceive in certain ways because of the grammatical structure and lexicon of our language.

Linguistic relativity The claim that the grammar and lexicon of our native language powerfully influence but do not imprison our thinking and perception.

Listening The process of receiving, constructing, and reconstructing meaning from, and responding to, spoken and/or nonverbal messages.

Logos Aristotle's conception of building arguments based on logic and evidence.

Love and intimacy touch Touch that is reserved for a very few special individuals that is not sexual but does express tenderness.

Low-context communication style Verbally precise, direct, and explicit method of communication usually found in individualistic cultures.

Low power-distance cultures Culture whose people value relatively equal power sharing and discourage attention to status differences and ranking in society.

Magic ratio Five positive for every one negative act to sustain a relationship.

Maintenance roles Group roles that address the social dimensions of small groups.

Manipulative communication An attempt by one person to maneuver another toward the manipulator's goal.

Manipulators Gestures made by one part of the body, usually the hands, that rub, pick, squeeze, clean. or groom another part of the body, and they have no specific meaning.

Margin of error A measure of the degree of sampling error accounted for by imperfections in sample selection.

Masculine culture A culture that exhibits stereotypic masculine traits such as male dominance, ambitiousness, assertiveness, competitiveness, and drive for achievement.

Masculine-feminine dimension Degree to which a culture expects either rigid adherence to gender role expectations or is flexible about gender role expectations.

Masculine-generic gender references The use of masculine nouns and pronouns to include references to both women and men.

Meaning The conscious pattern humans create out of their interpretation of experience; making sense of our world.

Mentors Knowledgeable individuals who have achieved some success in their profession or job and who assist people trying to get started in a line of work.

Message Stimulus that produces meaning.

Metaphor An implied comparison of two seemingly dissimilar things.

Metasearch engine An Internet tool that will send your keyword request to several search engines at once.

Mindfulness Thinking about ones communication with others and persistently working to improve it.

Mindlessness Not being cognizant of our communication with others and putting little or no effort into improving it.

Mixed messages Inconsistencies or outright contradictions between verbal and nonverbal messages.

Mixed metaphor The use of two or more vastly different metaphors in a single expression.

Morpheme The smallest unit of meaning in a language.

Morphology The part of grammar that describes how morphemes are constructed meaningfully from phonemes.

Multiculturalism Social-intellectual movement that promotes the value of diversity as a core principle and insists that all cultural groups be treated with respect and as equals.

Murphy's Law The assertion that anything that can go wrong likely will go wrong.

Muscle dysmorphia A preoccupation with one's body size and a perception that, though very muscular, one actually looks puny.

Myth A belief that is contradicted by fact.

Negative synergy The product of joint action of group members that produces a result worse than that expected based on perceived individual abilities and skills of members.

Negativity bias A strong tendency to weigh negative information more heavily than positive information, especially when forming perceptions of others.

Netiquette Etiquette (rules of proper conduct) when using the Internet.

Noise Any interference with effective transmission and reception of messages.

Nominal group technique Creative problem-solving method in which team members work alone to generate ideas, those ideas are announced to the group, and team members' ranking of ideas result in the group's top preferences.

Non sequitur Latin for "it does not follow." A conclusion that does not follow from its premises is a non sequitur fallacy.

Nonverbal communication Sharing meaning with others nonlinguistically.

Norm of reciprocity You give back what you get from others.

Norms The rules that indicate what group members have to do (obligation), should do (preference), and cannot do (prohibition) if they want to accomplish specific goals.

Oculesics The study of eye contact in human communication.

Openness A willingness to communicate.

Openness-closedness dialectic The tension in relationships between accessibility and privacy.

Operational definition Specifies measurable behaviors or experiences that indicate what a word means to the user.

Paralanguage Vocal cues.

Parallel processing Using both central and peripheral routes to persuasion.

Paraphrasing A concise response to the speaker which states the essence of the other's content in the listener's words.

Participative style (of leadership) Leaders encourage all group members to engage meaningfully in discussions and decision making.

Pathos Aristotle's conception of emotional appeals used for persuasion.

Perception The process of selecting, organizing, and interpreting sensory data.

Perception checking A behavior description followed by an interpretation of the behavior and finishing with a request for verification of your interpretation.

Performance An attempt to satisfy an audience of critics whose members are focused on evaluating your presentation.

Persuasion A communication process of converting, modifying, or maintaining the attitudes, beliefs, or behavior of others.

Phonemes The individual sounds that compose a specific spoken language.

Phonology A part of grammar that describes the patterns of sound in a language.

Physical noise External, environmental distractions, such as startling sounds, poorly heated rooms, and the like, that divert our attention from the message sent by a source.

Physiological noise Biological influences—such as sweaty palms, pounding heart, and butterflies in the stomach induced by speech anxiety, or feeling sick or exhausted at work—that interfere with sending and receiving messages.

Pitch Frequency is perceived as pitch—how high or low the sound is (e.g., how high or low a human voice is during conversation).

Power The ability to influence the attainment of goals sought by oneself or others.

Power-distance dimension Cultural variations in the acceptability of unequal distribution of power in relationships, institutions, and organizations.

Power resource Anything that enables individuals to achieve their goals, assist others to achieve their goals, or interferes with the goal attainment of others.

Predictability-novelty dialectic The desire for both stability and change in interpersonal relationships.

Prejudice Negative feelings about members of a group.

Prevention Power used to thwart the influence of others.

Primacy effect The tendency to be more influenced by initial information about a person than by information gathered later.

Principle of least interest The person who cares less about continuing a relationship usually has more power.

Principle of parsimony When competing explanations or theories fit the facts, the simplest is preferred.

Probing response A listener seeking more information from others by asking questions.

Productivity (in groups) The degree to which a group accomplishes its work efficiently and effectively.

Productivity (in language) The capacity of language to transform a small number of phonemes into whatever words, phrases, and sentences that we require to communicate our abundance of thoughts, ideas, and feelings.

Proposition The primary overriding claim for a persuasive speech.

Proposition of fact The primary overriding claim in a persuasive speech that alleges a truth.

Proposition of policy The primary overriding claim in a persuasive speech that calls for a significant change from how problems are currently handled.

Proposition of value A primary overriding claim in a persuasive speech that calls for a judgment that assesses the worth or merit of an idea, object, or practice.

Prototype The most representative or "best" example of something.

Provisionalism Qualifying our statements with words such as possibly, probably, perhaps, maybe, and could be, and avoiding absolutes such as always, never, must, can't, and won't.

Proxemics Study of the influence of distance and territoriality on human communication.

Pseudolistening When someone pretends to listen.

Psychological noise Preconceptions, biases, and assumptions that interfere with effective message transmission and reception.

Psychological reactance The more someone tries to control our behavior and restrict our choices, the more we are inclined to resist such efforts, even do the opposite behavior.

Quid pro quo sexual harassment When the more powerful person requires sexual favors from the less powerful person in exchange for keeping a job, getting a high grade in a class, landing an employment promotion, and the like.

Random sample Portion of the population chosen in such a manner that every member of the entire population has an equal chance of being selected.

Rationalization of disconfirmation Inventing superficial, even lame, alternative explanations for contradictory evidence.

Real examples Actual occurrences used to illustrate an idea, make a point, or identify a general principle.

Reasoning Thought process of drawing conclusions from evidence.

Rebid An attempt to connect with another person after an initial bid has been ignored.

Receiver Decoder of messages.

Referents The objects, events, ideas, or relationships referred to by words.

Reflected appraisal A term coined by Harry Stack Sullivan that refers to messages you receive from others that assess your self-concept.

Reflective thinking model John Dewey's sequence of logical steps that incorporates the scientific method of defining, analyzing, and solving problems.

Reframing (problem-solving technique) The creative process of breaking rigid thinking by placing a problem in a different frame of reference.

Refutation The process of answering opposing arguments in a debate or disagreement.

Relationship dimension (of messages) How the message defines or redefines the association between individuals.

Relevance Evidence used to support claims must relate directly to those claims.

Reliability Consistency of a source of information.

Resistance Covert, ambiguous noncompliance with the dictates of more powerful individuals.

Response styles The types of initial verbal reactions we make when another person comes to us with a problem, reveals a frustrating event, or is experiencing an emotional crisis.

Revelation-concealment dialectic The dilemma you face when wanting to share information about a relationship with those outside the relationship yet also wanting to conceal the relationship for various reasons.

Rhetorical question A question asked by a speaker that the audience answers mentally but not out loud.

Roast A purposely humorous tribute to a person.

Role fixation Playing a group role rigidly with little or no inclination to try other roles.

Roles Patterns of behavior that group members are expected to exhibit.

Rule A followable prescription that indicates what behavior is obligated, preferred, or prohibited in certain contexts.

Sapir-Whorf hypothesis A claim that we are either prisoners of our native language, unable to think certain thoughts or perceive in certain ways (linguistic determinism), or that our language powerfully influences but does not imprison our thinking and perceptions (linguistic relativity).

Schemas Mental frameworks that create meaningful patterns from stimuli.

Script A predictable sequence of events that indicates what we are expected to do in a given situation.

Search engine An Internet tool that computer generates indexes of web pages that match, or link with, keywords typed in a search window.

Segmenting A strategy to manage dialectics in which certain parts of a relationship are divided into separate domains and some of these domains are declared off limits.

Selecting A strategy for managing dialectics in which one contradictory impulse is given attention and another is ignored.

Selective memory bias The tendency to remember information that supports our stereotypes but to forget information that contradicts them.

Self-concept The sum total of everything that encompasses the self-referential term "me"; your identity or self-perception.

Self-deprecation Humor that makes gentle fun of one's own failings and limitations.

Self-disclosure The process of purposely revealing to others information about ourselves that they otherwise would not know.

Self-esteem The evaluative element of self-perception; self-appraisal or your perception of self-worth, attractiveness, and social competence.

Self-fulfilling prophecy Acting on an erroneous expectation that produces the expected behavior and confirms the original impression.

Self-justification The creation of excuses that absolve one of blame.

Self-reflexiveness The ability to use language to talk about language.

Self-selected sample A collection of individuals, usually the most committed, aroused, or motivated, who have chosen themselves to participate in a survey, poll, or study.

Self-serving bias The tendency to attribute our successful behavior to ourselves (personal traits) but to assign external circumstances (situations) to our unsuccessful behavior.

Semantic noise Confusing or distracting word choice that interferes with accurate message transmission and reception.

Semantic reaction A delayed, thoughtful response to language that seeks to decipher the users' intended meaning of a word.

Semantics The set of rules that governs the meaning of words and sentences.

Sender Initiator and encoder of messages.

Sensation The process by which our sense organs (eyes, ears, nose, skin, and tongue) that contain sense receptors change physical energy (light, sound waves, chemical substances) into neural impulses that are sent to our brains.

Sensitivity Receptive accuracy whereby we can detect, decode, and comprehend signals in our social environment.

Sensory acuity The level of sensitivity of our senses.

Sex Biological differences between males and females.

Sexual harassment Verbal or nonverbal communication of a sexual nature that is unwelcome by the recipient and is likely to interfere with the victim's work.

Sexual touch Intimate touch between individuals.

Shift response A competitive vying for attention and focus on oneself by shifting topics.

Shifting the burden of proof Inappropriately assuming the validity of a claim unless it is proven false by another person who never made the original claim.

Signal reaction An automatic, emotional response to a symbol (usually a word).

Signposts Organizational markers that indicate the structure of a speech and notify listeners that a particular point is about to be addressed.

Similarity attraction theory We are drawn to those who are similar to us.

Simile An explicit comparison of two seemingly dissimilar things using the word *like* or *as*.

Situational couple violence Individuals quarrel with their partners, anger and frustration erupt, and an assault occurs.

Skepticism The process of listening to claims, evaluating evidence and reasoning supporting those claims, and drawing conclusions based on probabilities.

Slang The highly informal words not in standard usage that are used by a group with a common interest.

Smoothing A collaborative strategy that attempts to calm the agitated feelings of those involved in a conflict.

Social cohesion That which binds us together in mutual liking.

Social comparison Evaluating yourself by comparing yourself to other people.

Social dimension (of groups) Relationships between group members and the impact these relationships have on the group.

Social judgment theory A theory of persuasion that focuses on how close or distant an audience's position on a controversial issue is from its anchor attitude.

Social loafing The tendency of individuals to reduce their work effort when they join groups.

Social-polite touch Touch communication that occurs during introductions, business relationships, and formal occasions.

Socialization The communication of shared cultural practices, beliefs, and values from generation to generation.

Spamming Sending unsolicited email, especially advertisements for products or activities.

Specific purpose statement (of speech) A concise, precise infinitive phrase composed of simple, clear language that encompasses both the general purpose and the central idea and indicates what the speaker hopes to accomplish with the speech.

Speech anxiety Fear of public speaking and the nervousness that accompanies that fear.

Speech of introduction Prepares an audience for a speech that is about to be presented.

Speech of presentation A brief speech that must communicate to an audience assembled the meaning and importance of an award being conferred.

Speech segmentation Process of discerning breaks between recognizable words.

Stages of relationship development There are five coming together stages and five coming apart stages of relationships.

Standard Agenda Structured method of decision making and problem solving based on the reflective thinking model.

Stereotype A generalization about a group or category of people.

Stereotype vulnerability A perceived threat from apprehension that a person will be evaluated based on a negative stereotype.

Stonewalling A form of the avoiding style of conflict management exhibited by refusing to discuss problems or by physically leaving when the other person is complaining, disagreeing, or attacking.

Stratification Various levels of cultural division based on power spanning the extremes of the haves and the have-nots.

Structure A form or shape characterized by an interrelationship among its parts.

Style (of speaking) Words chosen to express your thoughts and the ways you use language to bring your thoughts to life for an audience.

Stylistic similarity An identification strategy of persuasion in which a speaker tries to look and act similarly to listeners.

Substantive similarity Creates identification between a speaker and an audience by establishing common ground between the two.

Superordinate goal A goal that requires mutual effort by both groups to achieve a desired end.

Supporting materials Examples, statistics, and testimony used to bolster a speaker's viewpoint.

Supporting response Acknowledges the feelings of the speaker and tries to boost the person's confidence.

Supportiveness A confirmation of the worth and value of others and a willingness to help others succeed.

Support response A cooperative effort to focus attention on the other person, not oneself, during conversation.

Symbols Arbitrary representations of objects, events, ideas, or relationships.

Synergy By individuals working together as a group, the work of group members yields a greater total effect than the sum of the individual members' efforts could have produced.

Syntax The rules that govern appropriate combinations of words into phrases and sentences.

Systematic desensitization A technique used to control anxiety, even phobias, triggered by a wide variety of stimuli.

Task dimension (of groups) The work performed by a group and its impact on the group.

Task roles Group roles that advance the attainment of group goals.

Team A small number of people with complementary skills who are equally committed to a common purpose, goals, and working approach for which they hold themselves mutually accountable.

Telecommuting Pay for work at an alternate site.

Territoriality A predisposition to defend a fixed geographic area, or territory, as one's exclusive domain.

Testimonial Praising a product that you have used.

Threshold Minimum amount of energy that triggers a sensation for each human sensory system.

Toast A brief tribute to a person or couple.

Toulmin structure of argument Consists of six elements that constitute an argument: claim, grounds, warrant, backing, reservations, and qualifier.

Traits Relatively enduring characteristics of a person that highlight differences between people and are displayed in most situations.

Transitions They connect what was said in a speech with what will be said.

Triangular theory of love The interaction among three elements of love—intimacy, passion, and commitment—that determines seven different types of love between people.

Tribute speech A speech that praises or celebrates a living person.

True belief A willingness to accept claims without solid reasoning or valid evidence and to hold these beliefs tenaciously even if a googol of contradictory evidence disputes them.

True believers Those who willingly accept claims by authorities or valued sources without question and protect beliefs based on these claims by embracing confirmation bias.

Trustworthiness How truthful or honest an audience perceives a speaker to be.

Truth bias When you expect most messages are truthful.

Turning-against response An overtly negative rejection of a connecting bid.

Turning-away response Ignoring a connecting bid or acting preoccupied when a bid is offered.

Turning points (in relationships) Key moments that change a relationship, such as sharing an interest, disclosing a personal secret, or lending something important.

Turning-toward response Reacting positively to a connecting bid.

Twenty Percent Rule Discrimination decreases when at least 20% of group membership is composed of women or minorities.

Uncertainty Reduction Theory (URT) Posits that when strangers first meet, their principal goal is to reduce uncertainty and to increase predictability.

Understanding response A listener checking his or her perceptions for comprehension of the speaker's message or paraphrasing the message to check for accuracy.

Upward communication Messages that flow from subordinates to superordinates in an organization.

Validity Accuracy of a source of information.

Value dimensions Varying degrees of importance placed on those deeply felt views of what is right, good, and worthwhile.

Values The most deeply felt, generally shared views of what is good, right, or worthwhile behavior or thinking.

Variable Anything that can change.

Virtual groups Small groups whose members rarely interact face to face and who mostly communicate by using electronic technologies.

Virtual library An Internet search tool that combines Internet technology and standard library techniques for cataloguing and appraising information.

Visualization Countering negative thoughts of catastrophe with positive images of success.

Vocal fillers The insertion of *uhm, ah, like, you know, know what I mean, whatever,* and additional variants that substitute for pauses during speech and often draw attention to themselves.

Waist-to-hip ratio Universal measure of female attractiveness; the smaller the waist is compared to the hips (hourglass figure), the greater the perception of attractiveness.

Wedge shape Relatively broad shoulders and narrow waist and hips in men used as a measure of male attractiveness.

Workplace bullying Persistent verbal and nonverbal aggression at work that includes public humiliation, constant criticism, ridicule, gossip, insults, and social ostracism.

REFERENCES

Abbey, A. (1987). Misperceptions of friendly behavior as sexual interest: A survey of naturally occurring incidents. *Psychology of Women Quarterly*, 11, 173–194.

Abramson, J. (1994). *We, the jury*. New York: Basic Books.

Adam, D. (2001). Lifelines: Boom and bust. *Nature .com*. [Online]. Available at: http://www.nature .com/nsu/010118/010118-5.html

Adelmann, P. K., & Zajonc, R. B. (1989). Facial efference and the experience of emotion. *Annual Review of Psychology*, 40, 249–280.

Adler, J. E. (1998, January/February). Open minds and the argument from ignorance. *Skeptical Inquirer*, pp. 41–44.

Adler, R. (1977). *Confidence in communication: A guide to assertive and social skills*. New York: Holt, Rinehart & Winston.

Adler, R., & Elmhorst, J. M. (2008). *Communicating at work: Principles and practices for business and the professions*. New York: McGraw-Hill.

Adler, R., & Proctor, R. F. (2007). *Looking out, looking in*. Belmont, CA: Thomson/Wadsworth.

Afifi, T. D., McManus, T., Steuber, K., & Coho, A. (2009). Verbal avoidance and dissatisfaction in intimate conflict situations. *Human Communication Research*, 35, 357–383.

Afifi, W. A., Guerrero, L. K., & Egland, K. L. (1994, June). *Maintenance behaviors in same- and opposite-sex friendships: Connection to gender, relational closeness, and equity issues*. Paper presented at the annual meeting of the International Network on Personal Relationships, Iowa City.

Aguayo, R. (1990). *Dr. Deming: The American who taught the Japanese about quality*. New York: Simon & Schuster.

Ahrons, C. (1994). *The good divorce: Keeping your family together when your marriage comes apart*. New York: Harper Perennial.

Akert, R. M. (1998). *Terminating romantic relationships: The role of personal responsibility and gender*. Unpublished manuscript, Wellesley College.

Albada, K. F., Knapp, M. L., & Theune, K. E. (2002). Interaction Appearance Theory: Changing perceptions of physical attractiveness through social interaction. *Communication Theory*, 12, 8–40.

Albright, J. M. (2007). How do I love thee and thee and thee: Self-presentation, deception, and multiple relationships online. In M. T. Whitty, A. J. Baker, & J. A. Inman (Eds.), *Online matching*. Hampshire, England: Palgrave Macmillan.

Allan, K., & Burridge, K. (1991). *Euphemism and dysphemism: Language used as shield and weapon*. New York: Oxford University Press.

Allen, G. (1996). Military drug testing. *Winning Orations*, pp. 80–83.

Allen, M. (1998a). Comparing the persuasive effectiveness of one- and two-sided messages. In M. Allen & R. W. Preiss (Eds.), *Persuasion: Advances through meta-analysis*. Cresskill, NJ: Hampton Press.

Allen, M. (1998b). Methodological considerations when examining a gendered world. In D. J. Canary & K. Dindia (Eds.), *Handbook of sex differences and similarities in communication*. Mahwah, NJ: Erlbaum.

Allen, M., & Preiss, R. W. (1997). Comparing the persuasiveness of narrative and statistical evidence using meta-analysis. *Communication Research Reports*, 14, 125–131.

Allen, M., Bruflat, R., Fucilla, R., Kramer, M., McKellips, S., Ryan, D. J., & Spiegelhoff, M. (2000). Testing the persuasiveness of evidence: Combining narrative and statistical forms. *Communication Research Reports*, 17, 331–336.

Alley, M. (2005). *The craft of scientific presentations: Critical steps to succeed and critical errors to avoid*. Warren, MI: Springer.

Almond, E., & Gervas, L. (2003, July 23). A cultural curveball. *San Jose Mercury News*, pp. 1D, 8D.

Altman, I., & Taylor, D. (1973). *Social penetration: The development of interpersonal relationships*. New York: Holt, Rinehart & Winston.

AMA 2010 critical skills survey. (2010, April 27). *American Management Association*. [Online]. Available at: http://www.p21.org/documents/Critical%20Skills%20Survey%20Executive%20Summary.pdf

Amato, P., & Loomis, L. (1995). Parental divorce, marital conflicts, and offspring well-being during early adulthood. *Social Forces*, 73, 895–915.

Ambady, N., & Rosenthal, R. (1992). Thin slices of expressive behavior as predictors of interpersonal consequences: A meta-analysis. *Psychological Bulletin*, 111, 256–274.

Ambady, N., & Rosenthal, R. (1993). Half a minute: Predicting teacher evaluations from thin slices of nonverbal behavior and physical attractiveness. *Journal of Personality and Social Psychology*, 64, 431–441.

Ambady, N., Bernieri, F. J., & Richeson, J. A. (2000). Toward a histology of social behavior:

Judgmental accuracy from thin slices of the behavioral stream. In M. P. Zanna (Ed.), *Advances in experimental social psychology*. San Diego, CA: Academic Press.

Ambady, N., Koo, J., Lee, F., & Rosenthal, R. (1996). More than words: Linguistic and nonlinguistic politeness in two cultures. *Journal of Personality and Social Psychology*, 70, 996–1011.

Amen, D. G. (2007). *The brain in love*. New York: Three Rivers Press.

Amoral majority "fesses up." (1991, April 19). *San Jose Mercury News*, p. 1A.

Amour, S. (2007, May 22). Hi, I'm Joan, and I'm a workaholic. *USA Today*. [Online]. Available at: http://www.usatoday.com/money/workplace/2007-05-22-workaholic

Andersen, P. (1999). *Nonverbal communication: Forms and functions*. Mountain View, CA: Mayfield.

Andersen, P. A. (2006). The evolution of biological sex differences in communication. In K. Dindia & D. J. Canary (Eds.), *Sex differences and similarities in communication*. Mahwah, NJ: Erlbaum.

Andersen, P. A., Guerrero, L. K., & Jones, S. M. (2006). Nonverbal behavior in intimate interactions and intimate relationships. In V. Manusov & M. L. Patterson (Eds.), *The Sage handbook of nonverbal communication*. Thousand Oaks, CA: Sage.

Andersen, P. A., Murphy, M., & Wendt-Wasca, N. (1985). Teachers' reports of students' nonverbal communication in the classroom: A development study in grades K–12. *Communication Education*, 34, 292–307.

Andersen, P., Todd-Mancillas, W., & Di-Clemente, L. (1980). The effects of pupil dilation on physical, social, and task attraction. *Australian Scan: Journal of Human Communication*, 7 & 8, 89–95.

Anderson, C. A. (1999). Attributional style, depression, and loneliness: A cross-cultural comparison of American and Chinese students. *Personality and Social Psychology Bulletin*, 25, 482–499

Anderson, J. L., Crawford, C. B., Nadeau, J., & Lindberg, T. (1992). Was the Duchess of Windsor right? A cross-cultural review of the socioecology of ideals of female body shape. *Ethology and Sociobiology*, 13, 197–227.

Anderson, K., & Leaper, C. (1998). Meta-analyses of gender effects on conversational interruption: Who, what, when, where, and how. *Sex Roles*, 39, 225–252.

Anderson, R., & Killenberg, G. (1999). *Interviewing: Speaking, listening, and learning for professional life*. Mountain View, CA: Mayfield.

Anderson, R., & Ross, V. (1994). *Questions of communication: A practical introduction to theory*. New York: St. Martin's Press.

Andeweg, B. A., de Jong, J. C., & Hoeken, H. (1998). May I have your attention? Exordial techniques in informative oral presentations. *Technical Communication Quarterly*, 7, 271–284.

Angier, N. (2002, March 5). One lifetime is not enough for a trip to distant stars. *The New York Times*. [Online]. Available at: www.nytimes.com/2002/03/05/science/space/05TRAV.html

Anti-sweatshop activist brings delegates to their feet. (2002, March/April). *California Teacher*, p. 4.

Archer, D. (2000). *A world of food: Tastes and taboos in different cultures* (videotape). Berkeley: University of California Extension Center of Media and Independent Learning.

Archer, J. (2000). Sex differences in aggression between heterosexual partners: A meta-analytic review. *Psychological Bulletin*, 126, 651–680.

Archer, J. (2002). Sex differences in physically aggressive acts between heterosexual partners: A meta-analytic review. *Aggression and Violent Behavior*, 7, 213–351.

Aries, E. (2006). Sex differences in interaction: A reexamination. In K. Dindia & D. J. Canary (Eds.), *Sex differences and similarities in communication*. Mahwah, NJ: Erlbaum.

Arkowitz, H., & Lilienfeld, S. O. (2009, April/May). Road warriors. *Scientific American Mind*, pp. 64–65.

Armstrong, M. L., Roberts, A. E., Koch, J. R., Saunders, J. C., Owen, D. C., & Anderson, R. R., (2008). Motivation for contemporary tattoo removal: A shift in identity. *Archives of Dermatology*, 144, 879–884.

Aron, A., Aron, E. N., Norman, C. C., McKenna, C., & Heyman, R. E. (2000). Couples' shared participation in novel and arousing activities and experienced relationship quality. *Journal of Personality and Social Psychology*, 78, 273–284.

Aronson, E. (1999). *The social animal*. New York: Worth.

Aronson, E., Fried, C., & Stone, J. (1991). Overcoming denial and increasing the intentions to use condoms through the induction of hypocrisy. *American Journal of Public Health*, 81, 1636–1638.

Arrillaga, P. (2001, August 15). Trauma of "civilizing." *San Jose Mercury News*, p. 13A.

As "sexiest man alive," you'd think dating would be easier. (2006, December 12). *San Jose Mercury News*, p. 2A.

Atkinson, C. (2008). *Beyond bullet points: Using Microsoft Office PowerPoint 2007 to create presentations that inform, motivate, and inspire*. Redmond, WA: Microsoft Press.

Atkinson, R., & Flint, J. (2004). Fortress UK? Gated communities, the spatial revolt of the elites and time-space trajectories of segregation. *Housing Studies*, 19, 875–892.

Attridge, M., Bersheid, E., & Simpson, J. A. (1995). Predicting relationship stability from both partners versus one. *Journal of Personality and Social Psychology*, 69, 254–268.

Atwood, K. C. (2004, November/December). Bacteria, ulcers, and ostracism? *H. pylori* and the making of a myth. *Skeptical Inquirer*, pp. 27–34.

Aube, C., & Rousseau, V. (2005). Team goal commitment and team effectiveness: The role of task interdependence and supportive behaviors. *Group Dynamics: Theory, Research, and Practice*, 9, 189–204.

Aune, K. S., Kim, M., & Hu, A. (2000). *"Well I've been talking long enough about me. . . . What do you think of my accomplishments?" The relationship between self-construals, narcissism, compulsive talking, and bragging.* Paper presented at the meeting of the National Communication Association, Seattle, WA.

Autopsy report. (2005, May 18). *AIDSTruth.org.* [Online]. Available at: http://www.aidstruth.org/ejs-coroner-report.pdf

Avolio, B. J. (2007). Promoting more integrative strategies for leadership theory-building. *American Psychologist, 62,* 25–33.

Axtell, R. E. (1998). *Gestures: The do's and taboos of body language around the world.* New York: Wiley.

Ayres, J. (2005). Performance visualization and behavioral disruption: A clarification. *Communication Reports, 18,* 55–63.

Ayres, J., & Hopf, T. (1995). *Coping with speech anxiety.* Norwood, NJ: Ablex.

Ayres, J., Wongprasert, T. K., Silva, J., Story, T., & Sawant, D. D. (2001). Effects of performance visualization on employment interviews. *Communication Quarterly, 49,* 160–172.

Babcock, L. (2002). *Do graduate students negotiate their job offers?* Unpublished report, Carnegie Mellon University.

Babcock, L., & Laschever, S. (2003). *Women don't ask: Negotiation and the gender divide.* Princeton, NJ: Princeton University Press.

Babcock, L. M., Gelfand, M., Small, D., & Stayn, H. (2002). *Propensity to initiate negotiations: A new look at gender variation in negotiation behavior.* Unpublished manuscript, Carnegie Mellon University.

Bach, G., & Goldberg, H. (1972). *Creative aggression.* New York: Avon.

Bachman, G. F., & Guerrero, L. K. (2006). Forgiveness, apology, and communicative responses to hurtful events. *Communication Reports, 19,* 45–56.

Bahrick, H. P. (1984). Semantic memory content in permastore: Fifty years of memory for Spanish learned in school. *Journal of Experimental Psychology, 113,* 1–35.

Bailey, E. (2008, August 7). Celebrities with anxiety: Harrison Ford: fear of public speaking. *Healthcentral.com.* [Online]. Available at: http://www.healthcentral.com/anxiety/c/22705/36519/celebrities-public

Bailey, J. (2009, June 10). The Palin plagiarism scandal. *Plagiarism Today.* [Online]. Available at: http://www.plagiarismtoday.com/2009/06/10/the-palin-plagiarism-scandal/

Bailey, J. M., Gauline, S., Agyei, Y., & Gladue, B. A. (1994). Effects of gender and sexual orientation on evolutionarily relevant aspects of human mating psychology. *Journal of Personality and Social Psychology, 66,* 1081–1093.

Baker, L. A., & Emery, R. E. (1993). When every relationship is above average: Perceptions and expectations of divorce at the time of marriage. *Law and Human Behavior, 17,* 439–450.

Ball, A. L. (2010, May 28). Are 5001 Facebook friends one too many? *The New York Times.* [Online]. Available at: http://www.nytimes.com/2010/05/30/fashion/30FACEBOOK.html

Banaji, M. (2011, February). Harnessing the power of *Wikipedia* for scientific psychology: A call to action. *Observor,* pp. 5–6.

Baram, M. (2009, June 8). Stephen Colbert Iraq show: Gen. Odierno shaves his head. *Huffington Post.* [Online]. Available at: http://www.huffingtonpost.com/2009/06/08/stephen-colbert-iraq-show_n_212388.html

Bargh, J. A., & McKenna, K. Y. A. (2004). The Internet and social life. *Annual Review of Psychology, 55,* 573–590.

Barker, L., & Watson, K. (2000). *Listen up: How to improve relationships, reduce stress, and be more productive by using the power of listening.* New York: St. Martin's Press.

Barker, V. E., Abrams, J. R., Tiyaamornwong, V., Seibold, D. R., Duggan, A., Park, H. S., & Sebastian, M. (2000). New contexts for relational communication in groups. *Small Group Research, 31,* 470–503.

Barnes, P. M., Bloom, B., & Nahin, R. L. (2008, December 10). Complementary and alternative medicine use among adults and children: United States, 2007. *National Health Statistics Reports.* [Online]. Available at: http://nccam.nih.gov/news/2008/nhsr12.pdf

Barnes, S. B. (2001). *Online connections: Internet interpersonal relationships.* Cresskill, NJ: Hampton Press.

Baron, N. S. (2008). *Always on: Language in an online and mobile world.* New York: Oxford University Press.

Baron, R. A. (1988). Negative effects of destructive criticism: Impact on conflict, self-efficacy, and task performance. *Journal of Applied Psychology, 73,* 199–207.

Baron, R. A. (1990). Countering the effects of destructive criticism: The relative efficacy of four interventions. *Journal of Applied Psychology, 75,* 235–243.

Barreca, R. (1991). *They used to call me Snow White . . . but I drifted: Women's strategic use of humor.* New York: Viking Penguin.

Barron, L. A. (2003). Ask and you shall receive: Gender differences in negotiators' beliefs about requests for a higher salary. *Human Relations, 56,* 635–662.

Barry, D. (1991). *Dave Barry's guide to life.* New York: Wings Books.

Baruah, J., & Paulus, P. B. (2008). Effects of training on idea generation in groups. *Small Group Research, 39,* 523–541.

Bass, B. M., & Bass, R. (2008). *The Bass handbook of leadership: Theory, research, and managerial applications.* New York: Free Press.

Bauer, B. (1996, February 24). Undue pride tied to violence. *San Jose Mercury News,* p. 20A.

Baumeister, R. F., Campbell, J. D., Krueger, J. I., & Vohs, K. D. (2003). Does high self-esteem cause better performance, interpersonal success, happiness, or healthier lifestyles? *Psychological Science in the Public Interest, 4,* 1–44.

Baumeister, R. F., Catanese, K. R., & Vohs, K. D. (2001). Is there a gender difference in strength of sex drive? Theoretical vies, conceptual distinctions, and a review of relevant evidence. *Personality and Social Psychology Review*, 5, 242–273.

Baumeister, R. F., & Leary, M. R. (1995). The need to belong: Desire for interpersonal attachments as a fundamental human motivation. *Psychological Bulletin*, 117, 497–529.

Baumeister, R., Smart, L., & Boden, J. (1996). Relation of the threatened egotism to violence and aggressions: The dark side of high self-esteem. *Psychological Review*, 103, 5–33.

Baxter, L. (1990). Dialectical contradictions in relationship development. *Journal of Social and Personal Relationships*, 7, 69–88.

Baxter, L. (1994). A dialogic approach to relationship management. In D. Canary & L. Stafford (Eds.), *Communication and relational maintenance*. New York: Academic Press.

Baxter, L. A., & Bullis, C. (1986). Turning points in developing romantic relationships. *Human Communication Research*, 12, 469–494.

Baxter, L. A., & Erbert, L. A. (1999). Perceptions of dialectical contradictions in turning points of development in heterosexual romantic relationships. *Journal of Social and Personal Relationships*, 16, 547–569.

Baxter, L., & Montgomery, B. (1996). *Relating: Dialogues and dialect*. New York: Guilford Press.

Baxter, L. A., & Wilmot, W. W. (1984). "Secret tests": Social strategies for acquiring information about the state of the relationship. *Human Communication Research*, 11, 171–201.

Baxter, L., Braithwaite, D. O., & Nicholson, J. (1999). Turning points in the development of blended family relationships. *Journal of Social and Personal Relationships*, 16, 291–313.

Bazil, J. (1997). The ferrous wheel of death. In L. G. Schnoor & B. Wickelgren (Eds.), *Winning orations*. Northfield, MN: Interstate Oratorical Association.

Bazil, L. G. D. (1999). The effects of social behavior on fourth- and fifth-grade girls' perceptions of physically attractive and unattractive peers. *Dissertation Abstracts International*, 59, 4533B.

Beal, D. J., Cohen, R. R., Burke, M. J., & McLendon, C. I. (2003). Cohesion and performance in groups: A meta-analytic clarification of construct relations. *Journal of Applied Psychology*, 88, 989–1004.

Beating the odds. (2002, August 5). *People*, pp. 78–79.

Because we can, we must. (2004, May 17). *Almanac Between Issues*. [Online]. Available at: http://www.upenn.edu/almanac/between/2004/commence-b.html

Bechler, C., & Johnson, S. (1995). Leadership and listening: A study of member perceptions. *Small Group Research*, 26, 77–85.

Beck, A. J. (2010, August 26). Sexual victimization in prisons and jails reported by inmates. *Bureau of Justice Statistics*. [Online]. Available at: http://bjs.ojp.usdoj.gov/index.cfm?ty=pbdetail&iid=2202

Begley, S. (1998, July 13). You're OK, I'm terrific: Self-esteem backfires. *Newsweek*, p. 69.

Behnke, R. R., & Sawyer, C. R. (1999a). Milestones of anticipatory public speaking anxiety. *Communication Education*, 48, 1–8.

Behnke, R. R., & Sawyer, C. R. (1999b). Public speaking procrastination as a correlate of public speaking communication apprehension and self-perceived public speaking competence. *Communication Research Reports*, 16, 40–47.

Behnke, R. R., & Sawyer, C. R. (2004). Public speaking anxiety as a function of sensitization and habituation processes. *Communication Education*, 53, 164–173.

Belbin, R. (1996). *Team roles at work*. London: Butterworth-Heinemann.

Bellamy, R., & Walker, J. (1996). *Television and the remote control*. New York: Guilford Press.

Belle, D. (1987). Gender differences in the social moderators of stress. In R. C. Barnett, L. Biener, & G. K. Baruch (Eds.), *Gender and stress*. New York: Free Press.

Belle, D. (1989). Gender differences in children's social networks and supports. In D. Belle (Ed.), *Children's social networks and social supports*. New York: Wiley.

Benedetto, R. (2000, October 10). Poll: Bush more honest, likable. *USA Today*, p. 1A.

Benenson, J. F., Roy, R., Waite, A., Goldbaum, S., Linders, L., & Simpson, A. (2002). Greater discomfort as a proximate cause of sex differences in competition. *Merrill-Palmer Quarterly*, 48, 225–248.

Benfeld, K. (2010, January 14). "Gated communities" are not necessarily safer. *National Resources Defense Fund*. [Online]. Available at: http://switchboard.nrdc.org/blogs/kbenfield/gated_communities_are_not_nece.html

Benne, K., & Sheats, P. (1948). Functional roles of group members. *Journal of Social Issues*, 4, 41–49.

Bennett, A. (1995, January 10). Economics meeting: A zillion causes and effects. *The Wall Street Journal*, p. B1.

Bennis, W. (1976). *The unconscious conspiracy: Why leaders can't lead*. New York: AMACOM.

Bennis, W. (2007). The challenges of leadership in the modern world. *American Psychologist*, 62, 2–5.

Bennis, W., & Biederman, P. (1997). *Organizing genius: The secrets of creative collaboration*. New York: Addison-Wesley.

Bennis, W., & Nanus, B. (1985). *Leaders: The strategies for taking charge*. New York: Harper & Row.

Benoit, W. L. (1998). Forewarning and persuasion. In M. Allen & R. W. Preiss (Eds.), *Persuasion: Advances through meta-analysis*. Cresskill, NJ: Hampton Press.

Berdahl, J., & Moore, C. (2006). Workplace harassment: Double jeopardy for minority women. *Journal of Applied Psychology*, 91, 426–436.

Berger, C. R., & Calabrese, R. J. (1975). Some explorations in initial interaction and beyond: Toward a developmental theory of interpersonal communication. *Human Communication Research*, 1, 99–112.

Bergner, R. M., & Holmes, J. R. (2000). Self-concepts and self-concept change: A status dynamic approach. *Psychotherapy: Theory, Research, Practice, Training*, 37, 36–44.

Berlo, D. (1960). *The process of communication*. New York: Holt, Rinehart & Winston.

Bernieri, F. J. (2001). Toward a taxonomy of interpersonal sensitivity. In J. A. Hall & F. J. Bernieri, *Interpersonal sensitivity: Theory and measurement*. Mahwah, NJ: Erlbaum.

Berns, N. (2001). Degendering the problem and gendering the blame: Political discourse on women and violence. *Gender and Society*, 15, 262–281.

Berry, J. W. (1994). Acculturative stress. In W. J. Lonner & R. Malpass (Eds.), *Psychology and culture*. Boston: Allyn & Bacon.

Berry, J. W. (1997). Immigration, acculturation, and adaptation. *Applied Psychology: An International Review*, 46, 5–34.

Berscheid, E., & Walster, E. (1974). Physical attractiveness. In L. Berkowitz (Ed.), *Advances in experimental social psychology* (Vol. 7). New York: Academic Press.

Berscheid, E., Schneider, M., & Omoto, A. M. (1989). Issues in studying close relationships: Conceptualizing and measuring closeness. In C. Hendrick (Ed.), *Close relationships*. Newbury Park, CA: Sage.

Best English lesson. (1999, December 26). *Parade*, p. 8.

Bettancourt, B. A., & Miller, N. (1996). Gender differences in aggression as a function of provocation: A meta-analysis. *Psychological Bulletin*, 119, 422–447.

Billingsley, K. L. (2010, August 15). Twenty years later, self-esteem report looks foolish. *San Jose Mercury News*, p. A10.

Bingham, S. (1991). Communication strategies for managing sexual harassment in organizations: Understanding message options and their effects. *Journal of Applied Communication Research*, 19, 88–115.

Birdwhistell, R. (1970). *Kinesis and context*. Philadelphia: University of Pennsylvania Press.

Bjorkquist, K., Osterman, K., & Laberspetz, K. (1994). Sex differences in covert aggression among adults. *Aggressive Behavior*, 20, 27–33.

Black, K. (1990a, March). Can getting mad get the job done? *Working Women*, pp. 86–90.

Black, K. (1990b, March). The matter of tears. *Working Women*, p. 88.

Blake, R., & Mouton, J. (1964). *The managerial grid*. Houston, TX: Gulf Publishing.

Blakely, E., & Snyder, M. G. (1997). *Fortress America: Gated communities in the United States*. Washington, DC: Brookings Institute.

Blass, T. (2000). *Obedience to authority: Current perspectives on the Milgram paradigm*. Mahwah, NJ: Erlbaum.

Blecher, J. (2009, August 10). Survey says: Using a cell phone in a bathroom isn't as bad as you might think. *LetsTalk*. [Online]. Available at: http://www/letstalk.com/blog/post.htm?blogld=1052

Blenko, M. W., Mankins, M. C., & Rogers, P. (2010). *Decide & deliver: 5 steps to breakthrough performance in your organization*. Boston: Harvard Business Review Press.

Blond, A. (2008). Impacts of exposure to images of ideal bodies on male body dissatisfaction: A review. *Body Images*, 5, 244–250.

Bodley, H. (2003, July 28). Uecker keeps laughs coming at induction. *USA Today*, p. 5C.

Body art changes dress codes. (2006, October 19). *San Jose Mercury News*, p. 1A.

Bok, S. (1978). *Lying: Moral choice in public and private life*. New York: Random House.

Bollag, B. (2005, November 18). Consensus grows on basic skills that colleges should teach, but gauges of those abilities are poor, report says. *Chronicle of Higher Education*, 52, A38.

Bolton, R. (1979). *People skills: How to assert yourself, listen to others, and resolve conflicts*. New York: Simon & Schuster.

Bond, C. F., & DePaulo, B. M. (2006). Accuracy of deception judgments. *Personality and Social Psychology*, 10, 214–234.

Bond, C. F., & Rao, S. R. (2004). Lies travel: Mendacity in a mobile world. In P. A. Granhag & L. A. Stromwall (Eds.), *Deception detection in forensic contexts*. Cambridge, UK: Cambridge University Press.

Bond, C., & Uysal, A. (2007). On lie detection "wizards." *Law and Human Behavior*, 31, 109–115.

Bond, G. D., Malloy, D. M., Arias, E. A., Nunn, S. N., & Thompson, L. A. (2005). Lie-biased decision making in prison. *Communication Reports*, 18, 9–20.

Bono, J. E., & Judge, T. A. (2004). Personality and transformational and transactional leadership: A meta-analysis. *Journal of Applied Psychology*, 89, 901–910.

Boone, R. (2009, September 5). Court: Ashcroft can be held liable. *San Jose Mercury News*, p. A5.

Bor, J. (2001, January 3). Canadian smokers get stark warning: New labels depict harsh consequences. *San Jose Mercury News*, p. 6A.

Borkenau, P., Mauer, N., Riemann, R., Spinath, F. M., & Angleitner, A. (2004). Thin slices of behavior as cues of personality and intelligence. *Journal of Personality and Social Psychology*, 86, 599–614.

Bormann, E. (1990). *Small group communication: Theory and practice*. New York: Harper & Row.

Boroditsky, L. (2001). Does language shape thought? Mandarin and English speakers' conceptions of time. *Cognitive Psychology*, 43, 1–22.

Boroditsky, L. (2003). Linguistic relativity. *Encyclopedia of Cognitive Science*, pp. 917–921.

Bostrom, R. (1970). Patterns of communicative interaction in small groups. *Speech Monographs*, 37, 257–263.

Boudreau, J. (2007, August 12). Beijing brushes up on its English skills. *San Jose Mercury News*, p. 17A.

Bower, S., & Bower, G. (1976). *Asserting yourself*. Reading, MA: Addison-Wesley.

Bradbury, T. N., & Fincham, F. D. (1990). Attributions in marriage: Review and critique. *Psychological Bulletin*, 107, 3–33.

Bradbury, T. N., & Fincham, F. D. (1992). Attributions and behavior in marital interaction. *Journal of Personality and Social Psychology*, 63, 613–628.

Branan, N. (2007, November). Celebrating the bizarre. *Scientific American Mind*, p. 85.

Branton, S. (2006). In L. G. Schnoor & B. Wickelgren (Eds.), *Winning orations*. Mankato, MN: Interstate Oratorical Association.

Brehm, J. (1972). *Responses to loss of freedom: A theory of psychological resistance*. Morristown, NJ: General Learning Press.

Brembeck, W., & Howell, W. (1976). *Persuasion: A means of social influence*. Englewood Cliffs, NJ: Prentice Hall.

Brescoll, V. L., & Uhlmann, E. L. (2008). Can an angry woman get ahead? *Psychological Science*, 19, 268–275.

Brewer, M. B., & Brown, R. J. (1997). Intergroup relations. In D. T. Gilbert, S. T. Fiske, & G. Lindsey (Eds.), *The handbook of social psychology* (Vol. 2). Boston: McGraw-Hill.

Brin, D. (1998). *The transparent society: Will technology force us to choose between privacy and freedom?* Reading, MA: Addison-Wesley.

Brislin, R. (1993). *Understanding culture's influence on behavior*. Fort Worth, TX: Harcourt Brace Jovanovich.

British Association for the Advancement of Science. (2002). *LaughLab: The scientific quest for the world's funniest joke*. London: Arrow Books.

Brooks, D. (2011). *The social animal*. New York: Random House.

Brooks, L., & Perot, A. (1991). Reporting sexual harassment: Exploring a predicted model. *Psychology of Women Quarterly*, 15, 31–47.

Bross, I., Shapiro, P., & Anderson, B. (1972). How information is carried in scientific sub-language. *Science*, 176, 1303–1309.

Brown, A. Henningsen, D. D., Kartch, F. & Orr, N. (2009). The perceptions of verbal and nonverbal flirting cues in cross-sex interactions. *Human Communication*, 12, 371–381.

Brown, W. (2009). Listen up. *Professional Safety*, 54, 8.

Brownell, J. (2002). *Listening: Attitudes, principles, and skills*. Boston: Allyn & Bacon.

Brownlow, S. (2003). Gender-linked linguistic behavior in television interviews. *Sex Roles: A Journal of Research*. [Online]. Available at: www.findarticles.com

Bruess, C. J., & Pearson, J. C. (1996). Gendered patterns in family communication. In J. Wood (Ed.), *Gendered relationships*. Newbury Park, CA: Sage.

Bruskin & Goldring. (1993). America's number 1 fear: Public speaking. In Bruskin & Goldring (Eds.), *Bruskin & Goldring report*. Edison, NJ: Bruskin-Goldring.

Bryson, B. (1990). *The mother tongue: English and how it got that way*. New York: Avon Books.

Buchanan, J. (2010, December 1). Merck names first black CEO. *DiversityInc*. [Online]. Available at: http://www.diversityinc.com/article.8170/Merck-Names-First-Black-CEO/

Buckingham, M., & Coffman, C. (1999). *First, break all the rules: What the world's greatest managers do differently*. New York: Simon & Schuster.

Buckley, M., Laursen, J., & Otarola, V. (2009). Strengthening physician-nurse partnerships to improve quality and patient safety. *Physician Executive Journal*, 35, 24–28.

Buller, D., & Aune, K. (1992). The effects of speech rate similarity on compliance: Application of communication accommodations theory. *Western Journal of Communication*, 56, 37–53.

Bumiller, E. (2010, April 26). We have met the enemy and he is PowerPoint. *The New York Times*. [Online].Availableat:http://www.nytimes.com/2010/04/27/world/27powerpoint.html?partner=rss&emc=rss&pagewanted=print

Burfeind, M., & Witkemper, T. (2010, July 14). TeleNav-commissioned survey suggests both genders have similar views on abiding by and breaking the rules of the road. *TeleNav*. [Online]. Available: http://www.telenav.com/about/driving-behavior/

Burger, J. (2007, December). Replicating Milgram. *APS Observer*. [Online]. Available at: http://www.psychologicalscience.org/observer/getArticle.cfm?id=2264

Burgoon, J. K., & Dunbar, N. E. (2006). Nonverbal expressions of dominance and power in human relationships. In V. Manusov & M. L. Patterson (Eds.), *The Sage handbook of nonverbal communication*. Thousand Oaks, CA: Sage.

Burgoon, J. K., Blair, J. P., & Strom, R. E. (2008). Cognitive biases and nonverbal cue availability in detecting deception. *Human Communication Research*, 34, 572–599.

Burgoon, J. K., Buller, D. B., & Woodall, W. G. (1996). *Nonverbal communication: The unspoken dialogue*. New York: McGraw-Hill.

Burgoon, J., Manusou, V., Mineo, P., & Hale, J. (1985). Effects of gaze on hiring, credibility, attraction, and relational message interpretation. *Journal of Nonverbal Behavior*, 9, 133–146.

Burke, K. (1950). *A rhetoric of motives*. New York: Prentice Hall.

Burleson, B. R. (2003). Emotional support skills. In J. O. Greene & B. R. Burleson (Eds.), *Handbook of communication and social interaction skills*. Mahwah, NJ: Erlbaum.

Burleson, B. R., & Samter, W. (1996). Similarity in the communication skills of young adults: Foundations of attraction, friendship, and relationship satisfaction. *Communication Reports*, 9, 127–139.

Burleson, B. R., Holmstrom, A. J., & Gilstrap, C. M. (2005). "Gus can't say that to guys": Four experiments assessing the normative motivation account for deficiencies in the emotional support provided by men. *Communication Monographs*, 72, 468–501.

Burns, J. (1978). *Leadership*. New York: Harper & Row.

Burpitt, W., & Bigoness, W. (1997). Leadership and innovation among teams: The impact of empowerment. *Small Group Research*, 28, 414–423.

Bushman, B. J. (2002). Does venting anger feed or extinguish the flame? Catharsis, rumination, distraction, anger, and aggressive responding. *Personality and Social Psychology*, 28, 724–731.

Bushman, B. J., & Baumeister, R. F. (1998). Threatened egotism, narcissism, self-esteem, and direct and displaced aggression: Does self-love or self-hate lead to violence? *Journal of Personality and Social Psychology*, 75, 219–229.

Buss, D. M. (2003). *The evolution of desire: Strategies of human mating*. New York: Basic Books.

Buss, D. M., & Schmitt, D. P. (1993). Sexual strategies theory: An evolutionary perspective on human mating. *Psychological Review*, 100, 204–232.

Byers, E. S., & Heinlein, L. (1989). Predicting initiations and refusals of sexual activities in married and cohabiting heterosexual couples. *Journal of Sex Research*, 26, 210–231.

Byrne, D. (1997). An overview (and underview) of research and theory within the attraction paradigm. *Journal of Social and Personal Relationships*, 14, 417–431.

Byrne, D., & Clore, G. L. (1970). A reinforcement model of evaluative processes. *Personality*, 1, 103–128.

Cadinu, M., Maass, A., Rosabianca, A., & Kiesner, J. (2005). Why do women underperform under stereotype threat? Evidence for the role of negative thinking. *Psychological Science*, 16, 572–578.

Cafri, G., Van den Berg, P., & Thompson, J. K. (2006). Pursuit of muscularity in adolescent boys: Relations among biopsychosocial variables and clinical outcomes. *Journal of Clinical Child Adolescent Psychology*, 35, 283–291.

Cahn, D., & Lloyd, S. (1996). *Family violence from a communication perspective*. Thousand Oaks, CA: Sage.

Callahan, D. (2004). *The cheating culture: Why more Americans are doing wrong to get ahead*. New York: Harcourt.

Cameron, D. (2002, June 10). Flirty or dirty? The difference can be in the blink of an eye. *Sydney Morning Herald*. [Online]. Available at: http://www.smh.com.au/articles/2002/06/09/1022982798637.html

Cameron, D. (2007). *The myth of Mars and Venus: Do men and women really speak different languages?* New York: Oxford University Press.

Campbell, S. (2008). Perceptions of mobile phone use in public: The roles of individualism, collectivism, and focus of the setting. *Communication Reports*, 21, 70–81.

Canary, D. J., & Cupach, W. R. (1988). Relational and episodic characteristics associated with conflict tactics. *Journal of Social and Personal Relationships*, 5, 305–325.

Canary, D. J., & Hause, K. S. (1993). Is there any reason to research sex differences in communication? *Communication Quarterly*, 41, 129–144.

Canary, D. J., & Spitzberg, B. H. (1987). Appropriateness and effectiveness of perception of conflict strategies. *Human Communication Research*, 14, 96.

Canary, D. J., & Spitzberg, B. H. (1989). A model of perceived competence of conflict strategies. *Human Communication Research*, 15, 630–649.

Canary, D. J., Cupach, W. R., & Messman, S. J. (1995). *Relationship conflict: Conflict in parent-child, friendship, and romantic relationships*. Thousand Oaks, CA: Sage.

Canary, D. J., Stafford, L., Hause, K. S., & Wallace, L. A. (1993). An inductive analysis of relational maintenance strategies: Comparisons among lovers, relatives, friends, and others. *Communication Research Reports*, 10, 5–14.

Canfield, J., Hansen, M. V., & Kirberger, K. (1997). *Chicken soup for the teenage soul*. Deerfield Beach, FL: Health Communications.

Cannon, W. B. (1932). *The wisdom of the body*. New York: Norton.

Caplan, M., & Goldman, M. (1981). Personal space violations as a function of height. *Journal of Social Psychology*, 114, 167–171.

Card, N. A., Stucky, B. D., Sawalani, G. M., & Little, T. D. (2008). Direct and indirect aggression during childhood and adolescence: A meta-analytic review of gender differences, intercorrelations, and relations to maladjustment. *Child Development*, 79, 1185–229.

Carey, B. (2010, February 23). Evidence that little touches do mean so much. *The New York Times*. [Online]. Available at: http://www.nytimes.com/2010/02/23/health/23mind.html?_r=1&pagewanted=print

Carl, D., Gupta, V., & Javidan, M. (2004). Power distance. In R. J. House et al. (Eds.), *Culture, leadership, and organizations*. Thousand Oaks, CA: Sage.

Carli, L. L. (2001). Gender and social influence. *Journal of Social Issues*, 57, 725–742.

Carli, L. L., Ganley, R., & Pierce-Otay, A. (1991). Similarity and satisfaction in roommate relationships. *Personality and Social Psychology Bulletin*, 17, 419–426.

Carmany, E. (2006, November 17). Women voters made the difference in 2006 election. *Ms.* [Online]. Available at: www.msmagazine.com

Carnevale, A. (1996). *Workplace basics: The skills employers want*. Washington, DC: U.S. Department of Labor Employment and Training Administration.

Carnevale, P., & Probst, T. (1998). Social values and social conflict in creative problem solving.

Journal of Personality and Social Psychology, 74, 1300–1309.

Carpenter, N. (2004). What you don't know . . . In L. G. Schnoor & B. Wickelgren (Eds.), *Winning orations*. Mankato, MN: Interstate Oratorical Association.

Carroll, J. (2006, September 1). Americans prefer male boss to a female boss. *Brain.gallup.com*. [Online]. Available at: http://brain.gallup.com

Carroll, J. B. (Ed.). (1956). *Language, thought, and reality: Selected writings of Benjamin Lee Whorf*. Cambridge, MA: MIT Press.

Carroll, J. L., Volk, K. D., & Hyde, J. S. (1985). Differences between males and females in motives for engaging in sexual intercourse. *Archives of Sexual Behavior*, 14, 131–139.

Carter, T. J., Ferguson, M. J., & Hassin, R. R. (2011). A single exposure to the American flag shifts support toward Republicanism up to 8 months later. *Psychological Science*.

Carver, T. B., & Vondra, A. A. (1994, May/June). Alternative dispute resolution: Why it doesn't work and why it does. *Harvard Business Review*, pp. 120–130.

Cash, T. F., & Derlega, V. J. (1978). The matching hypothesis: Physical attractiveness among same-sex friends. *Personality and Social Psychology Bulletin*, 4, 240–243.

Cass, C., & Agiesta, J. (2011, September 21). Online slurs seen as jokes. *San Jose Mercury News*, p. A5.

Catholics for Choice. (2008). Truth and consequences: A look behind the Vatican's ban on contraception. [Online]. Available at: www.catholicsforchoice.org/topics/reform/documents/TruthConsequencesFINAL.pdf

Cebu airlines performs safety demo to Lady Gaga and Katy Perry. (2010, October 1). *Huffington Post*. [Online]. Available at: http://www.huffingtonpost.com/2010/01/cebu-airlines-safety-demonstration-n_746514.html?view=print

Cell phones and American adults. (2011). *Pew Internet*. [Online]. Available at: http://perinternet.org/Reports/2010/Cell-Phones-and-American-Adults/Overview.aspx

Celoria, J. (1997). The counterfeiting of airline safety: An examination of the dangers of bogus airline parts. In L. G. Schnoor & B. Wickelgren (Eds.), *Winning orations*. Mankato, MN: Interstate Oratorical Association.

Chabris, C., & Simons, D. (2010). *The invisible gorilla: And other ways our intuitions deceive us*. New York: Crown.

Chao, G. T., & Moon, H. (2005). The cultural mosaic: A metatheory for understanding the complexity of culture. *Journal of Applied Psychology*, 90, 1128–1140.

Chatman, J., & Barsade, S. (1995). Personality, organizational culture, and cooperation: Evidence from a business simulation. *Administrative Science Quarterly*, 40, 423–443.

Chatter box. (2007, July 1). *San Jose Mercury News*, p. 2C.

Chen, G. (1993). *A Chinese perspective of communication competence*. Paper presented at the annual convention of the Speech Communication Association, Miami Beach, FL.

Chen, G., & Starosta, W. (1998). *Foundations of intercultural communications*. Boston: Allyn & Bacon.

Chen, G., & Starosta, W. J. (1998a). Chinese conflict management and resolution: Overview and implications. *Intercultural Communication Studies*, 7, 1–16.

Chen, S., Geluykens, R., & Chong, J. C. (2006). The importance of language in global teams: A linguistic perspective. *Management International Review*, 46, 679–695.

Chen, Y., Tjosvold, D., & Fang, S. S. (2005). Working with foreign managers: Conflict management for effective leader relationships in China. *International Journal of Conflict Management*, 16, 265–286.

Chesebro, J. L. (2003). Effects of teacher clarity and nonverbal immediacy on student learning, receiver apprehension, and affect. *Communication Education*, 52, 135–147.

Cheung, B. Y., Chudek, M., & Heine, S. J. (2011). Evidence for a sensitive period for acculturation: Younger immigrants report acculturating at a faster pace. *Psychological Science*, 22, 147–152.

Chidambaram, L., & Tung, L. L. (2005). Is out of sight, out of mind? An empirical study of social loafing in technology-supported groups. *Information Systems Research*, 16, 149–160.

Childers, A. (1997). Hormone hell. In L. G. Schnoor & B. Wickelgren (Eds.), *Winning orations*. Northfield, MN: Interstate Oratorical Association.

Cho, H., & Witte, K. (2004). A review of fear-appeal effects. In J. S. Seiter & R. H. Gass (Eds.), *Perspectives on persuasion, social influence, and compliance gaining*. New York: Pearson.

Choi, I., Nisbett, R. E., & Norenzayan, A. (1999). Causal attribution across cultures: Variation and universality. *Psychological Bulletin*, 125, 47–63.

Choney, S. (2010, October 14). Average American teen sends and receives 3,339 texts a month. *Technolog.msnbc.com*. [Online]. Available at: http://technolog.msnbc.msn.com/_news/2010/10/14/5290191-average-american-teen-sends-and-receives-3339-texts-a-month

Choo, T. S. (2010, April 19). Need for a M'sian Ajay Banga. *Sun2Surf*. [Online]. Available at: http://www.sun2surf.com/articlePrint.cfm?id=45703

Christensen, A. J. (2004). *Patient adherence to medical treatment regimens: Bridging the gap between behavioral science and biomedicine*. New Haven, CT: Yale University Press.

Christopher, F. S., & Lloyd, S. A. (2000). Physical and sexual aggression in relationships. In C. Hendrick & S. Hendrick (Eds.), *Close relationships: A sourcebook*. Thousand Oaks, CA: Sage.

Chua-Eoan, H. (2009, April 1). The queen and Mrs. Obama: A breach in protocol. *Time*. [Online]. Available at: http://www.time.com/time/printout/0,8816,1888962,00.html

Cialdini, R. (1993). *Influence: Science and practice*. New York: HarperCollins.

Cialdini, R., & Trost (1998). Social influence: Social norms, conformity, and compliance. In D. T. Gilbert, S. T. Fiske, & G. Lindzey (Eds.), *Handbook of social psychology* (Vol. 2). Boston: McGraw-Hill.

Clark, D. G., Mendez, M. F., Farag, E., & Vinters, H. V. (2003). Clinicopathologic case report: Progressive aphasia in a 77-year-old man. *Journal of Neuropsychiatry and Clinical Neurosciences*, 15, 231–238.

Clark, H. D. (1990). The impact of AIDS on gender differences in willingness to engage in casual sex. *Journal of Applied Social Psychology*, 20, 771–782.

Clark, H. H. (1996). *Using language*. New York: Cambridge University Press.

Clark, J., & Barber, B. (1994). Adolescents in postdivorce and always married families: Self-esteem and perceptions of father's interest. *Journal of Marriage and the Family*, 56, 608–614.

Clark, R. D., & Hatfield, E. (1989). Gender differences in receptivity to sexual offers. *Journal of Psychology and Human Sexuality*, 2, 39–55.

Clarke, A. M., & Clarke, A. D. B. (2000). *Early experience and the life path*. London: Jessica Kingsley.

Clarke, C. (1995). Untitled. In L. G. Schnoor (Ed.), *Winning orations*. Northfield, MN: Interstate Oratorical Association.

Clay, R. A. (2002). Advertising as science. *Monitor on Psychology*, 33, 38–41.

Coates, J. (1993). *Women, men and language*. New York: Longman.

Cohen, A. B., & Tannenbaum, I. J. (2001). Lesbian and bisexual women's judgments of the attractiveness of different body types. *Journal of Sex Research*, 38, 226–232.

Cohen, S., & Bailey, D. (1997). What makes teams work: Group effectiveness research from the shop floor to the executive suite. *Journal of Management*, 23, 239–291.

Coleman, J. (2001, February 8). India's traditional social system is complicating distribution of relief to earthquake survivors. *San Jose Mercury News*, p. 7A.

Collingwood, H. (1997, January). Forget the Fortune 500: For big bucks, think smaller and smarter. *Working Woman*, pp. 24–25.

Collins, R., & Cooper, P. J. (1997). *The power of story: Teaching through storytelling*. Boston: Allyn & Bacon.

Collins, S. (2001). Men's voices and women's choices. *Animal Behaviour*, 60, 773–780.

Colt, G. (1997, August). The magic of touch. *LIFE*, pp. 53–62.

Columbia Accident Investigation Board. (2003, August). *Columbia accident investigation report* (Vol. 1). [Online]. Available at: http://caib.nasa.gove/news/report/pdf/vol1/chapters/.

Conlon, T. (2007, July 26). E-mail addiction: Battle of the sexes! *Switched.com*. [Online]. Available at: http://www.switched.com/2007/05/24/rise-of-the-blackberry-addicted

Connaughton, S. L., & Daly, J. A. (2005). Leadership in the new millennium: Communication beyond temporal, spatial, and geographical boundaries. In P. Kalbfleisch (Ed.), *Communication yearbook 29*. Mahwah, NJ: Erlbaum.

Connaughton, S. L., & Shuffler, M. (2007). Multinational and multicultural distributed teams: A review and future agenda. *Small Group Research*, 38, 387–412.

Coontz, S. (1997). *The way we really are: Coming to terms with America's changing families*. New York: Basic Books.

Coontz, S. (2009, January 18). Intimacy unstuck. *Boston Globe Sunday*. [Online]. Available at: http://www.stephaniecoontz.com/articles43.htm

Cooper, C. (2008). Elucidating the bonds of workplace humor: A relational process model. *Human Relations*, 61, 1087–1115.

Cooper, L. (1960). *The rhetoric of Aristotle: An expanded translation with supplementary examples for students of composition and public speaking*. New York: Appleton Century Crafts.

Cooper, M. L., Shapiro, C. M., & Powers, A. M. (1998). Motivations for sex and risky sexual behavior among adolescents and young adults: A functional perspective. *Journal of Personality and Social Psychology*, 75, 1528–1558.

Cooper, V. W. (1994). The disguise of self-disclosure: The relationship ruse of a Soviet spy. *Journal of Applied Communication Research*, 22, 338–347.

Correll, J., Park, B., Judd, C. M., Wittenbrink, B. (2002). The police officer's dilemma: Using ethnicity to disambiguate potentially threatening individuals. *Journal of Personality and Social Psychology*, 83, 1314–1329.

Costanzo, M., Archer, D., Aronson, E., & Pettigrew, T. (1986). Energy conservation behavior. *American Psychologist*, 41, 521–528.

Coste, J. K. (2003). *Learning to speak Alzheimer's: A groundbreaking approach for everyone dealing with the disease*. New York: Houghton Mifflin.

Covey, S. J. (1991). *The seven habits of highly effective people*. New York: Simon & Schuster

Cox, T., Lobel, S., & McLeod, P. (1991). Effects of ethnic groups' cultural differences on cooperative and competitive behavior on a group task. *Academy of Management Journal*, 34, 827–847.

Craig, K., & Rand, K. (1998). The perceptually "privileged" group member: Consequences of solo status for African Americans and whites in task groups. *Small Group Research*, 29, 339–358.

Cramer, D. (2002). Satisfaction with romantic relationships and a four-component model of conflict resolution. In S. P. Shohov (Ed.), *Advances in psychological research*. Hauppauge, NY: NOVA Science.

Cramton, C. (2001). The mutual knowledge problem and its consequences for dispersed collaboration. *Organizational Science*, 12, 346–371.

Cramton, C. (2002). Attribution in distributed work groups. In P. J. Hinds & S. Kiesler (Eds.), *Distributed work*. Cambridge, MA: MIT Press.

Crandall, C. (1988). Social contagion of binge eating. *Journal of Personality and Social Psychology*, 55, 588–598.

Crane, D. R. (1987). Diagnosing relationships with spatial distance: An empirical test of a clinical principle. *Journal of Marital and Family Therapy*, 13, 307–310.

Crary, D. (2010, May 7). Over 45 sex: Approval up, activity down. *San Jose Mercury News*, p. A6.

Crawford, J. (1996, March 21). *Anatomy of the English-only movememt; Social and ideological sources of language restrictionism in the United States*. Paper presented at a conference at University of Illinois at Urbana–Champaign, Illinois.

Crawford, M., & Kaufman, M. R. (2006). Sex differences versus social processes in the construction of gender. In K. Dindia & D. J. Canary (Eds.), *Sex differences and similarities in communication*. Mahwah, NJ: Erlbaum.

Crawford, W., & Gorman, M. (1996). Coping with electronic information. In J. Dock (Ed.), *The press of ideas: Readings for writers on print culture and the information age*. Boston: St. Martin's Press.

Crescenzo, S. (2005). It's time to admit the hard truth: We're not photographers. *Communication World*, 22, 12–14.

Crocker, J. (2002). Contingencies of self-worth: Implications for self-regulation and psychological vulnerability. *Self and Identity*, 1, 143–149.

Crocker, J. (2006). What is optimal self-esteem? In M. H. Kernis (Ed.), *Self-esteem: Issues and answers*. New York: Psychology Press.

Crocker, J., & Knight, K. M. (2005). Contingencies of self-worth. *Current Directions in Psychological Science*, 14, 200–203.

Crocker, J., & Park, L. E. (2004). The costly pursuit of self-esteem. *Psychological Bulletin*, 130, 392–414.

Crocker, J., & Wolfe, C. (2001). Contingencies of self-worth. *Psychological Review*, 108, 593–623.

Crocker, J., Brook, A. T., Niija, Y., & Villacorta, M. (2006). The pursuit of self-esteem: Contingencies of self-worth and self-regulation. *Journal of Personality*, 744, 1749–1772.

Crocker, J., Sommers, S., & Luhtanen, R. (2002). Hopes dashed and dreams fulfilled: Contingencies of self-worth in the graduate school admissions process. *Personality and Social Psychology Bulletin*, 28, 1275–1286.

Cronin, C., & Jreisat, S. (1995). Effects of modeling on the use of nonsexist language among high school freshpersons and seniors. *Sex Roles*, 33, 819–830.

Crooks, R., & Baur, K. (2011). *Our sexuality*. Belmont, CA: Wadsworth/Cengage.

Cross, S. E., & Madson, L. (1997). Models of the self: Self-construals and gender. *Psychological Bulletin*, 122, 5–37.

Crowley, G. (1995, March 6). Dialing the stress-meter down. *Newsweek*, p. 62.

Crown, D. F. (2007). The use of group and group-centric individual goals for culturally heterogeneous and homogeneous task groups: An assessment of European work teams. *Small Group Research*, 489–508.

Crumley, B. (2010, March 17). *The Game of Death:* France's shocking TV experiment. *Time*. [Online]. Availableat:http://www.time.com/time/printout/0,8816,1972981,00.html

Crusco, A., & Wetzel, C. (1984). The Midas touch: The effects of interpersonal touch on restaurant tipping. *Personality and Social Psychology*, 10, 512–517.

Crystal, D. (1997). *The Cambridge encyclopedia of language*. New York: Cambridge University Press.

Crystal, D. (2005). *How language works: How babies babble, words change meaning, and languages live or die*. New York: The Overlook Press.

Crystal, D. (2008). *Txtng: The gr8 db8*. New York: Oxford University Press.

Cuddy, A. J. C., Norton, M. I., & Fiske, S. T. (2005). This old stereotype: The pervasiveness and persistence of the elderly stereotype. *Journal of Social Issues*, 61, 267–285.

Cummings, E. M., & Keller, P. S. (2007). How interparental conflict affects children. *Directions in Mental Health Counseling*, 17, 85–96.

Cummings, E. M., Goeke-Morey, M. C., & Papp, L. M. (2003). Children's responses to everyday marital conflict tactics in the home. *Child Development*, 74, 1918–1929.

Cummings, E. M., Schermerhorn, A. C., Davies, P. T., Goeke-Morey, M. C., & Cummings, J. S. (2006). Interparental discord and child adjustment: Prospective investigations of emotional security as an explanatory mechanism. *Child Development*, 77, 132–152.

Cunningham, V, Lefkoe, M., & Sechrest, L. (2006). Eliminating fears: An intervention that permanently eliminates the fear of public speaking. *Clinical Psychology and Psychotherapy*, 13, 183–193.

Cupach, W. R., & Spitzberg, B. H. (Eds.). (2011). *The dark side of close relationships II*. New York: Routledge.

Cupach, W. R., & Spitzberg, B. H. (Eds.). (1994). *The dark side of interpersonal communication*. Hillsdale, NJ: Erlbaum.

Curbside recycling. (2010). *Earth 911.com*. [Online]. Available at: http://earth911.com/recycling/curbside-recycling

Cure for some baldness stumbled upon? (2011, February 17). *The Early Show-CBS News*. [Online]. Available at: http://www.cbsnews.com/stories/2011/02/17/earlyshow/health/main20032752.shtml

Curseu, P. L., & Schruijer, S. G. L. (2010). Does conflict shatter trust or does trust obliterate conflict? Revisiting the relationships between team diversity, conflict, and trust. *Group Dynamics: Theory, Research, and Practice*, 14, 66–79.

Curtis, K. (2002, March 8). Critics nip at attorney's trial tactics. *Santa Cruz Sentinel*, pp. A1, A4.

Curtis, R. C., & Miller, K. (1986). Believing another likes or dislikes you: Behaviors making the beliefs come true. *Journal of Personality and Social Psychology*, 51, 284–290.

Czopp, A. M., Monteith, M. J., & Mark, A. Y. (2006). Standing up for a change: Reducing bias through interpersonal confrontation. *Journal of Personality and Social Psychology*, 90, 784–803.

D'Souza, K. (2010, May 2). I got your four-letter words right here. *San Jose Mercury News*, pp. A1, A19.

Dahlberg, T. (2001, June 3). Violence in youth sports reaching an ugly point. *Santa Cruz Sentinel*, pp. C1, C2.

Dahlberg, T. (2010, February 20). Contrive script lacks soul. *Santa Cruz Sentinel*, p. C3).

Dainton, M. (2003). Equity and uncertainty in relational maintenance. *Western Journal of Communication*, 67, 164–186.

Daly, M. (2009, August 14). Palin stands by "death panel" health claim. *AARP Bulletin Today*. [Online]. Available at: http://bulletin.aarp.org/states/mi/2009/32/articles/palin_stand_by_death_panel_health_claim.html

Daly, M., & Wilson, M. (1998). The evolutionary social psychology of family violence. In C. B. Crawford & D. L. Krebs (Eds.), *Handbook of evolutionary psychology: Ideas, issues, and applications*. Mahwah, NJ: Erlbaum.

Damasio, A. R., & Damasio, H. (1999). Brain and language. In A. R. Damasio (Ed.), *The Scientific American book of the brain*. New York: Lyons Press.

Damasio, N. (2007, January 8). The marvelous and mysterious Marvin Harrison. *Sports Illustrated*, pp. 41–45.

Daniel, D. K. (2008, January 23). Bush falsehoods about war counted. *San Jose Mercury News*, p. 15A.

Daniels, L., & Johnson, A. (2007, March 29). The word on *Wikipedia:* Trust but verify. *MSNBC*. [Online]. Available at: http://www.msnbc.msn.com/id/17740041/print/1/displaymode/1098/

Darling, A. L., & Dannels, D. P. (2003). Practicing engineers talk about the importance of talk: A report on the role of oral communication in the workplace. *Communication Education*, 52, 1–16.

Dauble, J. (2010, November 30). CNBC-AP poll finds Americans concern over federal deficit has reached all-time high. CNBC. [Online]. Available at: http://www.cnbc.con/id/40338136/CNBC_AP_POLL_FINDS_AMERICANS_CONCERN_OVER_FEDERAL_DEFICIT_HAS_REACHED_ALL_TIME_HIGH

Davidoff, J., Davies, L., & Roberson, D. (1999). Colour categories in a Stone-age tribe. *Nature*, 398, 203–204.

Davidowitz, M., & Myricm, R. D. (1984). Responding to the bereaved: An analysis of "helping" statements. *Death Education*, 8, 1–10.

Davidson, C. (2007, March 19). We can't ignore the influence of digital technologies. *Chronicle of Higher Education*, p. B20.

Davies, P. T., Sturge-Apple, M. L., Winter, M. A., Cummings, E. M., & Farrell, D. (2006). Child adaptational development in contexts of interparental conflict over time. *Child Development*, 77, 218–233.

Davis, A. (2006, March 14). LetsTalk annual cell phone etiquette survey: More people find cell phone use in cars and supermarkets acceptable. *LetsTalk.com*. [Online]. Available at: http://www.letstalk.com/company/release_031406.htm

Dawes, R. M. (1994). *House of cards: Psychology and psychotherapy built on myth*. New York: Free Press.

De al Vina, M. (2008, February 24). Keeping it together while living apart. *San Jose Mercury News*, pp. 1D, 11D.

De Araujo, I. E., Rolls, E. T., Velazco, M. I., Margot, C., & Cayeux, I. (2005). Cognitive modulation of olfactory processing. *Neuron*, 4, 671–679.

De Klerk, U. (1991). Expletives: Men only? *Communication Monographs*, 58, 156–169.

De Waal, F. (2010). *The age of empathy: Nature's lessons for a kinder society*. New York: Three Rivers Press.

DeAndrea, D. C., Tong, S. T., & Walther, J. B. (2011). Dark sides of computer-mediated communication. In W. R. Cupach & B. H. Spitzberg (Eds.), *The dark side of close relationships II*. New York: Routledge.

DeBono, E. (1992). *Sur/petition: Going beyond competition*. New York: HarperCollins.

DeChurch, L. A., Hamilton, K. L., & Haas, C. (2007). Effects of conflict management strategies on perceptions of intragroup conflict. *Group Dynamics: Theory, Research, and Practice*, 11, 66–78.

Den Hartog, D. N. (2004). Assertiveness. In R. J. House et al. (Eds.), *Culture, leadership, and organizations*. Thousand Oaks, CA: Sage.

DePaulo, B., & Kasby, D. (1998). Everyday life in close and casual relationships. *Journal of Personality and Social Psychology*, 74, 63–79.

DePaulo, B., Kasby, D., Kirkendol, S., Wyer, M., & Epstein, J. (1996). Lying in everyday life. *Journal of Personal and Social Psychology*, 70, 979–995.

Derber, C. (1979). *The pursuit of attention: Power and individualism in everyday life*. New York: Oxford University Press.

Derks, P., Kalland, S., & Etgen, M. (1995). The effect of joke type and audience response on the reaction to a joker: Replication and extension. *Humor*, 8, 327–337.

Derlega, V. J. (1984). Self-disclosure and intimate relationships. In V. J. Derlega (Ed.), *Communication, intimacy, and close relationships*. New York: Academic Press.

DeSeve. K. (2003). Addicted to love. *Science Central.com*. [Online]. Available at: www.sciencentral.com/articles/view.php3?language=english&type=article&article_id=218392170

Devine, P. G. (1989). Stereotypes and prejudice: Their automatic and controlled components. *Journal of Personality and Social Psychology*, 56, 5–18.

DeVito, J. (1970). *The psychology of speech and language: An introduction to psycholinguistics*. New York: Random House.

DeVito, J. (1990). *Messages: Building interpersonal communication skills*. New York: Harper & Row.

Devos-Comby, L., & Salovey, P. (2002). Applying persuasion strategies to alter HIV-relevant thoughts and behavior. *Review of General Psychology*, 6, 287–304.

Dewey, J. (1910). *How we think*. Lexington, MA: D. C. Heath.

Dhawan, N., Roseman, I. J., Naidu, R. K., Thapa, K., & Rettek, S. I. (1995). Self-concepts across two cultures: India and the United States. *Journal of Cross-Cultural Psychology*, 26, 606–621.

Diamond, D. (1997a, January 31). Behind closed gates. *USA Weekend*, pp. 4–5.

Diamond, R. (1997b, August 1). Designing and assessing course and curricula. *Chronicle of Higher Education*, p. B7.

Dickerson, J. (2007, September 28). Bwah-ha-ha! *Slate.com*. [Online]. Available at: http://www.slate.com/toolbar.aspx?action=print&id=2174397

DiClaudio, D. (2006). *The hypochondriac's pocket guide to horrible diseases you probably already have*. New York: Bloomsbury.

Did HIV-positive mom's beliefs put her children at risk? (2005). *ABC News*. Available at: http://abcnews.go.com/Primetime/print?id=1386737

Dieckmann, L. E. (2000). Private secrets and public disclosure: The case of battered women. In S. Petronio (Ed.), *Balancing the secrets of private disclosures*. Mahwah, NJ: Erlbaum.

Diehl, M., & Stroebe, W. (1987). Productivity loss in brainstorming groups: Toward the solution of a riddle. *Journal of Personality and Social Psychology*, 53, 497–509.

Dillard, J. (1994). Rethinking the study of fear appeals: An emotional perspective. *Communication Theory*, 4, 195–323.

Dillard, J. P., & Nabi, R. L. (2006). The persuasive influence of emotion in cancer prevention and detection messages. *Journal of Communication*, 56, 123–139.

Dindia, K. (2000). Sex differences in self-disclosure, reciprocity of self-disclosure, and self-disclosure and liking: Three meta-analyses reviewed. In S. Petronio (Ed.), *Balancing the secrets of private disclosures*. Mahwah, NJ: Erlbaum.

Dindia, K. (2002). Self-disclosure research: Knowledge through meta-analysis. In M. Allen, R. W. Preiss, B. M. Gayle, & N. A. Burrell (Eds.), *Interpersonal communication research: Advances through meta-analysis*. Mahwah, NJ: Erlbaum.

Dindia, K. (2006). Men are from North Dakota, women are from South Dakota. In K. Dindia & D. J. Canary (Eds.), *Sex differences and similarities in communication*. Mahwah, NJ: Erlbaum.

Dindia, K., & Canary, D. J. (Eds.). (2006). *Sex differences and similarities in communication*. Mahwah, NJ: Erlbaum.

Dion, K. L., & Dion, K. K. (1987). Belief in a just world and physical attractiveness stereotyping. *Journal of Personality and Social Psychology*, 52, 775–780.

DiSalvo, D. (2010, January/February). Are social networks messing with your head? *Scientific American Mind*, pp. 48–55.

Dodd, C. (2012). *Managing business and professional communication*. Boston: Allyn & Bacon.

Domagalski, T. (1998). *Experienced and expressed anger in the workplace*. Unpublished doctoral dissertation, University of South Florida.

Donald and Rosie. (2007, January 8). *Newsweek*, p. 55.

Donald Trump tells FNC: "Rosie O'Donnell's a loser." (2007). *FoxNews.com*. [Online]. Available at: http://www.foxnews.com/printer_friendly_story/0,3566,237997,00.html

Donald, B. (2010, July 6). Apps to keep sidewalk texters safer. *San Jose Mercury News*, p. C2.

Donoghue, P. J., & Seigel, M. E. (2005). *Are you really listening? Keys to successful communication*. Notre Dame, IN: Sorin Books.

Donohue, W. A., & Kolt, R. (1992). *Managing interpersonal conflict*. Newbury Park, CA: Sage.

Dougherty, T., Turban, D., & Collander, J. (1994). Conforming first impressions in the employment interview. *Journal of Applied Psychology*, 79, 659–665.

Douglas, W. (1987). Affinity-testing in initial interactions. *Journal of Social and Personal Relationships*, 4, 3–16.

Dovidio, J. F., Saguy, T., & Shnabel, N. (2009). Cooperation and conflict within groups: Bridging intragroup and intergroup processes. *Journal of Social Issues*, 65, 429-449.

Dowd, E. T., Hughes, S., Brockbank, L., Halpain, D., Seibel, C., & Seibel, P. (1988). Compliance-based and defiance-based intervention strategies and psychological reactance in the treatment of free and unfree behavior. *Journal of Counseling Psychology*, 35, 363–369.

Downey, G., Freitas, A. L., Michaelis, B., & Khouri, H. (1998). The self-fulfilling prophecy in close relationships: Rejection sensitivity and rejection by romantic partners. *Journal of Personality and Social Psychology*, 75, 545–560.

Doyle, J. A. (1995). *The male experience*. Dubuque, IA: Brown & Benchmark.

Dressler, C. (1995, December 31). Please! End this meeting madness! *Santa Cruz Sentinel*, p. D1.

Driscoll, R., Davis, K., & Lipetz, M. (1972). Parental interference and romantic love: The Romeo and Juliet effect. *Journal of Personality and Social Psychology*, 24, 1–10.

Driskell, J., Radtke, P., & Salas, E. (2003). Virtual teams: Effects of technological mediation on team performance. *Group Dynamics: Theory, Research, and Practice*, 7, 297–323.

Driver, J. L., & Gottman, J. M. (2004). Daily marital interactions and positive affect during marital conflict among newlywed couples. *Family Process*, 43, 301–314.

D'Souza, K. (2010, May 2). I got your four-letter words right here. *San Jose Mercury News*, pp. A1, A19.

Duck, S. W. (1990). Relationships as unfinished business: Out of the frying pan and into the 1990s. *Journal of Social and Personal Relationships*, 7, 5–24.

Duck, S. (1991). Some evident truths about conventions in everyday relationships: All communications are not created equal. *Human Communication Research*, 18, 228–269.

Duck, S. (1994). Stratagems, spoils, and a serpent's tooth: On the delights and dilemmas of personal relationships. In W. R. Cupach & B. H. Spitzberg (Eds.), *The dark side of interpersonal communication*. Hillsdale, NJ: Erlbaum.

Duck, S. W., & Pittman, G. (1994). Social and personal relationships. In M. L. Knapp & G. R. Miller (Eds.), *Handbook of interpersonal communication*. Thousand Oaks, CA: Sage.

Dugosh, K. L, Paulus, P. B., Roland, E. J., & Yang, H. (2000). Cognitive stimulation in brainstorming. *Journal of Personality and Social Psychology*, 79, 722–735.

Dumont, S. (2010, October 22). Dress codes are changing. *Inside Business*. [Online]. Available at: http://www.insidebiz.com/news/dress-codes-are-changing

Dunleavy, K. N., Martin, M. M., Brann, M., Booth-Butterfield, M., Myers, S. A., & Weber, K. (2008). Student nagging behavior in the college classroom. *Communication Education*, 57, 1–19.

Dunn, G. (2009, June 6). Palin lifts from Gingrich in Anchorage speech. *Huffington Post*. [Online]. Available at: http://www.huffingtonpost.com/geoffrey-dunn/palin-plagiarizes-gingric_b_21228.html

Duran, R. L., Kelly, L., & Keaton, J. A. (2005). College faculty use and perceptions of electronic mail to communicate with students. *Communication Quarterly*, 53, 159–176.

Dux, P. E., Ivanoff, J., Asplund, C. L., & Marois, R. (2006). Isolation of a central bottleneck of information processing with time-resolved fMRI. *Neuron*, 52, 1109–1120.

Dyer, J. (2001, June 10). Ethics and orphans: The monster study. *San Jose Mercury News*, pp. 1A, 14A–16A.

Dziech, B. W., & Hawkins, M. W. (1998). *Sexual harassment in higher education: Reflections and new perspectives*. New York: Barland.

Eagly, A. H. (1995). The science and politics of comparing women and men. *American Psychologist*, 50, 145–158.

Eagly, A. H. (2007). Female leadership advantage and disadvantage: Resolving the contradictions. *Psychology of Women Quarterly*, 31, 1–12.

Eagly, A. H., & Carli, L. L. (2007). *Through the labyrinth: The truth about how women become leaders*. Boston: Harvard Business School Press.

Eagly, A. H., Ashmore, R. D., Makhijani, M. G., & Kennedy, L. C. (1991). What is beautiful is good, but . . . : A meta-analytic review of research on the physical attractiveness stereotype. *Psychological Bulletin*, 110, 109–128.

Eagly, A., Johannesen-Schmidt, M. C., & van Engen, M. L. (2003). Transformational, transactional, and laissez-faire leadership styles: A meta-analysis comparing women and men. *Psychological Bulletin*, 129, 569–591.

Early, C. (1989). Social loafing and collectivism: A comparison of the United States and People's Republic of China. *Administrative Science Quarterly*, 34, 555–581.

Edwards, J. (2002, May 8). Songwriter Otis Blackwell, "Don't Be Cruel" among hits. *Santa Cruz Sentinel*, p. A8.

Edwards, K., & Smith, E. E. (1996). A disconfirmation bias in the evaluation of arguments. *Journal of Personality and Social Psychology*, 71, 5–24.

Edwards, R. (1995, February). New tools help gauge marital success. *APA Monitor*, p. 6.

Ehrlich, P. (2000). *Human natures: Genes, culture, and the human prospect*. Washington, DC: Island Press.

Eichenberg, R. C. (2003). Gender differences in attitudes toward the use of force by the United States, 1990–2003. *International Security*, 28, 110–141.

Einarsen, S., Hoel, H., Zapf, D., & Cooper, C. L. (2003). The concept of bullying at work. In S. Einarsen, H. Hoel, D. Zapf, & C. L. Cooper (Eds.), *Bullying and emotional abuse in the workplace: International perspectives in research and practice*. London: Taylor & Francis.

Ekman, P. (1992). *Telling lies: Clues to deceit in the marketplace, politics, and marriage*. New York: Norton.

Ekman, P. (1993). Facial expression and emotion. *American Psychologist*, 48, 384–393.

Ekman, P. (1994). Strong evidence for universals in facial expressions: A reply to Russell's mistaken critique. *Psychological Bulletin*, 115, 268–287.

Ekman. P. (2003). *Emotions revealed: Recognizing faces and feelings to improve communication and emotional life*. New York: Holt.

Ekman, P., & Friesen, W. (1987). Universal and cultural differences in the judgment of facial expressions of emotion. *Journal of Personality and Social Psychology*, 53, 712–717.

Ekman, P., & O'Sullivan, M. (1991). Who can catch a liar? *American Psychologist*, 46, 913–920.

Ekman, P., Friesen, W., & Bear, J. (1984, May). The international language of gestures. *Psychology Today*, pp. 64–69.

El Nasser, H. (2002, December 15). Gated communities more popular, and not just for the rich. *USA Today*. [Online]. Available at: http://www

.usatoday.com/news/nation/2002-12-15-gated-usat_x.htm

Elder, L. (2000). *The ten things you can't say in America*. New York: St. Martin's Press.

Eldridge, N. S., & Gilbert, L. A. (1990). Correlates of relationship satisfaction in lesbian couples. *Psychology of Women Quarterly*, 14, 43–62.

Elfenbein, H. A., & Ambady, N. (2002). On the universality and cultural specificity of emotion recognition: A meta-analysis. *Psychological Bulletin*, 128, 203–235.

Elgin, S. H. (1989). *Success with the gentle art of verbal self-defense*. Englewood Cliffs, NJ: Prentice Hall.

Ellis, A. (1995). Thinking processes involved in irrational beliefs and their disturbed consequences. *Journal of Cognitive Psychotherapy*, 9, 105–116.

Ellis, A. (1996). How I learned to help clients feel better and get better. *Psychotherapy*, 33, 149–151.

Ellis, A. P. J., Bell, B. S., Ployhart, R. E., Hollenbeck, J. R., & Ilgen, D. R. (2005). An evaluation of generic teamwork skills training with action teams: Effects of cognitive and skill-based outcomes. *Personnel Psychology*, 58, 641–672.

Ellison, S. (2009). *Taking the war out of our words*. Deadwood, OR: Wyatt-MacKenzie.

Emanuel, R., Adams, J., Baker, K., Daufin, E. K., Ellington, C., Fitts, E., Himsel, J., Holladay, L., & Okeowo, D. (2008). How college students spend their time communicating. *International Journal of Listening*, 22, 13–28.

Emberson, L. L., Lupyan, G., Goldstein, M. H., & Spivey, M. J. (2010). Overheard cell-phone conversations: When less speech is more distracting. *Psychological Science*, 21, 1383–1388.

Emmons, M. (2005, April 10). Scholarship pressure changes youth sports. *San Jose Mercury News*, pp. 1A, 12A–13A.

Eng, S. (1997, May 14). Cover story. *San Jose Mercury News*, pp. 1, 8.

Eng, S. (1999, February 9). Love among the workstations. *San Jose Mercury News*, pp. C13, C14.

Engle, S. (2006, January 25). More college freshmen committed to social and civic responsibility, UCLA survey reveals. *UCLA News*. [Online]. Available at: www.newsroom.ucla.edu

Engleberg, I. (2002). Presentations in everyday life: Linking audience interest and speaker eloquence. *American Communication Journal*. [Online]. Available at: http://www.acjournal.org/holdings/vol5/iss2/special/engleberg.html

Epstein, R. (2006, February/March). Do gays have a choice? *Scientific American Mind*, pp. 51–57.

Epstein, R. (2007, February/March). The truth about online dating. *Scientific American Mind*, pp. 28–35.

Epstein, R. (2010, January/February). How science can help you fall in love. *Scientific American Mind*, pp. 26–33.

Erbert, L. A. (2000). Conflict and dialectics: Perceptions of dialectical contradictions in marital conflict. *Journal of Social and Personal Relationships*, 17, 638–659.

Ernst, E. (2010). Homeopathy: What does the "best" evidence tell us? *The Medical Journal of Australia*, 192, 458–460.

Escera, C., Alho, K., Winkler, I., & Naatanen, R. (1998). Neural mechanisms of involuntary attention to acoustic novelty and change. *Journal of Cognitive Neuroscience*, 10, 590–604.

Esser. J. K. (1998). Alive and well after 25 years: A review of groupthink research. *Organizational Behavior and Human Decision Processes*, 73, 116–141.

Evans, J. (1989). *Bias in human reasoning: Causes and consequences*. Hillsdale, NJ: Erlbaum.

Exline, J. J., & Baumeister, R. F. (2000). In M. E. McCullough, K. I. Pargament, & C. E. Thoresen (Eds.), *Forgiveness: Theory, research, and practice*. New York: Guilford Press.

Eyes wide open. (2000, October 30). *Newsweek*, p. 8.

Facebook: Measuring the cost to business of social networking. (2009, July). *Nucleus Research*. [Online]. Available at: http://nucleusresearch.com/research/notes-and-reports/facebook-measuring-the-cost-to-business-of-social-networking/

Fadiman, C. (Ed.). (1985). *The Little, Brown book of anecdotes*. Boston: Little, Brown.

Fairhurst, G. T., & Sarr, R. A. (1996). *The art of framing: Managing the language of leadership*. San Francisco: Jossey-Bass.

Famous quotes and authors. (2009). [Online]. Available at: http://www.famousquotesandauthors.com/authors/albert_einstein_quotes.html

Farhanghi, H. (2009, February 6). Facebook status update: I'm divorcing you! *ABC News*. [Online]. Available at: http://abcnews.go.com/International/story?id=6821042&page=1

Faria, M. A. (2002). Guns and violence. *Medical Sentinel*, 7, 112–118.

Farrell, E. (2005, February 4). More students plan to work to help pay for college. *Chronicle of Higher Education*, pp. A1, A34.

Fathi, N. (2009, June 23). Woman's death creates symbol of Iran protests. *San Jose Mercury News*, pp. 1A, 6A.

Fazio, R. H. (1986). How do attitudes guide behavior? In R. M. Sorrentino & E. T. Higgins (Eds.), *The handbook of motivation and cognition: Foundations of social behavior*. New York: Guilford Press.

Feeley, T. H., Marshall, H. M., & Reinhart, A. M. (2006). Reactions to narrative and statistical written messages promoting organ donation. *Communication Reports*, 19, 89–100.

Fein, M. L. (1993). *I. A. M. A common sense guide to coping with anger*. Westport, CT: Praeger.

Feingold, A. (1988). Matching for attractiveness in romantic partners and same-sex friends: A meta-analysis and theoretical critique. *Psychological Bulletin*, 104, 226–235.

Feingold, A. (1992). Good-looking people are not what we think. *Psychological Bulletin*, 111, 304–341.

Feldman, R. S., Forrest, J. A., & Happ, B. R. (2002). Self-presentation and verbal deception: Do self-presenters lie more? *Basic and Applied Social Psychology*, 24, 163–170.

Felps, W., Mitchell, T. R., & Byington, E. (2006). How, when, and why bad apples spoil the barrel: Negative group members and dysfunctional groups. *Research in Organizational Behavior*, 27, 175–222.

Fenell, D. L. (1993). Characteristics of long-term first marriages. *Journal of Mental Health Counseling*, 15, 446–460.

Festinger, L. (1957). *A theory of cognitive dissonance*. Stanford, CA: Stanford University Press.

Festinger, L. (1977). Cognitive dissonance. In E. Aronson (Ed.), *Readings about the social animal*. San Francisco: Freeman.

Fiedler, F., & House, R. (1988). Leadership theory and research: A report of progress. In C. Cooper & I. Robertson (Eds.), *International review of industrial and organizational psychology*. New York: Wiley.

Filkins, D. (2001, November 13). Letting their hair down. *San Jose Mercury News*, p. 14A.

Final report of the California task force to promote self-esteem and personal and social responsibility. (1990). Sacramento: California State Department of Education.

Fincham, F. D., Harold, G. T., & Gano-Phillips, S. (2000). The longitudinal association between attributions and marital satisfaction: Direction of effects and role of efficacy expectations. *Journal of Family Psychology*, 14, 267–285.

Fingerman, K. L., & Charles, S. T. (2010). It takes two to tango. *Current Directions in Psychological Science*, 19, 172–176.

Finn, A. N., Sawyer, C. R., & Schrodt, P. (2009). Examining the effect of exposure therapy on public speaking state anxiety. *Communication Education*, 58, 92–109.

Fisher, A. (2007, February 13). Cupid at work: 3 tips for office romances. *Fortune*. [Online]. Available at: http://money.cnn.com/2007/02/12/news/economy/cupid.fortune/index.htm

Fisher, H. E., Brown, L. L., Aron, A., Strong, G., & Mashek, D. (2010). Reward, addiction, and emotional regulation systems associated with rejection in love. *Journal of Neurophysiology*, 104, 51–60.

Fisher, K. (2000). *Leading self-directed work teams: A guide to developing new team leadership skills*. New York: McGraw-Hill.

Fisher, R. M. (2003, January/February). Beliefs on trial, and the legality of reasonableness. *Skeptical Inquirer*, pp. 29–34.

Fisher, R., & Brown, S. (1988). *Getting together: Building a relationship that gets to yes*. Boston: Houghton Mifflin.

Fisher, R., & Shapiro, D. (2005). *Beyond reason: Using emotions as you negotiate*. New York: Penguin Books.

Fiske, E. (1990, March 5). How to learn in college: Group study, many tests. *The New York Times*, p. A1.

Fitzhenry, R. I. (1993). *The Harper book of quotations*. New York: HarperCollins.

Fletcher, G., & Fincham, F. (1991). Attribution in close relationships. In G. Fletcher & F. Fincham (Eds.), *Cognition in close relationships*. Hillsdale, NJ: Erlbaum.

Fletcher, M. A. (1999). Study: Marriage rate is at its lowest ever. *San Jose Mercury News*, p. 25A.

Flowers, B. J., & Richardson, F. C. (1996). Why is multiculturalism good? *American Psychologist*, 51, 609–621.

Floyd, K. (1996). Meanings for closeness and intimacy in friendships. *Journal of Social and Personal Relationships*, 13, 85–107.

Floyd, K. (2006). An evolutionary approach to understanding nonverbal communication. In V. Manusov & M. L. Patterson (Eds.), *The Sage handbook of nonverbal communication*. Thousand Oaks, CA: Sage.

Flynn, J., Valikoski, T., & Grau, J. (2008). Listening in the business context: Reviewing the state of research. *International Journal of Listening*, 22, 141–151.

Foertsch, J., & Gernsbacher, M. A. (1997). In search of gender neutrality: Is singular *they* a cognitively efficient substitute for generic *he*? *Psychological Science*, 8, 106–111.

Foley, K. (2010, February 5). The award machine. *IN-Business*. [Online]. Available at: http://www.in-business.co.nz/the-award-machine/

Folger, J., Poole, M., & Stutman, R. (1993). *Working through conflict: Strategies for relationships, groups, and organizations*. New York: HarperCollins.

Fonner, K. L., Roloff, M. E. (2010). Why teleworkers are more satisfied with their jobs than are office-based workers: When less contact is beneficial. *Journal of Applied Communication Research*, 38, 336–361.

Forsyth, D., Heiney, M., & Wright, S. (1997). Biases in appraisals of women leaders. *Group Dynamics: Theory, Research, and Practices*, 1, 98–103.

Foulke, E. (2006). Listening comprehension as a function of word rate. *Journal of Communication*, 18, 198–206.

Fowers, B. J., Lyons, E., Montel, K. H., & Shaked, N. (2001). Positive illusions about marriage among married and single individuals. *Journal of Family Psychology*, 15, 95–109.

Fraley, R. C., & Shaver, P. R. (2000). Adult romantic attachment: Theoretical developments, emerging controversies, and unanswered questions. *Review of General Psychology*, 4, 132–154.

France, D. (2000, August 28). The HIV disbeliever. *Newsweek*, pp. 46–48.

Fredrickson, B. (2009a). *Positivity: Top-notch research reveals the 3-to-1 ratio that will change your life*. New York: Crown.

Fredrickson, B. (2009b). *Positivity: Groundbreaking research reveals how to embrace the hidden strength of positive emotions, overcome negativity, and thrive*. New York: Crown.

Freed, A. (1992). We understand perfectly: A critique of Tannen's view. In *Locating power*

(Proceedings of the 1992 Berkeley Women and Language Conference). Berkeley: University of California Press.

French, H. W. (2001, July 15). Equality is elusive for women in Japan. *San Jose Mercury News*, p. 11A.

Frerking, B. (1995, March 15). Question authority, parents say. *San Jose Mercury News*, p. A4.

Frey, K. P., & Eagley, A. H. (1993). Vividness can undermine the persuasiveness of messages. *Journal of Personality and Social Psychology*, 65, 32–44.

Froomkin, D. (2010, August 26). Inmate sexual victimization persists, while feds stall on new rules. *Huffington Post*. [Online]. Available at: http://www.huffingtonpost.com/2010/08/26/sexual-victimization-of-i_n_695640.html

Frost, J. H., Chance, Z., Norton, M. I., & Ariely, D. (2008). People are experience goods: Improving online dating with virtual dates. *Journal of Interactive Marketing*, 22, 51–62.

Fruhlinger, J. (2007, July 26). 43% of e-mail users sleep with their cell phones. *Switched*. [Online]. Available at: http://www.switched.com/2007/07/26/43-of-e-mail-users-sleep-with

Fry, D. P., & Fry, C. B. (1997). Culture and conflict resolution models: Exploring alternatives to violence. In D. P. Fry & K. Bjorkqvist (Eds.), *Cultural variation in conflict resolution: Alternatives to violence*. Mahwah, NJ: Erlbaum.

Frye, N. E., & Karney, B. R. (2006). The context of aggressive behavior in marriage: A longitudinal study of newlyweds. *Journal of Family Psychology*, 20, 12–20.

Frymier, A., & Shulman, G. (1996). The development of a learner empowerment measure. *Communication Education*, 45, 181–199.

Furnham, A., McClellan, A., & Omer, L. (2003). A cross-cultural comparison of ratings of perceived fecundity and sexual attractiveness as a function of body weight and waist-to-hip ratio. *Psychology, Health and Medicine*, 8, 219–230.

Gabrenya, W. (1985). Social loafing on an optimistic task: Cross-cultural differences among Chinese and Americans. *Journal of Cross-Cultural Psychology*, 16, 223–242.

Gabric, D., & McFadden, K. L. (2001). Student and employer perceptions of desirable entry-level operations management skills. *Mid-American Journal of Business*, 16, 51–59.

Gagne, F. (2004). Bias and accuracy in close relationships: An integrative review. *Personality and Social Psychology Review*, 8, 322–338.

Galanter, E. (1962). Contemporary psychophysics. In R. Brown, E. Galanter, E. H. Hess, & G. Mendler (eds.), *New directions in psychology*. New York: Holt, Rinehart & Winston.

Gamer, M. (2009, February/March). Portrait of a lie. *Scientific American Mind*, pp. 50–55.

Gammage, K. L., Carron, A. V., & Estabrooks, P. A. (2001). Team cohesion and individual productivity: The influence of the norm for productivity and the identifiability of individual effort. *Small Group Research*, 32, 3–18.

Gardner, L., & Leak, G. (1994). Characteristics and correlates of teacher anxiety among college psychology teachers. *Teaching of Psychology*, 21, 28–32.

Garfield, C. (1986). *Peak performers*. New York: Avon Books.

Garland-Thomson, R. (2009). *Staring: How we look*. New York: Oxford University Press.

Garrido, J. (2010, June 11). Minorities will be new American majority by 2050. *Hispanic News*. [Online]. Available at: http://hispanic.cc/minorities_will_be_the_new_american_majority_by-2050.htm

Gaschler, K. (2005, November 21). Judging Amy and Andy. *Scientific American Mind*, pp. 52–57.

Gass, R., & Seiter, J. (1999). *Persuasion, social influence, and compliance gaining*. Boston: Allyn & Bacon.

Gass, R., & Seiter, J. (2007). *Persuasion, social influence, and compliance gaining*. Boston: Allyn & Bacon.

Gastil, J. (1990). Generic pronouns and sexist language: The oxymoronic character of masculine generics. *Sex Roles*, 23, 629–643.

Gastil, J. (1994). A meta-analytic review of the productivity and satisfaction of democratic and autocratic leadership. *Small Group Research*, 25, 384–410.

Gates, D. (1993, March 29). White male paranoia. *Newsweek*, pp. 48–53.

Gayle, B. (1991). Sex equity in workplace conflict management. *Journal of Applied Communication Research*, 19, 152–169.

Gebhardt, L., & Meyers, R. (1995). Subgroups influence in decision-making groups: Examining consistency from a communication perspective. *Small Group Research*, 26, 147–168.

Geier, J. (1967). A trait approach in the study of leadership in small groups. *Journal of Communication*, 17, 316–323.

Gelles, R., & Straus, M. (1988). *Intimate violence: The causes and consequences of abuse in the American family*. New York: Simon & Schuster.

Gentner, D., & Goldin-Meadow, S. (2003). *Language in mind: Advances in the study of language and thought*. Cambridge, MA: MIT Press.

George, D. S. (2008, September 26). Women are gaining ground in family decision making. *Washington Post*. [Online]. Available at: http://www.washingtonpost.com/wp-dyn/content/article/2008/09/25/AR2008092504167.html

Gershon, I. (2010). *The breakup 2.0: Disconnecting over new media*. Ithaca, NY: Cornell University Press.

Getter, H., & Nowinski, I. (1981). A free response test of interpersonal effectiveness. *Journal of Personality Assessment*, 45, 301–308.

Gibb, J. (1961). Defensive communication. *Journal of Communication*, 11, 141–148.

Gibson, C. B., & McDaniel, D. M. (2010). Moving beyond conventional wisdom: Advancements in cross-cultural theories of leadership, conflict, and teams. *Perspectives on Psychological Science*, 5, 450–462.

Giles, H., & Le Poire, B. A. (2006). The ubiquity and social meaningfulness of nonverbal communication. In V. Manusov & M. L. Patterson (Eds.), *The Sage handbook of nonverbal communication*. Thousand Oaks, CA: Sage.

Giles, H., & Street, R. L. (1994). Communicator characteristics and behavior. In M. L. Knapp & G. R. Miller (Eds.), *Handbook of interpersonal communication*. Thousand Oaks, CA: Sage.

Gilligan, J., & Lee, B. (2004). Beyond the prison paradigm: From provoking violence to preventing it by creating "anti-prisons" (residential colleges and therapeutic communities). *Annals of the New York Academy of Sciences*. [Online]. Available at: http://www.annalsnyas.org/cgi/content/abstract/1036/1/300

Gilovich, T. (1991). *How we know what isn't so: The fallibility of human reason in everyday life*. New York: Free Press.

Girion, L. (2000, December 20). Americans losing their cool at work. *San Jose Mercury News*, pp. 1C, 6C.

Girl undergoes surgery for smile. (1995, December 16). *San Jose Mercury News*, p. B3.

Gladwell, M. (2005). *Blink: The power of thinking without thinking*. New York: Little, Brown.

Glassner, B. (2000). *The culture of fear: Why Americans are afraid of the wrong things*. New York: Basic Books.

Gleicher, F., & Petty, R. (1992). Expectations of reassurance influence the nature of fear-stimulated attitude change. *Journal of Experimental Social Psychology*, 28, 86–100.

Glick, P., & Fiske, S. T. (2001). An ambivalent alliance: Hostile and benevolent sexism as complementary justifications for gender inequality. *American Psychologist*, 56, 109–118.

Glick, P., et al. (2000). Beyond prejudice as simple antipathy: Hostile and benevolent sexism across cultures. *Journal of Personality and Social Psychology*, 79, 763–775.

Glick, P., Fiske, S. T., et al. (2004). Bad but bold: Ambivalent attitudes toward men predict gender inequality in 16 nations. *Journal of Personality and Social Psychology*, 86, 713–728.

Glick, P., Lameriras, M., Fiske, S. T., et al. (2004). Bad but bold: Ambivalent attitudes toward men predict gender inequality in 16 nations. *Journal of Personality and Social Psychology*, 86, 713–728.

Glomb, T. M. (2002). Workplace anger and aggression: Informing conceptual models with data from specific encounters. *Journal of Occupational Health Psychology*, 7, 20–36.

Godar, S. H., & Ferris, S. P. (2004). *Virtual and collaborative teams: Process, technologies and practice*. London: Idea Group.

Gold, J. A., Ryckman, R. M., & Mosley, N. R. (1984). Romantic mood induction and attraction to a dissimilar other: Is love blind? *Personality and Social Psychology Bulletin*, 10, 358–368.

Goldsmith, D. J. (2000). Soliciting advice: The role of sequential placement in mitigating face threat. *Communication Monographs*, 67, 1–19.

Goldsmith, D. J., & Fitch, K. (1997). The normative context of advice as social support. *Human Communication Research*, 23, 454–476.

Goldsmith, D. J., & MacGeorge, E. L. (2000). The impact of politeness and relationship on perceived quality of advice about a problem. *Human Communication Research*, 26, 234–263.

Goldston, L. (2007, June 8). Men test their best lines as women eat up attention. *San Jose Mercury News*, pp. 1B, 7B.

Goldwert, L. (2011, March 17). Americans hoarding potassium iodide pills due to radiation fears; pills protect thyroid, no cure-all. *New York Daily News*. [Online]. Available at: http://articles.nydailynews.com/2011-03-17/entertainment/29175582_1_potassium-iodide-radioactive-iodine-radiation-exposure

Goleman, D. (1995). *Emotional intelligence*. New York: Bantam.

Goleman, D. (1998). *Working with emotional intelligence*. New York: Bantam.

Gonzaga, G. C., Keltner, D., & Ward, D. (2008). Power in mixed-sex stranger interactions. *Cognition and Emotion*, 22, 1555–1568.

Gonzaga, G. C., Turner, R. A., Keltner, D., Campos, B., & Altemus, M. (2006). Romantic love and sexual desire in close relationships. *Emotion*, 6, 163–179.

Goodboy, A. K., Myers, S. A., & Members of Investigating Communication. (2010). Relational quality indicators and love styles as predictors of negative relational maintenance behaviors in romantic relationships. *Communication Reports*, 23, 65–78.

Goodman, E. (2009, July 16). Sotomayor takes one for the supreme team. *San Jose Mercury News*, p. A13.

Goodstein, L. (2008, November 6). Obama made gains among younger evangelical voters, data show. *The New York Times*. [Online]. Available at: www.nytimes.com/2008/11/07/us/politics/07religion.html

Goodwin, E. (2010, February 21). Primary reasons why kids drop out of community sports programs. *Youth Sports Quality Institute*. [Online]. Available at: http://ysqi4ed.wordpress.com/2010/02/

Gopnik, A., Meltzoff, A. N., & Kuhl, P. (2001). *The scientist in the crib: What early learning tells us about the mind*. New York: Perennial.

Gorlick, A. (2005, October 3). *Dictionary adds terms like chick flick*. Associated Press.

Gosling, S. D., Ko, S. J., Mannarelli, T., & Morris, M. E. (2002). A room with a cue: Personality judgments based on offices and bedrooms. *Journal of Personality and Social Psychology*, 82, 379–398.

Gottman, J. M. (1979). *Marital interaction: Experimental investigations*. New York: Academic Press.

Gottman, J. M. (1994). *What predicts divorce? The relationship between marital processes and marital outcomes*. Hillsdale, NJ: Erlbaum.

Gottman, J. M. (1994, May/June). Why marriages fail. *Family Therapy*, pp. 40–48.

Gottman, J. M., & Carrere, S. (1994). Why can't men and women get along? Developmental notes and marital inequities. In D. Canary & L. Stafford (Eds.), *Communication and relational maintenance*. New York: Academic Press.

Gottman, J. M., & DeClaire, J. (2001). *The relationship cure: A five-step guide for building better connections with family, friends, and lovers*. New York: Crown.

Gottman, J. M., & Gottman, J. S. (2006). *10 lessons to transform your marriage*. New York: Crown.

Gottman, J. M., & Levenson, R. W. (1999). Dysfunctional marital conflict: Women are being unfairly blamed. *Journal of Divorce and Remarriage*, 31, 1–7.

Gottman, J. M., & Silver, N. (1994). *Why marriages succeed and fail: And how you can make yours last*. New York: Simon & Schuster.

Gottman, J. M, & Silver, N. (1999). *The seven principles for making marriage work*. New York: Crown.

Gottman, J. M., Coan, J., Carrere, S., & Swanson, C. (1998). Predicting marital happiness and stability from newlywed interactions. *Journal of Marriage and the Family*, 60, 5–22.

Gould, S. J. (1981). *The mismeasure of man*. New York: Norton.

Grace, K. (2000). Unsanitary hotels. In L. G. Schnoor & B. Wickelgren (Eds.), *Winning orations*. Mankato, MN: Interstate Oratorical Association.

Gracely, E. J. (2003, July 24). *Why extraordinary claims demand extraordinary proof*. [Online]. Available at: http://www.quackwatch.org/01QuackeryRelatedTopics/extraproof.html

Grady, D. (2010, November 25). Study: Hospitals still not very safe. *San Jose Mercury News*, p. A6.

Grasz, J. (2009, August, 19). Forty-five percent of employers use social networking sites to research job candidates, CareerBuilder survey finds. *CareerBuilder*. [Online]. Available at: http://www.careerbuilder.com/share/aboutus/pressreleasesdetail.aspx?id=pr519&sd=8%2F19%2F2009&ed=12%F31%2F2009

Grasz, J. (2011, January 12). Employers reveal outrageous and common mistakes candidates make in job interviews. *CareerBuilder*. [Online]. Available at: http://www.careerbuilder.com/share/aboutus/pressreleasesdetail. aspx?id=pr614&sd=1/12/2011&ed=12/31/2011

Gray, J. (1992). *Men are from Mars, Women are from Venus: A practical guide to improving communication and getting what you want in your relationships*. New York: Harper Collins.

Graybar, S. R., Antonuccio, D. O., Boutilier, L. R., & Varble, D. L. (1989). Psychological reactance as a factor affecting patient compliance to physician advice. *Scandinavian Journal of Behavior Therapy*, 18, 43–51.

Green, M. C., & Brock, T. C. (2000). The role of transportation in the persuasiveness of public narratives. *Journal of Personality and Social Psychology*, 79, 701–721.

Green, W., & Lazarus, H. (1990). Are you meeting with success? *Executive Excellence*, 7, 1–12.

Greenberg, J. (1981, June/July). An interview with David Rosenhan. *APA Monitor*, pp. 4–5.

Grenny, J. (2009). Crucial conversations: The most potent force for eliminating disruptive behavior. *Physician Executive Journal*, 35, 30–33.

Griesinger, C. (2006). Untitled. In L. G. Schnoor & B. Wickelgren (Eds.), *Winning orations*. Mankato, MN: Interstate Oratorical Association.

Griffin, E. (1994; 2003). *A first look at communication theory*. New York: McGraw-Hill.

Grimes, B. F. (2004). *Ethnologue: Languages of the world*. Dallas, TX: SIL International.

Grogan, S., & Richards, H. (2002). Body image: Focus groups with boys and men. *Men and Masculinities*, 4, 219–232.

Gronbeck, B., German, K., Ehninger, D., & Monroe, A. (1998). *Principles of speech communication*. New York: Longman.

Gross, A. E., & Crofton, C. (1977). What is good is beautiful. *Sociometry*, 40, 85–90.

Grover, V. P., Keel, P. K., & Mitchell, J. P. (2003). Gender differences in implicit weight identity. *International Journal of Eating Disorders*, 34, 125–135.

Gruber, J. (2001). Heart disease in women. In L. G. Schnoor & B. Wickelgren (Eds.), *Winning orations*. Mankato, MN: Interstate Oratorical Association.

Grusec, J. E., & Redler, E. (1980). Attribution, reinforcement, and altruism: A developmental analysis. *Developmental Psychology*, 16, 525–534.

Grusec, J. E., Kuczynski, L., Rushton, J. P., & Simutis, Z. M. (1978). Modeling, direct instruction, and attributions: Effects on altruism. *Developmental Psychology*, 14, 51–57.

Grusky, O., Bonacich, P., & Webster, C. (1995). The coalition structure of the four-person family. *Current Research in Social Psychology*, pp. 16–29.

Gudykunst, W. B. (2005). An anxiety/uncertainty management (AUM) theory of effective communication: Making the mesh of the net finer. In W. B. Gudykunst (Ed.), *Theorizing about intercultural communication*. Thousand Oaks, CA: Sage.

Gudykunst, W. B., & Kim, Y. Y. (Eds.). (1992). *Readings on communicating with strangers*. New York: McGraw-Hill.

Guerrero, L. K. (1992). "I'm so mad I could scream": The effects of anger expression on relational satisfaction and communication competence. *Southern Communication Journal*, 59, 125–141.

Guerrero, L. K., & Chavez, A. M. (2005). Relational maintenance in cross-sex friendships characterized by different types of romantic intent: An exploratory study. *Western Journal of Communication*, 69, 339–358.

Guest, A. M. (2007). Cultures of childhood and psychosocial characteristics: Self-esteem and social comparison in two distinct communities. *Journal of the Society for Psychological Anthropology*, 35, 1–32.

Gustini, R. (2011, January 3). The rise and fall of Gov. Arnold Schwarzenegger. *Atlantic Wire*. [Online]. Available at: http://www.theatlanticwire.com/politics/2011/01/the-rise-and-fall-of-gov-arnold-schwarzenegger/21668/

Haas, S. M., & Stafford, L. (1998). An initial examination of maintenance behaviors in gay and lesbian relationships. *Journal of Social and Personal Relationships*, 15, 846–855.

Hackman, M., & Johnson, C. (2004). *Leadership: A communication perspective*. Prospect Heights, IL: Waveland Press.

Haefner, P. T., Notarius, C. I., & Pellegrini, D. S. (1991). Determinants of satisfaction with marital discussions: An exploration of husband-wife differences. *Behavioral Assessment*, 13, 67–82.

Hagensick, M. E. (2008). In L. G. Schnoor & D. Cronin-Mills (Eds.), *Winning orations*. Mankato, MN: Interstate Oratorical Association.

Hahner, J. C., Sokoloff, M. A., & Salesch, S. L. (1997). *Speaking clearly: Improving voice and diction*. New York: McGraw-Hill.

Hair salons. (2011). *Hoovers*. [Online]. Available at: http://www.hoovers.com/industry/hair-salons/1213-1.html

Haj-Yahia, M. M. (1999). Wife abuse and its psychological consequences as revealed by the first Palestinian national survey on violence against women. *Journal of Family Psychology*, 13, 642–662.

Haleta, L. L. (1996). Student perceptions of teachers' use of language: The effects of powerful and powerless language on impression formation and uncertainty. *Communication Education*, 45, 16–28.

Hall, E. (1969). *The hidden dimension*. New York: Doubleday

Hall, E. (1981). *Beyond culture*. New York: Doubleday.

Hall, J. A. (2006a). How big are nonverbal sex differences? The case of smiling and nonverbal sensitivity. In K. Dindia & D. J. Canary (Eds.), *Sex differences and similarities in communication*. Mahwah, NJ: Erlbaum.

Hall, J. A. (2006b). Women's and men's nonverbal communication. In V. Manusov & M. L. Patterson (Eds.), *The Sage handbook of nonverbal communication*. Thousand Oaks, CA: Sage.

Hall, J. A., & Bernieri, F. J. (2001). *Interpersonal sensitivity: Theory and measurement*. Mahwah, NJ: Erlbaum.

Hall, J. A., Coats, E. J., & LeBeau, L. S. (2005). Nonverbal behavior and the vertical dimension of social relations: A meta-analysis. *Psychological Bulletin*, 131, 898–924.

Hall, J. A., Park, N., Song, H., & Cody, M. J. (2010). Strategic misrepresentation in online dating: The effects of gender, self-monitoring, and personality traits. *Journal of Social and Personal Relationships*, 27, 117–135.

Hall, J., & Watson, W. (1970). The effects of normative intervention on group decision making. *Human Relations*, 23, 299–317.

Hamachek, D. (1982). *Encounters with others: Interpersonal relationships and you*. New York: Harcourt Brace.

Hamachek, D. (1992). *Encounters with the self*. Fort Worth, TX: Harcourt Brace Jovanovich.

Hamermesh, D. S., & Biddle, J. E. (1994). Beauty and the labor market. *American Economic Review*, 84, 174–194.

Hamermesh, D. S., & Parker, A. M. (2005). Beauty in the classroom: Professors' pulchritude and putative pedagogical productivity. *Economics of Education Review*, 24, 369–376.

Hample, D. (2006). Anti-comfort messages. In K. M. Galvin & P. J. Cooper (Eds.), *Making connections: Readings in relational communication*. Los Angeles: Roxbury.

Hampton, K., Sessions, L., Eun, J. H. (2009, November 4). Social isolation and new technology. *Pew Internet*. [Online]. Available at: http://www.pewinternet.org/Reports/2009/18--Social-Isolation-and-New-Technology.aspz

Hampton, K. N., Sessions, L. F., Eun, J. H., & Rainie, L. (2009, November). Social isolation and new technology: How the Internet and mobile phones impact Americans' social networks. *Pew Internet & American Life Project*. [Online]. Available at: http://pewinternet.org/~/media/Files/Reports/2009/PIP_Tech_and_Social_Isolation.pdf

Han, M. (2003). Body image dissatisfaction and eating disturbance among Korean college female students: Relationships to media exposure, upward comparison, and perceived reality. *Communication Studies*, 34, 65–78.

Han, S., & Shavitt, S. (1994). Persuasion and culture: Advertising appeals in individualistic and collectivistic societies. *Journal of Experimental Social Psychology*, 30, 326–350.

Haney, W. (1967). *Communication and organizational behavior*. Homewood, IL: Irwin.

Hanson, R. (2010, October 26). Your wise brain. *Psychology Today*. [Online]. Available at: http://www.psychologytoday.com/blog/your-wise-brain/201010/confronting-the-negativity-bias

Hardin, C., & Banaji, M. R. (1993). The influence of language on thought. *Social Cognition*, 11, 277–308.

Hardy, J., Eys, M. A., & Carron, A. V. (2005). Exploring the potential disadvantages of high cohesion in sports teams. *Small Group Research*, 36, 166–187.

Hare, W. (2009, March/April). What open-mindedness requires. *Skeptical Inquirer*, pp. 36–39.

Harrell, A. (2005, March 11). *Physical attractiveness of children and parental supervision in grocery stores: An evolutionary explanation of the neglect of ugly kids*. Paper presented at the Warren E. Kalbach Population Conference, Edmonton, Alberta.

Harris, J. (2009, November 16). Fact-checking critics of President Obama's bowing controversy. *San Diego City Buzz Examiner*. [Online]. Available at: http://www.examiner.com/city-buzz-in-san-diego/fact-checking-critics-on-president-obama-s-bowing-controversy

Harris, M. B. (1996). Aggressive experiences and aggressiveness: Relationship to ethnicity, gender, and age. *Journal of Applied Social Psychology*, 26, 843–870.

Harrison, D. A., Price, K. H., Gavin, J. H., & Florey, A. T. (2002). Time, teams, and task performance: Changing effects of surface- and deep-level diversity on group functioning. *Academy of Management Journal*, 45, 1029–1045.

Harrison, K., & Cantor, J. (1997). The relationship between media consumption and eating disorders. *Journal of Communication*, 47, 40–67.

Harrison, L. E. (2000). Introduction. In L. E. Harrison & S. P. Huntington (Eds.), *Culture matters: How values shape human progress*. New York: Basic Books.

Harrison, L. E., & Huntington, S. P. (Eds.). (2000). *Culture matters: How values shape human progress*. New York: Basic Books.

Hart, J. W., Bridgett, D. J., & Karau, S. J. (2001). Coworker ability and effort as determinants of individual effort on a collective task. *Group Dynamics: Theory, Research, and Practice*, 5, 181–190.

Hartshorne, J. K. (2011, March/April). Where are the talking robots? *Scientific American Mind*, pp. 44–51.

Haslam, S. A., Reicher, S. D., & Platow, M. J. (2011). *The new psychology of leadership: Identity, influence and power*. New York: Psychology Press.

Haslett, B. (1992). *The organization woman: Power and paradox*. Norwood, NJ: Ablex.

Hatfield, E., & Rapson, R. L. (1996). *Love and sex: Cross-cultural perspectives*. Boston: Allyn & Bacon.

Hatfield, E., & Sprecher, S. (1986). *Mirror, mirror . . . : The importance of looks in everyday life*. Albany: State University of New York Press.

Hatfield, E., Sprecher, S., Pillemer, J. T., Greenberge, D., & Wexler, P. (1989). Gender differences in what is desired in the sexual relationship. *Journal of Psychology and Human Sexuality*, 1, 39–52.

Hausmann, R., Tyson, L. D., & Zahidi, S. (2010). Global gender gap report 2010. *World Economic Forum*. [Online]. Available at: http://www3.weforum.org/docs/WEF_GenderGap_Report_2010.pdf

Hawkins, K. (1995). Effects of gender and communication content on leadership emergence in small task-oriented groups. *Small Group Research*, 26, 234–249.

Hawkley, L. C., Browne, M. W., & Cacioppo, J. T. (2005). How can I connect with thee? Let me count the ways. *Psychological Science*, 16, 798–804.

Hazan, C., & Shaver, P. R. (1994a). Attachment as an organizational framework for research on close relationships. *Psychological Inquiry*, 5, 1–22.

Hazan, C., & Shaver, P. R. (1994b). Deeper into attachment theory. *Psychological Inquiry*, 5, 68–79.

Heatherton, T. F., & Vohs, K. D. (2000). Personality processes and individual differences-interpersonal evaluations following threats to self: Role of self-esteem. *Journal of Personality and Social Psychology*, 78, 725–736.

Hebel, S. (2008, October 16). Presidential candidates apparently blink at their own peril. *Chronicle of Higher Education*. [Online]. Available at: http://chronicle.com/blogs/election/2533/presidential-candidates-apparently-blink-at-their-own-peril

Hecht, M., Collier, M., & Ribeau, S. (1993). *African American communication: Ethnic identity and cultural interpretation*. Newbury Park, CA: Sage.

Helfand, D. (2001, August 16). "Edspeak" is in a class by itself. *Los Angeles Times*. [Online]. Available at: www.latimes.com/news/education/la

Hellweg, S., Samovar, L., & Skow, L. (1994). Cultural variations in negotiation styles. In L. Samovar & R. Porter (Eds.), *Intercultural communication: A reader*. Belmont, CA: Wadsworth.

Hendricks, W., Holliday, M., Mobley, R., & Steinbrecher, K. (1996). *Secrets of power presentations*. Franklin Lakes, NJ: Career Press.

Henley, N. (1995). Body politics revised: What do we know today? In P. Kalbfleisch & M. Cody (Eds.), *Gender, power, and communication in human relationships*. Hillsdale, NJ: Erlbaum.

Henningsen, D. D., Henningsen, M. L., Eden, J., & Cruz, M. G. (2006). Examining the symptoms of groupthink and retrospective sensemaking. *Small Group Research*, 37, 36–64.

Henry, J. (1963). *Culture against man*. New York: Random House.

Hersey, P., Blanchard, K. H., & Johnson, D. E. (2007). *Management of organizational behavior: Leading human resources*. Upper Saddle River, NJ: Prentice Hall.

Hersey, T. (2000). *Soul gardening: Cultivating the good life*. Minneapolis, MN: Augsburg.

Hertenstein, M. J. (2002). Touch: Its communicative functions in infancy. *Human Development*, 45, 70–95.

Hertenstein, M. J., Holmes, R., McCullough, M., & Keltner, D. (2009). The communication of emotion via touch. *Emotion*, 9, 566–573.

Heslin, R. (1974, May). *Steps toward a taxonomy of touching*. Paper presented to the annual convention of the Midwestern Psychological Association.

Hess, E., & Goodwin, E. (1974). The present state of pupilometrics. In M. Janice (Ed.), *Pupillary dynamics and behavior*. New York: Plenum Press.

Hess, E., Seltzer, A., & Schlien, J. (1965). Pupil response of hetero- and homosexual males to pictures of men and women: A pilot study. *Journal of Abnormal Psychology*, 70, 165–168.

Hetherington, E., Bridges, M., & Insabella, G. (1998, February). What matters? What does not? Five perspectives on the association between marital transitions and children's adjustment. *American Psychologist*, 53, 167–184.

Hickson, M., Stacks, D. W., & Moore, N-J. (2004). *Nonverbal communication: Studies and applications*. Los Angeles: Roxbury.

Hill, C. T., Rubin, Z., & Peplau, L. A. (1976). Breakups before marriage: The end of 103 affairs. *Journal of Social Issues*, 32, 147–168.

Hines, T. (2003). *Pseudoscience and the paranormal*. New York: Prometheus Books.

Hingson, R., Heeren, T., Winter, M., & Wechsler, H. (2005). Magnitude of alcohol-related mortality and morbidity among U.S. college students ages 18-24: Changes from 1998 to 2001. *Annual Review of Public Health*, 26, 259–279.

Hingson, R. W., Heeren, T., Zakocs, R. C., Kopstein, A., & Wechsler, H. (2002). Magnitude of alcohol-related mortality and morbidity among U.S. college students ages 18-24. *Journal of Studies on Alcohol and Drugs*, 63, 136–144.

Hiramoto, M., & Anderson, V. (2006). Utterance-final position and projection of femininity in Japanese. *Journal of the Acoustical Society of America*, 120, 3294–3295.

Hitlan, R. T., Kelly, K. M., Schepman, S., Schneider, K. T., & Zarate, M. A. (2006). Language exclusion and the consequences of perceived ostracism in the workplace. *Group Dynamics: Theory, Research, and Practice*, 10, 56–70.

Hitsch, G. J., Hortacsu, A., & Ariely, D. (2010). Matching and sorting in online dating. *American Economic Review*, 100, 130–163.

Hodson, G. (2011). Do ideologically intolerant people benefit from intergroup contact? *Current Directions in Psychological Science*, 20, 154–159.

Hofstede, G. (1980). *Culture's consequences: International differences in work-related values*. Beverly Hills, CA: Sage.

Hofstede, G. (2012). Dimensionalizing cultures: The Hofstede model in context. In L. A. Samovar, R. E. Porter, & E. R. McDaniel (Eds.), *Intercultural communication: A reader*. Boston: Wadsworth/Cengage.

Hofstede, G., & Hofstede, G. J. (2005). *Cultures and organizations: Software of the mind*. New York: McGraw-Hill.

Hoge, W. (2002, July 20). Doctor is Britain's worst killer. *San Jose Mercury News*, p. 11A.

Hoigaard, R., Safvenbom, R., & Tonnessen, F. E. (2006). The relationship between group cohesion, group norms, and perceived social loafing in soccer teams. *Small Group Research*, 37, 217–232.

Holahan, P., Mooney, A., Mayer, R. C., & Paul, L. F. (2008). Do debates get more heated in cyberspace? Team conflict in the virtual environment. *Current Issues in Technology Management*, 12, 1–4.

Holan, A. D. (2009, December 18). PolitiFact's Lie of the Year: "Death panels." [Online]. Available at: http://www.politifact.com/truth-o-meter/article/2009/dec/18/politifact-lie-year-death-panels/

Hollander, E. (1985). Leadership and power. In G. Lindzey & E. Aronson (Eds.), *Handbook of social psychology*. New York: Random House.

Hollander, E., & Offerman, L. (1990, February). Power and leadership in organizations. *American Psychologist*, pp. 179–189.

Holman, T. B., & Jarvis, M. O. (2003). Hostile, volatile, avoiding, and validating couple-conflict types: An investigation of Gottman's couple-conflict types. *Personal Relationships*, 10, 267–282.

Holmes, E. A., & Mathews, A. (2005). Mental imagery and emotion: A special relationship? *Emotion*, 5, 489–497.

Holtgraves, T. (1997). Styles of language use: Individual and cultural variability in conversational indirectness. *Journal of Personality and Social Psychology*, 73, 624–637.

Holtgraves, T., & Dulin, J. (1994). The Muhammad Ali effect: Differences between African Americans and European Americans in their perceptions of a truthful braggart. *Language and Communication*, 14, 275–285.

Holtzman, S. (2010, November 8). Body piercings and tattoos messy for employers. *Jaffe Legal News Service*. [Online]. Available at: http://www.jlns.com/top-stories/2010/11/07/body-piercings-and-tattoos-messy-employers/30584

Home chores still a battle of the sexes. (1993, February 16). *San Jose Mercury News*, p. A5.

Honeycutt, J. M., Cantrill, J. G., & Allen, T. (1992). Memory structures for relational decay: A cognitive test of sequencing de-escalating actions and stages. *Human Communication Research*, 18, 528–562.

Honeycutt, J. M., Cantrill, J. G., & Greene, R. W. (1989). Memory structures for relational escalation: A cognitive test of the sequencing of relational actions and stages. *Human Communication Research*, 16, 62–90.

Hoover-Dempsey, K., Plas, J., & Wallston, B. (1986). Tears and weeping among professional women: In search of new understanding. *Psychology of Women Quarterly*, 10, 19–34.

Hoppes, S. (2008). Cross at your own risk: America's bridge safety neglect. In L. G. Schnoor & D. Cronin-Mills (Eds.), *Winning orations*. Mankato, MN: Interstate Oratorical Association.

Horner, T., Guyer, M., & Kalter, N. (1993). The biases of child sexual abuse experts: Believing is seeing. *Bulletin of the American Academy of Psychiatric Law*, 21, 281–292.

Hornsey, M. J., Robson, E., Smith, J., Esposo, S., & Sutton, R. M. (2008). Sugaring the pill: Assessing rhetorical strategies designed to minimize defensive reactions to group criticism. *Human Communication Research*, 34, 70–98.

Horowitz, B. (2002). *Communication apprehension: Origins and management*. Albany, NY: Singular.

Hoshino-Browne, E., Zanna, A. S., Spencer, S. J., Zanna, M. P., Kitayama, S., & Lackenbauer, S. (2005). On the cultural guises of cognitive dissonance: The case of Easterners and Westerners. *Journal of Personality and Social Psychology, 89,* 294–310.

Hosman, L. A. (2002). Language and persuasion. In J. P. Dillard & M. Pfau (Eds.), *The persuasion handbook: Developments in theory and practice.* Thousand Oaks, CA: Sage.

House Republicans dismiss constituents' ire toward proposed Medicare changes. (2011). *The Seattle Times.* [Online]. Available at: http://seattletimes.nwsource.com/html/health/2014903127_medicare29.html

House, R. J., & Javidan, M. (2004). Overview of GLOBE. In R. J. House, P. J. Hanges, M. Javidan, P. W. Dorfman, & V. Gupta (Eds.), *Culture, leadership, and organization: The GLOBE study of 62 societies.* Thousand Oaks, CA: Sage.

How Americans communicate. (1998). *National Communication Association.* [Online]. Available at: http//:www.natcom.org/research/Roper/how_americans-communicate.htm

How we got from 1 to 162 million websites on the Internet. (2008, April 4). *Royal Pingdom.* [Online]. Available at: http://royal.pingdom.com/2008/04/04/how-we-got-from-1-to-162-million-websites-on-the-internet

Howell, W. S. (1982). *The empathic communicator.* Belmont, CA: Wadsworth.

Hsu, F. L. K. (1981). The self in cross-cultural perspective. In A. J. Marsella, B. De Vos, & F. L. K. Hsu (Eds.), *Culture and self.* London: Tavistock. [Online]. Available at: http://www.jonwell.org/pubs/joboutlook/want.htm

Hsu, J. (2008, August/September). The secrets of storytelling: Our love for telling tales reveals the workings of the mind. *Scientific American Mind,* pp. 46–51.

Hughes, S. M., & Gallup, G. G. (2003). Sex differences in morphological predictors of sexual behavior: Shoulder to hip and waist to hip ratios. *Evolution and Human Behavior,* 24, 173–178.

Hui, C. H., & Triandis, H. C. (1986). Individualism-collectivism: A study of cross-cultural researchers. *Journal of Cross-Cultural Psychology,* 17, 225–248.

Hunt, M. (1982). *The universe within: New science explores the human mind.* New York: Simon & Schuster.

Hunt, S. (1997, February 28). Taste is not only relative, it's genetic. *Discovery Channel.* [Online]. Available at: http://www.exn.ca/Stories/1997/02/10/07.asp

Husband, R. (1992). Leading in organizational groups. In R. Cathcart & L. Samovar (Eds.), *Small group communication.* Dubuque, IA: Brown.

Huspek, M. (2000). Oppositional codes: The case of the penitentiary of New Mexico riot. *Journal of Applied Communication Research,* 28, 91–116.

Hutchinson, S. (2002, March 22). Jury's verdicts reaffirm court of public opinion. *San Jose Mercury News,* p. 9A.

Hyatt, J. (2010, May 21). Smarter, by design. *Newsweek.* [Online]. Available at: http://www.newsweek.com/2010/05/21/smarter-by-design.print.html

Hyde, J. S. (2005). The gender similarities hypothesis. *American Psychologist,* 60, 581–592.

Icon, E. (2011). Tattoos and piercings in the workplace. *Working World.* [Online]. Available at: http://www.workingworld.com/articles/Tattoos-and-Piercings-in-the-Workplace

Ilies, R., Hauserman, N., Schwochau, S., & Stibal, J. (2003). Reported incidence rates of work-related sexual harassment in the United States: Using meta-analysis to explain reported rate disparities. *Personnel Psychology,* 56, 607–631.

Impett, E. A., & Peplau, L. A. (2000, August). *Saying "yes" but thinking "no": Consensual participation in unwanted sex.* Paper presented at the annual meeting of the American Psychological Association, Washington, DC.

Impett, E. A., & Peplau, L. A. (2003). Sexual compliance: Gender, motivational, and relationship perspectives. *Journal of Sex Research,* 40, 87–100.

Impett, E. A., Gable, S. L., & Peplau, L. A. (2005). Giving up and giving in: The costs and benefits of daily sacrifice in intimate relationships. *Journal of Personality and Social Psychology,* 89, 327–344.

In U.S., religious prejudice stronger against Muslims. (2010, January 21). *Gallup.* [Online]. Available at: http://www.gallup.com/poll/125312/religious-prejudice-strong-against-muslims.aspx

Inagaki, Y. (1985). *Jiko Hyogen No Gijutsu (Skills in self-expression).* Tokyo: PHP Institute.

Inch, E., & Warnick, B. (1998). *Critical thinking and communication: The use of reason in argument.* Boston: Allyn & Bacon.

Infante, D. A., & Rancer, A. S. (1996). Argumentativeness and verbal aggressiveness: A review of recent theory and research. In B. R. Burleson (Ed.), *Communication yearbook 1996.* Thousand Oaks, CA: Sage.

Infante, D. A., Chandler, T. A., & Rudd, J. E. (1989). Test of an argumentative skill deficiency model of interpersonal violence. *Communication Monographs,* 56, 163–177.

Infante, D., Riddle, B., Horvatt, C., & Tumlin, S. (1992). Verbal aggressiveness: Messages and reasons. *Communication Quarterly,* 40, 116–126.

Infante, D. A., Sabourin, T., Rudd, J., & Sharron, E. (1990). Verbal aggression in violent and nonviolent marital disputes. *Communication Quarterly,* 4, 361–371.

Inman, C. (2010, February 20). Woods' scripted apology perfectly awkward. *San Jose Mercury News,* p. 1D.

International student enrollments rose modestly in 2009/2010, led by strong increase in students from China. (2010, November 15). *Institute of International Education.* [Online]. Available at: http://www.iie.org/en/Who-We-Are/News-and-Events/Press-Center/Press-Releases/

2010/2010-11-15-Open-Doors-International-Students-In-The-US

Internet 2010 in numbers. (2011, January 12). *Royal. Pingdom.com*. [Online]. Available at: http://royal.pingdom.com/2011/01/12/internet-2010-in-numbers/

Internet world statistics: Usage and population statistics. (2010, June 30). *Internet World Statistics*. [Online]. Available at: http://www.internetworldstats.com/top20.htm

Ireland,M. E., Slatcher, R. B., Eastwick, P. W., Scissors, L. E., Finkel, E. J., & Pennebaker, J. W. (2010). Language style matching predicts relationship initiation and stability. *Psychological Science*, 22, 39–44.

Is marriage bliss? Percentage very happy by marital status. (2011, April 7). *Pew Research Center*. [Online]. Available at: http://pewresearch.org/pubs/?ChartID=17

Is the letter Y a vowel or a consonant? (2011). *Oxford Dictionaries*. [Online]. Available at: http://www.oxforddictionaries.com/page/200

Isenhart, M. W., & Spangle, M. (2000). *Collaborative approaches to resolving conflict*. Thousand Oaks, CA: Sage.

Ishii, S., Klopf, D., & Cambra, R. (1984). The typical Japanese student as an oral communicator: A preliminary profile. *Otsuma Review*, 17, 39–63.

Italie, L. (2010, June 28). Facebook is divorce lawyers' new best friend. *MSNBC*. [Online]. Available at: http://www.msnbc.msn.com/cleanprint/CleanPrintProxy.aspx?1299709213011

Jackendoff, R. (1996). How language helps us think. *Pragmatics and Cognition*, 4, 1–34.

Jackson, D. (1997, November 24). It took way too long to lower the boom. *San Jose Mercury News*, p. B7.

Jacobson, N., & Gottman, J. (1998, March/April). Anatomy of a violent relationship. *Psychology Today*, pp. 61–65.

Jaffe, C. (1998). *Public speaking: Concepts and skills for a diverse society*. Belmont, CA: Wadsworth.

Jaffe, E. (2010). The psychological study of smiling. *Observer*, 23.

Jaksa, J., & Pritchard, M. (1994). *Communication ethics: Methods of analysis*. Belmont, CA: Wadsworth.

James, D., & Clarke, S. (1993). Women, men, and interruptions: A critical review. In D. Tannen (Ed.), *Gender and conversational interaction*. New York: Oxford University Press.

James, D., & Drakich, J. (1993). Understanding gender differences in amount of talk: A critical review of research. In D. Tannen (Ed.), *Gender and conversational interaction*. New York: Oxford University Press.

James, S. D. (2009, December 10). Manscapers mow more hair, even down there. *ABSNews/Health*. [Online]. Available at: http://abcnews.go.com/Health/GadgetGuide/manscaping-men-shave-wax-bodies/story?id=9293977

Jamieson, K. H. (1988). *Eloquence in an electronic age*. New York: Oxford University Press.

Janis, I. (1982). *Groupthink: Psychological studies of policy decisions and fiascoes*. Boston: Houghton Mifflin.

Janis, I. (1989). *Crucial decisions: Leadership in policy-making and crisis management*. New York: Free Press.

Jay, T. (1992). *Cursing in America: A psycholinguist's study of dirty language in the courts, in the movies, in the schoolyards and on the streets*. Philadelphia: Benjamin.

Jay, T. (2009). Do offensive words harm people? *Psychology, Public Policy, and Law*, 15, 81–101.

Jefferson, E. A. (2007, March 13). Americans are leaving gated communities. *Denverpost.com*. [Online]. Available at: http://www.denverpost.com/lifestyles/ci_5418726

Jeffries, V. (2002). The structure and dynamics of love: Toward a theory of marital quality and stability. *Humboldt Journal of Social Relations*, 27, 42–72.

Jemmott, J. B., Jemmott, L. S., & Fong, G. T. (2010). Efficacy of a theory-based abstinence-only intervention over months. *Archives of Pediatrics and Adolescent Medicine*, 164, 152–159.

Jensen, J. V. (1997). *Ethical issues in the communication process*. Prospect Heights, IL: Waveland Press.

Jensen-Campbell, L., Graziano, W., & West, S. (1995). Dominance, prosocial orientation, and female preferences: Do nice guys really finish last? *Journal of Personality and Social Psychology*, 68, 427–440.

Jill Bolte Taylor: Neuroanatomist. (2008, March). *TED*. [Online]. Available at: http://www.ted.com/speakers/jill_bolte_taylor.html

Jin, B., & Pena, J. F. (2010). Mobile communication in romantic relationships: Mobile phone use, relational uncertainty, love, commitment, and attachment styles. *Communication Reports*, 23, 39–51.

Job outlook (2007). [Online]. Available at: http://www.jobweb.com/joboutlook/2007/student2.htm

Job outlook 2009-student version. (2009). *National Association of Colleges and Employers*. [Online]. Available at: http://www.jobweb.org/studentarticles.aspx?id=2121

Johnson, C. (2009). Bad blood: Doctor-nurse behavior problems impact patient care. *Physician Executive Journal*, 35, 6–10.

Johnson, D. I., & Lewis, N. (2010). Perceptions of swearing in the work setting: An expectancy violations theory perspective. *Communication Reports*, 23, 106–118.

Johnson, D. W. (1971). Role-reversal: A summary and review of the research. *International Journal of Group Tensions*, 1, 318–334.

Johnson, D. W. (2003). Social interdependence: Interrelationships among theory, research, and practice. *American Psychologist*, 58, 934–945.

Johnson, D. W., & Johnson, R. T. (2000, June). Teaching students to be peacemakers: Results of twelve years of research. *CoopLearn.org*. [Online]. Available at: www.cooplearn.org/pages/peace-meta.html

Johnson, D. W., & Johnson, R. T. (2000, May). Civil political discourse in a democracy: The contribution of psychology. *Cooplearn.org*. [Online]. Available at: http://www.cooplearn.org/pages/contro-pol.html

Johnson, D. W., & Johnson, R. T. (2003). Field testing integrative negotiations. *Peace and Conflict: Journal of Peace Psychology*, 9, 39–68.

Johnson, D. W., & Johnson, R. T. (2003). Training for cooperative group work. In M. A. West, D. Tjosvold, & K. G. Smith (Eds.), *International handbook of organizational teamwork and cooperative working*. New York: Wiley.

Johnson, D. W., & Johnson, R. T. (2005). Learning groups. In S. A. Wheelan (Ed.), *The handbook of group research and practice*. Thousand Oaks, CA: Sage.

Johnson, K. G., Senatore, J. J., Liebig, M. C. & Minor, G. (1974). *Nothing never happens: Exercises to trigger group discussions and promote self discovery*. New York: Glencoe Press.

Johnson, M. P. (1995). Patriarchal terrorism and common couple violence: Two forms of violence against women. *Journal of Marriage and the Family*, 57, 283–294.

Johnson, M. P. (2006a). Conflict and control: Gender symmetry and asymmetry in domestic violence. *Violence Against Women*, 12, 1003–1018.

Johnson, M. P. (2006b). Gendered communication and intimate partner violence. In B. J. Dow & J. T. Wood (Eds.), *The Sage handbook of gender and communication*. Thousand Oaks, CA: Sage.

Johnson, S. (2009, June 18). Survey: Users irked by gadget gaffes. *San Jose Mercury News*, p. 13B.

Johnson, S., & Bechler, C. (1998). Examining the relationship between listening effectiveness and leadership emergence: Perceptions, behaviors, and recall. *Small Group Research*, 29, 452–471.

Johnson, W. (1946). *People in quandaries*. New York: Harper.

Johnstone, T., & Scherer, K. R. (2000). Vocal communication and emotion. In M. Lewis & J. Haviland (Eds.), *Handbook of emotion*. New York: Guilford Press.

Jonas, E., Schultz-Hardt, S., Frey, D., & Thelen, N. (2001). Confirmation bias in sequential information search after preliminary decisions: An expansion of dissonance theoretical research on selective exposure to information. *Journal of Personality and Social Psychology*, 80, 557–571.

Jonas, K. J., & Sassenberg, K. (2006). Knowing how to react: Automatic response priming from social categories. *Journal of Personality and Social Psychology*, 90, 709–721.

Jones, C. S., & Kaplan, M. F. (2003). The effects of racially stereotypical crimes on juror decision-making and information-processing strategies. *Basic and Applied Social Psychology*, 25, 1–13.

Jones, D. (2004, February 20). Contestant Amy Henry shines above the others. *USA Today*, p. 4B.

Jones, E. E., & Davis, K. E. (1965). From acts to dispositions: The attribution process in person perception. In L. Berkowitz (Ed.), *Advances in experimental social psychology* (Vol. 2). New York: Academic Press.

Jones, E. E., & Kelly, J. R. (2007). Contributions to a group discussion and perceptions of leadership: Does quantity always count more than quality? *Group Dynamics: Theory, Research, and Practice*, 11, 15–30.

Jones, S. (1994). *The right touch: Understanding and using the language of physical context*. Cresskill, NJ: Hampton Press.

Jorgenson, L. M., & Wahl, K. M. (2000). Psychiatrists as expert witnesses in sexual harassment cases under Daubert and Kumho. *Psychiatric Annals*, 30, 390–396.

Ju, L., & Cushman, D. (1995). *Organizational teamwork in high-speed management*. Albany: State University of New York Press.

Judge, T. A., & Piccolo, R. F. (2004). Transformational and transactional leadership: A meta-analytic test of their relative validity. *Journal of Applied Psychology*, 89, 755–768.

Just, M. A., Keller, T. A., & Cynkar, J. (2008). A decrease in brain activation associated with driving when listening to someone speak. *Brain Research*, 1205, 70–80.

Kalb, C., & McCormick, J. (1998, September 21). Bellying up to the bar. *Newsweek*, p. 89.

Kalbfleisch, P., & Cody, M. (Eds.). (1995). *Gender, power, and communication in human relationships*. Hillsdale, NJ: Erlbaum.

Kalbfleisch, P. J., & Herold, A. L. (2006). Sex, power, and communication. In K. Dindia & D. J. Canary (Eds.), *Sex differences and similarities in communication*. Mahwah, NJ: Erlbaum.

Kalof, L., Eby, K. K., Matheson, J. L., & Kroska, R. J. (2001). The influence of race and gender on student self-reports of sexual harassment by college professors. *Gender and Society*, 15, 282–302.

Kameda, N. (2003). Miscommunication factors in Japanese-US trade relationships. [Online]. Available at: http://www.rcwob.doshisha.ac.jp/review/5_2/5_2_011.pdf

Kameda, N. (2007). *Communicative challenges for Japanese companies: Strategies in the global marketplace*. Proceedings of the Association for Business Communication Seventh Asia-Pacific Conference.

Kane, M. J., Brown, L. H., McVay, J. C., Silvia, P. J., Myin-Germeys, I., & Kwapil, T. R. (2007). For whom the mind wanders, and when: An experience-sampling study of working memory and executive control in daily life. *Psychological Science*, 18, 559–656.

Kanner, B. (March/April, 1995). Ideal couples and romance. *Psychology Today*, pp. 46–49.

Kaplan, T. (1998, November 27). Few using health plan. *San Jose Mercury News*, p. B1.

Kaplowitz, R. A. (1986). *Selecting college and university personnel: The quest and the questions* (ASHE-ERIC Higher Education Report No. 8). Washington, DC: Association for the Study of Higher Education.

Karau, S. J., & Elsaid, A. M. M. K. (2009). Individual differences in beliefs about groups. *Group*

Dynamics: Theory, Research, and Practice, 13, 1–13.

Karau, S. J., & Hart, J. W. (1998). Group cohesiveness and social loafing: Effects of a social interaction manipulation on individual motivation within groups. *Group Dynamics: Theory, Research, and Practice*, 2, 185–191.

Karau, S., & Williams, K. (1993). Social loafing: A meta-analytic review and theoretical integration. *Journal of Personality and Social Psychology*, 65, 681–706.

Karremans, J. C., Frankenhuis, W. F., & Arons, S. (2010). Blind men prefer a low waist-to-hip ration. *Evolution and Human Behavior*, 31, 182–186.

Kates, D. B., Schaffer, H. E., Lattimer, J. K., Murray, G. B., & Cassem, E. H. (1994). Guns and public health: Epidemic of violence or pandemic of propaganda? *Tennessee Law Review*, 61, 513–596.

Katzenbach, J., & Smith, D. (1993a). *The wisdom of teams*. Boston: Harvard Business School Press.

Katzenbach, J., & Smith, D. (1993b, March/April). The discipline of teams. *Harvard Business Review*, pp. 111–120.

Kawatsu, H. (2009, May 25). *A mixed jury system for Japan*. Paper presented at the annual meeting of The Law and Society, Las Vegas, NV. [Online]. Available at: http://www.allacademic.com/meta/p18168_index.html

Keats, J. (2011). *Virtual words*. New York: Oxford University Press.

Keller, P. A. (1999). Converting the unconverted: The effect of inclination and opportunity to discount health-related fear appeals. *Journal of Applied Psychology*, 84, 403–415.

Kelley, T., & Littman, J. (2001). *The art of innovation: Lessons in creativity from IDEO, America's leading design firm*. New York: Doubleday.

Kelley, T., & Littman, J. (2005). *The ten faces of innovation: IDEO's strategies for beating the devil's advocate & driving creativity throughout your organization*. New York: Doubleday.

Kelly, J. R. (2005). The effect of nonverbal behaviors associated with sexual harassment proclivity on women's performance. *Sex Roles: A Journal of Research*, 53, 689–701.

Kelly, L., & Keaten, J. A. (2000). Treating communication anxiety: Implications of the communibiological paradigm. *Communication Education*, 49, 45–57.

Kelly, R. (2009, August 12). Twitter study reveals interesting results about usage-40% is "pointless babble." *Pearanalytics*. [Online]. Available at: http://www.pearanalytics.com/blog/2009/twitter-study-reveals

Kelsey, B. (1998). The dynamics of multicultural groups: Ethnicity as a determinant of leadership. *Small Group Research*, 29, 602–623.

Keltner, D. (2007). The power paradox. *Greatergood*. [Online]. Available at: http://greatergood.berkeley.edu/article/item/power_paradox/

Keltner, D., Gruenfeld, D. H., & Anderson, C. (2003). Power, approach, and inhibition. *Psychological Review*, 110, 265–284.

Kennedy, T. L. M., Smith, A., Wells, A. T., & Wellman, B. (2008, October 19). Networked families. *Pew Internet & American Life Project*. [Online]. Available at: http://www.pewinternet.org/~/media//Files/Reports/2008/PIP_Networked_Family.pdf.pdf

Kernis, M. H. (2003). High self-esteem: A differentiated perspective. In E. C. Chang & L. J. Sanna (Eds.), *Virtue, vice, and personality: The complexity of behavior*. Washington, DC: APA Books.

Kertesz, S. (2010, August 20). Physician's errors: How our health care system is failing us. *Huffington Post*. [Online]. Available at: http://www.huffingtonpost.com/stefan-kertesz/quality-eludes-doctors-wi_b_684221.html?view=print

Key survey findings. (2007, January). *MSNBC.com*. [Online]. Available at: http://www.msnbc.msn.com/id/17407725/

Keysar, B., & Henly, A. S. (2002). Speakers' overestimation of their effectiveness. *Psychological Science*, 13, 207–212.

Kiken, L. G., & Shook, N. J. (2011). Mindfulness increases positive judgments and reduces negativity bias. *Social Psychological and Personality Science*, 2, 425–431.

Killion, A. (1996, July 5). VanDerveer ordeal proves worth it for well-drilled team. *San Jose Mercury News*, pp. D1, D3.

Killion, A. (2004, August 16). Yet another "wake-up call" won't rouse this U.S. team. *San Jose Mercury News*, pp. 1D, 3D.

Kilmann, R., & Thomas, K. (1977). Developing a force-choice measure of conflict handling behavior: The "mode" instrument. *Educational Psychological Measurement*, 37, 309–325.

Kilpatrick, W. (1975). *Identity and intimacy*. New York: Dell.

Kim, H. S., & Markus, H. R. (1999). Deviance or uniqueness, harmony or conformity? A cultural analysis. *Journal of Personality and Social Psychology*, 77, 785–800.

Kim, J., LaRose, R., & Peng, W. (2009). Loneliness as the cause and the effect of problematic Internet use: The relationship between Internet use and psychological well-being. *CyberPsychology and Behavior*, 12, 451–455.

Kim, M. (1992). A comparative analysis of nonverbal expressions as portrayed by Korean and American print-media advertising. *Howard Journal of Communication*, 3, 321.

Kim, M. S., & Bresnahan, J. E. (1993). Attitude-behavior relations: A meta-analysis of attitudinal relevance and topic. *Journal of Communication*, 43, 101–142.

Kirn, W. (1997, October 3). Drinking to belong. *The New York Times*, p. A11.

King, E. B., Hebl, M. R., & Beal, D. J. (2009). Conflict and cooperation in diverse workgroups. *Journal of Social Issues*, 65, 261–285.

King, S. (1995, May 1). *Commentary-interpersonal cyberspace relationships*. Electronic message to Interpersonal Computing and Technology Discussion List. Georgetown University.

Kirkman, B. L., Rosen, B., Gibson, C. B., Tesluk, P. E., & McPherson, S. O. (2002). Five challenges to virtual team success: Lessons from Sabre, Inc. *Academy of Management Executive*, 16, 67–79.

Kitchen, P. (2007, August 25). Um, like, isn't the Internet wonderful? *San Jose Mercury News*, p. 3A.

Klapp, O. (1978). *Opening and closing: Strategies of information adaptation in society*. New York: Cambridge University Press.

Kleck, G. (2005). *Point blank: Guns and violence in America*. Somerset, NJ: Aldine Transaction.

Kleiman, C. (1991, July 28). A boost up the corporate ladder. *San Jose Mercury News*, p. PC1.

Klein, R. C. A., & Johnson, M. P. (1997). Strategies of couple conflict. In S. Duck (Ed.), *Handbook of personal relationships*. New York: Wiley.

Klein, S. (1996). Work pressure as a determinant of work group behavior. *Small Group Research*, 27, 299–315.

Klopf, D. (1998). *Intercultural encounters: The fundamentals of intercultural communication*. Englewood, CO: Morton.

Knapp, M. L. (2006). Lying and deception in close relationships. In A. Vangelisti & D. Perlman (Eds.), *The Cambridge handbook of personal relationships*. New York: Cambridge University Press.

Knapp, M., & Vangelisti, A. (1992). Stages of relationships. In M. Knapp & A. Vangelisti (Eds.), *Interpersonal communication and human relationships*. Needham Heights, MA: Allyn and Bacon.

Knapp, M., & Vangelisti, A. (2005). *Interpersonal communication and human relationships*. New York: Allyn & Bacon.

Knoll, K., & Jarvenpaa, S. L. (1998). Working together in global virtual teams. In M. Igbaria & M. Tan (Eds.), *The virtual workplace*. Hershey, PA: Idea Group.

Knutson, T. J., & Posirisuk, S. (2006). Thai relational development and rhetorical sensitivity as potential contributors to intercultural communication effectiveness: JAI YEN YEN. *Journal of Intercultural Communication Research*, 35, 205–217.

Knutson, T. J., Komolsevin, R., Chatiketu, P., & Smith, V. R. (2002). A comparison of Thai and U.S. American willingness to communicate. *Journal of Intercultural Commúnication Research*, 31, 1–16.

Knutson, T. J., Komolsevin, R., Chatiketu, P., & Smith, V. R. (2003). A cross-cultural comparison of Thai and US American rhetorical sensitivity: Implications for intercultural communication effectiveness. *International Journal of Intercultural Relations*, 27, 63–78.

Knutson, T. J., Komolsevin, R., Chatiketu, P., & Smith, V. R. (2002). A comparison of Thai and U.S. American willingness to communicate. *Journal of Intercultural Communication Research*, 31, 3–12.

Kohn, A. (1992). *No contest: The case against competition*. Boston: Houghton Mifflin.

Kohn, A. (1993). *Punished by rewards*. New York: Houghton Mifflin.

Konda, K. J. (2006). The war at home. In L. G. Schnoor & B. Wickelgren (Eds.), *Winning orations*. Mankato, MN: Interstate Oratorical Association.

Kopfman, J. E., Smith, S. W., Ah Yun, J. K., & Hodges, A. (1998). Affective and cognitive reactions to narrative versus statistical evidence organ donation messages. *Journal of Applied Communication Research*, 26, 279–300.

Korzybski, A. (1958). *Science and sanity*. Lakeville, CT: International Non-Aristotelian Literary.

Kotter, J. P. (1990). *A force for change: How leadership differs from management*. New York: Free Press.

Kottke, J. L., & MacLeod, C. D. (1989). Use of profanity in the counseling interview. *Psychological Reports*, 65, 627–634.

Kouri, K., & Lasswell, M. (1993). *Black–white marriages*. Binghamton, NY: Hayworth Press.

Kowalski, R. M. (1993). Inferring sexual interest from behavioral cues: Effects of gender and sexually relevant attitudes. *Sex Roles*, 29, 13–36.

Kozlowski, S. W. J., & Ilgen, D. R. (2006). Enhancing the effectiveness of work groups and teams. *Psychological Science in the Public Interest*, 7, 77–124.

Kozlowski, W. J., & Ilgen, D. R. (2007, June/July). The science of team success. *Scientific American Mind*, pp. 54–61.

Kramer, T. J., Fleming, G. P., & Mannis, S. M. (2001). Improving face-to-face brainstorming through modeling and facilitation. *Small Group Research*, 32, 533–557.

Kraul, C. (2006, December 20). Renowned for longevity, Ecuadorian town changing. *San Jose Mercury News*, p. 16A.

Kraus, M. W., & Keltner, D. (2009). Signs of socioeconomic status: A thin slicing approach. *Psychological Science*, 20, 99–106.

Kraus, M. W., Huang, C., & Keltner, D. (2010). Tactile communication, cooperation, and performance: An ethological study of the NBA. *Emotion*, 10, 745–749.

Krauss, R. M. (2001). The psychology of verbal communication. In N. Smelser & P. Baltes (Eds.), *International encyclopedia of the social and behavioral sciences*. London: Elsevier.

Krauss, R. M., & Chiu, C-Y. (1998). Language and social behavior. In D. T. Gilbert, S. T. Fiske, & G. Lindzey (Eds.), *The handbook of social psychology* (Vol. 2). New York: Oxford University Press.

Kraut, R. E. (1973). Effects of social labeling on giving to charity. *Journal of Experimental Social Psychology*, 9, 551–562.

Kraut, R., Kiesler, S., Boneva, B., Cummings, J., Helgeson, V., et al. (2002). Internet paradox revisited. *Journal of Social Issues*, 58, 49–74.

Kraut, R., Patterson, M., Lundmark, V., Kiesler, S., Mukopadhyay, T., & Scherlis, W. (1998). Internet paradox: A social technology that reduces social involvement and psychological well-being? *American Psychologist*, 53, 1017–1031.

Krebs, D. L., & Denton, K. (1997). Social illusions and self-deception: The evolution of biases in person perception. In J. A. Simpson & D. T. Kenrick (Eds.), *Evolutionary social psychology*. Mahwah, NJ: Erlbaum.

Krieger, L. M. (1999, February 5). Mystery rock injures woman asleep at home. *San Jose Mercury News*, pp. 1B, 4B.

Kristof, N. (1995, December 14). Sales pitch. *San Jose Mercury News*, p. A27.

Krucoff, C. (1998, November 11). When winning becomes the reason. *San Jose Mercury News*, p. D3.

Kruger, J. (2009, October 8). Survey finds 3 out of 10 city residents would give up sex before cellphones. *PMA Newsline*. [Online]. Available at: http://pmanewsline.com/2009/10/08.survey-finds-3-out-of-10-city-residents-would-give-up-sex-before-cellphones/

Kubicka, T. (1995). Traitorous transplants: The enemy within. In L. G. Schnoor (Ed.), *Winning orations*. Northfield, MN: Interstate Oratorical Association.

Kuhl, P. K. (1993). Developmental speech perception: Implications for models of language impairment. *Annals of the New York Academy of Sciences*, 682, 248–263.

Kuhl, P. K. (1994). Speech perception. In F. D. Minifie (Ed.), *Introduction to communication sciences and disorders*. San Diego, CA: Singular.

Kuhl, P. K. (2004). Early language acquisition: Cracking the speech code. *Nature Reviews Neuroscience*, 5, 831–843.

Kuhl, P. K., Conboy, B. T., Padden, D., Nelson, T., & Pruitt, J. (2005). Early speech perception and later language development: Implications for the "critical period." *Language Learning and Development*, 3, 237–264.

Kuhn, T., & Poole, M. S. (2000). Do conflict management styles affect group decision making? Evidence from a longitudinal field study. *Human Communication Research*, 26, 558–590.

Kunkel, A. W., & Burleson, B. R. (2006). Revisiting the different cultures thesis: An assessment of sex differences and similarities in supportive communication. In K. Dindia & D. J. Canary (Eds.), *Sex differences and similarities in communication*. Mahwah, NJ: Erlbaum.

Kuo, F. E., & Sullivan, W. C. (2001). Aggression and violence in the inner city: Effects of environment via mental fatigue. *Environment and Behavior*, 33, 543–571.

Kurdek, L. A. (1989). Relationship quality of gay and lesbian cohabiting couples: A 1-year follow-up study. *Journal of Social and Personal Relationships*, 6, 39–59.

Kurdek, L. A. (1998). Relationship outcomes and their predictors: Longitudinal evidence from heterosexual married, gay cohabiting, and lesbian cohabiting couples. *Journal of Marriage and the Family*, 60, 553–568.

Kurdek, L. A. (2005). What do we know about gay and lesbian couples? *Current Directions in Psychological Science*, 14, 251–254.

Kushner, H. (1981). *When bad things happen to good people*. New York: Avon.

Kutschera, U. (2008, January/February). The difference between Hahnemann and Darwin. *Skeptical Inquirer*, pp. 26–27.

Kuznia, R. (2010, April 2). Senator Menendez sparks controversy with Fortune 500 diversity survey. *HireDiversity.com*. [Online]. Available at: http://www.hirediversity.com/news/2010/4/2/senator_menendez_sparks_controversy_with_fortune.htm

Lacohee, H., & Anderson, B. (2001). Interacting with the telephone. *Journal of Human-Computer Studies*, 54, 665–699.

LaFasto, F., & Larson, C. (2001). *When teams work best: 6,000 team members and leaders tell what it takes to succeed*. Thousand Oaks, CA: Sage.

Lamberth, J. (1998, August 6). Driving while black: A statistician proves that prejudice still rules the road. *Washington Post*, p. C1.

Landers, A. (1995, February 25). Low-income families need fire protection too. *Santa Cruz Sentinel*, p. D5.

Landman, A., Ling, P. M., & Glantz, S. A. (2002). Tobacco industry youth smoking prevention programs: Protecting the industry and hurting tobacco control. *American Journal of Public Health*, 92, 917–930.

Landrum, R. E., & Harrold, R. (2003). What employers want from psychology graduates. *Teaching of Psychology*, 30, 131–133.

Lane, K., Balleweg, B. J., Suler, J. R., Fernald, P. S., & Goldstein, G. S. (2000). Acquiring skills-undergraduate students. In M. E. Ware & D. E. Johnson (Eds.), *Handbook of demonstrations and activities in the teaching of* psychology. *Vol. 3: Personality, abnormal, clinical-counseling, and social*. Mahwah, NJ: Erlbaum.

Langer, E. (1989). *Mindfulness*. Reading, MA: Addison-Wesley.

Langer, E., & Abelson, R. (1974). A patient by any other name . . . : Clinical group differences in labeling bias. *Journal of Consulting and Clinical Psychology*, 42, 4–9.

Langewitz, W., Denz, M., Keller, A., Ruttimann, S., & Wossmer, B. (2002). Spontaneous talking time at start of consultation in outpatient clinic: Cohort study. *Emergency Medical Journal*, 325, 682–683.

Langfred, C. (1998). Is group cohesiveness a double-edged sword? An investigation of the effects of cohesiveness on performance. *Small Group Research*, 29, 124–143.

Langlois, J. H., Kalakanis, L., Rubenstein, A. J., Larson, A., Hallam, M., & Smoot, M. (2000). Maxims and myths of beauty? A meta-analytic and theoretical review. *Psychological Review*, 126, 390–423.

Lanka, B. (1989). *I dream a world: Portraits of black women who changed America*. New York: Stewart, Tabori, & Chang.

Lapakko, D. (1997). Three cheers for language: A closer examination of a widely cited study of nonverbal communication. *Communication Education*, 46, 63–69.

Lapierre, L. M., & Allen, T. D. (2006). Work-supportive family, family-supportive supervision, use of organizational benefits, and problem-focused coping: Implications for work-family conflict and employee well-being. *Journal of Occupational Health Psychology*, 11, 169–181.

Lapinski, M. K., & Boster, F. J. (2001). Modeling the ego-defensive function of attitudes. *Communication Monographs*, 68, 314–324.

Larson, C. (1992). *Persuasion: Reception and responsibility*. Belmont, CA: Wadsworth.

Larson, C. U. (2007). *Persuasion: Reception and responsibility*. Belmont, CA: Thomson/Wadsworth.

Larson, C., & LaFasto, M. (1989). *Teamwork: What must go right, what can go wrong*. Newbury Park, CA: Sage.

Larson, J. R. (1989). The dynamic interplay between employees' feedback-seeking strategies and supervisors' delivery of performance feedback. *Academy of Management Review*, 14, 408–422.

Larson, J. R. (2007). Deep diversity and strong synergy: Modeling the impact of variability in members' problem-solving strategies on group problem-solving performance. *Small Group Research*, 38, 413–436.

Lassiter, G. D., & Munhall, P. J. (2001). The genius effect: Evidence for a nonmotivational interpretation. *Journal of Experimental Social Psychology*, 37, 349–355.

Latane, B., Williams, K., & Harkin, S. (1979). Many hands make light the work: The causes and consequences of social loafing. *Journal of Personality and Social Psychology*, 37, 822–832.

Laughlin, P. R., Hatch, E. C., Silver, J. S., & Boh, L. (2006). Groups perform better than the best individuals on letters-to-numbers problems: Effects of group size. *Journal of Personality and Social Psychology*, 90, 644–650.

Lavin, C. D., & Young, W. H. (2006). Mentoring in the virtual organization: Keys to building successful schools and businesses. *Mentoring and Tutoring: Partnership in Learning*, 14, 433–447.

Lazar, J. (1991). Ensuring productive meetings. In R. Swanson & B. Knapp (Eds.), *Innovative meeting management*. Austin, TX: Minnesota Mining and Manufacturing.

Lazarus, R. S. (1991). *Emotion and adaptation*. New York: Oxford University Press.

Leaper, C., & Ayres, M. M. (2007). A meta-analytic review of gender variations in adults' language use: Talkativeness, affiliative speech, and assertive speech. *Personality and Social Psychology Review*, 11, 328–363.

Leathers, D. (1970). The process effects of trust-destroying behaviors in the small group. *Speech Monographs*, 37, 181–187.

Leathers, D. (1979). The impact of multichannel message inconsistency on verbal and nonverbal decoding behavior. *Communication Monographs*, 46, 88–100.

Leathers, D. (1986). *Successful nonverbal communication: Principles and applications*. New York: Macmillan.

Lecheler, S., de Vreese, C., & Slothuus, R. (2009). Issue importance as a moderator of framing effects. *Communication Research*, 36, 400–425.

Lee, B. (1997). *The power principle: Influences with honor*. New York: Simon & Schuster.

Lee, Y-T, Jussim, L. J., & McCauley, C. R. (1995). *Stereotype accuracy: Toward appreciating group differences*. Washington, DC: American Psychological Association.

Leland, J., & Miller, M. (1998, August 17). Can gays "connect"? *Newsweek*, pp. 47–52.

Lenckus, D. (2005, November 28). Physician apologies, listening skills found to reduce medical malpractice claims. *Business Insurance*, p. 4.

Leonard, K. E., & Senchak, M. (1996). Prospective prediction of husband marital aggression within newlywed couples. *Journal of Abnormal Psychology*, 105, 369–380.

Lerner, J. S., & Tetlock, P. E. (1999). Accounting for the effects of accountability. *Psychological Bulletin*, 125, 255–275.

Lessmoellmann, A. (2006, October/November). Can we talk? *Scientific American Mind*, pp. 44–49.

Letellier, P. (1994). Gay and bisexual male domestic violence victimization: Challenges to feminist theory and responses to violence. *Violence and Victims*, 9, 95–106.

Levesque, M., & Kenny, D. (1993). Accuracy of behavioral predictions at zero acquaintance: A social relations analysis. *Journal of Personality and Social Psychology*, 65, 1178–1187.

Levine, K. (2001). The dentist's dirty little secret. In L. G. Schnoor & B. Wickelgren (Eds.), *Winning orations*. Mankato, MN: Interstate Oratorical Association.

Levine, M., & Shefner, J. (1991). *Fundamentals of sensation and perception*. Pacific Grove, CA: Brooks/Cole.

Levine, T. R., Feeley, T. H., McCornack, S. A., Hughes, M., & Harms, C. M. (2005). Testing the effects of nonverbal behavior training on accuracy in deception detection with the inclusion of a bogus training control group. *Western Journal of Communication*, 69, 203–217.

Levy, S. (2007, August 27). Facebook grows up. *Newsweek*, pp. 41–46.

Lewin, K., Lippitt, R., & White, R. K. (1939). Patterns of aggressive behavior in experimentally created social climates. *Journal of Social Psychology*, 10, 271–299.

Lewin, M. R., McNeil, D. W., & Lipson, J. M. (1996). Enduring without avoiding: Pauses and verbal dysfluencies in public speaking fear. *Journal of Psychopathology and Behavioral Assessment*, 18, 387–402.

Lewis, M. H., & Reinsch, N. L. (1988). Listening in organizational environments. *Journal of Business Communication*, 25, 49–67.

Lewis, R. D. (1996). *When cultures collide: Managing successfully across cultures*. London: Brealey.

Li, C. (1975). *Path analysis: A primer*. Pacific Grove, CA: Boxwood Press.

Li, N. P., Bailey, J. M., Kenrick, D. T., & Linsenmeier, J. A. W. (2002). The necessities and luxuries of mate preferences: Testing the tradeoffs. *Journal of Personality and Social Psychology*, 82, 947–955.

Liang, B., Tracy, A. J., Taylor, C. A., & Williams, L. M. (2002). Mentoring college-age women: A relational approach. *American Journal of Community Psychology*, 30, 271–288.

Lilienfeld, S. O., & Arkowitz, H. (2010, May/June). Are men the more belligerent sex? *Scientific American Mind*, pp. 64–65.

Linder, M., & Nygaard, I. (1998). *Void where prohibited: Rest breaks and the right to urinate on company time*. Ithaca, NY: Cornell University Press.

Lindsey, A. E., & Zakahi, W. R. (2006). Perceptions of men and women departing from conversational sex-role stereotypes. In K. Dindia & D. J. Canary (Eds.), *Sex differences and similarities in communication*. Mahwah, NJ: Erlbaum.

Lindsey, L. L. M., & Yun, K. A. (2003). Examining the persuasive effect of statistical messages: A test of mediating relationships. *Communication Studies*, 54, 306–322.

Linville, P. W., Fischer, G. W., & Fischoff, B. (1992). Perceived risk and decision-making involving AIDS. In J. B. Pryor & G. D. Reeder (Eds.), *The social psychology of HIV infection*. Hillsdale, NJ: Erlbaum.

Lipnack, J., & Stamps, J. (1997). *Virtual teams: Reaching across space, time, and organizations with technology*. New York: Wiley.

Lipstadt, D. (1993). *Denying the holocaust: The growing assault on truth and memory*. New York: Penguin.

Liptak, A. (2008, February 28). 1 in 100 U. S. adults behind bars, new study says. *The New York Times*. [Online]. Available at: http://www.nytimes.com/2008/02/28/us/28cnd-prison.html

Littlejohn, S. W., & Foss, K. A. (2008). *Theories of human communication*. Belmont, CA: Thomson/Wadsworth.

Liu, M. (2009). The intrapersonal and interpersonal effects of anger on negotiation strategies: A cross-cultural investigation. *Human Communication Research*, 35, 148–169.

Lock, C. (2004, July 31). Deception detection: Psychologists try to learn how to spot a liar. *Science News*, 166, 72–76.

Locke, J. (1998). *The de-voicing of society: Why we don't talk to each other anymore*. New York: Simon & Schuster.

Lodge, M., & Taber, C. S. (2005). The automaticity of affect for political candidates, parties, and issues: An experimental test of the hot cognition hypothesis. *Political Psychology*,.26, 455–482.

Loftus, E., & Palmer, J. (1974). Reconstruction of automobile destruction: An example of the interaction between language and memory. *Journal of Verbal Learning and Verbal Behavior*, 13, 585–589.

Loftus, E., & Zanni, G. (1975). Eyewitness testimony: The influence of the wording of a question. *Bulletin of the Psychonomic Society*, 5, 86–88.

Logan, J. S., Lively, S. E., & Pisoni, D. B. (1991). Training Japanese listeners to identify English /r/ and /1/: A first report. *Journal of the Acoustical Society of America*, 89, 874–876.

Lohr, J. M., Olatunji, B. O., Baumeister, R. F., & Bushman, B. J. (2007). The pseudopsychology of anger venting and empirically supported alternatives that do no harm. *Scientific Review of Mental Health Practice*, 5, 54–65.

Loots, G., & Devise, I. (2003). The use of visual-tactile communication strategies by deaf and hearing fathers and mothers of deaf infants. *Journal of Deaf Studies and Deaf Education*, 8, 31–43.

Lorenzo, G. L., Biesanz, J. C., & human, L. J. (2010). What is beautiful is good and more accurately understood: Physical attractiveness and accuracy in first impressions of personality. *Psychological Science*, 21, 1777–1782.

Loveday, L. (1986). *Explorations in Japanese sociolinguistics*. Philadelphia: Benjamins.

Lovett, F. (1997). Thinking about values. *Responsive Community*, 7, 87.

Lowry, P. B., Roberts, T. L., Romano, N. C., & Cheney, P. D. (2006). The impact of group size and social presence on small-group communication: Does computer-mediated communication make a difference? *Small Group Research*, 37, 631–661.

Lucas, S. E., & Medhurst, M. J. (2008). *Words of a century: The top 100 American speeches, 1900-1999*. New York: Oxford University Press.

Luck, S. J., & Vecera, S. P. (2002). Attention. In H. Pashler & S. Yantis (Eds.), *Steven's handbook of experimental psychology. Vol. 1: Sensation and perception*. New York: Wiley.

Luckmann, J. (1999). *Transcultural communication*. Albany, NY: Delmar.

Luckow, A., Reifman, A., & McIntosh, D. N. (1998, August). *Gender differences in coping: A meta-analysis*. Presented to the annual meeting of the American Psychological Association, San Francisco.

Lulofs, R. (1994). *Conflict: From theory to action*. Scottsdale, AZ: Gorsuch Scarisbrick.

Luong, A., & Rogelberg, S. G. (2005). Meetings and more meetings: The relationship between meeting load and the daily well-being of employees. *Group Dynamics: Theory, Research, and Practice*, 9, 58–67.

Lustig, M. W., & Koester, J. (2003). *Intercultural competence: Interpersonal communication across cultures*. New York: Longman.

Lutgen-Sandvik, P. (2006). Take this job and . . . : Quitting and other forms of resistance to workplace bullying. *Communication Monographs*, 73, 406–433.

Lutgen-Sandvik, P., & Sypher, B. D. (2009). Workplace bullying: Causes, consequences, and corrections. In P. Lutgen-Sandvik & B. D. Sypher (Eds.), *Destructive organizational communication*. New York: Routledge.

Lutgen-Sandvik, P., Tracy, S., & Alberts, J. (2005, February). *Burned by bullying in the American workplace: A first time study of U.S. prevalence and delineation of bullying "degree."* Paper presented at the Western States Communication Convention, San Francisco.

Lutgen-Sandvik, P., Tracy, S. J., & Alberts, J. K. (2007). Burned by bullying in the American workplace: Prevalence, perception, degree, and impact. *Journal of Management Studies, 44*(6), 837–862.

Lydgate, C. (2007, July 20). What the #$! Is Ramtha? *Willamette Week.* [Online]. Available at: http://www.wweek.com/popup/print.php?index-5860

Lying in America. (1987, February 23). *U.S. News & World Report,* pp. 54–61.

Lying is part of everyday life, research confirms. (1996). *Nando.net.* [Online]. Available at: http://www.nando.net/newsroom/ntm/health/061096/health 16_10972.html

Lynch, J. J. (2000). *A cry unheard: New insights into the medical consequences of loneliness.* Baltimore, MD: Bancroft Press.

Maass, A., Cadinu, M., Guarnieri, G., & Grasselli, A. (2003). Sexual harassment under social identity threat: The computer harassment paradigm. *Journal of Personality and Social Psychology,* 85, 853–870.

Maccoby, E. E. (1998). *The two sexes: Growing up apart, coming together.* Cambridge, MA: Harvard University Press.

Maccoby, E., & Mnookin, R. (1992). *Dividing the child: Social and legal dilemmas of custody.* Cambridge, MA: Harvard University Press.

MacDonald, G., Zanna, M. P., & Holmes, J. G. (2000). An experimental test of the role of alcohol in relationship conflict. *Journal of Experimental Social Psychology,* 36, 182–194.

Maddieson, I. (1984). *Patterns of sound.* Cambridge, UK: Cambridge University Press.

Magley, V. J. (2002). Coping with sexual harassment: Reconceptualizing women's resistance. *Journal of Personality and Social Psychology,* 83, 930–946.

Maher, S. (2011, May 24). Saturday was spiritual Rapture, predictor says. *San Jose Mercury News,* B1, B5.

Major, B., Kaiser, C. R., & McCoy, S. K. (2003). It's not my fault: When and why attributions to prejudice protect self-esteem. *Personality and Social Psychology Bulletin,* 29, 772–781.

Makau, J. M., & Marty, D. L. (2001). *Cooperative argumentation: A model for deliberative community.* Prospect Heights, IL: Waveland Press.

Making the grade: What American workers think should be done to improve education. (2001). *John J. Heldrich Center for Workforce Development.* [Online]. Available at: www.heldrich.rutgers.edu/worktrends.cfm

Mallory, J. (1999, November/December). Sexual assault in prison: The numbers are far from funny. *The Touchstone,* pp. 1–4.

Mancini, M. (2003). *Selling destinations: Geography for the travel professional.* Clifton Park, NY: Thomson/Selmar Learning.

Mandelbaum, D. G. (Ed.). (1949). *Selected writings of Edward Sapir.* Los Angeles: University of California Press.

Maner, J. K., Gailliot, M. T. & Miller, S. L. (2009). The implicit cognition of relationship maintenance: Inattention to attractive alternatives. *Journal of Experimental Social Psychology,* 45, 174–179.

Mannix, E., & Neale, M. A. (2005). What differences make a difference: The promise and reality of diverse teams in organizations. *Psychological Science in the Public Interest,* 6, 31–55.

Mansfield, M. (1990). Political communication in decision-making groups. In D. Swanson & D. Nimmo (Eds.), *New directions in political communication: A resource book.* Newbury Park, CA: Sage.

Manusov, V., & Patterson, M. L. (Eds.). (2006). *The Sage handbook of nonverbal communication.* Thousand Oaks, CA: Sage.

Marano, H. E. (1997, November). Gottman and Gray: The two Johns. *Psychology Today,* p. 6.

Marantz, A. (2005, November 21). The dreaded middle seat. *Scientific American Mind,* p. 9.

March 2010 web server survey. (2010, March). *Netcraft* [Online]. Available at: http://news.netcraft.com/

Marcus, D. (1999, March 22). When granny goes online. *U.S. News & World Report,* pp. 61–62.

Marcus-Newhall, A., Miller, N., Holtz, R., & Brewer, M. B. (1993). Cross-cutting category membership in role assignment: A means of reducing intergroup bias. *British Journal of Social Psychology,* 32, 125–145.

Marek, C. I, Wanzer, M. B., & Knapp, J. L. (2004). An exploratory investigation of the relationship between roommates' first impressions and subsequent communication patterns. *Communication Research Reports,* 21, 210–220.

Markey, C. N. (2005). Relations between body image and dieting behaviors: An examination of gender differences. *Sex Roles: A Journal of Research,* 53, 519–530.

Markey, C. N., Markey, P. M., & Birch, L. L. (2004). Understanding women's body satisfaction: The role of husbands. *Sex Roles: A Journal of Research,* 51, 209–216.

Marklein, M. B. (2007, December 18). College a time of seeking. *USA Today,* p. 6D.

Marklein, M. N. B. (2008, January 24). Study: Colleges shouldn't fret over hands-on parents. *USA Today,* p. 8D.

Markus, H., & Kitayama, S. (1991). Culture and the self: Implications for cognition, emotion, and motivation. *Psychological Review,* 98, 224–253.

Marsh, A. A., Elfenbein, H. A., & Ambady, N. (2007). Separated by a common language: Nonverbal accents and cultural stereotypes about Americans and Australians. *Journal of Cross-Cultural Psychology,* 38, 284–301.

Martell, R. F., Lane, D. M., & Emrich, C. (1996). Male-female differences: A computer simulation. *American Psychologist*, 51, 157–158.

Martin, J., & Nakayama, T. (2007). *Intercultural communication in contexts*. New York: McGraw-Hill.

Martin, J., & Nakayama, T. (2008). *Experiencing intercultural communication: An introduction*. New York: McGraw-Hill.

Martin, K. A., Moritz, S. E., & Hall, C. R. (1999). Imagery use in sport: A literature review and applied model. *Sport Psychologist*, 13, 245–268.

Martin, M. M., & Rubin, R. B. (1994). Development of a communication flexibility measure. *Southern Communication Journal*, 59, 171–178.

Mather, M., & Lavery, D. (2010, September). In U.S., proportion married at lowest recorded levels. *Population Reference Bureau*. [Online]. Available at: http://www.prb.org/Articles/2010/usmarriagedecline.aspx

Mathews, J. (2007, November 5). Poll elevates "helicopter parents." *San Jose Mercury News*, p. 5A.

Matlin, M. (1992). *Psychology*. Fort Worth, TX: Harcourt Brace Jovanovich.

Matsumoto, D. (1990). Cultural influences on facial expressions of emotion. *Southern Communication Journal*, 56, 128–137.

Matthews, R. A., Del Priore, R. E., Acitelli, L. K., & Barnes-Farrell, J. L. (2006). Work-to-relationship conflict: Crossover effects in dual-earner couples. *Journal of Occupational Health Psychology*, 11, 228–240.

Mattioli, D. (2010, March 23). More men make harassment claims. *The Wall Street Journal*. [Online]. Available at: http://online.wsj.com/article/SB10001424052748704117304575137881438719028.html#printMode

Maxfield, D., Grenny, J., McMillan, R., Patterson, K., & Switzler, A. (2005). Silence kills: The seven crucial conversations in healthcare. *VitalSmarts*. [Online]. Available at: http://www.silencekills.com/UPDL/SilenceKillsExecSummary.pdf

May, P. (2002, March 22). Jury says it's murder. *San Jose Mercury News*, p. 18A.

May, P. (2010, June 28). Tattoo nation. *San Jose Mercury News*, pp. A1, A8.

Mayer, R. E. (Ed.). (2005). *The Cambridge handbook of multimedia learning*. Cambridge, MA: Cambridge University Press.

Mayk, V. (2010, November 29). Wilkes University professors examine use of text messaging in the college classroom. *Latest Wilkes News Archives*. [Online]. Available at: http://www.wilkes.edu/pages/194.asp?item=61477

Mazer, J. P., & Hunt, S. K. (2008a). Cool communication in the classroom: A preliminary examination of student perceptions of instructor use of slang. *Qualitative Research Reports in Communication*, 9, 20–28.

Mazer, J. P., & Hunt, S. K. (2008b). The effects of instructor use of positive and negative slang on student motivation, affective learning, and classroom climate. *Communication Research Reports*, 25, 44–55.

Maznevski, M. L., & Chudoba, K. M. (2000). Bridging space over time: Global virtual team dynamics and effectiveness. *Organization Science*, 11, 473–492.

McAllister, S. (2008, December 12). Employment law: Excessive bathroom breaks. *AllExperts*. [Online]. Available at: http://en.allexperts.com/q/Employment-Law-924/2008/12/Excessive-bathroom-breaks.htm

McCabe, D. L., Trevino, L. K., & Butterfield, K. D. (2001). Cheating in academic institutions: A decade of research. *Ethics and Behavior*, 11, 219–232.

McCabe, M. P., & Ricciardelli, L. A. (2004). Weight and shape concerns of boys and men. In J. K. Thompson (Ed.), *Handbook of eating disorders and obesity*. Washington, DC: American Psychological Association.

McCall, W. (1996, June 25). The hand that holds the remote rules the most. *San Jose Mercury News*, p. D1.

McClure, R. (2007, June 3). A tip: American gratuities seen as excessive and rude abroad. *San Jose Mercury News*, pp. 1TR, 7TR.

McConnell, A. R., & Fazio, R. H. (1996). Women as men and people: Effects of gender marked language. *Personality and Social Psychology Bulletin*, 22, 1004–1013.

McConnell, J. H. (1995). *Are you communicating? You can't manage without it*. New York: McGraw-Hill.

McCoy, S. L., Tun, P. A., Cox, L. C., & Wingfield, A. (2005, July 12). Aging in a fast-paced world: Rapid speech and its effect on understanding. *ASHA Leader*, pp. 12, 30–31.

McCoy, S. L., Tun, P. A., & Wingfield, A. (2005, July 12). Aging in a fast-paced world: Rapid speech and its effect on understanding. *ASHA Leader*, pp. 12, 30–31.

McCrae, R. R., Martin, T. A., Hrebickove, M., Urbanek, T., Willemsen, G., & Costa, P. T. (2008). Personality trait similarity between spouses in four cultures. *Journal of Personality*, 76, 1137–1163.

McCroskey, J. C., & Richmond, V. P. (1992). Communication apprehension and small group communication. In R. S. Cathcart & L. A. Samovar (Eds.), *Small group communication: A reader*. Dubuque, IA: Brown.

McCroskey, J. C., Fayer, J. M., & Richmond, V. P. (1985). Don't speak to me in English: Communication apprehension in Puerto Rico. *Communication Quarterly*, 33, 185–192.

McCullough, M., Rochal, K. C., & Worthington, E. L. (1997). Interpersonal forgiving in close relationships. *Journal of Personality and Social Psychology*, 73, 321–336.

McDaniel, E. R. (2000). In L. A. Samovar & R. E. Porter (Eds.), *Intercultural communication: A reader*. Belmont, CA: Wadsworth.

McDaniel, E. R. (2003). Japanese nonverbal communication: A reflection of cultural themes. In L. A. Samovar & R. E. Porter (Eds.), *Intercultural communication: A reader*. Belmont, CA: Thomson/Wadsworth.

McDaniel, E. R., & Andersen, P. (1995, May). *Intercultural variations in tactile communication: An empirical field study*. Paper presented at a meeting of the International Communication Association, Albuquerque, NM.

McDonald, J. (1998, January/February). 200% probability and beyond: The compelling nature of extraordinary claims in the absence of alternative explanations. *Skeptical Inquirer*, pp. 45–49.

McGee, D. S., & Cegala, D. J. (1998). Patient communication skills training for improved competence in the primary care medical consultation. *Journal of Applied Communication Research*, 26, 412–430.

McGinn, D. (2000, October 16). Mired in meetings. *Newsweek*, pp. 52–54.

McGirk, J. (1998, February). You're not fat, you're in the wrong country. *Marie Claire*, pp. 52–56.

McGonagle, K. A., Kessler, R. C., & Gotlif, I. H. (1993). The effects of marital disagreement style, frequency, and outcome on marital disruption. *Journal of Social and Personal Relationships*, 9, 507–524.

McGrath, M. (2007, January). Methamphetamine in Montana: A preliminary report on trends and impact. *Montana Meth Project*. [Online]. Available at: http://www.montanameth.org/documents/MT_AG_Report

McGrath, M. (2008, April). *Methamphetamine in Montana: A follow-up report on trends and progress*. [Online]. Available at: http://www.doj.mt.gov/news/releases2008/20080331report.pdf

McGuinnies, E., & Ward, C. (1980). Better liked than right: Trustworthiness and expertise as factors in credibility. *Personality and Social Psychology Bulletin*, 6, 467–472.

McGuire, W. (1964). Inducing resistance to persuasion: Some contemporary approaches. In L. Berkowitz (Ed.), *Advances in experimental social psychology*. New York: Academic Press.

McKay, M., Rogers, P., & McKay, J. (1989). *When anger hurts: Quieting the storm within*. Oakland, CA: New Harbinger.

McKibben, W. F., Goetz, A. T., Shackelford, T. K., Schipper, L. D., Starratt, V. G., & Stewart-Williams, S. (2007). Why do men insult their intimate partners? *Personality and Individual Differences*, 43, 231–241.

McKimmie, B. M., Terry, D. J., Hogg, M. A., Manstead, A. S. R., Spears, R., & Doosje, B. (2003). I'm a hypocrite, but so is everyone else: Group support and the reduction of cognitive dissonance. *Group Dynamics: Theory, Research, and Practice*, 7, 214–224.

McLaughlin, S. (1996). The dirty truth about your kitchen: Using common sense to prevent food poisoning. In L. G. Schnoor (Ed.), *Winning orations*. Northfield, MN: Interstate Oratorical Association.

McLeod, P. L., Lobel, S. A., & Cox, T. H. (1996). Ethnic diversity and creativity in small groups. *Small Group Research*, 27, 248–264.

McNatt, D. B. (2000). Ancient Pygmalion joins contemporary management: A meta-analysis of the result. *Journal of Applied Psychology*, 85, 314–322.

McNeil, B. J., Pauker, S. G., Sox, H. C., & Tversky, A. (1982). On the elicitation of preferences for alternative therapies. *New England Journal of Medicine*, 306, 1259–1262.

McPherson, M., Smith-Lovin, L., & Brashears, M. E. (2006). Social isolation in America: Changes in core discussion networks over two decades. *American Sociological Review*, 71, 353–375.

McVay, J. C., & Kane, M. J. (2009). Conducting the train of thought: Working memory capacity, goal neglect, and mind wandering in an executive-control task. *Journal of Experimental Psychology: Learning, Memory, and Cognition*, 35, 196–204.

Mecca, S. J., & Rubin, L. J. (1999). Definitional research on African American students and sexual harassment. *Psychology of Women Quarterly*, 23, 813.

Meg Whitman spent fortune to come in 2nd in California governor's race. (2011, February 1). *Fox News.com*. [Online]. Available at: http://www.foxnews.com/politics/2011/02/01/meg-whitman-spent-fortune-come-nd-california-governors-race/

Mehl, M., & Pennebaker, J. (2002). *Mapping students' natural language use in everyday conversations*. Paper presented at the third annual meeting of the Society for Personality and Social Psychology, Savannah, GA.

Mehl, M. R., Vazire, S., Holleran, S. E., & Clark, C. S. (2010). Eavesdropping on happiness: Well-being is related to having less small talk and more substantive conversations. *Psychological Science*, 21, 539–541.

Mehrabian, A. (1971). *Silent messages*. Belmont, CA: Wadsworth.

Mehrabian, A. (1995). *Intercultural encounters: The fundamentals of intercultural communication*. Englewood, CO: Morton.

Meleis, A. F., & Meleis, M. (1998). Egyptian-Americans. In L. D. Purnell & B. J. Paulanka (Eds.), *Transcultural health care: A culturally competent approach*. Philadelphia: Davis.

Member FAQs. (2011). *Office of the Clerk, U. S. House of Representatives*. [Online]. Available at: http://clerk.house.gov/member_info/memberfaq.html

Menon, M., Tobin, D. D., Corby, B. C., Menon, M., Hodges, E. V., & Perry, D. G. (2007). The developmental costs of high self-esteem for antisocial children. *Child Development*, 78, 1627–1639.

Menzel, K. E., & Carrell, L. J. (1994). The relationship between preparation and performance in public speaking. *Communication Education*, 43, 17–26.

Mercer, G., & Benjamin, J. (1980). Spatial behavior of university undergraduates in double-occupancy residence room: An inventory of effects. *Journal of Applied Social Psychology*, 10, 32–44.

Merolla, A. J. (2008). Communicating forgiveness in friendships and dating relationships. *Communication Studies*, 59, 114–131.

Message of hope. (1998, July 24). *USA Weekend*, pp. 9–10.

Messman, S. J., Canary, D. J., & Hause, K. S. (2000). Motives to remain platonic, equity, and the use of maintenance strategies in opposite-sex friendships. *Journal of Social and Personal Relationships*, 17, 67–94.

Meston, C. M., & Buss, D. M. (2009). *Why women have sex: Understanding sexual motivations from adventure to revenge (and everything in between)*. New York: Times Books.

Metts, S., Cupach, N., & Imahori, T. (1992). Perceptions of sexual compliance resisting messages in three types of cross-sex relationships. *Western Journal of Communication*, 56, 1–17.

Micciche, T., Pryor, B., & Butler, J. (2000). A test of Monroe's Motivated Sequence for its effect on ratings of message organization and attitude change. *Psychological Reports*, 86, 1135–1138.

Mikulan, S. (2002). Downtown dog days. *LA Weekly*. [Online]. Available at: http://www.laweekly.com/ink/02/16/open-mikulan.shtml

Milbank, D. (2002, April 17). Bush gaffes get an official fix up. *San Jose Mercury News*, p. 8A.

Milgram, S. (1974). *Obedience to authority*. New York: Harper & Row.

Miller, A. G. (1986). *The obedience experiments: A case study of controversy in social science*. Westport, CT: Praeger.

Miller, A. G., Ashton, W., & Mishal, M. (1990). Beliefs concerning the features of constrained behavior: A basis for the fundamental attribution error. *Journal of Personality and Social Psychology*, 59, 635–650.

Miller, C. (1989). The social psychological effects of group decision rules. In P. Paulus (Ed.), *Psychology of group influence*. Hillsdale, NJ: Erlbaum.

Miller, J. G. (1984). Culture and the development of everyday social explanation. *Journal of Personality and Social Psychology*, 46, 961–978.

Miller, K. (2005). *Communication theories: Perspectives, processes, and contexts*. New York: McGraw-Hill.

Miller, N., Maruyama, G., Beaber, R. J., & Valone, K. (1976). Speed of speech and persuasion. *Journal of Personality and Social Psychology*, 34, 615–624.

Miller, P. J., Fung, H., & Mintz, J. (1996). Self-construction through narrative practices: A Chinese and American comparison of early socialization. *Ethos*, 24, 237–280.

Mitchell, T. R., & Lee, T. W. (2001). The unfolding model of voluntary turnover and job embeddedness: Foundations for a comprehensive theory of attachment. In B. M. Staw & R. I. Sutton (Eds.), *Research in Organizational Behavior*. Greenwich, CT: JAI Press.

Miura, A., & Hida, M. (2004). Synergy between diversity and similarity in group-idea generation. *Small Group Research*, 35, 540–564.

Mobius, M. M., & Rosenblat, T. S. (2006). Why beauty matters. *American Economic Review*, 96, 222–235.

Moghaddam, F. M. (1998). *Social psychology: Exploring universals across cultures*. New York: Freeman.

Moghaddam, F., Taylor, D., & Wright, S. (1993). *Social psychology in cross-cultural perspective*. New York: Freeman.

Mohamed, A., & Wiebe, F. (1996). Toward a process theory of groupthink. *Small Group Research*, 27, 416–430.

Mole, P. (2002, November/December). Are skeptics cynical? Popular misunderstandings of skepticism. *Skeptical Inquirer*, pp. 44–48.

Mongeau, P. A. (1998). Another look at fear-arousing persuasive appeals. In M. Allen & R. W. Weiss (Eds.), *Persuasion: Advances through meta-analysis*. Cresskill, NJ: Hampton Press.

Mongeau, P. A., Serewicz, M. C., Henningsen, M. L., & Davis, K. L. (2006). Sex differences in the transition to a heterosexual romantic relationship. In K. Dindia & D. J. Canary (Eds.), *Sex differences and similarities in communication*. Mahwah, NJ: Erlbaum.

Monmaney, T. (1993, September 20). Marshall's hunch. *The New Yorker*, pp. 64–72.

Monsour, M. (2002). *Women and men as friends: Relationships across the lifespan in the 21st century*. Mahwah, NJ: Erlbaum.

Montana Meth Project (2008). *Meth Project Organization*. [Online]. Available at: http://www.montanameth.org/About_Us/results.php

More Japanese think wives need not stay home. (2005, February 6). *Reuters UK*. [Online]. Available at: http://today.reuters.co.uk/News/newsArticle.aspx?type=oddlyEnough

More than one in four college students take courses online. (2010, January 28). *Education-Portal.com*. [Online]. Available at: http://education-portal.com/articles/More_Than_One_in_Four_College_Students_Take_Courses_Online.html

More than seven trillion SMS messages will be sent in 2011. *ABI Research*. [Online]. Available at: http://www.abiresearch.com/press/3584-More+than+Seven+Trillion+SMS_Messages+Will_Be+Sent+in+2011

More think it is important to give than to receive on Valentine's Day according to new survey. *Harris Interactive*. [Online]. Available at: http://www.harrisinteractive.com/news/allnewsbydate.asp?NewsID=1018

More women seeking tattoo removal than men: Survey. (2008, July 22). *The Med Guru*. [Online]. Available at: http://www.themedguru.com/articles/more_women_seeking_tattoo_removal_than_men_survey-8616555.html

Moreland, R. L. (2010). Are dyads really groups? *Small Group Research*, 41, 251–267.

Morelli, G. A., Rogoff, B., Oppenheim, D., & Goldsmith, D. (1992). Cultural variation in infants' sleeping arrangements: Questions of independence. *Developmental Psychology*, 28, 604–613.

Morreale, S. P. & Pearson, J. C. (2008). Why communication education is important: The centrality of the discipline in the 21st century. *Communication Education*, 57, 224–240.

Morris, D. (1977). *Manwatching: A field guide to human behavior*. New York: Abrams.

Morris, D. (1985). *Body watchers*. New York: Crown.

Morris, D., Collett, P., Marsh, P., & O'Shaughnessy, M. (1979). *Gestures: Their origins and distribution*. New York: Stein & Day.

Morris, M. W., & Peng, K. (1994). Culture and cause: American and Chinese attributions for social and physical events. *Journal of Personality and Social Psychology*, 67, 949–971.

Morris, T., & Gorham, J. (1996). Fashion in the classroom: Effects of attire on student perceptions of instructors in college classes. *Communication Education*, 45, 135–148.

Morrison, P. (2007, November 3). If "truthiness" trumps truth, we know we're in trouble. *San Jose Mercury News*, p. 17A.

Morse, C. R., & Metts, S. (2011). Situational and communicative predictors of foregiveness following a relational transgression. *Western Journal of Communication*, 75, 239–258.

Morse, S., & Gergen, K. (1970). Social comparison, self-consistency and the concept of self. *Journal of Personality and Social Psychology*, 16, 149–156.

Morton, J. B., & Trehub, S. E. (2001). Children's understanding of emotion in speech. *Child Development*, 72, 834–843.

Motley, M. T. (1995). *Overcoming your fear of public speaking: A proven method*. New York: McGraw-Hill.

Motley, M.T. (1997). COM therapy. In J.A. Daly, J. C. McCroskey, J. Ayres, T. Hopf, & D. M. Ayres (Eds.), *Avoiding communication*. Cresskill, NJ: Hampton Press.

Movie content. (1999, August 12). *The Gallup poll 1999*. New York: Gallup.

Mudrack, P., & Farrell, G. (1995). An examination of functional role behavior and its consequences for individuals in group settings. *Small Group Research*, 26, 542–571.

Muehlenhard, C., Koralewski, M., Andrews, S., & Burdick, C. (1986). Verbal and nonverbal cues that convey interest in dating: Two studies. *Behavior Therapy*, 17, 404–419.

Mulac, A. (2006). The gender-linked language effect: Do language differences really make a difference? In K. Dindia & D. J. Canary (Eds.), *Sex differences and similarities in communication*. Mahwah, NJ: Erlbaum.

Mulac, A., & Bradac, J. (1995). Women's style in problem solving interaction: Powerless, or simply feminine? In P. Kalbfleisch & M. Cody (Eds.), *Gender, power, and communication in human relationships*. Hillsdale, NJ: Erlbaum.

Mullen, B., Anthony, T., Salas, E., & Driskill, J. (1994). Group cohesiveness and quality decision making: An integration of tests of the groupthink hypothesis. *Small Group Research*, 25, 189–204.

Murray, B. (1997, May). How important is teaching style to students? *APA Monitor*, p. 103.

Murray-Johnson, L., Witte, K., Liu, W., Hubbell, A., Sampson, J., & Morrison, K. (2001). Addressing cultural orientations in fear appeals: Promoting AIDS-protective behaviors among Mexican immigrant and African American adolescents and American and Taiwanese college students. *Journal of Health Communication*, 6, 335–358.

Mussweiler, T., Ruter, K., & Epstude, K. (2004). The ups and downs of social comparison: Mechanisms of assimilation and contrast. *Journal of Personality and Social Psychology*, 87, 832–844.

Mydans, S. (2007, April 29). As English's dominance continues, linguists see few threats to its rule. *Boston Globe*. [Online]. Available at: http://www.boston.com/news/world/asia/articles/2007.04/29/as_englishs_dominance

Myers, D. G. (2002). *Intuition: Its power and perils*. New Haven, CT: Yale University Press.

Myers, D. G. (2004). *Psychology*. New York: Worth Publishers.

Myers, S. A., & Goodboy, A. K. (2005). A study of grouphate in a course on small group communication. *Psychological Reports*, 97, 381–386.

Myerson, J. (2001). *IDEO: Masters of innovation*. London: Calmann & King.

Na, E. Y., & Loftus, E. F. (1998). Attitudes toward law and prisoners, conservative authoritarianism, attribution, and internal locus of control: Korean and American law students and undergraduates. *Journal of Cross-Cultural Psychology*, 29, 595–615.

Na, J., & Kitayama, S. (2011). Spontaneous trait inference is culture-specific: Behavioral and neural evidence. *Psychological Science*, 20, 1–8.

Nabi, R. L. (2002). Discrete emotions and persuasion. In J. P. Dillard & M. Pfau (Eds.), *The persuasion handbook: Developments in theory and practice*. Thousand Oaks, CA: Sage.

Namie, G. (2007). 2007 U.S. workplace bullying survey. *Workplace Bullying Institute*. [Online]. Available at: http://bullyinginstitute.org/wbi-zogby2.html

Nanda, S., & Warms, R. L. (1998). *Cultural anthropology*. Belmont, CA: Wadsworth.

Narcisco, J., & Burkett, T. (1975). *Declare yourself*. Englewood Cliffs, NJ: Prentice Hall.

National Archives and Records Administration. (1987). *Kennedy's inaugural address of 1961*. Washington, DC: U.S. Government Printing Office.

National Geographic-Roper Public Affairs Geographic Literacy Study (2006, May). *Final Report*. [Online]. Available at: http://www.nationalgeographic.com/foundation/pdf/NGSRoper2006Report.pdf

National survey of student engagement, 2006 annual report. (2006). [Online]. Available at: http://nsse.iub.edu/NSSE_2006_Annual_Report

Nattrass, N. (2007, September/October). AIDS denialism vs. science. *Skeptical Inquirer*, pp. 31–37.

Navigating today's complex dating scene. (2011, June). *Spirit*, 61–63.

Neff, K. D., & Harter, S. (2002). The authenticity of conflict resolutions among adult couples: Does women's other-oriented behavior reflect their true selves? *Sex Roles*, 47, 403–412.

Nelson, M. (1998). *Embracing victory: Life lessons in competition and compassion*. New York: Morrow.

Nelson, T. F., Xuan, A., Lee, H., Weitzman, E. R., & Wechsler, H. (2009). Persistence of heavy drinking and ensuing consequences at heavy drinking colleges. *Journal of Studies on Alcohol and Drugs*, 70, 726–734.

Neuliep, J. W. (2000). *Intercultural communication: A contextual approach*. New York: Houghton Mifflin.

Neuliep, J. W., & Ryan, D. J. (1998). The influence of intercultural communication apprehension and sociocommunicative orientation on uncertainty reduction during initial cross-cultural interaction. *Communication Quarterly*, 46, 88–99.

Neumann, R., & Strack, F. (2000). "Mood contagion": The automatic transfer of mood between persons. *Journal of Personality and Social Psychology*, 79, 211–223.

Nevid, J. S. (2011, May/June). Teaching the Millenials. *Observor*, 24, 53–56.

New forms of violence at work on the rise worldwide says the International Labor Organization (ILO): Bullying is "epidemic." (2006, June 14). *Workplace Bullying Institute*. [Online]. Available at: http://www.bullyinginstitute.org/bbstudies/iloepidemic.html

Newman, D., Hocking, J., & Turk, D. (2000, February 27). *At last, redemption for the physically unattractive: An updated examination of physical attractiveness as a dependent variable*. Paper presented at the Western Communication Convention, Sacramento, CA.

Newport, F. (2007, September 28). Black of African American? *Gallup*. [Online]. Available at: http://www.gallup.com/poll/28816/black-african-american.aspx

Newport, F. (2010, November 8). In U.S., 64% support death penalty in cases of murder. *Gallup*. [Online]. Available at: http://www.gallup.com/poll/144284/Support-Death-Penalty-Cases-Murder.aspx

Newton, M. (2002). *Savage girls and wild boys: A history of feral children*. New York: St. Martin's Press.

Ng, S. H. (2001). Influencing through the power of language. In J. P. Forgas & D. W. Kipling (Eds.), *Social influence: Direct and indirect processes*. Philadelphia: Psychology Press.

Nicholson, C. (2010, May/June). The humor gap. *Scientific American Mind*, pp. 38–45.

Nickerson, R. S. (1998). Confirmation bias: A ubiquitous phenomenon in many guises. *Review of General Psychology*, 2, 175–220.

Nicotera, A., & Rancer, A. (1994). The influence of sex on self-perception and social stereotyping of aggressive communication predispositions. *Western Journal of Communication*, 58, 283–307.

Nishida, T. (1991). *Sequence patterns of self-disclosure among Japanese and North American students*. Paper presented at the Conference on Communication in Japan and the United States, California State University, Fullerton.

Noe, R. (1988). Women and mentoring. *Academy of Management Review*, 13, 65–78.

Noelle, D. (1999, January/February). World's longest firewalk: Physicist leads hot trek for science in Pennsylvania. *Skeptical Inquirer*, pp. 5–6.

Noguchi, S. (2006, June 13). Teens turn away from e-mail. *San Jose Mercury News*, p. 1A.

Noguchi, S. (2008, June 25). Lifted lines in grads' speeches. *San Jose Mercury News*, pp. 1B, 5B.

Noller, P. (1993). Gender and emotional communication in marriage: Different cultures or differential social power? *Journal of Language and Social Psychology*, 12, 132–152.

Nonnemaker, S. E. (2009). Living behind bars? An investigation of gated communities in New Tampa, Florida. *Theses and Dissertations*. Paper 2121. [Online]. Available at: http://scholarcommons.usf.edu/etd/2121

Noonan, P. (1998). *Simply speaking: How to communicate your ideas with style, substance, and clarity*. New York: HarperCollins.

Norman, A. (2006). Untitled. In L. G. Schnoor & B. Wickelgren (Eds.), *Winning orations*. Mankato, MN: Interstate Oratorical Association.

Northouse, P. (2007). *Leadership: Theory and practice*. Thousand Oaks, CA: Sage.

Norton, M. I., Monin, B., Cooper, J., & Hogg, M. A. (2003). *Journal of Personality and Social Psychology*, 85, 47–62.

Notarius, C., & Markman, H. (1993). *We can work it out: Making sense of marital conflict*. New York: Putnam's.

Nunberg, G. (2003, June 8). In Mideast, language of compromise does exist. *San Jose Mercury News*, pp. 1P, 3P.

Nussbaum, B. (2004, May 17). The power of design. *Business Week*, pp. 86–94.

O'Brien, C. (2008, August 30). Tug of war over Wiki entry on Palin. *San Jose Mercury News*, p. 1C.

O'Brien, T. (1995, November 5). No jerks allowed. *West*, pp. 8–14.

O'Brien, T. (2007, September 20). Sex less important than the web for many Americans. *Switched*. [Online]. Available at: http://www.switched.com/2007/09/20/sex-less-important-than-the-web-for-many-americans/

O'Donohue, W. T., & Fisher, J. E. (2008). *Cognitive behavior therapy: Applying empirically supported techniques in your practice*. Hoboken, NJ: Wiley.

O'Keefe, D. (1990). *Persuasion: Theory and research*. Newbury Park, CA: Sage.

O'Leary, K., Curley, A., & Clark, C. (1985). Assertion training for abused wives: A potentially hazardous treatment. *Journal of Marital and Family Therapy*, 11, 319–322.

O'Neil, J. M., Good, G. E., & Holmes, S. (1995). Fifteen years of theory and research on men's gender role conflict: New paradigms for empirical research. In R. Levant & W. Pollock (Eds.), *The new psychology of men*. New York: Basic Books.

O'Sullivan, L. F., & Byers, E. S. (1992). College students' incorporation of initiator and restrictor roles in sexual dating interactions. *Journal of Sex Research*, 29, 435–446.

O'Sullivan, M. (2005). Emotional intelligence and deception detection: Why most people can't "read" others, but a few can. In R. E. Riggio & R. S. Feldman (Eds.), *Applications of nonverbal communication*. Mahwah, NJ: Erlbaum.

Oakes, J. (1985). *Keeping track: How schools structure inequality*. New Haven, CT: Yale University Press.

Obama Michigan graduation speech: Full text. (2010, May 1). *Huffington Post*. [Online]. Available at: http://www.huffingtonpost.com/2010/05/01obama-michigan-graduation_n_559688.html?view=print

Obama shoe photo seen as "insult" by some Israelis. (2009, June 10). *Huffington Post*. [Online]. Available at: http://www.huffingtonpost.com/2009/06/10/obama-phone-seen-as_n_213693.html?view=print

Offner, A. K., Kramer, T. J., & Winter, J. P. (1996). The effects of facilitation, recording and pauses upon group brainstorming. *Small Group Research*, 27, 283–298.

Ohl, J. (2006). Untitled. In L. G. Schnoor & B. Wickelgren (Eds.), *Winning orations*. Mankato, MN: Interstate Oratorical Association.

Okami, P. (1992). Child perpetrators of sexual abuse: The emergence of a problematic deviant category. *Journal of Sex Research*, 29, 109–130.

Olivardia, R., Pope, H. G., Borowiecki, J. J., & Cohane, G. H. (2004). Biceps and body image: The relationship between muscularity and self-esteem, depression, and eating disorder symptoms. *Psychology of Men and Masculinity*, 5, 112–120.

Oliver, M. B., & Hyde, J. S. (1993). Gender differences in sexuality: A meta-analysis. *Psychological Bulletin*, 114, 29–51.

Olivola, C. Y., & Todorov, A. (2010). Elected in 100 milliseconds: Appearance-based trait inferences and voting. *Journal of Nonverbal Behavior*, 34, 83–110.

Olympic basketball/2008 Olympics. (2008). *InsideHoops.com*. [Online]. Available at: http://www.insidehoops.com/olympics.shtml

Omarzu, J. (2000). A disclosure decision model: Determining how and when individuals will self-disclose. *Personality and Social Psychology Review*, 4, 174–185.

Onishi, N. (2001, February 17). Fat is the ideal body shape in West Africa. *San Jose Mercury News*, p. 2A.

Onishi, N. (2007, July 16). Japanese wary as they prepare to join juries. *San Jose Mercury News*, p. 8A.

Oprah: A heavenly body? Survey finds talk-show host a celestial shoo-in. (1997, March 31). *U.S. News & World Report*, p. 18.

Orlowski, A. (2005, October 18). *Wikipedia* founder admits to serious quality problems. *The Register*. [Online]. Available at: http://www.theregister.co.uk/2005/10/18/wikipedia_quality_problem/print.html

Osgood, G. (1969). The nature of measurement of meaning. In J. Snider & C. Osgood (Eds.), *The semantic differential technique*. Chicago: Aldine.

Ostrom, M. (1999, March 18). Poll: Clinton disliked, but effective as ever. *San Jose Mercury News*, p. A10.

Oveis, C. (2010, January). *Thin slices of touch reveal affective style and relationship dynamics*. Paper presented at the 11th annual meeting of the Society for Personality and Social Psychology, Las Vegas, NV.

Owen, J. E., Boxley, L., Goldstein, M. S., Lee, J. H., Breen, N., & Rowland, J. H. (2010). Use of health-related online support groups: Population data from the California health interview survey complementarity and alternative medicine study. *Journal of Computer-Mediated Communication*, 15, 427–446.

Owen, W. F. (1987). The verbal expression of love by women and men as a critical communication event in personal relationships. *Women's Studies in Communication*, 10, 15–24.

Owens, L., Shute, R., & Slee, P. (2000). "Guess what I just heard!" Indirect aggression among teenage girls in Australia. *Aggressive Behavior*, 26, 57–66.

Oyserman, D., Coon, H. M., & Kemmelmeier, M. (2002). Rethinking individualism and collectivism: Evaluation of theoretical assumptions and meta-analyses. *Psychological Bulletin*, 128, 3–72.

Paetzold, R., & O'Leary-Kelly, A. (1993). Organizational communication and the legal dimensions of hostile work environment sexual harassment. In G. Kreps (Ed.), *Sexual harassment: Communication implications*. Cresskill, NJ: Hampton Press.

Paivio, A. (1969). Mental imagery in associative learning and memory. *Psychological Review*, 76, 241–263.

Palmer, P. (2000, October 9). Look closely at that bill. *Newsweek*, pp. 81–82.

Palomares, N. A. (2009). Women are sort of more tentative than men, aren't they? How men and women use tentative language differently, similarly, and counterstereotypically as a function of gender salience. *Communication Research*, 36, 538–560.

Park, D. C., & Huang, C-M. (2010). Culture wires the brain: A cognitive neuroscience perspective. *Perspectives on Psychological Science*, 5, 391–400.

Park, H., & Antonioni, D. (2007). Personality, reciprocity, and strength of conflict resolution strategy. *Journal of Research in Personality*, 41, 110–125.

Park, H. S., Levine, T. R., McCornack, S. A., Morrison, K., & Ferrara, M. (2002). How people really detect lies. *Communication Monographs*, 69, 144–157.

Park, R. (1997, September/October). Alternative medicine and the laws of physics. *Skeptical Inquirer*, pp. 21, 24–28.

Park, R. (2000). *Voodoo science: The road from foolishness to fraud.* New York: Oxford University Press.

Parker, E. S., Cahill, L., & McGaugh, J. I. (2006). A case of unusual autobiographical remembering. *Neurocase,* 12, 35–49.

Parker, S. K., & Griffin, M. A. (2002). What is so bad about a little name-calling? Negative consequences of gender harassment for overperformance demands and distress. *Journal of Occupational Health Psychology,* 7, 195–210.

Parker-Pope, T. (2010, May 10). The science of a happy marriage. *The New York Times.* [Online]. Available at: http://well.blogs.nytimes.com/2010/05/10/tracking-the-science-of-commitment/

Parks, C., & Vu, A. (1994). Social dilemma of individuals from highly individualist and collectivist cultures. *Journal of Conflict Resolution,* 3, 708–718.

Parks, M. R. (2007). *Personal relationships and personal networks.* Mahwah, NJ: Erlbaum.

Pashler, H. E. (1998). *The psychology of attention.* Cambridge, MA: MIT Press.

Passer, M. W., & Smith, R. E. (2004). *Psychology: The science of mind and behavior.* New York: McGraw-Hill.

Pasupathi, M., Cartensen, L. L., Levenson, R. W., & Gottman, J. M. (1999). Responsive listening in long-married couples: A psycholinguistic perspective. *Journal of Nonverbal Behavior,* 23, 173–193.

Patterson, M., Powell, J., & Lenihan, M. (1986). Touch, compliance, and interpersonal affects. *Journal of Nonverbal Behavior,* 10, 41–50.

Paulos, J. A. (1988). *Innumeracy: Mathematical illiteracy and its consequences.* New York: Hill & Wang.

Paulos, J. A. (1994, March). Counting on dyscalculia. *Discourse,* pp. 30–36.

Pavitt, C. (1999). Theorizing about the group communication-leadership relationship. In L. R. Frey, D. S. Gouran, & M. S. Poole (Eds.), *The handbook of group communication theory and research.* Thousand Oaks, CA: Sage.

Pavitt, C., & Curtis, E. (1994). *Small group discussion.* Scottsdale, AZ: Gorsuch Scarisbrick.

Pavitt, C., & Haight, L. (1985). The "competent communicator" as a cognitive prototype. *Human Communication Research,* 12, 225–241.

Pawlowski, D. R. (1998). Dialectical tensions in marital partners' accounts of their relationships." *Communication Quarterly,* 46, 396–416.

Pearson, C. M., Andersson, L. M., & Porath, C. L. (2000). Assessing and attacking workplace incivility. *Organizational Dynamics,* 29, 123–137.

Pearson, J. C., & Sessler, C. J. (1991, May). *Family communication and health: Maintaining marital satisfaction and quality of life.* Paper presented at the annual meeting of the International Communication Association, Chicago.

Pearson, P. (1997). *When she was bad: Women and the myth of innocence.* Toronto: Random House.

Penn, M. J., & Zalesne, E. K. (2007). *Microtrends: The small forces behind tomorrow's big changes.* New York: Twelve Press.

Peplau, L. A., & Spalding, L. R. (2000). The close relationships of lesbians, gay men, and bisexuals. In C. Hendrick & S. S. Hendrick (Eds.), *Close relationships: A sourcebook.* Thousand Oaks, CA: Sage.

Perloff, R. M. (2010). *The dynamics of persuasion: Communication and attitudes in the 21st century.* New York: Routledge.

Perret, G. (1994). *Classic one-liners.* New York: Sterling.

Pertaub, D., Slater, M., & Barker, C. (2002). An experiment on public speaking anxiety in response to three different types of virtual audiences. *Presence: Teleoperators and Virtual Environments,* 11, 670–678.

Peterson, C. (2000). The future of optimism. *American Psychologist,* 55, 44–55.

Peterson, M. S. (1997). Personnel interviewers' perception of the importance and adequacy of applicants' communication skills. *Communication Education,* 46, 287–291.

Petronio, S. (2002). *Boundaries of privacy: Dialectics of disclosure.* Albany: State University of New York Press.

Pettigrew, T., & Martin, J. (1987). Shaping the organizational context for black American inclusion. *Journal of Social Issues,* 43, 41–78.

Pettigrew, T. F., & Tropp, L. R. (2006). A meta-analytic test of intergroup contact theory. *Journal of Personality and Social Psychology,* 90, 751–783.

Petty, R., & Cacioppo, J. (1984). The effects of involvement on responses to argument quantity and quality: Central and peripheral routes to persuasion. *Journal of Personality and Social Psychology,* 46, 69–81.

Petty, R., & Cacioppo, J. (1986a). The elaboration likelihood model of persuasion. In L. Berkowitz (Ed.), *Advances in experimental social psychology* (Vol. 19). New York: Academic Press.

Petty, R., & Cacioppo, J. (1986b). *Communication and persuasion: Central and peripheral routes to attitude change.* New York: Springer-Verlag.

Petty, R., Kasmer, J., Haugtvedt, C., & Cacioppo, J. (1987). Source and message factors in persuasion: A reply to Stiff's critique of the elaboration likelihood model. *Communication Monographs,* 54, 233–249.

Petty, R. E., Rucker, D. D., Bizer, G. Y., & Cacioppo, J. T. (2004). The elaboration likelihood model in persuasion. In J. S. Seiter & R. H. Gass (Eds.), *Perspectives on persuasion, social influence, and compliance.* New York: Pearson.

Pew Internet & American Life Project. (2006, March 5). *Online dating: Americans who are seeking romance use the Internet to help them in their search, but there is still widespread public concern about the safety of online dating.* [Online]. Available at: www.pewinternet.org/pdfs/PIP_Online_Dating.pdf

Pew Research Center. (2007, July 1). *Generation gap in values, behaviors.* [Online]. Available at: http://pewresearch.org/assets/social/pdf/Marriage.pdf

Pew Research Center. (2009, June 29). *Growing old in America: Expectations vs. reality.*

[Online]. Available at: http://pewresearch.org/pubs/1296/aging-survey-expectations-versus-reality

Pfau, M., & Van Bockern, S. (1994). The persistence of inoculation in conferring resistance to smoking initiation among adolescents: The second year. *Human Communication Research*, 20, 413–430.

Pfau, M., Ivanov, B., Houston, B., Haigh, M., Sims, J., Gilchrist, E., Russell, J., Wigley, S., Eckstein, J., & Richert, N. (2005). Inoculation and mental processing: The instrumental role of associative networks in the process of resistance to counterattitudinal influence. *Communication Monographs*, 72, 414–441.

Pfau, M., Szabo, E. A., Anderson, J., Morrill, J., Zubric, J., & Wan, H. (2001). The role and impact of affect in the process of resistance to persuasion, *Human Communication Research*, 27, 216–252.

Pfeiffer, K., Cole, B., & Dada, M. K. (1998). Attributions for youth crime among British and Nigerian primary school children. *Journal of Social Psychology*, 138, 251–253.

Pileggi, S. (2010, January/February). The happy couple. *Scientific American Mind*, pp. 34–39.

Pinel, E. C. (1999). Stigma consciousness: The psychological legacy of social stereotypes. *Journal of Personality and Social Psychology*, 76, 114–128.

Pinel, E. C. (2002). Stigma consciousness in intergroup contexts: The power of conviction. *Journal of Experimental Social Psychology*, 38, 178–185.

Pinker, S. (1994). *The language instinct: How the mind creates language*. New York: Harper Collins.

Pinker, S. (1997). *How the mind works*. New York: Norton.

Pinker, S. (1999). *Words and rules: The ingredients of language*. New York: HarperCollins.

Pinker, S. (2007). *The stuff of thought: Language as a window into human nature*. New York: Viking Penguin.

Pinkley, R. L., & Northcraft, G. B. (2000). *Get paid what you're worth*. New York: St. Martin's Press.

Pitts, L. (2011, March 6). Prominent blogger dismisses accuracy as "no big deal." *San Jose Mercury News*, p. A13.

Plant, E. A., Kunstman, J. W., & Maner, J. K. (2010). You do not only hurt the one you love: Self-protective responses to attractive relationship alternatives. *Journal of Experimental Social Psychology*, 46, 474–477.

Plantronics study reveals how global professionals utilize new and traditional communication technologies to succeed at work. (2010, September 30). *Plantronics*. [Online]. Available at: http://press.plantronics.com/us/plantronics-study-reveals-how-the-global-professionals-utilize-new-and-traditional-communication-technologies-to-succeed-at-work/

Plester, B., Wood, C., & Bell, V. (2008). Txt msg n school literacy: Does mobile phone use adversely affect children's attainment? *Literacy*, 42, 137–144.

Pogrebin, L. C. (1987). *Among friends*. New York: McGraw-Hill.

Polidoro, M. (1999). It's all in the mind: On the mechanisms of deception in psychic fraud. In S. Della Sala (Ed.), *Mind myths: Exploring popular assumptions about the mind and brain*. Chichester, UK: Wiley.

Political bias affects brain activity, study finds. (2006, January 24). *MSNBC.com*. [Online]. Available at: http://www.msnbc.msn.com/id/11009379/

Politics. (2007). *MSNBC*. [Online]. Available at: www.msnbc.msn.com/id/105629041/

Poll: College students feel pressure to drink. (2000, June 20). *San Jose Mercury News*, p. 9A.

Poll: One in three aren't convinced Holocaust occurred. (1993, April 20). *San Jose Mercury News*, p. A1.

Pollack, I., & Pickett, J. M. (1964). Intelligibility of excerpts from fluent speech: Auditory vs. structural context. *Journal of Verbal Learning and Verbal Behavior*, 3, 79–84.

Poole, M. (2009, July 27). A's great Henderson cool at Cooperstown. *San Jose Mercury News*, pp. 1A, 6A.

Poole, M. S., & Zhang, H. (2005). Virtual teams. In S. A. Wheelan (Ed.), *The handbook of group research and practice*. Thousand Oaks, CA; Sage.

Poor sporting behavior incidents reported to NASO. (2007). *National Association of Sports Officials*. [Online]. Available at: http://www.naso.org/sportsmanship/badsports.html

Pope, H. G. (2004, March 28). The pressures behind steroid abuse: Young men-not just athletes-take risks for a big build. *San Jose Mercury News*, p. 1P.

Pope, H. G., Gruber, A. J., Mangweth, B., Bureau, B., deCol, C., Jouvent, R., & Hudson, J. I. (2000). Body image perception among men in three countries. *American Journal of Psychiatry*, 157, 1297–1301.

Pornpitakpan, C. (2004). The persuasiveness of source credibility: A critical review of five decades' evidence. *Journal of Applied Social Psychology*, 34, 243–281.

Porter, S., & ten Brinke, L. (2010). Truth about lies: What works in detecting high-stakes deception? *Legal and Criminological Psychology*, 15, 57–76.

Powell, G. N., & Graves, L. M. (2006). Gender and leadership: Perceptions and realities. In K. Dindia & D. J. Canary (Eds.), *Sex differences and similarities in communication*. Mahwah, NJ: Erlbaum.

Powell, J. L. (1988). A test of the knew-it-all-along effect in the 1984 presidential and statewide elections. *Journal of Applied Social Psychology*, 18, 760–773.

PowerPoint turns 20, as its creators ponder a dark side to success. (2007, June 20). *The Wall Street Journal*, p. B1.

Prager, K. J. (2000). Intimacy in personal relationships. In C. Hendrick & S. S. Hendrick (Eds.), *Close relationships: A sourcebook*. Thousand Oaks, CA: Sage.

Prager, K., & Buhrmester, D. (1998). Intimacy and need fulfillment in couple relationships. *Journal of Social and Personal Relationships*, 15, 435–469.

Praise thy employees survey says. (1994, September 13). *San Jose Mercury News*, p. E1.

Pratkanis, A., & Aronson, E. (2001). *Age of propaganda: The everyday use and abuse of persuasion*. New York: Freeman.

Pre-employment drug tests found almost 2% in state. (1990, May 24). *San Jose Mercury News*, p. 1A.

President Bush: Overall job rating. (2008, July 9). *PollingReport.com*. [Online]. Available at: http://www.pollingreport.com/BushJob.htm

President George W. Bush to the 300th graduating class of Yale University. (2001, May 22). *Everything2.com*. [Online]. Available at: http://www.everything2.com/index.pl?node_id=1056073

Price, B. H., Gurvit, S., Weintraub, C., Geula, E., Leimkuhler, E., & Mesulum, M. (1993). Neuropsychological patterns and language deficits in 20 consecutive cases of autopsy-confirmed Alzheimer's disease. *Archives of Neurology*, 50, 931–937.

Price, J., & Davis, B. (2008). *The woman who can't forget: The extraordinary story of living with the most remarkable memory known to science*. New York: Free Press.

Prop 8 Twitter reaction proves major support for ruling. (2010, August 5). *Huffington Post*. [Online]. Available at: http://www.huffingtonpost.com/2010/08/05/prop-8-twitter-reaction-p_n_671898.html

Provine, R. R. (2000). *Laughter: A scientific investigation*. New York: Viking.

Pruitt, D., & Rubin, J. (1986). *Social conflict: Escalation, stalemate, and settlement*. New York: Random House.

Purdy, M., & Borisoff, D. (1997). *Listening in everyday life*. Lanham, MD: University Press of America.

Putnam, F. W. (2010). Beyond sticks and stones. *American Journal of Psychiatry*, 167, 1422–1424.

Quinn, J. M., & Wood, W. (2004). Forewarnings of influence appeals: Inducing resistance and acceptance. In E. S. Knowles & J. A. Linn (Eds.), *Resistance and persuasion*. Mahwah, NJ: Erlbaum.

Raban, J. (1997, November 24). What the nanny trial tells us about transatlantic body language. *The New York Times*, p. 55.

Radford, B. (2001, January/February). Hotbed of skepticism: Firewalking held at Center for Inquiry International. *Skeptical Inquirer*, pp. 6–7.

Radmacher, K., & Azmitia, M. (2006). Are there gendered pathways to intimacy in early adolescents' and emerging adults' friendships? *Journal of Adolescent Research*, 21, 415–448.

Rainie, L. (2008, January 9). Pew Internet Project data memo. *Pew/Internet & American Life Project*. [Online]. Available at: http://www.pewinternet.org/pdfs/Pew_Videosharing

Rainie, L. Lenhart, A., Fox, S., Spooner, T., & Horrigan, J. (2000, May 10). Tracking online life. *Pew Internet*. [Online]. Available at: http://www.pewinternet.org/Reports/2000/Tracking-Online-Life/Summary-of-Findings/Findings.aspx

Rainie, L., Purcell, K., & Smith, A. (2011, January 18). The social side of the Internet. *Pew Internet*. [Online]. Available at: http://www.pewinternet.org/Reports/2011/The-Social-Side-of-the-Internet.aspx

Rains, S. A., & Young, V. (2009). A meta-analysis of research on formal computer-mediated support groups: Examining group characteristics and health outcomes. *Human Communication Research*, 35, 309–336.

Ramirez, A., & Broneck, K. (2009). IM me: Instant messaging as relational maintenance and everyday communication. *Journal of Social and Personal Relationships*, 26, 291–315.

Rampton, S., & Stauber, J. (2001). *Trust us, we're experts: How industry manipulates science and gambles with your future*. New York: Tarcher/Putnam.

Rathus, S. (1990). *Psychology*. Fort Worth, TX: Holt, Rinehart & Winston.

Ravitch, D. (2007). *EdSpeak: A glossary of education terms, phrases, buzzwords, and jargon*. Alexandria, VA: ASCD.

Ray, G. B., Ray, E. B., & Zahn, C. J. (1991). Speech behavior and social evaluation: An examination of medical messages. *Communication Quarterly*, 39, 119–129.

Ray, J. (2005, July 12). Censorship: Do teens bow to school control? *Gallup*. [Online]. Available at: http://www.galup.com/poll/17281/censorship-teens-bow-school-control.aspx

Reason, J., & Mycielska, K. (1982). *Absent-minded? The psychology of mental lapses and everyday errors*. Englewood Cliffs, NJ: Prentice Hall.

Regan, D., & Totten, J. (1975). Empathy and attribution: Turning observers into actors. *Journal of Personality and Social Psychology*, 32, 850–856.

Reicher, S. D., Haslam, S. A., & Platow, M. J. (2007, August/September). The new psychology of leadership. *Scientific American Mind*, pp. 22–29.

Reid, S. A., Byrne, S., Brundidge, J. S., Shoham, M. D., & Marlow, M. L. (2007). A critical test of self-enhancement, exposure, and self-categorization explanations for first- and third-person perceptions. *Human Communication Research*, 33, 143–162.

Reis, H. T., & Wheeler, L. (1991). Studying social interaction with the Rochester Interaction Record. In M. P. Zanna (Ed.), *Advances in experimental social psychology*. New York: Academic Press.

Reisberg, D. (1997). *Cognition: Exploring the science of the mind*. New York: Norton.

Remarks of Senator Barack Obama. (2008, January 3). *Obama News & Speeches*. [Online]. Available at: http://www.barackobama.com/2008/01/03/remarks_of_senator_barack_obam_39.php

Remland, M., Jones, T., & Brinkman, H. (1995). Interpersonal distance, body orientation, and touch: Effects of culture, gender, and age. *Journal of Social Psychology*, 135, 281–297.

Report: The media have debunked the death panels more than 40 times. (2009, August 15) *MediaMatters for America*. [Online]. Available at: http://mediamatters.org/research/200908150001

Results of the 2010 WBI U. S. workplace bullying survey. (2010). *Workplace Bullying Institute*. [Online]. Available at: http://www.workplacebullying.org/research/WBI-NatlSurvey2010.html

Rexroot, S. (2006). Untitled. In L. G. Schnoor & B. Wickelgren (Eds.), *Winning orations*. Mankato, MN: Interstate Oratorical Association.

Reyneri, A. (1984). The nose knows, but science doesn't. *Science*, 84, 26.

Reynolds, R. A., & Reynolds, J. L. (2002). Evidence. In J. E. Dillard & M. Pfau (Eds.), *The persuasion handbook: Developments in theory and practice*. Thousand Oaks, CA: Sage.

Rhodes, G., Yoshikawa, S., Clark, A., Lee, K., McKay, R., & Akamatsu, S. (2001). Attractiveness of facial averageness and symmetry in non-Western cultures: In search of biologically based standards of beauty. *Perception*, 30, 611–625.

Rhodes, T. (2010, November). Learning across the curriculum: Communication departments hold a vital role. *Spectra*, pp. 12–15.

Richards, G. (2010, September 26). Total cell phone ban in works for drivers? *San Jose Mercury News*, B1, B7.

Richmond, V. P., & McCroskey, J. C. (1995). *Communication: Apprehension, avoidance, and effectiveness*. Boston: Allyn & Bacon.

Richtel, M. (2007, November 4). Devices enforce silence of cellphones, illegally. *The New York Times*. [Online]. Available at: http://www.nytimes.com/2007/11/04/technology/04jammer.html?_r=3&ex=1351828800&en=e80e8e8d2c6a9275&ei=5088&partner=rssnyt&emc=rss&oref=slogin&oref=slogin

Ricks, D. (2000, February 4). Cancer likely to become leading U.S. killer. *San Jose Mercury News*, p. 10A.

Ridley, T. (2007). 2007 Vault employee tattoo and body piercing survey. *Vault*. [Online]. Available at: http://www.hawaii.edu/hivandaids/Vault_Employee_Tattoo_and_Body_Piercing_Survey._2007.pdf

Riechmann, D. (2001, August 17). Flight safety spiels really work. *Santa Cruz Sentinel*, pp. A1, A10.

Rieke, R. D., Sillars, M. O., & Peterson, T. R. (2005). *Argumentation and critical decision making*. New York: Pearson.

Rietzschel, E. F., Nijstad, B. A., & Strobe, W. (2006). Productivity is not enough: A comparison of interactive and nominal brainstorming groups on idea generation and selection. *Journal of Experimental Social Psychology*, 42, 244–251.

Riggio, R. E. (2006). Nonverbal skills and abilities. In V. Manusov & M. L. Patterson (Eds.), *The Sage handbook on nonverbal communication*. Thousand Oaks, CA: Sage.

Riggio, R. E., Riggio, H. R., Salinas, C., & Cole, E. J. (2003). The role of social and emotional communication skills in leader emergence and effectiveness. *Group Dynamics: Theory, Research, and Practice*, 7, 83–103.

Risman, B. J., & Johnson-Sumerford, D. (1998). Doing it fairly: A study of postgender marriages. *Journal of Marriage and the Family*, 60, 23–40.

Ritts, V., Patterson, M. L., & Tubbs, M. E. (1992). Expectations, impressions, and judgments of physically attractive students: A review. *Review of Educational Research*, 62, 413–426.

Roberts, S. (2007, January 16). Majority of women live without spouses. *San Jose Mercury News*, p. 1A.

Robinson, W. P., Shepherd, A., & Heywood, J. (1998). Truth, equivocation/concealment, and lies in job applications and doctor-patient communication. *Journal of Language and Social Psychology*, 17, 149–164.

Roby, D. E. (2009, Summer). Teacher leadership skills: An analysis of communication apprehension. *FindArticles*. [Online]. Available at: http://findarticles.com/p/articles/mi_qa3673/is_4_129/ai_n31948144/?tag=mantle_skin;content

Rochlen, A. B., & Mahalik, J. R. (2004). Women's perception of male partners' gender role conflict as predictors of psychological well-being and relationship satisfaction. *Psychology of Men and Masculinity*, 5, 147–157.

Rodkin, P. C., Farmer, T. W., Pearl, R., & Van Acker, R. (2000). Heterogeneity of popular boys: Antisocial and prosocial configurations. *Developmental Psychology*, 36, 14–24.

Rodriguez, J. (1995). *Confounds in fear arousing persuasive messages: Do the paths less traveled make all the difference?* Unpublished doctoral dissertation, Michigan State University, East Lansing.

Roediger, H., Capaldi, E., Paris, S., & Polivy, J. (1991). *Psychology*. New York: HarperCollins.

Rogelberg, S., & Rumery, S. (1996). Gender diversity, team decision quality, time on task, and interpersonal cohesion. *Small Group Research*, 27, 79–90.

Rogelberg, S. G., Leach, D. J., Warr, P. B., & Burnfield, J. L. (2006). "Not another meeting!" Are meeting time demands related to employee well-being? *Journal of Applied Psychology*, 91, 83–96.

Rogers, C., & Roethlisberger, F. (1952, July/August). Barriers and gateways to communication. *Harvard Business Review*, pp. 28–35.

Romano, D. (1988). *Intercultural marriage: Promises and pitfalls*. Yarmouth, ME: Intercultural Press.

Romig, D. (1996). *Breakthrough teamwork: Outstanding results using structured teamwork*. Chicago: Irwin.

Rooney, B. (2011, April 28). Exxon hits back at gas price anger. *CNN Money*. [Online]. Available at: http://money.cnn.com.2011/04/28/news/companies/exxon_earnings/index.htm

Roper Center Public Opinion Archives. (2007, September 21). Comparing past presidential performance. *Roper Center*. [Online]. Available at:

http://137.99.36.203/CFIDE/roper/presidential/webroot/presidential_rating.cfm

Rosch, E. (1973). On the internal structure of perceptual and semantic categories. In T. E. Moore (Ed.), *Cognitive development and the acquisition of language*. New York: Academic Press.

Rose, S. M. (1985). Same- and cross-sex friendships and the psychology of homosociality. *Sex Roles*, 12, 63–74.

Rose, V. (2001). The bowels of our nation. In L. G. Schnoor & B. Wickelgren (Eds.), *Winning orations*. Mankato, MN: Interstate Oratorical Association.

Rosen, D., Stefanone, M. A., & Lackaff, D. (2010). Online and offline social networks: Investigating culturally-specific behavior and satisfaction. In *Proceedings of IEEE's Hawaii International Conference on Systems Science*. Los Alamitos, CA: IEEE Press.

Rosenbaum, J. E. (2009). Patient teenagers? A comparison of the sexual behavior of virginity pledgers and matched nonpledgers. *Pediatrics*, 123, 110–120.

Rosenbaum, L., & Rosenbaum, W. (1985). Morale and productivity consequences of group leadership style, stress, and type of task. *Journal of Applied Psychology*, 55, 343–358.

Rosenblatt, J. S., Hinde, R. A., Beer, C., & Busnel, M. (1982). *Advances in the study of behavior*. New York: Academic Press.

Rosenfeld, L. (1983). Communication climate and coping mechanisms in the college classroom. *Communication Education*, 32, 169–174.

Rosenhan, D. L. (1973). On being sane in insane places. *Science*, 179, 250–258.

Rosenthal, D. B., & Hautaluoma, J. (1988). Effects of importance of issues, gender, and power of contenders on conflict management style. *Journal of Social Psychology*, 128, 699–701.

Rosenthal, N. (1997, July 15). How to prevent that "us vs. them" feeling within the family. *San Jose Mercury News*, p. E4.

Rosenthal, R. (Ed.). (1979). *Skill in nonverbal communication: Individual differences*. Cambridge, MA: Gunn & Hain.

Rosenthal, R., & Jacobson, L. (1968). *Pygmalion in the classroom: Teachers' expectations and pupils' intellectual development*. New York: Holt, Rinehart, & Winston.

Rosin, H. (2010, July/August). The end of men. *The Atlantic*, pp. 56–72.

Ross, L. (1977). The intuitive psychologist and his shortcomings: Distortions in the attribution process. In L. Berkowitz (Ed.), *Advances in experimental social psychology*. New York: Academic Press.

Ross, L., & Samuels, S. M. (1993). *The predictive power of personal reputation versus labels and construal in the prisoner's dilemma game*. Unpublished manuscript, Stanford University.

Rost, J. C. (1991). *Leadership for the twenty-first century*. New York: Praeger.

Rothwell, J. D. (1982). *Telling it like it isn't: Language misuse and malpractice*. Englewood Cliffs, NJ: Prentice Hall.

Rothwell, J. D. (2010, 2013). *In mixed company: Communicating in small groups and teams*. Boston: Wadsworth/Cengage.

Rottenberg, A. T. (2000). *The structure of argument*. New York: St. Martin's Press.

Rotundo, M., Nguyen, D., & Sackett, P. R. (2001). A meta-analytic review of gender differences in perceptions of sexual harassment. *Journal of Applied Psychology*, 86, 914–922.

Rovio, E., Eskola, J., Kozub, S. A., Duda, J. L., & Lintunen, T. (2009). Can high group cohesion be harmful? A case study of a junior ice-hockey team. *Small Group Research*, 40, 421–435.

Ruback, B. R., & Jweng, D. (1997). Territorial defense in parking lots: Retaliation against waiting drivers. *Journal of Applied Social Psychology*, 27, 821–834.

Rubin, D. L., Greene, K., & Schneider, D. (1994). Adopting gender-inclusive language reforms: Diachronic and synchronic variation. *Journal of Language and Social Psychology*, 13, 91–114.

Rubin, L. B. (1984). *Intimate strangers: Men and women together*. New York: Harper & Row.

Rubinstein, S., & Caballero, B. (2000). Is Miss America an undernourished role model? *Journal of the American Medical Association*, 282, 1569.

Ruch, W. (1989). *International handbook of corporate communication*. Jefferson, NC: McFarland.

Rucker, D. D., & Petty, R. E. (2004). When resistance is futile: Consequences of failed counterarguing for attitude certainty. *Journal of Personality and Social Psychology*, 86, 219–235.

Rudman, L. A., & Fairchild, K. (2004). Reactions to counterstereotypic behavior: The role of backlash in cultural stereotype maintenance. *Journal of Personality and Social Psychology*, 87, 157–176.

Ruet, B. (2006). Sudan's forgotten war. In L. G. Schnoor & B. Wickelgren (Eds.), *Winning orations*. Mankato, MN: Interstate Oratorical Association.

Ruggeiro, V. (1988). *Teaching thinking across the curriculum*. New York: Harper & Row.

Ruining it for the rest of us. (2008, December 19). *This American Life*. [Online]. Available at: http://www.thisamericanlife.org/radio-archives/episode/370/ruining-it-for-the-rest-of-us

Ruiter, R. A. C., Kessels, L. T. E., Jansma, B. M., & Brug, J. (2006). Increased attention for computer-tailored health communications: An event-related potential study. *Health Psychology*, 25, 300–306.

Rusbult, C. E., & Van Lange, P. A. M. (2003). Interdependence, interaction, and relationships. *Annual Review of Psychology*, 54, 351–375.

Rusting, C. L., & Nolen-Hoeksema, S. (1998). Regulating responses to anger: Effects of rumination and distraction on angry mood. *Journal of Personality and Social Psychology*, 74, 790–803.

Rutkowski, A-F, Saunders, C., Vogel, D., & van Genuchten, M. (2007). "Is it already 4 A.M. in your time zone?" Focus immersion and temporal dissociation in virtual teams. *Small Group Research*, 38, 98–129.

Rymer, R. (1993). *Genie: An abused child's flight from silence*. New York: HarperCollins.

Saal, F. E., Johnson, C. B., & Weber, N. (1989). Friendly or sexy? It may depend on whom you ask. *Psychology of Women Quarterly*, 13, 263–276.

Sabourin, T. C. (1995). The role of negative reciprocity in spouse abuse: A relational control analysis. *Journal of Applied Communication Research*, 23, 271–283.

Sabourin, T. C. (1996). The role of communication in verbal abuse between partners. In D. D. Cahn & S. A. Lloyd (Eds.), *Family violence from a communication perspective*. Thousand Oaks, CA: Sage.

Sacks, O. (1990). *Seeing voices: A journey into the world of the deaf*. New York: Vintage Books.

Sagan, C. (1996). *The demon-haunted world: Science as a candle in the dark*. New York: Random House.

Sagrestano, L. M. (1992). Power strategies in interpersonal relationships. *Psychology of Women Quarterly*, 16, 481–495.

Sahlstein, E. M. (2006). Making plans: Praxis strategies for negotiating uncertainty-certainty in long-distance relationships. *Western Journal of Communication*, 70, 147–165.

Said, C., Sebe, N., & Todorov, A. (2009). Structural resemblance to emotional expressions predicts evaluation of emotionally neutral faces. *Emotion*, 9, 260–264.

Saint, S., & Lawson, J. (1997). *Rules for reaching consensus*. San Diego, CA: Pfeiffer.

Salazar, A. (1995). Understanding the synergistic effects of communication in small groups. *Small Group Research*, 26, 169–199.

Salerno, S. (2005). *Sham: How the self-help movement made America helpless*. New York: Crown.

Samovar, L., & Porter, R. (2004). *Communication between cultures*. Belmont, CA: Thomson-Wadsworth.

Samovar, L. A., Porter, R. E., & McDaniel, E. R. (2010). *Communication between cultures*. Boston: Cengage Learning.

Sapir, E. (1931). Conceptual categories in primitive languages. *Science*, 74, 572–578.

Savage, D. G. (2011, March 3). Court: Speech that offends still protected. *San Jose Mercury News*, p. A3.

Savage-Rumbaugh, E. S., & Lewin, R. (1994, September). Ape at the brink. *Discover*, 15, 91–98.

Sawyer, K. (2007). *Group genius: The creative power of collaboration*. New York: Basic Books.

Sazer, L., & Kassinove, H. (1991). Effects of counselor's profanity and subject's religiosity on content acquisition of a counseling lecture and behavioral compliance. *Psychological Reports*, 69, 1059–1070.

Scanlon, J. (2003, August). 7 ways to squelch the net. *Wired*, p. 31.

Scherer, K. R. (2003). Vocal communication of emotion: A review of research paradigms. *Speech Communication*, 40, 227–256.

Schittekatte, M., & Van Hiel, A. (1996). Effects of partially shared information and awareness of unshared information on information sampling. *Small Group Research*, 27, 431–449.

Schlosser, E. (1997, September). A grief like no other. *The Atlantic Monthly*, pp. 37–76.

Schlosser, E. (2002). *Fast food nation*. New York: Penguin Books.

Schmidt, F. L., & Hunter, J. E. (1998). The validity and utility of selection methods in personnel psychology: Practical and theoretical implications of 85 years of research findings. *Psychological Bulletin*, 124, 262–274.

Schmidt, S., & Kipnis, D. (1987, November). The perils of persistence. *Psychology Today*, pp. 32–34.

Schmidt, W. (1991, October). *Oral communication across the curriculum: A critical review of literature*. Paper presented at the meeting of the Florida Communication Association Convention, Vero Beach.

Schmitt, D. P., & Allik, J. (2005). Simultaneous administration of the Rosenberg Self-Esteem Scale in 53 nations: Exploring the universal and culture-specific features of global self-esteem. *Journal of Personality and Social Psychology*, 89, 623–642.

Schmitt, D. P., & Buss, D. M. (2001). Human mate poaching: Tactics and temptations for infiltrating existing mateships. *Journal of Personality and Social Psychology*, 80, 894–917.

Schmitt, E. (2001, April 30). Census data finds major racial shift in largest cities. *San Jose Mercury News*, p. 9A.

Schneider, B. (2007, June 11). You don't have to be liked to be president . . . but it helps. *CNN.com*. [Online]. Available at: http://www.cnn.com/2007/POLITICS/06/13/schneider.likability/index.html

Schneider, K., & Levitt, S. (1996, June 3). Mission impossible. *People*, pp. 65–74.

Schoenbachler, D. D., & Whittler, T. E. (1996). Adolescent processing of social and physical threat communications. *Journal of Advertising*, 25, 37–54.

Scholtes, P. (1990). An elaboration of Deming's teachings on performance appraisal. In G. McLean, S. Damme, & R. Swanson (Eds.), *Performance appraisal: Perspectives on a quality management approach*. Alexandria, VA: American Society for Training and Development.

Scholz, M. (2005, June). A "simple" way to improve adherence. *RN*, 68, 82.

Schubert, S. (2006, October/November). A look tells all. *Scientific American Mind*, pp. 26–31.

Schultz, C. (1998, May 30). Message of peace from war photo. *San Jose Mercury News*, p. E3.

Schultz, E. A. (1990). *Dialogue at the margins: Whorf, Bakhtin, and linguistic relativity*. Madison: University of Wisconsin Press.

Schumacher, J. A., & Leonard, K. E. (2005). Husbands' and wives' marital adjustment, verbal aggression, and physical aggression as longitudinal predictors of physical aggression in early marriage. *Journal of Consulting and Clinical Psychology*, 73, 28–37.

Schwanhausser, M. (2007, October 16). In Silicon Valley, few women reach top jobs. *San Jose Mercury News*, pp. 1A, 12A.

Schwartz, J. (2003, October 20). *University of Washington press release*. [Online]. Available at: http://www.washington.edu/newsroom/news/2003archive/10-03archive/k102003.html

Schwartz, J. P., Magee, M. M., Griffin, L. D., & Dupuis, C. W. (2004). Effects of a group preventive intervention on risk and protective factors related to dating violence. *Group Dynamics: Theory, Research, and Practice*, 8, 221–231.

Sciolino, E. (1996, November 12). Subject of famous photograph lays wreath at Vietnam Memorial. *San Jose Mercury News*, pp. A1, A14.

Segall, M. H., Dasen, P. R., Berry, J. W., & Poortinga, Y. H. (1990). *Human behavior in global perspective: An introduction to cross-cultural psychology*. New York: Pergamon.

Seibold, D. R., & Spitzberg, B. H. (1982). Attribution theory and research: Review and implications for communication. In B. Dervin & M. J. Voight (Eds.), *Progress in communication sciences*. Norwood, NJ: Ablex.

Seidenberg, M. S., & Petitto, L. A. (1979). Signing behavior in apes: A critical review. *Cognition*, 7, 177–215.

Seigenthaler, J. (2005, November 29). A false *Wikipedia* "biography." *USA Today*.

Seligman, M. (1991). *Learned optimism*. New York: Knopf.

Sell, J., Lovaglia, M. J., Mannix, E. A., Samuelson, C. D., & Wilson, R. K. (2004). Investigating conflict, power, and status within and among groups. *Small Group Research*, 35, 44–72.

Senate Select Committee on Intelligence (2004). U.S. intelligence community's prewar intelligence assessments on Iraq: Conclusions. *Report of the 108th Congress*. [Online]. Available at: http://intelligence.senate.gov

Serdula, M. K., Collins, M. E., Williamson, D. F., Anda, R. F., Pamuk, E. R., & Byers, T. E. (1993). Weight control practices among U.S. adolescents and adults. *Annals of Internal Medicine*, 119, 667–671.

Seta, J. J., Wang, M. A., Crisson, J. E., & Seta, C. E. (1989). Audience composition and felt anxiety: Impact averaging and summation. *Basic and Applied Social Psychology*, 10, 57–72.

Seven little errors of Brian Williams' *Wikipedia* entry. (2007, April 9). *Popular Front All*. [Online]. Available at: http://gawker.com/news/brian-williams/the-seven-little-errors-of-brian-williams-wikipedia-entry-250792.php

Sever, J. M. (2003, October 8). A third of Americans with tattoos say they make them feel more sexy. *Harris Interactive*. [Online]. Available at: http://www.harrisinteractive.com/harris_poll/index.asp?PID=407

Sex in the digital age. (2010). *Men's Fitness*. [Online]. Available at: http://www.mensfitness.com/print/52160

Seyfarth, R. M., Cheney, D. L., & Marler, P. (1980). Vervet monkey alarm calls: Semantic communication in a free-ranging primate. *Animal Behavior*, 28, 1070–1094.

Shachtman, T. (1995). *The inarticulate society: Eloquence and culture in America*. New York: Free Press.

Shackelford, S., Wood, W., & Worchel, S. (1996). Behavioral styles and the influence of women in mixed-sex groups. *Social Psychology*, 59, 284–293.

Shadel, W. G., Niaura, R., & Abrams, D. B. (2001). How do adolescents process smoking and antismoking advertisements? A social cognitive analysis with implications for understanding smoking initiation. *Review of General Psychology*, 5, 429–444.

Shaffner, G. (1999). *The arithmetic of life and death*. New York: Ballantine Books.

Shafir, E. (1993). Choosing versus rejecting: Why some options are both better and worse than others. *Memory and Cognition*, 21, 546–556.

Shah, A. (2007, October 7). Global computer usage, cell phone ownership jump. *About.com*. [Online]. Available at: http://pcworld.about.com/od/researchreports/Global-computer-usage-cell-ph.htm

Sharpe, R. (2000, November 20). As leaders, women rule. *Business Week*, pp. 75–84

Shenk, D. (1997). *Data smog: Suriving the information glut*. New York: HarperCollins.

Shepela, S. T., & Levesque, L. L. (1998). Poisoned waters: Sexual harassment and the college climate. *Sex Roles*, 38, 589–611.

Sheppard, N. (2010, January 22). Stewart blasts Olbermann for Brown rants, defends Michelle Malkin. *NewsBusters*. [Online]. Available at: http://newsbusters.org/blogs/noel-sheppard/2010/01/22/stewart-blasts-olbermann-brown-rants-defends-michelle-malkin

Sherif, C. W., Kelly, M., Rodgers, H. L., Sarup, G., & Tittler, B. I. (1973). Personal involvement, social judgment and action. *Journal of Personality and Social Psychology*, 27, 311–328.

Sherif, M., Sherif, C., & Nebergall, R. (1965). *Attitude and attitude change: The social judgment-involvement approach*. Philadelphia: Saunders.

Sherrin, N. (1996). *The Oxford dictionary of humorous quotations*. New York: Oxford University Press.

Shih, M., Pittinsky, T. L., & Ambady, N. (1999). Stereotype susceptibility: Identity salience and shifts in quantitative performance. *Psychological Science*, 10, 80–83.

Shimanoff, S. (1992). Group interaction via communication rules. In R. Cathcart & L. Samovar (Eds.), *Small group communication: A reader*. Dubuque, IA: Brown.

Shimanoff, S. B. (1980). *Communication rule: Theory and research*. Beverly Hills, CA: Sage.

Shimanoff, S., & Jenkins, M. (1996). Leadership and gender: Challenging assumptions and recognizing resources. In R. Cathcart, L. Samovar, & L. Henman (Eds.), *Small group communication: Theory and practice*. Dubuque, IA: Brown & Benchmark.

Shirley, D. (1997). Managing creativity: Inventing, developing, and producing innovative products. [Online]. Available at: http://www.managingcreativity.com

Shockley, K., Richardson, D. C., & Dale, R. (2009). Conversation and coordinative structures. *Topics in Cognitive Science*, 1, 305–319.

Siebel, T. M., & Mange, S. A. (2009). The Montana Meth project: "Unselling" a dangerous drug. *Stanford Law and Policy Review*, 20, 405–416.

Sigelman, L., Tuch, S. A., & Martin, J. K. (2005). What's in a name? Preference for "black" versus "African-American" among Americans of African descent. *Public Opinion Quarterly*, 69, 429–438.

Sillars, A. L., Coletti, S. G., Parry, D., & Rogers, M. A. (1982). Coding verbal conflict tactics: Nonverbal and perceptual correlates of the "avoidance-distributive-integrative" distinction. *Human Communication Research*, 9, 83–95.

Sillars, M. L., Weisberg, J., Burggraf, C. S., & Zietlow, P. H. (1990). Communication and understanding revisited: Married couples' understanding and recall of conversations. *Communication Research*, 17, 500–532.

Silva, M. (2007, September 27). Cleaning up after Bush: It was "childrens do learn." *Baltimore Sun*. [Online]. Available at: http://weblogs.baltimoresun.com/news/politics/blog/2007/09/cleaning_up_after_bush

Simon, S. (2007, July 22). Catholic Church launches media blitz for marriage. *San Jose Mercury News*, p. 11A.

Simons, D. J., & Ambinder, M. S. (2005). Change blindness: Theory and consequences. *Current Directions in Psychological Science*, 14, 44–48.

Simons, D. J., & Levin, D. T. (1998). Failure to detect changes to people during a real-world interaction. *Psychonomic Bulletin and Review*, 5, 644–649.

Simons, L., & Zielenziger, M. (1996, March 3). Culture clash dims U.S. future in Asia. *San Jose Mercury News*, pp. A1, A22.

Simon-Thomas, E. R., Keltner, D. J., Sauter, D., Sinicropi-Yao, L., & Abramson, A. (2009). The voice conveys specific emotions: Evidence from vocal burst displays. *Emotion*, 9, 838–846.

Simpson, B., & Macy, M. W. (2001). Collective action and power inequality: Coalitions in exchange networks. *Social Psychology Quarterly*, 64, 88–100.

Simpson, M. D. (2006, September). Teach but don't touch: Practical advice for school employees on avoiding false allegations of improper conduct with students. *National Education Association*. [Online]. Available at: http://www.nea-nm.org/misc/TeachDon'tTouchColor.pdf

Simpson, P. A., & Stroh, L. K. (2004). Gender differences: Emotional expression and feelings of personal inauthenticity. *Journal of Applied Psychology*, 89, 715–721.

Singer, M. (1987). *Intercultural communication: A perceptual approach*. Englewood Cliffs, NJ: Prentice Hall.

Singh, D. (1993). Adaptive significance of female physical attractiveness: Role of waist-to-hip ratio. *Journal of Personality and Social Psychiatry*, 65, 293–307.

Singh, D. (1995). Female judgment of male attractiveness and desirability for relationships: Role of waist-to-hip ratio and financial status. *Journal of Personality and Social Psychology*, 69, 1089–1101.

Sion, M. (2011, February 11). In matters of the heart, it's all about the green. *San Jose Mercury News*, p. A11.

Smedes, L. B. (1984). *Forgive and forget: Healing the hurts we don't deserve*. New York: Harper & Row.

Smith, D., Gier, J., & Willis, F. (1982). Interpersonal touch and compliance with a marketing request. *Basic and Applied Social Psychology*, 3, 35–38.

Smith, M. J. (1982). *Persuasion and human interaction: A review and critique of social influence theories*. Belmont, CA: Wadsworth.

Smith, N. K., Larsen, J. T., Chartrand, T. L., Cacioppo, J. T., Katafiasz, H. A., & Moran, K. E. (2006). Being bad isn't always good: Affective context moderates the attention bias toward negative information. *Journal of Personality and Social Psychology*, 90, 210–220.

Smith, P., & Bond, M. (1994). *Social psychology across cultures: Analysis and perspective*. Boston: Allyn & Bacon.

Smith, P. B., Dugan, S., & Trompenaars, F. (1997). Locus of control and affectivity by gender and occupational status: A 14-nation study. *Sex Roles*, 36, 51–57.

Smith, S. M., & Shaffer, D. R. (1995). Speed of speech and persuasion: Evidence for multiple effects. *Personality and Social Psychology Bulletin*, 21, 1051–1060.

Smolowe, J. (2007, May 14). Caught in the middle. *People*, pp. 131–132.

Snyder, M. (2001). Self-fulfilling stereotypes. In A. Branaman (Ed.), *Self and society: Blackwell readers in sociology*. Malden, MA: Blackwell.

Snyder, M., & Swann, W. B. (1978). Hypothesis-testing processes in social interaction. *Journal of Personality and Social Psychology*, 36, 1202–1212.

Snyder, M., & Uranowitz, S. (1978). Reconstructing the past: Some cognitive consequences of person perception. *Journal of Personality and Social Psychology*, 36, 941–950.

Social isolation and new technology. (2010, January 21). *New Media Institute*. [Online]. Available at: http://www.newmedia.org/articles/social-isolation-and-new-technology-.html

Social media help make school, job ties, students say. (2011, April 20). *San Jose Mercury News*, D2.

Social networking sites in our lives (2011, June 16). *Pew Internet*. [Online]. Available at: http://

www.pewinternet.org/Reports/2011/Technology-and-Social-networks/summary.aspx

Solomon, C. (2010). The challenge of working in virtual teams: Virtual teams survey report-2010. *RW3 Culture Wizard*. [Online]. Available at: http://rw3.com/VTSReportsv7.pdf

Some tattoos a painful mistake. (2006, August 9). *San Jose Mercury News*, p. 2A.

Sommer, R. (1969). *Personal space: The behavioral basis of design*. Englewood Cliffs, NJ: Prentice Hall.

Sopory, P., & Dillard, J. P. (2002). Figurative language and persuasion. In J. P. Dillard & M. Pfau (Eds.), *The persuasion handbook: Developments in theory and practice*. Thousand Oaks, CA: Sage.

Sorensen, S. (1981, May). *Grouphate*. Paper presented at a meeting of the International Communication Association, Minneapolis, MN.

Souto, S. (2007, June 28). Topic: Employment law. *AllExperts.com*. [Online]. Available at: http://en.allexperts.com/q/Employment-Law-924/Bathroom-breaks.htm

Sparrow, B., Liu, J., & Wegner, D. M. (2011). Google effects on memory: Cognitive consequences of having information at our fingertips. *Science*. [Online]. Available at: http://www.sciencemag.org/content/early/2011/07/13/science.1207745

Spencer, L., & Spencer, S. (1993). *Competence at work: Models for superior performance*. New York: Wiley.

Spiegler, M. D., & Guevremont, D. C. (1998). *Contemporary behavior therapy*. Pacific Grove, CA: Brooks/Cole.

Spitzberg, B. H. (2000). A model of intercultural communication competence. In L. A. Samovar & R. E. Porter (Eds.), *Intercultural communication: A reader*.

Spitzberg, B. H. (2011). Intimate partner violence and aggression: Seeing the light in a dark place. In W. R. Cupach & B. H. Spitzberg (Eds.), *The dark side of close relationships II*. New York: Routledge.

Spitzberg, B., & Cupach, W. (1989). *Handbook of interpersonal competence research*. New York: Springer-Verlag.

Spitzberg, B., & Hecht, M. (1984). A component model of relational competence. *Human Communication Research*, 10, 575–599.

Sprecher, S. (2011). Internet matching services: The good, the bad, and the ugle (disguised as attractive). In W. R. Cupach & B. H. Spitzberg (Eds.), *The dark side of close relationships* II. New York: Routledge.

Sprecher, S., & Regan, P. C. (1998). Passionate and companionate love in courting and young married couples. *Sociological Inquiry*, 68, 163–185.

Springen, K. (1997, June 3). The biology of beauty. *Newsweek*, pp. 61–66.

Sriussadaporn-Charoenngam, N., & Jablin, F. M. (1999). An exploratory study of communication competence in Thai organizations. *Journal of Business Communication*, 36, 382–418.

Sroufe, L. A., Egeland, B., Carlson, E. A., & Collins, W. A. (2005). *The development of the person: The Minnesota study of risk and adaptation from birth to adulthood*. New York: Guilford Press.

Stafford, L., & Daly, J. A. (1984). Conversational memory: The effects of recall and memory expectations on remembrances of natural conversations. *Human Communication Research*, 10, 379–402.

Stallings, H. (2009). Prosecution deferred is justice denied. In L. G. Schnoor & D. Cronn-Mills (Eds.), *Winning orations*. Northfield, MN: Interstate Oratorical Association.

Stanford Institute for the Quantitative Study of Society. (2000). *SIQSS Internet Study*. [Online]. Available at: www.stanford.edu/group/siqss/Press_Release/InternetStudy.html

Stanne, M. B., Johnson, D. W., & Johnson, R. T. (1999). Does competition enhance or inhibit motor performance? A meta-analysis. *Psychological Bulletin*, 125, 133–154.

Statistics. (2011). *Telework Research Network*. [Online]. Available at: http://www.teleworkresearchnetwork.com/telecommuting-statistics

Steele, C. M. (1997). A threat in the air: How stereotypes shape intellectual identity and performance. *American Psychologist*, 52, 613–629.

Steele, C. M., Spencer, S. J., & Aronson, J. (2002). Contending with group image: The psychology of stereotype and social identity threat. In M. P. Zanna (Ed.), *Advances in experimental social psychology*. San Diego, CA: Academic Press.

Stefanone, M. A., Lackaff, D., & Rosen, D. (2011). Contingencies of self-worth and social-networking-site behavior. *Cyberpsychology, Behavior, and Social Networking*, 14, 41–49.

Steffins, S. (2001, May 12). Cupid in the cubicles. *San Jose Mercury News*, pp. 1F, 4F.

Stein, S. (2009, August 7). Obama-allied unions threatened with gun violence for town hall participation. *Huffington Post*. [Online]. Available at: http://www.huffingtonpost.com/2009/08/07/obama-allied-unions-threa_n_254204.html

Stephan, W. G., & Stephan, C. W. (1996). *Intergroup relations*. Boulder, CO: Westview Press.

Stephen Colbert's address to the graduates. (2006, June 5). *AlterNet*. [Online]. Available at: http://www.alternet.org/module/printversion/37144

Stephens, K. K., Houser, M. L., & Cowan, R. L. (2009). R U able to meat me: The impact of students' overly casual email messages to instructors. *Communication Education*, 58, 303–326.

Stern, N. (2004). Just say no to PowerPoint: Enough is enough. [Online]. Available at: http://www.eitforum.com/696.php

Sternberg, R. J. (1986). A triangular theory of love. *Psychological Review*, 93, 119–135.

Sternberg, R. J. (1988). *The triangle of love*. New York: Basic Books.

Sternberg, R. J. (1997). Construct validation of a triangular love scale. *European Journal of Social Psychology*, 27, 313–335.

Sternberg, R. J. (2004). WICS: A model of educational leadership. *Educational Forum*, 68, 108–114.

Sternberg, S. (2007, November 29). Unnecessary CT scans exposing patients to excessive radiation. *USA Today*, p. 1A.

Steward, A., & Lupfer, M. (1987). Touching as teaching: The effect of touch on students' perceptions and performing. *Journal of Applied Psychology*, 17, 800–809.

Steward, C. (2009a, July 24). Rickey takes his speech to school. *San Jose Mercury News*, pp. C1, C5.

Steward, C. (2009b, July 27). With the pressure on, Henderson once again steals the show. *San Jose Mercury News*, pp. 1A, 3A.

Stewart, E. C., & Bennett, M. J. (1991). *American cultural patterns: A cross-cultural perspective*. Yarmouth, ME: Intercultural Press.

Stewart, L., Cooper, P., Stewart, A., & Friedley, S. A. (1996). *Communication and gender*. Scottsdale, AZ: Gorsuch Scarisbrick.

Stewart, M. (2009). *The management myth: Debunking modern business philosophy*. New York: Norton.

Stiff, J., Dillard, I., Somera, H., & Sleight, C. (1988). Empathy, communication, and prosocial behavior. *Communication Monographs*, 55, 198–213.

Stone, D., Patton, B., & Heen, S. (1999). *Difficult conversations: How to discuss what matters most*. New York: Viking Press.

Stone, J., Aronson, E., Crain, A. L., Winslow, M. P., & Fried, C. B. (1994). Inducing hypocrisy as a means of encouraging young adults to use condoms. *Personality and Social Psychology Bulletin*, 20, 116–128.

Stone, J., Cooper, J., Wiegard, A. W., & Aronson, E. (1997). When exemplification fails: Hypocrisy and the motive for self-integrity. *Journal of Personality and Social Psychology*, 72, 54–65.

Strack, F., Martin, L. L., & Stepper, S. (1988). Inhibiting and facilitating conditions of facial expressions: A non-obtrusive test of the facial feedback hypothesis. *Journal of Personality and Social Psychology*, 54, 768–777.

Straus, M. A. (2001). Prevalence of violence against dating partners by male and female university students worldwide. *Violence Against Women*, 10, 790–811.

Straus, M. A. (2008). Dominance and symmetry in partner violence by male and female university students in 32 nations. *Children and Youth Services Review* (in press).

Straus, M. A., & Sweet, S. (1992). Verbal/symbolic aggression in couples: Incidence rates and relationship to personal characteristics. *Journal of Marriage and the Family*, 54, 346–357.

Street, M. (1997). Groupthink: An examination of theoretical issues, implications, and future research suggestions. *Small Group Research*, 28, 72–93.

Strong, W., & Cook, J. (1990). *Persuasion: Strategies for speakers*. Dubuque, IA: Kendall Hunt.

Study abroad by U.S. students slowed in 2008/09 with more students going to less traditional destinations. (2010, November 15). *Institute of International Education*. [Online]. Available at: http://www.iie.org/en/Who-We-Are/News-and-Events/Press-Center/Press-Releases/2010/2010-11-15-Open-Doors-US-Study-Abroad

Study tallies up total global digital data, finds looming storage shortage. (2007, March 7). [Online]. *FoxNews.com*. Available at: http://www.foxnews.com/story/0,2933,256957,00.html

Sturge-Apple, M. L., Davies, P. T., & Cummings, E. M. (2006a). Hostility and withdrawal in marital conflict: Effects on parental emotional unavailability and inconsistent discipline. *Journal of Family Psychology*, 20, 227–238.

Sturge-Apple, M. L., Davies, P. T., & Cummings, E. M. (2006b). The impact of hostility and withdrawal in interparental conflict on parental emotional unavailability and children's adjustment difficulties. *Child Development*, 77, 1623–1641.

Sudweeks, S., Gudykunst, W., Ting-Toomey, S., & Nishida, T. (1990). Developmental themes in Japanese–North American relationships. *International Journal of Intercultural Relations*, 14, 207–233.

Sugarmann, J. (2001). *Every handgun is aimed at you: The case for banning handguns*. New York: New Press.

Sulek, J. P. (2000, December 3). Harris latest in hit list of women ambushed for their appearance. *San Jose Mercury News*, p. 17A.

Sullivan, H. S. (1953). *The interpersonal theory of psychiatry*. New York: Norton.

Sunstein, C. R. (2006). *Infotopia: How many minds produce knowledge*. New York: Oxford University Press.

Sunstrom, J. (1997). A child's last hope. In L. G. Schnoor & B. Wickelgren (Eds.), *Winning orations*. Northfield, MN: Interstate Oratorical Association.

Sunwolf & Frey, L. R. (2005). Facilitating group communication. In S. A. Wheelan (Ed.), *The handbook of group research and practice*. Thousand Oaks, CA: Sage.

Superhuman heroes. (1998, June 6). *Economist*, pp. 10–12.

Surinder, K. S., & Cooper, R. B. (2003). Exploring the core concepts of media richness theory: The impact of cue multiplicity and feedback immediacy on decision quality. *Journal of Management Information Systems*, 20, 263–299.

Surk, B. (2008, October 16). Couple accused of sex on beach expose Dubai's cultural clash. *San Jose Mercury News*, p. 4A.

Surowiecki, J. (2005). *The wisdom of crowds: Why the many are smarter than the few and how collective wisdom shapes business, economics, societies, and nations*. New York: Anchor.

Survey says: Using a cell phone in a bathroom isn't as bad as you might think. (2009, August 10). *LetsTalk.com*. [Online]. Available at: http://www.letstalk.com/blog/post.htm?blogld=1052

Suter, E. A. (1994). Guns in the medical literature-a failure of peer review. *Journal of the Medical Association of Georgia*, 83, 133–159.

Sutton, R. I., & Hargadon, A. (1996). Brainstorming groups in context: Effectiveness in a product design firm. *Administrative Science Quarterly*, 41, 685–718.

Svoboda, E. (2009, February/March). Avoiding the big choke. *Scientific American Mind*, pp. 36–41.

Swain, S. (1989). Covert intimacy in men's friendships: Closeness in men's friendships. In B. J. Risman & P. Schwartz (Eds.), *Gender in intimate relationships: A microcultural approach*. Belmont, CA: Wadsworth.

Swaminathan, N. (2007, August 3). The sound track of our minds. *Scientific American*. [Online]. Available at: http://www.sciam.com/article.cfm?articleID=2CE5B31C-E7F2-99DF-3D96DEA33C219680

Swann, W. B., Rentfrow, P. J., & Gosling, S. D. (2003). The precarious couple effect: Verbally inhibited men + critical, disinhibited women = bad chemistry. *Journal of Personality and Social Psychology*, 85, 1095–1106.

Swann. W. B., Stein-Seroussi, A., & McNulty, S. E. (1992). Outcasts in a white-lie society: The enigmatic worlds of people with negative self-concepts. *Journal of Personality and Social Psychology*, 62, 618–624.

Swarns, R. L. (2004, August 29). Blacks debate "African-American." *San Jose Mercury News*, p. 4B.

Swift, J. S., & Huang, Y. (2004). The changing nature of international business relationships and foreign language competence. *International Journal of Management Practice*, 1, 21.

Swift, M. (2007, July 10). Education key to Latino majority. *San Jose Mercury News*, pp. 1B, 2B.

Swift, M. (2010, August 28). Grandma's on Facebook, and her friend list is bigger. *San Jose Mercury News*, p. A1.

Swift, M. (2011, February 20). Translator apps bridge global language gaps. *San Jose Mercury News*, pp. A1, A23.

Swift, M. (2011, June 5). Facebook study. *San Jose Mercury News*, E1, E7.

Swim, J. K., & Hyers, L. L. (1999). "Excuse me-what did you just say?" Women's public and private reactions to sexist remarks. *Journal of Experimental Social Psychology*, 35, 68–88.

Szabo, E. A., & Pfau, M. (2002). Nuances in inoculation: Theory and applications. In J. P. Dillard & M. Pfau (Eds.), *The persuasion handbook: Developments in theory and practice*. Thousand Oaks, CA: Sage.

Szivos, F. (2010, June 24). Anger in the workplace erupting. *Minuteman News Center*. [Online]. Available at: http://minutemannewscenter.com/articles/2010/06/24/westport/business/doc4c22643adebba882851574.txt

Tafoya, M. A., & Spitzberg, B. H. (2007). The dark side of infidelity: Its nature, prevalence, and communicative functions. In B. H. Spitzberg & W. R. Cupach (Eds.), *The dark side of interpersonal communication*. Mahwah, NJ: Erlbaum.

Tal, K. (1994, June 10). VWAR-L as a network community. *Network Observer*, 1, 6.

Talbot, M. M. (1998). *Language and gender: An introduction*. Malden, MA: Blackwell.

Tallmadge, A. (2007, Winter). When, not if. *Oregon Quarterly*, pp. 21–25.

Tamosaitis, N. (1995). *Net.sex*. Emerville, CA: Ziff-Davis Press.

Tannen, D. (1990). *You just don't understand: Women and men in conversation*. New York: Ballantine.

Tannen, D. (1994). *Talking from 9 to 5*. New York: Avon.

Tannen, D. (1998). *The argument culture: Moving from debate to dialogue*. New York: Random House.

Tannen, D. (2003, January 5). He, did you catch that? Why they're talking as fast as they can. *Washington Post*, pp. B1, B4.

Tannen, D. (2010, May/June). He said, she said. *Scientific American Mind*, pp. 55–59.

Tantleff-Dunn, S., Dunn, M. E., et al. (2002). Understanding faculty-student conflict: Student perceptions of precipitating events and faculty responses. *Teaching of Psychology*, 29, 197–202.

Taps, J., & Martin, P. (1990). Gender composition, attributional accounts, and women's influence and likability in task groups. *Small Group Research*, 4, 471–491.

Tapscott, D., & Williams, A. D. (2006). *Wikinomics: How mass collaboration changes everything*. New York: Penguin Group.

Taraban, C. B., Hendrick, S. S., & Hendrick, C. (1998). In P. A. Andersen & L. K. Guerrero (Eds.), *Handbook of communication and emotion*. New York: Academic Press.

Tarter, J. (2006, May/June). The cosmic haystack is large. *Skeptical Inquirer*, pp. 31–32.

Taste intensity. (1998, November). *Society for Neuroscience*. [Online]. Available at: http://www.sfn.org/index.cfm?pagename=brainBriefings_tasteIntensity

Tavris, C. (1989). *Anger: The misunderstood emotion*. New York: Simon & Schuster.

Tavris, C. (1992). *The mismeasure of women*. New York: Simon & Schuster.

Tavris, C., & Aronson, E. (2007). *Mistakes were made (but not by me)*. New York: Harcourt.

Taylor, L. S., Fiore, A. T., Mendelsohn, G. A., & Cheshire, C. (2011). "Out of my league": A real-world test of the matching hypothesis. *Personality and Social Psychology Bulletin*. [Online]. Available at: http://psp.sagepub.com/content/37/7/942

Taylor, S. (2002). *The tending instinct: Women, men, and the biology of relationships*. New York: Holt.

Tecce, J. J. (2004). *Body language in 2004 presidential debates*. [Online]. Available at: http://www.bc.edu/schools/cas/meta-elements/html/teece_analysis_2004.htm

Ted Kennedy's eulogy of brother Robert, St. Patrick's Cathedral, New York City, June 8, 1968. *New York Daily News*. [Online]. Available at: http://nydailynews.com/news/politics/2009/08/26/2009-08-26_ted_kennedys_eulogy_of_brother_robert_1968.html

Teicher, M. H., Samson, J. A., Polcari, A., & McGreenery, C. E. (2006). Sticks, stones, and hurtful words: Relative effects of various forms of childhood maltreatment. *American Journal of Psychiatry*, 163, 993–100.

Teicher, M. H., Samson, J. A., Sheu, Y-S, Polcari, A., & McGreenery, C. E. (2010). Hurtful words: Association of exposure to peer verbal abuse with elevated psychiatric symptom scores and corpus callosum abnormalities. *American Journal of Psychiatry*, 167, 1464–1471.

Telecommuting boosted in 1998 by Internet and economy. (1999). *Working Moms' Refuge*. [Online]. Available at: http://www.momsrefuge.com/telecommute/survey.html

Terrace, H. S. (1979). *Nim*. New York: Knopf.

Teven, J. J., & Comadena, M. E. (1996). The effects of office aesthetic quality on students' perceptions of teacher credibility and communicator style. *Communication Research Reports*, 13, 101–108.

Texting while walking, woman falls into fountain. (2011, January 20). *CBS News*. [Online]. Available at: http://www.cbsnews.com/stories/2011/01/20/earlyshow/main7265096.shtml

The dress-down revolution. (1996, May 12). *San Jose Mercury News*, p. A17.

The evidence that HIV causes AIDS. (2005, September 26). [Online]. Available at: http://www.niaid.gov/factsheets/evidhiv.htm

The fringe benefits of failure, and the importance of imagination. (2008, June 5). *Harvard Magazine*. [Online]. Available at: http://harvardmagazine.com/commencement/the-fringe-benefits-failure-the-importance-imagination

The gate debate: How you voted. (1997, February 28). *USA Weekend*, p. 9.

The week in perspective. (2006, December 31). *San Jose Mercury News*, p. 2P.

Thomas, K., & Velthouse, B. (1990). Cognitive elements of empowerment: An "interpretive" model of intrinsic task motivation. *Academy of Management Review*, 15, 666–681.

Thomas, L. S., Tod, D. A., & Lavallee, D. E. (2011). Variability in muscle dysmorphia symptoms: The influence of weight training. *Journal of Strength and Conditioning Research*, 25, 846–851.

Thompson, E. (1960). An experimental investigation of the relative effectiveness of organization structure in oral communication. *Southern Speech Journal*, 26, 59–69.

Thompson, J. (1986, April). Larger than life: Many women see themselves as roundfaced and pudgy, even when no one else does. *Psychology Today*, pp. 39–44.

Thompson, L., & Nadler, J. (2002). Negotiating via information technology: Theory and application. *Journal of Social Issues*, 58, 109–124.

Thompson, M., Zimbardo, P., & Hutchinson, G. (2005, March 9). *Consumers are having second thoughts about online dating*. [Online]. Available at: www.weattract.com/

Thoms, P., Pinto, J. K., Parente, D. H., & Druskat, V. U. (2002). Adaptation to self-managing work teams. *Small Group Research*, 33, 3–31.

Thomson, J. (2008, October 24). A quarter of people fear public speaking more than dying-here's how to beat your fear. *Smartcompany*. [Online]. Available at: http://www.smartcompany.com.au/Free-Articles/The-Briefing/20081024

Thourlby, W. (1978). *You are what you wear*. New York: New American Library.

Tibit, C. (2011). Understanding non-verbal insults from around the world. *Helium*. [Online]. Available at: http://www.helium.com/items/228168-understanding-non-verbal-insults-from-around-the-world/print

Ting-Toomey, S., & Chung, L. C. (2005). *Understanding intercultural communication*. Los Angeles: Roxbury.

Ting-Toomey, S., Gao, G., Yang, Z., Trubisky, P., Kim, H., Lin, S., & Nishida, T. (1991). Culture, face maintenance, and styles of handling interpersonal conflict: A study in five cultures. *International Journal of Conflict Management*, 2, 275–296.

Ting-Toomey, S., Yee-Jung, K. K., Shapiro, R. B., Garcia, W., Wright, T. J., & Oetzel, J. G. (2000). Ethnic/cultural identity salience and conflict styles in four U.S. ethnic groups. *International Journal of Intercultural Relations*, 24, 47–81.

Titsworth, B. S. (2004). Students' notetaking: The effects of teacher immediacy and clarity. *Communication Education*, 53, 305–320.

Tjosvold, D., Johnson, D. W., Johnson, R. T., & Sun, H. (2003). Can interpersonal competition be constructive within organizations? *Journal of Psychology*, 137, 63–84.

Tjosvold, D., Johnson, D. W., Johnson, R. T., & Sun, H. (2006). Competitive motives and strategies: Understanding constructive competition. *Group Dynamics: Theory, Research, and Practice*, 10, 87–99.

Today in labor history Oct 9 Smith Barney a tentative sexual harassment settlement (never finalized). (2010, October 9). *Democratic Underground*. [Online]. Available at: http://www.democraticunderground.com/discuss/duboard.php?az=view_all&address=367x28815

Tolhuizen, J. H. (1989). Communication strategies for intensifying dating relationships: Identification, use and structure. *Journal of Social and Personal Relationships*, 6, 413–434.

Tomasello, M., & Call, J. (1997). *Primate cognition*. New York: Oxford University Press.

Tomasello, M., Call, J., Nagell, K., Olguin, R., & Carpenter, M. (1994). The learning and use of gestural signals by young chimpanzees: A trans-generational study. *Primates*, 35, 137–154.

Top skills for job candidates. (2011). *National Association of Colleges and Employers*. [Online]. Available at: http://www.naceweb.org/PrinterFriendly.aspx?printpage=/Press/Releases/Top_Skills_for_Job_Candidates.aspx

Torbiorn, I. (1982). *Living abroad*. New York: Wiley.

Touching base with clichés, 24/7. (2004, March 24). *CNNInternational.com*. [Online]. Available at: http://edition.cnn.com/2004/WORLD/europe/03/24/plain.english/

Toulmin, S. E. (1958). *The uses of argument*. Cambridge, UK: Cambridge University Press.

Townsend, P. (1996, April 13). Face the truth. *Santa Cruz Sentinel*, p. D1.

Tracy, S. J., Lutgen-Sandvik, P., & Alberta, J. K. (2004, November). *Is it really bad? Exploring the emotional pain of workplace bullying through narratives, drawings and metaphors*. Paper presented at the annual convention of the National Communication Association, Chicago.

Transcript: Hillary Clinton's prime-time speech. (2009, July 24). *NPR*. [Online]. Available at: http://www.npr.org/templates/story/story.php?storyId=94003143

Trask, R. L. (1999). *Language: The basics*. New York: Routledge.

Triandis, H. C. (1989). The self and social behavior in differing cultural contexts. *Psychological Review*, 96, 506–520.

Triandis, H. C. (1990). Cross-cultural studies of individualism and collectivism. In J. J. Berman (Ed.), *Cross-cultural perspective*. Lincoln: University of Nebraska Press.

Triandis, H. C. (1994). *Culture and social behavior*. New York: McGraw-Hill.

Triandis, H. C. (1995). *Individualism and collectivism*. Boulder, CO: Westview Press.

Triandis, H. C. (1996). The psychological measurement of cultural syndromes. *American Psychologist*, 51, 407–415.

Triandis, H. C., Bontempo, R., Villareal, M. J., Asai, M., & Lucca, N. (1988). Individualism and collectivism: Cross-cultural perspectives on self-ingroup relationships. *Journal of Personality and Social Psychology*, 54, 323–338.

Tropman, J. (1996). *Making meetings work: Achieving high quality group decisions*. Thousand Oaks, CA: Sage.

Trosser, C. (1998, September/October). Obstacles to open discussion and critical thinking: The Grinnell College study. *Change Magazine*, pp. 44–49.

Trump Versus Rosie: The war continues. (2006, December 21). *The Showbuzz*. [Online]. Available at: http://www.showbuzz.cbsnews.com/stories/2006/12/21/people_hot_water/printable2287402.shtml

Tsapelas, I., Aron, A., & Orbuch, T. (2009). Marital boredom now predicts less satisfaction 9 years later. *Psychological Science*, 20, 543–545.

Tsapelas, I., Fisher, H. E., & Aron, A. (2011). Infidelity: When, where, why. In W. R. Cupach & B. H. Spitzberg (Eds.), *The dark side of close relationships*. New York: Routledge.

Tucker, P., & Aron, A. (1993). Passionate love and marital satisfaction at key transition points in the family life cycle. *Journal of Social and Clinical Psychology*, 12, 135–147.

Tufte, E. (2003, September). PowerPoint is evil: Power corrupts, PowerPoint corrupts absolutely. *Wired News*. [Online]. Available at: http://www.wired.com/wired/archive/11.09/ppt2_pr.html

Turnage, A. K. (2007). Email flaming behaviors and organizational conflict. *Journal of Computer-Mediated Communication*. [Online]. Available at: http://jcmc.indiana.edu/vol13/issue1/turnage.html

Turner, M. (2006). Using emotion in risk communication: The Anger Activism Model. *Public Relations Review*, 33, 114–119.

Turner, M., Bessarabova, E., Sipek, S., & Hambleton, K. (2007, May 23). *Does message-induced anger facilitate or debilitate persuasion? Two tests of the Anger Activism Model*. Paper presented at the annual meeting of the International Communication Association, San Francisco.

Turner, S. A., & Silvia, P. J. (2006). Must interesting things be pleasant? A test of competing appraisal structures. *Emotion*, 6, 670–674.

2006 sales, demographic and usage data: essential facts about the computer and video game industry. (2007). *Entertainment Software Association*. [Online]. Available at: http://www.theesa.com/archives/files/Essential%20Facts%202006.pdf

2011 office romance survey results. (2011). *Vault Career Intelligence*. [Online]. Available at: http://www.vault.com/wps/portal/usa/vcm/detail/Career-Advice/Office-Romance/2011-Office-Romance-Survey-Results?id=53933

Tyuasa, I. P. (2002). Empiricism and emotion: Representing and interpreting pitch ranges. In S. Benor, M. Rose, D. Sharma, J. Sweetland, & Q. Zhang (Eds.), *Gendered practices in language*. Stanford, CA: Center for the Study of Language and Information.

Understanding culture: Don't stare at a Navajo. (1974, June). *Psychology Today*, p. 107.

Unger, R., & Crawford, M. (1996). *Women and gender: A feminist psychology*. New York: McGraw-Hill.

Unnever, J. D., & Cullen, F. T. (2005). Executing the innocent and support for capital punishment: Implications for public policy. *Criminology and Public Policy*, 4, 3–38.

Urbina, I. (2009, August 8). Town hall forums on health care turn rowdy. *San Jose Mercury News*, p. A4.

Ury, W. (1993). *Getting past no: Negotiating your way from confrontation to cooperation*. New York: Bantam.

U.S. Department of Labor. (1991). *Skills and the new economy*. Washington, DC: U.S. Government Printing Office.

U.S. Equal Employment Opportunity Commission. (2006). *Sex-based discrimination*. [Online]. Available at: http://www.eeoc.gov/types/sex.html

Valacich, J. S., & Schwenk, C. (1995). Devil's advocacy and dialectical inquiry effects on face-to-face and computer-mediated group decision making. *Organizational Behavior and Human Decision Processes*, 63, 158–173.

Van de Vliert, E., Euwema, M. C., & Huismans, S. E. (1995). Managing conflict with a subordinate or a superior: Effectiveness of conglomerated behavior. *Journal of Applied Psychology*, 80, 271–281.

Van der Heijden, A. H. C. (1991). *Selective attention in vision*. New York: Routledge.

van der Kleij, R., Schraagen, J. M., & De Dreu, C. K. W. (2009). How conversations change over time in face-to-face and video-mediated communication. *Small Group Research*, 40, 355–381.

Van Dijke, M., & Poppe, M. (2004). Social comparison of power: Interpersonal versus intergroup effects. *Group Dynamics: Theory, Research, and Practice*, 8, 13–26.

Van Kleef, G. A. (2010). On angry leaders and agreeable followers: How leaders' emotions and followers' personalities shape motivation and team performance. *Psychological Science*, 21, 1827–1834.

Van Kleef, G. A., De Creu, C. K. W., & Manstead, A. S. R. (2004). The interpersonal effects of anger and happiness in negotiations. *Journal of Personality and Social Psychology*, 86, 57–76.

Van Oostrum, J., & Rabbie, J. (1995). Intergroup competition and cooperation within autocratic and democratic management regimes. *Small Group Research*, 26, 269–295.

Vandello, J. A., & Cohen, D. (1999). Patterns of individualism and collectivism across the United States. *Journal of Personality and Social Psychology*, 77, 279–292.

Vangelisti, A. L. (1994). "Couples" communication problems: The counselor's perspective. *Journal of Applied Communication Research*, 22, 106–126.

Vangelisti, A., Knapp, M., & Daly, J. (1990). Conversational narcissism. *Communication Monographs*, 57, 251–274.

Vargas, J. A. (2007, September 18). On *Wikipedia*, every fact is debatable in politics. *San Jose Mercury News*, pp. 1A, 13A.

Vault office romance 2007 survey: More employees caught canoodling. (2007, February 5). *Vault.com*. [Online]. Available at: http://www.vault.com/nr/newsmain.jsp?nr_page=3&ch_id=420&article_id=28739469

Vazire, S., & Gosling, S. D. (2004). E-perceptions: Personality impressions based on personal websites. *Journal of Personality and Social Psychology*, 87, 123–132.

Vecchio, R. P., Bullis, R. C., & Brazil, D. M. (2006). The utility of situational leadership theory. *Small Group Research*, 37, 407–424.

Vennochi, J. (2006, July 23). Bush, Merkel, and the quickie neck rub. *The Boston Globe*. [Online]. Available at: http://www.boston.com/news/globe/editorial_opinion/oped/articles/2006/07/23/bush_merkel_and_the_quickie_neck_rub/

Verlinden, J. (2005). *Critical thinking and everyday argument*. Belmont, CA: Wadsworth.

Vesselinov, E. (2008). Members only: Gated communities and residential segregation in metropolitan U.S. *Sociological Forum*, 23.

Victor, D. A. (2007, March 27–31). *What is the language of business? Affecting business outcome before you say a word*. Proceedings of the Association for Business Communication, Seventh Asia-Pacific Conference, City University of Hong Kong.

Victory, honor, sacrifice. (Henry H. Shelton address) (transcript) (2001, August 1). *Vital Speeches of the Day*. [Online]. Available at: http://www.accessmylibrary.com/coms2/summary_0286_28267884_ITM

Vitanza, S., & Marshall, L. (1993). *Dimensions of dating violence, gender and personal characteristics*. Unpublished manuscript.

Vito, D. (1999). Affective self-disclosure, conflict resolution and marital quality. *Dissertation Abstracts International*, 60, 1319.

Volkema, R. J., & Bergmann, T. J. (1989). Interpersonal conflict at work: An analysis of behavioral responses. *Human Relations*, 42, 757–770.

Vrij, A. (2000). *Detecting lies and deceit: The psychology of lying and its implications for professional practice*. Chichester, UK: Wiley.

Vrij, A. (2006). Nonverbal communication and deception. In V. Manusov & M. L. Patterson (Eds.), *The Sage handbook on nonverbal communication*. Thousand Oaks, CA; Sage.

Vrij, A., Granhad, P. A., & Porter, S. (2010). Pitfalls and opportunities in nonverbal and verbal lie detection. *Psychological Science in the Public Interest*, 11, 89–121.

Vroom, V. H., & Jago, A. G. (2007). The role of the situation in leadership. *American Psychologist*, 62, 17–24.

Wachsmuth, I. (2006, October/November). Gestures offer insight. *Scientific American Mind*, pp. 20–25.

Wade, C., & Tavris, C. (2008). *Invitation to psychology*. New York: Longman.

Wade, N. G., & Worthington, E. L. (2005). In search of a common core: A content analysis of interventions to promote forgiveness. *Psychotherapy: Theory, Research, Practice, Training*, 42, 160–177.

Wade, T. J. (1996). An examination of locus of control/fatalism for blacks, whites, boys, and girls over a two-year period of adolescence. *Social Behavior and Personality*, 24, 239–248.

Wagner, N. (2011, April 1). Medicalese turns patients' perception of common conditions into serious diseases. *Thedoctorwillseeyounow*. [Online]. Available at: http://www.thedoctorwillseeyounow.com/content/public_health/art2445.html

Wakefield, M., Terry-McElrath, Y., Emery, S., et al. (2006). Effect of televised, tobacco company–funded smoking prevention advertising on youth smoking-related beliefs, intentions, and behavior. *American Journal of Public Health*, 96, 1–7.

Waldner-Haugrud, L. K., Gratch, L. V., & Magruder, B. (1997). Victimization and perpetration rates of violence in gay and lesbian relationships:

Gender issues explored. *Violence and Victims*, 12, 173–184.

Wallace, D. S., Paulson, R. M., Lord, C. G., & Bond, C. F. (2005). Which behaviors do attitudes predict? Meta-analyzing the effects of social pressure and perceived difficulty. *Review of General Psychology*, 9, 214–227.

Wallace, P. (1999). *The psychology of the Internet*. New York: Cambridge University Press.

Waller, W., & Hill, R. (1951). *The family: A dynamic interpretation*. New York: Dryden.

Walsh, M. W. (2000, November 27). Many workers barred from trip to bathroom. *San Jose Mercury News*, p. 6E.

Walsh, M., & Vivona, M. (2010, October). International workplace productivity survey: White collar highlights. *LexisNexis*. [Online]. Available at: http://www.multivu.com/players/English/46619-LexisNexis-International-Workplace_Productivity-Survey/flexSwf/

Walter, C. (2006, December/January). Why do we cry? *Scientific American Mind*, pp. 44–51.

Walther, J. B. (2008). Computer-mediated communication and virtual groups. In E. A. Konijn, S. Utz, M. Tanis, & S. B. Barnes (Eds.), *Mediated interpersonal communication*. New York: Routledge.

Wanzer, M. B., Booth-Butterfield, M., & Booth-Butterfield, S. (1996). Humor and social attraction: Are funny people more popular? An examination of humor orientation, loneliness, and social attraction. *Communication Quarterly*, 44, 42–52.

Warschauer, M., El Said, G. R., & Zohry, A. (2002, July). Language choice online: Globalization and identity in Egypt. *Journal of Computer-Mediated Communication*, 7. [Online]. Available at: www.ascusc.org/jcmc/v017/issue4/warschauer.html

Warters, B. (2005, November). Changing patterns of roommate conflict fueled by the net. *Conflict Management in Higher Education Report*. [Online]. Available at: http://www.campus-adr.org/CMHER/ReportEvents/Edition6_1/roommates.html

Washington, J. (2009). Barriers slow black women's progress. *San Jose Mercury News*, p. 4C.

Watson, J. M., & Strayer, D. L. (2010). Supertaskers: Profiles in extraordinary multitasking ability. *Psychonomic Bulletin and Review*, 17, 479–485.

Watson, W., Kumar, K., & Michaelsen, L. (1993). Cultural diversity's impact on interaction process and performance: Comparing homogeneous and diverse task groups. *Academy of Management Journal*, 36, 590–602.

Watzlawick, P., Beavin, J., & Jackson, D. (1967). *Pragmatics of human communication*. New York: Norton.

Wayne, M. (1974). The meaning of silence in conversations in three cultures. In *Patterns of communication in and out of Japan*. Tokyo: ICU Communication Department.

WB lays down law on haircuts. (2000, June 8). *San Jose Mercury News*, p. 2A.

We met at the office. (1999, February 14). *Parade*, p. 25.

Weber, S. N. (1994). The need to be: The socio-cultural significance of black language. In L. A. Samovar & R. E. Porter (Eds.), *Intercultural communication: A reader*. Belmont, CA: Wadsworth.

Webster, E. (1964). *Decision making in the employment interview*. Montreal: Industrial Relations Center, McGill University Press.

Wechsler, H., & Nelson, T. F. (2008). What we have learned from the Harvard School of Public Health College Alcohol Survey: Focusing attention on college student alcohol consumption and the environmental conditions that promote it. *Journal of Studies on Alcohol and Drugs*, 69, 481–490.

Wechsler, H., & Wuethrich, B. (2003). *Dying to drink: Confronting binge drinking on college campuses*. New York: Rodale Books.

Wegner, D. M. (1989). *White bears and other unwanted thoughts*. New York: Viking/Penguin.

Weick, K. (1990). The vulnerable system: An analysis of the Tenerife air disaster. *Journal of Management*, 16, 571–593.

Weinberger, M. G., & Gulas, C. S. (1992). The impact of humor in advertising: A review. *Journal of Advertising*, 21, 35–59.

Weiner, B., Graham, S., Peter, D., & Zmuidinas, M. (1991). Public confession and forgiveness. *Journal of Personality*, 59, 281–312.

Weiner, R. (2009, December 27). Death panels lie on Factcheck.org's "Whoppers of 2009." *Huffington Post*. [Online]. Available at: http://www.huffingtonpost.com/2009/12/27/death-panels-lie-on-factc_n_404284.html

Weiner, S., Schwartz, A., Weaver, F., et al. (2010). Contextual errors and failures in individualizing patient care: A multicenter study. *Annals of Internal Medicine*, 153, 69–75.

Weingarten, G. (1994, September 27). I'm absolutely sure: You need a marshmallow enema. *San Jose Mercury News*, p. B7.

Weiss, B., & Feldman, R. S. (2006). Looking good and lying to do it: Deception as an impression management strategy in job interviews. *Journal of Applied Social Psychology*, 36, 1070–1056.

Welch, W. M. (2008, June 19). English-only laws gathering steam. *USA Today*, p. 3A.

Wellen, J. M., & Neale, M. (2006). Deviance, self-typicality, and group cohesion: The corrosive effects of the bad apples on the barrel. *Small Group Research*, 37, 165–186.

Wener, R. (2006). Effectiveness of the direct supervision system of correctional design and management. *Criminal Justice and Behavior*, 33, 392–410.

Wener, R., Frazier, W., & Farberstein, J. (1987, June). Building better jails. *Psychology Today*, pp. 40–49.

Werking, K. (1997). *We're just friends: Women and men in nonromantic relationships*. New York: Guilford Press.

Werner, S. (2005). Mandatory minimum sentencing. In L. G. Schnoor & B. Wickelgren (Eds.),

Winning orations. Mankato, MN: Interstate Oratorical Association.

West, C., & Zimmerman, D. H. (1987). Doing gender. *Gender and Society*, 1, 125–151.

West, R., & Turner, L. H. (2007). *Introducing communication theory: Analysis and application*. New York: McGraw-Hill.

Westen, D. (2007). *The political brain: The role of emotion in deciding the fate of the nation*. New York: Public Affairs Press.

Wetzel, P. (1988). Are "powerless" communication strategies the Japanese norm? *Language in Society*, 17, 555–564.

What a difference. (2005, November 27). *San Jose Mercury News*, p. 3P.

What social science can tell you about flirting and how to do it. (2007, March 16). *Social Issues Research Centre*. [Online]. Available at: http://www.sirc.org/publik/flirt.html

Wheelan, S. A. (2009). Group size, group development, and group productivity. *Small Group Research*, 40, 247–262.

Wheeler, T. L. (2004). Removing the obstruction for better health: A case for reversing the DSHEA act. In L. G. Schnoor & B. Wickelgren (Eds.), *Winning orations*. Mankato, MN: Interstate Oratorical Association.

White, D. (1998, December 30). Stupid things really said by famous people. *San Jose Mercury News*, p. E5.

White, J. E. (1997, May 5). I'm just who I am. *Time*, pp. 32–36.

White, M. M. (2002, September 4). Women to overtake men in management. *Santa Cruz Sentinel*, p. D5.

Whitkin, R. (1987, September 19). FAA says Delta had poor policies on crew training. *The New York Times*, p. 1.

WhowasNeda?Slainwomananunlikelymartyr.(2009, June 24). *CNN.com/world*. [Online]. Available at:http://www.cnn.com/2009/WORLD/meast/06/23/iran.neda.profile/

Whysall, M. (2011, March 18). Popularity of online dating sites. *ADI News*. [Online]. Available at: http://www.adi-news.com/popularity-of-online-dating-sites/29761/

Wiener, R. L., & Gutek, B. (1999). Advances in sexual harassment research, theory, and policy. *Psychology, Public Policy, and Law*, 5, 507–518.

Wierzbicka, A. (1986). Human emotions: Universal or culture-specific? *American Anthropologist*, 88, 584–594.

Wieselquist, J., Rusbult, C. E., Agnew, C. R., & Foster, C. A. (1999). Commitment, pro-relationship behavior, and trust in close relationships. *Journal of Personality and Social Psychology*, 77, 942–966.

Wilder, D. A., Simon, A. F., & Faith, M. (1996). Enhancing the impact of counterstereotypic information: Dispositional attributions for deviance. *Journal of Personality and Social Psychology*, 71, 276–287.

Wilgoren, J. (2002, October 31). Memorial for Wellstone assumes spirit of rally. *The New York Times*. [Online]. Available at: http://www.nytimes.com/2002/10/30/politics/30WELL.html?todaysheadlines

Willer, E. K., & Cupach, W. R. (2011). The meaning of girls' social aggression: Nasty or mastery? In W. R. Cupach & B. H. Spitzberg (Eds.), *The dark side of close relationships II*. New York: Routledge.

Williams, C. L., & Berry, J. W. (1991). Primary prevention of acculturative stress among refugees. *American Psychologist*, 46, 632–641.

Williams, J. E., & Best, D. L. (1990). *Measuring sex stereotypes: A multinational study*. Thousand Oaks, CA: Sage.

Williams, K. D. (2011, January/February). The pain of exclusion. *Scientific American Mind*, pp. 30–37.

Williams, R., & Williams, V. (1993). *Anger kills*. New York: Random House.

Williams, S. B., & Dilanni, P. (2006, April 3). With record numbers, Exxon tops Fortune 500 list for first time since 2001. *Fortune Press Center*. [Online]. Available at: http://www.timeinc.net/fortune/information/presscenter/fortune/press_releases/20060403

Willis, E. E. (2005). *How to be funny on purpose: Creating and consuming humor*. Toronto, Canada: Cybercom Publishing.

Willis, J., & Todorov, A. (2006). First impressions: Making up your mind after a 100-ms exposure to a face. *Psychological Science*, 17, 592–598.

Wilmot, W., & Hocker, J. (2011). *Interpersonal conflict*. New York: McGraw-Hill.

Wilson, C. (2008, June 19). Russert gets a final toast from Washington. *USA Today*, p. 2D.

Wilson, J. F. (2003). *Biological foundations of human behavior*. Belmont, CA: Wadsworth.

Wilson, T. D. (2002). *Strangers to ourselves: Discovering the adaptive unconscious*. Cambridge, MA: Harvard University Press.

Wilson-Doenges, G. (2000). An exploration of sense of community and fear of crime in gated communities. *Environment and Behavior*, 32, 597–611.

Winters, R. (2011, February 17). Telecommute jobs for people with degrees. *eHow*. [Online]. Available at: http://www.ehow.com/info_7952640_telecommute-jobs-people-degrees.html

Wiseman, R. (1997). *Deception and self-deception: Investigating psychics*. New York: Prometheus Books.

Wiseman, R., Sanders, J., Congalton, J., Gass, R., Sueda, K., & Ruiqing, D. (1995). A cross-cultural analysis of compliance gaining: China, Japan, and the United States. *Intercultural Communication Studies*, 1, 1–18.

Witt, C., & Fetherling, D. (2009). *Real leaders don't do PowerPoint: How to sell yourself and your ideas*. New York: Crown Forum.

Witt, P. L., & Behnke, R. R. (2006). Anticipatory speech anxiety as a function of public speaking assignment type. *Communication Education*, 55, 167–177.

Witt, P. L., Brown, K. C., Roberts, J. B., Weisel, J., Sawyer, C. R., & Behnke, R. R. (2006). Somatic anxiety patterns before, during, and after giving a public speech. *Southern Communication Journal*, 71, 87–100.

Witte, K. (1998). In P. A. Andersen & L. K. Guerrero (Eds.), *Handbook of communication and emotion*. New York: Academic Press.

Witte, K., & Allen, M. (1996, November). *When do scare tactics work? A meta-analysis of fear appeals*. Paper presented at the annual meeting of the Speech Communication Association, San Diego, CA.

Witte, K., Meyer, G., & Martell, D. (2001). *Effective health risk messages: A step-by-step guide*. Thousand Oaks, CA: Sage.

Witte, K., Murray-Johnson, L., Hubbell, A. P., Liu, W. Y., Sampson, J., & Morrison, K. (2000). Addressing cultural orientations in fear appeals: Promoting AIDS-protective behaviors among Hispanic immigrant and African-American adolescents, and American and Taiwanese college students. *Journal of Health Communication*, 6, 1023.

Witteman, H. (1993). The interface between sexual harassment and organizational romance. In G. Kreps (Ed.), *Sexual harassment: Communication implications*. Cresskill, NJ: Hampton Press.

Witvliet, C. V., Ludwig, T. E., & Wade, N. G. (2001). Granting foregiveness or harboring grudges: Implications for emotion, physiology, and health. *Psychological Science*, 12, 117, 123.

Woertz, P. A. (2010, April 22). Fortune 500 women CEOs. *CNNMoney*. [Online]. Available at: http://money.cnn.com/galleries/2010/fortune/1004/gallery.fortune500_women_ceos.fortune/index.html

Wojciszke, B., Baczynska, R., & Jaworski, M. (1998). On the dominance of moral categories in impression formation. *Personality and Social Psychology Bulletin*, 24, 1245–1257.

Wolf, S. (1979). Behavioral style and group cohesiveness as sources of minority influence. *European Journal of Social Psychology*, 9, 381–395.

Wolkomir, R., & Wolkomir, J. (1990, February). How to make smart choices. *Reader's Digest*, pp. 27–32.

Wolpe, J. (1990). *The practice of behavior therapy*. Tarrytown, NY: Pergamon Press.

Wolverton, T. (2011, February 5). No age limit on geeks. *San Jose Mercury News*, pp. A1, A6.

Wolvin, A., & Coakley, C. (1996). *Listening*. Dubuque, IA: Brown & Benchmark.

Wolvin, A., & Corley, D. (1984). The technical speech communication course: A view from the field. *Association for Communication Administration Bulletin*, 49, 83–91.

Woman angry over online time attacked computer, cops say. (1999, July 1). *San Jose Mercury News*, p. A11.

Women CEOs of the Fortune 1000. (2010, September). *Catalyst*. [Online]. Available at: http://www.catalyst.org/publication/322/women-ceos-of-the-fortune-1000

Women in government. (2010, October). *Catalyst*. [Online]. Available at: http://www.catalyst.org/publication/244/women-in-government

Women in the Senate. (2011). *Senate.gov*. [Online]. Available at: http://www.senate.gov/artandhistory/common/briefing/women_senators.htm

Women in U.S. management. (2010, December). *Catalyst*. [Online]. Available at: http://www.catalyst.org/publications/206/women-in-us-management

Wondrak, I., & Hoffman, J. (2007, April/May). A personal obsession: What drives stalkers to pursue their victims? *Scientific American Mind*, pp. 76–81.

Wong, N. C. (2003, April 7). Better not pout in P.A. *San Jose Mercury News*, pp. 1A, 14A.

Wong, Y. J., Pituch, K. A., & Rochlen, A. B. (2006). Men's restrictive emotionality: An investigation of associations with other emotion-related constructs, anxiety, and underlying dimensions. *Psychology of Men and Masculinity*, 7, 113–126.

Wood, A. F., & Smith, M. J. (2001). *Online communication: Linking technology, identity, and culture*. Mahwah, NJ: Erlbaum.

Wood, J. (1994). *Gendered lives: Communication, gender, and culture*. Belmont, CA: Wadsworth.

Wood, J. T. (1996). She says/he says: Communication, caring, and conflict in heterosexual relationships. In J. Wood (Ed.), *Gendered relationships*. Mountain View, CA: Mayfield.

Wood, J. T. (1998). *But I thought you meant . . . : Misunderstandings in human communication*. Mountain View, CA: Mayfield.

Wood, J. T. (2000). *Relational communication: Continuity and change in personal relationships*. Belmont, CA: Wadsworth.

Wood, J. T. (2001). A critical response to John Gray's Mars and Venus portrayals of men and women. *Southern Communication Journal*, 67, 201–210.

Wood, J. T. (2004). *Communication theories in action: An introduction*. Belmont, CA: Wadsworth/Thomson Learning.

Wood, J. T. (2007). *Gendered lives: Communication, gender, and culture*. Belmont, CA: Wadsworth.

Wood, J. T., & Inman, C. (1993). In a different mode: Recognizing male models of closeness. *Journal of Applied Communication Research*, 21, 279–295.

Wood, M. L. M. (2007). Rethinking the inoculation analogy: Effects on subjects with differing preexisting attitudes. *Human Communication Research*, 33, 357–378.

Woodman, T. (1991). *The role of forgiveness in marital adjustment*. Unpublished doctoral dissertation, Fuller Graduate School of Psychology, Pasadena, CA.

Workers lack verbal skills, survey finds. (1992, September 21). *San Jose Mercury News*, p. A2.

Worthington, D. L., Stallard, M. J., Price, J. M., & Gross, P. J. (2002). Hindsight bias, Daubert, and the silicone breast implant litigation: Making the case for court-appointed experts in complex medical and scientific litigation. *Psychology, Public Policy, and Law*, 8, 154–179.

Wright, N. S., & Drewery, G. P. (2006). Forming cohesion in culturally heterogeneous teams: Differences in Japanese, Pacific Islander and Anglo experiences. *Cross-Cultural Management*, 13, 43–53.

Wright, R. (1993, July 1). Women are taking center stage in the worldwide political arena. *San Jose Mercury News*, p. A10.

Wright, R. (2000). *Nonzero: The logic of human destiny*. New York: Vintage Books.

Wronge, Y., & Fernandez, L. (2000, December 19). Teenagers define "sex" too narrowly, study finds. *San Jose Mercury News*, pp. 1A, 14A.

Wurman, R. (1989). *Information anxiety*. New York: Doubleday.

Wyer, K. (2007, January 19). More college freshmen now show interest in politics, UCLA survey reveals. *UCLA News*. [Online]. Available at: http://www.newsroom.ucla.edu/page.asp?RelNum-7634

Yamashita, A. (2009). Native and foreign communication standards in colloquial Japanese language. *Dialectologia*, 3, 109–123.

Yang, J. L. (2006, June 12). The power of number 4.6. *Fortune*, p. 122.

Yardley, J., Rodcriguez, M. D., Bates, S. C., & Nelson, J. (2009). True confessions? Alumni's retrospective reports on undergraduate cheating behaviors. *Ethics and Behavior*, 19, 1–14.

Yaukey, J. (2000, July 4). Your e-mail can get you fired. *San Jose Mercury News*, p. 3C.

Yela, C. (2006). The evaluation of love: Simplified version of the scales for Yela's tetrangular model based on Sternberg's model. *European Journal of Psychological Assessment*, 22, 21–27.

Yelsma, P., & Athappilly, K. (1988). Marital satisfaction and communication practices: Comparisons among Indian and American couples. *Journal of Comparative Family Studies*, 19, 37–54.

Yen, H. (2010, May 27). Growth of interracial marriage slowing. *San Jose Mercury News*, p. A5.

Yerby, J., & Buerkel-Rothfuss, N. L. (1982, November). *Communication patterns, contradictions, and family functions*. Paper presented at the meeting of the Speech Communication Association, Louisville, KY.

Yingling, J. (1994). Constituting friendships in talk and metatalk. *Journal of Social and Personal Relationships*, 11, 411–426.

Yoder, J. D. (2002). 2001 Division 35 presidential address: Context matters: Understanding tokenism processes and their impact on women's work. *Psychology of Women Quarterly*, 26, 108.

Yoo, Y., & Alavi, M. (2004). Emergent leadership in virtual teams: What do emergent leaders do? *Information and Organization*, 14, 27–58.

Young, E. (2002, October 3). World's funniest joke revealed. *New Scientist*. [Online]. Available at: www.newscientist.com/article.ns?id=dn2876&print=true

Young, K. S. (1996, August 10). *Pathological Internet use: The emergence of a new clinical disorder*. Paper presented at the American Psychological Association's 104th annual convention, Toronto. [Online]. Available at: http://www.pitt.edu/~ksy/Welcome.html

Young, M. J., Behnke, R. R., & Mann, Y. M. (2004). Anxiety patterns in employment interviews. *Communication Reports*, 17, 49–57.

Yovetich, N. A., & Rusbult, C. E. (1994). Accommodative behavior in close relationships: Exploring transformation of motivation. *Journal of Experimental Social Psychology*, 30, 138–164.

Yu, X. (1997). The Chinese "nature" perspective on mao-dun (conflict) and mao-dun resolution strategies: A qualitative investigation. *Intercultural Communication Studies*, 7, 63–82.

Yukl, G. (2006). *Leadership in organizations*. Upper Saddle River, NJ: Prentice Hall.

Zaccaro, S. J. (2007). Trait-based perspectives of leadership. *American Psychologist*, 62, 6–16.

Zahahi, W. R., & Duran, R. L. (1984). Attraction, communicative competence, and communication satisfaction. *Communication Research Reports*, 1, 54–57.

Zander, A. (1982). The psychology of removing group members and recruiting new ones. *Human Relations*, 29, 1–8.

Zernike, K., & Thee-Brenan, M. (2010, April 14). Poll finds Tea Party backers wealthier and more educated. *The New York Times*. [Online]. Available at: http://www.nytimes.com/2010/04/15/us/politics/15poll.html

Zhang, Q. (2010). Asian Americans beyond the Model Minority stereotype: The nerdy and the left out. *Journal of International and Intercultural Communication*, 3, 20–37.

Zillmann, D. (1993). Mental control of angry aggression. In D. Wegner & J. Pennebaker (Eds.), *Handbook of mental control* (Vol. 5). Englewood Cliffs, NJ: Prentice Hall.

Zimbardo, P. (1992). *Psychology and life*. New York: HarperCollins.

Zimmerman, J. (2010, June 16). Walking while texting can be dangerous to your health. *Scripps News*. [Online]. Available at: http://www.scrippsnews.com/content/walking-while-texting-can-be-dangerous-your-health

Zinsser, W. (1985). *On writing well*. New York: Harper & Row.

Zormeier, S. M., & Samovar, L. A. (2000). Language as a mirror of reality: Mexican-American proverbs. In L. A. Samovar & R. E. Porter (Eds.), *Intercultural communication: A reader*. Belmont, CA: Wadsworth.

Zornoza, A., Ripoll, P., & Peiro, J. M. (2002). Conflict management in groups that work in two different communication contexts: Face-to-face and computer-mediated communication. *Small Group Research*, 33, 481–508.

Zuckerman, L. (1999, April 17). Words go right to the brain, but can they stir the heart? *The New York Times*, p. 9.

CREDITS

PHOTO CREDITS

CHAPTER 1

p. 2: ULTRA.F/Getty Images; p. 5: ©iStockphoto.com/izuseck; p. 13: Lou Toman/South Florida Sun-Sentinel; p. 17: Scott Olson/Getty Images; p. 20: AP Photo/Jason DeCrow; p. 27: AP Photo/Jon Minchillo; p. 30: AP Photo/David Josek; p. 30: Scott Heavey/Getty Images

CHAPTER 2

p.34;©iStockphoto.com/asiseeit:p.44:©iStockphoto.com/Spanic: p. 53: p. AP Photo/File; p. 53: Photo by Tom Donoghue/Picture Group via AP Images; p. 55: Peter Schols/Reuters/Landov; p. 57: Simon Marcus/Corbis

CHAPTER 3

p. 62: AP Photo/Chris Carlson; p. 66: Lindsay Miles-Pickup/Getty Images; p. 66: ©iStockphoto.com/bowdenimages; p. 68: Nicholas Kamm/Getty Images; p. 76: Hofstede, G., & Hofstede, G. J. (2005). Cultures and organizations: Software of the mind. New York: McGraw-Hill; p. 88: ©iStockphoto.com/contour99; p. 88: ©iStockphoto.com/4774344sean

CHAPTER 4

p. 94: Photo by Don Knuth; p. 98: Rick Gayle Studio / Corbis; p. 106; Optometric Extension Program Foundation, www.oefp.org; p. 109: © Momatiuk- Eastcott/Corbis; p. 111: AP photo / Carlos Osorio; p. 118: Photo by George Guajardo/NBC NewsWire via AP Images

CHAPTER 5

p. 126; © Digital Art/Corbis; p. 133: ©iStockphoto.com/mikkelwilliam; p. 133: ©iStockphoto.com/DorianGray; p. 134: Kevin Winter/Getty Images; p. 135: ©iStockphoto.com/clintspencer; p.139: Bill Aron/PhotoEdit; p. 144 (top left) ©iStockphoto.com/mikkelwilliam; p. 144 (top middle) ©iStockphoto.com/DorianGray; p. 144 (top right) ©iStockphoto.com/jeannehatch; p. 144 (bottom left) ©iStockphoto.com/cunfek; p. 144 (bottom middle) ©iStockphoto.com/LP7; p. 144 (bottom right) ©iStockphoto.com/TatyanaGI; p. 148: STRDEL / AFP / Getty Images

CHAPTER 6

p. 156: image100 / Corbis; p. 167: Bahrick, H. P. (1984). Semantic memory content in permastore: Fifty years of memory for Spanish learned in school. Journal of Experimental Psychology, 113, 1–35; p. 172: National Museum of American Art, Smithsonian Institute, USA / Photo © Bolton Picture Library/ The Bridgeman Art Library; p. 177: Steve Liss/Getty Images

CHAPTER 7

p. 186: Benelux / zefa / Corbis; p. 198: AP Photo/Lee Jinman; p. 201: Jack Star / PhotoLink / Getty Images; p. 205: Michael Newman / PhotoEdit; p. 208: AP photo / Jeff Widener

CHAPTER 8

p. 218: Corbis / © Deborah Feingold; p. 222: ©iStockphoto.com/Squaredpixels; p. 232: Ariel Shelley / Corbis; p. 245: Sean Locke/Getty Images; p. 249: Jeff Greenberg / PhotoEdit

CHAPTER 9

p. 252: Bob Daemmrich / The Image Works; p. 256: Robert Brenner / PhotoEdit; p. 259: ©iStockphoto.com/attator, ©iStockphoto.com/Sportstock; p. 268: p. Tom & Dee Ann McCarthy / Corbis: 269: AP Photo / Independent Florida Alligator, Andrew Stanfill; p. 275: © 1996, James A. Parcell / The Washington Post; p. 280: © Larry Dale Gordon/Corbis

CHAPTER 10

p. 286: ©iStockphoto.com/ihsanyildizli; p. 294: Mike Powell/Getty Images, Ethan Miller/Getty Images; p. 295: © Andrew Lichtenstein/Sygma/Corbis; p. 305 (left) Bloomberg/Getty Images; p. 305 (top right) AP Photo/Keystone, Walter Bieri; p. (bottom right) Donna Svennevik/Getty Images

CHAPTER 11

p. 310; Ap Photo/Marcio Jose Sanchez; p. 317: Bill Varie / Corbis; p. 327: ©iStockphoto.com/mediaphotos; p. 335: © David Madison/Corbis; p. 337: Check Six/Getty Images

CHAPTER 12

p. 340: © Scott Stulberg/Corbis; p. 347: Don Emmert/Getty Images; p. 355: Library of Congress John Neubauer / PhotoEdit; p. 362: Marwan Naamani/Getty Images

CHAPTER 13

p. 376: AP Photo/Reed Saxon; p. 387: Scott Barbour / Getty Images; p. 390: © 2008 Richard Koci Hernandez, San Jose Mercury News. Reprinted with permission from the YGS Group; p. 362: Photograph by Andrew Cutraro. Used with permission; p. 407: Carolyn Cole / AFP / Getty Images

CHAPTER 14

p. 410: Bob Daemmrich Photography; p. 414: Journal-Courier / Steve Warmowski / The Image Works; p. 415: Photograph by Katherine Domingo. Used with permission from My Stroke of Insight Inc; p. 426: Pam Panchak/Post-Gazette; p. 428: AP Photo / AJ Mast; p. 430: San Jose Mercury News, March 12, 2011 used with permission from The YGS Group; p. 437: RICK WILKING/Reuters /Landov

CHAPTER 15

p. 440: Peter Turnley / Corbis; p. 451: The Washington Post/Getty Images; p. 453: Manan Vatsyayana/Getty Images; p. 456: The Meth Project

CARTOON CREDITS

CHAPTER 1

p. 13: "Candorville" used with the permissions of Darrin Bell, the Washington Post Writers Group, and the Cartoonist Group. All rights reserved.; p. 19: Zits © 2009 Zits Partnership, King Features Syndicate; p. 28: CATHY © (1994) Cathy Guisewite. Reprinted with permission of UNIVERSAL UCLICK. All rights reserved.

CHAPTER 2

p. 40: CATHY © 1996 Cathy Guisewite. Reprinted with permission of UNIVERSAL UCLICK. All rights reserved.

CHAPTER 3

p. 78: Doonesbury © 1986 G.B. Trudeau. Reprinted with permission of UNIVERSAL UCLICK. All rights reserved.; p. 86: Luann © Greg Evans. Reprinted with permission of UNIVERSAL UCLICK. All rights reserved.

CHAPTER 4

p. 100; CALVIN AND HOBBES ©1992 Watterson. Dist. By UNIVERSAL UCLICK. Reprinted with permission. All rights reserved; p. 115: The New Yorker Collection, 1989 George Price from cartoonbank.com

CHAPTER 5

p. 129: Sally Forth © 2009 King Features Syndicate

CHAPTER 6

p. 159: Doonesbury © 2011 G.B. Trudeau. Reprinted with permission of UNIVERSAL UCLICK. All rights reserved;

p. 168: Non Sequitur © Wiley Miller. Reprinted with permission of UNIVERSAL UCLICK. All rights reserved; p. 181: CATHY © Cathy Guisewite. Reprinted with permission of UNIVERSAL UCLICK. All rights reserved.

CHAPTER 7

p. 195: DILBERT ©1995 Scott Adams. Used By permission of UNIVERSAL UCLICK. All rights reserved; p. 210: Zits © 2011 Zits Partnership, King Features Syndicate

CHAPTER 8

p. 231: CATHY © 2002 Cathy Guisewite. Reprinted with permission of UNIVERSAL UCLICK. All rights reserved; p. 236: The New Yorker Collection 1994 Mort Gerberg from cartoonbank.com; p. 241: Zits © 2009 Zits Partnership, King Features Syndicate; p. 245: Don Wright, June 6, 2001. Used with Permissions from TMS Reprints and the Palm Beach Post

CHAPTER 9

p. 267: © 1989, Scott Willis; p. 268: CALVIN AND HOBBES ©1995 Watterson. Dist. By UNIVERSAL UCLICK. Reprinted with permission. All rights reserved; p. 272: The New Yorker Collection 1997 J.B. Handelsman from cartoonbank.com

CHAPTER 10

p. 210: Dilbert ©1997 Scott Adams. Dist. By UNIVERSAL UCLICK. Reprinted with permission. All rights reserved

CHAPTER 11

p. 313: Cartoonstock.com

CHAPTER 12

p. 367; Dilbert ©2002 Scott Adams. Dist. By UNIVERSAL UCLICK. Reprinted with permission. All rights reserved

CHAPTER 13

p. 391: OFF THE MARK © 2004 Mark Parisi. Reprinted with permission of UNIVERSAL UCLICK. All rights reserved; p. 400: 2001 ZITS Partnership. Distributed by King Features Syndicate

INDEX